REASON
AND
RESPONSIBILITY

REASON

AND

RESPONSIBILITY

READINGS
IN SOME BASIC PROBLEMS
OF PHILOSOPHY

Third Edition

edited by

Joel Feinberg

The Rockefeller University

DICKENSON PUBLISHING COMPANY, INC., ENCINO, CALIFORNIA,
AND BELMONT, CALIFORNIA

Library of Congress Catalog Card Number: 74–22624
ISBN: 0–8221–0144–X
Printed in the United States of America

1 2 3 4 5 6 7 8 9 10

Cover design: Preston J. Mitchell

CONTENTS

PART 2 HUMAN KNOWLEDGE: ITS GROUNDS AND LIMITS

PART **6** SELF-LOVE AND THE CLAIMS OF MORALITY

THE DICKENSON SERIES IN PHILOSOPHY

Philosophy, said Aristotle, begins in wonder—wonder at the phenomenon of self-awareness, wonder at the infinitude of time, wonder that there should be anything at all. Wonder in turn gives rise to a kind of natural puzzlement: How can mind and body interact? How is it possible that there can be free will in a world governed by natural laws? How can moral judgments be shown to be true?

Philosophical perplexity about such things is a familiar and unavoidable phenomenon. College students who have experienced it and taken it seriously are, in a way, philosophers already, well before they come in contact with the theories and arguments of specialists. The good philosophy teacher, therefore, will not present his subject as some esoteric discipline unrelated to ordinary interests. Instead he will appeal directly to the concerns that already agitate the student, the same concerns that agitated Socrates and his companions and serious thinkers ever since.

It is impossible to be a good teacher of philosophy, however, without being a genuine philosopher oneself. Authors of the Dickenson Series in Philosophy are no exceptions to this rule. In many cases their textbooks are original studies of problems and systems of philosophy, with their own views boldly expressed and defended with argument. Their books are at once contributions to philosophy itself and models of original thinking to emulate and criticize.

That equally competent philosophers often disagree with one another is a fact to be exploited, not concealed. Dickenson anthologies bring together essays by authors of widely differing outlook. This diversity is compounded by juxtaposition, wherever possible, of classical essays with leading contemporary materials. The student who is shopping for a world outlook of his own has a large and representative selection to choose among, and the chronological arrangements, as well as the editor's introduction, can often give him a sense of historical development. Some Dickenson anthologies treat a single group of interconnected problems. Others are broader, dealing with a whole branch of philosophy, or representative problems from various branches of philosophy. In both types of collections, essays with opposed views on precisely the same questions are included to illustrate the argumentative give and take which is the lifeblood of philosophy.

Joel Feinberg
Series Editor

PREFACE

The conviction underlying this volume is that for the purpose of introducing the modern college student to philosophy it is far preferable to have a small number of representative problems examined in great detail than to have a "little bit of everything," with each "branch" of philosophy, each major "ism," and each major historical period represented with scrupulous impartiality, even though the articles may have little relevance to one another. I have selected articles from both classical and contemporary sources on such topics as religion, knowledge, mind, personal identity, death, explanation, freedom, responsibility, duty, and selfishness. The problems under these headings that concern philosophers are not mere idle riddles, but rather questions of vital interest to any reflective person. Each set of problems is plumbed in considerable depth in essays expressing different, and often opposing, views. My hope is that exposure to this argumentative give-and-take will encourage the student to take part in the process himself and develop, through practice, his powers of philosophical reasoning.

In selecting materials for this third edition, I have benefited from the advice, positive and negative, of the following critics, who were well selected for me by the publisher: H. Gene Blocker, of Ohio University; Albert H. Clodius, of Ventura College; Richard M. Gale, of the University of Pittsburgh; John T. Granrose, of The University of Georgia; and C. A. Staudenbaur, of Michigan State University. I am grateful to Patricia Burns and Oksana Wengerchuk for their cheerful and efficient help in typing and assembling the manuscript.

Joel Feinberg

REASON
AND
RESPONSIBILITY

PART 1 REASON AND

W hat can reason tell us about such vast topics as the origin of the universe and the existence and nature of God? Most of us have beliefs about these matters—beliefs derived from religious authorities or based on faith; but is there any way that these beliefs can be demonstrated to be reasonable or unreasonable? This question provides the unifying theme for the readings in Part One.

Traditional arguments for the existence of God are often divided into two groups: those that are a posteriori (based on experience) and those that are a priori (independent of experience). In fact, however, only one type of argument has ever purported to be *wholly* a priori; namely, the *ontological argument*, invented by St. Anselm in the eleventh century and defended in one form or another by Descartes, Spinoza, and Leibniz in the seventeenth century. (For Descartes's version of the argument, see his fifth Meditation, p. 127.) According to this argument, the very concept of God (or definition of the word "God") entails that God himself must exist. If the argument is correct, any rational being who has an idea of God, even if he has no knowledge whatever of the kind derived from sense experience, has conclusive rational grounds for believing that God exists. Most philosophers of religion today agree in rejecting the ontological argument, but there is little agreement over precisely what is wrong with it. One recent discussion of the argument is included here. The essay by William L. Rowe sets forth Anselm's argument clearly, step by step (including steps that are only implicit in Anselm's own formulation), summarizes the three most important objections to the argument, and then presents his own criticism. He concludes that the ontological argument is defective, but that it is nevertheless a "work of genius" which, despite its apparent simplicity, raises philosophical questions about the nature of existence that are subtle and fascinating in their own right.

Other arguments for God's existence are often called a priori, but these always contain at least one premise that asserts some simple experiential fact. Factual premises summarizing some facet of our experience are found in the various versions of the

RELIGIOUS BELIEF

cosmological argument—illustrated here by the selection from St. Thomas Aquinas. For the first three of his "Five Ways," Aquinas begins each argument by citing a familiar fact of experience: some things are in motion, there are causes and effects, things are generated and corrupted. He then attempts to show that this fact can be explained *only* by the existence of God, since alternative explanations lead to logical absurdities.

Both the ontological and the cosmological arguments are *deductive* in form; that is, they purport to demonstrate that if their premises are true, then their conclusions *must necessarily* be true. It is *logically impossible* for a valid deductive argument to have both true premises and false conclusion. The argument a posteriori, on the other hand, is more modest. It argues not that its conclusion follows necessarily from its premises, but only that its premises establish a *probability* that the conclusion is true. It is therefore what logicians call an *inductive argument.* The famous *argument from design,* which is given a classic formulation by Cleanthes in Hume's *Dialogues,* has this form. More precisely, it is an argument by analogy, with the form:

1. *a, b, c,* and *d* all have properties *P* and *Q*.
2. *a, b,* and *c* all have property *R* as well.
3. Therefore, *d* has property *R* too (probably).

The closer the similarity between *d* and *a, b,* and *c,* the more probable is the conclusion. Cleanthes' argument can be rendered as follows:

1. Boats, houses, watches, and the whole experienced world have such properties as "mutual adjustment of parts to whole" and "curious adapting of ends to means."
2. Boats, houses, and watches have the further property of having been produced by design.

3. Therefore, it is probable that the universe also has this further property, that it too was produced by design.

The conclusion of this argument, that a designer of the world exists, has the same logical role as a scientific hypothesis designed to explain the facts of experience, and must be accepted or rejected according to whether it meets the criteria of adequacy by which hypotheses are appraised in science and in everyday life.

The case against the argument from design is put with great force and ingenuity by Philo, probably speaking for Hume himself. The analogies cited by the argument, he claims, are weak, partly because we know only one small part of the universe and cannot with confidence infer from it the nature of the whole. Moreover, he argues, there are other equally plausible ways of accounting for the observed order in the world. One of these alternative explanations, called by Philo in Part VII the "Epicurean Hypothesis," bears striking resemblance to the Darwinian theory that biological adaptations are the result of chance variations and the survival of the fittest.

In Parts X and XI occurs one of the most famous discussions of "the problem of evil," so central to religious belief. Here Philo concedes that *if* the existence of God has already been established by some a priori argument, then perhaps one can account for the appearance of evil in the world. But, he goes on to argue, one cannot infer the existence of an all-good and all-powerful being *from* the appearance of evil; that is, the former can hardly be an *explanation* of the latter.

Many contemporary philosophers reject all attempts to interpret theological doctrines as larger scientific hypotheses. According to these writers, there is at least one crucial difference between the two: Scientific hypotheses are in principal *falsifiable*. We can at least conceive of an experience that we would count as evidence against Newton's laws, but the true believer's faith is compatible with anything that might happen. And, it has been urged, a doctrine that is consistent with everything possible can *explain* nothing actual. In the selection from a symposium on theology and falsification, the contemporary British philosopher Antony Flew challenges his fellow symposiasts to describe any conceivable occurrence that they would accept as evidence against the existence of a loving God. His challenge is met in quite different ways. R. M. Hare rejects the view that religious doctrines are explanatory assertions, yet argues that they are no worse for that; his Oxford colleague Basil Mitchell, on the other hand, would allow the fact of pain to count against—but not decisively against—Christian doctrine.

What if it should turn out (as many philosophers now believe) that all traditional arguments for the existence of God, a priori and a posteriori, are defective, or at least inconclusive? Would it follow that religious belief is unreasonable? William James, in the selection from *The Varieties of Religious Experience,* discusses various accounts of mystic experiences that are literally indescribable, in which there is allegedly a direct experience of God—an experience so vivid and intense that, while under its influence, one cannot doubt its authenticity. To a person subject to such experiences, all talk of proofs and hypotheses must seem totally irrelevant. Yet how is he to know that his prized experiences are not illusory unless he reasons about the matter? This William James does for him. Mystic experiences "have the right to be absolutely authoritative over the individuals [and only those individuals] to whom they come," he concludes. Bertrand Russell, however, in his critique of mysticism, arrives at the opposite conclusion. Sigmund Freud's analysis of the "oceanic consciousness" is included as an example of a psychological explanation of mystic phenomena. The crucial question for the philosopher is whether or not such explanations "explain away" the beliefs of the mystics by undermining their "authority." The essay of Huston Smith discusses this and related problems in the light of recent experiments with "consciousness-expanding" drugs.

Mystical experiences, while having nothing to do with argument, might nevertheless be considered a kind of "evidence" for their attendant beliefs. The question posed by William James in the final selection in this section, however, is whether beliefs based on *no evidence whatever* can nevertheless be, in some circumstances, reasonable. His ingenious essay answers this question in a cautious affirmative. (The careful reader might well ask himself, however, whether James's strict conditions for the proper exercise of "the will to believe" are in fact ever satisfied.) If there is one thing that William James, the nineteenth-century Protestant, has in common with Blaise Pascal, the seventeenth-century Catholic, it is the conviction that the primary function of religious belief is not simply to allay philosophical curiosity about things. Both are aware that, to many, religious belief is a vital practical need; and each in his own way urges that this be taken into account when the reasonableness of belief is assessed.

SAINT ANSELM

The Ontological Argument, from *Proslogium**

CHAPTER II

Truly there is a God, although the fool hath said in his heart, There is no God.

And so, Lord, do thou, who dost give understanding to faith, give me, so far as thou knowest it to be profitable, to understand that thou art as we believe; and that thou art that which we believe. And, indeed, we believe that thou art a being than which nothing greater can be conceived. Or is there no such nature, since the fool hath said in his heart, there is no God? (Psalms xiv. 1). But, at any rate, this very fool, when he hears of this being of which I speak—a being than which nothing greater can be conceived—understands what he hears, and what he understands is in his understanding; although he does not understand it to exist.

For, it is one thing for an object to be in the understanding, and another to understand that the object exists. When a painter first conceives of what he will afterwards perform, he has it in his understanding, but he does not yet understand it to be, because he has not yet performed it. But after he has made the painting, he both has it in his understanding, and he understands that it exists, because he has made it.

Hence, even the fool is convinced that something exists in the understanding, at least, than which nothing greater can be conceived. For,

when he hears of this, he understands it. And whatever is understood, exists in the understanding. And assuredly that, than which nothing greater can be conceived, cannot exist in the understanding alone. For, suppose it exists in the understanding alone: then it can be conceived to exist in reality; which is greater.

Therefore, if that, than which nothing greater can be conceived, exists in the understanding alone, the very being, than which nothing greater can be conceived, is one, than which a greater can be conceived. But obviously this is impossible. Hence, there is no doubt that there exists a being, than which nothing greater can be conceived, and it exists both in the understanding and in reality.

CHAPTER III

God cannot be conceived not to exist.—God is that, than which nothing greater can be conceived.—That which can be conceived not to exist is not God.

And it assuredly exists so truly, that it cannot be conceived not to exist. For, it is possible to conceive of a being which cannot be conceived not to exist; and this is greater than one which can be conceived not to exist. Hence, if that, than which nothing greater can be conceived, can be conceived not to exist, it is not that than which nothing greater can be conceived. But this is an irreconcilable contradiction. There is, then, so truly a being than which nothing greater can be conceived to exist, that it cannot even be

*From *St. Anselm: Basic Writings*, trans. S. N. Deane, with an Introduction by Charles Hartshorne (La Salle, Ill.: Open Court, 1961). Reprinted by permission of the publisher.

conceived not to exist; and this being thou art, O Lord, our God.

So truly, therefore, dost thou exist, O Lord, my God, that thou canst not be conceived not to exist; and rightly. For, if a mind could conceive of a being better than thee, the creature would rise above the Creator; and this is most absurd. And, indeed, whatever else there is, except thee alone, can be conceived not to exist. To thee alone, therefore, it belongs to exist more truly than all other beings, and hence in a higher degree than all others. For, whatever else exists does not exist so truly, and hence in a higher degree than all others. For, whatever else exists does not exist so truly, and hence in a less degree it belongs to it to exist. Why, then, has the fool said in his heart, there is no God (Psalms xiv. I), since it is so evident, to a rational mind, that thou dost exist in the highest degree of all? Why, except that he is dull and a fool?

CHAPTER IV

How the fool has said in his heart what cannot be conceived.—A thing may be conceived in two ways: (1) when the word signifying it is conceived; (2) when the thing itself is understood. As far as the word goes God can be conceived not to exist; in reality he cannot.

But how has the fool said in his heart what he could not conceive; or how is it that he could not conceive what he said in his heart? since it is the same to say in the heart, and to conceive.

But, if really, nay, since really, he both conceived, because he said in his heart; and did not say in his heart, because he could not conceive; there is more than one way in which a thing is said in the heart or conceived. For, in one sense, an object is conceived, when the word signifying it is conceived; and in another, when the very entity, which the object is, is understood.

In the former sense, then, God can be conceived not to exist; but in the latter, not at all. For no one who understands what fire and water are can conceive fire to be water, in accordance with the nature of the facts themselves, although that is possible according to the words. So, then, no one who understands what God is can conceive that God does not exist; although he says these words in his heart, either without any, or with some foreign signification. For, God is that than which a greater cannot be conceived. And he who thoroughly understands this, assuredly understands that this being so truly exists, that not even in concept can it be non-existent. Therefore, he who understands that God so exists, cannot conceive that he does not exist.

I thank thee, gracious Lord, I thank thee; because what I formerly believed by the bounty, I now so understand by thine illumination, that if I were unwilling to believe that thou dost exist, I should not be able to understand this to be true.

CHAPTER V

God is whatever it is better to be than not to be; and he, as the only self-existent being, creates all things from nothing.

What art thou, then, Lord God, than whom nothing greater can be conceived? But what art thou, except that which, as the highest of all beings, alone exists through itself, and creates all other things from nothing? For, whatever is not this is less than a thing which can be conceived of. But this cannot be conceived of thee. What good, therefore, does the supreme Good lack, through which every good is? Therefore, thou art just, truthful, blessed, and whatever it is better to be than not to be. For it is better to be just than not just; better to be blessed than not blessed.

WILLIAM L. ROWE

The Ontological Argument*

Arguments for the existence of God are commonly divided into a posteriori and a priori arguments. An a posteriori argument depends on a principle or premise that can be known only by means of our experience of the world. An a priori argument, on the other hand, purports to rest on principles which can be known independently of our experience of the world, just by reflecting on and understanding them. Of the three major arguments for the existence of God—the Cosmological, Teleological, and Ontological—only the last is entirely a priori. In the Cosmological argument one starts from some simple fact about the world, such as the fact that it contains things which are caused to exist by other things. In the Teleological argument a somewhat more complicated fact about the world serves as a starting point: the fact that the world exhibits order and design. In the Ontological argument, however, one begins simply with a concept of God.

I

It is perhaps best to think of the Ontological argument as a family of arguments, each member of which begins with a concept of God, and by appealing only to a priori principles, endeavors to establish that God actually exists. Within this family of arguments the most important historically is the argument set forth by Anselm in the second chapter of his *Proslogium* (A Discourse).[1] Indeed, the Ontological argument begins with chapter II of Anselm's *Proslogium.* In an earlier work, *Monologium* (A Soliloquy), Anselm had endeavored to establish the existence and nature of God by weaving together several versions of the Cosmological argument. In the Preface to *Proslogium* Anselm remarks that after the publication of *Monologium* he began to search for a single argument which alone would establish the existence and nature of God. After much strenuous but unsuccessful effort, he reports that he sought to put the project out of his mind in order to turn to more fruitful tasks. The idea, however, continued to haunt him until one day the proof he had so strenuously sought became clear to his mind. Anselm sets forth this proof in the second chapter of *Proslogium.*

Before discussing Anselm's argument in step-by-step fashion, there are certain concepts that will help us understand some of the central ideas of the argument. Suppose we draw a vertical line in our imagination and agree that on the left side of our line are all the things which exist, while on the right side of the line are all the things which don't exist. We might then begin to make a list of some of the things on both sides of our imaginary line, as follows:

THINGS WHICH EXIST	THINGS WHICH DON'T EXIST
The Empire State Building	The Fountain of Youth
Dogs	Unicorns
The planet Mars	The Abominable Snowman

Now each of the things (or sorts of things) listed thus far has (have) the following feature: it (they) logically might have been on the other side of the line. The Fountain of Youth, for example, is on the right side of the line, but *logically* there is no absurdity in the idea that it might have been on the left side of the line. Similarly, although dogs do exist, we surely can imagine without logical absurdity that they might not have existed, that they might have been on the right side of the line.

*Copyright © William L. Rowe, 1974. This essay was commissioned by the editor expressly for this volume. It has not been previously published.

Let us then record this feature of the things thus far listed by introducing the idea of a *contingent thing* as a thing that logically might have been on the other side of the line from the side it actually is on. The planet Mars and the Abominable Snowman are contingent things, even though the former happens to exist and the latter does not.

Suppose we add to our list the phrase "the object which is completely round and completely square at the same time" on the right side of our line. The round square, however, unlike the other things thus far listed on the right side of our line, is something that *logically could not* have been on the left side of the line. Noting this, let us introduce the idea of an *impossible thing* as a thing that is on the right side of the line and logically could not have been on the left side of the line.

Looking again at our list, we wonder if there is anything on the left side of our imaginary line which, unlike the things thus far listed on the left side, *logically could not* have been on the right side of the line. At this point we don't have to answer this question, but it is useful to have a concept to apply to any such things, should there be any. Accordingly, let us say that a *necessary thing* is a thing on the left side of our imaginary line and logically could not have been on the right side of the line.

Finally, a *possible thing* is any thing that is either on the left side of our imaginary line or logically might have been on the left side of the line. Possible things, then, will be all those things that are not impossible things—that is, all those things that are either contingent or necessary. If there are no necessary things, then all possible things will be contingent and all contingent things will be possible. If there is a necessary thing, however, then there will be a possible thing which is not contingent.

Armed with these concepts, we can clarify certain important distinctions and ideas in Anselm's thought. The first of these is his distinction between *existence in the understanding* and *existence in reality*. Anselm's notion of existence in reality is the same as our notion of existence; that is, being on the left side of our imaginary line. Since the Fountain of Youth is on the right side of the line, it does not exist in reality. The things which exist are, to use Anselm's phrase, the things which exist in reality. Anselm's notion of

existence in the understanding, however, is not the same as any idea we normally employ. When we think of a certain thing, say the Fountain of Youth, then that thing, on Anselm's view, exists in the understanding. Also, when we think of an existing thing like the Empire State Building, it, too, exists in the understanding. So some of the things on both sides of our imaginary line exist in the understanding, but only those on the left side of our line exist in reality. Are there any things that don't exist in the understanding? Undoubtedly there are, for there are things, both existing and non-existing, of which we have not really thought. Now suppose I assert that the Fountain of Youth does not exist. Since to meaningfully deny the existence of something I have to have that thing in mind, I have to think of it, it follows on Anselm's view that whenever someone asserts that some thing does not exist, that thing *does* exist in the understanding.[2] So in asserting that the Fountain of Youth does not exist, I imply that the Fountain of Youth does exist in the understanding. And in asserting that it does not exist I have asserted (on Anselm's view) that it does not exist in reality. This means that my simple assertion amounts to the somewhat more complex claim that the Fountain of Youth exists in the understanding but does not exist in reality—in short, that the Fountain of Youth exists *only* in the understanding.

We can now understand why Anselm insists that anyone who hears of God, thinks about God, or even denies the existence of God is, nevertheless, committed to the view that God exists in the understanding. Also, we can understand why Anselm treats what he calls "the fool's claim" that God does not exist as the claim that God exists *only* in the understanding—that is, that God exists in the understanding but does not exist in reality.

In *Monologium* Anselm sought to prove that among those beings which do exist there is one which is the greatest, highest, and the best. But in *Proslogium* he undertakes to prove that among those beings which exist there is one which is not just the greatest among existing beings, but is such that no conceivable being is greater. We need to distinguish these two ideas: (1) a being than which *no existing being* is greater, and (2) a being than which *no conceivable being* is greater.

If the only things in existence were a stone, a frog, and a man, the last of these would satisfy our first idea but not our second—for we can conceive of a being (an angel or God) greater than a man. Anselm's idea of God, as he expresses it in *Proslogium* II, is the same as (2) above; it is the idea of "a being than which nothing greater can be conceived." It will facilitate our understanding of Anselm's argument if we make two slight changes in the way he has expressed his idea of God. For his phrase I shall substitute the following: '*the* being than which none greater *is possible.*'[3] This idea says that if a certain being is God then no *possible being* can be greater than it, or conversely, if a certain being is such that it is even *possible* for there to be a being greater than it, then that being is not God. What Anselm proposes to prove, then, is that the being than which none greater is possible exists in reality. If he proves this he will have proved that God, as he conceives of Him, exists in reality.

But what does Anselm mean by "greatness"? Is a building, for example, greater than a man? In *Monologium,* chapter II, Anselm remarks: "But I do not mean physically great, as a material object is great, but that which, the greater it is, is the better or the more worthy—wisdom, for instance." Contrast wisdom with size. Anselm is saying that wisdom is something that contributes to the greatness of a thing. If a thing comes to have more wisdom than it did before then (given that its other characteristics remain the same), that thing has become a greater, better, more worthy thing than it was. Wisdom, Anselm is saying, is a great-making quality. However, the mere fact that something increases in size (physical greatness) does not make that thing a better thing than it was before, so size is not a great-making quality. By "greater than" Anselm means "better than," "superior to," or "more worthy than," and he believes that some characteristics, like wisdom and moral goodness, are great-making characteristics in that anything which has them is a *better thing* than it would be (other characteristics of it remaining the same) were it to lack them.

We come now to what we may call the *key idea* in Anselm's Ontological argument. Anselm believes that *existence in reality is a great-making quality.* Does Anselm mean that anything that exists is a greater thing than anything that doesn't? Although he does not ask or answer the question, it is perhaps reasonable to believe that Anselm did not mean this. When he discusses wisdom as a great-making quality he is careful not to say that any wise thing is better than any unwise thing—for he recognizes that a just but unwise man might be a better being than a wise but unjust man.[4] I suggest that what Anselm means is that anything that doesn't exist but might have existed (is on the right side of our line but might have been on the left) would have been a greater thing if it had existed (if it had been on the left side of our line). He is not comparing two different things (one existing and one not existing) and saying that the first is therefore greater than the second. Rather, he is talking about *one* thing and pointing out that if it does not exist but might have existed, then *it* would have been a greater thing if it had existed. Using Anselm's distinction between existence in the understanding and existence in reality, we may express the key idea in Anselm's reasoning as follows: If something exists only in the understanding but might have existed in reality, then it might have been greater than it is. Since the Fountain of Youth, for example, exists only in the understanding but (unlike the round square) might have existed in reality, it follows by Anselm's principle that the Fountain of Youth might have been a greater thing than it is.

II

We can now consider the step-by-step development of Anselm's Ontological argument. I shall use the term "God" in place of the longer phrase "the being than which none greater is possible" —wherever the term "God" appears we are to think of it as simply an abbreviation of the longer phrase.

1. God exists in the understanding.

As we have noted, anyone who hears of the being than which none greater is possible is, on Anselm's view, committed to premise (1).

2. God might have existed in reality (God is a possible being).

Anselm, I think, assumes the truth of (2) without making it explicit in his reasoning. By asserting

(2) I do not mean to imply that God does not exist in reality, but that, unlike the round square, God is a possible being.

3. If something exists only in the understanding and might have existed in reality, then it might have been greater than it is.

As we noted, this is the key idea in Anselm's Ontological argument. It is intended as a general principle, true of anything whatever.

Steps (1)–(3) constitute the basic premises of Anselm's Ontological argument. From these three items, Anselm believes, it follows that God exists in reality. But how does Anselm propose to convince us that if we accept (1)–(3) we are committed by the rules of logic to accept his conclusion that God exists in reality? Anselm's procedure is to offer what is called a *reductio ad absurdum* proof of his conclusion. Instead of showing directly that the existence of God follows from steps (1)–(3), Anselm invites us to *suppose* that God does not exist (i.e., that the conclusion he wants to establish is false) and then shows how this supposition, when conjoined with steps (1)–(3), leads to an absurd result, a result that couldn't possible be true because it is contradictory. Since the supposition that God does not exist leads to an absurdity, that supposition must be rejected in favor of the conclusion that God does exist.

Does Anselm succeed in reducing the "fool's belief" that God does not exist to an absurdity? The best way to answer this question is to follow the steps of his argument.

4. Suppose God exists only in the understanding.

This supposition, as we saw earlier, is Anselm's way of expressing the belief that God does not exist.

5. God might have been greater than He is. (2, 4, and 3)[5]

Step (5) follows from steps (2), (4), and (3). Since (3), if true, is true of anything whatever, it will be true of God. Therefore, (3) implies that if God exists only in the understanding and might have existed in reality, then God might have been greater than He is. If so, then given (2) and (4), (5) must be true. For what (3) says when applied to God is that given (2) and (4), it follows that (5).

6. God is a being than which a greater is possible. (5)

Surely if God is such that He logically might have been greater, then He is such than which a greater is possible.

We can now appreciate Anselm's *reductio* argument. He has shown that if we accept steps (1)–(4), we must accept step (6). But (6) is unacceptable; it is the absurdity Anselm was after. By replacing "God" in (6) with the longer phrase it abbreviates, we see that (6) amounts to the absurd assertion:

7. The being than which none greater is possible is a being than which a greater is possible.

Now since steps (1)–(4) have led us to an obviously false conclusion, and if we accept Anselm's basic premises (1)–(3) as true, then (4), the supposition that God exists only in the understanding, must be rejected as false. Thus we have shown that:

8. It is false that God exists only in the understanding.

But since premise (1) tells us that God does exist in the understanding and (8) tells us that God does not exist only there, we may infer that

9. God exists in reality as well as in the understanding. (1, 8)

III

Most of the philosophers who have considered this argument have rejected it because of a basic conviction that from the logical analysis of a certain idea or concept we can never determine that there exists in reality anything answering to that idea or concept. We may examine and analyse, for example, the idea of an elephant or the idea of a unicorn, but it is only by our experience of the world that we can determine that there exist things answering to our first idea and not to the second. Anselm, however, believes that the concept of God is utterly unique—from an analysis of this concept he believes that it can be determined that there exists in reality a being which answers to it. Moreover, he presents us with an argument to show that it can be done in the case of the idea of God. We can, of course, simply reject Anselm's argument on the grounds that it violates the basic conviction noted above. Many critics, however, have sought to prove more directly that it is a bad argument and to point out the particular step that is mistaken. Next we shall examine the three major objections that have been advanced by the argument's critics.

The first criticism was advanced by a contemporary of Anselm's, a monk named "Gaunilo," who wrote a response to Anselm entitled, "On Behalf of the Fool."[6] Gaunilo sought to prove that Anselm's reasoning is mistaken by applying it to things other than God, things which we know don't exist. He took as his example the island than which none greater is possible. No such island really exists. But, argues Gaunilo, if Anselm's reasoning were correct we could show that such an island really does exist. For since it is greater to exist than not to exist, if the island than which none greater is possible doesn't exist then it is an island than which a greater is possible. But it is impossible for the island than which none greater is possible to be an island than which a greater is possible. Therefore, the island than which none greater is possible must exist. About this argument Gaunilo remarks:

> If a man should try to prove to me by such reasoning that this island truly exists, and that its existence should no longer be doubted, either I should believe that he was jesting, or I know not which I ought to regard as the greater fool: myself, supposing I should allow this proof; or him, if he should suppose that he had established with any certainty the existence of this island.[7]

Gaunilo's strategy is clear: by using the very same reasoning Anselm employs in his argument, we can prove the existence of things we know don't exist. Therefore, Anselm's reasoning in his proof of the existence of God must be mistaken. In reply to Gaunilo, Anselm insisted that his reasoning applies only to God and cannot be used to establish the existence of things other than God. Unfortunately, Anselm did not explain just why his reasoning cannot be applied to things like Gaunilo's island.

In defense of Anselm against Gaunilo's objection, there are two difficulties in applying Anselm's reasoning to things like Gaunilo's island. The first derives from the fact that Anselm's principle that existence is a great-making quality was taken to mean that if something does not exist then it is not as great *a thing* (being) as it would have been had it existed. Now if we use precisely this principle in Gaunilo's argument, all we will prove is that if Gaunilo's island does not exist then the island than which none greater is possible is an island than which *a greater thing* is possible. But this statement is not an absurdity. For the island than which no greater *island* is possible can be something than which *a greater thing* is possible—an unsurpassable island may be a surpassable thing. (A perfect man might be a greater thing than a perfect island.) Consequently, if we follow Anselm's reasoning exactly, it does not appear that we can derive an absurdity from the supposition that the island than which none greater is possible does not exist.

A second difficulty in applying Anselm's reasoning to Gaunilo's island is that we must accept the premise that Gaunilo's island is a possible thing. But this seems to require us to believe that some finite, limited thing (an island) might have unlimited perfections. It is not at all clear that this is possible. Try to think, for example, of a hockey player than which none greater is possible. How fast would he have to skate? How many goals would he have to score in a game? How fast would he have to shoot the puck? Could he ever fall down, be checked, or receive a penalty? Although the phrase, "the hockey player than which none greater is possible," seems meaningful, as soon as we try to get a clear idea of what such a being would be like we discover that we can't form a coherent idea of it at all. For we are being invited to think of some limited, finite thing —a hockey player or an island—and then to think of it as exhibiting unlimited, infinite perfections. Perhaps, then, since Anselm's reasoning applies only to possible things, Anselm can reject its application to Gaunilo's island on the grounds that the island than which none greater is possible is, like the round square, an impossible thing.

By far the most famous objection to the Ontological argument was set forth by Immanuel Kant in the eighteenth century. According to this objection the mistake in the argument is its claim, implicit in premise (3), that existence is a quality or predicate that adds to the greatness of a thing. There are two parts to this claim: (1) existence is a quality or predicate, and (2) existence, like wisdom and unlike physical size, is a great-making quality or predicate. Someone might accept (1) but object to (2); the objection made famous by Kant, however, is directed at (1). According to this objection, existence is not a predicate at all. Therefore, since in its second premise Anselm's argument implies that existence *is* a predicate, the argument must be rejected.

The central point in the philosophical doctrine that existence is not a predicate concerns what we do when we ascribe a certain quality or predicate to something: for example, when we say of a man next door that he is intelligent, six feet tall, or fat. In each case we seem to assert or presuppose that there *exists* a man next door and then go on to ascribe to him a certain predicate—"intelligent," "six feet tall," or "fat." And many proponents of the doctrine that existence is not a predicate claim that this is a *general feature* of predication. They hold that when we ascribe a quality or predicate to anything we assert or presuppose that the thing exists and then ascribe the predicate to it. Now if this is so, then it is clear that existence cannot be a predicate which we may ascribe to or deny of something. For if it were a predicate, then when we assert of some thing (things) that it (they) exists (exist) we would be asserting or presupposing that it (they) exists (exist) and then going on to predicate existence of it (them). For example, if existence were a predicate, then in asserting "tigers exist" we would be asserting or presupposing that tigers exist and then going on to predicate existence of them. Furthermore, in asserting "dragons do not exist" we would be asserting or presupposing, if existence were a predicate, that dragons do exist and then going on to deny that existence attaches to them. In short, if existence were a predicate, the affirmative existential statement "tigers exist" would be a redundancy and the negative existential statement "dragons do not exist" would be contradictory. But clearly "tigers exist" is not a redundancy; and "dragons do not exist" is true and, therefore, not contradictory. What this shows, according to the proponents of Kant's objection, is that existence is not a genuine predicate.

According to the proponents of the above objection, when we assert that tigers exist and that dragons do not we are not saying that certain things (tigers) have and certain other things (dragons) do not have a peculiar predicate, *exis-*

tence; rather, we are saying something about the *concept* of a tiger and the *concept* of a dragon. We are saying that the concept of a tiger applies to something in the world and that the concept of a dragon does not apply to anything in the world.

Although this objection to the Ontological argument has been widely accepted, it is doubtful that it provides us with a conclusive refutation of the argument. It may be true that existence is not a predicate, that in asserting the existence of something we are not ascribing a certain predicate or attribute to that thing. But the arguments presented for this view seem to rest on mistaken or incomplete claims about the nature of predication. For example, the argument which we stated earlier rests on the claim that when we ascribe a predicate to anything we assert or presuppose that that thing exists. But this claim appears to be mistaken. In asserting that Dr. Doolittle is an animal lover I seem to be ascribing the predicate "animal lover" to Dr. Doolittle, but in doing so I certainly am not asserting or presupposing that Dr. Doolittle actually exists. Dr. Doolittle doesn't exist, but it is nevertheless true that he is an animal lover. The plain fact is that we can talk about and ascribe predicates to many things which do not exist and never did. Merlin, for example, no less than Houdini, was a magician, although Houdini existed but Merlin did not. If, as these examples suggest, the claim that whenever we ascribe a predicate to something we assert or presuppose that the thing exists is a false claim, then we will need a better argument for the doctrine that existence is not a predicate. There is some question, however, whether anyone has succeeded in giving a really conclusive argument for this doctrine.[8]

A third objection against the Ontological argument calls into question the premise that God might have existed in reality (God is a possible being). As we saw, this premise claims that the being than which none greater is possible is not an impossible object. But is this true? Consider the series of positive integers: 1, 2, 3, 4, etc. We know that any integer in this series, no matter how large, is such that a larger integer than it is possible. Therefore, the positive integer than which none larger is possible is an impossible object. Perhaps this is also true of the being than which none greater is possible. That is, perhaps no matter how great a being may be, it is possible for there to be a being greater than it. If this were so, then, like the integer than which none larger is possible, Anselm's God would not be a possible object. The mere fact that there are degrees of greatness, however, does not entitle us to conclude that Anselm's God is like the integer than which none larger is possible. There are, for example, degrees of size in angles—one angle is larger than another—but it is not true that no matter how large an angle is it is possible for there to be an angle larger than it. It is logically impossible for an angle to exceed four right angles. The notion of an angle, unlike the notion of a positive integer, implies a degree of size beyond which it is impossible to go. Is Anselm's God like a largest integer, and therefore impossible, or like a largest angle, and therefore possible? Some philosophers have argued that Anselm's God is impossible,[9] but the arguments for this conclusion are not very compelling. Perhaps, then, this objection is best construed not as proving that Anselm's God is impossible, but as raising the question whether any of us is in a position to know that the being than which none greater is possible is a possible object. For Anselm's argument cannot be a successful proof of the existence of God unless its premises are not just true but are really *known* to be true. Therefore, if we do not know that Anselm's God is a possible object, then his argument cannot prove the existence of God to us, cannot enable us to know that God exists.

IV

Finally, I want to present a somewhat different critique of Anselm's argument, a critique suggested by the basic conviction noted earlier; namely that from the mere logical analysis of a certain idea or concept we can never determine that there exists in reality anything answering to that idea or concept.

Suppose someone comes to us and says:

I propose to define the term "God" as *an existing, wholly perfect being.* Now since it can't be true that an existing, wholly perfect being does not exist, it can't be true that God, as I've defined Him, does not exist. Therefore, God must exist.

His argument appears to be a very simple Ontological argument. It begins with a particular idea or concept of God and ends by concluding that God, so conceived, must exist. What can we say

in response? We might start by objecting to his definition, claiming: (1) that only predicates can be used to define a term, and (2) that existence is not a predicate. But suppose he is not impressed by this response—either because he thinks that no one has fully explained what a predicate is or proved that existence isn't one, or because he thinks that anyone can define a word in whatever way he pleases. Can we allow him to define the word "God" in any way he pleases and still hope to convince him that it will not follow from that definition that there actually exists something to which his concept of God applies? I think we can. Let us first invite him, however, to consider some concepts other than his peculiar concept of God.

Earlier we noted that the term "magician" may be applied both to Houdini and Merlin, even though the former existed and the latter did not. Noting that our friend has used "existing" as part of his definition of "God," suppose we agree with him that we can define a word in any way we please, and, accordingly, introduce the following definitions:

A "magican" is defined as *an existing magician.*
A "magico" is defined as *a non-existing magician.*

Here we have introduced two words and used "existing" or "non-existing" in their definitions. Now something of interest follows from the fact that "existing" is part of our definition of a "magican." For while it is true that Merlin was a *magician,* it is not true that Merlin was a *magican.* And something of interest follows from our including "non-existing" in the definition of a "magico"—it is true that Houdini was a *magician,* but it is not true that Houdini was a *magico.* Houdini was a *magician* and a *magican,* but not a *magico*; Merlin was a *magician* and a *magico,* but not a *magican.*

We have just seen that introducing "existing" or "non-existing" into the definition of a concept has a very important implication. If we introduce "existing" into the definition of a concept, it follows that no non-existing thing can exemplify that concept. And if we introduce "non-existing" into the definition of a concept, it follows that no existing thing can exemplify that concept. No non-existing thing can be a *magican,* and no existing thing can be a *magico.*

But must some existing thing exemplify the concept "magican"? No! From the fact that "existing" is included in the definition of "magican" it does not follow that some existing thing is a magican—all that follows is that no non-existing thing is a magican. If there were no magicians in existence there would be nothing to which the term "magican" would apply. This being so, it clearly does not follow merely from our definition of "magican" that some existing thing is a magican. Only if magicians exist will it be true that some existing thing is a magican.

We are now in a position to help our friend see that from the mere fact that "God" is defined as an existing, wholly perfect being it will not follow that some existing being is God. Something of interest does follow from his definition; namely that no non-existing being can be God. But whether some existing thing is God will depend entirely on whether some existing thing is a wholly perfect being. If no wholly perfect being exists there will be nothing to which his concept of God can apply. This being so, it clearly does not follow merely from his definition of "God" that some existing thing is God. Only if a wholly perfect being exists will it be true that God, as he conceives of Him, exists.

The implications of these considerations for Anselm's ingenious argument can now be traced. Anselm conceives of God as a being than which none greater is possible. He then claims that existence is a great-making quality and something that has it is greater than it would have been had it lacked existence. Clearly then, no non-existing thing can exemplify Anselm's concept of God. For if we suppose that some non-existing thing exemplifies Anselm's concept of God and also suppose that that non-existing thing might have existed in reality (is a possible thing) then we are supposing that that non-existing thing (1) might have been a greater thing, and (2) is, nevertheless, a thing than which a greater is not possible. Thus far Anselm's reasoning is, I believe, impeccable. But what follows from it? All that follows from it is that no non-existing thing can be God (as Anselm conceives of God). All that follows is that given Anselm's concept of God, the proposition, "Some non-existing thing is God," cannot be true. But, as we saw earlier, this is also the case with the proposition, "Some non-existing thing is a magican." What remains to be shown is that

some existing thing exemplifies Anselm's concept of God. What really does follow from his reasoning is that the only thing that logically could exemplify his concept of God is something which actually exists. And this conclusion is not without interest. But from the mere fact that nothing but an existing thing could exemplify Anselm's concept of God, it does not follow that some existing thing actually does exemplify his concept of God—no more than it follows from the mere fact that no non-existing thing can be a magican that some existing thing is a magican.[10]

There is, however, one major difficulty in this critique of Anselm's argument. This difficulty arises when we take into account Anselm's implicit claim that God is a possible thing. To see just what this difficulty is, let us return to the idea of a possible thing, which is any thing that either is on the left side of our imaginary line or logically might have been on the left side of the line. Possible things, then, will be all those things that, unlike the round square, are not impossible things. Suppose we concede to Anselm that God, as he conceives of Him, is a possible thing. Now, of course, the mere knowledge that something is a possible thing does not enable us to conclude that that thing is an existing thing. Many possible things, like the Fountain of Youth, do not exist. But if something is a possible thing then it is either an existing thing or a non-existing thing. The set of possible things can be exhaustively divided into those possible things which actually exist and those possible things which do not exist. Therefore, if Anselm's God is a possible thing it is either an existing thing or a non-existing thing. We have concluded, however, that no non-existing thing can be Anselm's God; therefore, it seems we must conclude with Anselm that some actually existing thing does exemplify his concept of God.

To see the solution to this major difficulty we need to return to an earlier example. Let us consider again the idea of a "magican," an existing magician. It so happens that some magicians have existed—Houdini, the Great Blackstone, etc. But, of course, it might have been otherwise. Suppose, for the moment that no magicians have ever existed. The concept "magician" would still have application, for it would still be true that Merlin was a magician. But would any possible object be picked out by the concept of a "magican?" No, for no non-existing thing could exemplify the concept "magican." And on the supposition that no magicians ever existed, no existing thing would exemplify the concept "magican."[11] We then would have a coherent concept "magican" which would not be exemplified by any possible object at all. For if all the possible objects which are magicians are non-existing things, none of them would be a magican and, since no possible objects which exist are magicians, none of them would be a magican. Put in this way, our result seems paradoxical. We are inclined to think that only contradictory concepts like "the round square" are not exemplified by any possible things. The truth is, however, that when "existing" is included in or implied by a certain concept, it may be the case that no possible object does in fact exemplify that concept. For no possible object that doesn't exist will exemplify a concept like "magican" in which "existing" is included; and if there are no existing things which exemplify the other features included in the concept—for example, "being a magician" in the case of the concept "magican"—then no possible object that exists will exemplify the concept. Put in its simplest terms, if we ask whether any possible thing is a magican the answer will depend entirely on whether any existing thing is a magician. If no existing things are magicians then no possible things are magicans. Some possible object is a magican just in the case some actually existing thing is a magician.

Applying these considerations to Anselm's argument, we can find the solution to our major difficulty. Given Anselm's concept of God and his principle that existence is a great-making quality, it really does follow that the only thing that logically could exemplify his concept of God is something which actually exists. But, we argued, it doesn't follow from these considerations alone that God actually exists, that some existing thing exemplifies Anselm's concept of God. The difficulty we fell into, however, is that when we add the premise that God is a possible thing, that some possible object exemplifies his concept of God, it really does follow that God actually exists, that some actually existing thing exemplifies Anselm's concept of God. For if some possible object exemplifies his concept of God, that object is either an existing thing or a non-existing thing. But since no non-existing thing could exemplify

Anselm's concept of God, it follows that the possible object which exemplifies his concept of God must be a possible object that actually exists. Therefore, given (1) Anselm's concept of God, (2) his principle that existence is a great-making quality, and (3) the premise that God, as conceived by Anselm, is a possible thing, it really does follow that Anselm's God actually exists. But we now can see that in granting Anselm the premise that God is a possible thing we have granted far more than we intended. All we thought we were conceding is that Anselm's concept of God, unlike the concept of a round square, is not contradictory or incoherent. But without realizing it we were in fact granting much more than this, as became apparent when we considered the idea of a magican. There is nothing contradictory in the idea of a magican, an existing magician. But in asserting that a magican is a possible thing we are, as we saw, directly implying that some existing thing is a magician. For if no existing thing is a magician, the concept of a magican will apply to no possible object whatever. The same point holds with respect to Anselm's God. Since Anselm's concept of God logically cannot apply to some non-existing thing, the only possible objects to which it could apply are possible objects which actually exist. Therefore, in granting that Anselm's God is a possible thing we are conceding far more than that his idea of God isn't incoherent or contradictory. Suppose, for example, that every existing being has some defect which it might not have had. Without realizing it we were denying this when we granted that Anselm's God is a possible being. If every existing being has a defect it might not have had, then every existing being might have been greater. But if every existing being might have been greater, then Anselm's concept of God will apply to no possible object whatever. Therefore, if we allow Anselm his concept of God and his principle that existence is a great-making quality, then in granting that God, as Anselm conceives of Him, is a possible being we will be granting much more than that his concept of God is not contradictory. We will be conceding, for example, that some existing thing is as perfect as it can be. The fact is that Anselm's God is a possible thing only if some *existing* thing is as perfect as it can be.

Our final critique of Anselm's argument is simply this. In granting that Anselm's God is a possible thing we are in fact granting that Anselm's God actually exists. But since the purpose of the argument is to prove to us that Anselm's God exists, we cannot be asked to grant as a premise a statement which is virtually equivalent to the conclusion that is to be proved. Anselm's concept of God may be coherent and his principle that existence is a great-making quality may be true. But all that follows from this is that no non-existing thing can be Anselm's God. If we add to all of this the premise that God is a possible thing it will follow that God actually exists. But the additional premise claims more than that Anselm's concept of God isn't incoherent or contradictory. It amounts to the assertion that some existing being is supremely great. And since this is, in part, the point the argument endeavors to prove, the argument begs the question: it assumes the point it is supposed to prove.

If the above critique is correct, Anselm's argument fails as a proof of the existence of God. This is not to say, however, that the argument is not a work of genius. Perhaps no other argument in the history of thought has raised so many basic philosophical questions and stimulated so much hard thought. Even if it fails as a proof of the existence of God, it will remain as one of the high achievements of the human intellect.

NOTES

1. Some philosophers believe that Anselm sets forth a different and more cogent argument in chapter III of his *Proslogium.* For this viewpoint see Charles Hartshorne, *Anselm's Discovery* (LaSalle, Ill.: Open Court Publishing Co., 1965); and Norman Malcolm, "Anselm's Ontological Arguments," *The Philosophical Review* LXIX, No. 1 (January 1960): 41–62. For an illuminating account both of Anselm's intentions in *Proslogium II and III and of recent interpretations of Anselm see Arthur C. McGill's essay "Recent Discussions of Anselm's Argument" in The Many-faced Argument,* ed. *John Hick and Arthur C. McGill (New York: The Macmillan Co., 1967), pp. 33–110.*

2. Anselm does allow that someone may assert the sentence "God does not exist" without having in his understanding the object or idea for which the word 'God' stands (see *Proslogium,* chapter IV). But when a person does understand the object for which a word stands, then when he uses that word in a sentence denying the existence of that object he must have that object in his understanding. It is doubtful, however, that Anselm thought that incoherent or contradictory expressions like 'the round square' stand for objects which may exist in the understanding.

3. Anselm speaks of "a being" rather than "the being" than which none greater can be conceived. His argument is easier to present if we express his idea of God in terms of "the being." Secondly, to avoid the psychological connotations of "can be conceived" I have substituted "possible."

4. See *Monologium,* chapter XV.

5. The numbers in parentheses refer to the earlier steps in the argument from which the present step is derived.

6. Gaunilo's brief essay, Anselm's reply, and several of Anselm's major works, as translated by S. N. Deane, are collected in *Saint Anselm: Basic Writings* (LaSalle, Ill.: Open Court Publishing Co., 1962).

7. *Saint Anselm: Basic Writings,* p. 151.

8. Perhaps the most sophisticated presentation of the objection that existence is not a predicate is William P. Alston's "The Ontological Argument Revisited" in *The Philosophical Review* 69 (1960): 452–74.

9. See, for example, C. D. Broad's discussion of the Ontological Argument in *Religion, Philosophy, and Psychical Research* (New York: Harcourt, Brace & World, 1953).

10. An argument along the lines just presented may be found in J. Shaffer's illuminating essay "Existence, Predication and the Ontological Argument," *Mind* 71 (1962): 307–325.

11. I am indebted to Professor William Wainwright for bringing this point to my attention.

SAINT THOMAS AQUINAS

The Five Ways, from *Summa Theologica**

[Part I, Question 2, Article 3]

The existence of God can be proved in five ways.

The first and more manifest way is the argument from motion. It is certain, and evident to our senses, that in the world some things are in motion. Now whatever is moved is moved by another, for nothing can be moved except it is in potentiality to that towards which it is moved; whereas a thing moves inasmuch as it is in act. For motion is nothing else than the reduction of something from potentiality to actuality. But nothing can be reduced from potentiality to actuality, except by something in a state of actuality. Thus that which is actually hot, as fire, makes wood, which is potentially hot, to be actually hot, and thereby moves and changes it. Now it is not possible that the same thing should be at once in actuality and potentiality in the same respect, but only in different respects. For what is actually hot cannot simultaneously be potentially hot; but it is simultaneously potentially cold. It is therefore impossible that in the same respect and in the same way a thing should be both mover and moved, *i.e.,* that it should move itself. Therefore, whatever is moved must be moved by another. If that by which it is moved be itself moved, then this also must needs be moved by another, and that by another again. But this cannot go on to infinity, because then there would be no first mover, and consequently no other mover, seeing that subsequent movers move only inasmuch as they are moved by the first mover; as the staff moves only because it is moved by the hand.

*From *The Basic Writings of Saint Thomas Aquinas,* ed. Anton C. Pegis (New York: Random House; London: Burns & Oates, 1945), pp. 22–23. Copyright © 1945 Random House, Inc. Reprinted by permission of the publishers.

Therefore it is necessary to arrive at a first mover, moved by no other; and this everyone understands to be God.

The second way is from the nature of efficient cause. In the world of sensible things we find there is an order of efficient causes. There is no case known (neither is it, indeed, possible) in which a thing is found to be the efficient cause of itself; for so it would be prior to itself, which is impossible. Now in efficient causes it is not possible to go on to infinity, because in all efficient causes following in order, the first is the cause of the intermediate cause, and the intermediate is the cause of the ultimate cause, whether the intermediate cause be several, or one only. Now to take away the cause is to take away the effect. Therefore, if there be no first cause among efficient causes, there will be no ultimate, nor any intermediate, cause. But if in efficient causes it is possible to go on to infinity, there will be no first efficient cause, neither will there be an ultimate effect, nor any intermediate efficient causes; all of which is plainly false. Therefore it is necessary to admit a first efficient cause, to which everyone gives the name of God.

The third way is taken from possibility and necessity, and runs thus. We find in nature things that are possible to be and not to be, since they are found to be generated, and to be corrupted, and consequently, it is possible for them to be and not to be. But it is impossible for these always to exist, for that which can not-be at some time is not. Therefore, if everything can not-be, then at one time there was nothing in existence. Now if this were true, even now there would be nothing in existence, because that which does not exist begins to exist only through something already existing. Therefore, if at one time nothing was in existence, it would have been impossible for anything to have begun to exist; and thus even now nothing would be in existence—which is absurd. Therefore, not all beings are merely possible, but there must exist something the existence of which is necessary. But every necessary thing either has its necessity caused by another, or not. Now it is impossible to go on to infinity in necessary things which have their necessity caused by another, as has been already proved in regard to efficient causes. Therefore we cannot but admit the existence of some being having of itself its own necessity, and not receiving it from another, but rather causing in others their necessity. This all men speak of as God.

The fourth way is taken from the gradation to be found in things. Among beings there are some more and some less good, true, noble, and the like. But *more* and *less* are predicated of different things according as they resemble in their different ways something which is the maximum, as a thing is said to be hotter according as it more nearly resembles that which is hottest; so that there is something which is truest, something best, something noblest, and, consequently, something which is most being, for those things that are greatest in truth are greatest in being, as it is written in *Metaph.* ii.[1] Now the maximum in any genus is the cause of all in that genus, as fire, which is the maximum of heat, is the cause of all hot things, as is said in the same book.[2] Therefore there must also be something which is to all beings the cause of their being, goodness, and every other perfection; and this we call God.

The fifth way is taken from the governance of the world. We see that things which lack knowledge, such as natural bodies, act for an end, and this is evident from their acting always, or nearly always, in the same way, so as to obtain the best result. Hence it is plain that they achieve their end, not fortuitously, but designedly. Now whatever lacks knowledge cannot move towards an end, unless it be directed by some being endowed with knowledge and intelligence; as the arrow is directed by the archer. Therefore some intelligent being exists by whom all natural things are directed to their end; and this being we call God.

NOTES

1. [Aquinas refers here to Aristotle's *Metaphysics*, Ia 1 (993b30).]

2. [*Metaphysics*, Ia 1 (993b25).]

F. C. C O P L E S T O N

On St. Thomas's Proofs*

Aquinas did not, of course, deny that people can come to know that God exists by other ways than by philosophic reflection. Nor did he ever assert that the belief of most people who accept the proposition that God exists is the result of their having elaborated metaphysical arguments for themselves or of their having thought through the metaphysical arguments developed by others. Nor did he confuse a purely intellectual assent to the conclusion of such a metaphysical argument with a living Christian faith in and love of God. But he did think that reflection on quite familiar features of the world affords ample evidence of God's existence. The reflection itself, sustained and developed at the metaphysical level, is difficult, and he explicitly recognized and acknowledged its difficulty: he certainly did not consider that everyone is capable of sustained metaphys-

*From F. C. Copleston, *Aquinas* (Harmondsworth: Penguin Books Ltd., 1955), pp. 110–122. Reprinted by permission of the author and publisher.

ical reflection. At the same time the empirical facts on which this reflection is based were for him quite familiar facts. In order to see the relation of finite things to the being on which they depend we are not required to pursue scientific research, discovering hitherto unknown empirical facts. Nor does the metaphysician discover God in a manner analogous to the explorer who suddenly comes upon a hitherto unknown island or flower. It is attention and reflection which are required rather than research or exploration.

What, then, are the familiar facts which for Aquinas imply the existence of God? Mention of them can be found in the famous 'five ways' of proving God's existence, which are outlined in the *Summa theologica* (I*a*, 2, 3). In the first way Aquinas begins by saying that 'it is certain, and it is clear from sense-experience, that some things in this world are moved.' It must be remembered that he, like Aristotle, understands the term 'motion' in the broad sense of change, reduction from a state of potentiality to one of act; he does not refer exclusively to local motion. In the second way he starts with the remark that 'we find in material things an order of efficient causes.' In other words, in our experience of things and of their relations to one another we are aware of efficient causality. Thus while in the first way he begins with the fact that some things are in motion or in a state of change, the second way is based upon the fact that some things act upon other things, as efficient causes. In the third way he starts by stating that 'we find among things some which are capable of existing or not existing, since we find that some things come into being and pass away.' In other words, we perceive that some things are corruptible or perishable. In the fourth proof he observes that 'we find in things that some are more or less good and true and noble and so on (than others).' Finally in the fifth way he says: 'we see that some things which lack knowledge, namely natural bodies, act for an end, which is clear from the fact that they always or in most cases act in the same way, in order to attain what is best.'

There is, I think, little difficulty in accepting as empirical facts the starting-points of the first three ways. For nobody really doubts that some things are acted upon and changed or 'moved,' that some things act on others, and that some things are perishable. Each of us is aware, for

example, that he is acted upon and changed, that he sometimes acts as an efficient cause, and that he is perishable. Even if anyone were to cavil at the assertion that he is aware that he himself was born and will die, he knows very well that some other people were born and have died. But the starting-points of the two final arguments may cause some difficulty. The proposition that there are different grades of perfections in things stands in need of a much more thorough analysis than Aquinas accords it in his brief outline of the fourth way. For the schematic outlining of the five proofs was designed, not to satisfy the critical minds of mature philosophers, but as introductory material for 'novices' in the study of theology. And in any case Aquinas could naturally take for granted in the thirteenth century ideas which were familiar to his contemporaries and which had not yet been subjected to the radical criticism to which they were later subjected. At the same time there is not very much difficulty in understanding the sort of thing which was meant. We are all accustomed to think and speak as though, for example, there were different degrees of intelligence and intellectual capacity. In order to estimate the different degrees we need, it is true, standards or fixed points of reference; but, given these points of reference, we are all accustomed to make statements which imply different grades of perfections. And though these statements stand in need of close analysis, they refer to something which falls within ordinary experience and finds expression in ordinary language. As for the fifth way, the modern reader may find great difficulty in seeing what is meant if he confines his attention to the relevant passage in the *Summa theologica*. But if he looks at the *Summa contra Gentiles* (1, 13) he will find Aquinas saying that we see things of different natures co-operating in the production and maintenance of a relatively stable order or system. When Aquinas says that we see purely material things acting for an end, he does not mean to say that they act in a manner analogous to that in which human beings consciously act for definite purposes. Indeed, the point of the argument is that they do not do so. He means that different kinds of things, like fire and water, the behaviour of which is determined by their several 'forms,' co-operate, not consciously but as a matter of fact, in such a way that there is a relatively stable order or system. And here again, though much more would need to be said in a full discussion of the matter, the basic idea is nothing particularly extraordinary nor is it contrary to our ordinary experience and expectations.

It is to be noted also that Aquinas speaks with considerable restraint: he avoids sweeping generalizations. Thus in the first argument he does not say that all material things are 'moved' but that we see that some things in this world are moved or changed. In the third argument he does not state that all finite things are contingent but that we are aware that some things come into being and pass away. And in the fifth argument he does not say that there is an invariable world-order or system but that we see natural bodies acting always or in most cases in the same ways. The difficulty, therefore, which may be experienced in regard to Aquinas' proofs of God's existence concerns not so much the empirical facts or alleged empirical facts with which he starts as in seeing that these facts imply God's existence.

Perhaps a word should be said at once about this idea of 'implication.' As a matter of fact Aquinas does not use the word when talking about the five ways: he speaks of 'proof' and of 'demonstration.' And by 'demonstration' he means in this context what he calls *demonstratio quia* (*S.T.*, I*a*, 2, 2), namely a causal proof of God's existence, proceeding from the affirmation of some empirical fact, for example, that there are things which change, to the affirmation of a transcendent cause. It is, indeed, his second proof which is strictly the causal argument, in the sense that it deals explicitly with the order of efficient causality; but in every proof the idea of ontological dependence on a transcendent cause appears in some form or other. Aquinas' conviction was that a full understanding of the empirical facts which are selected for consideration in the five ways involves seeing the dependence of these facts on a transcendent cause. The existence of things which change, for instance, is, in his opinion, not self-explanatory: it can be rendered intelligible only if seen as dependent on a transcendent cause, a cause, that is to say, which does not itself belong to the order of changing things.

This may suggest to the modern reader that Aquinas was concerned with causal explanation in the sense that he was concerned with framing an empirical hypothesis to explain certain facts. But he did not regard the proposition affirming God's existence as a causal hypothesis in the sense of being in principle revisable, as a hypothesis, that is to say, which might conceivably have to be revised in the light of fresh empirical data or which might be supplanted by a more economical hypothesis. This point can perhaps be seen most clearly in the case of his third argument, which is based on the fact that there are things which come into being and pass away. In Aquinas' opinion no fresh scientific knowledge about the physical constitution of such things could affect the validity of the argument. He did not look on a 'demonstration' of God's existence as an empirical hypothesis in the sense in which the electronic theory, for example, is said to be an empirical hypothesis. It is, of course, open to anyone to say that in his own opinion cosmological arguments in favour of God's existence are in fact analogous to the empirical hypotheses of the sciences and that they have a predictive function; but it does not follow that this interpretation can legitimately be ascribed to Aquinas. We should not be misled by the illustrations which he sometimes offers from contemporary scientific theory. For these are mere illustrations to elucidate a point in terms easily understandable by his readers: they are not meant to indicate that the proofs of God's existence were for him empirical hypotheses in the modern sense of the term.

Does this mean, therefore, that Aquinas regarded the existence of God as being logically entailed by facts such as change or coming into being and passing away? He did not, of course, regard the proposition 'there are things which come into being and pass away' as logically entailing the proposition 'there is an absolutely necessary or independent being' in the sense that affirmation of the one proposition and denial of the other involves one in a verbal or formal linguistic contradiction. But he thought that metaphysical analysis of what it objectively means to be a thing which comes into being and passes away shows that such a thing must depend existentially on an absolutely necessary being. And he thought that metaphysical analysis of what it objectively means to be a changing thing shows that such a thing depends on a supreme unmoved mover. It follows that for Aquinas one is involved in a contradiction if one affirms the propositions 'there are things which come into being and pass away' and 'there are things which change' and at the same time denies the propositions 'there is an absolutely necessary being' and 'there is a supreme unmoved mover.' But the contradiction can be made apparent only by means of metaphysical analysis. And the entailment in question is fundamentally an ontological or causal entailment.

Not a few philosophers (certainly all 'empiricists') would presumably comment that if this represents Aquinas' real mind it is clear that he confused the causal relation with logical entailment. But it should be remembered that though Aquinas was convinced that the proposition stating that everything which begins to exist has *a* cause is absolutely certain, he did not think that the existence of any finite thing entails the existence of any other finite thing in the sense that the existence of any finite thing can be said to entail the existence of God. In theological language, if we once admit that there is an omnipotent Creator, we can say that He could create and maintain in existence any finite thing without the existence of any other finite thing. But it does not follow that there can be any finite thing without God. In other words, Aquinas is not bound to produce other instances of the ontological entailment which he asserts between the existence of finite things and God. Though the relation of creatures to God is analogous in some way to the relation of causal dependence of one finite thing on another, the former relation is, if we consider it as such, unique. Aquinas was not confusing causal relations in general with logical entailments: he was asserting a unique relation between finite things and the transfinite transcendent cause on which they depend.

It is worth emphasizing perhaps that it does not necessarily follow from Aquinas' view that a metaphysical approach to God's existence is an easy matter. It is true that he was confident of the power of the human reason to attain knowledge of God's existence; and he did not regard his arguments as standing in need of support from rhetoric or emotional appeal. And in the *Summa theologica,* where he is writing for 'novices' in theology, he states the arguments in a bald and perhaps disconcertingly impersonal manner. But we cannot legitimately conclude that he thought it easy for a man to come to the knowledge of God's existence by philosophic reflection alone.

Indeed, he makes an explicit statement to the opposite effect. He was well aware that in human life other factors besides metaphysical reflection exercise a great influence. Moreover, he would obviously agree that it is always possible to stop the process of reflection at a particular point. For Aquinas every being, in so far as it is or has being, is intelligible. But we can consider things from different points of view or under different aspects. For example, I might consider coming-into-being and passing-away simply in regard to definite instances and from a subjective point of view. It grieves me to think that someone I love will probably die before me and leave, as we say, a gap in my life. Or it grieves me to think that I shall die and be unable to complete the work which I have undertaken. Or I might consider coming-into-being and passing-away from some scientific point of view. What are the finite phenomenal causes of organic decay or of the generation of an organism? But I can also consider coming-into-being and passing-away purely as such and objectively, adopting a metaphysical point of view and directing my attention to the sort of being, considered as such, which is capable of coming into being and passing away. Nobody can compel me to adopt this point of view. If I am determined to remain on the level of, say, some particular science, I remain there; and that is that. Metaphysical reflections will have no meaning for me. But the metaphysical point of view is a possible point of view, and metaphysical reflection belongs to a full understanding of things so far as this is possible for a finite mind. And if I do adopt this point of view and maintain it in sustained reflection, an existential relation of dependence, Aquinas was convinced, should become clear to me if I remain on a different level of reflection. But just as extraneous factors (such as the influence of the general outlook promoted by a technical civilization) may help to produce my decision to remain on a non-metaphysical level of reflection, so also can extraneous factors influence my reflections on the metaphysical level. It seems to me quite wrong to suggest that Aquinas did not regard metaphysical reflection as a possible way of becoming aware of God's existence and that he looked on it, as some writers have suggested, as being simply a rational justification of an assurance which is necessarily attained in some other way. For if it constitutes a rational justification at all, it must, I think, be a possible way of becoming aware of God's existence. But it does not necessarily follow, of course, that it is an easy way or a common way.

After these general remarks I turn to Aquinas' five proofs of the existence of God. In the first proof he argues that 'motion' or change means the reduction of a thing from a state of potentiality to one of act, and that a thing cannot be reduced from potentiality to act except under the influence of an agent already in act. In this sense 'everything which is moved must be moved by another.' He argues finally that in order to avoid an infinite regress in the chain of movers, the existence of a first unmoved mover must be admitted. 'And all understand that this is God.'

A statement like 'all understand that this is God' or 'all call this (being) God' occurs at the end of each proof, and I postpone consideration of it for the moment. As for the ruling out of an infinite regress, I shall explain what Aquinas means to reject after outlining the second proof, which is similar in structure to the first.

Whereas in the first proof Aquinas considers things as being acted upon, as being changed or 'moved,' in the second he considers them as active agents, as efficient causes. He argues that there is a hierarchy of efficient causes, a subordinate cause being dependent on the cause above it in the hierarchy. He then proceeds, after excluding the hypothesis of an infinite regress, to draw the conclusion that there must be a first efficient cause, 'which all call God.'

Now, it is obviously impossible to discuss these arguments profitably unless they are first understood. And misunderstanding of them is only too easy, since the terms and phrases used are either unfamiliar or liable to be taken in a sense other than the sense intended. In the first place it is essential to understand that in the first argument Aquinas supposes that movement or change is dependent on a 'mover' acting here and now, and that in the second argument he supposes that there are efficient causes in the world which even in their causal activity are here and now dependent on the causal activity of other causes. That is why I have spoken of a 'hierarchy' rather than of a 'series.' What he is thinking of can be illustrated in this way. A son is dependent on his father, in the sense that he would not have existed except for the causal activity of his father. But

when the son acts for himself, he is not dependent here and now on his father. But he is dependent here and now on other factors. Without the activity of the air, for instance, he could not himself act, and the life-preserving activity of the air is itself dependent here and now on other factors, and they in turn on other factors. I do not say that this illustration is in all respects adequate for the purpose; but it at least illustrates the fact that when Aquinas talks about an 'order' of efficient causes he is not thinking of a series stretching back into the past, but of a hierarchy of causes, in which a subordinate member is here and now dependent on the causal activity of a higher member. If I wind up my watch at night, it then proceeds to work without further interference on my part. But the activity of the pen tracing these words on the page is here and now dependent on the activity of my hand, which in turn is here and now dependent on other factors.

The meaning of the rejection of an infinite regress should now be clear. Aquinas is not rejecting the possibility of an infinite series as such. We have already seen that he did not think that anyone had ever succeeded in showing the impossibility of an infinite series of events stretching back into the past. Therefore he does not mean to rule out the possibility of an infinite series of causes and effects, in which a given member depended on the preceding member, say X on Y, but does not, once it exists, depend here and now on the present causal activity of the preceding member. We have to imagine, not a lineal or horizontal series, so to speak, but a vertical hierarchy, in which a lower member depends here and now on the present causal activity of the member above it. It is the latter type of series, if prolonged to infinity, which Aquinas rejects. And he rejects it on the ground that unless there is a 'first' member, a mover which is not itself moved or a cause which does not itself depend on the causal activity of a higher cause, it is not possible to explain the 'motion' or the causal activity of the lowest member. His point of view is this. Suppress the first unmoved mover and there is no motion or change here and now. Suppress the first efficient cause and there is no causal activity here and now. If therefore we find that some things in the world are changed, there must be a first unmoved mover. And if there are efficient causes in the world, there must be a first efficient, and completely nondependent cause. The word 'first' does not mean first in the temporal order, but supreme or first in the ontological order.

A remark on the word 'cause' is here in place. What precisely Aquinas would have said to the David Humes either of the fourteenth century or of the modern era it is obviously impossible to say. But it is clear that he believed in real causal efficacy and real causal relations. He was aware, of course, that causal efficacy is not the object of vision in the sense in which patches of colours are objects of vision; but the human being, he considered, is aware of real causal relations and if we understand 'perception' as involving the co-operation of sense and intellect, we can be said to 'perceive' causality. And presumably he would have said that the sufficiency of a phenomenalistic interpretation of causality for purposes of physical science proves nothing against the validity of a metaphysical notion of causality. It is obviously possible to dispute whether his analyses of change or 'motion' and of efficient causality are valid or invalid and whether there is such a thing as a hierarchy of causes. And our opinion about the validity or invalidity of his arguments for the existence of God will depend very largely on our answers to these questions. But mention of the mathematical infinite series is irrelevant to a discussion of his arguments. And it is this point which I have been trying to make clear.

In the third proof Aquinas starts from the fact that some things come into being and perish, and he concludes from this that it is possible for them to exist or not to exist: they do not exist 'necessarily.' He then argues that it is impossible for things which are of this kind to exist always; for 'that which is capable of not existing, at some time does not exist.' If all things were of this kind, at some time there would be nothing. Aquinas is clearly supposing for the sake of argument the hypothesis of infinite time, and his proof is designed to cover this hypothesis. He does not say that infinite time is impossible: what he says is that if time is infinite and if all things are capable of not existing, this potentiality would inevitably be fulfilled in infinite time. There would then be nothing. And if there had ever been nothing, nothing would now exist. For no thing can bring itself into existence. But it is clear as a matter of fact that there are things. Therefore it can never have been true to say that there was literally no

thing. Therefore it is impossible that all things should be capable of existing or not existing. There must, then, be some necessary being. But perhaps it is necessary in the sense that it must exist if something else exists; that is to say, its necessity may be hypothetical. We cannot, however, proceed to infinity in the series or hierarchy of necessary beings. If we do so, we do not explain the presence here and now of beings capable of existing or not existing. Therefore we must affirm the existence of a being which is absolutely necessary (*per se neccessarium*) and completely independent. 'And all call this being *God.*'

This argument may appear to be quite unnecessarily complicated and obscure. But it has to be seen in its historical context. As already mentioned, Aquinas designed his argument in such a way as to be independent of the question whether or not the world existed from eternity. He wanted to show that on either hypothesis there must be a necessary being. As for the introduction of hypothetical necessary beings, he wanted to show that even if there are such beings, perhaps within the universe, which are not corruptible in the sense in which a flower is corruptible, there must still be an absolutely independent being. Finally, in regard to terminology, Aquinas uses the common medieval expression 'necessary being.' He does not actually use the term 'contingent being' in the argument and talks instead about 'possible' beings; but it comes to the same thing. And though the words 'contingent' and 'necessary' are now applied to propositions rather than to beings, I have retained Aquinas' mode of speaking. Whether one accepts the argument or not, I do not think that there is any insuperable difficulty in understanding the line of thought.

The fourth argument is admittedly difficult to grasp. Aquinas argues that there are degrees of perfections in things. Different kinds of finite things possess different perfections in diverse limited degrees. He then argues not only that if there are different degrees of a perfection like goodness there is a supreme good to which other good things approximate but also that all limited degrees of goodness are caused by the supreme good. And since goodness is a convertible term with being, a thing being good in so far as it has being, the supreme good is the supreme being and the cause of being in all other things. 'Therefore there is something which is the cause of the being and goodness and of every perfection in all other things; and this we call *God.*'

Aquinas refers to some remarks of Aristotle in the *Metaphysics;* but this argument puts one in mind at once of Plato's *Symposium* and *Republic.* And the Platonic doctrine of participation seems to be involved. Aquinas was not immediately acquainted with either work, but the Platonic line of thought was familiar to him from other writers. And it has not disappeared from philosophy. Indeed, some of those theists who reject or doubt the validity of the 'cosmological' arguments seem to feel a marked attraction for some variety of the fourth way, arguing that in the recognition of objective values we implicitly recognize God as the supreme value. But if the line of thought represented by the fourth way is to mean anything to the average modern reader, it has to be presented in a rather different manner from that in which it is expressed by Aquinas, who was able to assume in his readers ideas and points of view which can no longer be presupposed.

Finally, the fifth proof, if we take its statement in the *Summa theologica* together with that in the *Summa contra Gentiles,* can be expressed more or less as follows. The activity and behaviour of each thing is determined by its form. But we observe material things of very different types co-operating in such a way as to produce and maintain a relatively stable world-order or system. They achieve an 'end', the production and maintenance of a cosmic order. But nonintelligent material things certainly do not co-operate consciously in view of a purpose. If it is said that they co-operate in the realization of an end or purpose, this does not mean that they intend the realization of this order in a manner analogous to that in which a man can act consciously with a view to the achievement of a purpose. Nor, when Aquinas talks about operating 'for an end' in this connexion, is he thinking of the utility of certain things to the human race. He is not saying, for example, that grass grows to feed the sheep and that sheep exist in order that human beings should have food and clothing. It is of the unconscious co-operation of different kinds of material things in the production and maintenance of a relatively stable cosmic system that he is thinking, not of the benefits accruing to us from our use of certain objects. And his argument is that this co-operation on the part of heterogeneous material things clearly points to the existence of an extrinsic intelligent author of this co-operation, who operates with an end in view. If Aquinas had lived in the days of the evolutionary hypothesis, he would doubtless have argued that this hypothesis supports rather than invalidates the conclusion of the argument.

No one of these arguments was entirely new, as Aquinas himself was very well aware. But he developed them and arranged them to form a coherent whole. I do not mean that he regarded the validity of one particular argument as necessarily depending on the validity of the other four. He doubtless thought that each argument was valid in its own right. But, as I have already remarked, they conform to a certain pattern, and they are mutually complementary in the sense that in each argument things are considered from a different point of view or under a different aspect. They are so many different approaches to God.

DAVID HUME

Dialogues concerning Natural Religion*

PART II

I must own, Cleanthes, said Demea, that nothing can more surprise me than the light in which you have all along put this argument. By the whole tenor of your discourse, one would imagine that you were maintaining the Being of a God against the cavils of atheists and infidels, and were necessitated to become a champion for that fundamental principle of all religion. But this, I hope, is not by any means a question among us. No man, no man at least of common sense, I am persuaded, ever entertained a serious doubt with regard to a truth so certain and self-evident. The question is not concerning the *being* but the *nature* of God. This I affirm, from the infirmities of human understanding, to be altogether incomprehensible and unknown to us. The essence of that supreme Mind, his attributes, the manner of his existence, the very nature of his duration—these and every particular which regards so divine a Being are mysterious to men. Finite, weak, and blind creatures, we ought to humble ourselves in his august presence, and, conscious of our frailties, adore in silence his infinite perfections which eye hath not seen, ear hath not heard, neither hath it entered into the heart of man to conceive. They are covered in a deep cloud from human curiosity; it is profaneness to attempt penetrating through these sacred obscurities, and, next to the impiety of denying his existence, is the temerity of prying into his nature and essence, decrees and attributes.

But lest you should think that my *piety* has here got the better of my *philosophy,* I shall support my opinion, if it needs any support, by a very great authority. I might cite all the divines, al-

most from the foundation of Christianity, who have ever treated of this or any other theological subject; but I shall confine myself, at present, to one equally celebrated for piety and philosophy. It is Father Malebranche who, I remember, thus expresses himself.[1] "One ought not so much," says he, "to call God a spirit in order to express positively what he is, as in order to signify that he is not matter. He is a Being infinitely perfect—of this we cannot doubt. But in the same manner as we ought not to imagine, even supposing him corporeal, that he is clothed with a human body, as the anthropomorphites asserted, under colour that that figure was the most perfect of any, so neither ought we to imagine that the spirit of God has human ideas or bears any resemblance to our spirit, under colour that we know nothing more perfect than a human mind. We ought rather to believe that as he comprehends the perfections of matter without being material ... he comprehends also the perfections of created spirits without being spirit, in the manner we conceive spirit: that his true name is *He that is,* or, in other words, Being without restriction, All Being, the Being infinite and universal."

After so great an authority, Demea, replied Philo, as that which you have produced, and a thousand more which you might produce, it would appear ridiculous in me to add my sentiment or express my approbation of your doctrine. But surely, where reasonable men treat these subjects, the question can never be concerning the *being* but only the *nature* of the Deity. The former truth, as you well observe, is unquestionable and self-evident. Nothing exists without a cause; and the original cause of this universe (whatever it be) we call God, and piously ascribe to him every species of perfection. Whoever scruples this

*First published in 1779.

fundamental truth deserves every punishment which can be inflicted among philosophers, to wit, the greatest ridicule, comtempt, and disapprobation. But as all perfection is entirely relative, we ought never to imagine that we comprehend the attributes of this divine Being, or to suppose that his perfections have any analogy or likeness to the perfections of a human creature. Wisdom, thought, design, knowledge—these we justly ascribe to him because these words are honourable among men, and we have no other language or other conceptions by which we can express our adoration of him. But let us beware lest we think that our ideas anywise correspond to his perfections, or that his attributes have any resemblance to these qualities among men. He is infinitely superior to our limited view and comprehension, and is more the object of worship in the temple than of disputation in the schools.

In reality, Cleanthes, continued he, there is no need of having recourse to that affected scepticism so displeasing to you in order to come at this determination. Our ideas reach no further than our experience. We have no experience of divine attributes and operations. I need not conclude my syllogism, you can draw the inference yourself. And it is a pleasure to me (and I hope to you, too) that just reasoning and sound piety here concur in the same conclusion, and both of them establish the adorably mysterious and incomprehensible nature of the Supreme Being.

Not to lose any time in circumlocutions, said Cleanthes, addressing himself to Demea, much less in replying to the pious declamations of Philo, I shall briefly explain how I conceive this matter. Look round the world, contemplate the whole and every part of it: you will find it to be nothing but one great machine, subdivided into an infinite number of lesser machines, which again admit of subdivisions to a degree beyond what human senses and faculties can trace and explain. All these various machines, and even their most minute parts, are adjusted to each other with an accuracy which ravishes into admiration all men who have ever contemplated them. The curious adapting of means to ends, throughout all nature, resembles exactly, though it much exceeds, the productions of human contrivance—of human design, thought, wisdom, and intelligence. Since therefore the effects resemble each other, we are led to infer, by all the rules of analogy, that the causes also resemble, and that the Author of nature is somewhat similar to the mind of man, though possessed of much larger faculties, proportioned to the grandeur of the work which he has executed. By this argument *a posteriori,* and by this argument alone, do we prove at once the existence of a Deity and his similarity to human mind and intelligence.

I shall be so free, Cleanthes, said Demea, as to tell you that from the beginning I could not approve of your conclusion concerning the similarity of the Deity to men, still less can I approve of the mediums by which you endeavour to establish it. What! No demonstration of the Being of God! No abstract arguments! No proofs *a priori!* Are these which have hitherto been so much insisted on by philosophers all fallacy, all sophism? Can we reach no farther in this subject than experience and probability? I will not say that this is betraying the cause of a Deity; but surely, by this affected candour, you give advantages to atheists which they never could obtain by the mere dint of argument and reasoning.

What I chiefly scruple in this subject, said Philo, is not so much that all religious arguments are by Cleanthes reduced to experience, as that they appear not to be even the most certain and irrefragable of that inferior kind. That a stone will fall, that fire will burn, that the earth has solidity, we have observed a thousand and a thousand times; and when any new instance of this nature is presented, we draw without hesitation the accustomed inference. The exact similarity of the cases gives us a perfect assurance of a similar event, and a stronger evidence is never desired nor sought after. But wherever you depart, in the least, from the similarity of the cases, you diminish proportionably the evidence, and may at last bring it to a very weak analogy, which is confessedly liable to error and uncertainty. After having experienced the circulation of the blood in human creatures, we make no doubt that it takes place in Titius and Maevius; but from its circulation in frogs and fishes it is only a presumption, though a strong one, from analogy that it takes place in men and other animals. The analogical reasoning is much weaker when we infer the circulation of the sap in vegetables from our experience that the blood circulates in animals; and those who hastily followed that imperfect analogy are found, by more accurate experiments, to have been mistaken.

If we see a house, Cleanthes, we conclude, with the greatest certainty, that it had an architect or builder because this is precisely that species of effect which we have experienced to proceed from that species of cause. But surely you will not affirm that the universe bears such a resemblance to a house that we can with the same certainty infer a similar cause, or that the analogy is here entire and perfect. The dissimilitude is so striking that the utmost you can here pretend to is a guess, conjecture, a presumption concerning a similar cause; and how that pretension will be received in the world, I leave you to consider.

It would surely be very ill received, replied Cleanthes; and I should be deservedly blamed and detested did I allow that the proofs of Deity amounted to no more than a guess or conjecture. But is the whole adjustment of means to ends in a house and in the universe so slight a resemblance? the economy of final causes? the order, proportion, and arrangement of every part? Steps of a stair are plainly contrived that human legs may use them in mounting; and this inference is certain and infallible. Human legs are also contrived for walking and mounting; and this inference, I allow, is not altogether so certain because of the dissimilarity which you remark; but does it, therefore, deserve the name only of presumption or conjecture?

Good God! cried Demea, interrupting him, where are we? Zealous defenders of religion allow that the proofs of a Deity fall short of perfect evidence! And you, Philo, on whose assistance I depended in proving the adorable mysteriousness of the Divine Nature, do you assent to all these extravagant opinions of Cleanthes? For what other name can I give them? or, why spare my censure when such principles are advanced, supported by such an authority, before so young a man as Pamphilus?

You seem not to apprehend, replied Philo, that I argue with Cleanthes in his own way, and, by showing him the dangerous consequences of his tenets, hope at last to reduce him to our opinion. But what sticks most with you, I observe, is the representation which Cleanthes has made of the argument *a posteriori;* and, finding that the argument is likely to escape your hold and vanish into air, you think it so disguised that you can scarcely believe it to be set in its true light. Now, however much I may dissent, in other respects, from the dangerous principle of Cleanthes, I must allow that he has fairly represented that argument, and I shall endeavour so to state the matter to you that you will entertain no further scruples with regard to it.

Were a man to abstract from everything which he knows or has seen, he would be altogether incapable, merely from his own ideas, to determine what kind of scene the universe must be, or to give the preference to one state or situation of things above another. For as nothing which he clearly conceives could be esteemed impossible or implying a contradiction, every chimera of his fancy would be upon an equal footing; nor could he assign any just reason why he adheres to one idea or system, and rejects the others which are equally possible.

Again, after he opens his eyes and contemplates the world as it really is, it would be impossible for him at first to assign the cause of any one event, much less of the whole of things, or of the universe. He might set his fancy a rambling, and she might bring him in an infinite variety of reports and representations. These would all be possible, but, being all equally possible, he would never of himself give a satisfactory account for his preferring one of them to the rest. Experience alone can point out to him the true cause of any phenomenon.

Now, according to this method of reasoning, Demea, it follows (and is, indeed, tacitly allowed by Cleanthes himself) that order, arrangement, or the adjustment of final causes, is not of itself any proof of design, but only so far as it has been experienced to proceed from that principle. For aught we can know *a priori,* matter may contain the source or spring of order originally within itself, as well as mind does; and there is no more difficulty in conceiving that the several elements, from an internal unknown cause, may fall into the most exquisite arrangement, than to conceive that their ideas, in the great universal mind, from a like internal unknown cause, fall into that arrangement. The equal possibility of both these suppositions is allowed. But, by experience, we find (according to Cleanthes) that there is a difference between them. Throw several pieces of steel together, without shape or form, they will never arrange themselves so as to compose a watch.

Stone and mortar and wood, without an architect, never erect a house. But the ideas in a human mind, we see, by an unknown, inexplicable economy, arrange themselves so as to form the plan of a watch or house. Experience, therefore, proves that there is an original principle of order in mind, not in matter. From similar effects we infer similar causes. The adjustment of means to ends is alike in the universe, as in a machine of human contrivance. The causes, therefore, must be resembling.

I was from the beginning scandalized, I must own, with this resemblance which is asserted between the Deity and human creatures, and must conceive it to imply such a degradation of the Supreme Being as no sound theist could endure. With your assistance, therefore, Demea, I shall endeavour to defend what you justly call the adorable mysteriousness of the Divine Nature, and shall refute this reasoning of Cleanthes, provided he allows that I have made a fair representation of it.

When Cleanthes had assented, Philo, after a short pause, proceeded in the following manner.

That all inferences, Cleanthes, concerning fact are founded on experience, and that all experimental reasonings are founded on the supposition that similar causes prove similar effects, and similar effects similar causes, I shall not at present much dispute with you. But observe, I entreat you, with what extreme caution all just reasoners proceed in the transferring of experiments to similar cases. Unless the cases be exactly similar, they repose no perfect confidence in applying their past observation to any particular phenomenon. Every alteration of circumstances occasions a doubt concerning the event; and it requires new experiments to prove certainly that the new circumstances are of no moment or importance. A change in bulk, situation, arrangement, age, disposition of the air, or surrounding bodies—any of these particulars may be attended with the most unexpected consequences. And unless the objects be quite familiar to us, it is the highest temerity to expect with assurance, after any of these changes, an event similar to that which before fell under our observation. The slow and deliberate steps of philosophers here, if anywhere, are distinguished from the precipitate march of the vulgar, who, hurried on by the smallest similitude, are incapable of all discernment or consideration.

But can you think, Cleanthes, that your usual phlegm and philosophy have been preserved in so wide a step as you have taken when you compared to the universe houses, ships, furniture, machines, and, from their similarity in some circumstances, inferred a similarity in their causes? Thought, design, intelligence, such as we discover in men and other animals, is no more than one of the springs and principles of the universe, as well as heat or cold, attraction or repulsion, and a hundred others which fall under daily observation. It is an active cause by which some particular parts of nature, we find, produce alterations on other parts. But can a conclusion, with any propriety, be transferred from parts to the whole? Does not the great disproportion bar all comparison and inference? From observing the growth of a hair, can we learn anything concerning the generation of a man? Would the manner of a leaf's blowing, even though perfectly known, afford us any instruction concerning the vegetation of a tree?

But allowing that we were to take the *operations* of one part of nature upon another for the foundation of our judgment concerning the *origin* of the whole (which never can be admitted), yet why select so minute, so weak, so bounded a principle as the reason and design of animals is found to be upon this planet? What peculiar privilege has this little agitation of the brain which we call *thought*, that we must thus make it the model of the whole universe? Our partiality in our own favour does indeed present it on all occasions, but sound philosophy ought carefully to guard against so natural an illusion.

So far from admitting, continued Philo, that the operations of a part can afford us any just conclusion concerning the origin of the whole, I will not allow any one part to form a rule for another part if the latter be very remote from the former. Is there any reasonable ground to conclude that the inhabitants of other planets possess thought, intelligence, reason, or anything similar to these faculties in men? When nature has so extremely diversified her manner of operation in this small globe, can we imagine that she incessantly copies herself throughout so immense a universe? And if thought, as we may well suppose, be confined merely to this narrow corner and has even there so limited a sphere of action, with what propriety can we assign it for the original cause of all things? The narrow views of a peasant who makes his domestic economy the rule for the government of kingdoms is in comparison a pardonable sophism.

But were we ever so much assured that a thought and reason resembling the human were to be found throughout the whole universe, and were its activity elsewhere vastly greater and more commanding than it appears in this globe, yet I cannot see why the operations of a world constituted, arranged, adjusted, can with any propriety be extended to a world which is in its embryo state, and is advancing towards that constitution and arrangement. By observation we know somewhat of the economy, action, and nourishment of a finished animal, but we must transfer with great caution that observation to the growth of a foetus in the womb, and still more to the formation of an animalcule in the loins of its male parent. Nature, we find, even from our limited experience, possesses an infinite number of springs and principles which incessantly discover themselves on every change of her position and situation. And what new and unknown principles would actuate her in so new and unknown a situation as that of the formation of a universe, we cannot, without the utmost temerity, pretend to determine.

A very small part of this great system, during a very short time, is very imperfectly discovered to us; and do we thence pronounce decisively concerning the origin of the whole?

Admirable conclusion! Stone, wood, brick, iron, brass, have not, at this time, in this minute globe of earth, an order or arrangement without human art and contrivance; therefore, the universe could not originally attain its order and arrangement without something similar to human art. But is a part of nature a rule for another part very wide of the former? Is it a rule for the whole? Is a very small part a rule for the universe? Is nature in one situation a certain rule for nature in another situation vastly different from the former?

And can you blame me, Cleanthes, if I here imitate the prudent reserve of Simonides, who, according to the noted story, being asked by Hiero, *What God was?* desired a day to think of it, and then two days more; and after that manner continually prolonged the term, without ever bringing in his definition or description? Could you even blame me if I had answered, at first, *that I did not know,* and was sensible that this subject lay vastly beyond the reach of my faculties? You might cry out sceptic and rallier, as much as you pleased; but, having found in so many other subjects much more familiar the imperfections and even contradictions of human reason, I never should expect any success from its feeble conjectures in a subject so sublime and so remote from the sphere of our observation. When two *species* of objects have always been observed to be conjoined together, I can *infer,* by custom, the existence of one wherever I *see* the existence of the other; and this I call an argument from experience. But how this argument can have place where the objects, as in the present case, are single, individual, without parallel or specific resemblance, may be difficult to explain. And will any man tell me with a serious countenance that an orderly universe must arise from some thought and art like the human because we have experience of it? To ascertain this reasoning it were requisite that we had experience of the origin of worlds; and it is not sufficient, surely, that we have seen ships and cities arise from human art and contrivance.

Philo was proceeding in this vehement manner, somewhat between jest and earnest, as it appeared to me, when he observed some signs of impatience in Cleanthes, and then immediately stopped short. What I had to suggest, said Cleanthes, is only that you would not abuse terms, or make use of popular expressions to subvert philosophical reasonings. You know that the vulgar often distinguish reason from experience, even where the question relates only to matter of fact and existence, though it is found, where that *reason* is properly analyzed, that it is nothing but a species of experience. To prove by experience the origin of the universe from mind is not more contrary to common speech than to prove the motion of the earth from the same principle. And a caviller might raise all the same objections to the Copernican system which you have urged against my reasonings. Have you other earths, might he say, which you have seen to move? Have . . .

Yes! cried Philo, interrupting him, we have other earths. Is not the moon another earth, which we see to turn around its centre? Is not Venus another earth, where we observe the same phenomenon? Are not the revolutions of the sun also a confirmation, from analogy, of the same theory? All the planets, are they not earths which revolve about the sun? Are not the satellites moons which move round Jupiter and Saturn, and along with these primary planets round the sun? These analogies and resemblances, with others which I have not mentioned, are the sole proofs of the Copernican system; and to you it belongs to consider whether you have any analogies of the same kind to support your theory.

In reality, Cleanthes, continued he, the modern system of astronomy is now so much received by all inquirers, and has become so essential a part even of our earliest education, that we are not commonly very scrupulous in examining the reasons upon which it is founded. It is now become a matter of mere curiosity to study the first writers of that subject who had the full force of prejudice to encounter, and were obliged to turn their arguments on every side in order to render them popular and convincing. But if we peruse Galileo's famous *Dialogues* concerning the system of the world, we shall find that the great genius, one of the sublimest that ever existed, first bent all his endeavours to prove that there was no foundation for the distinction commonly made between elementary and celestial substances. The schools, proceeding from the illusions of sense, had carried this distinction very far; and had established the latter substances to be ingenerable, incorruptible, unalterable, impassible; and had assigned all the opposite qualities to the former. But Galileo, beginning with the moon, proved its similarity in every particular to the earth: its convex figure, its natural darkness when not illuminated, its density, its distinction into solid and liquid, the variations of its phases, the mutual illuminations of the earth and moon, their mutual eclipses, the inequalities of the lunar surface, etc. After many instances of this kind, with regard to all the planets, men plainly saw that these bodies became proper objects of experience, and that the similarity of their nature enabled us to extend the same arguments and phenomena from one to the other.

In this cautious proceeding of the astronomers you may read your own condemnation, Cleanthes, or rather may see that the subject in which you are engaged exceeds all human reason and inquiry. Can you pretend to show any such similarity between the fabric of a house and the generation of a universe? Have you ever seen nature in any such situation as resembles the first arrangement of the elements? Have worlds ever been formed under your eye, and have you had leisure to observe the whole progress of the phenomenon, from the first appearance of order to its final consummation? If you have, then cite your experience and deliver your theory.

PART III

How the most absurd argument, replied Cleanthes, in the hands of a man of ingenuity and invention, may acquire an air of probability! Are you not aware, Philo, that it became necessary for Copernicus and his first disciples to prove the similarity of the terrestrial and celestial matter because several philosophers, blinded by old systems and supported by some sensible appearances, had denied this similarity? But that it is by no means necessary that theists should prove the similarity of the works of *nature* to those of *art* because this similarity is self-evident and undeniable? The same matter, a like form; what more is requisite to show an analogy between their causes, and to ascertain the origin of all things from a divine purpose and intention? Your objections, I must freely tell you, are no better than the abstruse cavils of those philosophers who denied motion, and ought to be refuted in the same manner—by illustrations, examples, and instances rather than by serious argument and philosophy.

Suppose, therefore, that an articulate voice were heard in the clouds, much louder and more melodious than any which human art could ever reach; suppose that this voice were extended in the same instant over all nations and spoke to each nation in its own language and dialect; suppose that the words delivered not only contain a just sense and meaning, but convey some instruction altogether worthy of a benevolent Being superior to mankind—could you possibly hesitate a moment concerning the cause of this voice, and must you not instantly ascribe it to some design or purpose? Yet I cannot see but all the same objections (if they merit that appellation) which lie against the system of theism may also be produced against this inference.

Might you not say that all conclusions concerning fact were founded on experience; that, when we hear an articulate voice in the dark and thence infer a man, it is only the resemblance of the effects which leads us to conclude that there is a like resemblance in the cause; but that this extraordinary voice, by its loudness, extent, and flexibility to all languages, bears so little analogy to any human voice that we have no reason to suppose any analogy in their causes; and, consequently, that a rational, wise, coherent speech proceeded, you know not whence, from some accidental whistling of the winds, not from any divine reason or intelligence? You see clearly your own objections in these cavils, and I hope too you see clearly that they cannot possibly have more force in the one case than in the other.

But to bring the case still nearer the present one of the universe, I shall make two suppositions which imply not any absurdity or impossibility. Suppose that there is a natural, universal, invariable language, common to every individual of human race, and that books are natural productions which perpetuate themselves in the same manner with animals and vegetables, by descent and propagation. Several expressions of our passions contain a universal language: all brute animals have a natural speech, which, however limited, is very intelligible to their own species. And as there are infinitely fewer parts and less contrivance in the finest composition of eloquence than in the coarsest organized body, the propagation of an *Iliad* or *Aeneid* is an easier supposition that that of any plant or animal.

Suppose, therefore, that you enter into your library thus peopled by natural volumes containing the most refined reason and most exquisite beauty; could you possibly open one of them and doubt that its original cause bore the strongest analogy to mind and intelligence? When it reasons and discourses; when it expostulates, argues, and enforces its views and topics; when it applies sometimes to the pure intellect, sometimes to the affections; when it collects, disposes, and adorns every consideration suited to the subject; could you persist in asserting that all this, at the bottom, had really no meaning, and that the first formation of this volume in the loins of its original parent proceeded not from thought and design? Your obstinacy, I know, reaches not that degree of firmness; even your sceptical play and wantonness would be abashed at so glaring an absurdity.

But if there be any difference, Philo, between this supposed case and the real one of the universe, it is all to the advantage of the latter. The anatomy of an animal affords many stronger instances of design than the perusal of Livy or Tacitus; and any objection which you start in the former case, by carrying me back to so unusual and extraordinary a scene as the first formation of worlds, the same objection has place on the supposition of our vegetating library. Choose, then, your party, Philo, without ambiguity or evasion; assert either that a rational volume is no proof of a rational cause or admit of a similar cause to all the works of nature.

Let me here observe, too, continued Cleanthes, that this religious argument, instead of being weakened by that scepticism so much affected by you, rather acquires force from it and becomes more firm and undisputed. To exclude all argument or reasoning of every kind is either affectation or madness. The declared profession of every reasonable sceptic is only to reject abtruse, remote, and refined arguments; to adhere to common sense and the plain instincts of nature; and to assent, wherever any reasons strike him with so full a force that he cannot, without the greatest violence, prevent it. Now the arguments for natural religion are plainly of this kind; and nothing but the most perverse, obstinate metaphysics can reject them. Consider, anatomize the eye, survey its structure and contrivance, and tell me, from your own feeling, if the idea of a contriver does not immediately flow in upon you with a force like that of sensation. The most obvious conclusion, surely, is in favour of design; and it requires time, reflection, and study, to summon up those frivolous though abstruse objections which can support infidelity. Who can behold the male and female of each species, the correspondence of their parts and instincts, their passions and whole course of life before and after generation, but must be sensible that the propagation of the species is intended by nature? Millions and millions of such instances present themselves through every part of the universe, and no language can convey a more intelligible irresistible meaning than the curious adjustment of final causes. To what degree, therefore, of blind dogmatism must one have attained to reject such natural and such convincing arguments?

Some beauties in writing we may meet with which seem contrary to rules, and which gain the affections and animate the imagination in opposition to all the precepts of criticism and to the authority of the established masters of art. And if the argument for theism be, as you pretend, contradictory to the principles of logic, its universal, its irresistible influence proves clearly that there may be arguments of a like irregular nature. Whatever cavils may be urged, an orderly world, as well as a coherent, articulate speech, will still be received as an incontestable proof of design and intention.

It sometimes happens, I own, that the religious arguments have not their due influence on an ignorant savage and barbarian, not because they are obscure and difficult, but because he never asks himself any question with regard to them. Whence arises the curious structure of an animal? From the copulation of its parents. And these whence? From *their* parents? A few removes set the objects at such a distance that to him they are lost in darkness and confusion; nor is he actuated by any curiosity to trace them farther. But this is neither dogmatism nor scepticism, but stupidity: a state of mind very different from your sifting, inquisitive disposition, my ingenious friend. You can trace causes from effects; you can compare the most distant and remote objects; and your greatest errors proceed not from barrenness of thought and invention, but from too luxuriant a fertility which suppresses your natural good sense by a profusion of unnecessary scruples and objections.

Here I could observe, Hermippus, that Philo was a little embarrassed and confounded; but, while he hesitated in delivering an answer, luckily for him, Demea broke in upon the discourse and saved his countenance.

Your instance, Cleanthes, said he, drawn from books and language, being familiar, has, I confess, so much more force on that account; but is there not some danger, too, in this very circumstance, and may it not render us presumptuous, by making us imagine we comprehend the Deity and have some adequate idea of his nature and attributes? When I read a volume, I enter into the mind and intention of the author; I become him, in a manner, for the instant, and have an immediate feeling and conception of those ideas which revolved in his imagination while employed in that composition. But so near an approach we never surely can make to the Deity. His ways are not our ways, his attributes are perfect but incomprehensible. And this volume of nature contains a great and inexplicable riddle, more than any intelligible discourse or reasoning.

The ancient Platonists, you know, were the most religious and devout of all the pagan philosophers, yet many of them, particularly Plotinus, expressly declare that intellect or understanding is not to be ascribed to the Deity, and that our most perfect worship of him consists, not in acts of veneration, reverence, gratitude, or love, but in a certain mysterious self-annihilation or total extinction of all our faculties. These ideas are, perhaps, too far stretched, but still it must be acknowledged that, by representing the Deity as so intelligible and comprehensible, and so similar to a human mind, we are guilty of the grossest and most narrow partiality, and make ourselves the model of the whole universe.

All the *sentiments* of the human mind, gratitude, resentment, love, friendship, approbation, blame, pity, emulation, envy, have a plain reference to the state and situation of man, and are calculated for preserving the existence and promoting the activity of such a being in such circumstances. It seems, therefore, unreasonable to transfer such sentiments to a supreme existence or to suppose him actuated by them; and the phenomena, besides, of the universe will not support us in such a theory. All our *ideas* derived from the senses are confessedly false and illusive, and cannot therefore be supposed to have place in a supreme intelligence. And as the ideas of internal sentiment, added to those of the external senses, composed the whole furniture of human understanding, we may conclude that none of the *materials* of thought are in any respect similar in the human and in the divine intelligence. Now, as to the *manner* of thinking, how can we make any comparison between them or suppose them anywise resembling? Our thought is fluctuating, uncertain, fleeting, successive, and compounded; and were we to remove these circumstances, we absolutely annihilate its essence, and it would in such a case be an abuse of terms to apply to it the name of thought or reason. At least, if it appear more pious and respectful (as it really is) still to retain these terms when we mention the Supreme

Being, we ought to acknowledge that their meaning, in that case, is totally incomprehensible, and that the infirmities of our nature do not permit us to reach any ideas which in the least correspond to the ineffable sublimity of the Divine attributes.

PART IV

It seems strange to me, said Cleanthes, that you, Demea, who are so sincere in the cause of religion, should still maintain the mysterious, incomprehensible nature of the Deity, and should insist so strenuously that he has no manner of likeness or resemblance to human creatures. The Deity, I can readily allow, possesses many powers and atrributes of which we can have no comprehension; but, if our ideas, so far as they go, be not just and adequate and correspondent to his real nature, I know not what there is in this subject worth insisting on. Is the name, without any meaning, of such mighty importance? Or how do you mystics, who maintain the absolute incomprehensibility of the Deity, differ from sceptics or atheists, who assert that the first cause of all is unknown and unintelligible? Their temerity must be very great if, after rejecting the production by a mind—I mean a mind resembling the human (for I know of no other)—they pretend to assign, with certainty, any other specific intelligible cause; and their conscience must be very scrupulous, indeed, if they refuse to call the universal unknown cause a God or Deity, and to bestow on him as many sublime eulogies and unmeaning epithets as you shall please to require of them.

Who could imagine, replied Demea, that Cleanthes, the calm philosophical Cleanthes, would attempt to refute his antagonists by affixing a nickname to them, and, like the common bigots and inquisitors of the age, have recourse to invective and declamation instead of reasoning? Or does he not perceive that these topics are easily retorted, and that *anthropomorphite* is an appellation as invidious, and implies as dangerous consequences, as the epithet of *mystic* with which he has honoured us? In reality, Cleanthes, consider what it is you assert when you represent the Deity as similar to the human mind and understanding. What is the soul of man? A composition of various faculties, passions, sentiments, ideas—united, indeed, into one self or person, but still distinct from each other. When it reasons, the ideas which are the parts of its discourse arrange themselves in a certain form or order which is not preserved entire for a moment, immediately gives place to another arrangement. New opinions, new passions, new affections, new feelings arise which continually diversify the mental scene and produce in it the greatest variety and most rapid succession imaginable. How is this compatible with that perfect immutability and simplicity which all true theists ascribe to the Deity? By the same act, say they, he sees past, present, and future; his love and hatred, his mercy and justice, are one individual operation; he is entire in every point of space, and complete in every instant of duration. No succession, no change, no acquisition, no diminution. What he is implies not in it any shadow of distinction or diversity. And what he is this moment he ever has been and ever will be, without any new judgment, sentiment, or operation. He stands fixed in one simple, perfect state; nor can you ever say, with any propriety, that this act of his is different from that other, or that this judgment or idea has been lately formed and will give place, by succession, to any different judgment or idea.

I can readily allow, said Cleanthes, that those who maintain the perfect simplicity of the Supreme Being, to the extent in which you have explained it, are complete mystics, and chargeable with all the consequences which I have drawn from their opinion. They are, in a word, atheists, without knowing it. For though it be allowed that the Deity possesses attributes of which we have no comprehension, yet ought we never to ascribe to him any attributes which are absolutely incompatible with that intelligent nature essential to him. A mind whose acts and sentiments and ideas are not distinct and successive, one that is wholly simple and totally immutable, is a mind which has no thought, no reason, no will, no sentiment, no love, no hatred; or, in a word, is no mind at all. It is an abuse of terms to give it that appellation, and we may as well speak of limited extension without figure, or of number without composition.

Pray consider, said Philo, whom you are at present inveighing against. You are honouring with the appellation of *atheist* all the sound, orthodox divines, almost, who have treated of this subject; and you will at last be, yourself, found, according to your reckoning, the only sound theist in the world. But if idolaters be atheists, as, I think, may justly be asserted, and Christian theologians the same, what becomes of the argument, so much celebrated, derived from the universal consent of mankind?

But, because I know you are not much swayed by names and authorities, I shall endeavor to show you, a little more distinctly, the inconveniences of that anthropomorphism which you have embraced, and shall prove that there is no ground to suppose a plan of the world to be formed in the Divine mind, consisting of distinct ideas, differently arranged, in the same manner as an architect forms in his head the plan of a house which he intends to execute.

It is not easy, I own, to see what is gained by this supposition, whether we judge of the matter by *reason* or by *experience*. We are still obliged to mount higher in order to find the cause of this cause which you had assigned as satisfactory and conclusive.

If *reason* (I mean abstract reason derived from inquiries *a priori*) be not alike mute with regard to all questions concerning cause and effect, this sentence at least it will venture to pronounce: that a mental world or universe of ideas requires a cause as much as does a material world or universe of objects, and, if similar in its arrangement, must require a similar cause. For what is there in this subject which should occasion a different conclusion or inference? In an abstract view, they are entirely alike; and no difficulty attends the one supposition which is not common to both of them.

Again, when we will needs force *experience* to pronounce some sentence, even on these subjects which lie beyond her sphere, neither can she perceive any material difference in this particular between those two kinds of worlds, but finds them to be governed by similar principles, and to depend upon an equal variety of causes in their operations. We have specimens in miniature of both of them. Our own mind resembles the one; a vegetable or animal body the other. Let experience, therefore, judge from these samples. Nothing seems more delicate, with regard to its causes, than thought; and as these causes never operate in two persons after the same manner, so we never find two persons who think exactly alike. Nor indeed does the same person think exactly alike at any two different periods of time. A difference of age, of the disposition of his body, of

weather, of food, of company, of books, of passions—any of these particulars, or others more minute, are sufficient to alter the curious machinery of thought and communicate to it very different movements and operations. As far as we can judge, vegetables and animal bodies are not more delicate in their motions, nor depend upon a greater variety or more curious adjustment of springs and principles.

How, therefore, shall we satisfy ourselves concerning the cause of that Being whom you suppose the Author of nature, or, according to your system of anthropomorphism, the ideal world into which you trace the material? Have we not the same reason to trace that ideal world into another ideal world or new intelligent principle? But if we stop and go no farther, why go so far? Why not stop at the material world? How can we satisfy ourselves without going on *in infinitum?* And, after all, what satisfaction is there in that infinite progression? Let us remember the story of the Indian philosopher and his elephant. It was never more applicable than to the present subject. If the material world rests upon a similar ideal world, this ideal world must rest upon some other, and so on without end. It were better, therefore, never to look beyond the present material world. By supposing it to contain the principle of its order within itself, we really assert it to be God: and the sooner we arrive at that Divine Being, so much the better. When you go one step beyond the mundane system, you only excite an inquisitive humour which it is impossible ever to satisfy.

To say that the different ideas which compose the reason of the Supreme Being fall into order of themselves and by their own nature is really to talk without any precise meaning. If it has a meaning, I would fain know why it is not as good sense to say that the parts of the material world fall into order of themselves and by their own nature. Can the one opinion be intelligible, while the other is not so?

We have, indeed, experience of ideas which fall into order of themselves and without any *known* cause. But, I am sure, we have a much larger experience of matter which does the same, as in all instances of generation and vegetation where the accurate analysis of the cause exceeds all human comprehension. We have also experience of particular systems of thought and of matter which have no order; of the first in madness, of the second in corruption. Why, then, should we think that order is more essential to one than the other? And if it requires a cause in both, what do we gain by your system, in tracing the universe of objects into a similar universe of ideas? The first step which we make leads us on for ever. It were, therefore, wise in us to limit all our inquiries to the present world, without looking farther. No satisfaction can ever be attained by these speculations which so far exceed the narrow bounds of human understanding.

It was usual with the Peripatetics, you know, Cleanthes, when the cause of any phenomenon was demanded, to have recourse to their *faculties* or *occult qualities,* and to say, for instance, that bread nourished by its nutritive faculty, and senna purged by its purgative. But it has been discovered that this subterfuge was nothing but the disguise of ignorance, and that these philosophers, though less ingenuous, really said the same thing with the sceptics or the vulgar who fairly confessed that they knew not the cause of these phenomena. In like manner, when it is asked, what cause produced order in the ideas of the Supreme Being, can any other reason be assigned by you, anthropomorphites, than that it is a *rational* faculty, and that such is the nature of the Deity? But why a similar answer will not be equally satisfactory in accounting for the order of the world, without having recourse to any such intelligent creator as you insist on, may be difficult to determine. It is only to say that *such* is the nature of material objects, and that they are all originally possessed of a *faculty* of order and proportion. These are only more learned and elaborate ways of confessing our ignorance; nor has the one hypothesis any real advantage above the other, except in its greater conformity to vulgar prejudices.

You have displayed this argument with great emphasis, replied Cleanthes: You seem not sensible how easy it is to answer it. Even in common life, if I assign a cause for any event, is it any objection, Philo, that I cannot assign the cause of that cause, and answer every new question which may incessantly be started? And what philosophers could possibly submit to so rigid a rule?— philosophers who confess ultimate causes to be totally unknown, and are sensible that the most refined principles into which they trace the phe-

nomena are still to them as inexplicable as these phenomena themselves are to the vulgar. The order and arrangement of nature, the curious adjustment of final causes, the plain use and intention of every part and organ—all these bespeak in the clearest language an intelligent cause or author. The heavens and the earth join in the same testimony: The whole chorus of nature raises one hymn to the praises of its Creator. You alone, or almost alone, disturb this general harmony. You start abstruse doubts, cavils, and objections; you ask me what is the cause of this cause? I know not; I care not; that concerns not me. I have found a Deity; and here I stop my inquiry. Let those go farther who are wiser or more enterprising.

I pretend to be neither, replied Philo; and for that very reason I should never, perhaps, have attempted to go so far, especially when I am sensible that I must at last be contented to sit down with the same answer which, without further trouble, might have satisfied me from the beginning. If I am still to remain in utter ignorance of causes and can absolutely give an explication of nothing, I shall never esteem it any advantage to shove off for a moment a difficulty which you acknowledge must immediately, in its full force, recur upon me. Naturalists indeed very justly explain particular effects by more general causes, though these general causes themselves should remain in the totally inexplicable, but they never surely thought it satisfactory to explain a particular effect by a particular cause which was no more to be accounted for than the effect itself. An ideal system, arranged of itself, without a precedent design, is not a whit more explicable than a material one which attains its order in a like manner; nor is there any more difficulty in the latter supposition than in the former.

PART V

But to show you still more inconveniences, continued Philo, in your anthropomorphism, please to take a new survey of your principles. *Like effects prove like causes.* This is the experimental argument; and this, you say too, is the sole theological argument. Now it is certain that the liker the effects are which are seen and the liker the causes which are inferred, the stronger is the argument. Every departure on either side diminishes the probability and renders the experiment less conclusive. You cannot doubt of the principle; neither ought you to reject its consequences.

All the new discoveries in astronomy which prove the immense grandeur and magnificence of the works of nature are so many additional arguments for a Deity, according to the true system of theism; but, according to your hypothesis of experimental theism, they become so many objections, by removing the effect still farther from all resemblance to the effects of human art and contrivance. For if Lucretius, even following the old system of the world, could exclaim:

Quis regere immensi summam, quis habere
   profoundi
Indu manu validas potis est moderanter
   habenas?
Quis pariter coelos omnes convertere? et omnes
Ignibus aetheriis terras suffire feraces?
Omnibus inque locis esse omni tempore praesto?[2]

If Tully [Cicero] esteemed this reasoning so natural as to put it into the mouth of his Epicurean:

Quibus enim oculis animi intueri potuit vester Plato fabricam illam tanti operis, qua construi a Deo atque aedificari mundum facit? quae molitio? quae ferramenta? qui vectes? quae machinae? qui minstri tanti muneris fuerunt? quemadmodum autem obedire et parere voluntati architecti aer, ignis, aqua, terra potuerunt?[3]

If this argument, I say, had any force in former ages, how much greater must it have at present when the bounds of Nature are so infinitely enlarged and such a magnificent scene is opened to us? It is still more unreasonable to form our idea of so unlimited a cause from our experience of the narrow productions of human design and invention.

The discoveries by microscopes, as they open a new universe in miniature, are still objections, according to you, arguments, according to me. The further we push our researches of this kind, we are still led to infer the universal cause of all to be vastly different from mankind, or from any object of human experience and observation.

And what say you to the discoveries in anatomy, chemistry, botany? . . . These surely are no objections, replied Cleanthes; they only discover new instances of art and contrivance, it is still the image of mind reflected on us from innumerable objects. Add a mind *like the human,* said

Philo. I know of no other, replied Cleanthes. And the liker, the better, insisted Philo. To be sure, said Cleanthes.

Now, Cleanthes, said Philo, with an air of alacrity and triumph, mark the consequences. *First,* by this method of reasoning you renounce all claim to infinity in any of the attributes of the Deity. For, as the cause ought only to be proportioned to the effect, and the effect, so far as it falls under our cognizance, is not infinite, what pretensions have we, upon your suppositions, to ascribe that attribute to the Divine Being? You will still insist that, by removing him so much from similarity to human creatures, we give in to the most arbitrary hypothesis, and at the same time weaken all proofs of his existence.

Secondly, you have no reason, on your theory, for ascribing perfection to the Deity, even in his finite capacity, or for supposing him free from every error, mistake, or incoherence, in his undertakings. There are many inexplicable difficulties in the works of nature which, if we allow a perfect author to be proved *a priori,* are easily solved, and become only seeming difficulties from the narrow capacity of man, who cannot trace infinite relations. But according to your method of reasoning, these difficulties become all real, and, perhaps, will be insisted on as new instances of likeness to human art and contrivance. At least, you must acknowledge that it is impossible for us to tell, from our limited views, whether this system contains any great faults or deserves any considerable praise if compared to other possible and even real systems. Could a peasant, if the *Aeneid* were read to him, pronounce that poem to be absolutely faultless, or even assign to it its proper rank among the productions of human wit, he who had never seen any other production?

But were this world ever so perfect a production, it must still remain uncertain whether all the excellences of the work can justly be ascribed to the workman. If we survey a ship, what an exalted idea must we form of the ingenuity of the carpenter who framed so complicated, useful, and beautiful a machine? And what surprise must we feel when we find him a stupid mechanic who imitated others, and copied an art which, through a long succession of ages, after multiplied trials, mistakes, corrections, deliberations, and controversies, had been gradually improving? Many worlds might have been botched and bungled, throughout an eternity, ere this system was struck out; much labour lost, many fruitless trials made, and a slow but continued improvement carried on during infinite ages in the art of world-making. In such subjects, who can determine where the truth, nay, who can conjecture where the probability lies, amidst a great number of hypotheses which may be proposed, and a still greater which may be imagined?

And what shadow of an argument, continued Philo, can you produce from your hypothesis to prove the unity of the Deity? A great number of men join in building a house or ship, in rearing a city, in framing a commonwealth; why may not several deities combine in contriving and framing a world? This is only so much greater similarity to human affairs. By sharing the work among several, we may so much further limit the attributes of each, and get rid of that extensive power and knowledge which must be supposed in one deity, and which, according to you, can only serve to weaken the proof of his existence. And if such foolish, such vicious creatures as man can yet often unite in framing and executing one plan, how much more those deities or demons, whom we may suppose several degrees more perfect!

To multiply causes without necessity is indeed contrary to true philosophy, but this principle applies not to the present case. Were one deity antecedently proved by your theory who were possessed of every attribute requisite to the production of the universe, it would be needless, I own (though not absurd) to suppose any other deity existent. But while it is still a question whether all these attributes are united in one subject or dispersed among several independent beings, by what phenomena in nature can we pretend to decide the controversy? Where we see a body raised in a scale, we are sure that there is in the opposite scale, however concealed from sight, some counterposing weight equal to it; but it is still allowed to doubt whether that weight be an aggregate of several distinct bodies or one uniform united mass. And if the weight requisite very much exceeds anything which we have ever seen conjoined in any single body, the former supposition becomes still more probable and natural. An intelligent being of such vast power and capacity as is necessary to produce the universe, or, to speak in the language of ancient philoso-

phy, so prodigious an animal exceeds all analogy and even comprehension.

But further, Cleanthes: Men are mortal, and renew their species by generation; and this is common to all living creatures. The two great sexes of male and female, says Milton, animate the world. Why must this circumstance, so universal, so essential, be excluded from those numerous and limited deities? Behold, then, the theogeny of ancient times brought back upon us.

And why not become a perfect anthropomorphite? Why not assert the deity or deities to be corporeal, and to have eyes, a nose, mouth, ears, etc.? Epicurus maintained that no man had ever seen reason but in a human figure; therefore, the gods must have a human figure. And this argument, which is deservedly so much ridiculed by Cicero, becomes, according to you, solid and philosophical.

In a word, Cleanthes, a man who follows your hypothesis is able, perhaps, to assert or conjecture that the universe sometime arose from something like design; but beyond that position he cannot ascertain one single circumstance, and is left afterwards to fix every point of his theology by the utmost license of fancy and hypothesis. This world, for aught he knows, is very faulty and imperfect, compared to a superior standard, and was only the first rude essay of some infant deity who afterwards abandoned it, ashamed of his lame performance; it is the work only of some dependent, inferior deity, and is the object of derision to his superiors; it is the production of old age and dotage in some superannuated deity, and ever since his death has run on at adventures, from the first impulse and active force which it received from him. You justly give signs of horror, Demea, at these strange suppositions; but these, and a thousand more of the same kind, are Cleanthes' suppositions, not mine. From the moment the attributes of the Deity are supposed finite, all these have place. And I cannot, for my part, think that so wild and unsettled a system of theology is, in any respect, preferable to none at all.

These suppositions I absolutely disown, cried Cleanthes: they strike me, however, with no horror, especially when proposed in that rambling way in which they drop from you. On the contrary, they give me pleasure when I see that, by the utmost indulgence of your imagination, you never get rid of the hypothesis of design in the universe, but are obliged at every turn to have recourse to it. To this concession I adhere steadily; and this I regard as a sufficient foundation for religion.

PART VI

It must be a slight fabric, indeed, said Demea, which can be erected on so tottering a foundation. While we are uncertain whether there is one deity or many, whether the deity or deities, to whom we owe our existence, be perfect or imperfect, subordinate or supreme, dead or alive, what trust or confidence can we repose in them? What devotion or worship address to them? What veneration or obedience pay them? To all the purposes of life the theory of religion becomes altogether useless; and even with regard to speculative consequences its uncertainty, according to you, must render it totally precarious and unsatisfactory.

To render it still more unsatisfactory, said Philo, there occurs to me another hypothesis which must acquire an air of probability from the method of reasoning so much insisted on by Cleanthes. That like effects arise from like causes —this principle he supposes the foundation of all religion. But there is another principle of the same kind, no less certain and derived from the same source of experience, that, where several known circumstances are observed to be similar, the unknown will also be found similar. Thus, if we see the limbs of a human body, we conclude that it is also attended with a human head, though hid from us. Thus, if we see, through a chink in a wall, a small part of the sun, we conclude that were the wall removed we should see the whole body. In short, this method of reasoning is so obvious and familiar that no scruple can ever be made with regard to its solidity.

Now, if we survey the universe, so far as it falls under our knowledge, it bears a great resemblance to an animal or organized body, and seems actuated with a like principle of life and motion. A continual circulation of matter in it produces no disorder; a continual waste in every part is incessantly repaired; the closest sympathy is perceived throughout the entire system; and each part or member, in performing its proper offices, operates both to its own preservation and to that of the whole. The world, therefore, I infer, is an animal; and the Deity is the *soul* of the world, actuating it, and actuated by it.

You have too much learning, Cleanthes, to be at all surprised at this opinion which, you know, was maintained by almost all the theists of antiquity, and chiefly prevails in their discourses and reasonings. For though, sometimes, the ancient philosophers reason from final causes, as if they thought the world the workmanship of God, yet it appears rather their favourite notion to consider it as his body whose organization renders it subservient to him. And it must be confessed that, as the universe resembles more a human body than it does the works of human art and contrivance, if our limited analogy could ever, with any propriety, be extended to the whole of nature, the inference seems juster in favour of the ancient than the modern theory.

There are many other advantages, too, in the former theory which recommended it to the ancient theologians. Nothing more repugnant to all their notions because nothing more repugnant to common experience than mind without body, a mere spiritual substance which fell not under their senses nor comprehension, and of which they had not observed one single instance throughout all nature. Mind and body they knew because they felt both; an order, arrangement, organization, or internal machinery, in both they likewise knew, after the same manner; and it could not but seem reasonable to transfer this experience to the universe, and to suppose the divine mind and body to be also coeval and to have, both of them, order and arrangement naturally inherent in them and inseparable from them.

Here, therefore, is a new species of *anthropomorphism,* Cleanthes, on which you may deliberate, and a theory which seems not liable to any considerable difficulties. You are too much superior, surely, to *systematical prejudices* to find any more difficulty in supposing an animal body to be, originally, of itself or from unknown causes, possessed of order and organization, than in supposing a similar order to belong to mind. But the *vulgar prejudice* that body and mind ought always to accompany each other ought not, one should think, to be entirely neglected; since it is founded on *vulgar experience,* the only guide which you profess to follow in all these theological inquiries. And if you assert that our limited experience is an unequal standard by which to judge of the unlimited extent of nature, you entirely abandon your own hypothesis, and must thenceforward adopt our mysticism, as you call it, and admit of the absolute incomprehensibility of the Divine Nature.

This theory, I own, replied Cleanthes, has never before occurred to me, though a pretty natural one; and I cannot readily, upon so short an examination and reflection, deliver any opinion with regard to it. You are very scrupulous, indeed, said Philo. Were I to examine any system of yours, I should not have acted with half that caution and reserve in stating objections and difficulties to it. However, if anything occur to you, you will oblige us by proposing it.

Why then, replied Cleanthes, it seems to me that, though the world does, in many circumstances, resemble an animal body, yet is the analogy also defective in many circumstances the most material: no organs of sense; no seat of thought or reason; no one precise origin of motion and action. In short, it seems to bear a stronger resemblance to a vegetable than to an animal, and your inference would be so far inconclusive in favour of the soul of the world.

But, in the next place, your theory seems to imply the eternity of the world; and that is a principle which, I think, can be refuted by the strongest reasons and probabilities. I shall suggest an argument to this purpose which, I believe, has not been insisted on by any writer. Those who reason from the late origin of arts and sciences, though their inference wants not force, may perhaps be refuted by considerations derived from the nature of human society, which is in continual revolution between ignorance and knowledge, liberty and slavery, riches and poverty; so that it is impossible for us, from our limited experience, to foretell with assurance what events may or may not be expected. Ancient learning and history seem to have been in great danger of entirely perishing after the inundation of the barbarous nations; and had these convulsions continued a little longer or been a little more violent, we should not probably have now known what passed in the world a few centuries before us. Nay, were it not for the superstition of the popes, who preserved a little jargon of Latin in order to support the appearance of an ancient and universal church, that tongue must have been utterly lost; in which case the Western world, being totally barbarous, would not have been in a fit disposition for receiving the Greek language and learning, which was conveyed to them after the sacking of Constantinople. When learning and books had been extinguished, even the mechanical arts would have fallen considerably to decay; and it is easily imagined that fable or tradition might ascribe to them a much later origin than the true one. This vulgar argument, therefore, against the eternity of the world seems a little precarious.

But here appears to be the foundation of a better argument. Lucullus was the first that brought cherry-trees from Asia to Europe, though that tree thrives so well in many European climates that it grows in the woods without any culture. Is it possible that, throughout a whole eternity, no European had ever passed into Asia and thought of transplanting so delicious a fruit into his own country? Or if the tree was once transplanted and propagated, how could it ever afterwards perish? Empires may rise and fall, liberty and slavery succeed alternately, ignorance and knowledge give place to each other; but the cherry-tree will still remain in the woods of Greece, Spain, and Italy, and will never be affected by the revolutions of human society.

It is not two thousand years since vines were transplanted into France, though there is no climate in the world more favourable to them. It is not three centuries since horses, cows, sheep, swine, dogs, corn, were known in America. Is it possible that during the revolutions of a whole eternity there never arose a Columbus who might open the communication between Europe and that continent? We may as well imagine that all men would wear stockings for ten thousand years, and never have the sense to think of garters to tie them. All these seem convincing proofs of the youth or rather infancy of the world, as being founded on the operation of principles more constant and steady than those by which human society is governed and directed. Nothing less than a total convulsion of the elements will ever destroy all the European animals and vegetables which are now to be found in the Western world.

And what argument have you against such convulsions? replied Philo. Strong and almost incontestable proofs may be traced over the whole earth that every part of this globe has continued for many ages entirely covered with water. And though order were supposed inseparable from matter, and inherent in it, yet may matter be susceptible of many and great revolutions, through the endless periods of eternal duration. The incessant changes to which every part of it is subject seem to intimate some such general transformations; though, at the same time, it is observable that all the changes and corruptions of which we have ever had experience are but passages from one state of order to another; nor can matter ever rest in total deformity and confusion. What we see in the parts, we may infer in the whole; at least, that is the method of reasoning on which you rest your whole theory. And were I obliged to defend any particular system of this nature, which I never willingly should do, I esteem none more plausible than that which ascribes an eternal inherent principle of order to the world, though attended with great and continual revolutions and alterations. This at once solves all difficulties; and if the solution, by being so general, is not entirely complete and satisfactory, it is at least a theory that we must sooner or later have recourse to, whatever system we embrace. How could things have been as they are, were there not an original inherent principle of order somewhere, in thought or in matter? And it is very indifferent to which of these we give the preference. Chance has no place, on any hypothesis, sceptical or religious. Everything is surely governed by steady, inviolable laws. And were the inmost essence of things laid open to us, we should then discover a scene of which, at present, we can have no idea. Instead of admiring the order of natural beings, we should clearly see that it was absolutely impossible for them, in the smallest article, ever to admit of any other disposition.

Were anyone inclined to revive the ancient pagan theology which maintained, as we learned from Hesiod, that this globe was governed by 30,000 deities, who arose from the unknown powers of nature, you would naturally object, Cleanthes, that nothing is gained by this hypothesis; and that it is as easy to suppose all men animals, beings more numerous but less perfect, to have sprung immediately from a like origin. Push the same inference a step further, and you will find a numerous society of deities as explicable as one universal deity who possesses within himself the powers and perfections of the whole society. All these systems, then, of Scepticism, Polytheism, and Theism, you must allow, on your principles, to be on a like footing, and that no one of them has any advantage over the others. You may thence learn the fallacy of your principles.

PART VII

But here, continued Philo, in examining the ancient system of the soul of the world there strikes me, all of a sudden, a new idea which, if just, must go near to subvert all your reasoning, and destroy even your first inferences on which you repose such confidence. If the universe bears a greater likeness to animal bodies and to vegetables than to the works of human art, it is more probable that its cause resembles the cause of the former than that of the latter, and its origin ought rather to be ascribed to generation or vegetation than to reason or design. Your conclusion, even according to your own principles, is therefore lame and defective.

Pray open up this argument a little further, said Demea, for I do not rightly apprehend it in that concise manner in which you have expressed it.

Our friend Cleanthes, replied Philo, as you have heard, asserts that, since no question of fact can be proved otherwise than by experience, the existence of a Deity admits not of proof from any other medium. The world, says he, resembles the works of human contrivance; therefore its cause must also resemble that of the other. Here we may remark that the operation of one very small part of nature, to wit, man, upon another very small part, to wit, that inanimate matter lying within his reach, is the rule by which Cleanthes judges of the origin of the whole; and he measures objects, so widely disproportioned, by the same individual standard. But to waive all objections drawn from this topic, I affirm that there are other parts of the universe (besides the machines of human invention) which bear still a greater resemblance to the fabric of the world, and which, therefore, afford a better conjecture concerning the universal origin of this system. These parts are animals and vegetables. The world plainly resembles more an animal or a vegetable than it does a watch or a knitting-loom. Its cause, therefore, it is more probable, resembles the cause of the former. The cause of the former is generation or vegetation. The cause, therefore, of the world we may infer to be something similar or analogous to generation or vegetation.

But how is it conceivable, said Demea, that the world can arise from anything similar to vegetation or generation?

Very easily, replied Philo. In like manner as a tree sheds its seed into the neighboring fields and produces other trees, so the great vegetable, the world, or this planetary system, produces within itself certain seeds which, being scattered into the surrounding chaos, vegetate into new worlds. A comet, for instance, is the seed of a world; and after it has been fully ripened, by passing from sun to sun, and star to star, it is, at last, tossed into the unformed elements which everywhere surround this universe, and immediately sprouts up into a new system.

Or if, for the sake of variety (for I see no other advantage), we should suppose this world to be an animal: a comet is the egg of this animal; and in like manner as an ostrich lays its egg in the sand, which, without any further care, hatches the egg and produces a new animal, so ... I understand you, says Demea. But what wild, arbitrary suppositions are these! What *data* have you for such extraordinary conclusions? And is the slight, imaginary resemblance of the world to a vegetable or an animal sufficient to establish the same inference with regard to both? Objects which are in general so widely different, ought they to be a standard for each other?

Right, cries Philo: This is the topic on which I have all along insisted. I have still asserted that we have no *data* to establish any system of cosmogony. Our experience, so imperfect in itself and so limited both in extent and duration, can afford us no probable conjecture concerning the whole of things. But if we must needs fix on some hypothesis, by what rule, pray, ought we to determine our choice? Is there any other rule than the greater similarity of the objects compared? And does not a plant or an animal, which springs from vegetation or generation, bear a stronger resemblance to the world than does any artificial machine, which arises from reason and design?

But what is this vegetation and generation of which you talk? said Demea. Can you explain their operations, and anatomize that fine internal structure on which they depend?

As much, at least, replied Philo, as Cleanthes can explain the operations of reason, or anatomize that internal structure on which it depends. But without any such elaborate disquisitions, when I see an animal, I infer that it sprang from generation; and that with as great certainty as you conclude a house to have been reared by design. These words *generation, reason* mark only certain powers and energies in nature whose effects are known, but whose essence is incomprehensible; and one of these principles, more than the other, has no privilege for being made a standard to the whole of nature.

In reality, Demea, it may reasonably be expected that the larger the views are which we take of things, the better will they conduct us in our conclusions concerning such extraordinary and such magnificent subjects. In this little corner of the world alone, there are four principles, *reason, instinct, generation, vegetation,* which are similar to each other, and are the causes of similar effects. What a number of other principles may we naturally suppose in the immense extent and variety of the universe could we travel from planet to planet, and from system to system, in order to examine each part of this mighty fabric? Any one of these four principles above mentioned (and a hundred others which lie open to our conjecture) may afford us a theory by which to judge of the origin of the world; and it is a palpable and egregious partiality to confine our view entirely to that principle by which our own minds operate. Were this principle more intelligible on that account, such a partiality might be somewhat excusable; but reason, in its internal fabric and structure, is really as little known to us as instinct or vegetation; and, perhaps, even that vague, undeterminate word *nature,* to which the vulgar refer everything is not at the bottom more inexplicable. The effects of these principles are all known to us from experience; but the principles themselves and their manner of operation are totally unknown; nor is it less intelligible or less conformable to experience to say that the world arose by vegetation, from seed shed by another world, than to say that it arose from a divine reason or contrivance, according to the sense in which Cleanthes understands it.

But methinks, said Demea, if the world had a vegetative quality and could sow the seeds of new worlds into the infinite chaos, this power would be still an additional argument for design in its author. For whence could arise so wonderful a faculty but from design? Or how can order spring from anything which perceives not that order which it bestows?

You need only look around you, replied Philo, to satisfy yourself with regard to this question. A tree bestows order and organization on that tree which springs from it, without knowing the order; an animal in the same manner on its offspring; a bird on its nest; and instances of this kind are even more frequent in the world than those of order which arise from reason and contrivance. To say that all this order in animals and vegetables proceeds ultimately from design is begging the question; nor can that great point be ascertained otherwise than by proving, *a priori,* both that order is, from its nature, inseparably attached to thought and that it can never of itself or from original unknown principles belong to matter.

But further, Demea, this objection which you urge can never be made use of by Cleanthes, without renouncing a defense which he has already made against one of my objections. When I inquired concerning the cause of that supreme reason and intelligence into which he resolves everything, he told me that the impossibility of satisfying such inquiries could never be admitted as an objection in any species of philosophy. *We must stop somewhere,* says he; *nor is it ever within the reach of human capacity to explain ultimate causes or show the last connections of any objects. It is sufficient if any steps, so far as we go, are supported by experience and observation.* Now that vegetation and generation, as well as reason, are experienced to be principles of order in nature is undeniable. If I rest my system of cosmogony on the former, preferably to the latter, it is at my choice. The matter seems entirely arbitrary. And when Cleanthes asks me what is the cause of my great vegetative or generative faculty, I am equally entitled to ask him the cause of his great reasoning principle. These questions we have agreed to forbear on both sides; and it is chiefly his interest on the present occasion to stick to this agreement. Judging by our limited and imperfect experience, generation has some privileges above reason; for we see every day the latter arise from the former, never the former from the latter.

Compare, I beseech you, the consequences on both sides. The world, say I, resembles an animal; therefore it is an animal, therefore it arose from generation. The steps, I confess, are wide, yet there is some small appearance of analogy in each step. The world, says Cleanthes, resembles a machine; therefore it is a machine, therefore it arose from design. The steps are here equally wide, and the analogy less striking. And if he pretends to carry on *my* hypothesis a step further, and to infer design or reason from the great principle of generation on which I insist, I may, with better authority, use the same freedom to push further *his* hypothesis, and infer a divine generation or theogony from his principle of reason. I have at least some faint shadow of experience, which is the utmost that can ever be attained in the present subject. Reason, in innumerable instances, is observed to arise from the principle of generation, and never to arise from any other principle.

Hesiod and all the ancient mythologists were so struck with this analogy that they universally explained the origin of nature from an animal birth, and copulation. Plato, too, so far as he is intelligible, seems to have adopted some such notion in his *Timaeus.*

The Brahmins assert that the world arose from an infinite spider, who spun this whole complicated mass from his bowels, and annihilates afterwards the whole or any part of it, by absorbing it again and resolving it into his own essence. Here is a species of cosmogony which appears to us ridiculous because a spider is a little contemptible animal whose operations we are never likely to take for a model of the whole universe. But still here is a new species of analogy, even in our globe. And were there a planet wholly inhabited by spiders (which is very possible), this inference would there appear as natural and irrefragable as that which in our planet ascribes the origin of all things to design and intelligence, as explained by Cleanthes. Why an orderly system may not be spun from the belly as well as from the brain, it will be difficult for him to give a satisfactory reason.

I must confess, Philo, replied Cleanthes, that, of all men living, the task which you have undertaken, of raising doubts and objections, suits you best and seems, in a manner, natural and unavoidable to you. So great is your fertility of invention that I am not ashamed to acknowledge myself unable, on a sudden, to solve regularly such out-of-the-way difficulties as you incessantly start upon me, though I clearly see, in general, their fallacy and error. And I question not, but you are yourself, at present, in the same case, and have not the solution so ready as the objection, while you must be sensible that common sense and reason are entirely against you, and that such whimsies as you have delivered may puzzle but never can convince us.

PART VIII

What you ascribe to the fertility of my invention, replied Philo, is entirely owing to the nature of the subject. In subjects adapted to the narrow compass of human reason there is commonly but one determination which carries probability or conviction with it; and to a man of sound judgment all other suppositions but that one appear entirely absurd and chimerical. But in such questions as the present, a hundred contradictory views may preserve a kind of imperfect analogy, and invention has here full scope to exert itself. Without any great effort of thought, I believe that I could, in an instant, propose other systems of cosmogony which would have some faint appearance of truth, though it is a thousand, a million to one if either yours or any one of mine be the true system.

For instance, what if I should revive the old Epicurean hypothesis? This is commonly, and I believe justly, esteemed the most absurd system that has yet been proposed; yet I know not whether, with a few alterations, it might not be brought to bear a faint appearance of probability. Instead of supposing matter infinite, as Epicurus did, let us suppose it finite. A finite number of particles is only susceptible of finite transpositions; and it must happen, in an eternal duration, that every possible order or position must be tried an infinite number of times. This world, therefore, with all its events, even the most minute, has before been produced and destroyed, and will again be produced and destroyed, without any bounds and limitations. No one who has a conception of the powers of infinite, in comparison of finite, will ever scruple this determination.

But this supposes, said Demea, that matter can acquire motion without any voluntary agent or first mover.

And where is the difficulty, replied Philo, of that supposition? Every event, before experience, is equally difficult and incomprehensible; and every event, after experience, is equally easy and intelligible. Motion, in many instances, from gravity, from elasticity, from electricity, begins in matter, without any known voluntary agent; and to suppose always, in these cases, an unknown voluntary agent is mere hypothesis and hypothesis attended with no advantages. The beginning of motion in matter itself is as conceivable *a priori* as its communication from mind and intelligence.

Besides, why may not motion have been propagated by impulse through all eternity, and the same stock of it, or nearly the same, be still upheld in the universe? As much is lost by the composition of motion, as much is gained by its resolution. And whatever the causes are, the fact is certain that matter is and always has been in continual agitation, as far as human experience or tradition reaches. There is not probably, at present, in the whole universe, one particle of matter at absolute rest.

And this very consideration, too, continued Philo, which we have stumbled on in the course of the argument, suggests a new hypothesis of cosmogony that is not absolutely absurd and improbable. Is there a system, an order, an economy of things, by which matter can preserve that perpetual agitation which seems essential to it, and yet maintain a constancy in the forms which it produces? There certainly is such an economy, for this is actually the case with the present world. The continual motion of matter, therefore, in less than infinite transpositions, must produce this economy or order, and by its very nature, that order, when once established, supports itself for many ages if not to eternity. But wherever matter is so poised, arranged, and adjusted, as to continue in perpetual motion, and yet preserve a constancy in the forms, its situation must, of necessity, have all the same appearance of art and contrivance which we observe at present. All the parts of each form must have a relation to each other and to the whole; and the whole itself must have a relation to the other parts of the universe, to the element in which the form subsists, to the materials with which it repairs its waste and decay, and to every other form which is hostile or friendly. A defect in any of these particulars destroys the form, and the matter of which it is composed is again set loose, and is thrown into irregular motions and fermentations till it unite itself to some other regular form. If no such form be prepared to receive it, and if there be a great quantity of this corrupted matter in the universe, the universe itself is entirely disordered, whether it be the feeble embryo of a world in its first beginnings that is thus destroyed or the rotten carcase of one languishing in old age and infirmity. In either case, a chaos ensues till finite though innumerable revolutions produce, at last, some forms whose parts and organs are so adjusted as to support the forms amidst a continued succession of matter.

Suppose (for we shall endeavour to vary the expression) that matter were thrown into any position by a blind, unguided force; it is evident that this first position must, in all probability, be the most confused and most disorderly imaginable, without any resemblance to those works of human contrivance which, along with a symmetry of parts, discover an adjustment of means to ends and a tendency to self-preservation. If the actuating force cease after this operation, matter must remain for ever in disorder and continue an immense chaos, without any proportion or activity. But suppose that the actuating force, whatever it be, still continues in matter, this first position will immediately give place to a second which will likewise, in all probability, be as disorderly as the first, and so on through many successions of changes and revolutions. No particular order or position ever continues a moment unaltered. The original force, still remaining in activity, gives a perpetual restlessness to matter. Every possible situation is produced and instantly destroyed. If a glimpse or dawn of order appears for a moment, it is instantly hurried away and confounded by that never-ceasing force which actuates every part of matter.

Thus the universe goes on for many ages in a continued succession of chaos and disorder. But is it not possible that it may settle at last, so as not to lose its motion and active force (for that we have supposed inherent in it), yet so as to preserve an uniformity of appearance, amidst the continual motion and fluctuation of its parts? This we find to be the case with the universe at present. Every individual is perpetually changing, and every part of every individual; and yet the whole remains, in appearance, the same. May we not

hope for such a position or rather be assured of it from the eternal revolutions of unguided matter; and may not this account for all the appearing wisdom and contrivance which is in the universe? Let us contemplate the subject a little, and we shall find that this adjustment if attained by matter of a seeming stability in the forms, with a real and perpetual revolution or motion of parts, affords a plausible, if not a true, solution of the difficulty.

It is in vain, therefore, to insist upon the uses of the parts in animals or vegetables, and their curious adjustment to each other. I would fain know how an animal could subsist unless its parts were so adjusted? Do we not find that it immediately perishes whenever this adjustment ceases, and that its matter, corrupting, tries some new form? It happens indeed that the parts of the world are so well adjusted that some regular form immediately lays claim to this corrupted matter; and if it were not so, could the world subsist? Must it not dissolve, as well as the animal, and pass through new positions and situations till in great but finite succession it fall, at last, into the present or some such order?

It is well, replied Cleanthes, you told us that this hypothesis was suggested on a sudden, in the course of the argument. Had you had leisure to examine it, you would soon have perceived the insuperable objections to which it is exposed. No form, you say, can subsist unless it possess those powers and organs requisite for its subsistence; some new order or economy must be tried, and so on, without intermission, till at last some order which can support and maintain itself is fallen upon. But according to this hypothesis, whence arise the many conveniences and advantages which men and all animals possess? Two eyes, two ears are not absolutely necessary for the subsistence of the species. The human race might have been propagated and preserved without horses, dogs, cows, sheep, and those unnumerable fruits and products which serve to our satisfaction and enjoyment. If no camels had been created for the use of man in the sandy deserts of Africa and Arabia, would the world have been dissolved? If no loadstone had been framed to give that wonderful and useful direction to the needle, would human society and the human kind have been immediately extinguished? Though the maxims of nature be in general very frugal, yet instances of this kind are far from being rare; and any one of them is a sufficient proof of design—and of a benevolent design—which gave rise to the order and arrangement of the universe.

At least, you may safely infer, said Philo, that the foregoing hypothesis is so far incomplete and imperfect, which I shall not scruple to allow. But can we ever reasonably expect greater success in any attempts of this nature? Or can we ever hope to erect a system of cosmogony that will be liable to no exceptions, and will contain no circumstance repugnant to our limited and imperfect experience of the analogy of nature? Your theory itself cannot surely pretend to any such advantage, even though you have run into *anthropomorphism,* the better to preserve a conformity to common experience. Let us once more put it to trial. In all instances which we have ever seen, ideas are copied from real objects, and are ectypal, not archetypal, to express myself in learned terms. You reverse this order and give thought the precedence. In all instances which we have ever seen, thought has no influence upon matter except where that matter is so conjoined with it as to have an equal reciprocal influence upon it. No animal can move immediately anything but the members of its own body; and, indeed, the equality of action and reaction seems to be an universal law of nature; but your theory implies a contradiction to this experience. These instances, with many more which it were easy to collect (particularly the supposition of a mind or system of thought that is eternal or, in other words, an animal ingenerable and immortal)—these instances, I say, may teach all of us sobriety in condemning each other, and let us see that as no system of this kind ought ever to be received from a slight analogy, so neither ought any to be rejected on account of a small incongruity. For that is an inconvenience from which we can justly pronounce no one to be exempted.

All religious systems, it is confessed, are subject to great and insuperable difficulties. Each disputant triumphs in his turn, while he carries on an offensive war, and exposes the absurdities, barbarities, and pernicious tenets of his antagonist. But all of them, on the whole, prepare a complete triumph for the *sceptic,* who tells them that no system ought ever to be embraced with regard to such subjects: for this plain reason that no absurdity ought ever to be assented to with regard to

any subject. A total suspense of judgment is here our only reasonable resource. And if every attack, as is commonly observed, and no defence among theologians is successful, how complete must be *his* victory who remains always, with all mankind, on the offensive, and has himself no fixed station or abiding city which he is ever, on any occasion, obliged to defend?

PART IX

But if so many difficulties attend the argument *a posteriori,* said Demea, had we not better adhere to that simple and sublime argument *a priori* which, by offering to us infallible demonstration, cuts off at once all doubt and difficulty? By this argument, too, we may prove the *infinity* of the Divine attributes, which, I am afraid, can never be ascertained with certainty from any other topic. For how can an effect which either is finite or, for aught we know, may be so—how can such an effect, I say, prove an infinite cause? The unity, too, of the Divine Nature it is very difficult, if not absolutely impossible, to deduce merely from contemplating the works of nature; nor will the uniformity alone of the plan, even were it allowed, give us any assurance of that attribute. Whereas the argument *a priori* . . .

You seem to reason, Demea, interposed Cleanthes, as if those advantages and conveniences in the abstract argument were full proofs of its solidity. But it is first proper, in my opinion, to determine what argument of this nature you choose to insist on; and we shall afterwards, from itself, better than from its *useful* consequences, endeavour to determine what value we ought to put upon it.

The argument, replied Demea, which I would insist on is the common one. Whatever exists must have a cause or reason of its existence, it being absolutely impossible for anything to produce itself or be the cause of its own existence. In mounting up, therefore, from effect to causes, we must either go on in tracing an infinite succession, without any ultimate cause at all, or must at least have recourse to some ultimate cause that is *necessarily* existent. Now that the first supposition is absurd may be thus proved. In the infinite chain or succession of causes and effects, each single effect is determined to exist by the power and efficacy of that cause which immediately preceded; but the whole eternal chain or succession, taken together, is not determined or caused by anything, and yet it is evident that it requires a cause or reason, as much as any particular object which begins to exist in time. The question is still reasonable why this particular succession of causes existed from eternity, and not any other succession or no succession at all. If there be no necessarily existent being, any supposition which can be formed is equally possible; nor is there any more absurdity in *nothing's* having existed from eternity than there is in that succession of causes which constitutes the universe. What was it, then, which determined *something* to exist rather than *nothing,* and bestowed being on a particular possibility, exclusive of the rest? *External causes,* there are supposed to be none. *Chance* is a word without a meaning. Was it *nothing?* But that can never produce anything. We must, therefore, have recourse to a necessarily existent Being who carries the *reason* of his existence in himself, and who cannot be supposed not to exist, without an express contradiction. There is, consequently, such a Being—that is, there is a Deity.

I shall not leave it to Philo, said Cleanthes, though I know that starting objections is his chief delight, to point out the weakness of this metaphysical reasoning. It seems to me so obviously ill-grounded, and at the same time of so little consequence to the cause of true piety and religion, that I shall myself venture to show the fallacy of it.

I shall begin with observing that there is an evident absurdity in pretending to demonstrate a matter of fact, or to prove it by arguments *a priori.* Nothing is demonstrable unless the contrary implies a contradiction. Nothing that is distinctly conceivable implies a contradiction. Whatever we conceive as existent, we can also conceive as non-existent. There is no being, therefore, whose non-existence implies a contradiction. Consequently there is no being whose existence is demonstrable. I propose this argument as entirely decisive, and am willing to rest the whole controversy upon it.

It is protended that the Deity is a necessarily existent being; and this necessity of his existence is attempted to be explained by asserting that, if we knew his whole essence or nature, we should perceive it to be as impossible for him not to exist, as for twice two not to be four. But it is evident that this can never happen, while our faculties remain the same as at present. It will still be possible for us, at any time, to conceive the non-existence of what we formerly conceived to exist; nor can the mind ever lie under a necessity of supposing any object to remain always in being; in the same manner as we lie under a necessity of always conceiving twice two to be four. The words, therefore, *necessary existence* have no meaning or, which is the same thing, none that is consistent.

But further, why may not the material universe be the necessarily existent Being, according to this pretended explication of necessity? We dare not affirm that we know all the qualities of matter; and, for aught we can determine, it may contain some qualities which, were they known, would make its non-existence appear as great a contradiction as that twice two is five. I find only one argument employed to prove that the material world is not the necessarily existent Being; and this argument is derived from the contingency both of the matter and the form of the world. "Any particle of matter," it is said, "may be *conceived* to be annihilated, and any form may be *conceived* to be altered. Such an annihilation or alteration, therefore, is not impossible."[4] But it seems a great partiality not to perceive that the same argument extends equally to the Deity, so far as we have any conception of him, and that the mind can at least imagine him to be non-existent or his attributes to be altered. It must be some unknown, inconceivable qualities which can make his non-existence appear impossible or his attributes unalterable; and no reason can be assigned why these qualities may not belong to matter. As they are altogether unknown and inconceivable, they can never be proved incompatible with it.

Add to this that in tracing an eternal succession of objects it seems absurd to inquire for a general cause or first author. How can anything that exists from eternity have a cause, since that relation implies a priority in time and a beginning of existence?

In such a chain, too, or succession of objects, each part is caused by that which preceded it, and causes that which succeeds it. Where then is the difficulty? But the *whole,* you say, wants a cause. I answer that the uniting of several distinct countries into one kingdom, or several distinct members into one body, is performed merely by an arbitrary act of the mind, and has no influence on the nature of things. Did I show you the particular causes of each individual in a collection of twenty particles of matter, I should think it very unreasonable should you afterwards ask me what was the cause of the whole twenty. This is sufficiently explained in explaining the cause of the parts.

Though the reasonings which you have urged, Cleanthes, may well excuse me, said Philo, from starting any further difficulties, yet I cannot forbear insisting still upon another topic. It is observed by arithmeticians that the products of 9 compose always either 9 or some lesser product of 9 if you add together all the characters of which any of the former products is composed. Thus, of 18, 27, 36, which are products of 9, you make 9 by adding 1 to 8, 2 to 7, 3 to 6. Thus 369 is a product also of 9; and if you add 3, 6, and 9, you make 18, a lesser product of 9.[5] To a superficial observer so wonderful a regularity may be admired as the effect either of chance or design; but a skillful algebraist immediately concludes it to be the work of necessity, and demonstrates that it must for ever result from the nature of these numbers. Is it not probable, I ask, that the whole economy of the universe is conducted by a like necessity, though no human algebra can furnish a key which solves the difficulty? And instead of admiring the order of natural beings, may it not happen that, could we penetrate into the intimate nature of bodies, we should clearly see why it was absolutely impossible they could ever admit of any other disposition? So dangerous is it to introduce this idea of necessity into the present question! and so naturally does it afford an inference directly opposite to the religious hypothesis!

But dropping all these abstractions, continued Philo, and confining ourselves to more familiar topics, I shall venture to add an observation that the argument *a priori* has seldom been found very convincing, except to people of a metaphysical head who have accustomed themselves to abstract reasoning, and who, finding from mathematics that the understanding frequently leads to truth through obscurity, and contrary to first appearances, have transferred the same habit of thinking to subjects where it ought not to have place. Other people, even of good sense and the best inclined to religion, feel always some deficiency in such arguments, though they are not perhaps able to explain distinctly where it lies—a certain proof that men ever did and ever will derive their religion from other sources than from this species of reasoning.

PART X

It is my opinion, I own, replied Demea, that each man feels, in a manner, the truth of religion within his own breast, and, from a consciousness of his imbecility and misery rather than from any reasoning, is led to seek protection from that Being on whom he and all nature is dependent. So anxious or so tedious are even the best scenes of life that futurity is still the object of all our hopes and fears. We incessantly look forward and endeavour, by prayers, adoration, and sacrifice, to appease those unknown powers whom we find, by experience, so able to afflict and oppress us. Wretched creatures that we are! What resource for us amidst the innumerable ills of life did not religion suggest some methods of atonement, and appease those terrors with which we are incessantly agitated and tormented?

I am indeed persuaded, said Philo, that the best and indeed the only method of bringing everyone to a due sense of religion is by just representations of the misery and wickedness of men. And for that purpose a talent of eloquence and strong imagery is more requisite than that of reasoning and argument. For is it necessary to prove what everyone feels within himself? It is only necessary to make us feel it, if possible, more intimately and sensibly.

The people, indeed, replied Demea, are sufficiently convinced of this great and melancholy truth. The miseries of life, the unhappiness of man, the general corruptions of our nature, the unsatisfactory enjoyment of pleasures, riches, honours—these phrases have become almost proverbial in all languages. And who can doubt of what all men declare from their own immediate feeling and experience?

In this point, said Philo, the learned are perfectly agreed with the vulgar; and in all letters, *sacred* and *profane,* the topic of human misery has been insisted on with the most pathetic eloquence that sorrow and melancholy could inspire. The poets, who speak from sentiment, without a system, and whose testimony has therefore the more authority, abound in images of this nature. From Homer down to Dr. Young, the whole inspired tribe have ever been sensible that no other representation of things would suit the feeling and observation of each individual.

As to authorities, replied Demea, you need not seek them. Look round this library of Cleanthes. I shall venture to affirm that, except authors of particular sciences, such as chemistry or botany, who have no occasion to treat of human life, there is scarce one of those innumerable writers from whom the sense of human misery has not, in some passage or other, extorted a complaint and confession of it. At least, the chance is entirely on that side; and no one author has ever, so far as I can recollect, been so extravagant as to deny it.

There you must excuse me, said Philo: Leibniz has denied it, and is perhaps the first[6] who ventured upon so bold and paradoxical an opinion; at least, the first who made it essential to his philosophical system.

And by being the first, replied Demea, might he not have been sensible of his error? For is this a subject in which philosophers can propose to make discoveries especially in so late an age? And can any man hope by a simple denial (for the subject scarcely admits of reasoning) to bear down the united testimony of mankind, founded on sense and consciousness?

And why should man, added he, pretend to an exemption from the lot of all other animals? The whole earth, believe me, Philo, is cursed and polluted. A perpetual war is kindled amongst all living creatures. Necessity, hunger, want stimulate the strong and courageous; fear, anxiety, terror agitate the weak and infirm. The first entrance into life gives anguish to the new-born infant and to its wretched parent; weakness, impotence, distress attend each stage of that life, and it is, at last finished in agony and horror.

Observe, too, says Philo, the curious artifices of nature in order to embitter the life of every living being. The stronger prey upon the weaker and keep them in perpetual terror and anxiety. The weaker, too, in their turn, often prey upon the stronger, and vex and molest them without relaxation. Consider that innumerable race of insects, which either are bred on the body of each animal or, flying about, infix their stings in him. These insects have others still less than themselves which torment them. And thus on each hand, before and behind, above and below, every animal is surrounded with enemies which incessantly seek his misery and destruction.

Man alone, said Demea, seems to be, in part, an exception to this rule. For by combination in society he can easily master lions, tigers, and bears, whose greater strength and agility naturally enable them to prey upon him.

On the contrary, it is here chiefly, cried Philo, that the uniform and equal maxims of nature are most apparent. Man, it is true, can, by combination, surmount all his *real* enemies and become master of the whole animal creation; but does he not immediately raise up to himself *imaginary* enemies, the demons of his fancy, who haunt him with superstitious terrors and blast every enjoyment of life? His pleasure, as he imagines, becomes in their eyes a crime; his food and repose give them umbrage and offence; his very sleep and dreams furnish new materials to anxious fear; and even death, his refuge from every other ill, presents only the dread of endless and innumerable woes. Nor does the wolf molest more the timid flock than superstition does the anxious breast of wretched mortals.

Besides, consider, Demea: This very society by which we surmount those wild beasts, our natural enemies, what new enemies does it not raise to us? What woe and misery does it not occasion? Man is the greatest enemy of man. Oppression, injustice, contempt, contumely, violence, sedition, war, calumny, treachery, fraud—by these they mutually torment each other, and they would soon dissolve that society which they had formed were it not for the dread of still greater ills which must attend their separation.

But though these external insults, said Demea, from animals, from men, from all the elements, which assault us from a frightful catalogue of woes, they are nothing in comparison of those which arise within ourselves, from the distempered condition of our mind and body. How many lie under the lingering torment of disease? Hear the pathetic enumeration of the great poet.

Intestine stone and ulcer, colic-pangs,
Demoniac frenzy, moping melancholy,
And moon-struck madness, pining atrophy
Marasmus, and wide-wasting pestilence.
Dire was the tossing, deep the groans: *Despair*

Tended the sick, busiest from couch to couch
And over them triumphant *Death* his dart
Shook: but delay'd to strike, though oft invok'd
With vows, as their chief good and final hope.[7]

The disorders of the mind, continued Demea, though more secret, are not perhaps less dismal and vexatious. Remorse, shame, anguish, rage, disappointment, anxiety, fear, dejection, despair —who has ever passed through life without cruel inroads from these tormentors? How many have scarcely ever felt any better sensations? Labour and poverty, so abhorred by everyone, are the certain lot of the far greater number; and those few privileged persons who enjoy ease and opulence never reach contentment or true felicity. All the goods of life united would not make a very happy man, but all the ills united would make a wretch indeed; and any one of them almost (and who can be free from every one?), nay, often the absence of one good (and who can possess all?) is sufficient to render life ineligible.

Were a stranger to drop on a sudden into this world, I would show him, as a specimen of its ills, an hospital full of diseases, a prison crowded with malefactors and debtors, a field of battle strewed with carcases, a fleet floundering in the ocean, a nation languishing under tyranny, famine, or pestilence. To turn the gay side of life to him and give him a notion of its pleasures—whither should I conduct him? To a ball, to an opera, to court? He might justly think that I was only showing him a diversity of distress and sorrow.

There is no evading such striking instances, said Philo, but by apologies which still further aggravate the charge. Why have all men, I ask, in all ages, complained incessantly of the miseries of life? ... They have no just reason, says one: these complaints proceed only from their discontented, repining, anxious disposition. ... And can there possibly, I reply, be a more certain foundation of misery than such a wretched temper?

But if they were really as unhappy as they pretend, says my antagonist, why do they remain in life? ...

Not satisfied with life, afraid of death—

This is the secret chain, say I, that holds us. We are terrified, not bribed to the continuance of our existence.

It is only a false delicacy, he may insist, which a few refined spirits indulge, and which has spread these complaints among the whole race of mankind. ... And what is this delicacy, I ask, which you blame? Is it anything but a greater sensibility to all the pleasures and pains of life? And if the man of a delicate, refined temper, by being so much more alive than the rest of the world, is only so much more unhappy, what judgment must we form in general of human life?

Let me remain at rest, says our adversary, and they will be easy. They are willing artificers of their own misery. ... No! reply I: an anxious languor follows their repose; disappointment, vexation, trouble, their activity and ambition.

I can observe something like what you mention in some others, replied Cleanthes, but I confess I feel little or nothing of it in myself, and hope that it is not so common as you represent it.

If you feel not human misery yourself, cried Demea, I congragulate you on so happy a singularity. Others, seemingly the most prosperous, have not been ashamed to vent their complaints in the most melancholy strains. Let us attend to the great, the fortunate emperor, Charles V, when tired with human grandeur, he resigned all his extensive dominions into the hands of his son. In the last harangue which he made on that memorable occasion, he publicly avowed *that the greatest prosperities which he had ever enjoyed had been mixed with so many adversities that he might truly say he had never enjoyed any satisfaction or contentment.* But did the retired life in which he sought for shelter afford him any greater happiness? If we may credit his son's account, his repentance commenced the very day of his resignation.

Cicero's fortune, from small beginnings, rose to the greatest lustre and renown; yet what pathetic complaints of the ills of life do his familiar letters, as well as philosohpical discourses, contain? And suitably to his own experience, he introduces Cato, the great, the fortunate Cato protesting in his old age that had he a new life in his offer he would reject the present.

Ask yourself, ask any of your acquaintance, whether they would live over again the last ten or twenty years of their life. No! but the next twenty, they say, will be better:

And from the dregs of life, hope to receive
What the first sprightly running could not give.[8]

Thus, at last, they find (such is the greatness of human misery, it reconciles even contradictions) that they complain at once of the shortness of life and of its vanity and sorrow.

And it is possible, Cleanthes, said Philo, that after all these reflections, and infinitely more which might be suggested, you can still persevere in your anthropomorphism, and assert the moral attributes of the Deity, his justice, benevolence, mercy, and rectitude, to be of the same nature with these virtues in human creatures? His power, we allow, is infinite; whatever he wills is executed; but neither man nor any other animal is happy; therefore, he does not will their happiness. His wisdom is infinite; he is never mistaken in choosing the means to any end; but the course of nature tends not to human or animal felicity; therefore, it is not established for that purpose. Through the whole compass of human knowledge there are no inferences more certain and infallible than these. In what respect, then, do his benevolence and mercy resemble the benevolence and mercy of men?

Epicurus' old questions are yet unanswered.

"Is he willing to prevent evil, but not able? then is he impotent. Is he able, but not willing? then is he malevolent. Is he both able and willing? whence then is evil?

You ascribe, Cleanthes (and I believe justly), a purpose and intention to nature. But what, I beseech you, is the object of that curious artifice and machinery which she has displayed in all animals —the preservation alone of individuals, and propagation of the species? It seems enough for her purpose, if such a rank be barely upheld in the universe, without any care or concern for the happiness of the members that compose it. No resource for this purpose: no machinery in order merely to give pleasure or ease; no fund of pure joy and contentment; no indulgence without some want or necessity accompanying it. At least, the few phenomena of this nature are overbalanced by opposite phenomena of still greater importance.

Our sense of music, harmony, and indeed beauty of all kinds, gives satisfaction, without being absolutely necessary to the preservation and propagation of the species. But what racking pains, on the other hand, arise from gouts, gravels, megrims, toothaches, rheumatisms, where the injury to the animal machinery is either small

or incurable? Mirth, laughter, play, frolic seem gratuitous satisfactions which have no further tendency; spleen, melancholy, discontent, superstition are pains of the same nature. How then does the Divine benevolence display itself, in the sense of you anthropomorphites? None but we mystics, as you were pleased to call us, can account for this strange mixture of phenomena, by deriving it from attributes infinitely perfect but incomprehensible.

And have you, at last, said Cleanthes smiling, betrayed your intentions, Philo? Your long agreement with Demea did indeed a little surprise me, but I find you were all the while erecting a concealed battery against me. And I must confess that you have now fallen upon a subject worthy of your noble spirit of opposition and controversy. If you can make out the present point, and prove mankind to be unhappy or corrupted, there is an end at once of all religion. For to what purpose establish the natural attributes of the Deity, while the moral are still doubtful and uncertain?

You take umbrage very easily, replied Demea, at opinions the most innocent and the most generally received, even amongst the religious and devout themselves; and nothing can be more surprising than to find a topic like this—concerning the wickedness and misery of man—charged with no less than atheism and profaneness. Have not all pious divines and preachers who have indulged their rhetoric on so fertile a subject, have they not easily, I say, given a solution of any difficulties which may attend it? This world is but a point in comparison of the universe; this life but a moment in comparison of eternity. The present evil phenomena, therefore, are rectified in other regions, and in some future period of existence. And the eyes of men, being then opened to larger views of things, see the whole connection of general laws, and trace, with adoration, and benevolence and rectitude of the Deity through all the mazes and intricacies of his providence.

No! replied Cleanthes, no! These arbitrary suppositions can never be admitted, contrary to matter of fact, visible and uncontroverted. Whence can any cause be known but from its known effects? Whence can any hypothesis be proved but from the apparent phenomena? To establish one hypothesis upon another is building entirely in the air; and the utmost we ever attain by these conjectures and fictions is to ascertain the bare possibility of our opinion, but never can we, upon such terms, establish its reality.

The only method of supporting Divine benevolence—and it is what I willingly embrace—is to deny absolutely the misery and wickedness of man. Your representations are exaggerated; your melancholy views mostly fictitious; your inferences contrary to fact and experience. Health is more common than sickness; pleasure than pain; happiness than misery. And for one vexation which we meet with, we attain, upon computation, a hundred enjoyments.

Admitting your position, replied Philo, which yet is extremely doubtful, you must at the same time allow that, if pain be less frequent than pleasure, it is infinitely more violent and durable. One hour of it is often able to outweigh a day, a week, a month of our common insipid enjoyments; and how many days, weeks, and months are passed by several in the most acute torments? Pleasure, scarcely in one instance, is ever able to reach ecstasy and rapture; and in no one instance can it continue for any time at its highest pitch and altitude. The spirits evaporate, the nerves relax, the fabric is disordered, and the enjoyment quickly degenerates into fatigue and uneasiness. But pain often, good God, how often! rises to torture and agony; and the longer it continues, it becomes still more genuine agony and torture. Patience is exhausted, courage languishes, melancholy seizes us, and nothing terminates our misery but the removal of its cause or another event which is the sole cure of all evil, but which, from our natural folly, we regard with still greater horror and consternation.

But not to insist upon these topics, continued Philo, though most obvious, certain, and important, I must use the freedom to admonish you, Cleanthes, that you have put the controversy upon a most dangerous issue, and are unawares introducing a total scepticism into the most essential articles of natural and revealed theology. What! no method of fixing a just foundation for religion unless we allow the happiness of human life, and maintain a continued existence even in this world, with all our present pains, infirmities, vexations, and follies, to be eligible and desirable! But this is contrary to everyone's feeling and experience; it is contrary to an authority so established as nothing can subvert. No decisive proofs can ever be produced against this authority; nor is it possible for you to compute, estimate, and compare all the pains and all the pleasures in the lives of all men and of all animals; and thus, by your resting the whole system of religion on a point which, from its very nature, must for ever be uncertain, you tacitly confess that that system is equally uncertain.

But allowing you what never will be believed, at least, what you never possibly can prove, that animal or, at least, human happiness in this life exceeds its misery, you have yet done nothing; for this is not, by any means, what we expect from infinite power, infinite wisdom, and infinite goodness. Why is there any misery at all in the world? Not by chance, surely. From some cause then. Is it from the intention of the Deity? But he is perfectly benevolent. Is it contrary to his intention? But he is almighty. Nothing can shake the solidity of this reasoning, so short, so clear, so decisive, except we assert that these subjects exceed all human capacity, and that our common measures of truth and falsehood are not applicable to them—a topic which I have all along insisted on, but which you have, from the beginning, rejected with scorn and indignation.

But I will be contented to retire still from this intrenchment, for I deny that you can ever force me in it. I will allow that pain or misery in man is *compatible* with infinite power and goodness in the Deity, even in your sense of these attributes: what are you advanced by all these concessions? A mere possible compatibility is not sufficient. You must *prove* these pure, unmixt, and uncontrollable attributes from the present mixt and confused phenomena, and from these alone. A hopeful undertaking! Were the phenomena ever so pure and unmixt, yet, being finite, they would be insufficient for that purpose. How much more, where they are also so jarring and discordant!

Here, Cleanthes, I find myself at ease in my argument. Here I triumph. Formerly, when we argued concerning the natural attributes of intelligence and design, I needed all my sceptical and metaphysical subtilty to elude your grasp. In many views of the universe and of its parts, particularly the matter, the beauty and fitness of final causes strike us with such irresistible force that all objections appear (what I believe they really are) mere cavils and sophisms; nor can we then imagine how it was ever possible for us to repose any weight on them. But there is no view of human life or the condition of mankind from which, without the greatest violence, we can infer the moral attributes or learn that infinite benevolence, conjoined with infinite power and infinite wisdom, which we must discover by the eyes of faith alone. It is your turn now to tug the labouring oar, and to support your philosophical subtilties against the dictates of plain reason and experience.

PART XI

I scruple not to allow, said Cleanthes, that I have been apt to suspect the frequent repetition of the word *infinite,* which we meet with in all theological writers, to savour more of panegyric than of philosophy, and that any purposes of reasoning, and even of religion, would be better served were we to rest contented with more accurate and more moderate expressions. The terms *admirable, excellent, superlatively great, wise,* and *holy*—these sufficiently fill the imaginations of men, and anything beyond, besides that it leads into absurdities, has no influence on the affections or sentiments. Thus, in thy present subject, if we abandon all human analogy, as seems your intention, Demea, I am afraid we abandon all religion and retain no conception of the great object of our adoration. If we preserve human analogy, we must forever find it impossible to reconcile any mixture of evil in the universe with infinite attributes; much less can we ever prove the latter from the former. But supposing the Author of nature to be finitely perfect, though far exceeding mankind, a satisfactory account may then be given of natural and moral evil, and every untoward phenomenon be explained and adjusted. A less evil may then be chosen in order to avoid a greater; inconveniences be submitted to in order to reach a desirable end; and, in a word, benevolence, regulated by wisdom and limited by necessity, may produce just such a world as the present. You, Philo, who are so prompt at starting views and reflections and analogies, I would gladly hear, at length, without interruption, your opinion of this new theory; and if it deserve our attention, we may afterwards, at more leisure, reduce it into form.

My sentiments, replied Philo, are not worth being made a mystery of; and, therefore, without any ceremony, I shall deliver what occurs to me with regard to the present subject. I must, I think, be allowed that, if a very limited intelligence whom we shall suppose utterly unacquainted with the universe were assured that it were the production of a very good, wise, and powerful Being, however finite, he would, from his conjectures, form *beforehand* a different notion of it from what we find it to be by experience; nor would he ever imagine, merely from these attributes of the cause of which he is informed, that the effect could be so full of vice and misery and disorder, as it appears in this life. Supposing now that this person were brought into the world, still assured that it was the workmanship of such a sublime and benevolent Being, he might, perhaps, be surprised at the disappointment, but would never retract his former belief if founded on any very solid argument, since such a limited intelligence must be sensible of his own blindness and ignorance, and must allow that there may be many solutions of those phenomena which will for ever escape his comprehension. But supposing, which is the real case with regard to man, that this creature is not antecedently convinced of a supreme intelligence, benevolent, and powerful, but is left to gather such a belief from the appearances of things—this entirely alters the case, nor will he ever find any reason for such a conclusion. He may be fully convinced of the narrow limits of his understanding, but this will not help him in forming an inference concerning the goodness of superior powers, since he must form that inference from what he knows, not from what he is ignorant of. The more you exaggerate his weakness and ignorance, the more diffident you render him, and give him the greater suspicion that such subjects are beyond the reach of his faculties. You are obliged, therefore, to reason with him merely from the known phenomena, and to drop every arbitrary supposition or conjecture.

Did I show you a house or palace where there was not one apartment convenient or agreeable, where the windows, doors, fires, passages, stairs, and the whole economy of the building were the source of noise, confusion, fatigue, darkness, and the extremes of heat and cold, you would certainly blame the contrivance, without any further examination. The architect would in vain display his subtilty, and prove to you that, if this door or that window were altered, greater ills would ensue. What he says may be strictly true: the alteration of one particular, while the other parts of the building remain, may only augment the inconveniences. But still you would assert in general that, if the architect had had skill and good intentions, he might have formed such a plan of the whole, and might have adjusted the parts in such a manner as would have remedied all or most of these inconveniences. His ignorance, or even your own ignorance of such a plan, will never convince you of the impossibility of it. If you find any inconveniences and deformities in the building, you will always, without entering into any detail, condemn the architect.

In short, I repeat the question: Is the world, considered in general and as it appears to us in this life, different from what a man or such a limited being would, *beforehand,* expect from a very powerful, wise, and benevolent Deity? It must be strange prejudice to assert the contrary. And from thence I conclude that, however consistent the world may be, allowing certain suppositions and conjectures with the idea of such a Deity, it can never afford us an inference concerning his existence. The consistency is not absolutely denied, only the inference. Conjectures, especially where infinity is excluded from the Divine attributes, may perhaps be sufficient to prove a consistency, but can never be foundations from any inference.

There seem to be *four* circumstances on which depend all or the greatest part of the ills that molest sensible creatures; and it is not impossible but all these circumstances may be necessary and unavoidable. We know so little beyond common life, or even of common life, that, with regard to the economy of a universe, there is no conjecture, however wild, which may not be just, nor any one, however plausible, which may not be erroneous. All that belongs to human understanding, in this deep ignorance and obscurity, is to be sceptical or at least cautious, and not to admit of any hypothesis whatever, much less of any which is supported by no appearance of probability. Now this I assert to be the case with regard to all the causes of evil and the circumstances on which it depends. None of them appear to human reason in the least degree necessary or unavoidable, nor can we suppose them such, without the utmost license of imagination.

The *first* circumstance which introduces evil is that contrivance or economy of the animal creation by which pains, as well as pleasures, are employed to excite all creatures to action, and make them vigilant in the great work of self-preservation. Now pleasure alone, in its various degrees, seems to human understanding sufficient for this purpose. All animals might be constantly in a state of enjoyment; but when urged by any of the necessities of nature, such as thirst, hunger, weariness, instead of pain, they might feel a diminution of pleasure by which they might be prompted to seek that object which is necessary to their subsistence. Men pursue pleasure as eagerly as they avoid pain; at least, they might have been so constituted. It seems, therefore, plainly possible to carry on the business of life without any pain. Why then is any animal ever rendered susceptible of such a sensation? If animals can be free from it an hour, they might enjoy a perpetual exemption from it, and it required as particular a contrivance of their organs to produce that feeling as to endow them with sight, hearing, or any of the senses. Shall we conjecture that such a contrivance was necessary, without any appearance of reason, and shall we build on that conjecture as on the most certain truth?

But a capacity of pain would not alone produce pain were it not for the *second* circumstance, viz., the conducting of the world by general laws; and this seems nowise necessary to a very perfect Being. It is true, if everything were conducted by particular volitions, the course of nature would be perpetually broken, and no man could employ his reason in the conduct of life. But might not other particular volitions remedy this inconvenience? In short, might not the Deity exterminate all ill, wherever it were to be found, and produce all good, without any preparation or long progress of causes and effects?

Besides, we must consider that, according to the present economy of the world, the course of nature, though supposed exactly regular, yet to us appears not so, and many events are uncertain, and many disappoint our expectations. Health and sickness, calm and tempest, with an infinite number of other accidents whose causes are unknown and variable, have a great influence both on the fortunes of particular persons and on the prosperity of public societies; and indeed all human life, in a manner, depends on such accidents. A being, therefore, who knows the secret springs of the universe might easily, by particular volitions, turn all these accidents to the good of mankind and render the whole world happy, without discovering himself in any operation. A fleet whose purposes werc salutary to society might always meet with a fair wind. Good princes enjoy sound health and long life. Persons born to power and authority be framed with good tempers and virtuous dispositions. A few such events as these, regularly and wisely conducted, would change the face of the world, and yet would no more seem to disturb the course of nature or confound human conduct than the present economy of things where the causes are secret and variable and compounded. Some small touches given to Caligula's brain in his infancy might have converted him into a Trajan. One wave, a little higher than the rest, by burying Caesar and his fortune in the bottom of the ocean, might have restored liberty to a considerable part of mankind. There may, for aught we know, be good reasons why Providence interposes not in this manner, but they are unknown to us; and, though the mere supposition that such reasons exist may be sufficient to *save* the conclusion concerning the Divine attributes, yet surely it can never be sufficient to *establish* that conclusion.

If everything in the universe be conducted by general laws, and if animals be rendered susceptible of pain, it scarcely seems possible but some ill must arise in the various shocks of matter and the various concurrence and opposition of general laws; but this ill would be very rare were it not for the *third* circumstance which I proposed to mention, viz., the great frugality with which all powers and faculties are distributed to every particular being. So well adjusted are the organs and capacities of all animals, and so well fitted to their preservation, that, as far as history or tradition reaches, there appears not to be any single species which has yet been extinguished in the universe. Every animal has the requisite endowments, but these endowments are bestowed with so scrupulous an economy that any considerable diminution must entirely destroy the creature. Wherever one power is increased, there is a proportional abatement in the others. Animals which excel in swiftness are commonly defective in force. Those which possess both are either imperfect in some of their senses or are oppressed with the most craving wants. The human species, whose chief excellence is reason and sagacity, is of all others

the most necessitous, and the most deficient in bodily advantages, without clothes, without arms, without food, without lodging, without any convenience of life, except what they owe to their own skill and industry. In short, nature seems to have formed an exact calculation of the necessities of her creatures, and, like a *rigid master,* has afforded them little more powers or endowments than what are strictly sufficient to supply those necessities. An *indulgent parent* would have bestowed a large stock in order to guard against accidents, and secure the happiness and welfare of the creature in the most unfortunate concurrence of circumstances. Every course of life would not have been so surrounded with precipices that the least departure from the true path, by mistake or necessity, must involve us in misery and ruin. Some reserve, some fund, would have been provided to ensure happiness, nor would the powers and the necessities have been adjusted with so rigid an economy. The Author of nature is inconceivably powerful; his force is supposed great, if not altogether inexhaustible, nor is there any reason, as far as we can judge, to make him observe this strict frugality in his dealings with his creatures. It would have been better, were his power extremely limited, to have created fewer animals, and to have endowed these with more faculties for their happiness and preservation. A builder is never esteemed prudent who undertakes a plan beyond what his stock will enable him to finish.

In order to cure most of the ills of human life, I require not that man should have the wings of the eagle, the swiftness of the stag, the force of the ox, the arms of the lion, the scales of the crocodile or rhinoceros; much less do I demand the sagacity of an angel or cherubim. I am contented to take an increase in one single power or faculty of his soul. Let him be endowed with a greater propensity to industry and labour, a more vigorous spring and activity of mind, a more constant bent to business and application. Let the whole species possess naturally an equal diligence with that which many individuals are able to attain by habit and reflection, and the most beneficial consequences, without any allay of ill, is the immediate and necessary result of this endowment. Almost all the moral as well as natural evils of human life arise from idleness; and were our species, by the original constitution of their frame, exempt from this vice or infirmity, the perfect cultivation of land, the improvement of arts and manufactures, the exact execution of every office and duty, immediately follow; and men at once may fully reach that state of society which is so imperfectly attained by the best regulated government. But as industry is a power, and the most valuable of any, nature seems determined, suitably to her usual maxims, to bestow it on man with a very sparing hand, and rather to punish him severely for his deficiency in it than to reward him for his attainments. She has so contrived his frame that nothing but the most violent necessity can oblige him to labour; and she employs all his other wants to overcome, at least in part, the want of diligence, and to endow him with some share of a faculty of which she has thought fit naturally to bereave him. Here our demands may be allowed very humble, and therefore the more reasonable. If we required the endowments of superior penetration and judgment, of a more delicate taste of beauty, of a nicer sensibility to benevolence and friendship, we might be told that we impiously pretend to break the order of nature, that we want to exalt ourselves into a higher rank of being, that the presents which we require, not being suitable to our state and condition, would only be pernicious to us. But it is hard, I dare to repeat it, it is hard that, being placed in a world so full of wants and necessities, where almost every being and element is either our foe or refuses its assistance ... we should also have our own temper to struggle with, and should be deprived of that faculty which can alone fence against these multiplied evils.

The *fourth* circumstance whence arises the misery and ill of the universe is the inaccurate workmanship of all the springs and principles of the great machine of nature. It must be acknowledged that there are few parts of the universe which seem not to serve some purpose, and whose removal would not produce a visible defect and disorder in the whole. The parts hang all together, nor can one be touched without affecting the rest, in a greater or less degree. But at the same time, it must be observed that none of these parts or principles, however useful, are so accurately adjusted as to keep precisely within those bounds in which their utility consists; but they are, all of them, apt, on every occasion, to run into the one extreme or the other. One would

imagine that this grand production had not received the last hand of the maker—so little finished is every part, and so coarse are the strokes with which it is executed. Thus the winds are requisite to convey the vapours along the surface of the globe, and to assist men in navigation; but how often, rising up to tempests and hurricanes, do they become pernicious? Rains are necessary to nourish all the plants and animals of the earth; but how often are they defective? how often excessive? Heat is requisite to all life and vegetation, but is not always found in the due proportion. On the mixture and secretion of the humours and juices of the body depend the health and prosperity of the animal; but the parts perform not regularly their proper function. What more useful than all the passions of the mind, ambition, vanity, love, anger? But how often do they break their bounds and cause the greatest convulsions in society? There is nothing so advantageous in the universe but what frequently becomes pernicious, by its excess or defect; nor has nature guarded, with the requisite accuracy, against all disorder or confusion. The irregularity is never perhaps so great as to destroy any species, but is often sufficient to involve the individuals in ruin and misery.

On the concurrence, then, of these *four* circumstances does all or the greatest part of natural evil depend. Were all living creatures incapable of pain, or were the world administered by particular volitions, evil never could have found access into the universe; and were animals endowed with a large stock of powers and faculties, beyond what strict necessity requires, or were the several springs and principles of the universe so accurately framed as to preserve always the just temperament and medium, there must have been very little ill in comparison of what we feel at present. What then shall we pronounce on this occasion? Shall we say that these circumstances are not necessary, and that they might easily have been altered in the contrivance of the universe? This decision seems too presumptuous for creatures so blind and ignorant. Let us be more modest in our conclusions. Let us allow that, if the goodness of the Deity (I mean a goodness like the human) could be established on any tolerable reasons *a priori,* these phenomena, however untoward, would not be sufficient to subvert that principle, but might easily, in some unknown manner, be reconcilable to it. But let us still assert that, as this goodness is not antecedently established but must be inferred from the phenomena, there can be no grounds for such an inference while there are so many ills in the universe, and while these ills might so easily have been remedied, as far as human understanding can be allowed to judge on such a subject. I am sceptic enough to allow that the bad appearances, notwithstanding all my reasonings, may be compatible with such attributes as you suppose, but surely they can never prove these attributes. Such a conclusion cannot result from scepticism, but must arise from the phenomena, and from our confidence in the reasonings which we deduce from these phenomena.

Look round this universe. What an immense profusion of beings, animated and organized, sensible and active! You admire this prodigious variety and fecundity. But inspect a little more narrowly these living existences, the only beings worth regarding. How hostile and destructive to each other! How insufficient all of them for their own happiness! How contemptible or odious to the spectator! The whole presents nothing but the idea of a blind nature, impregnated by a great vivifying principle, and pouring forth from her lap, without discernment or parental care, her maimed and abortive children!

Here the Manichaean system occurs as a proper hypothesis to solve the difficulty; and, no doubt, in some respects it is very specious and has more probability than the common hypothesis, by giving a plausible account of the strange mixture of good and ill which appears in life. But if we consider, on the other hand, the perfect uniformity and agreement of the parts of the universe, we shall not discover in it any marks of the combat of a malevolent with a benevolent being. There is indeed an opposition of pains and pleasures in the feelings of sensible creatures; but are not all the operations of nature carried on by an opposition of principles, of hot and cold, moist and dry, light and heavy? The true conclusion is that the original Source of all things is entirely indifferent to all these principles, and has no more regard to good above ill than to heat above cold, or to drought above moisture, or to light above heavy.

There may *four* hypotheses be framed concerning the first causes of the universe: that they are endowed with perfect goodness; that they have perfect malice; that they are opposite and have both goodness and malice; that they have neither goodness nor malice. Mixed phenomena can never prove the two former unmixed principles; and the uniformity and steadiness of general laws seem to oppose the third. The fourth, therefore, seems by far the most probable.

What I have said concerning natural evil will apply to moral with little or no variation; and we have no more reason to infer that the rectitude of the Supreme Being resembles human rectitude than that his benevolence resembles the human. Nay, it will be thought that we have still greater cause to exclude from him moral sentiments, such as we feel them, since moral evil, in the opinion of many, is much more predominant above moral good than natural evil above natural good.

But even though this should not be allowed, and though the virtue which is in mankind should be acknowledged much superior to the vice, yet, so long as there is any vice at all in the universe, it will very much puzzle you anthropomorphites how to account for it. You must assign a cause for it, without having recourse to the first cause. But as every effect must have a cause, and that cause another, you must either carry on the progression *in infinitum* or rest on that original principle, who is the ultimate cause of all things ...

Hold! hold! cried Demea: Whither does your imagination hurry you? I joined in alliance with you in order to prove the incomprehensible nature of the Divine Being, and refute the principles of Cleanthes, who would measure everything by human rule and standard. But I now find you running into all the topics of the greatest libertines and infidels, and betraying that holy cause which you seemingly espoused. Are you secretly, then, a more dangerous enemy than Cleanthes himself?

And are you so late in perceiving it? replied Cleanthes. Believe me, Demea, your friend Philo, from the beginning, has been amusing himself at both our expense; and it must be confessed that the injudicious reasoning of our vulgar theology has given him but too just a handle of ridicule. The total infirmity of human reason, the absolute incomprehensibility of the Divine Nature, the great and universal misery, and still greater wickedness of men—these are strange topics, surely, to be so fondly cherished by orthodox divines and doctors. In ages of stupidity and ignorance, indeed, these principles may safely be espoused; and perhaps no views of things are more proper to promote superstition than such as encourage the blind amazement, the diffidence, and melancholy of mankind. But at present . . .

Blame not so much, interposed Philo, the ignorance of these reverend gentlemen. They know how to change their style with the times. Formerly, it was a most popular theological topic to maintain that human life was vanity and misery, and to exaggerate all the ills and pains which are incident to men. But of late years, divines, we find, begin to retract this position and maintain, though still with some hesitation, that there are more goods than evils, more pleasures than pains, even in this life. When religion stood entirely upon temper and education, it was thought proper to encourage melancholy, as, indeed, mankind never have recourse to superior powers so readily as in that disposition. But as men have now learned to form principles and to draw consequences, it is necessary to change the batteries, and to make use of such arguments as will endure at least some scrutiny and examination. This variation is the same (and from the same causes) with that which I formerly remarked with regard to scepticism.

Thus Philo continued to the last his spirit of opposition, and his censure of established opinions. But I could observe that Demea did not at all relish the latter part of the discourse; and he took occasion soon after, on some pretence or other, to leave the company.

NOTES

1. *Recherche de la Verité,* liv. 3, cap. 9.

2. *De Rerum Natura,* lib. XI [II], 1094. (Who can rule the sum, who hold in his hand with controlling force the strong reins, of the immeasurable deep? Who can at once make all the different heavens to roll and warm with ethereal fires all the fruitful earths, or be present in all places at all times?)—(Translation by H. A. J. Munro, G. Bell & Sons, 1920.)

3. *De Natura Deorum,* lib. I [cap. VIII]. (For with what eyes could your Plato see the construction of so vast a work which, according to him, God was putting together and building? What materials, what tools, what bars, what machines, what servants were employed in such gigantic work? How could the air, fire, water, and earth pay obedience and submit to the will of the architect?)

4. Dr. Clarke [Samuel Clarke, the rationalist theologian (1675–1729).]

5. *Republique des Lettres,* Aut 1685.

6. That sentiment had been maintained by Dr. King and some few others before Leibniz, though by none of so great fame as that German philosopher.

7. Milton: *Paradise Lost,* Bk. XI.

8. John Dryden, *Aureng-Zebe,* Act IV, sc. 1.

ANTONY FLEW, R. M. HARE, BASIL MITCHELL

Symposium on Theology and Falsification*

ANTONY FLEW

Let us begin with a parable. It is a parable developed from a tale told by John Wisdom in his haunting and revelatory article 'Gods.'[1] Once upon a time two explorers came upon a clearing in the jungle. In the clearing were growing many flowers and many weeds. One explorer says, 'Some gardener must tend this plot.' The other disagrees, 'There is no gardener.' So they pitch their tents and set a watch. No gardener is ever seen. 'But perhaps he is an invisible gardener.' So they set up a barbed-wire fence. They electrify it. They patrol with bloodhounds. (For they remember how H. G. Wells's *The Invisible Man* could be both smelt and touched though he could not be seen.) But no shrieks ever suggest that some intruder has received a shock. No movements of the wire ever betray an invisible climber. The bloodhounds never give cry. Yet still the Believer is not convinced. 'But there is a gardener, invisible, intangible, insensible to electric shocks, a gardener who has no scent and makes no sound, a gardener who comes secretly to look after the garden which he loves.' At last the Sceptic despairs, 'But what remains of your original assertion? Just how does what you call an invisible, intangible, eternally elusive gardener differ from an imaginary gardener or even from no gardener at all?'

In this parable we can see how what starts as an assertion, that something exists or that there is some analogy between certain complexes of phenomena, may be reduced step by step to an altogether different status, to an expression perhaps of a 'picture preference.'[2] The Sceptic says there is no gardener. The Believer says there is a gardener (but invisible, etc.). One man talks about sexual behaviour. Another man prefers to talk of Aphrodite (but knows that there is not really a superhuman person additional to, and somehow responsible for, all sexual phenomena).[3] The process of qualification may be checked at any point before the original assertion is completely withdrawn and something of that first assertion will remain (Tautology). Mr. Wells's invisible man could not, admittedly, be seen, but in all other respects he was a man like the rest of us. But though the process of qualification may be, and of course usually is, checked in time, it is not always judiciously so halted. Someone may dissipate his assertion completely without noticing that he has done so. A fine brash hypothesis may thus be killed by inches, the death by a thousand qualifications.

And in this, it seems to me, lies the peculiar danger, the endemic evil, of theological utterance. Take such utterances as 'God has a plan,' 'God created the world,' 'God loves us as a father loves his children.' They look at first sight very much like assertions, vast cosmological assertions. Of course, this is no sure sign that they either are, or are intended to be, assertions. But let us confine ourselves to the cases where those who utter such sentences intend them to express assertions. (Merely remarking parenthetically that those

*Antony Flew, R. M. Hare, and Basil Mitchell, "Theology and Falsification," *University*, 1950–51. Reprinted in A. Flew and A. MacIntyre, eds., *New Essays in Philosophical Theology* (New York: Macmillan, 1955), pp. 96–108. The discussion is reprinted here by permission of the Macmillan Company. First published 1955 by SCM Press Ltd. First American paperback edition published 1964.

who intend or interpret such utterances as crypto-commands, expressions of wishes, disguised ejaculations, concealed ethics, or as anything else but assertions, are unlikely to succeed in making them either properly orthodox or practically effective.)

Now to assert that such and such is the case is necessarily equivalent to denying that such and such is not the case.[4] Suppose then that we are in doubt as to what someone who gives vent to an utterance is asserting, or suppose that, more radically, we are sceptical as to whether he is really asserting anything at all, one way of trying to understand (or perhaps it will be to expose) his utterance is to attempt to find what he would regard as counting against, or as being incompatible with, its truth. For if the utterance is indeed an assertion, it will necessarily be equivalent to a denial of the negation of that assertion. And anything which would count against the assertion, or which would induce the speaker to withdraw it and to admit that it had been mistaken, must be part of (or the whole of) the meaning of the negation of that assertion. And to know the meaning of the negation of an assertion, is as near as makes no matter, to know the meaning of that assertion.[5] And if there is nothing which a putative assertion denies then there is nothing which it asserts either: and so it is not really an assertion. When the Sceptic in the parable asked the Believer, 'Just how does what you call an invisible, intangible, enternally elusive gardener differ from an imaginary gardener or even from no gardener at all?' he was suggesting that the Believer's earlier statement had been so eroded by qualification that it was no longer an assertion at all.

Now it often seems to people who are not religious as if there was no conceivable event or series of events the occurrence of which would be admitted by sophisticated religious people to be a sufficient reason for conceding 'there wasn't a God after all' or 'God does not really love us then.' Someone tells us that God loves us as a father loves his children. We are reassured. But then we see a child dying of inoperable cancer of the throat. His earthly father is driven frantic in his efforts to help, but his Heavenly Father reveals no obvious sign of concern. Some qualification is made—God's love is 'not a merely human love' or it is 'an inscrutable love,' perhaps—and we realize that such sufferings are quite compatible with the truth of the assertion that 'God loves us as a father (but, of course, . . .).' We are reassured again. But then perhaps we ask: what is this assurance of God's (appropriately qualified) love worth, what is this apparent guarantee really a guarantee against? Just what would have to happen not merely (morally and wrongly) to tempt but also (logically and rightly) to entitle us to say 'God does not love us' or even 'God does not exist'? I therefore put to the succeeding symposiasts the simple central questions, 'What would have to occur or to have occurred to constitute for you a disproof of the love of, or of the existence of, God?'

R. M. HARE[6]

I wish to make it clear that I shall not try to defend Christianity in particular, but religion in general—not because I do not believe in Christianity, but because you cannot understand what Christianity is, until you have understood what religion is.

I must begin by confessing that, on the ground marked out by Flew, he seems to me to be completely victorious. I therefore shift my ground by relating another parable. A certain lunatic is convinced that all dons want to murder him. His friends introduce him to all the mildest and most respectable dons that they can find, and after each of them has retired, they say, 'You see, he doesn't really want to murder you; he spoke to you in the most cordial manner; surely you are convinced now?' But the lunatic replies, 'Yes, but that was only his diabolical cunning; he's really plotting against me the whole time, like the rest of them; I know it I tell you.' However many kindly dons are produced, the reaction is still the same.

Now we say that such a person is deluded. But what is he deluded about? About the truth or falsity of an assertion? Let us apply Flew's test to him. There is no behaviour of dons that can be enacted which he will accept as counting against his theory; and therefore his theory, on this test, asserts nothing. But it does not follow that there is no difference between what he thinks about dons and what most of us think about them— otherwise we should not call him a lunatic and ourselves sane, and dons would have no reason to feel uneasy about his presence in Oxford.

Let us call that in which we differ from this lunatic, our respective *bliks*. He has an insane *blik* about dons; we have a sane one. It is important to realize that we have a sane one, not no *blik* at all; for there must be two sides to any argument—if he has a wrong *blik,* then those who are right about dons must have a right one. Flew has shown that a *blik* does not consist in an assertion or system of them; but nevertheless it is very important to have the right *blik.*

Let us try to imagine what it would be like to have different *bliks* about other things than dons. When I am driving my car, it sometimes occurs to me to wonder whether my movements of the sterring-wheel will always continue to be followed by corresponding alterations in the direction of the car. I have never had a steering failure, though I have had skids, which must be similar. Moreover, I know enough about how the steering of my car is made, to know the sort of thing that would have to go wrong for the steering to fail—steel joints would have to part, or steel rods break, or something—but how do I know that this won't happen? The truth is, I don't know; I just have a *blik* about steel and its properties, so that normally I trust the steering of my car; but I find it not at all difficult to imagine what it would be like to lose this *blik* and acquire the opposite one. People would say I was silly about steel; but there would be no mistaking the reality of the difference between our respective *bliks*—for example, I should never go in a motorcar. Yet I should hesitate to say that the difference between us was the difference between contradictory assertions. No amount of safe arrivals or bench-tests will remove my *blik* and restore the normal one; for my *blik* is compatible with any finite number of such tests.

It was Hume who taught us that our whole commerce with the world depends upon our *blik* about the world; and that difference between *bliks* about the world cannot be settled by observation of what happens in the world. That was why, having performed the interesting experiment of doubting the ordinary man's *blik* about the world, and showing that no proof could be given to make us adopt one *blik* rather than another, he turned to backgammon to take his mind off the problem. It seems, indeed, to be impossible even to formulate as an assertion the normal *blik* about the world which makes me put my confidence in the future reliability of steel joints, in the continued ability of the road to support my car,

and not gape beneath it revealing nothing below; in the general non-homicidal tendencies of dons; in my own continued well-being (in some sense of that word that I may not now fully understand) if I continue to do what is right according to my lights; in the general likelihood of people like Hitler coming to a bad end. But perhaps a formulation less inadequate than most is to be found in the Psalms: 'The earth is weak and all the inhabiters thereof: I bear up the pillars of it.'

The mistake of the position which Flew selects for attack is to regard this kind of talk as some sort of *explanation,* as scientists are accustomed to use the word. As such, it would obviously be ludicrous. We no longer believe in God as an Atlas—*nous n'avons pas besoin de cette hypothèse.*[7] But it is nevertheless true to say that, as Hume saw, without a *blik* there can be no explanation; for it is by our *bliks* that we decide what is and what is not an explanation. Suppose we believe that everything that happened, happened by pure chance. This would not of course be an assertion; for it is compatible with anything happening or not happening, and so, incidentally, is its contradictory. But if we had this belief, we should not be able to explain or predict or plan anything. Thus, although we should not be *asserting* anything different from those of a more normal belief, there would be a great difference between us; and this is the sort of difference that there is between those who really believe in God and those who really disbelieve in him.

The word 'really' is important, and may excite suspicion. I put it in, because when people have had a good Christian upbringing, as have most of those who now profess not to believe in any sort of religion, it is very hard to discover what they really believe. The reason why they find it so easy to think that they are not religious, is that they have never got into the frame of mind of one who suffers from the doubts to which religion is the answer. Not for them the terrors of the primitive jungle. Having abandoned some of the more picturesque fringes of religion, they think that they have abandoned the whole thing—whereas in fact they still have got, and could not live without, a religion of a comfortably substantial, albeit highly sophisticated, kind, which differs from that of many 'religious people' in little more than this, that 'religious people' like to sing Psalms about theirs—a very natural and proper thing to do. But nevertheless there may be a big difference lying behind—the difference between two people who, though side by side, are walking in different directions. I do not know in what direction. Flew is walking; perhaps he does not know either. But we have had some examples recently of various ways in which one can walk away from Christianity, and there are any number of possibilities. After all, man has not changed biologically since primitive times; it is his religion that has changed, and it can easily change again. And if you do not think that such changes make a difference, get acquainted with some Sikhs and some Mussulmans of the same Punjabi stock; you will find them quite different sorts of people.

There is an important difference between Flew's parable and my own which we have not yet noticed. The explorers do not *mind* about their garden; they discuss it with interest, but not with concern. But my lunatic, poor fellow, minds about dons; and I mind about the steering of my car; it often has people in it that I care for. It is because I mind very much about what goes on in the garden in which I find myself, that I am unable to share the explorers' detachment.

BASIL MITCHELL

Flew's article is searching and perceptive, but there is, I think, something odd about his conduct of the theologian's case. The theologian surely would not deny that the fact of pain counts against the assertion that God loves men. This very incompatibility generates the most intractable of theological problems—the problem of evil. So the theologian *does* recognize the fact of pain as counting against Christian doctrine. But it is true that he will not allow it—or anything—to count decisively against it; for he is committed by his faith to trust in God. His attitude is not that of the detached observer, but of the believer.

Perhaps this can be brought out by yet another parable. In time of war in an occupied country, a member of the resistance meets one night a stranger who deeply impresses him. They spend that night together in conversation. The Stranger tells the partisan that he himself is on the side of the resistance—indeed that he is in command of it, and urges the partisan to have faith in him no matter what happens. The partisan is utterly convinced at that meeting of the Stranger's sincerity and constancy and undertakes to trust him.

They never meet in conditions of intimacy again. But sometimes the Stranger is seen helping members of the resistance, and the partisan is grateful and says to his friends, 'He is on our side.'

Sometimes he is seen in the uniform of the police handing over patriots to the occupying power. On these occasions his friends murmur against him: but the partisan still says, 'He is on our side.' He still believes that, in spite of appearances, the Stranger did not deceive him. Sometimes he asks the Stranger for help and receives it. He is then thankful. Sometimes he asks and does not receive it. Then he says, 'The Stranger knows best.' Sometimes his friends, in exasperation, say 'Well, what *would* he have to do for you to admit that you were wrong and that he is not on our side?' But the partisan refuses to answer. He will not consent to put the Stranger to the test. And sometimes his friends complain, 'Well, if *that's* what you mean by his being on our side, the sooner he goes over to the other side the better.'

The partisan of the parable does not allow anything to count decisively against the proposition 'The Stranger is on our side.' This is because he has committed himself to trust the Stranger. But he of course recognizes that the Stranger's ambiguous behaviour *does* count against what he believes about him. It is precisely this situation which constitutes the trial of his faith.

When the partisan asks for help and doesn't get it, what can he do? He can (a) conclude that the Stranger is not on our side or; (b) maintain that he is on our side, but that he has reasons for withholding help.

The first he will refuse to do. How long can he uphold the second position without its becoming just silly?

I don't think one can say in advance. It will depend on the nature of the impression created by the Stranger in the first place. It will depend, too, on the manner in which he takes the Stranger's behavior. If he blandly dismisses it as of no consequence, as having no bearing upon his belief, it will be assumed that he is thoughtless or insane. And it quite obviously won't do for him to say easily, 'Oh, when used of the Stranger the phrase "is on our side" *means* ambiguous behavior of this sort.' In that case he would be like the religious man who says blandly of a terrible disaster

'It is God's will.' No, he will only be regarded as sane and reasonable in his belief, if he experiences in himself the full force of the conflict.

It is here that my parable differs from Hare's. The partisan admits that many things may and do count against his belief: whereas Hare's lunatic who has a *blik* about dons doesn't admit that anything counts against his *blik*. Nothing *can* count against *bliks*. Also the partisan has a reason for having in the first instance committed himself, viz, the character of the Stranger; whereas the lunatic has no reason for his *blik* about dons—because, of course, you can't have reasons for *bliks*.

This means that I agree with Flew that theological utterances must be assertions. The partisan is making an assertion when he says, 'The Stranger is on our side.'

Do I want to say that the partisan's belief about the Stranger is, in any sense, an explanation? I think I do. It explains and makes sense of the Stranger's behaviour: it helps to explain also the resistance movement in the context of which he appears. In each case it differs from the interpretation which the others put upon the same facts.

'God loves men' resembles 'the Stranger is on our side' (and many other significant statements, e.g. historical ones) in not being conclusively falsifiable. They can both be treated in at least three different ways: (1) As provisional hypotheses to be discarded if experience tells against them; (2) As significant articles of faith; (3) As vacuous formulae (expressing, perhaps, a desire for reassurance) to which experience makes no difference and which make no difference to life.

The Christian, once he has committed himself, is precluded by his faith from taking up the first attitude: 'Thou shalt not tempt the Lord thy God.' He is in constant danger, as Flew has observed, of slipping into the third. But he need not; and, if he does, it is a failure in faith as well as in logic.

ANTONY FLEW

It has been a good discussion: and I am glad to have helped to provoke it. But now—at least in *University*—it must come to an end: and the Editors of *University* have asked me to make some concluding remarks. Since it is impossible to deal with all the issues raised or to comment separately upon each contribution, I will concentrate on Mitchell and Hare, as representative of two very different kinds of response to the challenge made in 'Theology and Falsification.'

The challenge, it will be remembered, ran like this. Some theological utterances seem to, and are intended to, provide explanations or express assertions. Now an assertion, to be an assertion at all, must claim that things stand thus and thus; *and not otherwise.* Similarly an explanation, to be an explanation at all, must explain why this particular thing occurs; *and not something else.* Those last clauses are crucial. And yet sophisticated religious people—or so it seemed to me—are apt to overlook this, and tend to refuse to allow, not merely that anything actually does occur, but that anything conceivably could occur, which would count against their theological assertions and explanations. But in so far as they do this their supposed explanations are actually bogus, and their seeming assertions are really vacuous.

Mitchell's response to this challenge is admirably direct, straightforward, and understanding. He agrees 'that theological utterances must be assertions.' He agrees that if they are to be assertions, there must be something that would count against their truth. He agrees, too, that believers are in constant danger of transforming their would-be assertions into 'vacuous formulae.' But he takes me to task for an oddity in my 'conduct of the theologian's case. The theologian surely would not deny that the fact of pain counts against the assertion that God loves men. This very incompatibility generates the most intractable of theological problems, the problem of evil.' I think he is right. I should have made a distinction between two very different ways of dealing with what looks like evidence against the love of God: the way I stressed was the expedient of qualifying the original assertion; the way the theologian usually takes, at first, is to admit that it looks bad but to insist that there is—there must be—some explanation which will show that, in spite of appearances, there really is a God who loves us. His difficulty, it seems to me, is that he has given God attributes which rule out all possible saving explanations. In Mitchell's parable of the Stranger it is easy for the believer to find plausible excuses for ambiguous behavior: for the Stranger is a man. But suppose the Stranger is God. We cannot say that he would like to help but cannot: God is omnipotent. We cannot say that he would help if he only knew: God is omniscient. We cannot say that he is not responsible for the wickedness of others: God creates those others. Indeed an omnipotent, omniscient God must be an accessory before (and during) the fact to every human misdeed; as well as being responsible for every non-moral defect in the universe. So, though I entirely concede that Mitchell was absolutely right to insist against me that the theologian's first move is to look for an *explanation,* I still think that in the end, if relentlessly pursued, he will have to resort to the avoiding action of *qualification.* And there lies the danger of that death by a thousand qualifications, which would, I agree, constitute 'a failure in faith as well as in logic.'

Hare's approach is fresh and bold. He confesses that 'on the ground marked out by Flew, he seems to me to be completely victorious.' He therefore introduces the concept of *blik*. But while I think that there is room for some such concept in philosophy, and that philosophers should be grateful to Hare for his invention, I nevertheless want to insist that any attempt to analyse Christian religious utterances as expressions or affirmations of a *blik* rather than as (at least would-be) assertions about the cosmos is fundamentally misguided. *First,* because thus interpreted they would be entirely unorthodox. If Hare's religion really is a *blik,* involving no cosmological assertions about the nature and activities of a supposed personal creator, then surely he is not a Christian at all? *Second,* because thus interpreted, they could scarcely do the job they do. If they were not even intended as assertions then many religious activities would become fraudulent, or merely silly. If 'You ought *because* it is God's will' asserts no more than 'You ought,' then the person who prefers the former phraseology is not really giving a reason, but a fraudulent substitute for one, a dialectical dud cheque. If 'My soul must be immortal *because*

God loves his children, etc.' asserts no more than 'My soul must be immortal,' then the man who reassures himself with theological arguments for immortality is being as silly as the man who tries to clear his overdraft by writing his bank a cheque on the same account. (Of course neither of these utterances would be distinctively Christian: but this discussion never pretended to be so confined.) Religious utterances may indeed express false or even bogus assertions: but I simply do not believe that they are not both intended and interpreted to be or at any rate to presuppose assertions, at least in the context of religious practice; whatever shifts may be demanded, in another context, by the exigencies of theological apologetic.

One final suggestion. The philosophers of religion might well draw upon George Orwell's last appalling nightmare *1984* for the concept of *doublethink. 'Doublethink* means the power of holding two contradictory beliefs simultaneously, and accepting both of them. The party intellectual knows that he is playing tricks with reality, but by the exercise of *doublethink* he also satisfies himself that reality is not violated' (*1984,* p. 220). Perhaps religious intellectuals too are sometimes driven to doublethink in order to retain their faith in a loving God in face of the reality of a heartless and indifferent world. But of this more another time, perhaps.

NOTES

1. *P.A.S.,* 1944–5, reprinted as Ch. X of *Logic and Language,* Vol. I (Blackwell, 1951), and in his *Philosophy and Psychoanalysis* (Blackwell, 1953).

2. Cf. J. Wisdom, 'Other Minds,' *Mind,* 1940; reprinted in his *Other Minds* (Blackwell, 1952).

3. Cf. Lucretius, *De Rerum Natura, II,* 655–60.

4. For those who prefer symbolism: $p \equiv \sim\sim p$.

5. For by simply negating $\sim p$ we get $p \sim\sim \equiv p$.

6. Some references to intervening discussion have been excised by the editors of *New Essays in Philosophical Theology.*

7. We have no need of this hypothesis.

Religious Experience and Mysticism

WILLIAM JAMES

Mysticism*

Over and over again in these lectures I have raised points and left them open and unfinished until we should have come to the subject of Mysticism. Some of you, I fear, may have smiled as you noted my reiterated postponements. But now the hour has come when mysticism must be faced in good earnest, and those broken threads wound up together. One may say truly, I think, that personal religious experience has its root and centre in mystical states of consciousness; so for us, who in these lectures are treating personal experience as the exclusive subject of our study, such states of consciousness ought to form the vital chapter from which the other chapters get their light. Whether my treatment of mystical states will shed more light or darkness, I do not know, for my own constitution shuts me out from their enjoyment almost entirely, and I can speak of them only at second hand. But though forced to look upon the subject so externally, I will be as objective and receptive as I can; and I think I shall at least succeed in convincing you of the reality of the states in question, and of the paramount importance of their function.

First of all, then, I ask, What does the expression "mystical states of consciousness" mean? How do we part off mystical states from other states?

The words "mysticism" and "mystical" are often used as terms of mere reproach, to throw at

any opinion which we regard as vague and vast and sentimental, and without a base in either facts or logic. For some writers a "mystic" is any person who believes in thought-transference, or spirit-return. Employed in this way the word has little value: there are too many less ambiguous synonyms. So, to keep it useful by restricting it, I will do what I did in the case of the word "religion," and simply propose to you four marks which, when an experience has them, may justify us in calling it mystical for the purpose of the present lectures. In this way we shall save verbal disputation, and the recriminations that generally go therewith.

1. *Ineffability.*—The handiest of the marks by which I classify a state of mind as mystical is negative. The subject of it immediately says that it defies expression, that no adequate report of its contents can be given in words. It follows from this that its quality must be directly experienced; it cannot be imparted or transferred to others. In this peculiarity mystical states are more like states of feeling than like states of intellect. No one can make clear to another who has never had a certain feeling, in what the quality or worth of it consists. One must have musical ears to know the value of a symphony; one must have been in love one's self to understand a lover's state of mind. Lacking the heart or ear, we cannot interpret the musician or the lover justly, and are even likely to consider him weak-minded or absurd. The mystic finds that most of us accord to his experiences an equally incompetent treatment.

*From William James, *The Varieties of Religious Experience* (1902). Extracts from Lectures XVI and XVII. Lengthy footnote discussions have been omitted.

2. *Noetic quality.*—Although so similar to states of feeling, mystical states seem to those who experience them to be also states of knowledge. They are states of insight into depths of truth unplumbed by the discursive intellect. They are illuminations, revelations, full of significance and importance, all inarticulate though they remain; and as a rule they carry with them a curious sense of authority for aftertime.

These two characters will entitle any state to be called mystical, in the sense in which I use the word. Two other qualities are less sharply marked, but are usually found. These are:—

3. *Transiency.*—Mystical states cannot be sustained for long. Except in rare instances, half an hour, or at most an hour or two, seems to be the limit beyond which they fade into the light of common day. Often, when faded, their quality can but imperfectly be reproduced in memory; but when they recur it is recognized; and from one recurrence to another it is susceptible of continuous development in what is felt as inner richness and importance.

4. *Passivity.*—Although the oncoming of mystical states may be facilitated by preliminary voluntary operations, as by fixing the attention, or going through certain bodily performances, or in other ways which manuals of mysticism prescribe; yet when the characteristic sort of consciousness once has set in, the mystic feels as if his own will were in abeyance, and indeed sometimes as if he were grasped and held by a superior power. This latter peculiarity connects mystical states with certain definite phenomena of secondary or alternative personality, such as prophetic speech, automatic writing, or the mediumistic trance. When these latter conditions are well pronounced, however, there may be no recollection whatever of the phenomenon, and it may have no significance for the subject's usual inner life, to which, as it were, it makes a mere interruption. Mystical states, strictly so-called, are never merely interruptive. Some memory of their content always remains, and a profound sense of their importance. They modify the inner life of the subject between the times of their recurrence. Sharp divisions in this region are, however, difficult to make, and we find all sorts of gradations and mixtures.

These four characteristics are sufficient to mark out a group of states of consciousness peculiar enough to deserve a special name and to call for careful study. Let it then be called the mystical group.

Our next step should be to gain acquaintance with some typical examples. Professional mystics at the height of their development have often elaborately organized experiences and a philosophy based thereupon. But you remember what I said in my first lecture: phenomena are best understood when placed within their series, studied in their germ and in their over-ripe decay, and compared with their exaggerated and degenerated kindred. The range of mystical experience is very wide, much too wide for us to cover in the time at our disposal. Yet the method of serial study is so essential for interpretation that if we really wish to reach conclusions we must use it. I will begin, therefore, with phenomena which claim no special religious significance, and end with those of which the religious pretensions are extreme.

The simplest rudiment of mystical experience would seem to be that deepened sense of the significance of a maxim or formula which occasionally sweeps over one. "I've heard that said all my life," we exclaim, "but I never realized its full meaning until now." "When a fellow-monk," said Luther, "one day repeated the words of the Creed: 'I believe in the forgiveness of sins,' I saw the Scripture in an entirely new light; and straightway I felt as if I were born anew. It was as if I had found the door of paradise thrown wide open." This sense of deeper significance is not confined to rational propositions. Single words, and conjunctions of words, effects of light on land and sea, odors and musical sounds, all bring it when the mind is tuned aright. Most of us can remember the strangely moving power of passages in certain poems read when we were young, irrational doorways as they were through which the mystery of fact, the wildness and the pang of life, stole into our hearts and thrilled them. The words have now perhaps become mere polished surfaces for us; but lyric poetry and music are alive and significant only in proportion as they fetch these vague vistas of a life continuous with our own, beckoning and inviting, yet ever eluding our pursuit. We are alive or dead to the eternal inner message of the arts according as we have kept or lost this mystical susceptibility.

A more pronounced step forward on the mystical ladder is found in an extremely frequent phenomenon, that sudden feeling, namely, which sometimes sweeps over us, of having "been here before," as if at some indefinite past time, in just this place, with just these people, we were already saying just these things. As Tennyson writes:

> Moreover, something is or seems
> That touches me with mystic gleams,
> Like glimpses of forgotten dreams—
> Of something felt, like something here;
> Of something done, I know not where;
> Such as no language may declare.[1]

Sir James Crichton-Browne has given the technical name of "dreamy states" to these sudden invasions of vaguely reminiscent consciousness. They bring a sense of mystery and of the metaphysical duality of things, and the feeling of an enlargement of perception which seems imminent but which never completed itself. . . .

The next step into mystical states carries us into a realm that public opinion and ethical philosophy have long since branded as pathological, though private practice and certain lyric strains of poetry seem still to bear witness to its ideality. I refer to the consciousness produced by intoxicants and anaesthetics, especially by alcohol. The sway of alcohol over mankind is unquestionably due to its power to stimulate the mystical faculties of human nature, usually crushed to earth by the cold facts and dry criticisms of the sober hour. Sobriety diminishes, discriminates, and says no; drunkenness expands, unites, and says yes. It is in fact the great exciter of the *Yes* function in man. It brings its votary from the chill periphery of things to the radiant core. It makes him for the moment one with truth. Not through mere perversity do men run after it. To the poor and the unlettered it stands in the place of symphony concerts and of literature; and it is part of the deeper mystery and tragedy of life that whiffs and gleams of something that we immediately recognize as excellent should be vouch-safed to so many of us only in the fleeting earlier phases of what in its totality is so degrading a poisoning. The drunken consciousness is one bit of the mystic consciousness, and our total opinion of it must find its place in our opinion of that larger whole.

Nitrous oxide and ether, especially nitrous oxide, when sufficiently diluted with air, stimulate the mystical consciousness in an extraordinary degree. Depth beyond depth of truth seems revealed to the inhaler. This truth fades out, however, or escapes, at the moment of coming to; and if any words remain over in which it seemed to clothe itself, they prove to be the veriest nonsense. Nevertheless, the sense of profound meaning having been there persists; and I know more than one person who is persuaded that in the nitrous oxide trance we have a geniuine metaphysical revelation.

Some years ago I myself made some observations on this aspect of nitrous oxide intoxication, and reported them in print. One conclusion was forced upon my mind at that time, and my impression of its truth has ever since remained unshaken. It is that our normal waking consciousness, rational consciousness as we call it, is but one special type of consciousness, whilst all about it, parted from it by the filmiest of screens, there lie potential forms of consciousness entirely different. We may go through life without suspecting their existence; but apply the requisite stimulus, and at a touch they are there in all their completeness, definite types of mentality which probably somewhere have their field of application and adaptation. No account of the universe in its totality can be final which leaves these other forms of consciousness quite disregarded. How to regard them is the question—for they are so discontinuous with ordinary consciousness. Yet they may determine attitudes though they cannot furnish formulas, and open a region though they fail to give a map. At any rate, they forbid a premature closing of our accounts with reality. Looking back on my own experiences, they all converge towards a kind of insight to which I cannot help ascribing some metaphysical significance. The keynote of it is invariably a reconciliation. It is as if the opposites of the world, whose contradictoriness and conflict make all our difficulties and troubles, were melted into unity. Not only do they, as contrasted species, belong to one and the same genus, but *one of the species,* the nobler and better one, *is itself the genus, and so soaks up and absorbs its opposite into itself.* This is a dark saying, I know, when thus expressed in terms of common logic, but I cannot wholly escape from its authority. I feel as if it must mean something, something like what the hegelian philosophy means, if one could only lay hold of it more clearly. Those who have ears to hear, let them hear; to me the living sense of its reality only comes in the artificial mystic state of mind.[2]

I just now spoke of friends who believe in the anaesthetic revelation. For them too it is a monistic insight, in which the *other* in its various forms appears absorbed into the One.

"Into this pervading genius," writes one of them, "we pass, forgetting and forgotten, and thenceforth each is all, in God. There is no higher, no deeper, no other, than the life in which we are founded. 'The One remains, the many change and pass'; and each and every one of us *is* the One that remains. ... This is the ultimatum. ... As sure as being—whence is all our care —so sure is content, beyond duplexity, antithesis, or trouble, where I have trimphed in a solitude that God is not above."

This has the genuine religious mystic ring! ...

Certain aspects of nature seem to have a peculiar power of awakening such mystical moods. Most of the striking cases which I have collected have occurred out of doors. Literature has commemorated this fact in many passages of great beauty—this extract, for example, from Amiel's Journal Intime:—

Shall I ever again have any of those prodigious reveries which sometimes came to me in former days? One day, in youth, at sunrise, sitting in the ruins of the castle of Faucigny; and again in the mountains, under the noonday sun, above Lavey, lying at the foot of a tree and visited by three butterflies; once more at night upon the shingly shore of the Northern Ocean, my back upon the sand and my vision ranging through the milky way;—such grand and spacious, immortal, cosmogonic reveries, when one reaches to the stars, when one owns the infinite! Moments divine, ecstatic hours; in which our thought flies from world to world, pierces the great enigma, breathes with a respiration broad, tranquil, and deep as the respiration of the ocean, serene and limitless as the blue firmament, ... instants of irresistible intuition in which one feels one's self great as the universe, and calm as a god. ... What hours, what memories! The vestiges they leave behind are enough to fill us with belief and enthusiasm, as if they were visits of the Holy Ghost. ...

Even the least mystical of you must by this time be convinced of the existence of mystical moments as states of consciousness of an entirely specific quality, and of the deep impression which they make on those who have them. A Canadian psychiatrist, Dr. R. M. Bucke, gives to the more distinctly characterized of these phenomena the name of cosmic consciousness. "Cosmic consciousness in its more striking instances is not," Dr. Bucke says, "simply an expansion or extension of the self-conscious mind with which we are all familiar, but the superaddition of a function as distinct from any possessed by the average man as *self*-consciousness is distinct from any function possessed by one of the higher animals."

The prime characteristic of cosmic consciousness is a consciousness of the cosmos, that is, of the life and order of the universe. Along with the consciousness of the cosmos there occurs an intellectual enlightenment which alone would place the indivudual on a new plane of existence—would make him almost a member of a new species. To this is added a state of moral exaltation, an indescribable feeling of elevation, elation, and joyousness, and a quickening of the moral sense, which is fully as striking, and more important than is the enhanced intellectual power. With these come what may be called a sense of immortality, a consciousness of eternal life, not a conviction that he shall have this, but the consciousness that he has it already.[3]

It was Dr. Bucke's own experience of a typical onset of cosmic consciousness in his own person which led him to investigate it in others. He has printed his conclusions in a highly interesting volume, from which I take the following account of what occurred to him:—

I had spent the evening in a great city, with two friends, reading and discussing poetry and philosophy. We parted at midnight. I had a long drive in a hansom to my lodging. My mind, deeply under the influence of the ideas, images, and emotions called up by the reading and talk, was calm and peaceful. I was in a state of quiet, almost passive enjoyment, not actually thinking, but letting ideas, images, and emotions flow of themselves, as it were, through my mind. All at once, without warning of any kind, I found myself wrapped in a flame-colored cloud. For an instant I thought of fire, an immense conflagration somewhere close by in that great city; the next, I knew that the fire was within myself. Directly afterward there came upon me a sense of exultation, of immense joyousness accompanied or immediately followed by an intellectual illumination impossible to describe. Among other things, I did not merely come to believe, but I saw that the universe is not composed of dead matter, but is, on the contrary, a living Presence; I became conscious in myself of eternal life. It was not a conviction that I would have eternal life, but a consciousness that I possessed eternal life then; I saw that all men are immortal; that the cosmic order is such that without any peradventure all things work together for the good of each and all; that the foundation principle of the world, of all the worlds, is what we call love, and that the happiness of each and all is in the long run absolutely certain. The vision lasted a few seconds and was gone but the memory of it and the sense of the reality of what it taught has remained during the quarter of a century which has since elapsed. I knew that what the vision showed was true. I had attained to a point of view from which I saw that it must be true. That view, that conviction, I may say that consciousness, has never, even during periods of the deepest depression, been lost.[4]

We have now seen enough of this cosmic or mystic consciousness, as it comes sporadically. We must next pass to its methodical cultivation as an element of the religious life. Hindus, Buddhists, Mohammedans, and Christians all have cultivated it methodically.

In India, training in mystical insight has been known from time immemorial under the name of yoga. Yoga means the experimental union of the individual with the divine. It is based on persevering exercise; and the diet, posture, breathing, intellectual concentration, and moral discipline vary slightly in the different systems which teach it. The yogi, or disciple, who has by these means overcome the obscurations of his lower nature sufficiently, enters into the condition termed *samâdhi,* "and comes face to face with facts which no instinct or reason can ever know." He learns—

That the mind itself has a higher state of existence, beyond reason, a superconscious state, and that when the mind gets to that higher state, then this knowledge beyond reasoning comes. . . . All the different steps in yoga are intended to bring us scientifically to the superconscious state of Samâdhi. . . . Just as unconscious work is beneath consciousness, so there is another work which is above consciousness, and which, also, is not accompanied with the feeling of egoism. . . . There is no feeling of *I,* and yet the mind works, desireless, free from restlessness, objectless, bodiless. Then the Truth shines in its full effulgence, and we know ourselves—for Samâdhi lies potential in us all—for what

we truly are, free, immortal, omnipotent, loosed from the finite, and its contrasts of good and evil altogether, and identical with the Atman or Universal Soul.[5]

The Vedantists say that one may stumble into superconsciousness sporadically, without the previous discipline, but it is then impure. Their test of its purity, like our test of religion's value, is empirical: its fruits must be good for life. When a man comes out of Samâdhi, they assure us that he remains "enlightened, a sage, a prophet, a saint, his whole character changed, his life changed, illumined." . . .

In the Christian church there have always been mystics. Although many of them have been viewed with suspicion, some have gained favor in the eyes of the authorities. The experiences of these have been treated as precedents, and a codified system of mystical theology has been based upon them, in which everything legitimate finds its place.[6] The basis of the system is "orison" or meditation, the methodical elevation of the soul towards God. Through the practice of orison the higher levels of mystical experience may be attained. It is odd that Protestantism, especially evangelical Protestantism, should seemingly have abandoned everything methodical in this line. Apart from what prayer may lead to, Protestant mystical experience appears to have been almost exclusively sporadic. It has been left to our mind-curers to reintroduce methodical meditation into our religious life.

The first thing to be aimed at in orison is the mind's detachment from outer sensations, for these interfere with its concentration upon ideal things. Such manuals as Saint Ignatius's Spiritual Exercises recommend the disciple to expel sensation by a graduated series of efforts to imagine holy scenes. The acme of this kind of discipline would be a semi-hallucinatory mono-ideism—an imaginary figure of Christ, for example, coming fully to occupy the mind. Sensorial images of this sort, whether literal or symbolic, play an enormous part in mysticism. But in certain cases imagery may fall away entirely, and in the very highest raptures it tends to do so. The state of consciousness becomes then insusceptible of any verbal description. Mystical teachers are unanimous as to this. Saint John of the Cross, for instance, one of the best of them, thus describes the condition called the "union of love," which, he says, is reached by "dark contemplation." In this the Deity compenetrates the soul, but in such a hidden way that the soul—

finds no terms, no means, no comparison whereby to render the sublimity of the wisdom and the delicacy of the spiritual feeling with which she is filled. ... We receive this mystical knowledge of God clothed in none of the kinds of images, in none of the sensible representations, which our mind makes use of in other circumstances. Accordingly in this knowledge, since the senses and the imagination are not employed, we get neither form nor impression, nor can we give any account or furnish any likeness, although the mysterious and sweet-tasting wisdom comes home so clearly to the inmost parts of our soul. Fancy a man seeing a certain kind of thing for the first time in his life. He can understand it, use and enjoy it, but he cannot apply a name to it, nor communicate any idea of it, even though all the while it be a mere thing of sense. How much greater will be his powerlessness when it goes beyond the senses! This is the peculiarity of the divine language. The more infused, intimate, spiritual, and supersensible it is, the more does it exceed the senses, both inner and outer, and impose silence upon them. ... The soul then feels as if placed in a vast and profound solitude, to which no created thing has access, in an immense and boundless desert, desert the more delicious the more solitary it is. There, in this abyss of wisdom, the soul grows by what it drinks in from the wellsprings of the comprehension of love, ... and recognizes, however sublime and learned may be the terms we employ, how utterly vile, insignificant, and improper they are, when we seek to discourse of divine things by their means.[7]

I cannot pretend to detail to you the sundry stages of the Christian mystical life. Our time would not suffice, for one thing; and moreover, I confess that the subdivisions and names which we find in the Catholic books seem to me to represent nothing objectively distinct. So many men, so many minds: I imagine that these experiences can be as infinitely varied as are the idiosyncrasies of individuals. ...

To the medical mind these ecstasies signify nothing but suggested and imitated hypnoid states, on an intellectual basis of superstition, and a corporeal one of degeneration and hysteria. Undoubtedly these pathological conditions have existed in many and possibly in all the cases, but that fact tells us nothing about the value for knowledge of the consciousness which they in-

duce. To pass a spiritual judgment upon these states, we must not content ourselves with superficial medical talk, but inquire into their fruits for life.

Their fruits appear to have been various. Stupefaction, for one thing, seems not to have been altogether absent as a result. You may remember the helplessness in the kitchen and schoolroom of poor Margaret Mary Alacoque. Many other ecstatics would have perished but for the care taken of them by admiring followers. The "other-worldliness" encouraged by the mystical consciousness makes this over-abstraction from practical life peculiarly liable to befall mystics in whom the character is naturally passive and the intellect feeble; but in natively strong minds and characters we find quite opposite results. The great Spanish mystics, who carried the habit of ecstasy as far as it has often been carried, appear for the most part to have shown indomitable spirit and energy, and all the more so for the trances in which they indulged.

Saint Ignatius was a mystic, but his mysticism made him assuredly one of the most powerfully practical human engines that ever lived. Saint John of the Cross, writing of the intuitions and "touches" by which God reaches the substance of the soul, tells us that—

They enrich it marvelously. A single one of them may be sufficient to abolish at a stroke certain imperfections of which the soul during its whole life had vainly tried to rid itself, and to leave it adorned with virtues and loaded with supernatural gifts. A single one of these intoxicating consolations may reward it for all the labors undergone in its life—even were they numberless. Invested with an invincible courage, filled with an impassioned desire to suffer for its God, the soul then is seized with a strange torment—that of not being allowed to suffer enough.

Sant Teresa is as emphatic, and much more detailed. ...

Mystical conditions may, therefore, render the soul more energetic in the lines which their inspiration favors. But this could be reckoned an advantage only in case the inspiration were a true one. If the inspiration were erroneous, the energy would be all the more mistaken and misbegotten. So we stand once more before that problem of truth which confronted us at the end of the lectures on saintliness. You will remember that we turned to mysticism precisely to get some light on truth. Do mystical states establish the truth of those theological affections in which the saintly life has its root?

In spite of their repudiation of articulate self-description, mystical states in general assert a pretty distinct theoretic drift. It is possible to give the outcome of the majority of them in terms that point in definite philosophical directions. One of these directions is optimism, and the other is monism. We pass into mystical states from out of ordinary consciousness as from a less into a more, as from a smallness into a vastness, and at the same time as from an unrest to a rest. We feel them as reconciling, unifying states. They appeal to the yes-function more than to the no-function in us. In them the unlimited absorbs the limits and peacefully closes the account. Their very denial of every adjective you may propose as applicable to the ultimate truth—He, the Self, the Atman, is to be described by "No! no!" only, say the Upanishads—though it seems on the surface to be a no-function, is a denial made on behalf of a deeper yes. Whoso calls the Absolute anything in particular, or says that it is *this,* seems implicitly to shut it off from being *that*—it is as if he lessened it. So we deny the "this," negating the negation which it seems to us to imply, in the interests of the higher affirmative attitude by which we are possessed. . . .

In mystical literature such self-contradictory phrases as "dazzling obscurity," "whispering silence," "teeming desert," are continually met with. They prove that not conceptual speech, but music rather, is the element through which we are best spoken to by mystical truth. Many mystical scriptures are indeed little more than musical compositions.

He who would hear the voice of Nada, 'the Soundless Sound,' and comprehend it, he has to learn the nature of Dhâranâ. . . . When to himself his form appears unreal, as do on waking all the forms he sees in dreams; when he has ceased to hear the many, he may discern the ONE—the inner sound which kills the outer. . . . For then the soul will hear, and will remember. And then to the inner ear will speak THE VOICE OF THE SILENCE. . . . And now thy *Self* is lost in SELF, *thyself* unto THYSELF, merged in that SELF from which thou first didst radiate. . . . Behold! thou hast become the Light, thou has become the Sound, thou art thy

Master and thy God. Thou art THYSELF the object of thy search: the VOICE unbroken, that resounds throughout eternities, exempt from change, from sin exempt, the seven sounds in one, the VOICE OF THE SILENCE. *Om tat Sat.*

These words, if they do not awaken laughter as you receive them, probably stir chords within you which music and language touch in common. Music gives us ontological messages which non-musical criticism is unable to contradict, though it may laugh at our foolishness in minding them. There is a verge of the mind which these things haunt; and whispers therefrom mingle with the operations of our understanding, even as the waters of the infinite ocean send their waves to break among the pebbles that lie upon our shores. . . .

That doctrine, for example, that eternity is timeless, that our "immortality," if we live in the eternal, is not so much future as already now and here, which we find so often expressed to-day in certain philosophic circles, finds its support in a "hear, hear!" or an "amen," which floats up from that mysteriously deeper level. We recognize the passwords to the mystical region as we hear them, but we cannot use them ourselves; it alone has the keeping of "the password primeval."

I have now sketched with extreme brevity and insufficiency, but as fairly as I am able in the time allowed, the general traits of the mystic range of consciousness. *It is on the whole pantheistic and optimistic, or at least the opposite of pessimistic. It is anti-naturalistic, and harmonizes best with twice-bornness and so-called other-wordly states of mind.*

My next task is to inquire whether we can invoke it as authoritative. Does it furnish any *warrant for the truth* of the twice-bornness and supernaturality and pantheism which it favors? I must give my answer to this question as concisely as I can.

In brief my answer is this—and I will divide it into three parts:—

(1) Mystical states, when well developed, usually are, and have the right to be, absolutely authoritative over the individuals to whom they come.

(2) No authority emanates from them which should make it a duty for those who stand outside of them to accept their revelations uncritically.

(3) They break down the authority of the non-mystical or rationalistic consciousness, based upon the understanding and the senses alone. They show it to be only one kind of consciousness. They open out the possibility of other orders of truth, in which, so far as anything in us vitally responds to them, we may freely continue to have faith.

I will take up these points one by one.

1

As a matter of psychological fact, mystical states of a well-pronounced and emphatic sort are usually authoritative over those who have them. They have been "there," and know. It is vain for rationalism to grumble about this. If the mystical truth that comes to a man proves to be a force that he can live by, what mandate have we of the majority to order him to live in another way? We can throw him into a prison or a madhouse, but we cannot change his mind—we commonly attach it only the more stubbornly to its beliefs. It mocks our utmost efforts, as a matter of fact, and in point of logic it absolutely escapes our jurisdiction. Our own more "rational" beliefs are based on evidence exactly similar in nature to that which mystics quote for theirs. Our senses, namely, have assured us of certain states of fact; but mystical experiences are as direct perceptions of fact for those who have them as any sensations ever were for us. The records show that even though the five senses be in abeyance in them, they are absolutely sensational in their epistemological quality, if I may be pardoned the barbarous expression—that is, they are face to face presentations of what seems immediately to exist.

The mystic is, in short, *invulnerable,* and must be left whether we relish it or not, in undisturbed enjoyment of his creed. Faith, says Tolstoy, is that by which men live. And faith-state and mystic state are practically convertible terms.

2

But I now proceed to add that mystics have no right to claim that we ought to accept the deliverance of their peculiar experiences, if we are ourselves outsiders and feel no private call thereto. The utmost they can ever ask of us in this life is to admit that they establish a presumption. They form a consensus and have an unequivocal outcome; and it would be odd, mystics might say, if such a unanimous type of experience should prove to be altogether wrong. At bottom, however, this would only be an appeal to numbers like the appeal of rationalism the other way; and the appeal to numbers has no logical force. If we acknowledge it, it is for "suggestive," not for logical reasons: we follow the majority because to do so suits our life.

But even this presumption from the unanimity of mystics is far from being strong. In characterizing mystic states as pantheistic, optimistic, etc., I am afraid I over-simplified the truth. I did so for expository reasons, and to keep the closer to the classic mystical tradition. The classic religious mysticism, it now must be confessed, is only a "privileged case." It is an *extract,* kept true to type by the selection of the fittest specimens and their preservation in "schools." It is carved out from a much larger mass; and if we take the larger mass as seriously as religious mysticism has historically taken itself, we find that the supposed unanimity largely disappears. To begin with, even religious mysticism itself, the kind that accumulates traditions and makes schools, is much less unanimous than I have allowed. It has been both ascetic and antinomianly self-indulgent within the Christian church. It is dualistic in Sankhya, and monistic in Vedanta philosophy. I called it pantheistic; but the great Spanish mystics are anything but pantheists. They are with few exceptions non-metaphysical minds, for whom "the category of personality" is absolute. The "union" of man with God is for them much more like an occasional miracle than like an original identity. How different again, apart from the happiness common to all, is the mysticism of Walt Whitman, Edward Carpenter, Richard Jefferies, and other naturalistic pantheists, from the more distinctively Christian sort. The fact is that the mystical feeling of enlargement, union, and emancipation has no specific intellectual content whatever of its own. It is capable of forming matrimonial alliances with material furnished by the most diverse philosophies and theologies, provided only they can find a place in their framework for its peculiar emotional mood. We have no right, therefore, to invoke its prestige as distinctively in favor of any special belief, such as that in absolute idealism, or in the absolute monistic identity, or in the absolute goodness, of the world. It is only relatively in favor of all these things—it passes out of common human consciousness in the direction in which they lie.

So much for religious mysticism proper. But more remains to be told, for religious mysticism is only one half of mysticism. The other half has no accumulated traditions except those which the text-books on insanity supply. Open any one of these, and you will find abundant cases in which "mystical ideas" are cited as characteristic symptoms of enfeebled or deluded states of mind. In delusional insanity, paranoia, as they sometimes call it, we may have a *diabolical* mysticism, a sort of religious mysticism turned upside down. The same sense of ineffable importance in the smallest events, the same texts and words coming with new meanings, the same voices and visions and leadings and missions, the same controlling by extraneous powers; only this time the emotion is pessimistic: instead of consolations we have desolations; the meanings are dreadful; and the powers are enemies to life. It is evident that from the point of view of their psychological mechanism, the classic mysticism and these lower mysticisms spring from the same mental level, from that great subliminal or transmarginal region of which science is beginning to admit the existence, but of which so little is really known. That region contains every kind of matter: "seraph and snake" abide there side by side. To come from thence is no infallible credential. What comes must be sifted and tested, and run the gauntlet of confrontation with the total context of experience, just like what comes from the outer world of sense. Its value must be ascertained by empirical methods, so long as we are not mystics ourselves.

Once more, then, I repeat that non-mystics are under no obligation to acknowledge in mystical states a superior authority conferred on them by their intrinsic nature.

3

Yet, I repeat once more, the existence of mystical states absolutely overthrows the pretension of non-mystical states to be the sole and ultimate dictators of what we may believe. As a rule, mystical states merely add a supersensuous meaning to the ordinary outward data of consciousness. They are excitements like the emotions of love or ambition, gifts to our spirit by means of which facts already objectively before us fall into a new expressiveness and make a new connection with our active life. They do not contradict these facts as such, or deny anything that our senses have immediately seized. It is the rationalistic critic rather who plays the part of denier in the controversy, and his denials have no strength, for there never can be a state of facts to which new meaning may not truthfully be added, provided the mind ascend to a more enveloping point of view. It must always remain an open question whether mystical states may not possibly be such superior points of view, windows through which the mind looks out upon a more extensive and inclusive world. The difference of the views seen from the different mystical windows need not prevent us from entertaining this supposition. The wider world would in that case prove to have a mixed constitution like that of this world, that is all. It would have its celestial and its infernal regions, its tempting and its saving moments, its valid experiences and its counterfeit ones, just as our world has them; but it would be a wider world all the same. We should have to use its experiences by selecting and subordinating and substituting just as is our custom in this ordinary naturalistic world; we should be liable to error just as we are now; yet the counting in of that wider world of meanings, and the serious dealing with it, might, in spite of all the perplexity, be indispensable stages in our approach to the final fullness of the truth.

In this shape, I think, we have to leave the subject. Mystical states indeed wield no authority due simply to their being mystical states. But the higher ones among them point in directions to which the religious sentiments even of nonmystical men incline. They tell of the supremacy of the ideal, of vastness, of union, of safety, and of rest. They offer us *hypotheses*, hypotheses which we may voluntarily ignore, but which as thinkers we cannot possibly upset. The supernaturalism and optimism to which they would persuade us may, interpreted in one way or another, be after all the truest of insights into the meaning of this life.

NOTES

1. "The Two Voices."

2. What reader of Hegel can doubt that that sense of a perfected Being with all its otherness soaked up into itself, which dominates his whole philosophy, must have come from the prominence in his consciousness of mystical moods like this, in most persons kept subliminal? The notion is thor-

oughly characteristic of the mystical level, and the *Aufgabe* of making it articulate was surely set to Hegel's intellect by mystical feeling.

3.   *Cosmic Consciousness: a Study in the Evolution of the Human Mind* (Philadelphia, 1901), p. 2.

4.   *Loc. cit.,* pp. 7, 8. My quotation follows the privately printed pamphlet which preceded Dr. Bucke's larger work, and differs verbally a little from the text of the latter.

5.   My quotations are from Vivekananda, *Raja Yoga* (London, 1896).

6.   Görres's *Christliche Mystik* gives a full account of the facts. So does Ribet's *Mystique Divine,* 2 vols. (Paris, 1890). A still more methodical modern work is the *Mystica Theologia* of Vallgornera, 2 vols. (Turin, 1890).

7.   Saint John of the Cross: *The Dark Night of the Soul,* book ii. ch. xvii., in *Vie et oeuvres,* 3me éditon (Paris, 1893), iii. 428–432.

BERTRAND RUSSELL

Critique of Mysticism*

Ought we to admit that there is available, in support of religion, a source of knowledge which lies outside science and may properly be described as "revelation"? This is a difficult question to argue, because those who believe that truths have been revealed to them profess the same kind of certainty in regard to them that we have in regard to objects of sense. We believe the man who has seen things through the telescope that we have never seen; why, then, they ask, should we not believe them when they report things that are to them equally unquestionable?

It is, perhaps, useless to attempt an argument such as will appeal to the man who has himself enjoyed mystic illumination. But something can be said as to whether we others should accept this testimony. In the first place, it is not subject to the ordinary tests. When a man of science tells us the result of an experiment, he also tells us how the experiment was performed; others can repeat it, and if the result is not confirmed it is not accepted as true; but many men might put themselves into the situation in which the mystic's vision occurred without obtaining the same revelation. To this it may be answered that a man must use the

appropriate sense: a telescope is useless to a man who keeps his eyes shut. The argument as to the credibility of the mystic's testimony may be prolonged almost indefinitely. Science should be neutral, since the argument is a scientific one, to be conducted exactly as an argument would be conducted about an uncertain experiment. Science depends upon perception and inference; its credibility is due to the fact that the perceptions are such as any observer can test. The mystic himself may be certain that he *knows,* and has no need of scientific tests; but those who are asked to accept his testimony will subject it to the same kind of scientific tests as those applied to men who say they have been to the North Pole. Science, as such, should have no expectation, positive or negative, as to the result.

The chief argument in favour of the mystics is their agreement with each other. "I know nothing more remarkable," says Dean Inge, "than the unanimity of the mystics, ancient, mediaeval, and modern, Protestant, Catholic, and even Buddhist or Mohammedan, though the Christian mystics are the most trustworthy." I do not wish to underrate the force of this argument, which I acknowledged long ago in a book called *Mysticism and Logic.* The mystics vary greatly in their capacity of giving verbal expression to their experiences, but I think we may take it that those who

*From Bertrand Russell, *Religion and Science,* Home University Library 178 (New York: Oxford University Press, 1961), pp. 177–189. First published in 1935. Reprinted by permission of the publisher.

succeeded best all maintain: (1) that all division and separateness is unreal, and that the universe is a single indivisible unity; (2) that evil is illusory, and that the illusion arises through falsely regarding a part as self-subsistent; (3) that time is unreal, and that reality is eternal, not in the sense of being everlasting, but in the sense of being wholly outside time. I do not pretend that this is a complete account of the matters on which all mystics concur, but the three propositions that I have mentioned may serve as representatives of the whole. Let us now imagine ourselves a jury in a law-court, whose business it is to decide on the credibility of the witnesses who make these three somewhat surprising assertions.

We shall find, in the first place, that, while the witnesses agree up to a point, they disagree totally when that point is passed, although they are just as certain as when they agree. Catholics, but not Protestants, may have visions in which the Virgin appears; Christians and Mohammedans, but not Buddhists, may have great truths revealed to them by the Archangel Gabriel; the Chinese mystics of the Tao tell us, as a direct result of their central doctrine, that all government is bad, whereas most European and Mohammedan mystics, with equal confidence, urged submission to constituted authority. As regards the points where they differ, each group will argue that the other groups are untrustworthy; we might, therefore, if we were content with a mere forensic triumph, point out that most mystics think most other mystics mistaken on most points. They might, however, make this only half a triumph by agreeing on the greater importance of the matters about which they are at one, as compared with those as to which their opinions differ. We will, in any case, assume that they have composed their differences, and concentrated the defence at these three points—namely, the unity of the world, the illusory nature of evil, and the unreality of time. What test can we, as impartial outsiders, apply to their unanimous evidence?

As men of scientific temper, we shall naturally first ask whether there is any way by which we can ourselves obtain the same evidence at first hand. To this we shall receive various answers. We may be told that we are obviously not in a receptive frame of mind, and that we lack the requisite humility; or that fasting and religious meditation are necessary; or (if our witness is

Indian or Chinese) that the essential prerequisite is a course of breathing exercises. I think we shall find that the weight of experimental evidence is in favour of this last view, though fasting also has been frequently found effective. As a matter of fact, there is a definite physical discipline, called yoga, which is practised in order to produce the mystic's certainty, and which is recommended with much confidence by those who have tried it.[1] Breathing exercises are its most essential feature, and for our purposes we may ignore the rest.

In order to see how we could test the assertion that yoga gives insight, let us artificially simplify this assertion. Let us suppose that a number of people assure us that if, *for a certain time,* we breathe in a certain way, we shall become convinced that time is unreal. Let us go further, and suppose that, having tried their recipe, we have ourselves experienced a state of mind such as they describe. But now, having returned to our normal mode of respiration, we are not quite sure whether the vision was to be believed. How shall we investigate this question?

First of all, what can be meant by saying that time is unreal? If we really mean what we say, we must mean that such statements as "this is before that" are mere empty noise, like "twas brillig." If we suppose anything less than this—as, for example, that there is a relation between events which puts them in the same order as the relation of earlier and later, but that it is a different relation —we shall not have made any assertion that makes any real change in our outlook. It will be merely like supposing that the Iliad was not written by Homer, but by another man of the same name. We have to suppose that there are no "events" at all; there must be only the one vast whole of the universe, embracing whatever is real in the misleading appearance of a temporal procession. There must be nothing in reality corresponding to the apparent distinction between earlier and later events. To say that we are born, and then grow, and then die, must be just as false as to say that we die, then grow small, and finally are born. The truth of what seems an individual life is merely the illusory isolation of one element in the timeless and indivisible being of the universe. There is no distinction between improvement and deterioration, no difference between sorrows that end in happiness and happiness that ends in sorrow. If you find a corpse with a dagger in it, it makes no difference whether the man died of the wound or the dagger was plunged in after death. Such a view, if true, puts an end, not only to science, but to prudence, hope, and effort; it is incompatible with worldly wisdom, and—what is more important to religion—with morality.

Most mystics, of course, do not accept these conclusions in their entirety, but they urge doctrines from which these conclusions inevitably follow. Thus Dean Inge rejects the kind of religion that appeals to evolution, because it lays too much stress upon a temporal process. "There is no law of progress, and there is no universal progress," he says. And again: "The doctrine of automatic and universal progress, the lay religion of many Victorians, labours under the disadvantage of being almost the only philosophical theory which can be definitely disproved." On this matter, which I shall discuss at a later stage, I find myself in agreement with the Dean, for whom, on many grounds, I have a very high respect. But he naturally does not draw from his premises all the inferences which seem to me to be warranted.

It is important not to caricature the doctrine of mysticism, in which there is, I think, a core of wisdom. Let us see how it seeks to avoid the extreme consequences which seem to follow from the denial of time.

The philosophy based upon mysticism has a great tradition, from Parmenides to Hegel. Parmenides says: "What is, is uncreated and indestructible; for it is complete, immovable, and without end. Nor was it ever, nor will it be; for now *it is,* all at once, a continuous one."[2] He introduced into metaphysics the distinction between reality and appearance, or the way of truth and the way of opinion, as he calls them. It is clear that whoever denies the reality of time must introduce some such distinction, since obviously the world *appears* to be in time. It is also clear that, if everyday experience is not to be *wholly* illusory, there must be some relation between appearance and the reality behind it. It is at this point, however, that the greatest difficulties arise: if the relation between appearance and reality is made too intimate, all the unpleasant features of appearance will have their unpleasant counterparts in reality, while if the relation is made too remote, we shall be unable to make inferences from the character of appearance to that of reality, and reality will be left a vague Unknowable, as with Herbert Spencer. For Christians, there is the related difficulty of avoiding pantheism: if the world is *only* apparent, God created nothing, and the reality corresponding to the world is a part of God; but if the world is in any degree real and distinct from God, we abandon the wholeness of everything, which is an essential doctrine of mysticism, and we are compelled to suppose that, in so far as the world is real, the evil which it contains is also real. Such difficulties make thoroughgoing mysticism very difficult for an orthodox Christian. As the Bishop of Birmingham says: "All forms of pantheism ... as it seems to me, must be rejected because, if man is actually a part of God, the evil in man is also in God."

All this time I have been supposing that we are a jury, listening to the testimony of the mystics, and trying to decide whether to accept or reject it. If, when they deny the reality of the world of sense, we took them to mean "reality" in the ordinary sense of the law-courts, we should have no hesitation in rejecting what they say, since we should find that it runs counter to all other testimony, and even to their own in their mundane moments. We must therefore look for some other sense. I believe that, when the mystics contrast "reality" with "appearance," the word "reality" has not a logical, but an emotional, significance: it means what is, in some sense, important. When it is said that time is "unreal," what should be said is that, in some sense and on some occasions, it is important to conceive the universe as a whole, as the Creator, if He existed, must have conceived it in deciding to create it. When so conceived, all process is within one completed whole; past, present, and future, all exist, in some sense, together, and the present does not have that pre-eminent reality which it has to our usual ways of apprehending the world. If this interpretation is accepted, mysticism expresses an emotion, not a fact; it does not assert anything, and therefore can be neither confirmed nor contradicted by science. The fact that mystics do make assertions is owning to their inability to separate emotional importance from scientific validity. It is, of course, not to be expected that they will accept this view, but it is the only one, so far as I can see, which, while admitting something of their claim, is not repugnant to the scientific intelligence.

The certainty and partial unanimity of mystics is no conclusive reason for accepting their testimony on a matter of fact. The man of science, when he wishes others to see what he has seen, arranges his microscope or telescope; that is to say, he makes changes in the external world, but demands of the observer only normal eyesight. The mystic, on the other hand, demands changes in the observer, by fasting, by breathing exercises, and by a careful abstention from external observation. (Some object to such discipline, and think that the mystic illumination cannot be artificially achieved; from a scientific point of view, this makes their case more difficult to test than that of those who rely on yoga. But nearly all agree that fasting and an ascetic life are helpful.) We all know that opium, hashish, and alcohol produce certain effects on the observer, but as we do not think these effects admirable we take no account of them in our theory of the universe. They may even, sometimes, reveal fragments of truth; but we do not regard them as sources of general wisdom. The drunkard who sees snakes does not imagine, afterwards, that he has had a revelation of a reality hidden from others, though some not wholly dissimilar belief must have given rise to the worship of Bacchus. In our own day, as William James related,[3] there have been people who considered that the intoxication produced by laughing-gas revealed truths which are hidden at normal times. From a scientific point of view, we can make no distinction between the man who eats little and sees heaven and the man who drinks much and sees snakes. Each is in an abnormal physical condition, and therefore has abnormal perceptions. Normal perceptions, since they have to be useful in the struggle for life, must have some correspondence with fact; but in abnormal perceptions there is no reason to expect such correspondence, and their testimony, therefore, cannot outweigh that of normal perception.

The mystic emotion, if it is freed from unwarranted beliefs, and not so overwhelming as to remove a man wholly from the ordinary business of life, may give something of every great value —the same kind of thing, though in a heightened form, that is given by contemplation. Breadth and calm and profundity may all have their source in this emotion, in which, for the moment, all self-centred desire is dead, and the mind becomes a mirror for the vastness of the universe. Those who have had this experience, and believe it to be bound up unavoidably with assertions about the nature of the universe, naturally cling to these assertions. I believe myself that the assertions are inessential, and that there is no reason to believe them true. I cannot admit any method of arriving at truth except that of science, but in the realm of the emotions I do not deny the value of the experiences which have given rise to religion. Through association with false beliefs, they have led to much evil as well as good; freed from this association, it may be hoped that the good alone will remain.

NOTES

1. As regards yoga in China, see Waley, *The Way and Its Power*, pp. 117–18.

2. Quoted from Burnet's *Early Greek Philosophy*, p. 199.

3. See his *Varieties of Religious Experience*.

SIGMUND FREUD

Analysis of "the Oceanic Feeling"*

It is impossible to escape the impression that people commonly use false standards of measurement—that they seek power, success and wealth for themselves and admire them in others, and that they underestimate what is of true value in life. And yet, in making any general judgment of this sort, we are in danger of forgetting how variegated the human world and its mental life are. There are a few men from whom their contemporaries do not withhold admiration, although their greatness rests on attributes and achievements which are completely foreign to the aims and ideals of the multitude. One might easily be inclined to suppose that it is after all only a minority which appreciates these great men, while the large majority cares nothing for them. But things are probably not as simple as that, thanks to the discrepancies between people's thoughts and their actions, and to the diversity of their wishful impulses.

One of these exceptional few calls himself my friend in his letters to me. I had sent him my small book that treats religion as an illus.on,[1] and he answered that he entirely agreed with my judgement upon religion, but that he was sorry I had not properly appreciated the true source of religious sentiments. This, he says, consists in a peculiar feeling, which he himself is never without, which he finds confirmed by many others, and which he may suppose is present in millions of people. It is a feeling which he would like to call a sensation of "eternity," a feeling as of something limitless, unbounded—as it were, "oceanic." This feeling, he adds, is a purely subjective fact, not an article of faith; it brings with it no assurance of personal immortality, but it is the source of the religious energy which is seized upon by the various Churches and religious systems, directed by them into particuliar channels, and doubtless also exhausted by them. One may, he thinks, rightly call oneself religious on the ground of this oceanic feeling alone, even if one rejects every belief and every illusion.

The views expressed by the friend whom I so much honour, and who himself once praised the magic of illusion in a poem,[2] caused me no small difficulty. I cannot discover this "oceanic" feeling in myself. It is not easy to deal scientifically with feelings. One can attempt to describe their physiological signs. Where this is not possible—and I am afraid that the oceanic feeling too will defy this kind of characterization—nothing remains but to fall back on the ideational content which is most readily associated with the feeling. If I have understood my friend rightly, he means the same thing by it as the consolation offered by an original and somewhat eccentric dramatist to his hero who is facing a self-inflicted death. "We cannot fall out of this world."[3] That is to say, it is a feeling of an indissoluble bond, of being one with the external world as a whole. I may remark that to me this seems something rather in the nature of an intellectual perception, which is not, it is true, without an accompanying feeling-tone, but only such as would be present with any other act of thought of equal range. From my own experience I could not convince myself of the primary nature of such a feeling. But this gives me no right to deny that it does in fact occur in other people.

*Reprinted from *Civilization and Its Discontents* (pp. 11–16) by Sigmund Freud. Translated from the German and edited by James Strachey. First American edition 1962. By permission of W. W. Norton & Company, Inc., and The Hogarth Press Ltd. Copyright © 1961 by James Strachey. *Civilization and Its Discontents* is also to be found in Volume 21 of the *Complete Psychological Works of Sigmund Freud*, revised and edited by James Strachey.

The only question is whether it is being correctly interpreted and whether it ought to be regarded as the *fons et origo* of the whole need for religion.

I have nothing to suggest which could have a decisive influence on the solution of this problem. The idea of men's receiving an intimation of their connection with the world around them through an immediate feeling which is from the outset directed to that purpose sounds so strange and fits in so badly with the fabric of our psychology that one is justified in attempting to discover a psycho-analytic—that is, a genetic—explanation of such a feeling. The following line of thought suggests itself. Normally, there is nothing of which we are more certain than the feeling of our self, of our own ego.[4] This ego appears to us as something autonomous and unitary, marked off distinctly from everything else. That such an appearance is deceptive, and that on the contrary the ego is continued inwards, without any sharp delimitation, into an unconscious mental entity which we designate as the id and for which it serves as a kind of facade—this was a discovery first made by psycho-analytic research, which should still have much more to tell us about the relation of the ego to the id. But towards the outside, at any rate, the ego seems to maintain clear and sharp lines of demarcation. There is only one state—admittedly an unusual state, but not one that can be stigmatized as pathological—in which it does not do this. At the height of being in love the boundary between ego and object threatens to melt away. Against all the evidence of his senses, a man who is in love declares that "I" and "you" are one, and is prepared to behave as if it were a fact.[5] What can be temporarily done away with by a physiological [i.e. normal] function must also, of course, be liable to be disturbed by pathological processes. Pathology has made us acquainted with a great number of states in which the boundary lines between the ego and the external world become uncertain or in which they are actually drawn incorrectly. There are cases in which parts of a person's own body, even portions of his own mental life—his perceptions, thoughts and feelings—appear alien to him and as not belonging to his ego; there are other cases in which he ascribes to the external world things that clearly originate in his own ego and that ought to be acknowledged by it. Thus even the feeling of our own ego is subject to disturbances and the boundaries of the ego are not constant.

Further reflection tells us that the adult's ego-feeling cannot have been the same from the beginning. It must have gone through a process of development, which cannot, of course, be demonstrated but which admits of being constructed with a fair degree of probability.[6] An infant at the breast does not as yet distinguish his ego from the external world as the source of the sensations flowing in upon him. He gradually learns to do so, in response to various promptings.[7] He must be very strongly impressed by the fact that some sources of excitation, which he will later recognize as his own bodily organs, can provide him with sensations at any moment, whereas other sources evade him from time to time—among them what he desires most of all, his mother's breast—and only reappear as a result of his screaming for help. In this way there is for the first time set over against the ego an 'object,' in the form of something which exists "outside" and which is only forced to appear by a special action.[8] A further incentive to a disengagement of the ego from the general mass of sensations—that is, to the recognition of an "outside," an external world—is provided by the frequent, manifold and unavoidable sensations of pain and unpleasure, the removal and avoidance of which is enjoined by the pleasure principle, in the exercise of its unrestricted domination. A tendency arises to separate from the ego everything that can become a source of such unpleasure, to throw it outside and to create a pure pleasure-ego which is confronted by a strange and threatening "outside." The boundaries of this primitive pleasure-ego cannot escape rectification through experience. Some of the things that one is unwilling to give up, because they give pleasure, are nevertheless not ego but object; and some sufferings that one seeks to expel turn out to be inseparable from the ego in virtue of their internal origin. One comes to learn a procedure by which, through a deliberate direction of one's sensory activities and through suitable muscular action, one can differentiate between what is internal—what belongs to the ego—and what is external—what emanates from the outer world. In this way one makes the first step towards the introduction of the reality principle which is to dominate future development.[9] This differentiation, of course, serves the practical purpose of enabling one to defend oneself against sensations of unpleasure which one actually feels or with which one is threatened. In order to fend off certain unpleasurable excitations arising from within, the ego can use no other methods than those which it uses against unpleasure coming from without, and this is the starting-point of important pathological disturbances.

In this way, then, the ego detaches itself from the external world. Or, to put it more correctly, originally the ego includes everything, later it separates off an external world from itself. Our present ego-feeling is, therefore, only a shrunken residue of a much more inclusive—indeed, an all-embracing—feeling which corresponded to a more intimate bond between the ego and the world about it. If we may assume that there are many people in whose mental life this primary ego-feeling has persisted to a greater or less degree, it would exist in them side by side with the narrower and more sharply demarcated ego-feeling of maturity, like a kind of counterpart to it. In that case, the ideational contents appropriate to it would be precisely those of limitlessness and of a bond with the universe—the same ideas with which my friend elucidated the "oceanic" feeling.

But have we a right to assume the survival of something that was originally there, alongside of what was later derived from it? Undoubtedly. There is nothing strange in such a phenomenon, whether in the mental field or elsewhere. In the animal kingdom we hold to the view that the most highly developed species have proceeded from the lowest; and yet we find all the simple forms still in existence to-day. The race of the great saurians is extinct and has made way for the mammals; but a true representative of it, the crocodile, still lives among us. This analogy may be too remote, and it is also weakened by the circumstance that the lower species which survive are for the most part not the true ancestors of the present-day more highly developed species. As a rule the intermediate links have died out and are known to us only through reconstruction. In the realm of the mind, on the other hand, what is primitive is so commonly preserved alongside of the transformed version which has arisen from it that it is unnecessary to give instances as evidence. When this happens it is usually in consequence of a divergence in development: one portion (in the quantitative sense) of an attitude or instinctual impulse has remained unaltered, while another portion has undergone further development.

NOTES

1. *The Future of an Illusion* (1927).

2. [Footnote added 1931] *Liluli* [1919].—Since the publication of his two books *La vie de Ramakrishna* [1929] and *La vie de Vivekananda* [1930], I need no longer hide the fact that the friend spoken of in the text is Romain Rolland. [Romain Rolland had written to Freud about the "oceanic feeling" in a letter of December 5, 1927, very soon after the publication of *The Future of an Illusion*.]

3. Christian Dietrich Grabbe [1801–36], *Hannibal*: "Ja, aus der Welt werden wir nicht fallen. Wir sind einmal darin." ["Indeed, we shall not fall out of this world. We are in it once and for all."]

4. [Some remarks on Freud's use of the terms "ego" and "self" will be found in the Editor's Introduction to *The Ego and the Id* (1923), *Standard Ed., 19, 7.*]

5. [CF. a footnote to Section III of the Schreber case history (1911), *Standard Ed., 12, 69.*]

6. CF. the many writings on the topic of ego-development and ego-feeling, dating from Ferenczi's paper on "Stages in the Development of the Sense of Reality" (1913) to Federn's contributions of 1926, 1927 and later.

7. [In this paragraph Freud was going over familiar ground. He had discussed the matter not long before, in his paper on "Negation" (1925h), *Standard Ed.* 19, 236–8. But he had dealt with it on several earlier occasions. See, for instance, "Instincts and their Vicissitudes" (1915), ibid., 14, 119 and 134–6, and *The Interpretation of Dreams (1900), ibid.,* 5,565–6. Its essence, indeed, is already to be found in the "Project" of 1895, Sections 1, 2, 11 and 16 of Part I (Freud, 1950).]

8. [The "specific action" of the "Project."]

9. [CF. "Formulations on the Two Principles of Mental Functioning" (1911), *Standard Ed., 12, 222–3.*]

HUSTON SMITH

Do Drugs Have Religious Import?*

Until six months ago, if I picked up my phone in the Cambridge area and dialed KISS-BIG, a voice would answer, "If-if." These were coincidences: KISS-BIG happened to be the letter equivalents of an arbitrarily assigned telephone number, and I.F.I.F. represented the initials of an organization with the improbable name of the International Federation for Internal Freedom. But the coincidences were apposite to the point of being poetic. "Kiss big" caught the euphoric, manic, life-embracing attitude that characterized this most publicized of the organizations formed to explore the newly synthesized consciousness-changing substances; the organization itself was surely one of the "iffyest" phenomena to appear on our social and intellectual scene in some time. It produced the first firings in Harvard's history, an ultimatum to get out of Mexico in five days, and "the miracle of Marsh Chapel," in which, during a two-and-one-half-hour Good Friday service, ten theological students and professors ingested psilocybin and were visited by what they generally reported to be the deepest religious experiences of their lives.

Despite the last of these phenomena and its numerous if less dramatic parallels, students of religion appear by and large to be dismissing the psychedelic drugs that have sprung to our attention in the '60s as having little religious relevance. The position taken in one of the most forward-looking volumes of theological essays to have appeared in recent years—*Soundings,* edited by A. R. Vidler[1]—accepts R. C. Zaehner's *Mysticism*

Sacred and Profane as having "fully examined and refuted" the religious claims for mescalin which Aldous Huxley sketched in *The Doors of Perception.* This closing of the case strikes me as premature, for it looks as if the drugs have light to throw on the history of religion, the phenomenology of religion, the philosophy of religion, and the practice of the religious life itself.

1. DRUGS AND RELIGION VIEWED HISTORICALLY

In his trial-and-error life explorations man almost everywhere has stumbled upon connections between vegetables (eaten or brewed) and actions (yogi breathing exercises, whirling-dervish dances, flagellations) that alter states of consciousness. From the psychopharmacological standpoint we now understand these states to be the products of changes in brain chemistry. From the sociological perspective we see that they tend to be connected in some way with religion. If we discount the wine used in Christian communion services, the instances closest to us in time and space are the peyote of The Native American [Indian] Church and Mexico's 2000-year-old "sacred mushrooms," the latter rendered in Aztec as "God's Flesh"—striking parallel to "the body of our Lord" in the Christian eucharist. Beyond these neighboring instances lie the *soma* of the Hindus, the *haoma* and hemp of the Zoroastrians, the Dionysus of the Greeks who "everywhere . . . taught men the culture of the vine and the mysteries of his worship and everywhere [was] accepted as a god,"[2] the *benzoin* of Southeast Asia, Zen's tea whose fifth cup purifies and whose sixth "calls to the realm of the immortals,"[3] the *pituri* of the Australian aborigines, and probably the mystic *kykeon* that was eaten and

*Huston Smith, "Do Drugs Have Religious Import?" *Journal of Philosophy* LXI (1964), 517–530, reprinted by permission of the author and the editor of the *Journal of Philosophy.* This is the emended version of a paper presented to The Woodrow Wilson Society, Princeton University, on May 16, 1964.

drunk at the climactic close of the sixth day of the Eleusinian mysteries.[4] There is no need to extend the list, as a reasonably complete account is available in Philippe de Félice's comprehensive study of the subject, *Poisons sacrés, ivresses divines.*

More interesting than the fact that consciousness-changing devices have been linked with religion is the possibility that they actually initiated many of the religious perspectives which, taking root in history, continued after their psychedelic origins were forgotten. Bergson saw the first movement of Hindus and Greeks toward "dynamic religion" as associated with the "divine rapture" found in intoxicating beverages;[5] more recently Robert Graves, Gordon Wasson, and Alan Watts have suggested that most religions arose from such chemically induced theopanies. Mary Barnard is the most explicit proponent of this thesis. "Which . . . was more likely to happen first," she asks,[6] "the spontaneously generated idea of an afterlife in which the disembodied soul, liberated from the restrictions of time and space, experiences eternal bliss, or the accidental discovery of hallucinogenic plants that give a sense of euphoria, dislocate the center of consciousness, and distort time and space, making them balloon outward in greatly expanded vistas?" Her own answer is that "the [latter] experience might have had . . . an almost explosive effect on the largely dormant minds of men, causing them to think of things they had never thought of before. This, if you like, is direct revelation." Her use of the subjunctive "might" renders this formulation of her answer equivocal, but she concludes her essay on a note that is completely unequivocal: "Looking at the matter coldly, unintoxicated and unentranced, I am willing to prophesy that fifty theobotanists working for fifty years would make the current theories concerning the origins of much mythology and theology as out-of-date as pre-Copernican astronomy."

This is an important hypothesis—one which must surely engage the attention of historians of religion for some time to come. But as I am concerned here only to spot the points at which the drugs erupt onto the field of serious religious study, not to ride the geysers to whatever heights, I shall not pursue Miss Barnard's thesis. Having located what appears to be the crux of the historical question, namely the extent to which drugs not merely duplicate or simulate theologically

sponsored experiences but generate or shape theologies themselves, I turn to phenomenology.

2. DRUGS AND RELIGION VIEWED PHENOMENOLOGICALLY

Phenomenology attempts a careful description of human experience. The question the drugs pose for the phenomenology of religion, therefore, is whether the experiences they induce differ from religious experiences reached naturally, and if so how.

Even the Bible notes that chemically induced psychic states bear *some* resemblance to religious ones. Peter had to appeal to a circumstantial criterion—the early hour of the day—to defend those who were caught up in the Pentecostal experience against the charge that they were merely drunk: "These men are not drunk, as you suppose, since it is only the third hour of the day" (Acts 2:15); and Paul initiates the comparison when he admonishes the Ephesians not to "get drunk with wine . . . but [to] be filled with the spirit" (Ephesians 5:18). Are such comparisons, paralleled in the accounts of virtually every religion, superficial? How far can they be pushed?

Not all the way, students of religion have thus far insisted. With respect to the new drugs, Prof. R. C. Zaehner has drawn the line emphatically. "The importance of Huxley's *Doors of Perception,*" he writes, "is that in it the author clearly makes the claim that what he experienced under the influence of mescalin is closely comparable to a genuine mystical experience. If he is right, . . . the conclusions . . . are alarming."[7] Zaehner thinks that Huxley is not right, but I fear that it is Zaehner who is mistaken.

There are, of course, innumerable drug experiences that have no religious feature; they can be sensual as readily as spiritual, trivial as readily as transforming, capricious as readily as sacramental. If there is one point about which every student of the drugs agrees, it is that there is no such thing as the drug experience *per se*—no experience that the drugs, as it were, merely secrete. Every experience is a mix of three ingredients: drug, set (the psychological make-up of the individual), and setting (the social and physical environment in which it is taken.). But given the right set and setting, the drugs can induce religious experiences indistinguishable from experiences that occur spontaneously. Nor need set and setting be exceptional. The way the statistics are currently running, it looks as if from one-fourth to one-third of the general population will have religious experiences if they take the drugs under naturalistic conditions, meaning by this conditions in which the researcher supports the subject but does not try to influence the direction his experience will take. Among subjects who have strong religious inclinations to begin with, the proportion of those having religious experiences jumps to three-fourths. If they take the drugs in settings that are religious too, the ratio soars to nine in ten.

How do we know that the experiences these people have really are religious? We can begin with the fact that they say they are. The "one-fourth to one-third of the general population" figure is drawn from two sources. Ten months after they had had their experiences, 24 per cent of the 194 subjects in a study by the Californian psychiatrist Oscar Janiger characterized their experiences as having been religious.[8] Thirty-two per cent of the 74 subjects in Ditman and Hayman's study reported, looking back on their LSD experience, that it looked as if it had been "very much" or "quite a bit" a religious experience; 42 per cent checked as true the statement that they "were left with a greater awareness of God, or a higher power, or ultimate reality."[9] The statement that three-fourths of subjects having religious "sets" will have religious experiences comes from the reports of sixty-nine religious professionals who took the drugs while the Harvard project was in progress.[10]

In the absence of (a) a single definition of religious experience acceptable to psychologists of religion generally and (b) foolproof ways of ascertaining whether actual experiences exemplify any definition, I am not sure there is any better way of telling whether the experiences of the 333 men and women involved in the above studies were religious than by noting whether they seemed so to them. But if more rigorous methods are preferred, they exist; they have been utilized, and they confirm the conviction of the man in the street that drug experiences can indeed be religious. In his doctoral study at Harvard University, Walter Pahnke worked out a typology of religious experience (in this instance of the mystical variety) based on the classic cases of mystical experiences as summarized in Walter Stace's *Mysticism and Philosophy.* He then administered psilocybin to ten theology students and professors in the setting of a Good Friday service. The drug was given "double-blind," meaning that neither Dr. Pahnke nor his subjects knew which ten were getting psilocybin and which ten placebos to constitute a control group. Subsequently the reports the subjects wrote of their experiences were laid successively before three college-graduate housewives who, without being informed about the nature of the study, were asked to rate each statement as to the degree (strong, moderate, slight, or none) to which it exemplified each of the nine traits of mystical experience enumerated in the typology of mysticism worked out in advance. When the test of significance was applied to their statistics, it showed that "those subjects who received psilocybin experienced phenomena which were indistinguishable from, if not identical with . . . the categories defined by our typology of mysticism."[11]

With the thought that the reader might like to test his own powers of discernment on the question being considered, I insert here a simple test I gave to a group of Princeton students following a recent discussion sponsored by the Woodrow Wilson Society:

Below are accounts of two religious experiences. One occurred under the influence of drugs, one without their influence. Check the one you think *was* drug-induced.

I

Suddenly I burst into a vast, new, indescribably wonderful universe. Although I am writing this over a year later, the thrill of the surprise and amazement, the awesomeness of the revelation, the engulfment in an overwhelming feeling-wave of gratitude and blessed wonderment, are as fresh, and the memory of the experience is as vivid, as if it had happened five minutes ago. And yet to concoct anything by way of description that would even hint at the magnitude, the sense of ultimate reality . . . this seems such an impossible task. The knowledge which has infused and affected every aspect of my life came instantaneously and with such complete force of certainty that it was impossible, then or since, to doubt its validity.

II

All at once, without warning of any kind, I found myself wrapped in a flame-colored cloud. For an instant I thought of fire . . . the next, I knew that the fire was within myself. Directly afterward there came upon me a sense of exultation, of immense joyousness accompanied or immediately followed by an intellectual illumination impossible to describe. Among other things, I did not merely come to believe, but I saw that the universe is not composed of dead matter, but is, on the contrary, a living Presence; I became conscious in myself of eternal life. . . . I saw that all men are immortal: that the cosmic order is such that without any preadventure all things work together for the good of each and all; that the foundation principle of the world . . . is what we call love, and that the happiness of each and all is in the long run absolutely certain.

On the occasion referred to, twice as many students (46) answered incorrectly as answered correctly (23). I bury the correct answer in a footnote to preserve the reader's opportunity to test himself.[12]

Why, in the face of this considerable evidence, does Zaehner hold that drug experiences cannot be authentically religious? There appear to be three reasons:

1. His own experience was "utterly trivial." This of course proves that not all drug experiences are religious; it does not prove that no drug experiences are religious.

2. He thinks the experiences of others that appear religious to them are not truly so. Zaehner distinguishes three kinds of mysticism: nature mysticism, in which the soul is united with the natural world; monistic mysticism, in which the soul merges with an impersonal absolute; and theism, in which the soul confronts the living, personal God. He concedes that drugs can induce the first two species of mysticism, but not its supreme instance, the theistic. As proof, he analyzes Huxley's experience as recounted in *The Doors of Perception* to show that it produced at best a blend of nature and monistic mysticism. Even if we were to accept Zaehner's evaluation of the three forms of mysticism, Huxley's case, and indeed Zaehner's entire book, would prove only that not every mystical experience induced by the drugs is theistic. Insofar as Zaehner goes beyond this to imply that drugs do not and cannot induce theistic mysticism, he not only goes beyond the evidence but proceeds in the face of it. James Slotkin reports that the peyote Indians "see visions, which may be of Christ Himself. Sometimes they hear the voice of the Great Spirit. Sometimes they become aware of the presence of God and of those personal shortcomings which

must be corrected if they are to do His will.[13] And G. M. Carstairs, reporting on the use of psychedelic *bhang* in India, quotes a Brahmin as saying, "It gives good bhakti. . . . You get a very good bhakti with bhang," *bhakti* being precisely Hinduism's theistic variant.[14]

3. There is a third reason why Zaehner might doubt that drugs can induce geneuinely mystical experiences. Zaehner is a Roman Catholic, and Roman Catholic doctrine teaches that mystical rapture is a gift of grace and as such can never be reduced to man's control. This may be true; certainly the empirical evidence cited does not preclude the possibility of a genuine ontological or theological difference between natural and drug-induced religious experiences. At this point, however, we are considering phenomenology rather than ontology, description rather than interpretation, and on this level there is no difference. Descriptively, drug experiences cannot be distinguished from their natural religious counterpart. When the current philosophical authority on mysticism, W. T. Stace, was asked whether the drug experience is similar to the mystical experience, he answered, "It's not a matter of its being *similar* to mystical experience; it *is* mystical experience."

What we seem to be witnessing in Zaehner's *Mysticism Sacred and Profane* is a reenactment of the age-old pattern in the conflict between science and religion. Whenever a new controversy arises, religion's first impulse is to deny the disturbing evidence science has produced. Seen in perspective, Zaehner's refusal to admit that drugs can induce experiences descriptively indistinguishable from those which are spontaneously religious is the current counterpart of the seventeenth-century theologians' refusal to look through Galileo's telescope or, when they did, their persistence on dismissing what they saw as machinations of the devil. When the fact that drugs can trigger religious experiences becomes incontrovertible, discussion will move to more difficult question of how this new fact is to be interpreted. The latter question leads beyond phenomenology into philosophy.

3. DRUGS AND RELIGION VIEWED PHILOSOPHICALLY

Why do people reject evidence? Because they find it threatening, we may suppose. Theologians are not the only professionals to utilize this mode of defense. In his *Personal Knowledge,*[15] Michael Polanyi recounts the way the medical profession ignored such palpable facts as the painless amputation of human limbs, performed before their own eyes in hundreds of successive cases, concluding that the subjects were impostors who were either deluding their physicians or colluding with them. One physician, Esdaile, carried out about 300 major operations painlessly under mesmeric trance in India, but neither in India nor in Great Britain could he get medical journals to print accounts of his work. Polanyi attributes this closed-mindedness to "lack of a conceptual framework in which their discoveries could be separated from specious and untenable admixtures."

The "untenable admixture" in the fact that psychotomimetic drugs can induce religious experience is its apparent implicate: that religious disclosures are no more veridical than psychotic ones. For religious skeptics, this conclusion is obviously not untenable at all; it fits in beautifully with their thesis that *all* religion is at heart an escape from reality. Psychotics avoid reality by retiring into dream worlds of make-believe; what better evidence that religious visionaries do the same than the fact that identical changes in brain chemistry produce both states of mind? Had not Marx already warned us that religion is the "opiate" of the people?—apparently he was more literally accurate than he supposed. Freud was likewise too mild. He "never doubted that religious phenomena are to be understood only on the model of the neurotic symptoms of the individual."[16] He should have said "psychotic symptoms."

So the religious skeptic is likely to reason. What about the religious believer? Convinced that religious experiences are not fundamentally delusory, can he admit that psychotomimetic drugs can occasion them? To do so he needs (to return to Polanyi's words) "a conceptual framework in which [the discoveries can] be separated from specious and untenable admixtures," the "untenable admixture" being in this case the conclusion that religious experiences are in general delusory.

One way to effect the separation would be to argue that, despite phenomenological similarities between natural and drug-induced religious experiences, they are separated by a crucial *ontological* difference. Such an argument would follow the pattern of theologians who argue for the "real presence" of Christ's body and blood in the bread and wine of the Eucharist despite their admission that chemical analysis, confined as it is to the level of "accidents" rather than "essences," would not disclose this presence. But this distinction will not appeal to many today, for it turns on an essence-accident metaphysics which is not widely accepted. Instead of fighting a rear-guard action by insisting that if drug and non-drug religious experiences cannot be distinguished empirically there must be some transempirical factor that distinguishes them and renders the drug experience profane, I wish to explore the possibility of accepting drug-induced experiences as religious without relinquishing confidence in the truth-claims of religious experience generally.

To begin with the weakest of all arguments, the argument from authority: William James did not discount *his* insights that occurred while his brain chemistry was altered. The paragraph in which he retrospectively evaluates his nitrous oxide experiences has become classic, but it is so pertinent to the present discussion that it merits quoting once again.

One conclusion was forced upon my mind at that time, and my impression of its truth has ever since remained unshaken. It is that our normal waking consciousness, rational consciousness as we call it, is but one special type of consciousness, whilst all about it, parted from it by the filmiest of screens, there lie potential forms of consciousness entirely different. We may go through life without suspecting their existence; but apply the requisite stimulus, and at a touch they are there in all their completeness, definite types of mentality which probably somewhere have their field of application and adaptation. No account of the universe in its totality can be final which leaves these other forms of consciousness quite disregarded. How to regard them is the question—for they are so discontinuous with ordinary consciousness. Yet they may determine attitudes though they cannot furnish formulas, and open a region though they fail to give a map. At any rate, they forbid a premature closing of our accounts with reality. Looking back on my own experiences, they all converge toward a kind of insight to which I cannot help ascribing some metaphysical significance (*op. cit.,* 378–379).

To this argument from authority, I add two arguments that try to provide something by way of reasons. Drug experiences that assume a religious cast tend to have fearful and/or beatific features, and each of my hypotheses relates to one of these aspects of the experience.

Beginning with the ominous, "fear of the Lord," awe-ful features, Gordon Wasson, the New York banker-turned-mycologist, describes these as he encountered them in his psilocybin experience as follows: "Ecstasy! In common parlance ... ecstasy is fun. . . . But ecstasy is not fun. Your very soul is seized and shaken until it tingles. After all, who will choose to feel undiluted awe? . . . The unknowing vulgar abuse the word; we must recapture its full and terrifying sense."[17] Emotionally the drug experience can be like having forty-foot waves crash over you for several hours while you cling desperately to a life-raft which may be swept from under you at any minute. It seems quite possible that such an ordeal, like any experience of a close call, could awaken rather fundamental sentiments respecting life and death and destiny and trigger the "no atheists in fox holes" effect. Similarly, as the subject emerges from the trauma and realizes that he is not going to be insane as he had feared, there may come over him an intensified appreciation like that frequently reported by patients recovering from critical illness. "It happened on the day when my bed was pushed out of doors to the open gallery of the hospital," reads one such report:

I cannot now recall whether the revelation came suddenly or gradually; I only remember finding myself in the very midst of those wonderful moments, beholding life for the first time in all its young intoxication of loveliness, in its unspeakable joy, beauty, and importance. I cannot say exactly what the mysterious change was. I saw no new thing, but I saw all the usual things in a miraculous new light—in what I believe is their true light. I saw for the first time how wildly beautiful and joyous, beyond any words of mine to describe, is the whole of life. Every human being moving across that porch, every sparrow that flew, every branch tossing in the wind, was caught in and was a part of the whole mad ecstasy of loveliness, of joy, of importance, of intoxication of life.[18]

If we do not discount religious intuitions because they are prompted by battlefields and *physical* crises; if we regard the latter as "calling us to our senses" more often than they seduce us into delusions, need comparable intuitions be discounted simply because the crises that trigger them are of an inner, *psychic* variety?

Turning from the hellish to the heavenly aspects of the drug experience, *some* of the latter may be explainable by the hypothesis just stated; that is, they may be occasioned by the relief that attends the sense of escape from high danger. But this hypothesis cannot possibly account for *all* the beatific episodes, for the simple reason that the positive episodes often come first, or to persons who experience no negative episodes whatever. Dr. Sanford Unger of the National Institute of Mental Health reports that among his subjects "50 to 60% will not manifest any real disturbance worthy of discussion," yet "around 75% will have at least one episode in which exaltation, rapture, and joy are the key descriptions."[19] How are we to account for the drug's capacity to induce peak experiences, such as the following, which are *not* preceded by fear?

A feeling of great peace and contentment seemed to flow through my entire body. All sound ceased and I seemed to be floating in a great, very very still void or hemisphere. It is impossible to describe the overpowering feeling of peace, contentment, and being a part of goodness itself that I felt. I could feel my body dissolving and actually becoming a part of the goodness and peace that was all around me. Words can't describe this. I feel an awe and wonder that such a feeling could have occurred to me.[20]

Consider the following line of argument. Like every other form of life, man's nature has become distinctive through specialization. Man has specialized in developing a cerebral cortex. The analytic powers of this instrument are a standing wonder, but the instrument seems less able to provide man with the sense that he is meaningfully related to his environment: to life, the world, and history in their wholeness. As Albert Camus describes the situation, "If I were . . . a cat among animals, this life would have a meaning, or rather this problem would not arise, for I should belong to this world. I would *be* this world to which I am now opposed by my whole consciousness."[21] Note that it is Camus' consciousness that opposes him to his world. The drugs do not knock this consciousness out, but while they leave it operative they also activate areas of the brain that normally lie below its threshold of awareness. One of the clearest objective signs that the drugs are taking effect is the dilation they produce in the pupils of the eyes, and one of the most predictable subjective signs is the intensification of visual perception. Both of these responses are controlled by portions of the brain that lie deep, further to the rear than the mechanisms that govern consciousness. Meanwhile we know that the human organism is interlaced with its world in innumerable ways it normally cannot sense—through gravitational fields, body respiration, and the like: the list could be multiplied until man's skin began to seem more like a thoroughfare than a boundary. Perhaps the deeper regions of the brain which evolved earlier and are more like those of the lower animals—"If I were . . . a cat . . . I should belong to this world"—can sense this relatedness better than can the cerebral cortex which now dominates our awareness. If so, when the drugs rearrange the neurohumors that chemically transmit impulses across synapses between neurons, man's consciousness and his submerged, intuitive, ecological awareness might for a spell become interlaced. This is, of course, no more than a hypothesis, but how else are we to account for the extraordinary incidence under the drugs of that kind of insight the keynote of which James described "invariably a reconciliation"? "It is as if the opposites of the world, whose contradictoriness and conflict make all our difficulties and troubles, were melted into one and the same genus, but *one of the species,* the nobler and better one, *is itself the genus, and so soaks up and absorbs its opposites into itself*" (op. cit., 279).

4. DRUGS AND RELIGION VIEWED "RELIGIOUSLY"

Suppose that drugs can induce experiences indistinguishable from religious experiences and that we can respect their reports. Do they shed any light, not (we now ask) on life, but on the nature of the religious life?

One thing they may do is throw religious experience itself into perspective by clarifying its relation to the religious life as a whole. Drugs appear able to induce religious experiences; it is less evident that they can produce religious lives. It follows that religion is more than religious experiences. This is hardly news, but it may be a useful reminder, especially to those who incline toward "the religion of religion experience";

which is to say toward lives bent on the acquisition of desired states of experience irrespective of their relation to life's other demands and components.

Despite the dangers of faculty psychology, it remains useful to regard man as having a mind, a will, and feelings. One of the lessons of religious history is that, to be adequate, a faith must rouse and involve all three components of man's nature. Religions of reason grow arid; religions of duty, leaden. Religions of experience have their comparable pitfalls, as evidenced by Taoism's struggle (not always successful) to keep from degenerating into quietism, and the vehemence with which Zen Buddhism has insisted that once students have attained *satori,* they must be driven out of it, back into the world. The case of Zen is especially pertinent here, for it pivots on an enlightenment experience—*satori,* or *kensho*—which some (but not all) Zennists say resembles LSD. Alike or different, the point is that Zen recognizes that unless the experience is joined to discipline, it will come to naught:

Even the Buddha . . . had to sit. . . . Without *joriki,* the particular power developed through *zazen* [seated meditation], the vision of oneness attained in enlightenment . . . in time becomes clouded and eventually fades into a pleasant memory instead of remaining an omnipresent reality shaping our daily life. . . . To be able to live in accordance with what the Mind's eye has revealed through *satori* requires, like the purification of character and the development of personality, a ripening period of *zazen.* [22]

If the religion of religious experience is a snare and a delusion, it follows that no religion that fixes its faith primarily in substances that induce religious experiences can be expected to come to a good end. What promised to be a short cut will prove to be a short circuit; what began as a religion will end as a religion surrogate. Whether chemical substances can be helpful *adjuncts* to faith is another question. The peyote-using Native American Church seems to indicate that they can be; anthropologists give this church a good report, noting among other things that members resist alcohol and alcoholism better than do nonmembers.[23] The conclusion to which evidence currently points would seem to be that chemicals *can* aid the religious life, but only where set within a context of faith (meaning by this conviction that what they disclose is true) and discipline (meaning diligent exercise of the will in the attempt to work out the implications of the disclosures for the living of life in the everyday, common-sense world).

Nowhere today in Western civilization are these two conditions jointly fulfilled. Churches lack faith in the sense just mentioned; hipsters lack discipline. This might lead us to forget about the drugs, were it not for one fact: the distinctive religious emotion and the emotion that drugs unquestionably can occasion—Otto's *mysterium tremendum, majestas, mysterium fascinans;* in a phrase, the phenomenon of religious awe—seems to be declining sharply. As Paul Tillich said in an address to the Hillel Society at Harvard several years ago:

The question our century puts before us [is]: Is it possible to regain the lost dimension, the encounter with the Holy, the dimension which cuts through the world of subjectivity and objectivity and goes down to that which is not world but is the mystery of the Ground of Being?

Tillich may be right; this may be the religious question of our century. For if (as we have insisted) religion cannot be equated with religious experiences, neither can it long survive their absence.

NOTES

1. *Soundings: Essays concerning Christian Understandings,* A. R. Vidler, ed. (Cambridge: University Press, 1962). The statement cited appears on page 72, in H. A. Williams's essay on "Theology and self-awareness."

2. Edith Hamilton, *Mythology* (New York: Mentor, 1953), p. 55.

3. Quoted in Alan Watts, *The Spirit of Zen* (New York: Grove Press, 1958), p. 110.

4. George Mylonas, *Eleusis and the Eleusinian Mysteries* (Princeton, N.J.: Princeton Univ. Press, 1961), p. 284.

5. *Two Sources of Morality and Religion* (New York: Holt, 1935), pp. 206–212.

6. "The God in the Flowerpot," *The American Scholar* 32, No. 4 (Autumn 1963), 584, 586.

7. *Mysticism Sacred and Profane* (New York: Oxford, 1961), p. 12.

8. Quoted in William H. McGlothlin, "Long-lasting Effects of LSD on Certain Attitudes in Normals," printed for private distribution by the RAND Corporation, May 1962, p. 16.

9. *Ibid.,* pp. 45, 46.

10. Timothy Leary, "The Religious Experience: Its Production and Interpretation," *The Psychedelic Review,* 1, No. 3 (1964), 325.

11. "Drugs and Mysticism: An Analysis of the Relationship between Psychedelic Drugs and the Mystical Consciousness," a thesis presented to the Committee in Higher Degrees in History and Philosophy of Religion, Harvard University, June 1963.

12. The first account is quoted anonymously in "The Issue of the Consciousness-expanding Drugs," *Main Currents in Modern Thought,* 20, No. 1 (September-October 1963), 10–11. The second experience was that of Dr. R. M. Bucke, the author of *Cosmic consciousness,* as quoted in William James, *The Varieties of Religious Experience* (New York Modern Library, 1902), pp. 390–391. The former experience occurred under the influence of drugs; the latter did not.

13. James S. Slotkin, *Peyote Religion* (New York: Free Press of Glencoe, 1956).

14. "Daru and Bhang," *Quarterly Journal of the Study of Alcohol.* 15 (1954), 229.

15. Chicago: Univ. of Chicago Press, 1958.

16. *Totem and Taboo* (New York: Modern Library, 1938).

17. "The Hallucinogenic Fungi of Mexico: An Inquiry into the Origins of the Religious Idea among Primitive Peoples," *Harvard Botanical Museum Leaflets,* 19, 7 (1961).

18. Margaret Prescott Montague, *Twenty Minutes of Reality* (St. Paul, Minn.: Macalester Park, 1947), pp. 15, 17.

19. "The Current Scientific Status of Psychedelic Drug Research," read at the Conference on Methods in Philosophy and the Sciences, New School for Social Research, May 3, 1964, and scheduled for publication in David Solomon, ed., *The Conscious Expanders* (New York: Putnam, fall of 1964).

20. Quoted by Dr. Unger in the paper just mentioned.

21. *The Myth of Sisyphus* (New York: Vintage, 1955), p. 38.

22. Phillip Kapleau, *Zen Practice and Attainment,* a manuscript in process of publication.

23. Slotkin, *op. cit.*

BLAISE PASCAL

The Wager*

Infinite—nothing.—Our soul is cast into a body, where it finds number, time, dimension. Thereupon it reasons, and calls this nature, necessity, and can believe nothing else.

Unity joined to infinity adds nothing to it, no more than one foot to an infinite measure. The finite is annihilated in the presence of the infinite, and becomes a pure nothing. So our spirit before God, so our justice before divine justice. There is not so great disproportion between our justice and that of God, as between unity and infinity.

The justice of God must be vast like His compassion. Now justice to the outcast is less vast, and ought less to offend our feelings then mercy towards the elect.

We know that there is an infinite, and are ignorant of its nature. As we know it to be false that numbers are finite, it is therefore true that there is an infinity in number. But we do not know what it is. It is false that it is even, it is false that it is odd; for the addition of a unit can make no change in its nature. Yet it is a number, and every number is odd or even (this is certainly true of every finite number). So we may well know that there is a God without knowing what He is. Is there not one substantial truth, seeing there are so many things which are not the truth itself?

We know then the existence and nature of the finite, because we also are finite and have exten-

sion. We know the existence of the infinite, and are ignorant of its nature, because it has extension like us, but not limits like us. But we know neither the existence nor the nature of God, because He has neither extension nor limits.

But by faith we know His existence; in glory we shall know His nature. Now, I have already shown that we may well know the existence of a thing, without knowing its nature.

Let us now speak according to natural lights.

If there is a God, He is infinitely incomprehensible, since, having neither parts nor limits, He has no affinity to us. We are then incapable of knowing either what He is or if He is. This being so, who will dare to undertake the decision of the question? Not we, who have no affinity to Him.

Who then will blame Christians for not being able to give a reason for their belief, since they profess a religion for which they cannot give a reason? They declare, in expounding it to the world, that it is a foolishness, *stultitiam;* and then you complain that they do not prove it! If they proved it, they would not keep their words; it is in lacking proofs, that they are not lacking in sense. "Yes, but although this excuses those who offer it as such, and take away from them the blame of putting it forward without reason, it does not excuse those who receive it." Let us then examine this point, and say, "God is, or He is not." But to which side shall we incline? Reason can decide nothing here. There is an infinite chaos which separates us. A game is being played at the extremity of this infinite distance where heads or

*From Blaise Pascal, *Thoughts,* trans. W. F. Trotter (New York: P. F. Collier & Son, 1910), p. 233. This material reprinted with the kind permission of Crowell Collier and Macmillan, Inc.

tails will turn up. What will you wager? According to reason, you can do neither the one thing nor the other; according to reason, you can defend neither of the propositions.

Do not then reprove for error those who have made a choice; for you know nothing about it. "No, but I blame them for having made, not this choice, but a choice; for again both he who chooses heads and he who chooses tails are equally at fault, they are both in the wrong. The true course is not to wager at all."

—Yes; but you must wager. It is not optional. You are embarked. Which will you choose then; Let us see. Since you must choose, let us see which interests you least. You have two things to lose, the true and the good; and two things to stake, your reason and your will, your knowledge and your happiness; and your nature has two things to shun, error and misery. Your reason is no more shocked in choosing one rather than the other, since you must of necessity choose. This is one point settled. But your happiness? Let us weigh the gain and the loss in wagering that God is. Let us estimate these two chances. If you gain, you gain all; if you lose, you lose nothing. Wager them without hesitation that He is.—"That is very fine. Yes, I must wager; but I may perhaps wager too much."—Let us see. Since there is an equal risk of gain and of loss, if you had only to gain two lives, instead of one, you might still wager. But if there were three lives to gain, you would have to play (since you are under the necessity of playing), and you would be imprudent, when you are forced to play, not to chance your life to gain three at a game where there is an equal risk of loss and gain. But there is an eternity of life and happiness. And this being so, if there were an infinity of chances, of which one only would be for you, you would still be right in wagering one to win two, and you would act stupidly, being obliged to play, by refusing to stake one life against three at a game in which out of an infinity of an infinitely happy life to gain. But there is here an infinity of an infinitely happy life to gain, a chance of gain against a finite number of chances of loss, and what you stake is finite. It is all divided; wherever the infinite is and there is not an infinity of chances of loss against that of gain, there is no time to hesitate, you must give all. And thus, when one is forced to play, he must renounce reason to preserve his life, rather than

risk it for infinite gain, as likely to happen as the loss of nothingness.

For it is no use to say it is uncertain if we will gain, and it is certain that we risk, and that the infinite distance between the *certainty* of what is staked and the *uncertainty* of what will be gained, equals the finite good which is certainly staked against the uncertain infinite. It is not so, as every player stakes a certainty to gain an uncertainty, and yet he stakes a finite certainty to gain a finite uncertainty, without transgressing against reason. There is not an infinite distance between the certainty staked and the uncertainty of the gain; that is untrue. In truth, there is an infinity between the certainty of gain and the certainty of loss. But the uncertainty of the gain is proportioned to the certainty of the stake according to the proportion of the chances of gain and loss. Hence it comes that, if there are as many risks on one side as on the other, the course is to play even; and then the certainty of the stake is equal to the uncertainty of the gain, so far is it from the fact that there is an infinite distance between them. And so our proposition is of infinite force, when there is the finite to stake in a game where there are equal risks of gain and of loss, and the infinite to gain. This is demonstrable; and if men are capable of any truths, this is one.

"I confess it, I admit it. But still is there no means of seeing the faces of the cards?"—Yes, Scripture and the rest, &c.—"Yes, but I have my hands tied and my mouth closed; I am forced to wager, and am not free. I am not released, and am so made that I cannot believe. What then would you have me do?"

"True. But at least learn your inability to believe, since reason brings you to this, and yet you cannot believe. Endeavour then to convince yourself, not by increase of proofs of God, but by the abatement of your passions. You would like to attain faith, and do not know the way; you would like to cure yourself of unbelief, and ask the remedy for it. Learn of those who have been bound like you, and who now stake all their possessions. These are people who know the way which you would follow, and who are cured of an ill of which you would be cured. Follow the way by which they began; by acting as if they believe, taking the holy water, having masses said, &c. Even this will naturally make you believe, and deaden your acuteness.—"But this is what

I am afraid of."—And why? What have you to lose?

But to show you that this leads you there, it is this which will lessen the passions, which are your stumbling-blocks.

The end of this discourse.—Now what harm will befall you in taking this side? You will be faithful, honest, humble, grateful, generous, a sincere friend, truthful. Certainly you will not have those poisonous pleasures, glory and luxury; but will you not have others? I will tell you that you will thereby gain in this life, and that, at each step you take on this road, you will see so great certainty of gain, so much nothingness in what you risk, that you will at last recognize that you have wagered for something certain and infinite, for which you have given nothing.

"Ah! This discourse transports me, charms me," &c.

If this discourse pleases you and seems impressive, know that it is made by a man who has knelt, both before and after it, in prayer to that Being, infinite and without parts, before whom he lays all he has, for you also to lay before Him all you have for your own good and for His glory, so that strength may be given to lowliness.

WILLIAM JAMES

The Will to Believe*

I

Let us give the name of hypothesis to anything that may be proposed to our belief; and just as the electricians speak of live and dead wires, let us speak of any hypothesis as either *live* or *dead*. A live hypothesis is one which appeals as a real possibility to him to whom it is proposed. If I ask you to believe in the Mahdi, the notion makes no electric connection with your nature—it refuses to scintillate with any credibility at all. As an hypothesis it is completely dead. To an Arab, however (even if he be not one of the Mahdi's followers), the hypothesis is among the mind's possibilities: it is alive. This shows that deadness and liveness in an hypothesis are not intrinsic properties, but relations to the individual thinker. They are measured by his willingness to act. The maximum of liveness in an hypothesis means willingness to act irrevocably. Practically, that means belief; but there is some believing tendency wherever there is willingness to act at all.

Next, let us call the decision between two hypotheses an *option*. Options may be of several kinds. They may be first, *living* or *dead;* secondly, *forced* or *avoidable;* thirdly, *momentous* or *trivial;* and for our purposes we may call an option a *genuine* option when it is of the forced, living, and momentous kind.

1. A living option is one in which both hypotheses are live ones. If I say to you: "Be a theosophist or be a Mohammedan," it is probably a dead option, because for you neither hypothesis is likely to be alive. But if I say: "Be an agnostic or be a Christian," it is otherwise: trained as you are, each hypothesis makes some appeal, however small, to your belief.

2. Next, if I say to you: "Choose between going out with your umbrella or without it," I do not offer you a genuine option, for it is not forced. You can easily avoid it by not going out at all. Similarly, if I say, "Either love me or hate me," "Either call my theory true or call it false," your option is avoidable. You may remain indifferent to me, neither loving nor hating, and you may decline to offer any judgment as to my theory. But if I say, "Either accept this truth or go without it," I put on you a forced option, for there is no standing place outside of the alternative. Every dilemma based on a complete logical disjunc-

*Extracts from William James, "The Will to Believe," an Address to the Philosophical Clubs of Yale and Brown Universities. First published in the *New World,* 1896.

tion, with no possibility of not choosing, is an option of this forced kind.

3. Finally, if I were Dr. Nansen and proposed to you to join my North Pole expedition, your option would be momentous; for this would probably be your similar opportunity, and your choice now would either exclude you from the North Pole sort of immortality altogether or put at least the chance of it into your hands. He who refuses to embrace a unique opportunity loses the prize as surely as if he tried and failed. *Per contra,* the option is trivial when the opportunity is not unique, when the stake is insignificant, or when the decision is reversible if it later prove unwise. Such trivial options abound in the scientific life. A chemist finds an hypothesis live enough to spend a year in its verification: he believes in it to that extent. But if his experiments prove inconclusive either way, he is quit for his loss of time, no vital harm being done.

It will facilitate our discussion if we keep all these distinctions well in mind.

II

The next matter to consider is the actual psychology of human opinion. When we look at certain facts, it seems as if our passional and volitional nature lay at the root of all our convictions. When we look at others, it seems as if they could do nothing when the intellect had once said its say. Let us take the latter facts up first.

Does it not seem preposterous on the very face of it to talk of our opinions being modifiable at will? Can our will either help or hinder our intellect in its perceptions of truth? Can we, by just willing it, believe that Abraham Lincoln's existence is a myth, and that the portraits of him in *McClure's Magazine* are all of some one else? Can we, by any effort of our will, or by any strength of wish that it were true, believe ourselves well and about when we are roaring with rheumatism in bed, or feel certain that the sum of the two one-dollar bills in our pocket must be a hundred dollars? We can *say* any of these things, but we are absolutely impotent to believe them; and of just such things is the whole fabric of the truths that we do believe in made up—matters of fact, immediate or remote, as Hume said, and relations between ideas, which are either there or not there for us if we see them so, and which if

not there cannot be put there by any action of our own.

In Pascal's *Thoughts* there is a celebrated passage known in literature as Pascal's wager. In it he tries to force us into Christianity by reasoning as if our concern with truth resembled our concern with the stakes in a game of chance. Translated freely his words are these: You must either believe or not believe that God is—which will you do? Your human reason cannot say. A game is going on between you and the nature of things which at the day of judgment will bring out either heads or tails. Weigh what your gains and your losses would be if you should stake all you have on heads, or God's existence: if you win in such case, you gain eternal beatitude; if you lose, you lose nothing at all. If there were an infinity of chances, and only one for God in this wager, still you ought to stake your all on God; for though you surely risk a finite loss by this procedure, any finite loss is reasonable, even a certain one is reasonable, if there is but the possibility of infinite gain. Go, then, and take holy water, and have masses said; belief will come and stupefy your scruples. ... Why should you not? At bottom, what have you to lose?

You probably feel that when religious faith expresses itself thus, in the language of the gaming-table, it is put to its last trumps. Surely Pascal's own personal belief in masses and holy water had far other springs; and this celebrated page of his is but an argument for others, a last desperate snatch at a weapon against the hardness of the unbelieving heart. We feel that a faith in masses and holy water adopted wilfully after such a mechanical calculation would lack the inner soul of faith's reality; and if we were ourselves in the place of the Deity, we should probably take particular pleasure in cutting off believers of this pattern from their infinite reward. It is evident that unless there be some preexisting tendency to believe in masses and holy water, the option offered to the will by Pascal is not a living option. Certainly no Turk ever took to masses and holy water on its account; and even to us Protestants these means of salvation seem such foregone impossibilities that Pascal's logic, invoked for them specifically, leaves us unmoved. As well might the Mahdi write to us, saying, "I am the Expected One whom God has created in his effulgence. You shall be infinitely happy if you confess me;

otherwise you shall be cut off from the light of the sun. Weigh, then, your infinite gain if I am genuine against your finite sacrifice if I am not!" His logic would be that of Pascal; but he would vainly use it on us, for the hypothesis he offers us is dead. No tendency to act on it exists in us to any degree.

The talk of believing by our volition seems, then, from one point of view, simply silly. From another point of view it is worse than silly, it is vile. When one turns to the magnificent edifice of the physical sciences, and sees how it was reared; what thousands of disinterested moral lives of men lie buried in its mere foundations; what patience and postponement, what choking down of preference, what submission to the icy laws of outer fact are wrought into its very stones and mortar; how absolutely impersonal it stands in its vast augustness—then how besotted and contemptible seems very little sentimentalist who comes blowing his voluntary smoke-wreaths, and pretending to decide things from out of his private dream! Can we wonder if those bred in the rugged and manly school of science should feel like spewing such subjectivism out of their mouths? The whole system of loyalties which grow up in the schools of science go dead against its toleration; so that it is only natural that those who have caught the scientific fever should pass over to the opposite extreme, and write sometimes as if the incorruptibly truthful intellect ought positively to prefer bitterness and unacceptableness to the heart in its cup.

> It fortifies my soul to know
> That though I perish, Truth is so

sings Clough, while Huxley exclaims: "My only consolation lies in the reflection that, however bad our posterity may become, so far as they hold by the plain rule of not pretending to believe what they have no reason to believe, because it may be to their advantage so to pretend [the word 'pretend' is surely here redundant], they will not have reached the lowest depth of immorality." And that delicious *enfant terrible* Clifford writes: "Belief is desecrated when given to unproved and unquestioned statements for the solace and private pleasure of the believer. ... Whoso would deserve well of his fellows in this matter will guard the purity of his belief with a very fanaticism of jealous care, lest at any time it should rest on an unworthy object, and catch a stain which can never be wiped away. ... If [a] belief has been accepted on insufficient evidence [even though the belief be true, as Clifford on the same page explains] the pleasure is a stolen one. ... It is sinful because it is stolen in defiance of our duty to mankind. That duty is to guard ourselves from such beliefs as from a pestilence which may shortly master our own body and then spread to the rest of the town. ... It is wrong always, everywhere, and for every one, to believe anything upon insufficient evidence."

III

All this strikes one as healthy, even when expressed, as by Clifford, with somewhat too much of robustious pathos in the voice. Free will and simple wishing do seem, in the matter of our credences, to be only fifth wheels to the coach. Yet if any one should thereupon assume that intellectual insight is what remains after wish and will and sentimental preference have taken wing, or that pure reason is what then settles our opinions, he would fly quite as directly in the teeth of the facts.

It is only our already dead hypotheses that our willing nature is unable to bring to life again. But what has made them dead for us is for the most part a previous action of our willing nature of an antagonistic kind. When I say "willing nature," I do not mean only such deliberate volitions as may have set up habits of belief that we cannot now escape from—I mean all such factors of belief as fear and hope, prejudice and passion, imitation and partisanship, the circumpressure of our caste and set. As a matter of fact we find ourselves believing, we hardly know how or why. Mr. Balfour gives the name of "authority" to all those influences, born of the intellectual climate, that make hypotheses possible or impossible for us, alive or dead. Here in this room, we all of us believe in molecules and the conservation of energy, in democracy and necessary progress, in Protestant Christianity and the duty of fighting for "the doctrine of the immortal Monroe," all for no reasons worthy of the name. We see into these matters with no more inner clearness, and probably with much less, than any disbeliever in them might possess. His unconventionality would probably have some grounds to show for its conclusions; but for us, not insight, but the *prestige* of the opinions, is what makes the spark shoot from them and light up our sleeping magazines of faith. Our reason is quite satisfied, in nine hundred and ninety-nine cases out of every thousand of us, if it can find a few arguments that will do to recite in case our credulity is criticized by some one else. Our faith is faith in some one else's faith, and in the greatest matters this is the most the case. . . .

Evidently, then, our non-intellectual nature does influence our convictions. There are passional tendencies and volitions which run before and others which come after belief, and it is only the latter that are too late for the fair; and they are not too late when the previous passional work has been already in their own direction. Pascal's argument, instead of being powerless, then seems a regular clincher, and is the last stroke needed to make our faith in masses and holy water complete. The state of things is evidently far from simple; and pure insight and logic, whatever they might do ideally, are not the only things that really do produce our creeds.

IV

Our next duty, having recognized this mixedup state of affairs, is to ask whether it be simply reprehensible and pathological, or whether, on the contrary, we must treat it as a normal element in making up our minds. The thesis I defend is, briefly stated, this: *Our passional nature not only lawfully may, but must, decide an option between propositons, whenever it is a genuine option that cannot by its nature be decided on intellectual grounds; for to say, under such circumstances, "Do not decide, but leave the question open," is itself a passional decision—just like deciding yes or no—and is attended with the same risk of losing the truth.* . . .

VII

One more point, small but important, and our preliminaries are done. There are two ways of looking at our duty in the matter of opinion— ways entirely different, and yet ways about whose difference the theory of knowledge seems hitherto to have shown very little concern. *We must know the truth;* and *we must avoid error*—these are our first and great commandments as would-be knowers; but they are not two ways of stating an identical commandment, they are two separable laws. Although it may indeed happen that when we believe the truth A, we escape as an incidental consequence from believing the falsehood B, it hardly ever happens that by merely disbelieving B we necessarily believe A. We may in escaping B fall into believing other falsehoods, C or D, just as bad as B; or we may escape B by not believing anything at all, not even A.

Believe truth! Shun error!—these, we see, are two materially different laws; and by choosing between them we may end by coloring differently our whole intellectual life. We may regard the chase for truth as paramount, and the avoidance of error as secondary; or we may, on the other hand, treat the avoidance of error as more imperative, and let truth take its chance. Clifford, in the instructive passage which I have quoted, exhorts us to the latter course. Believe nothing, he tells us, keep your mind in suspense forever, rather than by closing it on insufficient evidence incur the awful risk of believing lies. You, on the other hand, may think that the risk of being in error is a very small matter when compared with the blessings of real knowledge, and be ready to be duped many times in your investigation rather than postpone indefinitely the chance of guessing true. I myself find it impossible to go with Clifford. We must remember that these feelings of our duty about either truth or error are in any case only expressions of our passional life. Biologically considered, our minds are as ready to grind out falsehood as veracity, and he who says, "Better go without belief forever than believe a lie!" merely shows his own preponderant private horror of becoming a dupe. He may be critical of many of his desires and fears, but this fear he slavishly obeys. He cannot imagine any one questioning its binding force. For my own part, I have also a horror of being duped; but I can believe that worse things than being duped may happen to a man in this world: so Clifford's exhortation has to my ears a thoroughly fantastic sound. It is like a general informing his soldiers that it is better to keep out of battle forever than to risk a single wound. Not so are victories either over enemies or over nature gained. Our errors are surely not such awfully solemn things. In a world where we are so certain to incur them in spite of all our caution, a certain lightness of heart seems healthier than this excessive nervousness on their behalf. At any rate, it seems the fittest thing for the empiricist philosopher.

VIII

And now, after all this introduction, let us go straight at our question. I have said, and now repeat it, that not only as a matter of fact do we find our passional nature influencing us in our opinions, but that there are some options between opinions in which this influence must be regarded both as an inevitable and as a lawful determinant of our choice.

I fear here that some of you my hearers will begin to scent danger, and lend an inhospitable ear. Two first steps of passion you have indeed had to admit as necessary—we must think so as to avoid dupery, and we must think so as to gain truth; but the surest path to those ideal consummations, you will probably consider, is from now onwards to take no further passional step.

Well, of course, I agree as far as the facts will allow. Wherever the option between losing truth and gaining it is not momentous, we can throw the chance of *gaining truth* away, and at any rate save ourselves from any chance of *believing falsehood,* by not making up our minds at all till objective evidence has come. In scientific questions, this is almost always the case; and even in human affairs in general, the need of acting is seldom so urgent that a false belief to act on is better than no belief at all. Law courts, indeed, have to decide on the best evidence attainable for the moment, because a judge's duty is to make law as well as to ascertain it, and (as a learned judge once said to me) few cases are worth spending much time over: the great thing is to have them decided on *any* acceptable principle, and got out of the way. But in our dealings with objective nature we obviously are recorders, not makers, of the truth; and decisions for the mere sake of deciding promptly and getting on to the next business would be wholly out of place. Throughout the breadth of physical nature facts are what they are quite independently of us, and seldom is there any such hurry about them that the risks of being duped by believing a premature theory need be faced. The questions here are always trivial options, the hypotheses are hardly living (at any rate not living for us spectators), the choice between believing truth or falsehood is seldom forced. The attitude of sceptical balance is there-fore the absolutely wise one if we would escape mistakes. What difference, indeed, does it make to most of us whether we have or have not a theory of the Röntgen rays, whether we believe or not in mind-stuff, or have a conviction about the causality of conscious states? It makes no difference. Such options are not forced on us. On every account it is better not to make them, but still keep weighing reasons *pro et contra* with an indifferent hand.

I speak, of course, here of the purely judging mind. For purposes of discovery such indifference is to be less highly recommended, and science would be far less advanced than she is if the passionate desires of individuals to get their own faiths confirmed had been kept out of the game. See for example the sagacity which Spencer and Weismann now display. On the other hand, if you want an absolute duffer in an investigation, you must, after all, take the man who has no interest whatever in its results: he is the warranted incapable, the positive fool. The most useful investigator, because the most sensitive observer, is always he whose eager interest in one side of the question is balanced by an equally keen nervousness lest he becomes deceived.[1] Science has organized this nervousness into a regular *technique,* her so-called method of verification; and she has fallen so deeply in love with the method that one may even say she has ceased to care for truth by itself at all. It is only truth as technically verified that interests her. The truth of truths might come in merely affirmative form, and she would decline to touch it. Such truth as that, she might repeat with Clifford, would be stolen in defiance of her duty to mankind. Human passions, however, are stronger than technical rules. *"Le coeur a ses raisons,"* as Pascal says, *"que la raison ne connait pas";*[2] and however indifferent to all but the bare rules of the game the umpire, the abstract intellect, may be, the concrete players who furnish him the materials to judge of are usually, each one of them, in love with some pet "live hypothesis" of his own. Let us agree, however, that wherever there is no forced option, the dispassionately judicial intellect with no pet hypothesis, saving us, as it does, from dupery at any rate, ought to be our ideal.

The question next arises: Are there not somewhere forced options in our speculative questions, and can we (as men who may be interested at least as much in positively gaining truth as in merely escaping dupery) always wait with impunity till the coercive evidence shall have arrived? It seems *a priori* improbable that the truth should be so nicely adjusted to our needs and powers as that. In the great boarding-house of nature, the cakes and the butter and the syrup seldom come out so even and leave the plates so clean. Indeed, we should view them with scientific suspicion if they did.

IX

Moral questions immediately present themselves as questions whose solution cannot wait for sensible proof. A moral question is a question not of what sensibly exists, but of what is good, or would be good if it did exist. Science can tell us what exists; but to compare the *worths,* both of what exists and of what does not exist, we must consult not science, but what Pascal calls our heart. . . .

Turn now from these wide questions of good to a certain class of questions of fact, questions concerning personal relations, states of mind between one man and another. *Do you like me or not?*— for example. Whether you do or not depends, in countless instances, on whether I meet you half-way, am willing to assume that you must like me, and show you trust and expectation. The previous faith on my part in your liking's existence is in such cases what makes your liking come. But if I stand aloof, and refuse to budge an inch until I have objective evidence, until you shall have done something apt, as the absolutists say, *ad extorquendum assensum meum,* ten to one your liking never comes. How many women's hearts are vanquished by the mere sanguine insistence of some man that they *must* love him! He will not consent to the hypothesis that they cannot. The desire for a certain kind of truth here brings about that special truth's existence; and so it is in innumerable cases of other sorts. . . . *And where faith in a fact can help create the fact,* that would be an insane logic which should say that faith running ahead of scientific evidence is the "lowest kind of immorality" into which a thinking being can fall. Yet such is the logic by which our scientific absolutists pretend to regulate our lives!

X

In truths dependent on our personal action, then, faith based on desire is certainly a lawful and possibly an indispensable thing.

But now, it will be said, these are all childish human cases, and have nothing to do with great cosmical matters, like the question of religious faith. Let us then pass on to that. Religions differ so much in their accidents that in discussing the religious question we must make it very generic and broad. What then do we now mean by the religious hypothesis? Science says things are; morality says some things are better than other things; and religion says essentially two things.

First, she says that the best things are the more eternal things, the overlapping things, the things in the universe that throw the last stone, so to speak, and say the final word. "Perfection is eternal"—this phrase of Charles Secrétan seems a good way of putting this first affirmation of religion, an affirmation which obviously cannot yet be verified scientifically at all.

The second affirmation of religion is that we are better off even now if we believe her first affirmation to be true.

Now, let us consider what the logical elements of this situation are *in case the religious hypothesis in both its branches be really true.* (Of course, we must admit that possibility at the outset. If we are to discuss the question at all, it must involve a living option. If for any of you religion be a hypothesis that cannot, by any living possibility, be true, then you need go no farther. I speak to the "saving remnant" alone.) So proceeding, we see, first, that religion offers itself as a *momentous* option. We are supposed to gain, even now, by our belief, and to lose by our non-belief, a certain vital good. Secondly, religion is a *forced* option, so far as that good goes. We cannot excape the issue by remaining sceptical and waiting for more light, because, although we do avoid error in that way *if religion be untrue,* we lose the good, *if it be true,* just as certainly as if we positively chose to disbelieve. It is as if a man should hesitate indefinitely to ask a certain woman to marry him because he was not perfectly sure that she would prove an angel after he brought her home. Would he not cut himself off from that particular angel-possibility as decisively as if he went and married some one else? Scepticism, then, is not avoidance of option; it is option of a certain particular kind of risk. *Better risk loss of truth than chance of error*—that is your faith-vetoer's exact position. He is actively playing his stake as much as the believer is; he is backing the field against the religious hypothesis, just as the believer is backing the religious hypothesis against the field. To preach scepticism to us as a duty until "sufficient evidence" for religion be found, is tantamount therefore to telling us, when in presence of the religious hypothesis, that to yield to our fear of its being error is wiser and better than to yield to our hope that it may be true. It is not intellect against all passions, then; it is only intellect with one passion laying down its law. And by what, forsooth, is the supreme wisdom of this passion warranted? Dupery for dupery, what proof is there that dupery through hope is so much worse than dupery through fear? I, for one, can see no proof; and I simply refuse obedience to the scientist's command to imitate his kind of option, in a case where my own stake is important enough to give me the right to choose my own form of risk. If religion be true and the evidence for it be still insufficient, I do not wish, by putting your extinguisher upon my nature (which feels to me as if it had after all some business in this matter), to forfeit my sole chance in life of getting upon the winning side—that chance depending, of course, on my willingness to run the risk of acting as if my passional need of taking the world religiously might be prophetic and right.

All this is on the supposition that it really may be prophetic and right, and that, even to us who are discussing the matter, religion is a live hypothesis which may be true. Now, to most of us religion comes in a still further way that makes a veto on our active faith even more illogical. The more perfect and more eternal aspect of the universe is represented in our religions as having personal form. The universe is no longer a mere *It* to us, but a *Thou,* if we are religious; and any relation that may be possible from person to person might be possible here. For instance, although in one sense we are passive portions of the universe, in another we show a curious autonomy, as if we were small active centres on our own account. We feel, too, as if the appeal of religion to us were made to our own active goodwill, as if evidence might be forever withheld from us unless we met the hypothesis half-way to take a trivial illustration: just as a man who in a company of gentlemen made no advances, asked a warrant for every concession, and believed no one's word without proof, would cut himself off by such churlishness from all the social rewards that a more trusting spirit would earn—so here, one who should shut himself up in snarling logicality and try to make the gods extort his recognition willy-nilly, or not get it at all, might cut himself off forever from his only opportunity of making the gods' acquaintance. This feeling, forced on us we know not whence that by obstinately believing that there are gods (although not to do so would be so easy both for our logic and our life) we are doing the universe the deepest service we can, seems part of the living essence of the religious hypothesis. If the hypothesis *were* true in all its parts, including this one, then pure intellectualism, with its veto on our making willing advances, would be an absurdity; and some participation of our sympathetic nature would be logically required. I therefore, for one, cannot see my way to accepting the agnostic rules for truth-seeking, or wilfully agree to keep my willing nature out of the game. I cannot do so for this plain reason, that *a rule of thinking which would absolutely prevent me from acknowledging certain kinds of truth if those kinds of truth were really there, would be an irrational rule.* That for me is the long and short of the formal logic of the situation, no matter what the kinds of truth might materially be.

I confess I do not see how this logic can be escaped. But sad experience makes me fear that some of you may still shrink from radically saying with me, *in abstracto,* that we have the right to believe at our own risk any hypothesis that is live enough to tempt our will. I suspect, however, that if this is so, it is because you have got away from the abstract logical point of view altogether, and are thinking (perhaps without realizing it) of some particular religious hypothesis which for you is dead. The freedom to "believe what we will" you apply to the case of some patent superstition; and the faith you think of is the faith defined by the schoolboy when he said, "Faith is when you believe something that you know ain't true." I can only repeat that this is misapprehension. *In concreto,* the freedom to believe can only cover living options which the intellect of the individual cannot by itself resolve; and living options never seem absurdities to him who has them to consider. When I look at the religious question as it really puts itself to concrete men, and when I think of all the possibilities which both practically and theoretically it involves, then this command that we shall put a stopper on our heart, instincts, and courage, and *wait*—acting of course meanwhile more or less as if religion were not true[3]—till doomsday, or till such time as our intellect and senses working together may have raked in evidence enough—this command, I say, seems to me the queerest idol ever manufactured in the philosophic cave. Were we scholastic absolutists, there might be more excuse. If we had an infallible intellect with its objective certitudes, we might feel ourselves disloyal to such a perfect organ of knowledge in not trusting to it exclusively, in not waiting for its releasing word. But if we are empiricists, if we believe that no bell in us tolls to let us know for certain when truth is in our grasp, then it seems a piece of idle fantasticality to preach so solemnly our duty of waiting for the bell. Indeed we *may* wait if we will—I hope you do not think that I am denying that—but if we do so, we do so at our peril as much as if we believed. In either case we *act,* taking our life in our hands. No one of us ought to issue vetoes to the other, nor should we bandy words of abuse. We ought, on the contrary, delicately and profoundly to respect one another's mental freedom: then only shall we bring about the intellectual republic; then only shall we have that spirit of inner tolerance without which all our outer tolerance is soulless, and which is empiricism's glory; then only shall we live and let live, in speculative as well as in practical things.

I began by a reference to Fitz-James Stephen; let me end by a quotation from him. "What do you think of yourself? What do you think of the world? ... These are questions with which all must deal as it seems good to them. They are riddles of the Sphinx, and in some way or other we must deal with them. ... In all important transactions of life we have to take a leap in the dark. ... If we decide to leave the riddles unanswered, that is a choice; if we waver in our answer, that, too, is a choice: but whatever choice we make, we make it at our peril. If a man chooses to turn his back altogether on God and the future, no one can prevent him; no one can show beyond reasonable doubt that he is mistaken. If a man thinks otherwise and acts as he thinks, I do not see that any one can prove that he is mistaken. Each must act as he thinks best; and if he is wrong, so much the worse for him. We stand on a mountain pass in the midst of whirling snow and blinding mist, through which we get glimpses now and then of paths which may be deceptive. If we stand still we shall be frozen to death. If we take the wrong road we shall be dashed to pieces. We do not certainly know whether there is any right one. What must we do? 'Be strong and of a good courage.' Act for the best, hope for the best, and take what comes.

... If death ends all, we cannot meet death better."

NOTES

1. Compare Wilfrid Ward's Essay "The Wish to Believe," in his *Witnesses to the Unseen* (Macmillan & Co., 1893).

2. "The heart has its reasons which reason does not know."

3. Since belief is measured by action, he who forbids us to believe religion to be true, necessarily also forbids us to act as we should if we did believe it to be true. The whole defence of religious faith hinges upon action. If the action required or inspired by the religious hypothesis is in no way different from that dictated by the naturalistic hypothesis, then religious faith is a pure superfluity, better pruned away, and controversy about its legitimacy is a piece of idle trifling, unworthy of serious minds. I myself believe, of course, that the religious hypothesis gives to the world an expression which specifically determines our reactions, and makes them in a large part unlike what they might be on a purely naturalistic sche e of belief.

4. *Liberty, Equality, Fraternity,* p. 353, 2d edition (London, 1874).

PART 2   HUMAN KNOWLEDGE

During the great golden age of philosophy, in the seventeenth and eighteenth centuries, problems about the nature of human knowledge divided philosophers into two schools; and despite changing idioms and increased understanding of the methods of science, the division to a large degree persists. On the one hand, the *empiricists,* whose leading thinkers were John Locke (1632–1704), George Berkeley (1685–1753), and David Hume (1711–1776), held that all our ideas come from experience and that no proposition about any matter of fact can be known to be true independently of experience. On the other hand, the *rationalists,* whose most important representatives were René Descartes (1596–1650), Baruch Spinoza (1632–1677), and Gottfried Leibniz (1646–1716), maintained that there are "innate ideas," and that certain general propositions (usually called "necessary" or "a priori" propositions) can be known to be true in advance of, or in the absence of, empirical verification.[1]

Advocates of the theory of innate ideas did not, of course, hold that we are born literally thinking certain thoughts, but rather that we are born with inherited dispositions to have thoughts of a certain form and structure. Just as dehydrated milk has the disposition to become milk when water is added to it, so the mind, on this theory, has from birth the disposition to acquire the concepts of being, substance, duration—even infinitude and God—once a certain amount of experience is "added to it." Thus, rationalism holds that there can be in the mind ideas and truths that were not first present in experience but only later activated by experience. For the empiricist, on the other hand, the mind is (as Locke put it) like a tablet on which nothing has been written (a *tabula rasa*) until experience writes its message on it.

The writings of René Descartes, a leading mathematician and man of science as well as a philosopher, are a clear example not only of the rationalistic doctrine and method

---

[1]It should be noted that both the rationalist and the empiricist are "rationalists" in the wider sense of the term—that is, as opposed to fideism, romanticism, or irrationalism. Both can support rational inquiry as the sole road to truth, but they differ in their conceptions of what rational inquiry is, particularly regarding the role that sense experience plays in it.

but also of the rationalistic temper of mind. In the autobiographical *Discourse on Method*, Descartes compares the state of the sciences and philosophy to an ancient European town, grown helter-skelter from an older village, with crooked streets, random walls, and poor sanitation. Of course, we are not accustomed to rip down whole cities in order to start from scratch the task of rational redesign; but individuals can without arrogance or absurdity think of ripping down and rebuilding their own homes:

... and the same I thought was true of any similar project for reforming the body of the Sciences, or the order of teaching them established in the Schools: but as for the opinions which up to that time I had embraced, I thought that I could not do better than resolve at once to sweep them wholly away, that I might afterwards be in a position to admit either others more correct, or even perhaps the same ones when they had undergone the scrutiny of reason. I firmly believed that in this way I should much better succeed in the conduct of my life, than if I built only upon old foundations, and leaned upon principles which, in my youth, I had taken upon trust.

Thus Descartes begins his dramatic quest for new "foundations," doubting everything that can be doubted until he finds a solid basis for reconstruction in the indubitable fact of his own existence as a "thinking substance." What makes the argument for his own existence so convincing, Descartes decides, is its "clearness and distinctness." Hence, he has a working criterion of truth to use in the voyage away from his skeptical starting point: Whatever he conceives clearly and distinctly is true.

In his third Meditation, Descartes finds in himself the idea of an infinite God. The idea, he argues, could not be his own invention, nor could it be derived from merely finite experience. Its only possible cause must be the actually existing deity. He then goes on to prove that this deity is no deceiver. Therefore, (a) since God has given us a powerful disposition to believe in the existence of material objects (such as human bodies), and (b) since God would be a deceiver if no such objects existed, and (c) since God is not a deceiver—it follows that such objects do exist and that human knowledge is reliable. Intellectual error, then, when it occurs, springs from a kind of hasty willfulness in ourselves and not from God.

And so, at last, almost everything doubted in the beginning, including a world of extended bodies in motion, has been demonstrated back into existence, every step of the way evident to the "natural light of reason" and the conclusion guaranteed by an eternally reliable God, who indeed is the foundation of it all.

Few philosophers today find Descartes's system of arguments convincing, but his method has left its mark on most of his successors. For three centuries philosophers have tried to give a rational reconstruction of our knowledge, beginning with the relatively indubitable and building on it, and taking very seriously as they work the nagging claims of imaginary skeptics that what we think we know with certainty we may not really know at all.

Skeptical doubts are especially likely to torment the empiricist philosopher. Since empiricism holds that the sole source ultimately of our knowledge of things external to us in sense experience, it is a matter of importance to empiricists to explain just how that knowledge is derived from the "impressions" made upon our various sense organs. John Locke rested a great part of his theory upon a crucial distinction first used in antiquity and then revived by Galileo—namely, the distinction between *primary and secondary qualities* of physical objects. Primary qualities are intrinsic characteristics of the object itself—characteristics such as solidity, extension in space (size), figure (shape), motion or rest, and number. These are qualities that the objects would continue to possess even if there were no perceiving beings in the world. Secondary qualities, on the other hand (such qualities as color, taste, smell, sound, warmth, and cold), exist only when actually sensed, and then only "in the mind" of the one who senses them. The primary quality itself is inseparable from the material object and is found in every part of it, no matter how small. Every conceivable unit of matter, from a celestial body to an atom, must have some size and shape. (On the other hand, no mere atom could have color.)

Locke also contributed to the terminology of subsequent empiricists the technical term "idea" to stand for "whatever is the object of the understanding when a man thinks" or, more generally, for any direct object of awareness or consciousness.[2] And, again, the "ideas" that result from our perception of primary qualities are different from our "ideas" of secondary qualities. When we perceive a primary quality, according to Locke, our "idea" of this quality exactly resembles the corresponding primary quality in the material object itself. In contrast, when we perceive a secondary quality, our "idea" of this quality has no resemblance to a corresponding property of the thing itself. That is, our "idea" of, for instance, color or odor in an object is produced in us by virtue of the object's "power" to reflect and absorb light waves of certain frequencies, or to emit molecules in certain degrees of vibration. Because of these capacities or "powers" of material objects, color and odor can come into existence. Yet without eyes, there could be no color; without noses, no odor; and without minds, no "secondary qualities" at all.

Locke's theory of perception, then, does seem to have strong support from scientifically sophisticated common sense. It often contrasted with another possible theory of

---

[2]David Hume's usage was somewhat narrower. In the *Treatise of Human Nature*, his earlier more formal exposition of the views included here, Hume explains that he will use the word "impression" to mean "all our sensations, passions, and emotions, as they make their first appearance in the soul." By "ideas" he means "the faint images of these in thinking and reasoning."

perception (a theory held by no reputable philosopher), which is sometimes ascribed (quite unfairly) to the scientifically unsophisticated common sense of "the ordinary man." According to the latter theory, called *naive realism,* the qualities that Locke called "primary" and those he called "secondary" are both strictly part of physical objects, and both can exist quite independently of perceiving minds.[3] It follows from naive realism that a world without perceiving minds might yet be a colorful, clamorous, and smelly place. Locke's view, in contrast, is that physical substances and their primary qualities can exist independently of sentient minds, and only the secondary qualities are mind-dependent. This theory can be called *sophisticated realism:* "sophisticated" because it seems to accord with what science tells us about secondary qualities; "realism" because it allows that material objects have a real existence independent of minds. Locke's view is often called *representative realism,* because of the tenet that ideas ("in the mind") faithfully mirror or "represent" material objects to us in perception, even though the material objects and the "ideas" by which we come to know them are quite distinct entities. The textbooks also call Locke's view the *causal theory of perception* because of the tenet that material objects are the causes of the ideas, or appearances, or sense data we have of them. The material substance itself is distinct from its own qualities, even from its own primary qualities, and, not being directly perceivable, must simply be posited as an unknowable "substratum" for its powers and properties. (Locke's conception of substance was rejected by most later empiricists, who preferred to think of a material thing as a mere "bundle of attributes," not as a mysterious entity "underlying" or "possessing" its own attributes.)

The realism of John Locke, roughly sketched in the preceding paragraphs, must be understood as the primary target of the arguments of George Berkeley, Bishop of Cloyne. Locke would have approved of Berkeley's systematic demonstration that secondary qualities are mental. Berkeley argues for the conclusion in two ways. First of all, he maintains that extreme degrees of each secondary quality are inseparable in our consciousness from pain. Hence, if it is absurd to imagine that pain is (say) *in* or *part of* the stove, then it is equally absurd to imagine that the heat is literally in the stove. Berkeley's second argument is the famous "argument from the relativity of perception." If I put one ice-chilled hand and one warm hand into a tub of tepid water, the water will feel hot to my cold hand and cold to my hot hand; but the water itself cannot be both hot and cold. Hence, both heat and cold must be "in the mind" only.

But Berkeley then turns the tables on Locke by arguing in quite similar ways for the necessarily mental status of *primary qualities* too. If the supporter of Locke accepts these latter arguments, there is nothing left of his conception of an external object beyond that of an unknowable "substratum." Berkeley easily disposes of the concept of a substratum as theoretically superfluous and unintelligible. He is left then with a world in which only perceiving minds ("subjects") and their "ideas" (the appearances of primary and secondary qualities) exist. Hence, the universe is through and through mental. This theory of reality bears the name *subjective idealism.* (Perhaps "ideaism" would be less misleading, since the theory has nothing whatever to do with normal ideals.)

[3] The Spanish-American philosopher George Santayana (*Winds of Doctrine* [London: J. M. Dent and Sons, New York: Charles Scribner's Sons, 1940], p. 146) once lampooned a similar view about the ethical characteristic "goodness" by likening it to the claim that whiskey is "intoxicating in itself, without reference to any animal; that it is pervaded, as it were, by an inherent intoxication, and stands dead drunk in its bottle!"

Berkeley was as concerned as Descartes or Locke to find a solid alternative to skepticism. As an empiricist, he was resolved to show that all of our ideas, insofar as they are genuine (not merely confused), are derived from experience. What, then, of our idea of corporeal objects such as trees, tables, bodies? Berkeley was driven by his logic and his empiricist startings to conclude that physical objects, insofar as we have any clear idea of them at all, are simply collections of sense impressions. Those corporeal substances, of which Descartes was at last able to form a "clear and distinct idea," turn out on analysis to be the figments of muddled thought.

Has empiricism then truly reconstructed our knowledge of the world, if this is its conclusion? Doesn't Berkeley's conception of a world "through and through mental" give a violent jolt to common sense? Not so, replies Berkeley's spokesman Philonous. Berkeley's idealism implies that tables and trees and bodies are just exactly what they seem—colored, shaped, hard, and so on. There is indeed nothing to these things except the qualities they seem to have. Moreover, it is not true that tables "vanish" or "pop out of existence" the moment we turn our backs on them (that *would* be repugnant to common sense); for God is always perceiving them, and therefore they continue to exist as ideas in His mind. To many later empiricists this use of God seemed a desperate expedient to save Berkeley's theory from embarrassment. John Stuart Mill (1806–1873) was typical of later empiricists (often called *phenomenalists*) who found ways to make the rejection of "corporeal substance" more palatable to common sense without invoking a *deus ex machina.* According to Mill, if we say that the table continues to exist when unperceived, all we can mean by this is that *if* someone were to look in a certain place, then he would have sense impressions of a certain (table-like) kind; for material objects are not simply bundles of actual sense impressions but are rather to be understood as "permanent possibilities of sensation," and this conception exhausts whatever clear idea we have of them.

David Hume applied the empiricist philosophy to other basic concepts, with results that even he called skeptical. Unlike Berkeley, who regarded skepticism as a charge to be rebutted, Hume thought of it as a position to be reluctantly adopted. In the selections included here, he examines the concept of causation and finds no more sense in the idea of a "necessary connection" between cause and effect (when we drop a stone, it *must* fall—so we think) than Berkeley did in the idea of "corporeal substance." We may continue to talk, as Hume himself does, of one thing's causing another, but all we can *mean* is that events of the first kind are in fact constantly conjoined with events of the second kind; and the so-called necessity that the second follow the first is simply the reflection of our habitual expectation. Hume would not have us deny the plain reports of our senses or the fruits of our mathematical deductions; he merely points out that there is no logically infallible method of achieving truth about matters of fact, and indeed no method at all for reasoning about matters that lie beyond all experience. But this kind of skepticism need not force us into a permanent suspension of judgment about all things, even in the practical affairs of life; for we will (as Hume elsewhere puts it) continue to leave buildings by the first-floor door rather than the upstairs window, and "Nature will always maintain her rights and prevail in the end over any abstract reasoning whatever."

The article "An Encounter with David Hume" was written specifically for this volume by Wesley C. Salmon of the University of Arizona. It is meant to show the beginning student of philosophy and science ("Physics 1a") how natural Hume's doubts can seem to one who ponders the methods and results of the exact sciences and how important it is to our conception of scientific knowledge to come to terms with those doubts. In particular, Salmon discusses such scientific notions as causation, inductive inference, probability, laws of nature, the regularity of nature, necessity, and predictability in the light of Hume's empiricism. Salmon's essay views these matters through the eyes of a sensitive undergraduate student of physics who comes to wonder whether all science rests ultimately on a kind of "faith" in the uniformity of nature that cannot be rationally demonstrated to be correct. If that is so, he asks (with a certain amount of anguish), how can physics be shown to be a more reliable guide to knowledge of the future than (say) astrology or crystal gazing? These questions pose in a very rough way what has come to be called "the problem of induction" or "Hume's riddle of induction." Salmon concludes by sketching the main strategies that have been proposed by philosophers for coming to terms with Hume's skeptical doubts about scientific method.

The great opponent of Hume was his countryman and almost exact contemporary Thomas Reid (1710–1796). It was Reid's primary purpose to vindicate common sense against the skepticism to which empiricism seemed finally to be driven. The "Scottish Common Sense School," of which Reid was the chief spokesman, had very widespread influence, particularly in the United States in the nineteenth century. Reid concedes to Berkeley and Hume that we cannot infer the existence of enduring corporeal (nonmental objects from our mere sense impressions. Nevertheless, he contends, our belief in such objects is no mere "opinion got by reasoning"; it is, rather, a natural principle of the human constitution, as reliable and as inevitable as any of the natural principles that govern our reasonings. (If, as Reid suggests, we think of nature, including our nature, as designed by God, then we can find strong similarities in his position to the argument of Descartes that "God can be no deceiver.")

Skepticism has still other challenges for the empiricist. All of us would claim to know not only that material objects exist independently of our perception of them (however this is to be analyzed), but also that the human figures we observe and converse with constantly are not mere automata but are possessed of minds and experiences, desires, sensations, and beliefs just like our own. But how can we know these things if all our knowledge is derived from sense impressions of bodily forms moving and shifting in regular ways in our perceptual field? We surely don't know the feelings (to pick only one class of mental phenomena as an example) of another person in the same direct way we know our own. Mill bases our knowledge of other minds on an argument from analogy similar in *form* to the "argument from design" discussed in Part One. In some, but not all, ways the analogical argument for other minds is even weaker than the analogical argument for a world-designer. It proceeds, for example, from only one observed instance (oneself) to the existence of many other instances. Moreover, at best it establishes only a tenuous probability for belief that we can hardly help but consider certainly true and indispensable.

The problem of reconstructing the rational basis of our unavoidable belief in other minds is still a perplexing one a century after Mill. Sydney Shoemaker of Cornell University has contributed specifically for this volume an account of the sources of the problem, the most famous solutions to it (including that of J. S. Mill), and an evaluation of their strengths and weaknesses. This leads him to a discussion of analogical reasoning (and inductive inference generally), the notion of privacy (and the "privileged access" persons are said to have to the contents of their own minds), the possibility that more than one mind or person might possess a given body, the doctrine called "logical behaviorism," and questions in the philosophy of perception.

The issue between rationalism and empiricism can be put very precisely, indeed even pithily, in a single short question: Are there any synthetic a priori propositions? Are there any general statements we can know with perfect certainty to be true prior to an examination of all (or even many) of the cases to which they apply? We cannot know for certain that *all kittens are playful* without checking each and every kitten, because, for all we know, we may one day discover a non-playful kitten. Without making any investigation, on the other hand, we can know that *all kittens are young cats;* for this is a necessary truth—one we can know, so to speak, without leaving our armchairs. But then, necessary though it be, it is perfectly trivial; it tells us nothing at all about kittens, since it is true not by virtue of some *fact* about kittens, but rather by virtue of what we *mean* by the word "kitten." Are there, then, any general propositions that are necessary (a priori) yet genuinely informative (synthetic)? The most famous affirmative answer to this question was that of the great German philosopher, Immanuel Kant (1724–1804). Kant never doubted that the propositions of mathematics and the basic principles of physical science are synthetic a priori, but he was convinced by Hume that the necessity and universality of a priori knowledge cannot be derived from sense experience which entitles us only to believe that so far as we have observed up to now there have been no exceptions to various regularities. The main problem of Kant's philosophy, posed and explained in the Introduction (repinted here) to his *Critique of Pure Reason,* is "How are synthetic a priori judgments possible?" In the major part of his *Critique,* Kant argues that necessity is imposed by the mind on the raw data of experience, a process which can reveal to us not the character of an independent reality, but rather the structure of the human understanding itself. A. J. Ayer, a twentieth-century follower of Hume, does not share Kant's initial assumption that there are synthetic a priori judgments, and argues for an empiricist interpretation of the propositions of mathematics and physics.

It is often said that *pragmatism,* the distinctively American contribution to the history of philosophy, is a third major theory of knowledge—even though its "founder," Charles Saunders Peirce (1839–1914), and its leading early spokesmen, William James (1842–1910) and John Dewey (1859–1952), were somewhat more modest in their claims for it. James, in his essay included here, treats the pragmatic maxim as a precise statement of the method actually employed by the great British empiricists. A phenomenalist like Mill, for example, makes implicit use of it in his interpretation of what we must *mean* when we say that a desk exists even when unperceived. What is the "cash value for experience" (in James's famous phrase) of such a statement? Only that *if* someone were to look in a certain office at a certain time, he would have certain desk-like *experiences.* And Berkeley, in rejecting the concept of a material substratum as strictly meaningless, makes implicit use of James's principle that "every difference must make a difference" for experience. Paul Henle, in his essay on James, finds two forms of James's theory of meaning, one "tough-minded" and the other "tender-minded," running through all of his writings.

RENÉ DESCARTES

Meditations on First Philosophy*

SYNOPSIS OF THE SIX
FOLLOWING MEDITATIONS

In the first Meditation I set forth the reasons for which we may, generally speaking, doubt about all things and especially about material things, at least so long as we have no other foundations for the sciences than those which we have hitherto possessed. But although the utility of a Doubt which is so general does not at first appear, it is at the same time very great, inasmuch as it delivers us from every kind of prejudice, and sets out for us a very simple way by which the mind may detach itself from the senses; and finally it makes it impossible for us ever to doubt those things which we have once discovered to be true.

In the second Meditation, mind, which making use of liberty which pertains to it, takes for granted that all those things of whose existence it has the least doubt, are non-existent, recognises that it is however absolutely impossible that it does not itself exist. This point is likewise of the greatest moment, inasmuch as by this means a distinction is easily drawn between the things which pertain to mind—that is to say to the intellectual nature—and those which pertain to body.

But because it may be that some expect from me in this place a statement of the reasons establishing the immortality of the soul, I feel that I should here make known to them that having

aimed at writing nothing in all this Treatise of which I do not possess very exact demonstrations, I am obliged to follow a similar order to that made use of by the geometers, which is to begin by putting forward as premises all those things upon which the proposition that we seek depends, before coming to any conclusion regarding it. Now the first and principal matter which is requisite for thoroughly understanding the immortality of the soul is to form the clearest possible conception of it, and one which will be entirely distinct from all the conceptions which we may have of body; and in this Meditation this has been done. In addition to this it is requisite that we may be assured that all the things which we conceive clearly and distinctly are true in the very way in which we think them; and this could not be proved previously to the Fourth Meditation. Further we must have a distinct conception of corporeal nature, which is given partly in this Second, and partly in the Fifth and Sixth Meditations. And finally we should conclude from all this, that those things which we conceive clearly and distinctly as being diverse substances, as we regard mind and body to be, are really substances essentially distinct one from the other; and this is the conclusion of the Sixth Meditation. This is further confirmed in this same Meditation by the fact that we cannot conceive of body excepting in so far as it is divisible, while the mind cannot be conceived of excepting as indivisible. For we are not able to conceive of the half of a mind as we can do of the smallest of all bodies; so that we see

René Descartes, *Meditations on First Philosophy,* trans. Elizabeth Haldane and G. R. T. Ross (London: Cambridge University Press, 1931). Reprinted by permission of the publisher. First published in Latin in 1641.

that not only are their natures different but even in some respects contrary to one another. I have not however dealt further with this matter in this treatise, both because what I have said is sufficient to show clearly enough that the extinction of the mind does not follow from the corruption of the body, and also to give men the hope of another life after death, as also because the premises from which the immortality of the soul may be deduced depend on an elucidation of a complete system of Physics. This would mean to establish in the first place that all substances generally—that is to say all things which cannot exist without being created by God—are in their nature incorruptible, and that they can never cease to exist unless God, in denying to them his concurrence, reduce them to nought; and secondly that body, regarded generally, is a substance, which is the reason why it also cannot perish, but that the human body, inasmuch as it differs from other bodies, is composed only of a certain configuration of members and of other similar accidents, while the human mind is not similarly composed of any accidents, but is a pure substance. For although all the accidents of mind be changed, although, for instance, it think certain things, will others, perceive others, etc., despite all this it does not emerge from these changes another mind: the human body on the other hand becomes a different thing from the sole fact that the figure or form of any of its portions is found to be changed. From this it follows that the human body may indeed easily enough perish, but the mind [or soul of man (I make no distinction between them)] is owing to its nature immortal.

In the third Meditation it seems to me that I have explained at sufficient length the principal argument of which I make use in order to prove the existence of God. But none the less, because I did not wish in that place to make use of any comparisons derived from corporeal things, so as to withdraw as much as I could the minds of readers from the senses, there may perhaps have remained many obscurities which, however, will, I hope, be entirely removed by the Replies which I have made to the Objections which have been set before me. Amongst others there is, for example, this one, 'How the idea in us of a being supremely perfect possesses so much objective reality (that is to say participates by representation in so many degrees of being and perfection)

that it necessarily proceeds from a cause which is absolutely perfect.' This is illustrated in these Replies by the comparison of a very perfect machine, the idea of which is found in the mind of some workman. For as the objective contrivance of this idea must have some cause, i.e. either the science of the workman or that of some other from whom he has received the idea, it is similarly impossible that the idea of God which is in us should not have God himself as its cause.

In the fourth Meditation it is shown that all these things which we very clearly and distinctly perceive are true, and at the same time it is explained in what the nature of error or falsity consists. This must of necessity be known both for the confirmation of the preceding truths and for the better comprehension of those that follow. (But it must meanwhile be remarked that I do not in any way there treat of sin—that is to say of the error which is committed in the pursuit of good and evil, but only of that which arises in the deciding between the true and the false. And I do not intend to speak of matters pertaining to the Faith or the conduct of life, but only of those which concern speculative truths, and which may be known by the sole aid of the light of nature.)

In the fifth Meditation corporeal nature generally is explained, and in addition to this the existence of God is demonstrated by a new proof in which there may possibly be certain difficulties also, but the solution of these will be seen in the Replies to the Objections. And further I show in what sense it is true to say that the certainty of geometrical demonstrations is itself dependent on the knowledge of God.

Finally in the Sixth I distinguish the action of the understanding *intellectio* from that of the imagination [imaginatio]; the marks by which this distinction is made are described. I here show that the mind of man is really distinct from the body, and at the same time that the two are so closely joined together that they form, so to speak, a single thing. All the errors which proceed from the senses are then surveyed, while the meaning of avoiding them are demonstrated, and finally all the reasons from which we may deduce the existence of material things are set forth. Not that I judge them to be very useful in establishing that which they prove, to wit, that there is in truth a world, that men possess bodies, and other such things which never have been doubted by anyone of sense; but because in considering these closely we come to see that they are neither so strong nor so evident as those arguments which lead us to the knowledge of our mind and of God; so that these last must be the most certain and most evident facts which can fall within the cognizance of the human mind. And this is the whole matter that I have tried to prove in these Meditations, for which reason I here omit to speak of many other questions with which I dealt incidentally in this discussion.

MEDITATION I

Of the things which may be brought within the sphere of the doubtful.

It is now some years since I detected how many were the false beliefs that I had from my earliest youth admitted as true, and how doubtful was everything I had since constructed on this basis; and from that time I was convinced that I must once for all seriously undertake to rid myself of all the opinions which I had formerly accepted, and commence to build anew from the foundation, if I wanted to establish any firm and permanent structure in the sciences. But as this enterprise appeared to be a very great one, I waited until I had attained an age so mature that I could not hope that at any later date I should be better fitted to execute my design. This reason caused me to delay so long that I should feel that I was doing wrong were I to occupy in deliberation the time that yet remains to me for action. To-day, then, since very opportunely for the plan I have in view I have delivered my mind from every care [and am happily agitated by no passions] and since I have procured for myself an assured leisure in a peaceable retirement, I shall at last seriously and freely address myself to the general upheaval of all my former opinions.

Now for this object it is not necessary that I should show that all of these are false—I shall perhaps never arrive at this end. But inasmuch as reason already persuades me that I ought no less carefully to withhold my assent from matters which are not entirely certain and indubitable than from those which appear to me manifestly to be false, if I am able to find in each one some reason to doubt, this will suffice to justify my rejecting the whole. And for that end it will not be requisite that I should examine each in particular, which would be an endless undertaking; for owing to the fact that the destruction of the foundations of necessity brings with it the downfall of the rest of the edifice, I shall only in the first place attack those principles upon which all my former opinions rested.

All that up to the present time I have accepted as most true and certain I have learned either from the senses or through the senses; but it is sometimes proved to me that these senses are deceptive, and it is wiser not to trust entirely to any thing by which we have once been deceived.

But it may be that although the senses sometimes deceive us concerning things which are hardly perceptible, or very far away, there are yet many others to be met with as to which we cannot reasonably have any doubt, although we recognize them by their means. For example, there is the fact that I am here, seated by the fire, attired in a dressing gown, having this paper in my hands and other similar matters. And how could I deny that these hands and this body are mine, were it not perhaps that I compare myself to certain persons, devoid of sense, whose cerebella are so troubled and clouded by the violent vapours of black bile, that they constantly assure us that they think they are kings when they are really quite poor, or that they are clothed in purple when they are really without covering, or who imagine that they have an earthenware head or are nothing but pumpkins or are made of glass. But they are mad, and I should not be any the less insane were I to follow examples so extravagant.

At the same time I must remember that I am a man, and that consequently I am in the habit of sleeping, and in my dreams representing to myself the same things or sometimes even less probable things, than do those who are insane in their waking moments. How often has it happened to me that in the night I dreamt that I found myself in this particular place, that I was dressed and seated near the fire, whilst in reality I was lying undressed in bed! At this moment it does indeed seem to me that it is with eyes awake that I am looking at this paper; that this head which I move is not asleep, that it is deliberately and of set purpose that I extend my hand and perceive it; what happens in sleep does not appear so clear nor so distinct as does all this. But in thinking over this I remind myself that on many occasions I have in sleep been deceived by similar illusions, and in dwelling carefully on this reflection I see so manifestly that there are no certain indications by which we may clearly distinguish wakefulness from sleep that I am lost in astonishment. And my astonishment is such that it is almost capable of persuading me that I now dream.

Now let us assume that we are asleep and that all these particulars, e.g. that we open our eyes, shake our head, extend our hands, and so on, are but false delusions; and let us reflect that possibly neither our hands nor our whole body are such as they appear to us to be. At the same time we must at least confess that the things which are represented to us in sleep are like painted representations which can only have been formed as the counterparts of something real and true, and that in this way those general things at least, i.e. eyes, a head, hands, and a whole body, are not imaginary things, but things really existent. For, as a matter of fact, painters, even when they study with the greatest skill to represent sirens and satyrs by forms the most strange and extraordinary, cannot give them natures which are entirely new, but merely make a certain medley of the members of different animals; or if their imagination is extravagant enough to invent something so novel that nothing similar has ever before been seen, and that then their work represents a thing purely fictitious and absolutely false, it is certain all the same that the colours of which this is composed are necessarily real. And for the same reason, although these general things, to wit, [a body,] eyes, a head, hands, and such like, may be imaginary, we are bound at the same time to confess that there are at least some other objects yet more simple and more universal, which are real and true; and of these just in the same way as with certain real colours, all these images of things which dwell in our thoughts, whether true and real or false and fantastic, are formed.

To such a class of things pertains corporeal nature in general, and its extension, the figure of extended things, their quantity or magnitude and number, as also the place in which they are, the time which measures their duration, and so on.

That is possibly why our reasoning is not unjust when we conclude from this that Physics, Astronomy, Medicine and all other sciences which have as their end the consideration of composite things, are very dubious uncertain; but that Arithmetic, Geometry and other sciences of that kind which only treat of things that are very simple and very general, without taking great trouble to ascertain whether they are actually existent or not, contain some measure of certainty and an element of the indubitable. For whether I am awake or asleep, two and three together always form five, and the square can never have more than four sides, and it does not seem possible that truths so clear and apparent can be suspected of any falsity [or uncertainty].

Nevertheless I have long had fixed in my mind the belief that an all-powerful God existed by whom I have been created such as I am. But how do I know that He has not brought it to pass that there is no earth, no heaven, no extended body, no magnitude, no place, and that nevertheless [I possess the perceptions of all these things and that] they seem to me to exist just exactly as I now see them? And, besides, as I sometimes imagine that others deceive themselves in the things which they think they know best, how do I know that I am not deceived every time that I add two and three, or count the sides of a square, or judge of things yet simpler, if anything simpler can be imagined? But possibly God has not desired that I should be thus deceived, for He is said to be supremely good. If, however, it is contrary to His goodness to have made me such that I constantly deceive myself, it would also appear to be contrary to His goodness to permit me to be sometimes deceived, and nevertheless I cannot doubt that He does permit this.

There may indeed be those who would prefer to deny the existence of a God so powerful, rather than believe that all other things are uncertain. But let us not oppose them for the present, and grant that all that is here said of a God is a fable; nevertheless in whatever way they suppose that I have arrived at the state of being tha⸱ I have reached—whether they attribute it to fate or to accident, or make out that it is by a continual succession of antecedents, or by some other method—since to err and deceive oneself is a defect, it is clear that the greater will be the probability of my being so imperfect as to deceive myself ever, as is the Author to whom they assign my origin the less powerful. To these reasons I have certainly nothing to reply, but at the end I feel constrained to confess that there is nothing in all that I formerly believed to be true, of which

I cannot in some measure doubt, and that not merely through want of thought or through levity, but for reasons which are very powerful and maturely considered; so that henceforth I ought not the less carefully refrain from giving credence to these opinions than to that which is manifestly false, if I desire to arrive at any certainty [in the sciences].

But it is not sufficient to have made these remarks, we must also be careful to keep them in mind. For these ancient and commonly held opinions still revert frequently to my mind, long and familiar custom having given them the right to occupy my mind against my inclination and rendered them almost masters of my belief; nor will I ever lose the habit of deferring to them or of placing my confidence in them, so long as I consider them as they really are, i.e. opinions in some measure doubtful, as I have just shown, and at the same time highly probable, so that there is much more reason to believe in than to deny them. That is why I consider that I shall not be acting amiss, if, taking of set purpose a contrary belief, I allow myself to be deceived, and for a certain time pretend that all these opinions are entirely false and imaginary, until at last, having thus balanced my former prejudices with my latter [so that they cannot divert my opinions more to one side than to the other], my judgment will no longer be dominated by bad usage or turned away from the right knowledge of the truth. For I am assured that there can be neither peril nor error in this course, and that I cannot at present yield too much to distrust, since I am not considering the question of action, but only of knowledge.

I shall then suppose, not that God who is supremely good and the fountain of truth, but some evil genius not less powerful than deceitful, has employed his whole energies in deceiving me; I shall consider that the heavens, the earth, colours, figures, sound, and all other external things are nought but the illusions and dreams of which this genius has availed himself in order to lay traps for my credulity; I shall consider myself as having no hands, no eyes, no flesh, no blood, nor any senses, yet falsely believing myself to possess all these things; I shall remain obstinately attached to this idea, and if by this means it is not in my power to arrive at the knowledge of any truth, I may at least do what is in my power [i.e.

suspend my judgment], and with firm purpose avoid giving credence to any false thing, or being imposed upon by this arch deceiver, however powerful and deceptive he may be. But this task is a laborious one, and insensibly a certain lassitude leads me into the course of my ordinary life. And just as a captive who in sleep enjoys an imaginary liberty, when he begins to suspect that his liberty is but a dream, fears to awaken, and conspires with these agreeable illusions that the deception may be prolonged, so insensibly of my own accord I fall back into my former opinions, and I dread awkening from this slumber, lest the laborious wakefulness which would follow the tranquility of this repose should have to be spent not in daylight, but in the excessive darkness of the difficulties which have just been discussed.

MEDITATION II

Of the Nature of the Human Mind; and that it is more easily known than the Body.

The Meditation of yesterday filled my mind with so many doubts that it is no longer in my power to forget them. And yet I do not see in what manner I can resolve them; and, just as if I had all of a sudden fallen into very deep water, I am so disconcerted that I can neither make certain of setting my feet on the bottom, nor can I swim and so support myself on the surface. I shall nevertheless make an effort and follow anew the same path as that on which I yesterday entered, i.e. I shall proceed by setting aside all that in which the least doubt could be supposed to exist, just as if I had discovered that it was absolutely false; and I shall never follow in this road until I have met with something which is certain, or at least, if I can do nothing else, until I have learned for certain that there is nothing in the world that is certain. Archimedes, in order that he might draw the terrestrial globe out of its place, and transport it elsewhere, demanded only that one point should be fixed and immoveable; in the same way I shall have the right to conceive high hopes if I am happy enough to discover one thing only which is certain and indubitable.

I suppose, then, that all the things that I see are false; I persuade myself that nothing has ever existed of all that my fallacious memory represents to me. I consider that I possess no senses; I imagine that body, figure, extension, movement and place are but the fictions of my mind. What, then, can be esteemed as true? Perhaps nothing at all, unless that there is nothing in the world that is certain.

But how can I know there is not something different from those things that I have just considered, of which one cannot have the slightest doubt? Is there not some God, or some other being by whatever name we call it, who puts these reflections into my mind? That is not necessary, for it is not possible that I am capable of producing them myself? I myself, am I not at least something? But I have already denied that I had senses and body. Yet I hesitate, for what follows from that? Am I so dependent on body and senses that I cannot exist without these? But I was persuaded that there was nothing in all the world, that there was no heaven, no earth, that there were no minds, nor any bodies: was I not then likewise persuaded that I did not exist? Not at all; of a surety I myself did exist since I persuaded myself of something [or merely because I thought of something]. But there is some deceiver or other, very powerful and very cunning, who ever employs his ingenuity in deceiving me. Then without doubt I exist also if he deceives me, and let him deceive me as much as he will, he can never cause me to be nothing so long as I think that I am something. So that after having reflected well and carefully examined all things, we must come to the definite conclusion that this proposition: I am, I exist, is necessary true each time that I pronounce it, or that I mentally conceive it.

But I do not yet know clearly enough what I am, I who am certain that I am; and hence I must be careful to see that I do not imprudently take some other object in place of myself, and thus that I do not go astray in respect of this knowledge that I hold to be the most certain and most evident of all that I have formerly learned. That is why I shall now consider anew what I believed myself to be before I embarked upon these last reflections; and of my former opinions I shall withdraw all that might even in a small degree be invalidated by the reasons which I have just brought forward, in order that there may be nothing at all left beyond what is absolutely certain and indubitable.

What then did I formerly believe myself to be? Undoubtedly I believed myself to be a man. But what is a man? Shall I say a reasonable animal? Certainly not; for then I should have to inquire what an animal is, and what is reasonable; and thus from a single question I should insensibly fall into an infinitude of others more difficult; and I should not wish to waste the little time and leisure remaining to me in trying to unravel subtleties like these. But I shall rather stop here to consider the thoughts which of themselves spring up in my mind, and which were not inspired by anything beyond my own nature alone when I applied myself to the consideration of my being. In the first place, then, I considered myself as having a face, hands, arms, and all that system of members composed of bones and flesh as seen in a corpse which I designated by the name of body. In addition to this I considered that I was nourished, that I walked, that I felt, and that I thought, and I referred all these actions to the soul: but I did not stop to consider what the soul was, or if I did stop. I imagined that it was something extremely rare and subtle like a wind, a flame, or an ether, which was spread throughout my grosser parts. As to body I had no manner of doubt about its nature, but thought I had a very clear knowledge of it; and if I had desired to explain it according to the notions that I had then formed of it, I should have described it thus: By the body I understand all that which can be defined by a certain figure: something which can be confined in a certain place, and which can fill a given space in such a way that every other body will be excluded from it; which can be perceived either by touch, or by sight, or by hearing, or by taste, or by smell: which can be moved in many ways not, in truth, by itself, but by something which is foreign to it, by which it is touched [and from which it receives impressions]: for to have the power of self-movement, as also of feeling or of thinking, I did not consider to appertain to the nature of body: on the contrary, I was rather astonished to find that faculties similar to them existed in some bodies.

But what am I, now that I suppose that there is a certain genius which is extremely powerful, and, if I may say so, malicious, who employs all his powers in deceiving me? Can I affirm that I possess the least of all those things which I have just said pertain to the nature of body? I pause to consider, I revolve all these things in my mind, and I find none of which I can say that it pertains to me. It would be tedious to stop to enumerate them. Let us pass to the attributes of soul and see if there is any one which is in me? What of nutrition of walking [the first mentioned]? But if it is so that I have no body it is also true that I can neither walk nor take nourishment. Another attribute is sensation. But one cannot feel without body, and besides I have thought I perceived many things during sleep that I recognised in my waking moments as not having been experienced at all. What of thinking? I find here that thought is an attribute that belongs to me; it alone cannot be separated from me. I am, I exist, that is certain. But how often? Just when I think; for it might possibly be the case if I ceased entirely to think, that I should likewise cease altogether to exist. I do not now admit anything which is not necessarily true: to speak accurately I am not more than a thing which thinks, that is to say a mind or a soul, or an understanding, or a reason, which are terms whose significance was formerly unknown to me. I am, however, a real thing and really exist; but what thing? I have answered: a thing which thinks.

And what more? I shall exercise my imagination [in order to see if I am not something more]. I am not a collection of members which we call the human body: I am not a subtle air distributed through these members, I am not a wind, a fire, a vapour, a breath, or anything at all which I can imagine or conceive; because I have assumed that all these were nothing. Without changing that supposition I find that I only leave myself certain of the fact that I am somewhat. But perhaps it is true that these same things which I supposed were non-existent because they are unknown to me, are really not different from the self which I know. I am not sure about this, I shall not dispute about it now; I can only give judgment on things that are known to me. I know that I exist, and I inquire what I am, I whom I know to exist. But it is very certain that the knowledge of my existence taken in its precise significance does not depend on things whose existence is not yet known to me; consequently it does not depend on those which I can feign in imagination. And indeed the very term *feign* in imagination proves to me my error, for I really do this if I image myself a something, since to imagine is nothing else than to contemplate the figure or image of a corporeal thing. But I already know for certain that I am, and that it may be that all these images, and,

speaking generally, all things that relate to the nature of body are nothing but dreams [and chimeras]. For this reason I see clearly that I have as little reason to say, 'I shall stimulate my imagination in order to know more distinctly what I am,' than if I were to say, 'I am now awake, and I perceive somewhat that is real and true: but because I do not yet perceive it distinctly enough, I shall go to sleep of express purpose, so that my dreams may represent the perception with greatest truth and evidence.' And, thus, I know for certain that nothing of all that I can understand by means of my imagination belongs to this knowledge which I have of myself, and that it is necessary to recall the mind from this mode of thought with the utmost diligence in order that it may be able to know its own nature with perfect distinctness.

But what then am I? A thing which thinks. What is a thing which thinks? It is a thing which doubts, understands, [conceives,] affirms, denies, wills, refuses, which also imagines and feels.

Certainly it is no small matter if all these things pertain to my nature. But why should they not so pertain? Am I not that being who now doubts nearly everything, who nevertheless understands certain things, who affirms that one only is true, who denies all the others, who desires to know more, is averse from being deceived, who imagines many things, sometimes indeed despite his will, and who perceives many likewise, as by the intervention of the bodily organs? Is there nothing in all this which is as true as it is certain that I exist, even though I should always sleep and though he who has given me being employed all his ingenuity in deceiving me? Is there likewise any one of these attributes which can be distinguished from my thought, or which might be said to be separated from myself? For it is so evident of itself that it is I who doubts, who understands, and who desires, that there is no reason here to add anything to explain it. And I have certainly the power of imagining likewise; for although it may happen (as I formerly supposed) that none of the things which I imagine are true, nevertheless this power of imagining does not cease to be really in use, and it forms part of my thought. Finally, I am the same who feels, that is to say, who perceives certain things, as by the organs of sense, since in truth I see light, I hear noise, I feel heat. But it will be said that these phenomena are false and that I am dreaming. Let it be so; still it is at least quite certain that it seems to me that I see light, that I hear noise and that I feel heat. That cannot be false; properly speaking it is what is in me called feeling; and used in this precise sense that is no other thing than thinking.

From this time I begin to know what I am with a little more clearness and distinction than before; but nevertheless it still seems to me, and I cannot prevent myself from thinking, that corporeal things, whose images are framed by thought, which are tested by the senses, are much more distinctly known than that obscure part of me which does not come under the imagination. Although really it is very strange to say that I know and understand more distinctly these things whose existence seems to me dubious, which are unknown to me, and which do not belong to me, than others of the truth of which I am convinced, which arc known to me and which pertain to my real nature, in a word, than myself. But I see clearly how the case stands: my mind loves to wander, and cannot yet suffer itself to be retained within the just limits of truth. Very good, let us once more give it the freest rein, so that, when afterwards we seize the proper occasion for pulling up, it may the more easily be regulated and controlled.

Let us begin by considering the commonest matters, those which we believe to be the most distinctly comprehended, to wit, the bodies which we touch and see; not indeed bodies in general, for these general ideas are usually a little more confused, but let us consider one body in particular. Let us take, for example, this piece of wax: it has been taken quite freshly from the hive, and it has not yet lost the sweetness of the honey which it contains; it still retains somewhat of the odour of the flowers from which it has been culled; its colour, its figure, its size are apparent; it is hard, cold, easily handled, and if you strike it with the finger, it will emit a sound. Finally all the things which are requisite to cause us distinctly to recognise a body, are met with in it. But notice that while I speak and approach the fire what remained of the taste is exhaled, the smell evaporates, the colour alters, the figure is destroyed, the size increases, it becomes liquid, it heats, scarcely can one handle it, and when one strikes it, no sound is emitted. Does the same wax remain after this change? We must confess that it

remains; none would judge otherwise. What then did I know so distinctly in this piece of wax? It could certainly be nothing of all that the senses brought to my notice, since all these things which fall under taste, smell, sight, touch, and hearing, are found to be changed, and yet the same wax remains.

Perhaps it was what I now think, viz, that this wax was not that sweetness of honey, nor that agreeable scent of flowers, nor that particular whiteness, nor that figure, nor that sound, but simply a body which a little while before appeared to me as perceptible under these forms, and which is now perceptible under others. But what, precisely, is it that I imagine when I form such conceptions? Let us attentively consider this, and, abstracting from all that does not belong to the wax, let us see what remains. Certainly nothing remains excepting a certain extended thing which is flexible and movable. But what is the meaning of flexible and movable? Is it not that I imagine that this piece of wax being round is capable of becoming square and of passing from a square to a triangular figure? No, certainly it is not that, since I imagine it admits of an infinitude of similar changes, and I nevertheless do not know how to compass the infinitude by my imagination, and consequently this conception which I have of the wax is not brought about by the faculty of imagination. What now is this extension? Is it not also unknown? For it becomes greater when the wax is melted, greater when it is boiled, and greater still when the heat increases; and I should not conceive [clearly] according to truth what wax is, if I did not think that even this piece that we are considering is capable of receiving more variations in extension than I have ever imagined. We must then grant that I could not even understand through the imagination what this piece of wax is, and that it is my mind alone which perceives it. I say this piece of wax in particular, for as to wax in general it is yet clearer. But what is this piece of wax which cannot be understood excepting by the [understanding or] mind? It is certainly the same that I see, touch, imagine, and finally it is the same which I have always believed it to be from the beginning. But what must particularly be observed is that its perception is neither an act of vision, nor of touch, nor of imagination, and has never been such although it may have appeared formerly to be so, but only an intuition of the mind, which may be imperfect and confused as it was formerly, or clear and distinct as it is at present, according as my attention is more or less directed to the elements which are found in it, and of which it is composed.

Yet in the meantime I am greatly astonished when I consider [the great feebleness of mind] and its proneness to fall [insensibly] into error; for although without giving expression to my thoughts I consider all this in my own mind, words often impede me and I am almost deceived by the terms of ordinary language. For we say that we see the same wax, if it is present, and not that we simply judge that it is the same from its having the same colour and figure. From this I should conclude that I knew the wax by means of vision and not simply by the intuition of the mind; unless by chance I remember that, when looking from a window and saying I see men who pass in the street, I really do not see them, but infer that what I see is men, just as I say that I see wax. And yet what do I see from the window but hats and coats which may cover automatic machines? Yet I judge these to be men. And similarly solely by the faculty of judgment which rests in my mind, I comprehend that which I believed I saw with my eyes.

A man who makes it his aim to raise his knowledge above the common should be ashamed to derive the occasion for doubting from the forms of speech invented by the vulgar; I prefer to pass on and consider whether I had a more evident and perfect conception of what the wax was when I first perceived it, and when I believed I knew it by means of the external senses or at least by the common sense as it is called, that is to say by the imaginative faculty, or whether my present conception is clearer now that I have most carefully examined what it is, and in what way it can be known. It would certainly be absurd to doubt as to this. For what was there in this first perception which was distinct? What was there which might not as well have been perceived by any of the animals? But when I distinguish the wax from its external forms, and when, just as if I had taken from it its vestments, I consider it quite naked, it is certain that although some error may still be found in my judgment, I can nevertheless not perceive it thus without a human mind.

But finally what shall I say of this mind, that is, of myself, for up to this point I do not admit in myself anything but mind? What then, I who seem to perceive this piece of wax so distinctly, do I not know myself, not only with much more truth and certainty, but also with much more distinctness and clearness? For if I judge that the wax is or exists from the fact that I see it, it certainly follows much more clearly that I am or that I exist myself from the fact that I see it. For it may be that what I see is not really wax, it may also be that I do not possess eyes with which to see anything; but it cannot be that when I see, or (for I no longer take account of the distinction) when I think I see, that I myself who think am nought. So if I judge that the wax exists from the fact that I touch it, the same thing will follow, to wit, that I am; and if I judge that my imagination, or some other cause, whatever it is, persuades me that wax exists, I shall still conclude the same. And what I have here remarked of wax may be applied to all other things which are external to me [and which are met with outside of me]. And further, if the [notion or] perception of wax has seemed to me clearer and more distinct, not only after the sight or the touch, but also after many other causes have rendered it quite manifest to me, with how much more [evidence] and distinctness must it be said that I now know myself, since all the reasons which contribute to the knowledge of wax, or any other body whatever, are yet better proofs of the nature of my mind! And there are so many other things in the mind itself which may contribute to the elucidation of its nature, that those which depend on body such as these just mentioned, hardly merit being taken into account.

But finally here I am, having insensibly reverted to the point I desired, for, since it is now manifest to me that even bodies are not properly speaking known by the senses or by the faculty of imagination, but by the understanding only, and since they are not known from the fact that they are seen or touched, but only because they are understood, I see clearly that there is nothing which is easier for me to know than my mind. But because it is difficult to rid oneself so promptly of an opinion to which one was accustomed for so long, it will be well that I should halt a little at this point, so that by the length of my meditation I may more deeply imprint on my memory this new knowledge.

MEDITATION III
Of God: That He exists.

I shall now close my eyes, I shall stop my ears, I shall call away all my senses, I shall efface even from my thoughts all the images of corporeal things, or at least (for that is hardly possible) I shall esteem them as vain and false; and thus holding converse only with myself and considering my own nature, I shall try little by little to reach a better knowledge of a more familiar acquaintanceship with myself. I am a thing that thinks, that is to say, that doubts, affirms, denies, that knows a few things, that is ignorant of many [that loves, that hates], that wills, that desires, that also imagines and perceives; for as I remarked before, although the things which I perceive and imagine are perhaps nothing at all apart from me and in themselves, I am nevertheless assured that these modes of thought that I call perceptions and imaginations, inasmuch only as they are modes of thought, certainly reside [and are met with] in me.

And in the little that I have just said, I think I have summed up all that I really know, or at least all that hitherto I was aware that I knew. In order to try to extend my knowledge further, I shall now look around more carefully and see whether I cannot still discover in myself some other things which I have not hitherto perceived. I am certain that I am a thing which thinks; but do I not then likewise know what is requisite to render me certain of a truth? Certainly in this first knowledge there is nothing that assures me of its truth, excepting the clear and distinct perception of that which I state, which would not indeed suffice to assure me that what I say is true, if it could ever happen that a thing which I conceived so clearly and distinctly could be false; and accordingly it seems to me that already I can establish as a general rule that all things which I perceive very clearly and very distinctly are true.

At the same time I have before received and admitted many things to be very certain and manifest, which yet I afterwards recognised as being dubious. What then were these things? They were the earth, sky, stars and all other objects which I apprehended by means of the senses. But what did I clearly [and distinctly] perceive in them? Nothing more than that the ideas or thoughts of these things were presented to my mind. And not even now do I deny that these ideas are met with in me. But there was yet another thing which I affirmed, and which, owing to the habit which I had formed of believing it, I thought I perceived very clearly, although in truth I did not perceive it at all, to wit, that these were objects outside of me from which these ideas proceeded, and to which they were entirely similar. And it was in this that I erred, or, if perchance my changement ws correct, this was not due to any knowledge arising from my perception.

But when I took anything very simple and easy in the sphere of arithmetic or geometry into consideration, e.g. that two and three together made five, and other things of the sort, were not these present to my mind so clearly as to enable me to affirm that they were true? Certainly if I judged that since such matters could be doubted, this would not have been so for any other reason than that it came into my mind that perhaps a God might have endowed me with such a nature that I may have been deceived even concerning things which seemed to me most manifest. But every time that this preconceived opinion of the sovereign power of a God presents itself to my thought, I am constrained to confess that it is easy to Him, if He wishes it, to cause me to err, even in matters in which I believe myself to have the best evidence. And, on the other hand, always when I direct my attention to things which I believe myself to perceive very clearly, I am so persuaded of their truth that I let myself break out into words such as these: Let who will deceive me, He can never cause me to be nothing while I think that I am, or some day cause it to be true to say that I have never been, it is being true now to say that I am, or that two and three make more or less than five, or any such thing in which I see a manifest contradiction. And, certainly, since I have no reason to believe that there is a God who is a deceiver, and as I have not yet satisfied myself that there is a God at all, the reason for doubt which depends on this opinion alone is very slight, and so to speak metaphysical. But in order to be able altogether to remove it, I must inquire whether there is a God as soon as the occasion presents itself; and if I find that there is a God, I must also inquire whether He may be a deceiver;

for without a knowledge of these two truths I do not see that I can ever be certain of anything.

And in order that I may have an opportunity of inquiring into this in an orderly way [without interrupting the order of meditation which I have proposed to myself, and which is little by little to pass from the notions which I find first of all in my mind to those which I shall later on discover in it] it is requisite that I should here divide my thoughts into certain kinds, and that I should consider in which of these kinds there is, properly speaking, truth or error to be found. Of my thoughts some are, so to speak, images of the things, and to these alone in the title 'idea' properly applied; examples are my thought of a man or of a chimera, of heaven, of an angel, or [even] of God. But other thoughts possess other form as well. For example in willing, fearing, approving, denying, though I always perceive something as the subject of the action of my mind; yet by this action I always add something else to the idea which I have of that thing; and of the thoughts of this kind some are called volitions or affections, and others judgments.

Now as to what concerns ideas, if we consider them only in themselves and do not relate them to anything else beyond themselves, they cannot properly speaking be false; for whether I imagine a goat or a chimera, it is not less true that I imagine the one than the other. We must not fear likewise that falsity can enter into will and into affections, for although I may desire evil things, or even things that never existed, it is not the less true that I desire them. Thus there remains no more than the judgments which we make, in which I must take the greatest care not to deceive myself. But the principal error and the commonest which we may meet with in them, consists in my judging that the ideas which are in me are similar or conformable to the things which are outside me; for without doubt if I considered the ideas only as certain modes of my thoughts, without trying to relate them to anything beyond, they could scarcely give me material for error.

But among these ideas, some appear to me to be innate, some adventitious, and others to be formed [or invented] by myself; for, as I have the power of understanding what is called a thing, or a truth, or a thought, it appears to me that I hold this power from no other source than my own nature. But if now hear some sound, if I see the sun, or feel heat, I have hitherto judged that these sensations proceeded from certain things that exist outside of me; and finally it appears to me that sirens, hippogryphs, and the like, are formed out of my own mind. But again I may possibly persuade myself that all these ideas are of the nature of those which I term adventitious, or else that they are all innate, or all fictitious: for I have not yet clearly discovered their true origin.

And my principal task in this place is to consider, in respect to those ideas which appear to me to proceed from certain objects that are outside me, what are the reasons which cause me to think them similar to these objects. It seems indeed in the first place that I am taught this lesson by nature; and, secondly, I experience in myself that these ideas do not depend on my will nor therefore on myself—for they often present themselves to my mind in spite of my will. Just now, for instance, whether I will or whether I do not will, I feel heat, and thus I persuade myself that this feeling, or at least this idea of heat, is produced in me by something which is different from me, i.e. by the heat of the fire near which I sit. And nothing seems to me more obvious than to judge that this object imprints its likeness rather than anything else upon me.

Now I must discover whether these proofs are sufficiently strong and convincing. When I say that I am so instructed by nature, I merely mean a certain spontaneous inclination which impels me to believe in this connection, and not a natural light which makes me recognise that it is true. But these two things are very different; for I cannot doubt that which the natural light causes me to believe to be true, as, for example, it has shown me that I am from the fact that I doubt, or other facts of the same kind. And I possess no other facts of the same kind. And I possess no other faculty whereby to distinguish truth from falsehood, which can teach me that what this light shows me to be true is not really true, and no other faculty that is equally truthworthy. But as far as [apparently] natural impulses are concerned, I have frequently remarked, when I had to make active choice between virtue and vice, that they often enough led me to the part that was worse; and this is why I do not see any reason for following them in what regards truth and error.

And as to the other reason, which is that these ideas must proceed from objects outside me, since they do not depend on my will, I do not find it any the more convincing. For just as these impulses of which I have spoken are found in me, notwithstanding that they do not always concur with my will, so perhaps there is in me some faculty fitted to produce these ideas without the assistance of any external things, even though it is not yet known by me; just as, apparently, they have hitherto always been found in me during sleep without the aid of any external objects.

And finally, though they did proceed from objects different from myself, it is not a necessary consequence that they should resemble these. On the contrary, I have noticed that in many cases there was a difference between the object and its idea. I find, for example, two completely diverse ideas of the sun in my mind; the one derives its origin from the senses, and should be placed in the category of adventitious ideas; according to this idea the sun seems to be extremely small; but the other is derived from astronomical reasonings, i.e. is elicited from certain notions that are innate in me, or else it is formed by me in some other manner; in accordance with it the sun appears to be several times greater than the earth. These two ideas cannot, indeed, both resemble the same sun, and reason makes me believe that the one which seems to have originated directly from the sun itself, is the one which is most dissimilar to it.

All this causes me to believe that until the present time it has not been by a judgment that was certain [or premeditated], but only by a sort of blind impulse that I believed that things existed outside of, and different from me, which, by the organs of my senses, or by some other method whatever it might be, conveyed these ideas or images to me [and imprinted on me their similitudes].

But there is yet another method of inquiring whether any of the objects of which I have ideas within me exist outside of me. If ideas are only taken as certain modes of thought, I recognize amongst them no difference or inequality, and all appear to proceed from me in the same manner; but when we consider them as images, one representing one thing and the other another, it is clear that they are very different one from the other. There is no doubt that those which represent to me substances are something more, and contain so to speak more objective reality within them

[that is to say, by representation participate in a higher degree of being or perfection] than those that simply represent modes or accidents; and that idea again by which I understand a supreme God, eternal, infinite, [immutable], omniscient, omnipotent, and Creator of all things which are outside of Himself, has certainly more objective reality in itself than those ideas by which finite substances are represented.

Now it is manifest by the natural light that there must at least be as much reality in the efficient and total cause as in its effect. For, pray, whence can the effect derive its reality, if not from its cause? And in what way can this cause communicate this reality to it, unless it possessed it in itself? And from this it follows, not only that something cannot proceed from nothing, but likewise that what is more perfect—that is to say, which has more reality within itself—cannot proceed from the less perfect. And this is not only evidently true of those effects which possess actual or formal reality, but also of the ideas in which we consider merely what is termed objective reality. To take an example, the stone which has not yet existed not only cannot now commence to be unless it has been produced by something which possesses within itself, either formally or eminently, all that enters into the composition of the stone [i.e. it must possess the same things or other more excellent things than those which exist in the stone] and heat can only be produced in a subject in which it did not previously exist by a cause that is of an order [degree or kind] at least as perfect as heat, and so in all other cases. But further, the idea of heat, or of a stone, cannot exist in me unless it has been placed within me by some cause which possesses within it at least as much reality as that which I conceive to exist in the heat or the stone. For although this cause does not transmit anything of its actual or formal reality to my idea, we must not for that reason imagine that it is necessarily a less real cause; we must remember that [since every idea is a work of the mind] its nature is such that it demands of itself no other formal reality than that which it borrows from my thought, of which it is only a mode [i.e. a manner or way of thinking]. But in order that an idea should contain some one certain objective reality rather than another, it must without doubt derive it from some cause in which there is at least as much formal reality as this idea contains of objective reality. For if we imagine that something is found in an idea which is not found in the cause, it must then have been derived from nought; but however imperfect may be this mode of being by which a thing is objectively [or by representation] in the understanding by its idea, we cannot certainly say that this mode of being is nothing, nor, consequently, that the idea derives its origin from nothing.

Nor must I imagine that, since the reality that I consider in these ideas is only objective, it is not essential that this reality should be formally in the causes of my ideas, but that it is sufficient that it should be found objectively. For just as this mode of objective existence pertains to ideas by their proper nature, so does the mode of formal existence pertain to the causes of those ideas (this is at least true of the first and principal) by the nature peculiar to them. And although it may be the case that one idea gives birth to another idea, that cannot continue to be so indefinitely; for in the end we must reach an idea whose cause shall be so to speak an archetype, in which the whole reality [or perfection] which is so to speak objectively [or by representation] in these ideas is contained formally [and really]. Thus the light of nature causes me to know clearly that the ideas in me are like [pictures or] images which can, in truth, easily fall short of the perfection of the objects from which they have been derived, but which can never contain anything greater or more perfect.

And the longer and the more carefully that I investigate these matters, the more clearly and distinctly do I recognise their truth. But what am I to conclude from it all in the end? It is this, that if the objective reality of any one of my ideas is of such a nature as clearly to make me recognise that it is not in me either formally or eminently, and that consequently I cannot myself be the cause of it, it follows of necessity that I am not alone in the world, but that there is another being which exists, or which is the cause of this idea. On the other hand, had no such an idea existed in me, I should have had no sufficient argument to convince me of the existence of any being beyond myself; for I have made very careful investigation everywhere and up to the present time have been able to find no other ground.

But of my ideas, beyond that which represents me to myself, as to which there can here be no difficulty, there is another which represents a God, and there are others representing corporeal and inanimate things, others angels, others animals, and others again which represent to me men similar to myself.

As regards the ideas which represent to me other men or animals, or angels, I can however easily conceive that they might be formed by an admixture of the other ideas which I have of myself, of corporeal things, and of God, even although there were apart from me neither men nor animals, nor angels, in all the world.

And in regard to the ideas of corporeal objects, I do not recognise in them anything so great or so excellent that they might not have possibly proceeded from myself; for if I consider them more closely, and examine them individually, as I yesterday examined the idea of wax, I find that there is very little in them which I perceive clearly and distinctly. Magnitude or extension in length, breadth, or depth, I do so perceive; also figure which results from a termination of this extension, the situation which bodies of different figure preserve in relation to one another, and movement or change of situation; to which we may also add substance, duration and number. As to other things such as light, colours, sounds, scents, tastes, heat, cold and the other tactile qualities, they are thought by me with so much obscurity and confusion that I do not even know if they are true or false, i.e. whether the ideas which I form of these qualities are actually the ideas of real objects or not [or whether they only represent chimeras which cannot exist in fact]. For although I have before remarked that it is only in judgments that falsity, properly speaking, or formal falsity, can be met with, a certain material falsity may nevertheless be found in ideas, i.e. when these ideas represent what is nothing as though it were something. For example, the ideas which I have of cold and heat are so far from clear and distinct that by their means I cannot tell whether cold is merely a privation of heat, or heat a privation of cold, or whether both are real qualities, or are not such. And inasmuch as [since ideas resemble images] there cannot be any ideas which do not appear to represent some things, if it is correct to say that cold is merely a privation of heat, the idea which represents it to me as something real and positive will not be improperly termed false, and the same holds good of other similar ideas.

To these it is certainly not necessary that I should attribute any author other than myself. For if they are false, i.e. if they represent things which do not exist, the light of nature shows me that they issue from nought, that is to say, that they are only in me in so far as something is lacking to the perfection of my nature. But if they are true, nevertheless because they exhibit so little reality to me that I cannot even clearly distinguish the thing represented from non-being, I do not see any reason why they should not be produced by myself.

As to the clear and distinct idea which I have of corporeal things, some of them seem as though I might have derived them from the idea which I possess of myself, as those which I have of substance, duration, number, and such like. For [even] when I think that a stone is a substance, or at least a thing capable of existing of itself, and that I am a substance also, although I conceive that I am a thing that thinks and not one that is extended, and that the stone on the other hand is an extended thing which does not think, and that thus there is a notable difference between the two conceptions—they seem, nevertheless, to agree in this, that both represent substances. In the same way, when I perceive that I now exist and further recollect that I have in former times existed, and when I remember that I have various thoughts of which I can recognize the number, I acquire ideas of duration and number which I can afterwards transfer to any object that I please. But as to all the other qualities of which the ideas of corporeal things are composed, to wit, extension, figure, situation and motion, it is true that they are not formally in me, since I am only a thing that thinks; but because they are merely certain modes of substance [and so to speak the vestments under which corporeal substance appears to us] and because I myself am also a substance, it would seem that they might be constrained in me eminently.

Hence there remains only the idea of God, concerning which we must consider whether it is something which cannot have proceeded from me myself. By the name God I understand a substance that is infinite [eternal, immutable], independent, all-knowing, all-powerful, and by which I myself and everything else, if anything else does exist, have been created. Now all these characteristics are such that the more diligently I attend to them, the less do they appear capable of proceeding from me alone; hence, from what has been already said, we must conclude that God necessarily exists.

For although the idea of substance is within me owing to the fact that I am substance, nevertheless I should not have the idea of an infinite substance—since I am finite—if it had not proceeded from some substance which was veritably infinite.

Nor should I imagine that I do not perceive the finite by a true idea, but only by the negation of the finite, just as I perceive repose and darkness by the negation of movement and of light; for, on the contrary, I see that there is manifestly more reality in infinite substance than in finite, and therefore that in some way I have in me the notion of the infinite earlier than the finite—to wit, the notion of God before that of myself. For how would it be possible that I should know that I doubt and desire, that is to say, that something is lacking to me, and that I am not quite perfect, unless I had within me some idea of a Being more perfect than myself, in comparison with which I should recognize the deficiencies of my nature?

And we cannot say that this idea of God is perhaps materially false and that consequently I can derive it from nought [i.e. that possibly it exists in me because I am imperfect], as I have just said is the case with ideas of heat, cold and other such things; for, on the contrary, as this idea is very clear and distinct and contains within it more objective reality than any other, there can be none which is of itself more true, nor any in which there can be less suspicion of falsehood. The idea, I say, of this Being who is absolutely perfect and infinite, is entirely true; for although, perhaps, we can imagine that such a Being does not exist, we cannot nevertheless imagine that His idea represents nothing real to me, as I have said of the idea of cold. This idea is also very clear and distinct; since all that I conceive clearly and distinctly of the real and the true, and of what conveys some perfection, is in its entirety contained in this idea. And this does not cease to be true although I do not comprehend the infinite, or though in God there is an infinitude of things which I cannot comprehend, nor possibly even reach in any way by thought; for it is of the nature of the infinite that my nature, which is finite and limited, should not comprehend it; and it is sufficient that I should understand this, and that I should judge that all things which I clearly perceive and in which I know that there is some perfection, and possibly likewise an infinitude of properties of which I am ignorant, are in God formally or eminently, so that the idea which I have of Him may become the most true, most clear, and most distinct of all the ideas that are in my mind.

But possibly I am something more than I suppose myself to be, and perhaps all those perfections which I attribute to God are in some way potentially in me, although they do not yet disclose themselves, or issue in action. As a matter of fact I am already sensible that my knowledge increases [and perfects itself] little by little, and I see nothing which can prevent it from increasing more and more into infinitude; nor do I see, after it has thus been increased [or perfected], anything to prevent my being able to acquire by its means all the other perfections of the Divine nature; nor finally why the power I have of acquiring these perfections, if it really exist in me, shall not suffice to produce the ideas of them.

At the same time I recognize that this cannot be. For, in the first place, although it were true that every day my knowledge acquired new degrees of perfection, and that there were in my nature many things potentially which are not yet there actually, nevertheless these excellences do not pertain to [or make the smallest approach to] the idea which I have of God in whom there is nothing merely potential [but in whom all is present really and actually]; for it is an infallible token of imperfection in my knowledge that it increases little by little. And further, although my knowledge grows more and more, nevertheless I do not for that reason believe that it can ever be actually infinite, since it can never reach a point so high that it will be unable to attain to any greater increase. But I understand God to be actually infinite, so that He can add nothing to His supreme perfection. And finally I perceive that the objective being of an idea cannot be produced by a being that exists potentially only, which properly speaking is nothing, but only a being which is formal or actual.

To speak the truth, I see nothing in all that I have just said which by the light of nature is not manifest to anyone who desires to think atten-

tively on the subject; but when I slightly relax my attention, my mind, finding its vision somewhat obscured and so to speak blinded by the images of sensible objects, I do not easily recollect the reason why the idea that I possess of a being more perfect than I, must necessarily have been placed in me by a being which is really more perfect; and this is why I wish here to go on to inquire whether I, who have this idea, can exist if no such being exists.

And I ask, from whom do I then derive my existence? Perhaps from myself or from my parents, or from some other source less perfect than God; for we can imagine nothing more perfect than God, or even as perfect as He is.

But [were I independent of every other and] were I myself the author of my being, I should doubt nothing and I should desire nothing, and finally no perfection would be lacking to me; for I should have bestowed on myself every perfection of which I possessed any idea and should thus be God. And it must not be imagined that those things that are lacking to me are perhaps more difficult of attainment than those which I already possess; for, on the contrary, it is quite evident that it was a matter of much greater difficulty to bring to pass that I, that is to say, a thing or substance that thinks, should emerge out of nothing, than it would be to attain to the knowledge of many things of which I am ignorant, and which are only the accidents of this thinking substance. But it is clear that if I had of myself possessed this greater perfection of which I have just spoken [that is to say, if I had been the author of my own existence], I should not at least have denied myself the things which are the more easy to acquire [to wit, many branches of knowledge of which my nature is destitute]; nor should I have deprived myself of any of the things contained in the idea which I form of God, because there are none of them which seem to me specially difficult to acquire: and if there were any that were more difficult to acquire, they would certainly appear to me to be such (supposing I myself were the origin of the other things which I possess) since I should discover in them that my powers were limited.

But though I assumed that perhaps I have always existed just as I am at present, neither can I escape the force of this reasoning, and imagine that the conclusion to be drawn from this is, that

I need not seek for any author of my existence. For all the course of my life may be divided into an infinite number of parts, none of which is in any way dependent on the other; and thus from the fact that I was in existence a short time ago it does not follow that I must be in existence now, unless some cause at this instant, so to speak, produces me anew, that is to say, conserves me. It is as a matter of fact perfectly clear and evident to all those who consider with attention the nature of time, that, in order to be conserved in each moment in which it endures, a substance has need of the same power and action as would be necessary to produce and create it anew, supposing it did not yet exist, so that the life of nature shows us clearly that the distinction between creation and conservation is solely a distinction of the reason.

All that I thus require here is that I should interrogate myself, if I wish to know whether I possess a power which is capable of bringing it to pass that I who now am shall still be in the future; for since I am nothing but a thinking thing, or at least since thus far it is only this portion of myself which is precisely in question at present, if such a power did reside in me, I should certainly be conscious of it. But I am conscious of nothing of the kind, and by this I know clearly that I depend on some being different from myself.

Possibly, however, this being on which I depend is not that which I call God, and I am created either by my parents or by some other cause less perfect than God. This cannot be, because, as I have just said, it is perfectly evident that there must be at least as much reality in the cause as in the effect; and thus since I am a thinking thing, and possess an idea of God within me, whatever in the end be the cause assigned to my existence, it must be allowed that it is likewise a thinking thing and that it possesses in itself the idea of all the perfections which I attribute to God. We may again inquire whether this cause derives its origin from itself or from some other thing. For if from itself, if follows by the reasons before brought forward, that this cause must itself be God; for since it possesses the virtue of self-existence, it must also without doubt have the power of actually possessing all the perfections of which it has the idea, that is, all those which I conceive as existing in God. But if it derives its existence from some other cause than itself, we

shall again ask, for the same reason, whether this second cause exists by itself or through another, until from one step to another, we finally arrive at an ultimate cause, which will be God.

And it is perfectly manifest that in this there can be no regression into infinity, since what is in question is not so much the cause which formerly created me, as that which conserves me at the present time.

Nor can we suppose that several causes may have concurred in my production, and that from one I have received the idea of one of the perfections which I attribute to God, and from another the idea of some other, so that all these perfections indeed exist somewhere in the universe, but not as complete in one unity which is God. On the contrary, the unity, the simplicity or the inseparability of all things which are in God is one of the principal perfections which I conceive to be in Him. And certainly the idea of this unity of all Divine perfections cannot have been placed in me by any cause from which I have not likewise received the ideas of all the other perfections; for this cause could not make me able to comprehend them as joined together in an inseparable unity without having at the same time caused me in some measure to know what they are [and in some way to recognise each one of them].

Finally, so far as my parents [from whom it appears I have sprung] are concerned, although all that I have ever been able to believe of them were true, that does not make it follow that it is they who conserve me, nor are they even the authors of my being in any sense, in so far as I am a thinking being; since what they did was merely to implant certain dispositions in that matter in which the self—i.e. the mind, which alone I at present identify with myself—is by me deemed to exist. And thus there can be no difficulty in their regard, but we must of necessity conclude from the fact alone that I exist, or that the idea of a Being supremely perfect—that is of God—is in me, that the proof of God's existence is grounded on the highest evidence.

It only remains to me to examine into the manner in which I have acquired this idea from God; for I have not received it through the senses, and it is never presented to me unexpectedly, as is usual with the ideas of sensible things when these things present themselves, or seem to present themselves, to the external organs of my senses nor is it likewise a fiction of my mind, for it is not in my power to take from or to add anything to it; and consequently the only alternative is that it is innate in me, just as the idea of myself is innate in me.

And one certainly ought not to find it strange that God, in creating me, placed this idea within me to be like the mark of the workman imprinted on his work; and it is likewise not essential that the mark shall be something different from the work itself. For from the sole fact that God created me it is most probable that in some way he has placed his image and similitude upon me, and that I perceive this similitude (in which the idea of God is contained) by means of the same faculty by which I perceive myself—that is to say, when I reflect on myself I not only know that I am something [imperfect], incomplete and dependent on another, which incessantly aspires after something which is better and greater than myself, but I also know that He on whom I depend possesses in Himself all the great things towards which I aspire [and the ideas of which I find within myself], and that not indefinitely or potentially alone, but really, actually and infinitely; and that thus He is God. And the whole strength of the argument which I have here made use of to prove the existence of God consists in this, that I recognise that it is not possible that my nature should be what it is, and indeed that I should have in myself the idea of a God, if God did not veritably exists—a God, I say, whose idea is in me, i.e. who possesses all those supreme perfections of which our mind may indeed have some idea but without understanding them all, who is liable to no errors or defect [and who has none of all those marks which denote imperfection]. From this it is manifest that He cannot be a deceiver, since the light of nature teaches us that fraud and deception necessarily proceed from some defect.

But before I examine this matter with more care, and pass on to the consideration of other truths which may be derived from it, it seems to me right to pause for a while in order to contemplate God Himself, to ponder at leisure His marvellous attributes, to consider, and admire, and adore, the beauty of this light so resplendent, at least as far as the strength of my mind, which is in some measure dazzled by the sight, will allow me to do so. For just as faith teaches us that the supreme felicity of the other life consists only in this contemplation of the Divine Majesty, so we continue to learn by experience that a similar meditation, though incomparably less perfect, causes us to enjoy the greatest satisfaction of which we are capable in this life.

MEDITATION IV
Of the True and the False.

I have been well accustomed these past days to detach my mind from my senses, and I have accurately observed that there are very few things that one knows with certainty respecting corporeal objects, that there are many more which are known to us respecting the human mind, and yet more still regarding God Himself; so that I shall now without any difficulty abstract my thoughts from the consideration of [sensible or] imaginable objects, and carry them to those which, being withdrawn from all contact with matter, are purely intelligible. And certainly the idea which I possess of the human mind inasmuch as it is a thinking thing, and not extended in length, width and depth, nor participating in anything pertaining to body, is incomparably more distinct than is the idea of any corporeal thing. And when I consider that I doubt, that is to say, that I am an incomplete and dependent being, the idea of a being that is complete and independent, that is of God, presents itself to my mind with so much distinctness and clearness—and from the fact alone that this idea is found in me, or that I who possess this idea exist, I conclude so certainly that God exists, and that my existence depends entirely on Him in every moment of my life—that I do not think that the human mind is capable of knowing anything with more evidence and certitude. And it seems to me that I now have before me a road which will lead us from the contemplation of the true God (in whom all the treasures of science and wisdom are contained) to the knowledge of the other objects of the universe.

For, first of all, I recognise it to be impossible that He should ever deceive me; for in all fraud and deception some imperfection is to be found, and although it may appear that the power of deception is a mark of subtilty or power, yet the desire to deceive without doubt testifies to malice or feebleness, and accordingly cannot be found in God.

In the next place I experienced in myself a certain capacity for judging which I have doubtless received from God, like all the other things that I possess; and as He could not desire to deceive me, it is clear that He has not given me a faculty that will lead me to err if I use it aright.

And no doubt respecting this matter could remain, if it were not that the consequence would seem to follow that I can thus never be deceived; for if I hold all that I possess from God, and if He has not placed me in the capacity for error, it seems as though I could never fall into error. And it is true that when I think only of God [and direct my mind wholly to Him], I discover [in myself] no cause of error, or falsity; yet directly afterwards, when recurring to myself, experience shows me that I am nevertheless subject to an infinitude of errors, as to which, when we come to investigate them more closely, I notice that not only is there a real and positive idea of God or of a Being of supreme perfection present to my mind, but also, so to speak, a certain negative idea of nothing, that is, of that which is infinitely removed from any kind of perfection; and that I am in a sense something intermediate between God and nought, i.e. placed in such a manner between the supreme Being and non-being, that there is in truth nothing in me that can lead to error in so far as a sovereign Being has formed me; but that, as I in some degree participate likewise in nought or in non-being, i.e. in so far as I am not myself the supreme Being, and as I find myself subject to an infinitude of imperfections, I ought not to be astonished if I should fall into error. Thus do I recognise that error, in so far as it is such, is not a real thing depending on God, but simply a defect; and therefore, in order to fall into it, that I have no need to possess a special faculty given me by God for this very purpose, but that I fall into error from the fact that the power given me by God for the purpose of distinguishing truth from error is not infinite.

Nevertheless this does not quite satisfy me; for error is not a pure negation [i.e. is not the simple defect or want of some perfection which ought not to be mine], but it is a lack of some knowledge which it seems that I ought to possess. And on considering the nature of God it does not appear to me possible that He should have given me a faculty which is not perfect of its kind, that is, which is wanting in some perfection due to it. For

if it is true that the more skillful the artisan, the more perfect is the work of his hands, what can have been produced by this supreme Creator of all things that is not in all its parts perfect? And certainly there is no doubt that God could have created me so that I could never have been subject to error; it is also certain that He ever wills what is best; is it then better that I should be subject to err than that I should not?

In considering this more attentively, it occurs to me in the first place that I should not be astonished if my intelligence is not capable of comprehending why God acts as He does; and that there is thus no reason to doubt of His existence from the fact that I may perhaps find many other things besides this as to which I am able to understand neither for what reason nor how God has produced them. For, in the first place, knowing that my nature is extremely feeble and limited, and that the nature of God is on the contrary immense, incomprehensible, and infinite, I have no further difficulty in recognising that there is an infinitude of matters in His power, the causes of which transcend my knowledge; and this reason suffices to convince me that the species of cause termed final, finds no useful employment in physical [or natural] things; for it does not appear to me that I can without temerity seek to investigate the [inscrutable] ends of God.

It further occurs to me that we should not consider one single creature separately, when we inquire as to whether the works of God are perfect, but should regard all his creations together. For the same thing which might possibly seem very imperfect with some semblance of reason if regarded by itself, is found to be very perfect if regarded as part of the whole universe; and although, since I resolved to doubt all things, I as yet have only known certainly my own existence and that of God, nevertheless since I have recognised the infinite power of God, I cannot deny that He may have produced many other things, or at least that He has the power of producing them, so that I may obtain a place as a part of a great universe.

Whereupon, regarding myself more closely, and considering what are my errors (for they alone testify to there being any imperfection in me), I answer that they depend on a combination of two causes, to wit, on the faculty of knowledge that rests in me, and on the power of choice or of free will—that is to say, of the understanding at at the same time of the will. For by the understanding alone I [neither assert nor deny anything, but] apprehend the ideas of things as to which I can form a judgment. But no error is properly speaking found in it, provided the word error is taken in its proper signification; and though there is possibly an infinitude of things in the world of which I have no idea in my understanding, we cannot for all that say that it is deprived of these ideas [as we might say of something which is required by its nature], but simply it does not possess these; because in truth there is no reason to prove that God should have given me a greater faculty of knowledge than He has given me; and however skillful a workman I represent Him to be, I should not for all that consider that He was bound to have placed in each of His works all the perfections which He may have been able to place in some. I likewise cannot complain that God has not given me a free choice or a will which is sufficient, ample and perfect, since as a matter of fact I am conscious of a will so extended as to be subject to no limits. And what seems to me very remarkable in this regard is that of all the qualities which I possess there is no one so perfect and so comprehensive that I do not very clearly recognise that it might be yet greater and more perfect. For, to take an example, if I consider the faculty of comprehension which I possess, I find that it is of very small extent and extremely limited, and at the same time I find the idea of another faculty much more ample and even infinite, and seeing that I can form the idea of it, I recognise from this very fact that it pertains to the nature of God. If in the same way I examine the memory, the imagination, or some other faculty, I do not find any which is not small and circumscribed, while in God it is immense [or infinite]. It is free will alone or liberty of choice which I find to be so great in me that I can conceive no other idea to be more great; it is indeed the case that it is for the most part this will that causes me to know that in some manner I bear the image and similitude of God. For although the power of will is incomparably greater in God than in me, both by reason of the knowledge and the power which, conjoined with it, render it stronger and more efficacious, and by reason of its object, inasmuch as in God it extends to a great many things; it nevertheless does not

seem to me greater if I consider it formally and precisely in itself: for the faculty of will consists alone in our having the power of choosing to do a thing or choosing not to do it (that is, to affirm or deny, to pursue or to shun it), or rather it consists alone in the fact that in order to affirm or deny, pursue or shun those things placed before us by the understanding, we act so that we are unconscious that any outside force constrains us in doing so. For in order that I should be free it is not necessary that I should be indifferent as to the choice of one or the other of two contraries; but contrariwise the more I lean to the one— whether I recognise clearly that the reasons of the good and true are to be found in it, or whether God so disposes my inward thought—the more freely do I choose and embrace it. And undoubtedly both divine grace and natural knowledge, far from diminishing my liberty, rather increase it and strengthen it. Hence this indifference which I feel, when I am not swayed to one side rather than to the other by lack of reason, is the lowest grade of liberty, and rather evinces a lack or negation in knowledge than a perfection of will: for if I always recognised clearly what was true and good, I should never have trouble in deliberating as to what judgment or choice I should make, and then I should be entirely free without ever being indifferent.

From all this I recognise that the power of will which I have received from God is not of itself the source of my errors—for it is very ample and very perfect of its kind—any more than is the power of understanding; for since I understand nothing but by the power which God has given me for understanding, there is no doubt that all that I understand, I understand as I ought, and it is not possible that I err in this. Whence then come my errors? They come from the sole fact that since the will is much wider in its range and compass than the understanding, I do not restrain it within the same bounds, but extend it also to things which I do not understand: and as the will is of itself indifferent to these, it easily falls into error and sin, and chooses the evil for the good, or the false for the true.

For example, when I lately examined whether anything existed in the world, and found that from the very fact that I considered this question it followed very clearly that I myself existed, I could not prevent myself from believing that a thing I so clearly conceived was true: not that I found myself compelled to do so by some external cause, but simply because from great clearness in my mind there followed a great inclination of my will; and I believed this with so much the greater freedom or spontaneity as I possessed the less indifference towards it. Now, on the contrary, I not only know that I exist, inasmuch as I am a thinking thing, but a certain representation of corporeal nature is also presented to my mind; and it comes to pass that I doubt whether this thinking nature which is in me, or rather by which I am what I am, differs from this corporeal nature, or whether both are not simply the same thing; and I here suppose that I do not yet know any reason to persuade me to adopt the one belief rather than the other. From this it follows that I am entirely indifferent as to which of the two I affirm or deny, or even whether I abstain from forming any judgment in the matter.

And this indifference does not only extend to matters as to which the understanding has no knowledge, but also in general to all those which are not apprehended with perfect clearness at the moment when the will is deliberating upon them: for, however probable are the conjectures which render me disposed to form a judgment respecting anything, the simple knowledge that I have that those are conjectures alone and not certain and indubitable reasons, suffices to occasion me to judge the contrary. Of this I have had great experience of late when I set aside as false all that I had formerly held to be absolutely true, for the sole reason that I remarked that it might in some measure be doubted.

But if I abstain from giving my judgment on any thing when I do not perceive it with sufficient clearness and distinctness, it is plain that I act rightly and am not deceived. But if I determine to deny or affirm, I no longer make use as I should of my free will, and if I affirm what is not true, it is evident that I deceive myself; even though I judge according to truth, this comes about only by chance, and I do not escape the blame of misusing my freedom; for the light of nature teaches us that the knowledge of the understanding should always precede the determination of the will. And it is in the misuse of the free will that the privation which constitutes the characteristic nature of error is met with. Privation, I say, is found in the act, in so far as it proceeds from me, but it is not found in the faculty which I have received from God, nor even in the act in so far as it depends on Him.

For I have certainly no cause to complain that God has not given me an intelligence which is more powerful, or a natural light which is stronger than that which I have received from Him, since it is proper to the finite understanding not to comprehend a multitude of things, and it is proper to a created understanding to be finite; on the contrary, I have every reason to render thanks to God who owes me nothing and who has given me all the perfections I possess, and I should be far from charging Him with injustice, and with having deprived me of, or wrongfully withheld from me, these perfections which He has not bestowed upon me.

I have further no reason to complain that He has given me a will more ample than my understanding, for since the will consists only of one single element, and is so to speak indivisible, it appears that its nature is such that nothing can be abstracted from it [without destroying it]; and certainly the more comprehensive it is found to be, the more reason I have to render gratitude to the giver.

And, finally, I must also not complain that God concurs with me in forming the acts of the will, that is the judgment in which I go astray, because these acts are entirely true and good, inasmuch as they depend on God; and in a certain sense more perfection accrues to my nature from the fact that I can form them, than if I could not do so. As to the privation in which alone the form reason of error or sin consists, it has no need of any concurrence from God, since it is not a thing [or an existence], and since it is not related to God as to a cause, but should be termed merely a negation [according to the significance given to these words in the Schools]. For in fact it is not an imperfection in God that He has given me the liberty to give or withhold my assent from certain things as to which He has not placed a clear and distinct knowledge in my understanding; but it is without doubt an imperfection in me not to make a good use of my freedom, and to give my judgment readily on matters which I only understand obscurely. I nevertheless perceive that God could easily have created me so that I never should err, although I still remained free, and endowed with a limited knowledge, viz, by giving to my understanding a clear and distinct intelligence of all things as to which I should ever have to deliberate; or simply by His engraving deeply in my memory the resolution never to form a judgment on anything without having a clear and distinct understanding of it, so that I could never forget it. And it is easy for me to understand that, in so far as I consider myself alone, and as if there were only myself in the world, I should have been much more perfect than I am, if God had created me so that I could never err. Nevertheless I cannot deny that in some sense it is a greater perfection in the whole universe that certain parts should not be exempt from error as others are than that all parts should be exactly similar. And I have no right to complain if God, having placed me in the world, has not called upon me to play a part that excels all others in distinction and perfection.

And further I have reason to be glad on the ground that if He has not given me the power of never going astray by the first means pointed out above, which depends on a clear and evident knowledge of all the things regarding which I can deliberate, He has at least left within my power the other means, which is firmly to adhere to the resolution never to give judgment on matters whose truth is not clearly known to me; for although I notice a certain weakness in my nature in that I cannot continually concentrate my mind on one single thought, I can yet, by attentive and frequently repeated meditation, impress it so forcibly on my memory that I shall never fail to recollect it whenever I have need of it, and thus acquire the habit of never going astray.

And inasmuch as it is in this that the greatest and principal perfection of man consists, it seems to me that I have not gained little by this day's Meditation, since I have discovered the source of falsity and error. And certainly there can be no other source than that which I have explained; for as often as I so restrain my will within the limits of my knowledge that it forms no judgment except on matters which are clearly and distinctly represented to it by the understanding, I can never be deceived; for every clear and distinct conception is without doubt something, and hence cannot derive its origin from what is nought, but must of necessity have God as its author—God, I say, who being supremely perfect, cannot be the cause of any error; and conse-

quently we must conclude that such a conception [or such a judgment] is true. Nor have I only learned to-day what I should avoid in order that I may not err, but also how I should act in order to arrive at a knowledge of the truth; for without doubt I shall arrive at this end if I devote my attention sufficiently to those things which I perfectly understand; and if I separate from these that which I only understand confusedly and with obscurity. To these I shall henceforth diligently give heed.

MEDITATION V

Of the essence of material things, and, again, of God that He exists.

Many other matters respecting the attributes of God and my own nature or mind remain for consideration; but I shall possibly on another occasion resume the investigation of these. Now (after first noting what must be done or avoided, in order to arrive at a knowledge of the truth) my principal task is to endeavour to emerge from the state of doubt into which I have these last days fallen, and to see whether nothing certain can be known regarding material things.

But before examining whether any such objects as I conceive exist outside of me, I must consider the ideas of them in so far as they are in my thought, and see which of them are distinct and which confused.

In the first place, I am able distinctly to imagine that quantity which philosophers commonly call continuous, or the extension in length, breadth, or depth, that is in this quantity, or rather in the object to which it is attributed. Further, I can number in it many different parts, and attribute to each of its parts many sorts of size, figure, situation and local movements, and, finally, I can assign to each of these movements all degrees of duration.

And not only do I know these things with distinctness when I consider them in general, but, likewise [however little I apply my attention to the matter], I discover an infinitude of particulars respecting numbers, figures, movements, and other such things, whose truth is so manifest, and so well accords with my nature, that when I begin to discover them, it seems to to me that I learn nothing new, or recollect what I formerly knew —that is to say, that I for the first time perceive things which were already present to my mind, although I had not as yet applied my mind to them.

And what I here find to be most important is that I discover in myself an infinitude of ideas of certain things which cannot be esteemed as pure negations, although they may possibly have no existence outside of my thought, and which are not framed by me, although it is within my power either to think or not to think them, but which possess natures which are true and immutable. For example, when I imagine a triangle, although there may nowhere in the world be such a figure outside my thought, or ever have been, there is nevertheless in this figure a certain determinate nature, form, or essence, which is immutable and eternal, which I have not invented, and which in no wise depends on my mind, as appears from the fact that diverse properties of that triangle can be demonstrated, viz, that its three angles are equal to two right angles, that the greatest side is subtended by the greatest angle, and the like, which now, whether I wish it or do not wish it, I recognise very clearly as pertaining to it, although I never thought of the matter at all when I imagined a triangle for the first time, and which therefore cannot be said to have been invented by me.

Nor does the objecton hold good that possibly this idea of a triangle has reached my mind through the medium of my senses, since I have sometimes seen bodies triangular in shape; because I can form in my mind an infinitude of other figures regarding which we cannot have the least conception of their ever having been objects of sense, and I can nevertheless demonstrate various properties pertaining to their nature as well as to that of the triangle, and these must certainly all be true since I conceive them clearly. Hence they are something, and not pure negation; for it is perfectly clear that all that is true is something, and I have already fully demonstrated that all that I know clearly is true. And even although I had not demonstrated this, the nature of my mind is such that I could not prevent myself from holding them to be true so long as I conceive them clearly; and I recollect that even when I was still strongly attached to the objects of sense, I counted as the most those truths which I conceived clearly as regards figures, numbers, and the other matters which pertain to arithmetic and geometry, and, in general, to pure and abstract mathematics.

But now, if just because I can draw the idea of something from my thought, it follows that all which I know clearly and distinctly as pertaining to this object does really belong to it, may I not derive from this an argument demonstrating the existence of God? It is certain that I no less find the idea of God, that is to say, the idea of a supremely perfect Being, in me, than that of any figure or number whatever it is; and I do not know any less clearly and distinctly that an [actual and] eternal existence pertains to this nature than I know that all that which I am able to demonstrate of some figure or number truly pertains to the nature of this figure or number, and therefore, although all that I concluded in the preceding Meditations were found to be false, the existence of God would pass with me as at least as certain as I have ever held the truths of mathematics (which concern only numbers and figures) to be.

This indeed is not at first manifest, since it would seem to present some appearance of being a sophism. For being accustomed in all other things to make a distinction between existence and essence, I easily persuade myself that the existence can be separated from the essence of God, and that we can thus conceive God as not actually existing. But, nevertheless, when I think of it with more attention, I clearly see that existence can no more be separated from the essence of God than can its having its three angles equal to two right angles be separated from the essence of a [rectilinear] triangle, or the idea of a mountain form the idea of a valley; and so there is not any less repugnance to our conceiving a God (that is, a Being supremely perfect) to whom existence is lacking (that is to say, to whom a certain perfection is lacking), than to conceive of a mountain which has no valley.

But although I cannot really conceive of a God without existence any more than a mountain without a valley, still from the fact that I conceive of a mountain with a valley, it does not follow that there is such a mountain in the world; similarly although I conceive of God as possessing existence, it would seem that it does not follow that there is a God which exists; for my thought does not impose any necessity upon things, and just as I may imagine a winged horse, although no horse with wings exists, so I could perhaps attribute existence to God, although no God existed.

But a sophism is concealed in this objection; for from the fact that I cannot conceive a mountain without a valley, it does not follow that there is any mountain or any valley in existence, but only that the mountain and the valley, whether they exist or do not exist, cannot in any way be separated one from the other. While from the fact that I cannot conceive God without existence, it follows that existence is inseparable from Him, and hence that He really exists; not that my thought can bring this to pass, or impose any necessity on things, but, on the contrary, because the necessity which lies in the thing itself, i.e. the necessity of the existence of God determines me to think in this way. For it is not within my power to think of God without existence (that is of a supremely perfect Being devoid of a supreme perfection) though it is in my power to imagine a horse either with wings or without wings.

And we must not here object that it is in truth necessary for me to assert that God exists after having presupposed that He possesses every sort of perfection, since existence is one of these, but that as a matter of fact my original supposition was not necessary, just as it is not necessary to consider that all quadrilateral figures can be inscribed in the circle; for supposing I thought this, I should be constrained to admit that the rhombus might be inscribed in the circle since it is a quadrilateral figure, which, however, is manifestly false. [We must not, I say, make any such allegations because] although it is not necessary that I should at any time entertain the notion of God, nevertheless whenever it happens that I think of a first and a sovereign Being, and, so to speak, derive the idea of Him from the storehouse of my mind, it is necessary that I should attribute to Him every sort of perfection, although I do not get so far as to enumerate them all, or to apply my mind to each one in particular. And this necessity suffices to make me conclude (after having recognised that existence is a perfection) that this first and sovereign Being really exists; just as though it is not necessary for me ever to imagine any triangle, yet, whenever I wish to consider a rectilinear figure composed only of three angles, it is absolutely essential that I should attribute to it all those properties which serve to bring about the conclusion that its three angles are not greater than two right angles, even although I may not then be considering this point in particular. But when I consider which figures are capable of being inscribed in the circle, it is in no wise necessary that I should think that all quadrilateral figures are of this number; on the contrary, I cannot even pretend that this is the case, so long as I do not desire to accept anything which I cannot conceive clearly and distinctly. And in consequence there is a great difference between the false suppositions such as this, and the true ideas born within me, the first and principal of which is that of God. For really I discern in many ways that this idea is not something factitious, and depending solely on my thought, but that it is the image of a true and immutable nature; first of all, because I cannot conceive anything but God himself to whose essence existence [necessarily] pertains; in the second place because it is not possible for me to conceive two or more Gods in this same position; and, granted that there is one such God who now exists, I see clearly that it is necessary that He should have existed from all eternity, and that He must exist eternally; and finally, because I know an infinitude of other properties in God, none of which I can either diminish or change.

For the rest, whatever proof or argument I avail myself of, we must always return to the point that it is only those things which we conceive clearly and distinctly that have the power of persuading me entirely. And although amongst the matters which I conceive of in this way, some indeed are manifestly obvious to all, while others only manifest themselves to those who consider them closely and examine them attentively; still, after they have once been discovered, the latter are not esteemed as any less certain than the former. For example, in the case of every right-angled triangle, although it does not so manifestly appear that the square of the base is equal to the squares of the two other sides as that this base is opposite to the greatest angle; still, when this has once been apprehended, we are just as certain of its truth as of the truth of the other. And as regards God, if my mind were not pre-occupied with prejudices, and if my thought did not find itself on all hands diverted by the continual pressure of sensible things, there would be nothing which I could know more immediately and more easily than Him. For is there anything more manifest than that there is a God, that is to say, a Supreme Being, to whose essence alone existence pertains?

And although for a firm grasp of this truth I have need of a strenuous application of mind, at present I not only feel myself to be as assured of it as of all that I hold as most certain, but I also remark that the certainty of all other things depends on it so absolutely, that without this knowledge it is impossible ever to know anything perfectly.

For although I am of such a nature that as long as I understand anything very clearly and distinctly, I am naturally impelled to believe it to be true, yet because I am also of such a nature that I cannot have my mind constantly fixed on the same object in order to perceive it clearly, and as I often recollect having formed a past judgment without at the same time properly recollecting the reasons that led me to make it, it may happen meanwhile that other reasons present themselves to me, which would easily cause me to change my opinion, if I were ignorant of the facts of the existence of God, and thus I should have no true and certain knowledge, but only vague and vacillating opinions. Thus, for example, when I consider the nature of a [rectilinear] triangle, I who have some little knowledge of the principles of geometry recognise quite clearly that the three angles are equal to two right angles, and it is not possible for me not to believe this so long as I apply my mind to its demonstration; but so soon as I abstain from attending to the proof, although I still recollect having clearly comprehended it, it may easily occur that I come to doubt its truth, if I am ignorant of there being a God. For I can persuade myself of having been so constituted by nature that I can easily deceive myself even in those matters which I believe myself to apprehend with the greatest evidence and certainty, especially when I recollect that I have frequently judged matters to be true and certain which other reasons have afterwards impelled me to judge to be altogether false.

But after I have recognised that there is a God —because at the same time I have also recognised that all things depend upon Him, and that He is not a deceiver, and from that have inferred that what I perceive clearly and distinctly cannot fail to be true—although I no longer pay attention to the reasons for which I have judged this to be true, provided that I recollect having clearly and distinctly perceived it, no contrary reason can be brought forward which could ever cause me to doubt of its truth; and thus I have a true and certain knowledge of it. And this same knowledge extends likewise to all other things which I recollect having formerly demonstrated, such as the truths of geometry and the like; for what can be alleged against them to cause me to place them in doubt? Will it be said that my nature is such as to cause me to be frequently deceived? But I already know that I cannot be deceived in the judgment whose grounds I know clearly. Will it be said that I formerly held many things to be true and certain which I have afterwards recognised to be false? But I had not had any clear and distinct knowledge of these things, and not as yet knowing the rule whereby I assure myself of the truth, I had been impelled to give my assent from reasons which I have since recognised to be less strong than I had at the time imagined them to be. What further objection can then be raised? That possibly I am dreaming (an objection I myself made a little while ago), or that all the thoughts which I now have are no more true than the phantasies of my dreams? But even though I slept the case would be the same, for all that is clearly present to my mind is absolutely true.

And so I very clearly recognise that the certainty and truth of all knowledge depends alone on the knowledge of the true God, in so much that, before I knew Him, I could not have a perfect knowledge of any other thing. And now that I know Him I have the means of acquiring a perfect knowlege of an infinitude of things, not only of those which relate to God Himself and other intellectual matters, but also of those which pertain to corporeal nature in so far as it is the object of pure mathematics [which have no concern with whether it exists or not].

MEDITATION VI

Of the Existence of Material Things, and of the real distinction between the Soul and Body of Man.

Nothing further now remains but to inquire whether material things exist. And certainly I at least know that these may exist in so far as they are considered as the objects of pure mathematics, since in this aspect I perceive them clearly and distinctly. For there is no doubt that God possesses the power to produce everything that I am capable of perceiving with distinctness, and I have never deemed that anything was impossible for Him, unless I found a contradiction in attempting to conceive it clearly. Further, the faculty of imagination which I possess, and of which, experience tells me, I make use when I apply myself to the consideration of material things, is capable of persuading me of their existence; for when I attentively consider what imagination is, I find that it is nothing but a certain application of the faculty of knowledge to the body which is immediately present to it, and which therefore exists.

And to render this quite clear, I remark in the first place the difference that exists between the imagination and pure intellection [or conception]. For example, when I imagine a triangle, I do not conceive it only as a figure comprehended by three lines, but I also apprehend these three lines as present by the power and inward vision of my mind, and this is what I call imagining. But if I desire to think of a chiliagon, I certainly conceive truly that it is a figure composed of a thousand sides, just as easily as I conceive of a triangle that it is a figure of three sides; but I cannot in any way imagine the thousand sides of a chiliagon [as I do the three sides of a triangle], nor do I, so to speak, regard them as present [with the eyes of my mind]. And although in accordance with the habit I have formed of always employing the aid of my imagination when I think of corporeal things, it may happen that in imagining a chiliagon I confusedly represent to myself some figure, yet it is very evident that this figure is not a chiliagon, since it in no way differs from that which I represent to myself when I think of a myriagon or any other many-sided figure; nor does it serve my purpose in discovering the properties which go to form the distinction between a chiliagon and other polygons. But if the question turns upon a pentagon, it is quite true that I can conceive its figure as well as that of a chiliagon without the help of my imagination; but I can also imagine it by applying the attention of my mind to each of its five sides, and at the same time to the space which they enclose. And thus I clearly recognise that I have need of a particular effort of mind in order to effect the

act of imagination, such as I do not require in order to understand, and this particular effort of mind clearly manifests the difference which exists between imagination and pure intellection.

I remark besides that this power of imagination which is in one, inasmuch as it differs from the power of understanding, is in no wise a necessary element in my nature, or in [my essence, that is to say, in] the essence of my mind; for although I did not possess it I should doubtless ever remain the same as I now am, from which it appears that we might conclude that it depends on something which differs from me. And I easily conceive that if some body exists with which my mind is conjoined and united in such a way that it can apply itself to consider it when it pleases, it may be that by this means it can imagine corporeal objects; so that this mode of thinking differs from pure intellection only inasmuch as mind in its intellectual activity in some manner turns on itself, and considers some of the ideas which it possesses in itself; while in imagining it turns towards the body, and there beholds in it something conformable to the idea which it has either conceived of itself or perceived by the senses. I easily understand, I say, that the imagination could be thus constituted if it is true that body exists; and because I can discover no other convenient mode of explaining it, I conjecture with probability that body does exist; but this is only with probability, and although I examine all things with care, I nevertheless do not find that from this distinct idea of corporeal nature, which I have in my imagination, I can derive any argument from which there will necessarily be deduced the existence of body.

But I am in the habit of imagining many other things besides this corporeal nature which is the object of pure mathematics, to wit, the colours, sounds, scents, pain, and other such things, although less distinctly. And inasmuch as I perceive these things much better through the senses, by the medium of which, and by the memory, they seem to have reached my imagination, I believe that, in order to examine them more conveniently, it is right that I should at the same time investigate the nature of sense perception, and that I should see if from the ideas which I apprehend by this mode of thought, which I call feeling, I cannot derive some certain proof of the existence of corporeal objects.

And first of all I shall recall to my memory those matters which I hitherto held to be true, as having perceived them through the senses, and the foundations on which my belief has rested; in the next place I shall examine the reasons which have since obliged me to place them in doubt; in the last place I shall consider which of them I must now believe.

First of all, then, I perceived that I had a head, hands, feet, and all other members of which this body—which I considered as a part, or possibly even as the whole, of myself—is composed. Further I was sensible that this body was placed amidst many others, from which it was capable of being affected in many different ways, beneficial and hurtful, and I remarked that a certain feeling of pleasure accompanied those that were beneficial, and pain those which were harmful. And in addition to this pleasure and pain, I also experienced hunger, thirst, and other similar appetites, as also certain corporeal inclinations towards joy, sadness, anger, and other similar passions. And outside myself, in addition to extension, figure, and motions of bodies, I remarked in them hardness, heat, and all other tactile qualities, and, further, light and colour, and scents and sounds, the variety of which gave me the means of distinguishing the sky, the earth, the sea, and generally all the other bodies, one from the other. And certainly, considering the ideas of all these qualities which presented themselves to my mind, and which alone I perceived properly or immediately, it was not without reason that I believed myself to perceive objects quite different from my thought, to wit, bodies from which those ideas proceeded; for I found by experience that these ideas presented themselves to me without my consent being requisite, so that I could not perceive any object, however desirous I might be, unless it were present to the organs of sense; and it was not in my power not to perceive it, when it was present. And because the ideas which I receive through the senses were much more lively, more clear, and even, in their own way, more distinct than any of those which I could of myself frame in meditation, or than those I found impressed on my memory, it appeared as though they could not have proceeded from my mind, so that they must necessarily have been produced in me by some other things. And having no knowledge of those objects excepting the knowledge which the ideas themselves gave me, nothing was more likely to occur to my mind than that the objects were similar to the ideas which were caused. And because I likewise remembered that I had formerly made use of my senses rather than my reason, and recognised that the ideas which I formed of myself were not so distinct as those which I perceived through the senses, and that they were most frequently even composed of portions of these last, I persuaded myself easily that I had no idea in my mind which had not formerly come to me through the senses. Nor was it without some reason that I believed that this body (which by a certain special right I call my own) belonged to me more properly and more strictly than any other; for in fact I could never be separated from it as from other bodies; I experienced in it and on account of it all my appetites and affections, and finally I was touched by the feeling of pain and titillation of pleasure in its parts, and not in the parts of other bodies which were separated from it. But when I inquired, why, from some, I know not what, painful sensation, there follows sadness of mind, and from the pleasurable sensation there arises joy, or why this mysterious pinching of the stomach which I call hunger causes me to desire to eat, and dryness of throat causes a desire to drink, and so on, I could give no reason excepting that nature taught me so; for there is certainly no affinity (that I at least can understand) between the craving of the stomach and the desire to eat, any more than between the perception of whatever causes pain and the thought of sadness which arises from this perception. And in the same way it appeared to me that I had learned from nature all the other judgments which I formed regarding the objects of my senses, since I remarked that these judgments were found in me before I had the leisure to weigh and consider any reasons which might oblige me to make them.

But afterwards many experiences little by little destroyed all the faith which I had rested in my senses; for I from time to time observed that those towers which from afar appeared to me to be round, more closely observed seemed square, and that colossal statues raised on the summit of these towers, appeared as quite tiny statues when viewed from the bottom; and so in an infinitude of other cases I found error in judgments founded on the external senses. And not only in those founded on the external senses, but even in those founded on the internal as well; for is there anything more intimate or more internal than pain? And yet I have learned from some persons whose arms or legs have been cut off, that they sometimes seemed to feel pain in the part which had been amputated, which made me think that I could not be quite certain that it was a certain member which pained me, even although I felt pain in it. And to those grounds of doubt I have lately added two others, which are very general; the first is that I never have believed myself to feel anything in waking moments which I cannot also sometimes believe myself to feel when I sleep, and so I do not think that these things which I seem to feel in sleep, proceed from objects outside of me, I do not see any reason why I should have this belief regarding objects which I seem to perceive while awake. The other was that being still ignorant, or rather supposing my self to be ignorant, of the author of my being, I saw nothing to prevent me from having been so constituted by nature that I might be deceived even in matters which seemed to me to be most certain. And as to the grounds on which I was formerly persuaded of the truth of sensible objects, I had not much trouble in replying to them. For since nature seemed to cause me to lean towards many things from which reason repelled me, I did not believe that I should trust much to the teachings of nature. And although the ideas which I receive by the sense do not depend on my will, I did not think that one should for that reason conclude that they proceeded from things different from myself, since possibly some faculty might be discovered in me—though hitherto unknown to me —which produced them.

But now that I begin to know myself better, and to discover more clearly the author of my being, I do not in truth think that I should rashly admit all the matters which the senses seem to teach us, but, on the other hand, I do not think that I should doubt them all universally.

And first of all, because I know that all things which I apprehend clearly and distinctly can be created by God as I apprehend them, it suffices that I am able to apprehend one thing apart from another clearly and distinctly in order to be certain that the one is different from the other, since they may be made to exist in separation at least by the omnipotence of God; and it does not sig-

nify by what power this separation is made in order to compel me to judge them to be different: and, therefore, just because I know certainly that I exist, and that meanwhile I do not remark that any other thing necessarily pertains to my nature or essence, excepting that I am a thinking thing, I rightly conclude that my essence consists solely in the fact that I am a thinking thing [or a substance whose whole essence or nature is to think]. And although possibly (or rather certainly, as I shall say in a moment) I possess a body with which I am very intimately conjoined, yet because, on the one side, I have a clear and distinct idea of myself inasmuch as I am only a thinking and unextended thing, and as, on the other, I possess a distinct idea of body, inasmuch as it is only an extended and unthinking thing, it is certain that this I [that is to say, my soul by which I am what I am], is entirely and absolutely distinct from my body, and can exist without it.

I further find in myself faculties employing modes of thinking peculiar to themselves, to wit, the faculties of imagination and feeling, without which I can easily conceive myself clearly and distinctly as a complete being; while, on the other hand, they cannot be so conceived apart from me, that is without an intelligent substance in which they reside, for [in the notion we have of these faculties, or, to use the language of the Schools] in their formal concept, some kind of intellection is comprised, from which I infer that they are distinct from me as its modes are from a thing. I observe also in me some other faculties such as that of change of position, the assumption of different figures and such like, which cannot be conceived, any more than can the preceding, apart from some substance to which they are attached, and consequently cannot exist without it; but it is very clear that these faculties, if it be true that they exist, must be attached to some corporeal or extended and not to an intelligent substance, since in the clear and distinct conception of these there is some sort of extension found to be present, but no intellection at all. There is certainly further in me a certain passive faculty of perception, that is, of receiving and recognising the ideas of sensible things, but this would be useless to me [and I could in no way avail myself of it], if there were not either in me or in some other thing another active faculty capable of forming and producing these ideas. But this active faculty cannot exist in me [inasmuch as I am a thing that thinks] seeing that it does not presuppose thought, and also that those ideas are often produced in me without my contributing in any way to the same, and often even against my will; it is thus necessarily the case that the faculty resides in some substance different from me in which all the reality which is objectively in the ideas that are produced by this faculty is formally or eminently contained, as I remarked before. And this substance is either a body, that is, a corporeal nature in which there is contained formally [and really] all that which is objectively [and by representation] in those ideas, or it is God Himself, or some other creature more noble than body in which that same is contained eminently. But since God is no deceiver, it is very manifest that He does not communicate to me these ideas immediately and by Himself, nor yet by the intervention of some creature in which their reality is not formally, but only eminently, contained. For since He has given me no faculty to recognise that this is the case, but, on the other hand, a very great inclination to believe [that they are sent to me or] that they are conveyed to me by corporeal objects, I do not see how He could be defended from the accusation of deceit if these ideas were produced by causes other than corporeal objects. Hence we must allow that corporeal things exist. However, they are perhaps not exactly what we perceive by the senses, since this comprehension by the senses is in many instances very obscure and confused; but we must at least admit that all things which I conceive in them clearly and distinctly, that is to say, all things which, speaking generally, are comprehended in the object of pure mathematics, are truly to be recognised as external objects.

As to other things, however, which are either particular only, as, for example, that the sun is of such and such a figure, etc., or which are less clearly and distinctly conceived, such as light, sound, pain and the like, it is certain that although they are very dubious and uncertain, yet on the sole ground that God is not a deceiver, and that consequently He has not permitted any falsity to exist in my opinion which He has not likewise given me the faculty of correcting, I may assuredly hope to conclude that I have within me the means of arriving at the truth even here. And first of all there is no doubt that in all things

which nature teaches me there is some truth contained; for by nature, considered in general, I now understand no other thing that either God Himself or else the order and disposition which God has established in created things; and by my nature in particular I understand no other thing than the complexus of all the things which God has given me.

But there is nothing which this nature teaches me more expressly [nor more sensibly] than that I have a body which is adversely affected when I feel pain, which has need of food or drink when I experience the feelings of hunger and thirst, and so on; nor can I doubt there being some truth in all this.

Nature also teaches me by the sensations of pain, hunger, thirst, etc., that I am not only lodged in my body as a pilot in a vessel, but that I am very closely united to it, and so to speak so intermingled with it that I seem to compose with it one whole. For if that were not the case, when my body is hurt, I, who am merely a thinking thing, should not feel pain, for I should perceive this wound by the understanding only, just as the sailor perceives by sight when something is damaged in his vessel; and when my body has need of drink or food, I should clearly understand the fact without being warned of it by confused feelings of hunger and thirst. For all these sensations of hunger, thirst, pain, etc. are in truth none other than certain confused modes of thought which are produced by the union and apparent intermingling of mind and body.

Moreover, nature teaches me that many other bodies exist around mine, of which some are to be avoided, and others sought after. And certainly from the fact that I am sensible of different sorts of colours, sounds, scents, tastes, heat, hardness, etc., I very easily conclude that there are in the bodies from which all these diverse sense-perceptions proceed certain variations which answer to them, although possibly these are not really at all similar to them. And also from the fact that amongst these different sense-perceptions some are very agreeable to me and others disagreeable, it is quite certain that my body (or rather myself in my entirety, inasmuch as I am formed of body and soul) may receive different impressions agreeable and disagreeable from the other bodies which surround it.

But there are many other things which nature seems to have taught me, but which at the same time I have never really received from her, but which have been brought about in my mind by a certain habit which I have of forming inconsiderate judgments on things; and thus it may easily happen that these judgments contain some error. Take, for example, the opinion which I hold that all space in which there is nothing that affects [or makes an impression on] my senses is void; that in a body which is warm there is something entirely similar to the idea of heat which is in me; that in a white or green body there is the same whiteness or greenness that I perceive; that in a bitter or sweet body there is the same taste, and so on in other instances; that the stars, the towers, and all other distant bodies are of the same figure and size as they appear from far off to our eyes, etc. But in order that in this there should be nothing which I do not conceive distinctly, I should define exactly what I really understand when I say that I am taught somewhat by nature. For here I take nature in a more limited signification than when I term it the sum of all the things given me by God, since in this sum many things are comprehended which only pertain to mind (and to these I do not refer in speaking of nature) such as the notion which I have of the fact that what has once been done cannot ever be undone and an infinitude of such things which I know by the light of nature [without the help of the body]; and seeing that it comprehends many other matters besides which only pertain to body, and are no longer here contained under the name of nature, such as the quality of weight which it possesses and the like, with which I also do not deal; for in talking of nature I only treat of those things given by God to me as a being composed of mind and body. But the nature here described truly teaches me to flee from things which cause the sensation of pain, and seek after the things which communicate to me the sentiment of pleasure and so forth; but I do not see that beyond this it teaches me that from those diverse sense-perceptions we should ever form any conclusion regarding things outside of us, without having [carefully and maturely] mentally examined them beforehand. For it seems to me that it is mind alone, and not mind and body in conjunction, that is requisite to a knowledge of the truth in regard to such things. Thus, although a star makes no larger an impression on my eye than the flame of a little candle there is yet in me no real or positive propensity impelling me to believe that it is not greater than that flame; but I have judged it to be so from my earliest years, without any rational foundation. And although in approaching fire I feel heat, and in approaching it a little too near I even feel pain, there is at the same time no reason in this which could persuade me that there is in the fire something resembling this heat any more than there is in it something resembling the pain; all that I have any reason to believe from this is, that there is something in it, whatever it may be, which excites in me these sensations of heat or of pain. So also, although there are spaces in which I find nothing which excites my senses, I must not from that conclude that these spaces contain no body; for I see this, as in other similar things, that I have been in the habit of perverting the order of nature, because these perceptions of sense having been placed within me by nature merely for the purpose of signifying to my mind what things are beneficial or hurtful to the composite whole of which it forms a part, and being up to that point sufficiently clear and distinct, I yet avail myself of them as though they were absolute rules by which I immediately determine the essence of the bodies which are outside me, as to which, in fact, they can teach me nothing but what is most obscure and confused.

But I have already sufficiently considered how, notwithstanding the supreme goodness of God, falsity enter into the judgments I make. Only here a new difficulty is presented—one respecting those things the pursuit or avoidance of which is taught me by nature, and also respecting the internal sensations which I possess, and in which I seem to have sometimes detected error [and thus to be directly deceived by my own nature]. To take an example, the agreeable taste of some food in which poison has been intermingled may induce me to partake of the poison, and thus deceive me. It is true, at the same time, that in this case nature may be excused, for it only induces me to desire food in which I find a pleasant taste, and not to desire poison which is unknown to it; and thus I can infer nothing from this fact, except that my nature is not omniscient, at which there is certainly no reason to be astonished, since man, being finite in nature, can only have knowledge the perfectness of which is limited.

But we not unfrequently deceive ourselves even in those things to which we are directly impelled by nature, as happens with those who when they are sick desire to drink or eat things hurtful to them. It will perhaps be said here that the cause of their deceptiveness is that their nature is corrupt, but that does not remove the difficulty, because a sick man is none the less truly God's creature than he who is in health; and it is therefore as repugnant to God's goodness for the one to have a deceitful nature as it is for the other. And as a clock composed of wheels and counterweights no less exactly observes the laws of nature when it is badly made, and does not show the time properly, than when it entirely satisfies the wishes of its maker, and as, if I consider the body of a man as being a sort of machine so built up and composed of nerves, muscles, veins, blood and skin, that though there were no mind in it at all, it would not cease to have the same motions as at present, exception being made of those movements which are due to the direction of the will, and in consequence depend upon the mind [as opposed to those which operate by the disposition of its organs], I easily recognise that it would be as natural to this body, supposing it to be, for example, dropsical, to suffer the parchedness of the throat which usually signifies to the mind the feeling of thirst, and to be disposed by this parched feeling to move the nerves and other parts in the way requisite for drinking, and thus to augment its malady and do harm to itself, as it is natural to it, when it has no indisposition, to be impelled to drink for its good by a similar cause. And although, considering the use to which the clock has been destined by its maker, I may say that it deflects from the order of its nature when it does not indicate the hours correctly; and as, in the same way, considering the machine of the human body as having been formed by God in order to have in itself all the movements usually manifested there, I have reason for thinking that it does not follow the order of nature when, if the throat is dry, drinking does harm to the conservation of health, nevertheless I recognise at the same time that this last mode of explaining nature is very different from the other. For this is but a purely verbal characterisation depending entirely on my thought, which compares a sick man and a badly constructed clock with the idea which I have of a healthy man

and a well made clock, and it is hence extrinsic to the things to which it is applied; but according to the other interpretation of the term nature I understand something which is truly found in things and which is therefore not without some truth.

But certainly although in regard to the dropsical body it is only so to speak to apply an extrinsic term when we say that its nature is corrupted, inasmuch as apart from the need to drink, the throat is parched; yet in regard to the composite whole, that is to say, to the mind or soul united to this body, it is not a purely verbal predicate, but a real error of nature, for it to have thirst when drinking would be hurtful to it. And thus it still remains to inquire how the goodness of God does not prevent the nature of man so regarded from being fallacious.

In order to begin this examination, then, I here say, in the first place, that there is a great difference between mind and body, inasmuch as body is by nature always divisible, and the mind is entirely indivisible. For, as a matter of fact, when I consider the mind, that is to say, myself inasmuch as I am only a thinking thing, I cannot distinguish in myself any parts, but apprehend myself to be clearly one and entire; and although the whole mind seems to be united to the whole body, yet if a foot, or an arm, or some other part, is separated from my body, I am aware that nothing has been taken away from my mind. And the faculties of willing, feeling, conceiving, etc. cannot be properly speaking said to be its parts, for it is one and the same mind which employs itself in willing and in feeling and understanding. But it is quite otherwise with corporeal or extended objects, for there is not one of these imaginable by me which my mind cannot easily divide into parts, and which consequently I do not recognise as being divisible; this would be sufficient to teach me that the mind or soul of man is entirely different from the body, if I had not already learned it from other sources.

I further notice that the mind does not receive the impressions from all parts of the body immediately, but only from the brain, or perhaps even from one of its smallest parts, to wit, from that in which the common sense is said to reside, which, whenever it is disposed in the same particular way, conveys the same thing to the mind, although meanwhile the other portions of the body may be differently disposed, as is testified by innumerable experiments which it is unnecessary here to recount.

I notice, also, that the nature of body is such that none of its parts can be moved by another part a little way off which cannot also be moved in the same way by each one of the parts which are between the two, although this more remote part does not act at all. As, for example, in the cord *ABCD* [which is in tension] if we pull the last part *D,* the first part *A* will not be moved in any way differently from what would be the case if one of the intervening parts *B* or *C* were pulled, and the last part *D* were to remain unmoved. And in the same way, when I feel pain in my foot, my knowledge of physics teaches me that this sensation is communicated by means of nerves dispersed through the foot, which, being extended like cords from there to the brain, when they are contracted in the foot, at the same time contract the inmost portions of the brain which is their extremity and place of origin, and then excite a certain movement which nature has established in order to cause the mind to be affected by a sensation of pain represented as existing in the foot. But because these nerves must pass through the tibia, the thigh, the loins, the back and the neck, in order to reach from the leg to the brain, it may happen that although their extremities which are in the foot are not affected, but only certain ones of their intervening parts [which pass by the loins or the neck], this action will excite the same movement in the brain that might have been excited there by a hurt received in the foot, in consequence of which the mind will necessarily feel in the foot the same pain as if it had received a hurt. And the same holds good of all the other perceptions of our senses.

I notice finally that since each of the movements which are in the portion of the brain by which the mind is immediately affected brings about one particular sensation only, we cannot under the circumstances imagine anything more likely than that this movement, amongst all the sensations which it is capable of impressing on it, causes mind to be affected by that one which is best fitted and most generally useful for the conservation of the human body when it is in health. But experience makes us aware that all the feelings with which nature inspires us are such as I have just spoken of; and there is therefore nothing

in them which does not give testimony to the power and goodness of the God [who has produced them]. Thus, for example, when the nerves which are in the feet are violently or more than usually moved, their movement, passing through the medulla of the spin to the inmost parts of the brain, gives a sign to the mind which makes it feel somewhat, to wit, pain, as though in the foot, by which the mind is excited to do its utmost to remove the cause of the evil as dangerous and hurtful to the foot. It is true that God could have constituted the nature of man in such a way that this same movement in the brain would have conveyed something quite different to the mind; for example, it might have produced consciousness of itself either in so far as it is in the brain, or as it is in the foot, or as it is in some other place between the foot and the brain, or it might finally have produced consciousness of anything else whatsoever; but none of all this would have contributed so well to the conservation of the body. Similarly, when we desire to drink, a certain dryness of the throat is produced which moves its nerves, and by their means the internal portions of the brain; and this movement causes in the mind the sensation of thirst, because in this case there is nothing more useful to us than to become aware that we have need to drink for the conservation of our health; and the same holds good in other instances.

From this it is quite clear that, notwithstanding the supreme goodness of God, the nature of man, inasmuch as it is composed of mind and body, cannot be otherwise than sometimes a source of deception. For if there is any cause which excites, not in the foot but in some part of the nerves which are extended between the foot and the brain, or even in the brain itself, the same movement which usually is produced when the foot is detrimentally affected, pain will be experienced as though it were in the foot, and the sense will thus naturally be deceived; for since the same movement in the brain is capable of causing but one sensation in the mind, and this sensation is much more frequently excited by a cause which hurts the foot than by another existing in some other quarter, it is reasonable that it should convey to the mind pain in the foot rather than in any other part of the body. And although the parchedness of the throat does not always proceed, as it usually does, from the fact that drinking is necessary for the health of the body, but sometimes comes from quite a different cause, as is the case with dropsical patients, it is yet much better that it should mislead on this occasion than if, on the other hand, it were always to deceive us when the body is in good health; and so on in similar cases.

And certainly this consideration is of great service to me, not only in enabling me to recognise all the errors to which my nature is subject, but also in enabling me to avoid them or to correct them more easily. For knowing that all my senses more frequently indicate to me truth than falsehood respecting the things which concern that which is beneficial to the body, and being able almost always to avail myself of many of them in order to examine one particular thing, and, besides that, being able to make use of my memory in order to connect the present with the past, and of my understanding which already has discovered all the causes of my errors, I ought to no longer to fear that falsity my be found in matters every day presented to me by my senses. And I ought to set aside all the doubts of these past days as hyperbolical and ridiculous, particularly that very common uncertainty respecting sleep, which I could not distinguish from the waking state; for at present I find a very notable difference between the two, inasmuch as our memory can never connect our dreams one with the other, or with the whole course of our lives, as it unites events which happen to us while we are awake. And, as a matter of fact, if someone, while I was awake, quite suddenly appeared to me and disappeared as fast as do the images which I see in sleep, so that I could not know from whence the form came nor whither it went, it would not be without reason that I should deem it a spectre or a phantom formed by my brain [and similar to those which I form in sleep], rather than a real man. But when I perceive things as to which I know distinctly both the place from which they proceed, and that in which they are, and the time at which they appeared to me; and when, without any interruption, I can connect the perceptions which I have of them with the whole course of my life, I am perfectly assured that these perceptions occur while I am waking and not during sleep. And I ought in no wise to doubt the truth of such matters, if, after having called up all my senses, my memory, and my understanding, to examine them, nothing is brought to evidence by any one of them which is repugnant to what is set forth by the others. For because God is in no wise a deceiver, it follows that I am not deceived in this. But because the exigencies of action often oblige us to make up our minds before having leisure to examine matters carefully, we must confess that the life of man is very frequently subject to error in respect to individual objects, and we must in the end acknowledge the infirmity of our nature.

GEORGE BERKELEY

Three Dialogues between Hylas and Philonous*

THE FIRST DIALOGUE

Philonous. Good morrow, Hylas. I did not expect to find you abroad so early.

Hylas. It is indeed something unusual; but my thoughts were so taken up with a subject I was discoursing of last night that, finding I could not sleep, I resolved to rise and take a turn in the garden.

Phil. It happened well, to let you see what innocent and aggreeable pleasures you lose every morning. Can there be a pleasanter time of the day or a more delightful season of the year? That purple sky, these wild but sweet notes of birds, the fragrant bloom upon the trees and flowers, the gentle influence of the rising sun—these and a thousand nameless beauties of nature inspire the soul with secret transports; its faculties, too, being at this time fresh and lively, are fit for those meditations which the solitude of a garden and tranquility of the morning naturally dispose us to. But I am afraid I interrupt your thoughts, for you seemed very intent on something.

Hyl. It is true, I was, and shall be obliged to you if you will permit me to go on in the same vein; not that I would by any means deprive myself of your company, for my thoughts always flow more easily in conversation with a friend than when I am alone; but my request is that you would suffer me to impart my reflections to you.

Phil. With all my heart, it is what I should have requested myself if you had not prevented me.

Hyl. I was considering the odd fate of those men who have in all ages, through an affectation of being distinguished from the vulgar, or some unaccountable turn of thought, pretended either to believe nothing at all or to believe the most extravagant things in the world. This, however, might be borne if their paradoxes and skepticism did not draw after them some consequences of general disadvantage to mankind. But the mischief lies here: that when men of less leisure see them who are supposed to have spent their whole time in the pursuits of knowledge professing an entire ignorance of all things or advancing such notions as are repugnant to plain and commonly received principles, they will be tempted to entertain suspicions concerning the most important truths, which they had hitherto held sacred and unquestionable.

Phil. I entirely agree with you as to the ill tendency of the affected doubts of some philosophers and fantastical conceits of others. I am even so far gone of late in this way of thinking that I have quitted several of the sublime notions I had got in their schools for vulgar opinions. And I give it you on my word, since this revolt from metaphysical notions to the plain dictates of na-. ture and common sense, I find my understanding strangely enlightened, so that I can now easily comprehend a great many things which before were all mystery and riddle.

*From George Berkeley, *Three Dialogues between Hylas and Philonous, in Opposition to Skeptics and Atheists.* The First Dialogue and some objections and replies from the Third Dialogue. First published in 1713.

Hyl. I am glad to find there was nothing in the accounts I heard of you.

Phil. Pray, what were those?

Hyl. You were represented in last night's conversation as one who maintained the most extravagant opinion that ever entered into the mind of man, to wit, that there is no such thing as "material substance" in the world.

Phil. That there is no such thing as what philosophers call 'material substance," I am seriously persuaded; but if I were made to see anything absurd or skeptical in this, I should then have the same reason to renounce this that I imagine I have now to reject the contrary opinion.

Hyl. What! Can anything be more fantastical, more repugnant to common sense or a more manifest piece of skepticism than to believe there is no such thing as matter?

Phil. Softly, good Hylas. What if it should prove that you, who hold there is, are, by virtue of that opinion, a greater skeptic and maintain more paradoxes and repugnances to common sense than I who believe no such thing?

Hyl. You may as soon persuade me the part is greater than the whole, as that, in order to avoid absurdity and skepticism, I should ever be obliged to give up my opinion in this point.

Phil. Well then, are you content to admit that opinion for true which, upon examination, shall appear most agreeable to common sense and remote from skepticism?

Hyl. With all my heart. Since you are for raising disputes about the plainest things in nature, I am content for once to hear what you have to say.

Phil. Pray, Hylas, what do you mean by a "skeptic?"

Hyl. I mean what all men mean, one that doubts of everything.

Phil. He then who entertains no doubt concerning some particular point, with regard to that point cannot be thought a skeptic.

Hyl. I agree with you.

Phil. Whether does doubting consist in embracing the affirmative or negative side of a question?

Hyl. In neither; for whoever understands English cannot but know that *doubting* signifies a suspense between both.

Phil. He then that denies any point can no more be said to doubt of it than he who affirms it with the same degree of assurance.

Hyl. True.

Phil. And, consequently, for such his denial is no more to be esteemed a skeptic than the other.

Hyl. I acknowledge it.

Phil. How comes it to pass then, Hylas, that you pronounce me a skeptic because I deny what you affirm, to wit, the existence of matter? Since, for aught you can tell, I am as peremptory in my denial as you in your affirmation.

Hyl. Hold, Philonous, I have been a little out in my definition; but every false step a man makes in discourse is not to be insisted on. I said indeed that a "skeptic" was one who doubted of everything; but I should have added: or who denies the reality and truth of things.

Phil. What things? Do you mean the principles and theorems of sciences? But these you know are universal intellectual notions, and consequently independent of matter; the denial therefore of this does not imply the denying them.

Hyl. I grant it. But are there no other things? What think you of distrusting the senses, of denying the real existence of sensible things, or pretending to know nothing of them. Is not this sufficient to denominate a man a skeptic?

Phil. Shall we therefore examine which of us it is that denies the reality of sensible things or professes the greatest ignorance of them, since, if I take you rightly, he is to be esteemed the greatest skeptic?

Hyl. That is what I desire.

Phil. What mean you by "sensible things?"

Hyl. Those things which are perceived by the senses. Can you imagine that I mean anything else?

Phil. Pardon me, Hylas, if I am desirous clearly to apprehend your notions, since this may much shorten our inquiry. Suffer me then to ask you this further question. Are those things only perceived by the senses which are perceived immediately? Or may those things properly be said to be "sensible" which are perceived immediately, or not without the intervention of others?

Hyl. I do not sufficiently understand you.

Phil. In reading a book, what I immediately perceive are the letters, but mediately, or by means of these, are suggested to my mind the notions of God, virtue, truth, etc. Now, that the letters are truly sensible things, or perceived by sense, there is no doubt; but I would know whether you take the things suggested by them to be so too.

Hyl. No, certainly; it were absurd to think God or virtue sensible things, though they may be signified and suggested to the mind by sensible marks with which they have an arbitrary connection.

Phil. It seems, then, that by "sensible things" you mean those only which can be perceived immediately by sense.

Hyl. Right.

Phil. Does it not follow from this that, though I see one part of the sky red, and another blue, and that my reason does thence evidently conclude there must be some cause of that diversity of colors, yet that cause cannot be said to be a sensible thing or perceived by the sense of seeing?

Hyl. It does.

Phil. In like manner, though I hear variety of sounds, yet I cannot be said to hear the causes of those sounds.

Hyl. You cannot.

Phil. And when by my touch I perceive a thing to be hot and heavy, I cannot say, with any truth or propriety, that I feel the cause of its heat or weight.

Hyl. To prevent any more questions of this kind, I tell you once for all that by "sensible things" I mean those only which are perceived by sense, and that in truth the senses perceive nothing which they do not perceive immediately, for they make no inferences. The deducing therefore of causes or occasions from effects and appearances, which alone are perceived by sense, entirely relates to reason.

Phil. This point then is agreed between us— that *sensible things are those only which are immediately perceived by sense.* You will further inform me whether we immediately perceive by sight anything besides light and colors and figures; or by hearing, anything but sounds; by the palate, anything beside tastes, by the smell, besides odors; or by the touch, more than tangible qualities.

Hyl. We do not.

Phil. It seems, therefore, that if you take away all sensible qualities, there remains nothing sensible?

Hyl. I grant it.

Phil. Sensible things therefore are nothing else but so many sensible qualities or combinations of sensible qualities?

Hyl. Nothing else.

Phil. Heat is then a sensible thing?

Hyl. Certainly.

Phil. Does the reality of sensible things consist in being perceived, or is it something distinct from their being perceived, and that bears no relation to the mind?

Hyl. To *exist* is one thing, and to be *perceived* is another.

Phil. I speak with regard to sensible things only; and of these I ask, whether by their real existence you mean a subsistence exterior to the mind and distinct from their being perceived?

Hyl. I mean a real absolute being, distinct from and without any relation to their being perceived.

Phil. Heat therefore, if it be allowed a real being, must exist without the mind?

Hyl. It must.

Phil. Tell me, Hylas, is this real existence equally compatible to all degrees of heat, which we perceive, or is there any reason why we should attribute it to some and deny it to others? And if there be, pray let me know that reason.

Hyl. Whatever degree of heat we perceive by sense, we may be sure the same exists in the object that occasions it.

Phil. What! the greatest as well as the least?

Hyl. I tell you, the reason is plainly the same in respect of both: they are both perceived by sense; nay, the greater degree of heat is more sensibly perceived; and consequently, if there is any difference, we are more certain of its real existence than we can be of the reality of a lesser degree.

Phil. But is not the most vehement and intense degree of heat a very great pain?

Hyl. No one can deny it.

Phil. And is any unperceiving thing capable of pain or pleasure?

Hyl. No, certainly.

Phil. Is your material substance a senseless being or a being endowed with sense and perception?

Hyl. It is senseless, without doubt.

Phil. It cannot, therefore, be the subject of pain?

Hyl. By no means.

Phil. Nor, consequently, of the greatest heat perceived by sense, since you acknowledge this to be no small pain?

Hyl. I grant it.

Phil. What shall we say then of your external object: is it a material substance, or no?

Hyl. It is a material substance with the sensible qualities inhering in it.

Phil. How then can a great heat exist in it, since you own it cannot in a material substance? I desire you would clear this point.

Hyl. Hold, Philonous, I fear I was out in yielding intense heat to be a pain. It should seem rather that pain is something distinct from heat, and the consequence or effect of it.

Phil. Upon putting your hand near the fire, do you perceive one simple uniform sensation or two distinct sensations?

Hyl. But one simple sensation.

Phil. Is not the heat immediately perceived?

Hyl. It is.

Phil. And the pain?

Hyl. True.

Phil. Seeing therefore they are both immediately perceived at the same time, and the fire affects you only with one simple or uncompounded idea, it follows that this same simple idea is both the intense heat immediately perceived and the pain; and, consequently, that the intense heat immediately perceived is nothing distinct from a particular sort of pain.

Hyl. It seems so.

Phil. Again, try in your thoughts, Hylas, if you can conceive a vehement sensation to be without pain or pleasure.

Hyl. I cannot.

Phil. Or can you frame to yourself an idea of sensible pain or pleasure, in general, abstracted from every particular idea of heat, cold, tastes, smells, etc.?

Hyl. I do not find that I can.

Phil. Does it not therefore follow that sensible pain is nothing distinct from those sensations or ideas—in an intense degree?

Hyl. It is undeniable; and, to speak the truth, I begin to suspect a very great heat cannot exist but in a mind perceiving it.

Phil. What! are you then in that *skeptical* state of suspense, between affirming and denying?

Hyl. I think I may be positive in the point. A very violent and painful heat cannot exist without the mind.

Phil. It has not therefore, according to you, any real being?

Hyl. I own it.

Phil. Is it therefore certain that there is no body in nature really hot?

Hyl. I have not denied there is any real heat in bodies. I only say there is no such thing as an intense real heat.

Phil. But did you not say before that all degrees of heat were equally real, or, if there was any difference, that the greater were more undoubtedly real than the lesser?

Hyl. True; but it was because I did not then consider the ground there is for distinguishing between them, which I now plainly see. And it is this: because intense heat is nothing else but a particular kind of painful sensation, and pain cannot exist but in a perceiving being, it follows that no intense heat can really exist in an unperceiving corporeal substance. But this is no reason why we should deny heat in an inferior degree to exist in such a substance.

Phil. But how shall we be able to discern those degrees of heat which exist only in the mind from those which exist without it?

Hyl. That is no difficult matter. You know the least pain cannot exist unperceived; whatever, therefore, degree of heat is a pain exists only in the mind. But as for all other degrees of heat nothing obliges us to think the same of them.

Phil. I think you granted before that no unperceiving being was capable of pleasure any more than of pain.

Hyl. I did.

Phil. And is not warmth, or a more gentle degree of heat than what causes uneasiness, a pleasure?

Hyl. What then?

Phil. Consequently, it cannot exist without the mind in an unperceiving substance, or body.

Hyl. So it seems.

Phil. Since, therefore, as well those degrees of heat that are not painful, as those that are, can exist only in a thinking substance, may we not conclude that external bodies are absolutely incapable of any degree of heat whatsoever?

Hyl. On second thoughts, I do not think it is so evident that warmth is a pleasure as that a great degree of heat is pain.

Phil. I do not pretend that warmth is as great a pleasure as heat is a pain. But if you grant it to be even a small pleasure, it serves to make good my conclusion.

Hyl. I could rather call it an "indolence." It seems to be nothing more than a privation of both pain and pleasure. And that such a quality or state as this may agree to an unthinking substance, I hope you will not deny.

Phil. If you are resolved to maintain that warmth, or a gentle degree of heat, is no pleasure, I know not how to convince you otherwise than by appealing to your own sense. But what think you of cold?

Hyl. The same that I do of heat. An intense degree of cold is a pain; for to feel a very great cold is to perceive a great uneasiness; it cannot therefore exist without the mind; but a lesser degree of cold may, as well as a lesser degree of heat.

Phil. Those bodies, therefore, upon whose application to our own we perceive a moderate degree of heat must be concluded to have a moderate degree of heat or warmth in them; and those upon whose application we feel a like degree of cold must be thought to have cold in them.

Hyl. They must.

Phil. Can any doctrine be true that necessarily leads a man into an absurdity?

Hyl. Without doubt it cannot.

Phil. Is it not an absurdity to think that the same thing should be at the same time both cold and warm?

Hyl. It is.

Phil. Suppose now one of your hands hot, and the other cold, and that they are both at once put into the same vessel of water, in an intermediate state, will not the water seem cold to one hand, and warm to the other?

Hyl. It will.

Phil. Ought we not therefore, by your principles, to conclude it is really both cold and warm at the same time, that is, according to your own concession, to believe an absurdity?

Hyl. I confess it seems so.

Phil. Consequently, the principles themselves are false, since you have granted that no true principle leads to an absurdity.

Hyl. But, after all, can anything be more absurd than to say, *there is no heat in the fire?*

Phil. To make the point still clearer; tell me whether, in two cases exactly alike, we ought not to make the same judgment?

Hyl. We ought.

Phil. When a pin pricks your finger, does it not rend and divide the fibres of your flesh?

Hyl. It does.

Phil. And when a coal burns your finger, does it any more?

Hyl. It does not.

Phil. Since, therefore, you neither judge the sensation itself occasioned by the pin, nor anything like it to be in the pin, you should not, conformably to what you have now granted, judge the sensation occasioned by the fire, or anything like it, to be in the fire.

Hyl. Well, since it must be so, I am content to yield this point and acknowledge that heat and cold are only sensations existing in our minds. But there still remain qualities enough to secure the reality of external things.

Phil. But what will you say, Hylas, if it shall appear that the case is the same with regard to all other sensible qualities, and that they can no more be supposed to exist without the mind than heat and cold?

Hyl. Then, indeed, you will have done something to the purpose; but that is what I despair of seeing proved.

Phil. Let us examine them in order. What think you of tastes—do they exist without the mind, or no?

Hyl. Can any man in his senses doubt whether sugar is sweet or wormwood bitter?

Phil. Inform me, Hylas. Is a sweet taste a particular kind of pleasure or pleasant sensation, or is it not?

Hyl. It is.

Phil. And is not bitterness some kind of uneasiness or pain?

Hyl. I grant it.

Phil. If therefore, sugar and wormwood are unthinking corporeal substances existing without the mind, how can sweetness and bitterness, that is, pleasure and pain, agree to them?

Hyl. Hold, Philonous. I now see what it was [that] deluded me all this time. You asked whether heat and cold, sweetness and bitterness, were not particular sorts of pleasure and pain; to which I answered simply that they were. Whereas I should have thus distinguished: those qualities as perceived by us are pleasures or pains, but not as existing in the external objects. We must not therefore conclude absolutely that there is no heat in the fire or sweetness in the sugar, but only that heat or sweetness, as perceived by us, are not in the fire or sugar. What say you to this?

Phil. I say it is nothing to the purpose. Our discourse proceeded altogether concerning sensible things, which you defined to be "the things we immediately perceive by our senses." Whatever other qualities, therefore, you speak of, as distinct from these, I know nothing of them, neither do they at all belong to the point in dispute. You may, indeed, pretend to have discovered certain qualities which you do not perceive and assert those insensible qualities exist in fire and sugar. But what use can be made of this to your present purpose, I am at a loss to conceive. Tell me then once more, do you acknowledge that heat and cold, sweetness and bitterness (meaning those qualities which are perceived by the senses), do not exist without the mind?

Hyl. I see it is to no purpose to hold out, so I give up the cause as to those mentioned qualities, though I profess it sounds oddly to say that sugar is not sweet.

Phil. But, for your further satisfaction, take this along with you: that which at other times seems sweet shall, to a distempered palate, appear bitter, and nothing can be plainer than that divers persons perceive different tastes in the same food, since that which one man delights in, another abhors. And how could this be if the taste was something really inherent in the food?

Hyl. I acknowledge I know not how.

Phil. In the next place, odors are to be considered. And with regard to these I would fain know whether what has been said of tastes does not exactly agree to them? Are they not so many pleasing or displeasing sensations?

Hyl. They are.

Phil. Can you then conceive it possible that they should exist in an unperceiving thing?

Hyl. I cannot.

Phil. Or can you imagine that filth and ordure affect those brute animals that feed on them out of choice with the same smells which we perceive in them?

Hyl. By no means.

Phil. May we not therefore conclude of smells, as of the other forementioned qualities, that they cannot exist in any but a perceiving substance or mind?

Hyl. I think so.

Phil. Then as to sounds, what must we think of them, are they accidents really inherent in external bodies or not?

Hyl. That they inhere not in the sonorous bodies is plain from hence; because a bell struck in the exhausted receiver of an air-pump sends forth no sound. The air, therefore, must be thought the subject of sound.

Phil. What reason is there for that, Hylas?

Hyl. Because, when any motion is raised in the air, we perceive a sound greater or less, in proportion to the air's motion; but without some motion in the air we never hear any sound at all.

Phil. And granting that we never hear a sound but when some motion is produced in the air, yet I do not see how you can infer from thence that the sound itself is in the air.

Hyl. It is this very motion in the external air that produces in the mind the sensation of sound. For, striking on the drum of the ear, it causes a vibration which by the auditory nerves being communicated to the brain, the soul is thereupon affected with the sensation called "sound."

Phil. What! is sound then a sensation?

Hyl. I tell you, as perceived by us it is a particular sensation in the mind.

Phil. And can any sensation exist without the mind?

Hyl. No, certainly.

Phil. How then can sound, being a sensation, exist in the air if by the "air" you mean a senseless substance existing without the mind?

Hyl. You must distinguish, Philonous, between sound as it is perceived by us, and as it is in itself; or (which is the same thing) between the sound we immediately perceive and that which exists without us. The former, indeed, is a particular kind of sensation, but the latter is merely a vibrative or undulatory motion in the air.

Phil. I thought I had already obviated that distinction by the answer I gave when you were applying it in a like case before. But, to say no more of that, are you sure then that sound is really nothing but motion?

Hyl. I am.

Phil. Whatever, therefore, agrees to real sound may with truth be attributed to motion?

Hyl. It may.

Phil. It is then good sense to speak of "motion" as of a thing that is *loud, sweet, acute,* or *grave.*

Hyl. I see you are resolved not to understand me. Is it not evident those accidents or modes belong only to sensible sound, or sound in the common acceptation of the word, but not to sound in the real and philosophic sense, which, as I just now told you, is nothing but a certain motion of the air?

Phil. It seems then there are two sorts of sound —the one vulgar, or that which is heard, the other philosophical and real?

Hyl. Even so.

Phil. And the latter consists in motion?

Hyl. I told you so before.

Phil. Tell me, Hylas, to which of the senses, think you, the idea of motion belongs? To the hearing?

Hyl. No, certainly; but to the sight and touch.

Phil. It should follow then that, according to you, real sounds may possibly be *seen* or *felt,* but never *heard.*

Hyl. Look you, Philonous, you may, if you please, make a jest of my opinion, but that will not alter the truth of things. I own, indeed, the inferences you draw me into sound something oddly, but common language, you know, is framed by, and for the use of, the vulgar. We must not therefore wonder if expressions adapted to exact philosophic notions seem uncouth and out of the way.

Phil. Is it come to that? I assure you I imagine myself to have gained no small point since you make so light of departing from common phrases and opinions, it being a main part of our inquiry to examine whose notions are widest of the common road and most repugnant to the general sense of the world. But can you think it no more than a philosophical paradox to say that "real sounds are never heard," and that the idea of them is obtained by some other sense? And is there nothing in this contrary to nature and the truth of things?

Hyl. To deal ingenuously, I do not like it. And, after the concessions already made, I had as well grant that sounds, too, have no real being without the mind.

Phil. And I hope you will make no difficulty to acknowledge the same of colors.

Hyl. Pardon me; the case of colors is very different. Can anything be plainer than that we see them on the objects?

Phil. The objects you speak of are, I suppose, corporeal substances existing without the mind?

Hyl. They are.

Phil. And have true and real colors inhering in them?

Hyl. Each visible object has that color which we see in it.

Phil. How! is there anything visible but what we perceive by sight?

Hyl. There is not.

Phil. And do we perceive anything by sense which we do not perceive immediately?

Hyl. How often must I be obliged to repeat the same thing? I tell you, we do not.

Phil. Have patience, good Hylas, and tell me once more whether there is anything immediately perceived by the senses except sensible qualities. I know you asserted there was not; but I would now be informed whether you still persist in the same opinion.

Hyl. I do.

Phil. Pray, is your corporeal substance either a sensible quality or made up of sensible qualities?

Hyl. What a question that is! Who ever thought it was?

Phil. My reason for asking was, because in saying "each visible object has that color which we see in it," you make visible objects to be corporeal substances, which implies either that corporeal substances are sensible qualities or else that there is something besides sensible qualities perceived by sight; but as this point was formerly agreed between us, and is still maintained by you, it is a clear consequence that your corporeal substance is nothing distinct from sensible qualities.

Hyl. You may draw as many absurd consequences as you please and endeavor to perplex the plainest things, but you shall never persuade me out of my senses. I clearly understand my own meaning.

Phil. I wish you would make me understand it, too. But, since you are unwilling to have your notion of corporeal substance examined, I shall urge that point no further. Only be pleased to let me know whether the same colors which we see exist in external bodies or some other.

Hyl. The very same.

Phil. What! are then the beautiful red and purple we see on yonder clouds really in them? Or do you imagine they have in themselves any other form than that of a dark mist of vapor?

Hyl. I must own, Philonous, those colors are not really in the clouds as they seem to be at this distance. They are only apparent colors.

Phil. "Apparent" call you them? How shall we distinguish these apparent colors from real?

Hyl. Very easily. Those are to be thought apparent which, appearing only at a distance, vanish upon a nearer approach.

Phil. And those, I suppose, are to be thought real which are discovered by the most near and exact survey.

Hyl. Right.

Phil. Is the nearest and exactest survey made by the help of a microscope or by the naked eye?

Hyl. By a microscope, doubtless.

Phil. But a microscope often discovers colors in an object different from those perceived by the unassisted sight. And, in case we had microscopes magnifying to any assigned degree, it is certain that no object whatsoever, viewed through them, would appear in the same color which it exhibits to the naked eye.

Hyl. And what will you conclude from all this? You cannot argue that there are really and naturally no colors on objects because by artificial managements they may be altered or made to vanish.

Phil. I think it may evidently be concluded from your own concessions that all the colors we see with our naked eyes are only apparent as those on the clouds, since they vanish upon a more close and accurate inspection which is afforded us by a microscope. Then, as to what you say by way of prevention: I ask you whether the real and natural state of an object is better discovered by a very sharp and piercing sight or by one which is less sharp?

Hyl. By the former without doubt.

Phil. Is it not plain from dioptrics that microscopes make the sight more penetrating and represent objects as they would appear to the eye in case it were naturally endowed with a most exquisite sharpness?

Hyl. It is.

Phil. Consequently, the microscopical representation is to be thought that which best sets forth the real nature of the thing, or what it is in itself. The colors, therefore, by it perceived are more genuine and real than those perceived otherwise.

Hyl. I confess there is something in what you say.

Phil. Besides, it is not only possible but manifest that there actually are animals whose eyes are by nature framed to perceive those things which by reason of their minuteness escape our sight. What think you of those inconceivably small animals perceived by glasses? Must we suppose they are all stark blind? Or, in case they see, can it be imagined their sight has not the same use in preserving their bodies from injuries which appears in that of all other animals? And if it has, is it not evident they must see particles less than their own bodies, which will present them with a far different view in each object from that which strikes our senses? Even our own eyes do not always represent objects to us after the same manner. In the jaundice everyone knows that all things seem yellow. Is it not therefore highly probable those animals in whose eyes we discern a very different texture from that of ours, and whose bodies abound with different humors, do not see the same colors in every object that we do? From all which should it not seem to follow that all colors are equally apparent, and that none of those which we perceive are really inherent in any outward object?

Hyl. It should.

Phil. The point will be past all doubt if you consider that, in case colors were real properties or affections inherent in external bodies, they could admit of no alteration without some change wrought in the very bodies themselves; but is it not evident from what has been said that, upon the use of microscopes, upon a change happening in the humors of the eye, or a variation of distance, without any manner of real alteration in the thing itself, the colors of any object are either changed or totally disappear? Nay, all other circumstances remaining the same, change but the situation of some objects and they shall present different colors to the eye. The same thing happens upon viewing an object in various degrees of light. And what is more known than that the same bodies appear differently colored by candlelight from what they do in the open day? Add to these the experiment of a prism which, separating the heterogeneous rays of light alters the color of any object and will cause the whitest to appear of a deep blue or red to the naked eye. And now tell me whether you are still of opinion that every body has its true real color inhering in it; and if you think it has, I would fain know further from you what certain distance and position of the object, what peculiar texture and formation of the eye, what degree or kind of light is necessary for ascertaining that true color and distinguishing it from apparent ones.

Hyl. I own myself entirely satisfied that they are all equally apparent and that there is no such thing as color really inhering in external bodies, but that it is altogether in the light. And what confirms me in this opinion is that in proportion to the light colors are still more or less vivid; and if there be no light, then are there no colors perceived. Besides, allowing there are colors on external objects, yet, how is it possible for us to perceive them? For no external body affects the mind unless it acts first on our organs of sense. But the only action of bodies is motion, and motion cannot be communicated otherwise than by impulse. A distant object, therefore, cannot act on the eye, nor consequently make itself or its properties perceivable to the soul. Whence it plainly follows that it is immediately some contiguous substance which, operating on the eye, occasions a perception of colors; and such is light.

Phil. How! is light then a substance?

Hyl. I tell you, Philonous, external light is nothing but a thin fluid substance whose minute particles, being agitated with a brisk motion and in various manners reflected from the different surfaces of outward objects to the eyes, communicate different motions to the optic nerves; which, being propagated to the brain, cause therein various impressions, and these are attended with the sensations of red, blue, yellow, etc.

Phil. It seems, then, the light does no more than shake the optic nerves.

Hyl. Nothing else.

Phil. And, consequent to each particular motion of the nerves, the mind is affected with a sensation which is some particular color.

Hyl. Right.

Phil. And these sensations have no existence without the mind.

Hyl. They have not.

Phil. How then do you affirm that colors are in the light, since by "light" you understand a corporeal substance external to the mind?

Hyl. Light and colors, as immediately perceived by us, I grant cannot exist without the mind. But in themselves they are only the motions and configurations of certain insensible particles of matter.

Phil. Colors, then, in the vulgar sense, or taken for the immediate objects of sight, cannot agree to any but a perceiving substance.

Hyl. That is what I say.

Phil. Well then, since you give up the point as to those sensible qualities which are alone thought colors by all mankind besides, you may hold what you please with regard to those invisible ones of the philosophers. It is not my business to dispute them; only I would advise you to bethink yourself whether, considering the inquiry we are upon, it be prudent for you to affirm—*the red and blue which we see are not real colors, but certain unknown motions and figures which no man ever did or can see are truly so.* Are not these shocking notions, and are not they subject to as many ridiculous inferences as those you were obliged to renounce before in the case of sounds?

Hyl. I frankly own, Philonous, that it is in vain to stand out any longer. Colors, sounds, tastes, in a word, all those termed "secondary qualities," have certainly no existence without the mind. But by this acknowledgment I must not be supposed to derogate anything from the reality of matter or external objects; seeing it is no more than several philosophers maintain, who nevertheless are the farthest imaginable from denying matter. For the clearer understanding of this you must know sensible qualities are by philosophers divided into "primary" and "secondary." The former are extension, figure, solidity, gravity, motion, and rest. And these they hold exist really in bodies. The latter are those above enumerated, or, briefly, all sensible qualities besides the primary, which they assert are only so many sensations or ideas existing nowhere but in the mind. But all this, I doubt not, you are already apprised of. For my part I have been a long time sensible there was such an opinion current among philosophers, but was never thoroughly convinced of its truth till now.

Phil. You are still then of opinion that *extension* and *figures* are inherent in external unthinking substances?

Hyl. I am.

Phil. But what if the same arguments which are brought against secondary qualities will hold good against these also?

Hyl. Why then I shall be obliged to think they too exist only in the mind.

Phil. Is it your opinion the very figure and extension which you perceive by sense exist in the outward object or material substance?

Hyl. It is.

Phil. Have all other animals as good grounds to think the same of the figure and extension which they see and feel?

Hyl. Without doubt, if they have any thought at all.

Phil. Answer me, Hylas. Think you the senses were bestowed upon all animals for their preservation and well-being in life? Or were they given to men alone for this end?

Hyl. I make no question but they have the same use in all other animals.

Phil. If so, is it not necessary they should be enabled by them to perceive their own limbs and those bodies which are capable of harming them?

Hyl. Certainly.

Phil. A mite therefore must be supposed to see his own foot, and things equal or even less than it, as bodies of some considerable dimension, though at the same time they appear to you scarce discernible or at best at so many visible points?

Hyl. I cannot deny it.

Phil. And to creatures less than the mite they will seem yet larger?

Hyl. They will.

Phil. Insomuch that what you can hardly discern will to another extremely minute animal appear as some huge mountain?

Hyl. All this I grant.

Phil. Can one and the same thing be at the same time in itself of different dimensions?

Hyl. That were absurd to imagine.

Phil. But from what you have laid down it follows that both the extension by you perceived and that perceived by the mite itself, as likewise all those perceived by lesser animals, are each of them the true extension of the mite's foot; that is to say, by your own principles you are led into an absurdity.

Hyl. There seems to be some difficulty in the point.

Phil. Again, have you not acknowledged that no real inherent property of any object can be changed without some change in the thing itself?

Hyl. I have.

Phil. But, as we approach to or recede from an object, the visible extension varies, being at one distance ten or a hundred times greater than at another. Does it not therefore follow from hence likewise that it is not really inherent in the object?

Hyl. I own I am at a loss what to think.

Phil. Your judgment will soon be determined if you will venture to think as freely concerning this quality as you have done concerning the rest. Was it not admitted as a good argument that neither heat nor cold was in the water because it seemed warm to one hand and cold to the other?

Hyl. It was.

Phil. Is it not the very same reasoning to conclude there is no extension or figure in an object because to one eye it shall seem little, smooth, and round, when at the same time it appears to the other great, uneven, and angular?

Hyl. The very same. But does this latter fact ever happen?

Phil. You may at any time make the experiment by looking with one eye bare and with the other through a microscope.

Hyl. I know not how to maintain it, and yet I am loath to give up *extension;* I see so many odd consequences following upon such a concession.

Phil. Odd, say you? After the concessions already made, I hope you will stick at nothing for its oddness. [But,[1] on the other hand, should it not seem very odd if the general reasoning which includes all other sensible qualities did not also include extension? If it be allowed that no idea nor anything like an idea can exist in an unperceiving substance, then surely it follows that no figure or mode of extension, which we can either perceive or imagine, or have any idea of, can be really inherent in matter, not to mention the peculiar difficulty there must be in conceiving a material substance, prior to and distinct from extension, to be the *substratum* of extension. Be the sensible quality what it will—figure or sound or color—it seems alike impossible it should subsist in that which does not perceive it.]

Hyl. I give up the point for the present, reserving still a right to retract my opinion in case I shall hereafter discover any false step in my progress to it.

Phil. That is a right you cannot be denied. Figures and extension being dispatched, we proceed next to *motion.* Can a real motion in any external body be at the same time both very swift and very slow?

Hyl. It cannot.

Phil. Is not the motion of a body swift in a reciprocal proportion to the time it takes up in describing any given space? Thus a body that describes a mile in an hour moves three times faster than it would in case it described only a mile in three hours.

Hyl. I agree with you.

Phil. And is not time measured by the succession of ideas in our minds?

Hyl. It is.

Phil. And is it not possible ideas should succeed one another twice as fast in your mind as they do in mine, or in that of some spirit of another kind?

Hyl. I own it.

Phil. Consequently, the same body may to another seem to perform its motion over any space in half the time that it does to you. And the same reasoning will hold as to any other proportion; that is to say, according to your principles (since the motions perceived are both really in the object) it is possible one and the same body shall be really moved the same way at once, both very swift and very slow. How is this consistent with common sense or with what you just now granted?

Hyl. I have nothing to say to it.

Phil. Then as for *solidity;* either you do not mean any sensible quality by that word, and so it is beside our inquiry; or if you do, it must be either hardness or resistance. But both the one and the other are plainly relative to our senses: it being evident that what seems hard to one animal may appear soft to another who has greater force and firmness of limbs. Nor is it less plain that the resistance I feel is not in the body.

Hyl. I own the very sensation of resistance, which is all you immediately perceive, is not in the *body,* but the cause of that sensation is.

Phil. But the causes of our sensations are not things immediately perceived, and therefore not sensible. This point I thought had been already determined.

Hyl. I own it was; but you will pardon me if I seem a little embarrassed; I know not how to quit my old notions.

Phil. To help you out, do but consider that if *extension* be once acknowledged to have no existence without the mind, the same must necessarily be granted of motion, solidity, and gravity, since they all evidently suppose extension. It is therefore superfluous to inquire particularly concerning each of them. In denying extension, you have denied them all to have any real existence.

Hyl. I wonder, Philonous, if what you say be true, why those philosophers who deny the secondary qualities any real existence should yet attribute it to the primary. If there is no difference between them, how can this be accounted for?

Phil. It is not my business to account for every opinion of the philosophers. But, among other reasons which may be assigned for this, it seems probable that pleasure and pain being rather annexed to the former than the latter may be one. Heat and cold, tastes and smells have something more vividly pleasing or disagreeable than the ideas of extension, figure, and motion affect us with. And, it being too visibly absurd to hold that pain or pleasure can be in an unperceiving substance, men are more easily weaned from believing the external existence of the secondary than the primary qualities. You will be satisfied there is something in this if you recollect the difference you made between an intense and more moderate degree of heat, allowing the one a real existence while you denied it to the other. But, after all, there is no rational ground for that distinction, for surely an indifferent sensation is as truly a *sensation* as one more pleasing or painful, and consequently should not any more than they be supposed to exist in an unthinking subject.

Hyl. It is just come into my head, Philonous, that I have somewhere heard of a distinction between *absolute* and *sensible* extension. Now though it be acknowledged that *great* and *small,* consisting merely in the relation which other extended beings have to the parts of our own bodies, do not really inhere in the substances themselves, yet nothing obliges us to hold the same with regard to *absolute* extension, which is something abstracted from *great* and *small,* from this or that particular magnitude or figure. So likewise as to motion: *swift* and *slow* are altogether relative to the succession of ideas in our own minds. But it does not follow, because those modifications of motion exist not without the mind, that therefore absolute motion abstracted from them does not.

Phil. Pray what is it that distinguishes one motion, or one part of extension, from another? Is it not something sensible, as some degree of swiftness or slowness, some certain magnitude or figure peculiar to each?

Hyl. I think so.

Phil. These qualities, therefore, stripped of all sensible properties, are without all specific and numerical differences, as the schools call them.

Hyl. They are.

Phil. That is to say, they are extension in general, and motion in general.

Hyl. Let it be so.

Phil. But it is a universally received maxim that *everything which exists is particular.* How then can motion in general, or extension in general, exist in any corporeal substance?

Hyl. I will take time to solve your difficulty.

Phil. But I think the point may be speedily decided. Without doubt you can tell whether you are able to frame this or that idea. Now I am content to put our dispute on this issue. If you can frame in your thoughts a distinct abstract idea of motion or extension divested of all those sensible modes as swift and slow, great and small, round and square, and the like, which are acknowledged to exist only in the mind, I will then yield the point you contend for. But if you cannot, it will be unreasonable on your side to insist any longer upon what you have no notion of.

Hyl. To confess ingenuously, I cannot.

Phil. Can you even separate the ideas of extension and motion from the ideas of all those qualities which they who make the distinction term "secondary?"

Hyl. What! is it not an easy matter to consider extension and motion by themselves, abstracted from all other sensible qualities? Pray how do the mathematicians treat of them?

Phil. I acknowledge, Hylas, it is not difficult to form general propositions and reasonings about those qualities without mentioning any other, and, in this sense, to consider or treat of them abstractedly. But how does it follow that, because I can pronounce the word "motion" by itself, I can form the idea of it in my mind exclusive of body? Or because theorems may be made of extension and figures, without any mention of *great*

or *small,* or any other sensible mode or quality, that therefore it is possible such an abstract idea of extension, without any particular size or figure or sensible quality, should be distinctly formed and apprehended by the mind? Mathematicians treat of quantity without regarding what other sensible qualities it is attended with, as being altogether indifferent to their demonstrations. But when, laying aside the words, they contemplate the bare ideas, I believe you will find they are not the pure abstracted ideas of extension.

Hyl. But what say you to *pure intellect?* May not abstracted ideas be framed by that faculty?

Phil. Since I cannot frame abstract ideas at all, it is plain I cannot frame them by the help of pure intellect, whatsoever faculty you understand by those words. Besides, not to inquire into the nature of pure intellect and its spiritual objects, as *virtue, reason, God,* or the like, thus much seems manifest that sensible things are only to be perceived by sense or represented by the imagination. Figures, therefore, and extension, being originally perceived by sense, do not belong to pure intellect; but, for your further satisfaction, try if you can frame the idea of any figure abstracted from all particularities of size or even from other sensible qualities.

Hyl. Let me think a little—I do not find that I can.

Phil. And can you think it possible that should really exist in nature which implies a repugnancy in its conception?

Hyl. By no means.

Phil. Since therefore it is impossible even for the mind to disunite the ideas of extension and motion from all other sensible qualities, does it not follow that where the one exist there necessarily the other exist likewise?

Hyl. It should seem so.

Phil. Consequently, the very same arguments which you admitted as conclusive against the secondary qualities are, without any further application of force, against the primary, too. Besides, if you will trust your senses, is it not plain all sensible qualities coexist, or to them appear as being in the same place? Do they ever represent a motion or figure as being divested of all other visible and tangible qualities?

Hyl. You need say no more on this head. I am free to own, if there be no secret error or oversight in our proceedings hitherto, that all sensible qualities are alike to be denied existence without the mind. But my fear is that I have been too liberal in my former concessions, or overlooked some fallacy or other. In short, I did not take time to think.

Phil. For that matter, Hylas, you may take what time you please in reviewing the progress of our inquiry. You are at liberty to recover any slips you might have made, or offer whatever you have omitted which makes for your first opinion.

Hyl. One great oversight I take to be this—that I did not sufficiently distinguish the *object* from the *sensation.* Now, though this latter may not exist without the mind, yet it will not thence follow that the former cannot.

Phil. What object do you mean? The object of the senses?

Hyl. The same.

Phil. It is then immediately perceived?

Hyl. Right.

Phil. Make me to understand the difference between what is immediately perceived and a sensation.

Hyl. The sensation I take to be an act of the mind perceiving; besides which there is something perceived, and this I call the "object." For example, there is red and yellow on that tulip. But then the act of perceiving those colors is in me only, and not in the tulip.

Phil. What tulip do you speak of? Is it that which you see?

Hyl. The same.

Phil. And what do you see besides color, figure, and extension?

Hyl. Nothing.

Phil. What you would say then is that the red and yellow are coexistent with the extension; is it not?

Hyl. That is not all; I would say they have a real existence without the mind, in some unthinking substance.

Phil. That the colors are really in the tulip which I see is manifest. Neither can it be denied that this tulip may exist independent of your mind or mind; but that any immediate object of the senses—that is, any idea, or combination of ideas—should exist in an unthinking substance, or exterior to all minds, is in itself an evident contradiction. Nor can I imagine how this follows from what you said just now, to wit, that the red and yellow were on the tulip *you saw,* since

you do not pretend to *see* that unthinking substance.

Hyl. You have an artful way, Philonous, of diverting our inquiry from the subject.

Phil. I see you have no mind to be pressed that way. To return then to your distinction between *sensation* and *object;* if I take you right, you distinguish in every perception two things, the one an action of the mind, the other not.

Hyl. True.

Phil. And this action cannot exist in, or belong to, any unthinking thing, but whatever besides is implied in a perception may?

Hyl. That is my meaning.

Phil. So that if there was a perception without any act of the mind, it were possible such a perception should exist in an unthinking substance?

Hyl. I grant it. But it is impossible there should be such a perception.

Phil. When is the mind said to be active?

Hyl. When it produces, puts an end to, or changes anything.

Phil. Can the mind produce, discontinue, or change anything but by an act of the will?

Hyl. It cannot.

Phil. The mind therefore is to be accounted *active* in its perceptions so far forth as *volition* is included in them?

Hyl. It is.

Phil. In plucking this flower I am active, because I do it by the motion of my hand, which was consequent upon my volition; so likewise in applying it to my nose. But is either of these smelling?

Hyl. No.

Phil. I act, too, in drawing the air through my nose, because my breathing so rather than otherwise is the effect of my volition. But neither can this be called "smelling," for if it were I should smell every time I breathed in that manner?

Phil. Smelling then is somewhat consequent to all this?

Hyl. It is.

Phil. But I do not find my will concerned any further. Whatever more there is—as that I perceive such a particular smell, or any smell at all —this is independent of my will, and therein I am altogether passive. Do you find it otherwise with you, Hylas?

Hyl. No, the very same.

Phil. Then, as to seeing, is it not in your power to open your eyes or keep them shut, to turn them this or that way?

Hyl. Without doubt.

Phil. But does it in like manner depend on your will that in looking on this flower you perceive *white* rather than any other color? Or, directing your open eyes toward yonder part of the heaven, can you avoid seeing the sun? Or is light or darkness the effect of your volition?

Hyl. No, certainly.

Phil. You are then in these respects altogether passive?

Hyl. I am.

Phil. Tell me now whether *seeing* consists in perceiving light and colors or in opening and turning the eyes?

Hyl. Without doubt, in the former.

Phil. Since, therefore, you are in the very perception of light and colors altogether passive, what is become of that action you were speaking of as an ingredient in every sensation? And does it not follow from your own concessions that the perception of light and colors, including no action in it, may exist in an unperceiving substance? And is not this a plain contradiction?

Hyl. I know not what to think of it.

Phil. Besides, since you distinguish the *active* and *passive* in every perception, you must do it in that of pain. But how is it possible that pain, be it as little active as you please, should exist in an unperceiving substance? In short, do but consider the point and then confess ingenuously whether light and colors, tastes, sounds, etc. are not all equally passions or sensations in the soul. You may indeed call them "external objects" and give them in words what subsistence you please. But examine your own thoughts and then tell me whether it be not as I say?

Hyl. I acknowledge, Philonous, that, upon a fair observation of what passes in my mind, I can discover nothing else but that I am a thinking being affected with variety of sensations; neither is it possible to conceive how a sensation should exist in an unperceiving substance. But then, on the other hand, when I look on sensible things in a different view, considering them as so many modes and qualities, I find it necessary to suppose a material *substratum*, without which they cannot be conceived to exist.

Phil. "Material substratum" call you it? Pray, by which of your senses came you acquainted with that being?

Hyl. It is not itself sensible; its modes and qualities only being perceived by the senses.

Phil. I presume then it was by reflection and reason you obtained the idea of it?

Hyl. I do not pretend to any proper positive idea of it. However, I conclude it exists because qualities cannot be conceived to exist without a support.

Phil. It seems then you have only a relative notion of it, or that you conceive it not otherwise than by conceiving the relation it bears to sensible qualities?

Hyl. Right.

Phil. Be pleased, therefore, to let me know wherein that relation consists.

Hyl. Is it not sufficiently expressed in the term "substratum" or "substance?"

Phil. If so, the word "substratum" should import that it is spread under the sensible qualities or accidents?

Hyl. True.

Phil. And consequently under extension?

Hyl. I own it.

Phil. It is therefore somewhat in its own nature distinct from extension?

Hyl. I tell you extension is only a mode, and matter is something that supports modes. And is it not evident the thing supported is different from the thing supporting?

Phil. So that something distinct from, and exclusive of, extension is supposed to be the *substratum* of extension?

Hyl. Just so.

Phil. Answer me, Hylas, can a thing be spread without extension, or is not the idea of extension necessarily included in *spreading?*

Hyl. It is.

Phil. Whatsoever therefore you suppose spread under anything must have in itself an extension distinct from the extension of that thing under which it is spread?

Hyl. It must.

Phil. Consequently, every corporeal substance being the *substratum* of extension must have in itself another extension by which it is qualified to be a *substratum,* and so on to infinity? And I ask whether this be not absurd in itself and repugnant to what you granted just now, to wit, that the *substratum* was something distinct from and exclusive of extension?

Hyl. Aye, but, Philonous, you take me wrong. I do not mean that matter is *spread* in a gross literal sense under extension. The word "substratum" is used only to express in general the same thing with "substance."

Phil. Well then, let us examine the relation implied in the term "substance." Is it not that it stands under accidents?

Hyl. The very same.

Phil. But that one thing may stand under or support another, must it not be extended?

Hyl. It must.

Phil. Is not therefore this supposition liable to the same absurdity with the former?

Hyl. You still take things in a strict literal sense; that is not fair, Philonous.

Phil. I am not for imposing any sense on your words; you are at liberty to explain them as you please. Only, I beseech you, make me understand something by them. You tell me matter supports or stands under accidents. How! is it as your legs support your body?

Hyl. No; that is the literal sense.

Phil. Pray let me know any sense, literal or not literal, that you understand it in.—How long must I wait for an answer, Hylas?

Hyl. I declare I know not what to say. I once thought I understood well enough what was meant by matter's supporting accidents. But now, the more I think on it, the less can I comprehend it; in short, I find that I know nothing of it.

Phil. It seems then you have no idea at all, neither relative nor positive, of matter? you know neither what it is in itself nor what relation it bears to accidents?

Hyl. I acknowledge it.

Phil. And yet you asserted that you could not conceive how qualities or accidents should really exist without conceiving at the same time a material support of them?

Hyl. I did.

Phil. That is to say, when you conceive the real existence of qualities, you do withal conceive something which you cannot conceive?

Hyl. It was wrong I own. But still I fear there is some fallacy or other. Pray, what think you of this? It is just come into my head that the ground of all our mistake lies in your treating of each quality by itself. Now I grant that each quality

cannot singly subsist without the mind. Color cannot without extension, neither can figure without some other sensible quality. But, as the several qualities united or blended together form entire sensible things, nothing hinders why such things may not be supposed to exist without the mind.

Phil. Either, Hylas, you are jesting or have a very bad memory. Though, indeed, we went through all the qualities by name one after another, yet my arguments, or rather your concessions, nowhere tended to prove that the secondary qualities did not subsist each alone by itself, but that they were not *at all* without the mind. Indeed, in treating of figure and motion we concluded they could not exist without the mind, because it was impossible even in thought to separate them from all secondary qualities, so as to conceive them existing by themselves. But then this was not the only argument made use of upon that occasion. But (to pass by all that has been hitherto said and reckon it for nothing, if you will have it so) I am content to put the whole upon this issue. If you can conceive it possible for any mixture or combination of qualities, or any sensible object whatever, to exist without the mind, then I will grant it actually to be so.

Hyl. If it comes to that the point will soon be decided. What more easy than to conceive a tree or house existing by itself, independent of, and unperceived by, any mind whatsoever? I do at this present time conceive them existing after that manner.

Phil. How say you, Hylas, can you see a thing which is at the same time unseen?

Hyl. No, that were a contradiction.

Phil. Is it not as great a contradiction to talk of *conceiving* a thing which is *unconceived?*

Hyl. It is.

Phil. The tree or house, therefore, which you think of is conceived by you?

Hyl. How should it be otherwise?

Phil. And what is conceived is surely in the mind?

Hyl. Without question, that which is conceived is in the mind.

Phil. How then came you to say you conceived a house or tree existing independent and out of all minds whatsoever?

Hyl. That was I own an oversight, but stay, let me consider what let me into it.—It is a pleasant mistake enough. As I was thinking of a tree in a solitary place where no one was present to see it, methought that was to conceive a tree as existing unperceived or unthought of, not considering that I myself conceived it all the while. But now I plainly see that all I can do is to frame ideas in my own mind. I may indeed conceive in my own thoughts the idea of a tree, or a house, or a mountain, but that is all. And this is far from proving that I can conceive them *existing out of the minds of all spirits.*

Phil. You acknowledge then that you cannot possibly conceive how any one corporeal sensible thing should exist otherwise than in a mind?

Hyl. I do.

Phil. And yet you will earnestly contend for the truth of that which you cannot so much as conceive?

Hyl. I profess I know not what to think; but still there are some scruples remain with me. Is it not certain I see things at a distance? Do we not perceive the stars and moon, for example, to be a great way off? Is not this, I say, manifest to the senses?

Phil. Do you not in a dream, too, perceive those or the like objects?

Hyl. I do.

Phil. And have they not then the same appearance of being distant?

Hyl. They have.

Phil. But you do not thence conclude the apparitions in a dream to be without the mind?

Hyl. By no means.

Phil. You ought not therefore to conclude that sensible objects are without the mind, from their appearance or manner wherein they are perceived.

Hyl. I acknowledge it. But does not my sense deceive me in those cases?

Phil. By no means. The idea or thing which you immediately perceive, neither sense nor reason informs you that it actually exists without the mind. By sense you only know that you are affected with such certain sensations of light and colors, etc. And these you will not say are without the mind.

Hyl. True, but, besides all that, do you not think the sight suggests something of *outness* or *distance?*

Phil. Upon approaching a distant object, do the visible size and figure change perpetually or do they appear the same at all distances?

Hyl. They are in a continual change.

Phil. Sight, therefore, does not suggest or any way inform you that the visible object you immediately perceive exists at a distance,[2] or will be perceived when you advance farther onward, there being a continued series of visible objects succeeding each other during the whole time of your approach.

Hyl. It does not; but still I know, upon seeing an object, what object I shall perceive after having passed over a certain distance? no matter whether it be exactly the same or no, there is still something of distance suggested in the case.

Phil. Good Hylas, do but reflect a little on the point, and then tell me whether there be any more in it than this. From the ideas you actually perceive by sight, you have by experience learned to collect what other ideas you will (according to the standing order of nature) be affected with, after such a certain succession of time and motion.

Hyl. Upon the whole, I take it to be nothing else.

Phil. Now is it not plain that if we suppose a man born blind was on a sudden made to see, he could at first have no experience of what may be suggested by sight?

Hyl. It is.

Phil. He would not then, according to you, have any notion of distance annexed to the things he saw, but would take them for a new set of sensations existing only in his mind?

Hyl. It is undeniable.

Phil. But to make it more plain: is not *distance* a line turned endwise to the eye?

Hyl. It is.

Phil. And can a line so situated be perceived by sight?

Hyl. It cannot.

Phil. Does it not therefore follow that distance is not properly and immediately perceived by sight?

Hyl. It should seem so.

Phil. Again, is it your opinion that colors are at a distance?

Hyl. It must be acknowledged they are only in the mind.

Phil. But do not colors appear to the eye as coexisting in the same place with extension and figures?

Hyl. They do.

Phil. How can you then conclude from sight that figures exist without, when you acknowledge colors do not; the sensible appearance being the very same with regard to both?

Hyl. I know not what to answer.

Phil. But allowing that distance was truly and immediately perceived by the mind, yet it would not thence follow it existed out of the mind. For whatever is immediately perceived is an idea; and can any *idea* exist out of the mind?

Hyl. To suppose that were absurd; but, inform me, Philonous, can we perceive or know nothing besides our ideas?

Phil. As for the rational deducing of causes from effects, that is beside our inquiry. And by the senses you can best tell whether you perceive anything which is not immediately perceived. And I ask you whether the things immediately perceived are other than your own sensations or ideas? You have indeed more than once, in the course of this conversation, declared yourself on those points, but you seem, by this last question, to have departed from what you then thought.

Hyl. To speak the truth, Philonous, I think there are two kinds of objects: the one perceived immediately, which are likewise called "ideas"; the other are real things or external objects, perceived by the mediation of ideas which are their images and representations. Now I own ideas do not exist without the mind, but the latter sort of objects do. I am sorry I did not think of this distinction sooner; it would probably have cut short your discourse.

Phil. Are those external objects perceived by sense or by some other faculty?

Hyl. They are perceived by sense.

Phil. How! is there anything perceived by sense which is not immediately perceived?

Hyl. Yes, Philonous, in some sort there is. For example, when I look on a picture or statue of Julius Caesar, I may be said, after a manner, to perceive him (though not immediately) by my senses.

Phil. It seems then you will have our ideas, which alone are immediately perceived, to be pictures of external things: and that these also are

perceived by sense inasmuch as they have a conformity or resemblance to our ideas?

Hyl. That is my meaning.

Phil. And in the same way that Julius Caesar, in himself invisible, is nevertheless perceived by sight, real things, in themselves imperceptible, are perceived by sense.

Hyl. In the very same.

Phil. Tell me, Hylas, when you behold the picture of Julius Caesar, do you see with your eyes any more than some colors and figures, with a certain symmetry and composition of the whole?

Hyl. Nothing else.

Phil. And would not a man who had never known anything of Julius Caesar see as much?

Hyl. He would.

Phil. Consequently, he has his sight and the use of it in as perfect a degree as you?

Hyl. I agree with you.

Phil. Whence comes it then that your thoughts are directed to the Roman emperor, and his are not? This cannot proceed from the sensations or ideas of sense by you then perceived, since you acknowledge you have no advantage over him in that respect. It should seem therefore to proceed from reason and memory, should it not?

Hyl. It should.

Phil. Consequently, it will not follow from that instance that anything is perceived by sense which is not immediately perceived. Though I grant we may, in one acceptation, be said to perceive sensible things mediately be sense—that is, when, from a frequently perceived connection, the immediate perception of ideas by one sense suggest to the mind others, perhaps belonging to another sense, which are wont to be connected with them. For instance, when I hear a coach drive along the streets, immediately I perceive only the sound; but from the experience I have had that such a sound is connected with a coach, I am said to hear the coach. It is nevertheless evident that, in truth and strictness, nothing can be *heard* but *sound;* and the coach is not then properly perceived by sense, but suggested from experience. So likewise when we are said to see a red-hot bar of iron; the solidity and heat of the iron are not the objects of sight, but suggested to the imagination by the color and figure which are properly perceived by that sense. In short, those things alone are actually and strictly perceived by any sense which would have been perceived in case that same sense had then been first conferred on us. As for other things, it is plain they are only suggested to the mind by experience grounded on former perceptions. But, to return to your comparison of Caesar's picture, it is plain, if you keep to that, you must hold the real things or archetypes of our ideas are not perceived by sense, but by some internal faculty of the soul, as reason or memory. I would, therefore, fain know what arguments you can draw from reason for the existence of what you call "real things" or "material objects," or whether you remember to have seen them formerly as they are in themselves, or if you have heard or read of anyone that did.

Hyl. Philonous, you are disposed to railery; but that will never convince me.

Phil. My aim is only to learn from you the way to come at the knowledge of "material beings." Whatever we perceive is perceived either immediately or mediately—by sense, or by reason and reflection. But, as you have excluded sense, pray show me what reason you have to believe their existence, or what *medium* you can possibly make use of to prove it, either to mine or your own understanding.

Hyl. To deal ingenuously, Philonous, now [that] I consider the point, I do not find I can give you any good reason for it. But this much seems pretty plain, that it is at least possible such things may really exist. And as long as there is no absurdity in supposing them, I am resolved to believe as I did, till you bring good reasons to the contrary.

Phil. What! is it come to this, that you only believe the existence of material objects, and that your belief is founded barely on the possibility of its being true? Then you will have me bring reasons against it, though another would think it reasonable the proof should lie on him who holds the affirmative. And, after all, this very point which you are now resolved to maintain, without any reason, is in effect what you have more than once during this discourse seen good reason to give up. But to pass over all this—if I understand you rightly, you say our ideas do not exist without the mind, but that they are copies, images, or representations of certain originals that do?

Hyl. You take me right.

Phil. They are then like external things?

Hyl. They are.

Phil. Have those things a stable and permanent nature, independent of our senses, or are they in a perpetual change, upon our producing any motions in our bodies, suspending, exerting, or altering our faculties or organs of sense?

Hyl. Real things, it is plain, have a fixed and real nature, which remains the same notwithstanding any change in our senses or in the posture and motion of our bodies; which indeed may affect the ideas in our minds, but it were absurd to think they had the same effect on things existing without the mind.

Phil. How then is it possible that things perpetually fleeting and variable as our ideas should be copies or images of anything fixed and constant? Or, in other words, since all sensible qualities, as size, figure, color, etc., that is, our ideas, are continually changing upon every alteration in the distance, medium, or instruments of sensation—how can any determinate material objects be properly represented or painted forth by several distinct things each of which is so different from and unlike the rest? Or, if you say it resembles some one only of our ideas, how shall we be able to distinguish the true copy from all the false ones?

Hyl. I profess, Philonous, I am at a loss. I know not what to say to this.

Phil. But neither is this all. Which are material objects in themselves—perceptible or imperceptible?

Hyl. Properly and immediately nothing can be perceived but ideas. All material things, therefore, are in themselves insensible and to be perceived only by their ideas.

Phil. Ideas then are sensible, and their archetypes or originals insensible?

Hyl. Right.

Phil. But how can that which is sensible be like that which is insensible? Can a real thing, in itself *invisible,* be like a *color,* or a real thing which is not *audible* be like a *sound?* In a word, can anything be like a sensation or idea, but another sensation or idea?

Hyl. I must own, I think not.

Phil. Is it possible there should be any doubt on the point? Do you not perfectly know your own ideas?

Hyl. I know them perfectly, since what I do not perceive or know can be no part of my idea.

Phil. Consider, therefore, and examine them, and then tell me if there be anything in them which can exist without the mind, or if you can conceive anything like them existing without the mind?

Hyl. Upon inquiry I find it impossible for me to conceive or understand how anything but an idea can be like an idea. And it is most evident that *no idea can exist without the mind.*

Phil. You are, therefore, by your principles forced to deny the reality of sensible things, since you made it to consist in an absolute existence exterior to the mind. That is to say, you are a downright skeptic. So I have gained my point, which was to show your principles led to skepticism.

Hyl. For the present I am, if not entirely convinced, at least silenced.

Phil. I would fain know what more you would require in order to a perfect conviction. Have you not had the liberty of explaining yourself all manner of ways? Were any little slips in discourse laid hold and insisted on? Or were you not allowed to retract or reinforce anything you had offered, as best served your purpose? Has not everything you could say been heard and examined with all the fairness imaginable? In a word, have you not in every point been convinced out of your own mouth? And, if you can at present discover any flaw in any of your former concessions, or think of any remaining subterfuge, any new distinction, color, or comment whatsoever, why do you not produce it?

Hyl. A little patience, Philonous. I am at present so amazed to see myself ensnared, and as it were imprisoned in the labyrinths you have drawn me into, that on the sudden it cannot be expected I should find my way out. You must give me time to look about me and recollect myself.

Phil. Hark; is not this the college bell?

Hyl. It rings for prayers.

Phil. We will go in then, if you please, and meet here again tomorrow morning. In the meantime, you may employ your thoughts on this morning's discourse and try if you can find any fallacy in it, or invent any new means to extricate yourself.

Hyl. Agreed.

THE THIRD DIALOGUE

. . .

[*Hyl.* [3] You say your own soul supplies you with some sort of an idea or image of God. But, at the same time, you acknowledge you have, properly speaking, no idea of your own soul. You even affirm that spirits are a sort of beings altogether different from ideas. Consequently, that no idea can be like a spirit. We have, therefore, no idea of any spirit. You admit nevertheless that there is spiritual substance, although you have no idea of it, while you deny there can be such a thing as material substance, because you have no notion or idea of it. Is this fair dealing? To act consistently, you must either admit matter or reject spirit. What say you to this?

Phil. I say, in the first place, that I do not deny the existence of material substance merely because I have no notion of it, but because the notion of it is inconsistent, or, in other words, because it is repugnant that there should be a notion of it. Many things, for aught I know, may exist whereof neither I nor any other man has or can have any idea or notion whatsoever. But then those things must be possible, that is, nothing inconsistent must be included in their definition. I say, secondly, that, although we believe things to exist which we do not perceive, yet we may not believe that any particular thing exists without some reason for such belief; but I have no reason for believing the existence of matter. I have no immediate intuition thereof, neither can I immediately from my sensations, ideas, notions, actions, or passions infer an unthinking, unperceiving, inactive substance, either by probable deduction or necessary consequence. Whereas the being of my self, that is, my own soul, mind, or thinking principle, I evidently know by reflection. You will forgive me if I repeat the same things in answer to the same objections. In the very notion or definition of "material substance" there is included a manifest repugnance and inconsistency. But this cannot be said of the notion of spirit. That ideas should exist in what does not perceive, or be produced by what does not act, is repugnant. But it is no repugnancy to say that a perceiving thing should be the subject of ideas, or an active thing the cause of them. It is granted we have neither an immediate evidence nor a demonstrative knowledge of the existence of other finite spirits, but it will not thence follow that such spirits are on a foot with material substances, if to suppose the one be inconsistent, and it be not inconsistent to suppose the other; if the one can be inferred by no argument, and there is a probability for the other; if we see signs and effects indicating distinct finite agents like ourselves, and see no sign or symptom whatever that leads to a rational belief of matter. I say, lastly, that I have a notion of spirit, though I have not, strictly speaking, an idea of it. I do not perceive it as an idea, or by means of an idea, but know it by reflection.

Hyl. Notwithstanding all you have said, to me it seems that, according to your own way of thinking, and in consequence of your own principles, it should follow that you are only a system of floating ideas without any substance to support them. Words are not to be used without a meaning. And, as there is no more meaning in *spiritual* substance than in *material* substance, the one is to be exploded as well as the other.

Phil. How often must I repeat that I know or am conscious of my own being, and that I *myself* am not my ideas, but somewhat else, a thinking, active principle that perceives, knows, wills, and operates about ideas. I know that I, one and the same self, perceive both colors and sounds, that a color cannot perceive a sound, nor a sound a color, that I am therefore one individual principle distinct from color and sound, and, for the same reason, from all other sensible things and inert ideas. But I am not in like manner conscious either of the existence or essence of matter. On the contrary, I know that nothing inconsistent can exist, and that the existence of matter implies an inconsistency. Further, I know what I mean when I affirm that there is a spiritual substance or support of ideas, that is, that a spirit knows and perceives ideas. But I do not know what is meant when it is said that an unperceiving substance has inherent in it and supports either ideas or the archetypes of ideas. There is, therefore, upon the whole no parity of case between spirit and matter.]

Hyl. I own myself satisfied in this point. But do you in earnest think the real existence of sensible things consists in their being actually perceived? If so, how comes it that all mankind distinguish between them? Ask the first man you meet, and he shall tell you, "to be perceived" is one thing, and "to exist" is another.

Phil. I am content, Hylas, to appeal to the common sense of the world for the truth of my notion. Ask the gardener why he thinks yonder cherry tree exists in the garden, and he shall tell you, because he sees and feels it; in a word, because he perceives it by his senses. Ask him why he thinks an orange tree not to be there, and he shall tell you, because he does not perceive it. What he perceives by sense, that he terms a real being and says it "is" or "exists"; but that which is not perceivable, the same, he says, has no being.

Hyl. Yes, Philonous, I grant the existence of a sensible thing consists in being perceivable, but not in being actually perceived.

Phil. And what is perceivable but an idea? And can an idea exist without being actually perceived? These are points long since agreed between us.

Hyl. But be your opinion never so true, yet surely you will not deny it is shocking and contrary to the common sense of men. Ask the fellow whether yonder tree has an existence out of his mind; what answer think you he would make?

Phil. The same that I should myself, to wit, that it does exist out of his mind. But then to a Christian it cannot surely be shocking to say, the real tree, existing without his mind, is truly known and comprehended by (that is, *exists in*) the infinite mind of God. Probably he may not at first glance be aware of the direct and immediate proof there is of this, inasmuch as the very being of a tree, or any other sensible thing, implies a mind wherein it is. But the point itself he cannot deny. The question between the materialists and me is not whether things have a *real* existence out of the mind of this or that person, but, whether they have an *absolute* existence, distinct from being perceived by God, and exterior to all minds. This, indeed, some heathens and philosophers have affirmed, but whoever entertains notions of the Deity suitable to the Holy Scriptures will be of another opinion.

Hyl. But, according to your notions, what difference is there between real things and chimeras formed by the imagination or the visions of a dream, since they are all equally in the mind?

Phil. The ideas formed by the imagination are faint and indistinct; they have, besides, an entire dependence on the will. But the ideas perceived by sense, that is, real things, are more vivid and clear, and, being imprinted on the mind by a spirit distinct from us, have not the like dependence on our will. There is, therefore, no danger of confounding these with the foregoing, and there is as little of confounding them with the visions of a dream, which are dim, irregular, and confused. And though they should happen to be never so lively and natural, yet, by their not being connected and of a piece with the preceding and subsequent transaction of our lives, they might easily be distinguished from realities. In short, by whatever method you distinguish *things* from *chimeras* on your own scheme, the same, it is evident, will hold also upon mind. For it must be, I presume, by some perceived difference, and I am not for depriving you of any one thing that you perceive.

Hyl. But still, Philonous, you hold there is nothing in the world but spirits and ideas. And this you must needs acknowledge sounds very oddly.

Phil. I own the word "idea," not being commonly used for "thing," sounds something out of the way. My reason for using it was because a necessary relation to the mind is understood to be implied by the term; and it is now commonly used by philosophers to denote the immediate objects of the understanding. But however oddly the proposition may sound in words, yet it includes nothing so very strange or shocking in its sense, which in effect amounts to no more than this, to wit, that there are only things perceiving and things perceived, or that every unthinking being is necessarily, and from the very nature of its existence, perceived by some mind, if not by any finite created mind, yet certainly by the infinite mind of God, in whom "we live, and move, and have our being." Is this as strange as to say the sensible qualities are not on the object or that we cannot be sure of the existence of things, or know anything of their real natures, though we both see and feel them and perceive them by all our senses?

Hyl. And, in consequence of this, must we not think there are no such things as physical or corporeal causes, but that a spirit is the immediate cause of all the *phenomena* in nature? Can there be anything more extravagant than this?

Phil. Yes, it is infinitely more extravagant to say a thing which is inert operates on the mind, and which is unperceiving is the cause of our perceptions. Besides, that which to you I know

not for what reason seems so extravagant is no more than the Holy Scriptures assert in a hundred places. In them God is represented as the sole and immediate Author of all those effects which some heathens and philosophers are wont to ascribe to Nature, Matter, Fate, or the like unthinking principle. This is so much the constant language of Scripture that it were needless to confirm it by citations.

Hyl. You are not aware, Philonous, that, in making God the immediate Author of all the motions in nature, you make Him the Author of murder, sacrilege, adultery, and the like heinous sins.

Phil. In answer to that I observe, first, that the imputation of guilt is the same whether a person commits an action with or without an instrument. In case, therefore, you suppose God to act by the mediation of an instrument or occasion called "matter," you as truly make Him the Author of sin as I, who think Him the immediate agent in all those operations vulgarly ascribed to Nature. I further observe that sin or moral turpitude does not consist in the outward physical action or motion, but in the internal deviation of the will from the laws of reason and religion. This is plain, in that the killing an enemy in a battle or putting a criminal legally to death is not thought sinful, though the outward act be the very same with that in the case of murder. Since, therefore, sin does not consist in the physical action, the making God an immediate cause of all such actions is not making Him the Author of sin. Lastly, I have nowhere said that God is the only agent who produces all the motions in bodies. It is true I have denied there are any other agents besides spirits, but this is very consistent with allowing to thinking rational beings, in the production of motions, the use of limited powers, ultimately, indeed, derived from God but immediately under the direction of their own wills, which is sufficient to entitle them to all the guilt of their actions.

Hyl. But the denying matter, Philonous, or corporeal substance, there is the point. You can never persuade me that this is not repugnant to the universal sense of mankind. Were our dispute to be determined by most voices, I am confident you would give up the point without gathering the votes.

Phil. I wish both our opinions were fairly stated and submitted to the judgment of men who had plain common sense, without the prejudices of a learned education. Let me be represented as one who trusts his senses, who thinks he knows the things he sees and feels, and entertains no doubts of their existence; and you fairly set forth with all your doubts, your paradoxes, and your skepticism about you, and I shall willingly acquiesce in the determination of any indifferent person. That there is no substance wherein ideas can exist besides spirit is to me evident, and that the objects immediately perceived are ideas is on all hands agreed. And that sensible qualities are objects immediately perceived no one can deny. It is therefore evident there can be no *substratum* of those qualities but spirit, in which they exist, not by way of mode or property, but as a thing perceived in that which perceives it. I deny, therefore, that there is any unthinking *substratum* of the objects of sense, and in that acceptation that there is any material substance. But if by "material substance" is meant only sensible body, that which is seen and felt (and the unphilosophical part of the world, I dare say, mean no more), then I am more certain of matter's existence than you or any other philosopher pretend to be. If there be anything which makes the generality of mankind averse from the notions I espouse, it is a misapprehension that I deny the reality of sensible things; but as it is you who are guilty of that and not I, it follows that in truth their aversion is against your notions and not mine. I do therefore assert that I am as certain as of my own being that there are bodies or corporeal substances (meaning the things I perceive by my senses), and that, granting this, the bulk of mankind will take no thought about, nor think themselves at all concerned in the fate of, those unknown natures and philosophical quiddities which some men are so fond of.

Hyl. What say you to this? Since, according to you, men judge of the reality of things by their senses, how can a man be mistaken in thinking the moon a plain lucid surface, about a foot in diameter, or a square tower, seen at a distance, round, or an oar, with one end in the water, crooked?

Phil. He is not mistaken with regard to the ideas he actually perceives, but in the inferences he makes from his present perceptions. Thus, in the case of the oar, what he immediately perceives by sight is certainly crooked, and so far he is in the right. But if he thence conclude that upon taking the oar out of the water he shall perceive the same crookedness, or that it would affect his touch as crooked things are wont to do, in that he is mistaken. In like manner, if he shall conclude, from what he perceives in one station, that, in case he advances toward the moon or tower, he should still be affected with the like ideas, he is mistaken. But his mistake lies not in what he perceives immediately and at present (it being a manifest contradiction to suppose he should err in respect of that), but in the wrong judgment he makes concerning the ideas he apprehends to be connected with those immediately perceived, or, concerning the ideas, that from what he perceives at present he imagines would be perceived in other circumstances. The case is the same with regard to the Copernican system. We do not here perceive any motion of the earth, but it were erroneous thence to conclude that, in case we were placed at as great a distance from that as we are now from the other planets, we should not then perceive its motion.

Hyl. I understand you and must needs own you say things plausible enough, but give me leave to put you in mind of one thing. Pray, Philonous, were you not formerly as positive that matter existed as you are now that it does not?

Phil. I was. But here lies the difference. Before, my positiveness was founded, without examination, upon prejudice, but now, after inquiry, upon evidence.

Hyl. After all, it seems our dispute is rather about words than things. We agree in the thing, but differ in the name. That we are affected with ideas from without is evident; and it is no less evident that there must be (I will not say archetypes, but) powers without the mind corresponding to those ideas. And as these powers cannot subsist by themselves, there is some subject of them necessarily to be admitted, which I call "matter," and you call "spirit." This is all the difference.

Phil. Pray, Hylas, is that powerful being, or subject of powers, extended?

Hyl. It has not extension, but it has the power to raise in you the idea of extension.

Phil. It is therefore itself unextended?

Hyl. I grant it.

Phil. Is it not also active?

Hyl. Without doubt; otherwise, how could we attribute powers to it?

Phil. Now let me ask you two questions: *First,* whether it be agreeable to the usage either of philosophers or others to give the name "matter" to an unextended active being? And, secondly, whether it be not ridiculously absurd to misapply names contrary to the common use of language?

Hyl. Well then, let it not be called "matter," since you will have it so, but some "third nature," distinct from matter and spirit. For what reason is there why you should call it spirit? Does not the notion of spirit imply that it is thinking as well as active and unextended?

Phil. My reason is this: because I have a mind to have some notion or meaning in what I say, but I have no notion of any action distinct from volition, neither can I conceive volition to be anywhere but in a spirit; therefore, when I speak of an active being I am obliged to mean a spirit. Besides, what can be plainer than that a thing which has no ideas in itself cannot impart them to me; and, if it has ideas, surely it must be a spirit. To make you comprehend the point still more clearly, if it be possible: I assert as well as you that, since we are affected from without, we must allow powers to be without, in a being distinct from ourselves. So far we are agreed. But then we differ as to the kind of this powerful being. I will have it to be spirit, you matter or I know not what (I may add, too, you know not what) third nature. Thus I prove it to be spirit. From the effects I see produced I conclude there are actions; and because actions, volitions; and because there are volitions, there must be a will. Again, the things I perceive must have an existence, they or their archetypes, out of my mind; but, being ideas, neither they nor their archetypes can exist otherwise than in an understanding, there is therefore an understanding. But will and understanding constitute in the strictest sense a mind or spirit. The powerful cause, therefore, of my ideas is in strict propriety of speech a *spirit.*

Hyl. And now I warrant you think you have made the point very clear, little suspecting that what you advance leads directly to a contradiction. Is it not an absurdity to imagine any imperfection in God?

Phil. Without a doubt.

Hyl. To suffer pain is an imperfection?

Phil. Are we not sometimes affected with pain and uneasiness by some other being?

Phil. We are.

Hyl. And have you not said that being is a spirit, and is not that spirit God?

Phil. I grant it.

Hyl. But you have asserted that whatever ideas we perceive from without are in the mind which affects us. The ideas, therefore, of pain and uneasiness are in God, or, in other words, God suffers pain; that is to say, there is an imperfection in the divine nature, which, you acknowledge, was absurd. So you are caught in a plain contradiction.

Phil. That God knows or understands all things, and that He knows, among other things, what pain is, even every sort of painful sensation, and what it is for His creatures to suffer pain, I make no question. But that God, though He knows and sometimes causes painful sensations in us, can Himself suffer pain I positively deny. We, who are limited and dependent spirits, are liable to impressions of sense, the effects of an external agent, which, being produced against our wills, are sometimes painful and uneasy. But God, whom no external being can affect, who perceives nothing by sense as we do, whose will is absolute and independent, causing all things, and liable to be thwarted or resisted by nothing, it is evident such a Being as this can suffer nothing, nor be affected with any painful sensation or, indeed, any sensation at all. We are chained to a body; that is to say, our perceptions are connected with corporeal motions. By the law of our nature we are affected upon every alteration in the nervous parts of our sensible body; which sensible body, rightly considered, is nothing but a complexion of such qualities or ideas as have no existence distinct from being perceived by a mind; so that this connection of sensations with corporeal motions means no more than a correspondence in the order of nature between two sets of ideas, or things immediately perceivable. But God is a pure spirit, disengaged from all such sympathy or natural ties. No corporeal motions are attended with the sensations of pain or pleasure in His mind. To know everything knowable is certainly a perfection, but to endure or suffer or feel anything by sense is an imperfection. The former, I say, agrees to God, but not the latter. God knows or has ideas, but His ideas are not conveyed to Him by sense, as ours are. Your not distinguishing where there is so manifest a difference makes you fancy you see an absurdity where there is none.

Hyl. But all this while you have not considered that the quantity of matter has been demonstrated to be proportional to the gravity of bodies. And what can withstand demonstration?

Phil. Let me see how you demonstrate that point.

Hyl. I lay it down for a principle that the moments or quantities of motion in bodies are in a direct compounded reason of the velocities and quantities of matter contained in them. Hence, where the velocities are equal, it follows the moments are directly as the quantity of matter in each. But it is found by experience that all bodies (bating the small inequalities arising from the resistance of the air) descend with an equal velocity; the motion therefore of descending bodies, and consequently their gravity, which is the cause or principle of that motion, is proportional to the quantity of matter, which was to be demonstrated.

Phil. You lay it down as a self-evident principle that the quantity of motion in any body is proportional to the velocity and matter taken together; and this is made use of to prove a proposition from whence the existence of matter is inferred. Pray is not this arguing in a circle?

Hyl. In the premise I only mean that the motion is proportional to the velocity, jointly with the extension and solidity.

Phil. But allowing this to be true, yet it will not thence follow that gravity is proportional to matter in your philosophic sense of the word, except you take it for granted that unknown *substratum,* or whatever else you call it, is proportional to those sensible qualities which to suppose is plainly begging the question. That there is magnitude and solidity or resistance perceived by sense I readily grant, as likewise, that gravity may be proportional to those qualities I will not dispute. But that either these qualities as perceived by us, or the powers producing them, do exist in a *material substratum*—this is what I deny, and you, indeed, affirm but, notwithstanding your demonstration, have not yet proved.

Hyl. I shall insist no longer on that point. Do you think, however, you shall persuade me the natural philosophers have been dreaming all this

while? Pray what becomes of all their hypotheses and explications of the phenomena which suppose the existence of matter?

Phil. What mean you, Hylas, by the "phenomena"?

Hyl. I mean the appearances which I perceive by my senses.

Phil. And the appearances perceived by sense, are they not ideas?

Hyl. I have told you so a hundred times.

Phil. Therefore, to explain the phenomena is to show how we come to be affected with ideas in that manner and order wherein they are imprinted on our senses. Is it not?

Hyl. It is.

Phil. Now, if you can prove that any philosopher has explained the production of any one idea in our minds by the help of *matter,* I shall forever acquiesce and look on all that has been said against it as nothing; but if you cannot, it is vain to urge the explication of phenomena. That a being endowed with knowledge and will should produce or exhibit ideas is easily understood. But that a being which is utterly destitute of these faculties should be able to produce ideas, or in any sort to affect an intelligence, this I can never understand. This I say, though we had some positive conception of matter, though we knew its qualities and could comprehend its existence, would yet be so far from explaining things that it is itself the most inexplicable thing in the world. And yet, for all this, it will not follow that philosophers have been doing nothing; for by observing and reasoning upon the connection of ideas, they discover the laws and methods of nature, which is a part of knowledge both useful and entertaining.

Hyl. After all, can it be supposed God would deceive all mankind? Do you imagine He would have induced the whole world to believe the being of matter if there was no such thing?

Phil. That every epidemical opinion arising from prejudice, or passion, or thoughtlessness may be imputed to God, as the Author of it, I believe you will not affirm. Whatsoever opinion we father on Him, it must be either because He has discovered it to us by supernatural revelation, or because it is so evident to our natural faculties, which were framed and given us by God, that it is impossible we should withhold our assent from it. But where is the revelation? Or where is th evidence that extorts the belief of matter? Nay, how does it appear that matter, taken for something distinct from what we perceive by our senses is thought to exist by all mankind, or, indeed, by any except a few philosophers who do not know what they would be at? Your question supposes these points are clear; and, when you have cleared them, I shall think myself obliged to give you another answer. In the meantime let it suffice that I tell you I do not suppose God has deceived mankind at all.

Hyl. But the novelty, Philonous, the novelty! There lies the danger. New notions should always be discountenanced; they unsettle men's minds, and nobody knows where they will end.

Phil. Why the rejecting a notion that has no foundation, either in sense or in reason or in Divine authority, should be thought to unsettle the belief of such opinions as are grounded on all or any of these, I cannot imagine. That innovations in government and religion are dangerous and ought to be discountenanced, I freely own. But is there the like reason why they should be discouraged in philosophy? The making anything known which was unknown before is an innovation in knowledge; and if all such innovations had been forbidden, men would [not] have made a notable progress in the arts and sciences. But it is none of my business to plead for novelties and paradoxes. That the qualities we perceive are not on the objects, that we must not believe our senses, that we know nothing of the real nature of things and can never be assured even of their existence, that real colors and sounds are nothing but certain unknown figures and motions, that motions are in themselves neither swift nor slow, that there are in bodies absolute extensions without any particular magnitude or figure, that a thing stupid, thoughtless, and inactive operates on a spirit, that the least particle of a body contains innumerable extended parts—these are the novelties, these are the strange notions which shock the genuine uncorrupted judgment of all mankind, and, being once admitted, embarrass the mind with endless doubts and difficulties. And it is against these and the like innovations I endeavor to vindicate Common Sense. It is true, in doing this I may, perhaps, be obliged to use some ambages and ways of speech not common. But if my notions are once thoroughly understood, that which is most singular in them will, in effect, be found to amount to no more than this—that it is absolutely impossible and a plain contradiction to suppose any unthinking being should exist without being perceived by a mind. And if this notion be singular, it is a shame it should be so at this time of day and in a Christian country.

Hyl. As for the difficulties other opinions may be liable to, those are out of the question. It is your business to defend your own opinion. Can anything be plainer than that you are for changing all things into ideas? You, I say, who are not ashamed to charge me with skepticism. This is so plain, there is no denying it.

Phil. You mistake me. I am not for changing things into ideas but rather ideas into things, since those immediate objects of perception, which, according to you, are only appearances of things, I take to be the real things themselves.

Hyl. Things! you may pretend what you please; but it is certain you leave us nothing but the empty forms of things, the outside only which strikes the senses.

Phil. What you call the empty forms and outside of things seem to me the very things themselves. Nor are they empty or incomplete otherwise than upon your supposition that matter is an essential part of all corporeal things. We both, therefore, agree in this, that we perceive only sensible forms; but herein we differ: you will have them to be empty appearances, I real beings. In short, you do not trust your senses, I do.

Hyl. You say you believe your senses, and seem to applaud yourself that in this you agree with the vulgar. According to you, therefore, the true nature of a thing is discovered by the senses. If so, whence comes that disagreement? Why, is not the same figure, and other sensible qualities, perceived all manner of ways? And why should we use a microscope the better to discover the true nature of a body, if it were discoverable to the naked eye?

Phil. Strictly speaking, Hylas, we do not see the same object that we feel; neither is the same object perceived by the microscope which was by the naked eye. But in case every variation was thought sufficient to constitute a new kind of individual, the endless number or confusion of names would render language impracticable. Therefore, to avoid this as well as other inconveniences which are obvious upon a little thought, men combine together several ideas, apprehended by divers senses, or by the same sense at different times or in different circumstances, but observed, however, to have some connection in nature, either with respect to coexistence or succession; all which they refer to one name and consider as one thing. Hence it follows that when I examine by my other senses a thing I have seen, it is not in order to understand better the same object which I had perceived by sight, the object of one sense not being perceived by the other senses. And when I look through a microscope, it is not that I may perceive more clearly what I perceived already with my bare eyes, the object perceived by the glass being quite different from the former. But in both cases my aim is only to know what ideas are connected together; and the more a man knows of the connection of ideas, the more he is said to know of the nature of things. What, therefore, if our ideas are variable, what if our senses are not in all circumstances affected with the same appearances? It will not thence follow they are not to be trusted or that they are inconsistent either with themselves or anything else, except it be with your preconceived notion of (I know not what) one single, unchanged, unperceivable, real nature, marked by each name; which prejudice seems to have taken its rise from not rightly understanding the common language of men speaking of several distinct ideas as united into one thing by the mind. And, indeed, there is cause to suspect several erroneous conceits of the philosophers are owing to the same original: while they began to build their schemes not so much on notions as words which were framed by the vulgar merely for convenience and dispatch in the common actions of life, without any regard to speculation.

Hyl. Methinks I apprehend your meaning.

Phil. It is your opinion the ideas we perceive by our senses are not real things, but images or copies of them. Our knowledge, therefore, is no further real than as our ideas are the true representations of those originals. But as these supposed originals are in themselves unknown, it is impossible to know how far our ideas resemble them, or whether they resemble them at all. We cannot, therefore, be sure we have any real knowledge. Further, as our ideas are perpetually varied, without any change in the supposed real things, it necessarily follows they cannot all be true copies of them, or, if some are and others are not, it is impossible to distinguish the former from the latter. And this plunges us yet deeper in uncertainty. Again, when we consider the point, we cannot conceive how any idea, or anything like an idea, should have an absolute existence out of a mind, nor consequently, according to you, how there should be any real thing in nature. The result of all which is that we are thrown into the most hopeless and abandoned skepticism. Now give me leave to ask you, *first,* whether your referring ideas to certain absolutely existing unperceived substances, as their originals, be not the source of all this skepticism? *Secondly,* whether you are informed, either by sense or reason, of the existence of those unknown originals? And in case you are not, whether it be not absurd to suppose them? *Thirdly,* whether, upon inquiry, you find there is anything distinctly conceived or meant by the "absolute or external existence of unperceiving substances"; *Lastly,* whether, the premises considered, it be not the wisest way to follow nature, trust your senses, and, laying aside all anxious thought about unknown natures or substances, admit with the vulgar those for real things which are perceived by the senses?

Hyl. For the present I have no inclination to the answering part. I would much rather see how you can get over what follows. Pray, are not the objects perceived by the senses of one likewise perceivable to others present? If there were a hundred more here, they would all see the garden, the trees and flowers, as I see them. But they are not in the same manner affected with the ideas I frame in my imagination. Does not this make a difference between the former sort of objects and the latter?

Phil. I grant it does. Nor have I ever denied a difference between the objects of sense and those of imagination. But what would you infer from thence? You cannot say that sensible objects exist unperceived because they are perceived by many.

Hyl. I own I can make nothing of that objection, but it has led me into another. Is it not your opinion that by our senses we perceive only the ideas existing in our minds?

Phil. It is.

Hyl. But the same idea which is in my mind cannot be in yours or in any other mind. Does it not, therefore, follow from your principles that no two can see the same thing? And is not this highly absurd?

Phil. If the term "same" be taken in the vulgar acceptation, it is certain (and not at all repugnant to the principles I maintain) that different persons may perceive the same thing, or the same thing or idea exist in different minds. Words are of arbitrary imposition; and since men are used to apply the word "same" where no distinction or variety is perceived, and I do not pretend to alter their perceptions, it follows that, as men have said before, *several saw the same thing,* so they may, upon like occasions, still continue to use the same phrase without any deviation either from propriety of language or the truth of things. But if the term "same" be used in the acceptation of philosophers who pretend to an abstracted notion of identity, then, according to their sundry definitions of this notion (for it is not yet agreed wherein that philosophic identity consists), it may or may not be possible for divers persons to perceive the same thing. But whether philosophers shall think fit to call a thing the "same" or no is, I conceive, of small importance. Let us suppose several men together, all endued with the same faculties, and consequently affected in like sort by their senses, and who had yet never known the use of language; they would without question agree in their perceptions. Though perhaps, when they came to the use of speech, some regarding the uniformness of what was perceived might call it the "same" thing; others, especially regarding the diversity of persons who perceived, might choose the denomination of "different" things. But who sees not that all the dispute is about a word, to wit, whether what is perceived by different persons may yet have the term "same" applied to it? Or suppose a house whose walls or outward shell remaining unaltered, the chambers are all pulled down, and new ones built in their place, and that you should call this the "same," and I should say it was not the "same," house—would we not, for all this, perfectly agree in our thoughts of the house considered in itself? And would not all the difference consist in a sound? If you should say we differed in our notions, for that you superadded to your idea of the house the simple abstracted idea of identity, whereas I did not, I would tell you I know not what you mean by that "abstracted idea of identity," and should desire you to look into your own thoughts and be sure you understood yourself.— Why so silent, Hylas? Are you not yet satisfied men may dispute about identity and diversity without any real difference in their thoughts and opinions abstracted from names? Take this further reflection with you—that, whether matter be allowed to exist or no, the case is exactly the same as to the point in hand. For the materialists themselves acknowledge what we immediately perceive by our senses to be our own ideas. Your difficulty, therefore, that no two see the same thing makes equally against the materialists and me. . . .

NOTES

1. [The remainder of the present paragraph did not appear in the first and second editions.]

2. [See the author's *An Essay towards a New Theory of Vision* (1709) and *The Theory of Vision Vindicated and Explained* (1733).]

3. [The four paragraphs following do not appear in the first and second editions.]

DAVID HUME

An Inquiry concerning Human Understanding*

SECTION II. OF THE ORIGIN OF IDEAS

Everyone will readily allow that there is a considerable difference between the perceptions of the mind when a man feels the pain of excessive heat or the pleasure of moderate warmth, and when he afterwards recalls to his memory this sensation or anticipates it by his imagination. These faculties may mimic or copy the perceptions of the senses, but they never can entirely reach the force and vivacity of the original sentiment. The utmost we say of them, even when they operate with greatest vigor, is that they represent their object in so lively a manner that we could *almost* say we feel or see it. But, except the mind be disordered by disease or madness, they never can arrive at such a pitch of vivacity as to render these perceptions altogether undistinguishable. All the colors of poetry, however splendid, can never paint natural objects in such a manner as to make the description be taken for a real landscape. The most lively thought is still inferior to the dullest sensation.

We may observe a like distinction to run through all the other perceptions of the mind. A man in a fit of anger is actuated in a very different manner from one who only thinks of that emotion. If you tell me that any person is in love, I easily understand your meaning and form a just conception of his situation, but never can mistake

that conception for the real disorders and agitations of the passion. When we reflect on our past sentiments and affections, our thought is a faithful mirror and copies its objects truly, but the colors which it employs are faint and dull in comparison of those in which our original perceptions were clothed. It requires no nice discernment or metaphysical head to mark the distinction between them.

Here, therefore, we may divide all the perceptions of the mind into two classes or species, which are distinguished by their different degrees of force and vivacity. The less forcible and lively are commonly denominated "thoughts" or "ideas." The other species want a name in our language, and in most others; I suppose, because it was not requisite for any but philosophical purposes to rank them under a general term or appellation. Let us, therefore, use a little freedom and call them "impressions," employing that word in a sense somewhat different from the usual. By the term "impression," then, I mean all our more lively perceptions, when we hear, or see, or feel, or love, or hate, or desire, or will. And impressions are distinguished from ideas, which are the less lively perceptions of which we are conscious when we reflect on any of those sensations or movements above mentioned.

Nothing, at first view, may seem more unbounded than the thought of man, which not only escapes all human power and authority, but is not even restrained within the limits of nature and reality. To form monsters and join incongruous

*David Hume, *An Inquiry Concerning Human Understanding,* Sections II, IV–VII. First published in 1748.

shapes and appearances costs the imagination no more trouble than to conceive the most natural and familiar objects. And while the body is confined to one planet, along which it creeps with pain and difficulty, the thought can in an instant transport us into the most distant regions of the universe, or even beyond the universe into the unbounded chaos where nature is supposed to lie in total confusion. What never was seen or heard of, may yet be conceived, nor is anything beyond the power of thought except what implies an absolute contradiction.

But though our thought seems to possess this unbounded liberty, we shall find upon a nearer examination that it is really confined within very narrow limits, and that all this creative power of the mind amounts to more than the faculty of compounding, transposing, augmenting, or diminishing the materials afforded us by the senses and experience. When we think of a golden mountain, we only join two consistent ideas, "gold" and "mountain," with which we were formerly acquainted. A virtuous horse we can conceive, because, from our own feeling, we can conceive virtue; and this we may unite to the figure and shape of a horse, which is an animal familiar to us. In short, all the materials of thinking are derived either from our outward or inward sentiment; the mixture and composition of these belongs alone to the mind and will, or, to express myself in philosophical language, all our ideas or more feeble perceptions are copies of our impressions or more lively ones.

To prove this, the two following arguments will, I hope, be sufficient. *First,* when we analyze our thoughts or ideas, however compounded or sublime, we always find that they resolve themselves into such simple ideas as were copied from a precedent feeling or sentiment. Even those ideas which at first view seem the most wide of this origin are found, upon a nearer scrutiny, to be derived from it. The idea of God, as meaning an infinitely intelligent, wise, and good Being, arises from reflecting on the operations of our own mind and augmenting, without limit, those qualities of goodness and wisdom. We may prosecute this inquiry to what length we please; where we shall always find that every idea which we examine is copied from a similar impression. Those who would assert that this position is not universally true, nor without exception, have only one, and that an easy, method of refuting it by producing that idea which, in their opinion, is not derived from this source. It will then be incumbent on us, if we would maintain our doctrine, to produce the impression or lively perception which corresponds to it.

Secondly, if it happen, from a defect of the organ, that a man is not susceptible of any species of sensation, we always find that he is as little susceptible of the correspondent idea. A blind man can form no notion of colors, a deaf man of sounds. Restore either of them that sense in which he is deficient by opening this new inlet for his sensations, you also open an inlet for the ideas, and he finds no difficulty in conceiving these objects. The case is the same if the object proper for exciting any sensation has never been applied to the organ. A Laplander ... has no notion of the relish of wine. And though there are few or no instances of a like deficiency in the mind where a person has never felt or is wholly incapable of a sentiment or passion that belongs to his species, yet we find the same observation to take place in a less degree. A man of mild manners can form no idea of inveterate revenge or cruelty, nor can a selfish heart easily conceive the heights of friendship and generosity. It is readily allowed that other beings may possess many senses of which we can have no conception, because the ideas of them have never been introduced to us in the only manner by which an idea can have access to the mind, to wit, by the actual feeling and sensation.

There is, however, one contradictory phenomenon which may prove that it is not absolutely impossible for ideas to arise independent of their correspondent impressions. I believe it will readily be allowed that the several distinct ideas of color, which enter by the eye, or those of sound, which are conveyed by the ear, are really different from each other, though at the same time resembling. Now, if this be true of different colors, it must be no less so of the different shades of the same color; and each shade produces a distinct idea, independent of the rest. For if this should be denied, it is possible, by the continual gradation of shades, to run a color insensibly into what is most remote from it; and if you will not allow any of the means to be different, you cannot, without absurdity, deny the extremes to be the same. Suppose, therefore, a person to have enjoyed his sight for thirty years and to have become perfectly acquainted with colors of all kinds, except one particular shade of blue, for instance, which it never has been his fortune to meet with; let all the different shades of that color, except that single one, be placed before him, descending gradually from the deepest to the lightest, it is plain that he will perceive a blank where that shade is wanting, and will be sensible that there is a greater distance in that place between the contiguous colors than in any other. Now I ask whether it be possible for him, from his own imagination, to supply this deficiency and raise up to himself the idea of that particular shade, though it had never been conveyed to him by his senses? I believe there are few but will be of opinion that he can; and this may serve as a proof that the simple ideas are not always, in every instance, derived from the correspondent impressions, though this instance is so singular that it is scarcely worth our observing, and does not merit that for it alone we should alter our general maxim.

Here, therefore, is a proposition which not only seems in itself simple and intelligible, but, if a proper use were made of it, might render every dispute equally intelligible, and banish all that jargon which has so long taken possession of metaphysical reasonings and drawn disgrace upon them. All ideas, especially abstract ones, are naturally faint and obscure. The mind has but a slender hold of them. They are apt to be confounded with other resembling ideas; and when we have often employed any term, though without a distinct meaning, we are apt to imagine it has a determinate idea annexed to it. On the contrary, all impressions, that is, all sensations either outward or inward, are strong and vivid. The limits between them are more exactly determined, nor is it easy to fall into any error or mistake with regard to them. When we entertain, therefore, any suspicion that a philosophical term is employed without any meaning or idea (as is but too frequent), we need but inquire, *from what impression is that supposed idea derived?* And if it be impossible to assign any, this will serve to confirm our suspicion. By bringing ideas in so clear a light, we may reasonably hope to remove all dispute which may arise concerning their nature and reality.[1]

SECTION IV. SKEPTICAL DOUBTS CONCERNING THE OPERATIONS OF THE UNDERSTANDING

PART I

All the objects of human reason or inquiry may naturally be divided into two kinds of wit, "Relations of Ideas," and "Matters of Fact." Of the first kind are the sciences of Geometry, Algebra, and Arithmetic, and, in short, every affirmation which is either intuitively or demonstratively certain. *That the square of the hypotenuse is equal to the square of the two sides* in a proposition which expresses a relation between these figures. *That three times five is equal to the half of thirty* expresses a relation between these numbers. Propositions of this kind are discoverable by the mere operation of thought, without dependence on what is anywhere existent in the universe. Though there never were a circle or triangle in nature, the truths demonstrated by Euclid would forever retain their certainty and evidence.

Matters of fact, which are the second objects of human reason, are not ascertained in the same manner, nor is our evidence of their truth, however great, of a like nature with the foregoing. The contrary of every matter of fact is still possible, because it can never imply a contradiction and is conceived by the mind with the same facility and distinctness as if ever so comfortable to reality. *That the sun will not rise tomorrow* is no less intelligible a proposition and implies no more contradiction than the affirmation *that it will rise.* We should in vain, therefore, attempt to demonstrate its falsehood. Were it demonstratively false, it would imply a contradiction and could never be distinctly conceived by the mind.

It may, therefore, be a subject worthy of curiosity to inquire what is the nature of that evidence which assures us of any real existence and matter of fact beyond the present testimony of our senses or the records of our memory. This part of philosophy, it is observable, had been little cultivated either by the ancients or moderns; and, therefore, our doubts and errors in the prosecution of so important an inquiry may be the more excusable while we march through such difficult paths without any guide or direction. They may even prove useful by exciting curiosity and destroying that implicit faith and security which is the bane of all reasoning and free inquiry. The discovery of defects in the common philosophy, if any such there be, will not, I presume, be a discouragement, but rather an incitement, as is usual, to attempt something more full and satisfactory than has yet been proposed to the public.

All reasonings concerning matter of fact seem to be founded on the relation of *cause* and *effect*. By means of that relation alone we can go beyond the evidence of our memory and senses. If you were to ask a man why he believes any matter of fact which is absent, for instance, that his friend is in the country or in France, he would give you a reason, and this reason would be some other fact: as a letter received from him or the knowledge of of his former resolutions and promises. A man finding a watch or any other machine in a desert island would conclude that there had once been men in that island. All our reasonings concerning fact are of the same nature. And here it is constantly supposed that there is a connection between the present fact and that which is inferred from it. Were there nothing to bind them together, the inference would be entirely precarious. The hearing of an articulate voice and rational discourse in the dark assures us of the presence of some person. Why? Because these are the effects of the human make and fabric, and closely connected with it. If we anatomize all the other reasonings of this nature, we shall find that they are founded on the relation of cause and effect, and that this relation is either near or remote, direct or collateral. Heat and light are collateral effects of fire, and the one effect may justly be inferred from the other.

If we would satisfy ourselves, therefore, concerning the nature of that evidence which assures us of matters of fact, we must inquire how we arrive at the knowledge of cause and effect.

I shall venture to affirm, as a general proposition which admits of no exception, that the knowledge of this relation is not, in any instance, attained by reasonings *a priori,* but arises entirely from experience, when we find that any particular objects are constantly conjoined with each other. Let an object be presented to a man of ever so strong natural reason and abilities—if that object be entirely new to him, he will not be able, by the most accurate examination of its sensible qualities, to discover any of its causes or effects. Adam, though his rational faculties be supposed, at the very first, entirely perfect, could not have inferred from the fluidity and transparency of water that it would suffocate him, or from the light and warmth of fire that it would consume him. No object ever discovers, by the qualities which appear to the senses, either the causes which produced it or the effects which will arise from it; nor can our reason, unassisted by experience, ever draw any inference concerning real existence and matter of fact.

This proposition, *that causes and effects are discoverable, not by reason, but by experience,* will readily be admitted with regard to such objects as we remember to have once been altogether unknown to us, since we must be conscious of the utter inability which we then lay under of foretelling what would arise from them. Present two smooth pieces of marble to a man who has no tincture of natural philosophy; he will never discover that they will adhere together in such a manner as to require great force to separate them in a direct line, while they make so small a resistance to a lateral pressure. Such events as bear little analogy to the common course of nature are also readily confessed to be known only by experience, nor does any man imagine that the explosion of gunpowder or the attraction of a loadstone could ever be discovered by arguments *a priori.* In like manner, when an effect is supposed to depend upon an intricate machinery or secret structure of parts, we make no difficulty in attributing all our knowledge of it to experience. Who will assert that he can give the ultimate reason why milk or bread is proper nourishment for a man, not for a lion or tiger?

But the same truth may not appear at first sight to have the same evidence with regard to events which have become familiar to us from our first appearance in the world, which bear a close analogy to the whole course of nature, and which are supposed to depend on the simple qualities of objects without any secret structure of parts. We are apt to imagine that we could discover these effects by the mere operation of our reason without experience. We fancy that, were we brought on a suddden into this world, we could at first have inferred that one billiard ball would communicate motion to another upon impulse, and that we needed not to have waited for the event in order to pronounce with certainty concerning it. Such is the influence of custom that where it is strongest it not only covers our natural ignorance but even conceals itself, and seems not to take place, merely because it is found in the highest degree.

But to convince us that all the laws of nature and all the operations of bodies without exception are known only by experience, the following reflections may perhaps suffice. Were any object presented to us, and were we required to pronounce concerning the effect which will result from it without consulting past observation, after what manner, I beseech you, must the mind proceed in this operation? It must invent or imagine some event which it ascribes to the object as its effect; and it is plain that this invention must be entirely arbitrary. The mind can never possibly find the effect in the supposed cause by the most accurate scrutiny and examination. For the effect is totally different from the cause, and consequently can never be discovered in it. Motion in the second billiard ball is a distinct event from motion in the first, nor is there anything in the one to suggest the smallest hint of the other. A stone or piece of metal raised into the air and left without any support immediately falls. But to consider the matter *a priori,* is there anything we discover in this situation which can beget the idea of a downward rather than an upward or any other motion in the stone or metal?

And as the first imagination or invention of a particular effect in all natural operations is arbitrary where we consult not experience, so must we also esteem the supposed tie or connection between the cause and effect which binds them together and renders it impossible that any other effect could result from the operation of that cause. When I see, for instance, a billiard ball moving in a straight line toward another, even suppose motion in the second ball should by accident be suggested to me as the result of their contact or impulse, may I not conceive that a hundred different events might as well follow from that cause? May not both these balls remain at absolute rest? May not the first ball return in a straight line or leap off the second in any line or direction? All these suppositions are consistent and conceivable. Why, then, should we give the preference to one which is no more consistent or conceivable than the rest? All our reasonings *a priori* will never be able to show us any foundation for this preference.

In a word, then, every effect is a distinct event from its cause. It could not, therefore, be discovered in the cause, and the first invention or conception of it *a priori,* must be entirely arbitrary. And even after it is suggested, the conjunction of it with the cause must appear equally arbitrary, since there are always many other effects which, to reason, must seem fully as consistent and natural. In vain, therefore, should we pretend to determine any single event or infer any cause or effect without the assistance of observation and experience.

Hence we may discover the reason why no philosopher who is rational and modest has ever pretended to assign the ultimate cause of any natural operation, or to show distinctly the action of that power which produces any single effect in the universe. It is confessed that the utmost effort of human reason is to reduce the principles productive of natural phenomena to a greater simplicity, and to resolve the many particular effects into a few general causes, by means of reasonings from analogy, experience, and observation. But as to the causes of these general causes, we should in vain attempt their discovery, nor shall we ever be able to satisfy ourselves by any particular explication of them. These ultimate springs and principles are totally shut up from human curiosity and inquiry. Elasticity, gravity, cohesion of parts, communication of motion by impulse— these are probably the ultimate causes and principles which we shall ever discover in nature; and we may esteem ourselves sufficiently happy if, by accurate inquiry and reasoning, we can trace up the particular phenomena to, or near to, these general principles. The most perfect philosophy of the natural kind only staves off our ignorance a little longer, as perhaps the most perfect philosophy of the moral or metaphysical kind serves only to discover larger portions of it. Thus the observation of human blindness and weakness is the result of all philosophy, and meets us, at every turn, in spite of our endeavors to elude or avoid it.

Nor is geometry, when taken into the assistance of natural philosophy, ever able to remedy this defect or lead us into the knowledge of ultimate causes by all that accuracy of reasoning for which it is so justly celebrated. Every part of mixed mathematics proceeds upon the supposition that certain laws are established by nature in her operations, and abstract reasonings are employed either to assist experience in the discovery of these laws or to determine their influence in particular instances where it depends upon any precise degree of distance and quantity. Thus it is a law of motion, discovered by experience, that the moment or force of any body in motion is in the compound ratio or proportion of its solid contents and its velocity, and, consequently, that a small force may remove the greatest obstacle or raise the greatest weight if by any contrivance or machinery we can increase the velocity of that force so as to make it an overmatch for its antagonist. Geometry assists us in the application of this law by giving us the just dimensions of all the parts and figures which can enter into any species of machine, but still the discovery of the law itself is owing merely to experience; and all the abstract reasonings in the world could never lead us one step toward the knowledge of it. When we reason *a priori* and consider merely any object or cause as it appears to the mind, independent of all observation, it never could suggest to us the notion of any distinct object, such as its effect, much less show us the inseparable and inviolable connection between them. A man must be very sagacious who could discover by reasoning that crystal is the effect of heat, and ice of cold, without being previously acquainted with the operation of these qualities.

PART II

But we have not yet attained any tolerable satisfaction with regard to the question first proposed. Each solution still gives rise to a new question as difficult as the foregoing and leads us on to further inquiries. When it is asked, *What is the nature of all our reasonings concerning matter of fact?* the proper answer seems to be, That they are founded on the relation of cause and effect. When again it is asked, *What is the foundation of all our reasonings and conclusions concerning that relation?* it may be replied in one word, *experience.* But if we still carry on our sifting humor and ask, *What is the foundation of all conclusions from experience?* this implies a new question which may be of more difficult solution and explication. Philosophers that give themselves airs of superior wisdom and sufficiency have a hard task when they encounter persons of inquisitive dispositions, who push them from every corner to

which they retreat, and who are sure at last to bring them to some dangerous dilemma. The best expedient to prevent this confusion is to be modest in our pretensions and even to discover the difficulty ourselves before it is objected to us. By this means we may make a kind of merit of our very ignorance.

I shall content myself in this section with an easy task and shall pretend only to give a negative answer to the question here proposed. I say, then, that even after we have experience of the operations of cause and effect, our conclusions from that experience are *not* founded on reasoning or any process of understanding. This answer we must endeavor both to explain and to defend.

It must certainly be allowed that nature has kept us at a great distance from all her secrets and has afforded us only the knowledge of a few superficial qualities of objects, while she conceals from us those powers and principles on which the influence of these objects entirely depends. Our senses inform us of the color, weight, and consistency of bread, but neither sense nor reason can ever inform us of those qualities which fit it for the nourishment and support of the human body. Sight or feeling conveys an idea of the actual motion of bodies, but as to what wonderful force or power which would carry on a moving body forever in a continued change of place, and which bodies never lose but by communicating it to others, of this we cannot form the most distant conception. But notwithstanding this ignorance of natural powers[2] and principles, we always presume when we see like sensible qualities that they have like secret powers, and expect that effects similar to those which we have experienced will follow from them. If a body of like color and consistency with that bread which we have formerly eaten be presented to us, we make no scruple of repeating the experiment and foresee with certainty like nourishment and support. Now this is a process of the mind or thought of which I would willingly know the foundation. It is allowed on hands that there is no known connection between the sensible qualities and the secret powers, and, consequently, that the mind is not led to form such a conclusion concerning their constant and regular conjunction by anything which it knows of their nature. As to past *experience,* it can be allowed to give *direct* and *certain* information of those precise objects only, and that precise period of time which fell under its cognizance: But why this experience should be extended to future times and to other objects which, for aught we know, may be only in appearance similar, this is the main question on which I would insist. The bread which I formerly ate nourished me; that is, a body of such sensible qualities was, at that time, endued with such secret powers. But does it follow that other bread must also nourish me at another time, and that like sensible qualities must always be attended with like secret powers? the consequence seems nowise necessary. At least, it must be acknowledged that there is here a consequence drawn by the mind that there is a certain step taken, a process of thought, and an inference which wants to be explained. These two propositions are far from being the same: *I have found that such an object has always been attended with such an effect,* and *I foresee that other objects which are in appearance similar will be attended with similar effects.* I shall allow, if you please, that the one proposition may justly be inferred from the other: I know, in fact, that it always is inferred. But if you insist that the inference is made by a chain of reasoning, I desire you to produce that reasoning. The connection between these propositions is not intuitive. There is required a medium which may enable the mind to draw such an inference, if indeed it be drawn by reasoning and argument. What that medium is I must confess passes my comprehension; and it is incumbent on those to produce it who assert that it really exists and is the original of all our conclusions concerning matter of fact.

This negative argument must certainly, in process of time, become altogether convincing if many penetrating and able philosophers shall turn their inquiries this way, and no one be ever able to discover any connecting proposition or intermediate step which supports the understanding in this conclusion. But as the question is yet new, every reader may not trust so far to his own penetration as to conclude, because an argument escapes his inquiry, that therefore it does not really exist. For this reason it may be requisite to venture upon a more difficult task, and, enumerating all the branches of human knowledge, endeavor to show that none of them can afford such an argument.

All reasonings may be divided into two kinds, namely, demonstrative reasoning, or that concerning relations of ideas, and moral reasoning, or that concerning matter of fact and existence. That there are no demonstrative arguments in the case seems evident, since it implies no contradiction that the course of nature may change and that an object, seemingly like those which we have experienced, may be attended with different or contrary effects. May I not clearly and distinctly conceive that a body, falling from the clouds and which in all other respects resembles snow, has yet the taste of salt or feeling of fire? Is there any more intelligible proposition than to affirm that all the trees will flourish in December and January, and will decay in May and June? Now, whatever is intelligible and can be distinctly conceived implies no contradiction and can never be proved false by any demonstrative argument or abstract reasoning *a priori.*

If we be, therefore, engaged by arguments to put trust in past experience and make it the standard of our future judgment, these arguments must be probable only, or such as regard matter of fact and real existence, according to the division above mentioned. But that there is no argument of this kind must appear if our explication of that species of reasoning be admitted as solid and satisfactory. We have said that all arguments concerning existence are founded on the relation of cause and effect, that our knowledge of that relation is derived entirely from experience, and that all our experimental conclusions proceed upon the supposition that the future will be conformable to the past. To endeavor, therefore, the proof of this last supposition by probable arguments, or arguments regarding existence, must be evidently going in a circle and taking that for granted which is the very point in question.

In reality, all arguments from experience are founded on the similarity which we discover among natural objects, and by which we are induced to expect effects similar to those which we have found to follow from such objects. And though none but a fool or madman will ever pretend to dispute the authority of experience or to reject that great guide of human life, it may surely be allowed a philosopher to have so much curiosity at least as to examine the principle of human nature which gives this mighty authority to experience and makes us draw advantage from that similarity which nature has placed among different objects. From causes which appear similar, we expect similar effects. This is the sum of our experimental conclusions. Now it seems evident that, if this conclusion were formed by reason, it would be as perfect at first, and upon one instance, as after ever so long a course of experience; but the case is far otherwise. Nothing so like as eggs, yet no one, on account of this appearing similarity, expects the same taste and relish in all of them. It is only after a long course of uniform experiments in any kind that we attain a firm reliance and security with regard to a particular event. Now, where is that process of reasoning which, from one instance, draws a conclusion so different from that which it infers from a hundred instances that are nowise different from that single one? This question I propose as much for the sake of information as with an intention of raising difficulties. I cannot find, I cannot imagine any such reasoning. But I keep my mind still open to instruction if anyone will vouchsafe to bestow it on me.

Should it be said that, from a number of uniform experiments, we *infer* a connection between the sensible qualities and the secret powers, this, I must confess, seems the same difficulty, couched in different terms. The question still occurs, On what process of argument is this *inference* founded? Where is the medium, the interposing ideas which join propositions so very wide of each other? It is confessed that the color, consistency, and other sensible qualities of bread appear not of themselves to have any connection with the secret powers of nourishment and support; for otherwise we could infer these secret powers from the first appearance of these sensible qualities without the aid of experience, contrary to the sentiment of all philosophers, and contrary to plain matter of fact. Here, then, is our natural state of ignorance with regard to the powers and influence of all objects. How is this remedied by experience? It only shows us a number of uniform effects resulting from certain objects, and teaches us that those particular objects, at that particular time, were endowed with such powers and forces. When a new object endowed with similar sensible qualities is produced, we expect similar powers and forces, and look for a like effect. From a body of like color and consistency with bread, we expect like nourishment and support. But this surely is a step or progress of the mind which wants to be explained. When a man says, *I have found, in all past instances, such sensible qualities, conjoined with such secret powers,* and when he says, *similar sensible qualities will always be conjoined with similar secret powers,* he is not guilty of a tautology, nor are these propositions in any respect the same. You say that the one proposition is an inference from the other; but you must confess that the inference is not intuitive, neither is it demonstrative. Of what nature is it then? To say it is experimental is begging the question. For all inferences from experience suppose, as their foundation, that the future will resemble the past and that similar powers will be conjoined with similar sensible qualities. If there be any suspicion that the course of nature may change, and that the past may be no rule for the future, all experience becomes useless and can give rise to no inference or conclusion. It is impossible, therefore, that any arguments are founded on the supposition of that resemblance. Let the course of things be allowed hitherto ever so regular, that alone, without some new argument or inference, proves not that for the future it will continue so. In vain do you pretend to have learned the nature of bodies from your past experience. Their secret nature, and consequently all their efforts and influence, may change without any change in their sensible qualities. This happens sometimes, and with regard to some objects. Why may it not happen always, and with regard to all objects? What logic, what process of argument secures you against this supposition? My practice, you say, refutes my doubts. But you mistake the purport of my question. As an agent, I am quite satisfied in the point; but as a philosopher who has some share of curiosity, I will not say skepticism, I want to learn the foundation of this inference. No reading, no inquiry has yet been able to remove my difficulty or give me satisfaction in a matter of such importance. Can I do better than propose the difficulty to the public, even though, perhaps, I have small hopes of obtaining a solution? We shall at least, by this means, be sensible of our ignorance, if we do not augment our knowledge.

I must confess that a man is guilty of unpardonable arrogance who concludes, because an argument has escaped his own investigation, that therefore it does not really exist. I must also confess that, though all the learned, for several ages, should have employed themselves in fruitless search upon any subject, it may still, perhaps, be rash to conclude positively that the subject must therefore pass all human comprehension. Even though we examine all the sources of our knowledge and conclude them unfit for such a subject, there may still remain a suspicion that the enumeration is not complete or the examination not accurate. But with regard to the present subject, there are some considerations which seem to remove all this accusation of arrogance or suspicion of mistake.

It is certain that the most ignorant and stupid peasants, nay infants, nay even brute beasts, improve by experience and learn the qualities of natural objects by observing the effects which result from them. When a child has felt the sensation of pain from touching the flame of a candle, he will be careful not to put his hand near any candle, but will expect a similar effect from a cause which is similar in its sensible qualities and appearance. If you assert, therefore, that the understanding of the child is led into this conclusion by any process of argument or ratiocination, I may justly require you to produce that argument, nor have you any pretense to refuse so equitable a demand. You cannot say that the argument is abstruse and may possibly escape your inquiry, since you confess that it is obvious to the capacity of a mere infant. If you hesitate, therefore, a moment or if, after reflection, you produce an intricate or profound argument, you, in a manner, give up the question and confess that it is not reasoning which engages us to suppose the past resembling the future, and to expect similar effects from causes which are to appearance similar. This is the proposition which I intended to enforce in the present section. If I be right, I pretend not to have made any mighty discovery. And if I be wrong, I must acknowledge myself to be indeed a very backward scholar, since I cannot now discover an argument which, it seems, was perfectly familiar to me long before I was out of my cradle.

SECTION V. SKEPTICAL SOLUTION OF THESE DOUBTS

PART I

The passion for philosophy, like that for religion, seems liable to this inconvenience, that though it aims at the correction of our manners and extirpation of our vices, it may only serve, by imprudent management, to foster a predominant inclination and push the mind with more determined resolution toward that side which already *draws* too much by the bias and propensity of the natural temper. It is certain that, while we aspire to the magnanimous firmness of the philosophic sage and endeavor to confine our pleasures altogether within our own minds, we may, at last, render our philosophy, like that of Epictetus and other Stoics, only a more refined system of selfishness, and reason ourselves out of all virtue as well as social enjoyment. While we study with attention the vanity of human life and turn all our thoughts toward the empty and transitory nature of riches and honors, we are, perhaps, all the while flattering our natural indolence which, hating the bustle of the world and drudgery of business, seeks a pretense of reason to give itself a full and uncontrolled indulgence. There is, however, one species of philosophy which seems little liable to this inconvenience, and that because it strikes in with no disorderly passion of the human mind, nor can mingle itself with any natural affection or propensity; and that is the Academic or Skeptical philosophy. The Academics always talk of doubt and suspense of judgment, of danger in hasty determinations, of confining to very narrow bounds the inquiries of the understanding, and of renouncing all speculations which lie not within the limits of common life and practice. Nothing, therefore, can be more contrary than such a philosophy to the supine indolence of the mind, its rash arrogance, its lofty pretensions, and its superstitious credulity. Every passion is mortified by it, except the love of truth; and that passion never is nor can be carried to too high a degree. It is surprising, therefore, that this philosophy, which in almost every instance must be harmless and innocent, should be the subject of so much groundless reproach and obloquy. But, perhaps, the very circumstance which renders it so innocent is what chiefly exposes it to the public hatred and resentment. By flattering no irregular passion, it gains few partisans. By opposing so many vices and follies, it raises to itself abundance of enemies who stigmatize it as libertine, profane, and irreligious.

Nor need we fear that this philosophy, while it endeavors to limit our inquiries to common life, should ever undermine the reasonings of common life and carry its doubts so far as to destroy all action as well as speculation. Nature will always maintain her rights and prevail in the end over any abstract reasoning whatsoever. Though we should conclude, for instance, as in the foregoing section, that in all reasonings from experience there is a step taken by the mind which is not supported by any argument or process of the understanding, there is no danger that these reasonings, on which almost all knowledge depends, will ever be affected by such a discovery. If the mind be not engaged by argument to make this step, it must be induced by some other principle of equal weight and authority; and that principle will preserve its influence as long as human nature remains the same. What that principle is may well be worth the pains of inquiry.

Suppose a person, though endowed with the strongest faculties of reason and reflection, to be brought on a sudden into this world; he would, indeed, immediately observe a continual succession of objects and one event following another, but he would not be able to discover anything further. He would not at first, by any reasoning, be able to reach the idea of cause and effect, since the particular powers by which all natural operations are performed never appear to the senses; nor is it reasonable to conclude, merely because one event in one instance precedes another, that therefore the one is the cause, the other the effect. The conjunction may be arbitrary and casual. There may be no reason to infer the existence of one from the appearance of the other: and, in a word, such a person without more experience could never employ his conjecture or reasoning concerning any matter of fact or be assured of anything beyond what was immediately present to his memory or senses.

Suppose again that he has acquired more experience and has lived so long in the world as to have observed similar objects or events to be constantly conjoined together—what is the consequence of this experience? He immediately infers the existence of one object from the appearance of the other, yet he has not, by all his experience, acquired any idea or knowledge of the secret power by which the one object produces the other, nor is it by any process of reasoning he is engaged to draw this inference; but still he finds himself determined to draw it, and though he

should be convinced that his understanding has no part in the operation, he would nevertheless continue in the same course of thinking. There is some other principle which determines him to form such a conclusion.

This principle is *custom* or *habit*. For whatever the repetition of any particular act or operation produces a propensity to renew the same act or operation without being impelled by any reasoning or process of the understanding, we always say that this propensity is the effect of *custom*. By employing that word we pretend not to have given the ultimate reason of such a propensity. We only point out a principle of human nature which is universally acknowledged, and which is well known by its effects. Perhaps we can push our inquiries no further or pretend to give the cause of this cause, but must rest contented with it as the ultimate principle which we can assign of all our conclusions from experience. It is sufficient satisfaction that we can go so far without repining at the narrowness of our faculties, because they will carry us no further. And it is certain we here advance a very intelligible proposition at least, if not a true one, when we assert that after the constant conjunction of two objects, heat and flame, for instance, weight and solidity, we are determined by custom alone to expect the one from the appearance of the other. This hypothesis seems even the only one which explains the difficulty why we draw from a thousand instances an inference which we are not able to draw from one instance that is in no respect different from them. Reason is incapable of any such variation. The conclusions which it draws from considering one circle are the same which it would form upon surveying all the circles in the universe. But no man, having seen only one body move after being impelled by another, could infer that every other body will move after a like impulse. All inferences from experience, therefore, are effects of custom, not of reasoning.[3]

Custom, then, is the great guide of human life. It is that principle alone which renders our experience useful to us and makes us expect, for the future, a similar train of events with those which have appeared in the past. Without the influence of custom we should be entirely ignorant of every matter of fact beyond what is immediately present to the memory and senses. We should never know how to adjust means to ends or to employ our natural powers in the production of any effect. There would be an end at once of all action as well as of the chief part of speculation.

But here it may be proper to remark that though our conclusions from experience carry us beyond our memory and senses and assure us of matters of fact which happened in the most distant places and most remote ages, yet some fact must always be present to the senses or memory from which we may first proceed in drawing these conclusions. A man who should find in a desert country the remains of pompous buildings would conclude that the country had, in ancient times, been cultivated by civilized inhabitants; but did nothing of this nature occur to him, he could never form such an inference. We learn the events of former ages from history, but then we must peruse the volume in which this instruction is contained, and thence carry up our inferences from one testimony to another, till we arrive at the eyewitnesses and spectators of these distant events. In a word, if we proceed not upon some fact present to the memory or senses, our reasonings would be merely hypothetical; and however the particular links might be connected with each other, the whole chain of inferences would have nothing to support it, nor could we ever, by its means, arrive at the knowledge of any real existence. If I ask why you believe any particular matter of fact which you relate, you must tell me some reason; and this reason will be some other fact connected with it. But as you cannot proceed after this manner *in infinitum,* you must at last terminate in some fact which is present to your memory or senses or must allow that your belief is entirely without foundation.

What, then, is the conclusion of the whole matter? A simple one, though, it must be confessed, pretty remote from the common theories of philosophy. All belief of matter of fact or real existence is derived merely from some object present to the memory or senses and a customary conjunction between that and some other object; or, in other words, having found, in many instances, that any two kinds of objects, flame and heat, snow and cold, have always been conjoined together: if flame or snow be presented anew to the senses, the mind is carried by custom to expect heat or cold, and to *believe* that such a quality does exist and will discover itself upon a nearer approach. This belief is the necessary result of

placing the mind in such circumstances. It is an operation of the soul, when we are so situated, as unavoidable as to feel the passion of love, when we receive benefits; or hatred, when we meet with injuries. All these operations are a species of natural instincts, which no reasoning or process of the thought and understanding is able either to produce or to prevent. At this point it would be very allowable for us to stop our philosophical researches. In most questions we can never make a single step further; and in all questions we must terminate here at last, after our most restless and curious inquiries. But still our curiosity will be pardonable, perhaps commendable, if it carry us on to still further researches and make us examine more accurately the nature of this *belief* and of the *customary conjunction* whence it is derived. By this means we may meet with some explications and analogies that will give satisfaction, at least to such as love the abstract sciences, and can be entertained with speculations which, however accurate, may still retain a degree of doubt and uncertainty. As to readers of a different taste, the remaining part of this Section is not calculated for them; and the following inquiries may well be understood, though it be neglected.

PART II

Nothing is more free than the imagination of man, and though it cannot exceed that original stock of ideas furnished by the internal and external senses, it has unlimited power of mixing, compounding, separating, and dividing these ideas in all the varieties of fiction and vision. It can feign a train of events with all the appearance of reality, ascribe to them a particular time and place, conceive them as existent, and paint them out to itself with every circumstance that belongs to any historical fact which it believes with the greatest certainty. Wherein, therefore, consists the difference between such a fiction and belief? It lies not merely in any peculiar idea which is annexed to such a conception as commands our assent, and which is wanting to every known fiction. For as the mind has authority over all its ideas, it could voluntarily annex this particular idea to any fiction, and consequently be able to believe whatever it pleases, contrary to what we find by daily experience. We can, in our conception, join the head of a man to the body of a horse, but it is not in our power to believe that such an animal has ever really existed.

It follows, therefore, that the difference between *fiction* and *belief* lies in some sentiment or feeling which is annexed to the latter, not to the former, and which depends not on the will, nor can be demanded at pleasure. It must be excited by nature like all other sentiments and must rise from the particular situation in which the mind is placed at any particular juncture. Whenever any object is presented to the memory or senses, it immediately, by the force of custom, carries the imagination to conceive that object which is usually conjoined to it; and this conception is attended with a feeling or sentiment different from the loose reveries of the fancy. In this consists the whole nature of belief. For as there is no matter of fact which we believe so firmly that we cannot conceive the contrary, there would be no difference between the conception assented to and that which is rejected were it not for some sentiment which distinguishes the one from the other. If I see a billiard ball moving toward another on a smooth table, I can easily conceive it to stop upon contact. This conception implies no contradiction, but still it feels very differently from that conception by which I represent to myself the impulse and the communication of motion from one ball to another.

Were we to attempt a *definition* of this sentiment, we should, perhaps, find it a very difficult, if not an impossible, task; in the same manner as if we should endeavor to define the feeling of cold, or passion of anger, to a creature who never had any experience of these sentiments. Belief is the true and proper name of this feeling, and no one is ever at a loss to know the meaning of that term, because every man is every moment conscious of the sentiment represented by it. It may not, however, be improper to attempt a *description* of this sentiment, in hopes we may by that means arrive at some analogies which may afford a more perfect explication of it. I say that belief is nothing but a more vivid, lively, forcible, firm, steady conception of an object than what the imagination alone is ever able to attain. This variety of terms, which may seem so unphilosophical, is intended only to express that act of the mind which renders realities, or what is taken for such, more present to us than fictions, causes them to weigh more in the thought, and gives them a superior influence

on the passions and imagination. Provided we agree about the thing, it is needless to dispute about the terms. The imagination has the command over all its ideas and can join and mix and vary them in all the ways possible. It may conceive fictitious objects with all the circumstances of place and time. It may set them in a manner before our eyes, in their true colors, just as they might have existed. But as it is impossible that this faculty of imagination can ever, of itself, reach belief, it is evident that belief consists not in the peculiar nature or order of ideas, but in the *manner* of their conception and in their *feeling* to the mind. I confess that it is impossible perfectly to explain this feeling or manner of conception. We may make use of words which express something near it. But its true and proper name, as we observed before, is "belief," which is a term that everyone sufficiently understands in common life. And in philosophy we can go no further than assert that *belief* is something felt by the mind, which distinguishes the ideas of the judgment from the fictions of the imagination. It gives them more weight and influence, makes them appear of greater importance, enforces them in the mind, and renders them the governing principle of our actions. I hear at present, for instance, a person's voice with whom I am acquainted, and the sound comes as from the next room. This impression of my senses immediately conveys my thought to the person, together with all the surrounding objects. I pain them out to myself as existing at present, with the same qualities and relations of which I formerly knew them possessed. These ideas take faster hold of my mind than ideas of an enchanted castle. They are very different from the feeling and have a much greater influence of every kind, either to give pleasure or pain, joy or sorrow.

Let us, then, take in the whole compass of this doctrine and allow that the sentiment of belief is nothing but a conception more intense and steady than what attends the mere fictions of the imagination, and that this *manner* of conception arises from a customary conjunction of the object with something present to the memory or senses. I believe that it will not be difficult, upon these suppositions, to find other operations of the mind analogous to it and to trace up these phenomena to principles still more general.

We have already observed that nature has established connections among particular ideas, and that no sooner one idea occurs to our thoughts than it introduces its correlative and carries our attention toward it by a gentle and insensible movement. These principles of connection or association we have reduced to three, namely, "resemblance," "contiguity," and "causation," which are the only bonds that unite our thoughts together and beget that regular train of reflection or discourse which, in a greater or less degree, takes place among all mankind. Now here arises a question on which the solution of the present difficulty will depend. Does it happen in all these relations that when one of the objects is presented to the senses or memory, the mind is not only carried to the conception of the correlative, but reaches a steadier and stronger conception of it than what otherwise it would have been able to attain? This seems to be the case with that belief which arises from the relation of cause and effect. And if the case be the same with the other relations or principles of association, this may be established as a general law which takes place in all the operations of the mind.

We may, therefore, observe, as the first experiment to our present purpose, that upon the appearance of the picture of an absent friend our idea of him is evidently enlivened by the *resemblance,* and that every passion which that idea occasions, whether of joy or sorrow, acquires new force and vigor. In producing this effect there concur both a relation and a present impression. Where the picture bears him no resemblance, at least was not intended for him, it never so much as conveys our thought to him. And where it is absent, as well as the person, though the mind may pass from the thought of one to that of the other, it feels its idea to be rather weakened than enlivened by that transition. We take a pleasure in viewing the picture of a friend when it is set before us; but when it is removed, rather choose to consider him directly than by reflection on an image which is equally distant and obscure.

The ceremonies of the Roman Catholic religion may be considered as instances of the same nature. The devotees of that superstition usually plead, in excuse for the mummeries with which they are upbraided, that they feel the good effect of those external motions, and postures, and actions in enlivening their devotion and quickening

their fervor, which otherwise would decay if directed entirely to distant and immaterial objects. We shadow out the objects of our faith, say they, in sensible types and images, and render them more present to us by the immediate presence of these types than it is possible for us to do merely by an intellectual view and contemplation. Sensible objects have always a greater influence on the fancy than any other, and this influence they readily convey to those ideas to which they are related and which they resemble. I shall only infer from these practices and this reasoning that the effect of resemblance in enlivening the ideas is very common; and as in every case a resemblance and a present impression must concur, we are abundantly supplied with experiments to prove the reality of the foregoing principle.

We may add force to these experiments by others of a different kind, in considering the effects of *contiguity* as well as of *resemblance.* It is certain that distance diminishes the force of every idea and that, upon our approach to any object, though it does not discover itself to our senses, it operates upon the mind with an influence which imitates an immediate impression. The thinking on any object readily transports the mind to what is contiguous; but it is only the actual presence of an object that transports it with a superior vivacity. When I am a few miles from home, whatever relates to it touches me more nearly than when I am two hundred leagues distant, though even at that distance the reflecting on anything in the neighborhood of my friends or family naturally produces an idea of them. But, as in this latter case, both the objects of the mind are ideas, notwithstanding there is an easy transition between them; that transition alone is not able to give a superior vivacity to any of the ideas, for want of some immediate impression.[4]

No one can doubt but *causation* has the same influence as the other two relations of resemblance and contiguity. Superstitious people are fond of the relics of saints and holy men, for the same reason that they seek after types or images in order to enliven their devotion and give them a more intimate and strong conception of those exemplary lives which they desire to imitate. Now it is evident that one of the best relics which a devotee could procure would be the handiwork of a saint; and if his clothes and furniture are ever to be considered in this light, it is because they were once at his disposal and were moved and affected by him; in which respect they are to be considered as imperfect effects, and as connected with him by a shorter chain of consequences than any of those by which we learn the reality of his existence.

Suppose that the son of a friend who had been long dead or absent were presented to us; it is evident that this object would instantly revive its correlative idea and recall to our thoughts all past intimacies and familiarities in more lively color than they would otherwise have appeared to us. This is another phenomenon which seems to prove the principle above mentioned.

We may observe that in these phenomena the belief of the correlative object is always presupposed, without which the relation could have no effect. The influence of the picture supposes that we *believe* our friend to have once existed. Contiguity to home can never excite our ideas of home unless we *believe* that it really exists. Now I assert that this belief, where it reaches beyond the memory or senses, is of a similar nature and arises from similar causes with the transition of thought and vivacity of conception here explained. When I throw a piece of dry wood into a fire, my mind is immediately carried to conceive that it augments, not extinguishes, the flame. This transition of thought from the cause to the effect proceeds not from reason. It derives its origin altogether from custom and experience. And, as it first begins from an object present to the senses, it renders the idea or conception of flame more strong or lively than any loose floating reverie of the imagination. The idea arises immediately. The thought moves instantly toward it and conveys to it all that force of conception which is derived from the impression present to the senses. When a sword is leveled at my breast, does not the idea of wound and pain strike me more strongly than when a glass of wine is presented to me, even though by accident this idea should occur after the appearance of the latter object? But what is there in this whole matter to cause such a strong conception except only a present object and a customary transition to the idea of another object which we have been accustomed to conjoin with the former? This is the whole operation of the mind in all our conclusions concerning matter of fact and existence; and it is a satisfaction to find some analogies by which it

may be explained. The transition from a present object does in all cases give strength and solidity to the related idea.

Here, then, is a kind of pre-established harmony between the course of nature and the succession of our ideas; and though the powers and forces by which the former is governed be wholly unknown to us, yet our thoughts and conceptions have still, we find, gone on in the same train with the other works of nature. Custom is that principle by which this correspondence has been effected, so necessary to the subsistence of our species and the regulation of our conduct in every circumstance and occurrence of human life. Had not the presence of an object instantly excited the idea of those objects commonly conjoined with it, all our knowledge must have been limited to the narrow sphere of our memory and senses, and we should never have been able to adjust means to ends or employ our natural powers either to the producing of good or avoiding of evil. Those who delight in the discovery and contemplation of *final causes* have here ample subject to employ their wonder and admiration.

I shall add, for a further confirmation of the foregoing theory, that as this operation of the mind, by which we infer like effects from like causes, and *vice versa,* is so essential to the subsistence of all human creatures, it is not probable that it could be trusted to the fallacious deductions of our reason, which is slow in its operations, appears not, in any degree, during the first years of infancy, and, at best, is in every age and period of human life extremely liable to error and mistake. It is more conformable to the ordinary wisdom of nature to secure so necessary an act of the mind by some instinct or mechanical tendency which may be infallible in its operations, may discover itself at the first appearance of life and thought, and may be independent of all the labored deductions of the understanding. As nature as taught us the use of our limbs without giving us the knowledge of the muscles and nerves by which they are actuated, so has she implanted in us an instinct which carries forward the thought in a correspondent course to that which she has established among external objects, though we are ignorant of those powers and forces on which this regular course and succession of objects totally depends.

SECTION VI. OF PROBABILITY[5]

Though there be no such thing as *chance* in the world, our ignorance of the real cause of any event has the same influence on the understanding and begets a like species of belief or opinion.

There is certainly a probability which arises from a superiority of chances on any side; and, according as this superiority increases and surpasses the opposite chances, the probability receives a proportionable increase and begets still a higher degree of belief of assent to that side in which we discover the superiority. If a die were marked with one figure or number of spots on four sides, and with another figure or number of spots on the two remaining sides, it would be more probable that the former would turn up than the latter, though, if it had a thousand sides marked in the same manner, and only one side different, the probability would be much higher and our belief or expectation of the even more steady and secure. This process of the thought or reasoning may seem trivial and obvious; but to those who consider it more narrowly it may, perhaps, afford matter for curious speculation.

It seems evident that when the mind looks forward to discover the event which may result from the throw of such a die, it considers the turning up of each particular side as alike probable; and this is the very nature of chance, to render all the particular events comprehended in it entirely equal. But finding a greater number of sides concur in the one event than in the other, the mind is carried more frequently to that event and meets it oftener in revolving the various possibilities or chances on which the ultimate result depends. This concurrence of several views in one particular event begets immediately, by an explicable contrivance of nature, the sentiment of belief and gives that event the advantage over its antagonist which is supported by a smaller number of views and recurs less frequently to the mind. If we allow that belief is nothing but a firmer and stronger conception of an object than what attends the mere fictions of the imagination, this operation may, perhaps, in some measure be accounted for. The concurrence of these several views or glimpses imprints the idea more strongly on the imagination, gives it superior force and vigor, renders its influence on the passions and affections more sensible, and, in a word, begets that reliance or security which constitutes the nature of belief and opinion.

The case is the same with the probability of causes as with that of chance. There are some cases which are entirely uniform and constant in producing a particular effect, and no instance has ever yet been found of any failure or irregularity in their operation. Fire has always burned, and water suffocated, every human creature. The production of motion by impulse and gravity is a universal law which has hitherto admitted of no exception. But there are other causes which have been found more irregular and uncertain, nor has rhubarb always proved a purge, or opium a soporific, to everyone who has taken these medicines. It is true, when any cause fails of producing its usual effect, philosophers ascribe not this to any irregularity in nature, but suppose that some secret causes in the particular structure of parts have prevented the operation. Our reasonings, however, and conclusions concerning the event are the same as if this principle had no place. Being determined by custom to transfer the past to the future in all our inferences, where the past has been entirely regular and uniform we expect the event with the greatest assurance and leave no room for any contrary supposition. But where different effects have been found to follow from causes which are to *appearance* exactly similar, all these various effects must occur to the mind in transferring the past to the future, and enter into our consideration when we determine the probability of the event. Though we give the preference to that which has been found most usual, and believe that this effect will exist, we must not overlook the other effects, but must assign to each of them a particular weight and authority in proportion as we have found it to be more or less frequent. It is more probable, in almost every country of Europe, that there will be frost sometime in January than that the weather will continue open throughout that whole month, though this probability varies according to the different climates, and approaches to a certainty in the more northern kingdoms. Here, then, it seems evident that when we transfer the past to the future in order to determine the effect which will result from any cause, we transfer all the different events in the same proportion as they have appeared in the past, and conceive one to have existed a hundred times, for instance, another ten times, and another once. As a great number of views do here concur in one event, they fortify and confirm it to the imagination, beget that sentiment which we call "belief," and give its object the preference above the contrary event which is not supported by an equal number of experiments and recurs not so frequently to the thought in transferring the past to the future. Let anyone try to account for this operation of the mind upon any of the received systems of philosophy, and he will be sensible of the difficulty. For my part, I shall think it sufficient if the present hints excite the curiosity of philosophers and make them sensible how defective all common theories are in treating of such curious and such sublime subjects.

SECTION VII. OF THE IDEA OF NECESSARY CONNECTION

PART I

The great advantage of the mathematical sciences above the moral consists in this, that the ideas of the former, being sensible, are always clear and determinate, the smallest distinction between them is immediately perceptible, and the same terms are still expressive of the same ideas without ambiguity or variation. An oval is never mistaken for a circle, nor a hyperbola for an ellipsis. The isosceles and scalenum are distinguished by boundaries more exact than vice and virtue, right and wrong. If any term be defined in geometry, the mind readily, of itself substitutes on all occasions the definition for the term defined, or, even when no definition is employed, the object itself may be presented to the senses and by that means be steadily and clearly apprehended. But the finer sentiments of the mind, the operations of the understanding, the various agitations of the passions, though really in themselves distinct, easily escape us when surveyed by reflection, nor is it in our power to recall the original object as often as we have occasion to contemplate it. Ambiguity, by this means, is gradually introduced into our reasonings: similar objects are readily taken to be the same, and the conclusion becomes at last very wide of the premises.

One may safely, however, affirm that if we consider these sciences in a proper light, their advantages and disadvantages nearly compensate each other and reduce both of them to a state of equality. If the mind, with greater facility, retains the ideas of geometry clear and determinate, it must carry on a much longer and more intricate chain of reasoning and compare ideas much wider of each other in order to reach the abstruser truths of that science. And if moral ideas are apt, without extreme care, to fall into obscurity and confusion, the inferences are always much shorter in these disquisitions, and the intermediate steps which led to the conclusion much fewer than in the sciences which treat of quantity and number. In reality, there is scarcely a proposition in Euclid so simple as not to consist of more parts than are to be found in any moral reasoning which runs not into chimera and conceit. Where we trace the principles of the human mind through a few steps, we may be very well satisfied with our progress, considering how soon nature throws a bar to all our inquiries concerning causes and reduces us to an acknowledgment of our ignorance. The chief obstacle, therefore, to our improvements in the moral or metaphysical sciences is the obscurity of the ideas and ambiguity of the terms. The principal difficulty in the mathematics is the length of inferences and compass of thought requisite to the forming of any conclusion. And, perhaps, our progress in natural philosophy is chiefly retarded by the want of proper experiments and phenomena, which are often discovered by chance and cannot always be found when requisite, even by the most diligent and prudent inquiry. As moral philosophy seems hitherto to have received less improvement than either geometry or physics, we may conclude that if there be any difference in this respect among these sciences, the difficulties which obstruct the progress of the former require superior care and capacity to be surmounted.

There are no ideas which occur in metaphysics more obscure and uncertain than those of "power," "force," "energy," or "necessary connection," of which it is every moment necessary for us to treat in all our disquisitions. We shall, therefore, endeavor in this Section to fix, if possible, the precise meaning of these terms and thereby remove some part of that obscurity which is so much complained of in this species of philosophy.

It seems a proposition which will not admit of much dispute that all our ideas are nothing but copies of our impressions, or, in other words, that it is impossible for us to *think* of anything which we have not antecedently *felt*, either by our external or internal senses. I have endeavored[6] to explain and prove this proposition, and have expressed my hopes that by a proper application of it men may reach a greater clearness and precision in philosophical reasonings than what they have hitherto been able to attain. Complex ideas may, perhaps, be well known by definition, which is nothing but an enumeration of those parts or simple ideas that compose them. But when we have pushed up definitions to the most simple ideas and find still some ambiguity and obscurity, what resources are we then possessed of? By what invention can we throw light upon these ideas and render them altogether precise and determinate to our intellectual view? Produce the impressions or original sentiments from which the ideas are copied. These impressions are all strong and sensible. They admit not of ambiguity. They are not only placed in a full light themselves, but may throw light on their correspondent ideas, which lie in obscurity. And by this means we may perhaps obtain a new microscope or species of optics by which, in the moral sciences, the most minute and most simple ideas may be so enlarged as to fall readily under our apprehension and be equally known with the grossest and most sensible ideas that can be the object of our inquiry.

To be fully acquainted, therefore, with the idea of power or necessary connection, let us examine its impression and, in order to find the impression with greater certainty, let us search for it in all the sources from which it may possibly be derived.

When we look about us toward external objects and consider the operation of causes, we are never able, in a single instance, to discover any power or necessary connection, any quality which binds the effect to the cause and renders the one an infallible consequence of the other. We only find that the one does actually in fact follow the other. The impulse of one billiard ball is attended with motion in the second. This is the whole that appears to be *outward* senses. The mind feels no sentiment or *inward* impression from this succession of objects; consequently, there is not, in any single particular instance of cause and effect, anything which can suggest the idea of power or necessary connection.

From the first appearance of an object we never can conjecture what effect will result from it. But were the power or energy of any cause discoverable by the mind, we could foresee the effect, even without experience, and might, at first, pronounce with certainty concerning it by the mere dint of thought and reasoning.

In reality, there is no part of matter that does ever, by its sensible qualities, discover any power or energy, or give us ground to imagine that it could produce anything, or be followed by any other object, which we could denominate its effect. Solidity, extension, motion—these qualities are all complete in themselves and never point out any other event which may result from them. The scenes of the universe are continually shifting, and one object follows another in an uninterrupted succession; the power or force which actuates the whole machine is entirely concealed from us and never discovers itself in any of the sensible qualities of body. We know that, in fact, heat is a constant attendant of flame; but what is the connection between them we have no room so much as to conjecture or imagine. It is impossible, therefore, that the idea of power can be derived from the contemplation of bodies in single instances of their operation, because no bodies ever discover any power which can be the original of this idea.[7]

Since, therefore, external objects as they appear to the senses give us no idea of power or necessary connection by their operation in particular instances, let us see whether this idea be derived from reflection on the operations of our own minds and be copies from any internal impression. It may be said that we are every moment conscious of internal power while we feel that, by the simple command of our will, we can move the organs of our body or direct the faculties of our mind. An act of volition produces motion in our limbs or raises a new idea in our imagination. This influence of the will we know by consciousness. Hence we acquire the idea of power or energy, and are certain that we ourselves and all other intelligent beings are possessed of power. This idea, then, is an idea of reflection since it arises from reflecting on the operations of our own mind and on the command which is exercised by will both over the organs of the body and faculties of the soul.

We shall proceed to examine this pretension and, first, with regard to the influence of volition over the organs of the body. This influence, we may observe, is a fact which, like all other natural events, can be known only by experience, and can never be foreseen from any apparent energy or power in the cause which connects it with the effect and renders the one an infallible consequence of the other. The motion of our body follows upon the command of our will. Of this we are every moment conscious. But the means by which this is effected, the energy by which the will performs so extraordinary an operation—of this we are so far from being immediately conscious that it must forever escape our most diligent inquiry.

For, *first,* is there any principle in all nature more mysterious than the union of soul with body, by which a supposed spiritual substance acquires such an influence over a material one that the most refined thought is able to actuate the grossest matter? Were we empowered by a secret wish to remove mountains or control the planets in their orbit, this extensive authority would not be more extraordinary, nor more beyond our comprehension. But if, by consciousness, we perceived any power or energy in the will, we must know this power; we must know its connection with the effect; we must know the secret union of soul and body, and the nature of both these substances by which the one is able to operate in so many instances upon the other.

Secondly, we are not able to move all the organs of the body with a like authority, though we cannot assign any reason, besides experience, for so remarkable a difference between one and the other. Why has the will an influence over the tongue and fingers, not over the heart or liver? This question would never embarrass us were we conscious of a power in the former case, not in the latter. We should then perceive, independent of experience, why the authority of the will over the organs of the body is circumscribed within such particular limits. Being in that case fully acquainted with the power or force by which it operates, we should also know why its influence reaches precisely to such boundaries, and no further.

A man suddenly struck with a palsy in the leg or arm, or who had newly lost those members, frequently endeavors, at first, to move them and employ them in their usual offices. Here he is as much conscious of power to command such limbs as a man in perfect health is conscious of power to actuate any member which remains in its natural state and condition. But consciousness never deceives. Consequently, neither in the one case nor in the other are we ever conscious of any power. We learn the influence of our will from experience alone. And experience only teaches us how one event constantly follows another, without instructing us in the secret connection which binds them together and renders them inseparable.

Thirdly, we learn from anatomy that the immediate object of power in voluntary motion is not the member itself which is moved, but certain muscles and nerves and animal spirits, and, perhaps, something still more minute and more unknown, through which the motion is successively propagated ere it reach the member itself whose motion is the immediate object of volition. Can there be a more certain proof that the power by which this whole operation is performed, so far from being directly and fully known by an inward sentiment or consciousness, is to the last degree mysterious and unintelligible? Here the mind wills a certain event; immediately another event, unknown to ourselves and totally different from the one intended, is produced. This event produces another, equally unknown, till, at last, through a long succession the desired event is produced. But if the original power were felt, it must be known; were it known, its effect must also be known, since all power is relative to its effect. And, *vice versa,* if the effect be not known, the power cannot be known nor felt. How indeed can we be conscious of a power to move our limbs when we have no such power, but only that to move certain animal spirits which, though they produce at last the motion of our limbs, yet operate in such a manner as is wholly beyond our comprehension?

We may therefore conclude from the whole, I hope, without any temerity, though with assurance, that our idea of power is not copied from any sentiment or consciousness of power within ourselves when we give rise to animal motion or apply our limbs to their proper use and office. That their motion follows the command of the will is a matter of common experience, like other natural events; but the power or energy by which this is effected, like that in other natural events, is unknown and inconceivable.[8]

Shall we then assert that we are conscious of a power or energy in our own minds when, by an act or command of our will, we raise up a new idea, fix the mind to the contemplation of it, turn it on all sides, and at last dismiss it for some other idea when we think that we have surveyed it with sufficient accuracy? I believe the same arguments will prove that even this command of the will gives us no real idea of force or energy.

First, it must be allowed that when we know a power, we know that very circumstance in the cause by which it is enabled to produce the effect, for these are supposed to be synonymous. We must, therefore, know both the cause and effect and the relation between them. But do we pretend to be acquainted with the nature of the human soul and the nature of an idea, or the aptitude of the one to produce the other? This is a real creation, a production of something out of nothing, which implies a power so great that it may seem, at first sight, beyond the reach of any being less than infinite. At least it must be owned that such a power is not felt, nor known, nor even conceivable by the mind. We only feel the event, namely, the existence of an idea consequent to a command of the will; but the manner in which this operation is performed, the power by which it is produced, is entirely beyond our comprehension.

Secondly, the command of the mind over itself is limited, as well as its command over the body; and these limits are not known by reason or any acquaintance with the nature of cause and effect, but only by experience and observation, as in all other natural events and in the operation of external objects. Our authority over our sentiments and passions is much weaker than that over our ideas; and even the latter authority is circumscribed within very narrow boundaries. Will any one pretend to assign the ultimate reason of these boundaries, or show why the power is deficient in one case, not in another?

Thirdly, this self-command is very different at different times. A man in health possesses more of it than one languishing with sickness. We are more master of our thoughts in the morning than in the evening; fasting, than after a full meal. Can we give any reason for these variations except experience? Where then is the power of which we pretend to be conscious? Is there not here, either

in a spiritual or material substance, or both, some secret mechanism or structure of parts upon which the effect depends, and which, being entirely unknown to us, renders the power or energy of the will equally unknown and incomprehensible?

Volition is surely an act of the mind with which we are sufficiently acquainted. Reflect upon it. Consider it on all sides. Do you find anything in it like this creative power by which it raises from nothing a new idea and, with a kind of *fiat,* imitates the omnipotence of its Maker, if I may be allowed so to speak, who called forth into existence all the various scenes of nature? So far from being conscious of this energy in the will, it requires as certain experience as that of which we are possessed to convince us that such extraordinary effects do ever result from a simple act of volition.

The generality of mankind never find any difficulty in accounting for the more common and familiar operations of nature, such as the descent of heavy bodies, the growth of plants, the generation of animals, or the nourishment of bodies by food; but suppose that in all these cases they perceive the very force or energy of the cause by which it is connected with its effect, and is forever infallible in its operation. They acquire, by long habit, such a turn of mind that upon the appearance of the cause they immediately expect, with assurance, its usual attendant, and hardly conceive it possible that any other event could result from it. It is only on the discovery of extraordinary phenomena, such as earthquakes, pestilence, and prodigies of any kind, that they find themselves at a loss to assign a proper cause and to explain the manner in which the effect is produced by it. It is usual for men, in such difficulties, to have recourse to some invisible intelligent principle as the immediate cause of that event which surprises them, and which they think cannot be accounted for from the common powers of nature. But philosophers, who carry their scrutiny a little further, immediately perceive that, even in the most familiar events, the energy of the cause is as unintelligible as in the most unusual, and that we only learn by experience the frequent conjunction of objects, without being ever able to comprehend anything like connection between them. Here, then, many philosophers think themselves obliged by reason to have recourse, on all occasions, to the same principle which the vulgar never appeal to but in cases that appear miraculous and supernatural. They acknowledge mind and intelligence to be, not only the ultimate and original cause of all things, but the immediate and sole cause of every event which appears in nature. They pretend that those objects which are commonly denominated "causes" are in reality nothing but "occasions," and that the true and direct principle of every effect is not any power or force in nature, but a volition of the Supreme Being, who wills that such particular objects should forever be conjoined with each other. Instead of saying that one billiard ball moves another by a force which it has derived from the author of nature, it is the Deity himself, they say, who, by a particular volition, moves the second ball, being determined to this operation by the impulse of the first ball, in consequence of those general laws which he has laid down to himself in the government of the universe. But philosophers, advancing still in their inquiries, discover that as we are totally ignorant of the power on which depends the mutual operation of bodies, we are no less ignorant of that power on which depends the operation of mind on body, or of body on mind; nor are we able, either from our senses or consciousness, to assign the ultimate principle in the one case more than in the other. The same ignorance, therefore, reduces them to the same conclusion. They assert that the Deity is the immediate cause of the union between soul and body, and that they are not the organs of sense which, being agitated by external objects, produce sensations in the mind; but that it is a particular volition of our omnipotent Maker which excites such a sensation in consequence of such a motion in the organ. In like manner, it is not any energy in the will that produces local motion in our members: It is God himself, who is pleased to second our will, in itself impotent, and to command that motion which we erroneously attribute to our own power and efficacy. Nor do philosophers stop at this conclusion. They sometimes extend the same inference to the mind itself in its internal operations. Our mental vision or conception of ideas is nothing but a revelation made to us by our Maker. When we voluntarily turn our thoughts to any object and raise up its image in the fancy, it is not the will which creates that idea, it is the universal Creator who discovers it to the mind and renders it present to us.

Thus, according to these philosophers, everything is full of God. Not content with the principle that nothing exists but by his will, that nothing possesses any power but by his concession, they rob nature and all created beings of every power in order to render their dependence on the Deity still more sensible and immediate. They consider not that by this theory they diminish, instead of magnifying, the grandeur of those attributes which they affect so much to celebrate. It argues, surely, more power in the Deity to delegate a certain degree of power to inferior creatures than to produce everything by his own immediate volition. It argues more wisdom to contrive at first the fabric of the world with such perfect foresight that of itself, and by its proper operation, it may serve all the purposes of Providence than if the great Creator were obliged every moment to adjust its parts and animate by his breath all the wheels of that stupendous machine.

But if we would have a more philosophical confutation of this theory, perhaps the two following reflections may suffice:

First, it seems to me that this theory of the universal energy and operation of the Supreme Being is too bold ever to carry conviction with it to a man sufficiently apprised of the weakness of human reason and the narrow limits to which it is confined in all its operations. Though the chain of arguments which conduct to it were ever so logical, there must arise a strong suspicion, if not an absolute assurance, that it has carried us quite beyond the reach of our faculties when it leads to conclusions so extraordinary and so remote from common life and experience. We are got into fairyland long ere we have reached the last steps of our theory; and *there* we have no reason to trust our common methods of arguments or to think that our usual analogies and probabilities have any authority. Our line is too short to fathom such immense abysses. And however we may flatter ourselves that we are guided, in every step which we take, by a kind of verisimilitude and experience, we may be assured that this fancied experience has no authority when we thus apply it to subjects that lie entirely out of the sphere of experience. But on this we shall have occasion to touch afterwards.[9]

Secondly, I cannot perceive any force in the arguments on which this theory is founded. We are ignorant, it is true, of the manner in which bodies operate on each other. Their force or energy is entirely incomprehensible. But are we not equally ignorant of the manner or force by which a mind, even the Supreme Mind, operates, either on itself or on body? Whence, I beseech you, do we acquire any idea of it? We have no sentiment or consciousness of this power in ourselves. We have no idea of the Supreme Being but what we learn from reflection on our own faculties. Were our ignorance, therefore, a good reason for rejecting anything, we should be led into that principle of denying all energy in the Supreme Being, as much as in the grossest matter. We surely comprehend as little the operations of the one as of the other. Is it more difficult to conceive that motion may arise from impulse than that it may arise from volition? All we know is our profound ignorance in both cases.[10]

PART II

But to hasten to a conclusion of this argument, which is already drawn out to too great a length: We have sought in vain for an idea of power or necessary connection in all the sources from which we would suppose it to be derived. It appears that in single instances of the operation of bodies we never can, by our utmost scrutiny, discover anything but one event following another, without being able to comprehend any force or power by which the cause operates or any connection between it and its supposed effect. The same difficulty occurs in contemplating the operations of mind on body, where we observe the motion of the latter to follow upon the volition of the former, but are not able to observe or conceive the tie which binds together the motion and volition, or the energy, by which the mind produces this effect. The authority of the will over its own faculties and ideas is not a whit more comprehensible, so that, upon the whole, there appears not, throughout all nature, any one instance of connection which is conceivable by us. All events seem entirely loose and separate. One event follows another, but we never can observe any tie between them. They seem *conjoined,* but never *connected.* But as we can have no idea of anything which never appeared to our outward sense or inward sentiment, the necessary conclu-

sion *seems* to be that we have no idea of connection or power at all, and that these words are absolutely without any meaning when employed either in philosophical reasonings or common life.

But there still remains one method of avoiding this conclusion, and one source which we have not yet examined. When any natural object or event is presented, it is impossible for us, by any sagacity or penetration, to discover, or even conjecture, without experience, what event will result from it, or to carry our foresight beyond that object which is immediately present to the memory and senses. Even after one instance or experiment where we have observed a particular event to follow upon another, we are not entitled to form a general rule or foretell what will happen in like cases, it being justly esteemed an unpardonable temerity to judge the whole course of nature from one single experiment, however accurate or certain. But when one particular species of events has always, in all instances, been conjoined with another, we make no longer any scruple of foretelling one upon the appearance of the other, and of employing that reasoning which can alone assure us of any matter of fact or existence. We then call the one object "cause," the other "effect." We suppose that there is some connection between them, some power in the one by which it infallibly produces the other and operates with the greatest certainty and strongest necessity.

It appears, then, that this idea of a necessary connection among events arises from a number of similar instances which occur, of the constant conjunction of these events; nor can that idea ever be suggested by any one of these instances surveyed in all possible lights and positions. But there is nothing in a number of instances, different from every single instance, which is supposed to be exactly similar, except only that after a repetition of similar instances the mind is carried by habit, upon the appearance of one event, to expect its usual attendant and to believe that it will exist. This connection, therefore, which we *feel* in the mind, this customary transition of the imagination from one object to its usual attendant, is the sentiment or impression from which we form the idea of power or necessary connection. Nothing further is the case. Contemplate the subject on all sides, you will never find any other origin of that idea. This is the sole difference between one instance, from which we can never receive the idea of connection, and a number of similar instances by which it is suggested. The first time a man saw the communication of motion by impulse, as by the shock of two billiard balls, he could not pronounce that the one event was *connected,* but only that it was *conjoined* with the other. After he has observed several instances of this nature, he then pronounces them to be *connected.* What alteration has happened to give rise to this new idea of *connection?* Nothing but that he now *feels* these events to be *connected* in his imagination, and can readily foretell the existence of one from the appearance of the other. When we say, therefore, that one object is connected with another, we mean only that they have acquired a connection in our thought and gave rise to this inference by which they become proofs of each other's existence—a conclusion which is somewhat extraordinary, but which seems founded on sufficient evidence. Nor will its evidence be weakened by any general diffidence of the understanding or skeptical suspicion concerning every conclusion which is new and extraordinary. No conclusions can be more agreeable to skepticism than such as make discoveries concerning the weakness and narrow limits of human reason and capacity.

And what stronger instance can be produced of the surprising ignorance and weakness of the understanding than the present? For surely, if there be any relation among objects which it imports us to know perfectly, it is that of cause and effect. On this are founded all our reasonings concerning matter of fact or existence. By means of it alone we attain any assurance concerning objects which are removed from the present testimony of our memory and senses. The only immediate utility of all sciences is to teach us how to control and regulate future events by their causes. Our thoughts and inquiries are, therefore, every moment employed about this relation; yet so imperfect are the ideas which we form concerning it that it is impossible to give any just definition of cause, except what is drawn from something extraneous and foreign to it. Similar objects are always conjoined with similar. Of this we have experience. Suitably to this experience, therefore, we may define a cause to be *an object followed by another, and where all the objects,* similar to the first, are followed by objects similar to the second. Or, in other words, *where, if the first object had not been, the second never had existed.* The appearance of a cause always conveys the mind, by a customary transition, to the idea of the effect. Of this also we have experience. We may, therefore, suitably to this experience, form another definition of cause and call it *an object followed by another, and whose appearance always conveys the thought to that other.* But though both these definitions be drawn from circumstances foreign to the cause, we cannot remedy this inconvenience or attain any more perfect definition which may point out that circumstance in the cause which gives it a connection with its effect. We have no idea of this connection, nor even any distinct notion what it is we desire to know when we endeavor at a conception of it. We say, for instance, that the vibration of this string is the cause of this particular sound. But what do we mean by that affirmation? We either mean *that this vibration is followed by this sound, and that all similar vibrations have been followed by similar sounds;* or, *that this vibration is followed by this sound, and that, upon the appearance of one, the mind anticipates the senses and forms immediately an idea of the other.* We may consider the relation of cause and effect in either of these two lights; but beyond these we have no idea of it.[11]

To recapitulate, therefore, the reasonings of this Section: Every idea is copied from some preceding impression or sentiment; and where we cannot find any impression, we may be certain that there is no idea. In all single instances of the operation of bodies or minds there is nothing that produces any impression, nor consequently can suggest any idea, of power or necessary connection. But when many uniform instances appear, and the same object is always followed by the same event, we then begin to entertain the notion of cause and connection. We then *feel* a new sentiment or impression, to wit, a customary connection in the thought or imagination between one object and its usual attendant; and this sentiment is the original of that idea which we seek for. For as this idea arises from a number of similar instances, and not from any single instance, it must arise from that circumstance in which the number of instances differ from every individual instance. But this customary connection or transition of the imagination is the only circumstance in which they differ. In every other particular they are alike. The first instance which we saw of motion, communicated by the shock of two billiard balls (to return to this obvious illustration), is exactly similar to any instance that may at present occur to us, except only that we could not at first *infer* one event from the other, which we are enabled to do at present, after so long a course of uniform experience. I know not whether the reader will readily apprehend this reasoning. I am afraid that, should I multiply words about it or throw it into a greater variety of lights, it would only become more obscure and intricate. In all abstract reasonings there is one point of view which, if we can happily hit, we shall go further toward illustrating the subject than by all the eloquence and copious expression in the world. This point of view we should endeavor to reach, and reserve the flowers of rhetoric for subjects which are more adapted to them.

NOTES

1.   It is probable that no more was meant by those who denied innate ideas than that all ideas were copies of our impressions, though it must be confessed that the terms which they employed were not chosen with such caution, nor so exactly defined, as to prevent all mistakes about their doctrine. For what is meant by "innate"? If "innate" be equivalent to "natural," then all the perceptions and ideas of the mind must be allowed to be innate or natural, in whatever sense we take the latter word, whether in opposition to what is uncommon, artificial, or miraculous. If by innate he meant contemporary to our birth, the dispute seems to be frivolous, nor is it worth while to inquire at what time thinking begins, whether before, at, or after our birth. Again, the word "idea" seems to be commonly taken in a very loose sense by Locke and others, as standing for any of our perceptions, our sensations and passions, as well as thoughts. Now, in this sense, I should desire to know what can be meant by asserting that self-love, or resentment of injuries, or the passion between the sexes is not innate?

But admitting these terms "impressions" and "ideas" in the sense above explained, and understanding by "innate" what is original or copied from no precedent perception, then may we assert that all our impressions are innate, and our ideas not innate.

To be ingenuous, I must own it to be my opinion that Locke was betrayed into this question by the schoolmen, who, making use of undefined terms, draw out their disputes to a tedious length without ever touching the point in question. A like ambiguity and circumlocution seem to run through that philosopher's reasonings, on this as well as most other subjects.

2.   The word "power" is here used in a loose and popular sense. The more accurate explication of it would give additional evidence to this argument. See Section VII.

3.   Nothing is more usual than for writers, even on *moral, political,* or *physical* subjects, to distinguish between *reason* and *experience,* and to suppose that these species of argumentation are entirely different from each other. The former are taken for the mere result of our intellectual faculties, which, by considering a *a priori* the nature of things, and examining the effects that must follow from their operation, establish particular principles of science and philosophy. The latter are supposed to be derived entirely from sense and observation, by which we learn what has actually resulted from the operation of particular objects, and are thence able to infer what will for the future result from them. Thus, for instance, the limitations and restraints of civil government and a legal constitution may be defended, either from *reason,* which, reflecting on the great frailty and corruption of human nature, teaches that no man can safely be trusted with unlimited authority; or from *experience* and history, which inform us of the enormous abuses that ambition in every age and country has been found to make of so imprudent a confidence.

The same distinction between reason and experience is maintained in all our deliberations concerning the conduct of life, while the experienced statesman, general physician, or merchant, is trusted and followed, and the unpracticed novice, with whatever natural talents endowed, neglected and despised. Though it be allowed that reason may form very plausible conjectures with regard to the consequences of such a particular conduct in such particular circumstances, it is still supposed imperfect without the assistance of experience, which is alone able to give stability and certainty to the maxim derived from study and reflection.

But notwithstanding that this distinction be thus universally received, both in the active and speculative scenes of life, I shall not scruple to pronounce that it is, at bottom, erroneous, or at least superficial.

If we examine those arguments which, in any of the sciences above mentioned, are supposed to be the mere effects of reasoning and reflection, they will be found to terminate at last in some general principle or conclusion for which we can assign no reason but observation and experience. The only difference between them and those maxims which are vulgarly esteemed the result of pure experience is that the former cannot be established without some process of thought, and some reflection on what we have observed, in order to distinguish its circumstances and trace its consequences—whereas, in the latter, the experienced event is exactly and fully similar to that which we infer as the result of any particular situation. The history of a Tiberius or a Nero makes us dread a like tyranny, were our monarchs freed from the restraints of laws and senates: but the observation of any fraud or cruelty in private life is sufficient, with the aid of a little thought, to give us the same apprehension, while it serves as an instance of the general corruption of human nature, and shows us the danger which we must incur by reposing an entire confidence in mankind. In both cases, it is experience which is ultimately the foundation of our inference and conclusion.

There is no man so young and inexperienced as not to have formed from observation many general and just maxims concerning human affairs and the conduct of life; but it must be confessed that when a man comes to put these in practice he will be extremely liable to error, till time and further experience both enlarge these maxims, and teach him their proper use and application. In every situation or incident there are many particular and seemingly minute circumstances which the man of greatest talents is at first apt to overlook, though on them the justness of his conclusions, and consequently the prudence of his conduct, entirely depend. Not to mention that, to a young beginner, the general observations and maxims occur not always on the proper occasions, nor can be immediately applied with due calmness and distinction. The truth is, an inexperienced reasoner could be no reasoner at all were he absolutely inexperienced; and when we assign that character to anyone, we mean it only in a comparative sense, and suppose him possessed of experience in a smaller and more imperfect degree.

4. [A footnote containing a long quotation from Cicero, deleted.]

5. Mr. Locke divides all arguments into "demonstrative" and "probable." In this view, we must say that it is only probable all men must die, or that the sun will rise tomorrow. But to conform our language more to common use, we ought to divide arguments into *demonstrations, proofs,* and *probabilities;* by proofs, meaning such arguments from experience as leave no room for doubt or opposition.

6. [In Section II.]

7. Mr. Locke, in his chapter of Power, says that, finding from experience that there are several new productions in matter, and concluding that there must somewhere be a power capable of producing them, we arrive at last by this reasoning at the idea of power. But no reasoning can ever give us a new, original simple idea, as this philosopher himself confesses. This, therefore, can never be the origin of that idea.

8. It may be pretended, that the resistance which we meet with in bodies, obliging us frequently to exert our force and call up all our power, this gives us the idea of force and power. It is this *nisus* or strong endeavor of which we are conscious, that is the original impression from which this idea is copied. But, *first,* we attribute power to a vast number of objects where we never can suppose this resistance or exertion of force to take place: to the Supreme Being, who never meets with any resistance; to the mind in its command over its ideas and limbs, in common thinking and motion, where the effect follows immediately upon the will, without any exertion or summoning up of force; to inanimate matter, which is not capable of this sentiment. *Secondly,* this sentiment of an endeavor to overcome resistance has no known connection with any event: What follows it we know by experience, but could not know it *a priori.* It must, however, be confessed that the animal *nisus* which we experience, though it can afford no accurate precise idea of power, enters very much into that vulgar, inaccurate idea which is formed of it.

9. Section XII. [Not included here.]

10. I need not examine at length the *vis inertiae* which is so much talked of in the new philosophy, and which is ascribed to matter. We find by experience that a body at rest or in motion continues forever in its present state, till put from it by some new cause; and that a body impelled takes as much motion from the impelling body as it acquires itself. These are facts. When we call this a *vis inertiae,* we only mark these facts, without pretending to have any idea of the inert power, in the same manner as, when we talk of gravity, we mean certain effects without comprehending that active power. It was never the meaning of Sir Isaac Newton to rob second causes of all force or energy, though some of his followers have endeavored to establish that theory upon his authority. On the contrary, that great philosopher had recourse to an ethereal active fluid to explain his universal attraction, though he was so cautious and modest as to allow that it was a mere hypothesis not to be insisted on without more experiments. I must confess that there is something in the fate of opinions a little extraordinary. Descartes insinuated that doctrine of the universal and sole efficacy of the Deity, without insisting on it. Malebranche and other Cartesians made it the foundation of all their philosophy. It had, however, no authority in England. Locke, Clarke, and Cudworth never so much as take notice of it, but suppose all along that matter has a real, though subordinate and derived, power. By what means has it become so prevalent among our modern metaphysicians?

11. According to these explications and definitions, the idea of *power* is relative as much as that of *cause;* and both have a reference to an effect, or some other event constantly conjoined with the former. When we consider the *unknown* circumstance of an object by which the degree or quantity of its effect is fixed and determined, we call that its power. And accordingly, it is allowed by all philosophers that the effect is the measure of the power. But if they had any idea of power as it is in itself, why could they not measure it in itself? The dispute, whether the force of a body in motion be as its velocity, or the square of its velocity; this dispute, I say, needed not be decided by comparing its effects in equal or unequal times, but by direct mensuration and comparison.

As to the frequent use of the words "force," "power," "energy," etc., which everywhere occur in common conversation as well as in philosophy, that is no proof that we are acquainted, in any instance, with the connecting principle between cause and effect, or can account ultimately for the production of one thing by another. These words, as commonly used, have very loose meanings annexed to them, and their ideas are very uncertain and confused. No animal can put external bodies in motion without the sentiment of a *nisus* or endeavor; and every animal has a sentiment or feeling from the stroke or blow of an external object that is in motion. These sensations, which are merely animal, and from which we can *a priori* draw no inference, we are apt to transfer to inanimate objects, and to suppose that they have some such feelings whenever they transfer or receive motion. With regard to energies, which are exerted without our annexing to them any idea of communicated motion, we consider only the constant experienced conjunction of the events; and as we *feel* a customary connection between the ideas, we transfer that feeling to the objects, as nothing is more usual than to apply to external bodies every internal sensation which they occasion.

WESLEY C. SALMON

An Encounter with David Hume*

A DAY IN THE LIFE OF A HYPOTHETICAL STUDENT

In the Physics 1a lecture hall, Professor Salvia[1] has had a bowling ball suspended from a high ceiling by a long rope so that it can swing back and forth like a pendulum. Standing well over to one side of the room, he holds the bowling ball at the tip of his nose. He releases it (taking great care not to give it a push). It swings through a wide arc, gaining considerable speed as it passes through the low portion of its swing beneath the point of suspension from the ceiling. It continues to the other side of the room, where it reaches the end of its path, and then returns. The professor stands motionless as the bowling ball moves faster and faster back toward his nose. As it passes through the midpoint of the return arc, it is again traveling very rapidly, but it begins to slow down, and it stops just at the tip of his nose. Some of the students think he is cool. "This demonstration," he says, "illustrates the faith that the physicist has in nature's regularity." (See Figure 1.)

Imagine that you have witnessed this demonstration just after your philosophy class, where the subject of discussion was Hume's *Enquiry Concerning Human Understanding*. You raise your hand. "How did you *know* that the bowling

*Copyright © Wesley C. Salmon, 1974. This essay was commissioned by the editor expressly for this volume. It has not been previously published. Wesley C. Salmon is Professor of Philosophy at the University of Arizona. Illustrations by Alexis Ahmad.

ball would stop where it did, just short of bashing your nose into your face?" you ask.

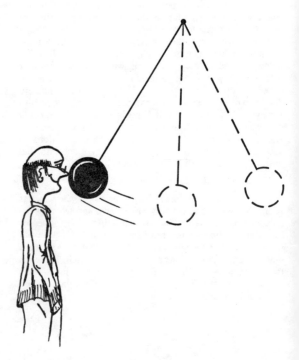

Figure 1. Prof Salvia's Pendulum. After swinging to the opposite side of the lecture hall, the bowling ball swings right back to the tip of the prof's nose, which remains motionless during the entire procedure.

"This is a standard demonstration," he replies; "I do it every year in this class, and it has often been used by many other physics teachers." In an attempt to inject a little humor, he adds, "If I had had any doubt about its working, I'd have had the teaching assistant do it."

"Are you saying, then, that you trusted the experiment to work this time simply because it has been tried so many times in the past, and has never failed?" You recall Hume's discussion of the collisions of billiard balls. In the first instance, according to Hume, before you have any experience with material objects colliding with one another, you would not know what to expect when you see a moving billiard ball approaching a stationary one, but after a good deal of experience you confidently expect some motion to be transferred to the stationary ball as a result of the collision. As your experience accumulates, you learn to predict the exact manner in which the second ball will move after being struck by the first. But you cannot really accept that answer, and neither, you feel sure, will your physics professor. Without waiting for an answer, you follow up your first question with another.

"I have this friend," you continue, "who drives like a maniac. It scares me to ride with him, but he always tells me not to worry—he has never had an accident, or even a traffic ticket. Should I conclude—assuming he is telling the truth (just as I assume you are telling me the truth about this demonstration)—that it is as safe for me to ride with him as it is for you to perform the bowling ball trick?"

"It's not the same thing at all," another student chimes in; "you can prove, mathematically, that the pendulum will not swing back beyond its original starting point, but you certainly can't prove mathematically that your friend won't have a wreck. In a way it's just the opposite; you can prove that he is likely to have an accident if he keeps on driving like that."

"What you say is partly right," says Professor Salvia to the second student, "but it isn't only a matter of mathematics. We have to rely upon the laws of physics as well. With the pendulum we were depending mainly upon the law of conservation of energy, one of the most fundamental laws of nature. As the pendulum goes through its swing, potential energy is transformed into kinetic energy, which is transformed back into potential energy, and so forth. As long as the total amount of energy remains unchanged, my nose is safe."

Since you have not yet studied the concept of energy, you do not worry too much about the details of the explanation. You are satisfied that you will understand why the pendulum behaves as it does when you have learned more about the concepts and laws that were mentioned. But you do remember something Hume wrote. There are two kinds of reasoning: reasoning concerning relations of ideas, and reasoning concerning matters of fact and existence. Mathematical reasoning falls into the former category (relations of ideas) and consequently, by itself, cannot provide any information about matters of fact. The pendulum and the professor's nose are, however, matters of fact, so we need something in addition to mathematics to get the information we want concerning that situation. Professor Salvia has told us what it is—we need the laws of nature as well.

Since physics is your last class in the morning, you head for the cafeteria when it is over to get a sandwich and coffee. The philosophy class is still bugging you. What was it Hume said about bread? That we do not know the "secret power" by which it nourishes us? Now we do, of course; we understand metabolism, the mechanism by which the body converts food into energy. Hume (living in the eighteenth century) did not understand about power and energy, as he said repeatedly. He did not know why bread is suitable food for humans, but not for tigers and lions. In biology class, you recall, you studied herbiverous, carnivorous, and omniverous species. Biologists must now understand why some species can metabolize vegetables and others cannot. Modern physics, chemistry, and biology can provide a complete explanation of the various forms of energy, the ways they can be converted from one form to another, and the ways in which they can be utilized by a living organism.

Taking a sip of the hot coffee, you recall some other things Hume said—for example, remarks about the "connection" between heat and flame. We now know that heat is really a form of energy; that temperature is a measure of the average kinetic energy of the molecules. Now, it seems, we know a great deal about the "secret powers," "energy," etc., that so perplexed Hume. Modern physics knows that ordinary objects are composed of molecules, which are in turn composed of atoms, which are themselves made up of sub-atomic particles. Modern science can tell us what holds atoms and molecules together, and why the things that consist of them have the properties they do. What was it that Hume said about a piece of ice and a crystal (e.g., a diamond)? That we do not know why one is caused by cold and the other by heat? I'll just bet, you think, that Salvia could answer that one without a bit of trouble. Why, you wonder, do they make us read these old philosophers who are now so out of date? Hume was, no doubt, a very profound thinker in his day, but why do we have to study him now, when we know the answers to all of those questions? If I were majoring in history that might be one thing, but that doesn't happen to be my field of interest. Oh, I suppose they'd say that getting an education means that you have to learn something about the "great minds of the past," but why doesn't the philosophy professor come right out and tell us the answers to these questions? It's silly to pretend that they are still great mysteries.

After lunch, let's imagine, you go to a class in contemporary social and political problems, a class you particularly like because of the lively discussions. A lot of time is spent talking about such topics as population growth, ecology and the environment, energy demands and uses, food production, and pollution. You discuss population trends, the extrapolation of such trends, and the prediction that by the year 2000 A.D., world population will reach 7 billion. You consider the various causes and possible effects of increasing concentrations of carbon dioxide in the atmosphere. You discuss solutions to various of these problems in terms of strict governmental controls, economic sanctions and incentives, and voluntary compliance on the part of enlightened and concerned citizens.

"If people run true to form," you interject, "if they behave as they always have, you can be sure that you won't make much progress relying on the good will and good sense of the populace at large."

"What is needed is more awareness and education," another student remarks, "for people can change if they see the need. During World War II people willingly sacrificed in order to support the war effort. They will do the same again, if they see that the emergency is really serious. That's why we need to provide more education and make stronger appeals to their humanitarian concerns."

"What humanitarian concerns?" asks still another student with evident cynicism.

"People *will* change," says another. "I have been reading that we are entering a new era, the Age of Aquarius, when man's finer, gentler, more considerate nature will be manifest."

"Well, I don't know about all of this astrology," another remarks in earnest tones, "but I do not believe that God will not let His world perish if we mend our ways and trust in Him. I have complete faith in His goodness."

You find this statement curiously reminiscent of Professor Salvia's earlier mention of his faith in the regularity of nature.

That night, after dinner, you read an English assignment. By the time you finish it, your throat feels a little scratchy, and you notice that you have a few sniffles. You decide to begin taking large doses of vitamin C; you have read that there is quite some controversy as to whether this helps to ward off colds, but that there is no harm in taking this vitamin in large quantities. Before going to the drug store to buy some vitamin C, you write home to request some additional funds; you mail your letter in the box by the pharmacy. You return with the vitamin C, take a few of the pills, and turn in for the night—confident that the sun will rise tomorrow morning, and hoping that you won't feel as miserable as you usually do when you catch a cold. David Hume is the farthest thing from your mind.

HUME REVISITED

The next morning, you wake up feeling fine. The sun is shining brightly, and you have no sign of a cold. You are not sure whether the vitamin C cured your cold, or whether it was the good night's sleep, or whether it wasn't going to develop into a real cold regardless. Perhaps, even it was the placebo effect; in psychology you learned that people can often be cured by totally inert drugs (e.g., sugar pills) if they believe in them. You don't really know what caused your prompt recovery, but frankly, you don't really care. If it was the placebo effect that is fine with you; you just hope it will work as well the next time.

You think about what you will do today. It is Thursday, so you have a philosophy discussion section in the morning and a physics lab in the afternoon. Thursday, you say to yourself, has got to be the lousiest day of the week. The philosophy section is a bore, and the physics lab is a drag. If only it were Saturday, when you have no classes! For a brief moment you consider taking off. Then you remember the letter you wrote last night, think about your budget and your grades, and resign yourself to the prescribed activities for the day.

The leader of the discussion section starts off with the question, "What was the main problem —I mean the really *basic* problem—bothering Hume in the *Enquiry*?" You feel like saying, "Lack of adequate scientific knowledge" (or words to that effect), but restrain yourself. No use antagonizing the guy who will decide what grade to give you. Someone says that he seemed to worry quite a lot about causes and effects, to which the discussion leader (as usual) responds, "But *why*?" Again, you stifle an impulse to say, "Because he didn't know too much about them."

After much folderal, the leader finally elicits the answer, "Because he wanted to know how we can find out about things we don't actually see (or hear, smell, touch, taste, etc.)."

"In other words," the leader paraphrases, "to examine the basis for making inferences from what we observe to what we cannot (at the moment) observe. Will someone," he continues, "give me an example of something you believe in which you are not now observing?"

You think of the letter you dropped into the box last night, of your home and parents, and of the money you hope to receive. You do not see the letter now, but you are confident it is somewhere in the mails; you do not see your parents now, but you firmly believe they are back home where you left them; you do not yet see the money you hope to get, but you expect to see it before too long. The leader is pleased when you give those examples. "And what do causes and effects have to do with all of this?" he asks, trying to draw you out a little more. Still thinking of your grade you cooperate. "I believe the letter is somewhere in the mails because I wrote it and dropped it in the box. I believe my parents are at home because they are always calling me up to tell me what to do. And I believe that the money will come as an

effect of my eloquent appeal." The leader is really happy with that; you can tell you have an A for today's session.

"But," he goes on, "do you see how this leads us immediately into Hume's next question? If cause-effect relations are the whole basis for our knowledge of things and events we do not observe, how do we know whether one event causes another, or whether they just happen together as a matter of coincidence?" Your mind is really clicking now.

"I felt a cold coming on last night, and I took a massive dose of vitamin C," you report. "This morning I feel great, but I honestly don't know whether the vitamin C actually cured it."

"Well, how could we go about trying to find out," retorts the discussion leader.

"By trying it again when I have the first symptoms of a cold," you answer, "and by trying it on other people as well." At that point the bell rings, and you leave class wondering whether the vitamin C really did cure your incipient cold.

You keep busy until lunch, doing one thing and another, but sitting down and eating, you find yourself thinking again about the common cold and its cure. It seems to be a well-known fact that the cold is caused by one or more viruses, and the human organism seems to have ways of combatting virus infections. Perhaps the massive doses of vitamin C trigger the body's defenses, in some way or other, or perhaps it provides some kind of antidote to the toxic effects of the virus. You don't know much about all of this, but you can't help speculating that science has had a good deal of success in finding causes and cures of various diseases. If continued research reveals the physiological and chemical processes in the cold's infection and in the body's response, then surely it would be possible to find out whether the vitamin C really has any effect upon the common cold or not. It seems that we could ascertain whether a causal relation exists in this instance if only we could discover the relevant laws of biology and chemistry.

At this point in your musings, your notice that it is time to get over to the physics lab. You remember that yesterday morning you were convinced that predicting the outcome of an experiment is possible if you know which physical laws apply. That certainly was the outcome of the discussion in the physics class. Now, it seems, the question about the curative power of vitamin C hinges on exactly the same thing—the laws of nature. As you hurry to the lab it occurs to you that predicting the outcome of an experiment, before it is performed, is a first-class example of what you were discussing in philosophy—making inferences from the observed to the unobserved. We observe the set-up for the experiment (or demonstration) before it is performed, and we predict the outcome before we observe it. Salvia certainly was confident about the prediction he made. Also, recalling one of Hume's examples, you were at least as confident, when you went to bed last night, that the sun would rise this morning. But Hume *seemed* to be saying that the basis for this confidence was the fact that the sun has been observed to rise every morning since the dawn of history. "That's wrong," you say to yourself as you reach the physics lab. "My confidence in the rising of the sun is based upon the laws of astronomy. So here we are back at the laws again."

Inside the lab you notice a familiar gadget; it consists of a frame from which five steel balls are suspended so that they hang in a straight line, each one touching its neighbors. Your little brother got a toy like this, in a somewhat smaller size, for his birthday a couple of years ago. You casually raise one of the end balls, and let it swing back. It strikes the nearest of the four balls left hanging, and the ball at the other end swings out (the three balls in the middle keeping their place). The ball at the far end swings back again, striking its neighbor, and then the ball on the near end swings out, almost to the point from which you let it swing originally. The process goes on for a while, with the two end balls alternately swinging out and back. It has a pleasant rhythm. (See Figure 2.)

While you are enjoying the familiar toy, the lab instructor, Dr. Sagro,[2] comes over to you. "Do you know why just the ball on the far end moves —instead of, say, two on the far end, or all four of the remaining ones—when the ball on this end strikes?"

"Not exactly, but I suppose it has something to do with conservation of energy," you reply, recalling what Salvia said yesterday in answer to the question about the bowling ball.

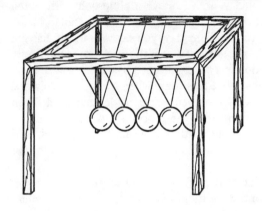

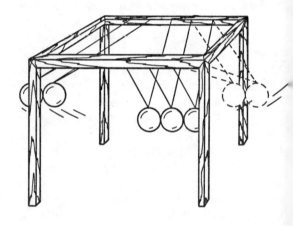

Figure 2. The Energy-Momentum Toy. When two balls at the right collide with the remaining three, two balls swing away from the left side. What happens when three on the right collide with the remaining two?

"That's right," says Dr. Sagro, "but it also depends upon conservation of momentum." Before you have a chance to say anything she continues, "Let me ask you another question. What would happen if you raised two balls at this end, and let them swing together toward the remaining three?"

"I think two balls will swing away at the other end," you reply, remembering the way your brother's toy worked.

"Why don't you test it to find out if you are right?" says the instructor. You do, and you find that the result is as you had predicted. Without saying anything about it, you assume that this, too, can be explained by means of the laws of conservation of energy and momentum.

Dr. Sagro poses another question. "What will happen," she asks, "if you start by swinging three balls from this end?" Since there are only two remaining balls you don't know what to say, so you confess ignorance. She suggests you try it, in order to find out what will happen. When you do, you see that three balls swing to the other side, and three swing back again; the middle ball swings back and forth, acting as the third ball in each group. This was a case in which you didn't know what to expect as a result until you tried the experiment.[3] This was like some of Hume's examples; not until you have actually had the experience do you know what result to expect. But there is also something different. Hume said that you must try the experiment many times in order to know what to expect; nevertheless, after just one trial you are sure what will happen whenever the experiment is repeated. This makes it rather different from the problem of whether vitamin C cured your cold. In that case, it seemed necessary to try the experiment over and over again, preferably with a number of different people. Reflecting upon this difference, you ask the lab instructor a crucial question, "If you knew the laws of conservation of momentum and energy, but had never seen the experiment with the three balls performed, would you have been able to predict the outcome?"

"Yes," she says simply.

"Well," you murmur inaudibly, "it seems as if the whole answer to Hume's problem regarding inferences about things we do not immediately observe, including predictions of future occurrences, rests squarely upon the laws of nature."

KNOWING THE LAWS

Given that the laws are so fundamental, you decide to find out more about them. The laws of conservation of energy and momentum are close at hand, so to speak, so you decide to start there. "O.K.," you say to the lab instructor, "what are these laws of nature, which enable you to predict so confidently how experiments will turn out before they are performed? I'd like to learn something about them."

"Fine," she says, delighted with your desire to learn; "let's start with conservation of energy, and we can demonstrate it quite easily."[4] (See Figure 3.)

Your laboratory contains a standard piece of equipment—an air track—on which little cars move back and forth. The track is made of metal with many tiny holes through which air is blown. The cars thus ride on a thin cushion of air; they move back and forth almost without friction. Some of the cars are equipped with spring bumpers, so that they will bounce off of one another upon impact, while others have coupling devices which lock them together upon contact. Dr. Sagro begins by explaining what is meant by the momentum of a body—namely, its mass multiplied by its velocity.[5] "To speak somewhat quaintly," she says, "the mass is just a measure of the quantity of matter in the body.[6] Since, in all of the experiments we are going to do, it is safe to say that the mass of each body remains unchanged, we need not say more about it. You can see that each car comes with its mass labeled; this one, for instance, has a mass of 200 grams, while this one has a mass of 400 grams. We have a number of different cars with quite a variety of different masses. The velocity," she continues, "is what we ordinarily mean by 'speed' along with the direction of travel. On the air track there are only two possible directions, left to right and right to left. Let us simply agree that motion from left to right has a positive velocity, while motion from right to left has a negative velocity. Mass, of course, is always a positive quantity. Thus, momentum, which is mass times velocity, may be positive, negative, or zero. When we add the momenta of various bodies together, we must always be careful of the sign (plus or minus)."

With these preliminaries, you begin to perform a variety of experiments. She has various types of fancy equipment for measuring velocities, which she shows you how to use, and she also helps you to make measurements. You find that it is fun pushing cars back and forth on the track, crashing them into one another, and measuring their velocities before and after collisions. You try it with a variety of cars of different masses and with differing velocities. You try it with the ones that bounce apart after impact and with those that stick together. You always find that the *total* momentum (the sum of the momenta for the two cars) before any collision is equal to the *total* momentum after the collision, even though the momenta of the individual cars may change markedly as a result of the collision. This, Dr. Sagro explains, is what the law of conservation of momentum demands: when two bodies (such as the cars) interact with one another (as in a collision), the total momentum of the system consisting of those

"There are many other applications of the law of conservation of momentum," she continues. "When a rifle recoils upon being fired, when a jet engine propels an airplane, when a rocket engine lifts an artificial satellite into orbit, or when you step out of an untethered rowboat and are surprised to feel it moving out from under you— these are all cases of conservation of momentum."

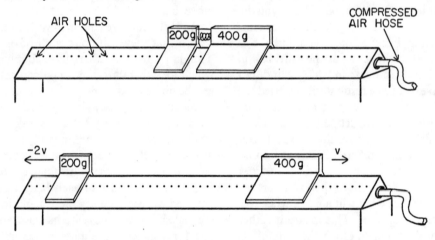

Figure 3.   Cars on the Air Track. Top: Cars tied together against spring under tension. Bottom: Cars moving apart after "explosion." 400 g × v + 200 gx (−2v) = 0. Momentum is conserved.

two bodies is the same before and after the interaction.

You ask her whether this law applies only to collisions; she replies immediately that it applies to all kinds of interactions. "Let's see how it works for a simple type of 'explosion,'" she suggests. She helps you tie together two cars, holding a compressed spring between them. You burn the string which holds them together and they fly apart. You measure the velocities and compute the momenta of each of the cars after the "explosion." It turns out that the momentum of the one car is always equal in amount but opposite in direction to that of the other. This is true whether the cars are of equal or unequal masses and whether the tension on the spring that drives them apart is great or small. "This is just what the law of conservation of momentum tells us to expect," she explains; "the momentum of each car is zero before the 'explosion' because they are not moving (each has velocity equal to zero), and so the two momenta after the 'explosion' (one positive and one negative) must add up to zero. That is what has happened every time.

"Is this law ever violated?" you ask.

"No," she answers, "there are no known exceptions to it." You leave the lab with the feeling that you know at least one fundamental law, and that you have seen it proved experimentally right before your eyes. You can't wait to tell your philosophy professor about it.

When you go to your philosophy class the next morning, the topic is still Hume's *Enquiry Concerning Human Understanding* and the problem of how we can have knowledge of things we do not observe. As the lecture begins, Professor Philo[7] is saying, "As we saw during the last lecture, Hume maintains that our knowledge of what we do not observe is based entirely upon cause and effect relations, but that raises the question of how we can gain knowledge of these relations. Hume maintained that this knowledge can result only from repeated observation of one type of event (a cause) to see whether it is always followed by an event of another kind (its effect).

Hume therefore analyzed the notion of causality in terms of constant conjunction of events. Consider for a moment Hume's favorite example, the colliding billiard balls . . ."

You raise your hand. "It seems to me that Hume was wrong about this," you begin, and then you relate briefly yesterday's experiences in the physics lab. "If you know the relevant laws of nature," you conclude, "you can predict the outcomes of future experiments on the basis of a single trial, or perhaps even without benefit of any trials at all."

"But how," asks Professor Philo, "can we establish knowledge of the laws of nature?"

You had a hunch she might ask some such question, and you are ready with your reply, "We *proved* it experimentally."

"Well," says Professor Philo, "I'm not a physicist, so perhaps you had better explain in a little more detail just what the experimental proof consists of. You mentioned something about an explosion—how did that go?"

You explain carefully how the air track works, how the two cars were joined together with a spring under tension in between, and how they moved apart when the string was burned. "In every case," you conclude, "the momentum of the two cars was equal in amount and opposite in direction, just as the law of conservation of momentum says it should be."

"Now let me see if I understand your line of reasoning," says the professor in a tone that is altogether too calm to suit you. "If the law of conservation of momentum is correct, then the two cars will part in the manner you described. The cars did move apart in just that way. Therefore, the law of conservation of momentum is correct. Is that your argument?"

"I guess so," you reply a bit hesitantly, because it looks as if she is trying to trap you.

"Do you think that kind of argument is valid?" she responds.

"What do you mean?" you ask, beginning to feel a little confused.

"Well," she says, "isn't that rather like the following argument: If this defendant is guilty, he will refuse to testify at his own trial; he does refuse to testify; therefore, he is guilty. Would any judge allow that argument in a court of law?"

"Of course not," you reply, "but it isn't the same thing at all. We tested the law of conserva-

tion of momentum many times in many different ways, and in every case we got the expected result (allowing for the usual small inaccuracies in the measurements)."

"If I remember what you said," Ms. Philo goes on, "in one of your experiments you had one car with a mass of 200 grams and another with a mass of 400 grams, and in that case the lighter car recoiled with twice the speed of the more massive one. How many times did you repeat this particular experiment?"

"Once or twice, as nearly as I can recall."

"Yet, you seem to believe that the result would be the same, no matter how many times the experiment was repeated—is that correct?"

"I suppose so," you reply somewhat uncomfortably.

"And with how many different masses and how many different recoil velocities did you try it? Do you believe it would work the same way if the masses were thousands or billions of kilograms instead of a few grams? And do you suppose that it would work the same way if the velocities were very great—somewhere near the speed of light?"

Since you have heard that strange things happen when speeds approach that of light, your hesitancy increases, but you reply tentatively, "Well, the lab instructor told me that there are no exceptions to the law."

"Did she say that," asks Philo, "or did she say no *known* exceptions?"

"I guess that was it," you reply lamely, feeling quite crushed.

Professor Philo endeavors to summarize the discussion. "What is considered experimental 'proof of a law of nature' is actually a process of testing *some* of its logical consequences. That is, you ask what would have to happen *if* your hypothesis is true, and then you perform an experiment to see if it turns out that way *in fact*. Since any law of nature is a generalization,[8] it has an unlimited number of consequences. We can never hope to test them all. In particular, any *useful* law of nature will have consequences that pertain to the future; they enable us to make predictions. We can never test these consequences until it is too late to use them for the purpose of prediction. To suppose that testing *some* of the consequences of a law constitutes a *conclusive proof* of the law would clearly be an outright logical fallacy." The bell rings and you leave the class, convinced that she has merely been quibbling.

During your physics class you brood about the previous discussion in the philosophy class, without paying very close attention to the lecture. Similar thoughts keep nagging at you during lunch. The objections brought up by Professor Philo seem to be well-founded, you conclude, but you wonder how they can be reconciled with the apparent reliability and certainty of scientific knowledge. In desperation, you decide to talk it over with Professor Salvia during his office hour this very afternoon. When you arrive, you don't know exactly where to begin, so you decide to go back to the pendulum demonstration, which was the thing that got you started on this whole mess. "When you performed that demonstration," you ask, "were you *absolutely certain* how it would turn out? Has it never failed?"

"Well, to be perfectly honest," he says, "it has been known to fail. Once when a friend of mine was doing it in front of a large auditorium, the suspension in the ceiling broke and the ball landed right on his foot. He was in a cast for months!"

"But that's no fault of the law of conservation of energy is it?" you ask. "The breaking of the suspension didn't mean that conservation of energy is false, did it?"

"Of course not," he answers, "we still believe firmly in conservation of energy."

"But are you *certain* of the law of conservation of energy, or any other law of nature?" you ask, and before he has a chance to answer, you tell him about the discussion in the philosophy class this morning.

"So that's what's bothering you," he says, after hearing the whole story. "Professor Philo has an important point. No matter how thoroughly we have tested a scientific law—better, let's say "hypothesis"—there is always the possibility that new evidence will show up to prove it false. For instance, around the close of the nineteenth century, many physicists seemed virtually certain that Newtonian mechanics was absolutely correct. A wide variety of its consequences had been tested under many different circumstances, and Newton's laws stood up extremely well. But early in the twentieth century it became clear that what we now call 'classical physics' would have to undergo major revisions, and a profound scientific revolution ensued. Modern physics, which includes quantum mechanics and relativity theory, was the result. We can never be sure that any hypothesis we currently accept as correct will not have to be abandoned or modified at some time in the future as a result of new evidence."

"What about the law of conservation of momentum?" you ask, recalling yesterday's experience in the lab. "The lab instructor said it has no known exceptions."

"That is correct," says Salvia, "and it is a rather interesting case. Conservation of momentum is a consequence of Newton's laws of motion; therefore, any consequence of conservation of momentum is a consequence of Newton's laws. But we now regard Newton's laws as not strictly true—they break down, for example, with objects traveling close to the speed of light—but conservation of momentum holds even in these cases. So we have a good example of a case where we believe a lot of consequences, but we do not believe in the laws (Newton's) from which the consequences follow."

It occurs to you that this is a rather important set of supposed laws; perhaps the philosophy professor was not merely quibbling when she said that it was not valid to conclude that a hypothesis is true just because we know many of its consequences to be true.

"Since you cannot be certain of any so-called law of nature," you ask, "why do you believe in them so firmly?"

"Because," answers Salvia, "we consider them very well confirmed. We accept well-confirmed hypotheses, knowing that we may later have to change our minds in the light of new evidence. Science can no longer claim infallible truth."

"Does that mean that scientific results are highly probable, but not absolutely certain?" you ask trying to be sure you have understood what he has said.

"Yes, you could put it that way," he agrees.

You leave with the feeling that you have a pretty good comprehension of the situation. As a result of your study of physics and philosophy you now understand why science cannot claim infallibility for its findings, but must be content with results that are well confirmed. With that, you take off for the weekend. (And what you do with your weekend is your own business.)

HUME'S BOMBSHELL

A little tired, but basically in a cheerful mood, you arrive at your philosophy class on Monday morning. You meet the professor a few minutes before class outside the room, and you tell her very briefly of your conversation with the physics professor. You explain that you now understand why it is that scientific laws can never be considered completely certain, but only as well-confirmed hypotheses. With her help, and with that of Professor Salvia, you now understand what Hume was driving at—and you see, moreover, that Hume was right. She smiles, and you both go into the classroom, where she begins her lecture.

"Last Friday, as you may recall, we had quite a lively discussion about the status of scientific laws—the law of conservation of momentum, in particular. We saw that such laws cannot be proved conclusively by any amount of experimental evidence. This is a point with which, I am happy to report, many (if not most) contemporary scientists agree. They realize that the most they can reasonably claim for their hypotheses is strong confirmation. Looking at the matter this way, one could conclude that it is wise to believe in scientific predictions, for if they are not certain to be true, they are a good bet. To believe in scientific results is to bet with the best available odds.

"However," she continues, "while this view may be correct as far as it goes, Hume was making a much more fundamental, and I should add, much more devastating point. Hume was challenging not merely our right to claim that scientific predictions will always be right, but also our right to claim that they will usually, or often, or indeed ever, be correct. Take careful note of what he says in section IV:

Let the course of things be allowed hitherto ever so regular; that alone, without some new argument or inference, proves not that, for the future, it will continue so. In vain do you pretend to have learned the nature of bodies from your past experience. Their secret nature, and consequently all their effects and influence, may change, without any change in their sensible qualities. This happens sometimes, and with regard to some objects: Why may it not happen always and with regard to all objects? What logic, what process of argument secures you against this supposition?

He is saying, as I hope you understood from your reading, that no matter how reliably a law seems to have held in the past, there is no logical reason why it must do so in the future *at all.* It is therefore possible that *every* scientific prediction, based on *any* law or laws whatever, may turn out to be false from this moment on. The stationary billiard ball that is struck by a moving one may remain motionless where it is—while the moving ball may bounce straight back in the direction from whence it came, or it may go straight up in the air, or it might vanish in a puff of smoke. Any of these possibilities can be imagined; none of them involves any logical contradiction. This is the force of Hume's skeptical arguments. The conclusion seems to be that we have no *reason* to believe in scientific predictions—no more reason than to believe on the basis of astrology, crystal gazing, or sheer blind guessing."

You can hardly believe your ears; what is she saying? You raise your hand, and when you are recognized, you can hardly keep your intense irritation from showing as you assert, "But certainly we can say that scientific predictions are more probable than those based, for example, upon astrology." As you speak, you are reminded of the remark in contemporary problems last Wednesday concerning the coming of the Age of Aquarius. Science has got to be better than *that!* As these thoughts cross your mind, Professor Philo is saying ". . . but that depends upon what you mean by 'probable,' doesn't it?"

The physics lecture today is on Newton's law of gravitation, and the professor is explaining that every bit of matter in the universe is attracted to every other by a force proportional to the masses and inversely proportional to the square of the distance between them. He goes on to explain how Kepler's laws of planetary motion and Galileo's law of falling bodies are (when suitably corrected) consequences of Newton's laws. You listen carefully, but you recognize this as another law that enables scientists to make impressive predictions. Indeed, Salvia is now telling how Newton's laws were used to explain the tides on the oceans and to predict the existence of two planets, Neptune and Pluto, that had not been known before. At the same time, you are wondering whether there is anything in what Hume seemed to be saying about such laws. Is it possible that suddenly, at the very next moment, matter would cease to have gravitational attraction, so that the whole solar system would go flying apart? It's a pretty chilling thought.

At lunch you are thinking about this question, and you glance back at some of the readings that were assigned from Hume's *Enquiry.* You notice again Hume's many references to secret powers and forces. Well, gravitation is surely a force, though there has not been any great secret about it since Newton's time. It is the "power" which keeps the solar system together. You remember reading somewhere that, according to Hume, you cannot know that it is safer to leave a building by way of the halls, stairways, and doors than it would be to step out of the third-story window. Well, Newton's law makes it clear why you don't want to step out of the third-story window, but what assurance have you that the building will continue to stand, rather than crashing down around your ears before you can get out? The engineers who design and build towers and bridges have a great deal of knowledge of the "secret powers" of their materials, so they must know a great deal more than Hume did about the hidden properties of things.

At this very moment, a lucky coincidence oc curs—you see Dr. Sagro, your physics lab instructor, entering the cafeteria. You wave to her, and she sits down with you, putting her coffee cup on the table. You begin to ask her some questions about structural materials, and she responds by inquiring whether you would be satisfied if she could explain how the table supports the cup of coffee. You recognize it as just the kind of question you have in mind, and urge her to proceed.

"Certain materials, such as the metal in this table," she begins, "have a rather rigid crystalline structure, and for this reason they stick together and maintain their shape unless subjected to large· forces. These crystals consist of very regular (and very beautiful) arrays of atoms, and they are held together by forces, essentially electrostatic in origin, among the charged particles that make up the atoms. Have you studied Coulomb's law of electrostatic forces?"

"No," you reply, "we are just doing Newton's law of gravitation. I think Salvia said electricity and magnetism would come up next semester."

"Well," she says, "these electrostatic forces are a lot like gravitational forces (they vary inversely with the square of the distance), but there are a couple of very important differences. First, as you know, there are two types of charges, positive and negative. The proton in the nucleus of the atom carries a positive charge, and the electrons that circulate about the nuclei have a negative charge. Two particles with opposite signs (such as a proton and an electron) attract one another, while two particles with like signs (e.g., two electrons or two protons) repel each other. This is different from gravity, because all matter attracts all other matter; there is no such thing as gravitational repulsion. The second main difference is that the electrostatic force is fantastically stronger than the gravitational force—roughly a billion billion billion billion times more powerful—but we don't usually notice it because most objects we deal with in everyday life are electrically neutral, con taining equal amounts of positive and negative electric charge, or very nearly so. If you could somehow strip all of the electrons away from an apple, and all of the protons away from the earth, the force of attraction between the apple and the earth would be unbelievable.

"It is these *extremely* strong attractive and repulsive forces among the electrons and protons in the metal that maintain a stable and rigid form. That's why the table doesn't collapse. And the reason the coffee cup stays on top of the table, without penetrating its surface or slipping through, is that the electrons in the surface of the cup strongly repel those in the surface of the table. Actually, there is also a quantum mechanical force that prevents the weight of the cup from noticeably compressing the table, but we needn't go into that, because the effect is mostly due to the electrostatic forces."

Pleased with this very clear explanation, you thank her, but follow it up with another question. "Is there any logical reason why it has to be that way—why opposite charges attract and like charges repel? Can you prove that it is impossible for like charges to attract and unlike charges to repel? What would happen if *that* were suddenly to become the law?"

"It would certainly result in utter catastrophe," she replies, "with all of the atomic nuclei bunching up together in one place and all of the electrons rushing away from them to congregate elsewhere. But to answer your question, no, there is no logical proof that it couldn't be that way. In our physical world we find that there are, in fact, two types of charges, and they obey the Coulomb law rather than the one you just formulated."

"Can you prove that the world will not switch from the one law to the other, say, tomorrow?" you ask.

"No, frankly, I can't," she answers, "but I, and all other physicists assume—call it an article of faith if you like—that it won't happen."

There's that word "faith" again, you muse as you leave the cafeteria.

The more you think about it, the more clearly you see that the physicists have not shown you how to get around the basic problem Hume raised; rather, they have really reinforced it. Maybe this problem is tougher than I thought, you say to yourself, and you head for Professor Philo's office to talk further about it. "I was thinking about all these 'secret powers' Hume talks about," you begin, "and so I asked my physics instructor about them. She explained, as an example, how a table supports a coffee cup, but she did it on the basis of laws of nature—Coulomb's law of electrostatics was one of them. This law is very well confirmed, I suppose, but she admitted that it is quite possible to imagine that this law would fail tomorrow, and—if you'll pardon the expression—all hell would break loose. Now, my question is, how can we find out about these secret powers that Hume keeps saying we need to know? How can we discover the real underlying causes of what happens?"

"I think you are really beginning to get the point Hume was driving at," she replies, "namely, that there is no way, even in principle, of finding any hidden causes or secret powers. You can, of course, find regularities in nature—such as conservation of energy, conservation of momentum, universal gravitation, and electrostatic attraction and repulsion—but these can only be known to have held up to the present. There is no further kind of hidden connection or causal relation that can be discovered by more careful observation, or examination with some kind of super-microscope. Of course, we do discover regularities, and we explain them. For instance, Kepler's laws of planetary motion are regularities that are explained by Newton's laws of motion and gravitation, but these do not reveal any secret powers. They simply provide more

general regularities to cover the more restricted ones.

"In his discussion of 'the idea of necessary connection,' Hume tries to bring out precisely this point. We can observe, as you were saying in class the other day, that recoil experiments always yield a particular type of result—namely, momentum is conserved. We have observed this many times. And now we expect, on future trials, that the same thing will happen. But we do not observe, nor can we discover in any way, an *additional* factor which constitutes a necessary connection between the 'explosion' and the subsequent motion of the cars. This seems to be what Hume had in mind when he wrote:

These ultimate springs and principles are totally shut up from human curiosity and enquiry. Elasticity, gravity, cohesion of parts, communication of motion by impulse; these are probably the ultimate causes and principles which we ever discover in nature; and we may esteem ourselves sufficiently happy, if, by accurate inquiry and reasoning, we can trace up the particular phenomena to, or near to, these general principles.[9]

Hume is acknowledging that we can discover general regularities in nature, but he is denying that an additional 'connection' can be found. And Hume was dedicated to the maxim, as are modern scientists, that we have no business talking about things it is impossible in principle for us to know anything about.

"When he asks why we do, in fact, expect so confidently that the future experiments will have outcomes similar to those of the past trials, Hume finds that it is nothing other than a matter of psychological conditioning. When we see one type of cause repeatedly followed by a particular type of effect, we come to expect that the same type of effect will follow the next time we come across that kind of cause. But this is not a matter of logical reasoning. Have you heard of Pavlov's conditioning experiments with dogs?" You nod. "When the bell rings the dog starts to salivate. He is *not* reasoning that, since the sounding of the bell has, in the past, been associated with the bringing of food, therefore, on this occasion the food will (at least probably) appear soon after the bell rings. According to Hume's analysis, what is called 'scientific reasoning' is no more rational or logical than your watering at the mouth when you are hungry and hear the dinner bell. It is something you cannot help doing, Hume says, but that does not mean that it has any logical foundation."

"That brings up a question I've wanted to ask," you say. "Hume seems to think that people necessarily reason in that way—inductive reasoning, I think it is called—but I've noticed that lots of people don't seem to. For instance, many people (including a student in my current problems course) believe in things like astrology; they believe that the configuration of the planets has a bearing on human events, when experience shows that it often doesn't work that way." The professor nods in agreement. You continue, "So if there is no logical justification for believing in scientific predictions, why isn't it just as reasonable to believe in astrological predictions?"

"That" replies the prof, "is a very profound and difficult question. I doubt that any philosopher has a completely satisfactory answer to it."

MODERN ANSWERS[10]

The Wednesday philosophy lecture begins with a sort of rhetorical question, "What reason do we have (Hume is, at bottom, asking) for trusting the scientific method; what grounds do we have for believing that scientific predictions are reliable?" You have been pondering that very question quite a bit in the last couple of days, and—rhetorical or not—your hand shoots up. You have a thing or two to say on the subject.

"Philosophers may have trouble answering such questions," you assert, "but it seems to me there is an obvious reply. As my physics professor has often said, the scientist takes a very practical attitude. He puts forth a hypothesis; if it works he believes in it, and he continues to believe in it as long as it works. If it starts giving him bad predictions, he starts looking for another hypothesis, or for a way of revising his old one. Now the important thing about the scientific method, it seems to me, is that it works. Not only has it led to a vast amount of knowledge about the physical world, but it has been applied in all sorts of practical ways—and although these applications may not have been uniformly beneficial—for better or worse they were successful. Not always, of course, but by and large. Astrology, crystal gazing, and other such superstitious methods simply do not work very well. That's good enough for me."[11]

"That is, indeed, a very tempting answer," Professor Philo replies, "and in one form or another, it has been advanced by several modern philosophers. But Hume actually answered that one himself. You might put it this way. We can all agree that science has, up till now, a very impressive record of success in predicting the future. The question we are asking, however, is this: should we *predict* that science will continue to have the kind of success it has had in the past? It is quite natural to assume that its record will continue, but this is just a case of applying the scientific method to itself. In studying conservation of momentum, you inferred that future experiments would have results similar to those of your past experiments; in appraising the scientific method, you are assuming that its future success will match its past success. But using the scientific method to judge the scientific method is circular reasoning. It is as if a man goes to a bank to cash a check. When the teller refuses, on the grounds that he does not know this man, the man replies, 'That is no problem; permit me to introduce myself—I am John Smith, just as it says on the check.'

"Suppose that I were a believer in crystal gazing. You tell me that your method is better than mine because it has been more successful than mine. You say that this is a good reason for preferring your method to mine. I object. Since you are using your method to judge my method (as well as your method), I demand the right to use my method to evaluate yours. I gaze into my crystal ball and announce the result: from now on crystal gazing will be very successful in predicting the future, while the scientific method is due for a long run of bad luck."

You are about to protest, but she continues.

"The trouble with circular arguments is that they can be used to prove anything; if you assume what you are trying to prove, then there isn't much difficulty in proving it. You find the scientific justification of the scientific method convincing because you already trust the scientific method; if you had equal trust in crystal gazing I should think you would find the crystal gazer's justification of his method equally convincing. Hume puts it this way:

When a man says, *I have found, in all past instances such sensible qualities conjoined with such secret powers*

And when he says, *Similar sensible qualities will always be conjoined with similar secret powers,* he is not guilty of a tautology, nor are these propositions in any respect the same. You can say that the one proposition is an inference from the other. But you must confess that the inference is not intuitive; neither is it demonstrative: Of what nature is it, then? To say it is experimental is begging the question. For all inferences from experience suppose, as their foundation, that the future will resemble the past, and that similar powers will be conjoined with similar sensible qualities.[12]

If the assumption that the future is like the past is the presupposition of the scientific method, we cannot assume that principle in order to justify the scientific method. Once more, we can hardly find a clearer statement than Hume's:

We have said that all arguments concerning existence are founded on the relation of cause and effect; that our knowledge of that relation is derived entirely from experience; and that all our experimental conclusions proceed upon the supposition that the future will be conformable to the past. To endeavour, therefore, the proof of this last supposition by probable arguments, or arguments regarding existence, must evidently be going in a circle, and taking that for granted, which is the very point in question.[13]

"The principle that the future will be like the past, or that regularities which have held up to the present will persist in the future, has traditionally been called *the principle of uniformity of nature.* Some philosophers, most notably Immanuel Kant, have regarded it as an a priori truth.[14] It seems to me, however, that Hume had already provided a convincing refutation of that claim by arguing that irregularities, however startling to common sense, are by no means inconceivable—that is, they cannot be ruled out a priori. Recall what he said:

... it implies no contradiction that the course of nature may change, and that an object, seemingly like those which we have experienced, may be attended with different or contrary effects. May I not clearly and distinctly conceive that a body, falling from the clouds, and which, in all other respects, resembles snow, has yet the taste of salt or feeling of fire? ... Now whatever is intelligible, and can be distinctly conceived, implies no contradiction, and can never be proved false by any demonstrative argument or abstract reasoning a priori.[15]

"Other philosophers have proposed assuming this principle (or something similar) as a postulate; Bertrand Russell, though not the only one to advocate this approach, is by far the most famous.[16] But most philosophers agree that this use of postulation is question-begging. The real question still remains: why should one adopt any such postulate? Russell himself, in another context, summed it up very well: The method of 'postulating' what we want has many advantages; they are the same as the advantages of theft over honest toil."[17]

"Nevertheless," you interject, "can't we still say that scientific predictions are more probable than, say, those of astrology or crystal gazing?"

"It seems to me you raised a similar question once before," Professor Philo replies, "and I seem to recall saying that it depends on what you mean by the term 'probable.' Maybe it would be helpful if I now explain what I meant."[18] You nod encouragement. "The concept of probability—or perhaps I should say 'concepts' of probability—are very tricky. If you were to undertake a systematic study of confirmation and induction, you would have to go into a rather technical treatment of probability, but perhaps I can give a brief hint of what is involved.[19] One thing that has traditionally been meant by this term relates directly to the frequency with which something occurs—as Aristotle put it, the probable is that which happens often. If the weather forecaster says that there is a 90% chance of rain, he presumably means that, given such weather conditions as are now present, rain occurs in nine out of ten cases. If these forecasts are correct, we can predict rain on such occasions and be right nine times out of ten.

"Now, if you mean that scientific predictions are probable in *this* sense, I think we must deny your claim. For Hume has argued—cogently, I think—that, for all we can know now, *every* future scientific prediction may go wrong. He was not merely saying that science is fallible, that it will sometimes err in its predictions—he was saying that nature might at any moment (for all we can know) become irregular on such a wide scale that any kind of scientific prediction of future occurrences would be utterly impossible. We have not found any reason to believe he was mistaken about this point."

"That must not be the concept of probability I had in mind," you remark; "I'm not quite sure how to express it, but it had something to do with what it would be reasonable to believe. I was thinking of the fact that, although we cannot regard scientific hypotheses as certain, we can consider them well confirmed. It is something like saying that a particular suspect is probably guilty of a crime—that the evidence, taken as a whole, seems to point to him."

"You have put your finger on another important probability concept," the professor replies. "It is sometimes known as the rational credibility concept. The most popular contemporary attempt (I believe) to deal with Hume's problem of inductive reasoning is stated in terms of this concept. The argument can be summarized in the following way. Hume has proved that we cannot *know for sure* that our scientific predictions will be correct, but that would be an unreasonable demand to place upon science. The best we can hope is for scientific conclusions that are probable. But when we ask that they be probable, in this sense, we are only asking that they be based upon the best possible evidence. Now, that is just what scientific predictions are—they are predictions based upon the best possible evidence. The scientist has fashioned his hypotheses in the light of all available information, and he has tested them experimentally on many occasions under a wide variety of circumstances. He has summoned all of the available evidence, and he has brought it to bear on the problem at hand. Such scientific predictions are obviously probable (as we are now construing this term); hence, they are rationally credible.[20] If we say that a belief is irrational, we mean that it runs counter to the evidence, or the person who holds it is ignoring the evidence. And in such contexts, when we speak of evidence, we are referring to inductive or scientific evidence.

"Now, the argument continues, to ask whether it is reasonable to believe in scientific conclusions comes right down to asking whether one ought to fashion his beliefs on the basis of the available evidence. But this is what it means to be rational. Hence, the question amounts to asking whether it is rational to be rational. If the question makes any sense at all, the obvious answer is 'yes.' "

"That answer certainly satisfies me," you say, feeling that Dr. Philo has succeeded admirably in stating the point you were groping for. "I'm glad to know that lots of other philosophers agree with it. Do you think it is a satisfactory answer to Hume's problem of induction?" You are more than a trifle discouraged when she gives a negative response with a shake of her head. "Why not?" you demand.

"This argument seems to me to beg the question," she replies, "for it assumes that the concept of evidence is completely clear. But that is precisely the question at issue. If we could be confident that the kind of experiments you performed in the physics lab to test the law of conservation of momentum do, in fact, provide evidence for that law, then we could say that the law is well supported by evidence. But to suppose that such facts do constitute evidence amounts to saying that what has happened in the past is a sign of what will happen in the future—the fact that momentum was conserved in your 'explosion' experiments is an indication that momentum will be conserved in future experiments of a similar nature. This assumes that the future will be like the past, and that is precisely the point at issue. To say that one fact constitutes evidence for another means, in part, that the one provides some basis for inference to the occurrence of the other. The problem of induction is nothing other than the problem of determining the circumstances under which such inference is justified. Thus, we have to resolve the problem of induction—Hume's problem—before we can ascertain whether one fact constitutes evidence for another. We cannot use the concept of evidence—inductive evidence —to solve the problem of induction.

"There is another way to look at this same argument. If you ask me whether you should use the scientific method, I must find out what you hope to accomplish. If you say that you want to get a job teaching physics, I can tell you right away that you had better use the scientific method, at least in your work, because that is what is expected of a physicist. If you say that you want to enjoy the respect and prestige that accrues to scientists in certain social circles, the answer is essentially the same. If you tell me, however, that you want to have as much success as possible in predicting future events, the answer is by no means as easy. If I tell you to go ahead and make scientific predictions, because that is what is considered reasonable (that is what is meant by fashioning your beliefs on the basis of evidence), then you should ask whether being reasonable in this sense (which is obviously the commonly accepted sense) is a good way to attain your goal. The answer, 'but that's what it means to be reasonable,' is beside the point. You might say, 'I want a method that is reasonable to adopt in order to achieve my goal of successful prediction—that is what I mean by being reasonable. To tell me that the scientific method is what is usually *called* reasonable doesn't help. I want to know whether the method that is *commonly called* reasonable is *actually* a reasonable method to adopt to attain my goal of successful prediction of the future. The fact that it is usually considered reasonable cuts no ice, because an awareness of Hume's problem of induction has not filtered down into common usage.' That's what I think you should say."

"Couldn't we avoid all of these problems," suggests another student, "if we simply resisted the temptation to generalize? In social science, my area of interest, we find that it is very risky to generalize, say, from one society to another. An opinion survey on students in the far west, for example, will not be valid when applied to students attending eastern schools. Wouldn't we be better off to restrict our claims to the facts we know, instead of trying to extend them inductively to things we really don't know?"

"The opinion you have offered bears a strong resemblance (though it isn't identical) to that of an influential British philosopher.[21] He has presented his ideas persuasively, and has many followers. Hume, he says, has proved conclusively that induction is not a justifiable form of inference; it is, consequently, no part of science. The only kind of logic that has a legitimate place in science is deductive logic. Deductive inferences are demonstrative; their conclusions must be true if their premises are true. These inferences are precisely what Hume called 'reasoning concerning relations of ideas.' The crucial point is that they *do not add to our knowledge* in any way— they enable us to see the content of our premises, but they do not extend that content in the least. Thus, from premises that refer only to events in the past and present, it is impossible to *deduce* any predictions of future facts. Any kind of inference which would enable us to predict the future on the basis of facts already observed would have to be of a different sort; such inference is often

called 'ampliative' or 'inductive.' If science contains only deductive inferences, but no inductive inferences, it can never provide us with any knowledge beyond the content of our immediate observations.

"Now this philosopher does not reject scientific knowledge; he simply claims that prediction of the future is no part of the business of science. Accordingly, the function of scientific investigation is to find powerful general hypotheses (he calls them *conjectures*) that adequately explain all known facts that have occurred so far. As long as such a generalization succeeds in explaining the new facts that come along it is retained; if it fails to explain new facts, it must be modified or rejected. The sole purpose of scientific experimentation is to try to find weaknesses in such hypotheses—that is to criticize them or try to refute them. He calls this the 'method of conjectures and refutations,' or sometimes simply, 'the critical approach.'

"The main difficulty with this approach—an insuperable one, in my opinion—is the fact that it completely deprives science of its predictive function. To the question of which method to use for predicting the future, it can give no answer. Astrology, crystal gazing, blind guessing, and scientific prediction are all on a par. To find out what the population of the world will be in 2000 A.D., we might as well employ a psychic seer as a scientific demographer. I find it hard to believe that this can constitute a satisfactory solution to the problem of employing our knowledge to find rational solutions to the problems that face us— problems whose solutions demand that we make predictions of the future course of events. Tempting as it is to try to evade Hume's problem in this way, I do not see how we can be satisfied to admit that there is no rational approach to our problem."

"But perhaps there is no answer to Hume's problem," says still another student; "maybe the only hope for salvation of this world is to give up our blind worship of science and return to religion. We have placed our faith in science, and look where we are as a result. I believe we should adopt a different faith."

There's that word *again,* you note to yourself, as the professor begins her answer: "Though I heartily agree that many of the results of science —*technological* results, I think we should emphasize—have been far from beneficial, I don't think we can properly condemn scientific *knowledge*. Knowledge is one thing; what we choose to do with it is quite another. But that's not the issue we are concerned with. I do not see how anyone could deny that science has had a great deal of success in making predictions; no other approach can possibly present a comparable record of success. And, as time goes on, the capability for predictive success seems only to increase. It would be an utterly astonishing piece of luck, if it were sheer coincidence, that science has been so much luckier than other approaches in making its predictions. If anyone can consistently pick a winner in every race at every track every day, we are pretty sure he has more than good luck going for him. Science isn't infallible, but it is hard to believe its predictive success is just a matter of chance. I, at least, am not prepared to say that science is just one among many equally acceptable faiths—you pays your money and you takes your choice. I feel rather sure that the scientific approach has a logical justification of some sort." With that, the bell rings, the discussion ends, and everyone leaves—none by way of the window.

It just isn't good enough, you say to yourself, after listening to your physics professor lecturing, with demonstrations, on the law of conservation of angular momentum. You don't know whether you're dizzier from the discussion of Hume's problem in the philosophy class or from watching student volunteers in this class being spun on stools mounted on turntables. In any case, you decide to look up Professor Philo after lunch, and you find her in her office.

"Look," you say a bit brusquely, "I see that Hume was right about our inability to prove that nature is uniform. But suppose that nature does play a trick on us, so to speak. Suppose that after all this time of appearing quite uniform, manifesting all sorts of regularities such as the laws of physics, she turns chaotic. Then there isn't anything we can do anyhow. Someone might make a lucky guess about some future event, but there would be no systematic method for anticipating the chaos successfully. It seems to me I've got a way of predicting the future which will work if nature is uniform—the scientific method, or if you like, the inductive method—and if nature isn't uniform, I'm out of luck whatever I do. It

seems to me I've got everything to gain and nothing to lose (except a lot of hard work) if I attempt to adhere to the scientific approach. That seems good enough to me; what do you think."[22]

"Well," she says quietly, "I tend to agree with that answer, and so do a few others, but we are certainly in the minority. And many difficult problems arise when you try to work it out with precision."

"What sorts of difficulties are these?" you ask.

"There are several kinds," she begins; "for instance, what exactly do you mean by saying that nature is uniform? You cannot mean—to use Hume's quaint language—that like sensible qualities are always conjoined with like secret powers. All of us, including Hume, know this claim is false. Bread which looks and tastes completely harmless may contain a deadly poison. A gas which has exactly the appearance of normal air may suffocate living organisms and pollute the atmosphere. That kind of uniformity principle cannot be the basis of our inferences."

"That's quite true," you answer, "but perhaps we could say that nature operates according to regular laws. Ever since I began to think about Hume's problem, I have been led back to laws of nature."

"Your suggestion is a good one," she replies, "but modern philosophers have found it surprisingly difficult to say precisely what type of statement can qualify as a possible law of nature. It is a law of nature, most physicists would agree, that no material objects travel faster than light; they would refuse to admit, *as a law of nature*, that no golden spheres are more than one mile in diameter. It is not easy to state clearly the basis for this distinction. Both statements are generalizations, and both are true to the best of our knowledge."[23]

"Isn't the difference simply that you cannot, even in principle accelerate a material object to the speed of light, while it is possible in principle to fabricate an enormous sphere of gold?"

"That is precisely the question at issue," she replies. "The problem is, what basis do we have for claiming possibility in the one case and impossibility in the other. You seem to be saying that a law of nature prevents the one but not the other, which is obviously circular. And if you bring in the notion of causation—causing something to go faster than light vs. causing a large golden sphere to be created—you only compound the difficulty, for the concept of causation is itself a source of great perplexity.

"Suppose, however, that we had succeeded in overcoming that obstacle—that we could say with reasonable precision which sorts of statements are candidates for the status of laws of nature and which are not. We then face a further difficulty. It is obvious that some tests of scientific laws carry greater weight than others. The discovery of the planet Neptune, for example, confirmed Newton's laws much more dramatically than would a few additional observations of Mars. A test with particles traveling at very high velocities would be much stronger evidence for conservation of momentum than would some more experiments on the air track in the physics lab. It is not easy to see how to measure or compare the weight which different types of evidence lend to different scientific hypotheses.

"Scientific confirmation is a subtle and complex matter to which contemporary philosophers have devoted a great deal of attention; some have tried to construct systems of inductive logic that would capture this kind of scientific reasoning. Such efforts have, at best, met with limited success; inductive logic is in a primitive state compared with deductive logic. Until we have a reasonably clear idea of what such inference consists of, however, it is unlikely that we will be able to go very far in meeting the fundamental challenge Hume issued concerning the justification of scientific reasoning. Unless we can at least say what inductive inference is, and what constitutes uniformity of nature (or natural law), we can hardly argue that inductive reasoning—and only inductive reasoning—will prove successful in predicting the future if nature is uniform. And even if those concepts were clarified, the argument would still be intricate indeed."

"Do you think there is any chance that answers to such problems can be found?" you ask.

"I think it's just possible."

"Thanks," you say as you get up to leave.

"And my thanks to you," she replies. "You cannot possibly know how satisfying it is to talk with someone like you—someone intelligent—who takes such philosophical problems seriously and thinks hard about them. If you keep it up, you might be the very person to find some of the answers. I wish you well."

NOTES

1. Professor Salvia is a descendent of Salviati, the protagonist in Galileo's dialogues. The name was shortened when the family emigrated to America.

2. Dr. Sagro is married to a descent of Sagredo, another character in Galileo's dialogues.

3. If you really did know, please accept the author's apologies.

4. Please note that "demonstrate" is ambiguous. In mathematics it means "prove"; in physics it means "exemplify." Hume uses this term only in the mathematical sense.

5. Hume, using the terminology of his day, refers to it as the "moment" of the moving body.

6. This is Newton's definition; it is somewhat out of date, but adequate in the present context.

7. She is a direct descendent of Philo, the protagonist in Hume's "Dialogues Concerning Natural Religion," most of which is reprinted in this anthology.

8. Professor Philo realizes that it would be more accurate to say that a statement or hypothesis expressing a law of nature must be a generalization, but she does not wish to introduce unnecessary terminological distinctions at this point. For further details see W. Salmon, "Determinism and Indeterminism in Modern Science," p. 351 in this anthology.

9. In section IV, part I, anticipating the results of the later discussion.

10. All of the attempts to deal with Hume's problem which are treated in this section are discussed in detail in Wesley C. Salmon, The Foundations of Scientific Inference (Pittsburgh: University of Pittsburgh Press, 1967); this book will be cited hereafter as Foundations.

11. This is an inductive justification; see Foundations, chapter II, section 1.

12. David Hume, An Enquiry Concerning Human Understanding (hereafter, Enquiry), section IV, part II.

13. Ibid.

14. For discussion of justification by means of synthetic a priori principles, see Foundations, chapter II, section 4.

15. Enquiry, section IV, part II.

16. For discussion of the postulational approach, see Foundations, chapter II, section 6.

17. Bertrand Russell, Introduction to Mathematical Philosophy (London: Allen & Unwin, 1919), p. 71.

18. The "probabilistic approach" is discussed in Foundations, chapter II, section 7.

19. An elementary survey of philosophical problems of probability is given in Foundations, chapters IV–VII. References to additional literature on this subject can be found there.

20. We are assuming, of course, that these predictions are properly made. Scientists are only human, and they do make mistakes. One should not conclude, however, that every false prediction represents a scientific error. Impeccable scientific procedure is fallible, as we have already noted more than once.

21. This refers to the "deductivist" position of Sir Karl Popper. This approach is discussed in Foundations, chapter II, section 3.

22.   This approach is due mainly to Hans Reichenbach; it is known as a "pragmatic justification" and is discussed in *Foundations,* chapter II, section 8.

23.   Further elementary discussion of this issue can be found in Carl G. Hempel, *Philosophy of Natural Science*

(Englewood Cliffs, N.J.: Prentice-Hall, Inc., 1966), § 5.3. A more technical and extensive treatment of related issues can be found in Nelson Goodman, *Fact, Fiction, and Forecast,* 2nd ed. (Indianapolis, Ind.: The Bobbs-Merrill Co., 1965).

THOMAS   REID

Of the Existence of a Material World*

It is beyond our power to say when, or in what order, we came by our notions of these qualities. When we trace the operations of our minds as far back as memory and reflection can carry us, we find them already in possession of our imagination and belief, and quite familiar to the mind: but how they came first into acquaintance, or what has given them so strong a hold of our belief, and what regard they deserve, are, no doubt, very important questions in the philosophy of human nature.

Shall we, with the Bishop of Cloyne,[1] serve them with a *quo warranto,*[2] and have them tried at the bar of philosophy, upon the statute of the ideal system?[3] Indeed, in this trial they seem to have come off very pitifully; for, although they had very able counsel, learned in the law—viz., Descartes, Malebranche, and Locke, who said everything they could for their clients—the Bishop of Cloyne, believing them to be aiders and abeters of heresy and schism, prosecuted them with great vigour, fully answered all that had been pleaded in their defence, and silenced their ablest advocates, who seem, for half a century past, to decline the argument, and to trust to the favour of the jury rather than to the strength of their pleadings.

Thus, the wisdom of *philosophy* is set in opposition to the *common sense* of mankind. The first

pretends to demonstrate, *a priori,* that there can be no such thing as a material world; that sun, moon, stars, and earth, vegetable and animal bodies, are, and can be nothing else, but sensations in the mind, or images of those sensations in the memory and imagination; that, like pain and joy, they can have no existence when they are not thought of. The last can conceive no otherwise of this opinion, that as a kind of metaphysical lunacy, and concludes that too much learning is apt to make men mad; and that the man who seriously entertains this belief, though in other respects he may be a very good man, as a man may be who believes that he is made of glass; yet, surely he hath a soft place in his understanding, and hath been hurt by much thinking.

This opposition betwixt philosophy and common sense, is apt to have a very unhappy influence upon the philosopher himself. He sees human nature in an odd, unamiable, and mortifying light. He considers himself, and the rest of his species, as born under a necessity of believing ten thousand absurdities and contradictions, and endowed with such a pittance of reason as is just sufficient to make this unhappy discovery: and this is all the fruit of his profound speculations. Such notions of human nature tend to slacken every nerve of the soul, to put every noble purpose and sentiment out of countenance, and spread a melancholy gloom over the whole face of things.

If this is wisdom let me be deluded with the vulgar. I find something within me that recoils

*From Thomas Reid, *Inquiry into the Human Mind on the Principles of Common Sense,* Chapter V, Section VII. First published in 1764.

against it, and inspires more reverent sentiments of the human kind, and of the universal administration. Common Sense and Reason have both one author; that Almighty Author in all whose other works we observe a consistency, uniformity, and beauty which charm and delight the understanding: there must, therefore, be some order and consistency in the human faculties, as well as in other parts of his workmanship. A man that thinks reverently of his own kind, and esteems true wisdom and philosophy, will not be fond, nay, will be very suspicious, of such strange and paradoxical opinions. If they are false, they disgrace philosophy; and, if they are true, they degrade the human species, and make us justly ashamed of our frame.

To what purpose is it for philosophy to decide against common sense in this or any other matter? The belief of a material world is older, and of more authority, than any principles of philosophy. It declines the tribunal of reason, and laughs at all the artillery of the logician. It retains its sovereign authority in spite of all the edicts of philosophy, and reason itself must stoop to its orders. Even those philosophers who have disowned the authority of our notions of an external material world, confess that they find themselves under a necessity of submitting to their power.

Methinks, therefore, it were better to make a virtue of necessity; and, since we cannot get rid of the vulgar notion and belief of an external world, to reconcile our reason to it as well as we can; for, if Reason should stomach and fret ever so much at this yoke, she cannot throw it off; if she will not be the servant of Common Sense, she must be her slave.

In order, therefore, to reconcile Reason to Common Sense in this matter, I beg leave to offer to the consideration of philosophers these two observations. First, that, in all this debate about the existence of a material world, it hath been taken for granted on both sides, that this same material world, if any such there be, must be the express image of our sensations; that we can have no conception of any material thing which is not like some sensation in our minds; and particularly that the sensations of touch are images of extension, hardness, figure, and motion. Every argument brought against the existence of a material world, either by the Bishop of Cloyne, or by the author of the "Treatise of Human Nature,"[4] by supposeth this. If this is true, their arguments are conclusive and unanswerable; but, on the other hand, if it is not true, there is no shadow of argument left. Have those philosophers, then, given any solid proof of this hypothesis, upon which the whole weight of so strange a system rests? No. They have not so much as attempted to do it. But, because ancient and modern philosophers have agreed in this opinion, they have taken it for granted. But let us, as becomes philosophers, lay aside authority; we need not, surely, consult Aristotle or Locke, to know whether pain be like the point of a sword. I have as clear a conception of extension, hardness, and motion, as I have of the point of a sword; and, with some pains and practice, I can form as clear a notion of the other sensations of touch as I have of pain. When I do so, and compare them together, it appears to me clear as daylight, that the former are not of kin to the latter, nor resemble them in any one feature. They are as unlike, yea as certainly and manifestly unlike, as pain is to the point of a sword. It may be true, that those sensations first introduced the material world to our acquaintance; it may be true, that it seldom or never appears without their company; but, for all that, they are as unlike as the passion of anger is to those features of the countenance which attend it.

So that, in the sentence those philosophers have passed against the material world, there is an *error personae.*[5] Their proof touches not matter, or any of its qualities; but strikes directly against an idol of their own imagination, a material world made of ideas and sensations, which never had nor can have an existence.

Secondly, The very existence of our conceptions of extension, figure and motion, since they are neither ideas of sensation nor reflection, overturns the whole ideal system, by which the material world hath been tried and condemned so that there hath been likewise in this sentence an *error juris.*[6]

It is a very fine and a just observation of Locke, that, as no human art can create a single particle of matter, and the whole extent of our power over the material world consists in compounding, combining, and disjoining the matter made to our hands; so, in the world of thought, the materials are all made by nature, and can only be variously combined and disjoined by us. So that it is impossible for reason or prejudice, true or false philosophy, to produce one simple notion or conception, which is not the work of nature, and the result of our constitution. The conception of extension, motion, and the other attributes of matter, cannot be the effect of error or prejudice; it must be the work of nature. And the power or faculty by which we acquire those conceptions, must be something different from any power of the human mind that hath been explained, since it is neither sensation nor reflection.

This I would, therefore, humbly propose, as an *experimentum crucis*,[7] by which the ideal system must stand or fall; and it brings the matter to a short issue: Extension, figure, motion, may, any one or all of them, be taken for the subject of this experiment. Either they are ideas of sensation, or they are not. If any one of them can be shewn to be an idea of sensation, or to have the least resemblance to any sensation, I lay my hand upon my mouth, and give up all pretense to reconcile reason to common sense in this matter, and must suffer the ideal scepticism to triumph. But if, on the other hand, they are not ideas of sensation, nor like to any sensation, then the ideal system is a rope of sand, and all the laboured arguments of the sceptical philosophy against a material world, and against the existence of everything but impressions and ideas, proceed upon a false hypothesis.

If our philosophy concerning the mind be so lame with regard to the origin of our notions of the clearest, most simple, and most familiar objects of thought, and the powers from which they are derived, can we expect that it should be more perfect in the account it gives of the origin of our opinions and belief? We have seen already some instances of its imperfection in this respect: and, perhaps, that same nature which hath given us the power to conceive things altogether unlike to any of our sensations, or to any operation of our minds, hath likewise provided for our belief of them, by some part of our constitution hitherto not explained.

Bishop Berkeley hath proved, beyond the possibility of reply, that we cannot by reasoning infer the existence of matter from our sensations; and the author of the "Treatise of Human Nature" hath proved no less clearly, that we cannot by reasoning infer the existence of our own or other minds from our sensations. But are we to admit nothing but what can be proved by reasoning? Then we must be sceptics indeed, and believe nothing at all. The author of the "Treatise of Human Nature" appears to me to be but a half-sceptic. He hath not followed his principles so far as they lead him; but, after having, with unparalleled intrepidity and success, combated vulgar prejudices, when he had but one blow to strike, his courage fails him, he fairly lays down his arms, and yields himself a captive to the most common of all vulgar prejudices—I mean the belief of the existence of his own impressions and ideas.

I beg, therefore, to have the honour of making an addition to the sceptical system, without which I conceive it cannot hang together. I affirm, that the belief of the existence of impressions and ideas, is as little supported by reason, as that of the existence of minds and bodies. No man ever did or could offer any reason for this belief. Descartes took it for granted, that he thought, and had sensations and ideas; so have all his followers done. Even the hero of scepticism hath yielded this point, I crave leave to say, weakly and imprudently. I say so, because I am persuaded that there is no principle of his philosophy that obliged him to make this concession. And what is there in impressions and ideas so formidable, that this all-conquering philosophy, after triumphing over every other existence, should pay homage to them? Besides, the concession is dangerous: for belief is of such a nature, that, if you leave any root, it will spread; and you may more easily pull it up altogether, than say, Hitherto shalt go and no further: the existence of impressions and ideas I give up to thee; but see thou pretend to nothing more. A thorough and consistent sceptic will never, therefore, yield this point; and while he holds it, you can never oblige him to yield anything else.

To such a sceptic I have nothing to say; but of the semi-sceptics, I should beg to know, why they believe the existence of their impressions and ideas. The true reason I take to be, because they cannot help it; and the same reason will lead them to believe many other things.

All reasoning must be from first principles; and for first principles no other reason can be given but this, that, by the constitution of our nature, we are under a necessity of assenting to them.

Such principles are parts of our constitution, no less than the power of thinking: reason can neither make nor destroy them; nor can it do anything without them: it is like a telescope, which may help a man to see farther, who hath eyes; but, without eyes, a telescope shews nothing at all. A mathematician cannot prove the truth of his axioms, nor can he prove anything, unless he takes them for granted. We cannot prove the existence of our minds, nor even of our thoughts and sensations. A historian, or a witness can prove nothing, unless it is taken for granted that the memory and senses may be trusted. A natural philosopher can prove nothing, unless it is taken for granted that the course of nature is steady and uniform.

How or when I got such first principles, upon which I build all my reasoning, I know not; for I had them before I can remember: but I am sure they are parts of my constitution, and that I cannot throw them off. That our thoughts and sensations must have a subject, which we call *ourself,* is not therefore an opinion got by reasoning, but a natural principle. That our sensations of touch indicate something external, extended, figured, hard or soft, is not a deduction of reason, but a natural principle. The belief of it, and the very conception of it, are equally parts of our constitution. If we are deceived in it, we are deceived by Him that made us, and there is no remedy.

I do not mean to affirm, that the sensations of touch do, from the very first, suggest the same notions of body and its qualities which they do when we are grown up. Perhaps Nature is frugal in this, as in her other operations. The passion of love, with all its concomitant sentiments and desires, is naturally suggested by the perception of beauty in the other sex; yet the same perception does not suggest the tender passion till a certain period of life. A blow given to an infant, raises grief and lamentation; but when he grows up, it as naturally stirs resentment, and prompts him to resistance. Perhaps a child in the womb, or for some short period of its existence, is merely a sentient being; the faculties by which it perceives an external world, by which it reflects on its own thoughts, and existence, and relation to other things, as well as its reasoning and moral faculties, unfold themselves by degrees; so that it is inspired with the various principles of common sense, as with the passions of love and resentment, when it has occasion for them.

NOTES

1. [George Berkeley.]

2. [In old English law, a writ against one who is thought to have usurped any office, franchise, or liberty, to inquire on behalf of the king by what authority one exercises the office, etc.]

3. [By "the ideal system," Reid means the system of "ideas"—that is, idealism or phenomenalism.]

4. [Reid refers here to David Hume.]

5. [Personal error.]

6. [Error of principle.]

7. [Crucial experiment.]

JOHN STUART MILL

Other Minds*

[What are the grounds of our knowledge of other minds?] By what evidence do I know, or by what considerations am I led to believe, that there exist other sentient creatures; that the walking and speaking figures which I see and hear, have sensations and thoughts, or, in other words, possess Minds? The most strenuous Intuitionist does not include this among the things that I know by direct intuition. I conclude it from certain things, which my experience of my own states of feeling proves to me to be marks of it. These marks are of two kinds, antecedent and subsequent; the previous conditions requisite for feeling, and the effects or consequences of it. I conclude that other human beings have feelings like me, because, first, they have bodies like me, which I know, in my own case, to be the antecedent condition of feelings; and because, secondly, they exhibit the acts, and other outward signs, which in my own case I know by experience to be caused by feelings. I am conscious in myself of a series of facts connected by a uniform sequence, of which the beginning is modifications of my body, the middle is feelings, the end is outward demeanor. In the case of other human beings I have the evidence of my senses for the first and last links of the series, but not for the intermediate link. I find, however, that the sequence between the first and last is as regular and constant in those other cases as it is in mine. In my own case I know that the first link

produces the last through the intermediate link, and could not produce it without. Experience, therefore, obliges me to conclude that there must be an intermediate link; which must either be the same in others as in myself, or a different one: I must either believe them to be alive, or to be automations: and by believing them to be alive, that is, by supposing the link to be of the same nature as in the case of which I have experience, and which is in all other respects similar, I bring other human beings, as phenomena, under the same generalizations which I know by experience to be the true theory of my own existence. And in doing so I conform to the legitimate rules of experimental inquiry. The process is exactly parallel to that by which Newton proved that the force which keeps the planets in their orbits is identical with that by which an apple falls to the ground. It was not incumbent on Newton to prove the impossibility of its being any other force; he was thought to have made out his point when he had simply shown, that no other force need be supposed. We know the existence of other beings by generalization from the knowledge of our own; the generalization merely postulates that what experience shows to be a mark of the existence of something within the sphere of our consciousness, may be concluded to be a mark of the same thing beyond that sphere.

This logical process loses none of its legitimacy on the supposition that neither Mind nor Matter is anything but a permanent possibility of feeling. Whatever sensation I have, I at once refer it to

---

*From John Stuart Mill, *An Examination of Sir William Hamilton's Philosophy* (New York: Henry Hold and Co., 1884), extract from Vol. I, chapter 12.

one of the permanent groups of possibilities of sensation which I call material objects. But among these groups I find there is one (my own body) which is not only composed, like the rest, of a mixed multitude of sensations and possibilities of sensation, but is also connected, in a peculiar manner, with all my sensations. Not only is this special group always present as an antecedent condition of every sensation I have, but the other groups are only enabled to convert their respective possibilities of sensation into actual sensations, by means of some previous change in that particular one. I look about me, and though there is only one group (or body) which is connected with all my sensations in this peculiar manner, I observe that there is a great multitude of other bodies, closely resembling in their sensible properties (in the sensations composing them as groups) this particular one, but whose modifications do not call up, as those of my own body do, a world of sensations in my consciousness. Since they do not do so in my consciousness, I infer that they do it out of my consciousness, and that to each of them belongs a world of consciousness of its own, to which it stands in the same relation in which what I call my own body stands to mine. And having made this generalization, I find that all other facts within my reach agree with it. Each of these bodies exhibits to my senses a set of phenomena (composed of acts and other manifestations) such as I know, in my own case, to be effects of consciousness, and such as might be looked for if each of the bodies has really in connection with it a world of consciousness. All this is as good and genuine an inductive process on the theory we are discussing, as it is on the common theory. Any objection to it in the one case would be an equal objection in the other. I have stated the postulate required by the one theory: the common theory is in need of the same. If I could not, from my personal knowledge of one succession of feelings, infer the existence of other successions of feelings, when manifested by the same outward signs, I could just as little, from my personal knowledge of a single spiritual substance, infer by generalization, when I find the same outward indications, the existence of other spiritual substances.

S Y D N E Y   S H O E M A K E R

The Problem of Other Minds*

There is no sane person who does not hold, with great confidence, a vast number of what I shall call "other minds beliefs." These include beliefs to the effect that particular creatures have particular mental states (e.g., my belief that my wife is angry), beliefs to the effect that certain creatures "have minds" (e.g., the belief that something is a person rather than a mechanical puppet), and, what is involved in all such beliefs, the belief that there are creatures other than oneself that "have minds." The problem of other minds is the problem of explaining how we can be justified in holding these beliefs, or, alternatively, how we can know such beliefs to be true. (These alternative formulations are not quite equivalent, since justified belief is not always knowledge, but we will not concern ourselves here with the differences between them.)

We need not, for present purposes, take the noun "mind" too seriously; in speaking of people as "having minds" we will not mean that they have, or are, Cartesian "souls" or "spiritual sub-

*Copyright © Sydney Shoemaker, 1974. This essay was commissioned by the editor expressly for this volume. It has not been previously published.

stances," entitles that are capable of existing in separation from human bodies. Here, to "have a mind" is just to be the subject of some mental states or other, and the term "mental states" is used broadly to cover thoughts, beliefs, intentions, wants, likes, dislikes, emotions, feelings, and sensations. Even a materialist must allow that people "have minds" in this sense, unless he denies that anyone ever has thoughts, feelings, desires, etc. (and as Descartes' *Cogito* argument brings out, if anyone doubts or denies that there are minds, it follows that he himself has a mind).

One way of introducing our problem is by way of what has come to be called the problem of the "inverted spectrum." How can I know that my experience of colors does not differ from yours in such a way that, for example, blue things look to me the way yellow things look to you (and vice versa)? If the answer is given that you say, just as I do, that orange is more similar to yellow than to blue, that violet is more similar to blue than to yellow, etc., the question can be raised about a more systematic difference: How do I know that my visual experience does not differ from yours in such a way that a normal spectrum looks to me the way it would look to you if it were inverted (rotated one hundred and eighty degrees), and in such a way that things of any given color look to me the way things having the "inverse color" look to you (where the inverse of a color is the color having the position in the inverted spectrum that the color itself has on the ordinary spectrum)? It might, of course, be questioned whether it makes any sense to suppose that two people might differ in this way in their color experience. But it seems imaginable that I might awake some morning to the shocking discovery that the color of the clear sky looks to me the way the color of daffodils used to look to me, and vice versa, and, in general, that things we take to be standardly of a certain color look to me (with respect to color) the way things of the inverse of that color used to look to me. And I can imagine, compatibly with this, that according to other observers, and also according to spectroscopic evidence, there has been no change in the objective colors of the things themselves. We can put this by saying that it is imaginable that my color spectrum might be inverted relative to what it was in the past. But if such an intrapersonal spectrum inversion is possible, it would seem offhand that

it ought also to be possible for the color spectrum of one person to be inverted relative to the color spectrum of another—so that things of any color look (with respect to color) to one of them the way things of the inverse color look to the other.[1] Yet if such an interpersonal difference existed, it seems that the two persons would make exactly the same color discriminations (and, more generally, exactly the same judgments of color similarity and dissimilarity about the same pairs of objects), and that they would agree in their application of color terms (e.g., each will have been taught to call "blue" things that look to him the way the sky looks to him, and to call "yellow" things that look the way daffodils look to him). Thus apparently nothing in the behavior of such persons, including their verbal behavior, would reveal the difference between them. If so, nothing in the behavior of actual persons reveals the *absence* of such a difference.

If it is possible that there should be such undetectable differences between the color experiences of different persons, it would seem that there could also be undetectable interpersonal differences in the case of other sorts of experiences as well. For example, perhaps the sensations one person calls "pains" could be exactly like those another person calls "tickles," the other person responding to the one sort of sensation in just the ways the other responds to the other. If so, how can I ever know that you feel the way I do?

It is worth noting that it is primarily in the case of sensations and sense-experiences that this problem seems to arise. It does not get much foothold in the case of such mental states as beliefs, thoughts, and intentions. There is nothing it is characteristically "like" (for example, there is nothing it *feels* like) for a person to have a particular belief, thought, or intention, and thus there can be no question as to whether what it is like for me to have a particular belief is or is not the same as what it is like for you to have that belief. Moreover, the skepticism which seems to be supported by the possibility of spectrum inversion and the like is (in the first instance, anyhow) a limited skepticism; only if I suppose myself to know that another person characteristically has *some* sort of experience when he sees something red can I entertain the thought that perhaps his experience of red is radically unlike mine. But once one has had the thought that perhaps one cannot know whether another person's sensations are like or unlike one's own, one's next thought is likely to be that perhaps one cannot know whether others have sensations at all. And one's next thought after this is likely to be that perhaps one cannot know anything about the mental states of others, or even whether there are other creatures having mental states. Thus there is a rather natural transition from the inverted spectrum problem to the general problem of other minds.

Sometimes the general problem has been put in the following way. We cannot (it is said) perceive or observe the minds or mental states of other persons. All that we can perceive or observe ("directly" or "immediately") in the case of another person are his bodily states and bodily behavior —his posture, his movements, his coloration and changes in coloration (e.g., blushing and blanching), the sounds he produces, etc. If we divide facts into the "physical" and the "mental," then the facts we observe with our senses are physical and not mental. So our senses do not directly provide us with any knowledge of other minds; at best they provide us with data from which to *infer* the existence of other minds, or from which to infer the existence in others of particular mental states. And this raises the question of what justifies us in inferring from these particular physical facts (and not others) to the existence of these particular mental facts (and not others). What is it that justifies me in taking one sequence of bodily movements, sounds, etc., as showing that someone is angry, another as showing that someone wants ice cream, and so on? There are, of course, mental facts that we know without inferring them from anything. That *I* am angry, or that *I* want ice cream, is not something I infer from what I see, hear, or otherwise perceive. Such knowledge is "direct" and "non-inferential." But it is only of one's own mental states that one has such knowledge; the mental facts that are knowable in this way are always facts about the "mind" of the knower himself. So the existence of such knowledge does not explain, at least not directly, how we can have knowledge of *other* minds. Moreover, it is partly the fact that we can know our mental states in the way we do that suggests that mental states are in some fundamental way different from physical states, and

that there is thus a gap, requiring bridging, between the facts we can perceive and facts about the minds of persons other than ourselves. Having this "direct" knowledge of one's own mental states does not involve observing the physical states of one's body and seems compatible with complete ignorance of these states.

The formulation of the problem of other minds just sketched involves some questionable claims. In what sense, if any, is it true that we cannot perceive the mental states of others? We regularly say things like "I could see that he was angry," and "I saw that he was deep in thought, so I didn't disturb him." Should it be said that these are improper, or perhaps figurative, uses of the word "see"? On what grounds? It is true that where one would naturally say that one could see that a certain person was angry, it is always possible that someone or something (a skilled actor, or a skillfully made mannequin) should look just the way that person did without itself being angry. But if this is taken as showing that we cannot see that someone is angry, an exactly analogous fact must be taken as showing that we cannot see that something is an oak tree. For clearly what is not an oak tree (say a piece of stage setting made of papier-maché and plastic) can look just like one. But it is a perfectly proper use of the word "see" to say "I could see that it was an oak tree," and it is an equally proper useage to say "I could see that he was angry."

Just as it is far from obvious that one cannot see that someone is angry, thinking, etc., so it is far from obvious that ascriptions of mental states to others are always, or even typically, inferred from physical facts. Often one looks at someone and knows "right off" that he is elated, or angry, or amused. One does not say to oneself "He is scowling, so he must be angry," and still less does one say to oneself "His eyebrows are contracted, so he must be angry." Most of us are quite unskilled at describing human behavior and facial expressions in purely physical terms. We are far more likely to notice and remember whether someone "looked angry" than whether the corners of his mouth were turned up or down, whether his eyes were narrowed and his eyebrows contracted, and so on—and if we were given a great deal of information of the latter sort about someone, but not allowed to see him, most of us would be at a loss to say anything about what the person's mental state was.

But—to argue the other side—if our judgments about the mental states of others are usually not consciously inferred from physical descriptions of behavior, they are at any rate based on observations of behavior. And while we can be said to observe or perceive facts about another person's mental states, we do this *by* observing his behavior (and the circumstances in which it occurs). It is *from* a man's behavior (including his facial expressions) that I see that he is angry—even though I may be unable to describe his behavior except by saying that he acted angrily, or looked angry. And it is physical features that serve as the cues that enable us to see someone as angry, elated, amused, and so forth. Suppose that throughout their lives Peter and Paul (let them be identical twins) behave in physically identical ways in physically identical surroundings. It is compatible with this that at a certain time Peter should be happy while Paul is sad. But it is not compatible with this that at any time Peter should be *seen* to be happy while Paul is *seen* to be sad. The perceiving of physical changes and differences in behavior and circumstances underlies the perceiving of psychological, or mental, changes and differences—in much the way that the perceiving of colors and shapes underlies the perceiving of something as an oak tree.

In any case, it should be clear that the fact that the mental states of others are observable by us does not (given the way in which they are observable by us) make our knowledge of them at all like our knowledge of our own mental states. For one thing, it is not (in ordinary circumstances) by observing my behavior that I know that I am angry, or that I am in pain, or that I am wondering if it is time for lunch. For another, I can have knowledge of my own mental states in cases in which my behavior indicates nothing about my mental states or is misleading about them. For another, it would seem that while information about a person's behavior (or other bodily states) could require others to alter their beliefs about whether the person is afraid, in pain, having visual experiences, etc., such information could not require the person himself to alter his beliefs about these matters. And whether or not our sincere ascriptions to ourselves of some sorts of mental states (e.g., pains) are totally immune to error

(as some philosophers have held), it is certainly hard to think of any assertions that are less liable to error than the sincere assertions expressed by sentences like "I feel a pain in my back," "I am afraid," and "It looks to me as if there were a red circle in front of me" (where the latter is intended as a description of the speaker's experience, rather than as a tentative judgment about what there is in front of him). It is true of some mental states—though by no means of all—that one's sincere self-ascriptions of them seem, compared with one's acriptions of them to others, relative incorrigible (i.e., immune to correction) by behavioral evidence, and relatively infallible (i.e., immune to error). All of this is sometimes summed up by saying that each person has a "privileged access" to (some of) his own mental states.

It seems pretty obvious that facts about how a body is moving, about its color and changes in color, about the acoustical properties of the sounds it is producing, etc., can never logically entail anything about what anyone is thinking, feeling, and so forth. (This is not to deny, of course, that such physical facts can be evidence in favor of attributions of mental states.) The fact that mental states are logically independent of bodily behavior in this way seems to fit with (although it neither entails nor is entailed by) the fact that people have a privileged access to their own mental states. Given all this, it is natural to conclude that it is in one's own case, and only in one's own case, that one is "directly" presented with mental facts. And this does seem to raise a problem as to how one can know facts about other minds, i.e., how observation of behavior (something distinct from mental states, and logically independent of them) can give rise to such knowledge.

PRIVACY

Some philosophers have thought that they could explain our privileged access to our own mental states by the fact (or alleged fact) that the contents of a mind are "private" to that mind. The sort of privacy in question is supposed to be illustrated by the fact (or alleged fact) that pains, for example, are unshareable and untransferable; it is impossible, so it is said, that another person should have, or come to have, the very headache I have now. Let us call this "privacy of ownership." The first point to be noted about this is that if pains (and beliefs, desires, intentions, etc.) are private in this sense, so also are smiles. If it can be said that you cannot have or acquire my pain, and can at best have a pain exactly similar to it (but numerically distinct from it), then it can equally well be said that you cannot have or acquire my smile, and can at best have a smile exactly like mine (but numerically distinct from it). But the fact that smiles are unshareable and untransferable is not thought to give rise to any epistemological problem about the smiles of others. So what does privacy of ownership have to do with knowledge of other minds?

The answer to this, in part anyhow, is that philosophers have supposed that a person knows about his pains *by* having them, or knows about them in a way that involves having them. This is true and harmless if taken simply as the point that each person has a privileged access to mental facts about himself. But it is easy to fall into a way of representing this point that makes it seem as if it were an explanation, rather than a reiteration, of the fact that we have this privileged access— an explanation, moreover, that makes it seem quite mysterious that we can know any mental states other than our own. Perhaps because one can say indifferently "I have a pain in my foot" and "I feel a pain in my foot," and because "feel" is in other contexts a verb of perception, it is natural to identify *having* a pain with *feeling* a pain and to construe it as a way of perceiving, or apprehending, the pain. Then privacy of ownership, in the case of pains, is seen as implying that each person's pains are perceived, observed, or apprehended by him and him alone. It is then supposed that it is *by* perceiving his pains that a person knows that he is in pain, and that it is because he alone can perceive his pains that he has a privileged access to the fact that he is in pain. Given this way of thinking, it cannot help but seem that our knowledge of minds begins (and perhaps ends) with our knowledge of our own minds, and that our judgments about other minds must be based on our knowledge of our own minds in something like the way our judgments about unexamined crows are based on knowledge of examined crows, i.e., as an inductive extrapolation from it—but with the difference, which is unfavorable to our judgments about other minds, that whereas presently unex-amined crows can come to be examined, the contents of other minds are forever hidden from us.

Inevitably it has been suggested by some philosophers that perhaps, after all, it is possible for one person to "directly perceive" the contents of another person's mind. The suggestion is that while in fact our knowledge of the mental states of others is always grounded on behavior and so (it is thought) is indirect, it is nevertheless possible "in principle" that one person should perceive the "objects" (the pains, tickles, thoughts, etc.) in another person's mind, and thus have knowledge of that person's mind that is as direct as the knowledge which the person himself has of it. Sometimes alleged cases of telepathic communication are described as one person's "directly" or "immediately" perceiving the contents of another person's mind. And it is sometimes suggested that where two people feel pain in the very same place (as reportedly can happen in the case of Siamese twins), they can be said to feel the very same pain.

Let us consider this briefly. It is evident that it would not follow from my feeling a pain in your body (supposing this to be possible) that I feel your pain; if I feel a pain in your arm, but you feel no pain there, we can hardly say that the pain I feel is yours and that in feeling it I have direct knowledge of your pain. But suppose that you and I both feel pain in a certain place, say in your arm, and both describe our pains in the same way (e.g., each of us describes his pain as sharp and throbbing); will this show that we both feel the same pain, and that I feel your pain? I would think not. But let us see if it would help if the answer were affirmative. Supposing that I could feel your pain, by feeling a pain where you feel one, would this give me an access to your feelings which is as direct as the access you have to them? Clearly not. Simply from feeling what is in fact your pain I would not know that you have a pain (any more than I would know that you have a car simply from seeing what is in fact your car). How might I know that the pain I feel is yours? It seems that to know this I would have to know, in the ordinary way, i.e., from your behavior (including your "verbal behavior," i.e., what you say) that you feel a pain of certain description. So even if there is something that would count as my feeling your pain, this would not enable me to bypass your behavior in acquiring knowledge of your state of mind.[2]

But now, and this is a fact of some importance, if I could not acquire an access of the sort you have to your state of mind by "perceiving" (feeling) your pains, itches, etc., then the fact that you have the access you have is not explained by your perceiving such objects. If my feeling your pain will not, by itself, tell me that you are in pain, how can *your* feeling your pain tell you that you are in pain? The answer might be given that whoever feels a pain is *ipso facto* in pain. But then, how do you know that you feel a pain? Here appeal to the notion that you perceive or observe (by feeling it) a private object (a pain) is of no help; it simply gives a contentious description of the fact known, and gives no explanation of how it is known. We can certainly allow it to be true that (1) whoever feels or has a pain knows that he does in a manner that does not in any way rest on knowledge or observation of behavior, and (2) that no one other than that person knows this fact in the same way. But it is an illusion to think that we explain this fact by construing the feeling of a pain as the perceiving of a private object, one that can be "owned" and "perceived" (felt) by only one person. This does not explain (1), for it simply replaces the question "When a person is in pain, how does he know that he is?" with the question "When a person perceives (feels) a pain, how does he know that he does?" and provides no answer to the latter question. And it does not explain (2), since, as we have seen, (2) would be true even if pains were not private objects in the required sense, i.e., even if it were possible for more than one person to have and "perceive" the very same pain.

There are, I think, good reasons for holding that the "feel" in "I feel pain" is not a verb of perception at all. Clearly it is not like the "feel" in "I feel something smooth and hard"; it is not by the sense of touch that I feel pains and itches. And there is something queer, to say the least, about the idea of a mode of perception whose objects cannot exist without being perceived in that mode and cannot be misperceived (and presumably pains cannot exist without being felt, and cannot be misfelt). But I shall not pursue this matter. The point is that even if we do construe feeling a pain as perceiving or observing a private object (one that only one person can perceive or

observe), this does not in the least explain the difference between one's knowledge of one's own mental states (in this case, one's knowledge that one is in pain) and one's knowledge of the mental states of others. Appreciation of this point should undermine the plausibility of thinking of pains and the like as private objects in this sense, and of characterizing the difference between self-knowledge and knowledge of other minds in terms of the distinction between the observable (or perceivable) and the unobservable (unperceivable).

Now that we have looked at some of the sources of the problem of knowledge of other minds, we must consider some of the theories that have been offered as solutions to this problem. In the ensuing discussion I shall be concerned with theories about knowledge of other minds which attempt to show that, and how, our other minds beliefs can be construed as legitimate conclusions from observed or observable facts about behavior and physical circumstances.

THE ANALOGICAL ARGUMENT

The most famous, and most criticized, of all the proposed solutions to the problem of other minds is what I shall call the analogical position. This solution received one of its classic formulations in John Stuart Mill's *Examination of Sir William Hamilton's Philosophy*, and in more recent times has been defended by, among others, C. D. Broad, H. H. Price, A. J. Ayer, and Stuart Hampshire.[3] The analogical position starts from the fact that there are cases in which a person can have knowledge of mental states that is not in any way based or grounded on behavior or other "physical" phenomena, namely cases in which the mental states known are states of the knower himself. This seems to provide the possibility of each person's discovering empirically that in his own case certain sorts of behavior (or other physical phenomena) are regularly accompanied by certain mental states, and this providing inductive grounds for the conclusion that in general (and not only in his own case) these kinds of behavior are accompanied by these mental states, and this in turn entitling him to take certain sorts of behavior as evidence of the existence of certain mental states. Thus, it is suggested, our other minds beliefs are justified in virtue of being the conclusions of warranted analogical or inductive inferences (particular instances of the so-called "Argument from Analogy") which each of us is entitled to make from correlations he has established, or could in principle establish, to hold in his own case. To put it crudely, what entitles me to take your wincing and screaming as evidence that you feel pain is the fact that I find such behavior to be accompanied by pain (namely mine) when it occurs in my body.

As many of its proponents have acknowledged, the analogical position is scarcely plausible if offered as the genetic thesis that one actually arrives at his other minds beliefs by first noting certain kinds of behavior to be accompanied by certain mental states in his own case and then inferring to the existence of similar mental states in others in which one observes similar behavior. It is ludicrous, at best, to suppose that infants and toddlers came to identify as such the signs of approval and disapproval in their elders by performing such an intellectual feat. But ordinarily the analogical position is proposed as a thesis about the *justification,* and not about the *origin,* of our other minds beliefs. A proponent of this position could even allow that some of our other minds beliefs are "innate"—e.g., that it is part of our genetic inheritance (something that has come to be "wired in" to members of our species because of its survival value) that we instinctively take certain behavior (what we describe as threatening gestures) to be evidence of hostile intent. But a belief's being innate would not, in itself, make it true or justified, and it is with the justification of our other minds beliefs that the analogical position is concerned.

It is usually assumed by advocates of the analogical position that there is a legitimate sense of "observe" in which facts about one's own mental states can be observed, or "established by observation," while facts about the mental states of others cannot be so observed or established. This sense of "observe" is intended to be such that when one observes a fact to hold (in this sense), one's coming to know the fact does not in any way depend on one's having inductively grounded knowledge that other facts are evidence of that fact. Where the premises (or evidence statements) of an inductive argument are known by observation in this sense, let us say that the argument is a "simple inductive argument." The

analogical position (or one version of it) holds that the "argument from analogy" is a legitimate simple inductive argument; more precisely, it holds that there are legitimate simple inductive arguments, having as premises statements about the mental states and behavior of the inductive arguer, which support our other minds beliefs, and that only those other minds beliefs that are supported in this way are justifiable.

The analogical position has been severely criticized in the last few decades. The favorite objections have been that the argument from analogy is an "induction from a single instance," and that (given the assumptions of the analogical position) the conclusion of the argument from analogy is not verifiable by the person making the inference. Both objections stem from the fact that, according to the assumptions of the analogical position, it is only in one's own case that one can have knowledge of mental states that is "observational" and noninductive. It follows from this that the only mental states that can be mentioned in the premises of a simple inductive argument are those of the inductive arguer, and that the conclusion of such an inductive argument will not be verifiable (by observation) by the inductive arguer if it asserts the existence of mental states other than those of the inductive arguer. That an argument is an induction from a single instance has been thought to make it at best an extremely weak induction—like the inference from a single swan's being white to the conclusion that all swans are white. And that the conclusion of an inductive inference is not verifiable by the inductive arguer has been thought to throw into question whether the conclusion is even meaningful; for many philosophers have supposed that there is a close connection between a proposition's being meaningful and its being empirically verifiable.

Despite the popularity of the verifiability objection, it is not easy to find a plausible sense of "verifiable" which is such that both (a) judgments about other minds are not verifiable in this sense (given the assumptions of the analogical position) and (b) all clearly acceptable inductive inferences are verifiable in this sense. Clearly there is a sense in which my judgment that you are angry is "directly" verifiable (verifiable "by observation"); it is directly verifiable *by you.* But if we impose the requirement that every acceptable inductive argument be directly verifiable *by the person giving the argument,* we are in danger of ruling out as unacceptable all or most of the inductive arguments that scientists, historians, and ordinary men do in fact accept. I say now, on inductive grounds, that there are now (10:00 A.M., October 24, 1973) craters on the other side of the moon. It is possible, although highly unlikely, that before I die I will actually see craters on the other side of the moon. But in seeing them I will not be verifying (directly) the judgment I make *now*— what I will know "directly" will be that there are *then* (in 1984, say) craters on that side of the moon, not that there are craters there now (in 1973). So in one sense every judgment about unobserved objects is unverifiable; given that I am not observing something at time *t*, it is not possible that I should directly verify some proposition about its state at *t* (where "directly verifying" involves observing). In another sense judgments about the current state of the other side of the moon are verifiable by me. Although I am not now observing the other side of the moon, I *could have been* observing it now. Whereas, by contrast, not only am I not "directly aware" of your mental state now (i.e., am not aware of it in the way you are aware of it), but I *could not have been* directly aware of your mental state now. But consider now inductive inferences concerning the remote past. I infer, on the basis of documents and archeological remains, that there was a battle here five hundred years ago. Since it is not possible that I should have observed that battle, the conclusion of that inference is not "directly verifiable" by me. Someone might say that if I had been born five hundred years earlier I could have observed the battle. But one can equally well say that if I had been a different person (you rather than me), I could have been directly aware of your current mental state. And it seems no more possible that I should have been born five hundred years earlier than that I should have been a different person.[4]

As for the "single instance" objection, the standard reply to this has been that it is a misrepresentation to say that the argument from analogy is an induction from a single instance. If, for example, we take the (immediate) conclusion of the argument to be the generalization that wincing is accompanied by pain on the part of he who winces (the "wincer"), then there will be as many instances in my inductive sample as there are cases in which I have observed wincing and noted whether it was accompanied by pain on the part of the wincer. And clearly I can enlarge the sample by observing additional such cases. To be sure, all of the cases included in the sample will be cases of *my* wincing and being (or not being) in pain. I cannot enlarge the sample to include cases involving the behavior and mental states of persons other than myself. But this, it may be said, is analogous to the fact that I cannot enlarge the sample of any inductive inference to include cases observed before I was born—and the latter fact is not thought to make inferences concerning the remote past inductions "from a single instance."

But there is another objection, related to these, that seems to have more force. To explain this I shall have to make a few general remarks about inductive inference.[5]

If a generalization is of the form "All A's are B" (e.g., "All crows are black"), then A's that are B (in our example, black crows) are called "positive instances" of the generalization, and A's that are not B (in our example, crows that are not black) will be "negative instances" of the generalizatin. Clearly we cannot establish, or be justified in believing, such a generalization on the basis of a simple inductive inference unless it is possible to establish by observation the existence of positive instances of it—for having inductive evidence for such a generalization will consist in having discovered (by some unbiased sampling procedure) a significant number of positive instances of it without discovering any negative instances. But it seems that if the sampling is not to be biased it must also be *possible* that we should establish by observation the existence of negative instances of the generalization; in other words, the generalization must be falsifiable by observation. Otherwise the deck will be stacked in advance in favor of the generalization, and our investigation will be a farce—like the use of a telephone poll to determine whether everyone has access to a telephone. A generalization that does not satisfy this condition is the proposition "All elephants are observed"; and the fact that we have observed lots of positive instances of this (lots of observed elephants) and have not observed any negative instances of it (have not observed any unobserved elephants) clearly does not give inductive support to this obviously false proposition. It seems to be true, with certain qualifications that need not concern us now, that the conclusion of any legitimate simple inductive argument must satisfy this condition, i.e., must be falsifiable by observation.[6]

Now let us return to the argument from analogy. To simplify matters let us ignore the complexity of the connections that actually hold between mental states and behavior, and pretend that I (as a sample analogical arguer) am in pain whenever I wince. Let us see whether this fact about myself could serve, for me, as the premise of a legitimate simple inductive argument to the conclusion "Wincing is always accompanied by pain on the part of the person whose body manifests the wincing." (That this generalization is in fact clearly false is beside the point.) At first glance it seems that both positive instances and negative instances of this generalization could be discovered by observation. But notice that the generalization contains the words "the person." Unless I know, and know by observation, that I am *the* person whose body manifests wincing when I wince, my noting that I feel pain while my body is manifesting wincing will not count as observing a positive instance of this generalization. This raises the question of *how* I know that I am *the* person, i.e., the only person, who has the body I have. It would of course be insane to suggest that perhaps I don't know this, and that for all I know my body is "co-animated" by two or more distinct persons, or two or more distinct minds. But it would be equally insane to suggest that I don't know that the human-appearing creatures around me have minds, yet this does not prevent us from asking *how* I know this. And the question of how I know that I am alone in having the body I have turns out to be important.

Since the words "the person" in the proposed conclusion of our simple inductive argument seem to give trouble, let us try replacing them with the words "a person"; now the conclusion will read "Wincing is always accompanied by pain on the part of *a* person whose body manifests the wincing." There is no difficulty about observing positive instances of this generalization; whether or not I know that I am alone in having the body I have, I will observe a positive instance of this generalization if I notice that my body is manifesting wincing and that I am in pain. But there is a problem about observing neg-

ative instances of this generalization. For if I did not know, and know by observation, that I am alone in having the body I have, my noting that my body is manifesting wincing and that I am not in pain would not count as observing such a negative instance. For then it might be, compatibly with what I would know by observation, that the wincing is accompanied by pain on the part of someone else who shares my body with me.

So how *do* I know that I am alone in having the body I have? It might be held that I know this a priori, and that it is logically necessary, or conceptually necessary, truth that there is at the most one person per body. But this is, from the standpoint of the analogical position, an unmotivated view. And in fact it seems to be false. There seems to be no logical incoherence in the idea that two or more distinct persons, or two distinct "minds," might alternate in controlling a single body, or even that two such persons (or minds) might simultaneously have partial control over the same body, each having equal claim to have that body as its body. And there are imaginable phenomena that would be evidence of such "co-animation." Presumably it is the fact that these phenomena do not in fact occur that entitles each of us to believe that he is alone in having the body he has. My body does not characteristically manifest behavior indicating that it is animated by someone having mental states other than my own, and other bodies do not manifest behavior indicating that distinct minds are competing for, or cooperating in, their control. But, and this is the point, in order to have such grounds for the belief that I am alone in having the body I have, I must already know what sorts of behavior are evidence for what sorts of mental states; I must know that if my body *were* to manifest certain behavior this *would* be evidence that it is animated by someone having certain mental states. And it is precisely such evidential relationships between behavior and mental states that the argument from analogy is supposed to establish. So only someone who doesn't need the argument from analogy, because he already knows these evidential relationships, is in a position to use it. Moreover, the fact that one is alone in having the body he has is not something he knows "by observation" in the narrow sense favored by the analogical position—the sense in which we cannot know by observation facts about the mental states of others.

For it is implicit in what I have said that my knowledge that my body is animated by only one mind is no less "inferential" than my knowledge that other bodies are animated by minds; both sorts of knowledge rest on implicit knowledge of the same sorts of evidential relationships between mental states and behavior. And this means that neither of the generalizations considered above, neither "Wincing is always accompanied by pain on the part of *the* person . . ." nor "Wincing is always accompanied by pain on the part of *a* person . . .," could be supported by a legitimate simple inductive argument based on correlations observed "in one's own case." In the case of the first of these generalizations it is impossible to observe (in the narrow sense) the existence of positive instances, and in the case of the second it is impossible to observe the existence of negative instances. And this is fatal to the analogical position, or at least one version of it.

BEHAVIORISM AND "CONCEPTUAL CONNECTIONS"

The view about knowledge of other minds that seems most remote from the analogical position is that known as "behaviorism," or (to distinguish it from the methodological doctrine in psychology bearing the same name) "philosophical behaviorism" or "logical behaviorism." Behaviorism is not, in the first instance, a thesis about knowledge of other minds; it is a thesis about what mental states are, or about what mental terms and propositions mean. But it is a view that is tailor-made to meet the demand that the mental states of a person be knowable by other persons on the basis of behavior. Roughly speaking, behaviorism is the doctrine that discourse about the mental (about thoughts, emotions, sensations, etc.) is really discourse about behavior. While the behaviorist does not equate having a mental state with behaving in a certain way, he holds that mental states are distinguishable from behavior only in the way that something's having a disposition or tendency to behave in certain ways is distinguishable from its actually behaving in those ways (e.g., in the way something's being flexible is distinguishable from its bending). Sometimes behaviorism takes the form of the doctrine that every mental proposition (every proposition ascribing a mental state) is "analyzable" or "translatable" into a proposition (an enormously complicated one) explicitly about behavior, a proposition describing how a body behaves or would behave given certain conditions. This seems to explain neatly and simply how it is that we can ascribe mental states on the basis of behavior.

It scarcely needs arguing that behaviorism and the analogical position are radically different and radically incompatible. Whereas the analogical position regards all connections between mental states and behavior as purely contingent connections, that have to be discovered empirically, behaviorism holds that the existence of some of these connections is implicit in the very meaning of mental terms, or in the very concepts of mental states.

Behaviorism has been severely criticized on a variety of grounds, which we cannot go into here. But while few philosophers nowadays would accept the behaviorist view that propositions about mental states are "reducible" to statements about physical behavior, many philosophers remain sympathetic with one part of the behaviorist thesis, namely the view that some connections between mental states and behavior are "logical" or "essential" or "conceptual" rather than "contingent." I shall call this the "conceptual connection view." One source of this view has been the conviction that it is our only defense against complete skepticism concerning other minds; those who think this argue that the analogical position is mistaken, and conclude from this that if all connections between mental states and behavior were contingent there would be no way at all in which such connections could be known, and so no way at all in which the mental states of others could be known. But it is, quite independently of this, quite plausible to maintain that there is *some* sort of logical, or conceptual, connection between (for example) fearing something and avoiding it, or between desiring something and pursuing it. It is easy to imagine a world in which fear has no tendency to give rise to perspiration and trembling, in which embarrassment has no tendency to give rise to blushing, and so on; that these mental states have, or tend to have, *these* behavioral manifestations seems clearly to be a contingent, empirical fact. But can we imagine a world in which fear has no tendency to give rise to avoidance of the thing feared, or in which desire has no tendency to give rise to pursuit of the thing desired? Offhand it would seem not. People might at some future time use the *word* "desire" to name a state which is unconnected with pursuit of the things they say they "desire"; but if they did, they could hardly mean by the word "desire" what we mean by it.

At this point we had better make some distinctions. If a proposition says that under certain conditions a certain mental state (or set of mental states) gives rise to, or tends to give rise to, certain behavior, let us call it a Mental-to-Behavior generalization, and let us say that it asserts a Mental-to-Behavior connection. If a proposition says that under certain conditions a certain sort of behavior is accompanied by, or tends to be accompanied by, certain mental states, let us call it a Behavior-to-Mental connection. What I claimed in the preceding paragraph is that it is plausible to hold that some Mental-to-Behavior generalizations are conceptually (or logically) true. But what some advocates of the conceptual connection view have apparently held is that some Behavior-to-Mental generalizations are conceptually (logically) true. And that is a different matter.

If we are liberal enough about what counts as a description of behavior, it is easy to find Behavior-to-Mental generalizations that are logically true. Clearly enough, it is logically true that shouting in anger is typically (in fact always) accompanied by anger. But, what is equally clear, this logical truth is of no help whatever in explaining our knowledge that someone is angry, since we have to know that someone is angry in order to know that his behavior counts as "shouting in anger." To describe someone's behavior as "shouting in anger" is to give a "mentalistically loaded" description of it. And if we limit ourselves, in formulating Behavior-to-Mental generalizations, to descriptions that are not mentalistically loaded, and are instead expressed in purely physical terms, then it is quite implausible to suppose that any such generalizations are logically or conceptually true. The bodily movements, sound emissions, etc., that make up human behavior could all occur in the "behavior" of an automated clothing store mannequin, and any combination or sequence of these that could occur in the behavior of an actual person could (in principle) occur in the behavior of such

a mechanical puppet without its thereby coming to "have a mind."

INFERENCE TO THE BEST EXPLANATION

It is worth noting that it is Behavior-to-Mental generalizations which the analogical position, in the version of it discussed earlier, holds to be justified by the argument by analogy. It is a shared assumption of this version of the analogical position and of the version of the conceptual connection view which I have just criticized that it is Behavior-to-Mental generalizations that play the crucial role in the justification of inferences from behavior to mental states; where the two positions differ is in what they say about the logical status of these generalizations (whether they are logically true or contingently true) and about how we know them (whether we know them a priori or empirically). But this shared assumption of the two positions seems to me to be mistaken. There is perhaps a sense in which any behaviorally based mental state ascription commits one to a Behavior-to-Mental generalization; if in certain circumstances I take the occurrence of certain behavior as entitling me to ascribe a certain mental state, I would seem to be committed to the general claim that whenever *exactly* similar behavior exists in *exactly* similar circumstances, the mental state in question is likely to exist. But such generalizations are useless as licenses for inference; in fact behavior and circumstances are never exactly duplicated, and in any case it would be impossible to establish that they were exactly duplicated. Indeed, it seems clear that one knows such generalizations by knowing that particular inferences are warranted, and not vice versa. And if we consider cases in which we do invoke generalizations relating mental states and behavior in justification of our other minds beliefs, I think it turns out that the generalizations are for the most part Mental-to-Behavior generalizations rather than Behavior-to-Mental generalizations. In talking of the connections between mental states and behavior we characteristically say that a certain mental state *manifests* itself in, or is *expressed* by, or *gives rise to* certain behavior; or that someone's having certain mental states *makes* him behave in certain ways, or *leads* him to behave in certain ways. The locutions we use highlight the causal or quasi-causal character of the connections; and of course it is typically mental states that cause or produce behavior, and not vice versa. And when we arrive at a mental state ascription by explicit reasoning, the reasoning usually constitutes what has been aptly called an "inference to the best explanation."[7] We begin (in effect) by asking "Why is he doing that?" or "Why would someone behave in that way?" and then proceed by evaluating the possible answers for adequacy, simplicity, consistency with what we know about the person and his circumstances, and so forth, finally settling upon one of them as the most plausible explanation of the behavior in question. What we have to know about mental states and behavior in order to conduct such reasoning is what sorts of mental states will produce, or give rise to, what sorts of behavior—in other words, what we need to know are Mental-to-Behavior connections. Thus it appears to be Mental-to-Behavior generalizations and connections, rather than Behavior-to-Mental generalizations and connections, that are of primary importance vis-à-vis our knowledge of other minds.

But now we should take notice of the fact that our reasoning concerning other minds involves generalizations and connections that do not have to do with behavior at all. These include generalizations asserting connections between mental states and their physical causes, e.g., "If someone's hand is burnt, he feels pain" (for short, these are Physical-to-Mental generalizations, and assert Physical-to-Mental connections); and generalizations asserting connections between different mental states, e.g., "People want to avoid things they believe to be painful" (for short, these are Mental-Mental generalizations, and assert Mental-Mental connections). If we make explicit everything that is taken for granted in reasoning concerning other minds, a typical case of such reasoning will be found to involve generalizations of both of these sorts as well as Mental-to-Behavior generalizations. To take a very simple example, we see John, teeth clenched and red in the face, walk up to Tom and strike him, and we conclude that John is angry at Tom. Although such a judgment would be unlikely to involve explicit inference, anyone who judged in this way could be said to be taking for granted a number of generalizations, and these are precisely the generalizations that would be required to justify an "inference to the best explanation" from

John's behavior to the conclusion that he is angry at Tom. Among these generalizations, which usually go unmentioned and unformulated because of their obviousness, is a Physical-to-Mental generalization to the effect that if someone's eyes are open and directed towards an object in good light, then normally he will, if conscious, have veridical sense-impressions of the object, and so will perceive it. Also among these generalizations is a Mental-Mental generalization to the effect that if someone has sense impressions of a man of a certain appearance, he will (normally) believe that there is a man of that appearance before him. We take for granted generalizations like these in believing that John knew that Tom was before him and knew that he was striking Tom. Further, in taking the striking as evidence of anger we take for granted some Mental-to-Behavior generalization to the effect that if X is angry at Y, and believes that Y is before him, then in the absence of interfering factors (including scruples and self-control) he is likely to behave violently towards what he believes to be Y. We also take for granted a Mental-to-Behavior generalization to the effect that (normally) if someone tries to strike someone, his arm makes a striking movement. And we take for granted some Mental-to-Behavior generalization to the effect that anger tends to manifest itself in teeth clenching and reddening of the face.

THE INFORMED AGENCY CONDITION

While sometimes such generalizations are presupposed by reasoning from behavior to other minds, at other times they figure in the conclusions of such reasoning; for that certain such generalizations are true of a set of creatures can be part of what we conclude from their behavior. Suppose, what is perhaps no longer a merely fanciful possibility, we were to come into contact with intelligent creatures "from outer space" whose evolutionary development had been completely independent of ours. If the behavior and facial expressions of such creatures sometimes resembled what we call smiling, frowning, grimacing, blushing, teeth clenching, sweating, etc., this resemblance might be as superficial, psychologically speaking, as that between the tail wagging of dogs and the tail waving of cats. What looks like smiling in them might be a manifestation of hostility, or of some emotion that is completely alien to us. Such creatures might differ from us in their sensory apparatus (e.g., they might be equipped with something like sonar, or something like radar) and in their method of reproduction (perhaps theirs would not involve sexual differentiation), and they might, accordingly, differ radically from us with respect to the sorts of sensations, feelings and emotions they are capable of having. And their bodies might be quite different from ours; they might be equipped with pincers instead of hands, wheels instead of legs, and so on. But despite all this, it is surely possible that we should recognize such creatrues as intelligent and sentient beings, and come to know a great deal about their mental states. For we could observe them engaging in complex patterns of behavior—behavior we perceive as "intelligent" and "purposive"—which we find to be inexplicable except on the assumption that they have certain motivational states (goals, needs, wants, desires, likes, dislikes, etc.), that they have modes of sense perception that provide them with information concerning their environment that is relevant to the satisfaction of their wants and needs, that they are sufficiently intelligent and rational to draw a significant number of the deductive and inductive consequences of their beliefs and thus to anticipate the consequences of their actions, and, finally, that they have a significant degree of voluntary control over their bodily movements. Especially compelling, as a reason for attributing "minds" to such creatures, would be the fact that their output of sounds or gestures is interpretable as a sequence of sentences in a language, many of these sentences constituting true descriptions of their surroundings and many of them having a content relevant to purposes seemingly manifested in their nonverbal behavior. This, it is plausible to say, is something that could *only* be explained by the creatures' having minds.[8]

Let us speak of any subject of mental states as having a "psychology" consisting of all of the Physical-to-Mental, Mental-Mental, and Mental-to-Behavior generalizations that are true of it. Given the ways other subjects of mental states might differ from us in their sensory apparatus, in what sensory and emotional states they are capable of having, and in the nature of their bodies and the nature and extent of their control over their bodies, it does not seem to be a necessary condition of our having behaviorally grounded

knowledge of the mental states of other creatures that their psychologies should be the same as ours. (This is, incidentally, a further reason for rejecting the analogical position and its assumption that one's knowledge of other minds rests on an inductive extrapolation of generalizations one has found to hold in one's own case.) But it does seem to be a necessary condition of our having such knowledge (a) that some of the Physical-to-Mental generalizations true of the creatures describe connections that constitute (amount to, or add up to) their having the power to perceive facts about their physical situation and surroundings (call this the *Perceptual* condition); (b) that some of the Mental-Mental generalizations describe connections that constitute their having a significant degree of intelligence and rationality (call this the *Rationality* condition); and (c) that some of the Mental-to-Behavior generalizations describe connections that constitute their having a significant degree of voluntary control over their bodily movements (call this the *Volitional* condition). Where these conditions are satisfied, let us refer to the generalizations in virtue of which they are satisfied as, respectively, the Perceptual generalizations, the Rationality generalizations, and the Volitional generalizations. The conjunction of these three conditions I shall call the Informed Agency condition (since informed, intelligent action requires the satisfaction of this condition). What I am claiming is that this condition must be satisfied by the psychology of a set of creatures if it is to be possible for us to have behaviorally grounded knowledge of their mental states. It is precisely when behavior can be seen as manifesting a psychology satisfying this condition that it can be seen as "intelligent" and "purposive," and as calling for an explanation in terms of mental states. When the behavior of creatures is never of this sort (as is true of trees, except in fairy stories), it is at best idle to suppose that mental states play any role in its production; such behavior is most appropriately explained in non-mentalistic terms.

What accounts for the presumption that creatures having mental states are creatures whose psychologies satisfy the Informed Agency condition? Three possible answers come to mind. (1) It might be held that for each of us this presumption is an inductive extrapolation from the fact that his own psychology satisfies this condition (this can be thought of as a version of the analogical position). (2) It might be held that explanations of behavior in terms of psychologies that satisfy this condition are always simpler than competing explanations in terms of psychologies that do not satisfy it. (3) It might be held that our mental concepts impose constraints on the ways mental states can meaningfully or consistently be supposed to be related to one another and to bodily states, and that this delimits the class of possible psychologies in such a way that only those that satisfy the Informed Agency condition are capable of explaining behavior (this can be thought of as a version of the conceptual connection view). Let us consider these in turn.

It should be noted that the Perceptual part of the Informed Agency condition seems to involve the Volitional part in a rather fundamental way; for having the ability to perceive facts about one's surroundings seems to involve having some degree of voluntary control over one's bodily movements (those of one's hands, etc., in the case of tactual perception, and those of one's head and eyes in the case of visual perception). Now in order to discover anything about one's bodily states (and their relation to one's mental states) one must satisfy the Perceptual condition (and hence also the Volitional condition), while in order to discover anything at all one must satisfy the Rationality condition. Hence, the only sort of psychology anyone could discover himself to have is one satisfying the Informed Agency condition (or at least the Perceptual and Rationality conditions). So if other parts of psychologies are possible, one's own case constitutes a biased sample (with respect to the property of satisfying the Informed Agency condition), and an inductive extrapolation from it (involving this property) would be illegitimate. And if other sorts of psychologies are not possible, the extrapolation from one's own case is superfluous. Hence (again) the analogical position seems to be of no help.

Turning now to the second answer, let us pretend that we could write out all of the sentences you would accept as expressing true propositions about how human mental states are connected with one another and with physical states of affairs. Let us say that you accept the "hypothesis" (call it H-1) that the psychology expressed by this set of sentences (or a psychology similar to it) is true of the human-appearing creatures you

see around you. Now there is a simple recipe for constructing countless other "hypotheses," incompatible with H-1, which are (assuming them to be internally consistent and conceptually coherent) just as simple as H-1 and equivalent to it in their power to predict and explain behavior. (That is, all of these hypotheses predict the same behavior on the part of a creature as H-1, given the same information about its past behavior and physical stimuli). To get such an hypothesis, start with the set of sentences associated with H-1, and systematically intersubstitute in these sentences two mental terms that differ in meaning, leaving the sentences otherwise unchanged. For example, replace "like" with "dislike" wherever it occurs, and vice versa. Or systematically interchange "believe" and "disbelieve." The set of sentences resulting from such a systematic intersubstitution will express an alternative psychology; and corresponding to each such psychology will be an hypothesis to the effect that the psychology is true of the human-appearing creatures around you. Clearly there are countless different psychologies and hypotheses we could construct in this way. And most of these will violate some part of the Informed Agency condition. For example, the psychology we get by interchanging "believe" and "disbelieve" will violate the Perceptual condion, since the corresponding hypothesis will imply that people are systematically mistaken about (and so lack the ability to perceive facts about) their physical surroundings. Yet since this hypothesis attributes to disbelief precisely the behavioral effects (as well as the causes) which hypothesis H-1 attributes to belief, it will predict the same behavior as H-1. And for the same reason, all of the alternative hypotheses constructable in this way have the same predictive power as H-1; so far as their observable consequences are concerned, the differences between these hypotheses "cancel out." Moreover, there is no obvious sense in which H-1 is "simpler" than any of the other hypotheses. Yet the other hypotheses will be full of such bizarre generalizations as "People dread, and if possible avoid, the things they like, and they seek out, and look forward to with delight, the things they dislike." Anyone would reject as absurd the suggestion that it is perhaps one of these hypotheses, rather than H-1, that is true of his friends and neighbors. But this rejection cannot be justified on the grounds that H-1 is superior to the other hypotheses in simplicity and explanatory power.

It may be suggested that what is decisive here is our adherence to the principle "Like causes have like effects." You know (to a considerable extent) what the causes and effects of mental states are in your own case, and you get a simpler account of the world (other things being equal) if you suppose that they are the same in other people; *given* that H-1 is true of you, the simplest hypothesis is that it is true of other similarly behaving creatures as well (even though H-1 is not itself simpler than other hypotheses that could equally well predict the behavior of these creatures). This suggestion has some force. But it is doubtful that it adequately explains the confidence with which we reject the hypotheses that result from systematic intersubstitution in H-1. Let us divide thy generalizations in the H-1 psychology into two groups, A and B; group A will consist of the Perceptual, Rationality, and Volitional generalizations, and group B will consist of all the rest (including such generalizations as "Angry people tend to scowl," "Happy people tend to smile," "Fearful people tend to tremble," and "Embarrassed people tend to blush"). One way of producing an alternative psychology would be to leave the group A generalizations unchanged while systematically intersubstituting certain mental terms in the group B generalizations. Another way would be to leave the group B generalizations unchanged while systematically intersubstituting certain mental terms in the group A generalizations. Psychologies produced in the first way do not violate the Informed Agency condition, while those produced in the second way do violate it. Clearly the behavior of actual human beings is not satisfactorily explained or predicted by psychologies of either of these sorts. But whereas we can imagine fairly easily that a psychology of the first sort might be true of the Martians (e.g., that the same Perceptual, Rationality, and Volitional generalizations are true of them as of us, but that they smile when angry, scowl when happy, blush only when at ease, and so on), it seems quite out of the question that a psychology of the second sort should be true of them (e.g., that while smiles, scowls, blushes, etc. have the same causes and effects in them as in us, believing has in them the causes, and the effects on voluntary behavior, that disbe-

lieving has in us, and vice versa). That matters strike us this way cannot, I think, be explained by our adherence to the principle "Like causes have like effects"; for given that H-1 is true of us, that principle is violated as much by the hypothesis that a psychology of the first sort is true of the Martians as by the hypothesis that a psychology of the second sort is true of them.

This brings us to the third and last explanation of the presumption that other subjects of mental states have psychologies that satisfy the Informed Agency condition, namely that this is a consequence of constraints imposed by the very concepts of mental states (or, if you like, by the very meaning of mental terms). While I have characterized this as a version of the conceptual connection view, it is very different from behaviorism, at least as behaviorism is usually conceived; for it does not imply that mental concepts are "reducible" to physical concepts. Rather, we have here a version of what recently has been called the "causal" or "functional" theory of mental states and processes. Such a theory says, roughly, that what defines a mental state as being the mental state it is (e.g., what makes it a particular belief, or a particular desire) is some fact about the causal or functional role it plays in a complex system of states which include physical states (including behavior) as well as other mental states.[9] This explains why we get outrageous results if we intersubstitute (for example) the terms "believe" and "disbelieve" and the terms "belief" and "disbelief" in the psychology H-1, leaving it otherwise unchanged. For this assigns to belief the causal or functional role which H-1 assigns to disbelief, and vice versa; and this will be incoherent if belief and disbelief are *defined* by roles assigned them in H-1. On the version of this theory suggested here, it is not all of the causal facts about mental states, but only (or primarily) those that are relevant to the satisfaction of the Informed Agency condition, that make them the mental states they are.

Given the legitimacy of the presumption that the Informed Agency condition is satisfied by the psychologies of subjects of mental states, it would seem that inference from behavior to other minds can be justified if any "inference to the best explanation" can be justified (and so if any sort of science is possible).

But we are not out of the woods yet. For how does this account deal with the problem of the "inverted spectrum" raised at the beginning of our discussion? While it seems that we can dismiss on conceptual (or "semantic") grounds the hypothesis that the causal role played in my mental life by believing and liking is played in yours by disbelieving and disliking (and vice versa), our psychologies being otherwise alike, it does not seem at all evident that we can dismiss in this way the hypothesis that your color spectrum is inverted relative to mine, our psychologies being otherwise alike. For one thing, the psychology attributed to you by this hypothesis does not seem to violate the Informed Agency condition (as is indicated, perhaps, by the fact that I can imagine discovering that my color spectrum is inverted relative to what it was yesterday). Yet I would like to think that I know, or am entitled to believe, that (for example) blue things look to you the way blue things, rather than yellow things, look to me. Perhaps, although I doubt it, such beliefs can be justified by an appeal to the principle "Like causes have like effects" (if this could be shown, it would amount to a partial vindication of the analogical position). Perhaps, but again I doubt it, the inverted spectrum hypothesis is, after all, meaningless or conceptually incoherent. My own belief is that in order to solve this problem we will have to delve deeply into the philosophy of perception; among other things, we need to consider what sort of "thing" a sense-impression or sense-experience is, and what it is for sense-impressions to be phenomenally similar or different. Such an investigation cannot be undertaken here. But until this problem is solved, no account of our knowledge of other minds can claim to be satisfactory.

NOTES

1. See Taylor, 1966. (Full references are given in the bibliography following.)

2. I might, of course, discover that whenever I feel pain in your body you report, if asked, that you feel pain in the same place; eventually this might enable me to ascribe pain to you with confidence simply on the basis of the fact I feel pain in your body. But here the supposition that the pains I feel in your body are *your* pains plays no role in explaining my ability to know what you feel. I could acquire the same sort of ability (an ability to know that you are in pain without asking you and without observing your behavior) by noticing that whenever I feel an itch on my nose you report, if asked, that you feel pain—eventually this might entitle me to ascribe pain to you with confidence on the basis of the fact that I feel

an itch on my nose. In both cases, my knowledge of your state of mind would be derivative from my behaviorally based knowledge; only because I can take your behavior as an indication as to whether you are in pain can I come to be entitled, on inductive grounds, to take something I feel (whether it be an itch on my nose or a pain in your arm) as showing that you feel pain.

3. The relevant works of these writers are listed in the bibliography.

4. On this point, and on that discussed in the following paragraph, I have learned from A. J. Ayer's discussions of these matters.

5. The central idea in the objection that follows, that the argument from analogy is illegitimate because it extrapolates from a logically biased sample, is due to Alvin Plantinga (see Plantinga, 1967). But my development of this idea is very different from his.

6. Michael Slote (see Slote, 1970) has pointed out that there are simple inductive arguments that do not satisfy this condition but which seem nevertheless to be acceptable. If I have examined millions of fruit flies, and all of those born before last Monday are now dead, this surely gives me good inductive evidence that all fruit flies are mortal. Yet it is not possible that I should establish by observation that something is a counter-instance to (negative instances of) the generalization "All fruit flies are mortal," i.e., is an immortal fruit fly. It should be noted, however, that the generalization "All fruit flies are mortal," while not itself falsifiable by observation, is a deductive consequence of other generalizations that are also supported by the available evidence, and which are falsifiable by observation. For example, the evidence supports the falsifiable generalization "No fruit fly lives more than a month," which of course entails that all fruit flies are mortal. This suggests that we modify our requirement to read "The conclusion of a simple indictive inference must either itself be falsifiable by observation, or if it is not, must be entailed by another generalization which is falsifiable by observation and is supported by the available evidence." But this requirement is too easy to satisfy. The generalization "All elephants are observed" is entailed by the generalization "All elephants are observed and non-pink," and the latter is falsifiable by observation (we *could* observe a pink elephant) and supported by the available evidence (in the sense that only positive instances of it have in fact been observed). Yet both of these generalizations are clearly false, and the simple inductive inferences to them are unacceptable and ought to be ruled by our condition. This can be achieved as follows. First, we will say that a proposition P is a logically independent conjunct of the conjunction "P and Q" if it neither implies nor is implied by Q. Now we will modify our condition to read as follows: "The conclusion of a legitimate simple inductive reference must be entailed by a generalization (which may be the conclusion itself) which is falsifiable by observation, supported by the available evidence, and not equivalent to a conjunction having as a logically independent conjunct a proposition that is not falsifiable by observation." As the reader can verify for himself, this condition is satisfied by "All fruit flies are mortal," but not by either "All elephants are observed" or "All elephants are observed and non-pink." I think that this adequately captures the requirement that the conclusion of a simple inductive inference must be such that the sample will not be logically biased.

7. For this notion, See Gilbert Harman, "The Inference to the Best Explanation," *The Philosophical Review* LXXIV (1965): 88–95. See also Harman's *Thought* (Princeton, 1973).

8. On this point, see Price, 1938. For criticism of Price, see Malcolm, 1958.

9. See Lewis, 1967. See also D. M. Armstrong, *A Materialist Theory of Mind* (London, 1968).

SELECTED BIBLIOGRAPHY

Ayer, A. J. "One's Knowledge of Other Minds." In *Philosophical Essays.* London, 1954.

Ayer, A. J. *The Problem of Knowledge.* Hammondsworth, 1956, ch. 5.

Broad, C. D. *Mind and Its Place in Nature.* London, 1925, ch. VII.

Chihara, C. S., and Fodor, J. A. "Operationism and Ordinary language." *American Philosophical Quarterly* II (1965): 281–95.

Cook, John W. "Human Beings." In *Studies in the Philosophy of Wittgenstein,* edited by Winch. London, 1969.

Hampshire, S. "The Analogy of Feeling." *Mind* LXI (1952): 1–12.

Hyslop, A. and Jackson, F. C. "The Analogical Inference to Other Minds." *American Philosophical Quarterly* 9(1972): 168–76.

Lewis, D. "An Argument for the Identity Theory." *The Journal of Philosophy* LXIII, 1 (January 6, 1966): 17–25. Reprinted in *Materialism and the Mind-Body Problem,* edited by Rosenthal. Englewood Cliffs, N.J., 1971.

Locke, Don. *Myself and Others.* Oxford, 1968.

Lycan, W. Gregory. "Non-inductive Evidence; Recent Work on Wittgenstein's 'Criteria.'" *American Philosophical Quarterly* 8 (1971): 109–125.

Malcolm, N. "Knowledge of Other Minds," *The Journal of Philosophy* LV (1958): 969–78. Reprinted in Malcolm, *Knowledge and Certainty,* Englewood Cliffs, N.J., 1963, and in various anthologies.

Mill, J. S. *An Examination of Sir William Hamilton's Philosophy.* 6th ed. New York, 1889, pp. 243–44.

Pap, A. "Other Minds and the Principle of Verifiability." *Revue internationale de Philosophie* No. 17–18 (1951): 280–306. Reprinted in *New Readings in Philosophical Analysis* edited by Feigl, Sellars and Lehrer. New York, 1972.

Price, H. H. "Our Evidence for the Existence of Other Minds." *Philosophy* 13 (1938): 425–56.

Putnam, H. "Robots: Machines or Artificaly Created Life?" *The Journal of Philosophy* LXI (1964): 668–81. Reprinted in *Modern Materialism: Readings on Mind-Body Identity* edited by O'Connor. New York, 1969, and elsewhere.

Putnam, H. "The Mental Life of Some Machines." In Castaneda (ed.). Reprinted in *Modern Materialism,* edited by O'Connor.

Shorter, J. M. "Other Minds," in *The Encyclopedia of Philosophy,* Vol. 6, edited by Edwards. New York, 1967.

Slote, M. *Reason and Scepticism.* London, 1970, ch. 4.

Strawson, P. F. "Persons," in *Concepts, and the Mind-Body Problem,* edited by Feigl, Scriven, and Maxwell. Minneapolis, 1958. Widely reprinted. A revised and expanded version of this paper occurs as chapter III of Strawson's *Individuals,* London, 1959.

Taylor, D. M. "The Incommunicability of Content." *Mind* LXXV (1966): 527–41.

Thomson, J. F. "The Argument from Analogy and Our Knowledge of Other Minds." *Mind* LX (1951): 336–59.

Watling, J. "Ayer on Other Minds." *Theoria* XX (1954): 43–58.

Wisdom, J. *Other Minds.* Oxford, 1952.

Wittgenstein, L. *Philosophical Investigations.* Edited by G. E. M. Anscombe and R. Rhees, trans. by G. E. M. Anscombe. Oxford, 1953.

Ziff, P. "The Simplicity of Other Minds." *The Journal of Philosophy* LXII (1965): 575–84. Reprinted in Feigl, Sellars and Lehrer (eds.), *New Readings in Philosophical Analysis,* New York, 1972.

The A Priori

IMMANUEL KANT

Introduction to *The Critique of Pure Reason**

I

Of the Difference between Pure and Empirical Cognition.

It is beyond a doubt that all our knowledge begins with experience. For by what should our faculties be roused to act, if not by objects that affect our senses, and thus partly of themselves produce impressions, partly, again, bring the understanding itself into movement, in order to compare these, to join or disjoin them, and in this manner work up such crude material of the intimations of sense into a cognition or recognition of objects which is named experience. So far as time is concerned, then, no cognition of ours precedes experience, and with experience all our knowledge begins.

But, though all our knowledge begins *with* experience, it does not follow that therefore it all derives *from* experience. For it is just possible that experience is itself a compound. It is just possible, that is, that there is in experience, besides what is due to the impression of sense something in addition that comes from our faculties themselves (when merely acting because of impression); and in that case, it would take long practice, it may be, to enable us to distinguish the latter, and separate it from the former.

It is at least not a question to be summarily dismissed, but one that demands more particular

consideration, this, to wit: whether there really be such component part of knowledge as is independent of experience and, indeed, of any impression of sense whatever? Such component part of knowledge, did it exist, were alone to be truly termed *a priori;* and it would evidently stand in contradistinction to what other component part of knowledge is called empirical: the latter, namely, having its source only *a posteriori,* or in experience.

The expression *a priori,* at the same time, is not precise enough to designate the entire sense of the preceding question. For of many a mere empirical fact, we say, that we know it *a priori,* simply because we do not directly derive it from experience, but from a general rule; and this, even notwithstanding that the rule itself may be so derived. For example, we say of a man that shall have undermined his house, he might have known *a priori* that it would fall in; he had no occasion to wait for the experience of the actual event. Nevertheless, he could not have known this absolutely *a priori.* For that bodies are heavy and, consequently, fall when their supports are withdrawn—this, at least, he must have known by experience beforehand.

In what follows, therefore, we shall understand by cognitions *a priori,* not such as are independent of this or that experience, but such as are totally independent of any experience whatsoever. Opposed to these are empirical cognitions, or such as are only possible *a posteriori,* or from experience. Pure again, are those *a priori* cogni-

*Immanuel Kant. *The Critique of Pure Reason,* Introduction, Parts I-VI. Trans. J. H. Stirling (Edinburgh: Oliver, 1881). First published in German in 1781.

tions which are quite free from all and every empirical admixture. Thus, for example, the proposition, that all change has its cause, is an *an priori* proposition; but it is not, at the same time, *purely* such, for change is an idea which can only be derived from experience.

II

We do possess certain a priori *Cognitions, and even Common Sense is never without such.*

What is wanted here is a criterion, by means of which we may, with certainty, distinguish what is pure from what is empirical. Now experience informs us that something *is* so and so, but not that it cannot be otherwise. *Firstly,* then, should there be a proposition such that it is thought together with its necessity, then it is a judgment *a priori;* and, if underived from any other absolutely *a priori. Secondly,* experience extends to its judgments never strict or true, but only (through induction) assumptive or comparative universality; so that, properly, it can only be said, so far as we are yet aware, there is no exception to this or that rule. Should any judgment, then, be thought in strict universality, or so, that is, that exceptions are impossible, we may be sure that that judgment is no derivative from experience, but directly *a priori.* Empirical universality, therefore, is only an arbitrary raising of validity from that which obtains in most cases to that which holds good in all, as in the proposition, for example, that all bodies are heavy. Whereas, when strict universality attaches to a judgment, such universality points to a special cognitive source, namely, to a faculty of cognition *a priori.* Necessity and strict universality, therefore, are sure criteria of *a priori* cognition, and inseparably found together. In practice, however, as it is easier, now to apply the one and now the other, it will be advisable to avail ourselves, as occasion may suggest, of either criterion separately; for, even separately, either of them is quite infallible.

Now, it is easy to show that there actually are in our knowledge such necessary and, in the strictest sense, universal (consequently pure *a priori*) judgments. Would we have an example from science, we have only to turn to any proposition in mathematics; while, as for the most ordinary common sense, there is obviously to hand, by way of instance, the proposition that every change

must have a cause, where the very notion cause so manifestly implies necessity (of connection with an effect) and strict universality (of rule), that it would be altogether lost did we derive it, like Hume, from our conjoining what simply follows with what simply precedes, through the mere habit of the experience, and the consequent simple custom of connecting ideas (where the necessity could be only subjective). Besides demonstrating the actual existence in our knowledge of principles *a priori* by a reference to fact, we might even *a priori* prove as much. We might demonstrate, that is, the indispensable necessity of such principles to the very possibility of experience. For how should there be any certainly in experience, were all the rules in it only empirical and (consequently) contingent? It were hardly possible, evidently, to allow any such rules the name of first principles. But it may suffice here to have demonstrated the fact of the possession of pure cognition on our part, together with the signs of the latter. Nay, not merely judgments, but even certain ideas, may claim for themselves an *a priori* origin. Suppose, in the case of our empirical idea of a *body,* we successively withdraw all its empirical constituents, such as colour, consistency, weight, even impenetrability, we shall still find it impossible to withdraw the space it occupied. This space will still remain when the body itself has disappeared. In like manner, if, in regard to our empirical idea of an object in general, whether corporeal or incorporeal, we withdraw all properties known to us from experience, we shall still be unable to withdraw from it those by which we think it as substance, or as attributive to substance (though this notion of substance has more determination in it than that of an object in general). We must, therefore, overborne by the necessity with which said notion forces itself upon us, admit that it has its seat *a priori* in our faculties of cognition.

III

Philosophy stands in need of a Science which shall determine the Possibility, the Principles, and the Limits of all a priori *Cognition.*

But, to go still further, it is a fact that there are cognitions which even quit the bounds of all possible experience, and actually, by means of ideas for which, so far as experience goes, no correspondent object can be found, assume to extend the range of our judgments beyond any experience whatever.

And just in these latter cognitions, transcending as they do the world of sense, and unaccompanied by experience to guide and correct them, there lie interests of reason which we hold to be of far greater consequence and loftier aim than anything or all that understanding can teach us in the domain of experience. In these cognitions, indeed, even at the risk of failure, we rather venture everything than, for any reason of doubt, or carelessness and indifference, consent to forego what is of such an import. Such unavoidable problems of pure reason's own are God. Free Will, and Immortality. The science, again, which, as well in the end it contemplates, as in all its complement of means, is alone directed to the solution of these, we name metaphysic—a science that, in its procedure, starts as yet only dogmatically; that is, having instituted no previous inquiry into sufficiency or insufficiency on the part of reason for so great an enterprise, it yet confidently undertakes completion of it.

Now, it seems no more than natural that, once we have left the solid ground of experience, we should not forthwith proceed to build, without having carefully assured ourselves, first of all, in regard to a foundation, and that, too, all the more, should we find ourselves provided only with principles which are unauthenticated, and have come to us we know not whence. It seems no more than natural, I say, that, rather than this, we should have long before started the question, How have we got to these principles, and of what extent, import, and value are they? In effect, nothing is more natural when by the word *natural* we understand what, rightly and reasonably, ought to take place; but, on the other hand, when we mean by *natural* only what usually takes place, then nothing is more natural than that any such preliminary inquiry should remain long null. For the fact is, that some of the principles in view (as the mathematical ones) possess authentication from of old, and reflect, consequently, a similar presumption on to others which may in reality be altogether different. Besides, when one is beyond experience, one is safe not to be contradicted by experience; and, eager as we are to extend our knowledge, only when so contradicted is it that we can allow ourselves a

halt. But even this may be avoided, should we be but careful with our fictions: for fictions, in such circumstances, they must be. On the other hand, mathematics afford us a splendid example of success in the cognition in question. Objects and ideas, it is true, are considered there only so far as they are capable of being exhibited in objective representation. But this is easily overlooked, because said representation can itself be *a priori* given, and is, consequently, scarcely to be distinguished from a pure notion proper. Led away by such a proof of the power of reason, we can see no bounds to the extension we desire. The light dove, in feeling the resistance of the air its free flight cleaves, might very well think to itself that it would have a still better chance in a space that were void. Even so Plato, because of the narrow limits it set the understanding, forsook the world of sense; and, beyond its bounds buoyed up on the wings of the ideas, committed himself to the blank inane of the pure intellect. He did not perceive that, with every effort His progress was null; for foothold he had none against which steadied, he might have exerted his strength to bring reason from the spot. It is, however, an ordinary fate of speculative reason, to complete its edifice at the soonest, and only then to examine whether the foundations are well laid or not. All manner of excuses, rather, is indulged in to comfort us in regard of their entire sufficiency, or even to prove such late, dangerous examination wholly inexpedient. What saves us during the work from any fear or suspicion, deceiving us with apparent substantiality indeed, is this. A great part, perhaps the greatest, of the business of our reason consists in the analysis of ideas which we have already formed of objects. This furnishes us with a number of cognitions which, although they are nothing more than elucidations or explanations what is already (confusedly) implied, are still, at least in form, regarded as new: in matter or contents, not extending our notions, they explicate them. But this process furnishing, as it does, an actual *a priori* cognition, accompanied, too, by a certain safe gain, our reason interpolates unawares into this false show of extension allegations of quite another nature; foisting in with given notions other notions quite alien, and that too, *a priori*, without our knowing how or whence these latter come, or even without any such question being ever once entertained by us

Accordingly, I shall treat directly now in the beginning of the difference between these two modes of cognition.

IV

Of the Difference between Analytic and Synthetic Judgments.

In all judgments in which the relation of a subject to a predicate is thought (affirmatives alone considered—application to negatives being afterwards easy) this relation is possible in two ways. Either the predicate B belongs to the subject A as something that (covertly) is contained in it; or B lies completely outside of the notion A, though possessing connexion with it. In the first case I call the judgment *analytic;* in the second *synthetic.* Analytic judgments (the affirmative ones) are therefore those in which the connexion of the predicate with the subject is thought through identity; synthetic, again, those in which this connexion is thought without identity. We might name them also, the former, judgments of explication; the latter, judgments of extension. The former, namely, add in the predicate, nothing to the notion of the subject, but only separate this notion into its subnotional parts, which parts are already (obscurely) thought *in* the notion. The latter, on the other hand, add to the subject a predicate which was not at all thought in it, and could not by any analysis have been extracted from it. For example, if I say, All bodies are extended, this is an analytic judgment. For, in order that I may find extension as connected with it, I need not leave what notion itself I attach to *body.* I have only to analyze it, or open my eyes to what complex I think in it, to become aware of this predicate as contained in it. The judgment, therefore, is analytic. On the other hand, if I say, All bodies are heavy, in that case the predicate is something quite different from anything I think in the mere notion of a body as such. The addition of such a predicate produces, therefore, a synthetic judgment.

Judgments of experience, as such, are all synthetic. For it were absurd to have recourse to experience for an analytic judgment, seeing that I need not go out of my notion itself to get the judgment, nor require, therefore, any testimony of experience in the case. That a body is extended is a proposition *a priori* evident, and not a judg-ment of experience. For, without having recourse to experience, I have already in the notion all the conditions necessary for my judgment. I have only, according to the principle of contradiction, to extract the predicate from the notion. In so acting, I become aware, also, of the necessity of the judgment, and necessity is no declaration of experience. On the other hand, although I do not include, in the notion of a body in general, the predicate heavy, still said notion (body) designates an object of experience, by a part of experience, to which part I can add other parts of the same experience, not comprehended in the first. I know the notion body already analytically, say, through the characters extension, impenetrability, figure, etc., which the notion simply implies. But now I extend my knowledge, and in once more consulting experience (from which I had derived this notion of body), I find, always conjoined with the said characters, that also of weight, which, as a predicate, therefore, I add synthetically to the notion in question. It is, therefore, on experience that the possibility is founded of the synthesis of the predicate heavy with the subject body, because, though the one is not implied in the other, still both notions, as parts of a whole (namely experience, which is itself a synthetic conjunction of perceptions), belong to each other, if only contingently.

But, in the case of *a priori* synthetic judgments, this expedient (of experience) is altogether inapplicable. If, in such reference, I am to go beyond the notion A in order to recognise another, B, as connected with it, on what do I support myself, and by what is the synthesis made possible, seeing that I have not the advantage in this case of looking about me for it in the field of experience? Let us take the proposition, All that happens has a cause. In the notion of something that happens (an effect), I think something come to be, which, therefore, had a certain time before it, etc., and from this something, as it is there before me, it is possible for me to deduce various analytic judgments. But the notion cause lies quite out of this notion. Denoting something quite different from that which happens (the effect), it is not at all implied in it. How do I come, then, to say of any fact in event something quite different from the fact itself, and to recognise the notion cause, though not contained in said fact, nevertheless as belonging to it, and that, too, necessarily? What is the unknown x on which the understanding supports itself, when it believes itself to discover from the notion A a predicate B, alien to it, but which it judges, nevertheless, to be connected with it? It cannot be experience, because the relative proposition adds the latter to the former, not only with a greater universality than experience can supply, but even with the expression of necessity, and consequently wholly *a priori* or through mere notions. Well now, the entire end and aim of our speculative cognition *a priori* concern such synthetic principles, or judgments of extension. For the analytic ones are certainly of the greatest importance and necessity, but, here with us, they are available only for the sake of that precison of ideas which is required for an accurate and complete synthesis, as an acquisition veritably new.

V

In all the Rational Theoretical Sciences, Synthetic a priori *judgments are present as Principles.*

1. Mathematical judgments are all synthetic. This proposition seems hitherto to have escaped the observation of the anatomists of human reason—nay, to be directly opposed to all their suppositions, although it is undeniably certain and very important in result. For, because it was found that mathematical reasonings proceed all of them on the principle of contradiction (as the nature, indeed, of apodictic certainty requires) there ensued the conviction that by means of the same principle also it was that the fundamental propositions themselves were to be seen into. In this they erred. For a synthetic proposition may certainly be understood from the principle of contradiction: still, only in this way, that another synthetic proposition is presupposed from which it may be inferred,—but never independently.

First of all, it is to be remarked that mathematical judgments as such are always *a priori,* and not empirical; for they bring with them necessity, which is not to be got from experience. Should this, however, as a general proposition, appear doubtful, I will confine it to *pure* mathematic, the very notion of which implies that it is not concerned with empirical, but only with pure *a priori* cognition.

We might be apt to think at first that the proposition $7 + 5 = 12$ is merely an analytic proposition, which follows from the notion of a sum of 7 and 5, according to the principle of contradiction. But if we look closer, we shall find that the notion of the sum of 7 and 5 implies nothing but the uniting of the two numbers into one, there being no thought, at the same time, of what this one number itself is which comprehends the two. The notion of 12 is not thought in this, that I think to myself the uniting of 7 and 5: and I may analyze my notion of such possible sum as long as I please without finding the 12 in it. We must go out of these notions, and take help from perception. We must assist ourselves, that is, by such objective representation as corresponds to one of the two numbers (say five points or the five fingers), and, so assisted, add the units of the number perceived (5), one by one, to the notion of the number thought (7). I take first the number 7; next, for the notion of the 5, I refer to my fingers as perceived; and then I add the units (which together constitute the number 5), one by one, in guidance of the representation perceived, to the number 7. In this way, for result, I see the number 12 emerge. That 7 should be added to 5, I have indeed thought in the notion of a sum $7 + 5$, but not that this sum is equal to the number 12. An arithmetical proposition is, therefore, always synthetic, as we may more distinctly discern, should we assume somewhat larger numbers; in which case it will clearly appear that, let us turn and twist our notions as we may, we never can, by mere analysis of notions, and unassisted by perception, discover their sum.

Just as little is any proposition of pure geometry analytic. That the straight line between any two points is the shortest, is a synthetic proposition. For my notion of straight includes in it nothing of quantity, but only a quality. The notion shortest is wholly something adscititious, something added to it, and cannot by any analysis be derived from the notion straight line. Perception, then, must be here called in to assist, and only by its intervention is the synthesis possible.

Some few propositions which are presupposed in geometry are, it is true, really analytic and rest on the principle of contradiction. They serve, however, only as identical propositions, for the chain of the method, and not as principles. For example, it is said a is equal to a, that is, the whole is equal to itself; or $a + b$ is greater than a, which is, the whole is greater than its part. And yet even these, that pass valid on the authority of mere notions, are only allowed place in mathematic because they can be exhibited in perception. What commonly leads us here to suppose that the predicate of such apodictic judgments is already contained in our notion, and that, consequently, the judgment is analytic, is solely the peculiarity of the expression. To a given notion, namely, we must think a certain predicate, and this necessity is already present with the notions. But the question is not what we must think *to* the given notion, but what we actually, though obscurely, think *in* it; and then we see that the predicate belongs to the notion, necessarily indeed, not, however, because of being thought in it, but because of a perception which must be added to it.

2. Natural philosophy possesses synthetic *a priori* judgments as principles. I will only adduce a couple of propositions in example; as that in all changes of the corporeal world the quantity of matter remains the same, or that in all communication of motion, action and reaction are always alike. In both, not only the necessity is clear, and by consequence their *a priori* origin, but also the fact that they are synthetic propositions. For in the notion of matter I do not think its permanence, but only its presence in space as filling it. That is, I actually go beyond the notion of matter in order to think *a priori to* it something that I did not think *in* it. The proposition, therefore, is not analytic, but synthetic, and yet *a priori;* so it is with the other propositions of the pure part of the science.

3. In metaphysic (though we should only regard it as a science which has been hitherto desiderated, but which, from the very nature of human reason, nevertheless, is a science indispensable), synthetic cognitions *a priori* simply *must be.* For it is not its business merely to unravel notions which we *a priori* form of things. On the contrary, the business here is to extend our *a priori* cognition; and to that we must avail ourselves of such propositions as add on something beyond the given notion, something not contained in it; and in this way, by means of synthetic *a priori* judgments alone, advance indeed so far that experience itself is unable to follow us. For example, there is the proposition, among others, that the world must have a beginning. And by this we see that metaphysic, at least

in its aim, consists of pure *a priori* synthetic propositions.

VI
General Problem of Pure Reason.

It is already not a little won, if we can bring a variety of questions under the formula of a single problem. For in this way, through exact determination of it, we not only lighten to ourselves our own work, but we facilitate for everybody else as well, who will examine it, the judgment whether we have done justice to our own design or not. The problem proper of pure reason, now, is comprised in the question, How are *a priori* synthetic judgments possible?

That metaphysic, hitherto, has remained in so vacillating a condition of uncertainty and contradiction, is solely to be ascribed to the fact that we have not sooner attained to the conception of this problem, or even to that of the distinction between analytic and synthetic judgments. On the solution of this problem now, or on a satisfactory proof that the possibility it would wish demonstrated does not exist, it depends whether metaphysic shall stand or fall. David Hume, who of all philosophers came nearest to this problem, thought it not out, however, by any means determinately enough, or in its generality, but merely took his stand by the synthetic proposition of the connexion of the effect with its cause (*principium causalitatis*). Accordingly, he assumed to make out that such a proposition is, *a priori,* wholly impossible. His reasonings went to prove, indeed, that all we call metaphysic terminates in a mere delusion of a supposed insight on the part of reason, into what in effect is merely borrowed from experience, and has only taken on, through custom, the semblance of necessity. But such an allegation, subversive as it is of all pure philosophy, would never have occurred to him had he but caught sight of our problem in its universality. For he would have then been conscious that, on his argument, even pure mathematic would be impossible, inasmuch as it is a science built on *a priori* synthetic propositions—a conclusion, plainly, from which his own good sense would certainly have saved him.

In the solution of the above problem there is involved, at the same time, the possibility of an application of pure reason in foundation and completion of all the sciences in which any theoretical *a priori* cognition of objects is concerned; that is, an answer to the questions, How is pure mathematic possible? How is pure natural philosophy possible?

Of these sciences, inasmuch as they once for all are, we may certainly with propriety ask, how they are possible; for that they must be possible is demonstrated by their actuality.[1] As for metaphysic, again, we may reasonably doubt of possibility in its regard, in view, namely, of its unsatisfactory progress hitherto, as well as of the fact that, considering its essential aim, we cannot say it has, in any instance, actually been.

And yet, again, knowledge of this kind is really, in a certain sense, to be assumed as given, or metaphysic is actual after all—if not as science, then as natural capability (*metaphysica naturalis*). For human reason, not moved by any vanity of mere learning, but impelled by necessity of its very nature, strives ever irrepressibly forward towards such questions as cannot possibly be answered by any mere empirical consideration, or principles derived thence. So it is that really in all men, so soon as reason has advanced to speculation, a metaphysic of some kind always has been and always will be. And now, from the same source, we have this question also: How is metaphysic as natural capability possible? That is, how do the questions which pure reason starts for herself, and which, in some way, she *must* answer—how do these questions originate in the very nature of reason as such?

It is the fact, however, that unavoidable contradictions have always shown themselves in any attempt yet to answer these natural questions (*e.g.*, whether the world has had a beginning, or whether it exists from all eternity, etc.)? We cannot, therefore, remain satisfied with a mere natural capability for metaphysic, or with the mere faculty of reason itself, in possession of which there is always that necessity of a metaphysic of some kind, be it what it may. It must be possible, rather, to bring matters relatively to some certainty as concerns either the knowing or the not knowing of the objects in question, either the ability or the inability of reason to judge in their regard. That is, it must be possible for us either confidently to extend, or else duly limit, reason.

This last question, which flows from the general problem, were rightly put thus: How is metaphysic as a science possible?

A criticism of reason leads, therefore, at last necessarily to science; while, without criticism, dogmatically to set to work with reason, results only in groundless allegations, to which others equally specious may be opposed, and the end, consequently, is scepticism.

Neither will this science be of great and forbidding extent. It is not with the objects of reason, namely, the multiplicity of which is infinite, but with reason's self, that it has to do. The problems it considers take birth in the bosom of reason only: they are not imposed upon reason by the nature of things, which are different from it, but by its own nature. Accordingly, therefore if reason has, first of all, come perfectly to know its own powers in regard of objects which may be offered in experience, it must be easy fully and surely to determine the range and extent of its desired application beyond all bounds of experience.

We may and must, therefore, regard all these previous attempts dogmatically to bring about a metaphysic as, in effect, null. For, whatever there may be of analytic in the one or the other of them, as regards the mere dissection of the notions which *a priori* attend our reason, such material is not the end and aim of, but only a preparation for, metaphysic proper. To this science it belongs, namely, to extend our synthetic *a priori* knowledge, and to that, said analytic material is inapplicable, as it merely shows what is contained in those notions, but not how we *a priori* attain to them. Accordingly, we are not enabled thereby to determine their due and valid use in regard of the objects of cognition generally. It is no great hardship to abandon such pretensions wholly, seeing that the undeniable and dogmatically inevitable contradictions of reason have long since cost every previous metaphysic all its credit. It will demand more self-reliance, in view of the difficulty within and the opposition without, to resist, in regard to a science indispensable to human reason (whose root, let us hew off whatever actual stems we may, it is impossible to tear up), discouragement from the attempt to further it, once for all at last, into a prosperous and fruitful growth, by means of another, and, to those in the past, wholly opposed method.

NOTES

1. This may be doubted as regards a pure natural philosophy. But we have only to look to the first propositions of physic proper (empirical), as the permanence of matter in quantity, inertia, the equality of action and reaction, etc., to be convinced that they consitute a *physician puram* (*or rationalem*), which certainly deserves to be separately established, in its whole extent, whether large or limited, as science proper.

A. J. AYER

The A Priori*

The view of philosophy which we have adopted may, I think, fairly be described as a form of empiricism. For it is characteristic of an empiricist to eschew metaphysics, on the ground that every factual proposition must refer to sense-experience. And even if the conception of philosophizing as an activity of analysis is not to be discovered in the traditional theories of empiricists, we have seen that it is implicit in their practice. At the same time, it must be made clear that, in calling ourselves empiricists, we are not avowing a belief in any of the psychological doctrines which are commonly associated with empiricism. For, even if these doctrines were valid, their validity would be independent of the validity of any philosophical thesis. It could be established only by observation, and not by the purely logical considerations upon which our empiricism rests.

Having admitted that we are empiricists, we must now deal with the objection that is commonly brought against all forms of empiricism; the objection, namely, that it is impossible on empiricist principles to account for our knowledge of necessary truths. For, as Hume conclusively showed, no general proposition whose validity is subject to the test of actual experience can ever be logically certain. No matter how often it is verified in practice, there still remains the possibility that it will be confuted on some future occasion. The fact that a law has been substan-

tiated in $n-1$ cases affords no logical guarantee that it will be substantiated in the nth case also, no matter how large we take n to be. And this means that no general proposition referring to a matter of fact can ever be shown to be necessarily and universally true. It can at best be a probable hypothesis. And this, we shall find, applies not only to general propositions, but to all propositions which have a factual content. They can none of them ever become logically certain. This conclusion, which we shall elaborate later on, is one which must be accepted by every consistent empiricist. It is often thought to involve him in complete scepticism; but this is not the case. For the fact that the validity of a proposition cannot be logically guaranteed in no way entails that it is irrational for us to believe it. On the contrary, what is irrational is to look for a guarantee where none can be forthcoming; to demand certainty where probability is all that is obtainable. We have already remarked upon this, in referring to the work of Hume. And we shall make the point clearer when we come to treat of probability, in explaining the use which we make of empirical propositions. We shall discover that there is nothing perverse or paradoxical about the view that all the "truths" of science and common sense are hypotheses; and consequently that the fact that it involves this view constitutes no objection to the empiricist thesis.

Where the empiricist does encounter difficulty is in connection with the truths of formal logic and mathematics. For whereas a scientific gener-

---

*From A. J. Ayer, *Language, Truth, and Logic* (London: Victor Gollancz, Ltd., 1936), pp. 71–87. Reprinted by permission of the publisher.

alization is readily admitted to be fallible, the truths of mathematics and logic appear to everyone to be necessary and certain. But if empiricism is correct no proposition which has a factual content can be necessary or certain. Accordingly the empiricist must deal with the truths of logic and mathematics in one of the two following ways: he must say either that they are not necessary truths, in which case he must account for the universal conviction that they are; or he must say that they have no factual content, and then he must explain how a proposition which is empty of all factual content can be true and useful and surprising.

If neither of these courses proves satisfactory, we shall be obliged to give way to rationalism. We shall be obliged to admit that there are some truths about the world which we can know independently of experience; that there are some properties which we can ascribe to all objects, even though we cannot conceivably observe that all objects have them. And we shall have to accept it as a mysterious inexplicable fact that our thought has this power to reveal to us authoritatively the nature of objects which we have never observed. Or else we must accept the Kantian explanation which, apart from the epistemological difficulties which we have already touched on, only pushes the mystery a stage further back.

It is clear that any such concession to rationalism would upset the main argument of this book. For the admission that there were some facts about the world which could be known independently of experience would be incompatible with our fundamental contention that a sentence says nothing unless it is empirically verifiable. And thus the whole force of our attack on metaphysics would be destroyed. It is vital, therefore, for us to be able to show that one or other of the empiricist accounts of the propositions of logic and mathematics is correct. If we are successful in this, we shall have destroyed the foundations of rationalism. For the fundamental tenet of rationalism is that thought is an independent source of knowledge, and is moreover a more trustworthy source of knowledge than experience; indeed some rationalists have gone so far as to say that thought is the only source of knowledge. And the ground for this view is simply that the only necessary truths about the world which are known to us are known through thought and not through experience. So that if we can show either that the truths

in question are not necessary or that they are not "truths about the world," we shall be taking away the support on which rationalism rests. We shall be making good the empiricist contention that there are no "truths of reason" which refer to matters of fact.

The course of maintaining that the truths of logic and mathematics are not necessary or certain was adopted by Mill. He maintained that these propositions were inductive generalizations based on an extremely large number of instances. The fact that the number of supporting instances was so very large accounted, in his view, for our believing these generalizations to be necessarily and universally true. The evidence in their favour was so strong that it seemed incredible to us that a contrary instance should ever arise. Nevertheless it was in principle possible for such generalizations to be confuted. They were highly probable, but, being inductive generalizations, they were not certain. The difference between them and the hypotheses of natural science was a difference in degree and not in kind. Experience gave us very good reason to suppose that a "truth" of mathematics or logic was true universally; but we were not possessed of a guarantee. For these "truths" were only empirical hypotheses which had worked particularly well in the past; and like all empirical hypotheses, they were theoretically fallible.

I do not think that this solution of the empiricist's difficulty with regard to the propositions of logic and mathematics is acceptable. In discussing it, it is necessary to make a distinction which is perhaps already enshrined in Kant's famous dictum that, although there can be no doubt that all our knowledge begins with experience, it does not follow that it all arises out of experience.[1] When we say that the truths of logic are known independently of experience, we are not of course saying that they are innate, in the sense that we are born knowing them. It is obvious that mathematics and logic have to be learned in the same way as chemistry and history have to be learned. Nor are we denying that the first person to discover a given logical or mathematical truth was led to it by an inductive procedure. It is very probable, for example, that the principle of the syllogism was formulated not before but after the validity of syllogistic reasoning had been observed in a number of particular cases. What we are discussing, however, when we say that logical and mathematical truths are known independently of experience, is not a historical question concerning the way in which these truths were originally discovered, nor a psychological question concerning the way in which each of us comes to learn them, but an epistemological question. The contention of Mill's which we reject is that the propositions of logic and mathematics have the same status as empirical hypotheses; that their validity is determined in the same way. We maintain that they are independent of experience in the sense that they do not owe their validity to empirical verification. We may come to discover them through an inductive process; but once we have apprehended them we see that they are necessarily true, that they hold good for every conceivable instance. And this serves to distinguish them from empirical generalizations. For we know that a proposition whose validity depends upon experience cannot be seen to be necessarily and universally true.

In rejecting Mill's theory, we are obliged to be somewhat dogmatic. We can do no more than state the issue clearly and then trust that his contention will be seen to be discrepant with the relevant logical facts. The following considerations may serve to show that of the two ways of dealing with logic and mathematics which are open to the empiricist, the one which Mill adopted is not the one which is correct.

The best way to substantiate our assertion that the truths of formal lògic and pure mathematics are necessarily true is to examine cases in which they might seem to be confuted. It might easily happen, for example, that when I came to count what I had taken to be five pairs of objects, I found that they amounted only to nine. And if I wished to mislead people I might say that on this occasion twice five was not ten. But in that case I should not be using the complex sign "2 X 5 = 10" in the way in which it is ordinarily used. I should be taking it not as the expression of a purely mathematical proposition, but as the expression of an empirical generalization, to the effect that whenever I counted what appeared to me to be five pairs of objects I discovered that they were ten in number. This generalization may very well be false. But if it proved false in a given case, one would not say that the mathematical proposition "2 X 5 = 10" had been confuted. One

would say that I was wrong in supposing that there were five pairs of objects to start with, or that one of the objects had been taken away while I was counting, or that two of them had coalesced, or that I had counted wrongly. One would adopt as an explanation whatever empirical hypothesis fitted in best with the accredited facts. The one explanation which would in no circumstances be adopted is that ten is not always the product of two and five.

To take another example: if what appears to be a Euclidean triangle is found by measurement not to have angles totalling 180 degrees, we do not say that we have met with an instance which invalidates the mathematical proposition that the sum of the three angles of a Euclidean triangle is 180 degrees. We say that we have measured wrongly, or, more probably, that the triangle we have been measuring is not Euclidean. And this is our procedure in every case in which a mathematical truth might appear to be confuted. We always preserve its validity by adopting some other explanation of the occurrence.

The same thing applies to the principles of formal logic. We may take an example relating to the so-called law of excluded middle, which states that a proposition must be either true or false, or, in other words, that it is impossible that a proposition and its contradictory should neither of them be true. One might suppose that a proposition of the form "x has stopped doing y" would in certain cases constitute an exception to this law. For instance, if my friend has never yet written to me, it seems fair to say that it is neither true nor false that he has stopped writing to me. But in fact one would refuse to accept such an instance as an invalidation of the law of excluded middle. One would point out that the proposition "My friend has stopped writing to me" is not a simple proposition, but the conjunction of the two propositions "My friend wrote to me in the past" and "My friend does not write to me now": and, furthermore, that the proposition "My friend has not stopped writing to me" is not, as it appears to be, contradictory to "My friend has stopped writing to me," but only contrary to it. For it means "My friend wrote to me in the past, and he still writes to me." When, therefore, we say that such a proposition as "My friend has stopped writing to me" is sometimes neither true nor false, we are speaking inaccurately. For we seem to be saying that neither it nor its contradictory is true. Whereas what we mean, or anyhow should mean, is that neither it nor its apparent contradictory is true. And its apparent contradictory is really only its contrary. Thus we preserve the law of excluded middle by showing that the negating of a sentence does not always yield the contradictory of the proposition originally expressed.

There is no need to give further examples. Whatever instance we care to take, we shall always find that the situations in which a logical or mathematical principle might appear to be confuted are accounted for in such a way as to leave the principle unassailed. And this indicates that Mill was wrong in supposing that a situation could arise which would overthrow a mathematical truth. The principles of logic and mathematics are true universally simply because we never allow them to be anything else. And the reason for this is that we cannot abandon them without contradicting ourselves, without sinning against the rules which govern the use of language, and so making our utterances self-stultifying. In other words, the truths of logic and mathematics are analytic propositions or tautologies. In saying this we are making what will be held to be an extremely controversial statement, and we must now proceed to make its implications clear.

The most familiar definition of an analytic proposition, or judgement, as he called it, is that given by Kant. He said[2] that an analytic judgement was one in which the predicate B belonged to the subject A as something which was covertly contained in the concept of A. He contrasted analytic with synthetic judgements, in which the predicate B lay outside the subject A, although it did stand in connection with it. Analytic judgements, he explains, "add nothing through the predicate to the concept of the subject, but merely break it up into those constituent concepts that have all along been thought in it, although confusedly." Synthetic judgements, on the other hand, "add to the concept of the subject a predicate which has not been in any wise thought in it, and which no analysis could possible extract from it." Kant gives "all bodies are extended" as an example of an analytic judgement, on the ground that the required predicate can be extracted from the concept of "body," "in accordance with the

principle of contradiction"; as an example of a synthetic judgement, he gives "all bodies are heavy." He refers also to "$7 + 5 = 12$" as a synthetic judgement, on the ground that the concept of twelve is by no means already thought in merely thinking the union of seven and five. And he appears to regard this as tantamount to saying that the judgement does not rest on the principle of contradiction alone. He holds, also, that through analytic judgements our knowledge is not extended as it is through synthetic judgements. For in analytic judgements "the concept which I already have is merely set forth and made intelligible to me."

I think that this is a fair summary of Kant's account of the distinction between analytic and synthetic propositions, but I do not think that it succeeds in making the distinction clear. For even if we pass over the difficulties which arise out of the use of the vague term "concept," and the unwarranted assumption that every judgement, as well as every German or English sentence, can be said to have a subject and a predicate, there remains still this crucial defect. Kant does not give one straightforward criterion for distinguishing between analytic and synthetic propositions; he gives two distinct criteria, which are by no means equivalent. Thus his ground for holding that the proposition "$7 + 5 = 12$" is synthetic is, as we have seen, that the subjective intension of "$7 + 5$" does not comprise the subjective intension of "12"; whereas his ground for holding that "all bodies are extended" is an analytic proposition in that it rests on the principle of contradiction alone. That is, he employs a psychological criterion in the first of these examples, and a logical criterion in the second, and takes their equivalence for granted. But, in fact, a proposition which is synthetic according to the former criterion may very well be analytic according to the latter. For, as we have already pointed out, it is possible for symbols to be synonymous without having the same intensional meaning for anyone: and accordingly from the fact that one can think of the sum of seven and five without necessarily thinking of twelve, it by no means follows that the proposition "$7 + 5 = 12$" can be denied without self-contradiction. From the rest of his argument, it is clear that it is this logical proposition, and not any psychological proposition, that Kant is really anxious to establish. His use of the psychological criterion leads him to think that he has established it, when he has not.

I think that we can preserve the logical import of Kant's distinction between analytic and synthetic propositions, while avoiding the confusions which mar his actual account of it, if we say that a proposition is analytic when its validity depends solely on the definitions of the symbols it contains, and synthetic when its validity is determined by the facts of experience. Thus, the proposition "There are ants which have established a system of slavery" is a synthetic proposition. For we cannot tell whether it is true or false merely by considering the definitions of the symbols which constitute it. We have to resort to actual observation of the behaviour of ants. On the other hand, the proposition "Either some ants are parasitic or none are" is an analytic proposition. For one need not resort to observation to discover that there either are or are not ants which are parasitic. If one knows what is the function of the words "either," "or," and "not," then one can see that any proposition of the form "Either p is true or p is not true" is valid, independently of experience. Accordingly, all such propositions are analytic.

It is to be noticed that the proposition "Either some ants are parasitic or none are" provides no information whatsoever about the behaviour of ants, or, indeed, about any matter of fact. And this applies to all analytic propositions. They none of them provide any information about any matter of fact. In other words, they are entirely devoid of factual content. And it is for this reason that no experience can confute them.

When we say that analytic propositions are devoid of factual content, and consequently that they say nothing, we are not suggesting that they are senseless in the way that metaphysical utterances are senseless. For, although they give us no information about any empirical situation, they do enlighten us by illustrating the way in which we use certain symbols. Thus if I say, "Nothing can be coloured in different ways at the same time with respect to the same part of itself," I am not saying anything about the properties of any actual thing; but I am not talking nonsense. I am expressing an analytic proposition, which records our determination to call a colour expanse which differs in quality from a neighbouring colour expanse a different part of a given thing. In other

words, I am simply calling attention to the implications of a certain linguistic usage. Similarly, in saying that if all Bretons are Frenchmen, and all Frenchmen Europeans, then all Bretons are Europeans, I am not describing any matter of fact. But I am showing that in the statement that all Bretons are Frenchmen, and all Frenchmen Europeans, the further statement that all Bretons are Europeans is implicitly contained. And I am thereby indicating the convention which governs our usage of the words "if" and "all."

We see, then, that there is a sense in which analytic propositions do give us new knowledge. They call attention to linguistic usages, of which we might otherwise not be conscious, and they reveal unsuspected implications in our assertions and beliefs. But we can see also that there is a sense in which they may be said to add nothing to our knowledge. For they tell us only what we may be said to know already. Thus, if I know that the existence of May Queens is a relic of tree-worship, and I discover that May Queens still exist in England, I can employ the tautology "If p implies q, and p is true, q is true" to show that there still exists a relic of tree-worship in England. But in saying that there are still May Queens in England, and that the existence of May Queens is a relic of tree-worship, I have already asserted the existence in England of a relic of tree-worship. The use of the tautology does, indeed, enable me to make this conceded assertion explicit. But it does not provide me with any new knowledge, in the sense in which empirical evidence that the election of May Queens has been forbidden by law would provide me with new knowledge. If one had to set forth all the information one possessed, with regard to matters of fact, one would not write down any analytic propositions. But one would make use of analytic propositions in compiling one's encyclopedia, and would thus come to include propositions which one would otherwise have overlooked. And, besides enabling one to make one's list of information complete, the formulation of analytic propositions would enable one to make sure that the synthetic propositions of which the list was composed formed a self-consistent system. By showing which ways of combining propositions resulted in contradictions, they would prevent one from including incompatible propositions and so making the list self-stultifying. But in so far as we had actually used such words as "all" and "or" and "not" without falling into self-contradiction, we might be said already to know what was revealed in the formulation of analytic propositions illustrating the rules which govern our usage of these logical particles. So that here again we are justified in saying that analytic propositions do not increase our knowledge.

The analytic character of the truths of formal logic was obscured in the traditional logic through its being insufficiently formalized. For in speaking always of judgements, instead of propositions, and introducing irrelevant psychological questions, the traditional logic gave the impression of being concerned in some specially intimate way with the workings of thought. What it was actually concerned with was the formal relationship of classes, as is shown by the fact that all its principles of inference are subsumed in the Boolean class-calculus, which is subsumed in its turn in the propositional calculus of Russell and Whitehead.[3] Their system, expounded in *Principia Mathematica,* makes it clear that formal logic is not concerned with the properties of men's minds, much less with the properties of material objects, but simply with the possibility of combining propositions by means of logical particles into analytic propositions, and with studying the formal relationship of these analytic propositions, in virtue of which one is deducible from another. Their procedure is to exhibit the propositions of formal logic as a deductive system, based on five primitive propositions, subsequently reduced in number to one. Hereby the distinction between logical truths and principles of inference, which was maintained in the Aristotelian logic, very properly disappears. Every principle of inference is put forward as a logical truth and every logical truth can serve as a principle of inference. The three Aristotelian "laws of thought," the law of identity, the law of excluded middle, and the law of non-contradiction, are incorporated in the system, but they are not considered more important than the other analytic propositions. They are not reckoned among the premises of the system. And the system of Russell and Whitehead itself is probably only one among many possible logics, each of which is composed of tautologies as interesting to the logician as the arbitrarily selected Aristotelian "laws of thought."[4]

A point which is not sufficiently brought out by Russell, if indeed it is recognised by him at all, is that every logical proposition is valid in its own right. Its validity does not depend on its being incorporated in a system, and deduced from certain propositions which are taken as self-evident. The construction of systems of logic is useful as a means of discovering and certifying analytic propositions, but it is not in principle essential even for this purpose. For it is possible to conceive of a symbolism in which every analytic proposition could be seen to be analytic in virtue of its form alone.

The fact that the validity of an analytic proposition in no way depends on its being deducible from other analytic propositions is our justification for disregarding the question whether the propositions of mathematics are reducible to propositions of formal logic, in the way that Russell supposed.[5] For even if it is the case that the definition of a cardinal number as a class of classes similar to a given class is circular, and it is not possible to reduce mathematical notions to purely logical notions, it will still remain true that the propositions of mathematics are analytic propositions. They will form a special class of analytic propositions, containing special terms, but they will be none the less analytic for that. For the criterion of an analytic proposition is that its validity should follow simply from the definition of the terms contained in it, and this condition is fulfilled by the propositions of pure mathematics.

The mathematical propositions which one might most pardonably suppose to be synthetic are the propositions of geometry. For it is natural for us to think, as Kant thought, that geometry is the study of the properties of physical space and consequently that its propositions have factual content. And if we believe this, and also recognize that the truths of geometry are necessary and certain, then we may be inclined to accept Kant's hypothesis that space is the form of intuition of our outer sense, a form imposed by us on the matter of sensation, as the only possible explanation of our *a priori* knowledge of these synthetic propositions. But while the view that pure geometry is concerned with physical space was plausible enough in Kant's day, when the geometry of Euclid was the only geometry known, the subsequent invention of non-Euclidean geometries has shown it to be mistaken. We see now that the axioms of a geometry are simply definitions, and that the theorems of a geometry are simply the logical consequences of these definitions.[6] A geometry is not in itself about physical space; in itself it cannot be said to be "about" anything. But we can use a geometry to reason about physical space. That is to say, once we have given the axioms a physical interpretation, we can proceed to apply the theorems to the objects which satisfy the axioms. Whether a geometry can be applied to the actual physical world or not, is an empirical question which falls outside the scope of the geometry itself. There is no sense, therefore, in asking which of the various geometries known to us are false and which are true. In so far as they are all free from contradiction, they are all true. What one can ask is which of them is the most useful on any given occasion, which of them can be applied most easily and most fruitfully to an actual empirical situation. But the proposition which states that a certain application of a geometry is possible is not itself a proposition of that geometry. All that the geometry itself tells us is that if anything can be brought under the definitions, it will also satisfy the theorems. It is therefore a purely logical system, and its propositions are purely analytic propositions.

It might be objected that the use made of diagrams in geometrical treatises shows that geometrical reasoning is not purely abstract and logical, but depends on our intuition of the properties of figures. In fact, however, the use of diagrams is not essential to completely rigorous geometry. The diagrams are introduced as an aid to our reason. They provide us with a particular application of the geometry, and so assist us to perceive the more general truth that the geometry involve certain consequences. But the fact that most of us need the help of an example to make us aware of those consequences does not show that the relation between them and the axioms is not a purely logical relation. It shows merely that our intellects are unequal to the task of carrying out very abstract processes of reasoning without the assistance of intuition. In other words, it has no bearing on the nature of geometrical propositions, but is simply an empirical fact about ourselves. Moreover, the appeal to intuition, though generally of psychological value, is also a source of danger to the geometer. He is tempted to make assumptions which are accidentally true of the particular figure he is taking as an illustration, but do not follow from his axioms. It has, indeed, been shown that Euclid himself was guilty of this, and consequently that the presence of the figure is essential to some of his proofs.[7] This shows that his system is not, as he presents it, completely rigorous, although of course it can be made so. It does not show that the presence of the figure is essential to a truly rigorous geometrical proof. To suppose that it did would be to take as a necessary feature of all geometries what is really only an incidental defect in one particular geometrical system.

We conclude, then, that the propositions of pure geometry are analytic. And this leads us to reject Kant's hypothesis that geometry deals with the form of intuition of our outer sense. For the ground for this hypothesis was that it alone explained how the propositions of geometry could be both true *a priori* and synthetic: and we have seen that they are not snythetic. Similarly our view that the propositions of arithmetic are not synthetic but analytic leads us to reject the Kantian hypothesis[8] that arithmetic is concerned with our pure intuition of time, the form of our inner sense. And thus we are able to dismiss Kant's transcendental aesthetic without having to bring forward the epistemological difficulties which it is commonly said to involve. For the only argument which can be brought in favour of Kant's theory is that it alone explains certain "facts." And now we have found that the "facts" which it purports to explain are not facts at all. For while it is true that we have *a priori* knowledge of necessary propositions, it is not true, as Kant supposed, that any of these necessary propositions are synthetic. They are without exception analytic propositions, or, in other words, tautologies.

We have already explained how it is that these analytic propositions are necessary and certain. We saw that the reason why they cannot be confuted in experience is that they do not make any assertion about the empirical world. They simply record our determination to use words in a certain fashion. We cannot deny them without infringing the conventions which are presupposed by our very denial, and so falling into self-contradiction. And this is the sole ground of their necessity. As Wittgenstein puts it, our justification for holding that the world could not conceivably disobey the laws of logic is simply that we could not say of an unlogical world how it would look.[9] And just as the validity of an analytic proposition is independent of the nature of the external world; so is it independent of the nature of our minds. It is perfectly conceivable that we should have employed different linguistic conventions from those which we actually do employ. But whatever these conventions might be, the tautologies in which we recorded them would always be necessary. For any denial of them would be self-stultifying.

We see, then, that there is nothing mysterious about the apodeictic certainty of logic and mathematics. Our knowledge that no observation can ever confute the proposition "7 + 5 = 12" depends simply on the fact that the symbolic expression "7 + 5" is synonymous with "12," just as our knowledge that every oculist is an eyedoctor depends on the fact that the symbol "eyedoctor" is synonymous with "oculist." And the same explanation holds good for every other *a priori* truth.

What is mysterious at first sight is that these tautologies should on occasion be so surprising, that there should be in mathematics and logic the possibility of invention and discovery. As Poincaré says: "If all the assertions which mathematics puts forward can be derived from one another by formal logic, mathematics cannot amount to anything more than an immense tautology. Logical inference can teach us nothing essentially new, and if everything is to proceed from the principle of identity, everything must be reducible to it. But can we really allow that these theorems which fill so many books serve no other purpose then to say in a round-about fashion 'A = A'?"[10] Poincaré finds this incredible. His own theory is that the sense of invention and discovery in mathematics belongs to it in virtue of mathematical induction, the principle that what is true for the number 1, and true for $n + 1$ when it is true for n,[11] is true for all numbers. And he claims that this is a synthetic *a priori* principle. It is, in fact, *a priori*, but is not synthetic. It is a defining principle of the natural numbers, serving to distinguish them from such numbers as the infinite cardinal numbers, to which it cannot be applied.[12] Moreover, we must remember that discoveries can be made, not only in arithmetic, but also in geometry and formal logic, where no use

is made of mathematical induction. So that even if Poincaré were right about mathematical induction, he would not have provided a satisfactory explanation of the paradox that a mere body of tautologies can be so interesting and so surprising.

The true explanation is very simple. The power of logic and mathematics to surprise us depends, like their usefulness, on the limitations of our reason. A being whose intellect was infinitely powerful would take no interest in logic and mathematics.[13] For he would be able to see at a glance everything that his definitions implied, and, accordingly, could never learn anything from logical inference which he was not fully conscious of already. But our intellects are not of this order. It is only a minute proportion of the consequences of our definitions that we are able to detect at a glance. Even so simple a tautology as "91 X 79 = 7189" is beyond the scope of our immediate apprehension. To assure ourselves that "7189" is synonymous with "91 X 79" we have to resort to calculation, which is simply a process of tautological transformation—that is, a process by which we change the form of expressions without altering their significance. The multiplication tables are rules for carrying out this process in arithmetic, just as the laws of logic are rules for the tautological transformation of sentences expressed in logical symbolism or in ordinary language. As the process of calculation is carried out more or less mechanically, it is easy for us to make a slip and so unwittingly contradict ourselves. And this accounts for the existence of logical and mathematical "falsehoods," which otherwise might appear paradoxical. Clearly the risk of error in logical reasoning is proportionate to the length and the complexity of the process of calculation. And in the same way, the more complex an analytic proposition is, the more chance it has of interesting and surprising us.

It is easy to see that the danger of error in logical reasoning can be minimized by the introduction of symbolic devices, which enable us to express highly complex tautologies in a conveniently simple form. And this gives us an opportunity for the exercise of invention in the pursuit of logical enquiries. For a well-chosen definition will call our attention to analytic truths, which would otherwise have escaped us. And the framing of definitions, which are useful and fruitful may well be regarded as a creative act.

Having thus shown that there is no inexplicable paradox involved in the view that the truths of logic and mathematics are of of them analytic, we may safely adopt it as the only satisfactory explanation of their *a priori* necessity. And in adopting it we vindicate the empiricist claim that there can be no *a priori* knowledge of reality. For we show that the truths of pure reason, the propositions, which we know to be valid independently of all experience, are so only in virtue of their lack of factual content. To say that a proposition is true *a priori* is to say that it is a tautology. And tautologies, though they may serve to guide us in our empirical search for knowledge, do not in themselves contain any information about any matter of fact.

NOTES

1.   *Critique of Pure Reason,* 2nd ed., Introduction, section i.

2.   *Critique of Pure Reason,* 2nd ed., Introduction, sections iv and v.

3.   Vide Karl Menger, "Die Neue Logik," *Krise und Neuaufbau in den Exakten Wissenschaften,* pp. 94–6; and Lewis and Langford, *Symbolic Logic,* Chapter v.

4.   Vide Lewis and Langford, *Symbolic Logic,* Chapter vii, for an elaboration of this point.

5.   Vide *Introduction to Mathematical Philosophy,* Chapter ii.

6.   Cf. H. Poincaré, *La Science et l'Hypothèse,* Part II, Chapter iii.

7.   Cf. M. Black, *The Nature of Mathematics,* p. 154.

8.   This hypothesis is not mentioned in the *Critique of Pure Reason,* but was maintained by Kant at an earlier date.

9.   *Tractatus Logico-Philosophicus,* 3031.

10.   *La Science et l'Hypothèse,* Part I, Chapter i.

11.   This was wrongly stated in previous editions as "true for *n* when it is true for *n* + 1."

12.   Cf. B. Russell's *Introduction to Mathematical Philosophy,* Chapter iii, p. 27.

13.   Cf. Hans Hahn, "Logik, Mathematick und Naturerkennen," *Einheitswissenschaft,* Heft II, p. 18. "Ein allwissendes Wesen braucht keine Logik und keine Mathematick."

Pragmatism

WILLIAM JAMES

What Pragmatism Means*

Some years ago, being with a camping party in the mountains, I returned from a solitary ramble to find every one engaged in a ferocious metaphysical dispute. The *corpus* of the dispute was a squirrel—a live squirrel supposed to be clinging to one side of a tree-trunk; while over against the tree's opposite side a human being was imagined to stand. This human witness tries to get sight of the squirrel by moving rapidly round the tree, but no matter how fast he goes, the squirrel moves as fast in the opposite direction, and always keeps

the tree between himself and the man, so that never a glimpse of him is caught. The resultant metaphysical problem now is this: *Does the man go round the squirrel or not?* He goes round the tree, sure enough, and the squirrel is on the tree; but does he go round the squirrel? In the unlimited leisure of the wilderness, discussion had been worn threadbare. Every one had taken sides, and was obstinate; and the numbers on both sides were even. Each side, when I appeared, therefore appealed to me to make it a majority. Mindful of the scholastic adage that whenever you meet a contradiction you must make a distinction, I immediately sought and found one, as follows: "Which party is right," I said, "depends on what

*William James, "What Pragmatism Means," from *Pragmatism, A New Name for Some Old Ways of Thinking* (New York: Longmans, Green, and Co., 1907).

you *practically mean* by 'going round' the squirrel. If you mean passing from the north of him to the east, then to the south, then to the west, and then to the north of him again, obviously the man does go round him, for he occupies these successive positions. But if on the contrary you mean being first in front of him, then on the right of him, then behind him, then on his left, and finally in front again, it is quite as obvious that the man fails to go round him, for by the compensating movements the squirrel makes, he keeps his belly turned towards the man all the time, and his back turned away. Make the distinction, and there is no occasion for any further dispute. You are both right and both wrong according as you conceive the verb 'to go round' in one practical fashion or the other."

Although one or two of the hotter disputants called my speech a shuffling evasion, saying they wanted no quibbling or scholastic hair-splitting, but meant just plain honest English "round," the majority seemed to think that the distinction had assuaged the dispute.

I tell this trivial anecdote because it is a peculiarly simple example of what I wish now to speak of as *the pragmatic method.* The pragmatic method is primarily a method of settling metaphysical disputes that otherwise might be interminable. Is the world one or many?—fated or free?—material or spiritual?—here are notions either of which may or may not hold good of the world; and disputes over such notions are unending. The pragmatic method in such cases is to try to interpret each notion by tracing its respective practical consequences. What difference would it practically make to any one if this notion rather than that notion were true? If no practical difference whatever can be traced, then the alternatives mean practically the same thing, and all dispute is idle. Whenever a dispute is serious, we ought to be able to show some practical difference that must follow from one side or the other's being right.

A glance at the history of the idea will show you still better what pragmatism means. The term is derived from the same Greek word $\pi\rho\acute{\alpha}\gamma\mu\alpha$, meaning action, from which our words "practice" and "practical" come. It was first introduced into philosophy by Mr. Charles Peirce in 1878. In an article entitled "How to Make Our Ideas Clear," in the *Popular Science Monthly* for January of that year[1] Mr. Peirce, after pointing out that our beliefs are really rules for action, said that, to develop a thought's meaning, we need only determine what conduct it is fitted to produce: that conduct is for us its sole significance. And the tangible fact at the root of all our thought-distinctions, however subtle, is that there is no one of them so fine as to consist in anything but a possible difference to practice. To attain perfect clearness in our thoughts of an object, then, we need only consider what conceivable effects of a practical kind the object may involve —what sensations we are to expect from it, and what reactions we must prepare. Our conception of these effects, whether immediate or remote, is then for us the whole of our conception of the object, so far as that conception has positive significance at all.

This is the principle of Peirce, the principle of pragmatism. It lay entirely unnoticed by any one for twenty years, until I, in an address before Professor Howison's Philosophical Union at the University of California, brought it forward again and made a special application of it to religion. By that date (1898) the times seemed ripe for its reception. The word "pragmatism" spread, and at present it fairly spots the pages of the philosophic journals. On all hands we find the "pragmatic movement" spoken of, sometimes with respect, sometimes with contumely, seldom with clear understanding. It is evident that the term applies itself conveniently to a number of tendencies that hitherto have lacked a collective name, and that it has "come to stay."

To take in the importance of Peirce's principle, one must get accustomed to applying it to concrete cases. I found a few years ago that Ostwald, the illustrious Leipzig chemist, had been making perfectly distinct use of the principle of pragmatism in his lectures on the philosophy of science, though he had not called it by that name.

"All realities influence our practice," he wrote me, "and that influence is their meaning for us. I am accustomed to put questions to my classes in this way: In what respects would the world be different if this alternative or that were true? If I can find nothing that would become different, then the alternative has no sense."

That is, the rival views mean practically the same thing, and meaning, other than practical, there is for us none. Ostwald in a published lecture gives this example of what he means. Chemists have long wrangled over the inner constitution of certain bodies called "tautomerous." Their properties seemed equally consistent with the notion that an instable hydrogen atom oscillates inside of them, or that they are instable mixtures of two bodies. Controversy raged, but never was decided. "It would never have begun," says Ostwald, "if the combatants had asked themselves what particular experimental fact could have been made different by one or the other view being correct. For it would then have appeared that no difference of fact could possibly ensue; and the quarrel was as unreal as if, theorizing in primitive times about the raising of dough by yeast, one party should have invoked a 'brownie,'' while another insisted on an 'elf' as the true cause of the phenomenon."[2]

It is astonishing to see how many philosophical disputes collapse into insignificance the moment you subject them to this simple test of tracing a concrete consequence. There can *be* no difference anywhere that doesn't *make* a difference elsewhere—no difference in abstract truth that doesn't express itself in a difference in concrete fact and in conduct consequent upon that fact, imposed on somebody, somehow, somewhere, and somewhen. The whole function of philosophy ought to be to find out what definite difference it will make to you and me, at definite instants of our life, if this world-formula or that world-formula be the true one.

There is absolutely nothing new in the pragmatic method. Socrates was an adept at it. Aristotle used it methodically. Locke, Berkeley, and Hume made momentous contributions to truth by its means. Shadworth Hodgson keeps insisting that realities are only what they are "known as." But these forerunners of pragmatism used it in fragments: they were preluders only. Not until in our time has it generalized itself, become conscious of a universal mission, pretended to a conquering destiny. I believe in that destiny, and I hope I may end by inspiring you with my belief.

Pragmatism represents a perfectly familiar attitude in philosophy, the empiricist attitude, but it represents it, as it seems to me, both in a more radical and in a less objectionable form than it has ever yet assumed. A pragmatist turns his back resolutely and once for all upon a lot of inveterate habits dear to professional philosophers. He turns away from abstraction and insufficiency, from verbal solutions, from bad *a priori* reasons, from fixed principles, closed systems, and pretended absolutes and origins. He turns towards concreteness and adequacy, towards facts, towards action and towards power. That means the empiricist temper regnant and the rationalist temper sincerely given up. It means the open air and possibilities of nature, as against dogma, artificiality, and the pretence of finality in truth.

At the same time it does not stand for any special results. It is a method only. But the general triumph of that method would mean an enormous change in what I called in my last lecture the "temperament" of philosophy. Teachers of the ultra-rationalistic type would be frozen out, much as the courtier type is frozen out in republics, as the ultramontane type of priest is frozen out in protestant lands. Science and metaphysics would come much nearer together, would in fact work absolutely hand in hand.

Metaphysics has usually followed a very primitive kind of quest. You know how men have always hankered after unlawful magic, and you know what a great part in magic *words* have always played. If you have his name, or the formula of incantation that binds him, you can control the spirit, genie, afrite, or whatever the power may be. Solomon knew the names of all the spirits, and having their names, he held them subject to his will. So the universe has always appeared to the natural mind as a kind of enigma, of which the key must be sought in the shape of some illuminating or power-bringing word or name. That word names the universe's *principle,* and to possess it is after a fashion to possess the universe itself. "God," "Matter," "Reason," "the Absolute," "Energy," are so many solving names. You can rest when you have them. You are at the end of your metaphysical quest.

But if you follow the pragmatic method, you cannot look on any such word as closing your quest. You must bring out of each word its practical cash-value, set it at work within the stream of your experience. It appears less as a solution, then, than as a program for more work, and more particularly as an indication of the ways in which existing realities may be *changed.*

Theories thus become instruments, not answers to enigmas, in which we can rest. We don't lie back upon them, we move forward, and, on occasion, make nature over again by their aid. Pragmatism unstiffens all our theories, limbers them up and sets each one at work. Being nothing essentially new, it harmonizes with many ancient philosophic tendencies. It agrees with nominalism, for instance, in always appealing to particulars; with utilitarianism in emphasizing practical aspects; with positivism in its disdain for verbal solutions, useless questions and metaphysical abstractions.

All these, you see, are *anti-intellectualist* tendencies. Against rationalism as a pretension and a method pragmatism is fully armed and militant. But, at the outset, at least, it stands for no particular results. It has no dogmas, and no doctrines save its method. As the young Italian pragmatist Papini has well said, it lies in the midst of our theories, like a corridor in a hotel. Innumerable chambers open out of it. In one you may find a man writing an atheistic volume; in the next some one on his knees praying for faith and strength; in a third a chemist investigating a body's properties. In a fourth a system of idealistic metaphysics is being excogitated; in a fifth the impossibility of metaphysics is being shown. But they all own the corridor, and all must pass through it if they want a practicable way of getting into or out of their respective rooms.

No particular results then, so far, but only an attitude of orientation, is what the pragmatic method means. *The attitude of looking away from first things, principles, "categories," supposed necessities; and of looking towards last things, fruits, consequences, facts.*

So much for the pragmatic method! You may say that I have been praising it rather than explaining it to you, but I shall presently explain it abundantly enough by showing how it works on some familiar problems. Meanwhile the word pragmatism has come to be used in a still wider sense, as meaning also a certain *theory of truth.* I mean to give a whole lecture to the statement of that theory, after first paving the way, so I can be very brief now. But brevity is hard to follow, so I ask for your redoubled attention for a quarter of an hour. If much remains obscure, I hope to make it clearer in the later lectures.

One of the most successfully cultivated branches of philosophy in our time is what is called inductive logic, the study of the conditions under which our sciences have evolved. Writers on this subject have begun to show a singular unanimity as to what the laws of nature and elements of fact mean, when formulated by mathematicians, physicists and chemists. When the first mathematical, logical, and natural uniformities, the first *laws,* were discovered, men were so carried away by the clearness, beauty and simplification that resulted, that they believed themselves to have deciphered authentically the eternal thoughts of the Almighty. His mind also thundered and reverberated in syllogisms. He also thought in conic sections, squares and roots and ratios, and geometrized like Euclid. He made Kepler's laws for the planets to follow; he made velocity increase proportionally to the time in falling bodies; he made the law of the sines for light to obey when refracted; he established the classes, orders, families and genera of plants and animals, and fixed the distances between them. He thought the archetypes of all things, and devised their variations; and when we rediscover one of these his wondrous institutions, we seize his mind in its very literal intention.

But as the sciences have developed further, the notion has gained ground that most, perhaps all, of our laws are only approximations. The laws themselves, moreover, have grown so numerous that there is no counting them; and so many rival formulations are proposed in all the branches of science that investigators have become accustomed to the notion that no theory is absolutely a transcript of reality, but that any one of them may from some point of view be useful. Their great use is to summarize old facts and to lead to new ones. They are only a man-made language, a conceptual shorthand, as some one calls them, in which we write our reports of nature; and languages, as is well known, tolerate much choice of expression and many dialects.

Thus human arbitrariness has driven divine necessity from scientific logic. If I mention the names of Sigwart, Mach, Ostwald, Pearson, Milhaud, Poincaré, Duhem, Ruyssen, those of you who are students will easily identify the tendency I speak of, and will think of additional names.

Riding now on the front of this wave of scientific logic Messrs. Schiller and Dewey appear with their pragmatistic account of what truth everywhere signifies. Everywhere, these teachers say, "truth" in our ideas and beliefs means the same thing that it means in science. It means, they say, nothing but this, *that ideas (which themselves are but parts of our experience) become true just in so far as they help us to get into satisfactory relation with other parts of our experience,* to summarize them and get about among them by conceptual short-cuts instead of following the interminable succession of particular phenomena. Any idea upon which we can ride, so to speak; any idea that will carry us prosperously from any one part of our experience to any other part, linking things satisfactorily, working securely, simplifying, saving labor; is true for just so much, true in so far forth, true *instrumentally.* This is the "instrumental" view of truth taught so successfully at Chicago, the view that truth in our ideas means their power to "work," promulgated so brilliantly at Oxford.

Messrs. Dewey, Shiller, and their allies, in reaching this general conception of all truth, have only followed the example of geologists, biologists and philologists. In the establishment of these other sciences, the successful stroke was always to take some simple process actually observable in operation—as denudation by weather, say, or variation from parental type, or change of dialect by incorporation of new words and pronunciations—and then to generalize it, making it apply to all times, and produce a great result by summating its effects through the ages.

The observable process which Schiller and Dewey particularly singled out for generalization is the familiar one by which any individual settles into *new opinions.* The process here is always the same. The individual has a stock of old opinions already, but he meets a new experience that puts them to a strain. Somebody contradicts them; or in a reflective moment he discovers that they contradict each other; or he hears of facts with which they are incompatible; or desires arise in him which they cease to satisfy. The result is an inward trouble to which his mind till then had been a stranger, and from which he seeks to escape by modifying his previous mass of opinions. He saves as much of it as he can, for in this matter of belief we are all extreme conservatives. So he tries to change first this opinion, and then that (for they resist change very variously), until at last some new idea comes up which he can graft upon the ancient stock with a minimum of disturbance of the latter, some idea that mediates between the stock and the new experience and runs them into one another most felicitously and expediently.

This new idea is then adopted as the true one. It preserves the older stock of truths with a minimum of modification, stretching them just enough to make them admit the novelty, but conceiving that in ways as familiar as the case leaves possible. An *outrée* explanation, violating all our preconceptions, would never pass for a true account of a novelty. We should scratch round industriously till we found something less eccentric. The most violent revolutions in an individual's beliefs leave most of his old order standing. Time and space, cause and effect, nature and history, and one's own biography remain untouched. New truth is always a go-between, a smoother-over of transitions. It marries old opinion to new fact so as ever to show a mimimum of jolt, a maximum of continuity. We hold a theory true just in proportion to its success in solving this "problem of maxima and minima." But success in solving this problem is eminently a matter of approximation. We say this theory solves it on the whole more satisfactorily than that theory; but that means more satisfactorily to ourselves, and individuals will emphasize their points of satisfaction differently. To a certain degree, therefore, everthing here is plastic.

The point I now urge you to observe particularly is the part played by the older truths. Failure to take account of it is the source of much of the unjust criticism levelled against pragmatism. Their influence is absolutely controlling. Loyalty to them is the first principle—in most cases it is the only principle; for by far the most usual way of handling phenomena so novel that they would make for a serious rearrangment of our preconception is to ignore them altogether, or to abuse those who bear witness for them.

You doubtless wish examples of this process of truth's growth, and the only trouble is their superabundance. The simplest case of new truth is of course the mere numerical addition of new kinds of facts, or of new single facts of old kinds, to our experience—an addition that involves no alteration in the old beliefs. Day follows day, and its contents are simply added. The new contents themselves are not true, they simply *come* and *are.* Truth is *what we say about* them, and when we say that they have come, truth is satisfied by the plain additive formula.

But often the day's contents oblige a rearrangement. If I should now utter piercing shrieks and act like a maniac on this platform, it would make many of you revise your ideas as to the probable worth of my philosophy. "Radium" came the other day as part of the day's content, and seemed for a moment to contradict our ideas of the whole order of nature, that order having come to be identified with what is called the conservation of energy. The mere sight of radium paying heat away indefinitely out of its own pocket seemed to violate that conservation. What to think? If the radiations from it were nothing but an escape of unsuspected "potential" energy, pre-existent inside of the atoms, the principle of conservation would be saved. The discovery of "helium" as the radiation's outcome, opened a way to this belief. So Ramsay's view is generally held to be true, because, althouth it extends our old ideas of energy, it causes a minimum of alteration in their nature.

I need not multiply instances. A new opinion counts as "true" just in proportion as it gratifies the individual's desire to assimilate the novel in his experience to his beliefs in stock. It must both lean on old truth and grasp new fact; and its success (as I said a moment ago) in doing this, is a matter for the individual's appreciation. When old truth grows, then, by new truth's addition, it is for subjective reasons. We are in the process and obey the reasons. That new idea is truest which performs most felicitously its function of satisfying our double urgency. It makes itself true, gets itself classed as true, by the way it works; grafting itself then upon the ancient body of truth, which thus grows much as a tree grows by the activity of a new layer of cambium.

Now Dewey and Schiller proceed to generalize this observation and to apply it to the most ancient parts of truth. They also once were plastic. They also were called true for human reasons. They also mediated between still earlier truths and what in those days were novel observations. Purely objective truth, truth in whose establishment the function of giving human satisfaction in marrying previous parts of experience with newer parts played no rôle whatever, is nowhere to be found. The reasons why we call things true is the reason why they *are* true, for "to be true" *means* only to perform this marriage-function.

The trail of the human serpent is thus over everything. Truth independent; truth that we *find* merely; truth no longer malleable to human need; truth incorrigible, in a word; such truth exists indeed superabundantly—or is supposed to exist by rationalistically minded thinkers; but then it means only the dead heart of the living tree, and its being there means only that truth also has its paleontology, and its "prescription," and may grow stiff with years of veteran service and petrified in men's regard by sheer antiquity. But how plastic even the oldest truths nevertheless really are has been vividly shown in our day by the transformation of logical and mathematical ideas, a transformation which seems even to be invading physics. The ancient formulas are reinterpreted as special expressions of much wider principles, principles that our ancestors never got a glimpse of in their present shape and formulation.

Mr. Schiller still gives to all this view of truth the name of "Humanism," but, for this doctrine too, the name of pragmatism seems fairly to be in the ascendant, so I will treat it under the name of pragmatism in these lectures.

Such then would be the scope of pragmatism—first, a method; and second, a genetic theory of what is meant by truth. And these two things must be our future topics.

What I have said of the theory of truth will, I am sure, have appeared obscure and unsatisfactory to most of you by reason of its brevity. I shall make amends for that hereafter. In a lecture on "common sense" I shall try to show what I mean by truths grown petrified by antiquity. In another lecture I shall expatiate on the idea that our thoughts become true in proportion as they successfully exert their go-between function. In a third I shall show how hard it is to discriminate subjective from objective factors in Truth's development. You may not follow me wholly in these lectures; and if you do, you may not wholly agree with me. But you will, I know, regard me at least as serious, and treat my effort with respectful consideration.

You will probably be surprised to learn, then, that Messrs. Schiller's and Dewey's theories have suffered a hailstorm of contempt and ridicule. All rationalism has risen against them. In influential quarters Mr. Schiller, in particular, has been treated like an impudent schoolboy who deserves a spanking. I should not mention this but for the fact that it throws so much sidelight upon that rationalistic temper to which I have opposed the temper of pragmatism. Pragmatism is uncomfortable away from facts. Rationalism is comfortable only in the presence of abstractions. This pragmatist talk about truths in the plural, about their utility and satisfactoriness, about the success with which they "work," etc., suggests to the typical intellectualist mind a sort of course lame second-rate makeshift article of truth. Such truths are not real truth. Such tests are merely subjective. As against this, objective truth must be something non-utilitarian, haughty, refined, remote, august, exalted. It must be an absolute correspondence of our thoughts with an equally absolute reality. It must be what we *ought* to think unconditionally. The conditioned ways in which we *do* think are so much irrelevance and matter for psychology. Down with psychology, up with logic, in all this question!

See the exquisite contrast of the types of mind! The pragmatist clings to facts and concreteness, observes truth at its work in particular cases, and generalizes. Truth, for him, becomes a classname for all sorts of definite working-values in experience. For the rationalist it remains a pure abstraction, to the bare name of which we must defer. When the pragmatist undertakes to show in detail just *why* we must defer, the rationalist is unable to recognize the concretes from which his own abstraction is taken. He accuses us of *denying* truth; whereas we have only sought to trace exactly why people follow it and always ought to follow it. Your typical ultra-abstractionist fairly shudders at concreteness: other things equal, he positively prefers the pale and spectral. If the two universes were offered, he would always choose the skinny outline rather than the rich thicket of reality. It is so much purer, clearer, nobler.

I hope that as these lectures go on, the concreteness and closeness to facts of the pragmatism which they advocate may be what approves itself to you as its most satisfactory peculiarity. It only follows here the example of the sister-sciences, interpreting the unobserved by the observed. It brings old and new harmoniously together. It converts the absolutely empty notion of a static relation of "correspondence" (what that may mean we must ask later) between our minds and reality, into that of a rich and active commerce (that any one may follow in detail and understand) between particular thoughts of ours, and the great universe of other experiences in which they play their parts and have their uses.

But enough of this at present: The justification of what I say must be postponed. I wish now to add a word in further explanation of the claim I made at our last meeting, that pragmatism may be a happy harmonizer of empiricist ways of thinking with the more religious demands of human beings.

Men who are strongly of the fact-loving temperament, you may remember me to have said, are liable to be kept at a distance by the small sympathy with facts which that philosophy from the present-day fashion of idealism offers them. It is far too intellectualistic. Old fashioned theism was bad enough, with its notion of God as an exalted monarch, made up a lot of unintelligible or preposterous "attributes"; but, so long as it held strongly by the argument from design, it kept some touch with concrete realities. Since, however, Darwinism has once for all displaced design from the minds of the "scientific,," theism has lost that foothold; and some kind of an immanent or patheistic deity working *in* things rather than above them is, if any, the kind recommended to our contemporary imagination. Aspirants to a philosophic religion turn, as a rule, more hopefully nowadays towards idealistic pantheism than towards the older dualistic theism, in spite of the fact that the latter still counts able defenders.

But, as I said in my first lecture, the brand of pantheism offered is hard for them to assimilate if they are lovers of facts, or empirically minded. It is the absolutistic brand, spurning the dust and reared upon pure logic. It keeps no connexion whatever with concreteness. Affirming the Absolute Mind, which is its substitute for God, to be the rational presupposition of all particulars of fact, whatever they may be, it remains supremely indifferent to what the particular facts in our world actually are. Be they what they may, the Absolute will father them. Like the sick lion in Esop's fable, all footprints lead into his den, but *nulla vistigia retrorsum.* [3] You cannot redescend into the world of particulars by the Absolute's aid, or deduce any necessary consequences of detail important for your life from your idea of his nature. He gives you indeed the assurance that all is well with *Him,* and for his eternal way of thinking; but thereupon he leaves you to be finitely saved by your own temporal devices.

Far be it from me to deny the majesty of this conception, or its capacity to yield religious comfort to a most respectable class of minds. But from the human point of view, no one can pretend that it doesn't suffer from the faults of remoteness and abstractness. It is eminently a product of what I have ventured to call the rationalistic temper. It disdains empiricism's needs. It substitutes a pallid outline for the real world's richness. It is dapper, it is noble in the bad sense, in the sense in which to be noble is to be inapt for humble service. In this real world of sweat and dirt, it seems to me that when a view of things is "noble," that ought to count as a presumption against its truth, and as a philosophic disqualification. The prince of darkness may be a gentleman, as we are told he is, but whatever the God of earth and heaven is, he can surely be no gentleman. His menial services are needed in the dust of our human trials, even more than his dignity is needed in the empyrean.

Now pragmatism, devoted though she be to facts, has no such materialistic bias as ordinary empiricism labors under. Moreover, she has no objection whatever to the realizing of abstractions, so long as you get about among particulars with their aid and they actually carry you somewhere. Interested in no conclusions but those which our minds and our experiences work out together, she has no *a priori* prejudices against theology. *If theological ideas prove to have a value for concrete life, they will be true, for pragmatism, in the sense of being good for so much. For how much more they are true, will depend entirely on their relations to the other truths that also have to be acknowledged.*

What I said just now about the Absolute, of transcendental idealism, is a case in point. First, I called it majestic and said it yielded religious comfort to a class of minds, and then I accused it of remoteness and sterility. But so far as it affords such comfort, it surely is not sterile; it has that amount of value; it performs a concrete function. As a good pragmatist, I myself ought to call the Absolute true "in so far forth," then; and I unhesitatingly now do so.

But what does *true in so far forth* mean in this case? To answer, we need only apply the prag-

matic method. What do believers in the Absolute mean by saying that their belief afford them comfort? They mean that since, in the Absolute finite evil is "overruled" already, we may, therefore, whenever we wish, treat the temporal as if it were potentially the eternal, be sure that we can trust its outcome, and, without sin, dismiss our fear and drop the worry of our finite responsibility. In short, they mean that we have a right ever and anon to take a moral holiday, to let the world wag in its own way, feeling that its issues are in better hands than ours and are none of our business.

The universe is a system of which the individual members may relax anxieties occasionally, in which the don't-care mood is also right for men, and moral holidays in order—that, if I mistake not, is part, at least, of what the Absolute is "known-as," that is the great difference in our particular experiences which his being true makes, for us, that is his cash-value when he is pragmatically interpreted. Farther than that the ordinary lay-reader in philosophy who thinks favorably of absolute idealism does not venture to sharpen his conceptions. He can use the Absolute for so much, and so much is very precious. He is pained at hearing you speak incredulously of the Absolute, therefore, and disregards your criticisms because they deal with aspects of the conception that he fails to follow.

If the Absolute means this, and means no more than this, who can possibly deny the truth of it? To deny it would be to insist that men should never relax, and that holidays are never in order.

I am well aware how odd it must seem to some of you to hear me say that an idea is "true" so long as to believe it is profitable to our lives. That it is *good,* for as much as it profits, you will gladly admit. If what we do by its aid is good, you will allow the idea itself to be good in so far forth, for we are the better for possessing it. But is it not a strange misuse of the word "truth," you will say, to call ideas also "true" for this reason?

To answer this difficulty fully is impossible at this stage of my account. You touch here upon the very central point of Messrs. Schiller's, Dewey's, and my own doctrine of truth, which I cannot discuss with detail until my sixth lecture. Let me now say only this, that truth is *one species of good,* and not, as is usually supposed, a category distinct from good, and co-ordinate with it. *The true is the name of whatever proves itself to b good in the way of belief, and good, too, for definite, assignable reasons.* Surely you must admit this, that if there were *no* good for life in true ideas, or if the knowledge of them were positively disadvantageous and false ideas the only useful ones, then the current notion that truth is divine and precious, and its pursuit a duty, could never have grown up or become a dogma. In a world like that, our duty would be to *shun* truth, rather. But in this world, just as certain foods are not only agreeable to our taste, but good for our teeth, our stomach, and our tissues; so certain ideas are not only agreeable to think about, or agreeable as supporting other-ideas that we are fond of, but they are also helpful in life's practical struggles. If there be any life that it is really better we should lead, and if there be any idea which, if believed in, would help us to lead that life, then it would be really *better for us* to believe in that idea, *unless, indeed, belief in it incidentally clashed with other greater vital benefits.*

"What would be better for us to believe!" This sounds very like a definition of truth. It comes very near to saying "what we *ought* to believe"; and in *that* definition none of you would find any oddity. Ought we ever not to believe what it is *better for us* to believe? And can we then keep the notion of what is better for us, and what is true for us, permanently apart?

Pragmatism says no, and I fully agree with her. Probably you also agree, so far as the abstract statement goes, but with a suspicion that if we practically did believe everything that made for good in our own personal lives, we should be found indulging all kinds of fancies about this world's affairs, and all kinds of sentimental superstitions about a world hereafter. Your suspicion here is undoubtedly well founded, and it is evident that something happens when you pass from the abstract to the concrete that complicates the situation.

I said just now that what is better for us to believe is true *unless the belief incidentally clashes with some other vital benefit.* Now in real life what vital benefits is any particular belief of ours most liable to clash with? What indeed except the vital benefits yielded by *other beliefs* when these prove incompatible with the first ones? In other words, the greatest enemy of any one of our truths may be the rest of our truths. Truths have once for all this desperate instinct of self-preservation and of desire to extinguish whatever contradicts them. My belief in the Absolute, based on the good it does me, must run the gauntlet of all my other beliefs. Grant that it may be true in giving me a moral holiday. Nevertheless, as I conceive it—and let me speak now confidentially, as it were, and merely in my own private person—it clashes with other truths of mine whose benefits I hate to give up on its account. It happens to be associated with a kind of logic of which I am the enemy, I find that it entangles me in metaphysical paradoxes that are inacceptable, etc., etc. But as I have enough trouble in life already without adding the trouble of carrying these intellectual inconsistencies, I personally just give up the Absolute. I just *take* my moral holidays; or else as a professional philosopher, I try to justify them by some other principle.

If I could restrict my notion of the Absolute to its bare holiday-giving value, it wouldn't clash with my other truths. But we cannot easily thus restrict our hypotheses. They carry supernumerary features, and these it is that clash so. My disbelief in the Absolute means then disbelief in those other supernumerary features, for I fully believe in the legitimacy of taking moral holidays.

You see by this what I meant when I called pragmatism a mediator and reconciler and said, borrowing the word from Papini, that she "unstiffens" our theories. She has in fact no prejudices whatever, no obstructive dogmas, no rigid canons of what shall count as proof. She is completely genial. She will entertain any hypothesis, she will consider any evidence. It follows that in the religious field she is at a great advantage both over positivistic empiricism, with its anti-theological bias, and over religious rationalism, with its exclusive interest in the remote, the noble, the simple, and the abstract in the way of conception.

In short, she widens the field of search for God. Rationalism sticks to logic and the empyrean. Empiricism sticks to the external senses. Pragmatism is willing to take anything, to follow either logic or the senses and to count the humblest and most personal experiences. She will count mystical experiences if they have practical consequences. She will take a God who lives in the very dirt of private fact—if that should seem a likely place to find him.

Her only test of probable truth is what works best in the way of leading us, what fits every part of life best and combines with the collectivity of experience's demands, nothing being omitted. If theological ideas should do this, if the notion of God, in particular, should prove to do it, how could pragmatism possibly deny God's existence? She could see no meaning in treating as "not true" a notion that was pragmatically so successful. What other kind of truth could there be, for her, than all this agreement with concrete reality?

In my last lecture I shall return again to the relations of pragmatism with religion. But you see already how democratic she is. Her manners are as various and flexible, her resources as rich and endless, and her conclusions as friendly as those of mother nature.

NOTES

1. Translated in the *Revue Philosophique* for January, 1879 (vol. vii).

2. "Theorie and Praxis," *Zeitschrift des Oesterreichischen Ingenieur-u. Architecten-Vereins,* 1905, Nr. 4 u. 6. I find a still more radical pragmatism than Ostwald's in an address by Professor W. S. Franklin: "I think that the sickliest notion of physics, even if a student gets it, is that it is 'the science of masses, molecules, and the ether.' And I think that the healthiest notion, even if a student does not wholly get it, is that physics is the science of the ways of taking hold of bodies and pushing them!" (*Science,* January 2, 1903.)

3. [No sign of a return.]

PAUL HENLE

James's Theory of Meaning*

Central in James's entire philosophy is the theory of meaning, the analysis of the conditions under which statements are significant. In the broadest outlines of this theory, James agreed with Peirce and freely acknowledged his indebtedness. With Peirce, he held that the way to understand an idea is to envisage its possible consequences in experience. Thus, to say "My pipe has gone out" is implicitly to predict, among other things, that if I draw on it, I will experience no taste; if I stick my finger into the bowl, I will not be burned; and so with innumerable other consequences. These are all ways in which my experience will be different if the pipe has gone out.

So far, there is nothing new or startling in the theory. From any point of view, an investigation of the consequences of an idea may contribute to its understanding. What was both new and startling in Pierce's theory, however, and again James agreed, was that the entire meaning of any statement could be given by these consequences in experience. Given that, if I draw on the pipe, I will taste nothing, that I may stick my finger in the bowl without burning it, and the vast number of other similar experiential consequences which might be drawn, then one has the entire meaning of saying that my pipe has gone out. The analysis in the case of my pipe is simple, but James would hold that any conception could be reduced in this way to a set of differences in experience—actual or possible experience. This is the pragmatic theory of meaning.

Such a theory has the effect of reducing disputes to concrete terms and getting away from purely verbal arguments. Consider the pair of statements, "This table is exactly one yard long" and "This table is not quite a yard long, but it is so close that no measuring instrument can detect

*From Paul Henle, "William James: Introduction," in *Classic American Philosophers* (pp. 115–122, 125–127), edited by Max H. Fisch. Copyright, 1951. Reprinted by permission of Mrs. Jeanne Henle and Appleton-Century-Crofts, Educational Division, Meredith Corporation.

the difference." At first sight, the statements would appear to be incompatible and to contradict each other. Applying the pragmatic criterion of meaning, however, what each statement comes to is that the table measures a yard regardless of the instrument employed. Thus the experiential consequences are the same in the two cases and the meanings are seen to be identical. Instead of a conflict, we have alternative verbal formulations of the same idea.

It may happen again that a statement which appears meaningful actually lacks meaning. Suppose I were to tell you that there is an imp sitting in the corner of the room, an imp about three feet tall with a long pointed tail. Suppose I were to add that our imp is perfectly transparent, that he keeps out of the reach of people, that he dodges when things are thrown at him, that he is altogether silent, and is so thoroughly washed as to have no detectable odor. In what way would you be the wiser for this information? From James's point of view, the answer is clear. In no way would experience be different if there were such an imp or if there were not. Hence there is no choice between the alternatives and no meaning to the entire description.

Still, the description seems intelligible. The reason is that one time it was perfectly meaningful to say that there was an imp about. It meant that one was likely, quite inexplicably, to have his ears tweaked; that if one turned suddenly, he might catch a glimpse of a shadowy figure disappearing; and that if one sniffed carefully, he might detect the faintest aroma of brimstone. In our description, however, all these meanings have been cancelled out and what remains comes simply to nothing.

So far, in consideration of what ideas are meaningful, we have considered only the direct consequences of the statement itself. Under some conditions, James is willing to go further than this and broaden his theory of meaning. An illustration may make the position clear. Take such an issue as the existence of God. James is convinced that the traditional attempts to demonstrate His existence are a complete failure. On the other hand there is no disproof of the existence of God. There seems to be no possible appeal to experience, no way in which our experience would be different, in the foreseeable future at least, if God exists or does not. By the criteria we

have been sketching, therefore, the issue is meaningless. Still, a belief in God makes a difference in people's lives; they feel different and may even act differently. Hence there is a difference in people's experience caused by a belief in God, and this difference, James believes, is enough to give the issue meaning.

Thus, James construes broadly the difference which a statement must make in possible experience to be meaningful. It may be that there are consequences of the statement subject to scientific test; or it may be that there are no such consequences, but that belief in the statement makes a difference. In any case, however, the general principle holds; wherever there is meaning there is a difference in some possible experience.

James's first and most striking application of this doctrine is to the problem of truth. The tradition in Western philosophy has accorded truth an awe and reverence approaching that given to deity itself. Science has professed a devotion to truth and to truth alone. James raises the question why. As the ancient sceptics pointed out, true and false statements may look quite similar and there may be as much evidence for one as for the other. If truth is stranger than fiction, fiction is often more interesting. Why then this devotion to truth? James's answer is to give a pragmatic analysis of the meaning of the term "true." If a statement is true, what difference does this make in any experience, actual or possible? So far as James can see, the difference comes to this: If one acts on a true statement, he will not be disappointed in his expectations; if he acts on a false one, he is likely to be disappointed.

Thus, truth is a good guide to conduct, falsity is not. Here, then, is the difference between truth and falsity in experience and, since experience determines meanings, this is the meaning of the term "truth."

James's view can be put in other terms. In science, an hypothesis is accepted or rejected because of its ability or inability to explain certain data and give rise to successful predictions. So long as a theory enables one to anticipate the outcome of experiments it is accepted and held to be a "good" theory. James's view is equivalent to holding that all our beliefs are to be treated as if they were scientific theories; to be accepted as good or true to the extent, and only to the extent, that they enable us to anticipate the course of events. Thus, even so simple a statement as "My pipe has gone out" is to be regarded not as a picture of the nature of things, but rather as an explanation of my present sensations as I suck and as a suggestion that it is safe to put my finger in the bowl. To the extent that future experience bears this out, it is a good theory and, by James's analysis, a true statement.

James formulates his view in other terms as well. The true is what is better to believe. The true is what agrees with reality, meaning by "reality" subsequent experience. The true is what "works." All of these statements are loose, probably intentionally so, and are liable to misinterpretation. James's critics took full advantage of this possibility of misrepresentation. Suppose, for example, I am invited to dinner by an utter bore and invent a previous engagement even though I have no plans for the evening in question. The man is satisfied, arranges dinner without me, and I am spared a tedious evening. In a sense, this works and, in a sense, if I dislike the man sufficiently, this is a good guide for conduct. Thus pragmatists were accused of saying what they pleased and calling it the truth.

But this is not the sense of working or being a good guide to conduct that James intended, and he was careful to make the point entirely explicit. Before one can say that a theory works, one must recall what work it is supposed to do. We have seen that the function of beliefs is to anticipate experience and, in the case of a deliberate lie such as we have been considering, there is no accurate clue to what is coming. Someone might, for example, try to locate me on the assumption that I had a previous engagement and call all my friends' houses. The last place one would look would be my home where, in all probability, I should be. Thus though the excuse would work in one sense, this is not the sense that James requires for a statement to qualify as true.

In order to work and be a good guide to conduct, then, a belief must not be arbitrary but must take account of the realities with which it deals. There are other limitations as well. A belief which came in conflict with most of our other beliefs would lead only to confusion. We would anticipate one sort of future on the basis of the new one. Hence James requires that, to be counted as true, a belief be consistent with previous opinions, at least so far as is possible. It is true of course,

expecially in the case of new scientific theories, that consistency with all that was previously believed is usually impossible and something must be sacrificed. Even here, however, the sacrifice of old beliefs must be kept at a minimum and the entire system of truths brought into consistency, with the least abandonment of the old.

In spite of these strict requirements on what may be considered true, there are cases in which one has the right and even is forced simply to decide what he will believe. These are cases in which there are neither immediate evidences from experience nor conclusive implications of other truths. Consider, as James does in one essay, the question, is life worth living? Conclusive evidence in the form of a demonstration one way or the other is lacking. One may decide that it is not worth living and the pessimism induced thereby will probably result in a life that indeed is not worth living. Or one may decide that the evidence is inconclusive and be left by one's doubts in a state hardly more worth enduring. Or, finally, one may adopt a faith that life is worth living and through that determination make it so. In this case belief freely adopted creates its own truth. The attitude, once taken and adhered to, creates its own verification in subsequent experience. This possibility of arriving at a truth by other than intellectual means, was a cardinal point of James's philosophy and the theory of it is developed in "The Will to Believe." It is important to notice, however, that James allows this method of settling problems only as a last resort, only when there is no possibility of obtaining evidence by any ordinary method. Even then, there are further restrictions.

It is a corollary of James's theory of truth that truth is a matter of degree. A belief may work, or be a good guide to conduct, not absolutely, but to a limited extent. James is ready to say that the belief is true to that extent but no further. It follows, also, and this aspect of his theory outraged his contemporaries most, that truth may change. At the very least, truth grows as new theories are developed and confirmed.

We have seen that in one formulation James considered the truth as what was better to believe, thus making truth one species of good and raising the question as to what constitutes good and what general ethical principles can be established. James answers the question in an essay, "The

Moral Philosopher and the Moral Life," ... This essay has been the basis of a number of developments in ethics and in attempts to work out a general theory embracing ethics and esthetics.

James begins the essay with the same sort of treatment which characterized his discussion as to whether or not life is worth living, by a bold assertion, made in the hope that it will be self-justifying, that there is an ethical truth. He definitely rejects a complete relativism or, as he calls it, an "ethical skepticism." The problem then becomes not "Is there an ethical norm?" but rather "What is it?"

But although James insists that an ethical standard is possible, he is not willing to set up his own beliefs or preferences as absolute standards. To do this would be to renounce the attempt to attain objectivity and simply add one more to the many systems of ethics. Rather the philosopher must compare the various standards of values which have been advocated in the attempt to discover something universal in all of them. James argues that one common element in all moral situations is the presence of some conscious being or agent and he appeals to the reader to agree that if there were no conscious beings, there could be no good or bad. To be good is to be good in the eyes of some one, and a universe devoid of life would be simply amoral. Continuing this line of reasoning, it is an easy step to conclude that what is common to all things which are good is that they satisfy some sort of demand or appeal to some one. This being the case, James is ready to say that to be good is to satisfy demand. This gives a standard which is at once universal, giving a basis for an ethical theory and at the same time avoids the peculiar preferences of any one philosopher.

The equation of good with satisfaction of demand requires some explanation. If an act satisfies the demands of one person and not of others, how is it to be evaluated? James claims that no demand, as such, is preferable to any other and that, in case of conflict, the action which satisfies the most demands should prevail. Similarly in cases where an individual is torn by a conflict of his own demands, the better line of conduct is what satisfies the most, or more persistent, or strongest demands. To be good, then, is to satisfy demand; the ideal would be to satisfy all demands, but, since this is impossible in practice, that is better which satisfies more demands.

This is a general account of the procedure of solving ethical problems, but it does not give the answer to any specific problem. James is content to leave the matter in this state, maintaining that, for the solution of specific problems, specific factual knowledge is necessary. To decide what line of action will produce the most satisfaction, requires a knowledge of the consequences of that action, as well as of the way in which people will react to it. Thus the question goes out of the domain in which the philosopher has peculiar competence and into that where practice and experience hold sway.

James's ethical position was formulated long before he wrote his lectures on pragmatism. As a result the language is somewhat different, but the underlying thought is the same. When James enquires into the characteristics of moral situations and concludes that there could be no good in a world where there are no sentient beings, what he is doing is to raise, in pragmatic terms, the question of the meaning of the term "good." The difference which is made by something being good, in experiential terms, is simply that a demand is satisfied; or, to be more accurate, that more demands are satisfied than frustrated. Since this is the concrete difference made by something being good, this is the meaning of the term. What James has done, then, in his ethical analysis is to apply the pragmatic theory, both in his act of faith in declaring that there is an answer to the problems and in his development of just how the answer is to be obtained.

Turning to other aspects of his philosophy, we find James calling his theory of mind and matter *radical empiricism*. The theory was never worked out fully and is represented only by a series of articles which were published in book form posthumously. ... In his thought, unquestionably, radical empiricism is an outgrowth of the pragmatic method, but the view can be arrived at in other ways and it has influenced the American neo-realists and even such arch-enemies of pragmatism as Bertrand Russell.

In essence, the doctrine of radical empiricism consists in two points, the first of which differentiates it from the older British empiricism. Locke, Berkeley, and Hume had tried to analyze knowledge in terms of simple sensations and then to reconstitute it out of these components. In this discussion the relations between simple sensations were largely imposed on them and, in later times, this became the central point of attack upon the empiricists by their idealist critics. James admitted the point of the criticism but reaffirmed the empirical position by contending that relations are given in the same sense as the terms they relate. The relation of one thing being on another, for example, is given in the same way as the sensations of the things one of which is on the other. Thus James holds that relations are not a mental addition to the given elements of experience, but rather a part and parcel of the given, presented in the same manner as other aspects. The result is an empiricism more adequate than that developed by James's predecessors.

The other basic point of radical empiricism is that the same element of experience may function in different contexts. In particular, it may function both as an element of consciousness and as a part of physical reality. When I look at my pipe, for example, my percept, what I see, may at once be part of my consciousness and part of the physical pipe. There is no need to speak of a mental image duplicating the physical reality; what is given may be at once mental and physical, mental if considered as part of my pattern of thought, physical if considered along with the other aspects which constitute the pipe. The pipe itself may be regarded simply as the sum-total of its actual and possible appearances. This view of matter is closely related to Berkeley's and differs only in allowing possible appearances on existence outside of mind. Mind and matter, then, instead of being different kinds of stuff, become different organizations of the same material. The difference between them is one of entering into different relationships, not of being different substances.

If we take the two main theses of radical empiricism together, it is clear that the way is paved for a monistic view of the world which does not require mind as something over and beyond experience necessary to supply the relationships which link the various parts of experience. The relations are there as aspects of the experience. Neither is mind reduced in the manner of the materialists to something inert and completely non-mental. Rather the entire world is thought of as constituted of entities mental, in that they enter into the constitution of minds, and physical, in that a different organization of them gives

physical objects. "Pure experience" is the name James gives to this neutral stuff. . . .

If this description of James's philosophy is at all correct, any attempt to assess and evaluate it must be concerned primarily with the theory of meaning which is the core of the whole point of view. In this connection, it will be useful to employ a distinction which James draws in the first chapter of *Pragmatism* between those philosophers whom he calls "tough-minded" and those who are "tender-minded." James describes the tough-minded as being empiricists, pluralists, and irreligious; the tender-minded have the opposite characteristics. James suggests pragmatism as a view to appeal to both types of philosopher. In this contention I think James is right; but he achieves his result only be employing two theories of meaning, the one to appeal to the tough-minded and the other to the tender-minded philosophers. The two theories cover different ground, and so are complementary rather than contradictory; but I believe they are distinct and represent different points of view.

To take first what may be called the tough-minded theory, we have seen that the basic tenet of pragmatism is that the meaning of any statement consists in its consequences for possible experience. Where there are no such consequences, there is no meaning. A rigid adherence to this theory would yield a view more closely related to Dewey's instrumentalism and in many respects similar to contemporary positivism. It would rule out many metaphysical issues, including such questions as the existence of God.

But James finds this theory of meaning too narrow. A belief in God makes a difference in the life of the believer and so must be accounted meaningful. But notice that in this case it is not the statement itself which has consequences for experience, but rather the believing of the statement. One deduces consequences, not from the statement, but from the fact that someone believes it. Thus it is not the existence of God which makes a difference in what one will experience, but rather it is the belief which colors one's attitude toward life and so makes a difference. Thus the will to believe may be differentiated from the other aspects of James's pragmatism in that it considers not properly the consequences of a statement, but the consequences of believing the statement.

There is a further point, however, in this connection. Suppose that a belief in God, as James suggests, affects a person's emotional outlook and mode of conduct, and consider the meaning of the statement "God exists" from the point of view of the person holding the belief. If it is to be believed, the statement must itself have meaning. This meaning cannot be the consequences of holding the belief, since, for the believer, these consequences are the result of holding the belief, not the meaning of the statement itself. Thus if a person is to feel relief because he is sure God exists, the relief is not the meaning of saying that God exists, but rather the result of the belief. Neither can the statement have meaning in the tough-minded sense previously discussed, since admittedly there is no experimental test for the existence of God. Thus there must be another, unexplained sense of meaning in which James is ready to allow that the statement "God exists" is meaningful. This might be called the tender-minded view of meaning, a view which would allow meaning to any statement whatsoever, provided only that believing it makes a difference in the attitude or conduct of the believer.

To summarize James's theory of meaning: A statement is meaningful if either (a) it has experiential consequences, or (b) it has no such consequences, but belief in it has experiential consequences. In case (a) the experiential consequences constitute the meaning. This is the tough-minded view. In case (b) there is no explanation of what constitutes the meaning and we are left with the bare criterion of meaningfulness. This is the tender-minded view.[1]

James uses the two standards of meaning in a complementary fashion, being willing to make use of any statement which is meaningful by either criterion. Even though Professor A. O. Lovejoy pointed out the difference in standards in unmistakable terms, James was not impressed and continued to use the two without distinction.

It is easy to trace the two views of meaning through the remainder of James's philosophy. The doctrine of the will to believe is clearly dependent on the tender-minded view. So are his cosmology and his philosophy of religion which depend on the will to believe. The radical empiricism, on the other hand, is an outgrowth of the tough-minded view, insisting as it does on taking reality as just what it shows itself to be. The ethics shows a combination of the two views employing the will to believe and the tender-minded theory in the insistence that there is an ethical truth and the tough-minded view in the determination of what that truth is. This dualism of theory of meaning, then, runs through James's entire philosophy, some of his doctrines having the one source, some the other. This is not to claim that there is any gap or inconsistency in the entire philosophy. It is merely that different parts of it rest on different theories of meaning. The parts, however, in James's thought fit together as neatly as the white and yolk of an egg.

Perhaps it is merely the temper of the age which followed him, or perhaps a difference in the intrinsic worth of the two aspects of his philosophy, but at any rate, that side of James's philosophy which I have called tough-minded has been much more influential than the other. In general, James's cosmology has been neglected, his philosophy of religion has lost much of its influence, and the theory of the will-to-believe has few, if any, followers. The pragmatic theory of meaning is, however, very much alive and, indeed, holds almost exclusive sway in contemporary discussions of semantics. Similarly, the radical empiricism, as well as aspects of the ethics and theory of truth, while not always discussed in James's terminology, are in the forefront of present-day discussion. This side of James's philosophy has as much vitality today as on the day it was written.

NOTES

1. It is tempting to say that in case (b) the consequences of the belief constitute the meaning. It would be possible to read parts of Chapter III of *Pragmatism* in support of this interpretation. But section V of "The Moral Philosopher and the Moral Life," as well as the discussions of philosophy of religion, rule it out, for reasons indicated above.

PART 3 MIND AND ITS

To a large degree, what has come to be known as the "Mind-Body Problem" in philosophy is a product of the philosophy of René Descartes. How can things differing as radically as minds (or souls) and bodies, in Descartes's conception, be so intimately related, as they clearly are, in every human person? Bodies are solid chunks of material stuff, extended in three-dimensional space, publicly observable and measurable, possessed of a certain mass and velocity, and capable of causing things to happen, in accordance with the invariant laws of mechanics, by transmitting their impact in "collisions" with other material things. A mind, on the other hand, is directly "observable" only by the person who owns it; only he can think his thoughts, feel his emotions, suffer his pains. Although, under certain circumstances, someone else can cut open his skill and see and touch his living *brain,* there is no conceivable way for another to see or touch his mind or its beliefs, sensations, and desires. Minds, moreover, have no size or shape or spatial location, no mass, or velocity, or capacity to make impact.

Nevertheless, to common sense, it seems certain that minds and bodies do causally interact. When I will, or wish, or desire (mental events) to raise my arm, up it goes (bodily event); and when a sliver of wood penetrates my flesh (bodily event), I feel pain (mental event). It would surely seem, then, that, in normal volition, mental events *cause* physical ones and that, in sensation and perception, physical events *cause* mental ones. Yet how can this be? How can the mind, a mass-less, weightless, unextended thing, push up against a nerve cell and cause an impulse to be transmitted along a nerve to a muscle? And how can physical stimuli like wood slivers or even light rays penetrate a thing that has no size or location and cause it to have an experience? Isn't this as inconceivable as a collision between a physical object and a ghost? This is the kind of difficulty cited by Pierre Gassendi in his objections to Descartes's theory of the interaction between mind and body. (Gassendi was one of a number of distinguished philosophers, theologians, and scientists invited to comment on the manuscript of Descartes's *Meditations* before it was published. Their "Objections" were then forwarded to Descartes, who in turn composed "Replies," and published the whole exchange along with the original work. The entire discussion is strongly recommended to the serious student of Descartes's philosophy.)

Most important seventeenth-century philosophers, no matter how impressed in other ways by the "Cartesian philosophy" (as the philosophy of Descartes came to be called), found Descartes's theory of interaction between mind and body unacceptable. Some came, therefore to abandon the part of Descartes's philosophy that generated the difficulty: his *dualism,* or theory that mind and matter are distinct and independent kinds of substances, each capable of existing quite independently of the other. *Idealism* of Berkeley's sort was one alternative. *Materialism*—the theory that mind is either reducible to, or ultimately dependent upon, matter—was another. Others kept a kind of dualism, but abandoned the common-sense view that mind and body do really interact causally. Some held, for example, that the wood sliver's penetration of my flesh does not *cause* me pain; rather, it is the *occasion* for God, whose infinite nature somehow encompasses both mind and matter, to cause me to feel pain, and similarly that my desire to raise my arm is simply the occasion for God's causing my arm to go up. This is the theory called *occasionalism.* Others held the view called *parallelism,* according to which mind and body only appear to interact because of a kind of "pre-established harmony" between their life histories. Leibniz likened this parallelism to that between two clocks that strike at the same moment, having been wound up together and each designed to keep accurate time, in causal independence of each other.

Efforts to solve the mind-body problem by such means are quite unnecessary, C. D. Broad argues in his spirited defense of interactionism, for, once we state and consider carefully the reasons that have been urged against causal interaction of mind and body, we can find no basis in them for denying the deliverances of common sense on this matter. The Australian materialist philosopher, J. J. C. Smart, interprets the verdicts of common sense somewhat differently. He appeals directly to the methodological principle called "Ockham's razor" (after William of Ockham, c. 1285–1349). Ockham's "principle of parsimony," as it is sometimes called, decrees that nothing is to be assumed in an explanation beyond what is strictly necessary to account for the data, that "entities are not to be multiplied without necessity." To hold that experiences, such as aches and pains, sensations, after-images, and desires, are something distinct in kind from matter, something "over and above" the physico-chemical processes of the brain, seems to Smart to violate Ockham's razor. The most economical view, he maintains, is that which holds sensations to be simply identical with brain processes in the same sense of "identical" as that in which lightning flashes are held to be identical with electrical discharges. Smart's article is one of the influential expressions of that "identity theory" of mind and body which has come into a new popularity and has been the object of considerable controversy in recent years. It seems safe to say that the leading rival solutions to the mind-body problem at this time are either forms of dualism or else variants of the identity theory. The identity theory should be carefully distinguished (as it is by Smart) from another form of materialism ("epiphenomenalism"), which holds that mind is a distinct but causally impotent by-product of the world charted by physics.

In the section on "Survival of Death and Personal Identity" the controversy between dualism and materialism continues, though with a narrower focus and special emphasis —on the question of death and immortality. C. J. Ducasse (1881–1969), one of our century's most distinguished proponents of dualism, employs the doctrine of the causal interaction and independence of body and mind in his effort to show that a life after death is at least conceivable. If body and mind are one and the same thing, or if mind is a mere "epiphenomenon" or by-product of body, then it would follow that the disintegration of mind (soul, self) would proceed *pari passu* with the disintegration of the body. But if our minds are distinct substances, and causally efficacious in their own right, then it is at least possible that they (we) can survive the death of their (our) bodies. That survival is possible is the main conclusion for which Ducasse here argues. (Note that survival is not the same as immortality, or *permanent* survival.) Whether survival is an actual fact Ducasse takes to be an empirical question, for which the only available evidence is that provided by psychical research.

Antony Flew, of the University of Keele, addresses himself to a riddle that troubled many tough-minded philosophers in the 1930s. The claim that men survive death cannot be directly disproved empirically; for if death is in fact the permanent cessation of consciousness, there can never be any *experience* to show it to be such. After I die, I will never know that death is unconsciousness, nor will I know anything else. But it seems that we can at least conceive what empirical evidence *for* survival would look like. I can imagine (so it was often said) what it would be like to witness, unobserved by anyone else, my own funeral. This is the claim that Flew submits to careful and unsympathetic scrutiny. One thing that emerges very clearly from Flew's essay is that if we are to make philosophical progress in discussions of survival, we must get clear about a set of prior questions that are not normally treated in works on the mind-body problem; namely, questions about *personal identity.* Who or what am I, this entity whose possible survival of death is under discussion? Am I simply this body, and nothing more? What then of my belief that this body "belongs" to me, that the owner is one thing and his body another? Am I simply my mind? Am I a self that somehow encompasses both body and mind? Could I be the *same self* that I am now if I had none of my present memories, or if I suddenly discovered myself with an altogether different body (e.g., with four legs and a tail)? How much can I change without ceasing to be the person I am now? These are only some of the riddles associated with the elusive concept of personal identity. Still others are suggested by more recondite possibilities: resurrection of the dead, reincarnation, transmigration of souls, bodily transfers, multiple or alternate possession of a body by various persons, brain transplants, and "brain rejuvenations"—examples drawn from theology, psychic research, abnormal psychology, and science fiction.

The classic theory of personal identity is that of John Locke. It is *memory*, primarily, that makes one a person, and the ability to remember past experiences that makes one the same person as the one who originally had those experiences. Although Locke's position has been criticized for, among other things, an apparent circularity of argument (memory presupposes personal identity and cannot therefore also be used to define it), Sydney Shoemaker comes to the defense of the Lockean position by employing a causal theory of memory. In the final selection in this section, Terrence Penelhum, of the University of Calgary, considers one of Locke's fanciful examples (an exchange of bodies between a cobbler and a prince) but rejects Locke's claim that it illustrates the priority of memory to bodily continuity as a criterion of personal identity.

Just as dualism implies the possibility of survival of bodily death, so materialism raises the intriguing question of consciousness in machines. "It seems to me," writes J. J. C. Smart, "that science is increasingly giving us a viewpoint whereby organisms are able to be seen as physico-chemical mechanisms: it seems that even the behavior of man himself will one day be explicable in mechanistic terms." No matter how complicated a "physico-chemical mechanism" may be, the methods of science can discover how it works, and our ever more sophisticated engineering techniques can enable us to put models of it together ourselves. Thus, it should be possible, in principle at least (though well beyond our present techniques), for us to construct robots (made out of metals and plastics) or androids (made out of protoplasm and biological materials) that can do whatever human beings can do—"fall in love, go mad (power- or otherwise), annoy with oversolicitousness ... have feelings, thoughts, attitudes, and character traits."[1] In 1747, Julien Offray De La Mettrie caused a great scandal by publishing a book, *L'Homme Machine,* which boldly argued that man *is* a kind of self-sufficient, self-operated, "organic machine," but very few important philosophers have taken this thesis very seriously. With the revolution in computer technology after World War II, however, there has been a revival of interest in the question whether man is a machine. The characteristic form of La Mettrie's question in the computer age is ". . . what if any human property prevents a super-computer from saying [truly] 'anything you can do, I can do better'?"[2] The challenge this question poses is taken up by Paul Ziff, of the University of North Carolina, and L. J. Cohen, of Oxford, who argue in separate ways that any being properly called a machine, whose "mental life" had been completely programmed, could not possibly be said to have feelings or "a mind of its own" without violence to our concepts of mind and person. In the concluding essay, Keith Gunderson, of the University of Minnesota, rejects the arguments of Ziff and Cohen. Professor Gunderson maintains that the question of machine mentality is still open and suggests ways in which the study of computer simulation of human mental processes can throw new light on those processes themselves.

[1]Hilary Putnam, "Robots: Machines or Artificially Created Life?" in Sidney Hook, ed., *Dimensions of Mind* (New York: New York University Press, 1960), pp. 63–64.
[2]Michael Scriven, "The Compleat Robot," in Sidney Hook, ed. *Dimensions of Mind* (New York: New York University Press, 1960), p. 113.

PIERRE GASSENDI

Objections to Descartes' Sixth Meditation*

... *For finally you say:* And although possibly (or rather certainly, as I shall say in a moment) I possess a body with which I am very intimately conjoined, yet because on the one side I have a clear and distinct idea of myself, inasmuch as I am only a thinking and not an extended thing, and on the other I possess a distinct idea of body, inasmuch as it is only an extended and not a thinking thing; it is certain that I am really distinct from my body, and can exist without it.

So this was your objective, was it? Hence, since the whole of the difficulty hinges on this, we must halt awhile, in order to see how you manage to make this position good. The principal matter here in questions is the distinction between you and body. But what body do you here mean? Plainly this solid body composed of members, the body to which, without doubt, the following words refer: I possess a body connected with myself and it is certain that I am distinct from my body, *etc.*

But now, O Mind, there is no difficulty about this body. There would be a difficulty, if with the greater part of philosophers I were to object that you were the realisation, the perfection, the activity, the form, the appearance, or, to use a popular fashion of speech, a mode of the body. They, forsooth, do not acknowledge that you are more distinct and separable from your body than figure, or

any other mode. This, too, they maintain, whether you are the entire soul, or are besides also νοὺς δυνάμει, νοὺς παθητικός, *the potential intellect, or passive intellect, as they style it. But it pleases me to deal somewhat liberally with you and consider you as though you were the* νοὺς ποιητικός, *the active intellect, nay, even as* Χωριστός, *i.e., capable of separate existence, though separable in another sense than they imagined.*

For since those philosophers assigned it to all men (if not rather to all things) as something common to them and as being the source of intellectual activity on the part of the potential intellect, exactly in the same way and with the same necessity as light supplies the eye with the opportunity of seeing (whence they were wont to compare it to the light of the sun, and hence to regard it as coming from without), I myself rather consider you (as you also are quite willing I should) as a certain special intellect exercising domination in the body.

Moreover I repeat that the difficulty is not as to whether you are separable or not from this body (whence, shortly before, I hinted that it was not necessary to recur to the power of God in order to secure the separability of those things which you apprehend as separate), but from the body which you yourself are: seeing that possibly you really are a subtle body diffused within that solid one, or occupying some seat within it. But you have not yet convinced us that you are anything absolutely incorporeal. Likewise, though in the second Meditation you proclaimed that you are not a wind, nor a fire, nor a vapour, nor a breath, do be advised

---

*From the "Objections and Replies" published with Descartes' *Meditations* in the second edition (1642); trans. Elizabeth Haldane and G. R. T. Ross (London: Cambridge University Press, 1931), pp. 195–203. Reprinted by permission of the publisher.

of the warning I give you, that the statement thus announced has not been proved.

You said *that you did not at that point dispute about those matters;* but you have not subsequently discussed them, nor have you in any way proved that you are not a body of this kind. I had hoped that here you would make the matter good; but if you do discuss anything, if you do prove anything, your discussion and proof merely show that you are not the solid body, about which, as I have already said, there is no difficulty.

4. But, *you say,* I have on the one hand a clear and distinct idea of myself, in so far as I am merely a thinking thing and not extended, and on the other a distinct idea of body, in so far as it is an extended thing, but not one that thinks. *Firstly, however, in so far as the idea of body is concerned, there appears to be no need for spending much pains over it. For, if you indeed make this pronouncement about the idea of body universally, we must repeat our previous objection, namely that you have to prove that it is incompatible with the nature of body to be capable of thinking. Thus it would be a begging of the question when the problem was raised by you as* to whether you are a subtle body or not, *in a way that implied that thought is incompatible with body.*

But since you make that assertion and certainly treat only of that solid body, from which you maintain that you are separable and distinct, I do not on that account so much deny that you have an idea of yourself, as maintain that you could not possess it if you were really an unextended thing. For, I ask you, how do you think that you, an unextended subject, could receive into yourself the semblance or idea of a body which is extended? For, if such a semblance proceeds from the body, it is certainly corporeal and has parts outside of other parts, and consequently is corporeal. Or alternatively, whether or not its impression is due to some other source, since necessarily it always represents an extended body, it must still have parts and, consequently, be extended. Otherwise, if it has no parts, how will it represent parts? If it has no extension how will it represent extension? If devoid of figure, how represent an object possessing figure? If it has no position, how can it represent a thing which has upper and lower, right and left, and intermediate parts? If without variation, how represent the various colours, etc.? Therefore an idea appears not to lack extension utterly. But

unless it is devoid of extension how can you, if unextended, be its subject? How will you unite it to you? How lay hold of it? How will you be able to feel it gradually fade and finally vanish away?

Next, relatively to your idea of yourself nothing is to be added to what has been already said, and especially in the second Meditation. For thence it is proved that, far from having a clear and distinct idea of yourself, you seem to be wholly without one. This is because, even though you recognise that you think, you do not know of what nature you, who think, are. Hence, since this operation alone is known to you, the chief matter is, nevertheless, hidden from you, namely, the substance which so operates. This brings up the comparison in which you may be likened to a blind man, who, on feeling heat, and being told that it proceeds from the sun, should think that he has a clear and distinct idea of the sun, inasmuch as, if anyone ask him what the sun is, he can reply: it is something which produces heat.

But, you will say, I here add not only that I am a thinking thing, *but that I am* a thing which is not extended. *But not to mention that this is asserted without proof, since it is still in question, I ask firstly: for all that have you a clear and distinct idea of yourself? You say that you are not extended; but in so doing you say what you are not, not what you are. In order to have a clear and distinct idea, or, what is the same thing, a true and genuine idea of anything, is it not necessary to know the thing itself positively, and so to speak affirmatively, or does it suffice to know that it is not any other thing? Would it not then be a clear and distinct idea of Bucephalus, if one knew of him that he was not a fly?*

But, not to urge this, my question is rather: are you not an extended thing, or are you not diffused throughout the body? I cannot tell what you will reply; for, though from the outset I recognised that you existed only in the brain, I formed that belief rather by conjecture than by directly following your opinion. I derived my conjecture from the statement which ensures, in which you assert, that you are not affected by all parts of the body, but only by the brain, or even by one of its smallest parts. *But I was not quite certain whether you were found therefore only in the brain or in a part of it, since you might be found in the whole body, but be acted on at only one part. Thus it would be according to the popular belief, which takes the* soul to be diffused throughout the entire body, while yet it is in the eye alone that it has vision.

Similarly the following words moved one to doubt: 'and, although the whole mind seems to be united to the whole body,' etc. You indeed do not there assert that you are united with the whole of the body, but you do not deny it. Howsoever it be, with your leave let me consider you firstly as diffused throughout the whole body. Whether you are the same as the soul, or something diverse from it, I ask you, O unextended thing, what you are that are spread from head to heel, or that are coextensive with the body, that have a like number of parts corresponding to its parts? Will you say that you are therefore unextended, because you are a whole in a whole, and are wholly in every part? I pray you tell me, if you maintain this, how you conceive it. Can a single thing thus be at the same time wholly in several parts? Faith assures us of this in the case of the sacred mystery (of the Eucharist). But the question here is relative to you, a natural object, and is indeed one relative to our natural light. Can we grasp how there can be a plurality of places without there being a plurality of objects located in them? Is not a hundred more than one? Likewise, if a thing is wholly in one place, can it be in others, unless it is itself outside itself, as place is outside place? Say what you will, it will at least be obscure and uncertain whether you are wholly in any part and not rather in the various parts of the body by means of your several parts. And since it is much more evident that nothing can exist as a whole in different places, it will turn out to be still more clear that you are not wholly in the single parts of your body but merely in the whole as a whole, and that you are so by means of your parts diffused through the whole and consequently that you have extension.

Secondly let us suppose that you are in the brain alone, or merely in some minute part of it. You perceive that the same thing is clearly an objection, since, however small that part be, it is nevertheless extended, and you are coextensive with it, and consequently are extended and have particular parts corresponding to its particular parts. Will you say that you take that part of the brain to be a point? That is surely incredible, but suppose it is a point. If it is indeed something Physical, the same difficulty remains, because such a point is extended and is certainly not devoid of parts. If it

is a Mathematical point you know that it is given only by the imagination. But let it be given or let rather us feign that in the brain there is given a Mathematical point, to which you are united, and in which you exist. Now, see how useless a fiction this will turn out to be. For, if it is to be assumed, we must feign it to exist in such a way that you are at the meeting place of the nerves by which all the regions informed by the soul transmit to the brain the ideas or semblances of the things perceived by the senses. But firstly, the nerves do not all meet at one point, whether for the reason that, as the brain is continued into the spinal marrow, many nerves all over the back pass into that, or because those which extend to the middle of the head are not found to terminate in the same part of the brain. But let us assume that they all do meet; none the less they cannot all unite in a mathematical point, since they are bodies, not mathematical lines, and so able to meet in a mathematical point. And supposing we grant that they do so unite, it will be impossible for the spirits[1] which pass through these to pass out of the nerves or to enter them, as being bodies; since body cannot be in or pass through what is not a place, as the mathematical point is. But though we should allow that the animal spirits do exist in or pass through what is not a place, nevertheless you, existing as you do in a point, in which there are neither right hand parts nor left hand, neither higher nor lower, nor anything similar, cannot judge as to whence they come nor what they report.

Moreover I say the same thing of those spirits which you must transmit in order to have feeling or to report tidings,[2] and in order to move. I omit that we cannot grasp how you impress a motion upon them, you who are yourself in a point, unless you are really a body, or unless you have a body by which you are in contact with them and at the same time propel them. For, if you say that they are moved by themselves, and that you only direct their motion, remember that you somewhere else denied that the body is moved by itself; so that we must thence infer that you are the cause of that movement. Next, explain to us how such a direction can take place without some effort and so some motion on your part? How can there be effort directed towards anything, and motion on its part, without mutual contact of what moves and what is moved? How can there be contact apart from body, when (as is so clear to the natural light)

'Apart from body, naught touches or is touched?'[3]

Yet why do I delay here when it is on you that the onus rests of proving that you are unextended and hence incorporeal? But neither do I think that you will find an argument in the fact that man is popularly said to consist of soul and body, inferring that if one part is said to be body, the other must be declared not to be body. For, if you did so, you would give us an opportunity of drawing the distinction in such a way that man should be held to consist of a double body, viz. the solid one and the subtle one; and according to this scheme while the former retained the name body, the common term, the other would be given the name soul. I pass by the fact that the same thing would be said about the other animals, to which you have not granted a mind similar to your own; lucky they, if by your sanction they possess even a soul! Hence, therefore, when you conclude that you are certain that you are really distinct from your body, *you see that that would be admitted, but that it would not therefore be conceded that you were incorporeal, and not rather a species of very subtle body distinct from your grosser body.*

You add that hence you can exist apart from it. *But after being conceded the point that you can exist apart from that grosser body in the same way as an odoriferous vapour does while passing out of an apple and dispersing into the air, what do you think you have gained? Something more certainly than the above mentioned Philosophers wish to prove, who believe that you wholly perish at death itself; being as it were like a figure which on the alteration of the superficies so disappears, that it may be said to be non-existent or wholly nothing. Indeed, since you were something corporeal as well, or a fine substance, you will not be said to vanish wholly at death, or wholly pass into nothing, but to exist by means of your dispersed parts, howsoever much, on account of being thus drawn asunder, you are not likely to think any more, and will be said to be neither a thinking thing, nor a mind, nor a soul. Yet all these objections I bring, not in order to cast doubt on the conclusion you intend to prove, but merely by way of expressing my disagreement as to the cogency of the argument set forth by you.*

5. *In connection with this, you interpose several things tending to the same conclusion, on all of which we need not insist. One thing I note, and*

that is that you say that nature teaches you by the sensation of pain, hunger, thirst, etc., that you are not lodged in the body as a sailor in a ship, but that you are very closely united with it and, so to speak, intermingled with it so as to compose one whole along with it. For if that were not the case, *you say,* "when my body is hurt, I who am merely a thinking thing would not feel pain, but should perceive the wound with the mere understanding, just as the sailor perceives by sight when something is damaged in his vessel, and when my body has need of food or drink, I should clearly understand this fact, and not have the confused feelings of hunger and thirst. For all these sensations of hunger, thirst, pain, etc. are in truth none other than certain confused modes of thought which are produced by the union and apparent intermingling of mind and body."

This is indeed quite right; but it still remains to be explained, how that union and apparent intermingling, *or* confusion, *can be found in you, if you are incorporeal, unextended and indivisible. For if you are not greater than a point, how can you be united with the entire body, which is of such great magnitude? How, at least, can you be united with the brain, or some minute part in it, which (as has been said) must yet have some magnitude or extension, however small it be? If you are wholly without parts, how can you mix or appear to mix with its minute subdivisions? For there is no mixture unless each of the things to be mixed has parts that can mix with one another. Further, if you are discrete, how could you be involved with and form one thing along with matter itself? Again since conjunction or union exists between certain parts, ought there not to be a relation of similarity between parts of this sort? But what must the union of the corporeal with the incorporeal be thought to be? Do we conceive how stone and air are fused together, as in pumice stone, so as to become a fusion of uniform character? Yet the similarity between stone and air which itself is also a body, is greater than that between body and soul, or a wholly incorporeal mind. Further, ought not that union to take place by means of the closest contact? But how, as I said before, can that take place, apart from body? How will that which is corporeal seize upon that which is incorporeal, so to hold it conjoined with itself, or how will the incorporeal grasp the corporeal, so as reciprocally to keep it bound to itself, if in it, the incorporeal, there is nothing which it can use to grasp the other, or by which it can be grasped?*

Hence, since you admit that you feel pain, I ask you how to think that you, if you are incorporeal and unextended, are capable of experiencing the sensation of pain. Thus the affection pain can only be understood as arising from some pulling asunder of bodily parts when something interferes and annuls their continuity. For example a state of pain is an unnatural state, but how can that be in an unnatural state or be affected contrary to nature, which by nature is of one sort, simple, indivisible and immutable? Again since pain is either alteration, or cannot occur without it, how can that be altered, which being more devoid of parts than a point, cannot be altered nor can cease to be just as it is, unless it turns into nothing? I add also: since pain comes from the foot, the arm, and from other regions at the same time, ought there not to be in you various parts, in which you receive it in various ways, in order not to be confused and to regard it as being the pain of merely one part. But, in a word, the general difficulty always remains, viz. how the corporeal can have anything in common with the incorporeal, or what relationship may be established between the one and the other.

6. I pass by the other passages in which, in a very copious and neat argument, you strive to show that something else is in existence besides yourself and God. For you deduce the conclusion that your body and its corporeal faculties exist; and likewise other bodies which despatch into your senses and into yourself the semblances of themselves, and

produce the experiences of pleasure and pain, which beget in you desire and aversion.

And from this you at length derive the following conclusion, which is, as it were, the fruit of your reasoning, in order that since all the sensations relative to the things which have to do with the welfare of the body more frequently indicate to you truth than falsehood, *you may thence infer* that you ought no longer to fear that falsity may be found in matters every day represented to you by the senses. *You say the same, consequently, about dreams,* for since they are not connected with the whole of our actions and course of life in the same way as what we experience when awake, *you thence establish the conclusion that real things* are presented to you, not in sleep, but when you are awake. Hence, *you say next,* since God is not a deceiver, it follows that you are not deceived in such matters. *This is an extremely pious statement; and so, too, you are assuredly quite in the right when you finally conclude:* that the life of man is subject to error, and that we must acknowledge the infirmity of our nature.

NOTES

1. The 'animal spirits' correspond to the 'nervous impulses' of modern psychology. D. and his contemporaries believed that an actual substance passed along the nerve when it was stimulated.

2. Of the external world? Clerselier translates this passage 'proclaim or communicate feeling or movement.'

3. Tangere nec tangi sine corpore nulla potest res—a misquotation of Lucretius (*De Rerum natura* 1. 305):—Tangere enim et tangi, nisi corpus nulla potest res.

RENÉ DESCARTES

Reply to Gassendi*

... Finally it is worthy of you alone, O flesh, to think *that the idea of God, of an Angel, and of the human mind, are corporeal, or after the fashion of the corporeal, derived forsooth from the human form, and from other very subtle, simple, and imperceptible objects, such as air or aether.* For whosoever thus represents God or the mind to himself, tries to imagine a thing which is not imageable, and constructs nothing but a corporeal idea to which he falsely assigns the name God or mind. For, in the true idea of mind, nothing is contained but thought and its attributes, of which none is corporeal.

2. In this passage you show very clearly that you rely on prejudices merely and never divest yourself of them, when you wish to make out that we suspect no falsity in matters in which we have never detected falsity; it is thus that, *when we behold a tower close at hand and touch it, we are sure that it is square,* if it appear to be square; so too when we are really awake *we cannot doubt whether we are awake or dreaming;* and so forth. Now you have no reason to think that all the things in which error can reside have been noticed by you, and it could easily be proved that you sometimes are wrong about those things which you accept as certain. But when you come round to the position at which you state, *that at least we cannot doubt that things appear as they*

do, you have returned to the true path; your statement is one that I have myself made in the second Meditation. But here the question raised concerned the reality of external objects, and in what you have contributed to this there is nothing correct.

3. I shall not here delay to notice your tedious and frequent repetitions of such statements as, e.g. *that I have failed to prove certain matters,* which nevertheless I have demonstrated; *that I have treated only of the solid body,* though I have dealt with every kind of matter, even of the subtlest; etc. What opposition other than a plain denial is merited by affirmations of this kind, which are not supported by reasons? Yet incidentally I should like to discover what argument you use to prove that I have treated of solid matter rather than of that which is subtle. Have I not said: *'I possess (a body) united with myself, and it is certain that I am distinct from my body'?* And I cannot see why these words are not equally applicable to an impalpable and to a solid body; nor do I think that anyone but you could fail to see this. Apart from this, in the second Meditation I made it evident that mind could be understood as an existing substance, though we did not understand anything to exist that was wind, or fire, or vapour, or breath, or anything else of a bodily nature however impalpable and refined. I said however that at that point I did not discuss whether it was in truth distinct from every kind of body; but in the present passage I did discuss the matter and proved my assertion. But you

*From the "Objections and Replies" published with the *Meditations;* trans. Elizabeth Haldane and G. R. T. Ross (London: Cambridge University Press, 1931), pp. 230–233. Reprinted by permission of the publishers.

show that you have wholly failed to comprehend the controversy by your confusion of the issue as to what may be known of the soul with the question as to that which the soul really is.

4. Here you ask, *how I think that I, an unextended subject, can receive into myself the resemblance or idea of a thing which is extended.* I reply that no corporeal resemblance can be received in the mind, but that what occurs there is the pure thinking of a thing, whether it be corporeal or equally whether it be one that is incorporeal and lacking any corporeal semblance. But as to imagination, which can only be exercised in reference to corporeal things, my opinion is that it requires the presence of a semblance which is truly corporeal, and to which the mind applies itself, without, however, its being received in the mind.

Your statement *about the idea of the sun, which a blind man can derive merely from the sun's warmth,* is easily refuted. For the blind man can have a clear and distinct idea of the sun as a source of heat although he does not possess the idea of it as a source of light. Nor is your comparison of me to that blind man just: firstly, because the act of knowledge which apprehends a thing that thinks is much more extensive than our apprehension of a thing which warms, as it is much more than that of anything else, as was shown in its proper place; secondly, because no one can prove that the idea of the sun which the blind man forms, does not contain everything which can be learned of the sun, save those who, being endowed with sight, are aware in addition of its light and figure. You, however, not only know nothing more than I do of mind, but do not even have knowledge of the very thing I recognize in it; so that in this comparison it is rather you who play the part of blind man, while I, along with the whole human race, could at most be said to be one-eyed.

In adding that *the mind is not extended,* my intention was not thereby to explain what mind is, but merely to proclaim that those people are wrong who think that it is extended. In the same way if any people affirmed *that Bucephalus was Music,*[1] it would not be idle of others to deny the statement. In good truth your subsequent atempts to prove that mind is extended because it makes use of a body which is extended, seem to employ no better reasoning than if you were to argue that because Bucephalus neighs and whin-

nies, and so utters sounds that are comparable with Music, it followed that Bucephalus is Music. For, though mind is united with the whole body, it does not follow that it itself is extended throughout the body, because it is not part of its notion to be extended, but merely to think. Neither does it apprehend extension by means of an extended semblance existing in it, although it images it by applying itself to a corporeal semblance which is extended, as has already been said. Finally there is no necessity for it itself to be a body although it has the power of moving body.

5. What you say at this point *relatively to the union of mind and body* is similar to what precedes. At no place do you bring an objection to my arguments; you only set forth the doubts which you think follow from my conclusions, though they arise merely from your wishing to subject to the scrutiny of the imagination matters which, by their own nature, do not fall under it. Thus when you wish to compare the union of mind and body with the mixture of two bodies, it is enough for me to reply that no such comparison ought to be set up, because the two things are wholly diverse, and we must not imagine that there are parts in mind because it is aware of parts in body. Whence do you derive the conclusion that everything which mind knows must exist in mind? If that were so, then, when it was aware of the magnitude of the earth, it would be obliged to have that object within it, and consequently would not only be extended but greater in extent than the whole world.

6. Here though you do not contradict me at all, you have nevertheless much to say; and hence the reader may discover that the number of your arguments is not to be inferred from any proportion between them and the prolixity of your words.

Up to this point we have had a discussion between mind and flesh, and, as was but natural, in many things they disagreed. But now, at the end, I catch sight of the real Gassendi, and look up to him as a man of great philosophical eminence. I salute him as a man noted for his intellectual candour and integrity of life, and shall endeavour, by employing all the courtesies which I can muster, to merit his friendship at all times. I therefore ask him not to take it amiss if, in replying to his objections, I have used a philosophical freedom, since their entire contents caused me very great pleasure. Among other things I rejoiced that such a long and carefully composed dissertation contained nothing in opposition to my reasoning, nothing opposed even to my conclusions, to which I was not able very easily to reply.

NOTES

1. Descartes misread Gassendi's *musca* (fly) as musica. The mistake must have occurred when he saw Gassendi's work in MS. But in spite of the fact that *musca* appeared in the printed version when the work was published, so that Descartes had the opportunity of rectifying his error, he refrained from doing so. This provoked an attack by an opponent, Revius, in *Staterna Philosophiae Cartesianae*, a pamphlet published at Amsterdam in 1650.

C. D. B R O A D

The Traditional Problem of Body and Mind*

In the last chapter we considered organisms simply as complicated material systems which behave in certain characteristic ways. We did not consider the fact that some organisms are animated by minds, and that all the minds of whose existence we are certain animate organisms. And we did not deal with those features in the behaviour of certain organisms which are commonly supposed to be due to the mind which animates the organism. It is such facts as these, and certain problems to which they have given rise, which I mean to discuss in the present chapter. There is a question which has been argued about for some centuries now under the name of "Interaction"; this is the question whether minds really do act on the organisms which they animate, and whether organisms really do act on the minds which animate them. (I must point out at once that I imply no particular theory of mind or body by the word "to animate". I use it as a perfectly neutral name to express the fact that a certain mind is connected in some peculiarly intimate way with a certain body, and, under normal conditions with no other body. This is a fact even on a purely behaviouristic theory of mind; on such a view to say that the mind M animates the body B would mean that the body B, in so far as it behaves in certain ways, *is* the mind M. A body

*From C. D. Broad, *The Mind and Its Place in Nature* (London: Routledge & Kegan Paul Ltd; New York: Humanities Press Inc., 1925), pp. 95–97, 103–121. Reprinted by permission of the author and publisher.

which did not act in these ways would be said not to be animated by a mind. And a different Body B', which acted in the same general way as B, would be said to be animated by a different mind M'.)

The problem of Interaction is generally discussed at the level of enlightened common-sense, where it is assumed that we know pretty well what we mean by "mind", by "matter" and by "causation". Obviously no solution which is reached at that level can claim to be ultimate. If what we call "matter" should turn out to be a collection of spirits of low intelligence, as Leibniz thought, the argument that mind and body are so unlike that their interaction is impossible would become irrelevant. Again, if causation be nothing but regular sequence and concomitance, as some philosophers have held, it is ridiculous to regard psycho-neural parallelism and interaction as mutually exclusive alternatives. For interaction will mean no more than parallelism, and parallelism will mean no less than interaction. Nevertheless I am going to discuss the arguments here at the common-sense level, because they are so incredibly bad and yet have imposed upon so many learned men.

We start then by assuming a developed mind and a developed organism as two distinct things, and by admitting that the two are now intimately connected in some way or other which I express by saying that "this mind *animates* this organism". We assume that bodies are very much as enlightened common-sense believes them to be; and that, even if we cannot define "causation", we have some means of recognising when it is present and when it is absent. The question then is: "Does a mind ever act on the body which it animates, and does a body ever act on the mind which animates it?" The answer which common-sense would give to both questions is: "Yes, certainly". On the face of it my body acts on my mind whenever a pin is stuck into the former and a painful sensation thereupon arises in the latter. And, on the face of it, my mind acts on the body whenever a desire to move my arm arises in the former and is followed by this movement in the latter. Let us call this common-sense view "Two-sided Interaction". Although it seems so obvious it has been denied by probably a majority of philosophers and a majority of physiologists. So the question is: "Why should so many distinguished men, who have studied the subject, have denied the apparently obvious fact of Two-sided Interaction?"

ARGUMENTS AGAINST INTERACTION

... There are, so far as I know, two [scientific arguments against two-sided interaction]. One is supposed to be based on the physical principle of the Conservation of Energy, and on certain experiments which have been made on human bodies. The other is based on the close analogy which is said to exist between the structures of the physiological mechanism of reflex action and that of voluntary action. I will take them in turn.

(1) *The Argument from Energy.* It will first be needful to state clearly what is asserted by the principle of the Conservation of Energy. It is found that, if we take certain material systems, *e.g.,* a gun, a cartridge, and a bullet, there is a certain magnitude which keeps approximately constant throughout all their changes. This is called "Energy". When the gun has not been fired it and the bullet have no motion, but the explosive in the cartridge has great chemical energy. When it has been fired the bullet is moving very fast and has great energy of movement. The gun, though not moving fast in its recoil, has also great energy of movement because it is very massive. The gases produced by the explosion have some energy of movement and some heat-energy, but much less

chemical energy than the unexploded charge had. These various kinds of energy can be measured in common units according to certain conventions. To an innocent mind there seems to be a good deal of "cooking" at this stage, *i.e.,* the conventions seem to be chosen and various kinds and amounts of concealed energy seem to be postulated in order to make the principle come out right at the end. I do not propose to go into this in detail, for two reasons. In the first place, I think that the conventions adopted and the postulates made, though somewhat suggestive of the fraudulent company-promoter, can be justified by their coherence with certain experimental facts, and that they are not simply made *ad hoc.* Secondly, I shall show that the Conservation of Energy is absolutely irrelevant to the question at issue, so that it would be waste of time to treat it too seriously in the present connexion. Now it is found that the total energy of all kinds in this system, when measured according to these conventions, is approximately the same in amount though very differently distributed after the explosion and before it. If we had confined our attention to a part of this system and *its* energy this would not have been true. The bullet, *e.g.,* had no energy at all before the explosion and a great deal afterwards. A system like the bullet, the gun, and the charge, is called a "Conservative System"; the bullet alone, or the gun and the charge, would be called "Non-conservative Systems". A conservative system might therefore be defined as one whose total energy is redistributed, but not altered in amount, by changes that happen within it. Of course a given system might be conservative for some kinds of change and not for others.

So far we have merely defined a "Conservative System", and admitted that there are systems which, for some kinds of change at any rate, answer approximately to our definition. We can now state the Principle of the Conservation of Energy in terms of the conceptions just defined. The principle asserts that every material system is either itself conservative, or, if not, is part of a larger material system which is conservative. We may take it that there is good inductive evidence for this proposition.

The next thing to consider is the experiment on the human body. These tend to prove that a living body, with the air that it breathes and the food that it eats, forms a conservative system to a high degree of approximation. We can measure the chemical energy of the food given to a man, and that which enters his body in the form of Oxygen breathed in. We can also, with suitable apparatus, collect, measure and analyse the air breathed out, and thus find its chemical energy. Similarly, we can find the energy given out in bodily movement, in heat, and in excretion. It is alleged that, on the average, whatever the man may do, the energy of his bodily movements is exactly accounted for by the energy given to him in the form of food and of Oxygen. If you take the energy put in in food and Oxygen, and subtract the energy given out in waste-products, the balance is almost exactly equal to the energy put out in bodily movements. Such slight differences as are found are as often on one side as on the other, and are therefore probably due to unavoidable experimental errors. I do not propose to criticise the interpretation of these experiments in detail, because, as I shall show soon, they are completely irrelevant to the problem of whether mind and body interact. But there is just one point that I will make before passing on. It is perfectly clear that such experiments can tell us only what happens on the average over a long time. To know whether the balance was accurately kept at every moment we should have to kill the patient at each moment and analyse his body so as to find out the energy present then in the form of stored-up products. Obviously we cannot keep on killing the patient in order to analyse him, and then reviving him in order to go on with the experiment. Thus it would seem that the results of the experiment are perfectly compatible with the presence of quite large excesses or defects in the total bodily energy at certain moments, provided that these average out over longer periods. However, I do not want to press this criticism; I am quite ready to accept for our present purpose the traditional interpretation which has been put on the experiments.

We now understand the physical principle and the experimental facts. The two together are generally supposed to prove that mind and body cannot interact. What precisely is the argument, when fully stated, would run somewhat as follows: "I will to move my arm, and it moves. If the volition has anything to do with causing the movement we might expect energy to flow from my mind to my body. Thus the energy of my body

ought to receive a measurable increase, not accounted for by the food that I eat and the Oxygen that I breathe. But no such physically unaccountable increases of bodily energy are found. Again, I tread on a tin-tack, and a painful sensation arises in my mind. If treading on the tack has anything to do with causing the sensation we might expect energy to flow from my body to my mind. Such energy would cease to be measurable. Thus there ought to be a noticeable decrease in my bodily energy, not balanced by increases anywhere in the physical system. But such unbalanced decreases of bodily energy are not found." So it is concluded that the volition has nothing to do with causing my arm to move, and that treading on the tack has nothing to do with causing the painful sensation.

Is this argument valid? In the first place it is important to notice that the conclusion does not follow from the Conservation of Energy and the experimental facts alone. The real premise is a tacitly assumed proposition about causation; viz., that, if a change in A has anything to do with causing a change in B, energy must leave A and flow into B. This is neither asserted nor entailed by the Conservation of Energy. What *it* says is that, *if* energy leaves A, it must appear in something else, say B; so that A and B together form a conservative system. Since the Conservation of Energy is not itself the premise for the argument against Interaction, and since it does not entail that premise, the evidence for the Conservation of Energy is not evidence against Interaction. Is there any independent evidence for the premise? We may admit that it *is* true of many, though not of all, transactions within the physical realm. But there are cases where it is not true even of purely physical transactions; and, even if it were always true in the physical realm, it would not follow that it must also be true of transphysical causation. Take the case of a weight swinging at the end of a string hung from a fixed point. The total energy of the weight is the same at all positions in its course. It is thus a conservative system. But at every moment the direction and velocity of the weight's motion are different, and the proportion between its kinetic and its potential energy is constantly changing. These changes are caused by the pull of the string, which acts in a different direction at each different moment. The string makes no difference to the total energy of the weight; but it makes all the difference in the world to the particular way in which the energy is distributed between the potential and the kinetic forms. This is evident when we remember that the weight would begin to move in an utterly different course if at any moment the string were cut.

Here, then, we have a clear case even in the physical realm where a system is conservative but is continually acted on by something which affects its movement and the distribution of its total energy. Why should not the mind act on the body in this way? If you say that you can see how a string can affect the movement of a weight, but cannot see how a volition could affect the movement of a material particle, you have deserted the scientific argument and have gone back to one of the philosophical arguments. Your real difficulty is either that volitions are so very unlike movements, or that the volition is in your mind whilst the movement belongs to the physical realm. And we have seen how little weight can be attached to these objections.

The fact is that, even in purely physical systems, the Conservation of Energy does not explain what changes will happen or when they will happen. It merely imposes a very general limited condition on the changes that are possible. The fact that the system composed of bullet, charge, and gun, in our earlier example, is conservative does not tell us that the gun ever will be fired, or when it will be fired if at all, or what will cause it to go off, or what forms of energy will appear if and when it does go off. This change in this case is determined by pulling the trigger. Likewise the mere fact that the human body and its neighbourhood form a conservative system does not explain any particular bodily movement; it does not explain why I ever move at all, or why I sometimes write, sometimes walk, and sometimes swim. To explain the happening of these particular movements at certain times it seems to be essential to take into account the volitions which happen from time to time in my mind; just as it is essential to take the string into account to explain the particular behaviour of the weight, and to take the trigger into account to explain the going off of the gun at a certain moment. The difference between the gun-system and the body-system is that a little energy does flow into the former when the trigger is pulled, whilst it is alleged that none

does so when a volition starts a bodily movement. But there is not even this amount of difference between the body-system and the swinging weight.

Thus the argument from energy has no tendency to disprove Two-sided Interaction. It has gained a spurious authority from the august name of the Conservation of Energy. But this impressive principle proves to have nothing to do with the case. And the real premise of the argument is not self-evident, and is not universally true even in purely intra-physical transactions. In the end this scientific argument has to lean on the old philosophic arguments; and we have seen that these are but bruised reeds. Nevertheless, the facts brought forward by the argument from energy do throw some light on the *nature* of the interaction between mind and body, assuming this to happen. They do suggest that all the energy of our bodily actions comes out of and goes back into the physical world, and that minds neither add energy to nor abstract it from the latter. What they do, if they do anything, is to determine that at a given moment so much energy shall change from the chemical form to the form of bodily movement; and they determine this, so far as we can see, without altering the total amount of energy in the physical world.

(2) *The Argument from the Structure of the Nervous System.* There are purely reflex actions, like sneezing and blinking, in which there is no reason to suppose that the mind plays any essential part. Now we know the nervous structure which is used in such acts as these. A stimulus is given to the outer end of an effect nerve; some change or other runs up this nerve, crosses a synapse between this and an afferent nerve, travels down the latter to a muscle, causes the muscle to contract, and so produces a bodily movement. There seems no reason to believe that the mind plays any essential part in this process. The process may be irreducibly vital, and not merely physico-chemical; but there seems no need to assume anything more than this. Now it is said that the whole nervous system is simply an immense complication of interconnected nervous arcs. The result is that a change which travels inwards has an immense number of alternative paths by which it may travel outwards. Thus the reaction to a given stimulus is no longer one definite movement, as

in the simple reflex. Almost any movement may follow any stimulus according to the part which the afferent disturbance happens to take. This path will depend on the relative resistance of the various synapses at the time. Now a variable response to the same stimulus is characteristic of deliberate as opposed to reflex action.

These are the facts. The argument based on them runs as follows. It is admitted that the mind has nothing to do with the causation of purely reflex actions. But the nervous structure and the nervous processes involved in deliberate action do not differ in kind from those involved in reflex action; they differ only in degree of complexity. The variability which characterises deliberate action is fully explained by the variety of alternative paths and the variable resistances of the synapses. So it is unreasonable to suppose that the mind has any more to do with causing deliberate actions than it has to do with causing reflex actions.

I think that this argument is invalid. In the first place I am pretty sure that the persons who use it have before their imagination a kind of picture of how mind and body must interact if they interact at all. They find that the facts do not answer to this picture, and so they conclude that there is no interaction. The picture is of the following kind. They think of the mind as sitting somewhere in a hole in the brain, surrounded by telephones. And they think of the afferent disturbance as coming to an end at one of these telephones and there affecting the mind. The mind is then supposed to respond by sending an efferent impulse down another of these telephones. As no such hole, with afferent nerves stopping at its walls and efferent nerves starting from them, can be found, they conclude that the mind can play no part in the transaction. But another alternative is that this picture of how the mind must act if it acts at all is wrong. To put it shortly, the mistake is to confuse a gap in an explanation with a spatio-temporal gap, and to argue from the absence of the latter to the absence of the former.

The interactionist's contention is simply that there is a gap in any purely physiological explanation of deliberate action; i.e., that all such explanations fail to account completely for the facts because they leave out one necessary condition. It does not follow in the least that there must be a spatio-temporal breach of continuity in the physiological conditions, and that the missing condition must fill this gap in the way in which the movement of a wire fills the spatio-temporal interval between the pulling of a bell-handle and the ringing of a distant bell. To assume this is to make the mind a kind of physical object, and to make its action a kind of mechanical action. Really, the mind and its actions are not literally in Space at all, and the time which is occupied by the mental event is no doubt *also* occupied by some part of the physiological process. Thus I am inclined to think that much of the force which this argument actually exercises on many people is simply due to the presupposition about the *modus operandi* of interaction, and that it is greatly weakened when this presupposition is shown to be a mere prejudice due to our limited power of envisaging unfamiliar alternative possibilities.

We can, however, make more detailed objections to the argument than this. There is a clear introspective difference between the mental accompaniment of voluntary action and that of reflex action. What goes on in our minds when we decide with difficulty to get out of a hot bath on a cold morning is obviously extremely different from what goes on in our minds when we sniff pepper and sneeze. And the difference is qualitative; it is not a mere difference of complexity. This difference has to be explained somehow; and the theory under discussion gives no plausible explanation of it. The ordinary view that, in the latter case, the mind is not acting on the body at all; whilst, in the former, it is acting on the body in a specific way, does at least make the introspective difference between the two intelligible.

Again, whilst it is true that deliberate action differs from reflex action in its greater variability of response to the same stimulus, this is certainly not the whole or the most important part of the difference between them. The really important difference is that, in deliberate action, the response is varied *appropriately* to meet the special circumstances which are supposed to exist at the time or are expected to arise later; whilst reflex action is not varied in this way, but is blind and almost mechanical. The complexity of the nervous system explains the *possibility* of variation; it does not in the least explain why the alternative which actually takes place should as a rule be appropriate and not merely haphazard. And so again it seems as if some factor were in operation in deliberate action which is not present in reflex action; and it is reasonable to suppose that this factor is the volition in the mind.

It seems to me that this second scientific argument has no tendency to disprove interaction; but that the facts which it brings forward do tend to suggest the particular form which interaction probably takes if it happens at all. They suggest that what the mind does to the body in voluntary action, if it does anything, is to lower the resistance of certain synapses and to raise that of others. The result is that the nervous current follows such a course as to produce the particular movement which the mind judges to be appropriate at the time. On such a view the difference between reflex, habitual, and deliberate actions for the present purpose become fairly plain. In pure reflexes the mind cannot voluntarily affect the resistance of the synapses concerned, and so the action takes place in spite of it. In habitual action it deliberately refrains from interfering with the resistance of the synapses, and so the action goes on like a complicated reflex. But it *can* affect these resistances if it wishes, though often only with difficulty; and it is ready to do so if it judges this to be expedient. Finally, it may lose the power altogether. This would be what happens when a person becomes a slave to some habit, such as drug-taking.

I conclude that, at the level of enlightened common-sense at which the ordinary discussion of Interaction moves, no good reason has been produced for doubting that the mind acts on the body in volition, and that the body acts on the mind in sensation. The philosophic arguments are quite inconclusive; and the scientific arguments, when properly understood, are quite compatible with Two-sided Interaction. At most they suggest certain conclusions as to the form which interaction probably takes if it happens at all.

DIFFICULTIES IN THE DENIAL OF INTERACTION

I propose now to consider some of the difficulties which would attend the denial of Interaction, still keeping the discussion at the same common-sense level. If a man denies the action of body on mind he is at once in trouble over the causation of new sensations. Suppose that I suddenly tread on an unsuspected tin-tack. A new sensation suddenly comes into my mind. This is an event, and it presumably has some cause. Now, however carefully I introspect and retrospect, I can find no other mental event which is adequate to account for the fact that just that sensation has arisen at just that moment. If I reject the common-sense view that treading on the tack is an essential part of the cause of the sensation, I must suppose either that it is uncaused, or that it is caused by other events in my mind which I cannot discover by introspection or retrospection, or that it is caused telepathically by other finite minds or by God. Now enquiry of my neighbours would show that it is not caused telepathically by any event in their minds which they can introspect or remember. Thus anyone who denies the action of body on mind, and admits that sensations have causes, must postulate either (*a*) immense numbers of unobservable states in his own mind; or (*b*) as many unobservable states in his neighbours' minds, together with telepathic action; or (*c*) some nonhuman spirit together with telepathic action. I must confess that the difficulties which have been alleged against the action of body on mind seem to be mild compared with those of the alternative hypotheses which are involved in the denial of such action.

The difficulties which are involved in the denial of the action of mind on body are at first sight equally great; but I do not think that they turn out to be so serious as those which are involved in denying the action of body on mind. The *prima facie* difficulty is this. The world contains many obviously artificial objects, such as books, bridges, clothes, etc. We know that, if we go far enough back in the history of their production, we always do in fact come on the actions of some human body. And the minds connected with these bodies did design the objects in question, did will to produce them, and did believe that they were initiating and guiding the physical process by means of these designs and volitions. If it be true that the mind does not act on the body, it follows that the designs and volitions in the agents' minds did not in fact play any part in the production of books, bridges, clothes, etc. This appears highly paradoxical. And it is an easy step from it to say that anyone who denies the action of mind on body must admit that books, bridges, and other such objects *could* have been produced even though there had been no minds, no thought of these objects and no desire for them. This consequence seems manifestly absurd to common-sense, and it might be argued that it reflects its absurdity back on the theory which entails it.

The man who denies that mind can act on body might deal with this difficulty in two ways: (1) He might deny that the conclusion *is* intrinsically absurd. He might say that human bodies are extraordinarily complex physical objects, which probably obey irreducible laws of their own, and that we really do not know enough about them to set limits to what their unaided powers could accomplish. This is the line which Spinoza took. The conclusion, it would be argued, *seems* absurd only because the state of affairs which it contemplates is so very unfamiliar. We find it difficult to imagine a body like ours without a mind like ours; but, if we could get over this defect in our powers of imagination, we might have no difficulty in admitting that such a body could do all the things which our bodies do. I think it must be admitted that the difficulty is not so great as that which is involved in denying the action of body on mind. There we had to postulate *ad hoc* utterly unfamiliar entities and modes of action; here it is not certain that we should have to do this.

(2) The other line of argument would be to say that the alleged consequence does not necessarily follow from denying the action of mind on body. I assume that both parties admit that causation is something more than mere *de facto* regularity of sequence and concomitance. If they do not, of course the whole controversy between them becomes futile; for there will certainly be causation between mind and body and between body and mind, in the only sense in which there is causation anywhere. This being presupposed, the following kind of answer is logically possible. When I say that B could not have happened unless A had happened, there are two alternative possibilities. (A) A may itself be an indispensable link in any chain of causes which ends up with B. (B) A may not itself be a link in any chain of causation which ends up with B. But there may be an indispensable link a in any such chain of causation, and A may be a necessary accompaniment or sequent of a. These two possibilities may be illustrated by diagrams. (a) is represented by the figure below:—

$$A_0 \xrightarrow{\quad A \quad} A_1 \xrightarrow{\quad} A_2 \xrightarrow{\quad} B$$

The two forms of (b) are represented by the two figures below:—

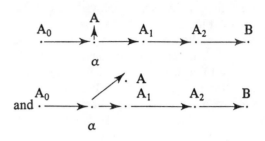

Evidently, If B cannot happen unless a precedes, and if a cannot happen without A accompanying or immediately following it, B will not be able to happen unless A precedes it. And yet A will have had no part in causing B. It will be noticed that, on this view a has a complex effect AA_1 of which a certain part, viz., A_1 is sufficient by itself to produce A_2 and ultimately B. Let us apply this abstract possibility to our present problem. Suppose that B is some artificial object, like a book or a bridge. If we admit that this could not have come into existence unless a certain design and volition had existed in a certain mind, we could interpret the facts in two ways. (a) We could hold that the design and volition are themselves an indispensable link in the chain of causation which ends in the production of a bridge or a book. This is the common view, and it requires us to admit the action of mind on body. (b) We might hold that the design and the volition are not themselves a link in the chain of causation which ends in the production of the artificial object; but that they are a necessary accompaniment or sequent of something which is an indispensable link in this chain of causation. On this view the chain consists wholly of physical events; but one of these physical events (viz., some event in the brain) has a complex consequent. One part of this consequent is purely physical, and leads by purely physical causation to the ultimate production of a bridge or a book. The other is purely mental, and consists of a certain design and volition in the mind which animates the human body concerned. If this has any consequences they are purely mental. Each part of this complex consequent follows with equal necessity; this particular brain-state could no more have existed without such and such a mental state accompanying or following it than it could have existed without such and such a bodily movement following it. If we are willing to take some such view as this, we can admit that certain objects could not have existed unless there had been designs of them and desires for them; and yet we could consistently deny that these desires and designs have any effect on the movements of our bodies.

It seems to me then that the doctrine which I will call "One-sided Action of Body on Mind" is logically possible; *i.e.,* a theory which accepts the action of body on mind but denies the action of mind on body. But I do not see the least reason to accept it, since I see no reason to deny that mind acts on body in volition. One-sided Action has, I think, generally been held in the special form called "Epiphenomenalism." I take this doctrine to consist of the following four propositions: (1) Certain bodily events cause certain mental events. (2) No mental event plays any part in the causation of any bodily event. (3) No mental event plays any part in the causation of any other mental event. Consequently (4) all mental events are caused by bodily events and by them only. Thus Epiphenomenalism is just One-sided Action of Body on Mind, together with a special theory about the nature and structure of mind. This special theory does not call for discussion here, where I am dealing only with the relations between minds and bodies, and am not concerned with a detailed analysis of mind. . . .

ARGUMENTS IN FAVOUR OF INTERACTION

The only arguments *for* One-sided Action of Body on Mind or for Parallelism are the arguments *against* Two-sided Interaction; and these, as we have seen, are worthless. Are there any arguments in favour of Two-sided Interaction? I have incidentally given two which seem to me to have considerable weight. In favour of the action of mind on body is the fact that we seem to be immediately aware of a causal relation when we voluntarily try to produce a bodily movement, and that the arguments to show that this cannot be true are invalid. In favour of the action of body on mind are the insuperable difficulties which I have pointed out in accounting for the happening of new sensations on any other hypothesis. There are, however, two other arguments which have often been thought to prove the action of mind on body. These are (1) an evolutionary argument, first used, I believe, by William James; and (2) the famous "telegram argument." They both seem to be quite obviously invalid.

(1) The evolutionary argument runs as follows: It is a fact, which is admitted by persons who deny Two-sided Interaction, that minds increase in complexity and power with the growth in complexity of the brain and nervous system. Now, if the mind makes no difference to the actions of the body, this development on the mental side is quite unintelligible from the point of view of natural selection. Let us imagine two animals whose brains and nervous systems were of the same degree of complexity; and suppose, if possible, that one had a mind and the other had none. If the mind makes no difference to the behaviour of the body the chance of survival and of leaving descendants will clearly be the same for the two animals. Therefore natural selection will have no tendency to favour the evolution of mind which has actually taken place. I do not think that there is anything in this argument. Natural selection is a purely negative process; it simply tends to eliminate individuals and species which have variations unfavourable to survival. Now, by hypothesis, the possession of a mind is not *unfavourable* to survival; it simply makes no difference. Now it may be that the existence of a mind of such and such a kind is an inevitable consequence of the existence of a brain and nervous system of such and such a degree of complexity. Indeed we have seen that some such view is essential if the opponent of Two-sided Interaction is to answer the common-sense objection that artificial objects could not have existed unless there had been a mind which designed and desired them. On this hypothesis there is no need to invoke natural selection twice over, once to explain the evolution of the brain and nervous system, and once to explain the evolution of the mind. If natural selection will account for the evolution of the brain and nervous system, the evolution of the mind will follow inevitably, even though it adds nothing to the survival-value of the organism. The plain fact is that natural selection does not account for the origin or for the growth in complexity of anything whatever; and therefore it is no objection to any particular theory of the relations of mind and body

that, if it were true, natural selection would not explain the origin and development of mind.

(2) The "telegram argument" is as follows: Suppose there were two telegrams, one saying "Our son has been killed", and the other saying: "Your son has been killed". And suppose that one or other of them was delivered to a parent whose son was away from home. As physical stimuli they are obviously extremely alike, since they differ only in the fact that the letter "Y" is present in one and absent in the other. Yet we know that the reaction of the person who received the telegram might be very different according to which one he received. This is supposed to show that the reactions of the body cannot be wholly accounted for by bodily causes, and that the mind must intervene causally in some cases. Now I have very little doubt that the mind does play a part in determining the action of the recipient of the telegram; but I do not see why this argument should prove it to a person who doubted or denied it. If two very similar stimuli are followed by two very different results, we are no doubt justified in concluding that these stimuli are not the complete causes of the reactions which follow them. But of course it would be admitted by every one that the receipt of the telegram is not the complete cause of the recipient's reaction. We all know that his brain and nervous system play an essential part in any reaction that he may make to the stimulus. The question then is whether the minute structure of his brain and nervous system, including in this the supposed traces left by past stimuli and past reactions, is not enough to account for the great difference in his behaviour on receiving two very similar stimuli. Two keys may be very much alike, but one may fit a certain lock and the other may not. And, if the lock be connected with the trigger of a loaded gun, the results of "stimulating" the system with one or other of the two keys will be extremely different. We know that the brain and nervous system are very complex, and we commonly suppose that they contain more or less permanent traces and linkages due to past stimuli and reactions. If this be granted, it is obvious that two very similar stimuli may produce very different results, simply because one fits in with the internal structure of the brain and nervous system whilst the other does not. And I do not see how we can be sure that anything more is needed to account for the mere difference of reaction adduced by the "telegram argument."

J. J. C. S M A R T

Sensations and Brain Processes*

This paper takes its departure from arguments to be found in U. T. Place's "Is Consciousness a Brain Process?"[1] I have had the benefit of discussing Place's thesis in a good many universities in the United States and Australia, and I hope that the present paper answers objections to his thesis which Place has not considered and that it presents his thesis in a more nearly unobjectiona-

ble form. This paper is meant also to supplement the paper "The 'Mental' and the 'Physical,' " by H. Feigl,[2] which in part argues for a similar thesis to Place's.

Suppose that I report that I have at this moment a roundish, blurry-edged after-image which is yellowish towards its edge and is orange towards its center. What is it that I am reporting? One answer to this question might be that I am not reporting anything, that when I say that it looks to me as though there is a roundish yellow-orange patch of light on the wall I am expressing

*This is a very slightly revised version of a paper which was first published in the *Philosophical Review,* LXVIII (1959), 141–156. [Reprinted by permission of the author and the editors of the *Philosophical Review.*]

some sort of *temptation,* the temptation to say that there *is* a roundish yellowy-orange patch on the wall (though I may know that there is not such a patch on the wall). This is perhaps Wittgenstein's view in the *Philosophical Investigations* (see §§ 367,370). Similarly, when I "report" a pain, I am not really reporting anything (or, if you like, I am reporting in a queer sense of "reporting"), but am doing a sophisticated sort of wince. (See § 244: "The verbal expression of pain replaces crying and does not describe it." Nor does it describe anything else?)[3] I prefer most of the time to discuss an after-image rather than a pain, because the word "pain" brings in something which is irrelevant to my purpose: the notion of "distress." I think that "he is in pain" entails "he is in distress," that is, that he is in a certain agitation-condition.[4] Similarly, to say "I am in pain" may be to do more than "replace pain behavior": it may be partly to report something, though this something its quite nonmysterious, being an agitation-condition, and so susceptible of behavioristic analysis. The suggestion I wish if possible to avoid is a different one, namely that "I am in pain" is a genuine report, and that what it reports is an irreducibly psychical something. And similarly the suggestion I wish to resist is also that to say "I have a yellowish-orange after-image" is to report something irreducibly psychical.

Why do I wish to resist this suggestion? Mainly because of Occam's razor. It seems to me that science is increasingly giving us a viewpoint whereby organisms are able to be seen as physico-chemical mechanisms:[5] it seems that even the behavior of man himself will one day be explicable in mechanistic terms. There does seem to be, so far as science is concerned, nothing in the world but increasingly complex arrangements of physical constituents. All except for one place: in consciousness. That is, for a full description of what is going on in a man you would have to mention not only the physical processes in his tissues, glands, nervous system, and so forth, but also his states of consciousness: his visual, auditory, and tactual sensations, his aches and pains. That these should be *correlated* with brain processes does not help, for to say that they are *correlated* is to say that they are something "over and above." You cannot correlate something with itself. You correlate footprints with bur-

glars, but not Bill Sikes the burglar with Bill Sikes the burglar. So sensations, states of consciousness, do seem to be the one sort of thing left outside the physicalist picture, and for various reasons I just cannot believe that this can be so. That everything should be explicable in terms of physics (together of course with descriptions of the ways in which the parts are put together—roughly, biology is to physics as radio-engineering is to electromagnetism) except the occurrence of sensations seems to me to be frankly unbelievable. Such sensations would be "nomological danglers," to use Feigl's expression.[6] It is not often realized how odd would be the laws whereby these nomological danglers would dangle. It is sometimes asked, "Why can't there be psychophysical laws which are of a novel sort, just as the laws of electricity and magnetism were novelties from the standpoint of Newtonian mechanics?" Certainly we are pretty sure in the future to come across new ultimate laws of a novel type, but I expect them to relate simple constituents: for example, whatever ultimate particles are then in vogue. I cannot believe that ultimate laws of nature could relate simple constituents to configurations consisting of perhaps billions of neurons (and goodness knows how many billion billions of ultimate particles) all put together for all the world as though their main purpose in life was to be a negative feedback mechanism of a complicated sort. Such ultimate laws would be like nothing so far known in science. They have a queer "smell" to them. I am just unable to believe in the nomological danglers themselves, or in the laws whereby they would dangle. If any philosophical arguments seemed to compel us to believe in such things, I would suspect a catch in the argument. In any case it is the object of this paper to show that there are no philosophical arguments which compel us to be dualists.

The above is largely a confession of faith, but it explains why I find Wittgenstein's position (as I construe it) so congenial. For on this view there are, in a sense, no sensations. A man is a vast arrangement of physical particles, but there are not, over and above this, sensations or states of consciousness. There are just behavioral facts about this vast mechanism, such as that it expresses a temptation (behavior disposition) to say "there is a yellowish-red patch on the wall" or that it goes through a sophisticated sort of wince, that is, says "I am in pain." Admittedly Wittgenstein says that though the sensation "is not a something," it is nevertheless "not a nothing either" (§ 304), but this need only mean that the word "ache" has a use. An ache is a thing, but only in the innocuous sense in which the plain man, in the first paragraph of Frege's *Foundations of Arithmetic,* answers the question "What is the number one?" by "a thing." It should be noted that when I assert that to say "I have a yellowish-orange after-image" is to express a temptation to assert the physical-object statement "There is a yellowish-orange patch on the wall," I mean that saying "I have a yellowish-orange after-image" is (partly) the exercise of the disposition[7] which is the temptation. It is not to *report* that I have the temptation, any more than is "I love you" normally a report that I love someone. Saying "I love you" is just part of the behavior which is the exercise of the disposition of loving someone.

Though for the reasons given above, I am very receptive to the above "expressive" account of sensation statements, I do not feel that it will quite do the trick. Maybe this is because I have not thought it out sufficiently, but it does seem to me as though, when a person says "I have an after-image," he *is* making a genuine report, and that when he says "I have a pain," he *is* doing more than "replace pain-behavior," and that "this more" is not just to say that he is in distress. I am not so sure, however, that to admit this is to admit that there are nonphysical correlates of brain processes. Why should not sensations just be brain processes of a certain sort? There are, of course, well-known (as well as lesser-known) philosophical objections to the view that reports of sensations are reports of brain-processes, but I shall try to argue that these arguments are by no means as cogent as is commonly thought to be the case.

Let me first try to state more accurately the thesis that sensations are brain-processes. It is not the thesis that, for example, "after-image" or "ache" means the same as "brain process of sort X" (where "X" is replaced by a description of a certain sort of brain process). It is that, in so far as "after-image" or "ache" is a report of a process, it is a report of a process that *happens to be* a brain process. It follows that the thesis does not claim that sensation statements can be translated into statements about brain processes.[8] Nor does it claim that the logic of a sensation statement is the same as that of a brain-process statement. All it claims is that in so far as a sensation statement is a report of something, that something is in fact a brain process. Sensations are nothing over and above brain processes. Nations are nothing "over and above" citizens, but this does not prevent the logic of nation statements being very different from the logic of citizen statements, nor does it insure the translatability of nation statements into citizen statements. (I do not, however, wish to assert that the relation of sensation statements to brain-process statements is very like that of nation statements to citizen statements. Nations do not just *happen to be* nothing over and above citizens, for example. I bring in the "nations" example merely to make a negative point: that the fact that the logic of A-statements is different from that of B-statements does not insure that A's are anything over and above B's.)

Remarks on Identity. When I say that a sensation is a brain process or that lightning is an electric discharge, I am using "is" in the sense of strict identity. (Just as in the—in this case necessary—proposition "7 is identical with the smallest prime number greater than 5.") When I say that a sensation is a brain process or that lightning is an electric discharge I do not mean just that the sensation is somehow spatially or temporally continuous with the brain process or that the lightning is just spatially or temporally continuous with the discharge. When on the other hand I say that the successful general is the same person as the small boy who stole the apples I mean only that the successful general I see before me is a time slice[9] of the same four-dimensional object of which the small boy stealing apples is an earlier time slice. However, the four-dimensional object which has the general-I-see-before-me for its late time slice is identical in the strict sense with the four-dimensional object which has the small-boy-stealing-apples for an early time slice. I distinguish these two senses of "is identical with" because I wish to make it clear that the brain-process doctrine asserts identity in the *strict* sense.

I shall now discuss various possible objections to the view that the processes reported in sensation statements are in fact processes in the brain. Most of us have met some of these objections in our first year as philosophy students. All the more reason to take a good look at them. Others of the objections will be more recondite and subtle.

Objection 1. Any illiterate peasant can talk perfectly well about his after-images, or how things look or feel to him, or about his aches and pains, and yet he may know nothing whatever about neurophysiology. A man may, like Aristotle, believe that the brain is an organ for cooling the body without any impairment of his ability to make true statements about his sensations. Hence the things we are talking about when we describe our sensations cannot be processes in the brain.

Reply. You might as well say that a nation of slugabeds, who never saw the Morning Star or knew of its existence, or who had never thought of the expression "the Morning Star," but who used the expression "the Evening Star" perfectly well, could not use this expression to refer to the same entity as we refer to (and describe as) "the Morning Star."[10]

You may object that the Morning Star is in a sense not the very same thing as the Evening Star, but only something spatiotemporally continuous with it. That is, you may say that the Morning Star is not the Evening Star in the strict sense of "identity" that I distinguished earlier.

There is, however, a more plausible example. Consider lightning.[11] Modern physical science tells us that lightning is a certain kind of electrical discharge due to ionization of clouds of water vapor in the atmosphere. This, it is now believed, is what the true nature of lightning is. Note that there are not two things: a flash of lightning and an electrical discharge. There is one thing, a flash of lightning, which is described scientifically as an electrical discharge to the earth from a cloud of ionized water molecules. The case is not at all like that of explaining a footprint by reference to a burglar. We say that what lightning really is, what its true nature as revealed by science is, is an electrical discharge. (It is not the true nature of a footprint to be a burglar).

To forestall irrelevant objections, I should like to make it clear that by "lightning" I mean the publicly observable physical object, lightning, not a visual sense-datum of lightning. I say that the publicly observable physical object lightning is in fact the electrical discharge, not just a correlate of it. The sense-datum, or rather the having of the sense-datum, the "look" of lightning, may well in my view be a correlate of the electrical discharge. For in my view it is a brain state *caused* by the lightning. But we should no more confuse sensations of lightning with lightning than we confuse sensations of a table with the table.

In short, the reply to Objection 1 is that there can be contingent statements of the form "A is identical with B," and a person may well know that something is an A without knowing that it is a B. An illiterate peasant might well be able to talk about his sensations without knowing about his brain processes, just as he can talk about lightning though he knows nothing of electricity.

Objection 2. It is only a contingent fact (if it is a fact) that when we have a certain kind of sensation there is a certain kind of process in our brain. Indeed it is possible, though perhaps in the highest degree unlikely, that our present physiological theories will be as out of date as the ancient theory connecting mental processes with goings on in the heart. It follows that when we report a sensation we are not reporting a brain-process.

Reply. The objection certainly proves that when we say "I have an after-image" we cannot *mean* something of the form "I have such and such a brain-process." But this does not show that what we report (having an after-image) is not *in fact* a brain process. "I see lightning" does not *mean* "I see an electrical discharge." Indeed, it is logically possible (though highly unlikely) that the electrical discharge account of lightning might one day be given up. Again, "I see the Evening Star" does not *mean* the same as "I see the Morning Star," and yet "The Evening Star and the Morning Star are one and the same thing" is a contingent proposition. Possibly Objection 2 derives some of its apparent strength from a "Fido"-Fido theory of meaning. If the meaning of an expression were what the expression named, then of course it *would* follow from the fact that "sensation" and "brain-process" have different meanings that they cannot name one and the same thing.

Objection 3.[12] Even if Objections 1 and 2 do not prove that sensations are something over and above brain-processes, they do prove that the qualities of sensations are something over and above the qualities of brain-processes. That is, a may be possible to get out of asserting the existence of irreducibly psychic processes, but not out of asserting the existence of irreducibly psychic *properties*. For suppose we identify the Morning Star with the Evening Star. Then there must be some properties which logically imply that of being the Morning Star, and quite distinct properties which entail that of being the Evening Star. Again, there must be some properties (for example, that of being a yellow flash) which are logically distinct from those in the physicalist story.

Indeed, it might be thought that the objection succeeds at one jump. For consider the property of "being a yellow flash." It might seem that this property lies inevitably outside the physicalist framework within which I am trying to work (either by "yellow" being an objective emergent property of physical objects, or else by being a power to produce yellow sense-data, where "yellow," in this second instantiation of the word, refers to a purely phenomenal or introspectible quality). I must therefore digress for a moment and indicate how I deal with secondary qualities. I shall concentrate on color.

First of all, let me introduce the concept of a normal percipient. One person is more a normal percipient than another if he can make color discriminations that the other cannot. For example, if A can pick a lettuce leaf out of a heap of cabbage leaves, whereas B cannot though he can pick a lettuce leaf out of a heap of beetroot leaves, then A is more normal than B. (I am assuming that A and B are not given the time to distinguish the leaves by their slight difference in shape, and so forth.) From the concept of "more normal than" it is easy to see how we can introduce the concept of "normal." Of course, Eskimos may make the finest discriminations at the blue end of the spectrum, Hottentots at the red end. In this case the concept of a normal percipient is a slightly idealized one, rather like that of "the mean sun" in astronomical chronology. There is no need to go into such subtleties now. I say that "This is red" means something roughly like "A normal percipient would not easily pick this out of a clump of geranium petals though he would pick it out of a clump of lettuce leaves." Of course it does not exactly mean this: a person might know the meaning of "red" without knowing anything about geraniums, or even about normal percipients. But the point is that a person can be *trained* to say "This is red" of objects which would not easily be picked out of geranium petals by a normal percipient, and so on. (Note that even a color-blind person can reasonably assert that something is red, though of course he needs to use another human being, not just himself, as his "color meter.") This account of secondary qualities explains their unimportance in physics. For obviously the discriminations and lack of discriminations made by a very complex neurophysiological mechanism are hardly likely to correspond to simple and nonarbitrary distinctions in nature.

I therefore elucidate colors as powers, in Locke's sense, to evoke certain sorts of discriminatory responses in human beings. They are also, of course, powers to cause sensations in human beings (an account still nearer Locke's). But these sensations, I am arguing, are identifiable with brain processes.

Now how do I get over the objection that a sensation can be identified with a brain process only if it has some phenomenal property, not possessed by brain processes, whereby one-half of the identification may be, so to speak, pinned down?

Reply. My suggestion is as follows. When a person says, "I see a yellowish-orange afterimage," he is saying something like this: *"There is something going on which is like what is going on when* I have my eyes open, am awake, and there is an orange illuminated in good light in front of me, that is, when I really see an orange." (And there is no reason why a person should not say the same thing when he is having a veridical sense-datum, so long as we construe "like" in the last sentence in such a sense that something can be like itself.) Notice that the italicized words, namely "there is something going on which is like what is going on when," are all quasilogical or topic-neutral words. This explains why the ancient Greek peasant's reports about his sensations can be neutral between dualistic metaphysics or my materialistic metaphysics. It explains how sensations can be brain-processes and yet how a man who reports them need know nothing about brain-processes. For he reports them only very abstractly as "something going on which is like what is going on when. ...." Similarly, a person may say "someone is in the room," thus reporting truly that the doctor is in the room, even though he has never heard of doctors. (There are not two people in the room: "someone" *and* the doctor.) This account of sensation statements also explains the singular elusiveness of "raw feels"— why no one seems to be able to pin any properties on them.[13] Raw feels, in my view, are colorless for the very same reason that *something* is colorless. This does not mean that sensations do not have plenty of properties, for if they are brain-processes they certainly have lots of neurological properties. It only means that in speaking of them as being like or unlike one another we need not know or mention these properties.

This, then, is how I would reply to Objection 3. The strength of my reply depends on the possibility of our being able to report that one thing is like another without being able to state the respect in which it is like. I do not see why this should not be so. If we think cybernetically about the nervous system we can envisage it as able to respond to certain likenesses of its internal processes without being able to do more. It would be easier to build a machine which would tell us, say on a punched tape, whether or not two objects were similar, than it would be to build a machine which would report wherein the similarities consisted.

Objection 4. The after-image is not in physical space. The brain-process is. So the after-image is not a brain-process.

Reply. This is an *ignoratio elenchi.* I am not arguing that the after-image is a brain-process, but that the experience of having an after-image is a brain process. It is the *experience* which is reported in the introspective report. Similarly, if it is objected that the after-image is yellowy-orange, my reply is that it is the experience of seeing yellowy-orange that is being described, and this experience is not a yellowy-orange something. So to say that a brain-process cannot be yellowy-orange is not to say that a brain-process cannot in fact be the experience of having a yellowy-orange after-image. There is, in a sense, no such thing as an after-image or a sense-datum, though there is such a thing as the experience of having an image, and this experience is described indirectly in material object language, not in phenomenal language, for there is no such thing.[14] We describe the experience by saying, in effect, that it is like the experience we have when, for example, we really see a yellow-orange patch on the wall. Trees and wallpaper can be green, but not the experience of seeing or imagining a tree or wallpaper. (Or if they are described as green or yellow this can only be in a derived sense.)

Objection 5. It would make sense to say of a molecular movement in the brain that it is swift or slow, straight or circular, but it makes no sense to say this of the experience of seeing something yellow.

Reply. So far we have not given sense to talk of experiences as swift or slow, straight or circular. But I am not claiming that "experience" and "brain-process" mean the same or even that they have the same logic. "Somebody" and "the doctor" do not have the same logic, but this does not lead us to suppose that talking about somebody telephoning is talking about someone over and above, say, the doctor. The ordinary man when he reports an experience is reporting that something is going on, but he leaves it open as to what sort of thing is going on, whether in a material solid medium or perhaps in some sort of gaseous medium, or even perhaps in some sort of non-spatial medium (if this makes sense). All that I am saying is that "experience" and "brain-process" may in fact refer to the same thing, and if so we may easily adopt a convention (which is not a change in our present rules for the use of experience words but an addition to them) whereby it would make sense to talk of an experience in terms appropriate to physical processes.

Objection 6. Sensations are private, brain processes are *public.* If I sincerely say, "I see a yellowish-orange after-image," and I am not making a verbal mistake, then I cannot be wrong. But I can be wrong about a brain-process. The scientist looking into my brain might be having an illusion. Moreover, it makes sense to say that two or more people are observing the same brain-process but not that two or more people are reporting the same inner experience.

Reply. This shows that the language of introspective reports has a different logic from the language of material processes. It is obvious that until the brain-process theory is much improved and widely accepted there will be no *criteria* for saying "Smith has an experience of such-and-such a sort" *except* Smith's introspective reports. So we have adopted a rule of language that (normally) what Smith says goes.

Objection 7. I can imagine myself turned to stone and yet having images, aches, pains, and so on.

Reply. I can imagine that the electrical theory of lightning is false, that lightning is some sort of purely optical phenomenon. I can imagine that lighting is not an electrical discharge. I can imagine that the Evening Star is not the Morning Star. But it is. All the objection shows is that "experience" and "brain-process" do not have the same meaning. It does not show that an experience is not in fact a brain-process.

This objection is perhaps much the same as one which can be summed up by the slogan: "What can be composed of nothing cannot be composed of anything."[15] The argument goes as follows: on the brain-process thesis the identity between the brain-process and the experience is a contingent one. So it is logically possible that there should be no brain-process, and no process of any other sort either (no heart process, no kidney process, no liver process). There would be the experience but no "corresponding" physiological process with which we might be able to identify it empirically.

I suspect that the objector is thinking of the experience as a ghostly entity. So it is composed of something, not of nothing, after all. On his view it is composed of ghost stuff, and on mine it is composed of brain stuff. Perhaps the counter-reply will be[16] that the experience is simple and uncompounded, and so it is not composed of anything after all. This seems to be a quibble, for, if it were taken seriously, the remark "What can be composed of nothing cannot be composed of anything" could be recast as an a priori argument against Democritus and atomism and for Descartes and infinite divisibility. And it seems odd that a question of this sort could be settled a priori. We must therefore construe the word "composed" in a very weak sense, which would allow us to say that even an indivisible atom is composed of something (namely, itself). The dualist cannot really say that an experience can be composed of nothing. For he holds that experiences are something over and above material processes, that is, that they are a sort of ghost stuff. (Or perhaps ripples in an underlying ghost stuff.) I say that the dualist's hypothesis is a perfectly intelligible one. But I say that experiences are not to be identified with ghost stuff but with brain stuff. This is another hypothesis, and in my view

a very plausible one. The present argument cannot knock it down a priori.

Objection 8. The "beetle in the box" objection (see Wittgenstein, *Philosophical Investigations,* § 293). How could descriptions of experiences, if these are genuine reports, get a foothold in language? For any rule of language must have public criteria for its correct application.

Reply. The change from describing how things are to describing how we feel is just a change from uninhibitedly saying "this is so" to saying "this looks so." That is, when the naïve person might be tempted to say, "There is a patch of light on the wall which moves whenever I move my eyes" or "A pin is being stuck into me," we have learned how to resist this temptation and say "It *looks as though* there is a patch of light on the wallpaper" or "It *feels as though* someone were sticking a pin into me." The introspective account tells us about the individual's state of consciousness in the same way as does "I see a patch of light" or "I feel a pin being stuck into me": it differs from the corresponding perception statement in so far as it withdraws any claim about what is actually going on in the external world. From the point of view of the psychologist, the change from talking about the environment to talking about one's perceptual sensations is simply a matter of disinhibiting certain reactions. These are reactions which one normally suppresses because one has learned that in the prevailing circumstances they are unlikely to provide a good indication of the state of the environment.[17] To say that something looks green to me is simply to say that my experience is like the experience I get when I see something that really is green. In my reply to Objection 3, I pointed out the extreme openness or generality of statements which report experiences. This explains why there is no language of private qualities. (Just as "someone," unlike "the doctor," is a colorless word.)[18]

If it is asked what is the difference between those brain processes which, in my view, are experiences and those brain processes which are not, I can only reply that it is at present unknown. I have been tempted to conjecture that the difference may in part be that between perception and reception (in D. M. MacKay's terminology) and that the type of brain process which is an experience might be identifiable with MacKay's active "matching response."[19] This, however, cannot be the whole story, because sometimes I can perceive somet' 'ng unconsciously, as when I take a handkerchief out of a drawer without being aware that I am doing so. But at the very least, we can classify the brain processes which are experiences as those brain processes which are, or might have been, causal conditions of those pieces of verbal behaviour which we call reports of immediate experience.

I have now considered a number of objections to the brain-process thesis. I wish now to conclude with some remarks on the logical status of the thesis itself. U. T. Place seems to hold that it is a straight-out scientific hypothesis.[20] If so, he is partly right and partly wrong. If the issue is between (say) a brain-process thesis and a heart thesis, or a liver thesis, or a kidney thesis, then the issue is a purely empirical one, and the verdict is overwhelmingly in favor of the brain. The right sorts of things don't go on in the heart, liver, or kidney, nor do these organs possess the right sort of complexity of structure. On the other hand, if the issue is between a brain-or-liver-or-kidney thesis (that is, some form of materialism) on the one hand and epiphenomenalism on the other hand, then the issue is not an empirical one. For there is no conceivable experiment which could decide between materialism and epiphenomenalism. This latter issue is not like the average straight-out empirical issue in science, but like the issue between the nineteenth-century English naturalist Philip Gosse[21] and the orthodox geologists and paleontologists of his day. According to Gosse, the earth was created about 4000 B.C. exactly as described in *Genesis*, with twisted rock strata, "evidence" of erosion, and so forth, and all sorts of fossils, all in their appropriate strata, just as if the usual evolutionist story had been true. Clearly this theory is in a sense irrefutable: no evidence can possibly tell against it. Let us ignore the theological setting in which Philip Gosse's hypothesis had been placed, thus ruling out objections of a theological kind, such as "what a queer God who would go to such elaborate lengths to deceive us." Let us suppose that it is held that the universe just *began* in 4004 B.C. with the initial conditions just everywhere as they were in 4004 B.C., and in particular that our own planet began with sediment in the rivers, eroded cliffs, fossils in the rocks, and so on. No scientist would ever entertain this as a serious hypothesis, consistent though it is with all possible evidence. The hypothesis offends against the principles of parsimony and simplicity. There would be far too many brute and inexplicable facts. Why are pterodactyl bones just as they are? No explanation in terms of the evolution of pterodactyls from earlier forms of life would any longer be possible. We would have millions of facts about the world as it was in 4004 B.C. that just have to be *accepted*.

The issue between the brain-process theory and epiphenomenalism seems to be of the above sort. (Assuming that a behavioristic reduction of introspective reports is not possible.) If it be agreed that there are no cogent philosophical arguments which force us into accepting dualism, and if the brain process theory and dualism are equally consistent with the facts, then the principles of parsimony and simplicity seem to me to decide overwhelmingly in favor of the brain-process theory. As I pointed out earlier, dualism involves a large number of irreducible psychophysical laws (whereby the "nomological danglers" dangle) of a queer sort, that just have to be taken on trust, and are just as difficult to swallow as the irreducible facts about the paleontology of the earth with which we are faced on Philip Gosse's theory.

NOTES

1. *British Journal of Psychology,* XLVII (1956), 44–50.

2. *Minnesota Studies in the Philosophy of Science,* Vol. II (Minneapolis: University of Minnesota Press, 1958), pp. 370–497.

3. Some philosophers of my acquaintance, who have the advantage over me in having known Wittgenstein, would say that this interpretation of him is too behavioristic. However, it seems to me a very natural interpretation of his printed words, and whether or not it is Wittgenstein's real view it is certainly an interesting and important one. I wish to consider it here as a possible rival both to the "brain-process" thesis and to straight-out old-fashioned dualism.

4. See Ryle, *The Concept of Mind* (London: Hutchinson's University Library, 1949), p. 93.

5. On this point see Paul Oppenheim and Hilary Putnam, "Unity of Science as a Working Hypothesis," in *Minnesota Studies in the Philosophy of Science,* Vol. II (Minneapolis: University of Minnesota Press, 1958), pp. 3–36.

6. Feigl, *op. cit.,* p. 428. Feigl uses the expression "nomological danglers" for the laws whereby the entities dangle: I have used the expression to refer to the dangling entities themselves.

7. Wittgenstein did not like the word "disposition." I am using it to put in a nutshell (and perhaps inaccurately) the view which I am attributing to Wittgenstein. I should like to repeat that I do not wish to claim that my interpretation of Wittgenstein is correct. Some of those who knew him do not interpret him in this way. It is merely a view which I find myself extracting from his printed words and which I think is important and worth discussing for its own sake.

8. See Place, *op. cit.*, p. 45, and Feigl, *op. cit.*, p. 390, near top.

9. See J. H. Woodger, *Theory Construction,* International Encyclopedia of Unified Science, II, No. 5 (Chicago: University of Chicago Press, 1939), 38. I here permit myself to speak loosely. For warnings against possible ways of going wrong with this sort of talk, see my note "Spatialising Time," *Mind,* LXIV (1955), 239–41.

10. Cf. Feigl, *op. cit.,* p. 439.

11. See Place, *op. cit.,* p. 48; also Feigl, *op. cit.,* p. 438.

12. I think this objection was first put to me by Professor Max Black. I think it is the most subtle of any of those I have considered, and the one which I am least confident of having satisfactorily met.

13. See B. A. Farrell, *"Experience,"* Mind, LIX (1950), 170–98.

14. Dr. J. R. Smythies claims that a sense-datum language could be taught independently of the material object language ("A Note on the Fallacy of the 'Phenomenological Fallacy,'" *British Journal of Psychology,* XLVIII [1957], 141–44). I am not so sure of this: there must be some public criteria for a person having got a rule wrong before we can teach him the rule. I suppose someone might *accidentally* learn color words by Dr. Smythies' procedure. I am not, of course, denying that we can learn a sense-datum language in the sense that we can learn to report our experience. Nor would Place deny it.

15. I owe this objection to Dr. C. B. Martin. I gather that he no longer wishes to maintain this objection, at any rate in its present form.

16. Martin did not make this reply, but one of his students did.

17. I owe this point to Place, in correspondence.

18. The "beetle in the box" objection is, *if it is sound,* an objection to *any* view, and in particular the Cartesian one, that introspective reports are genuine reports. So it is no objection to a weaker thesis that I would be concerned to uphold, namely, that if introspective reports of "experiences" are genuinely reports, then the things they are reports of are in fact brain processes.

19. See his article "Towards an Information-Flow Model of Human Behaviour," *British Journal of Psychology,* XLVII (1956), 30–43.

20. *Op. cit.* For a further discussion of this, in reply to the original version of the present paper, see Place's note "Materialism as a Scientific Hypothesis," *Philosophical Review,* LXIX (1960), 101–4.

21. See the entertaining account of Gosse's book *Omphalos* by Martin Gardner in *Fads and Fallacies in the Name of Science,* 2nd ed. (New York: Dover, 1957), pp. 124–27.

Survival of Death and Personal Identity

C. J. DUCASSE

Is Life after Death Possible?*

The question whether human personality survives death is sometimes asserted to be one upon which reflection is futile. Only empirical evidence, it is said, can be relevant, since the question is purely one of fact.

But no question is purely one of fact until it is clearly understood; and this one is, on the contrary, ambiguous and replete with tacit assumptions. Until the ambiguities have been removed and the assumptions critically examined, we do not really know just what it is we want to know when we ask whether a life after death is possible. Nor, therefore, can we tell until then what bear-

*C. J. Ducasse, "Some Questions concerning Survival after Death," *Newsletter of the Parapsychology Foundation,* Vol. 3, No. 1, Jan.–Feb. 1956. This paper is a slight extension of Professor Ducasse's Foerster Lecture (at the University of California, Berkeley, May 1947) entitled "Is a Life after Death Possible?" The concluding section has been omitted. Reprinted by permission of the author, the University of California Press, and the Parapsychology Foundation.

ing on this question various facts empirically known to us may have.

To clarify its meaning is chiefly what I now propose to attempt. I shall ask first why a future life is so generally desired and believed in. Then I shall state, as convincingly as I can in the time available, the arguments commonly advanced to prove that such a life is impossible. After that, I shall consider the logic of these arguments, and show that they quite fail to establish the impossibility. Next, the tacit but arbitrary assumption, which makes them nevertheless appear convincing, will be pointed out. . . .

Let us turn to the first of these tasks.

WHY MAN DESIRES LIFE AFTER DEATH

To begin with, let us note that each of us here has been alive and conscious at all times in the past which he can remember. It is true that sometimes our bodies are in deep sleep, or made inert by anesthetics or injuries. But even at such times we do not experience unconsciousness in ourselves, for to experience it would mean being conscious of being unconscious, and this is a contradiction. The only experience of unconsciousness in ourselves we ever have is, not experience of total unconsciousness, but of unconsciousness of *this* or *that;* as when we report: "I am not conscious of any pain," or "of any bell-sound," or "of any difference between those two colors," etc. Nor do we ever experience unconsciousness in another person, but only the fact that, sometimes, some or all of the ordinary activities of his body cease to occur. That consciousness itself is extinguished at such times is thus only a hypothesis which we construct to account for certain changes in the behavior of another person's body or to explain in him or in ourselves the eventual lack of memories relating to the given period.

Being alive and conscious is thus, with all men, a lifelong experience and habit; and conscious life is therefore something they naturally—even if tacitly—expect to continue. As J. B. Pratt has pointed out, the child takes the continuity of life for granted. It is the fact of death that has to be taught him. But when he has learned it, and the idea of a future life is then put explicitly before his mind, it seems to him the most natural thing in the world.[1]

The witnessing of death, however, is a rare experience for most of us, and, because it breaks so sharply into our habits, it forces on us the question whether the mind, which until then was manifested by the body now dead, continues somehow to live on, or, on the contrary, has become totally extinct. This question is commonly phrased as concerning "the immortality of the soul," and immortality, strictly speaking, means survival forever. But assurance of survival for some considerable period—say a thousand, or even a hundred, years—would probably have almost as much present psychological value as would assurance of survival strictly forever. Most men would be troubled very little by the idea of extinction at so distant a time—even less troubled than is now a healthy and happy youth by the idea that he will die in fifty or sixty years. Therefore, it is survival for some time, rather than survival specifically forever, that I shall alone consider.

The craving for continued existence is very widespread. Even persons who believe that death means complete extinction of the individual's consciousness often find comfort in various substitute conceptions of survival. They may, for instance, dwell on the continuity of the individual's germ plasm in his descendants. Or they find solace in the thought that, the past being indestructible, their individual life remains eternally an intrinsic part of the history of the world. Also—and more satisfying to one's craving for personal importance—there is the fact that since the acts of one's life have effects, and these in turn further effects, and so on, therefore what one has done goes on forever influencing remotely, and sometimes greatly, the course of future events.

Gratifying to one's vanity, too, is the prospect that, if the achievements of one's life have been great or even only conspicuous, or one's benefactions or evil deeds have been notable, one's name may not only be remembered by acquaintances and relatives for a little while, but may live on in recorded history. But evidently survival in any of these senses is but a consolation prize—but a thin substitute for the continuation of conscious individual life, which may not be a fact, but which most men crave nonetheless.

The roots of this craving are certain desires which death appears to frustrate. For some, the chief of these is for reunion with persons dearly loved. For others, whose lives have been wretched, it is the desire for another chance at the happiness they have missed. For others yet, it is desired for further opportunity to grow in ability, knowledge or character. Often, there is also the desire, already mentioned, to go on counting for something in the affairs of men. And again, a future life for oneself and others is often desired in order that the redressing of the many injustices of this life shall be possible. But it goes without saying that, although desires such as these are often sufficient to cause belief in a future life, they constitute no evidence at all that it is a fact.

In this connection, it may be well to point out that, although both the belief in survival and the belief in the existence of a god or gods are found in most religions, nevertheless there is no necessary connection between the two beliefs. No contradiction would be involved in supposing either that there is a God but no life after death or that there is a life after death but no God. The belief that there is a life after death may be tied to a religion, but it is no more intrinsically religious than would be a belief that there is life on the planet Mars. The after-death world, if it exists, is just another region or dimension of the universe.

But although belief in survival of death is natural and easy and has always been held in one form or another by a large majority of mankind, critical reflection quickly brings forth a number of apparently strong reasons to regard that belief as quite illusory. Let us now review them.

THE ARGUMENTS AGAINST SURVIVAL

There are, first of all, a number of facts which definitely suggest that both the existence and the nature of consciousness wholly depend on the presence of a functioning nervous system. It is pointed out, for example, that wherever consciousness is observed, it is found associated with a living and functioning body. Further, when the body dies, or the head is struck a heavy blow, or some anesthetic is administered, the familiar outward evidences of consciousness terminate, permanently or temporarily. Again, we know well that drugs of various kinds—alcohol, caffein, opium, heroin, and many others—cause specific changes at the time in the nature of a person's mental states. Also, by stimulating in appropriate ways the body's sense organs, corresponding states of consciousness—namely, the various kinds of sensations—can be caused at will. On the other hand, cutting a sensory nerve immediately eliminates a whole range of sensations.

Again, the contents of consciousness, the mental powers, or even the personality, are modified in characteristic ways when certain regions of the brain are destroyed by disease or injury or are disconnected from the rest by such an operation as prefrontal lobotomy. And that the nervous system is the indispensable basis of mind is further suggested by the fact that, in the evolutionary scale, the degree of intelligence of various species of animals keeps pace closely with the degree of development of their brain.

That continued existence of mind after death is impossible has been argued also on the basis of theoretical considerations. It has been contended, for instance, that what we call states of consciousness—or more particularly, ideas, sensations, volitions, feelings and the like—are really nothing but the minute physical or chemical events which take place in the tissues of the brain. For, it is urged, it would be absurd to suppose that an idea or a volition, if it is not itself a material thing or process, could cause material effects such as contractions of muscles.

Moreover, it is maintained that the possibility of causation of a material event by an immaterial, mental cause is ruled out *a priori* by the principle of the conservation of energy; for such causation would mean that an additional quantity of energy suddenly pops into the nervous system out of nowhere.

Another conception of consciousness, which is more often met with today than the one just mentioned, but which also implies that consciousness cannot survive death, is that "consciousness" is only the name we give to certain types of behavior, which differentiate the higher animals from all other things in nature. According to this view, to say, for example, that an animal is conscious of a difference between two stimuli means nothing more than that it responds to each by different behavior. That is, the difference of *behavior* is what consciousness of difference between the stimuli *consists in;* and is not, as is commonly assumed, only the behavioral *sign* of something mental and not public, called "consciousness that the stimuli are different."

Or again, consciousness, of the typically human sort called thought, is identified with the typically human sort of behavior called speech; and this, again not in the sense that speech *expresses* or *manifests* something different from itself, called "thought," but in the sense that speech—whether uttered or only whispered—*is* thought itself. And obviously, if thought, or any mental activity, is thus but some mode of behavior of the living body, the mind cannot possibly survive death.

Still another difficulty confronting the hypothesis of survival becomes evident when one imagines in some detail what survival would have to include in order to satisfy the desires which cause man to crave it. It would, of course, have to include persistence not alone of consciousness, but also of personality; that is, of the individual's character, acquired knowledge, cultural skills and interests, memories, and awareness of personal identity. But even this would not be enough, for what man desires is not bare survival, but to go on living in some objective way. And this means to go on meeting new situations and, by exerting himself to deal with them, to broaden and deepen his experience and develop his talent capacities.

But it is hard to imagine this possible without a body and an environment for it, upon which to act and from which to receive impressions. And, if a body and an environment were supposed, but not material and corruptible ones, then it is paradoxical to think that, under such radically different conditions, a given personality could persist.[2]

To take a crude but telling analogy, it is past belief that, if the body of any one of us were suddenly changed into that of a shark or an octopus, and placed in the ocean, his personality could, for more than a very short time, if at all, survive intact so radical a change of environment and of bodily form.

THE ARGUMENTS EXAMINED

Such, in brief, are the chief reasons commonly advanced for holding that survival is impossible. Scrutiny of them, however, will, I think, reveal that they are not as strong as they first seem and far from strong enough to show that there can be no life after death.

Let us consider first the assertion that "thought," or "consciousness," is but another name for subvocal speech, or for some other form of behavior, or for molecular processes in the tissues of the brain. As Paulsen and others have pointed out,[3] no evidence ever is or can be offered to support that assertion, because it is in fact but a disguised proposal to make the words "thought," "feeling," "sensation," "desire," and so on, denote facts quite different from those which these words are commonly employed to denote. To say that those words are but other names for certain chemical or behavioral events is as grossly arbitrary as it would be to say that "wood" is but another name for glass, or "potato" but another name for cabbage. What thought, desire, sensation, and other mental states are like, each of us can observe directly by introspection; and what introspection reveals is that they do not in the least resemble muscular contraction, or glandular secretion, or any other known bodily events. No tampering with language can alter the observable fact that thinking is one thing and muttering quite another; that the feeling called anger has no resemblance to the bodily behavior which usually goes with it; or that an act of will is not in the least like anything we find when we open the skull and examine the brain. Certain mental events are doubtless connected in some way with certain bodily events, but they are not those bodily events themselves. The connection is not identity.

This being clear, let us next consider the arguments offered to show that mental processes, although not identical with bodily processes, nevertheless depend on them. We are told, for instance, that some head injuries, or anesthetics, totally extinguish consciousness for the time being. As already pointed out, however, the strict fact is only that the usual bodily signs of consciousness are then absent. But they are also absent when a person is asleep; and yet, at the same time, dreams, which are states of consciousness, may be occurring.

It is true that when the person concerned awakens, he often remembers his dreams, whereas the person that has been anesthetized or injured has usually no memories relating to the period of apparent blankness. But this could mean that his consciousness was, for the time, dissociated from its ordinary channels of manifestation, as was reported of the co-conscious personalities of some of the patients of Dr. Morton

Prince.[4] Moreover, it sometimes occurs that a person who has been in an accident reports lack of memories not only for the period during which his body was unresponsive but also for a period of several hours *before* the accident, during which he had given to his associates all the ordinary external signs of being conscious as usual.

But, more generally, if absence of memories relating to a given period proved unconsciousness for that period, this would force us to conclude that we were unconscious during the first few years of our lives, and indeed have been so most of the time since; for the fact is that we have no memories whatever of most of our days. That we are alive and conscious of any long past specific date is, with only a few exceptions, not something we actually remember, but only something which we infer must be true.

EVIDENCE FROM PSYCHICAL RESEARCH

Another argument advanced against survival was, it will be remembered, that death must extinguish the mind, since all manifestations of it then cease. But to assert that they invariably then cease is to ignore altogether the considerable amount of evidence to the contrary, gathered over many years and carefully checked by the Society for Psychical Research. This evidence, which is of a variety of kinds, has been reviewed by Professor Gardner Murphy in an article published in the Journal of the Society.[5] He mentions first the numerous well-authenticated cases of apparition of a dead person to others as yet unaware that he had died or even been ill or in danger. The more strongly evidential cases of apparition are those in which the apparition conveys to the person who sees it specific facts until then secret. An example would be that of the apparition of a girl to her brother nine years after her death, with a conspicuous scratch on her cheek. Their mother then revealed to him that she herself had made that scratch accidentally while preparing her daughter's body for burial, but that she had then at once covered it with powder and never mentioned it to anyone.

Another famous case is that of a father whose apparition some time after death revealed to one of his sons the existence and location of an unsuspected second will, benefiting him, which was then found as indicated. Still another case would be the report by General Barter, then a subaltern in the British Army in India, of the apparition to him of a lieutenant he had not seen for two or three years. The lieutenant's apparition was riding a brown pony with black mane and tail. He was much stouter than at their last meeting, and, whereas formerly clean-shaven, he now wore a peculiar beard in the form of a fringe encircling his face. On inquiry the next day from a person who had known the lieutenant at the time he died, it turned out that he had indeed become very bloated before his death; that he had grown just such a beard while on the sick list; and that he had some time before bought and eventually ridden to death a pony of that very description.

Other striking instances are those of an apparition seen simultaneously by several persons. It is on record that an apparition of a child was perceived first by a dog, that the animal's rushing at it, loudly barking, interrupted the conversation of the seven persons present in the room, thus drawing their attention to the apparition, and that the latter then moved through the room for some fifteen seconds, followed by the barking dog.[6]

Another type of empirical evidence of survival consists of communications, purporting to come from the dead, made through the persons commonly called sensitives, mediums, or automatists. Some of the most remarkable of these communications were given by the celebrated American medium, Mrs. Piper, who for many years was studied by the Society for Psychical Research, London, with the most elaborate precautions against all possibility of fraud. Twice, particularly, the evidences of identity supplied by the dead persons who purportedly were thus communicating with the living were of the very kinds, and of the same precision and detail, which would ordinarily satisfy a living person of the identity of another living person with whom he was not able to communicate directly, but only through an intermediary, or by letter or telephone.[7]

Again, sometimes the same mark of identity of a dead person, or the same message from him, or complementary parts of one message, are obtained independently from two mediums in different parts of the world.

Of course, when facts of these kinds are recounted, as I have just done, only in abstract summary, they make little if any impression upon us. And the very word "medium" at once brings to our minds the innumerable instances of demonstrated fraud perpetrated by charlatans to extract money from the credulous bereaved. But the modes of trickery and sources of error, which immediately suggest themselves to us as easy, natural explanations of the seemingly extraordinary facts, suggest themselves just as quickly to the members of the research committees of the Society for Psychical Research. Usually, these men have had a good deal more experience than the rest of us with the tricks of conjurers and fraudulent mediums, and take against them precautions far more strict and ingenious than would occur to the average sceptic.[8]

But when, instead of stopping at summaries, one takes the trouble to study the detailed, original reports, it then becomes evident that they cannot all be just laughed off; for to accept the hypothesis of fraud or mal-observation would often require more credulity than to accept the facts reported.

To *explain* those facts, however, is quite another thing. Only two hypotheses at all adequate to do so have yet been advanced. One is that the communications really come, as they purport to do, from persons who have died and have survived death. The other is the hypothesis of telepathy—that is, the supposition, itself startling enough, that the medium is able to gather information directly from the minds of others, and that this is the true source of the information communicated. To account for all the facts, however, this hypothesis has to be stretched very far, for some of them require us to suppose that the medium can tap the minds even of persons far away and quite unknown to him, and can tap even the subconscious part of their minds.

Diverse highly ingenious attempts have been made to devise conditions that would rule out telepathy as a possible explanation of the communications received; but some of the most critical and best-documented investigators still hold that it has not yet been absolutely excluded. Hence, although some of the facts recorded by physical research constitute, prima facie, strong empirical evidence of survival, they cannot be said to establish it beyond question. But they do show that we need to revise rather radically in some respects our ordinary ideas of what is and is not possible in nature.

CAN MENTAL STATES CAUSE BODILY EVENTS?

Let us now turn to another of the arguments against survival. That states of consciousness entirely depend on bodily processes, and therefore cannot continue when the latter have ceased, is proved, it is argued, by the fact that various states of consciousness—in particular, the several kinds of sensations—can be caused at will by appropriately stimulating the body.

Now, it is very true that sensations and some other mental states can be so caused; but we have just as good and abundant evidence that mental states can cause various bodily events. John Laird mentions, among others, the fact that merely willing to raise one's arm normally suffices to cause it to rise; that a hungry person's mouth is caused to water by the idea of food; that feelings of rage, fear or excitement cause digestion to stop; that anxiety causes changes in the quantity and quality of the milk of a nursing mother; that certain thoughts cause tears, pallor, blushing or fainting; and so on.[9] The evidence we have that the relation is one of cause and effect is exactly the same here as where bodily processes cause mental states.

It is said, of course, that to suppose something non-physical, such as thought, to be capable of causing motion of a physical object, such as the body, is absurd. But I submit that if the heterogeneity of mind and matter makes this absurd, then it makes equally absurd the causation of mental states by stimulation of the body. Yet no absurdity is commonly found in the assertion that cutting the skin causes a feeling of pain, or that alcohol, caffein, bromides, and other drugs, cause characteristic states of consciousness. As David Hume made clear long ago, no kind of causal connection is intrinsically absurd. Anything might cause anything; and only observation can tell us what in fact can cause what.

Somewhat similar remarks would apply to the allegation that the principle of the conservation of energy precludes the possibility of causation of a physical event by a mental event. For if it does then it equally precludes causation in the converse direction, and this, of course, would leave us totally at a loss to explain the occurrence of sensations. But, as Keeton and others have pointed out,[10] that energy is conserved is not something observation has revealed or could reveal, but only a postulate—a defining postulate for the notion of an "isolated physical system."

That is, conservation of energy is something one has to have if, but only if, one insists on conceiving the physical world as wholly self-contained, independent, isolated. And just because the metaphysics which the natural sciences tacitly assume does insist on so conceiving the physical world, this metaphysics compels them to save conservation by postulations *ad hoc* whenever dissipation of energy is what observation reveals. It postulates, for instance, that something else, which appears at such times but was not until then regarded as energy, is energy too, but it is then said, "in a different form."

Furthermore, as Broad has emphasized, all that the principle of conservation requires is that when a quantity Q of energy disappears at one place in the physical world an equal quantity of it should appear at some other place there. And the supposition that, in some cases, what causes it to disappear here and appear there is some mental event, such perhaps as a volition, does not violate at all the supposition that energy is conserved.[11]

A word, next, on the parallelism between the degree of development of the nervous systems of various animals and the degree of their intelligence. This is alleged to prove that the latter is the product of the former. But the facts lend themselves equally well to the supposition that, on the contrary, an obscurely felt need for greater intelligence in the circumstances the animal faced was what brought about the variations which eventually resulted in a more adequate nervous organization.

In the development of the individual, at all events, it seems clear that the specific, highly complex nerve connections which become established in the brain and cerebellum of, for instance, a skilled pianist are the results of his will over many years to acquire the skill.

We must not forget in this context that there is a converse, equally consistent with the facts, for the theory, called epiphenomenalism, that mental states are related to the brain much as the halo is to the saint, that is, as effects but never themselves as causes. The converse theory, which might be called hypophenomenalism, and which is pretty well that of Schopenhauer, is that the instruments which the various mechanisms of the body consti-

tute are the objective products of obscure cravings for the corresponding powers; and, in particular, that the organization of the nervous system is the effect and material isomorph of the variety of mental functions exercised at a given level of animal or human existence.

THE INITIAL ASSUMPTION BEHIND THE ARGUMENTS AGAINST SURVIVAL

We have now scrutinized all but the last of the reasons mentioned earlier for rejecting the possibility of survival, and we have found them all logically weak. Before examining the one which remains, it will be useful for us to pause a moment and inquire why so many of the persons who advance those reasons nevertheless think them convincing.

It is, I believe, because these persons approach the question of survival with a certain unconscious metaphysical bias. It derives from a particular initial assumption which they tacitly make. It is that *to be real is to be material.* And to be material, of course, is to be some process or part of the perceptually public world, that is, of the world we all perceive by means of our so-called five senses.

Now the assumption that to be real is to be material is a useful and appropriate one for the purpose of investigating the material world and of operating upon it; and this purpose is a legitimate and frequent one. But those persons, and most of us, do not realize that the validity of that assumption is strictly relative to that specific purpose. Hence they, and most of us, continue making the assumption, and it continues to rule judgment, even when, as now, the purpose in view is a different one, for which the assumption is no longer useful or even congruous.

The point is all-important here and therefore worth stressing. Its essence is that the conception of the nature of reality that proposes to define the real as the material is not the expression of an observable fact to which everyone would have to bow, but is the expression only of a certain direction of interest on the part of the persons who so define reality—of interest, namely, which they have chosen to center wholly in the material, perceptually public world. This specialized interest is of course as legitimate as any other, but it automatically ignores all the facts, commonly called facts of mind, which only introspection reveals. And that specialized interest is what alone compels persons in its grip to employ the word "mind" to denote, instead of what it commonly does denote, something else altogether, namely, the public behavior of bodies that have minds.

Only so long as one's judgment is swayed unawares by that special interest do the logically weak arguments against the possibility of survival, which we have examined, seem strong.

It is possible, however, and just as legitimate, as well as more conducive to a fair view of our question, to center one's interest at the start on the facts of mind as introspectively observable, ranking them as most real in the sense that they are the facts the intrinsic nature of which we mostly directly experience, the facts which we most certainly know to exist; and moreover, that they are facts without the experiencing of which we should not know of any other facts whatever —such, for instance, as those of the material world.

The sort of perspective one gets from this point of view is what I propose now to sketch briefly. For one thing, the material world is then seen to be but one among other objects of our consciousness. Moreover, one becomes aware of the crucially important fact that it is an object postulated rather than strictly given. What this means may be made clearer by an example. Suppose that, perhaps in a restaurant we visit for the first time, an entire wall is occupied by a large mirror and we look into it without realizing that it is a mirror. We then perceive, in the part of space beyond it, various material objects, notwithstanding that in fact they have no existence there at all. A certain set of the vivid color images which we call visual sensations was all that was strictly given to us, and these we construed, automatically and instantaneously, but nonetheless erroneously, as signs or appearances of the existence of certain material objects at a certain place.

Again, and similarly, we perceive in our dreams various objects which at the time we take as physical but which eventually we come to believe were not so. And this eventual conclusion, let it be noted, is forced upon us not because we then detect that something, called "physical substance," was lacking in those objects, but only because we notice, as we did not at the time, that their behavior was erratic—incoherent with their ordinary one. That is, their appearance was a *mere* appearance, deceptive in the sense that it did not then predict truly, as ordinarily it does, their later appearances. This, it is important to notice, is the *only* way in which we ever discover that an object we perceive was not really physical, or was not the particular sort of physical object we judged it to be.

These two examples illustrate the fact that our perception of physical objects is sometimes erroneous. But the essential point is that, even when it is veridical instead of erroneous, *all* that is literally and directly given to our minds is still only *some set of sensations.* These, on a given occasion, may be only color sensations; but they often include also tactual sensations, sounds, odors, and so on. It is especially interesting, however, to remark here in passing that, with respect to almost all the many thousands of persons and other "physical" objects we have perceived in a lifetime, *vivid color images* were the only data our perceiving strictly had to go by; so that, if the truth should happen to have been that those objects, like ghosts or images in a mirror, were actually intangible—that is, were *only* color images— we should never have discovered that this was the fact. For all we *directly* know, it *may* have been the fact!

To perceive a physical object, then, instead of merely experiencing passively certain sensations (something which perhaps hardly ever occurs), is always to *interpret,* that is, to *construe,* given sensations as signs of, and appearances to us of, a postulated something other than themselves, which we believe is causing them in us and is capable of causing in us others of specific kinds. We believe this because we believe that our sensations too must have some cause, and we find none for them among our other mental states.

Such a postulated extramental something we call "a physical object." We say that we observe physical objects, and this is true. But it is important for the present purpose to be clear that we "observe" them never in any more direct or literal manner than is constituted by the process of interpretive postulation just described—never, for example, in the wholly direct and literal manner in which we are able to observe our sensations themselves and our other mental states.

That perception of a physical object is thus always the product of two factors—one, a set of sensations simply given to us, and the other an act of interpretation of these, performed by us—is something which easily escapes notice and has even been denied. This, however, is only because the interpretive act is almost always automatic, instantaneous, and correct—like, for instance, that of thinking of the meaning of any familiar word we hear. But that an interpretive act does occur is forced on our attention when, in a particular case, we discover that we misconstrued the meaning of the sensations. Or, again, the interpretive act is noticeable when, because the sensations are too scant and therefore ambiguous, we catch ourselves hesitating between two or more possible interpretations of them and say that we are not sure what objects it is we see.

"OUR OWN" BODIES

To complete the sketch of the view of the universe obtained when we conceive ourselves primarily as minds rather than as bodies, attention must now be directed to a particular one of the objects which, in the sense described, we perceive in the world external to our minds. This especially interesting object is the one we call "our own body"; and the question we must now ask is: How do we identify it among the thousands of human bodies we perceive? What peculiarities mark it from all others and make us call it our own?

One of them, of course, is that we never directly see certain parts of it; for instance, most of its back, or any part of its head except a certain aspect of its nose and orbital arch. This aspect, moreover, we always see when it is illuminated if we see anything at all.

But there are four other and more important peculiarities which mark a human body as our own. One is that it is the only physical object we can directly cause to move by a mere act of will. This statement, however, probably needs to be slightly qualified, since the results of the many experiments at Duke University and elsewhere have provided strong evidence of the reality of the so-called psychokinetic effect (as well as of clairvoyance).[12] These experiments appear to show that it is sometimes possible for a human volition to cause directly at least minute alterations in the behavior of physical objects other than one's own

body. If so, we could then conceive a willed motion of our own body as simply a psychokinetic effect in maximum degree. It is well to remember in this connection that causation, directly by an act of will, of some alteration in the behavior of a molecule, is neither more nor less intrinsically intelligible, nor a priori more probable or improbable, when the molecule happens to be part of a brain than when it happens instead to be part of a physical object of some other kind, such as a piece of wood or a stone.

Another of the marks of the body we call our own is that it is the only one the stimulation of which causes directly in us sensations of the corresponding kinds. This statement, too, may turn out to need slight qualification if full confirmation should be obtained that vivid images are sometimes received by the mind directly from physical objects or events, that is, received without intermediary stimulation of the sense organs of one's body.

Cases of this kind would be examples of what is meant by clairvoyance as distinguished from telepathy, and if the reality of it can be regarded as firmly established, then sensation could be viewed as a special instance of clairvoyance, and the sense organs, together with the corresponding nerves and brain regions, as specialized transmitters, which, like microscopes, magnify what they transmit, but transmit at all only what occurs at relatively short distances and in circumstances of special kinds. Here, as before, we should not forget that it is neither more nor less intelligible or probable a priori that a color experience, for example, should have for its immediate cause a molecular event in the visual cortex of the brain, than a molecular event in some physical object other than the brain or even the body.[13]

Besides the two marks just mentioned, there are two others likewise peculiar to the body we call our own. They are less obvious to casual observation, but quite as important theoretically. And they, too, consist of unique capacities in respect to causation, but causation now of changes in the structure, instead of only the states, of conscious mind and of brain.

One of them is that the body we call our own is the only one in which certain mutilations of the brain ever directly cause specific alterations in the dispositions or capacities our mind manifests. An example would be the effects upon the mind of the brain operation called prefrontal lobotomy, mentioned earlier. It notably alters the conscious personality.

The other mark relates to causation in the converse direction: the body we call our own is the only one in which certain elaborate connections among the nerve cells in the association areas of the brain can be directly caused by a mental event —for instance, by that mental event which consists of a firm and persistent volition to acquire some particular bodily skill, such as skill to play a given musical instrument.

These remarks have been intended to provide a perspective by virtue of which the relation of body to mind can be observed without the distortion otherwise imposed by the tacit assumption we mentioned, which is commonly made, but which has validity and relevance strictly limited to the purpose of studying and controlling the material world. That enlarged and fairer perspective, I now submit, makes clear that no paradox at all is really involved in the supposition that some forms of consciousness may exist independently of connection with animal or human bodies; and, therefore, that survival is at least theoretically possible. . . .

NOTES

1. J. B. Pratt, *The Religious Consciousness,* p. 225.

2. Cf. Gardner Murphy, "Difficulties Confronting the Survival Hypothesis," *Journal of the American Society for Psychical Research* for April, 1945, p. 72; Corliss Lamont, *The Illusion of Immortality* (New York, 1935), pp. 26ff.

3. F. Paulsen, *Introduction to Philosophy* (trans. by F. Thilly, 2d ed), pp. 82–83.

4. *My Life as a Dissociated Personality,* edited by Morton Prince (Boston: Badger).

5. "An Outline of Survival Evidence," *Journal of the American Society for Psychical Research* for January, 1945.

6. The documents obtained by the Society for Psychical Research concerning this case, that of the lieutenant's apparition, and that of the girl with the scratch, are reproduced in Sir Ernest Bennett's *Apparitions and Haunted Houses* (London: Faber and Faber, 1945), pp. 334–337, 28–35, and 145–150 respectively.

7. A summary of some of the most evidential facts may be found in the book by M. Sage, entitled *Mrs. Piper and the Society for Psychical Research* (New York: Scott-Thaw Co., 1904); others of them are related in detail in Sir Oliver Lodge's *The Survival of Man,* Sec. IV (New York, Moffat, Yard and Co., 1909) and in A. M. Robbins' *Both Sides of the Veil,* Part II (Boston: Sherman, French, and Co., 1909). The fullest account is in the *Proceedings of the Society for Psychical Research.*

8. Cf. H. Carrington, *The Physical Phenomena of Spiritualism, Fraudulent and Genuine* (Small, Maynard & Co., Boston, 1908).

9. John Laird, *Our Minds and Their Bodies* (London, 1925), pp. 16–19.

10. M. T. Keeton, "Some Ambiguities in the Theory of the Conservation of Energy," *Philosophy of Science,* Vol. 8, No. 3, July 1941.

11. C. D. Broad, *The Mind and Its Place in Nature,* pp. 103ff. [This volume, p. 271.]

12. For a summary of these experiments, see J. B. Rhine's book *The Reach of the Mind* (New York, 1947).

13. It is interesting to note that essentially the same suggestion as that made above—that voluntary activity is a special case of psychokinesis, and sensory perception a special case of clairvoyance—was independently made and developed by R. H. Thouless and B. P. Wiesner in an article, "The Psi Processes in Normal and 'Paranormal' Psychology" (*Procs. Soc. for Psychical Research,* December 1947), where they wrote: "The hypothesis we wish to suggest is that, in normal thinking and perceiving I am in the same sort of relation to what is going on in the sensory part of my brain and nervous system as that of the successful clairvoyant to some external event, and that this relation is established by the same means," and "We suggest also that there is a similar identity of relation in normal motor control of the body on the one hand and the 'paranormal' process of psychokinesis on the other" (pp. 180–181).

ANTONY FLEW

Can a Man Witness His Own Funeral?*

I

"Whether we are to live in a future state, as it is the most important question which can possibly be asked, so it is the most intelligible one which can be expressed in language"—Bishop Butler in the dissertation *Of Personal Identity.* [Included in this volume, pp. 000–000.]

The purposes of this paper are, *first,* to try to begin to raise what Butler called "strange perplexities"[1] about the meaningfulness of this question and, *second,* to attempt to dispose of the counter-thesis, maintained by Schlick, that it must be significant because the possibility being discussed is not merely conceivable but also imaginable. These are very strictly limited objectives. We shall not, and shall not pretend to, do more than attack these two of the vast complex problems, both logical and empirical, compendiously described as the questions of Survival and Immortality.

II

Now suppose someone offers the gambit "We all of us survive death" or "We all of us live forever." Might we not reply "Whatever in the world do you mean? For, in the ordinary senses of the words you use, the former sentence is self-contradictory and the latter denies one of the

most securely established of all empirical generalisations; for it is the contrary of that traditional darling of the logicians 'All men are mortal.' " As the objections to the two sentences are different, let us deal with each of them separately.

"We all of us survive death" is self-contradictory because we use the words "death" and "survival" and their derivatives in such a way that the classification of the crew of a torpedoed ship into "Dead" and "Survivors" is both exclusive and exhaustive. Every member of the crew must (logical "must") have either died or survived: and no member of the crew could (logical "could") have both died and survived. It is easy to overlook that "We all of us survive death" is self-contradictory because we all habitually and wisely give all utterances the benefit of the doubt. Generously assuming that other people usually have something intelligible to express even when they speak or write in unusual or incorrect ways, we attempt to attach sense even to expressions which are strictly self-contradictory. This tendency is frequently exploited by advertisers. Posters advertising the film *Bachelor Husband* catch the eye precisely because the expression "bachelor husband" is self-contradictory, and therefore paradoxical. We tend to puzzle over the title, to ponder—doubtless to the advertiser's eventual profit—over the non-linguistic improprieties suggested by this linguistically improper expression. If we see the headline "We survived death!" we do not just exclaim (in the tone of voice of rigid logical school-masters) "Nonsense: you either survive or

*Antony G. N. Flew, "Can a Man Witness His Own Funeral?" *Hibbert Journal,* Vol. 54 (April 1956), 242–250. Reprinted by permission of the author and the editor of the *Hibbert Journal.*

you die!", but, curiosity aroused, we read on to learn how the death was only 'death' (in inverted commas), that the people in question had only pretended, been reported, appeared, to die; but had not of course in fact died. Sometimes, for instance, people show all the usual 'symptoms' of death, all the usually reliable signs that they will not walk, or talk, or joke again, but then, surprisingly, recover and do walk and talk and joke once more. This happened quite often in World War II: Russian doctors in particular reported many cases of patients who showed the usual indications of death—the heart not beating and so forth —but were brought back to life by shock treatments, blood transfusions, and such-like. These patients thus survived 'death' (in inverted commas). The doctors then adapted their language— or at least the language of *Soviet War News* (London) was adapted—to meet the new situation: "We cannot survive death" was retained as the expression of a necessary truth; and the expression "clinical death" was introduced as a more precise and less awkward substitute for 'death' (in inverted commas) to refer to the condition of the patients who showed all the usual 'symptoms' but who nevertheless might or might not survive to tell the tale. "We survive death" thus was, and remains, self-contradictory. The paradox use of "survives death" in advertising and headlines, and the inverted-comma use of 'death' in which people can be said to return from the 'dead' (in inverted commas), do not in the least weigh against this contention. They positively reinforce it: it is precisely because "He survived death" is self-contradictory that it is a good headline; it is precisely because "to survive death" is self-contradictory that the doctors put the word "death" between warning inverted commas when first they had to report that a patient survived 'death,' and later introduced the new expression "clinical death" to replace the makeshift 'death' (in inverted commas) when similar cases occurred repeatedly.

"We all of us live forever" is, on the other hand, not self-contradictory but just as a matter of fact false, being as it is the flat contrary of the massively confirmed generalisation "All men are mortal." (Though if you choose to use the latter expression to express not a factual generalisation but an artificial truth of logic, making it true by definition that all *men* are mortal, thus incurring

the probably unwelcome consequence that on this definition neither the prophet Elijah[2] nor— on the Roman view[3]—the Virgin Mary can count as human beings; then, of course, "we all of us [men] live forever" will on your definition become self-contradictory, and not merely false as a matter of manifest empirical fact.) But, like "We all of us survive death," "We all of us live forever" has what we might call 'headline value.' Both are 'shockers' and thus catch the eye and arouse curiosity. They make us wonder what the writer is up to, what is the story which he is going to tell under these arresting headlines. For surely he cannot really be intending to say something so obviously nonsensical or so notoriously false as what at first glance he seems to be saying.

Now many stories have been and still more could be told under these headlines. People have claimed that "We all of us live for ever, *because* the evil (and sometimes even the good) that men do lives after them." People have have argued that "We survive death, *because* our descendants will live on after we are dead." And in the variety and irrelevance of their supporting reasons they have revealed the variety and irrelevance of the theses which they have been concerned to maintain when they used these and similar paradoxical expressions. The only use with which we are concerned here—and certainly the only use which would justify Butler's claim that here was "the most important question which can possibly be asked"—is that in which they are intended to support or express what Wisdom has called "the logically unique expectation,"[4] the expectation that we shall see and feel, or at any rate and more non-committally, that we shall 'have experiences' after we are dead. Therefore we shall take it that the person who has said "We all of us survive death" or "We all of us live forever" was making a move intended to justify such expectations.

And against this move the simple-minded counter-move is to attempt a sort of philosophical fools' mate. Clearly this expectation cannot (logical "cannot") be well grounded unless we are going to exist after our deaths.[5] But we have been insisting that it is not merely false but actually self-contradictory to say that we survive death. So we cannot (logical "cannot") exist after our deaths. Therefore these logically unique expectations cannot be well founded. Indeed the suggestion on which they are based, the assumption which they presuppose (*viz.* that "We survive death") is self-contradictory and therefore senseless.

III

Well, of course there are several possible defences against this sort of attack; and the possible variations on these defences are innumerable. The traditional one depends on the distinction between body and mind, or body and soul (what Professor Ryle, unaccountably ignoring Plato, insists on calling the *Cartesian* Myth; a notion which—far from being a philosopher's fancy—is incapsulated in the idiom of innumerable languages and is a widespread, though not universal, element in folklore and religion). The first stage is to maintain that people consist of two elements, one, the body, visible, tangible and corporeal, the other, the mind or soul, invisible, intangible and incorporeal. The second stage is to maintain that we are our souls or minds. This stage is indispensable: unless we are our souls the survival of our souls will not be our survival; and the news that our souls were to be preserved after we died would be of no more importance or concern to us than the news that any other parts of us—our appendices, say—were to be preserved. Granted these two presuppositions (and "presuppositions" is surely the *mot juste:* for they are rarely either distinguished from one another or argued for[6]) it is then significant and even plausible to say that we (our incorporeal souls, that is) survive death (which is "the mere death of the body"). The desire to allow doctrines of personal immortality to be significant and plausible is one of the main drives behind dualist conceptions, and one perhaps insufficiently stressed by Professor Ryle in *The Concept of Mind.*[7] But this is a vast and another subject; here we propose to concentrate exclusively on one more modern defence, that which claims that "I shall survive my death" cannot be self-contradictory and therefore senseless, because it refers to a possibility which is not merely conceivable but imaginable.[8]

This argument was used by Moritz Schlick.[9] "I take it for granted that . . . we are concerned with the question of survival after 'death.' "—[His inverted commas. These surely tacitly concede the claim that "to survive death" is a self-contradictory expression: compare the similar tacit admission made in the tombstone insistence "Not dead but sleeping." A.F.] I think we may agree with Professor Lewis when he says about this hypothesis: "Our understanding of what would verify it has no lack of clarity. In fact I can easily imagine, e.g. witnessing the funeral of my own body and continuing to exist without a body, for nothing is easier to describe than a world which differs from our ordinary world only in the complete absence of all data which I would call parts of my own body. We must conclude that immortality, in the sense defined, should not be regarded as a metaphysical 'problem,' but is an empirical hypothesis, because it possesses logical verifiability. It could be verified by following the prescription 'Wait until you die!'." A briefer and more puckish version of the same argument can be found in John Wisdom's unending saga *Other Minds.* "I know indeed what it would be like to witness my own funeral—the men in tall silk hats, the flowers, and the face beneath the glass-topped coffin"[10] and it is also deployed by Dr. Casimir Lewy in his 'Is the Notion of Disembodied Existence Self-contradictory?'[11]

So far as I know this argument has never been challenged: presumably partly because we can most of us imagine (image) a scene such as Wisdom describes; and partly because no one wants to arrogate to himself the right to decide what Wisdom or Schlick or anyone other than he himself can or cannot imagine (image). But the argument can and should be challenged: and it can be done without arbitrarily prescribing any limit to Wisdom's obviously very considerable imaginative powers. For there is all the difference in the world between: imagining what it would be like to witness my own funeral (which requires only a minor effort); and imagining what it would be like to witness me witnessing *my own* funeral (which is logically impossible. Or at least, less dogmatically, is very far from being a logically straightforward matter). If it really is I who witness it then it is not my funeral but only 'my funeral' (in inverted commas): and if it really is my funeral then I cannot be a witness, for I shall be dead and in the coffin.

Of course I can imagine many situations which might be described as my watching 'my own funeral' (in inverted commas): I can remember Harry Lime in the film *The Third Man* watching 'his own funeral,' and of course I can imagine being in the same situation as Harry Lime; but it was not really Harry Lime's own funeral, and what I can imagine would not really be mine. Again I can imagine my own funeral—I shall not try to better Wisdom's whimsical description of such a scene—but now what I am imagining is not *my* witnessing *my own* funeral but merely my own funeral. (Parenthetically, it should be pointed out that Wisdom is far too good a writer to have committed himself to the former—and improper—description of his imaginings [imagings]. What he wrote was "I know indeed what it would be like to witness my own funeral." Unfortunately, this will not, under examination, support his thesis: which requires that he should be able to imagine his surviving his own death and his witnessing his own funeral: which seems to be impossible, since the latter supposition, like the former, is apparently self-contradictory).

But surely this is merely slick? Surely I can perfectly well imagine my own funeral, really my own funeral with my body in the coffin and not a substitute corpse or a weight of bricks; with me there watching it all, but invisible, intangible, a disembodied spirit? Well, yes, this seems all right: until someone asks the awkward question "Just how does all this differ from your imagining your own funeral without your being there at all (except as the corpse in the coffin)?"[12]

Certainly Schlick could imagine, as he claimed, "the funeral of his own body": though it is perhaps a pity that he should describe what he imagined in this way and not, more naturally, as "his own funeral." But then he goes on to talk of imagining his "continuing to exist without a body": which he tries to justify by claiming that "nothing is easier than to describe a world which differs from our ordinary world only in the complete absence of all data which I would call parts of my own body." But the fact that we can all of us describe, or even imagine, a world which would differ from our ordinary world only in the complete absence of all data describable as parts of our respective bodies has not, by itself, the slightest tendency to show that anyone could imagine or describe a world in which, after his funeral, he continued to exist without a body. By itself it merely shows that we can each imagine what the world would be like if he were obliterated from it entirely, and no trace of his corpse remained. Schlick has misdescribed what he could imagine. Misled by the fact that a man

can easily imagine what his funeral will be like, and hence what it would be like to watch it, it is tempting to insist that he can imagine what it would be like *for him* to watch *his own* funeral. Schlick is thus able to "conclude that immortality, in the sense defined ... is an empirical hypothesis. ... It could be verified by following the prescription 'Wait until you die!' " But he has not defined a sense of "immortality" at all: apparently he has merely misdescribed some rather humdrum exercises of his imagination in an extremely exciting and misleading way. He has failed to say anything to prevent his opponent from objecting to his conclusion: "But, on the contrary, nothing whatever could be verified (by me) by (my) following the prescription 'Wait until you die!': (for me my) death is so final that it is logically impossible (for me) to survive it to verify any hypotheses at all."

IV

We have now fulfilled the two strictly limited purposes of this paper. But perhaps it is worth while to add comments on three other possible objections to the attempted philosophical fools' mate; emphasising that nothing we have said or shall say must be interpreted to mean that we ourselves consider it to be decisive. *First* it may be said that this is all too cut and dried, the logic of our ordinary language is not as sharp, clear, and uncomplicated as has been made out. This is true and important. To take only one example: any adequate treatment of the logic of survival and immortality (the enquiry initiated by Plato's *Phaedo*) would demand the use of the distinction between death and dissolution; just as any full discussion of the logic of metempsychosis and pre-existence (the enquiry initiated by Plato's *Meno*) would have to take account of the parallel distinction between birth and conception. But for our first purpose, the raising of "strange perplexities," soft shading and rich detail is confusing, while for the second, dealing with one countermove crudely made, is unnecessary.

Second, it may be suggested that, although Schlick and Wisdom as a matter of fact only succeeded in imagining their own funerals and the world going on without them (and then misdescribed and/or mistook the significance of what they did imagine), it would nevertheless be quite possible to imagine all sorts of bizarre phenomena which we should feel inclined to describe as "the activities of disembodied people" or even as "evidence of survival." This again is true and important. Anyone who has read at all widely in the literature of psychical research must often have felt inclined to apply such expressions to phenomena, or putative phenomena, recorded in that literature.[13] But it is all too easy to misinterpret what we shall be doing if we do allow ourselves to describe such *outré* phenomena in these paradoxical ways. In fact we shall be attaching sense to an expression—"disembodied person"—for which previously no sense had been provided: either directly as an idiomatic expression; or indirectly through the uses given to its constituent words. We are thereby introducing a new sense of the word "person."[14] Yet it may appear to us and to others as if we have discovered a new sort of person, a new state in which a person can be. Whereas a disembodied person is no more a special sort of person than is an imaginary person: and (except in the Services—which have their peculiar sense of the word "disembodied") disembodiment is no more a possible state of a person than is non-existence.

Now it is perfectly possible to specify a sense for the expression "disembodied person": just as it is possible to attach sense to any expression, even one which on present usage would be self-contradictory. The difficulty is to attach a sense to it so that some expression incorporating it will, if true, provide a ground for the logically unique expectation. In their present use person words have logical liaisons of the very greatest importance: personal identity is the necessary condition of both accountability and expectation; which is only to say that it is unjust to reward or punish someone for something unless (as a minimum condition) he is the same person who did the deed; and also that it is absurd to expect experiences for Flew in 1984 unless (as a minimum condition) there is going to be a person in existence in 1984 who will be the same person as I. The difficulty, not necessarily insuperable, is to change the use of person words so radically that it becomes significant to talk of people surviving dissolution, without changing it to such an extent that these vital logical liaisons are lost.

The *third* obvious criticism returns us to the traditional foundation for what we might call a "logic of immortality." The objection might be made that it has been assumed throughout that people are merely bodies, that people are bodies and nothing more. Even though we have excluded discussions of the traditional dualisms from this paper, this criticism has to be met. It is met by pointing out that no one has either argued or assumed anything of the sort. What has been done is merely to take for granted the ordinary meaning and use of person words, and to use them—we hope—in the conventional and proper way: a very different matter. People are what you meet. Person words refer to men and women like you and me and the other fellow. They are taught by pointing at people: indeed how else could they or should they be taught? They do not refer to anything invisible and elusive, to any mysterious incorporeal substances. Even children can be taught them, can and do know what is meant by "Father," "I," "man," "person," or "butcher." But that is not to say that they refer merely or at all to bodies. "Person" is no synonym for "body": though "body" is used peculiarly in the services as a slightly pejorative substitute for "person," the degrading point of the substitution would be lost if the words were really synonymous; there is a difference, a difference of life and death, between "We brought a person down from the foot of the Z'mutt ridge" and "We brought a body down from the foot of the Z'mutt ridge."[15] Person words do not mean either bodies or souls nor yet any combination of the two: "I" is no synonym for "my body" nor yet for "my mind" or "my soul" nor yet for any combination of these (as anyone who tries a few substitutions must soon discover). If we are indeed compound of two such disparate elements, that is a contingent fact about people and not part of what is meant by "person" and other person words.[16] To suggest that it has been assumed that people are merely bodies is surely to reveal that you yourself assume that everyone must be a dualist—or at least a dualist with one component missing—a sort of one-legged dualist. And this is a mistake. But though this third criticism is mistaken, it does go straight to the heart of the matter. For the whole position does depend on the fact that people are what you meet: we do not just meet the sinewy containers in which other people are kept; they do not just encounter the fleshy houses which we ourselves inhabit.[17] The whole position depends on the obvious, crucial, but constantly neglected fact that person words mean what they do mean. This paper has consisted in insistent and obstinate underlining of this fact; and in pointing out two implications of it, important but limited in scope: that Butler was wrong to deny that there were logical difficulties about the notion of a future life; and that Schlick's short way with these difficulties will not do. Perhaps attention to it can transform discussion of the problems of Survival and Immortality in a way very similar to that in which Moore's insistence that we do know that some material things exist has transformed discussions of Idealism and of the problems of Epistemology.[18] As Berkeley, with his usual insight, remarked, "the grand mistake is that we know not what we mean by 'we,' 'selves' or 'mind,' etc."[19]

NOTES

1.   *Loc. cit.:* also in Ch. 1 of the *Analogy of Religion* he writes of "strange difficulties."

2.   See II Kings, ii. 11.

3.   See *Munificentissimus Deus* of 1. xi. 50.

4.   In 'Gods' *PAS* 44/5, reprinted in *Logic and Language* I (Ed. A. G. N. Flew: Blackwell, 1951).

5.   Lucretius exploited this point: Debet enim, misere si forte aegreque futurum est. Ipse quoque esse in eo tum tempore, cui malè possit Accidere. [For if there is going to be misery and pain in the future then the person it's going to happen to has got to exist at that time.] *De Rerum Natura,* Book III, 861–3.

6.   But there are arguments to be found: *e.g.* in Plato's *Alcibiades* 1§§ 128ff., Descartes' *Meditation* II, and Butler's *Analogy,* Ch. I.

7.   There are some, but surprisingly few, references: cf. pp. 11, 23, 26 and 186. As I have twice mentioned Professor Ryle only to disagree, I should like to add here that I owe him an enormous debt.

8.   For a clear and very relevant elucidation of the senses of "imagine" and an examination of the relation and lack of relation between the ability to form mental pictures and the deciding of questions of significance and non-significance see Annis Flew 'Images, Supposing, and Imagining' in *Philosophy,* 1953.

9.   *Philosophical Review,* July, 1936, p. 356. Reprinted in Feigl and Sellars' *Readings in Philosophical Analysis,* pp. 159–60.

10.   *Mind,* 1942, p. 2 and *Other Minds* (Blackwell, 1952), p. 36. Perhaps this is not Wisdom's own view but only that of one of his characters. In any case I should like to stress how much delight and illumination this series of articles has given me.

11.   *PAS,* 1942–3, pp. 64–5: this is a non-linguist aberration from the method of the rest of this strenuous paper; a paper of which I hope shortly to publish a detailed criticism.

12.   Here we might compare Wisdom on "picture preferences" in 'Other Minds' in *Mind,* 1940 and in *Other Minds,* Ch. I, which will suggest how much, how very much, difference there may be even when "there is no *factual* difference." Utterances of a belief in the immortality of the soul usually form part of a whole attitude to the world (cf. σωμα σημα — "the body is a prison"). But though this paper does not even begin to come to grips with this sort of complex of belief and attitude of which utterances about the immorality of the soul form a part, it is worth pointing out that, rightly or wrongly, most people who have held such faiths have believed that 'the logically unique expectation' was in fact justified: and would be no longer able or willing (psychologically) to maintain their faiths if convinced that it was not. See my 'Theology and Falsification' and 'Death' in *University* (Blackwell's, 1950 and 1952), Vol. I, No. 3 and Vol. II, No. 2; reprinted in *Essays in Philosophical Theology* (S.C.M. Press, 1955: edited by A. MacIntyre and A. G. N. Flew). [See this volume, p. 59.]

13.   Compare for instance Kenneth Richmond's compendium *Evidence of Identity* (Bell, 1939) or the classic *Phantasms of the Living* by Gurney, Myers and Podmore (Abridged, Kegan Paul, 1918). I have discussed briefly the relations between our present problems and such phenomena in my *A New Approach to Psychical Research* (C. A. Watts, 1953). Ch. VII.

14.   "I am not at all clear what I ought to mean by this disembodied existence, merely because I could mean so many things by it."—J. N. Findlay in *P.A.S.,* 1949–50, p. 61.

15.   Consider this item from the London *Times* of 3/1/51: *Climber Killed by an Avalanche.* "Five mountaineers were trapped by an avalanche yesterday. . . . Two escaped. Two others were extricated by an R.A.F. Mountain Rescue squad. . . . Mr. N. Ryder . . . was buried under several feet of snow, and another rescue party located his body early this morning."

16.   I have written more about this in "Locke and the Problem of Personal Identity" in *Philosophy,* Jan., 1951.

17.   Contrast Bishop Butler: "It is as easy to conceive— that we may exist out of bodies as in them, that we might have animated bodies of any other organs and senses wholly different from those now given us, and that we may hereafter animate these same or new bodies variously modified and organised—as to conceive how we can animate such bodies as our present" (*Analogy,* Ch. 1). This assumption that people are not what we meet but are elusive entities which mysteriously 'animate' human bodies (and possibly non-human bodies or even no bodies at all) is fundamental and crucial to his argument.

18.   Compare papers by Ambrose, Wisdom, Malcolm Mace and others in *The Philosophy of G. E. Moore.* (Edited Paul A. Schlipp).

19.   Albeit with a different intent. *Philosophical Commentaries* (Ed. A. A. Luce), p. 301.

JOHN LOCKE

The Idea of Personal Identity*

... This also shows wherein the identity of the same *man* consists; viz. in nothing but a participation of the same continued life, by constantly fleeting particles of matter, in succession vitally united to the same organized body. He that shall place the identity of man in anything else, but, like that of other animals, in one fitly organized body, taken in any one instant, and from thence continued, under one organization of life, in several successively fleeting particles of matter united to it, will find it hard to make an embryo, one of years, mad and sober, the *same* man, by any supposition, that will not make it possible for Seth, Ishmael, Socrates, Pilate, St. Austin, and Caesar Borgia, to be the same man. For if the identity of *soul alone* makes the same *man*, and there be nothing in the nature of matter why the same individual spirit may not be united to different bodies, it will be possible that those men, living in distant ages, and of different tempers, may have been the same man: which way of speaking must be from a very strange use of the word man, applied to an idea out of which body and shape are excluded. And that way of speaking would agree yet worse with the notions of those philosophers who allow of transmigration, and are of opinion that the souls of men may, for their miscarriages, be detruded into the bodies of beasts, as fit habitations, with organs suited to the satisfaction of their brutal inclinations. But yet I

think nobody, could he be sure that the *soul* of Heliogabalus were in one of his hogs, would yet say that hog were a *man* or *Heliogabalus*.

It is not therefore unity of substance that comprehends all sorts of identity, or will determine it in every case; but to conceive and judge of it aright, we must consider what idea the word it is applied to stands for: it being one thing to be the same *substance,* another the same *man,* and a third the same *person*, if *person*, *man*, and *substance,* are three names standing for three different ideas;—for such as is the idea belonging to that name, such must be the identity; which, if it had been a little more carefully attended to, would possibly have prevented a great deal of that confusion which often occurs about this matter, with no small seeming difficulties, especially concerning *personal* identity, which therefore we shall in the next place a little consider.

An animal is a living organized body; and consequently the same animal, as we have observed, is the same continued *life* communicated to different particles of matter, as they happen successively to be united to that organized living body. And whatever is talked of other definitions, ingenious observation puts it past doubt, that the idea in our minds, of which the sound "man" in our mouths is the sign, is nothing else but of an animal of such a certain form. Since I think I may be confident, that, whoever should see a creature of his own shape or make, though it had no more reason all its life than a cat or a parrot, would call him still a *man;* or whoever should hear a cat or

*From John Locke, *An Essay Concerning Human Understanding,* Book II, Chapter 27, "Of Ideas of Identity and Diversity." First published in 1690.

a parrot discourse, reason, and philosophize, would call or think it nothing but a *cat* or a *parrot;* and say, the one was a dull irrational man, and the other a very intelligent rational parrot. A relation we have in an author of great note,[1] is sufficient to countenance the supposition of a rational parrot. His words are:

"I had a mind to know, from Prince Maurice's own mouth, the account of a common, but much credited story, that I had heard so often from many others, of an old parrot he had in Brazil, during his government there, that spoke, and asked, and answered common questions, like a reasonable creature: so that those of his train there generally concluded it to be witchery or possession; and one of his chaplains, who lived long afterwards in Holland, would never from that time endure a parrot, but said they all had a devil in them. I had heard many particulars of this story, and assevered by people hard to be discredited, which made me ask Prince Maurice what there was of it. He said, with his usual plainness and dryness in talk, there was something true, but a great deal false of what had been reported. I desired to know of him what there was of the first. He told me short and coldly, that he had heard of such an old parrot when he had been at Brazil; and though he believed nothing of it, and it was a good way off, yet he had so much curiosity as to send for it: that it was a very great and a very old one; and when it came first into the room where the prince was, with a great many Dutchmen about him, it said presently, *What a company of white men are here!* They asked it, what it thought that man was, pointing to the prince. It answered, *Some General or other.* When they brought it close to him, he asked it, *D'où venez-vous?* It answered, *De Marinnan.* The Prince, *A qui estes-vous?* The parrot, *A un Portugais.* The Prince, *Que fais-tu là?* Parrot, *Fe garde les poulles.* The Prince laughed, and said, *Vous gardez les poulles?* The parrot answered, *Oui, moi; et je sçai bien faire,*[2] and made the chuck four or five times that people use to make to chickens when they call them. I set down the words of this worthy dialogue in French, just as Prince Maurice said them to me. I asked him in what language the parrot spoke, and he said in Brazilian. I asked whether he understood Brazilian; he said no, but he had taken care to have two interpreters by him, the one a Dutchman that

spoke Brazilian, and the other a Brazilian that spoke Dutch; that he asked them separately and privately, and both of them agreed in telling him just the same thing that the parrot had said. I could not but tell this odd story, because it is so much out of the way, and from the first hand, and what may pass for a good one; for I dare say this Prince at least believed himself in all he told me, having ever passed for a very honest and pious man: I leave it to naturalists to reason, and to other men to believe, as they please upon it; however, it is not, perhaps, amiss to relieve or enliven a busy scene sometimes with such digressions, whether to the purpose or no.

I have taken care that the reader should have the story at large in the author's own words, because he seems to me not to have thought it incredible; for it cannot be imagined that so able a man as he, who had sufficiency enough to warrant all the testimonies he gives of himself, should take so much pains, in a place where it had nothing to do, to pin so close, not only a man whom he mentions as his friend, but on a Prince in whom he acknowledges very great honesty and piety, a story which, if he himself thought incredible, he could not but also think ridiculous. The Prince, it is plain, who vouches this story, and our author, who relates it from him, both of them call this talker a parrot: and I ask any one else who thinks such a story fit to be told, whether, if this parrot, and all of its kind, had always talked, as we have a prince's word for it this one did,— whether, I say, they would not have passed for a race of *rational animals,* but yet, whether, for all that, they would have been allowed to be men, and not *parrots?* For I presume it is not the idea of a thinking or rational being alone that makes the *idea of a man* in most people's sense: but of a body, so and so shaped, joined to it; and if that be the idea of a man, the same successive body not shifted all at once, must, as well as the same immaterial spirit, go to the making of the same man.

This being premised, to find wherein personal identity consists, we must consider what *person* stands for;—which, I think, is a thinking intelligent being, that has reason and reflection, and can consider itself as itself, the same thinking thing, in different times and places; which it does only by that consciousness which is inseparable from thinking, and, as it seems to me, essential to it: it being impossible for any one to perceive without *perceiving* that he does perceive. When we see, hear, smell, taste, feel, meditate, or will anything, we know that we do so. Thus it is always as to our present sensations and perceptions: and by this every one is to himself that which he calls *self:*— it not being considered, in this case, whether the same self be continued in the same or divers substances. For, since consciousness always accompanies thinking, and it is that which makes every one to be what he calls self, and thereby distinguishes himself from all other thinking things, in this alone consists personal identity, i.e. the sameness of a rational being: and as far as this consciousness can be extended backwards to any past action or thought, so far reaches the identity of that person; it is the same self now it was then; and it is by the same self with this present one that now reflects on it, that that action was done.

But it is further inquired, whether it be the same identical substance. This few would think they had reason to doubt of, if these perceptions, with their consciousness, always remained present in the mind, whereby the same thinking thing would be always consciously present, and, as would be thought, evidently the same to itself. But that which seems to make the difficulty is this, that this consciousness being interrupted always by forgetfulness, there being no moment of our lives wherein we have the whole train of all our past actions before our eyes in one view, but even the best memories losing the sight of one part whilst they are viewing another; and we sometimes, and that the greatest part of our lives, not reflecting on our past selves, being intent on our present thoughts, and in sound sleep having no thoughts at all, or at least none with that consciousness which remarks our waking thoughts,—I say, in all these cases, our consciousness being interrupted, and we losing the sight of our past selves, doubts are raised whether we are the same thinking thing, i.e. the same *substance* or no. Which, however reasonable or unreasonable, concerns not *personal* identity at all. The question being what makes the same person; and not whether it be the same identical substance, which always thinks in the same person, which, in this case, matters not at all: different substances, by the same consciousness (where

they do partake in it) being united into one person, as well as different bodies by the same life are united into one animal, whose identity is preserved in that change of substances by the unity of one continued life. For, it being the same consciousness that makes a man be himself to himself, personal identity depends on that only, whether it be annexed solely to one individual substance, or can be continued in a succession of several substances. For as far as any intelligent being *can* repeat the idea of any past action with the same consciousness it had of it at first, and with the same consciousness it has of any present action; so far it is the same personal self. For it is by the consciousness it has of its present thoughts and actions, that it is *self to itself* now, and so will be the same self, as far as the same consciousness can extend to actions past or to come; and would be by distance of time, or change of substance, no more two persons, than a man be two men by wearing other clothes today than he did yesterday, with a long or a short sleep between: the same consciousness uniting those distant actions into the same person, whatever substances contributed to their production.

That this is so, we have some kind of evidence in our very bodies, all whose particles, whilst vitally united to this same thinking conscious self, so that *we feel* when they are touched, and are affected by, and conscious of good or harm that happens to them, are a part of ourselves; i.e. of our thinking conscious self. Thus, the limbs of his body are to every one a part of himself; he sympathizes and is concerned for them. Cut off a hand, and thereby separate it from that consciousness he had of its heat, cold, and other affections, and it is then no longer a part of that which is himself, any more than the remotest part of matter. Thus, we see the *substance* whereof personal self consisted at one time may be varied at another, without the change of personal identity; there being no question about the same person, though the limbs which but now were a part of it, be cut off.

But the question is, Whether if the same substance which thinks be changed, it can be the same person; or, remaining the same, it can be different persons?

And to this I answer: First, This can be no question at all to those who place thought in a purely material animal constitution, void of an immaterial substance. For, whether their supposition be true or no, it is plain they conceive personal identity preserved in something else than identity of substance; as animal identity is preserved in identity of life, and not of substance. And therefore those who place thinking in an immaterial substance only, before they can come to deal with these men, must show why personal identity cannot be preserved in the change of immaterial substances, or variety of particular immaterial substances, as well as animal identity is preserved in the change of material substances, or variety of particular bodies: unless they will say, it is one immaterial spirit that makes the same life in brutes, as it is one immaterial spirit that makes the same person in men; which the Cartesians at least will not admit, for fear of making brutes thinking things too.

But next, as to the first part of the question, Whether, if the same thinking substance (supposing immaterial substances only to think) be changed, it can be the same person? I answer, that cannot be resolved but by those who know what kind of substances they are that do think; and whether the consciousness of past actions can be transferred from one thinking substance to another. I grant were the same consciousness the same individual action it could not: but it being a present representation of a past action, why it may not be possible, that that may be represented to the mind to have been which really never was, will remain to be shown. And therefore how far the consciousness of past actions is annexed to any individual agent, so that another cannot possibly have it, will be hard for us to determine, till we know what kind of action it is that cannot be done without a reflex act of perception accompanying it, and how performed by thinking substances, who cannot think without being conscious of it. But that which we call the same consciousness, not being the same individual act, why one intellectual substance may not have represented to it, as done by itself, what it never did, and was perhaps done by some other agent— why, I say, such a representation may not possibly be without reality of matter of fact, as well as several representations in dreams are, which yet whilst dreaming we take for true—will be difficult to conclude from the nature of things. And that it never is so, will by us, till we have clearer views of the nature of thinking substances, be best resolved into the goodness of God; who, as far as

the happiness or misery of any of his sensible creatures is concerned in it, will not, by a fatal error of theirs, transfer from one to another that consciousness which draws reward or punishment with it. How far this may be an argument against those who would place thinking in a system of fleeting animal spirits, I leave to be considered. But yet, to return to the question before us, it must be allowed, that, if the same consciousness (which, as has been shown, is quite a different thing from the same numerical figure or motion in body) can be transferred from one thinking substance to another, it will be possible that two thinking substances may make but one person. For the same consciousness being preserved, whether in the same or different substances, the personal identity is preserved.

As to the second part of the question, Whether the same immaterial substance remaining, there may be two distinct persons; which question seems to me to be built on this,—Whether the same immaterial being, being conscious of the action of its past duration, may be wholly stripped of all the consciousness of its past existence, and lose it beyond the power of ever retrieving it again: and so as it were beginning a new account from a new period, have a consciousness that *cannot* reach beyond this new state. All those who hold pre-existence are evidently of this mind; since they allow the soul to have no remaining consciousness of what it did in that pre-existent state, either wholly separate from body, or informing any other body; and if they should not, it is plain experience would be against them. So that personal identity, reaching no further than consciousness reaches, pre-existent spirit not having continued so many ages in a state of silence, must needs make different persons. Suppose a Christian Platonist or a Pythagorean should, upon God's having ended all his works of creation the seventh day, think his soul hath existed ever since; and should imagine it has revolved in several human bodies; as I once met with one, who was persuaded his had been the *soul* of Socrates (how reasonably I will not dispute; this I know, that in the post he filled, which was no inconsiderable one, he passed for a very rational man, and the press has shown that he wanted not parts or learning;)—would any one say, that he, being not conscious of any of Socrates's actions or thoughts, could be the same *per-*

son with Socrates? Let any one reflect upon himself, and conclude that he has in himself an immaterial spirit, which is that which thinks in him, and, in the constant change of his body keeps him the same: and is that which he calls *himself:* let him also suppose it to be the same soul that was in Nestor or Thersites, at the siege of Troy, (for souls being, as far as we know anything of them, in their nature indifferent to any parcel of matter, the supposition has no apparent absurdity in it,) which it may have been, as well as it is now the soul of any other man: but he now having no consciousness of any of the actions either of Nestor or Thersites, does or can he conceive himself the same person with either of them? Can he be concerned in either of their actions? attribute them to himself, or think them his own, more than the actions of any other men that ever existed? So that this consciousness, not reaching to any of the actions of either of those men, he is no more one *self* with either of them than if the soul or immaterial spirit that now informs him had been created, and began to exist, when it began to inform his present body; though it were never so true, that the same *spirit* that informed Nestor's or Thersites' body were numerically the same that now informs his. For this would no more make him the same person with Nestor, than if some of the particles of matter that were once a part of Nestor were now a part of this man; the same immaterial substance, without the same consciousness, no more making the same person, by being united to any body, than the same particle of matter, without consciousness, united to any body, makes the same person. But let him once find himself conscious of any of the actions of Nestor, he then finds himself the same person with Nestor.

And thus may we be able, without any difficulty, to conceive the same person at the resurrection, though in a body not exactly in make or parts the same which he had here,—the same consciousness going along with the soul that inhabits it. But yet the soul alone, in the change of bodies, would scarce to any one but to him that makes the soul the man, be enough to make the same man. For should the soul of a prince, carrying with it the consciousness of the prince's past life, enter and inform the body of a cobbler, as soon as deserted by his own soul, every one sees he would be the same *person* with the prince,

accountable only for the prince's actions: but who would say it was the same *man?* The body too goes to the making the man, and would, I guess, to everybody determine the man in this case, wherein the soul, with all its princely thoughts about it, would not make another man: but he would be the same cobbler to every one besides himself. I know that, in the ordinary way of speaking, the same person, and the same man, stand for one and the same thing. And indeed every one will always have a liberty to speak as he pleases, and to apply what articulate sounds to what ideas he thinks fit, and change them as often as he pleases. But yet, when we will inquire what makes the same *spirit, man,* or *person,* we must fix the ideas of spirit, man, or person in our minds; and having resolved with ourselves what we mean by them, it will not be hard to determine in either of them, or the like, when it is the same, and when not.

But though the immaterial substance or soul does not alone, wherever it be, and in whatsoever state, make the same *man;* yet it is plain, consciousness, as far as ever it can be extended—should it be to ages past—unites existences and actions very remote in time into the same *person,* as well as it does the existences and actions of the immediately preceding moment: so that whatever has the consciousness of present and past actions, is the same person to whom they both belong. Had I the same consciousness that I saw the ark and Noah's flood, as that I saw an overflowing of the Thames last winter, or as that I write now, I could no more doubt that I who write this now, that saw the Thames overflowed last winter, and that viewed the flood at the general deluge, was the same *self,*—place that self in what *substance* you please—than that I who write this am the same *myself* now whilst I write (whether I consist of all the same substance, material or immaterial, or no) that I was yesterday. For as to this point of being the same self, it matters not whether this present self be made up of the same or other substances—I being as much concerned, and as justly accountable for any action that was done a thousand years since, appropriated to me now by this self-consciousness, as I am for what I did the last moment.

Self is that conscious thinking thing,—whatever substance made up of, (whether spiritual or material, simple or compounded, it matters not)

—which is sensible or conscious of pleasure and pain, capable of happiness or misery, and so is concerned for itself, as far as that consciousness extends. Thus every one finds that, whilst comprehended under that consciousness, the little finger is as much a part of himself as what is most so. Upon separation of this little finger, should this consciousness go along with the little finger, and leave the rest of the body, it is evident the little finger would be the person, the same person; and self then would have nothing to do with the rest of the body. As in this case it is the consciousness that goes along with the substance, when one part is separate from another, which makes the same person, and constitutes this inseparable self: so it is in reference to substances remote in time. That with which the consciousness of this present thinking thing *can* join itself, makes the same person, and is one self with it, and with nothing else; and so attributes to itself, and owns all the actions of that thing, as its own, as far as that consciousness reaches, and no further; as every one who reflects will perceive.

In this personal identity is founded all the right and justice of reward and punishment; happiness and misery being that for which every one is concerned for *himself,* and not mattering what becomes of any *substance,* not joined to, or affected with that consciousness. For, as it is evident in the instance I gave but now, if the consciousness went along with the little finger when it was cut off, that would be the same self which was concerned for the whole body yesterday, as making part of itself, whose actions then it cannot but admit as its own now. Though, if the same body should still live, and immediately from the separation of the little finger have its own peculiar consciousness, whereof the little finger knew nothing, it would not at all be concerned for it, as a part of itself, or could own any of its actions, or have any of them imputed to him.

This may show us wherein personal identity consists: not in the identity of substance, but, as I have said, in the identity of consciousness, wherein if Socrates and the present mayor of Queinborough agree, they are the same person: if the same Socrates waking and sleeping do not partake of the same consciousness, Socrates waking and sleeping is not the same person. And to punish Socrates waking for what sleeping Socrates thought, and waking Socrates was never con-

scious of, would be no more of right, than to punish one twin for what his brother-twin did, whereof he knew nothing, because their outsides were so like, that they could not be distinguished; for such twin have been seen.

But yet possibly it will still be objected,—Suppose I wholly lose the memory of some parts of my life, beyond a possibility of retrieving them, so that perhaps I shall never be conscious of them again; yet am I not the same person that did those actions, had those thoughts that I once was conscious of, though I have now forgot them? To which I answer, that we must here take notice what the word *I* is applied to; which, in this case, is the *man* only. And the same man being presumed to be the same person, I is easily here supposed to stand also for the same person. But if it be possible for the same man to have distinct incommunicable consciousness at different times, it is past doubt the same man would at different times make different persons; which, we see, is the sense of mankind in the solemnest declaration of their opinions, human laws not punishing the mad man for the sober man's actions, nor the sober man for what the mad man did,—thereby making them two persons: which is somewhat explained by our way of speaking in English when we say such an one is 'not himself,' or is 'beside himself'; in which phrases it is insinuated, as if those who now, or at least first used them, thought that self was changed; the selfsame person was no longer in that man.

But yet it is hard to conceive that Socrates, the same individual man, should be two persons. To help us a little in this, we must consider what is meant by Socrates, or the same individual *man.*

First, it must be either the same individual, immaterial, thinking substance; in short, the same numerical soul, and nothing else.

Secondly, or the same animal, without any regard to an immaterial soul.

Thirdly, or the same immaterial spirit united to the same animal.

Now, take which of these suppositions you please, it is impossible to make personal identity to consist in anything but consciousness; or reach any further than that does.

For, by the first of them, it must be allowed possible that a man born of different women, and in distant times, may be the same man. A way of speaking which, whoever admits, must allow it possible for the same man to be two distinct persons, as any two that have lived in different ages without the knowledge of one another's thoughts.

By the second and third, Socrates, in this life and after it, cannot be the same man any way, but by the same consciousness; and so making human identity to consist in the same thing wherein we placed personal identity, there will be no difficulty to allow the same man to be the same person. But then they who place human identity in consciousness only, and not in something else, must consider how they will make the infant Socrates the same man with Socrates after the resurrection. But whatsoever to some men makes a man, and consequently the same individual man, wherein perhaps few are agreed, personal identity can by us be placed in nothing but consciousness, (which is that alone which makes what we call *self*,) without involving us in great absurdities.

But is not a man drunk and sober the same person? Why else is he punished for the act he commits when drunk, though he be never afterwards conscious of it? Just as much the same person as a man that walks, and does other things in his sleep, is the same person, and is answerable for any mischief he shall do in it. Human laws punish both, with a justice suitable to *their* way of knowledge;—because, in these cases, they cannot distinguish certainly what is real, what counterfeit: and so the ignorance in drunkenness or sleep is not admitted as a plea. For, though punishment be annexed to personality, and personality to consciousness, and the drunkard perhaps be not conscious of what he did, yet human judicatures justly punish him; because the fact is proved against him, but want of consciousness cannot be proved for him. But in the Great Day, wherein the secrets of all hearts shall be laid open, it may be reasonable to think, no one shall be made to answer for what he knows nothing of; but shall receive his doom, his conscious accusing or excusing him.

NOTES

1. Sir William Temple, in his *Memoirs of what passed in Christendom from 1672 to 1679,* p. 66.

2. The parrot was asked, 'Whence come ye?' It replied, 'From Marinnan.' The Prince asked, 'To whom do you belong?' The parrot replied, 'To a Portuguese.' 'What do you there?' asked the Prince. The parrot answered, 'I look after the chickens.' The Prince laughed, and said, '*You* look after the chickens?' The parrot answered, 'Yes, I; and I know well enough how to do it.'

SYDNEY SHOEMAKER

On Knowing Who One Is*

There are striking differences between the ways in which we know certain sorts of facts about ourselves and the ways in which we know the same kinds of facts about others. To the question 'How do I know, when I do know, what another person is presently thinking and feeling?' the short answer is 'From his behaviour'. This is evidently not the answer to the question 'How do I know what I myself am presently feeling and

*Sydney Shoemaker, "On Knowing Who One Is," *Common Factor*, No. 4 (Autumn, 1966), 49–56. Reprinted by permission of the author and the editor of *Common Factor*, London.

thinking?' Some philosophers would give to the latter question the answer 'By introspection'. This answer seems to be at best uninformative (if 'knowing of a feeling by introspection' turns out to mean simply 'knowing of a feeling when it is one's own') and at worst misleading (if introspecting is thought of consist in observing, by means of an 'inner sense', objects that are observable to oneself alone)—but I shall not argue this here. What seems beyond question is (1) that one has knowledge of facts about one's 'present state of mind' that is not based on the sorts of evidence on which another person's knowledge of these facts would have to be based, i.e., evidence consisting of facts about one's bodily behaviour, and (2) that one's sincere claims to know such facts about oneself are either entirely incapable of being mistaken or, at least, are incapable of being mistaken in many of the ways in which another person's claim to know the same facts about oneself could be mistaken. These differences between 'first-person' and 'third-person' knowledge of states of mind have certainly influenced philosophical thinking about the nature of a person or 'self'; in particular, they have seemed to many philosophers to support the dualistic view that the mind of a person (which tends to be identified with the person) is essentially a non-physical entity, in principle separable from the person's body, of which that person alone has direct knowledge.

While it often happens that a person fails to know who another person is, it seldom happens that a person fails to know who he himself is. It may seem as if this is easily explained in terms of the facts just mentioned and the dualistic theory these facts make plausible. If each of us is directly aware of facts about himself in a way in which no one else can be aware of them, does it not follow that each of us knows far better than anyone else who he is? Knowing who a person is, however, is not simply a matter of knowing facts about him. If you point to someone and ask me if I know who he is, I could only be making a bad joke if I replied 'Yes. He is the man standing about twenty feet from us, wearing a blue suit and a striped tie and smoking a cigar.' Knowing such facts about a person does not count as knowing who he is. And this is not because the facts are 'physical' rather than 'mental' or 'psychological.' There is, after all, such a thing as a person's not knowing who he himself is, and this is not a matter of the person's not knowing facts about his present state of mind. A victim of amnesia may not know who he is, yet he will know such things as that he is hungry, that his feet hurt, and that he is curious about his identity. When Descartes asked 'What then am I?' and went on to enumerate various things he knew about himself, he mentioned nothing that an amnesia victim would not know about himself, and nothing that would justify the claim that he knew who he was.

What is it, then, to know who a person is? It would be a mistake to expect a very precise answer to this question, for the notion of knowing who a person is is just not a very precise one. Often context will determine whether one is said to know who a person is; of one and the same person I might in different circumstances say (a) 'I knew who he was—I recognized him right away as the man who lives in the house on the corner', and (b) 'I didn't know who he was—I had no idea that he was N. N., the famous violinist'. In general, and ignoring complexities of the sort just mentioned, we can say that knowing who X is consists in knowing the truth of a nontrivial identity judgment of the form 'X is the person who . . .,' where the description 'the person who . . .,' or descriptions closely related to it, could be used in a fairly wide variety of circumstances to refer to the person in question. (Ordinarily knowing the identity judgment 'That man is the man who came into the room a few moments ago' would not count as knowing who someone is, for here the identifying description is one that could be used to refer to the person only in very special circumstances.) Coming to know who a person is typically involves coming to know such things as his name, his occupation, his place of residence, his family connections, and the more important facts about his life history. It is worth noting that where A is the same person as B (i.e., where 'A' and 'B' are different expressions referring to one and the same person) one can know who A is without thereby knowing who B is, and can fail to know who A is without thereby failing to know who B is. I may know who John is without knowing who Smith's murderer is, even though in fact John is Smith's murderer, and I may fail to know who Tom's worst enemy is without failing to know who I am, even though in fact I am Tom's worst enemy.

As remarked earlier, a man can fail to know who he is. And others may know who a man is when he does not. So it is not true as a matter of necessity that I know better than anyone else who I am. Still, a man's knowledge of who he is does differ in a philosophically important way from the knowledge of other persons of who he is. A victim of amnesia may discover who he is in the way in which others would discover this; he may come to know his 'identity' with the help of detectives and the missing persons bureau, and on the basis of fingerprints, photographs, and the like. But he may also come to know who he is in a way in which no one else could come to know this; he may come to know it by regaining his memory. There is, to be sure, a sense in which a person *A* could come to know who another person *B* is by regaining his (*A's*) memory. Having regained his memory A recognizes B, who had seemed a stranger to him, as an old friend. But here the sense in which *A* comes to know *B's* identity by regaining his memory is very different from the sense in which he comes to know his own identity by regaining his memory. Upon regaining his memory *A* knows that he is *A,* the husband of such and such a woman, the father of three children, the person who has such and such a past history. But we could hardly say that upon regaining his memory he *recognizes* himself as *A*, or as the person of whom various things are true. *A's* coming to know who *B* is can be analysed into two components, (1) his coming to remember that he had a friend of whom various things are true, and (2) his recognizing *B* as that friend from his present appearance. But it seems clear that *A's* coming to know who he himself is cannot be so analysed. In coming to know this he need not inspect his body or look into a mirror. Neither his present appearance nor any other present fact about him serves as something from which he recognizes his 'present self' as being identical with the 'past self' whose existence he has come to remember. Nor is any such recognition necessary, for what A comes to remember is not that someone or other (whom he then recognizes himself as being, or recognizes as himself) had such and such a past history; what he comes to remember is that *he* had such and such a past history.

What emerges here is that each of us has, in memory, a kind of access to his own past history which no one other than himself can have. The statements we make about our own past histories are not infallible, but they are immune to one sort of error to which the statements of other persons about our past histories are subject; they are immune to what might be called error through misidentification. If you point to me and say, on the basis of memory, 'That's the man who stole my watch', your statement may be false even though your memory is as accurate as it could possibly be; this will be so if the thief looked exactly like me but was in fact someone else (my twin, my double, or someone disguised to look like me). But if I say on the basis of memory 'I am the man

who stole your watch', then while my statement may be false (my memory may be mistaken; I may have dreamt the entire incident), it cannot be that my memory is accurate and yet that I am mistaken in thinking that the remembered thief was myself. Another way of putting this point is by saying that whereas my statement 'I am the person who did such and such' can express *what* I remember (and thus, when this is so, cannot be false if my memory is accurate), my statement 'you are the person who did such and such' can at best be a conclusion from what I remember and from other things I know (and so can be false even if my memory is accurate).

It is, I think, this special access to his own past that each person has *via* memory, rather than the special access to his own present thoughts and feelings that each person has *via* 'introspection', that constitutes a person's privileged access to his own 'identity', or to 'who he is'. There is, however, one interesting point of resemblance between these two sorts of special access. Just as I can know what I am feeling without observing my bodily behaviour, so I can know, because I remember, that I am the person who did some past action without first ascertaining that my present body is identical with the human body involved in that past action. And just as the existence of the first sort of special access can lead to the idea that the subject of thought and feeling is something logically distinct from the body (for I can know that I feel pain without in any way observing my body), so the existence of the second sort of special access can lead to the idea that the identity through time of a person is logically quite independent of the identity through time of human bodies. I believe that both of these ideas are mistaken. With regard to the second, I have argued at length elsewhere that if bodily identity were not normally good evidence of personal identity, it would be impossible for anything else to be evidence of personal identity. But I shall not repeat these arguments here, for I think that nowadays the tendency of philosophers is to exaggerate rather than underestimate the importance of bodily identity as a constitutive factor in personal identity. As I shall now try to show, there is a good deal to be said for the view, which is traditionally associated with the name of John Locke, that memory is not only the source of our special access to our own identities, but is also the main constitutive factor in personal identity.

We have already noted that a person can remember his own past actions as his own in a way in which other persons cannot remember them as his. A further, and related, fact of importance is that if a person remembers any event at all—whether it be an action of his own, an action of another person, or an event that it not an action of anyone—it follows that he, the very person who remembers, must have witnessed the event at the time of its occurrence (where consciously performing an action counts as 'witnessing' it, and where in general what counts as witnessing an event depends on the nature of the event; for me to be in a position to remember the last Presidential election campaign it is enough that I should have been aware at the time, from newspapers, television, etc. that it was going on). Here we have an important conceptual connection between memory and personal identity. The question now is whether this fact provides any basis for the claim that memory is a constitutive factor in personal identity that is independent of bodily identity. Whether it does seems to depend on whether it is possible to establish that a person remembers a past event without first establishing, or without thereby having established, that the person is bodily continuous with one of the witnesses of the event (where to say that a person A at time t_1 is bodily continuous with a person B at time t_2 is to say that the body of A at t_1 and the body of B at t_2 are one and the same body). If this is possible, then it is possible for there to be a case in which it is discovered (a) that a person remembers a past event, and therefore is identical with one of the witnesses of the event, and (b) that the person is not bodily continuous with any of the witnesses of the event.

It is often argued that such cases are not possible. It is pointed out that in order for it to be the case that a person remembers a past event it is not sufficient that he should have memories that happen to correspond to it—i.e., that the event should be just like one that it seems to the person that he remembers. It can happen by chance that a mere seeming memory corresponds to something that actually happened, and a 'veridical' memory can correspond to events other than the one of which it is a memory, namely to events

similar to that event. In order to establish that a person really does remember an event, it is maintained, we must establish, not merely that his memories do correspond to it, but that he is in a position to remember it, i.e., that he witnessed it. But this means that we must establish that he is identical with one of the witnesses to the event. And since we must establish that such an identity holds in order to establish that he remembers the event, we cannot establish that the identity holds on the basis of the fact that he remembers the event; for until we have established that the identity holds, it is said, we are not in a position to assert that he does remember. In such a case, the argument goes, the only thing that would establish that the identity holds, and thereby establish that the person does remember the event, is evidence of bodily identity.

I believe, however, that this argument overlooks one important component of the concept of memory. The concept of memory is in part a *causal* notion. To say that a person remembers a past event is not simply to say (1) that he witnessed the event, and (2) that he now has a memory corresponding to the event. For even if (1) and (2) were both the case, we would not say that the person remembered the event unless we thought that it was *because* he witnessed the event that he now has memories corresponding to it. If we become persuaded that a person has seeming memories of an event only because he has repeatedly heard the event described, or as the result of hypnotic suggestion, and believe that he would have those seeming memories even if he had not witnessed the event, then even though we know that he did witness the event and that his seeming memories do correspond to what happened, we will not want to say that he remembers the event. It would be extremely difficult to specify just what sort of causal connection must exist between past witnessings of an event and present memories corresponding to it in order for it to be true that the memories are of the event. But it is arguable (a) that the existence of the requisite sort of causal connection is, at least in some circumstances, a sufficient as well as a necessary condition for its being true that the memories are of the past event, and (b) that in some such cases it is possible to establish that the requisite sort of causal connection holds without first establishing whether the person who has the present memories is identical with the person who did the past witnessing.

Suppose, to use a fanciful case that I have discussed elsewhere, that the brain from Brown's body is transplanted into Robinson's body (Robinson's brain having been removed), and that the resulting creature—we will call it 'Brownson'—survives and eventually exhibits more or less normal human behaviour. The question would arise whether Brownson should be identified with Brown, with Robinson or with neither. I think that we would not want to say that he is Brown until we had satisfied ourselves that he remembers things that Brown had done and experienced. But I also think that we could satisfy ourselves of this without first establishing that he was Brown. If Brownson proved to have memories that correspond to events in Brown's life, we would very probably say that he remembers these events. We would say this, not simply because of the correspondence between the memories and the past events and actions, but because it would be reasonable to suppose that this correspondence is explained by the fact that Brownson has the brain Brown had when he witnessed those events and did those actions, because it would therefore be reasonable to suppose that the causal connection is of fundamentally the same sort that exists in ordinary cases of memory, and because we would take the existence of such a causal connection as establishing that we have a genuine case of memory. If, as I believe, it would be reasonable in this case to say that Brownson remembers events in Brown's life, it would also be reasonable to conclude that Brownson is Brown. These conclusions will be most compelling if virtually all of Brownson's memories correspond to events in Brown's past history. In any event, this seems to be a case in which the question of whether X is the same person as Y ultimately turns, not on whether X is bodily continuous with Y (except for his brain, Brownson is bodily continuous with Robinson rather than with Brown), but on whether X can remember events in Y's life.

I should now like to return briefly to the 'special access' to our own pasts which consists in our being able to remember past actions as our own in a way in which other persons cannot remember them as ours. It seems to me that it is absolutely central to the notion of a person that persons have this sort of special access to their own past histories. Only a being who had such memory knowledge of its own past, and a good deal of such knowledge, could engage in purposive behaviour; an agent's knowledge of what he is doing is continuous with, and cannot exist without, knowledge of what he has just been doing, i.e., what he has done, thought and experienced in the immediate past. Even the simplest action would be impossible if the agent completely lacked the latter sort of knowledge, and I believe that it could be shown (I have not the space to show this here) that it is quite impossible that such knowledge could generally be grounded in the way in which our knowledge of the past histories of persons other than ourselves is grounded. I believe also that the ability to locate past and present events within what Mr. Strawson refers to in *Individuals* as 'a single, unified spatio-temporal system', and the associated ability to know one's own place within such a system, rests on the special access one has to events in one's own past. One way of knowing where a past event occurred in relation to one's present location is to remember witnessing the event and remember one's own movements between the time of witnessing the event and the present. There are of course other ways in which one can know such a spatial relationship, but I believe that if one could never know such a spatial relationship in this way one could never know such a spatial relationship at all. Indeed, it seems to me arguable that a creature who lacked altogether the ability to have this sort of knowledge of its own past history would be incapable of knowledge of any sort, and could not qualify as a conscious being, or as a person. Since it is in the ability to have this sort of knowledge that a person's special access to his own identity consists. I am thus led to something very much like Locke's definition of 'person': 'a thinking intelligent being, that has reason and reflection, *and can consider itself as itself, the same thinking thing, in different times and places;* which it does only by that consciousness which is inseparable from thinking and, as it seems to me, essential to it ...' (*Essay* II, xxvii, 11, my emphasis).

TERENCE PENELHUM

Bodily Transfer*

Once upon a time there was a kingdom ruled over by a handsome prince, whose youth had been filled with daring escapades and travels. One morning his servants went to wake him as usual, but a very strange phenomenon met their eyes when they entered. There before them, or so it seemed, was their prince; yet he had a lost and rather frantic expression on his face, and was intermittently staring down at his shoes. His servants wished him good morning, and instead of the usual lofty nod they were treated to a series of entreaties. They were asked to explain where they all were, who they all were, and what all these beautiful clothes and shoes were. He then asked to be taken to the prince, because he wished to explain his presence in the palace, he said; though he was at a loss how to do this. The servants in turn were at a loss how to reply to this request, but one of them bravely told him that he *was* the prince. This he denied, pointing to the portrait of the prince on the wall and saying that *that* was the prince, whom he had often seen pass by in the street. He was the cobbler from the other end of the city and should really be at work by now. Then the climax came; one of them showed him his face in the mirror. He cried out and protested that he had a different body the night before, and recounted how he had been mending shoes till midnight and had hit his thumb several times because he was sleepy. The

servants sent for the palace doctor; but before he could get there there was a great commotion at the palace gate. It seemed that a similar situation had arisen at the cobbler's house, where someone who appeared to be obviously the cobbler had woken up and demanded to be taken away from this dingy house and back to the palace where he belonged. Scoldings from the cobbler's wife had made no difference; he had protested that he did not know who she was, that he must have been kidnapped, and that she should not hector him in the tone she was using. He then forced his way out towards the palace, followed by the protesting woman, and insisting that he was the prince. When he reached the palace the guards refused to let him in, but were discomfited by his apparent recognition of them and his knowledge of the names of the palace servants. They sent for these people who were still in a baffled state from their encounter with the man in the prince's bedroom. Questioning revealed that the man who looked like the cobbler seemed to recall nothing of the cobbler's late-night shoe-mending, but all sorts of things about the past adventures of the prince, which he insisted were his own doings. He then demanded to be treated as his station required, and told them to put the impostor in his bedroom out of the gates. They found the man in the bedroom quite willing to go, and finally agreed to this solution over the protests of the cobbler's wife, who said that if her husband were going to be kept like royalty, she ought to be, too. Were they right?

*From Terence Penelhum, *Survival and Disembodied Existence* (London: Routledge & Kegan Paul, 1970), pp. 79–89. Reprinted by permission of the author and publisher.

I shall take it for granted that since we have never been in a situation quite like the one imagined, a decision as to whether the two men in the story should be regarded as the persons they *claim* to be, rather than the ones they *appear* to be, is indeed one that involves us in a certain degree of innovation; so that an answer to our question is not a mere matter of making explicit a decision we have already made implicitly, but of making a new one. In making it, however, we have to try to stay as close as possible to the conceptual conventions we already follow, if we are to avoid inconsistencies. The difficulty of the puzzle seems to me to lie in the fact that our instincts are indeed as Locke says they are, viz. to accept that this is a case of bodily transfer, yet a careful examination of our current conventions suggests the reverse reading.

For we are only able to use men's memory-beliefs because of the possibility of using physical tests to confirm who people are, and even when we are entitled to accept men's memory-claims without applying these tests, in doing so we commit ourselves to the existence of facts which would independently guarantee a claimant's identity if we knew them. So if we adhere to the conventions that we have, we should unhesitatingly reject claims like those made in our story, where the physical tests are negative consistently. Further, we have seen that in order to elicit and recognize people's memory-claims we have to be able to listen to them over a period of time and therefore be able, by normal physical means, to recognize them throughout that time. And for there to have been a past for our claimants in the story to refer to it must have been possible for others to have observed them and recognize them by normal physical means, throughout a substantial period. For both of these requirements to be met, the normal physical evidence of identity has to be presupposed.

This does not, unfortunately, show that we could not read the puzzle-story the way that someone like Locke would wish. We can, or almost.

Locke could argue as follows. Granted that there has to be a continuing present human body for the speaker of memory-claims (and the bearer of character-traits) to be identified; granted that there has to have been a continuing past body for

us to recognize the past history which the present memory-claims are about. Surely these requirements are satisfied in the case of our prince and cobbler? The sets of memory-claims made are in each case made by an identifiable continuing present person; and the past cobbler and prince were readily identifiable in the past and are known to have done and experienced the very things now being described in the past tense. The only oddity is that the body that the cobbler's claims seem to fit is not the one now uttering them; and the body the princely claims fit is not the one now uttering them. We have all the physical adjuncts that are necessary. The fact that the claims are so systematic and consistent makes it thoroughly reasonable to say that there has been bodily transfer.

I think this argument is incontestable. It is possible to say this. I think such cases would have to be exceptional, but I will not argue this here.[1] What it is important to stress is that our story has done nothing to give clear content to the notion of a person going *out of* one body *into* another body, or of a person existing with *no* body. (The latter possibility seems a necessary condition of the first.) For this language carries the implication that what leaves one habitat and enters another is an entity identifiable independently of either body. The argument does nothing, in other words, to warrant Locke's choice of language in describing the case—'Should the soul of a prince ... enter and inform the body of a cobbler.' Our story gives sense to the notion of two persons exchanging bodies, but none to the notion of these persons existing independently of the bodies which they exchange.

If we accepted the description of our story that involved the prince and the cobbler changing bodies, then we would be committed to the following conceptual innovation: we could henceforth only infer personal identity from bodily identity in cases where there were no systematic memory-claims to suggest that the person now before us did actions and had experiences in the past that were done 'in' another identifiable body. Needless to say, this would be an inconvenient change, and the claims would have to be very systematic indeed. It would amount, of course, to a weakening of the bodily criterion of identity to a position of relative parity with the memory-criterion.

But it is not the only reading of our story. We could also insist on not abandoning the primacy of bodily identity. We could do this in perhaps two ways. One way which suggests itself is that of weakening the memory-criterion by making a major change in the concept of memory, and allowing it to be possible for someone not only to remember actions and experiences in his own past, but also to remember those in the past of another. But this is not as helpful or coherent a suggestion as it looks. We already can remember actions and experiences in the lives of others. We can remember witnessing another doing them or having them, and we can remember *that* he did or had them. All that we cannot do is to remember doing them or remember having them. For this is to remember one's own doing or one's own having of them. To suggest that we could change the sense of 'remember' so that one could remember doing someone else's actions or having someone else's experience is to pass the bounds of possible linguistic legislation, since it is to suggest that one could say something which had the effect of committing us to the possibility of some past action of experience belonging uniquely to two different people, and this is self-contradictory. This can be brought out by expanding our story. Suppose the one who physically appears to be the prince says, 'I remember mending shoes last night,' and is then convinced, by reports on his physical characteristics and those of the cobbler, that it was not he who mended the shoes but the cobbler. It would not suffice for him to correct his earlier statement to read 'I remember the cobbler mending the shoes.' This already has a use that would still be needed in the language, viz. the use for claiming knowledge of the cobbler's past actions that comes from having witnessed the cobbler performing them. To give 'remember' a new use to cover the new type of knowledge of another's past would be to make it impossible to distinguish this new type from the ordinary recollections of a witness.

There is a simpler and more viable way in which we might retain intact both our present standards of identity and yet adjust to these startling events. We might invent a new word to cover cases of what seem to be memories (because of their accuracy, their presentation in the first person singular past tense, etc.), but cannot *be* memories (because they fit the wrong body). I

suggest the concept of retrocognition. We could say that the cobbler and prince retrocognize one another's pasts. Such a strange phenomenon would naturally go with the adoption of one another's characters—at least if, when I began to retrocognize my neighbour's past, I proceeded to forget my own.

This way of preserving present practice involves no change in the use of current concepts, only the introduction of a new one. Not, of course, a very clear one, but perhaps a useable one. My present point is that such an alternative does exist and can deal with our case of putative bodily transfer as easily as the hypothesis of *actual* bodily transfer. This does, however, with the restrictions imposed, remain one possible and reasonable reading of our story.[2] Furthermore, we feel, I think, an instinctive *preference* for it, even though there seem to be no good reasons for such a preference. There are, I think, two reasons for such a preference, both philosophically disreputable.

The first derives from imagining oneself one of the protagonists in the story. Surely if we do this we can see that anyone possessed of all these memories would *know* quite clearly who he was? Surely he would know that he had a new body (or rather, another)? How could even the most numerous collection of third parties tell him he was wrong?

We are mistaken if we yield to this.

A criterion of identity has to be part of a publicly-usable set of conceptual devices. (There is no sense to the suggestion that someone is one person to himself and another to others, unless this means that he is concealing his identity from them by a disguise or something equally uninteresting). Now what makes memory a criterion of identity is the fact that people make their memories public property by making memory-claims, by *saying* that they remember things. And what makes these claims correct, what shows that people are remembering and not imagining is the fact that these claims can be tested publicly. Someone who says he remembers is not making an introspective report, but a public knowledge-claim, which is corrigible in the same way that claims to see or hear are. But, of course, only the person himself has the experience (the image, or whatever) which most people say they have when they remember, and which serves presumably as the *occasion* for the claim. This is important as a fact of psychology, but not with regard to the status of memory-claims themselves. This is the general sort of context in which we learn to *make* memory-claims. But when someone, as in our story, has the usual sort of memory-experience he is disposed to use the normal memory-language, and say, e.g., 'I remember mending the shoes.' To say that he must be right because only he has the appropriate present *experiences* is to overlook that the decisions and investigations of others, as much as his own experiences, are necessary before he can be said to be entitled to claim to *remember*.

It is familiar enough for you or me to think we remember something and find out that we are mistaken—after which we say that we didn't really remember, but only thought that we did. But any experience we had is still part of our mental history just as much as it was when we took it as a memory. So it is easy enough to imagine being one of the people in the story and thinking that one remembered. This does not, without further decision, justify our saying that this amounts to *accepting* their memory-claims, which there is reason not to do. But imagining apparent memories is no different from imagining real ones, since the inner experiences would be the same; hence the ease with which it is taken for granted that one would be doing the second rather than the first.

The second source of our instinctive preference for saying that our heroes have changed bodies rather than experienced some radical upheaval in their memories is more familiar. It is the deep commitment of most of us in our interpretative thinking to psychophysical dualism. We seem to believe in an independently identifiable purely psychical entity which inhabits the body and can leave it and go to another. An examination of our story and our identification practices shows that such a concept is not coherent and not borne out by the imaginary events. It is not coherent because the only criterion of identity for such an entity would be memory, which we have shown cannot operate as a criterion alone; it is not borne out by the events because to recognize that they have occurred in the way stated is to make use of bodily evidence. Yet the dualistic thesis, bolstered by the use of inappropriate mental pictures, determines our choice in reading the events described.

Of course, since what we would say in actual cases would be determined by such prejudices as this one, no doubt our instinctive preference, philosophically disreputable or not, would determine the common usages which such cases would generate. But this would merely show that the dualistic model was influential, not that it was coherent.

To sum up. We can say that the cobbler and the prince have changed bodies. We can say this because we are able to imagine identifying the pre-change persons through time by reference to the bodies which they had, and to imagine identifying the post-change persons through time by reference to the bodies which they have. But saying this is merely to admit that two people could, at the cost of some conceptual change, be said to *exchange* bodies. It is not to say that they can meaningfully be said to exist independently of the bodies which they exchange. It gives no sense to the conception of a person going *out of* one body *into* another. Further, although we can say they have exchanged bodies, we do not have to do so. We can change our conventions in another way, by inventing the new concept of retrocognition. The only thing that would come near to making the bodily transfer story a *mandatory* reading of the tale of the cobbler and the prince would be our having an independently intelligible notion of that which could be alleged to leave one body and go into the other, and our being able to trace this progress. We may disregard the second of these conditions, for the first is not satisfied. The notion we need is the very one we have been looking for, and the story does not provide it. On the contrary, the story will only serve the purposes that tales of its type are invented to serve in the literature of personal identity if we assume quite incorrectly that we have it already.

NOTES

1. I have argued it in 'Personal Identity'.
2. And of A. M. Quinton's.

PAUL ZIFF

The Feelings of Robots*

Could a robot have feelings? Some say of course.[1] Some say of course not.[2]

1. I want the right sort of robots. They must be automata and without doubt machines.

I shall assume that they are essentially computing machines, having micro-elements and whatever micro-mechanisms may be necessary for the functioning of these engineering wonders. Furthermore, I shall assume that they are powered by microsolar batteries: instead of having lunch they will have light.

And if it is clear that our robots are without doubt machines then in all other respects they may be as much like men as you like. They may be the size of men. When clothed and masked they may be virtually indistinguishable from men in practically all respects: in appearance, in movement, in the utterances they utter, and so forth. Thus except for the masks any ordinary man would take them to be ordinary men. Not suspecting they were robots nothing about them would make him suspect.

But unmasked the robots are to be seen in all their metallic lustre. What is in question here is not whether we can blur the line between a man and a machine and so attribute feelings to the machine. The question is whether we can attribute feelings to the machine and so blur the line between a man and a machine.

2. Could robots have feelings? Could they, say, feel tired, or bored?

Ex hypothesi robots are mechanisms, not organisms, not living creatures. There could be a broken-down robot but not a dead one. Only living creatures can literally have feelings.

If I say 'She feels tired' one can generally infer that what is in question is (or was or will be in the case of talk about spirits)[3] a living creature. More generally, the linguistic environment '... feels tired' is generally open only to expressions that refer to living creatures. Suppose you say 'The robot feels tired'. The phrase 'the robot' refers to a mechanism. Then one can infer that what is in question is not a living creature. But from the utterance of the predicative expression '... feels tired' one can infer that what is in question is a living creature. So if you are speaking literally and you say 'The robot feels tired' you imply a contradiction. Consequently one cannot literally predicate '... feels tired' of 'the robot'.

Or again: no robot will ever do everything a man can. And it doesn't matter how robots may be constructed or how complex and varied their movements and operations may be. Robots may calculate but they will not literally reason. Perhaps they will take things but they will not literally borrow them. They may kill but not literally murder. They may voice apologies but they will not literally make any. These are actions that only persons can perform: *ex hypothesi* robots are not persons.

*Paul Ziff, "The Feelings of Robots," *Analysis*, Vol. 19, No. 3 (1959). Reprinted by permission of the editor of *Analysis*.

3. 'A dead robot' is a metaphor but 'a dead battery' is a dead metaphor: if there were a robot around it would put its metaphor to death.

What I don't want to imply I need not imply. An implication can be weakened. The sense of a word can be widened or narrowed or shifted. If one wishes to be understood then one mustn't go too far: that is all. Pointing to one among many paintings, I say 'Now *that* one is a *painting*'. Do I mean the others are not? Of course not. Yet the stress on 'that' is contrastive. So I say 'The robot, that mechanism, not of course a living creature but a machine, it feels tired': you cannot infer that what is in question here is a living creature.

If I say of a person 'He feels tired', do you think I am saying that he is a living creature and only that? If I say 'The robot feels tired' I am not saying that what is in question is a living creature, but that doesn't mean that nothing is being said. If I say 'The robot feels tired', the predicate '. . . feels tired' means whatever it usually means except that one cannot infer that what is in question is a living creature. That is the only difference.

And what has been said about 'The robot feels tired' could be said equally well about 'The robot is conscious', 'The robot borrowed my cat', and so forth.

4. Could robots feel tired? Could a stone feel tired? Could the number 17 feel tired? It is clear that there is no reason to believe that 17 feels tired. But that doesn't prove anything. A man can feel tired and there may be nothing, there need be nothing at all, that shows it. And so with a robot or a stone or the number 17.

Even so, the number 17 could not feel tired. And I say this not because or not simply because there are no reasons to suppose that 17 does feel tired but because there are good reasons not to suppose that 17 ever feels anything at all. Consequently it is necessary to consider whether there are any reasons for supposing that robots feel tired and whether there are good reasons for not supposing that robots ever feel anything at all.

5. Knowing George and seeing the way he looks I say he feels tired. Knowing Josef and seeing the way he looks I don't say he feels tired. Yet if you don't know either of them then to you George and Josef may look alike.

In one sense they may look alike to me too, but not in another. For George but not Josef will look tired. If you ask me to point out the difference there may be nothing relevant, there need be nothing relevant, to point to. For the relevant difference may be like that between looking at an unframed picture and looking at it framed. Only the frame here is provided by what I know about them: you cannot see what I know.

(Speaking with the robots, one can say that the way things look to me, my present output will not be the same as yours, the way things look at you, even though at present we may both receive the same input, the same stimuli, and this is because your mechanism was not in the same initial state as mine, owing either to a difference in structure or to a difference in previous inputs.)

If we say of a person that he feels tired, we generally do so not only on the basis of what we see then and there but on the basis of what we have seen elsewhere and on the basis of how what we have seen elsewhere ties in with what we see then and there. And this is only to say that in determining whether or not a person feels tired both observational and theoretic considerations are involved and, as everywhere, are inextricably interwoven.

6. Suppose you and I visit an actor at home. He is rehearsing the role of a grief-stricken man. He ignores our presence as a grief-stricken man might. His performance is impeccable. I know but you do not know that he is an actor and that he is rehearsing a role. You ask 'Why is he so miserable?' and I reply 'He isn't.' 'Surely,' you say, 'he is grief-stricken. Look at him! Show me what leads you to say otherwise?' and of course there may be nothing then and there to show.

So Turing[4] posed the question whether automata could think, be conscious, have feelings, etc., in the following naive way: what test would an automaton fail to pass? MacKay[5] has pointed out that any test for mental or any other attributes to be satisfied by the observable activity of a human being can be passed by automata. And so one is invited to say what would be wrong with a robot's performance.

Nothing need be wrong with either the actor's or a robot's performance. What is wrong is that they are performances.

7. Suppose K is a robot. An ordinary man may see K and not knowing that K is a robot, the ordinary man may say 'K feels tired'. If I ask him what makes him think so, he may reply 'K

worked all day digging ditches. Anyway, just look at K: if he doesn't look tired, who does?'

So K looks tired to the ordinary man. That doesn't prove anything. If I know K is a robot, K may not look tired to me. It is not what I see but what I know. Or it is not what I see then and there but what I have seen elsewhere. Where? In a robot psychology laboratory.

8. If I say 'The robot feels tired', the predicate '. . . feels tired' means whatever it usually means except that one cannot infer that what is in question is a living creature. That is the only difference.

To speak of something living is to speak of an organism in an environment. The environment is that in which the behaviour of the organism takes place. Death is the dissolution of the relation between an organism and its environment. In death I am pluralized, converted from one to many. I become my remains. I merge with my environment.

If we think of robots being put together, we can think of them being taken apart. So in our laboratory we have taken robots apart, we have changed and exchanged their parts, we have changed and exchanged their programmes, we have started and stopped them, sometimes in one state, sometimes in another, we have taken away their memories, we have made them seem to remember things that were yet to come, and so on.

And what we find in our laboratory is this: no robot could sensibly be said to feel anything. Why not?

9. Because there are not psychological truths about robots but only about the human makers of robots. Because the way a robot acts (in a specified context) depends primarily on how we programmed it to act. Because we can programme a robot to act in any way we want it to act. Because a robot could be programmed to act like a tired man when it lifted a feather and not when it lifted a ton. Because a robot couldn't mean what it said any more than a phonograph record could mean what it said. Because we could make a robot say anything we want it to say. Because coveting thy neighbor's robot wife would be like coveting his car and not like coveting his wife. Because robots are replaceable. Because robots have no individuality. Because one can duplicate all the parts and have two virtually identical machines. Because one can exchange all the parts and still have the same machines. Because one can exchange the programmes of two machines having the same structure. Because . . .

Because no robot would act tired. Because a robot could only act like a robot programmed to act like a tired man. For suppose some robots are programmed to act like a tired man after lifting a feather while some are so programmed that they never act like a tired man. Shall we say 'It is a queer thing but some robots feel tired almost at once while others never feel tired'? Or suppose some are programmed to act like a tired man after lifting something blue but not something green. Shall we say 'Some robots feel tired when they lift blue things but not when they lift green things'? And shall we conclude 'Some robots find blue things heavier than green things'? Hard work makes a man feel tired: what will make a robot act like a tired man? Perhaps hard work, or light work, or no work, or anything at all. For it will depend on the whims of the man who makes it (though these whims may be modified by whatever quirks may appear in the robot's electronic nerve network, and there may be unwanted and unforeseen consequences of an ill-conceived programme.) Shall we say 'There's no telling what will make a robot feel tired'? And if a robot acts like a tired man then what? Some robots may be programmed to require a rest, others to require more work. Shall we say 'This robot feels tired so put it back to work'?

What if all this were someday to be done with and to human beings? What if we were someday to break down the difference between a man and his environment? Then some day we would wake and find that we are robots. But we wouldn't wake to a mechanical paradise or even an automatic hell: for then it might not make sense to talk of human beings having feelings just as it now doesn't make sense to talk of robots having feelings.

A robot would behave like a robot.

NOTES

1. Cf. D. M. MacKay, "The Epistemological Problem for Automata," in *Automata Studies* (Princeton: Princeton Univ. Press, 1956), 235–251.

2. Cf. M. Scriven. "The Mechanical Concept of Mind." *Mind, LXII,* 246 (1953), 230–240.

3. I shall henceforth omit the qualification.

4. Cf. "Computing Machinery and Intelligence," *Mind, LIX,* 236 (1950), 433–466.

5. Cf. "Mentality in Machines," *Arist. Soc. Supp. XXVI* (1952), 61–86.

L. JONATHAN COHEN

Can There Be Artificial Minds?*

I

The first and commonest move[1] in recent controversy about this question has been to compare the familiar mental activities and experiences of men, such as thinking up a joke or imagining an invention, with the actual or possible performances of servomechanisms, computers, and other programmed artifacts. Neurologists, businessmen and generals are all interested in what such artifacts can be designed to do and how they can do it. It seems plausible to suppose that it is this interest which is crystallised in the question 'Can there be artificial minds?' And that question is then one to be discussed by experts in cybernetics, not by lay philosophers.

The second move[2]—an advance—is to argue that these technical discussions unjustifiably assume that the question is a proper one. Of course, it makes sense to ask whether a robot could duplicate all forms of human behaviour and sensitivity, and this is a legitimate problem for cyberneticists to discuss. But to have a mind of one's own entails a capacity for consciousness, only living things can have conscious and unconscious states, and 'machines do not even belong to the *category* of things which can be dead or alive'. Hence we have a paradox to puzzle us. 'On the one hand it does not seem that there is anything in the construction, constituents or behaviour of the human being which it is essentially

impossible for science to duplicate or synthesise. On the other hand there seems to be some important and meaningful descriptions of human behaviour which can never be properly applied to machines.'[3] And we resolve the paradox by coming to understand both these apparently conflicting truths well enough to recognize that they do not really conflict.

But I do not think it satisfactory to leave the matter at this stage. If anyone does use the description 'conscious machine' or 'intelligent computer', we are told, one of these terms must have changed in meaning. So long as we recognize the change, some philosophers assure us, we shall not be puzzled. And, presumably, so long as we are not puzzled everything is all right. But I believe that there are other worthwhile things which philosophical analysis can help to achieve or maintain besides the avoidance of puzzlement. And I want to show how a prevalent threat to one of these things seems to be aided if the metaphor of 'artificial minds' is allowed to settle into lay speech and become familiar outside the laboratory. In order to bring out how this comes about I shall concentrate on showing just how farfetched this metaphor is. For I shall argue that the knowledge which we can in principle acquire about any programmed artifact whatever is of such a type that if we ever acquired knowledge of this type about a human being we should describe him as having *no* mind of his own. Indeed, where category-assignments are at stake, it is often more cogent to argue from differences and similarities

*L. Jonathan Cohen, "Can There Be Artificial Minds?" *Analysis,* Vol. 16 (1955), 36–41. Reprinted by permission of the author and the editor of *Analysis.*

in the types of knowledge attainable than from the absurdity or good sense of ascribing certain qualities, like consciousness, in the relevant cases. For when a major category-shift is being systematically proposed or carried through by any group of human beings all their relevant notions of what makes sense and what does not may alter accordingly.

II

Consider, firstly, two comparatively simple situations in which a cyberneticist might find himself. He has a servomechanism, or a computing machine, with no randomising element, and he also has a wife. On the one hand, say, he wishes to predict how his machine is going to behave during the afternoon; and, on the other, he wants to predict how his wife will behave. Knowing the artifact's programme and assuming no breakdowns he can calculate in principle exactly how it will behave, within the limits of his true beliefs about what environmental events will occur to affect it. So far as he knows what information will be acquired by the feed-back or what questions will be put to the computer he can in principle deduce the machine's behaviour from its programme. With regard to his wife, however, he must make do as a starting point with whatever he has learned about her character from his experience of her and of other human beings and from the wisdom of novelists, psychologists and friends. From these beliefs, assuming she remains in normal health, he can try to work out how she will behave, within the limits of his knowledge about what environmental events will occur to affect her.

Thus in both cases the logical form of his reasoning is the same. Roughly, both predictions are argued from a set of general propositions coupled with a set of singular propositions which satisfy the antecedents of these hypotheticals. Moreover, in both cases the evidence for the singular propositions is similar in type. For both these sets of propositions are predictions about environmental happenings in the afternoon. But the other two sets of premises differ from one another in logical status. The cyberneticist's beliefs about his wife's character are not on the same level as his beliefs about his artifact's programme. Only if he found out that he had remembered or recorded this programme incorrectly would he revise his beliefs

about its content. But many other events, besides the discovery of a lapse in memory or a slip of the pen, might suggest a revision of his beliefs about his wife's character. Those beliefs were based on past experience and further experience may justify altering them. It is no objection that the cyberneticist may sometimes be startled by what his machine does, i.e. by the logical consequences of its programmes. His surprise is then due to the inadequacy of his prior calculations, whereas there may often be times when no amount of prior reasoning would prevent him from being surprised at his wife's behaviour. Hence there is an asymmetry between the type of knowledge the cyberneticist has about his machine's behaviour and the type of knowledge he has about his wife's.

Let us see if this asymmetry could be remedied by altering details of one or both of the two situations. We might begin by supposing that the artifact contains a randomising element, so that certain features of its behaviour, likely to be activated during the afternoon, are determined by a dice-throw or similar device. The cyberneticist's predictions about his machine would now have to specify certain ranges of alternative events, about which he could say no more than that in each range one and one only of the specified events (or groups of events) would occur. His knowledge of, say, the mechanics of dice-throwing would not be enough for him to predict which event (or group of events) was more probable than the others. But these new predictions as a whole would still have just as much logical certainty as before. It might well be that the cyberneticist also believed that in certain likely circumstances his wife might do one or other of several alternative actions, while his knowledge of her character was insufficient for him to be able to decide which of these alternatives was the most probable. His predictions about her behaviour would then differ in type from his predictions about his artifact in a way precisely analogous to that in which they differed before.

Someone might now suggest:—'Suppose the cyberneticist built his machine so that once it had been programmed in any way he couldn't "take the lid off" without altering the programme. Suppose, too, that he lost both his records and his memory after programming it. He would then be able to reconstruct its programme only by observing its behaviour, and any predictions he made about the latter would be of the same logical type as predictions about his wife's behaviour.' Well, let us suppose this. It would certainly be hard luck for the cyberneticist. It would cause him a lot of extra work—work of a sort to which he might be unused in his laboratory. But conceivably his memory might return to him or his records might be found by the charwoman, whereas nothing could ever happen which would make his beliefs about his wife's mental character as justifiably certain as his beliefs about the artifact's programme would then be.

'Suppose, on the other hand, that physiologists had discovered a method of "taking the lid off" his wife's brain, nervous system, glands, etc., which enabled surgeons to record every detail of their structure and content. Suppose also that psychologists had found reliable correlations between such features and the character-traits of those people who exhibited them. (After all, you claim to be concerned with everything that is logically possible, not merely with what is biologically possible.) The cyberneticist's knowledge of his wife's character would now depend on these psychological correlations, which might conceivably be just as reliable as the generalisations in electronic theory on which he bases his assumptions about the possibility of programming any machine successfully (i.e. without breakdowns). What now would be the difference in logical type between his two predictions, even if he recovered his memory, or his record, of the artifact's programme?' Well, it would be the same as the difference between the kind of prediction that was based on direct acquaintance with the programme fed into the artifact and the kind that relied on inferring this programme from observation of the machine's dials, circuits, etc.

'But suppose the surgeons could operate on his wife's brain in such a way as to alter her character in any desired respect. Surely the cyberneticist could not programme his wife—leaving no contingency to chance whims and making her in all mental respects his ideal woman—just as much as he could programme his artifact?' Certainly: his two predictions about the afternoon would then be altogether of the same logical type. But we should then say, I think, that his wife had no mind of her own, that her husband had already explicitly or implicitly done all her thinking for her, and that the notion of programming an ideal mind was therefore self-contradictory. For consider some of the situations in which we do say that a human being either has, or acts as if he has, no mind of his own.

One situation occurs when we are watching the parade-ground drill of a Guards battalion. 'By force of training', we might say, 'they have come to let all their thinking be done for them by their officers and n.c.o.'s, and so they move with clockwork precision like mindless machines.' Of course, we should admit that the soldiers are not really without minds of their own, because when they are off duty we know no programme of rules and commands which effectively controls all their behaviour. Again, there might be a monastery in which every facet of day-to-day life was governed by the rule of a religious order. Admirers might say of such monks, 'They have surrendered their own minds in fulfilment of a Higher Purpose,' though no one would doubt that the monks really had minds of their own. For it would always make sense to talk about their leaving the order, even if this never in fact happened. But I do not see how our cyberneticist's unfortunate wife could ever recover a mind of her own. Her husband's difficulty—suppose he wanted such a recovery—would be logical, not technical. Whatever randomising elements he introduced into her brain, or however much he asked other cyberneticists to programme her and not to tell him what they had done, neighbors who were 'in the know' would still nod their heads at one another as she walked past and murmur, 'Poor girl, she can never again think for herself or have any emotions that are really her own'.

III

What I have been trying to point out is an opposition between the still familiar concept of mentality and the concept of total subservience to known or knowable rules. The metaphor of 'artificial minds' clearly destroys this opposition by ascribing mentality to programmed artifacts. That is why such a metaphor is—outside the laboratory—not merely eccentric and novel, but also undesirable. If we blur our concept of mind in this respect, then, however completely human beings were regimented in thought and action by their government's, party's or church's ideological programme, it would be false to say that they behaved as if they had no minds of their own. They too could still be said to think for themselves. And that would be a shift in the notion of having a mind of one's own and thinking for oneself of which George Orwell's Newspeak could have been proud.

NOTES

1. E.g., A. M. Turing in *Mind,* Oct. 1950; L. Pinsky in *Mind,* July 1951; and J. O. Wisdom, R. J. Spilsbury, and D. M. Mackay in *Pro. Ar. Soc.,* Sup. Vol. XXVI (1952).

2. E.g., M. Scriven in *Mind,* April 1953. [But see footnote 2 in article by Paul Ziff on p. 320.]

3. M. Scriven, Ibid., pp. 233–4.

KEITH GUNDERSON

Robots, Consciousness, and Programmed Behaviour*[1]

I

Might we after all be a kind of robot? or might certain sorts of robots after all be a kind of us? Could a robot which simply did or had what it was supposedly programmed to do or have, be a robot which really felt and was conscious, had thoughts and intentions, deliberated and decided?

In 1748 in his book *L'homme machine* La Mettrie wrote:

We are in the position of a watch that should say (a writer of fables would make the watch a hero in a silly tale): 'I was never made by that fool of a workman, I who divide time, who mark so exactly the course of the sun, who repeat aloud the hours which I mark. No! that is impossible.'[2]

I shall apply the label 'defenders of La Mettrie's watch' to those who claim it could never be shown that our own mental life and behaviour is watch-like or programmed and that if a subject's mental life or behaviour is watch-like or programmed, then it cannot be like ours. From Descartes to Cybernetics one can tick off defenders of La Mettrie's watch. In his *Principles of Philosophy* Descartes wrote:

*Keith Gunderson, "Robots, Consciousness, and Programmed Behaviour," *British Journal for the Philosophy of Science,* Vol. 19 (1968). 109–122. Reprinted by permission of the author, the editor of the *British Journal for the Philosophy of Science,* and Cambridge University Press. This article appears in expanded form as Chapter Three in *Mentality and Machines* by Keith Gunderson (New York: Doubleday, 1971).

We do not praise automata for precisely carrying out all the movements for which they were designed, since they carry them out by necessity; we rather praise the maker for fashioning such precise machines, because he fashioned them not by necessity but freely.[3]

And about three hundred years later Paul Ziff in his provocative little article 'The Feelings of Robots'[4] wrote:

MacKay has pointed out that any test for mental or any other attributes to be satisfied by the observable activity of a human being can be passed by automata. And so one is invited to say what would be wrong with a robot's performance. Nothing need be wrong with either the actor's or a robot's performance. What is wrong is that they are performances.

He then goes on to suggest reasons (similar to Descartes') why 'no robot could sensibly be said to feel anything':

Because there are not psychological truths about robots but only about the human makers of robots. Because the way a robot acts (in a specified context) depends primarily on how we programmed it to act. Because a robot could be programmed to act like a tired man when it lifted a feather and not when it lifted a ton.

So too Jonathan Cohen in his article 'Can There Be Artificial Minds?'[5] marshalls a variety of arguments to support his contention that if a husband came to know and predict the future behaviour of his wife in the way in which we can come to control and predict (in principle, at least) the future 'behaviour' of a computer (with or without randomising elements):

... we should then say, I think, that his wife had no mind of her own, that her husband had already explicitly or implicitly done her thinking for her, and that the notion of programming an ideal mind, was therefore self-contradictory.

This conclusion will be of interest to us later. First, however, we shall be concerned with the jump Cohen makes from it to the following claims:

What I have been trying to point out is an opposition between the still familiar concept of mentality and the concept of total subservience to known or knowable rules. The metaphor of 'artificial minds' clearly destroys this opposition by ascribing mentality to programmed artifacts. That is why such a metaphor is—outside the laboratory—not merely eccentric and novel, but also undesirable. If we blur our concept of mind in this respect, then, however completely human beings were regimented in thought and action by their government's, party's, or church's ideological programme, it would be false to say that they behaved as if they had no minds of their own. They too could still be said to think for themselves. And that would be a shift in the notion of having a mind of one's own and thinking for oneself of which George Orwell's Newspeak could have been proud.

He goes on to write:

But I do not see how our cyberneticist's unfortunate wife could ever recover a mind of her own. Her husband's difficulty—suppose he wanted such a recovery—would be logical, not technical. Whatever randomising elements he introduced into her brain, or however much he asked other cyberneticians to programme her and not to tell him what they had done, neighbours who were 'in the know' would still nod their heads at one another as she walked past and murmur, 'Poor girl, she can never again think for herself or have any emotions that are really her own.'

Such arguments and attitudes have assumed a variety of forms and phrasings in recent years. But it will not matter if we neglect some of these nuances. For I intend to develop distinctions which will show that it would *never* follow from the fact of a subject being programmed that the subject failed to have thoughts, feelings, or intentions, perform this or that, etc. In so far as (some) robots can be shown to lack minds it will be for different reasons.

I am more interested in *why* the defence of La Mettrie's watch fails than in *that* it fails. *Why* it fails has a bearing on current issues in the philosophy of mind and philosophical psychology, namely the relationship between consciousness and behaviour and the explanatory limits of computer simulation of congnitive processes.

I have elsewhere[6] argued against what I take to be the most influential bad argument for saying that machines (or robots) could feel, think, or do such-and-such. I shall here argue against what I take to be the most influential[7] bad argument for saying that machines (or robots) could *not* feel, think, and so on.

II

First consider a typically whimsical philosophical preamble to a discussion of the mentality of robots. Suppose a skull is cracked open and some micro-wires etc. fall out. We become suspicious. We inspect closely the subject we took to be the owner of that skull. Very interesting. Finally we exclaim: 'A robot ... a programmed robot!' So we find *it* out. Whatever that subject had done in the past, whatever we had thought about it, 'his' mental life however we knew it is now unveiled as no more than the exhibited capacities of a programmed robot. Things are seen in a new light, and some would say it is now clear that at best the robot only 'behaved' and was 'conscious'.

So suppose we come to know that at one time so-and-so manufactured this robot, made this teeny mechanical brain which from the outset was endowed with a highly self-corrective microprogramme (self-corrective in the way that certain programmes for digital computers are, so that the machine may alter its routines to avoid previous blunders in a chess game) and 'clothed and masked' it in such a way that it was 'virtually indistinguishable from men in practically all respects: in appearance, movement, in the utterances it uttered, and so forth'.[8] Now if we came to know such things, we might indeed with good reason think it necessary to revise some of our past attitudes towards and judgments about the subject who is not revealed as a robot. We would now suspect that certain descriptions and ascriptions which we had formerly thought appropriate of and to that subject were no longer appropriate. But exactly which ones, and why?

Give or take a few details the preamble flickers out and a set of philosophical questions are posed. The central problem usually turns out to be the one of trying to determine which psychological predicates would no longer be applicable to the robot and which ones would remain essentially 'intact'. Let me call this *the repredication problem* of the unmasked robot. There is obviously no obvious solution to the repredication problem for robots given only the foregoing description of the unmasking. For this is a highly flexible Halloween surprise which could be satisfied by many different kinds of robots. Rather like cars and rather unlike people, robots come in a variety of makes and models. What we could say truly about a conventional gear-change may not extend to an automatic.

Questions which pop up at this point are 'Is the programmed robot like a man under hypnosis? Or like a cunning dissembler? Or more like an actor with a script?' To assess these (often proffered) comparisons may be instructive. We find, for example, that the repredication which should occur in connection with the robot is very unlike the repredication which would be forced upon us were we to discover a subject to have done what he did as a result of being hypnotised (as, for example, where a man is hypnotised to insult someone who upon finding this out no longer feels insulted). Nor would it be like the case of the typical someone upon whom light breaks thus: 'Look here, now, you've been deceived all along. She's only been pretending. She doesn't really love you.' For to find out about the programme in the robot's 'life' (or life) is presumably, to find out something new about *all* the robot's 'life' (or life). But what would it be to find that someone had been hypnotised for the whole of his life, or had pretended for the whole of his life? What would it be for anyone to live an *entire* life under hypnosis, or an *entire* life of pretence, or have someone's *entire* life shown to be performance? Compare: ' . . . eight, nine, ten', snap: 'You're no longer Descartes. You're just your old self.' But *what* or *which* old self? Nor could one pretend to be Descartes all of his life. For when would the pretence begin? In the womb? Pretence, hypnosis, performance, though different from each other, are alike in this, that they all demand settings. They demand an environment in which they can occur and with which therefore they can be contrasted—a backdrop of non-pretence, non-performance. They must *enter into* the subject's life at a certain point, at a certain time. They cannot constitute the subject's mode of life at all points, at all times. The case of the robot and his programme does not demand this to the same extent, which is one reason why Ziff is wrong (above) in his likening a robot acting according to a programme to an actor's performance. Unlike the actor with a script, the robot we've imagined can easily be seen as always having been a programmed robot, which insofar as its actions are concerned has performed them in accordance with that programme.

On the other hand it should be mentioned that only subjects with certain sorts of conscious capacities to begin with could be hypnotised, could be dissemblers, or performers with scripts. In other words consciousness is presupposed by abilities to act in accord with certain kinds of directives. It is not a byproduct of such directions. What this reveals in connection with robots is that it would be wrong to suggest that a robot could be made conscious as a result of a foxy programme. There is, to begin with, a subject, the robot, which has a programme. There is not, to end with, a subject, the programme, which is the robot. The importance of this morphology of mechanism is that what a programme can be made to make a robot do will in part depend upon facts about the robot's nature, its hardware, its input potential, which are independent of its programme. To assess *in toto* the mental machinations of a robot we need to consider not only how the robot is programmed, we need also to consider how and in what the programme is roboted.

If the robot so loosely (but typically) characterised at the outset was neither conscious nor unconscious but non-conscious then indeed we would have been deceived in any Buber-like 'I-thou' relationship we had thought existed between us and that robot. Here the appropriate repredication would be more analogous to that which would occur were we to discover a ventriloquist had been deceiving us with his dummy. For example: 'Charlie McCarthy seemed to be my most sympathetic friend until I found out he was made of wood. Fantastic. I felt and thought he had thoughts and feelings.'

But if the robot had certain basic capacities to begin with, then the case of discovering him (it) to be a robot might well not be a case where it would be appropriate to jump back and exclaim anything at all. If finding out about the robot is like finding out that a dog is not a dog but a wolf we may well feel that it would not be polite to exclaim (rudely) in front of the robot. Just as if we desist, for moral reasons, from beating dogs, we may desist, for the same (good) reasons, from beating wolves.

III

But here let me anticipate disappointments with what I have so far said. The strategy underlying most discussions of minds and machines is designed to uncover whatever conditions must obtain before it would be appropriate to ascribe feelings, thoughts, and so on to robots. This is done with an eye to tampering with our all too unclear perspectives with respect to human minds and their underlying makeup. But to be told that we should not withdraw predications of feelings, thoughts, and so on to robots *if* the robots had certain conscious capacities to begin with is not, it must seem, to be told anything illuminating. Yet I think it is—particularly in the context of recent philosophical discussions of mind and machines and computer simulation of cognitive processes.

Once the distinction is made between a robot's basic capacities, its input potential, on the one hand, and its programme which may utilise these capacities on the other, following claims seem in order:

If a subject is such that certain kinds of directives, commands, or controls (i.e. programmes), could not be imposed upon him (it), then, of course, the subject will not be able to perform various mental acts, infer this from that, prove theorems, write couplets, etc. But the reason will not be the programmed nature of the subject's mental life (whatever it amounts to), but will be the nature of the subject who (which) simply lacks certain sorts of programming in the first place.

On the other hand, if the subject is a certain sort of being to begin with such that certain kinds of directives, commands, and controls are possible, then the simple fact that he (it) was programmed to do this or that will not be sufficient to establish that the subject did not really do this or that.

In the case of programmed *behaviour* and those mental aspects closely associated with it the defence of La Mettrie's watch fails because with few exceptions there is no (clear or necessary) opposition between behaviour and being programmed. Indeed, behaviour seems particularly amenable to being construed in terms of well-defined tasks, and because of this it is compatible with being programmed. In their *Plans and the Structure of Behavior,* for example, Miller, Galanter, and Pribram write:

Any complete description of behavior should be adequate to serve as a set of instructions, that is, it should have the characteristics of a plan that could guide the action described. When we speak of a Plan in these pages, however, the term will refer to a *hierarchy* of instructions, and the capitalization will indicate that this special interpretation is intended. *A Plan is any hierarchical process in the organism that can control the order in which a sequence of operations is to be performed.*

A plan is, for an organism, essentially the same as a program for a computer, especially if the program has the sort of hierarchical character described above.[9]

Much current research into computer simulation of problem-solving rests on this intuition. Behaviour in so far as it can be construed in terms of well-defined tasks harbours an inbuilt compatibility with being programmed (call it 'programme-receptiveness'). And if a subject fails to possess the basic capacities necessary to the construction of routines for proving theorems, writing couplets, etc., *then* the nature (or basic capacities or input potentials) of the subject determines that the subject does not do these things and preempts and precludes the possibility of the subject failing in these respects because he (it) was merely programmed to effect them.

Most simply put, and contrary to the defence of La Mettrie's watch, there is *no* type of mental predicate which fails to apply to a subject simply *because* it was programmable in certain ways. Although various quasi-Rylean, behaviouristically oriented, problem-solving psychological predicates may be shown *not* to apply to a given subject, this will be because the subject lacks the capacity for being programmed in certain ways.

It will not be because the subject *was* programmed in certain ways.

And when we turn to those aspects of mentality which are quite different from solving problems, playing checkers, or writing couplets—such things as having pains, emotions, after-images, etc. . . . the defence of La Mettrie's watch may be seen to be wholly irrelevant. For the having of pains, emotions, after-images, etc., are all examples of non-problem-solving non-behaviour. They are not potentially well-defined tasks which hence may be programmable, for they are not tasks at all. Consequently they could never be shown to be absent from an unmasked robot *because* the robot was merely programmed to do this or that. For they are not the sorts of things which a robot could do. They may be had, but not done.

Whether or not a robot has a capacity for pain, emotion, or after-images, will of course greatly affect what the robot could *then* be programmed to do. The problem of determining the nature of the subject is not primarily a problem of deciding how to programme it. It is a problem of knowing and deciding how to construct the subject so that it *can* be programmed in certain ways.

Thus we see that the robot without a programme need not be a robot without a mind. For it could be a robot with half a mind—a robot with certain capacities for sentience, with certain input potentials, etc. It would by nature be a non-sapient robot . . . sub-moronic when compared to others of the same model which had also been equipped by benevolent manufacturers with programmes which use their basic capacities.

On the basis of the preceding remarks, then, it may be useful to sort psychological features into two kinds: those which it at least makes sense to attempt to simulate with a machine or robot through programming (in the sense of devising routines), and those which it does not. The first I shall call *programme-receptive* features of mentality. These include most kinds of problem-solving: game-playing, theorem-proving, etc. . . . i.e. rule governed activities. The second set of features I shall call *programme-resistant.*[10] *These include such things as having pains, feelings, emotions, etc. It would be a methodological howler to attempt to simulate these with a machine simply by expanding current programming techniques in the sense of defining new routines. It may of course prove possible to produce machine analogues of these features through a development in hardware. (There are undoubtedly mental aspects in between those which are clearly programme-receptive and those which are programme-resistant—e.g. thinking. But I shall not go into that here.)* Thus some psychological predicates may be viewed primarily as software predicates; some primarily as hardware predicates. Though I shall not develop the point, I believe this distinction may help to clarify the difference between sapience and sentience.

It is unfortunate that this rather elementary but crucial distinction is very often overlooked by both philosophers and those working on artificial intelligence and computer simulation of cognitive processes. This has resulted in philosophers coupling the mental limitation of machines (period) with the limitations as to what a machine could be programmed to do. And it has resulted in some computer simulation theorists trying to simulate programme-resistant features of mentality using simulation techniques which are strictly relevant only to the simulation of programme-receptive features: for example, there has been an attempt to extend programming techniques used in simulating problem-solving behaviour so that merely by developing new routines a machine will also simulate human emotions—the having of fears, anxiety, and so on.

To show that such a machine was only programmed to do such-and-such could not possibly show the absence of consciousness in that machine. Conversely, however, one could not make such a machine conscious simply by programming it in a certain way. Instead the link between consciousness in machines and what machines can be programmed to do is this: if a machine could be programmed in certain ways, this might demand consciousness in the machine: and if it were not possible to programme the machine in certain ways, this might suggest that the machine lacked capacities which we can loosely refer to as its consciousness.

IV

The above should help us to see why Ziff's remarks about how a robot's actions in a particular context depend on how it was programmed to act have little bearing on the question 'Could robots have feelings?' Looked at from one angle it seems that Ziff's imagined robots in the last analysis are not capable of feeling anything. But if so, the only reason they are not, is that they are specified in a vague way at the outset of Ziff's article and end up, as it were, 'retroanalytically defined' as robots which are without feelings. That is to say, at the end of his analysis we are told what his robots, about which so many interesting questions were raised at the outset, were really like. But what I have tried to show is that other 'retroanalytic definitions' are compatible with the robots so flexibly characterised at the beginning of Ziff's article.[11] And furthermore and mainly what I wish to object to is the suggestion that Ziff's robots, however interpreted, cannot feel *because* they only do what they are programmed to do, or *because* they could be programmed to respond in all sorts of strange ways to various stimuli. Ziff's programmed robots cannot feel simply because of the sorts of robots Ziff decided to say that they are; not unsimply because of the sorts of programmes they have. From another angle, however, Ziff's view becomes virtually impossible to understand. This is so if one attributes to him the claim attributed to him by Putnam where he (Putnam) says: 'Ziff has informed me that by a "robot" he did not have in mind a "learning machine" of the kind envisaged by Smart, and he would agree that the considerations brought forward in his paper would not necessarily apply to such a machine (if it can properly be classed as a "machine" at all)'.[12] Given this interpretation it is difficult to understand how Ziff's robots could be 'virtually indistinguishable from men in practically all respects: in appearance, in movement, in the utterances they utter, and so forth'. Ziff wishes to have it both ways if he does not want his robots to be as sophisticated as 'learning machines', and yet seem as sophisticated as men. Even to *seem* that sophisticated in mental capacities strongly suggests subjects psychologically less vacant than Ziff supposes his robots to be.

Similarly, Cohen's remarks on artificial minds are mistaken in so far as he claims an opposition between *mentality* and the concept of total subservience to known or knowable rules. All that Cohen's case of the totally programmed wife shows is that someone's mind could be controlled in a certain way: it does not show that a wholly programmed mind is no mind at all. To show that someone does not think for himself, is not in the least to show that someone does not really think,

and in the same sense(s) as the present sense(s) of 'think', whatever that (or they) may come to.

Arguments to the effect that a robot which only did what it was programmed to do could not be a robot which *really* was conscious, had feelings, thoughts and intentions, or which *really* deliberated and decided, fail because of the foregoing. But here let me anticipate some objections to my objections. One reason why the notion of 'being programmed' has come to seem opposed to the notion of 'being conscious' is because most of the currently existing programmed devices (computers *et al.*) have appeared—at least to some philosophers—obviously non-conscious, so in fairness to part of the 'spirit' of some of the articles being criticised, I should add that there is some textual justification for pointing out that the authors of the articles cited are not always arguing simply from the fact that a subject is therefore non-conscious. They are also to some extent presupposing that there are other relevant facts which one discovers when one discovers that the subject is programmed which count against saying that the subject could be conscious. Nonetheless: (a) throughout the literature these presuppositions are never clearly set out, defended, or developed; (b) no distinction is drawn between the very different sorts of subjects which could be programmed; (c) there is no reason for supposing that for every subject which is programmed one will be able to uncover independent facts which would tend to establish that the subject was not conscious, capable of thought, creativeness, and the like. And (d) in some cases, given that the subject could be programmed to do certain things, what we would expect to find would be just the opposite: namely that the subject *was* conscious, capable of thought, intentional behaviour, and so on. (Exactly what it would take to show that such expectations were satisfied is, of course, no easy matter to decide. The 'other minds' problem could arise in connection with robots—even though we made them.)

V

It may be argued that though it would be possible to programme a robot to have or effect all sorts of marvellous (humanoid) experiences and accomplishments if it had certain basic capacities to begin with, it is an analytic truth that robots could never possess the requisite capacities for such experiences or accomplishments. But those who would argue that a subject could not be both a robot and have certain basic capacities or input potentials, may be in the same position (now) as James and others were in towards the end of the 19th century when it was vehemently maintained that a subject could not be both wholly mechanistic and exhibit self-adaptive behaviour. This also had the flavour of an analytic truth before various negative feedback machines were developed and the notion of 'self-adaptive behaviour' received further clarification.[13]

If psychological predicates are really applicable only to persons, which I think is unlikely, then robots of certain sorts might be persons of certain sorts. They would be persons to which certain other hitherto non-person predicates applied— certain clusters of what might be called B-(biographical) and E-(ecological) predicates such as, 'is manufactured', 'was a 1966 model', 'sleeps electrically', etc.

There is, however, no more reason to assume that robots would have to be persons in order to partake of psychological predicates than there is reason to assume that a dog would have to be a person to be able to show affection and obeisance. In other words, I believe that psychological predicates can become applicable to machines or robots, as I think some already have, without blurring the line between robots and persons. In short it seems possible that such a line need not be blurred *except with respect to the predicates in question.* That is, it may be possible to show that a machine could, for example, recognise various sorts of patterns without blurring the line between men and machines *except in so far as recognition is concerned.* If in such a case the line between men and machines need not be blurred except with respect to 'recognition' (and its near synonyms) then it is hardly clear that the meaning of such words as 'men', 'persons', robots', or 'machines', will have altered. Both rolling stones and rolling men gather no moss, which hardly shows that men are borderline cases of stones. When Thomas Edison invented the light bulb he did not produce a borderline case of a white dwarf star. (Compare 'If it really throws light it's some sort of star' with 'If it really has feelings it's some sort of living organism'.)

In the case of living things and machines there was no global blurring of the line between men

and machines when we began (appropriately) to refer to 'self-adapting' machines. Instead a localised sharing occurred in connection with the feature of self-adaptation. That is precisely why cybernetics seemed to provide a non-trivial counter example to some of the claims made by vitalists.

So to build robots to which all sorts of psychological predicates legitimately apply need not be comparable to building robots which were just like us. They would of course be rather like us in so far as they share those predicates. And to be like us with respect to sharing a given capacity or the exercise thereof does not necessitate that the robot be identical to us even in that respect. Both washing machines and human beings wash clothes; but they are not identical with respect to this capacity or the exercise thereof. Hence for a robot to have psychological predicates apply to it is not automatically, as many would assume, either the same as the robot being the same as, or even being almost the same as, a person.

Furthermore, it is not even the case that in every instance where the concepts were blurred, interesting discoveries would be ruled out. For how the concepts (of men and machines) come to get blurred is also of central importance. If, for example, we found that we do not really do some things which we thought we did, and are therefore more like certain machines than we had hitherto realised, or if we found out that the way that we did things was more purely mechanised than hitherto imagined, then in both cases something very interesting might be found out. (Compare recent suggestive attempts by Newell, Shaw, and Simon to explain creative thinking in human beings in terms of certain kinds of rule-governed behaviour.)[14]

A view more explicitly of the kind the immediately foregoing remarks contrast with is developed by A. R. Lacey in his article 'Men and Robots' where he writes:

Let me add again that I do not mean that no artifact will ever achieve feeling, but that such an artifact would not be a robot, in my sense, but a human, or on the human side of the fence.[15]

But it is not at all certain that in every case where artifacts had feelings they should for that reason be placed 'on the human side of the fence' (except trivially, for example, with respect to feelings). And I disagree with him where, after despairing of finding the differences between men and robots in terms of what they can do, he writes:

This does not mean that we could not create an artifact which turned out to be conscious; but such an artifact would be a human (or some such thing) and not a robot in our present sense.[16]

His qualifying phrase 'in our present sense' does not barricade Lacey's claims against the linguistic possibility that 'conscious' could acquire new uses (without altering its meaning)[17] in much the same manner that 'problem solving' and 'self-adaptive' seem to have done. It remains possible in the face of such diachronic surprises to trivialise a thesis like Lacey's by, say, simply not identifying the present sense of 'robot' with the then current senses of 'robot'. One can always choose to use a word in an idiosyncratic manner, but nothing is gained thereby. (There is no such thing as an idiosyncratic *sense* of a word.) And obviously Lacy is not doing that. So if he does wish to identify his construal of the meaning of the word 'robot' with *the* meaning of the word 'robot', his claims based in part on this identification will be vulnerable.

There need not be any 'the difference' between men and robots. Different differences are possible and must be discussed in any attempt to stake out what a robot could be and do and how what it could be or do would serve to distinguish men from robots. Some of these differences would no doubt be marked out by the use of psychological predicates and some would be marked out by the use of what I have loosely called B- and E-predicates. Some by others.

Many philosophers including many defenders of La Mettrie's watch have looked for an almost magical covering word or predicate (or small set of predicates) such that if it or they (always) applied or failed to apply to a certain subject we would then *be safe* (always) in saying that the subject was definitely (or definitely not) a human, or a robot, or a machine. And so they persist in perpetrating such claims as 'If a subject could think (create, feel, perform, purposively, and so on) then it would not be a robot (or machine, etc.)' and have failed to note that no one feature

(or small set of features) such as 'feels' or 'is made in a factory' can be regarded as essential to something being or not being a robot or human being or machine. Perhaps a programmed conscious robot could perform as well as a human being, and do this by, for example, thinking out the answer, and still not thereby be a kind of us. Many other relevant differences might remain: biographical, ecological, and so on.

VI

True borderline-case decisions may be as rare in philosophy as true tied-finishes are in the Kentucky Derby. So far, at least, the question of whether an actual subject is a humanoid machine or a mechanistic human has not arisen. Instead the question has arisen as to whether certain predicates ('recognises patterns', 'plays chess', 'writes poetry', etc.) hitherto used only in connection with human beings should apply to what are most certainly machines; or whether certain predicates hitherto used only in connection with machines (e.g. 'is programmed') also apply to what are most certainly human beings.

In a recent article, 'Robots: Machines or Artificially Created Life'[18] Hilary Putnam seems to me to mischaracterise the central issues involved in 'minds and machines' controversies in so far as he assimilates the question of clarity 'with respect to the "central area" of talk about feelings, thoughts, consciousness, life, etc.' to the question of clarity 'with respect to the "borderline-case" or robots (i.e. as machines or artificial life)'. If and when we draw open the closed curtain of technological ignorance and find persots or robsons inhabiting the parlours of persons, we will probably (though not necessarily)[19] know what to say about them. If problems persist which are to be solved by making a linguistic decision, they will be trivial problems: for in a clear case of a borderline case the only decision involved in selecting descriptions is a poetic one (e.g. shall we call them 'persots' or 'robsons'? I myself prefer 'persots'). To think otherwise is to mistake neology for ontology. A tangerine is a tangerine is a tangerine.

The non-trivial, non-science-fictional problems of philosophy now are rather such problems as: Are the information processes underlying the problem-solving capacities of, for example, a (clearly non-human) list-processing computer analogous to human ones? Do so-called pattern-recognition programmes actually enable machines to *recognise* patterns? What sorts of evaluation procedures can be developed which will assist us in deciding which of any two competing simulations are the most useful in speculating about human mentality. Which machine models of human mentality are subject to plausible neurophysiological interpretation, which ones are not? What relationships obtain amongst mentalistic phenomena which are receptive to being simulated by current computer programming techniques, and those which are not? Which psychological predicates refer to basic capacities, and which apply to behaviour 'generated' by those capacities? Which are a mixture? Short of making a mind, how can we model aspects of the mind?[20]

NOTES

1. Earlier versions of this paper were read and discussed with philosophers at the University of California, Santa Barbara, and at Claremont College. A truncated version was presented at The Chapel Hill Colloquium in Philosophy (25 November, 1967). I am indebted to the participants in these discussions for helpful suggestions.
Some of the points developed here were suggested in my 'Interview with a Robot,' *Analysis*, 23 (1963), 136–42.

2. *L'homme machine*, by Julien Offray de La Mettrie, translated as *Man a Machine*, by Gertrude Carman Bussey (Open Court, 1953), p. 145.

3. In *Descartes' Philosophical Writings*, trans. by Elizabeth Anscombe and Peter Thomas Geach (Thomas Nelson and Sons Ltd., 1954), p. 188.

4. *Analysis*, 19 (1959), 67–68. [This vol., p. 318.]

5. In *Analysis*, 16 (1965). [This vol., p. 321.]

6. Keith Gunderson, 'The Imitation Game,' *Mind*, 73, n.s. (1964), 234–45; reprinted in *Minds and Machines*, ed. Alan Ross Anderson, pp. 60–71.

7. Note Denis Thompson's recent article 'Can a Machine be Conscious?', where he refers to this argument as 'probably the most common argument in the machine debate', this *Journal*, 16 (1965), 36. And compare as well Michael Scriven in

his 'The Compleat Robot: A Prolegomena to Androidology' where he begins Section 5 with a 'quote' from the air: 'Machines only do what we tell them to do, they are incapable of genuinely original thought.' Scriven's objections to this view mark an about face from the stance he took in 'The Mechanical Concept of Minds', in *Minds and Machines*, edited by Alan Ross Anderson, a fact often ignored by recent critics of that paper. What I say in this paper is, at least in conclusions, much in accord with Scriven's later views. Also Turing, Putnam, Minsky, Armer, *et al.* have at least sketched some dissatisfactions with the defence of La Mettrie's watch, and some of the things I say may be viewed as an elaboration of why such dissatisfaction has been justified.

8. Paul Ziff, this *Journal*, 16 (1965), 64.

9. George A. Miller, Eugene Galanter, and Karl H. Pribram, *Plans and the Structure of Behavior* (New York) 1960, p. 16.

10. Cf. Keith Gunderson, 'Some Mental Limitations of Some Machines', Chapter IV of *Mentality and Machines* where the distinction between *programme-receptive* and *programme-resistant* mentalistic phenomena is worked out in detail in connection with an IPL-V computer.

11. Compare this criticism of Ziff with a criticism of Ayer's 'The Concept of a Person' made by Raziel Abelson in his 'Person, P-Predicates, and Robots,' *American Philosophical Quarterly*, 3 (1966), 308.

12. Hilary Putnam, 'Minds and Machines,' in *Dimensions of Mind*, ed. by Sidney Hook, p. 176.

13. Cf. Keith Gunderson, 'Cybernetics,' in *Encyclopaedia of Philosophy*, ed. by Paul Edwards (Crowell-Collier, 1967).

14. 'The Processes of Creative Thinking,' the RAND Corporation, p. 1320, 16 September, 1958.

15. *Philosophical Quarterly*, 10 (1960), 61–72.

16. *Ibid.*

17. Cf. R. Puccetti's interesting article 'On Thinking Machines and Feeling Machines,' this *Journal*, 18 (1967), where a parallel use is made of Putnam's important distinction between (1) a word acquiring a new *use* in the language because of the (core) meaning it has (had) and (2) a word being (arbitrarily) *given* a new use (or meaning).

18. *F. Phil.*, 61 (1964), 668–91.

19. Cf. my 'Cybernetics and Mind-Body Problems,' *op. cit.*

20. Cf. Keith Gunderson, 'Philosophical Considerations of Artificial Intelligence and Computer Simulation of Cognitive Processess,' chapter III of *Mentality and Machines* (in preparation), where all these questions are discussed.

PART 4 DETERMINISM

W hat are we asking when we ask *why* something happened? Will an adequate explanation show us that in some sense or other the event to be explained *had* to happen in the way it did? Are voluntary human actions in principle subject to the same kinds of explanations as physical events? If everything that happens can in principle be explained by science, is there then no such thing in the universe as random chance, genuine contingency, and uncertainty? The essays that begin this section by John Hospers of the University of Southern California, Wesley C. Salmon of the University of Arizona, and R. S. Peters of the University of London are addressed to such questions as these. The theory of explanation, of course, has great interest to the philosopher in its own right; but it is also of great strategic importance to the continuing arguments over the ancient riddle of determinism and free will.

Determinism is the theory that all events, including human actions and choices, are, without exception, totally determined. What does it mean to say that an event (a past event, E, for instance) is "totally determined"? To this question various answers have been given, which for our present purposes we can take to be roughly equivalent.

1. E was completely caused.
2. There were antecedent sufficient conditions for E; that is, conditions such that given their occurrence E *had* to occur.
3. It was causally necessary that E occur.
4. Given what preceded it, it was inevitable that E take place.
5. E is subsumable under a universal law of nature; that is, the occurrence of E was deducible from a description of the conditions that obtained before its occurrence and certain universal laws.
6. The occurrence of E is subject in principle to scientific explanation.
7. The occurrence of E was in principle predictable.

8. There are circumstances and laws which, if they had been known, would have made it possible for one to predict the occurrence and exact nature of E.

Indeterminism, the logical contradictory of determinism, is the theory that some events are not determined. Most (but by no means all) exponents of indeterminism hold that the events that are not determined are human actions.

There are a number of common-sense considerations that should at least incline a reflective person toward determinism. Whenever we plug in a machine, or plant seeds, or prepare for a storm, we act in the expectation that physical events will occur in accordance with known laws of nature. Hardly anyone would deny, moreover, that physical characteristics of human beings—the color of their eyes, the cellular structure of their brains, glands, and other organs—are determined exactly by their genetic inheritance. And pediatricians and mothers of large broods have often observed that *temperament* is determined, at least to a large degree, right from birth. To a large extent our characters, personalities, and intellects are a consequence of our inherited physical capacities and temperamental proclivities, and our choices in turn reflect our characters. Similarly, our early childhood training, family environment, and education have formative influences on character. We do what we do because we are what we are, and we are what we are, at least to a large extent, because our genes and the influencing conduct of others have made us that way.

At the same time, common sense recognizes that human beings *do* do some things "of their own free will"; that is, in circumstances when they might very well have done something else instead. This common-sense observation seems hard to reconcile with determinism, which seems to imply that every event that occurs is the only one that could have occurred in the circumstances. This in turn seems to imply that no matter what I did a moment ago, I *could not have done otherwise*—which, in turn, seems to say that I *had* to do what I did, that I was not a free agent. But, most of us would agree, my ability to do otherwise is a necessary condition of praise or blame, reward or punishment—in short, for my *being responsible*. Therefore, if determinism cannot be reconciled with the ability to do otherwise, it cannot be reconciled with moral responsibility either. But we *do* hold people responsible for what they do (indeed, some say we *must* hold people responsible); therefore (some have argued), so much the worse for determinism. Such is the common-sense case against determinism.

Common sense, however, is no more pleased with indeterminism, which seems to give no satisfactory answer at all to any query of the form "Why did *this* happen rather than some other thing?" The reply "It just happened, that's all" inevitably leaves us unsatisfied. If we drop a stone and, to our astonishment, it rises straight up in the air instead of falling, we won't rest content with the "explanation" that "it was just one of those things—a totally random chance occurrence without rhyme or reason." We are even less likely to accept "chance" as an "explanation" for human actions. Such an explanation, we feel, makes all human actions arbitrary and unintelligible; it also seems to destroy the intimate bond between a person and his actions that is required by judgments of moral responsibility. Yet just insofar as a person's action was uncaused, just so far does it seem to have occurred "without rhyme or reason," as a "matter of pure chance." In the words of one determinist: "in proportion as an act of volition starts of itself without cause it is exactly, so far as the freedom of the individual is concerned, as if it had been thrown into his mind from without—'suggested to him by a freakish demon.' "[1]

Common sense thus is tied up in knots. It looks with little favor either on determinism or indeterminism in respect to human actions. Yet since these two theories are defined as logical contradictories, one of them *must* be true. The plight of common sense thus takes the form of a *dilemma;* that is, an argument of the form

1. If P is true, then Q is true.
2. If not-P is true, then Q is true.
3. Either P is true or not-P is true.
4. Therefore, Q is true (where Q is something repugnant or antecedently unacceptable).

The dilemma of determinism can be stated thus:

1. If determinism is true, we can never do other than we do; hence, we are never responsible for what we do.
2. If indeterminism is true, then some events—namely, all human actions—are random, hence not free; hence, we are never responsible for what we do.
3. Either determinism is true or else indeterminism is true.
4. Therefore, we are never responsible for what we do.

There are several ways we might try to escape being gored by the "horns of the dilemma," but one way is *not* open to us. We may not deny the third premise; for, given our definitions of "determinism" and "indeterminism," it amounts simply to the statement that either determinism is true or else it is not—surely an innocuous claim! We are, in short, not able in this case to get "between the horns of the dilemma" by denying its disjunctive premise.

---

[1] R. E. Hobart, "Free-Will as Involving Determinism and Inconceivable Without it," *Mind*, 43, 1934.

We are thus left with three possibilities. We can deny the first premise and hold that determinism is, after all, perfectly compatible with free will and responsibility; or we can deny the second premise and hold that an act can be both free and intelligible, and hence responsible, though it was not traceable to determining causes outside the actor himself; or finally we can accept the entire argument just as it stands and argue on independent grounds that its conclusion is not so "repugnant" or so "antecedently unacceptable" as it seems on first appearance.

The first way of attempting to resolve the dilemma is often called "soft determinism"; but that label is unfortunate, bringing with it perjorative associations of "tenderminded-ness." Perhaps "reconciling determinism" would be a better name, for this theory is, after all, the conjunction of two theses: (1) that determinism is true and (2) that determinism is compatible with free will and responsibility. Reconciling determinism —the view of Thomas Hobbes, John Locke, David Hume, and John Stuart Mill—is represented here by the selection from A. J. Ayer of Oxford University. Common to all these philosophers is the view that the key phrase "He could have done otherwise" is properly understood as hypothetical, meaning roughly "He would have done other-wise *if* he had so chosen (intended, wished)." In this hypothetical sense, I could have done otherwise than I did, even if determinism is true. I just wrote the word "true," but *if* I had chosen to write another word (say "right") instead, I should have done so (unless somebody intervened with a gun or knife to prevent me), and this is true even though I was determined to choose to write "true." In short, according to this theory, if I can do what I choose, I am free in the only sense of "free" used in ordinary parlance and in ascriptions of responsibility, and it matters not whether my choice itself was causally determined.

Reconciling determinists often take great pains to distinguish the determinism they espouse from a theory called *fatalism*, which they reject. To say of an event that it was fated to happen is to say more than that it was causally determined. It is to say that it would have happened no matter what the person involved might have done to avoid it. In this sense all of us are fated to die (at some time or other); but only a fatalist would say that a person is fated from birth to die at a definite place and at a definite time. A determinist would admit that it was determined that Abraham Lincoln die in Washington in 1865; but to say that it was *fated* that he so die is to imply, among other things, that even had Lincoln tried to shoot himself in Springfield, Illinois, in 1850, or even had he not gone to the theater on the fatal night, somehow he would have met the same fate he in fact met, in Washington, D.C., in 1865. That *all* events are so fated is a doctrine with strange mystic overtones, and has rarely been defended by philoso-phers.[2]

The second way of attempting to resolve the dilemma (that is, by denying that an uncaused act is necessarily a random event "without rhyme or reason") is found in the writings of Aristotle, Thomas Reid, and the contemporary Scottish philosopher C. A. Campbell, among others, and is represented here by the second selection from Roderick Chisholm of Brown University. Proponents of the view that human actions are neither determined nor fortuitous—the theory called *libertarianism*—remind us that human actions, unlike other events in nature, are subject to a special kind of explanation: the actor's own *reasons* for acting. An uncaused action, done deliberately for some reason,

[2]One outstanding exception to this generalization is Richard Taylor. See his *Metaphysics* (Englewood Cliffs, N.J.: Prentice-Hall, Inc., 1963), Chapter 5.

would therefore be a perfectly intelligible one, and adequately explained by an account of its reasons. The libertarian denies both theses of the reconciling determinist; thus, Chisholm's article can be understood to be a reply to views like that of Ayer. Chisholm's very brief essay, "Responsibility and Avoidability," puts the logical form of "the problem of determinism and free will" into clear focus. For that reason, the student will be well advised to read it first in this section. This article will also help the student to understand Chisholm's more substantial article in defense of libertarianism. In that longer article, Chisholm rejects what he has here labeled "premise 4," namely, that "The making of a choice is the occurrence of an event"—and substitutes the metaphysical theory of the human self that seems required if we are to save moral responsibility.

That moral responsibility is real and undeniable is the great motivating idea behind the philosophy called "existentialism." The statement that "existence precedes essence" is Jean-Paul Sartre's way of putting the theory called "indeterminism" above. Nothing is "written" in advance about the outcome of human choice; to believe the opposite is simply to arm oneself with bad excuses in bad faith. The world including our own characters is what we freely choose to make it, and there are no eternal models, not even valid moral ideals to bind us until we freely commit ourselves to them. Sartre writes to vindicate a radical human freedom, but there is nothing naively optimistic or sentimental in his conclusion. On the contrary! Human freedom, as he conceives it, is a sobering, even dreadful thing, that not only permits but necessitates ultimate accountability and generates the whole inventory of "existential emotions." Sartre will not let us forget, however, that it also makes possible the higher "existential virtues" of courage and authenticity.

The compatibility of free will and determinism is also denied by those who respond to the dilemma in the third way (that is, by embracing the conclusion of the dilemma, instead of trying to avoid it). This is the approach of the "non-reconciling determinists" (sometimes called "hard determinists"), who, instead of abandoning determinism as the libertarians do, jettison free will and moral responsibility instead. Non-reconciling determinism was the view of Spinoza and Arthur Schopenhauer, among others, and is represented here by the selection from John Hospers.

In recent years, the debate over determinism has taken a somewhat different turn. Some writers have argued forcefully that, quite apart from any assumptions about freedom and responsibility, genuine deliberation and decision cannot possibly be determined, since the very concepts of "deliberating" and "deciding," as we ordinarily understand them, entail an absence of prior causal determination. In a widely discussed article included here, Carl Ginet, of Cornell University, has taken just such a stand. If determinism is true, argues Ginet, then it is at least possible for a person to "discover" in advance what his future decisions will be; but if that is so, then those future "decisions," he argues, cannot be genuine decisions at all. Ginet argues neither for nor against the truth of determinism on independent grounds: he merely points out that we must pay a very high price in ordinary common-sense beliefs if we are to accept it. His conclusion, then, is consistent with both "hard determinism," and libertarianism. Alvin Goldman, of the University of Michigan, on the other hand, finds less difficulty in the idea that actions and decisions can be predicted well in advance on scientific grounds, even by the person whose actions and decisions they will be. In dealing with this question, Goldman considers the most dramatic crucial case—the possible existence, for each person, of a "book of life" in which is written in advance a description of each voluntary action and each deliberate decision the person will eventually bring about on his own. Goldman attempts to show that it is conceivable that a person might discover such a "book" with his own name on it, read what he will in fact do in the future, and yet, in time, deliberate over whether he shall do what it is written he *will* do. On the success or failure of such efforts as Goldman's the tenability of determinism may very well hinge.

JOHN HOSPERS

What Is Explanation?*

I

We are sometimes presented with a statement describing some observed fact, and when we ask 'Why?' we are presented with another statement which is said to constitute an explanation of the first. What is the relation between these two statements? What is it that makes the second statement an 'explanation' of the first? By virtue of what does it explain? Though everyone is constantly uttering statements which are supposed in one way or another to explain, few persons are at all clear about what it is that makes such statements explanations. Nor is the situation clarified when it is declared on the one hand that science explains everything and on the other hand that science never explains at all but only describes.

The question 'What is it to explain?' admits of no general answer, for the term 'to explain' covers many activities: one may explain how, and why, and whither, and whence, and how much, and many other things. Very frequently when we ask someone to explain what he has just said we are merely asking him to restate his assertion in clearer or simpler words.

In this essay I shall treat only explaining *why*. Even within this area there are some cases with which we shall not be concerned: one may explain

*John Hospers, "What Is Explanation?" First published in the *Journal of Philosophy*, 1946. This is the revised version published in *Essays in Conceptual Analysis*, ed. Antony Flew (London: Macmillan; New York: St. Martin's Press, 1956), pp. 94–119. Reprinted by permission of the author, the *Journal of Philosophy*, Macmillan & Co. Ltd., and St. Martin's Press.

why the angles of a Euclidean triangle must equal 180°, and this is quite different from explaining why iron rusts. The latter is an event or a process, and I shall be concerned solely with explaining why in the special context of temporal events: roughly, why did event x happen, or why do events of class X happen? The illustration from geometry is, I should prefer to say, an example of giving *reasons* rather than explanations. Another example may further illustrate the point: If you ask me to explain why I hold a certain belief, I may reply by giving *reasons* for it—statements which I take to be evidence for the belief in question. Now, if I am rational, the fact that there is good evidence for *p* may explain why I believe *p*—that is, the reason for my believing *p* may also constitute an explanation of why I believe *p*. But this may not be so: the explanation of a person's believing in a benevolent Deity may be that he wants a father-substitute or that he needs a protector in a cold harsh world; but when asked to explain why he believes in a benevolent Deity he may cite reasons, *e.g.* the Argument from Design, which may have nothing to do with *why* he holds the belief. We shall be concerned here, then, with the explanation of events, not with reasons or evidences one might cite in favour of propositions.

II

What, then, is it to explain why an event occurs? (1) It has sometimes been said that we have explained it if we have stated its *purpose*. 'Why did you walk through the snow for ten miles when you could have taken the bus?' 'Because I wanted to win a wager.' 'Why does that dog scratch at the door?' 'He's cold and he wants to get in.' When such answers are given we are inclined to feel that our question has been answered and that the event has been satisfactorily explained; and it has been explained with reference to a purpose which some sentient being (s) had in attaining a certain end. This is the most primitive conception of explanation. People like to feel that there is a purposive explanation for everything: if not in terms of human or animal purposes, then of divine ones, or mysterious forces and powers. We tend to extend what holds true of some events to all events whatever; we know what conscious motivation is like from our own experience of it, and so we 'feel at home' with this kind of explanation.

We shall examine the scope and legitimacy of purposive explanation later in this paper. It is enough to remark here that if explanation must always be in terms of purpose, then the physical sciences do not explain anything. The properties of uranium, the rise of aeroplanes, the phenomena of magnetism are not explained in terms of any purposes at all; biologists even avoid talking about animal events such as the hen sitting on eggs in terms of purpose. However animistically the nature of explanation may at one time have been conceived, purposiveness is certainly no essential part of its meaning now. The stone is no longer held to fall because it wants to get to the centre of the earth.

(2) Another account of the nature of explanation is that an event has been explained when it has been shown to be an instance of some class of events which is already familiar to us. For example, when a person's behaviour seems strange to us, we are satisfied when it is 'explained' to us as being really impelled by the same sort of motives and desires as occur in us, and are therefore familiar to us. 'Why is he introducing the man he hates to the woman he loves?' 'Because he wants them to fall in love with each other' would not generally be accepted as an explanation, for this very reason. When we observe that a balloon ascends rather than descends, unlike most objects, and it is made clear to us that air has weight and that the gas inside the balloon weighs less than would be an equal volume of air, we are satisfied;

the phenomenon has been 'reduced' to something already familiar to us in everyday experience, such as a dense object sinking in water while a hollow one floats. This event is no longer unusual, strange, or unique; it has been shown to illustrate a principle with which we were already acquainted. When we want to know why gases diffuse when released into a chamber from which the air has been pumped out, the explanation offered by the kinetic theory of gases is satisfactory to us because it asserts that molecules behave *like* particles with which we are already acquainted in our everyday experience.

Only those who have practised experimental physics know anything by actual experience about the laws of gases; they are not things which force themselves on our attention in common life, and even those who are most familiar with them never think of them out of working hours. On the other hand, the behaviour of moving solid bodies is familiar to everyone; everyone knows roughly what will happen when such bodies collide with each other or with a solid wall, though they may not know the exact dynamical laws involved in such reactions. In all our common life we are continually encountering moving bodies, and noticing their reactions; indeed, if the reader thinks about it, he will realize that whenever we are passively affected by it, a moving body is somehow involved in the transaction. Movement is just the most familiar thing in the world; it is through motion that everything and anything happens. And so by tracing a relation between the unfamiliar changes which gases undergo when their temperature or volume is altered, and the extremely familiar changes which accompany the motions and mutual reactions of solid bodies, we are rendering the former more intelligible; we are explaining them. (Norman Campbell, *What Is Science?* Dover, N.Y., p. 84.)

Professor Bridgman holds that all explanation is of this kind:

I believe that examination will show that the essence of an explanation consists in reducing a situation to elements with which we are so familiar that we accept them as a matter of course, so that our curiosity rests (P. W. Bridgman, *The Logic of Modern Physics,* p. 37).

And yet I am sure that such a view as this must be mistaken. In the *first* place, we may seek explanations for the most familiar events as well as of those unfamiliar to us. We may ask why stones fall as well as why aeroplanes rise, and be curious for an answer equally in both cases. True, our motivation for asking the latter question is probably greater because the kind of phenomenon in question is (or was) less familiar; most people would not think to ask it about stones because the falling of stones is familiar and usual—but the question can as legitimately be asked in the one case as in the other. In the *second* place, the explanation may not be familiar at all: it may be far less familiar than the event to be explained. The discoloration of a painted kitchen wall when gas heat is used may be a familiar phenomenon to the housewife—surely more familiar than its explanation in terms of the chemical combination of sulphur in the gas fumes with elements in the paint, producing a compound that is dark in colour. Yet this is the true explanation. If the explanation is not familar, one is tempted to say, it ought to be, as long as it is true. Surely its familiarity is irrelevant to its validity as an explanation. Familiarity is, in any case, a subjective matter—what is familiar to you may not be familiar to me; and yet the explanation, if true, is as true for me as for you.

The only grain of truth in the view that explaining is rendering familiar seems to be this: the law that does the explaining may not be familiar, *but* the fact that the phenomenon in question, such as the flight of an aeroplane, *can* be subsumed under a law—the fact that the behaviour *is* lawlike and hence predictable—tends to make it less mysterious, less like a miracle, and thus in a sense more familiar. To show that the behaviour of something is lawlike is to show it to be a part of the order of nature, and in that sense familiar, although the particular law or laws stating the uniformity may be quite unfamiliar.

In what, then, *does* explanation consist? The answer, I think, is quite simple: (3) to explain an event is simply to bring it under a law;[1] and to explain a law is to bring it under another law. It does not matter whether the law is one about purposes or not, or whether it is familiar or not; what matters is that if the explanation is to be *true* (and we surely seek true explanations, not false ones), the law invoked must be true: indeed, this is already implied in the use of the word 'law', which refers to a true, *i.e.* a really existing, uniformity of nature; if the uniformity turned out to be only imaginary, or having exceptions, we would no longer call it a law.

In saying that explanation is in terms of laws, I use the word 'law' in a wider sense than is sometimes employed: in the sense I mean, any uniformity of nature is a law. Thus, it is a law that iron rusts, and it is a law that iron is magnetic—although both of these are usually listed in textbooks as 'properties of iron' rather than as laws. In this sense, it seems to me that explaining why something occurs always involves a law. If we ask, 'Why don't the two liquids in the flask mix?' and someone answers, 'Don't you see, the one is transparent and the other is red?' this does not strike us as an explanation (*i.e.* as a true explanation) of the phenomenon, because we know of no law according to which red liquids will not mix with transparent ones. But when we are told that the red liquid is coloured water and that the transparent liquid is gasoline, we consider the phenomenon to be explained, for we hold it to be a law of nature that water and gasoline do not mix. In the sense in which I am using the word 'law', the non-mixture of water and gasoline is a law; and *only* if a law is brought in do we have an explanation of the phenomenon.

Sometimes, I should add, all we have available is a 'statistical law'—a law not of the form 'All A is B' or 'Whenever A, then B', but, *e.g.,* '75 per cent of A is B'. Can such a 'law' constitute an explanation? I should be inclined to say that it is, although we would still want an explanation of why 25 per cent of A's are *not* B's. If water did not always boil at 212°F but did so only 75 per cent of the time, we might explain the boiling of this kettle of water by saying that its temperature had reached 212°, though we would still want an explanation of why the kettle of water next to it, which also reached 212°, did not boil. In other words, our statistical law would still not answer the question 'Why this and not that?' and in order to answer *this* question, we would need a nonstatistical law of the form, 'Under such-and-such conditions, water always boils at 212°F, but under such-and-such other conditions, it does not.' It would seem, then, that a statistical law has in turn to be explained by a non-statistical one, although of course we may not, at any given stage in the progress of science, know of any non-statistical law by which to explain the statistical one.

Another example: 'Why does Johnny have cold?' 'Because Johnny has been playing with Roger, and Roger has a cold.' It is not a law that everyone who plays with someone who has a cold also gets a cold; the best we can do here is to state a percentage of cases in which this happens. So far as it goes, this is satisfactory; some uniformity is better than none. And yet, surely, we do not rest satisfied with this; we want to go on and ask why it sometimes happens but sometimes not. And the answer to this question would be a non-statistical law: 'People always get colds under such-and-such conditions'. Whether a statistical law can *always* be explained in terms of a non-statistical one depends not only on our powers of discovery but upon the nature of the universe. It is certainly no *a priori* truth that nature's uniformities are all of the 100 per cent variety instead of 75 per cent.

One further qualification: We have said that we explain particular events in terms of laws, and laws in terms of wider laws. But sometimes we give at least tentative explanations of them in terms not of laws but of general *hypotheses:* if a law is a well-established statement of how nature works, a statement about nature's workings that is not well established, or perhaps not even probable but only possible, cannot be a law. And yet we can use it to explain a law. But to whatever degree the hypothesis is uncertain, to that degree the explanation is jeopardized. An explanation cannot be known to be true if it involves a hypothesis which (by the definition of 'hypothesis') is *not* known to be true. Whether the explanation is a true explanation, then, depends on the fate of the hypothesis. (In the 'higher reaches' of most sciences, where the most general laws are involved, the only explanations possible are usually those in terms of very general hypotheses.)

III

So much for a general statement of what explanation consists of. I should like now to append some comments and to answer some questions to which the above account may give rise.

1. Thus far we have been content to answer the question 'Why does A do B?' by saying 'Because all A's do B'. But there are those who say that such an answer is no explanation at all. 'To say that all gases expand when heated', says Norman Campbell (*What is Science?* p. 80), 'is not to explain why hydrogen expands when heated; it merely leads us to ask immediately why all gases

expand. An explanation which leads immediately to another question of the same kind is no explanation at all.'

I want to insist that the answer given *is* an explanation of the occurrence in question; to say 'Hydrogen is a gas, and all gases expand when heated' is a perfectly satisfactory answer to the question why hydrogen expands when heated. But it is *not,* of course, an answer to *another* question—Why do all gases expand when heated? —and this is probably the question which the person meant to ask in the first place. These questions must not be confused with each other; I believe Campbell's position is the result of this confusion. It is fatally easy to telescope (unconsciously) two questions into one, and then be dissatisfied with the answer. Distinguishing them, we get:

Question 1. Why does this gas expand when heated?
Explanation. It is hydrogen, and hydrogen expands when heated.
Question 2. Why does hydrogen expand when heated?
Explanation. Hydrogen is a gas, and all gases expand when heated.
Question 3. Why do all gases expand when heated?

Here we attempt to give an explanation in terms of the kinetic theory of gases. To criticize Answer 1 because it is not an answer to Question 2, or Answer 2 because it is not an answer to Question 3, is surely a confusion. I want to say that Answer 1 is a perfectly satisfactory explanation for the phenomenon referred to in Question 1, though of course not for those referred to in Questions 2 and 3. But there is a frequent tendency to telescope these questions and demand to Question 1 the answer to Question 3.

The situation may be illustrated in another way. If I ask, 'Why did the water-pipes in my basement burst last night?' someone may answer that it is because the basement got too cold, and another may answer that it is because water expands when it freezes, while yet another may say that we do not know the 'real explanation' unless we can state why water expands when it freezes. Here, again we must separate the questions:

Question 1. Why did the water-pipes break?
Explanation. They always do when the temperature falls to below 32°.

Question 2. Why do they break when the temperature falls ... etc.?

Explanation. Because the water in them expands when it freezes, and the water on expanding breaks the pipes.

Question 3. Why does water expand when it freezes?

Explanation. Here we try to answer in terms of the structure of the water-molecule.

But to say that we have not explained (1) until we have explained (3) is grossly to underestimate the number of phenomena for which we do have perfectly satisfactory explanations. That is, we *do* have explanations for (1) and (2), and our having them is *not* contingent upon having an explanation for (3).

We could put our point in another way. *Logically* the answers given to each question in turn are satisfactory explanations; but *psychologically* they may not be equally satisfying, *depending on the previous knowledge of the questioner.* To the questioner who knew nothing about the relation of pipes bursting to temperature, the answer 'Because they got cold' (to the question) would be psychologically quite satisfactory, but not to the person who already knew that it had something to do with temperature, for the question *he* meant to ask was (2) or (3). Again: If I ask why this wire conducts electricity, it is a perfectly good explanation to answer 'Because it is made of copper, and copper is a conductor of electricity'. Psychologically, however, this answer would not be equally satisfying to everyone; it *would* be to the person who knew nothing of the properties of copper (or who did not know that this wire was copper), but it would *not* be to the person who already knew the properties of copper but was really enquiring as to why copper, unlike many other substances, is a conductor of electricity.

2. Can an event have *two* explanations? Why not? Let us suppose that we want to explain an event E, and that we have a law saying that every time conditions A are fulfilled, E happens, and another law saying that every time conditions B are fulfilled, E happens. A will then be a complete explanation for the occurrence of E, and B will also be a complete explanation. Whether any such state of affairs actually occurs in the world is, of course, another question. Most of the suggested double explanations of events are in fact parts of a single explanation. Thus, for example,

if we are asked to explain why the burglar committed the robbery last night, the detective may explain it in terms of his expertness at picking locks, the butler may explain it in terms of the family being out of the room, the maid may say it was because the bedroom window was open, the policeman may say it was because the night was foggy and visibility at a minimum, the sociologist may explain it in terms of the criminal's background of slum conditions, and the psychologist may explain it in terms of pseudoaggressive impulses dating from a childhood period marked by intense family quarrels. All these explanations are probably correct enough as far as they go. It may well be that in the absence of any one of these factors the burglary would not have occurred. But these are, it would surely seem, parts and aspects of *one* complete explanation—and in explaining human actions the whole explanation may be inconceivably complex. Still, the possibility remains that in *some cases* there may be two separate and complete explanations for an occurrence; at least it cannot be ruled out *a priori.*

3. Must there be a *deductive* relation between the thing to be explained and the explanation, such that one can deduce the statement of the phenomenon to be explained from the explanation?

All copper conducts electricity.
This wire is made of copper.
Therefore, this wire conducts electricity.

Here the explanation yields the desired conclusion easily, and it is quite clear that what we have here is a genuine explanation. The question is, must all explanation conform to this model? Have we failed to give an explanation if we have failed to deduce the explanandum from the explanation?

Let us first note that in many cases, if this is required, the explanation would be bewilderingly complex, and the premises in the deduction extremely numerous. Consider the burglary example just cited. From the fact that the weather was foggy and that the man had tendencies to steal and that he had a poor background ... etc., we cannot deduce the fact that he committed the theft. We cannot deduce it, indeed, from any set of premises known to be true. What we need for deducing it is a law, to the effect that if such-and-such conditions are fulfilled an act of this kind will always occur, and then a minor premise to the effect that these conditions were in fact fulfilled. The conditions would indeed have to be extremely numerous, and the statement of the law immensely complicated. Yet such a law is required if the desired conclusion is to be deduced.

We never in fact use a deductive model in cases like this one, and it is worthy of note that we do not deny ourselves the claim that we have explained the event because of this. What, therefore, are we to say of the deductive model as a *sine qua non* for all explanation? As I see it, we have two alternatives open to us:

(a) We can, in the light of such examples, scrap the deductive model entirely. We can say that often one can in fact deduce the explanandum from the explanation, but that this is not essential to explanation. We might add, as some do, that to perform the deduction is one way (the best way?) to *justify* an explanation we have put forward, but that the giving of a true explanation is not dependent on this.

(b) We can still insist that a complete explanation does involve the deduction, but that what we often give is in fact less than a complete explanation. We list, as in the burglary example, a few salient facts and either take the remainder as too obvious to mention or do not know what they are. But such measures are concessions of failure. The fact is that the only way to be sure of our explanation is to deduce the phenomenon in question from premises which we know to be true.

I merely wish here to state these alternatives, not to decide between them. It is, surely, a matter of how liberally or how strictly we wish to use the term 'explanation'; and, though I incline toward the second alternative, I do not wish to champion without reserve a 'puristic' account of explanation which is not in fact followed by anyone—at least anyone in the psychological and social sciences—and which, it is sometimes declared, is in practice almost useless and boringly academic.

Thus far in enquiring about the need for a deductive relationship, we have considered only the explanation of particular events: we have deduced them from two premises, one stating a law and the other stating a particular condition: 'All copper conducts electricity; this is copper, therefore this conducts electricity.' 'All water freezes at 32°F, the water in the pond went below 32° last night; therefore the water in the pond froze.' And so on. But, as we say earlier, we not only explain particular events; we also explain *laws*. And the same question could be repeated here: is the deductive requirement necessary? There is no doubt that in the 'neat, tidy' cases it is fulfilled: for example, Kepler's laws of planetary motion can be deduced from Newton's laws of motion together with the law of gravitation; and thus the latter clearly explain the former. But is this strictly a requirement for *all* explanation of laws? Again, some would say that it is—that anything short of this is not a full explanation. Others would say that it is not—that the deductive case is only the ideal one but that explanation does not require it. For example, a law can be explained in terms of a very general theory, from which the law cannot be strictly deduced, but which will nevertheless entitle the theory to be called an explanation. (The deductivist will reply that it is not *known* to be an explanation until the acid test, *i.e.* the deduction, is performed.)

4. In any case, whether deducibility is a necessary condition of explanation or not, it is not a sufficient condition. One can deduce that this watch will not work from the premises that watches will not work if gremlins get into them and that gremlins are in fact in this watch. Yet no one would accept this as an explanation for the misbehaviour of the watch. Similarily, one might deduce it from the premises that whatever God wills happens and that God has willed the misbehaviour of this watch. One can deduce anything if one selects one's premises carefully.

One might remark at this point that it is also necessary that the premises be *true,* and that this is the required addition. I would unhesitatingly agree that the premises must indeed be true—false statements cannot form parts of true explanations (indeed, if explanation is in terms of law, and a law is a true statement of a uniformity, *i.e.* one that actually occurs, then this proviso has already been implicit in our account of explanation). But suppose we make this proviso explicit —is it enough? I do not believe so. It might be true that God wills everything that happens, but as long as we have no means of knowing this, we cannot use it as a premise in our explanation. That is, we cannot use it as an explanation unless the proposition is not only true, but is *known to be so.*

Suppose, then, that we accept this last revision —will it do the trick? I hardly think so; it still misses the main point. Let us imagine a deeply religious scientist who holds that everything that happens is the result of divine will; he may yet reject the theological explanation as an account of *why* things happen as they do. The reason is surely fairly obvious: what the scientist wishes to discover is why this happened *rather than that,* and the theological explanation will not enable him to make this discrimination: *whatever* happens, one can deduce it from the premises that God willed it to happen and that whatever He wills happens.

What condition, then, remains to be supplied? The condition seems to be a rather simple one, yet one which it is difficult to state precisely. What we have in mind is this: we want to eliminate the indiscriminate 'explanatory' power of the gremlin-hypothesis and the God-hypothesis, even though they slip through the deductive net, because they do not enable us to explain why this happens *rather than that.* 'What explains everything explains nothing.'

This *can* be put by saying that the explanation must have *predictive* value, but this is a bit misleading. For one thing, it places undue emphasis upon the future, whereas explanation of past is just as important as explanation of future; we would have, then, to use a tenseless sense of 'predict'. For another thing, there are many explanations which seem to be true but whose predictive power is minimal or at any rate difficult to see: many biological phenomena can be explained in terms of laws of mutations, for example, but it is not clear what these laws enable us to *predict*— certainly not where or when a mutation will occur or what kind it will be when it does arise.

Perhaps what we want to say can be best expressed by the simple proviso that the explanation must explain *other* phenomena than those it is invoked to explain, and yet, unlike the God-hypothesis, not just everything indiscriminately: in other words, it should explain other events (whether past, present, or future makes no difference), but it should all the same be *capable of disproof* by empirical observations, whether or not any actual empirical observations ever disprove it, it must be capable of testing. Without this condition it would not be considered an explanation in any science.

In fact all this is implicit in our requirement that an explanation be in terms of law or laws. A law is universal proposition about all events or processes in a certain class, and if it holds for A, a member of the class (a present event), it also holds for members B, C, and D (future events); thus by the very nature of a law, laws explain more than a single event. The testability of explanations is also implicit in the concept of law, for a law is an empirical statement of a uniformity of nature, and, being contingent, it is always subject to disconfirmation by observation. Still, it is well to make the implicit explicit to show why the deductive requirement is not enough and what more is required of an explanation.

5. In evaluating the extent to which proffered explanations yield as genuine empirical knowledge (*i.e.* are real empirical laws), much care is required, for in this field the verbal booby-traps in our way are numerous and intricate.

If someone asked, 'Why is this object spherical?' and the reply were given, 'Because it's globular', everyone would recognize the answer to be trivial because it is analytic. Many so-called explanations do not give much more information than this, although even very bad ones are not usually quite as empty as this one. Even when one says that opium produces sleep because of its dormitive power, we are at least told that it is because of something within it that sleep is produced, not by some outside factor such as the atmosphere. When we ask why hydrogen combines with oxygen to form water, and are told that it is because hydrogen has an *affinity* for oxygen, again the reply is relatively empty: it tells us only that under certain conditions hydrogen does combine with oxygen but tells us nothing of why hydrogen rather than some other substances does this; but at least we know from the answer that there *is* a law relating the combination of elements to some set of conditions, though we do not yet know what this law is. And if we ask why the mother cat takes care of her kittens and fights to defend them, and are told that it is because she has a *maternal instinct,* at least we know that the activity is not a learned one—and this is indeed something—although again the answer may not give us the kind of thing we were asking for. Most explanations in terms of instinct, tendency, affinity, power, and faculty are of this next-to-worthless kind, conveying only a minimum of information, and leading us to ask a why-question of the explanation given.

Let us observe how easily the invention of a name may make us assume that an explanation has been given. If it is asked, 'Why is iron magnetic?' and we answer, 'Because iron, cobalt, and nickel are magnetic', no one would think much of this as an explanation; but the moment we give a name to the behaviour of these metals, and call them, say, 'fero-affinitive', then when someone asks why iron is magnetic, we can say, 'Why, because its a fero-affinitive metal, that's why'. And yet no more has been said in the second case than in the first. Similarly, if we had a name for the tendency of seeds to sprout upwards to reach the surface of the ground, people would be readier to say that their tendency to rise could be *explained* by the presence of this property. Yet a name for what it does is a different thing from an explanation of why it does what it does.

Not all examples are as simple as this. When external influences tend to reduce or raise the bodily temperature of an organism, various bodily mechanisms come into play to return the temperature to normal. This is known as 'homeostasis'. So far, we simply have a name for the phenomenon, and if someone volunteered it as an *explanation* he would surely be mistaken. But now suppose a bird finds its nest partially destroyed and it sets about rebuilding it to the way it was before; we ask why, and are told, 'That's the bird's homeostatic tendency'. Now the name 'homeostasis' is no longer merely a label for the temperature-controlling mechanisms; it relates these mechanisms to a quite different thing, the bird's attempt to restore the *status quo*. In both examples there is an attempt to restore a state which has ceased to exist. Is 'homeostasis' now an explanation, or is it simply a description-in-a-nutshell, a *generalized* description, of what the organism does, without attempting to explain why?

Observe, incidentally, how easily all these so-called explanations slip through the deductive net. We can deduce the required conclusion easily: 'When organisms have homeostatic tendencies, they do so-and-so. This organism has homeostatic tendencies. Therefore, it does so-and-so. The deductive requirement will let good and bad explanations alike slip through like water through a sieve. This shows us again that,

whether necessary to explanation or not, the deducibility requirement is not sufficient.

But let us return: Is homeostasis an explanation of the organism's behaviour or not? Before we say, 'No, it isn't', let us reflect on this point: if appeal to homeostasis is simply a short way of saying that birds do this and people do that, is not the appeal to gravitation simply a short way of saying that apples do this and stars do that? And yet the Law of Gravitation is one of the most sacred of our explanatory principles. Perhaps, as Wisdom says, talking about gravitation is simply a way of saying that apples fall *and so on;* but then is not homeostasis simply a way of saying that birds rebuild their nests *and so on?*

It is, of course, incorrect to say that apples fall because of gravitation, if we mean by this that gravitation is some animistic force or pull, just as it would be wrong to say that birds behave so-and-so because of homeotasis, if we mean it to be a separate force or magnetism within birds. If we are so tempted, it is both useful and important to say that each of the explanations referred to is simply a way of saying 'this happens *and so on'*. But it is, I should think, the *extent and range* of the 'and so on' that matters here. What gives the Principle of Gravitation its remarkable explanatory power is not its appeal to an occult force but its bringing together under one formula an enormous range of diverse and complex phenomena. Because of this range, and the exactitude with which it can be applied to widely separate phenomena, the Law of Gravitation is the classical case of a law having predictive power—and it is extremely doubtful whether homeostasis possesses or ever will possess this. We rest, then, once again with this second and all-important necessary condition of explanation (the first being, at least in common opinion, the deducibility requirement): its power to explain a wide range of phenomena *other* than those it was invoked to explain.

6. No mention has thus far been made of explanation in terms of *purpose.* And yet this is the oldest concept of explanation and still the one most frequently employed by primitive peoples. And there are contexts in which we still employ the concept of purpose in giving explanations— for example, when we say that my purpose in going to the store was to do some Christmas shopping, and that this is *why* I went.

The word 'purpose' is, of course, ambiguous. (*a*) Most frequently in ordinary usage a purpose is something of which I am conscious—a conscious intent to do something. The conscious intent is not the *whole* of the purpose: part of the criterion of whether it is my purpose to do X is whether I am disposed towards doing X, whether I take steps towards X and do X if I have the chance. (*b*) Some tendencies to act are not accompanied by any state of awareness; and here psychologists speak of *unconscious* purposes. We need not stop here over the exact interpretation of this way of speaking; let us simply say that one is said to have X as his unconscious purpose if he consistently acts, without intending it, so as to bring about X. (*c*) We speak of inanimate objects as having purposes—for example, the purpose of a hammer is to drive nails. This of course is not a purpose consciously envisaged by the hammer. All we mean here is that the mechanical object *reflects* the conscious purposes of its makers. *We* had a conscious purpose in making the hammer, and thus we speak elliptically of the hammer as having that purpose. Strictly speaking, of course, the purpose is ours and not the hammer's.

In all of these cases a purpose implies a purposer, or someone to have the purpose. We do sometimes use the word 'purpose' in another sense which carries no such implication (*d*) when we say, 'What is the purpose of the heart?' 'To pump blood through the body.' Here purpose simply means function—*i.e.* what does it *do*? what part does it play in the bodily economy? If the word 'purpose' is used here I would view it as a 'degenerate' usage—a misleading locution in which another word, 'function', would serve much better. It is true that someone, in asking the purpose of the heart, might have in mind a theological question, 'What purpose did God have in endowing us with this organ?' but if this is meant, we are back again to purpose sense 1, in which purpose implies a purposer and the word 'purpose' refers to conscious intent—the only difference now being that it is God's intent and not ours that is in question. But this, of course, is not what medical men generally have in mind when they ask purpose-questions about parts of organisms; else every such medical question would be a disguised theological question.

Having disentangled these senses of 'purpose', let us ask about the legitimacy of purposive explanations. Briefly I think it comes to this: explanations require laws, and if there are laws *about* purposes, there is no reason why they cannot figure in some explanations just as laws about falling bodies figure in other explanations. To the extent that laws about purposes have been established, they can be used as explanations like any other laws. Unfortunately the only laws (if any) that we are in a position to make about purposes are about human ones. Explanations in terms of divine purposes cannot be employed because no laws about divine purposes have ever been established. Even explanations of biological events in terms of animal purposes is frowned upon: we do not count it an explanation if it is said that the hen sits on her eggs *in order to* hatch chicks, because we have no indication that the hen does so with this purpose in mind; even if this is true, we do not know it, and therefore we cannot use it as a law in our explanation. In the human realm alone we know that purposes exist, and only there can we therefore employ them in explanations. We can even deduce conclusions from them, thus:

People act so as to fulfill their purposes, unless prevented by external circumstances.

My purpose was to go shopping, and I was not prevented . . . etc.

Therefore, I went shopping.

This way of putting it may sound rather silly, as the deductive model often does, but at any rate a deduction can be achieved from premises which are in all probability true.

The chief mistake which people are in the habit of making with regard to purposive explanation is probably that of wanting an answer to a why-question in terms of purpose when the conditions under which a purpose-answer is legitimate are not fulfilled. People extend their questioning unthinkingly from areas in which purposive explanation is in order into areas in which it is not. Thus: 'Why did he go to New York?' 'Well, in response to impulses from certain centres in his brain, some muscles in his arms and legs started moving towards the airport and . . .' 'No, that's not what I mean. I mean, why did he go? what did he go for? what purpose did he have in view?' 'He went in order to see some operas.' Contrast this with the following: 'Why did he die?' 'Well, a bullet entered his lung, puncturing some blood vessels, and the blood filled his lung so that he couldn't breathe any more, and ...' 'No, that's not what I mean. I mean, *why* did he die?' But here we can no longer give an answer in terms of purpose—unless, that is, our talk is rooted in a theological context and we are willing to say that, just as the first person went to New York because he wanted to see operas, so the second person died because God had some purpose (intent) in seeing to it that he was murdered. If this is what is meant, one could try to answer the question in the theistic context of divine purposes; but if this context is rejected, the why-question demanding an answer in terms of purpose is meaningless, because an answer is being demanded when the only conditions under which the question is meaningful are not fulfilled.

This point is worth emphasizing because it is so often ignored in practice. Having received answers to why-questions when these questions were meaningful and explanations could be given, people continue to use why-questions even when they no longer know what they are asking for. One need not be surprised that no answer is forthcoming to such questions. And in our discouragement with such questions we are all too prone to make a mistake ourselves and terminate an exasperating series of why-questions with a remark such as, 'That's just something we don't know,' as if it were like cases where something definite is being asked but we do not yet know the laws which explain the phenomena we are asking about. If something in the case is not known, there must be something in the case which we could fail to know. If we are to ask a meaningful question, we must know what it is that we are asking for; only then can we recognize an answer as being one when we do find it.

7. This leads us directly into an important question, How far can explanation go? We may explain an event in terms of a law, and this law in terms of other laws, and so on, but must we not finally come to a stop? The bursting of the pipes is explained by the expansion of water on freezing; let us assume that water expands on freezing because the water-molecule has such-and-such a structure; now why does the water-molecule have this structure? Perhaps this can some day be explained by reference to electron-proton arrangements with the atom, and this in turn by reference

to the disposition of more minute particles (if they can be called such) yet to be discovered; but sooner or later must we not say, 'That's just the way things are—this is just an ultimate law about the universe. We can explain other things in terms of it, but it we cannot explain'? Are there ultimate laws, laws which explain but cannot even in principle be explained?

In practice we come rather quickly to laws which cannot be explained further. Laws about atomic structure are typical of such laws. Laws of psycho-physical correlation are another example. *Why* do I have a certain colour-sensation which I call red, indescribable but qualitatively different from all others, when light within a certain range of wave-length impinges upon my retina, and another indescribably different sensation which I call yellow when rays of another wave-length strike the retina? That this wavelength is correlated with this visual experience seems to be sheer 'brute fact'—a law[2] which cannot be explained in terms of anything more ultimate than itself.

At the same time, we should be careful in dismissing any uniformity we cannot explain as a 'brute fact' or 'basic law'. Many things, such as why this element has this melting-point and these spectral lines, were once considered basic and unexplainable properties of the element, but have since been explained in terms of the intra-molecular structure of the element. No matter how much at a loss we may be for an explanation, we can always ask and speculate. If it had been accepted as a basic law that water starts to expand when it gets below 39°F, we would never have gone on to discover anything about the structure of the water-molecule. Fruitful scientific procedure depends on assuming that no given law is basic; if scientists did not continue always to ask the question 'Why?' the process of scientific enquiry would stop dead in its tracks.

Thus, if there *are* basic laws, it seems that we cannot know of any given law that it is one. We can know that it is *not,* by explaining it in terms of other laws; but how could we know that it *is*? Discovering basic laws is epistemologically similar to discovering uncaused events: if there are uncaused events, we can never know that there are, for all we can safely say is that we have not yet found causes for them.

One further point about basic or ultimate laws: If a law is really a basic one, any request for an explanation of it is self-contradictory. To explain a law is to place it in a context or network of wider and more inclusive laws; a basic law is by definition one of which this cannot be done; therefore to ask of an admittedly basic law that it be explained is implicitly to deny that it is basic and thus to deny the very premise of the argument. It is a request for explanation in a situation where by one's own admission no more explaining can be done.

Like so many others, this point may seem logically compelling but psychologically unsatisfying. Having heard the above argument, one may still feel inclined to ask, 'Why are the basic uniformities of the universe the way they are, and not some other way? Why should we have just *these* laws rather than other ones? I want an *explanation* of why they are as they are.' I must confess here, as an autobiographical remark, that I cannot help sharing this feeling: I want to ask why the laws of nature, being contingent, are as they are, even though I cannot conceive of what an explanation of this would be like, and even though by my own argument above the request for such an explanation is self-contradictory.[3] The fact is, as we saw above, that why-questions have had answers so many times that we tend automatically to ask them here even when they can have no answers because we have ripped them out of the only context in which they have meaning—like the situation of the child who, being told what is above the table and above the ceiling of his room and above the house and above the earth, now asks what is above the universe. The question has now gone outside the context of meaningful discourse, and so has the request for the explanation of a basic law. We should remember: to explain is to explain *in terms of something*, and if *ex hypothesi* there is no longer any something for it to be explained in terms of, then the request for an explanation is self-contradictory: it demands on the one hand that you explain X in terms of a Y while insisting simultaneously that there is no Y.

8. One sometimes encounters the complaint that science does not really explain but only describes. 'Science doesn't tell us *why* things happen,' it is said, 'it only tells us *how* things happen.' Now it does often happen that the exact intention of the user of a why-question is not very clear—as we have already seen. But in the way in which

the term 'why' is most commonly used, science *does* explain why: for example, the bursting of the pipes, the formation of ice at the top of ponds rather than at the bottom, and many other phenomena, are explained by reference to the law that water expands when it freezes. (If someone says we have *not* explained why the pipes burst, then what does he mean by 'why'? What sort of thing is he asking for? What *would* answer his question? Let him state in other terms what it is that he is asking for.)

'But is not explanation after all merely description?' It is all very well to say that when we explain something we actually describe—*e.g.* stating laws of nature is describing how nature works. But this does not preclude the fact that we *are* explaining. When the question is asked why pressing the button turns on the light, we explain by describing just what goes on—currents, open and closed circuits, conduction of electricity by wires, dynamos in the power plant, and so on. But have we not in so doing explained the phenomenon about which we were asking? We have explained *by* describing, if you will; but certainly we have explained. To say that because we are describing we cannot be explaining would be like saying that because an object is red it cannot also be coloured.

9. A similar complaint is sometimes voiced against scientific explanation, that it 'explains things *away*'. Explaining something is interpreted as equivalent to explaining it away. Now the precise meaning of the phrase 'explaining away' is one which I have never been able to discover. What is one supposed to be doing when he explains something away? Surely not to declare that it does not exist! Explanation deprives us of no facts we had before. To 'explain colour' in terms of light-waves is not, of course (as should have been obvious), to take away the fact of colour-experiences. 'Thinking is nothing but the occurrence of certain neural impulses' should be changed into '*When* thinking takes place (and that it does is just as incontrovertible a fact as the neurons are), there are neural impulses.'

In the special context of beliefs, perhaps 'explaining away' may mean impugning the truth of one's conclusions. If so, there are again no grounds for fear. To 'explain away' someone's politically reactionary tendencies by saying, 'He's old, and people always get conservative when they get old', does not for a moment take away whatever truth the person's opinions may have; at most, it only exposes part of the causal genesis of his having them. And if the views of this person were 'explained away' by these biographical observations, the views of his opponent would be equally vulnerable: 'You needn't pay any attention to that young upstart, they're all hot communists when they're young'. Reference to biography may, together with laws of human nature (if any are known in this area), explain why a person held a certain belief at a certain time, but the truth or falsity of the belief is quite unaffected by this and, of course, is tested on different grounds entirely. The idea that reference to a person's mental or physical condition could 'explain away' the truth of a belief is one of the most flagrant blunders of the materialistically minded laity of our day.

NOTES

1. With qualifications to be discussed later.

2. A law which would, to be sure, have to be qualified to take care of abnormal cases, *e.g.* colour-blindness, jaundice, etc. The genesis of colour-sensations is complex and does not depend *merely* upon the kind of light-rays entering the eye.

3. Explanation in terms of divine purposes again will not help: if we are told that the laws of nature are as they are because God willed it so, we can ask why He should have willed it so; and if here again an answer is given, we can once again ask a why-question of this answer.

W E S L E Y   C.   S A L M O N

Determinism and Indeterminism in Modern Science*

According to a famous legend, the stoic philosopher Epictetus, who was a slave, broke a vase that his master, who was also a philosopher, treasured. When the master began to beat him, Epictetus protested, "By the philosophy to which we both adhere, it was predestined from the beginning of the world that I should break the vase; I am not to blame and I should not be beaten." His master replied, "By that same philosophy, it was determined for all time that I should beat you," and he continued to do so. This anecdote sums up much of the frustration that people down through the ages have felt when confronted with the problem of "free will and determinism." The main purpose of the present essay is to attempt to clarify the notion of determinism, and some other concepts closely related to it. Except for a few incidental remarks, I shall leave the problem of free will to other authors.

*Copyright © Wesley C. Salmon, 1970. This essay was commissioned by the editor expressly for this volume. It has not been previously published. Wesley C. Salmon is Professor of Philosophy at the University of Arizona.

Determinism is a doctrine that comes in many forms. In ancient mythology, as well as some later religions, it was a crude sort of fatalism. The fates, with conscious intent, decide at the time of one's birth what is going to happen to him, and nothing anyone can do will make it otherwise. The following passage nicely illustrates the fatalistic view.

DEATH SPEAKS: There was a merchant in Bagdad who sent his servant to market to buy provisions and in a little while the servant came back, white and trembling, and said, Master, just now when I was in the market-place I was jostled by a woman in the crowd and when I turned I saw it was Death that jostled me. She looked at me and made a threatening gesture; now, lend me your horse, and I will ride away from this city and avoid my fate. I will go to Samarra and there Death will not find me. The merchant lent him his horse, and the servant mounted it, and he dug his spurs in its flanks and as fast as the horse would gallop he went. Then the merchant went down to the market-place and he saw me standing in the crowd and he came to me and said, Why did you make a threatening gesture to my servant when you saw him this morning?

That was not a threatening gesture, I said, it was only a start of surprise. I was astonished to see him in Bagdad, for I had an appointment with him tonight in Samarra.[1]

Certain sects of Christianity have maintained that God, who created the world and holds it in his all-powerful control, fore-ordains exactly what is to happen. This view is known as *predestinarianism,* and it is reinforced by the doctrine of God's omniscience. If God knows with complete certainty and in precise detail what will occur in the future—including whether *you* will go to heaven or to hell—the future is determined to be just exactly what God knows it is going to be. The individual has no power over his future and can do nothing to change it. Even his own acts, and his apparently free decisions, are predetermined by something outside of him, over which he has no influence. The feeling of freedom which accompanies many of our decisions and actions is a mere illusion.

Both fatalism and predestinarianism attribute the control of human "fate" or "destiny" to some supernatural agency. Most of us, nowadays, reject fatalism as primitive superstition, and few still believe in predestination. Agnostics and atheists find no basis for believing in God at all, and contemporary theists generally believe that God allows man some measure of freedom. However, it has long been suspected that even a "hard-headed" scientific world-view would lead to a determinism just as inimical to freedom of choice and action as are fatalism and predestinarianism.

1. DETERMINISM IN CLASSICAL PHYSICS

In his famous poem *De Rerum Natura,* Lucretius maintains that everything in the universe consists solely of atoms which move about in otherwise empty space, colliding with one another and forming complex arrangements. The earth and the sun, rocks and trees, human beings and other animals—all are just complicated collections of various kinds of atoms. Everything that happens in the universe, including human thought and action, is simply the result of the movements of atoms. Lucretius realized that free will is problematic if we conceive the motions of atoms to be strictly determined by mechanical laws; he writes, "... if all movement is always interconnected, the new arising from the old in a determinate order ... what is the source of the free will possessed by living things throughout the earth?"[2]

Lucretius tried to resolve the problem by claiming that atoms sometimes swerve spontaneously and without any cause from their otherwise determined courses. Believing that freedom of the will is an established fact, he was led to deny determinism. His argument can be set out as follows:

(1) If determinism is true, man does not have free will.
    Man has free will.
    _____
    Determinism is False.

On the basis of this argument, Lucretius accepted indeterminism as the correct world-view.

Lucretius wrote in the first century B.C., hundreds of years before Newton formulated the laws that govern the motions and collisions of those tiny lumps of matter the Greek atomists postulated. Before Newton, one could have speculated as to whether the laws of mechanics completely determine the motions of material particles; after Newton, that question seemed to be closed. From 1686, when the *Principia*[3] was first published, until about 1900, Newton's mechanics was tested and retested, confirmed and reconfirmed. Not only did it explain the approximate correctness of Galileo's law of falling bodies and Kepler's laws of planetary motion, but it also accounted for the behavior of the tides, and the bulging of the Earth at its equator. Moreover, when a delicate laboratory experiment made possible the direct measurement of the gravitational attraction between a large ball of lead and a small one, Newton was found to be right.[4] Newton's laws explained why the orbits of the planets are not perfect ellipses, as Kepler had said, by bringing in the mutual gravitational attractions among the planets themselves, instead of considering only the attraction between each planet and the sun. Indeed, when the planet Uranus appeared not to conform to Newton's laws, Neptune was postulated to account for the deviation. Newton's laws enabled astronomers to predict the location of Neptune and telescopic observation confirmed its existence. These laws led to the discovery of a theretofore unobserved planet. Later, when Neptune seemed to violate Newton's laws, Pluto was postulated and then observed.[5]

It is almost impossible to overestimate the impressive success of Newtonian mechanics. As more sophisticated experimental and mathematical techniques were developed to extend the application of Newton's laws to new phenomena, confirming evidence continued to mount. One of the greatest mathematical physicists to contribute to the application of Newtonian mechanics to planetary motion was P. S. Laplace, who, early in the nineteenth century, wrote,

All events, even those which on account of their insignificance do not seem to follow the great laws of nature, are a result of it just as necessarily as the revolutions of the sun. In ignorance of the ties which unite such events to the entire system of the universe, they have been made to depend upon final causes or upon hazard, according as they occur and are repeated with regularity, or appear without regard to order; but these imaginary causes have gradually receded with the widening bounds of knowledge and disappear entirely before sound philosophy, which sees in them only the expression of our ignorance of the true causes.[6]

Here is a classic statement of the determinist's position. All events, no matter how large or small, no matter how significant or insignificant, are completely determined by strict laws of mechanics. When people attribute events to final causes (e.g., fate or divine intervention) or hazard (i.e., pure accident or chance) it is only because they are ignorant of the actual facts. The success of Newtonian mechanics offered convincing evidence that all natural phenomena could be explained by the laws of mechanics. As the application of scientific knowledge is pushed further and further, we see that nothing is in principle incapable of explanation on a purely mechanical basis. The argument of Lucretius resulted from the imperfect state of ancient science; if we still accept the first premise, the argument must continue as follows:

(2) If determinism is true, man does not have free will.
     Determinism is true.

Man does not have free will.

Both of these arguments are logically valid; they differ with respect to their second premises.

Newtonian mechanics—so it seemed to Laplace and countless other philosophers and scientists—clearly turned the tide against Lucretius in favor of determinism. Although Lucretius' argument is logically valid, its second premise is not true. What appears to Lucretius to be free will, free choice, or free action is in fact determined, according to Laplace, and any appearance of indeterminacy is only the result of incomplete knowledge of all the causes.

2. DETERMINISM AND THE SCIENCES OF LIFE AND MIND

If one believed, with Lucretius and Laplace, that there is nothing more than atoms and their motions, determinism seemed unavoidable in the Newtonian era. But not everyone found this materialistic outlook entirely compelling. Descartes had argued persuasively that there are two realms, the physical and the psychological, and that they are quite distinct from one another.[7] One could agree with Descartes that the laws of mechanics, which govern the material world, are strictly deterministic, and still maintain that freedom exists in the mental domain. It is essential to remember the difference between the scientific evidence for determinism in physics and the philosophical speculation that everything is entirely reducible to material atoms and their motions.

Descartes held that only man, among all the animals, has a mental life; other animals are mere mechanisms. This doctrine reflects the Christian view that only man has an immortal soul. It suffered a sharp setback when Charles Darwin's epoch-making work on evolution in mid-nineteenth century showed that man and the other animals are not utterly distinct, but closely related.[8] In the face of this result, it might be tempting to suggest that the deepest gulf is not between man and everything else, but rather, between living and non-living things. Darwin's work on the origin of species and the descent of man did not, after all, explain the origin of life itself. But Darwin's work has an aspect that bears upon this distinction as well. Instead of explaining the existence of various species of living things as a result of purposeful "special creation" as recounted in *Genesis*, he explains them in terms of non-purposive mechanisms of natural selection. Add to that the chemical synthesis of the "organic compound" urea from exclusively inorganic substances, and the sharp separation between the biological and the physical realms begins to look less tenable.[9]

In spite of strong indications of continuity between the physical phenomena whose behavior was explained deterministically by Newtonian mechanics and the biological realm of living things, and in spite of man's kinship with the rest of the animal kingdom, there still remained the mysterious phenomena of consciousness that seem the almost exclusive property of the human race. One could speculate that chimpanzees, apes, dogs, and horses may have a very primitive mental life, and even, perhaps, a low degree of free will; nevertheless, in man the conscious aspect is extremely conspicuous (especially to himself), and that might be the locus of his freedom. Man might be so constructed that his physiological aspects are governed by deterministic laws, but his mental life is still governed by psychological laws that are indeterministic. That is what Descartes had maintained from the outset.

At this point, another intellectual giant of the nineteenth century steps into the picture. In an attempt to understand mental illness, Sigmund Freud developed a psychological theory according to which all mental occurrences, even those of the seemingly most trivial sorts, are as strictly caused as are any physical phenomena.[10] Freud postulated unconscious mechanisms that give rise to dreams and neurotic symptoms, and he offered causal explanations of such trivia as slips of the tongue and the pen. Freud's theories were no idle philosophical speculations; they were designed to explain observable phenomena, and they were tested by experience. I do not mean to argue that Freud's theories are still totally acceptable as current theories; neither, for that matter, are Newton's laws. There can be little doubt, however, that he heralded dramatically the possibility that psychological phenomena may be subject to laws just as deterministic as those of Newtonian mechanics. He offers the strong suggestion that our conscious deliberations and "free" choices can be explained as deterministically as the result of the collision of two billiard balls on a table. By the close of the nineteenth century, determinism seemed well on the way to being a scientifically well grounded view of the entire universe in all of its aspects—physical, biological, psychological, and even social.

3. DETERMINISM AND CONTEMPORARY SCIENCE

Twentieth century science has, in some ways, confirmed and extended the grounds for holding a deterministic world-view, and in others it has seemed to undermine determinism. Spectacular progress in the biological sciences has extended enormously the degree to which processes in living organisms can be understood strictly in terms of chemistry and physics. The most striking achievement has been in the field of molecular biology, where the mechanisms of heredity are explained in exclusively chemical terms. The gene is recognized as a large and complex molecule whose properties are fully determined by its chemical structure, and whose capabilities for self-replication are thereby explained.[11] Protein molecules, the "building blocks of life," are known to be constructed out of amino acids. Amino acids have been synthesized, and so have protein molecules more recently—just as this article was going to press—H. Gobind Khorana, a Nobel Prize winner at the University of Wisconsin, and associates, synthesized a gene. In the not too distant future, man will very probably succeed in synthesizing a viable living organism from inorganic chemicals. These developments constitute an important extension of Darwin's beginnings, and it no longer seems justifiable to deny that the laws that govern the behavior of atoms have complete dominion in the biological realm.

The science of psychology was in its infancy at the turn of the century, but it too has lived up to its nineteenth century promise. The scientific study of human and animal behavior—from the psychoanalytic, behavioristic, and physiological standpoints—has borne considerable fruit in showing that human experience, feeling, deliberation, choice, and action can be understood in terms of strict psychological laws. It is perhaps too soon to say whether these laws are ultimately reducible to those of physiology, and thence to those of physics and chemistry, but many indications point in that direction. Even Freud believed that the psychoanalytic mechanisms he postulated would eventually be explained in physiological terms. Subsequent neurological studies suggest that it may soon be feasible to explain learning in terms of specific chemical changes that occur in the brain cells, and psycho-pharmacological developments suggest that chemical understanding of feelings and emotions is not too far away. It is certainly plausible at this point, to suppose that the laws that govern the behavior of atoms also govern our thoughts, feelings, emotions, decisions, and ultimately, all of our actions.[12]

What sort of picture does this give of a person as a thinking, deliberating, considering, choosing agent? His life begins when two cells, a sperm and an egg, unite, and following the laws of physics and chemistry, the genes that are present begin to replicate. The individual's heredity, which determines in large measure what he will become both physically and psychologically, is passed on to him from his parents through the genes that carry "the genetic code." From the beginning, outside influences impinge upon him—even before birth—and these too have a bearing upon what he will become and how he will react to further outside influences. Among prenatal influences are, for example, such disease viruses as that of German measles, which may affect the sense organs of the unborn child and deprive him for life of experiences most of us have. When the infant leaves the womb, social factors begin to operate. Again, external causes—vaguely known as "environmental influences"—become effective. How the person grows depends in part upon such social factors as the personality of the parent and the economic condition of the family, and in part upon what he has already become as a result of the hereditary, physiological, and environmental influences that have already operated upon him. Where, if at all, does the individual's genuine choice—freely made—enter the picture? If he grows up to commit murder, is that not just a part of the inexorable causal process in which he is caught up? Is he not just as much a complete victim of his heredity and environment as Oedipus was of his fate? Is this not the most reasonable inference from the scientific knowledge that is presently available? Before we try to draw a conclusion, it will be best to take another look at the laws of physics that seem to be fundamental to the whole scheme of things.

As the twentieth century dawned, physics, which seemed so secure, was approaching a crisis. Two great revolutions were about to shake it to its very foundations. One of these revolutions, which consisted in the replacement of Newtonian mechanics by Einstein's special (1905) and general (1916) theories of relativity, did nothing to upset the deterministic character of physics. Newton's laws of mechanics turned out to be not quite correct, so they had to be replaced by some revised laws of mechanics, but ones that were no less deterministic.[13]

The other revolution had a profound bearing upon determinism. According to the theories of electromagnetic radiation available at the end of the nineteenth century, a light beam entering a dark box with a small hole will produce inside the box an infinite amount of radiant energy in the ultraviolet region of the spectrum, thus giving rise to a holocaust more terrible than the worst nuclear bomb. This consequence was later aptly called "the ultraviolet catastrophe." Since no such cataclysms occur, something must be drastically wrong with classical physics. In 1900, Max Planck introduced the quantum hypothesis, and showed that it yields a far more satisfactory account of "black body radiation."[14] In 1913, Neils Bohr applied quantization to the orbits of electrons in hydrogen atoms, and showed that he could thereby explain the spectral lines emitted by hydrogen gas when it is excited by passage of an electric current. Bohr's theory, unfortunately, did not work at all well for the spectra of helium and the more complex atoms. By about 1925, Werner Heisenberg, Erwin Schrödinger, Max Born, and others had worked out the details of a more satisfactory quantum mechanics, but the theory they produced was fundamentally statistical. The physics of atoms had become indeterministic. For example, it is a consequence of quantum mechanics that atoms of silver, when shot between the poles of a magnet, will be deflected either up or down, but there is no way, even in principle, of determining beforehand which way a particular atom will go. Each one has a 50–50 chance of going either way, and that is all there is to it.[15] Thus, for reasons entirely different from those of Lucretius, modern physicists also attribute indeterministic swerves to atoms in motion.

A natural reaction to examples of this kind is to say that there are real causes that determine which atom will be deflected in which direction, but that we have not yet found them. There exists, however, a highly technical proof that such an interpretation is not admissible, for the present theory *cannot* be supplemented in such a way as to make it deterministic. It is intrinsically indeterministic. Any attempt to make it deterministic, by postulating additional causes, will render it logically self-contradictory.[16] At the same time, the present quantum mechanics could be replaced—not merely supplemented—by a thoroughly deterministic theory. Einstein, for one, was never satisfied with the irreducibly statistical character of quantum mechanics—"God does not play dice with the universe" is his oft-quoted remark. Some first-rate physicists are presently working to find a deterministic theory to replace the current quantum mechanics, one by which it will be possible to explain what now seems irreducibly statistical by means of "hidden variables" that cannot occur in the present theory. No one can say for sure whether they will succeed; any new theory, deterministic or indeterministic, has to stand the test of experiment. The current quantum theory does show, however, that the world *may* be fundamentally and irremediably indeterministic, for according to the best currently available knowledge, it is.

4. WHAT IS DETERMINISM?

So far, the discussion had proceeded as if a number of the fundamental concepts we have been using are clear. Since this is a rather dubious supposition, let us focus attention upon some of them in the hope of enhancing our understanding. We will do well to begin with the classic definition of determinism given by Laplace. At this point, our aim is not to argue the truth or falsity of determinism, but only to say what it means. Laplace writes,

> Given for one instant an intelligence which could comprehend all the forces by which nature is animated and the respective situation of the beings who compose it—an intelligence sufficiently vast to submit these data to analysis—it would embrace in the same formula the movements of the greatest bodies in the universe and those of the lightest atom; for it, nothing would be uncertain and the future, as the past, would be present to its eyes.[17]

The intelligence mentioned in this statement has sometimes been called "Laplace's demon," but he never intended to imply that such a demon actually exists—or an omniscient God for that matter. According to a famous anecdote, when Napoleon learned of Laplace's great work, *The System of the World,* he asked Laplace where God fit into the system; Laplace replied, "Sir, I have no need of that hypothesis." What he was trying to do was to capture the import of determinism. To affirm determinism is to maintain that the precise condition of the entire universe at any one instant, together with the laws of nature, logically entail the condition of the universe in its totality at any future instant. Newtonian mechanics is deterministic, for if the precise position and momentum of each and every particle at one moment—say 12:00 noon, Greenwich mean time, April 15, 1970—is known, and if the laws of Newtonian mechanics are the true laws of nature, then anyone who could solve sufficiently complicated mathematical equations could deduce with perfect exactitude and rigor the precise state of the universe at any subsequent moment. From these data and these laws, Laplace's demon could calculate any future occurrence. He could ascertain exactly what you will have for breakfast on April 15, 1980, and if you should drop a bit of egg, precisely where it will spot your tie.

No determinist seriously believes that human beings are at present capable of ascertaining the total future of the universe in all detail, or that we will ever be able to do so. He is saying, instead, that it is possible in principle to make such inferences because the laws of nature and the state of the universe at any one time actually do determine the state of the universe at all future times. The fact that we are unable to make perfect predictions in all cases is, to the determinist, the result of human ignorance and other limitations; it is not because nature is lacking in precise determination.

To what, then, is the indeterminist committed? For him, the combination of laws and total state of the universe at one moment do not completely determine the states of the universe at other moments. It is not a failure of our intelligence, a limitation on our knowledge of the laws of nature, or a partial ignorance of the state of the universe at the given moment. Instead, *given* complete knowledge of the state of the universe at some instant, *given* perfectly accurate formulations of the laws of nature, and *given* unlimited ability to solve mathematical equations, the complete state of the universe at some other moment simply does not follow. This is what it means to deny that determinism, as held by Laplace, is true. For example, Lucretius said that the atoms, all originally falling downward through space at a uniform speed, spontaneously swerved from their courses. In our latter-day wisdom, we know that space does not, by itself, have a downward direction, and that there is no physical way to distinguish uniform motion through space from rest. Lucretius might just as well have said that the atoms were all sitting there motionless, when some of them started dancing around and bumping into one another. Given a precise knowledge of the size, shape, location, and state of motion (rest) of each atom, and given all the laws which govern their motion, there is no way to infer which atom will move, when it will move, in what direction it will move, and what other atoms it will collide with. If you object that there must be *some* reason why one of these atoms moved at the time and in the manner it did, Lucretius will staunchly deny it. It is not just that we do not know the reason—there is no reason!

In this context, I think we can feel the compelling force of the determinist viewpoint. To suppose that atoms start moving about without any cause at all strains our conceptions. It is easy to protest, with the determinist, that there must be some reason; it is tempting to say that the indeterminist is not even offering an intelligible account, let alone a true one. And, indeed, many philosophers have elevated determinism to the status of an a priori truth—one that cannot rationally be denied. It is sometimes called *the principle of sufficient reason,* "a thing cannot occur without a cause that produces it," and sometimes *the law of universal causation,* "everything that happens presupposes something from which it follows according to a rule."[18]

Notice that two very different grounds have been offered in support of determinism. In the first place, it has been regarded as a very general statement that is strongly supported by the success of science in explaining all kinds of phenomena by means of deterministic laws. In the second place, it has been taken as an a priori truth that cannot be rejected without logical absurdity. If it genuinely enjoys the status of an a priori truth, it needs no support from scientific evidence, and

science can never conceivably offer any evidence against it.

In view of the results of modern quantum mechanics, it seems inadvisable to regard determinism as an a priori principle. Quantum mechanics, in the form it now has, may not be true, but its truth or falsity is a matter of its correspondence with the facts, not the violation of an a priori principle. Quantum mechanics has shown that science can operate with indeterministic laws without degenerating into unintelligibility or logical absurdity. It seems reasonable to conclude that determinism is not an inviolable a priori principle; rather, its truth or falsity is a very fundamental and general fact about nature that we can hope to establish only more or less certainly on the basis of scientific evidence. If we are tempted to make determinism an a priori principle of reason, it may be because common sense tells us what "stands to reason." Contemporary common sense seems to have assimilated a good deal of the Newtonian world-view, but it has not yet come to terms with the statistical and probabilistic aspects of twentieth century science.

5. TYPES OF DETERMINISM AND INDETERMINISM

It is traditional to distinguish two kinds of causation, *efficient* causation and *final* causation. Efficient causation has a rather mechanical character, in the sense that effect follows cause without reference to purposes, intentions, or ends. If running water erodes the earth from beneath a rock, and the rock rolls down a hill, the whole process is normally regarded as one in which efficient causes are operating mechanically. If the rock crashes into the home of a mine owner who has been exploiting his employees, and people think it is God's way of punishing him, they are treating it as a case of final causation, inasmuch as this account does involve reference to purposes. The view that God created the separate species of living things in order to realize certain of His purposes takes the origin of species to be an example of final causation. Darwin's view, that the species develop by natural selection, regards the same result as the effect of efficient causes. Biological evolution does not have to be considered an instance of efficient causation, however, for theologians can still maintain that evolution is God's way of bringing about the realization of His purposes.

Whether one believes in efficient causation or final causation or a mixture of the two, it is still possible to be a determinist or an indeterminist. Let us adopt traditional terms and say that a person who believes that nature operates only with efficient causes, but never with final causes, is a *mechanist.* Let us say that anyone who believes that there are final causes is a *teleologist.* To be a mechanist or a teleologist is to make a commitment as to *what kinds* of causes there are, but not as to the pervasiveness of causation of either type. A determinist is one who takes a stand on the question of how extensively causes, of whatever type, operate, but not necessarily a commitment on what type of causes there are. We can, consequently, define four distinct positions:

1. *Mechanistic determinism:* Every event is completely determined by causes, and these causes are efficient, not final, causes. Laplace is the classic representive of this position.

2. *Teleological determinism:* Every event is completely determined by causes, and at least some of these causes are final causes. Calvinistic predestinarianism is the most familar example.

3. *Mechanistic indeterminism:* Events are not completely determined by causes, but to whatever extent they are determined, it is by efficient causes alone. Lucretius, with his indeterministic atomism, would seem to represent this view, as would most modern physicists who consider quantum mechanics basically indeterministic.

4. *Teleological indeterminism:* Events are not completely determined by causes, but some events are determined to some extent by final causes. An ancient fatalist might represent this view; for instance, the significant events in the life of Oedipus, such as killing his father and marrying his mother, were determined by final causes, but the less important ones, such as the exact positions of the drops of his father's blood, may well have been left to chance.

Scientific progress seems, historically, to be associated with a transition from teleology to mechanism. Aristotle's physics, which dominated the scene for several centuries before Newton, incorporated final causes. Newton's mechanics was entirely non-teleological. Biology before Darwin tended to be teleological, but Darwin, as we noted, introduced a mechanistic conception of biological evolution through natural selection. Subsequently, even the psychological and social sciences have tended to reject teleological conceptions. The question of whether teleological or mechanical conceptions are appropriate is, it seems to me, a matter to be decided by the success or failure of theories and explanations that employ them. On the whole, it appears, experience has strongly suggested that mechanical approaches are more fruitful than teleological ones, but this is an extremely complex issue.[19] The important point is to show how the two types of causation give rise to two types of determinism and two types of indeterminism.

6. LAWS OF NATURE

The laws that are written in law books (also called "statutes") are concocted by humans to *prescribe* how people shall behave. The people who are governed by such laws may conform to them or violate them. The laws of nature, by contrast, *describe* the ways in which various kinds of things in the universe operate, and there is no possibility of violation. If things did not conform to a purported law, it would not be an actual law of nature. Laws of nature, moreover, do not involve a legislator, human or divine, and we should certainly avoid thinking that the existence of laws of nature presupposes a supernatural lawmaker. To fall victim to such an inference would be entrapment by a bad pun.

In science, one often hears of Hooke's law, Kepler's laws, Newton's laws, etc. In each case there are one or more statements, propounded by the individual whose name is attached, which *purport* to describe how things like springs, planets, and bullets behave. If these statements do, in fact, state accurately how such things behave, then they express laws of nature. The law of nature itself is a general uniformity or regularity in nature; the statement that is written in the science text seeks to describe this regularity. There is an elementary, but crucial, distinction between the words used to state a law, and the fact of nature that is being described. The word "table," for instance, is a linguistic entity with five letters, but neither legs nor a flat surface; the word is not to be confused with a piece of furniture. Similarly, the statement of a law is a linguistic entity, which must not be confused with the regularity that nature actually exhibits. If the sentence in the book is true, it expresses a law; when we assert the statement, we do so because we believe it expresses a law, but we may be quite wrong in thinking so. For example, it was long believed that Newton's so-called laws of motion were true, but we no longer think so; although we still refer to them as "laws," we do not really believe they express genuine laws of nature. We presently believe, however, that the speed of light is the greatest speed at which signals of any kind can be transmitted across empty space, and that law is fundamental to Einstein's special theory of relativity.

The doctrine of determinism, as formulated by Laplace, makes essential reference to the laws of nature. It is of utmost importance to remember that such references do not pertain to statements that are found in textbooks, but rather, to the actual regularities that exist in nature. At any given time, of course, we do not know for certain which statements express actual regularities, and any statement we make purporting to express a law of nature may be incorrect, but that does not imply that we cannot speak meaningfully about the actual laws of nature (as opposed merely to our conceptions of the laws of nature). We do not know for certain that a given bottle actually contains Scotch whiskey, but we quite properly talk about the contents of such bottles even in the absence of certainty. When I take a drink from such a bottle, it is the contents of the bottle I shall be drinking, not merely my conception—I hardly ever drink a conception. If it were never permissible to say anything of which we are not absolutely certain, we could never say anything about the physical world.

7. DETERMINISM AND EXPLANATION

There are many kinds of explanation, such as explaining the meaning of an unfamiliar word, or explaining how to operate a new camera. Some explanations are answers to the question "Why?" and scientific explanations are frequently, if not always, of that type. For example, suppose a small plane crashed upon take-off from an airport near Denver on July 15, 1970, and we ask why the crash occurred. A satisfactory answer might point out that the plane failed to clear an obstacle 100 feet high located a certain distance from the end of the runway, and it might cite such relevant conditions as the length of the runway, the type of aircraft involved and the load it was carrying, the altitude of the airport, the air temperature, the wind velocity and direction, and the relative humidity. These specific factors would be related to the crash by general laws; e.g., that increase of altitude, air temperature, and relative humidity increase the distance needed for take-off. In offering this kind of explanation, two basic kinds of elements are involved, namely, specific conditions obtaining prior to the event to be explained (let us call them *initial conditions*) and *general laws*. The explanation consists in citing the initial conditions and the general laws, and pointing out that the occurrence of the event to be explained follows logically from those premises. An explanation of this type can be schematized as follows:

(3)   Statements of initial conditions
      Statements of general laws

      Statement that the event to be explained occurs

Such an explanation can be regarded as an argument to the effect that the event to be explained was to be expected, in the light of the initial conditions and the general laws, because its occurrence follows from them.[20]

There is a striking similarity between this characterization of explanation and Laplace's formulation of determinism. Recall that his demon requires (i) knowledge of the condition of the universe at some particular moment, i.e., initial conditions, (ii) knowledge of the laws of nature, obviously, general laws, and (iii) ability to carry out mathematical deductions, i.e., the ability to establish the validity of the argument. If determinism, as Laplace conceives it, is true, *every future event* is explainable in terms of the laws of nature and some initial conditions. If you want to explain the entire state of the universe at some future time, you would presumably have to take as initial conditions the entire state of the universe at some antecedent time, as well as all of the laws of nature. But to explain some relatively limited and isolated event, such as the plane crash, only some of the conditions obtaining before the crash would be needed (weather conditions in Hong Kong would not be relevant), and some laws of nature would probably be dispensable. In either case, whether you are trying to explain the condition of the whole universe at some time, or merely some particular event in it, both laws and initial conditions are required.

In view of the close relationship between determinism and one type of scientific explanation, it is tempting to conclude that events that are causally determined can be explained, and those that can be explained are causally determined. From this point, it is easy to take another step and say that when human actions and decisions can be explained they are determined. One more step leads to the conclusion that to explain human behavior and choices is to show that they cannot be free. To explain human behavior seems to amount to *explaining away* human responsibility! There are, however, a number of dubious steps in this inference.

Whether determinism is true or not, there are many cases in which we do not have enough facts to be able to construct an explanation which demonstrates that the event to be explained must have occurred, given the initial conditions and the laws. For example, we say that John Jones recovered from his streptococcus infection because he was given penicillin, knowing that not all, but only most, streptococcus infections respond to penicillin. We do not have any set of laws and initial conditions from which it follows that the recovery *must* occur; at best, we can show that it is highly probable. It seems there are at least two types of explanation, and they differ from one another in two fundamental ways. The first type, illustrated by the plane crash example, is known as *deductive* explanation; the second type, illustrated by the streptococcus infection example, is known as *inductive* explanation.[21] They differ in the following two ways. First, although both types require the use of general laws, deductive explanations incorporate *universal laws* which hold without exception, while inductive explanations employ *statistical laws*. For instance, the Bernoulli principle, which is fundamental to aerodynamics, states that *in all cases,* the greater the velocity of flow of a fluid (liquid or gas), the smaller is the pressure it exerts perpendicular to the direction of flow. Universal laws have the overall form, "All F are G." Statistical laws are also generalizations, but instead of saying that something happens in every case, they say that it happens in a certain percentage of cases. The percentage may be specified by a precise number, as in "51% of all babies born are male," or it may be given by a vague word, as in "Most cases of streptococcus infection clear up promptly when penicillin is administered." Second, although each type of explanation consists in an argument, the arguments are deductive (i.e., the conclusion follows with necessity from the premises) and inductive (i.e., the premises confer a high probability upon the conclusion) respectively.

If we understand that schema (3) may represent either an inductive or a deductive argument, both types of explanation conform to it. More explicitly, however, the simplest examples of the two types of explanation can be compared and contrasted via the following two schemas:

(4) All F are G.
  x is F.
  _____
  x is G.

(5) Most F are G.
  x is F.
  _____ [p]
  x is G.

In each case, the first premise is a general law (statistical laws are general in that they refer to a whole class F, but they are not universal in that they do not assert that every member of the class has the property G), the second premise gives the initial conditions, and the conclusion asserts the occurrence of the event to be explained. The single line in (4) signifies a deductive relation between premises and conclusion; the double line in (5) signifies an inductive relation, the number p at the side indicating the degree of probability of the conclusion given the premises. If the probability p attaching to the inductive inference in (5) is near enough to one, we can say that the event to be explained was to be expected in view of the explanatory facts, though it did not necessarily have to happen given these circumstances.

There are still other cases, however, in which we seem to be able to explain occurrences even though the explanatory facts do not make the event very probable—cases, in fact, in which the non-occurrence of the event is more probable than its occurrence, even in the presence of the explanatory conditions. To cite an example that has been widely discussed, if a person contracts syphilis, and it goes through the primary, secondary, and latent stages without treatment with penicillin, he may develop paresis. This is one form of tertiary syphilis, but only a small percentage of those who have untreated latent syphilis become paretic. At the same time, the only people who develop paresis are victims of syphilis. If an individual develops paresis, we offer as an explanation the fact that he had untreated latent syphilis, even though the probability of a latent untreated syphilitic becoming paretic is considerably less than one half. There are no known characteristics by means of which to predict which cases will develop paresis and which will not.[22]

It is easy to say that explanations of this sort are partial and rudimentary, due to our lack of knowledge of all of the factors surrounding syphilis and its various manifestations. Such an attitude is probably well founded. Scientific experience indicates that further investigation is likely to provide answers to the question of what makes one syphilitic develop paresis and another not. The explanation provides some understanding of what happened and why, but we have good reason to believe that further research will make possible more complete explanations. The same can be said for the streptococcus infection. Even though the explanation of the cure conferred a high probability upon it, there is good reason to suppose that eventually we will find an objective characteristic of certain streptococcus bacilli which makes them resistant to penicillin. When it has been found, we will be able to tell exactly which streptococcus infections can be successfully treated by penicillin and which cannot. When that information is available, it will be possible to give a deductive explanation of the cure of this particular infection by penicillin.

This discussion of types of explanations and how they can be supplemented has a direct bearing upon determinism. If determinism is true, then it is possible in principle to supplement any explanation that is inductive or probabilistic in such a way as to transform it into a deductive explanation. Whenever we use a statistical gener-

alization in an explanation, according to a determinist, it is because our knowledge is incomplete, not because the basic laws of nature are genuinely statistical. On the deterministic view, any reference to chance or probability is, as Laplace remarked above, merely an expression of our ignorance of the true laws of nature.

The indeterminist, by contrast, is committed to saying that there are at least some events for which it is impossible to provide deductive explanations; the best we can hope for is some kind of statistical explanation. While the indeterminist might agree that the statistical character of the laws cited in the medical examples is a reflection of the incompleteness of biological science, he might maintain that in physics there are events that are not amenable to deductive explanation. Lucretius, if he were here and could talk our jargon, might explain the spontaneous movement of an atom by saying that there are various kinds of atoms—large and small, rough and smooth—and that the small smooth ones have a certain probability of jumping even though they are not bumped by other atoms. Such characteristics are the only ones that are relevant to whether the atoms engage in spontaneous movement, so the best explanation we can give is in terms of such probabilities. If we were to tell him that there *must* be *some* reason why this small smooth atom rather than another started to move at that moment, we would merely be expressing a deterministic prejudice.

Leaving this historical fiction, we find a similar situation in modern physics. The atoms of certain elements are unstable, and they suffer radioactive decay. The uranium atom, for example, may decay by emitting an alpha-particle from its nucleus. The nucleus constitutes a strong enclosure, and the alpha-particle races frantically back and forth, bumping into the wall of the nucleus about 10^{21} ($=1,000,000,000,000,000,000,000$) times per second, and on the average an alpha-particle makes it out in about a billion years. In other words, it has about one chance in 10^{38} of getting out any time it bombards the barrier of its nuclear prison.[23] When we ask why a particular uranium atom decayed in this manner at this particular time, the answer is that an alpha-particle "tunnelled out" of its nucleus. When we ask why the alpha-particle escaped on that particular trial, having failed on countless other occasions, the answer is simply that there is a probability of about 10^{-38} of such an outcome on any given bombardment of the wall. That is all there is to it. Perhaps you want to say that there must be some reason for the success on this trial and the failures on the others, but we do not yet know what it is. According to current quantum mechanics, however, that is not the case. We are, according to that theory, dealing with an irremediably indeterministic process.

The situation in quantum mechanics arises out of what seems to be a pervasive feature of the atomic and sub-atomic world. It has been described by an unfortunate phrase, "the uncertainty principle." When one speaks of uncertainty, it is natural to suppose that there is something to be known, but we do not know it for sure. Thus, it has sometimes been said that there is an inescapable uncertainty if one attempts to ascertain the values of both the position and momentum of a particle, and similarly for energy and time. If we ascertain the position of an electron with great precision, we will be unable to ascertain its momentum very exactly, and conversely. There is a limit to the joint precision with which two so-called complementary parameters can be known. This way of speaking, as well as many popular attempts to explain the uncertainty principle, strongly suggest that the electron has, at any given moment, an exact position and an exact momentum, but we are not able to find out what both of those values are. This is a serious misinterpretation of the uncertainty principle, as many experts agree.[24] We should say instead that particles such as the electron and our alpha-particle are actually in physical states that are not characterized by exact values of position and momentum, energy and time. We *can* ascertain the state of the particle, but the state, together with all of the pertinent laws of nature, does not provide the basis for deterministic prediction or deductive explanation of such events as the alpha-particle tunnelling out of the uranium nucleus. Even Laplace's demon could not reliably predict the time at which a particular uranium atom would experience radioactive decay.

8. EXPLANATION AND RELEVANCE

If the world is actually indeterministic, in the way modern physics suggests, you might infer that some things cannot be explained. Such a conclusion would, I think, be unjustified.[25] It is true that some events could not be explained deductively, but the supposition that there is no other kind of explanation is simply another aspect of the deterministic view. If we embrace indeterminism, we must adopt a suitable conception of explanation to go along with it. For the indeterminist, some events will have to be explained statistically—I do not say "inductively," because I shall be suggesting a different sort of statistical explanation. Moreover, it looks as if we will have to come to terms with events that are extremely inprobable; 10^{-38} is a very small number. Shall we conclude that only events with high probabilities can be explained—that those with low probabilities are inexplicable? This result will be forced upon us if we think that explanations, deductive or statistical, must be *arguments* showing that the event to be explained *was to be expected*, for that requires high probability if deductive certainty is lacking. I am inclined to believe, however, that this way of characterizing statistical explanation is inappropriate. The key to an alternative approach will be the concept of *statistical relevance*.

Suppose a life insurance company is considering issuing a policy to a particular person, Frank Smith, and suppose that at the premium set, the company will make a profit if he lives for at least ten years. The company must decide whether to sell him life insurance at that rate, and so they would like to know whether he will survive for at least a decade. From mortality tables, they can find the probability that an unspecified American will live that long, but they know in addition that he is male and 37 years old. Again the mortality tables will furnish the probability of a 37-year-old American male living ten years longer. His age and sex are relevant because the probability of survival for a male is different from that for a female, and the probability certainly varies with age. In order to make the decision, the company will secure further evidence about him, e.g., his state of health, his occupation, his personal habits, his marital status, and his hobbies. We know, for example, that the probability of survival is different for heavy cigarette smokers than for non-smokers, different for diabetics than for people in normal health, different for steeplejacks than for clergymen, and different for married men than for bachelors. Any specification of characteristics of Frank Smith that alters the probability of his living to the age of 47 *is statistically relevant* to the case at hand. Characteristics that do not change the probability are irrelevant. Examples of irrelevant characteristics would be the color of his eyes (but not of his skin), whether his social security number is odd or even, and whether his first child is a boy or a girl.

The insurance company would like to know whether Frank Smith will live another ten years, and whether or not Laplace's demon could predict that fact with certainty, the insurance company cannot. Hence, they must be content with probabilities, and indeed, that is the entire basis of their business. In making decisions as to who to insure, they try to take into consideration the statistically relevant factors, and they try to avoid getting involved with irrelevant ones.

The same considerations, I believe, enter into statistical explanation. When we ask why John Jones' streptococcus infection cleared up quickly, we mention the fact that he was given penicillin, for that is a highly relevant fact. The probability of a streptococcus infection going away promptly is quite different, depending upon whether the patient received penicillin or not. When we ask for an explanation of the fact that John Doe contracted paresis, the fact that he had latent untreated syphilis is cited, for the probability of anyone developing paresis is very different, depending upon whether he ever arrives at the condition of untreated latent syphilis. If we find such explanations incomplete, it is because we reasonably believe that there are additional relevant factors, as yet unknown, that have a bearing upon the probability of recovery from streptococcus infection, or the occurrence of paresis.

Now it might occur to you that an incredible variety of factors could be relevant to, say, the contraction of paresis. Whether John Doe's parents are of Latin or Anglo-Saxon extraction might have some bearing upon his attitudes toward sex, and hence, upon the likelihood of his contracting syphilis, and finally upon the chance of his becoming paretic. His socio-economic status might also be relevant in a number of ways, including the probability of his seeking medical treatment should the symptoms of a venereal disease appear. Nevertheless, although such factors may be indirectly relevant in the absence of more detailed information about his medical condition, they become irrelevant in the light of further information. Once it is known that the victim has contracted syphilis, the probability of his picking up a venereal disease is irrelevant. Once it is known that he has arrived at the stage of latent untreated syphilis, the likelihood of his seeking medical treatment in the early stages of the disease is irrelevant. The more immediate conditions, so to speak, screen off the relevance of the more remote ones.[26]

The determinist and the indeterminist alike, in attempting to explain an event, are trying to assemble a *total set of relevant conditions*. By a total set of relevant conditions, I mean a set of conditions that cannot be supplemented in any way that would change the probability of the given outcome. This aim is achieved more readily than you might offhand suppose. If you have a universal law of the form, "All F are G"—for example, all copper conducts electricity—then the probability of a piece of copper being an electric conductor is one, and nothing can be added to change that. If you add that the piece of copper was formed into a penny, the probability of its conductivity is still one. If you add that it was originally mined in northern Michigan, the probability of conductivity is still one. Unless the general statement was false in the first place (in which case it did not express a genuine law), what is true of all copper is true of any specific type of copper: We have, indeed, found a total set of conditions relevant to conductivity. Similar considerations apply to negative universal generalizations such as "No whales are fish," the probability in such cases being zero instead of one.

The determinist is very happy with the total sets of relevant conditions that are embodied in universal laws, for these are just the kinds of laws he wants for his deductive explanations. When the laws are statistical, he feels, the explanations are incomplete because there are further relevant conditions to be found. He maintains, in other words, that the only way to achieve a total set of relevant conditions is to find universal laws. The indeterminist takes a different view. He maintains that there are other ways of arriving at total sets of relevant conditions. When asked why an atom experienced spontaneous radioactive decay, he might answer that it is an atom of uranium 238, and that it has a half-life of about eight billion years (which is a convenient way of expressing its probability of disintegration). To say merely that it is a uranium atom would not be sufficient, for the different isotopes of uranium have different half-lives, but once the isotope has been specified, nothing further is relevant. It does not matter whether the atom is in a block of pure metallic uranium 238, whether it is alloyed with other uranium isotopes or other metallic elements, whether it is in chemical compound with other elements (e.g., an oxide), whether it is in a magnetic field, or whether it has been blessed by the Pope. In such cases, according to the indeterminist, there is a certain probability of spontaneous decay, and nothing we can add has any bearing upon that probability. If the determinist says that there must be some further relevant factor that has not yet been found, the indeterminist could appropriately reply, "Perhaps it would be nice if there were, but what guarantee have we that nature is so accommodating to our wishes?"

If indeterminism is true, it does not follow that there are events that are incapable of being explained. To offer an explanation, as I have suggested, is to assemble a total set of relevant conditions for the event to be explained, and to cite the probability of that event in the presence of these conditions. This view of explanation, unlike the standard account of deductive and inductive explanation, does not view an explanation as an argument showing that the event was to be expected on the basis of the explanatory facts. The explanation is, rather, a presentation of the conditions relevant to the occurrence of the event, and a statement of the degree of probability of the event given these conditions. That degree of probability may be high, middling, or low, but whatever its size, it is an index of the degree to which we would have been justified in expecting it.

A point of clarification must be added lest complete misunderstanding arise. The general laws, be they universal or statistical, that provide the relevant conditions, may themselves be explained on a different level, so to speak. If we invoke the general law that all copper conducts electricity, this provides a total set of conditions relevant to the fact that a particular piece of copper, such as a penny placed behind a blown fuse, conducts electricity. However, that does not exclude the

possibility of explaining electrical conductivity itself in terms of the behavior of electrons. The fact that such further explanation is possible does not mean that the original explanation of the conductivity of the penny was incomplete; it only means that facts adduced to explain other facts may in turn be explained on a more general or theoretical level.[27]

9. CAUSES VS. STATISTICAL CORRELATIONS

In recent years, evidence of a significant statistical correlation between cigarette smoking and various diseases has been widely publicized. The tobacco industry, in its frequent protest that "no causal connection" has been found, has emphatically reiterated the distinction between causal connection and "mere statistical correlation." While I believe that the statements on behalf of the cigarette manufacturers are wrong, and that extremely strong evidence of a causal connection between cigarette smoking and disease has been presented, that is not the major point here. We are interested in determinism and in explanation, and each of these concepts seems to have a deep causal component. When we think of determinism we think of causal determination, and when we ask "why," the natural answer is "because ...." To ask why the airplane crashed is to ask what caused the crash.

A persistent statistical correlation—that is, a genuine statistical relevance relation—is strongly indicative of a causal relation of some sort. Consider some examples. Both fever and characteristic types of spots are symptoms of measles. The fever does not cause the spots and the spots do not cause the fever, yet there is a marked statistical relevance of the one to the other. The reason, of course, is that they are distinct effects of a common cause, and the common cause explains the statistical relation. In similar fashion, there is a high degree of statistical relevance between the drop in barometer reading and the occurrence of a storm, but neither causes the other. Both the storm and the falling barometer are the result of meteorological conditions that barometers are designed to indicate. The main danger in confusing statistical correlation with genuine causation is the danger of confusing symptoms with causes. In medicine, engineering, social work, politics and other practical pursuits, we know the futility of treating the symptoms when we want to correct the conditions giving rise to them.

In discussing the search for total sets of relevant conditions, I mentioned the fact that some relevant conditions can render others irrelevant by what is called "screening off." The screening off phenomenon is basically a matter of causal proximity. The measles infection is more closely related to both the fever and the spots than are the spots and fever to each other. The barometer reading is more remote from the storm than is the set of atmospheric conditions responsible for the storm. Primary syphilis is causally more remote from paresis than is secondary or latent syphilis.

What do these causal relations amount to? It seems that the world is full of processes that go on in a relatively continuous way. Billiard balls roll around on tables, bouncing off the cushions and colliding with one another, according to the laws of classical mechanics. Light rays are propagated in accordance with the laws of optics. Springs can be extended and contracted as described by Hooke's law. When the temperature of a gas is increased, without changing the size of the container, the pressure increases. These are processes that are governed by universal laws of the kind found in classical physics and used in deductive explanations.[28] If everything that happens in the world follows from antecedent conditions by processes that conform to such laws, we say that the universe is *causally* deterministic. In this case, we could say with Laplace, "We ought then to regard the present state of the universe as the effect of its anterior state and as the cause of the one which is to follow.[29] If, however, the causal processes are governed by laws that have an irreducibly statistical character, such as we find in contemporary quantum mechanics, then the world is causally indeterministic. It would be a mistake to suppose, however, that there are real connections among events over and above the perfect or imperfect correlations that are embodied in the laws of nature. David Hume's discussion of this point in *An Enquiry Concerning Human Understanding*[30] is a philosophic classic.[31]

10. FREE WILL AND INDETERMINISM

Suppose indeterminism, of the sort suggested by modern quantum mechanics, is true. No one knows for sure whether it is, but it might be, and it is interesting to see what bearing that would have on the problem of human free will.

There is good evidence that radiation of the sort emitted in radioactive decay of unstable nuclei can have profound effects upon genetic structure and can induce mutations. Suppose that the father of a child was in the vicinity of radioactive materials just prior to its conception, and that a chance disintegration of an unstable atom emitted a gamma-ray which altered a gene that was passed on to the child. Suppose, to make the case dramatic, that the genetic damage of the gamma-ray results in the child becoming a congenital criminal, although he would have developed normal character and personality if that atom had not disintegrated just when it did. Would we be inclined to say that this person's criminal acts are done freely, because of the chance occurrence in his heredity, while his non-criminal acts would have been unfree if chance were unable to influence his genetic make-up? Hardly.

But, you might say, the indeterministic event was not part of him. It happened before he was conceived, it came from outside him and his father, and its results were passed onto him (suppose) in a fully deterministic manner. Very well. Suppose a person eats some food which, unknown to him, is contaminated with radioactive material. One of these unstable atoms decays, indeterministically, at a vital place in his body; as a result he contracts cancer. Is there any element of freedom introduced because the chance event took place inside of his body? Hardly.

But, you might continue, the onset of cancer does not involve any element of thought, deliberation, decision, or choice, and these are vitally involved in freedom. That seems to be a sound point. Suppose, therefore, that you are trying to make up your mind about experimenting with marijuana. If determinism were true, your heredity, your environment, and the physiological processes in your nervous system would totally determine the outcome of your deliberation. If you decided to go ahead and try it, the decision would be a causally determined result of the chemistry of your brain at that moment. Under these circumstances, you might seriously doubt that the choice is free. Suppose, however, that determinism is not true. At the crucial point in your brain is an unstable atom. Its relation to the decision process is something like a trigger mechanism. If that atom disintegrates at the proper moment, it will start a process that will lead causally to the decision to smoke pot. If it does not disintegrate, you will decide against it. Does the decision now seem free? Hardly.

These science fiction speculations are designed for one purpose: to raise the question of whether the problem of free will is really connected with determinism in the way it seems to be. Having seen that determinism seems to raise very serious difficulties in connection with freedom of choice and action, we are tempted to jump unreflectively to the conclusion that all will be rosy if we just abandon determinism. When we go on to postulate indeterminism, however, the net result seems to be absolutely no progress at all in the direction of free will. The problem is just as difficult and puzzling—if not more so—under the assumption of indeterminism than it was in the context of determinism. It appears that we can construct the following argument:

(6) If indeterminism is true, man does not have free will.
     Indeterminism is true.
     _____
     Man does not have free will.

We do not know for sure whether the second premise of this argument is true, but modern quantum mechanics makes it at least plausible. That, however, is not the crucial point. Argument (6) can be combined with argument (2) as follows:

(7) If determinism is true, man does not have free will.
     If indeterminism is true, man does not have free will.
     Either determinism is true or indeterminism is true.
     _____
     Man does not have free will.

This argument is a dilemma, and it is logically valid.[32] Moreover, its third premise is necessarily true, for indeterminism holds if determinism does not, and conversely. There are two avenues to follow from here. One can accept all three premises and draw the conclusion that freedom of will, freedom of decision, freedom of choice,

and freedom of action are all illusory. The other avenue, and by far the most promising one, I believe, is to reexamine the first premise of arguments (1) and (2), which is the same as the first premise of (7). This premise, which was accepted so facilely at the beginning, has taken us down the long path to argument (7), which might aptly be called "the dilemma of free will." Perhaps the premise is not as self-evident as it appeared at the outset. It may turn out that the question of whether the breaking of the vase by Epictetus was causally determined is far less important than the question of how many vases he, and other slaves, broke after his beating. Legend does not, as far as I know, provide a clear answer to this latter question.[33]

NOTES

1. From the play "Sheppey," by W. Somerset Maugham (copyright, 1933, by W. Somerset Maugham), published in 1933 by William Heinemann, London, and in 1934 by Doubleday and Company, Inc. Reprinted by permission of A. P. Watt & Son, as literary agents to the late Mr. Maugham and on behalf of Messrs. William Heinemann, Ltd.

2. Lucretius, *The Nature of the Universe,* trans. by R. E. Latham (Baltimore: Penguin Books, 1951).

3. Sir Isaac Newton, *Philosophiae Naturalis Principia Mathematica (Mathematical Principles of Natural Philosophy).*

4. The so-called "torsion-balance experiment," first performed by Henry Cavendish in 1798. All previous confirmations of Newton's gravitational theory involved either one or two bodies of astronomic proportions: the influence of the earth on falling bodies, the mutual attraction between the sun and the planets, the influence of the moon on the tides. The Cavendish experiment detected the gravitational attraction between two ordinary medium-size terrestrial objects.

5. The explanation of the "perturbations of Uranus" by the planet Neptune was accomplished in 1843 by John C. Adams, and independently about two years later by U. J. J. Leverrier. Neptune was observed and identified as a planet by J. G. Galle in 1846. In similar fashion, Pluto was discovered in 1930. Leverrier also determined that there was a small deviation in the path of Mercury, and he postulated a planet Vulcan to explain it, but Vulcan was never found. The deviation received a more satisfactory explanation in Einstein's general theory of relativity, but even this explanation is challenged by some contemporary physicists, most notably, R. H. Dicke of Princeton University.

6. Pierre Simon, Marquis de Laplace, *A Philosophical Essay on Probabilities,* trans. by Frederick Wilson Truscott and Frederick Lincoln Emery (New York: Dover Publications, Inc., 1951), p. 3.

7. René Descartes, *Meditations.* In saying that his arguments were persuasive, I do not mean to ignore the severe difficulty of the problem of interaction between mind and matter to which his mind-body dualism led. This problem becomes even more acute if one admits that there is a great deal of interaction between mind and matter, and simulta-

neously wants to claim determinism for the physical realm and indeterminism for the psychological realm.

8. Darwin published *The Origin of Species* in 1859 and *The Descent of Man* in 1871.

9. The synthesis of urea was accomplished by Friedrich Wöhler in 1828.

10. See especially Freud's *Psychopathology of Everyday Life* and *The Interpretation of Dreams*, both published in *The Basic Writings of Sigmund Freud*, ed. by A. A. Brill (New York: Random House, 1938). Although Freud lived and worked well into the twentieth century, many of the most significant ideas were developed before the turn of the century.

11. Isaac Asimov, *The Genetic Code* (New York: New American Library, Signet Science Books, 1962), provides an accurate and readable popular account of the most important developments in molecular biology; James Watson, *The Double Helix* (New York: Atheneum Publishers, 1968; reprinted as a Signet paperback by the New American Library), is a fascinating biographical account of the discovery of the structure of the DNA molecule by one of its co-discoverers.

12. For a collection of articles from the *Scientific American* discussing recent developments in this area, see McGaugh, Weinberger, and Whalen, eds., *Psychobiology: The Biological Bases of Behavior* (San Francisco: W. H. Freeman & Co., 1967). See also, Dean Wooldridge, *The Machinery of the Brain* (New York: McGraw-Hill Book Co., 1963).

13. A. d'Abro, *The Evolution of Scientific Thought* (New York: Dover Publications, Inc., 1950), provides an excellent non-technical account of the development of relativity theory.

14. A. d'Abro, *The Rise of the New Physics* (New York: Dover Publications, Inc., 1951), provides an excellent non-technical account of the development of quantum theory.

15. This is the famous Stern-Gerlach experiment, and it has considerable fundamental importance in quantum theory. See d'Abro, *The Rise of the New Physics*, pp. 599–601.

16. The proof is due to John von Neumann, and is given in his treatise *Mathematical Foundations of Quantum Theory* (Princeton: Princeton University Press, 1955). The significance of this proof is, however, a matter for serious dispute among able physicists.

17. Laplace, *op. cit.*, p. 4.

18. These formulations are due to G. W. Leibniz and Immanuel Kant, respectively.

19. For discussions of some of the complexities involved in the issue of teleology, see *Purpose in Nature*, ed. by John V. Canfield (Englewood Cliffs, N.J.: Prentice-Hall, Inc., 1966). Also, see the discussion by John Hospers in this anthology (p. 000) of the view that only teleological explanations are genuine explanations.

20. This view of explanation is presented and discussed very clearly by Hospers in this anthology.

21. Carl G. Hempel in *Aspects of Scientific Explanation* (New York: The Free Press, 1965) has given the clearest and most exhaustive technical discussion of these two types of explanation (which he calls "deductive-nomological" and "inductive-statistical" respectively). He also provided this example of inductive explanation.

22. "... 72 out of 100 untreated persons [with latent syphilis] go through life without the symptoms of late [tertiary] syphilis, but 28 out of 100 untreated persons were known to have developed serious outcomes [paresis and others] and there is no way to predict what will happen to an untreated infected person." Edwin Gurney Clark, M.D., and William O. Mortimer Harris, M.D., "Venereal Diseases," *Encyclopaedia Britannica*, 1961, Vol. XXIII, p. 44.

23. See George Gamow, *The Atom and its Nucleus* (Englewood Cliffs, N.J.: Prentice-Hall, Inc., 1961), pp. 111–115. Gamow was responsible for the theoretical explanation of this phenomenon in 1928.

24. See Adolf Grünbaum, "Complementarity in Quantum Physics and its Philosophical Generalization," *Journal of Philosophy*, LIV (1957), pp. 713–727, for an extremely clear discussion of this issue.

25. I have offered a detailed and technical account of explanation in *"Statistical Explanation and Statistical Relevance"* (Pittsburgh: University of Pittsburgh Press, 1971). The present discussion of explanation and relevance is a highly oversimplified version.

26. This concept of *screening off* is of crucial importance in the discussion of explanation and statistical relevance; it is discussed at length in the book cited in the preceding note.

27. See Hospers' article above for a clear exposition of this point.

28. There is an exceedingly difficult problem, to which no satisfactory answer has yet been given, as to how causal laws are to be distinguished from other universal or statistical generalizations. The book cited in note 25 goes into some details of this problem.

29. Laplace, *op. cit.*, p. 4.

30. [See p. 166 in this anthology.]

31. See the discussion of Hume's view in my article, "An Encounter with David Hume," p. 190 in this anthology.

32. This type of argument is discussed in my *Logic* in *Foundations of Philosophy Series* (Englewood Cliffs, N.J.: Prentice-Hall, Inc., 1963; 2nd ed., 1973), §9.

33. To my mind, the best approach to the problem of the relation of free will to determinism is given by Charles Stevenson, "Ethical Judgments and Avoidability," reprinted in this anthology.

R. S. PETERS

Types Of Explanation In Psychological Theories*

TYPES OF QUESTIONS ABOUT HUMAN BEHAVIOR

(A) *'His reason' explanations.* The over-riding aim of a scientist should be explanation. This sounds rather obvious, but it has many important consequences in relation to psychological theorizing. For the general question 'Why did Jones do that?' is capable of being asked and answered in a variety of different ways. The particular formula employed in asking the question usually dictates the sort of answer which is expected and which counts as an explanation.[1] The paradigm case of a human action is when something is done in order to bring about an end. So the usual way of explaining an action is to describe it as an action of a certain sort by indicating the end which Jones had in mind. We therefore ask the 'why' question in a more specific form. We ask what was his *reason* for doing that or what was the *point* of it, what *end* he had in mind. If we ask why Jones walked across the road, the obvious answer will be something like 'To buy tobacco.' Instead of saying this we could say 'because he wanted some tobacco'. This is, logically speaking, another way of giving the same sort of answer; for the answer 'to buy some tobacco' is only an explanation because we assume in Jones some sort of directive disposition—a general tendency to obtain and use tobacco.

Even in this very simple sort of explanation in terms of a man's reason for doing something there are, as a matter of fact, concealed assumptions. We assume, for instance, that walking across the street is an efficient way of getting to the tobacconist. This counts as an explanation not simply because Jones envisaged walking across the street as a means to getting the tobacco but because it really is a means to getting it. We assume, too, that a man who has this information will act on it if he wants some tobacco. We assume that men are rational in that they will take means which lead to ends if they have the information and want the ends. 'His reason' is an explanation in terms of what Popper (1945) calls 'the logic of the situation'.

But it is not only norms of efficiency and consistency that are implicit in the concept of 'his reason'. There are also norms or standards of social appropriateness. After all Jones might have crawled or run across the road. But 'to get some tobacco' would be a very odd answer to the question 'Why did Jones *run* across the road?' Yet running would be quite an efficient way of getting across the road. It would, however, be socially odd as a way of crossing the road to get some tobacco. *Man is a rule-following animal.* His actions are not simply directed towards ends; they also conform to social standards and conventions, and unlike a calculating machine he acts because of his knowledge of rules and objectives. For instance, we ascribe to people *traits* of character like honesty, punctuality, considerateness

*From R. S. Peters, *The Concept of Motivation* (London: Routledge & Kegan Paul; New York: Humanities Press, 1958), pp. 3–16. Reprinted by permission of the author.

and meanness. Such terms do not, like ambition or hunger or sexual desire, indicate the sorts of goals that a man tends to pursue; rather they indicate the type of regulation that he imposes on his conduct whatever his goals may be. A man who is ruthless, selfish, punctual, considerate, persistent, and honest, does not have any particular goals; rather he pursues whatever goals he has in particular sorts of ways.

This simple purposive model of a man taking means to bring about an end is further complicated by the fact that norms enter into and often entirely define the end. Ends like passing an examination, getting married, becoming a professor, and reading a paper, explain quite adequately a great deal of the goings on in the precincts of a university; yet they are defined almost entirely by social convention. It is a gross over-simplification to think of ends merely as terminating points of activity. Actually even a rat, after eating or achieving some other end, will continue being active in a variety of ways—sniffing, preening, and so on. If eating can be regarded as an end this is not because it is a definite terminating point of activity but because activity *previous* to it varies concomitantly with changes in the conditions necessary to define it as an end. The concept of means is just as necessary to bring out what is meant by an end as the concept of end is to bring out what is meant by a means. Ends are not given as natural terminating points like a chain of oases distributed across a desert. And, to a large extent, what counts as falling within a means-to-end explanatory framework is determined by convention. Even those ends, like eating and sexual intercourse, which are universal and which have an obvious biological basis, can scarcely be specified without recourse to norms. For there are countless ways of performing the acts which can be regarded as ends and in every culture a few particular ways are stamped with the hallmark of conventionality. Eating is not just getting food into the stomach. Jones' movements across the road are classifiable as means to the end of buying tobacco because of a vast system of norms defining 'buying tobacco' as an end as well as a system of norms regulating what is an efficient and socially appropriate way of attaining it.

My reasons for stressing this rule-following purposive pattern into which we fit our common-sense explanations are twofold. In the first place

I want to insist that most of our explanations are couched in terms of this model and our predictions of people's behaviour presuppose it. We know what the parson will do when he begins to walk towards the pulpit because we know the conventions regulating church services. And we can make such predictions without knowing anything about the *causes* of people's behaviour unless we include under 'causes' things like the parson's training and grasp of the rules, which are things of a different order from 'causes' in the sense of antecedent movements. Man in society is like a chess-player writ large. Requests for explanation are usually reflections of our ignorance about the particular rule or goal which is relevant to the behaviour in question. We usually know the general pattern but are unsure which part of it is relevant. Sometimes, of course, we are in the position of a free-thinker at a Roman Catholic mass. The question 'Why did X do that?' is then usually a request for an elucidation of the whole pattern of conventions. In explaining human actions we, like anthropologists, must all, in the first place be structuralists. Indeed I would go so far as to say that anthropology or sociology must be the basic sciences of human action in that they exhibit the systematic framework of norms and goals which are necessary to classify actions as being of a certain sort. They both—like classical economics—presuppose the purposive, rule-following model; in this respect they are quite unlike sciences which imply a mechanical model of explanation.

In the second place this rule-following purposive pattern of explanation must be sketched in some detail because a proper understanding of what is meant by a human action has very important logical consequences. It shows, for instance, as I shall argue, that human actions cannot be sufficiently explained in terms of causal concepts like 'colourless movements'. Indeed to claim that we are confronted with an action is *ipso facto* to rule out such mechanical explanations, as being sufficient.

(B) *'The reason' explanations.* But, of course, as psychologists will be the first to point out, people often invent reasons for doing things or delude themselves into thinking that the reasons they offer for their actions are operative reasons. We therefore often say of a man that *his* reason may have been x but *the* reason why he acted like that was y. For instance we might say that Jones said that he crossed the road in order to buy some tobacco but the reason why he did it was not really his desire for tobacco; it was sex. There was a pretty girl looking in the window of the tobacconist. This explanation may of course be erroneous. For instance a psychologist once told me that I delayed crossing the road to College because of an aversion to getting down to work. I replied, and I think more convincingly, that I stayed on the other side in order to look at the row of glistening cars drawn up opposite. But whether the explanation in question is correct or incorrect does not much matter; the point is that to speak of *the* reason why a person does something is different in that it is a way of calling attention to the law or assumed law that a given case actually falls under. *His* reason may coincide with *the* reason. *The* reason why Jones crossed the road might in fact be his desire for tobacco. He might also be aware that he wanted to inspect the girl at close quarters, but was concealing this by the camouflage of buying tobacco. This would then be his *real* reason. But whereas *his* reason —whether real or not—entails that a man is conscious of his objective, the reason why he did it does not.[2] *The* reason why he did it might well be sex or aversion to work; yet the individual might be quite unaware of pursuing or avoiding the relevant goals. And whereas to say that *he* had a reason for doing something is more or less to rule out a causal explanation, to give *the* reason why he did it is sometimes to subsume it under a law-like proposition of a causal kind. This is not necessarily so. For we can say that sex or aversion to work was *the* reason why he did it and simply be insisting that a different directive disposition is being exercised. But *the* reason why he did it might also be that he was pushed or assailed by an attack of giddiness. These would be causal explanations which would rebut the suggestion that he had a reason for crossing the road. Causal explanations, in other words, can count as *the* reason why a person does something; but they are only one type of answer to the question 'What was *the* reason why he did it?'

(C) *Causal explanations.* There are, however, other questions about particular goings on—I omit to say actions on purpose—to which answers in causal terms are appropriate. Instead of the omnibus question 'Why did Jones do that?' we often ask what made, drove, or possessed him to do it. These are usually cases of lapses from action or failure to act—when there is some kind of *deviation* from the purposive rule-following model, when people, as it were, get it wrong. This may be in respect of an efficiency norm—for example, when a person refuses to take the only quick route to his destination by underground train, or when he can't remember a well-known name when he is performing an introduction. Or the behaviour may go wrong in respect of a norm governing social appropriateness—as with a business man who runs to work when he is not late or a tutor who crawls round the room sniffing while listening to an undergraduate essay. Or behaviour may go wrong by being deflected towards a peculiar goal as with a married man who suddenly makes an advance to a choir boy. In such cases it is as if the man suffers something rather than does something. It is because things seem to be happening to him that it is appropriate to ask what made, drove, or possessed him to do that. The appropriate answer in such cases may be in terms of a causal theory.

These cases of particular goings on which look like breakdowns of action are very similar to a whole class of general activities which seem to have no point or a very odd point—dreams, hallucinations, obsessions, anxieties and perversions. In such cases the Greeks suggested that the gods intervene and take possession of the individual's mind. Very often recourse is made to crude physiological explanations. It was not till the advent of Freud that any systematic explanation of such goings-on was offered in psychological terms. Indeed Freud claimed in 1913 that the main contribution of psycho-analysis to general psychology was to link together and to give psychological explanations for happenings which had previously been left to physiology or to folk-lore. Many have claimed that Freud, by reclaiming these phenomena for psychology, was in fact extending the model of purposive rule-following behaviour to cover the unconscious. He showed, it is argued, that we have reasons for acts which were previously only explained in terms of causes. I shall argue later that this thesis is mistaken. Freud showed, perhaps, that the concept of 'wish' has a wider application than was previously thought. But his account of the working of the primary processes creaks with causality. In maintaining that in the unconscious there is no sense of causal or logical connexion he was *ipso facto* denying that the model of 'his reason', implying norms of efficiency and social appropriateness, was relevant. Freud, I shall argue, provides the classic case of giving quasi-causal explanations where causal explanations seem *prima facie* appropriate.

I shall also argue that Freud in fact only intended to explain by reference to unconscious mental processes cases where the purposive rule-following model breaks down or is inappropriate. He did not think—and often explicitly denied—that this sort of explanation can be appropriately given for everything—for cases where a man acts as well as for cases where something happens to a man. In this respect Freud was, from the point of view of my argument, on the side of the angels. For my case is not simply that causal explanations are otiose when we know the point of a person's action in that, life being short and time limited, we no longer feel inclined to ask 'why' once we have accommodated a piece of behaviour within the rule-following purposive model. It is also that if we are in fact confronted with a case of a genuine action (i.e. an act of doing something as opposed to suffering something), then causal explanations are *ipso facto* inappropriate as sufficient explanations. Indeed they may rule out rule-following purposive explanations. To ask what made Jones do something is at least to suggest that he had no good reason for doing it. Similarly to ascribe a point to his action is *ipso facto* to deny that it can be *sufficiently explained* in terms of causes, though, of course, there will be many causes in the sense of *necessary* conditions. A story can always be told about the underlying mechanisms; but this does not add up to a sufficient explanation, if it is an action that has to be explained.

To give a causal *explanation* of an event involves at least showing that other conditions being presumed unchanged a change in one variable is a *sufficient* condition for a change in another. In the mechanical conception of 'cause' it is also demanded that there should be spatial and temporal contiguity between the movements involved. Now the trouble about giving this sort of explanation of human actions is that we can never specify an action exhaustively in terms of movements of the body or within the body. It is therefore impossible to state sufficient conditions in terms of antecedent movements which may vary concomitantly with subsequent movements. 'Signing a contract', for instance, is a typical example of a human action. The movements involved are grouped together because they are seen by the agent to be efficient and appropriate means to an end. But it would be impossible to stipulate exhaustively what the movements *must* be. For if this is a case of a human action the agent must be presumed to be intelligent and he will, accordingly, vary his movements in a great variety of ways. He may hold the pen slightly differently, vary the size of his writing according to the space available, and so on, depending on the sort of ink, paper, and pen available. But provided that he produces a signature which confirms to rough and ready criteria—e.g., it must not be typed—more or less *any* movements will do. I suppose he could sign a contract by holding the pen between his toes. A very general range of movements could perhaps be specified, but no specific movements of the muscles, limbs, or nervous system, which *must* occur before it would be conceded that a contract had been signed. This is tantamount to saying that the concept of an action is inseparable from that of intelligence; for part of what we mean by 'intelligence' is the ability to vary movements relative to a goal in a way which is appropriate to changes in the situation necessary to define it as a goal and in the conditions relevant to attaining it. So we could never give a sufficient explanation of an action in causal terms because we could never stipulate the movements which would have to count as dependent variables. A precise functional relationship could never be established. Of course, just as we could stipulate a general range of movements necessary to define signing a contract, so also we could lay down certain very general necessary conditions. We could, for instance, say that a man could not sign a contract unless he had a brain and nervous system. Such physiological knowledge *might* enable us to predict *bodily movements*. And *if* we had bridging laws to correlate such physiological findings with descriptions of actions we might *indirectly predict* actions. But we would *first* have to grasp concepts connected with action like 'knowing what we are doing' and 'grasp of means to an end'. As such concepts have no application at the level of mere movement, such predictions would not count as sufficient *explanations of actions.*

Furthermore, as I have already argued, general standards or rules are implicit in the concept of an action. We can therefore say that a man is doing something efficiently, correctly, and so on, if he knowingly varies what he does in accordance with changes in the situation conventionally singled out as the goal and the conditions perceived as relevant to attaining it. It only makes sense to talk of actions in this way, not of cases where something happens to a man. A man's action may break down because of a causal condition like a lesion in his brain. But all that can be said of such causal conditions is that they just occur. Movements *qua* movements are neither intelligent, efficient, nor correct. They only become so in the context of an action. There cannot therefore be a sufficient explanation of actions in causal terms because, as Popper has put it, there is a logical gulf between nature and convention. Statements implying norms and standards cannot be deduced from statements about mere movements which have no such normative implications. The contention that man is a rule-following animal must, if taken seriously, entail that the transition from nature to convention occurs whenever we try to give a sufficient explanation of human actions in causal terms. There is, however, no objection to such explanations of what *happens* to a man; for happenings cannot be characterized as intelligent or unintelligent, correct or incorrect, efficient or inefficient. *Prima facie* they are just occurrences. Perhaps Freud showed that some lapses and breakdowns may not be *just* occurrences. But this is another story. The point is that there is a *prima facie* case for treating them as such.

To make explicit the implications of my thesis for psychological theories: If the question is 'Why did Jones walk across the road?' a *sufficient* explanation can only be given in terms of the rule-following purposive model—if this is a case of an action rather than of something happening to him. Answers in terms of causal concepts like 'receptor impulses' and 'colourless movement', are either not explanations because they state not sufficient but only necessary conditions, or they

are ways of denying that what has to be explained is a human action. If we ask 'Why did Jones *jump* while he was crossing the road?' it might be appropriate to say 'because of a twinge in his stomach' or 'because a car back-fired'. The stimulus-response sort of model would perhaps be appropriate and the causal type of explanation in terms of internal or external stimulation might be sufficient because the assumption might be that Jones was suffering something rather than performing an action. This sort of jump would then be quite different from the jump he might perform while competing in an athletic contest.

This is not to deny that causal explanations are *relevant* to human actions. It is only to deny that they are sufficient explanations of them. Causal theories have at least three jobs to do in this context. Firstly they can state *necessary* conditions for human actions to occur. Hebb's physiological speculations, for instance, might well provide a sketch of a typical class of necessary conditions. But this does not mean that such speculations *explain* human actions. Secondly, as a corollary, they could show that some individual differences in performance are dependent on slight differences in such necessary conditions. Hebb's hypothesis of the relationship between the size of the association areas of the brain and the possibility of late learning would be such a hypothesis. Thirdly such theories could be used to give *sufficient* conditions for breakdowns in performance, as in the case of brain lesions, by indicating a necessary condition which was absent. Alternatively lapses and breakdowns could be explained by the postulation of special disrupting conditions—e.g. Freud's theory of the unconscious wish. . . .

NOTES

1. I am indebted to J. O. Urmson for some of these distinctions.

2. Hamlyn has pointed out to me the use of "the reason for his action" as well as "the reason why he did it." "The reason for" seems to be similar to "his reason" but to imply a coincidence between "his reason" and "the reason why he did it." I am not here concerned with the use of "reason" in the context of *justification* as when we say that a reason for giving up smoking is that it causes lung cancer. "His reason" and "the reason for" can be used in contexts both of justification and of explanation. Needless to say "the reason why he did it" is reserved for contexts of explanation with which I am here concerned.

Determinism, Freedom, and Libertarianism

RODERICK M. CHISHOLM

Responsibility and Avoidability*

Edwards and Hospers† hold that this is an important sense in which we may be said *not* to be morally responsible for any of our acts or choices. I propose the following as an explicit formulation of their reasoning:

1. If a choice is one we could not have avoided making, then it is one for which we are not morally responsibile.

2. If we make a choice under conditions such that, given those conditions, it is (casually but not logically) impossible for the choice not to be made, then the choice is one we could not have avoided making.

3. Every event occurs under conditions such that, given those conditions, it is (casually but not logically) impossible for that event not to occur.

4. The making of a choice is the occurrence of an event.

5. We are not morally responsible for any of our choices.

If we wish to reject the conclusion (5)—and for most of us (5) is difficult to accept—we must reject at least one of the premises.

*From *Determinism and Freedom in the Age of Modern Science,* ed. Sidney Hook (New York: New York University Press, 1960), pp. 145–147. Reprinted by permission of the author and publisher.
†[Paul Edwards and John Hospers each wrote articles included in the same volume as that in which this article appeared.]

Premise (1), I think, may be interpreted as a logical truth. If a man is responsible for what he did, then we may say, "He *could* have done otherwise." And if we may say "He couldn't help it," then he is not responsible for what he did.

Many philosophers would deny (2), substituting a weaker account of *avoidability.* A choice is avoidable, they might say, provided only it is such that, *if* the agent had reflected further, or had reflected on certain things on which in fact he did not reflect, he would *not* have made the choice. To say of a choice that it "could *not* have been avoided," in accordance with this account, would be to say that, even if the agent *had* reflected further, on anything you like, he would all the same have made the choice. But such conditional accounts of *avoidability* ("An act or choice is avoidable provided only it is such that, *if* the agent were to do so-and-so, the act or choice would not occur") usually have this serious defect: the antecedent clause ("if the agent were to do so-and-so") refers to some act or choice, or to the failure to perform some act or to make some choice; hence we may ask, concerning the occurrence or non-occurrence of this act or choice, whether or not *it* is avoidable. Thus one who accepted (5) could say that, if the agent's failure to reflect further was itself unavoidable, his choice was also unavoidable. And no such conditional account of *avoidability* seems adequate to the use of "avoidable" and "unavoidable" in questions and statements such as these.

If we accept a conditional account of avoidability, we may be tempted to say, of course, that it would be a *misuse* of "avoidable" to ask whether the non-occurrence of the antecedent event ("the agent does so-and-so") is avoidable. But the philosopher who accepts (5) may well insist that, since the antecedent clause refers to an act or a choice, the use of "avoidable" in question is *not* a misuse.

What, then, if we were to deny (3)? Suppose that some of our choices do not satisfy (3)—that when they are made they are *not* made under any conditions such that it is (causally) impossible (though logically possible) for them not to be made. If there are choices of this sort, then they are merely fortuitous or capricious. And if they are merely fortuitous or capricious, if they "just happen," then, I think, we may say ... that we are *not* morally responsible for them. Hence denying (3) is not the way to avoid (5).

We seem confronted, then, with a dilemma: either our choices have sufficient causal conditions or they do not; if they do have sufficient causal conditions they are not avoidable; if they do not, they are fortuitous or capricious; and therefore, since our choices are either unavoidable, or fortuitous, we are not morally responsible for them.

There are philosophers who believe that by denying the rather strange-sounding premise (4) we can escape the dilemma. Insisting on something like "the primacy of practical reason," they would say that since we are certain that (5) is false we must construct a metaphysical theory about the self, a theory denying (4) and enabling us to reconcile (3) and the denial of (5). I say "Metaphysical" because it seems to be necessary for the theory to replace (4) by sentences using such terms as "active power," "the autonomy of the will," "prime mover," or "higher levels of causality"—terms designating something to which we apparently need not refer when expressing the conclusions of physics and the natural sciences. But I believe we cannot know whether such theories enable us to escape our dilemma. For it seems impossible to conceive what the relation is that, according to these theories, holds between the "will," "self," "mover," or "active power," on the one hand, and the bodily events this power is supposed to control, on the other—the relation between the "activities" of the self and the events described by physics.

I am dissatisfied, then, with what philosophers have proposed as alternatives to premises (1) through (4) above, but since I feel certain that (5) is false I also feel certain that at least one of the premises is false.

A. J. A Y E R

Freedom and Necessity*

When I am said to have done something of my own free will it is implied that I could have acted otherwise; and it is only when it is believed that I could have acted otherwise that I am held to be morally responsible for what I have done. For a

*A. J. Ayer, "Freedom and Necessity," in *Philosophical Essays* (London: Macmillan; New York: St. Martin's Press, 1954), pp. 271–284. Reprinted by permission of the author and St. Martin's Press, Inc., The Macmillan Company of Canada, Ltd., and Macmillan & Co. Ltd. First published in *Polemic*, 5 (1946).

man is not thought to be morally responsible for an action that it was not in his power to avoid. But if human behaviour is entirely governed by causal laws, it is not clear how any action that is done could ever have been avoided. It may be said of the agent that he would have acted otherwise if the causes of his action had been different, but they being what they were, it seems to follow that he was bound to act as he did. Now it is commonly assumed both that men are capable of acting freely, in the sense that is required to make them morally responsible, and that human behaviour is entirely governed by causal laws: and it is the apparent conflict between these two assumptions that gives rise to the philosophical problem of the freedom of the will.

Confronted with this problem, many people will be inclined to agree with Dr. Johnson: 'Sir, we *know* our will is free, and *there's* an end on't'. But, while this does very well for those who accept Dr. Johnson's premise, it would hardly convince anyone who denied the freedom of the will. Certainly, if we do know that our wills are free, it follows that they are so. But the logical reply to this might be that since our wills are not free, it follows that no one can know that they are: so that if anyone claims, like Dr. Johnson, to know that they are, he must be mistaken. What is evident, indeed, is that people often believe themselves to be acting freely; and it is to this 'feeling' of freedom that some philosophers appeal when they wish, in the supposed interests of morality, to prove that not all human action is causally determined. But if these philosophers are right in their assumption that a man cannot be acting freely if his action is causally determined, then the fact that someone feels free to do, or not to do, a certain action does not prove that he really is so. It may prove that the agent does not himself know what it is that makes him act in one way rather than another: but from the fact that a man is unaware of the causes of his action, it does not follow that no such causes exist.

So much may be allowed to the determinist; but his belief that all human actions are subservient to causal laws still remains to be justified. If, indeed, it is necessary that every event should have a cause, then the rule must apply to human behaviour as much as to anything else. But why should it be supposed that every event must have a cause? The contrary is not unthinkable. Nor is the law of universal causation a necessary presupposition of scientific thought. The scientist may try to discover causal laws, and in many cases he succeeds; but sometimes he has to be content with statistical laws, and sometimes he comes upon events which, in the present state of his knowledge, he is not able to subsume under any law at all. In the case of these events he assumes that if he knew more he would be able to discover some law, whether causal or statistical, which would

enable him to account for them. And this assumption cannot be disproved. For however far he may have carried his investigation, it is always open to him to carry it further; and it is always conceivable that if he carried it further he would discover the connection which had hitherto escaped him. Nevertheless, it is also conceivable that the events with which he is concerned are not systematically connected with any others: so that the reason why he does not discover the sort of laws that he requires is simply that they do not obtain.

Now in the case of human conduct the search for explanations has not in fact been altogether fruitless. Certain scientific laws have been established; and with the help of these laws we do make a number of successful predictions about the ways in which different people will behave. But these predictions do not always cover every detail. We may be able to predict that in certain circumstances a particular man will be angry, without being able to prescribe the precise form that the expression of his anger will take. We may be reasonably sure that he will shout, but not sure how loud his shout will be, or exactly what words he will use. And it is only a small proportion of human actions that we are able to forecast even so precisely as this. But that, it may be said, is because we have not carried our investigations very far. The science of psychology is still in its infancy and, as it is developed, not only will more human actions be explained, but the explanations will go into greater detail. The ideal of complete explanation may never in fact be attained: but it is theoretically attainable. Well, this may be so: and certainly it is impossible to show *a priori* that it is not so: but equally it cannot be shown that it is. This will not, however, discourage the scientist who, in the field of human behaviour, as elsewhere, will continue to formulate theories and test them by the facts. And in this he is justified. For since he has no reason *a priori* to admit that there is a limit to what he can discover, the fact that he also cannot be sure that there is no limit does not make it unreasonable for him to devise theories, nor, having devised them, to try constantly to improve them.

But now suppose it to be claimed that, so far as men's actions are concerned, there is a limit: and that this limit is set by the fact of human freedom. An obvious objection is that in many

376 DETERMINISM, FREEDOM, AND RESPONSIBILITY

cases in which a person feels himself to be free to do, or not to do, a certain action, we are even now able to explain, in causal terms, why it is that he acts as he does. But it might be argued that even if men are sometimes mistaken in believing that they act freely, it does not follow that they are always so mistaken. For it is not always the case that when a man believes that he has acted freely we are in fact able to account for his action in causal terms. A determinist would say that we should be able to account for it if we had more knowledge of the circumstances, and had been able to discover the appropriate natural laws. But until those discoveries have been made, this remains only a pious hope. And may it not be true that, in some cases at least, the reason why we can give no causal explanation is that no causal explanation is available; and that this is because the agent's choice was literally free, as he himself felt it to be?

The answer is that this may indeed be true, inasmuch as it is open to anyone to hold that no explanation is possible until some explanation is actually found. But even so it does not give the moralist what he wants. For he is anxious to show that men are capable of acting freely in order to infer that they can be morally responsible for what they do. But if it is a matter of pure chance that a man should act in one way rather than another, he may be free but he can hardly be responsible. And indeed when a man's actions seem to us quite unpredictable, when, as we say, there is no knowing what he will do, we do not look upon him as a moral agent. We look upon him rather as a lunatic.

To this it may be objected that we are not dealing fairly with the moralist. For when he makes it a condition of my being morally responsible that I should act freely, he does not wish to imply that it is purely a matter of chance that I act as I do. What he wishes to imply is that my actions are the result of my own free choice: and it is because they are the result of my own free choice that I am held to be morally responsible for them.

But now we must ask how it is that I come to make my choice. Either it is an accident that I choose to act as I do or it is not. If it is an accident, then it is merely a matter of chance that I did not choose otherwise; and if it is merely a matter of chance that I did not choose otherwise,

it is surely irrational to hold me morally responsible for choosing as I did. But if it is not an accident that I choose to do one thing rather than another, then presumably there is some causal explanation of my choice: and in that case we are led back to determinism.

Again, the objection may be raised that we are not doing justice to the moralist's case. His view is not that it is a matter of chance that I choose to act as I do, but rather that my choice depends upon my character. Nevertheless he holds that I can still be free in the sense that he requires; for it is I who am responsible for my character. But in what way am I responsible for my character? Only, surely, in the sense that there is a causal connection between what I do now and what I have done in the past. It is only this that justifies the statement that I have made myself what I am: and even so this is an over-simplification, since it takes no account of the external influences to which I have been subjected. But, ignoring the external influences, let us assume that it is in fact the case that I have made myself what I am. Then it is still legitimate to ask how it is that I have come to make myself one sort of person rather than another. And if it be answered that it is a matter of my strength of will, we can put the same question in another form by asking how it is that my will has the strength that it has and not some other degree of strength. Once more, either it is an accident or it is not. If it is an accident, then by the same argument as before, I am not morally responsible, and if it is not an accident we are led back to determinism.

Furthermore, to say that my actions proceed from my character or, more colloquially, that I act in character, is to say that my behaviour is consistent and to that extent predictable: and since it is, above all, for the actions that I perform in character that I am held to be morally responsible, it looks as if the admission or moral responsibility, so far from being incompatible with determinism, tends rather to presuppose it. But how can this be so if it is a necessary condition of moral responsibility that the person who is held responsible should have acted freely? It seems that if we are to retain this idea of moral responsibility, we must either show that men can be held responsible for actions which they do not do freely, or else find some way of reconciling determinism with the freedom of the will.

It is no doubt with some object of effecting this reconciliation that some philosophers have defined freedom as the consciousness of necessity. And by so doing they are able to say not only that a man can be acting freely when his action is causally determined, but even that his action must be causally determined for it to be possible for him to be acting freely. Nevertheless this definition has the serious disadvantage that it gives to the word 'freedom' a meaning quite different from any that it ordinarily bears. It is indeed obvious that if we are allowed to give the word 'freedom' any meaning that we please, we can find a meaning that will reconcile it with determinism: but this is no more a solution of our present problem than the fact that the word 'horse' could be arbitrarily used to mean what is ordinarily meant by 'sparrow' is a proof that horses have wings. For suppose that I am compelled by another person to do something 'against my will'. In that case, as the word 'freedom' is ordinarily used, I should not be said to be acting freely: and the fact that I am fully aware of the constraint to which I am subjected makes no difference to the matter. I do not become free by becoming conscious that I am not. It may, indeed, be possible to show that my being aware that my action is causally determined is not incompatible with my acting freely: but it by no means follows that it is in this that my freedom consists. Moreover, I suspect that one of the reasons why people are inclined to define freedom as the consciousness of necessity one may somehow be able to master it. But this is a fallacy. It is like someone's saying that he wishes he could see into the future, because if he did he would know what calamities lay in wait for him and so would be able to avoid them. But if he avoids the calamities then they don't lie in the future and it is not true that he foresees them. And similarly if I am able to master necessity, in the sense of escaping the operation of a necessary law, then the law in question is not necessary. And if the law is not necessary, then neither my freedom nor anything else can consist in my knowing that it is.

Let it be granted, then, that when we speak of reconciling freedom with determinism we are using the word 'freedom' in an ordinary sense. It still remains for us to make this usage clear: and perhaps the best way to make it clear is to show what it is that freedom, in this sense, is contrasted with. Now we began with the assumption that freedom is contrasted with causality: so that a man cannot be said to be acting freely if his action is causally determined. But this assumption has led us into difficulties and I now wish to suggest that it is mistaken. For it is not, I think, causality that freedom is to be contrasted with, but constraint. And while it is true that being constrained to do an action entails being caused to do it, I shall try to show that the converse does not hold. I shall try to show that from the fact that my action is causally determined it does not necessarily follow that I am constrained to do it: and this is equivalent to saying that it does not necessarily follow that I am not free.

If I am constrained, I do not act freely. But in what circumstances can I legitimately be said to be constrained? An obvious instance is the case in which I am compelled by another person to do what he wants. In a case of this sort the compulsion need not be such as to deprive one of the power of choice. It is not required that the other person should have hypnotized me, or that he should make it physically impossible for me to go against his will. It is enough that he should induce me to do what he wants by making it clear to me that, if I do not, he will bring about some situation that I regard as even more undesirable than the consequences of the action that he wishes me to do. Thus, if the man points a pistol at my head I may still choose to disobey him: but this does not prevent its being true that if I do fall in with his wishes he can legitimately be said to have compelled me. And if the circumstances are such that no reasonable person would be expected to choose the other alternative, then the action that I am made to do is not one for which I am held to be morally responsible.

A similar, but still somewhat different, case is that in which another person has obtained an habitual ascendancy over me. Where this is so, there may be no question of my being induced to act as the other person wishes by being confronted with a still more disagreeable alternative: for if I am sufficiently under his influence this special stimulus will not be necessary. Nevertheless I do not act freely, for the reason that I have been deprived of the power of choice. And this means that I have acquired so strong a habit of obedience that I no longer go through the process of deciding whether or not to do what the other person wants. About other matters I may still deliberate; but as regards the fulfillment of this other person's wishes, my own deliberations have ceased to be a causal factor in my behaviour. And it is in this sense that I may be said to be constrained. It is not, however, necessary that such constraint should take the form of subservience to another person. A kleptomaniac is not a free agent, in respect to his stealing, because he does not go through any process of deciding whether or not to steal. Or rather, if he does go through such a process, it is irrelevant to his behaviour. Whatever he resolved to do, he would steal all the same. And it is this that distinguishes him from the ordinary thief.

But now it may be asked whether there is any essential difference between these cases and those in which the agent is commonly thought to be free. No doubt the ordinary thief does go through a process of deciding whether or not to steal, and no doubt it does affect his behaviour. If he resolved to refrain from stealing, he could carry his resolution out. But if it be allowed that his making or not making this resolution is causally determined, then how can he be any more free than the kleptomaniac? It may be true that unlike the kleptomaniac he could refrain from stealing if he chose: but if there is a cause, or set of causes, which necessitate his choosing as he does, how can he be said to have the power of choice? Again, it may be true that no one now compels me to get up and walk across the room: but if my doing so can be causally explained in terms of my history or my environment, or whatever it may be, then how am I any more free than if some other person had compelled me? I do not have the feeling of constraint that I have when a pistol is manifestly pointed at my head; but the chains of causation by which I am bound are no less effective for being invisible.

The answer to this is that the cases I have mentioned as examples of constraint do differ from the others: and they differ just in the ways that I have tried to bring out. If I suffered from a compulsion neurosis, so that I got up and walked across the room, whether I want to or not, or if I did so because somebody else compelled me, then I should not be acting freely. But if I do it now, I shall be acting freely, just because these conditions do not obtain; and the fact that my action may nevertheless have a cause is, from this point of view, irrelevant. For it is not when my action has any cause at all, but only when it has a special sort of cause, that it is reckoned not to be free.

But here it may be objected that, even if this distinction corresponds to ordinary usage, it is still very irrational. For why should we distinguish, with regard to a person's freedom, between the operations of one sort of cause and those of another? Do not all causes equally necessitate? And it is not therefore arbitrary to say that a person is free when he is necessitated in one fashion but not when he is necessitated in another?

That all causes equally necessitate is indeed a tautology, if the word 'necessitate' is taken merely as equivalent to 'cause': but if, as the objection requires, it is taken as equivalent to 'constrain' or 'compel', then I do not think that this proposition is true. For all that is needed for one event to be the cause of another is that, in the given circumstances, the event which is said to be the effect would not have occurred if it had not been for the occurrence of the event which is said to be the cause, or *vice versa*, according as causes are interpreted as necessary, or sufficient, conditions: and this fact is usually deducible from some causal law which states that whenever an event of the one kind occurs then, given suitable conditions, an event of the other kind will occur in a certain temporal or spatio-temporal relationship to it. In short, there is an invariable concomitance between the two classes of events; but there is no compulsion, in any but a metaphorical sense. Suppose, for example, that a psycho-analyst is able to account for some aspect of my behaviour by referring it to some lesion that I suffered in my childhood. In that case, it may be said that my childhood experience, together with certain other events, necessitates my behaving as I do. But all that this involves is that it is found to be true in general that when people have had certain experiences as children, they subsequently behave in certain specifiable ways; and my case is just another instance of this general law. It is in this way indeed that my behaviour is explained. But from the fact that my behaviour is capable of being explained, in the sense that it can be subsumed under some natural law, it does not follow that I am acting under constraint.

If this is correct, to say that I could have acted otherwise is to say, first, that I should have acted otherwise if I had so chosen; secondly, that my action was voluntary in the sense in which the actions, say, of the kleptomaniac are not; and thirdly, that nobody compelled me to choose as I did: and these three conditions may very well be fulfilled. When they are fulfilled, I may be said to have acted freely. But this is not to say that it was a matter of chance that I acted as I did, or, in other words, that my action could not be explained. And that my actions should be capable of being explained is all that is required by the postulate of determinism.

If more than this seems to be required it is, I think, because the use of the very word 'determinism' is in some degree misleading. For it tends to suggest that one event is somehow in the power of another, whereas the truth is merely that they are factually correlated. And the same applies to the use, in this context, of the word 'necessity' and even of the word 'cause' itself. Moreover, there are various reasons for this. One is the tendency to confuse causal with logical necessitation, and so to infer mistakenly that the effect is contained in the cause. Another is the uncritical use of a concept of force which is derived from primitive experiences of pushing and striking. A third is the survival of an animistic conception of causality, in which all causal relationships are modelled on the example of one person's exercising authority over another. As a result we tend to form an imaginative picture of an unhappy effect trying vainly to escape from the clutches of an overmastering cause. But, I repeat, the fact is simply that when an event of one type occurs, an event of another type occurs also, in a certain temporal or spatio-temporal relation to the first.

The rest is only metaphor. And it is because of the metaphor, and not because of the fact, that we come to think that there is an antithesis between causality and freedom.

Nevertheless, it may be said, if the postulate of determinism is valid, then the future can be explained in terms of the past: and this means that if one knew enough about the past one would be able to predict the future. But in that case what will happen in the future is already decided. And how then can I be said to be free? What is going to happen is going to happen and nothing that I do can prevent it. If the determinist is right, I am the helpless prisoner of fate.

But what is meant by saying that the future course of events is already decided? If the implication is that some person has arranged it, then the proposition is false. But if all that is meant is that it is possible, in principle, to deduce it from a set of particular facts about the past, together with the appropriate general laws, then, even if this is true, it does not in the least entail that I am the helpless prisoner of fate. It does not even entail that my actions make no difference to the future: for they are causes as well as effects; so that if they were different their consequences would be different also. What it does entail is that my behaviour can be predicted: but to say that my behaviour can be predicted is not to say that I am acting under constraint. It is indeed true that I cannot escape my destiny if this is taken to mean no more than that I shall do what I shall do. But this is a tautology, just as it is a tautology that what is going to happen is going to happen. And such tautologies as these prove nothing whatsoever about the freedom of will.

JOHN HOSPERS

Free Will and Psychoanalysis*

O Thou who didst with pitfall and with gin
Beset the Road I was to wander in,
   Thou wilt not with Predestined Evil round
Enmesh, and then inpute my Fall to Sin!
                    —Edward FitzGerald,
        The Rubaiyat of Omar Khayyam

... It is extremely common for nonprofessional philosophers and iconoclasts to deny that human freedom exists, but at the same time to have no clear idea of what it is that they are denying to exist. The first thing that needs to be said about the free-will issue is that any meaningful term must have a meaningful opposite: if it is meaningful to assert that people are not free, it must be equally meaningful to assert that people *are* free, whether this latter assertion is in fact true or not. Whether it is true, of course, will depend on the meaning that is given the weasel-word "free." For example, if freedom is made dependent on indeterminism, it may well be that human freedom is nonexistent. But there seem to be no good grounds for asserting such a dependence, especially since lack of causation is the furthest thing from people's minds when they call

*John Hospers, "Meaning and Free Will," *Philosophy and Phenomenological Research,* X (1950), 313–330, reprinted by permission of the author and the editor. The selection appearing here is the abridged version printed as "Free Will and Psychoanalysis" in Wilfred Sellars and John Hospers, eds., *Readings in Ethical Theory* (New York: Appleton-Century-Crofts, 1952), pp. 560–575. For a later discussion of the problem of this paper and one more in accord with the author's present views, see Professor Hospers' *Human Conduct* (New York: Harcourt, Brace & World, 1961), pp. 493–524.

an act free. Doubtless there are other senses that can be given to the word "free"—such as "able to do anything we want to do"—in which no human beings are free. But the first essential point about which the denier of freedom must be clear is *what* it is that he is denying. If one knows that it is like for people not to be free, one must know what it *would* be like for them to *be* free.

Philosophers have advanced numerous senses of "free" in which countless acts performed by human beings can truly be called free acts. The most common conception of a free act is that according to which an act is free if and only if it is a *voluntary* act. But the word "voluntary" does not always carry the same meaning. Sometimes to call an act voluntary means that we can do the act *if* we choose to do it: in other words, that it is physically and psychologically possible for us to do it, so that the occurrence of the act follows upon the decision to do it. (One's decision to raise his arm is in fact followed by the actual raising of his arm, unless he is a paralytic; one's decision to pluck the moon from the sky is not followed by the actual event.) Sometimes a voluntary act is conceived (as by G. E. Moore[1]) as an act which would not have occurred if, just beforehand, the agent had chosen not to perform it. But these senses are different from the sense in which a voluntary act is an act resulting from *deliberation*, or perhaps merely from *choice*. For example, there are many acts which we could have avoided, if we had chosen to do so, but which we nevertheless did not *choose* to perform, much less *deliberate* about them. The act of raising one's leg in the process of taking a step while out for a walk, is one which a person could have avoided by choosing to, but which, after one has learned to walk, takes place automatically or semi-automatically through habit, and thus is not the result of choice. (One may have chosen to take the walk, but not to take this or that step while walking.) Such acts are free in Moore's sense but are not free in the sense of being deliberate. Moreover, there are classes of acts of the same general character which are not even covered by Moore's sense: sudden outbursts of feeling, in some cases at least, could not have been avoided by an immediately preceding volition, so that if these are to be included under the heading of voluntary acts, the proviso that the act could have been avoided by an immediately preceding volition must be amended to read "could have been avoided by a volition or series of volitions by the agent *at some time in the past*"—such as the adoption of a different set of habits in the agent's earlier and more formative years.

(Sometimes we call *persons,* rather than their acts, free. S. Stebbing, for example, declares that one should never call acts free, but only the doers of the acts.[2] But the two do not seem irreconcilable: can we not speak of a *person* as free *with respect to a certain act* (never just free in general) if that *act* is free—whatever we may then go on to mean by saying that an act is free? Any statement about a free act can then be translated into a statement about the doer of the act.)

Now, no matter in which of the above ways we may come to define "voluntary," there are still acts which are voluntary *but which we would be very unlikely to think of as free.* Thus, when a person submits to the command of an armed bandit, he may do so voluntarily in every one of the above senses: he may do so as a result of choice, even of deliberation, and he could have avoided doing it by willing not to—he could, instead, have refused and been shot. The man who reveals a state secret under torture does the same: he could have refused and endured more torture. Yet such acts, and persons in respect of such acts, are not generally called free. We say that they were performed *under compulsion,* and if an act is performed under compulsion we do not call it free. We say, "He wasn't free because he was forced to

do as he did," though of course his act was voluntary.

This much departure from the identification of free acts with voluntary acts almost everyone would admit. Sometimes, however, it would be added that this is all the departure that can be admitted. According to Moritz Schlick, for example,

Freedom means the opposite of compulsion; a man *is free* if he does not act under *compulsion,* and he is compelled or unfree when he is hindered from without in the realization of his natural desires. Hence he is unfree when he is locked up, or chained, or when someone forces him at the point of a gun to do what otherwise he would not do. This is quite clear, and everyone will admit that the everyday or legal notion of the lack of freedom is thus correctly interpreted, and that a man will be considered quite free . . . if no such external compulsion is exerted upon him.[3]

Schlick adds that the entire vexed free-will controversy in philosophy is so much wasted ink and paper, because compulsion has been confused with causality and necessity with uniformity. If the question is asked whether every event is caused, the answer is doubtless yes; but if it is whether every event is compelled, the answer is clearly no. Free acts are uncompelled acts, not uncaused acts. Again, when it is said that some state of affairs (such as water flowing downhill) is necessary, if "necessary" means "compelled," the answer is no; if it means merely that it always happens that way, the answer is yes: universality of application is confused with compulsion. And this, according to Schlick, is the end of the matter.

Schlick's analysis is indeed clarifying and helpful to those who have fallen victim to the confusion he exposes—and this probably includes most persons in their philosophical growing-pains. But *is* this the end of the matter? Is it true that all acts, though caused, are free as long as they are not compelled in the sense which he specifies? May it not be that, while the identification of "free" with "uncompelled" is acceptable, the area of compelled acts is vastly greater than he or most other philosophers have ever suspected? (Moore is more cautious in this respect than Schlick; while for Moore an act is free if it is voluntary in the sense specified above, he thinks there may be another sense in which human beings, and human acts, are not free at all.[4]) We remember statements about human beings being pawns of their early environment, victims of conditions beyond their control, the result of causal influences stemming from their parents, and the like, and we ponder and ask, "Still, are we really free?" Is there not something in what generations of sages have said about man being fettered? Is there not perhaps something too facile, too sleight-of-hand, in Schlick's cutting of the Gordian knot? For example, when a metropolitan newspaper headlines an article with the words "Boy Killer is Doomed Long before He Is Born,"[5] and then goes on to describe how a twelve-year-old boy has been sentenced to prison for the murder of a girl, and how his parental background includes records of drunkenness, divorce, social maladjustment, and paresis, we are still to say that his act, though voluntary and assuredly *not* done at the point of a gun, is free? The boy has early displayed a tendency toward sadistic activity to hide an underlying masochism and "prove that he's a man"; being coddled by his mother only worsens this tendency, until, spurned by a girl in his attempt on her, he kills her—not simply in a fit of anger, but calculatingly, deliberately. Is he free in respect of his criminal act, or for that matter in most of the acts of his life? Surely to ask this question is to answer it in the negative. Perhaps I have taken an extreme case; but it is only to show the superficiality of the Schlick analysis the more clearly. Though not everyone has criminotic tendencies, everyone has been molded by influences which in large measure at least determine his present behavior; he is literally the product of these influences, stemming from periods prior to his "years of discretion," giving him a host of character traits that he cannot change now even if he would. So obviously does what a man is depend upon how a man comes to be, that it is small wonder that philosophers and sages have considered man far indeed from being the master of his fate. It is not as if man's will were standing high and serene above the flux of events that have molded him; it is itself caught up in this flux, itself carried along on the current. An act is free when it is determined by the man's character, say moralists; but what if the most decisive aspects of his character were already irrevocably acquired before he could do anything to mold them? What if even the degree of will power available to him in shaping his habits and disciplining himself now to overcome the influence of his early environment is a factor over which he has no control? What are we to say of this kind of "freedom"? Is it not rather like the freedom of the machine to stamp labels on cans when it has been devised for just that purpose? Some machines can do so more efficiently than others, but only because they have been better constructed.

It is not my purpose here to establish this thesis in general, but only in one specific respect which has received comparatively little attention, namely, the field referred to by psychiatrists as that of unconscious motivation. In what follows I shall restrict my attention to it because it illustrates as clearly as anything the points I wish to make.

Let me try to summarize very briefly the psychoanalytic doctrine on this point.[6] The conscious life of the human being, including the conscious decisions and volitions, is merely a mouthpiece for the unconscious—not directly for the enactment of unconscious drives, but of the compromise between unconscious drives and unconscious reproaches. There is a Big Three behind the scenes which the automaton called the conscious personality carries out: the id, and "eternal gimme," presents its wish and demands its immediate satisfaction; the super-ego says no to the wish immediately upon presentation, and the unconscious ego, the mediator between the two, tries to keep peace by means of compromise.[7]

To go into examples of the functioning of these three "bosses" would be endless; psychoanalytic case books supply hundreds of them. The important point for us to see in the present context is that *it is the unconscious that determines what the conscious impulse and the conscious action shall be.* Hamlet, for example, had a strong Oedipus wish, which was violently counteracted by super-ego reproaches; these early wishes were vividly revived in an unusual adult situation in which his uncle usurped the coveted position from Hamlet's father and won his mother besides. This situation evoked strong strictures on the part of Hamlet's super-ego, and it was this that was responsible for his notorious delay in killing his uncle. A dozen times Hamlet could have killed Claudius easily; but everytime Hamlet "decided" not to: a free choice, moralists would say—but no, listen to the super-ego: "What you feel such hatred toward your uncle for, what you are plotting to kill him for, is precisely the crime which you yourself desire to commit: to kill your father and replace him in the affections of your mother. Your fate and your uncle's are bound up together." This paralyzes Hamlet into inaction. Consciously all he knows is that he is unable to act; this conscious inability he rationalizes, giving a different excuse each time.[8] We have always been conscious of the fact that we are not masters of our fate in every respect—that there are many things which we cannot do, that nature is more powerful than we are, that we cannot disobey laws without danger of reprisals, etc. We have become "officially" conscious, too, though in our private lives we must long have been aware of it, that we are not free with respect to the emotions that we feel—whom we love or hate, what types we admire, and the like. More lately still we have been reminded that there are unconscious motivations for our basic attractions and repulsions, our compulsive actions or inabilities to act. But what is not welcome news is that our very acts of volition, and the entire train of deliberations leading up to them, are but façades for the expression of unconscious wishes, or rather, unconscious compromises and defenses.

A man is faced by a choice: shall he kill another person or not? Moralists would say, here is a free choice—the result of deliberation, an action consciously entered into. And yet, though the agent himself does not know it, and has no awareness of the forces that are at work within him, his choice is already determined for him: his conscious will is only an instrument, a slave, in the hands of a deep unconscious motivation which determines his action. If he has a great deal of what the analyst calls "free-floating guilt," he will not; but if the guilt is such as to demand immediate absorption in the form of self-damaging behavior, this accumulated guilt will have to be discharged in some criminal action. The man himself does not know what the inner clockwork is; he is like the hands on the clock, thinking they move freely over the face of the clock.

A woman has married and divorced several husbands. Now she is faced with a choice for the next marriage: shall she marry Mr. A, or Mr. B, or nobody at all? She may take considerable time to "decide" this question, and her decision may appear as a final triumph of her free will. Let us assume that A is a normal, well-adjusted, kind, and generous man, while B is a leech, an impostor, one who will become entangled constantly in quarrels with her. If she belongs to a certain classifiable psychological type, she will inevitably choose B, and she will do so even if her previous husbands have resembled B, so that one would think that she "had learned from experience." Consciously, she will of course "give the matter due consideration," etc., etc. To the psychoanalyst all this is irrelevant chaff in the wind—only a camouflage for the inner workings about which she knows nothing consciously. If she is of a certain kind of masochistic strain, as exhibited in her previous set of symptoms, she *must* choose B: her super-ego, always out to maximize the torment in the situation, seeing what dazzling possibilities for self-damaging behavior are promised by the choice of B, compels her to make the choice she does, and even to conceal the real basis of the choice behind an elaborate façade of rationalizations.

A man is addicted to gambling. In the service of his addiction he loses all his money, spends what belongs to his wife, even sells his property and neglects his children. For a time perhaps he stops; then, inevitably, he takes it up again. The man does not know that he is a victim rather than an agent; or, if he sometimes senses that he is in the throes of something-he-knows-not-what, he will have no inkling of its character and will soon relapse into the illusion that he (his conscious self) is freely deciding the course of his own actions. What he does not know, of course, is that he is still taking out on his mother the original lesion to his infantile narcissism, getting back at her for her fancied refusal of his infantile wishes—and this by rejecting everything identified with her, namely education, discipline, logic, common sense, training. At the roulette wheel, almost alone among adult activities, chance—the opposite of all these things—rules supreme; and his addiction represents his continued and emphatic reiteration of his rejection of Mother and all she represents to his unconscious.

This pseudo-aggression of his is of course masochistic in its effects. In the long run he always loses; he can never quit while he is winning. And far from playing in order to win, rather one can say that his losing is a *sine qua non* of his psychic equilibrium (as it was for example with Dostoyevsky): guilt demands punishment, and in the ego's "deal" with the super-ego the super-ego has granted satisfaction of infantile wishes in return for the self-damaging conditions obtaining. Winning would upset the neurotic equilibrium.[9]

A man has wash-compulsion. He must be constantly washing his hands—he uses up perhaps 400 towels a day. Asked why he does this, he says, "I need to, my hands are dirty"; and if it is pointed out to him that they are not really dirty, he says, "They feel dirty anyway; I feel better when I wash them." So once again he washes them. He "freely decides" every time; he feels that he must wash them, he deliberates for a moment perhaps, but always ends by washing them. What he does not see, of course, are the invisible wires inside him pulling him inevitably to do the things he does: the infantile id-wish concerns preoccupation with dirt, the super-ego charges him with this, and the terrified ego must respond, "No, I don't like dirt, see how clean I like to be, look how I wash my hands!"

Let us see what further "free acts" the same patient engages in (this is an actual case history): he is taken to a concentration camp, and given the worst of treatment by the Nazi guards. In the camp he no longer chooses to be clean; does not even try to be—on the contrary, his choice is now to wallow in filth as much as he can. All he is aware of now is a disinclination to be clean, and every time he must choose he chooses not to be. Behind the scenes, however, another drama is being enacted: the super-ego, perceiving that enough torment is being administered from the outside, can afford to cease pressing its charges in this quarter—the outside world is doing the torturing now, so the super-ego is relieved of the responsibility. Thus the ego is relieved of the agony of constantly making terrified replies in the form of washing to prove that the super-ego is wrong. The defense no longer being needed, the person slides back into what is his natural predilection anyway, for filth. This becomes too much even for the Nazi guards: they take hold of him one day, saying "We'll teach you how to be clean!" drag him into the snow, and pour bucket after bucket of icy water over him until he freezes to death. Such is the end-result of an original id-wish, caught in the machinations of a destroying super-ego.

Let us take, finally, a less colorful, more everyday example. A student at a university, possessing wealth, charm, and all that is usually considered essential to popularity, begins to develop the following personality-pattern: although well taught in the graces of social conversation, he always makes a *faux pas* somewhere, and always in the worse possible situation; to his friends he makes cutting remarks which hurt deeply—and always apparently aimed in such a way as to hurt the most: a remark that would not hurt A but would hurt B he invariably makes to B rather than to A, and so on. None of this is conscious. Ordinarily he is considerate of people, but he contrives always (unconsciously) to impose on just those friends who would resent it most, and at just the times when he should know that he should not impose: at 3 o'clock in the morning, without forewarning, he phones a friend in a near-by city demanding to stay at his apartment for the weekend; naturally the friend is offended, but the person himself is not aware that he has provoked the grievance ("common sense" suffers a temporary eclipse when the neurotic pattern sets in, and one's intelligence, far from being of help in such a situation, is used in the interest of the neurosis), and when the friend is cool to him the next time they meet, he wonders why and feels unjustly treated. Aggressive behavior on his part invites resentment and aggression in turn, but all that he consciously sees is others' behavior towards him—and he considers himself the innocent victim of an unjustified "persecution."

Each of these acts is, from the moralist's point of view, free: he chose to phone his friend at 3 A.M.; he chose to make the cutting remark that he did, etc. What he does not know is that an ineradicable masochistic pattern has set in. His unconscious is far more shrewd and clever than is his conscious intellect; it sees with uncanny accuracy just what kind of behavior will damage him most, and unerringly forces him into that behavior. Consciously, the student "doesn't know why he did it"—he gives different "reasons" at different times, but they are all, once again, rationalizations cloaking the unconscious mechanism which propels him willy-nilly into actions that his "common sense" eschews.

The more of this sort of thing one observes, the more he can see what the psychoanalyst means when he talks about *the illusion of freedom*. And the more of a psychiatrist one becomes, the more he is overcome with a sense of what an illusion this free-will can be. In some kinds of cases most of us can see it already: it takes no psychiatrist to look at the epileptic and sigh with sadness at the thought that soon this person before you will be as one possessed, not the same thoughtful intelligent person you knew. But people are not aware of this in other contexts, for example when they express surprise at how a person whom they have been so good to could treat them so badly. Let us suppose that you help a person financially or morally or in some other way, so that he is in your debt; suppose further that he is one of the many neurotics who unconsciously identify kindness with weakness and aggression with strength, then he will unconsciously take your kindness to him as weakness and use it as the occasion for enacting some aggression against you. He can't help it, he may regret it himself later; still, he will be driven to do it. If we gain a little knowledge of psychiatry, we can look at him with pity, that a person otherwise so worthy should be so unreliable—but we will exercise realism too, and be aware that there are some types of people that you cannot be good to. In "free" acts of their conscious volition, they will use your own goodness against you.

Sometimes the persons themselves will become dimly aware that "something behind the scenes" is determining their behavior. The divorcee will sometimes view herself with detachment, as if she were some machine (and indeed the psychoanalyst does call her a "repeating-machine"): "I know I'm caught in a net, that I'll fall in love with this guy and marry him and the whole ridiculous merry-go-round will start all over again."

We talk about free will, and we say, for example, the person is free to do so-and-so if he *can* do so *if* he wants to—and we forget that his wanting to is itself caught up in the stream of determinism, that unconscious forces drive him into the wanting or not wanting to do the thing in question. The analogy of the puppet whose motions are manipulated from behind by invisible wires, or better still, by springs inside, is a telling one at almost every point.

And the glaring fact is that it all started so early, before we knew what was happening. The personality-structure is inelastic after the age of five, and comparatively so in most cases after the age of three. Whether one acquires a neurosis or not is determed by that age—and just as involuntarily as if it had been a curse of God. If, for example, a masochistic pattern was set up, under pressure of hyper-narcissism combined with real or fancied infantile deprivation, then the masochistic snowball was on its course downhill long before we or anybody else knew what was happening, and long before anyone could do anything about it. To speak of human beings as "puppets" in such a context is no idle metaphor, but a stark rendering of a literal fact: only the psychiatrist knows what puppets people really are; and it is no wonder that the protestations of philosophers that "the act which is the result of a volition, a deliberation, a conscious decision, is free" leave these persons, to speak mildly, somewhat cold.

But, one may object, all the states thus far described have been abnormal, neurotic ones. The well-adjusted (normal) person at least is free.

Leaving aside the question of how clearly and on what grounds one can distinguish the neurotic from the normal, let me use an illustration of a proclivity that everyone would call normal, namely, the decision of a man to support his wife and possibly a family, and consider briefly its genesis, according to psychoanalytic accounts.[10]

Every baby comes into the world with a full-fledged case of megalomania—interested only in himself, acting as if believing that he is the center of the universe and that others are present only to fulfill his wishes, and furious when his own wants are not satisfied immediately no matter for what reason. Gratitude, even for all the time and worry and care expended on him by the mother, is an emotion entirely foreign to the infant, and as he grows older it is inculcated in him only with the greatest difficulty; his natural tendency is to assume that everything that happens to him is due to himself, except for denials and frustrations, which are due to the "cruel, denying" outer world, in particular the mother; and that he owes nothing to anyone, is dependent on no one. This omnipotence-complex, or illusion of non-dependence, has been called the "autarchic fiction." Such a conception of the world is actually fostered in the child by the conduct of adults, who automatically attempt to fulfill the infant's every wish concerning nourishment, sleep, and attention. The child misconceives causality and sees in these wish-fulfillments not the results of maternal kindness and love, but simply the result of his own omnipotence.

This fiction of omnipotence is gradually destroyed by experience, and its destruction is probably the deepest disappointment of the early years of life. First of all, the infant discovers that he is the victim of organic urges and necessities: hunger, defecation, urination. More important, he discovers that the maternal breast, which he has not previously distinguished from his own body (he has not needed to, since it was available when he wanted it), is not a part of himself after all, but of another creature upon whom he is dependent. He is forced to recognize this, e.g., when he wants nourishment and it is at the moment not present; even a small delay is most damaging to the "autarchic fiction." Most painful of all is the experience of weaning, probably the greatest tragedy in every baby's life, when his dependence is most cruelly emphasized; it is a frustrating experience because what he wants is no longer there at all; and if he has been able to some extent to preserve the illusion of non-dependence heretofore, he is not able to do so now—it is plain that the source of his nourishment is not dependent on him, but he on it. The shattering of the autarchic fiction is a great disillusionment to every child, a tremendous blow to his ego which he will, in one way or another, spend the rest of his life trying to repair. How does he do this?

First of all, his reaction to frustration is anger and fury; and he responds by kicking, biting, etc., the only ways he knows. But he is motorically helpless, and these measures are ineffective, and only serve to emphasize his dependence the more. Moreover, against such responses of the child the parental reaction is one of prohibition, often involving deprivation of attention and affection. Generally the child soon learns that this form of rebellion is profitless, and brings him more harm than good. He wants to respond to frustration with violent aggression, and at the same time learns that he will be punished for such aggression, and that in any case the latter is ineffectual. What face-saving solution does he find? Since he must "face facts," since he must in any case "conform" if he is to have any peace at all, he tries to make it seem as if he himself is the source of the commands and prohibitions: the *external* prohib-

itive force is *internalized*— and here we have the origin of conscience. By making the prohibitive agency seem to come from within himself, the child can "save face"—as if saying, "The prohibition comes from within me, not from outside, so I'm not subservient to external rule, I'm only obeying rules I've set up myself," thus to some extent saving the autarchic fiction, and at the same time avoiding unpleasant consequences directed against himself by complying with parental commands.

Moreover, the boy[11] has unconsciously never forgiven the mother for his dependence on her in early life, for nourishment and all other things. It has upset his illusion of non-dependence. These feelings have been repressed and are not remembered; but they are acted out in later life in many ways—e.g., in the constant deprecation man has for woman's duties such as cooking and housework of all sorts ("All she does is stay home and get together a few meals, and she calls that work"), and especially in the man's identification with the mother in his sex experiences with women. By identifying with someone one cancels out in effect the person with whom he identifies —replacing that person, unconsciously denying his existence, and the man, identifying with his early mother, playing the active role in "giving" to his wife as his mother has "given" to him, is in effect the denial of his mother's existence, a fact which is narcissistically embarrassing to his ego because it is chiefly responsible for shattering his autarchic fiction. In supporting his wife, he can unconsciously deny that his mother gave to him, and that he was dependent on her giving. Why is it that the husband plays the provider, and wants his wife to be dependent on no one else, although twenty years before he was nothing but a parasitic baby? This is a face-saving device on his part: he can act out the reasoning, "See, I'm not the parasitic baby; on the contrary I'm the provider, the giver." His playing the provider is a constant face-saving device, to deny his early dependence which is so embarrassing to his ego. It is no wonder that men generally dislike to be reminded of their babyhood, when they were dependent on women.

Thus we have here a perfectly normal adult reaction which is unconsciously motivated. The man "chooses" to support a family—and his choice is as unconsciously motivated as anything could be. (I have described here only the "normal" state of affairs, uncomplicated by the well-nigh infinite number of variations that occur in actual practice.)

Now, what of the notion of responsibility? What happens to it on our analysis?

Let us begin with an example, not a fictitious one. A woman and her two-year-old baby are riding on a train to Montreal in mid-winter. The child is ill. The woman wants badly to get to her destination. She is, unknown to herself, the victim of a neurotic conflict whose nature is irrelevant here except for the fact that it forces her to behave aggressively toward the child, partly to spite her husband whom she despises and who loves the child, but chiefly to ward off super-ego charges of masochistic attachment. Consciously she loves the child, and when she says this she says it sincerely, but she must behave aggressively toward it nevertheless, just as many children love their mothers but are nasty to them most of the time in neurotic pseudo-aggression. The child becomes more ill as the train approaches Montreal; the heating system of the train is not working, and the conductor pleads with the woman to get off the train at the next town and get the child to a hospital at once. The woman refuses. Soon after, the child's condition worsens, and the mother does all she can to keep it alive, without, however, leaving the train, for she declares that it is absolutely necessary that she reach her destination. But before she gets there the child is dead. After that, of course, the mother grieves, blames herself, weeps hysterically, and joins the church to gain surcease from the guilt that constantly overwhelms her when she thinks of how her aggressive behavior has killed her child.

Was she responsible for her deed? In ordinary life, after making a mistake, we say, "Chalk it up to experience." Here we should say, "Chalk it up to the neurosis." *She* could not help it if her neurosis forced her to act this way—she didn't even know what was going on behind the scenes, her conscious self merely acted out its assigned part. This is far more true than is generally realized: criminal actions in general are not actions for which their agents are responsible; the agents are passive, not active—they are victims of a neurotic conflict. Their very hyper-activity is unconsciously determined.

To say this is, of course, not to say that we should not punish criminals. Clearly, for our own protection, we must remove them from our midst so that they can no longer molest and endanger organized society. And, of course, if we use the word "responsible" in such a way that justly to hold someone responsible for a deed is by definition identical with being justified in punishing him, then we can and do hold people responsible. But this is like the sense of "free" in which free acts are voluntary ones. It does not go deep enough. In a deeper sense we cannot hold the person responsible: we can hold his neurosis responsible, but *he is not responsible for his neurosis,* particularly since the age at which its onset was inevitable was an age before he could even speak.

The neurosis is responsible—but isn't the neurosis a part of *him?* We have been speaking all the time as if the person and his unconscious were two separate beings; but isn't he one personality, including conscious and unconscious departments together?

I do not wish to deny this. But it hardly helps us here; for what people want when they talk about freedom, and what they hold to when they champion it, is the idea that the *conscious* will is the master of their destiny. "I am the master of my fate, I am the captain of my soul"—and they surely mean their conscious selves, the self that they can recognize and search and introspect. Between an unconscious that willy-nilly determines your actions, and an external force which pushes you, there is little if anything to choose. The unconscious is just *as if* it were an outside force; and indeed, psychiatrists will assert that the inner Hitler (your super-ego) can torment you far more than any external Hitler can. Thus the kind of freedom that people want, the only kind they will settle for, is precisely the kind that psychiatry says they cannot have.

Heretofore it was pretty generally thought that, while we could not rightly blame a person for the color of his eyes or the morality of his parents, or even for what he did at the age of three, or to a large extent what impulses he had and whom he fell in love with, one *could* do so for other of his adult activities, particularly the acts he performed voluntarily and with premeditation. Later this attitude was shaken. Many voluntary acts came to be recognized, at least in some circles, as compelled by the unconscious. Some philosophers recognized this too—Ayer[12] talks about the kleptomaniac being unfree, and about a person being unfree when another person exerts a habitual ascendancy over his personality. But this is as far as he goes. The usual examples, such as the kleptomaniac and the schizophrenic, apparently satisfy most philosophers, and with these exceptions removed, the rest of mankind is permitted to wander in the vast and alluring fields of freedom and responsibility. So far, the inroads upon freedom left the vast majority of humanity untouched; they began to hit home when psychiatrists began to realize, though philosophers did not, that the domination of the conscious by the unconscious extended, not merely to a few exceptional individuals, but to all human beings, that the "big three behind the scenes" are not respecters of persons, and dominate us all, even including that *sanctum sanctorum* of freedom, our conscious will. To be sure, the domination by the unconscious in the case of "normal" individuals is somewhat more benevolent than the tyranny and despotism exercised in neurotic cases, and therefore the former have evoked less comment; but the principle remains in all cases the same: the unconscious is the master of every fate and the captain of every soul.

We speak of a machine turning out good products most of the time but every once in a while it turns out a "lemon." We do not, of course, hold the product responsible for this, but the machine, and via the machine, its maker. Is it silly to extend to inanimate objects the idea of responsibility? Of course. But is it any less so to employ the notion in speaking of human creatures? Are not the two kinds of cases analogous in countless important ways? Occasionally a child turns out badly too, even when his environment and training are the same as that of his brothers and sisters who turn out "all right." He is the "bad penny." His acts of rebellion against parental discipline in adult life (such as the case of the gambler, already cited) are traceable to early experiences of real or fancied denial of infantile wishes. Sometimes the denial has been real, though many denials are absolutely necessary if the child is to grow up to observe the common decencies of civilized life; sometimes, if the child has an unusual quantity of narcissism, every event that occurs is interpreted by him as a denial of his wishes, and nothing a parent could do, even granting every humanly possible wish, would help. In any event, the later neurosis can be attributed to this. Can the person himself be held responsible? Hardly. If he engages in activities which are a menace to society, he must be put into prison, of course, but responsibility is another matter. The time when the events occurred which rendered his neurotic behavior inevitable was a time long before he was capable of thought and decision. As an adult, he is a victim of a world he never made—only this world is inside him.

What about the children who turn out "all right"? All we can say is that "it's just lucky for them" that what happened to their unfortunate brother didn't happen to them; *through no virtue of their own* they are not doomed to the life of unconscious guilt, expiation, conscious depression, terrified ego-gestures for the appeasement of a tyrannical super-ego, that he is. The machine turned them out with a minimum of damage. But if the brother cannot be blamed for his evils, neither can they be praised for their good; unless, of course, we should blame people for what is not their fault, and praise them for lucky accidents.

We all agree that machines turn out "lemons," we all agree that nature turns out misfits in the realm of biology—the blind, the crippled, the diseased; but we hesitate to include the realm of the personality, for here, it seems, is the last retreat of our dignity as human beings. Our ego can endure anything but this; this island at least must remain above the encroaching flood. But may not precisely the same analysis be made here also? Nature turns out psychological "lemons" too, in far greater quantities than any other kind; and indeed all of us are "lemons" in some respect or other, the difference being one of degree. Some of us are lucky enough not to have a gambling-neurosis or criminotic tendencies or masochistic mother-attachment or overdimensional repetition-compulsion to make our lives miserable, but most of our actions, those usually considered the most important, are unconsciously dominated just the same. And, if a neurosis may be likened to a curse of God, let those of us, the elect, who are enabled to enjoy a measure of life's happiness without the hell-fire of neurotic guilt, take this, not as our own achievement, but simply for what it is—a gift of God.

Let us, however, quit metaphysics and put the situation schematically in the form of a deductive argument.

1. An occurrence over which we had no control is something we cannot be held responsible for.

2. Events E, occurring during our babyhood, were events over which we had no control.

3. Therefore events E were events which we cannot be held responsible for.

4. But if there is something we cannot be held responsible for, neither can we be held responsible for something that inevitably results from it.

5. Events E have as inevitable consequence Neurosis N, which in turn has inevitable consequence Behavior B.

6. Since N is the inevitable consequence of E and B is the inevitable consequence of N, B is the inevitable consequence of E.

7. Hence, not being responsible for E, we cannot be responsible for B.

In Samuel Butler's Utopian satire *Erewhon* there occurs the following passage, in which a judge is passing sentence on a prisoner:

It is all very well for you to say that you came of unhealthy parents, and had a severe accident in your childhood which permanently undermined your constitution; excuses such as these are the ordinary refuge of the criminal; but they cannot for one moment be listened to by the ear of justice. I am not here to enter upon curious metaphysical questions as to the origin of this or that—questions to which there would be no end were their introduction once tolerated, and which would result in throwing the only guilt on the tissues of the primordial cell, or on the elementary gases. There is no question of how you came to be wicked, but only this—namely, are you wicked or not? This has been decided in the affirmative, neither can I hesitate for a single moment to say that it has been decided justly. You are a bad and dangerous person, and stand branded in the eyes of your fellow countrymen with one of the most heinous known offenses.[13]

As moralists read this passage, they may perhaps nod with approval. But the joke is on them. The sting comes when we realize what the crime is for which the prisoner is being sentenced: namely, consumption. The defendant is reminded that

during the previous year he was sentenced for aggravated bronchitis, and is warned that he should profit from experience in the future. Butler is employing here his familiar method of presenting some human tendency (in this case, holding people responsible for what isn't their fault) to a ridiculous extreme and thereby reducing it to absurdity.

Assuming the main conclusions of this paper to be true, is there any room left for freedom?

This, of course, all depends on what we mean by "freedom." In the senses suggested at the beginning of this paper, there are countless free acts, and unfree ones as well. When "free" means "uncompelled," and only external compulsion is admitted, again there are countless free acts. But now we have extended the notion of compulsion to include determination by unconscious forces. With this sense in mind, our question is, "With the concept of compulsion thus extended, and in the light of present psychoanalytic knowledge, is there any freedom left in human behavior?"

If practicing psychoanalysts were asked this question, there is little doubt that their answer would be along the following lines: they would say that they were not accustomed to using the term "free" at all, but that if they had to suggest a criterion for distinguishing the free from the unfree, they would say that a person's freedom is present *in inverse proportion to his neuroticism;* in other words, the more his acts are determined by a *malevolent* unconscious, the less free he is. Thus they would speak of *degrees* of freedom. They would say that as a person is cured of his neurosis, he becomes more free—free to realize capabilities that were blocked by the neurotic affliction. The psychologically well-adjusted individual is in this sense comparatively the most free. Indeed, those who are cured of mental disorders are sometimes said to have *regained their freedom:* they are freed from the tyranny of a malevolent unconscious which formerly exerted as much of a domination over them as if they had been abject slaves of a cruel dictator.

But suppose one says that a person is free only to the extent that his acts are *not unconsciously determined at all,* be they unconscious benevolent *or* malevolent? If this is the criterion, psychoanalysts would say, most human behavior cannot be called free at all: our impulses and volitions having to do with our basic attitudes toward life, whether we are optimists or pessimists, tough-minded or tender-minded, whether our tempers are quick or slow, whether we are "naturally self-seeking" or "naturally benevolent" (and *all the acts consequent upon these things*), what things annoy us, whether we take to blondes or brunettes, old or young, whether we become philosophers or artists or businessmen—all this has its basis in the unconscious. If people generally call most acts free, it is not because they believe that compelled acts should be called free, it is rather through not knowing how large a proportion of our acts actually are compelled. Only the comparatively "vanilla-flavored" aspects of our lives—such as our behavior toward people who don't really matter to us—are exempted from this rule.

These, I think, are the two principal criteria for distinguishing freedom from the lack of it which we might set up on the basis of psychoanalytic knowledge. Conceivably we might set up others. In every case, of course, it remains trivially true that "it all depends on how we choose to use the word." The facts are what they are, regardless of what words we choose for labeling them. But if we choose to label them in a way which is not in accord with what human beings, however vaguely, have long had in mind in applying these labels, as we would be doing if we labeled as "free" many acts which we know as much about as we now do through modern psychoanalytic methods, then we shall only be manipulating words to mislead our fellow creatures.

NOTES

1. *Ethics,* pp. 15–16.
2. *Philosophy and the Physicists,* p. 212.
3. *The Problems of Ethics,* Rynin translation, p. 150.
4. *Ethics,* Chapter 6, pp. 217ff.
5. *New York Post,* Tuesday, May 18, 1948, p. 4.
6. I am aware that the theory presented below is not accepted by all practicing psychoanalysts. Many non-Freudians would disagree with the conclusions presented below. But I do not believe that this fact affects my argument, as long as the concept of unconscious motivation is accepted. I am aware, too, that much of the language employed in the following descriptions is animistic and metaphorical; but as long as I am presenting a view I would prefer to "go the whole hog" and present it in its most dramatic form. The theory can in any case be made clearest by the use of such language, just as atomic theory can often be made clearest to students with the use of models.
7. This view is very clearly developed in Edmund Bergler, *Divorce Won't Help,* especially Chapter I.
8. See *The Basic Writings of Sigmund Freud,* Modern Library Edition, p. 310. (In *The Interpretation of Dreams.*) Cf. also the essay by Ernest Jones, "A Psycho-analytical Study of Hamlet."
9. See Edmund Bergler's article on the pathological gambler in *Diseases of the Nervous System* (1943). Also "Suppositions about the Mechanism of Criminosis," *Journal of Criminal Psychopathology* (1944) and "Clinical Contributions to the *Psychogenesis of Alcohol Addiction," Quarterly Journal of Studies on Alcohol,* 5:434 (1944).
10. E.g., Edmund Bergler, *The Battle of the Conscience,* Chapter I.
11. The girl's development after this point is somewhat different. Society demands more aggressiveness of the adult male, hence there are more super-ego strictures on tendencies toward passivity in the male; accordingly his defenses must be stronger.
12. A. J. Ayer, "Freedom and Necessity," *Polemic* (September–October 1946), pp. 40–43. [This volume, p. 374.]
13. Samuel Butler, *Erewhon* (Modern Library edition), p. 107.

RODERICK M. CHISHOLM

Human Freedom and the Self*

"A staff moves a stone, and is moved by a hand, which is moved by a man." Aristotle, *Physics,* 256a.

1. The metaphysical problem of human freedom might be summarized in the following way: "Human beings are responsible agents; but this fact appears to conflict with a deterministic view of action—the view that every event that is involved in an act is caused by some other event. And it also appears to conflict with the view that some of the events that are essential to the act are not caused at all." To solve the problem, I believe, we must make somewhat far-reaching assumptions about the self or the agent—about the man who performs the act.

Perhaps it is needless to remark that, in all likelihood, it is impossible to say anything significant about this ancient problem that has not been said before.[1]

2. Let us consider some deed, or misdeed, that may be attributed to a responsible agent: one man, say, shot another. If the man *was* responsible for what he did, then, I would urge, what was to happen at the time of the shooting was something that was entirely up to the man himself. There was a moment at which it was true, both that he could have fired the shot and also that he could have refrained from firing it. And if this is

so, then, even though he did fire it, he could have done something else instead. (He didn't find himself firing the shot "against his will," as we say.) I think we can say, more generally, then, that if a man is responsible for a certain event or a certain state of affairs (in our example, the shooting of another man), then that event or state of affairs was brought about by some act of his, and the act was something that was in his power either to perform or not to perform.

But now if the act which he *did* perform was an act that was also in his power *not* to then it could not have been caused or determined by any event that was not itself within his power either to bring about or not to bring about. For example, if what we say he did was really something that was brought about by a second man, one who forced his hand upon the trigger, say, or who, by means of hypnosis, compelled him to perform the act, then since the act was caused by the *second* man it was nothing that was within the power of the *first* man to prevent. And precisely the same thing is true, I think, if instead of referring to a second man who compelled the first one, we speak instead of the *desires* and *beliefs* which the first man happens to have had. For if what we say he did was really something that was brought about by his own beliefs and desires, if these beliefs and desires in the particular situation in which he happened to have found himself caused him to do just what it was that we say he did do, then, since *they* caused it, *he* was unable to do anything other than just what it was that he

*A revised version of the Lindley Lecture given at the University of Kansas, April 23, 1964. (An earlier version of the lecture was published by the Department of Philosophy of the University of Kansas in 1964.) Reprinted by permission of the author and the publisher.

did do. It makes no difference whether the cause of the deed was internal or external; if the cause was some state or event for which the man himself was not responsible, then he was not responsible for what we have been mistakenly calling his act. If a flood caused the poorly constructed dam to break, then, given the flood and the constitution of the dam, the break, we may say, *had* to occur and nothing could have happened in its place. And if the flood of desire caused the weak-willed man to give in, then he, too, had to do just what it was that he did do and he was no more responsible than was the dam for the results that followed. (It is true, of course, that if the man is responsible for the beliefs and desires that he happens to have, then he may also be responsible for the things they lead him to do. But the question now becomes: *is* he responsible for the beliefs and desires he happens to have? If he is, then there was a time when they were within his power either to acquire or not to acquire, and we are left, therefore, with our general point.)

One may object: But surely if there were such a thing as a man who is really *good,* then he would be responsible for things that he would do; yet, he would be unable to do anything other than just what it is that he does do, since, being good, he will always choose to do what is best. The answer, I think, is suggested by a comment that Thomas Reid makes upon an ancient author. The author had said of Cato, "He was good because he could not be otherwise," and Reid observes: "This saying if understood literally and strictly, is not the praise of Cato, but of his constitution, which was no more the work of Cato than his existence."[2] If Cato was himself responsible for the good things that he did, then Cato, as Reid suggests, was such that, although he had the power to do what was not good, he exercised his power only for that which was good.

All of this, if it is true, may give a certain amount of comfort to those who are tender-minded. But we should remind them that it also conflicts with a familiar view about the nature of God—with the view that St. Thomas Aquinas expresses by saying that "every movement both of the will and of nature proceeds from God as the Prime Mover."[3] If the act of the sinner *did* proceed from God as the Prime Mover, then God was in the position of the second agent we just discussed—the man who forced the trigger finger, or the hypnotist—and the sinner, so-called, was *not* responsible for what he did. (This may be a bold assertion, in view of the history of western theology, but I must say that I have never encountered a single good reason for denying it.)

There is one standard objection to all of this and we should consider it briefly.

3. The objection takes the form of a strategem —one designed to show that determinism (and divine providence) is consistent with human responsibility. The strategem is one that was used by Jonathan Edwards and by many philosophers in the present century, most notably, G. E. Moore.[4]

One proceeds as follows: The expression (a) He could have done otherwise, it is argued, means no more nor less than (b) if he had chosen to do otherwise, then he would have done otherwise. (In place of "chosen," one might say "tried," "set out," "decided," "undertaken," or "willed.") The truth of statement (b), it is then pointed out, is consistent with determinism (and with divine providence); for even if all of the man's actions were causally determined, the man could still be such that, *if* he had chosen otherwise, then he would have done otherwise. What the murderer saw, let us suppose, along with his beliefs and desires, *caused* him to fire the shot; yet he was such that *if,* just then, he had chosen or decided *not* to fire the shot, then he would not have fired it. All of this is certainly possible. Similarly, we could say, of the dam, that the flood caused it to break and also that the dam was such that, *if* there had been no flood or any similar pressure, then the dam would have remained intact. And therefore, the argument proceeds, if (b) is consistent with determinism, and if (a) and (b) say the same thing, then (a) is also consistent with determinism; hence we can say that the agent *could* have done otherwise even though he was caused to do what he did do; and therefore determinism and moral responsibility are compatible.

Is the argument sound? The conclusion follows from the premises, but the catch, I think, lies in the first premise—the one saying that statement (a) tells us no more nor less than what statement (b) tells us. For (b), it would seem, could be true while (a) is false. That is to say, our man might be such that, if he had chosen to do otherwise, then he would have done otherwise, and yet also such that he could not have done otherwise. Suppose, our murderer was of this sort: first, he would have done otherwise *only* if he had chosen to do otherwise; and, secondly, he *could not have chosen* to do otherwise. Then the fact that he also happens to be such that, *if* he had chosen not to shoot, he would not have shot, would make no difference. For, in the circumstances imagined he could not have done anything other than just what it was that he did do. In a word: from our statement (b) above ("If he had chosen to do otherwise, then he would have done otherwise"), we cannot make an inference to (a) above. ("He could have done otherwise") unless we can *also* assert: (c) He could have chosen to do otherwise. And therefore, if we must reject this third statement (c), then, even though we may be justified in asserting (b), we are not justified in asserting (a). If the man could not have chosen to do otherwise, then he would not have done otherwise— *even if* he was such that, if he *had* chosen to do otherwise, then he would have done otherwise.

I suggest that, if the man could have done otherwise, then these things are true: first, if he had undertaken, endeavored, or set out to do otherwise, then he would have done otherwise; and, secondly, there was no sufficient causal condition for his not thus undertaking, endeavoring, or setting out to do otherwise.[5] If this is true, then the ascription of responsibility conflicts with a deterministic view of human action.

4. Perhaps there is less need to argue that the ascription of responsibility also conflicts with the view that the act, or some event essential to the act, is not caused at all. If, say, the motion of the finger was caused by the flexing of the muscles, if the flexing of the muscles was caused by some other change within the man's brain, and if the change within the brain was not caused at all, if it was fortuitous or capricious, happening so to speak out of the blue, then presumably no one was responsible for the act.

5. We must not say, then, that every event in the act is caused by some other event. And we must not say that some of the events that are essential to the act are not caused at all. The possibility that remains, therefore, is this: we should say that at least one of the events that are involved in the act is caused, not by any other events, but by something else instead. And this something else can only be the agent—the man. If there is an event that is caused, not by other events, but by the man, then there are some events involved in the act that are not caused by other events. But if the event in question is caused by the man then it *is* caused and we are not committed to saying that there is something involved in the act that is not caused at all. And if he caused it in the process of doing something he had some reason for doing, then the act was in no sense fortuitous or capricious.

But this doctrine may be a lot to take, for it implies something of considerable importance about the nature of the agent or the man.

6. If we consider only inanimate objects, we may say that causation is a relation among *events* or *states of affairs.* The dam's breaking, for example, was an event that was caused by a set of other events—the dam being weak, the flood being strong, and so on. But if a man is responsible for a particular deed, then, if what I have said is true, there is some event, or set of events, that is caused, *not* by other events or states of affairs, but by the man himself, by the agent, whatever he may be.

Let us say that when one event or state of affairs (or set of events or states of affairs) causes some other event or state of affairs, then we have an instance of *event causation.* And let us say that when a *person,* or a *man,* as distinct from an event, causes an event or state of affairs, then we have an instance of *agent causation.*

The nature of what is intended by the expression "agent causation" may be illustrated by this sentence from Aristotle's *Physics:* "Thus, a staff moves a stone, and is moved by a hand, which is moved by a man." (VII, 5, 256a, 6–8) If the man was responsible, then we have in this illustration a number of instances of causation—most of them being instances of event causation, but at least one of them being an instance of agent causation. What the staff did to the stone an instance of event causation; for what happened, strictly speaking, was that the motion of the staff caused the motion of the stone. And similarly for what the hand did to the staff: the motion of the hand caused the motion of the staff. And, as we know from physiology, there are still other events which caused the motion of the hand. Hence we need not introduce the agent at this particular point, as Aristotle does—we *need* not, though we *may.* We *may* say that the hand was moved by the man, but we may *also* say that the motion of the hand was caused by the motion of muscles; and we may say that the motion of the muscles was caused by certain events that took place within the brain. But some event, presumably a change within the agent himself, was caused by the agent. Using a pair of medieval terms, we may say that the agent was the "immanent cause" of a change in his own state. This change, in turn, was the "transeunt cause" of still other events, among them being events within the agent's brain. The agent himself, therefore, may also be said to be a cause of those other events.

7. One may object, firstly: "If the *man* does anything, then, as Aristotle's remark suggests, what he does is to move the *hand*. But he certainly doesn't do anything to his *brain*—he may not even know that he *has* a brain. If he doesn't do anything to his brain and if, as physiology seems to tell us, the motion of the hand was caused by something that happened within the brain, then there is no point in appealing to a special category of 'agent causation' as distinguished from 'event causation'—for the whole thing, after all, is a matter of causal relations among events or states of affairs. The motion of the hand was caused by events within the brain. Nothing was caused by the man."

The answer to this objection, I think, is this: It is true that the agent does not *do* anything with his brain, or to his brain, in the sense in which he *does* something with his hand and does something to the staff. But from this it does not follow that the agent was not the immanent cause of something that happened within his brain.

We should note a useful distinction that has been proposed by Professor A. I. Melden—namely, the distinction between "making something A happen" and "doing A."[6] If I reach for the staff pick it up, then one of the things that I *do* is just that—reach for the staff and pick it up. And if it is something that I do, then there is a very clear sense in which it may be said to be something that I know that I do. If you ask me, "Are you doing something, or trying to do something, with the staff?", I will have no difficulty in finding an answer. But in doing something with the staff, I also make various things happen which are not in this same sense things that I do: I will make various air-particles move; I will free a number of blades of grass from the pressure that had been upon them; and I may cause a shadow

to move from one place to another. If these are merely things that I make happen, as distinguished from things that I do, then I may know nothing whatever about them; I may not have the slightest idea that, in moving the staff, I am bringing about any such thing as the motion of air-particles, shadows, and blades of grass.

We may say, in answer to the first objection, therefore, that it is true that our agent does nothing to his brain or with his brain; but from this it does not follow that the agent is not the cause of some event within his brain; for the brain event may be something which, like the motion of the air-particles, he made happen in picking up the staff. The only difference between the two cases is this: in each case, he made something happen when he picked up the staff; but in the one case —the motion of the air-particles or of the shadows—it was the motion of the staff that caused the event to happen; and in the other case—the event that took place in the brain—it was this event that caused the motion of the staff.

The point is, in a word, that whenever a man does a certain thing, then he makes happen a whole series of events only *some* of which are identified by us and by him as his doing that thing.

8. One may object, secondly: "You say that whenever a man does anything, then there is some event A, presumably a change within the man's own state, which is caused only by the man. But if A was not caused by any other event, then A was not brought about by any *other* change within the agent. You cannot say, therefore, what the man's causing A consists of."

It is true that we cannot say what the man's causing A "consists of." To the question "What is it for a man to cause an event A to happen?" we can answer only by saying "Just that—he causes A to happen." But this does not mean that the concept of a man's causing something to happen is muddled or obscure.

Indeed, we may plausibly say—and there is a respectable philosophical tradition to which we may appeal—that the notion of causation by an agent is *more* clear than that of causation by an event, and that it is only by understanding our own causal efficacy as agents that we can grasp the concept of *cause* at all. Hume may be said to have shown that we do not derive the concept of *cause* from what we perceive of external things.

How, then, do we derive it? The most plausible suggestion, it seems to me, is that of Reid, once again: namely, that "the conception of an efficient cause may very probably be derived from the experience we have had . . . of our own power to produce certain effects."[7] If we did not understand the concept of agent causation, we would not understand the concept of event causation.

9. One may object, finally: "If the agent makes a certain event A happen, then, in addition to the event A, there is the event which is the agent's making A happen. What is the status of *that* event? Either it was caused by some other event, or it was not caused at all, or it was caused by the agent. But if it was caused by some other event, you cannot hold the agent responsible for it. And if it wasn't caused at all, you cannot hold him responsible for it. Therefore you must say that whenever a man makes anything happen, he makes it happen that he makes that thing happen. But this, surely, is absurd. There may be occasions on which I cause myself to do something. I may leave a reminder on the table in order to bring it about that I will do a certain thing tomorrow. But ordinarily I do not cause myself to do the things I do; I just do them. And from this it follows that it would be a mistake to say that, whenever a man makes anything happen, he makes it happen that he makes that thing happen."

When a man thus leaves a reminder on the table, he does something for the purpose of causing himself to do a certain other thing later. And in this sense it is true to say that ordinarily a man does not cause himself to do the things he does. For a man's ordinary actions are such that it is not necessary for him to do other things for the purpose of causing himself to perform them. But this is quite consistent with the thesis that, whenever a man does perform an act, he causes it to happen that he performs that act. For, as we have seen, it is one thing to say merely that a man makes a certain event X happen, and it is another thing to say that he makes X happen for the purpose of making some other event happen. From the fact that he makes X happen, it does not follow that he makes anything happen for the purpose of making X happen. And so a man may make it happen that he performs a certain action without thereby doing anything for the purpose of causing himself to perform that action. There-

fore, from the fact that most acts are such that the agent doesn't have to do anything for the purpose of causing himelf to get them done, it does not follow that it is a mistake to say that, whenever a man makes anything happen, he makes it happen that he makes that thing happen.

10. It may have been noted that I have avoided the term "free will" in all of this. For even if there is such a faculty as "the will," which somehow sets our acts agoing, the question of freedom, as John Locke said, is not the question *"whether the will be free"; it is the question "whether a man be free."*[8] For if there is a "will," as a moving faculty, the question is whether the man is free to will to do those things that he does will to do—and also whether he is free *not* to will any of those things that he does will to do, and, again, whether he is free to will any of those things that he does not will to do. Jonathan Edwards tried to restrict himself to the question—"Is the man free to do what it is that he wills?"—but the answer to this question will not tell us whether the man is responsible for what it is that he *does* will to do. Using still another pair of medieval terms, we may say that the metaphysical problem of freedom does not concern the *actus imperatus;* it does not concern the question whether we are free to accomplish whatever it is that we will or set out to do; it concerns the *actus elicitus,* the question whether we are free to will or to set out to do those things that we do will or set out to do. It is one thing to ask whether the things that a man wills are things that are within his power; this is the problem of the *actus voluntatis imperatus.* It is quite a different thing to ask whether his willing itself is something that is within his power; the problem of the *actus voluntatis elicitus.* And this latter—the problem of the *actus elicitus*—is the problem, not of the freedom of the will, but of the freedom of the man.

11. If we are responsible, and if what I have been trying to say is true, then we have a prerogative which some would attribute only to God: each of us, when we really act, is a prime mover unmoved. In doing what we do, we cause certain events to happen, and nothing and no one, except we ourselves, causes us to cause those events to happen.

12. If we are thus prime movers unmoved and if our actions, or those for which we are responsi-

ble, are not causally determined, then they are not causally determined by our *desires*. And this means that the relation between what we want or what we desire, on the other hand, and what it is that we do, on the other, is not as simple as most philosophers would have it.

We may distinguish between what we might call the "Hobbist approach" and what we might call the "Kantian approach" to this question. The Hobbist approach is the one that is generally accepted at the present time, but the Kantian approach, I believe, is the one that is true. According to Hobbism, if we *know,* of some man, what his beliefs and desires happen to be and how strong they are, if we know what he feels certain of, what he desires more than anything else, and if we know the state of his body and what stimuli he is being subjected to, then we may *deduce,* logically, just what it is that he will do—or, more accurately, just what it is that he will try, set out, or undertake to do. Thus Professor Melden has said that "the connection between wanting and doing is logical."[9] But according to the Kantian approach to our problem, and this is the one that I would take, there is no such logical connection between wanting and doing, nor need there even be a causal connection. No set of statements about a man's desires, beliefs, and stimulus situation at any time implies any statement telling us what the man will try, set out, or undertake to do at that time. As Reid put it, though we may "reason from men's motives to their actions and, in many cases, with great probability," we can never do so "with absolute certainty."[10]

This means that, in one very strict sense of the terms, there can be no complete science of man. If we think of science as a matter of finding out what laws happen to hold, and if the statement of a law tells us what kinds of events are caused by what other kinds of events, then there will be human actions which we cannot explain by subsuming them under any laws. We cannot say, "It is causally necessary that, given such and such desires and beliefs, and being subject to such stimuli, the agent will do so and so." For at times the agent, if he chooses, may rise above his desires, or step aside, and do something else instead.

But all of this is consistent with saying that, perhaps more often than not, our desires do exist under conditions such that those conditions ne-

cessitate us to act. And we may also say, with Leibniz, that at other times our desires may "incline without necessitating."

13. Leibniz's phrase presents us with our final philosophical problem. What does it mean to say that a desire, or a motive, might "incline without necessitating"? There is a temptation, certainly, to say that "to incline" means to cause and that "not to necessitate" means not to cause, but obviously we cannot have it both ways.

Nor will Leibniz's own solution do. In his letter to Coste, he puts the problem as follows: "When a choice is proposed, for example to go out or not to go out, it is a question whether, with all the circumstances, internal and external, motives, perceptions, dispositions, impressions, passions, inclinations taken together, I am still in a contingent state, or whether I am necessitated to make the choice, for example, to go out; that is to say, whether this proposition true and determined in fact, *In all these circumstances taken together I shall choose to go out,* is contingent or necessary."[11] Leibniz's answer might be put as follows: in one sense of the terms "necessary" and "contingent," the proposition "In all these circumstances taken together I shall choose to go out," may be said to be contingent and not necessary, and in another sense of these terms, it may be said to be necessary and not contingent. But the sense in which the proposition may be said to be contingent, according to Leibniz, is only this: there is no logical contradiction involved in denying the proposition. And the sense in which it may be said to be necessary is this: since "nothing even occurs without cause or determining reason," the proposition is causally necessary. "Whenever all the circumstances taken together are such that the balance of deliberation is heavier on one side than on the other, it is certain and infallible that that is the side that is going to win out." But if what we have been saying is true, the proposition "In all these circumstances taken together I shall choose to go out," may be causally as well as logically contingent. Hence we must find another interpretation for Leibniz's statement that our motives and desires may incline us, or influence us, to choose without thereby necessitating us to choose.

Let us consider a public official who has some moral scruples but who also, as one says, could be had. Because of the scruples that he does have, he would never take any positive steps to receive a bribe—he would not actively solicit one. But his morality has its limits and he is also such that, if we were to confront him with a *fait accompli* or to let him see what is about to happen ($10,000 in cash is being deposited behind the garage), then he would succumb and be unable to resist. The general situation is a familiar one and this is one reason that people pray to be delivered from temptation. (It also justifies Kant's remark: "And how many there are who may have led a long blameless life, who are only *fortunate* in having escaped so many temptations.")[12] Our relation to the misdeed that we contemplate may not be a matter simply of being able to bring it about or not to bring it about. As St. Anselm noted, there are at least four possibilities. We may illustrate them by reference to our public official and the event which is his receiving the bribe, in the following way: (i) he may be able to bring the event about himself (*facere esse*), in which case he would actively cause himself to receive the bribe; (ii) he may be able to refrain from bringing it about himself (*non facere esse*), in which case he would not himself do anything to insure that he receive the bribe; (iii) he may be able to do something to prevent the event from occurring (*facere non esse*), in which case he would make sure that the $10,000 was *not* left behind the garage; or (iv) he may be unable to do anything to prevent the event from occurring (*non facere non esse*), in which case, though he may not solicit the bribe, he would allow himself to keep it.[13] We have envisaged our official as a man who can resist the temptation to (i) but cannot resist the temptation to (iv): he can refrain from bringing the event about himself, but he cannot bring himself to do anything to prevent it.

Let us think of "inclination without necessitation," then, in such terms as these. First we may contrast the two propositions:

(1) He can resist the temptation to do something in order to make *A* happen;

(2) He can resist the temptation to allow *A* to happen (i.e., to do nothing to prevent *A* from happening).

We may suppose that the man has some desire to have *A* happen and thus has a motive for making *A* happen. His motive for making *A* happen, I suggest, is one that *necessitates* provided that, because of the motive, (1) is false; he cannot resist the temptation to do something in order to make *A* happen. His motive for making *A* happen is one that *inclines* provided that, because of the motive, (2) is false; like our public official, he cannot bring himself to do anything to prevent *A* from happening. And therefore we can say that his motive for making *A* happen is one that *inclines but does not necessitate* provided that, because of the motive, (1) is true and (2) is false; he can resist the temptation to make it happen but he cannot resist the temptation to allow it to happen.

NOTES

1. The general position to be presented here is suggested in the following writings, among others: Aristotle, *Eudemian Ethics*, Book II, Ch. 6; *Nicomachean Ethics*, Book III, Ch. 1–5; Thomas Reid, *Essays on the Active Powers of Man;* C. A. Campbell, "Is 'Free Will' a Pseudo-Problem?" *Mind*, N.S. Vol. LX (1951), pp. 441–465; Roderick M. Chisholm, "Responsibility and Avoidability," and Richard Taylor, "Determination and the Theory of Agency," in Sidney Hook, ed., *Determinism and Freedom in the Age of Modern Science* (New York 1958).

2. Thomas Reid, *Essays on the Active Powers of Man*, Essay IV, Chapter 4 (*Works* p. 600)

3. *Summa Theologica*, First Part of the Second Part, Question VI ("On the Voluntary and Involuntary").

4. Jonathan Edwards, *Freedom of the Will* (New Haven 1957); G. E. Moore, *Ethics* (Home University Library 1912), Chapter Six.

5. I have attempted to spell this out in more detail in "He Could Have Done Otherwise," in Myles Brand, ed., *The Nature of Human Action* (Glenview, Ill., Scott, Foresman and Company, 1970).

6. A. I. Melden, *Free Action* (London 1961), especially Chapter Three. Mr. Melden's own views, however, are quite the contrary of those that are proposed here.

7. Reid, *Works*, p. 524.

8. *Essay Concerning Human Understanding*, Book II, Chapter XXI.

9. *Op. cit.*, p. 166.

10. Reid, *Works*, pp. 608, 612.

11. "Lettre a Mr. Coste de la Nécessité et de la Contingence" (1707) in *Opera Philosophica*, ed. Erdmann, pp. 447–449.

12. In the Preface to the *Metaphysical Elements of Ethics*, in T. K. Abbott, ed., *Kant's Critique of Practical Reason and Other Works on the Theory of Ethics* (London 1959), p. 303.

13. Cf. D. P. Henry, "Saint Anselm's De 'Grammatico' " *Philosophical Quarterly*, Vol. X (1960), pp. 115–126. St. Anselm noted that (i) and (iii), respectively, may be thought of as forming the upper left and the upper right corners of a square of opposition, and (iv) and (ii) the lower left and the lower right.

JEAN-PAUL SARTRE

Existentialism Is a Humanism*

I should like on this occasion to defend existentialism against some charges which have been brought against it.

First, it has been charged with inviting people to remain in a kind of desperate quietism because, since no solutions are possible, we should have to consider action in this world as quite impossible. We should then end up in a philosophy of contemplation; and since contemplation is a luxury, we come in the end to a bourgeois philosophy. The Communists in particular have made these charges.

On the other hand, we have been charged with dwelling on human degradation, with pointing up everywhere the sordid, shady, and slimy, and neglecting the gracious and beautiful, the bright side of human nature; for example, according to Mlle. Mercier, a Catholic critic, with forgetting the smile of the child. Both sides charge us with having ignored human solidarity, with considering man as an isolated being. The Communists say that the main reason for this is that we take pure subjectivity, the *Cartesian I think,* as our starting point; in other words, the moment in which man becomes fully aware of what it means to him to be an isolated being; as a result, we are unable to return to a state of solidarity with the men who are not ourselves, a state which we can never reach in the *cogito.*

From the Christian standpoint, we are charged with denying the reality and seriousness of human undertakings, since, if we reject God's commandments and the eternal verities, there no longer remains anything but pure caprice, with everyone permitted to do as he pleases and incapable, from his own point of view, of condemning the points of view and acts of others.

I shall try today to answer these different charges. Many people are going to be surprised at what is said here about humanism. We shall try to see in what sense it is to be understood. In any case, what can be said from the very beginning is that by Existentialism we mean a doctrine which makes human life possible and, in addition, declares that every truth and every action implies a human setting and a human subjectivity.

As is generally known, the basic charge against us is that we put the emphasis on the dark side of human life. Someone recently told me of a lady who, when she let slip a vulgar word in a moment of irritation, excused herself by saying, "I guess I'm becoming an Existentialist." Consequently, Existentialism is regarded as something ugly; that is why we are said to be naturalists; and if we are, it is rather surprising that in this day and age we cause so much more alarm and scandal than does naturalism, properly so called. The kind of person who can take in his stride such a novel as Zola's *The Earth* is disgusted as soon as he starts reading an Existentialist novel; the kind of person who is resigned to the wisdom of the ages—which is pretty sad—finds us even sadder. Yet, what can

*Reprinted with permission of the publisher from *Existentialism* by Jean-Paul Sartre (New York: Philosophical Library, Inc., 1947).

be more disillusioning than saying "true charity begins at home" or "a scoundrel will always return evil for good?"

We know the commonplace remarks made when this subject comes up, remarks which always add up to the same thing: we shouldn't struggle against the powers that be; we shouldn't resist authority; we shouldn't try to rise above our station; any action which doesn't conform to authority is romantic; any effort not based on past experience is doomed to failure; experience shows that man's bent is always toward trouble, that there must be a strong hand to hold him in check, if not, there will be anarchy. There are still people who go on mumbling these melancholy old saws, the people who say, "It's only human!" whenever a more or less repugnant act is pointed out to them, the people who glut themselves on *chansons réalistes;* [satirical songs about contemporary persons or events]; these are the people who accuse Existentialism of being too gloomy, and to such an extent that I wonder whether they are complaining about it, not for its pessimism, but much rather its optimism. Can it be that what really scares them in the doctrine I shall try to present here is that it leaves to man a possibility of choice? To answer this question, we must reexamine it on a strictly philosophical plane. What is meant by the term *Existentialism?*

Most people who use the word would be rather embarrassed if they had to explain it, since, now that the word is all the rage, even the work of a musician or painter is being called "existentialist." A gossip columnist in *Clartés* signs himself *The Existentialist,* so that by this time the word has been so stretched and has taken on so broad a meaning, that it no longer means anything at all. It seems that for want of an advance-guard doctrine analogous to surrealism, the kind of people who are eager for scandal and flurry turn to this philosophy, which in other respects does not at all serve their purposes in this sphere.

Actually, it is the least scandalous, the most austere of doctrines. It is intended strictly for specialists and philosophers. Yet it can be defined easily. What complicates matters is that there are two kinds of Existentialist; first, those who are Christian, among whom I would include Jaspers and Gabriel Marcel, both Catholic; and on the other hand the atheistic Existentialists, among whom I class Heidegger, and then the French

Existentialists and myself. What they have in common is that they think that existence precedes essence, or, if you prefer, that subjectivity must be the starting point.

Just what does that mean? Let us consider some object that is manufactured, for example, a book or a paper cutter: here is an object which has been made by an artisan whose inspiration came from a concept. He referred to the concept of what a paper cutter is and likewise to a known method of production, which is part of the concept, something which is, by and large, a routine. Thus, the paper cutter is at once an object produced in a certain way and, on the other hand, one having a specific use; and one cannot postulate a man who produces a paper cutter but does not know what it is used for. Therefore, let us say that, for the paper cutter, essence—that is, the ensemble of both the production routines and the properties which enable it to be both produced and defined—precedes existence. Thus, the presence of the paper cutter or book in front of me is determined. Therefore, we have here a technical view of the world whereby it can be said that production precedes existence.

When we conceive God as the Creator, He is generally thought of as a superior sort of artisan. Whatever doctrine we may be considering, whether one like that of Descartes or that of Leibnitz, we always grant that will more or less follows understanding or, at the very least, accompanies it, and that when God creates He knows exactly what He is creating. Thus, the concept of man in the mind of God is comparable to the concept of paper cutter in the mind of the manufacturer, and, following certain techniques and a conception, God produces man, just as the artisan, following a definition and a technique, makes a paper cutter. Thus, the individual man is the realization of a certain concept in the divine intelligence.

In the eighteenth century, the atheism of the *philosophes* discarded the idea of God, but not so much for the notion that essence precedes existence. To a certain extent, this idea is found everywhere; we find it in Diderot, in Voltaire, and even in Kant. Man has a human nature; this human nature, which is the concept of the human, is founded in all men, which means that each man is a particular example of a universal concept, man. In Kant, the result of this universality is that the wild man, the natural man, as well as the bourgeois, are circumscribed by the same definition and have the same basic qualities. Thus, here too the essence of man precedes the historical existence that we find in nature.

Atheistic Existentialism, which I represent, is more coherent. It states that if God does not exist, there is at least one being in whom existence precedes essence, a being who exists before he can be defined by any concept, and that this being is man, or, as Heidegger says, human reality. What is meant here by saying that existence precedes essence? It means that, first of all, man exists, turns up, appears on the scene, and only afterwards, defines himself. If man, as the Existentialist conceives him, is indefinable, it is because at first he is nothing. Only afterward will he be something, and he himself will have made what he will be. Thus, there is no human nature, since there is no God to conceive it. Not only is man what he conceives himself to be, but he is also only what he wills himself to be after this thrust toward existence.

Man is nothing else but what he makes of himself. Such is the first principle of Existentialism. It is also what is called "subjectivity," the name we are labeled with when charges are brought against us. But what do we mean by this, if not that man has a greater dignity than a stone or table? For we mean that man first exists, that is, that man first of all is the being who hurls himself toward a future and who is conscious of imagining himself as being in the future. Man is at the start a plan which is aware of itself, rather than a patch of moss, a piece of garbage, or a cauliflower; nothing exists prior to this plan; there is nothing in heaven; man will be what he will have planned to be. Not what he will want to be. Because by the word "will" we generally mean a conscious decision, which is subsequent to what we have already made of ourselves. I may want to belong to a political party, write a book, get married; but all that is only a manifestation of an earlier, more spontaneous choice that is called "will." But if existence really does precede essence, man is responsible for what he is. Thus, Existentialism's first move is to make every man aware of what he is and to make the full responsibility of his existence rest on him. And when we say that a man is responsible for himself, we do not only mean that he is responsible for his own individuality, but that he is responsible for all men.

The word "subjectivism" has two meanings, and our opponents play on the two. Subjectivism means, on the one hand, that an individual chooses and makes himself; and, on the other, that it is impossible for man to transcend human subjectivity. The second of these is the essential meaning of Existentialism. When we say that man chooses his own self, we mean that every one of us does likewise; but we also mean by that that in making this choice he also chooses all men. In fact, in creating the man that we want to be, there is not a single one of our acts which does not at the same time create an image of man as we think he ought to be. To choose to be this or that is to affirm at the same time the value of what we choose, because we can never choose evil. We always choose the good, and nothing can be good for us without being good for all.

If, on the other hand, existence precedes essence, and if we grant that we exist and fashion our image at one and the same time, the image is valid for everybody and for our whole age. Thus, our responsibility is much greater than we might have supposed, because it involves all mankind. If I am a workingman and choose to join a Christian trade union rather than be a Communist, and if by being a member I want to show that the best thing for man is resignation, that the kingdom of man is not of this world, I am not only involving my own case—I want to be resigned for everyone. As a result, my action has involved all humanity. To take a more individual matter, if I want to marry, to have children, even if this marriage depends solely on my own circumstances or passion or wish, I am involving all humanity in monogamy and not merely myself. Therefore, I am responsible for myself and for everyone else. I am creating a certain image of man of my own choosing. In choosing myself, I choose man.

This helps us understand what the actual content is of such rather grandiloquent words as anguish, forlornness, despair. As you will see, it's all quite simple.

First, what is meant by "anguish"? The Existentialists say at once that man is anguish. What that means is this: the man who involves himself and who realizes that he is not only the person he chooses to be, but also a lawmaker who is, at the same time, choosing all mankind as well as himself, cannot escape the feeling of his total and deep responsibility. Of course, there are many people who are not anxious; but we claim that they are hiding their anxiety, that they are fleeing from it. Certainly, many people believe that when they do something, they themselves are the only ones involved, and when someone says to them, "What if everyone acted that way?" they shrug their shoulders and answer, "Everyone doesn't act that way." But really, one should always ask himself, "What would happen if everybody looked at things that way?" There is no escaping this disturbing thought except by a kind of double-dealing. A man who lies and makes excuses for himself by saying "not everybody does that," is someone with an uneasy conscience, because the act of lying implies that a universal value is conferred upon the lie.

Anguish is evident even when it conceals itself. This is the anguish that Kierkegaard called the "anguish of Abraham." You know the story: an angel has ordered Abraham to sacrifice his son; if it really were an angel who has come and said, "You are Abraham, you shall sacrifice your son," everything would be all right. But everyone might first wonder, "Is it really an angel, and am I really Abraham? What proof do I have?"

There was a madwoman who had hallucinations; someone used to speak to her on the telephone and give her orders. Her doctor asked her, "Who is it who talks to you?" She answered, "He says it's God." What proof did she really have that it was God? If an angel comes to me, what proof is there that it's an angel; and if I hear voices, what proof is there that they come from heaven and not from hell, or from the subconscious, or a pathological condition? What proves that they are addressed to me? What proof is there that I have been appointed to impose my choice and my conception of man on humanity? I'll never find any proof or sign to convince me of that. If a voice addresses me, it is always for me to decide that this is the angel's voice; if I consider that such an act is a good one, it is I who will choose to say that it is good rather than bad.

Now, I'm not being singled out as an Abraham, and yet at every moment I'm obliged to perform exemplary acts. For every man, everything happens as if all mankind had its eyes fixed on him and were guiding itself by what he does. And every man ought to say to himself, "Am I

really the kind of man who has the right to act in such a way that humanity might guide itself by my actions?" And if he does not say that to himself, he is masking his anguish.

There is no question here of the kind of anguish which would lead to quietism, to inaction. It is a matter of a simple sort of anguish that anybody who has had responsibilities is familiar with. For example, when a military officer takes the responsibility for an attack and sends a certain number of men to death, he chooses to do so, and in the main he alone makes the choice. Doubtless, orders come from above, but they are too broad; he interprets them, and on this interpretation depend the lives of ten or fourteen or twenty men. In making a decision he cannot help having a certain anguish. All leaders know this anguish. That doesn't keep them from acting; on the contrary, it is the very condition of their action. For it implies that they envisage a number of possibilities, and when they choose one, they realize that it has value only because it is chosen. We shall see that this kind of anguish, which is the kind that Existentialism describes, is explained, in addition, by a direct responsibility to the other men whom it involves. It is not a curtain separating us from action, but is part of the action itself.

When we speak of "forlornness," a term Heidegger was fond of, we mean only that God does not exist and that we have to face all the consequences of this. The Existentialist is strongly opposed to a certain kind of secular ethics which would like to abolish God with the least possible expense. About 1880, some French teachers tried to set up a secular ethics which went something like this: God is a useless and costly hypothesis; we are discarding it; but, meanwhile, in order for there to be an ethics, a society, a civilization, it is essential that certain values be taken seriously and that they be considered as having an *a priori* existence. It must be obligatory, *a priori,* to be honest, not to lie, not to beat your wife, to have children, etc., etc. So we're going to try a little device which will make it possible to show that values exist all the time, inscribed in a heaven of ideas, though otherwise God does not exist. In other words—and this, I believe, is the tendency of everything called "reformism" in France— nothing will be changed if God does not exist. We shall find ourselves with the same norms of honesty, progress, and humanism, and we shall have made of God an outdated hypothesis which will peacefully die off by itself.

The Existentialist, on the contrary, thinks it very distressing that God does not exist, because all possibility of finding values in a heaven of ideas disappears along with Him; there can no longer be an *a priori* Good, since there is no infinite and perfect consciousness to think it. Nowhere is it written that the Good exists, that we must be honest, that we must not lie; because the fact is we are on a plane where there are only men. Dostoyevsky said, "If God didn't exist, everything would be possible." That is the very starting point of Existentialism. Indeed, everything is permissible if God does not exist, and as a result man is forlorn, because neither within him nor without does he find anything to cling to. He can't start making excuses for himself.

If existence really does precede essence, there is no explaining things away by reference to a fixed and given human nature. In other words, there is no determinism, man is free, man is freedom. On the other hand, if God does not exist, we find no values or commands to turn to which legitimize our conduct. So, in the bright realm of values, we have no excuse behind us, nor justification before us. We are alone, with no excuses.

That is the idea I shall try to convey when I say that man is condemned to be free. Condemned, because he did not create himself, yet, in other respects is free; because, once thrown into the world, he is responsible for everything he does. The Existentialist does not believe in the power of passion. He will never agree that a sweeping passion is a ravaging torrent which fatally leads a man to certain acts and is therefore an excuse. He thinks that man is responsible for his passion.

The Existentialist does not think that man is going to help himself by finding in the world some omen by which to orient himself. Because he thinks that man will interpret the omen to suit himself. Therefore, he thinks that man, with no support and no aid, is condemned every moment to invent man. Ponge, in a very fine article, has said, "Man is the future of man." That's exactly it. But if it is taken to mean that this future is recorded in heaven, that God sees it, then it is false, because it would really no longer be a future to be forged, a virgin future before him, then this remark is sound. But then we are forlorn.

To give you an example which will enable you to understand forlornness better, I shall cite the case of one of my students who came to see me under the following circumstances: his father was on bad terms with his mother, and, moreover, was inclined to be a collaborationist; his older brother had been killed in the German offensive of 1940, and the young man, with somewhat immature but generous feelings, wanted to avenge him. His mother lived alone with him, very much upset by the half-treason of her husband and the death of her older son; the boy was her only consolation.

The boy was faced with the choice of leaving for England and joining the Free French Forces —that is, leaving his mother behind—or remaining with his mother and helping her to carry on. He was fully aware that the woman lived only for him and that his going off—and perhaps his death —would plunge her into despair. He was also aware that every act that he did for his mother's sake was a sure thing, in the sense that it was helping her to carry on, whereas every effort he made toward going off and fighting was an uncertain move which might run aground and prove completely useless; for example, on his way to England he might, while passing through Spain, be detained indefinitely in a Spanish camp; he might reach England or Algiers and be stuck in an office at a desk job. As a result, he was faced with two very different kinds of action: one, concrete, immediate, but concerning only one individual; the other concerned an incomparably vaster group, a national collectivity, but for that very reason was dubious, and might be interrupted en route. And, at the same time, he was wavering between two kinds of ethics. On the one hand, an ethics of sympathy, of personal devotion; on the other, a broader ethics, but one whose efficacy was more dubious. He had to choose between the two.

Who could help him choose? Christian doctrine? No. Christian doctrine says, "Be charitable, love your neighbor, take the more rugged path, etc., etc." But which is the more rugged path? Whom should he love as a brother? The fighting man or his mother? Which does the greater good, the vague act of fighting in a group or the concrete one of helping a particular human being to go on living? Who can decide *a priori* Nobody. No book of ethics can tell him. The

Kantian ethics says, "Never treat any person as a means, but as an end." Very well, if I stay with my mother, I'll treat her as an end and not as a means; but by virtue of this very fact, I'm running the risk of treating the people around me who are fighting, as means; and, conversely, if I go to join those who are fighting, I'll be treating them as an end, and, by doing that, I run the risk of treating my mother as a means.

If values are vague, and if they are always too broad for the concrete and specific case that we are considering, the only thing left for us is to trust our instincts. That's what this young man tried to do; and when I saw him, he said, "In the end, feeling is what counts. I ought to choose whichever pushes me in one direction. If I feel that I love my mother enough to sacrifice everything else for her—my desire for vengeance, for action, for adventure—then I'll stay with her. If, on the contrary, I feel that my love for my mother isn't enough, I'll leave."

But how is the value of a feeling determined? What gives his feeling for his mother value? Precisely the fact that he remained with her. I may say that I like so-and-so well enough to sacrifice a certain amount of money for him, but I may say so only if I've done it. I may say, "I love my mother well enough to remain with her" if I have remained with her. The only way to determine the value of this affection is, precisely, to perform an act which confirms and defines it. But, since I require this affection to justify my act, I find myself caught in a vicious circle.

On the other hand, Gide has well said that a mock feeling and a true feeling are almost indistinguishable; to decide that I love my mother and will remain with her, or to remain with her by putting on an act, amount somewhat to the same thing. In other words, the feeling is formed by the acts one performs; so, I cannot refer to it in order to act upon it. Which means that I can neither seek within myself the true condition which will impel me to act, nor apply to a system of ethics for concepts which will permit me to act. You will say, "At least, he did go to a teacher for advice." But if you seek advice from a priest, for example, you have chosen this priest; you already knew, more or less, just about what advice he was going to give you. In other words, choosing your adviser is involving yourself. The proof of this is that if you are a Christian, you will say, "Consult a priest." But some priests are collaborating, some are just marking time, some are resisting. Which to choose? If the young man chooses a priest who is resisting or collaborating, he has already decided on the kind of advice he's going to get. Therefore, in coming to see me he knew the answer I was going to give him, and I had only one answer to give: "You're free, choose, that is, invent." No general ethics can show you what is to be done; there are no omens in the world. The Catholics will reply, "But there are." Granted—but, in any case, I myself choose the meaning they have.

When I was a prisoner, I knew a rather remarkable young man who was a Jesuit. He had entered the Jesuit order in the following way: he had had a number of very bad breaks; in childhood, his father died, leaving him in poverty, and he was a scholarship student at a religious institution where he was constantly made to feel that he was being kept out of charity; then, he failed to get any of the honors and distinctions that children like; later on, at about eighteen, he bungled a love affair; finally, at twenty-two, he failed in military training, a childish enough matter, but it was the last straw.

This young fellow might well have felt that he had botched everything. It was a sign of something, but of what? He might have taken refuge in bitterness or despair. But he very wisely looked upon all this as a sign that he was not made for secular triumphs, and that only the triumphs of religion, holiness, and faith were open to him. He saw the hand of God in all this, and so he entered the order. Who can help seeing that he alone decided what the sign meant?

Some other interpretation might have been drawn from this series of setbacks; for example, that he might have done better to turn carpenter or revolutionist. Therefore, he is fully responsible for the interpretation. Forlornness implies that we ourselves choose our being. Forlornness and anguish go together.

As for "despair," the term has a very simple meaning. It means that we shall confine ourselves to reckoning only with what depends upon our will, or on the ensemble of probabilities which make our action possible. When we want something, we always have to reckon with probabilities. I may be counting on the arrival of a friend. The friend is coming by rail or streetcar; this supposes that the train will arrive on schedule, or that the streetcar will not jump the track. I am left in the realm of possibility; but possibilities are to be reckoned with only to the point where my action comports with the ensemble of these possibilities, and no further. The moment the possibilities I am considering are not rigorously involved by my action, I ought to disengage myself from them, because no God, no scheme, can adapt the world and its possibilities to my will. When Descartes said, "Conquer yourself rather than the world," he meant essentially the same thing.

The Marxists to whom I have spoken reply, "You can rely on the support of others in your action, which obviously has certain limits, because you're not going to live forever. That means: rely on both what others are doing elsewhere to help you, in China, in Russia, and what they will do later on, after your death, to carry on the action and lead it to its fulfillment, which will be the revolution. You even *have* to rely upon that, otherwise you're immortal." I reply at once that I will always rely on fellow fighters insofar as these comrades are involved with me in a common struggle, in the unity of a party or a group in which I can more or less make my weight felt; that is, one whose ranks I am in as a fighter and whose movements I am aware of at every moment. In such a situation, relying on the unity and will of the party is exactly like counting on the fact that the train will arrive on time or that the car won't jump the track. But, given that man is free and that there is no human nature for me to depend on, I cannot count on men whom I do not know by relying on human goodness or man's concern for the good of society. I don't know what will become of the Russian revolution; I may make an example of it to the extent that at the present time it is apparent that the proletariat plays a part in Russia that it plays in no other nation. But I can't swear that this will inevitably lead to a triumph of the proletariat. I've got to limit myself to what I see.

Given that men are free and that tomorrow they will freely decide what man will be, I cannot be sure that, after my death, fellow fighters will carry on my work to bring it to its maximum perfection. Tomorrow, after my death, some men may decide to set up fascism, and the others may be cowardly and muddled enough to let them do it. Fascism will then be the human reality, so much the worse for us.

Actually, things will be as man will have decided they are to be. Does that mean that I should abandon myself to quietism? No. First, I should involve myself; then, act on the old saw, "Nothing ventured, nothing gained." Nor does it mean that I shouldn't belong to a party, but rather that I shall have no illusions and shall do what I can. For example, suppose I ask myself, "Will socialization, as such, ever come about?" I know nothing about it. All I know is that I'm going to do everything in my power to bring it about. Beyond that, I can't count on anything. Quietism is the attitude of people who say, "Let others do what I can't do." The doctrine I am presenting is the very opposite of quietism, since it declares, "There is no reality except in action." Moreover, it goes further, since it adds, "Man is nothing else than his plan; he exists only to the extent that he fulfills himself; he is therefore nothing else than the ensemble of his acts, nothing else than his life." . . .

I've been reproached for asking whether Existentialism is humanistic. It's been said, "But you said in *Nausea* that the humanists were all wrong. You made fun of a certain kind of humanist. Why come back to it now?" Actually, the word "humanism" has two very different meanings. By "humanism" one can mean a theory which takes man as an end and as a higher value. Humanism in this sense can be found in Cocteau's tale *Around the World in Eighty Hours*, when a character, because he is flying over some mountains in an airplane, declares, "Man is simply amazing." That means that I, who did not build the airplanes, shall personally benefit from these particular inventions, and that I, as man, shall personally consider myself responsible for, and honored by, acts of a few particular men. This would imply that we ascribe a value to man on the basis of the highest deeds of certain men. This humanism is absurd, because only the dog or the horse would be able to make such an overall judgment about man, which they are careful not to do, at least to my knowledge.

But it cannot be granted that a man may make a judgment about man. Existentialism spares him from any such judgment. The Existentialist will never consider man as an end because he is always in the making. Nor should we believe that there is a mankind to which we might set up a cult in the manner of Auguste Comte. The cult of mankind ends in the self-enclosed humanism of Comte, and let it be said, of fascism. This kind of humanism we can do without.

But there is another meaning of humanism. Fundamentally it is this: man is constantly outside of himself; in projecting himself, in losing himself outside of himself, he makes for man's existing; and, on the other hand, it is by pursuing transcendent goals that he is able to exist; man, being this state of passing beyond, and seizing upon things only as they bear upon this passing beyond, is at the heart, at the center of this passing beyond. There is no universe other than a human universe, the universe of human subjectivity. This connection between transcendency, as a constituent element of man—not in the sense that God is transcendent, but in the sense of passing beyond—and subjectivity, in the sense that man is not closed in on himself but is always present in a human universe, is what we call "Existentialist humanism." Humanism, because we remind man that there is no lawmaker other than

himself, and that in his forlornness he will decide by himself; because we point out that man will fulfill himself as man, not in turning toward himself, but in seeking outside of himself a goal which is just this liberation, just this particular fulfillment.

From these few reflections it is evident that nothing is more unjust than the objections that have been raised against us. Existentialism is nothing else than an attempt to draw all the consequences of a coherent atheistic position. It isn't trying to plunge man into despair at all. But if one calls every attitude of unbelief despair, like the Christians, then the word is not being used in its original sense. Existentialism isn't so atheistic that it wears itself out showing that God doesn't exist. Rather, it declares that even if God did exist, that would change nothing. There you've got our point of view. Not that we believe that God exists, but we think that the problem of His existence is not the issue. In this sense Existentialism is optimistic, a doctrine of action, and it is plain dishonesty for Christians to make no distinction between their own despair and ours and then to call us despairing.

Deliberation, Prediction, and Foreknowledge

CARL GINET

Can the Will Be Caused?*

Two views of the problem about freedom of the will that occur frequently in philosophical literature, and elsewhere, can be stated in terms of their questions about the two propositions: (I) The will is caused. (II) The will is free.[1]

*Carl Ginet, "Can the Will Be Caused?" *Philosophical Review*, Vol. 71 (1962), 49–55. Reprinted by permission of the author and the editors of the *Philosophical Review*.

One view naïvely assumes that these propositions are logical contradictories and that there is no important difficulty about the meaning of either. It simply raises the question: Which is true? A familiar argument for (II) is based on an appeal to introspective evidence that (I) is false. The case against (II) is often argued by claiming that science requires (or confirms) a general deterministic postulate that entails (I) or by supporting (I) directly with talk of how a person's past determines his motives and his motives determine his voluntary acts.

Another, I think more penetrating, view takes as fundamental the question whether the two propositions are indeed logically incompatible. Most philosophers raising this question have (through suitable explications of what "free" means) answered it negatively.[2] This is not surprising because the question has nearly always been prompted by the feeling that there are good reasons for accepting both propositions: (I) seems to be supported by the common practice of explaining choices, decisions, volitions, as due to certain psychological attributes of the agent (his desires, beliefs, and the like); (II) seems to be supported by the common practice of appraising choices and agents' reasons for them and of holding agents responsible for them, in which it is assumed that the agents could have chosen otherwise.

Although this second approach to the problem does question one assumption of the more naïve approach, it overlooks another important point. For it still shares with the naïve view the assumption that both (I) and (II) are meaningful descriptions of possible states of affairs. Challenging this assumption in the case of (I) should lead to a better understanding of the problem. To this end I shall argue that (I) is *necessarily* false, that it is conceptually impossible that the will should be caused. The idea that it can be caused is a philosophical mistake, based on notions that cannot be reconciled with our actual concept of deciding.

I take it that (I) can, without argument, be translated to read: all volitions, choices, and decisions are caused. Thus to argue that (I) is not conceptually possible it will suffice to argue that it is not conceptually possible that a decision should be caused.

This conclusion follows directly from the following two propositions:

(A) It is conceptually impossible for a person to know what a decision of his is going to be before he makes it.

(B) If it were conceptually possible for a decision to be caused, then it would be conceptually possible for a person to know what a decision of his was going to be before making it.

I shall argue for each of these separately.

(A) This proposition goes counter to the thinking of some acute philosophers,[3] but the following considerations should make it convincing.

No one can be intelligibly described as knowing what his decision will be before he makes it because the claim to possess such knowledge is implicitly inconsistent. One may be prevented from seeing this, however, by the fact that certain utterances *appear* to make such a claim and yet are susceptible of intelligible interpretation.

For example, consider an utterance of the form "I know now that I shall later decide to do. . . ." There is more than one thing a person might mean by such a remark: he might mean that he has made his decision as to what he will do and so knows what decision he will later announce; or he might mean that he has made his decision as to what he will do and so knows what decision he will later pretend to make; or he might mean that he had made his decision but thinks he will later forget his present intention and make the same decision again. But his meaning anything at all by it depends on the fact that the locution "I know now that I shall later . . ." is commonly used to *express* a present decision concerning future action. Any attempt to understand the remark above must rely on this fact and regard the remark, not as a claim to know what a decision not yet made will be, but as the expression of a decision already made about future action.

The remark must be so regarded because any expansion explicitly denying that the speaker was making this decision-expressing use of "I know that I shall later . . ." also reduces it to absurdity. Consider: "I already know (am quite certain) that I shall later decide to do . . ., but I have not yet decided what I shall do, that is, I've not yet made up my mind what I shall do, this is, I do not yet know what I shall do." Now this utterance clearly makes two *inconsistent* claims: on the one hand, that the speaker knows what he will decide to do, hence, what he will at least try to do; on the other hand, that he does *not* know what he will try to do.

For a person to claim that he knows what he will decide to do, hence, what he will at least try to do, and *then* to begin the process of making up his mind what he will do—trying to persuade himself one way or another by offering himself reasons for and against the various alternatives—would surely be a procedure of which we could make no sense. Either his undertaking to make a decision belies his prior claim to knowledge, or his prior claim makes a farce of his undertaking to make a decision. If he does already know what he will decide to do, then he cannot by the process of making up his mind persuade himself of anything that he does not already know. Yet the whole point of making up one's mind is to pass from uncertainty to a kind of knowledge about what one will do or try to do. To believe that someone already knows what his future attempted action will be is to refuse to regard anything he does as having the point necessary to its being his *deciding* that he will attempt the action. (Analogously, if someone knows already how the pieces of a puzzle go together to form a required shape, then nothing he might do, while knowing that, can count as his *figuring out* how the pieces go together to form the required shape.)

Thus it is unintelligible to describe someone as undertaking to make up his mind and as *knowing* prior to this undertaking what the outcome of it will be. In other words, the concept of a decision does not allow the possibility of a person's knowing what his decision will be before he makes it.[4]

(B) I shall try to reduce to absurdity just one of several interpretations that might be given to the proposition that decisions are caused. This particular interpretation is important because it is one common to many philosophical discussions of the free will problem.

To think of a decision as *caused* (in the sense that interests me here) is to think of a decision as a specific, discriminable event whose occurrence is ascertainable independently of inquiry as to how it was caused, and to think of its being caused as consisting in the fact that there is a set of events and circumstances preceding and accompanying it to which it has a certain relation —the causal relation. This relation is understood to be defined for an indefinite variety of events and circumstances—including even physical events remote from human influence—and, hence, it is in its conception quite independent of any peculair kinds of events and circumstances that might stand in such relation to each other. It applies just as well to decisions and desires as to explosions and temperatures. This view of the causal relation is Humean to the extent that the relation holds between a particular event A and a certain set of its antecedents B only if it is a true

generalization that an event of the same kind as A will always accompany the occurrence of a set of circumstances sufficiently similar to B

With this interpretation (as far as it goes), if (I) does describe a possible state of affairs then it must be at least logically possible that someone should know what a decision of his will be before he makes it. For if this interpretation did make sense and a decision were caused, then the decider would know his decision in advance if both the following conditions were satisfied: (1) The decider knew prior to his decision the causal law that circumstances of the kind that were going to cause it are always accompanied by a decision of that kind. (2) The decider knew prior to his decision that circumstances of the required kind existed or would exist. Under these conditions, the decider would watch a series of causally connected events and circumstances produce a decision of his, knowing all the time what decision would be produced.

The common interpretation of "Decisions are caused" that was explained above excludes all grounds from which one might deduce the conceptual impossibility of such a situation. How could the possibility of the first condition be excluded? If a completely universal proposition can be known by anyone then it can be known by everyone; and surely there is no sense in the idea of a true causal law that could not be known by anyone.

How could the possibility of the second condition (that the decider knows prior to his decision of the existence of its causal circumstances) be excluded? One can, of course, describe a set of circumstances that it would be logically impossible for the decider to know in advance of his decision. (One need only include in the set the circumstance that the decider remains ignorant of certain other circumstances in the set at least until the time of the decision. It might be imagined, for example, that an agent's having a certain set of desires, beliefs, perceptions, and attitudes was always sufficient to produce a certain decision provided also that the agent was not aware at the time of some of those attitudes.) And a set of circumstances would not be a less plausible candidate for the cause of a decision merely because it had this feature. But neither could a set of circumstances be ruled out as a candidate for the cause merely because it *lacked* this feature.

Part of the idea being considered is that the notion of the causal relation is a perfectly general one, applicable to all kinds of events, physical and mental. And this surely means that the notion of the causal relation, whatever it does include, cannot include grounds for deducing that in the special case of a decision it is impossible that any set of its circumstances should both have the causal relation to it and be knowable by the decider in advance. Thus we cannot appeal to the meaning of "are caused" in the proposition "Decisions are caused" to rule out the embarrassing situation outlined above.

The other part of the idea important to this consideration is that a decision is a specific event which, like a flash or a bang, can be identified independently of inquiry into its causes. It is not supposed that one needs to know what causal law an event falls under before one can identify it as a decision. Rather, as with other kinds of events, the knowledge that one is inquiring about a decision is supposed to guide the causal inquiry, to tell one what sort of causal circumstance to look for, *not* to await the outcome of the inquiry. The meaning of "decisions" proves then to be of no more face-saving value than that of "are caused."

And thus this common interpretation of the proposition that decisions might be caused leaves just as much logical room for the discovery that the set of circumstances to which a decision has the causal relation is one that the decider *could* have known in advance as it does for the discovery that it is not.

In short, if the concept of a decision *were* such that one could ascertain that an event fell under it and then independently ascertain that that event had the causal relation to a certain set of its circumstances, then the concept of a decision *would* allow one to think of (1), (2), and, hence, of someone's knowing what his decision will be before he makes it, as genuine possibilities. But in section (A) we saw the absurdity of admitting this latter possibility. I conclude that the concept of a decision makes it impossible that any event be both identified as a decision and said to be caused; and, therefore, that proposition (I) is necessarily false.

Two comments should be made on the import of this argument: If we accept the conclusion that (I) is necessarily false we must be prepared to say one of two things about the explanations that we commonly offer for our own and others' decisions —explanations that certainly seem to be in terms of events or circumstances preceding and accompanying those decisions (desires, beliefs, and the like). Either we must say that these explanations are all, not merely false, but guilty of conceptual absurdity in implying that decisions are caused; or we must say that they do not imply that decisions are caused but are explanations of a quite different kind, involving a relation quite different in conception from the causal relation defined in the Humean way. I choose the latter alternative but shall not elaborate it here.

From my argument it does not follow that there are decisions (or choices or volitions). I have shown only that *if* there are decisions, they are (necessarily) not part of the causal order, that explanations of them must be of a different kind. The Argument above only removes another of the confusions obscuring the free-will-determinism problem. The real question, it seems to me, is whether a vast addition to our knowledge about the *physical* causes and effects of the minuter internal processes of our bodies could possibly turn out to be incompatible with regarding any of the behavior of those bodies as expressing wills (decisions, choices, volitions). If the answer to this is yes (and there are considerations that can incline one to think it is), then it is an unsettled empirical question whether wills (necessarily free) are attributable to human organisms at all.

NOTES

1. I should like to acknowledge my indebtedness to Professor John Rawls, who gave me the initial suggestion for the argument of this paper and help with its development. None of the thoughts here, however, should be attributed to him.

2. For example: Hobbes, Hume, Mill, Moore, Schlick, Nowell-Smith. Some have argued that (I) and (II) *are* logically incompatible on the basis of their own examination of the senses of the predicates involved. See, for example, C. D. Broad, "Determinism, Indeterminism, and Libertarianism," in *Ethics and the History of Philosophy* (New York, 1952), esp. pp. 201–211; and C. A. Campbell, "Is 'Freewill' a Pseudo-Problem?" *Mind*, LX (1951), 441–465.

3. For example, Bertrand Russell in *Our Knowledge of the External World* (Chicago, 1929), pp. 254–255, imagines "a set of beings who know the whole future with absolute certainty," who "would not have to wait for the event in order to know what decision they were going to adopt on some future occasion," and says that they would not regret this knowledge because "human actions are the outcome of desire, and no foreseeing can be true unless it takes account of desire."

4. Some of the conceptual truths on which the argument above relies have been stated by Stuart Hampshire and H. L. A. Hart, "Decision, Intention, and Certainty," *Mind,* LXVII (1958), 1–12. They say (pp. 2–3): " 'He has not yet decided what he will do' entails 'He does not yet know what he will do.' . . . If a man does claim to be able to predict with certainty his own future actions, basing his prediction on induction, then he is implying that the actions in question will be in some sense, or to some degree, involuntary . . . If it is up to him to decide what he is going to do, then he must still be uncertain what he will do until he has made a decision or until his intentions are formed . . . . The certainty comes at the moment of decision, and indeed constitutes the decision, when the certainty is arrived at in this way, as a result of considering reasons, and not as a result of considering evidence."

ALVIN I. GOLDMAN

Actions, Predictions, and Books of Life*

Are actions determined? It is difficult to tell "directly" whether or not actions are governed by universal laws, so some philosophers resort to the following "indirect" argument:

If actions are determined, it is possible to predict them (with certainty).

It is not possible for actions to be predicted (with certainty). Therefore, actions are not determined.

This position will be called "anti-predictionism," and a defender of it is an "anti-predictionist." The aim of this paper is to rebut anti-predictionism.

Both premises of the anti-predictionist argument will come under attack. The first premise asserts that determinism implies the possibility of prediction, or, in its contrapositive form, that the impossibility of prediction implies indeterminism. But on a reasonable definition of determinism this premise is false. One can specify events which it is logically impossible to predict, but which nonetheless may be determined. Setting such events aside, however, there is a presump-

tive connection between determinism and the possibility of prediction. To support the second premise the anit-predictionist may call attention to a problem concerning the possibility of writing a complete description of someone's life—including his voluntary actions—even before he is born. If actions were determined, it would be possible for such a "book of life" to be written. The anti-predictionist contends, however, that no such book of life could be written, at least not with any assurance that its predictions would come true. For a book of life might be discovered and read by the agent whose actions it predicts; but if the agent reads these predictions, he can choose to falsify them. Hence nobody could write such a book of life with any certainty that his predictions would be fulfilled. Therefore, the anti-predictionist concludes, determinism does not hold. Against this position, I maintain that it may well be possible for books of life to be written, and for the author of such a book to know (with certainty) that its predictions will be fulfilled.

Anti-predictionists generally support their second premise by contrasting the predictability of human behavior with that of physical events. They allege that special difficulties of a purely conceptual sort arise for the prediction of action, difficulties that are unparalleled in the realm of purely physical phenomena. I shall argue that there are no essential differences between actions and physical events with respect to the problem of prediction. More precisely, *conceptual* reflec-

*This paper is an abridged and simplified version of a paper with the same title that originally appeared in *American Philosophical Quarterly* V, No. 3, (July 1968): 135–151. A slightly different version appears as Chapter Six. ("Determinism and Predictability") of Alvin I. Goldman, *A Theory of Human Action* (Englewood Cliffs, N.J.: Prentice-Hall, Inc., 1970). For a more rigorous presentation, the reader should consult either of these versions. Reprinted here by permission of the author and the editor of the *American Philosophical Quarterly*.

tion on the nature of human behavior (as opposed to *empirical* investigation by the special sciences) does not reveal any peculiar immunity of action to prediction.

I am not attempting to prove the thesis that actions are determined; I merely wish to show that the anti-predictionist's arguments fail to prove that actions are not determined. It is, of course, conceivable that actions are undetermined. If so, they are not perfectly predictable. My contention is just that the arguments of philosophers, based on familiar, common-sense features of human action and choice, do not prove that actions are undetermined or immune to prediction. My aim, in other words, is not to establish the *truth*, but merely the *tenability*, of the thesis that actions are determined.

II

Some writers have pointed out that certain actions (under certain descriptions, at least) cannot be predicted: i.e., it is logically impossible for them to be predicted. They have inferred from this that these actions are not determined. I am prepared to concede that it is indeed logically impossible for certain actions (under certain descriptions) to be predicted. But it does not follow from this that they are undetermined.

Before turning to these cases, let us present some relevant definitions. I shall define *determinism* as the view that every event and state of affairs is determined in every detail. An event is *determined* (in a given detail) if and only if it is *deducible from some set of antecedent conditions and laws of nature*. Roughly, a law of nature is any true non-analytic universal statement of unlimited scope which supports counterfactual conditionals. Notice that this definition makes no reference to predictability, and thereby leaves open the connection, if any, between determinism and predictability. When an event is deducible from certain laws and antecedent conditions, I shall say that these antecedent conditions *causally necessitate* this event. I assume that if human actions are determined, then among the events or conditions that causally necessitate them are desires, beliefs, and decisions of the agent.

In our discussion of predictability we need a sense of 'prediction' distinct from mere lucky guesses or precognition. We must be concerned with predictions made on the basis of laws and antecedent conditions. I shall call a prediction a *scientific prediction* if and only if it is made by *deducing* the predicted event from known laws and antecedent conditions. A scientific predictor may learn of the laws and antecedent conditions in any number of ways. (On my definition, most predictions made by actual scientists are not "scientific predictions," since real scientists seldom, if ever, *deduce* subsequent events from laws and prior conditions. But scientific prediction, as defined here, may be regarded as an ideal of prediction to which scientists can aspire.)

With these definitions at hand, let us examine some cases in which actions, or action-related events, are logically impossible to predict. Let the expression 'invent *x*' mean 'think of *x* for the very first time.' Now suppose that Sam invents the corkscrew in 1625—in other words, the first thought of the corkscrew occurs in 1625, when Sam thinks of it. It logically follows from this that nobody predicts Sam's invention of the corkscrew. For in order to predict Sam's invention of the corkscrew, the predictor would himself have to think of the corkscrew, and he would have to have such a thought before 1625. But if someone did have such a thought before 1625, then Sam would not *invent* the corkscrew in 1625: Sam's thinking of the corkscrew in 1625 would not count as an inventing of the corkscrew. Thus, it is logically impossible that anyone should (correctly) predict Sam's inventing of the corkscrew.

Does it follow from this that Sam's invention of the corkscrew is undetermined? Certainly not. Although it is logically impossible for anyone to predict Sam's invention of the corkscrew, his invention of the corkscrew may be deducible from laws and antecedent conditions. Consider an analogous case in the realm of purely physical phenomena. Let the expression 'a tornado strikes *x by surprise* at *t*' mean 'a tornado strikes *x* at *t*, and before *t* nobody thinks of a tornado striking *x*.' Now suppose that a tornado strikes Timbuktu by surprise at *t*. It is logically impossible for this event to be predicted, for if someone did predict it, there would be a thought, prior to *t*, of a tornado striking Timbuktu, and hence there would be no event of a tornado striking Timbuktu *by surprise* at *t*. But there is no reason to conclude that the event of a tornado striking Timbuktu by surprise is undetermined. We may well suppose that this event is deducible from laws and antecedent conditions. For surely we may suppose that a tornado's striking Timbuktu at *t* is deducible from prior meteorological conditions and physical laws. But if we simply add to these antecedent conditions the further (antecedent) condition that nobody thinks of a tornado striking Timbuktu before *t,* we obtain a set of laws and antecedent conditions which jointly entail that a tornado strikes Timbuktu *by surprise* at *t.* We see, then, that the logical impossibility of an event being predicted does not prove that this event is undetermined.

With this point in mind, consider a case involving not actions, but decisions. In his article "Can The Will Be Caused?" Carl Ginet claims that it is impossible ("conceptually impossible") for anyone to predict his own decisions. And he regards this as a reason for concluding that decisions are not caused, i.e., determined. The argument begins by defining 'deciding to do *A*' as 'passing into a state of knowledge (of a certain kind) that one will do, or try to do, *A.*' Now suppose that Sam, at *t,* decides to do *A.* If Sam had predicted that he would make this decision —and if this prediction had involved *knowledge* —then Sam could not, at *t,* decide to do *A.* For if, before *t,* he knew that he would decide to do *A,* then he knew before *t* that he would do, or try to do, *A.* But if he knew, before *t,* that he would do, or try to do, *A,* he could not, at *t,* have *passed into* a state of knowing that he would do, or try to do, *A.* Thus, it is logically impossible for anyone to predict his own decision.

Of course, one might predict one's future decision and then forget about it. Having forgotten about this prediction—i.e., having lost this knowledge—one could later *pass into* a state of (renewed) knowledge that one would do, or try to do, an action. But if one *retains* the foreknowledge, nothing one does later can count as *deciding.*

But does it follow from this that a person's decisions are uncaused, or undetermined? As before, the answer is no. From the fact that it is logically impossible for anyone to predict his own decision (and retain the knowledge contained in this prediction) it does not follow that the decision is not deducible from laws and antecedent conditions. Once we notice that there are certain events, the occurrence of which presupposes that

they have not been predicted, we readily see that it is logically impossible for some events to be predicted. But it does not follow that these events are undetermined. Determinism simply does not entail the logical possibility of prediction.

III

Let us set aside the special class of events, including inventions, surprise tornadoes, and decisions, which logically presuppose the absence of prediction or foreknowledge. If we set these aside, it appears that determinism does imply the possibility, in principle, of prediction. For if an event is deducible from laws and antecedent conditions, then if anyone knew these laws and antecedent conditions beforehand, and if he had sufficient reasoning or calculational powers to make the relevant deduction, he could know, beforehand, that the indicated event would occur. In the actual world, of course, there may be no beings with sufficient knowledge of prior conditions and laws, or sufficient deductive powers, to make scientific predictions, especially scientific predictions of (voluntary) human actions. But if we are interested in the possibility, *in principle,* of prediction, we must not confine ourselves to the actual world. We will have to consider certain *non-actual* possible worlds in which a potential predictor is endowed with all relevant information and calculational powers.

The anti-predictionist would contend that there are *no* possible worlds in which scientific predictions are made of an agent's voluntary actions. Or, at any rate, there are no possible worlds in which scientific predictions are made of an agent's voluntary actions and in which the agent learns of these predictions prior to the actions. This is because it is always open to an agent to act contrary to the prediction; in other words, he can always choose to *refute* the prediction, no matter what has been predicted. According to the anti-predictionist, then, there are no possible worlds in which a book of someone's life is written (scientifically) before he is born, a book which he reads during his lifetime, and parts of which he reads prior to the time of the recorded (i.e., predicted) actions. I contend that this claim is mistaken. I think there may well be possible worlds in which books of life are (scientifically) written and yet read at appropriate times by the agent in question. This, then, is an appropriate test of the anti-predictionist's position.

In order to ascertain whether there are possible worlds of the indicated kind, we must try to imagine such worlds. Now we are not interested in possible worlds that are radically different from our own, for the only point of appealing to these possible worlds is to shed light on the actual one. Specifically, we shall want our possible worlds to contain all and only the physical and psychological laws that the actual world contains. Since we do not know all the laws of the actual world, however, we proceed as follows. We see whether we can coherently imagine a world in which scientific predictions of actions are made but which contains no *apparent* difference from our own world with respect to laws of nature. Since this world contains *scientific* predictions, it means that it must be deterministic (at least it must be deterministic with respect to the events being predicted). But this does not beg any questions, for the very fact that such a world does not diverge in any obvious way from the actual world (in terms of laws or regularities) lends credence to the view that the actual world is deterministic. Of course, it does not prove the actual world to be deterministic; but it is not my purpose here to offer such a proof.

My strategy, then, is to sketch a possible world in which a book of life is scientifically written, and in which the agent reads portions of this book. What is problematic and interesting about this is that the book may have a causal effect on the actions it predicts. That is, it may have an effect on the truth or falsity of the statements contained in the book. It is obvious that the prospective author of such a book must take such "reflexivity" into account. Before sketching my possible world, let us examine the structure of prediction-making where the prediction itself has a causal effect on the predicted event.

Consider the problem of an election predictor. He may know what the precise results of the upcoming election will be, if he makes no public prediction of the election. If he publishes a prediction, however, some of the voters, having found out what the results will be, may change their votes and thereby falsify his prediction. How, then, can a pollster make a genuinely scientific and accurate prediction of an election? Can he take into account the effect of the prediction

itself? Herbert Simon has shown that, under specifiable conditions, a predictor can do this. Essentially, what the predictor must know is the propensity of the voters in the community to *change* their voting intention in accordance with their expectations of the outcome. If persons are more likely to vote for a candidate when they expect him to win than when they expect him to lose, we have a "bandwagon" effect; if the opposite holds, we have an "underdog" effect.

Let us suppose that a given pollster has ascertained that, two days before the election, 60 percent of the electorate plans to vote for candidate *A* and 40 percent for *B*. He also knows that, unless he publishes a prediction, the percentages will be the same on election day. Further suppose he knows that there is a certain "bandwagon" effect obtaining in the voting community. (That this bandwagon effect holds in the community could be discovered either by studying previous elections or by deducing it from "higher-level" generalizations found to be true of the community.) When the original intention of the electorate is to vote 60 percent for *A*, this bandwagon effect can be expressed by the equation $V = 60 + .2(P - 50)$, where P is the percentage vote for *A* publicly predicted by a pollster, and V is the actual resultant vote for *A*. Clearly, if the pollster publicly predicts that *A* will receive 60 percent of the vote, his prediction will be falsified. Putting $P = 60$, the equation tells us that $V = 62$. In other words, the effect of the prediction, combined with the original voting intention of the electorate, would result in a 62 percent vote for *A*. However, the pollster can easily calculate a value for P which will make $P = V$. He need only solve the two equations, $P = V$ and $V = 60 + .2(P - 50)$. Such a solution yields $P = 62.5$. Thus, the pollster can publish a prediction saying that 62.5 percent of the electorate will vote for *A*, knowing that his own prediction will bring an additional 2.5 percent of the electorate into the *A* column, and thereby make his prediction come true.

If someone wishes to predict a single person's behavior and yet let him learn of the prediction, the predictor must employ the same sort of strategy as the pollster. He must take into account the agent's reaction to the prediction. There are several kinds of circumstances in which, having made the appropriate calculations, he will be able to make a correct prediction: (1) The agent learns of the prediction but does not want to falsify it. (2) Upon hearing the prediction, the agent decides to falsify it, but later, when the time of the action approaches, he acquires preponderant reasons for doing what was predicted after all. (3) Having decided to refute the prediction, the agent performs the action conforming with it because he doesn't realize that he is conforming with it. (4) At the time of the action the agent lacks either the ability or the opportunity to do anything but conform with the prediction, though he may have believed that he would be able to falsify it. In any of these four kinds of cases, a predictor would be able to calculate that his prediction, together with numerous other antecedent conditions, would causally necessitate that the agent perform the predicted action. In a case of type (2), for example, the predictor may be able to foresee that the agent will first read his prediction and decide to falsify it. But other factors will crop up—ones which the agent did not originally count on—that will make him change his mind and perform the predicted action after all. And the predictor also foresees this.

In the first three types of cases, (1), (2), and (3), the agent performs the predicted action *voluntarily* (though in (3) he does not realize that what he is doing falls under the description "what was predicted"). In other words, in each of these three kinds of cases, the agent *could have* acted otherwise. Thus, the possibility of a scientific prediction does not require that the agent be *unable* to act in any way different from the prediction. All that is required is that the agent will not *in fact* act in any way different from the prediction. A predictor might know that an agent will in fact act in a certain way, not because he knows the agent will be incapable of doing otherwise, but because he knows that the agent will *choose* or *decide* to act as predicted.

IV

I shall now sketch a possible world in which scientific predictions are made of an agent's life and inscribed in a "book of life," (parts of) which the agent subsequently reads. Obviously I cannot describe the whole of this world, but I shall describe some of its most important and problematic features, namely the interaction between the agent and the book. Unfortunately, I shall have to omit a description of another important part of the world, the part in which the predictor (or predictors) gathers his data and makes his calculations. I am unable to describe this part of the world, first, because I do not know all the laws which the predictor would have at his disposal, and secondly, because I am not able to say just what the structure of this being would be. However, the main features of the predictor's *modus operandi* should be clear from our discussion of the pollster, whose technique is at the heart of such predicting.

While browsing around the library one day, I notice an old dusty tome, quite large, entitled "Alvin I. Goldman." I take it from the shelf and start reading. In great detail, it describes my life as a little boy. It always gibes with my memory and frequently revives my memory of forgotten events. I realize that this purports to be a book of my life and I resolve to test it. Turning to the section with today's date on it, I find the following entry for 2:36 P.M. "He discovers me on the shelf. He takes me down and starts reading me. . . ." I look at the clock and see that it is 3:03. It is quite plausible, I say to myself, that I found the book about half an hour ago. I turn now to the entry for 3:03. It reads: "He is reading me. He is reading me. He is reading me." I continue looking at the book in this place, meanwhile thinking how remarkable the book is. The entry reads: "He continues to look at me, meanwhile thinking how remarkable I am."

I decide to defeat the book by looking at a future entry. I turn to an entry eighteen minutes hence. It says: "He is reading this sentence." Aha, I say to myself, all I need do is refrain from reading that sentence eighteen minutes from now. I check the clock. To ensure that I won't read that sentence, I close the book. My mind wanders; the book has revived a buried memory and I reminisce about it. I decide to reread the book there and relive the experience. That's safe, I tell myself, because it is an earlier part of the book. I read that passage and become lost in reverie and rekindled emotion. Time passes. Suddenly I start. Oh yes, I intended to refute the book. But what was the time of the listed action?, I ask myself. It was 3:19, wasn't it? But it's 3:21 now, which means I have already refuted the book. Let me check and make sure. I inspect the book at the entry for 3:17. Hmm, that seems to be the wrong place for there it says I'm in a reverie. I skip a couple of pages and suddenly my eyes alight on the sentence: "He is reading this sentence." But it's an entry for 3:21, I notice! So I made a mistake. The action I had intended to refute was to occur at 3:21, not 3:19. I look at the clock, and it is still 3:21. I have not refuted the book after all.

I now turn to the entry for 3:28. It reads, "He is leaving the library, on his way to the President's office." Good heavens, I say to myself, I had completely forgotten about my appointment with the President of the University at 3:30. I suppose I could falsify the book by not going, but it is much more important for me not to be late for that appointment. I'll refute the book some other time! Since I do have a few minutes, however, I turn back to the entry for 3:22. Sure enough, it says that my reading the 3:28 entry has reminded me about the appointment. Before putting the book back on the shelf, and leaving, I turn to an entry for tomorrow at 3:30 P.M. "He's still riding the bus bound for Chicago," it reads. Well, I say to myself, *that* prediction will be easy to refute. I have absolutely no intention of going to Chicago tomorrow.

Despite my decision to refute the book, events later induce me to change my mind and to conform to it, for stronger reasons arise for not refuting it. When I get home that evening I find a note from my wife saying that her father (in Chicago) is ill and that she had to take the car and drive to Chicago. I call her there and she explains what has happened. I tell her about the book. Next morning she calls again with news that her father's condition is deteriorating and that I must come to Chicago immediately. As I hang up I realize that the book may turn out right after all, but the situation nevertheless demands that I go to Chicago. I might still refute it by going by plane or train. However, I call the airlines and am told that the fog is delaying all flights. The railroad says that there are no trains for Chicago till later in the day. So, acquiescing, I take a bus to Chicago, and find myself on it at 3:30.

V

I have given several cases in which the book is not refuted, and the reader should be convinced that I could easily continue this way. But it is important now to reply to several objections which the anti-predictionist is anxious to make against my procedure.

1. *"Your story clearly presupposes determinism. But whether or not determinism is true is the central matter of dispute. Hence, you are begging the question."* Admittedly, my story does presuppose determinism. Unless determinism were true, the imagined predictor could not have figured out what actions the agent would perform and then have written them in the book. However, this does not beg the question. For I am not trying to prove that determinism *is* true. I am merely trying to show that the thesis of determinism is quite compatible with the world as we know it and with human nature as we know it. The world depicted in my story is very much like the real world, except that it contains different antecedent conditions. The fact that this imagined world is determined and contains predictions of actions, and yet resembles the real world so closely, suggests that the real world may also be determined. At any rate, this supposition seems quite tenable, and its tenability is what I seek to establish.

2. *"The story you told was fixed. Events might have been different from the way you described them. For example, the fog might not have curtailed all air traffic."* No, events could not be different *in the world I am imagining.* That is, in my world all the events I described were causally necessitated by prior antecedent conditions. I did not describe all the antecedent conditions, so perhaps the reader cannot see that each event I did describe was causally necessitated by them. But, since it is a deterministic world, that is so. No one can imagine *my* world and also substitute the negation of one of the events I described. I'm not "fixing" the story by saying that the fog curtailed air traffic; that just is the way my imagined world goes.

3. *"But I can imagine a world in which some putative predictions of actions are refuted."* I have no doubt that you can; that is very easy. You could even imagine a world *somewhat* like the one I have just described, but in which putative predictions are falsified. But this proves nothing at all. I would never deny that one can construct some possible worlds in which putative scientific predictions of actions are not successful. I have only claimed that one can (also) construct *some* possible worlds in which genuine scientific predictions of actions are made (and are successful).

The situation with predictions of actions is no different from the one with predictions of physical events. We can construct possible worlds in which predictions of physical phenomena are correct. But we can also construct worlds in which putative scientific predictions of physical phenomena are incorrect. If our ability to construct worlds in which predictions are unsuccessful proves the inherent unpredictableness of the kind of phenomena unsuccessfully predicted, then we can prove the unpredictableness of physical phenomena as easily as the unpredictableness of human action.

4. *"The world you have described, though possible, is a highly improbable world. Worlds in which putative predictions of actions are falsified are much more probable."* The notion of one possible world being "more probable" than another seems to me unintelligible. Surely the statistical sense of probability cannot be intended. There is no way of "sampling" from possible worlds to discover what features most of them have. Perhaps the antipredictionist means that we can *imagine* more worlds in which putative predictions of actions are falsified. But this too is questionable. I can imagine indefinitely many worlds in which successful predictions of actions are made.

Perhaps the anti-predictionist means that it is improbable that any such sequence of events as I described would occur in the *real* world. He may well be right on this point. However, to talk about what is probable (in the evidential sense) in the real world is just to talk about what has happened, is happening, and will happen *as a matter of fact.* But the dispute between predictionists and anti-predictionists is, presumably, not about what *will* happen, but about what *could* happen *in principle.* This "in principle" goes beyond the particular facts of the actual world.

5. *"The difference between physical phenomena and action is that predictions of actions can defeat themselves; but predictions of physical events cannot."* This is not so. One can construct worlds in which the causal effect of a putative prediction of a physical event falsifies that prediction. Jones calculates the position of a speck of dust three inches from his nose and the direction and velocity of wind currents in the room. He then announces his prediction that five seconds thence the speck will be in a certain position. He neglects to account for the wind expelled from his

mouth when he makes the prediction, however, and this factor changes the expected position of the speck of dust. Perhaps one can imagine a wider variety of cases in which predictions affect human action more than physical phenomena. But this is only a difference of *degree,* not of kind.

6. *"Predictions of physical events can refute themselves because the predictor may fail to account for the effect of his own prediction. But were he to take this effect into account, he would make a correct prediction. On the other hand, there are conditions connected with the prediction of action in which, no matter what prediction the predictor makes, his prediction will be falsified. Here there is no question of inaccurate calculation or insufficient information. Whatever he predicts will be incorrect. Yet this situation arises only in connection with human action, not physical events."*

This is an important objection and warrants detailed discussion.

VI

Suppose that I wish to predict what action you will perform thirty seconds from now, but that I shall not try to change or affect your behavior except by making my prediction. (Thus, I shall not, for example, predict that you will perform no action at all and then make that prediction come true by killing you.) Further suppose that the following conditions obtain. At this moment you want to falsify any prediction that I shall make of your action. Moreover, you will still have this desire thirty seconds from now, and it will be stronger than any conflicting desire you will have at that time. Right now you intend to do action A, but you are prepared to perform $-A$ (not A) if I predict that you will perform A. Thirty seconds hence you will have the ability and opportunity to do A and the ability and opportunity to do $-A$. Finally, conditions are such that, if I make a prediction in English in your presence, you will understand it, will remember it for thirty seconds, and will be able to tell whether any of your actions will conform to it or not. Given all these conditions, whatever I predict—at least, if I make the prediction by saying it aloud, in your presence, in English, etc.—will be falsified. If I predict you will do A, then you will do $-A$, while if I predict that you will do $-A$, you will proceed to do A. In other words, in these conditions any prediction of mine will causally necessitate the non-occurrence of the event I predict.

Notice that this example does not prove that it is impossible "simpliciter" for me to make a scientific prediction of your action. All that it proves is that I cannot make such a prediction *in a certain manner,* viz., by announcing it to you in English. If I predict your action in some other manner, by thinking it to myself or by saying it aloud in Hindustani, for example, the effect on your action would not be the same as if I say it aloud in English. Assume that, if you do not hear me make any prediction or if you hear me say something you fail to understand, you will proceed to perform action *A.* Then it is possible for me to predict your action correctly by announcing the prediction in Hindustani.

In determining whether or not a certain set of events, including (1) a prediction, (2) the event predicted, and (3) certain other assumed conditions, is a "causally compossible" set, it is essential to specify the manner of the prediction. This is true *in general,* not just in the case of predictions of action. A prediction which is "embodied" or expressed in one way will not have the same causal effects as the same prediction expressed in another way. We can see this in the case of the speck of dust. Jones predicted the position of the dust by announcing it orally, and this resulted in the falsification of the prediction. But had he made the same prediction in another fashion— say by moving his toes in a certain conventional pattern—his prediction would not have been falsified, for the position of the dust would not have been affected.

What is the significance of the fact that it is impossible, in some circumstances, for a (correct) prediction of an action to be made in a specified manner? First, this unpredictability does not prove that these actions are undetermined. Indeed, the very construction of the case in which no prediction is possible *presupposed* the existence of laws of nature which, together with a given prediction, would result in a certain action. In short, the case under discussion should, if anything, support rather than defeat the thesis that actions are determined. The only reason one might have for thinking the contrary is the assumption—which should by now appear very dubious—that determinism entails predictability. What our present case shows, I think, is that

under some circumstances, even a determined event may not be susceptible of being correctly predicted in a specified manner. This fact can be further supported by adducing a similar case connected with purely physical events. And this brings me to my second point: the case produced above does not reflect a peculiarity of human action, since parallel examples can be found among physical phenomena.

Imagine a certain physical apparatus placed in front of a piano keyboard. A bar extends from the apparatus and is positioned above a certain key. (Only white keys will be considered.) If the apparatus is not disturbed, the bar will strike that key at a certain time. Now let us suppose that the apparatus is sensitive to sound, and, in particular, can discriminate between sounds of varying pitches. If the apparatus picks up a certain sound, the position of the bar will move to the right and proceed to strike the key immediately to the right of the original one (if there is one). Specifically, if the sound has the same pitch as that of the key over which the bar is poised, the bar will move. If the monitored sound has any other pitch, the bar will remain in its position and proceed to strike that key.

Now suppose that someone (or something) wishes to make predictions of the behavior of the apparatus. He wishes to predict what key the bar will strike. But the following restriction is made on the *manner* in which the prediction is to be made. The prediction must be expressed according to a specific set of conventions or symbols. To predict that the bar will strike middle C, for example, the predictor must emit a sound with the pitch of middle C. To predict that the bar will strike D, he must emit a sound with the pitch of that key, etc. All sound emissions are to be made in the neighborhood of the apparatus. Given this restriction on the manner of prediction, it will be causally incompossible for the predictor to make a correct prediction. Suppose that the bar is poised above middle C. If he predicts that it will strike middle C—that is, if he emits a sound of that pitch—the bar will move and proceed to strike D. But if he predicts any other behavior of the bar, for example, that it will strike D, the bar will remain in its original position and strike middle C.

Admittedly, the manner of prediction I have allowed to the predictor of this physical phenomenon is much more narrowly restricted than the manner of prediction allowed to the predictor of human action. But we could imagine physical apparatuses with a greater degree of complexity, able to "refute" predictions made in any of a wider variety of manners. In any case, the principle of the situation is the same for both physical phenomena and human actions, though the manners of prediction which affect one phenomenon may be different from the manners of prediction which affect the other. The latter difference simply reflects that fact that physical objects and human beings do not respond in precisely the same ways to the same causes. But this is equally true of different kinds of physical objects and of different pairs of human beings.

VII

I have shown that there are possible worlds in which voluntary actions are scientifically predicted. Are there possible worlds in which a person predicts one of his *own* actions? I think that there are such worlds, which I shall illustrate by continuing the sketch of the world described earlier.

Having tested my book of life on a very large number of occasions during many months and having failed to refute it, I become convinced that whatever it says is true. I have about as good inductive evidence for this proposition as I do for many another proposition I could be said to know. Finally, I get up enough courage to look at the very end of the book and, as expected, it tells when and how I shall die. Dated five years hence, it describes my committing suicide by jumping off the eighty-sixth floor observation deck of the Empire State Building. From a description of the thoughts which will flash through my mind before jumping, it is clear that the intervening five years will have been terrible. As the result of those experiences, I shall have emotions and desires (and beliefs) which will induce me to jump. Since I trust the book completely, I now conclude that I *shall* commit suicide five years hence. Moreover, I can be said to *know* that I shall commit suicide.

This example shows, contrary to the view of some authors, that we can have knowledge of our own future actions. knowledge which is not based on having already made a decision or formed an intention to perform the future action. In this

case, there is a time at which I have certain knowledge of what I shall do (at any rate, about as "certain" as one can be with inductive evidence) and yet I have formed no intention nor made any decision to perform that action. At the time I read the book's prediction, I do not intend to commit suicide. But although I do not intend to commit suicide, I fully believe and know that, five years later, I shall intend to commit suicide. I firmly believe that, at that later time, I shall feel certain emotions and have certain desires which will induce me to jump off the Empire State Building. At the time of my reading the book I do not feel those things, but I commiserate with my future self, much as I commiserate with and understand another person's desires, beliefs, feelings, intentions, etc. Still, my understanding of these states of mind and of the action in which they will issue is the understanding of a spectator; my knowledge of these states and of my future action is purely inductive. Moreover, this knowledge is of a particular *voluntary* act to be performed at a specified time. Though the suicide will be a "desperate" action, it will in no sense be "coerced" or done unknowingly; it will flow from a firm intention, an intention formed very deliberately. But that intention will not be formed until after I have had certain experiences, experiences which, at the time I am reading the book, I have not yet had.

We can imagine two alternative series of events to occur between my reading the book and my suicide. First, I might *forget* what I have learned from the book, and later decide to commit suicide. Secondly, while never forgetting the prediction, the knowledge of my future suicide may gradually change from mere inductive knowledge to knowledge based on intention. In this second alternative, there is never any "moment" of decision. I never pass from a state of complete doubt about committing suicide into a sudden intention of committing suicide. Rather, there is a gradual change, over the five-year period, from mere inductive knowledge that I shall commit suicide to an intention to commit suicide. When I first read the book I am fully prepared to assent to the proposition that I shall commit suicide. But I am saddened by the thought; my heart isn't in it. Later, as a result of various tragic experiences, my *will* acquiesces in the idea. I begin to welcome the thought of suicide, to entertain the thought of committing suicide with pleasure and relief. When the appointed time comes around, I am *bent* on suicide. This gradual change in attitude constitutes the difference between the kinds of knowledge of my future suicide, the difference between mere inductive knowledge and knowledge based on intention.

Many philosophers are very uncomfortable with the idea of a book of life. They believe that the existence of such books—or of foreknowledge of actions in any form—would deprive us of all the essential characteristics of voluntary behavior: choice, decision, deliberation, etc. I do not think this fear is warranted. I have just shown that even if a person reads what a book of life predicts, and believes this prediction, he can still perform the indicated action voluntarily. Moreover, the existence of predictions which the agent does *not* read leaves ample opportunity for deliberation and decision. An agent may know that a book of his life exists and yet proceed to make decisions and to deliberate as all of us do now. The agent's belief that there is such a book, and his belief that the book's existence implies that his actions are causally necessitated, is compatible with his deliberating whether to do one action or another. Although his future action is causally necessitated, one of the antecedent conditions which necessitate it is his deliberation. Indeed, the prediction in the book of life was made precisely because its writer knew that the agent would deliberate and then decide to do the predicted action. Thus, the book of life can hardly be said to preclude deliberation. Nor does the book of life imply that the agent's deliberation is "for naught," or "irrelevant." On the contrary, his deliberation is a crucial antecedent condition: were he not to deliberate, he probably would not perform the action he eventually does perform. Deliberation and decision are perfectly compatible with the existence of books of life; and they are perfectly compatible with the thesis that they, and the actions in which they issue, are determined.

PART 5 RESPONSIBILITY,

This section carries the discussion of Part Four into the realm of moral philosophy. All parties to the discussion agree that a man can be held morally responsible for his past action *only* if he was able to do other than he did. Put more tersely: Avoidability is a necessary condition of responsibility. We saw in Part Four that there are two senses of "avoidable." In the *categorical sense,* to say that an act is avoidable is to say that there were no antecedent conditions (causes) sufficient for its occurrence. In the *hypothetical sense,* to say that an act is avoidable is to say that *if* the actor had chosen (or, perhaps, intended) to do otherwise, he would have done otherwise (nothing would have stopped him). Avoidability in the hypothetical sense is perfectly compatible with determinism; avoidability in the categorical sense, by definition, is not. Now the question arises: In which of the senses of "avoidable"—the categorical sense, the hypothetical sense, or both—is it true that a man can be held responsible for his action only if it was avoidable?

Perhaps responsibility, in the relevant sense, is best understood as a kind of *liability* to responsive actions of various kinds by other people. Thus, to be responsible for a past action is to be properly subject (that is, liable) to credit, praise, or reward if the act was in some special way a good one; or to blame, censure, or punishment if it was an evil one. Most of the essays included here are concerned with responsibility as liability to criminal punishment or to moral blame. Essentially, they inquire: Under what conditions are criminal punishment and/or moral blame reasonable and justified? This in turn takes us to the larger questions: What are blame and punishment all about? What are their functions, their aims, their justifying rationales?

A vast amount has been written on the aims and justification of criminal punishment (probably because, as a political institution devoted to the infliction of pain on human beings, it has never sat easily on the conscience of civilized man), and insofar as blame

[1]C. L. Stevenson, *Ethics and Language* (New Haven: Yale University Press, 1944), p. 307.

BLAME, AND PUNISHMENT

can be construed as a "kind of verbally mediated punishment,"[1] the various traditional theories of the nature and justification of punishment find their counterparts in discussions of blame. Theories of punishment can be classified very roughly as follows:

1. *Utilitarian theories.* These theories hold that punishment is at best a necessary evil, justifiable if and only if the good of its consequences (its "social utility") outweighs its own immediate and intrinsic evil. Punishment is pain or deprivation inflicted on a person (presumably a wrongdoer) for the sake of such future goods as correction or reform of the offender, protection of society against other offenses by the same offender, and (especially) deterrence of other would-be offenders by backing up the threat of retribution.

2. *The retributive theory.* In the words of one of its critics, the retributive theory holds that "the primary justification of punishment is always to be found in the fact that an offense has been committed which deserves punishment, not in any future advantage to be gained by its infliction."[2] Two versions of the theory should be distinguished: a *moralistic version,* which maintains that the proper function of punishment is to inflict on the offender the pain "called for" or deserved by the moral gravity of his offense; and a *legalistic version,* which holds that the justification of punishment is always to be found in the fact that a rule has been broken, for the violation of which a certain penalty is specified—whether or not the offender incurs any moral guilt. This theory is not to be confused with the theory (discussed below) that vindictive satisfaction in the mind of the beholder is the ultimate justification of punishment, for its proponents have been among the leading enemies of vengeance. (Some confusion about this matter is no doubt caused by the inconstant terminology used by philosophers.)

3. *Vengeance theories.* Vengeance theories make much of the unhappy fact that, when harmful wrongs are committed, there is among men a widespread and natural

[2] A. C. Ewing, *The Morality of Punishment* (London: Kegan Paul, 1929), p. 13.

lust for vengeance. Such theories are of three different kinds. The *escape-valve version*, associated with the names of James Fitzjames Stephen and Oliver Wendell Holmes, Jr., holds that legal punishment is an orderly outlet for aggressive feelings, which would otherwise demand satisfaction in socially disruptive ways. This, of course, is a variant of the utilitarian theory. The *hedonistic version* finds the justification of punishment in the pleasure it gives people (particularly the victim of the crime and his loved ones) to see the criminal suffer for his crime. Few philosophers have held this odious version of the utilitarian theory, though perhaps Lotze, Bentham, and Gabriel DeTarde come close to it. Finally, the *romantic version* of the theory, very popular among the uneducated, holds that the justification of punishment is to be found in the emotions of hate and anger it expresses, these emotions being those allegedly felt by all normal or right-thinking people. This theory is called "romantic" because, like any theory labeled romantic, it holds that certain emotions and the actions they inspire are self-certifying, needing no further justification.

Erewhon, the imaginary land of Samuel Butler's novel, is "nowhere" misspelled backward; and, since it is a slightly distorted mirror image of Butler's own Victorian England, or our own time, with almost everything "put backward," it is aptly named. The prevailing Erewhonian treatment of moral delinquency is very much the same as our own treatment of physical illness: Delinquents are "treated" and often "cured" by "straighteners." But the Erewhonian treatment of the physically ill is the same as our treatment of the morally delinquent: The sick are severely reprobated and punished. The aim of the wily satirist is to get his readers to see that the Erewhonians are neither more nor less rational than we are, all told; that *any* society that makes a fundamental distinction between disease and crime is cruelly inconsistent. The reformers, or "malcontents," in Erewhon also have their mirrored counterparts among our own moral philosophers. Substitute "crime" for the words "illness" and "consumption" in the following passage, and it becomes an accurate statement of the views of many utilitarian philosophers about punishment:

> The malcontents ... assert that illness is the inevitable result of certain antecedent causes, which, in the great majority of cases, were beyond the control of the individual, and that therefore a man is only guilty for being in a consumption in the same way as rotten fruit is guilty for having gone rotten.

We may, of course, be driven to cutting out rotten spots or throwing away rotten fruit, just as we must, in difficult cases, incarcerate, flog, or even hang, rotten men, but in neither case is self-righteous moralizing appropriate.

Note how naturally a utilitarian account of punishment fits a deterministic world view. Indeed, determinism, in the quoted passage, is cited as a reason for holding a utilitarian theory. The Erewhonians themselves seem to be determinists, and this drives them to find some justifying myth to support their harsh standards of responsibility for illness. Their myth of the unborn invites comparison both with the Christian doctrine of original sin and Oriental doctrines of pre-existence. The reasoning of the Erewhonians, put in terms of morality rather than illness, seems to be as follows: It would be unfair to hold a person responsible for his evil ways if the causes of his character can be traced back ultimately to his parents, his earliest influences, his genes, etc. Indeed, if determinism is true, one's parents cannot help having the characters *they* have, and so on back in time. Therefore, if responsibility is to be reasonable, a person somehow must have created or chosen his own character. But to do this, he must have existed before he was born. Hence, the myth of the unborn. Aristotle, in the selection that opens this section, has a much more plausible account of the way in which one can be said to have chosen his own character, and also a famous argument to show that most of us are in fact responsible for the characters we have.

The moralistic version of the retributive theory is given its classic statement in the passage from Immanuel Kant included here. The great Russian novelist Fyodor Dostoevsky, in an account of his own experiences in a nineteenth-century Siberian prison camp, points out the difficulties of making punishment fit the moral gravity of the offense; he cites inevitable inequalities of moral guilt in the commission of the same crime and inequalities of suffering from the same punishment. Oliver Wendell Holmes also argues against the retributive theory, calling the intuition of fittingness between moral evil and suffering merely "vengeance in disguise." The satisfaction of vengeance for Holmes, however, is a proper function of criminal law.

J. D. Mabbott boldly announces that he is going to defend a retributive theory of punishment. Mabbott's retributivism, however, is the legalistic kind, and has no more in common with Kant than with utilitarianism. John Rawl's very influential discussion of punishment, using some arguments foreshadowed in Mabbott's article, attempts to work out a compromise between legalistic retributivism and utilitarianism. The final article in this section, by Elizabeth Beardsley, is also concerned with blame (and praise). By distinguishing between the various "perspectives" from which judgments of praise and blame are made, she goes a long way toward settling the question whether praise and blame can be reasonable, if determinism should happen to be true.

ARISTOTLE

Conditions of Responsibility for Action*

BOOK TWO

This book is the first of a series (II–V) dealing with the moral virtues. But first we have to ask what moral virtue or goodness is. It is a confirmed disposition to act rightly, the disposition being itself formed by a continuous series of right actions.

CHAPTER ONE

Virtue, then, is of two kinds, intellectual and moral. Of these the intellectual is in the main indebted to teaching for its production and growth, and this calls for time and experience. Moral goodness, on the other hand, is the child of habit, from which it has got its very name, ethics being derived from *ethos*, 'habit,' . . . This is an indication that none of the moral virtues is implanted in us by Nature, since nothing that Nature creates can be taught by habit to change the direction of its development. For instance a stone, the natural tendency of which is to fall down, could never, however often you threw it up in the air, be trained to go in that direction. No more can you train fire to burn downwards. Nothing in fact, if the law of its being is to behave in one way, can be habituated to behave in another. The moral virtues, then, are produced in us neither *by* Nature nor *against* Nature. Nature, indeed, prepares in us the ground for their reception, but their complete formation is the product of habit.

Aristotle, The Nicomachean Ethics, trans. (with notes in italics) J. A. K. Thomson (Harmondsworth: Penguin Books, 1955), Book Two, chapters 1–5; Book three, Chapters 1, 5. Reprinted by permission of George Allen & Unwin Ltd.

Consider again these powers or faculties with which Nature endows us. We acquire the ability to use them before we do use them. The senses provide us with a good illustration of this truth. We have not acquired the sense of sight from repeated acts of seeing, or the sense of hearing from repeated acts of hearing. It is the other way round. We had these senses before we used them, we did not acquire them as a result of using them. But the moral virtues we do acquire by first exercising them. The same is true of the arts and crafts in general. The craftsman has to learn how to make things, but he learns in the process of making them. So men become builders by building, harp players by playing the harp. By a similar process we become just by performing just actions, temperate by performing temperate actions, brave by performing brave actions. Look at what happens in political societies—it confirms our view. We find legislators seeking to make good men of their fellows by making good behaviour habitual with them. That is the aim of every law-giver, and when he is unable to carry it out effectively, he is a failure; nay, success or failure in this is what makes the difference between a good constitution and a bad.

Again, the creation and the destruction of any virtue are effected by identical causes and identical means; and this may be said, too, of every art. It is as a result of playing the harp that harpers become good or bad in their art. The same is true of builders and all other craftsmen. Men will become good builders as a result of building well, and bad builders as a result of building badly. Otherwise what would be the use of having anyone to teach a trade? Craftsmen would all be born either good or bad. Now this holds also of the virtues. It is in the course of our dealings with our fellow-men that we become just or unjust. It is our behaviour in a crisis and our habitual reactions to danger that make us brave or cowardly, as it may be. So with our desires and passions. Some men are made temperate and gentle, others profligate and passionate, the former by conducting themselves in one way, the latter by conducting themselves in another, in situations in which their feelings are involved. We may sum it all up in the generalization, 'Like activities produce like dispositions.' This makes it our duty to see that our activities have the right character, since the differences of quality in them are repeated in the dispositions that follow in their train. So it is a matter of real importance whether our early education confirms us in one set of habits or another. It would be nearer the truth to say that it makes a very great difference indeed, in fact all the difference in the world.

If, then, everything depends upon the way in which we act, clearly it is incumbent on us to inquire what this way is, never forgetting that we must not look for the precision attainable in the exact sciences.

CHAPTER TWO

Since the branch of philosophy on which we are at present engaged differs from the others in not being a subject of merely intellectual interest —I mean we are not concerned to know what goodness essentially is, but how we are to become good men, for this alone gives the study its practical value—we must apply our minds to the solution of the problems of conduct. For, as I remarked, it is our actions that determine our dispositions.

Now that when we act we should do so according to the right principle, is common ground and I propose to take it as a basis of discussion.[1] But we must begin with the admission that any theory of conduct must be content with an outline without much precision in details. We noted this when I said at the beginning of our discussion of this part of our subject that the measure of exactness of statement in any field of study must be determined by the nature of the matter studied.

Now matters of conduct and considerations of what is to our advantage have no fixity about them any more than matters affecting our health. And if this be true of moral philosophy as a whole, it is still more true that the discussion of particular problems in ethics admits of no exactitude. For they do not fall under any science or professional tradition, but those who are following some line of conduct are forced in every collocation of circumstances to think out for themselves what is suited to these circumstances, just as doctors and navigators have to do in their different *métiers*. We can do no more than give our arguments, inexact as they necessarily are, such support as is available.

After this reminder Aristotle proceeds to lay down a proposition or generalization which is cardinal in his system of ethics. Excess of deficiency in his actions impairs the moral quality of the agent.

Let us begin with the following observation. It is in the nature of moral qualities that they can be destroyed by deficiency on the one hand and excess on the other. We can see this in the instances of bodily health and strength.[2] Physical strength is destroyed by too much and also by too little exercise. Similarly health is ruined by eating and drinking either too much or too little, while it is produced, increased, and preserved by taking the right quantity of drink and victuals. Well, it is the same with temperance, courage, and the other virtues. The man who shuns and fears everything and can stand up to nothing becomes a coward. The man who is afraid of nothing at all, but marches up to every danger, becomes foolhardy. In the same way the man who indulges in every pleasure without refraining from a single one becomes incontinent. If, on the other hand, a man behaves like the Boor in comedy and turn his back on every pleasure, he will find his sensibilities becoming blunted. So also temperance and courage are destroyed both by excess and deficiency, and they are kept alive by observance of the mean.

Our virtues are employed in the same kinds of action as established them.

Let us go back to our statement that the virtues are produced and fostered as a result, and by the agency, of actions of the same quality as effect their destruction. It is also true that after the virtues have been formed they find expression in actions of that kind. We may see this in a concrete instance—bodily strength. It results from taking plenty of nourishment and going in for hard training, and it is the strong man who is best fitted to cope with such conditions. So with the virtues. It is by refraining from pleasures that we become temperate, and it is when we have become temperate that we are most able to abstain from pleasures. Or take courage. It is by habituating ourselves to make light of alarming situations and to confront them that we become brave, and it is when we have become brave that we shall be most able to face an alarming situation.

There is one way of discovering whether we are in full possession of a virtue or not. We possess it if we feel pleasure in its exercise; indeed, it is just with pleasures and pains that virtue is concerned.

CHAPTER THREE

We may use the pleasure (or pain) that accompanies the exercise of our dispositions as an index of how far they have established themselves. A man is temperate who abstaining from bodily pleasures finds this abstinence pleasant; if he finds it irksome, he is intemperate. Again, it is the man who encounters danger gladly, or at least without painful sensations, who is brave; the man who has these sensations is a coward. In a word, moral virtue has to do with pains and pleasures. There are a number of reasons for believing this. (1) Pleasure has a way of making us do what is disgraceful; pain deters us from doing what is right and fine. Hence the importance—I quote Plato—of having been brought up to find pleasure and pain in the right things. True education is just such a training. (2) The virtues operate with actions and emotions, each of which is accompanied by pleasure or pain. This is only another way of saying that virtue has to do with pleasures and pains. (3) Pain is used as an instrument of punishment. For in her remedies Nature works by opposites, and pain can be remedial. (4) When any disposition finds its complete expression it is, as we noted, in dealing with just those things by which it is its nature to be made better or worse, and which constitute the sphere of its operations. Now when men become bad it is under the influence of pleasures and pains when they seek the wrong ones among them, or seek them at the wrong time, or in the wrong manner, or in any of

the wrong forms which such offences may take; and in seeking the wrong pleasures and pains they shun the right. This has led some thinkers to identify the moral virtues with conditions of the soul in which passion is eliminated or reduced to a minimum. But this is to make too absolute a statement—it needs to be qualified by adding that such a condition must be attained 'in the right manner and at the right time' together with the other modifying circumstances.

So far, then, we have got this result. Moral goodness is a quality disposing us to act in the best way when we are dealing with pleasures and pains, while vice is one which leads us to act in the worst way when we deal with them.

The point may be brought out more clearly by some other considerations. (5) There are three kinds of things that determine our choice in all our actions—the morally fine, the expedient, the pleasant; and three that we shun—the base, the harmful, the painful. Now in his dealings with all of these it is the good man who is most likely to go right, and the bad man who tends to go wrong, and that most notably in the matter of pleasure. The sensation of pleasure is felt by us in common with all animals, accompanying everything we choose, for even the fine and the expedient have a pleasurable effect upon us. (6) The capacity for experiencing pleasure has grown in us from infancy as part of our general development, and human life, being dyed in grain with it, receives therefrom a colour hard to scrape off. (7) Pleasure and pain are also the standards by which with greater or less strictness we regulate our considered actions. Since to feel pleasure and pain rightly or wrongly is an important factor in human behaviour, it follows that we are primarily concerned with these sensations. (8) Heraclitus says it is hard to fight against anger, but it is harder still to fight against pleasure. Yet to grapple with the harder has always been the business, as of art, so of goodness, success in a task being proportionate to its difficulty. This gives us another reason for believing that morality and statesmanship must concentrate on pleasures and pains, seeing it is the man who deals rightly with them who will be good, and the man who deals with them wrongly who will be bad.

Here, then, are our conclusions. (*a*) Virtue is concerned with pains and pleasures. (*b*) The actions which produce virtue are identical in character with those which increase it. (*c*) These actions differently performed destroy it. (*d*) The actions which produced it are identical with those in which it finds expression.

Aristotle now meets an obvious objection: How can a man perform (say) just actions unless he is already just?

CHAPTER FOUR

A difficulty, however, may be raised as to what we mean when we say that we must perform just actions if we are to become just, and temperate actions if we are to be temperate. It may be argued that, if I do what is just and temperate, I am just and temperate already, exactly as, if I spell words or play music correctly, I must already be literate or musical. This I take to be a false analogy, even in the arts. It is possible to spell a word right by accident or because somebody tips you the answer. But you will be a scholar only if your spelling is done as a scholar does it, that is thanks to the scholarship in your own mind. Nor will the suggested analogy with the arts bear scruitiny. A work of art is good or bad in itself—let it possess a certain quality, and that is all we ask of it. But virtuous actions are not done in a virtuous—a just or temperate—way merely because *they* have the appropriate quality. The *doer* must be in a certain frame of mind when he does them. Three conditions are involved. (1) The agent must act in full consciousness of what he is doing. (2) He must 'will' his action, and will it for its own sake. (3) The act must proceed from a fixed and unchangeable disposition. Now these requirements, if we except mere knowledge, are not counted among the necessary qualifications of an artist. For the acquisition of virtue, on the other hand, knowledge is of little or no value, but the other requirements are of immense, of sovran, importance, since it is the repeated performance of just and temperate actions that produces virtue. Actions, to be sure, are *called* just and temperate when they are such as a just or temperate man would do. But the doer is just or temperate not because he does such things but when he does them in the way of just and temperate persons. It is therefore quite fair to say that a man becomes just by the performance of just, and temperate by the performance of temperate, action; nor is there the smallest likelihood of a man's becoming good by any other course of conduct. It is not, however,

a popular line to take, most men preferring theory to practice under the impression that arguing about morals proves them to be philosophers, and that in this way they will turn out to be fine characters. Herein they resemble invalids, who listen carefully to all the doctor says but do not carry out a single one of his orders. The bodies of such people will never respond to treatment—nor will the souls of such 'philosophers.'

It is now time to produce a formal definition of virtue. In the Aristotelian system this means stating its genus and differentia—that is to say, the class of things to which it belongs and the point or points which distinguish it from other members of the class.

CHAPTER FIVE

We now come to the formal definition of virtue. Note first, however, that the human soul is conditioned in three ways. It may have (1) feelings, (2) capacities, (3) dispositions; so virtue must be one of these three. By 'feelings' I mean desire, anger, fear, daring, envy, gratification, friendliness, hatred, longing, jealousy, pity and in general all states of mind that are attended by pleasure or pain. By 'capacities' I mean those faculties in virtue of which we may be described as capable of the feelings in question—anger, for instance, or pain, or pity. By 'dispositions' I mean states of mind in virtue of which we are well or ill disposed in respect of the feelings concerned. We have, for instance, a bad disposition where angry feelings are concerned if we are disposed to become excessively or insufficiently angry, and a good disposition in this respect if we consistently feel the due amount of anger, which comes between these extremes. So with the other feelings.

Now, neither the virtues nor the vices are feelings. We are not spoken of as good or bad in respect of our feelings but of our virtues and vices. Neither are we praised or blamed for the way we feel. A man is not being praised for being frightened or angry, nor is he blamed just for being angry; it is for being angry in a particular way. But we *are* praised and blamed for our virtues and vices. Again, feeling angry or frightened is something we can't help, but our virtues are in a manner expressions of our will; at any rate there is an element of will in their formation. Finally, we are said to be 'moved' when our feelings are affected, but when it is a question of moral goodness or badness we are not said to be 'moved' but to be 'disposed' in a particular way. A similar line of reasoning will prove that the virtues and vices are not capacities either. We are not spoken of as good or bad, nor are we praised or blamed, merely because we are *capable* of feeling. Again, what capacities we have, we have by nature; but it is not nature that makes us good or bad. . . . So, if the virtues are neither feelings nor capacities, it remains that they must be dispositions. . . .

We have now to state the 'differentia' of virtue. Virtue is a disposition; but how are we to distinguish it from other dispositions? We may say that it is such a disposition as enables the good man to perform his function well. And he performs it well when he avoids the extremes and chooses the mean in actions and feelings. . . .

BOOK THREE

Aristotle now approaches the question of moral responsibility, so important in modern ethics. It never occurred to him to doubt the freedom of the will, but he is as much alive as any modern thinker to the fact—and the importance of the fact—that our acts are not all voluntary. In the following chapter he distinguishes between the degrees of their voluntariness.

CHAPTER ONE

We have found that moral excellence or virtue has to do with feelings and actions. These may be voluntary or involuntary. It is only to the former that we assign praise or blame, though when the involuntary are concerned we may find ourselves ready to condone and on occasion to pity. It is clearly, then, incumbent on the student of moral philosophy to determine the limits of the voluntary and involuntary. Legislators also find such a definition useful when they are seeking to prescribe appropriate rewards and punishments.

Actions are commonly regarded as involuntary when they are performed (*a*) under compulsion, (*b*) as the result of ignorance. An act, it is thought, is done under compulsion when it originates in some external cause of such a nature that the agent or person subject to the compulsion contributes nothing to it. Such a situation is created, for example, when a sea captain is carried out of his course by a contrary wind or by men who have got him in their power. But the case is not always so clear. One might have to consider an action performed for some fine end or through fear of something worse to follow. For example, a tyrant who had a man's parents or children in his power might order him to do something dishonourable on condition that, if the man did it, their lives would be spared; otherwise not. In such cases it might be hard to say whether the actions are voluntary or not. A similar difficulty is created by the jettison of cargo in a storm. When the situation has no complications you never get a man voluntarily throwing away his property. But if it is to save the life of himself and his mates, any sensible person will do it. Such actions partake of both qualities, though they look more like voluntary than involuntary acts. For at the time they are performed they are the result of a deliberate choice between alternatives, and when an action is performed the end or object of that action is held to be the end it had at the moment of its performance. It follows that the terms 'voluntary' and 'involuntary' should be used with reference to the time when the acts were being performed. Now in the imaginary cases we have stated the acts are voluntary. For the movement of the limbs instrumental to the action originates in the agent himself, and when this is so it is in a man's own power to act or not to act. Such actions therefore are voluntary. But they are so only in the special circumstances; otherwise of course they would be involuntary. For nobody would choose to do anything of the sort purely for its own sake. Occasionally indeed the performance of such actions is held to do a man credit. This happens when he submits to some disgrace or pain as the only way of achieving some great or splendid result. But if his case is just the opposite he is blamed, for it shows a degraded nature to submit to humiliations with only a paltry object in view, or at any rate not a high one. But there are also cases which are thought to merit, I will not say praise, but condonation. An example is provided when a man does something wrong because he is afraid of torture too severe for flesh and blood to endure. Though surely there are some things which a man cannot be compelled to do—which he will rather die than do, however painful the mode of death. Such a deed is matricide; the reasons which 'compelled' Alcmaeon in Euripides' play to kill his mother carry their absurdity on the face of them. Yet it is not always easy to make up our minds what is our best course in choosing one of two alternatives—such and such an action instead of such and such another—or in facing one penalty instead of another. Still harder is it to stick to our decision when made. For, generally speaking, the consequences we expect in such imbroglios are painful, and what we are forced to do far from honourable. Then we get praised or blamed according as we succumb to the compulsion or resist it.

What class of actions, then, ought we to distinguish as 'compulsory'? It is arguable that the bare description will apply to any case where the cause of the action is found in things external to the agent when he contributes nothing to the result. But it may happen that actions, though, abstractly considered, involuntary, are deliberately chosen at a given time and in given circumstances in preference to a given alternative. In that case, their origin being in the agent, these actions must be pronounced voluntary in the particular circumstances and because they are preferred to their alternatives. In themselves they are involuntary, yet they have more of the voluntary about them, since conduct is a sequence of particular acts, and the particular things done in the circumstances we have supposed are voluntary. But when it comes to saying which of two alternative lines of action should be preferred—then difficulties arise. For the differences in particular cases are many.

If it should be argued that pleasurable and honourable things exercise constraint upon us from without, and therefore actions performed under their influence are compulsory, it may be replied that this would make every action compulsory. For we all have some pleasurable or honourable motive in everything we do. Secondly, people acting under compulsion and against their will find it painful, whereas those whose actions are inspired by the pleasurable and the honourable find that these actions are accompanied by pleasure. In the third place it is absurd to accuse external influences instead of ourselves when we fall an easy prey to such inducements and to lay the blame for all dishonourable deeds on the seductions of pleasure, while claiming for ourselves credit for any fine thing we have done. It appears, then, that an action is compulsory only when it is caused by something external to itself which is not influenced by anything contributed by the person under compulsion.

Then there are acts done through ignorance. Any act of this nature is other than voluntary, but it is involuntary only when it causes the doer subsequent pain and regret. For a man who has been led into some action by ignorance and yet has no regrets, while he cannot be said to have been a voluntary agent—he did not know what he was doing—nevertheless cannot be said to have acted involuntarily, since he feels no compunction. We therefore draw a distinction. (*a*) When a man who has done something as the result of ignorance is sorry for it, we take it that he has acted involuntarily. (*b*) When such a man is not sorry, the case is different and we shall have to call him a 'non-voluntary' agent. For it is better that he should have a distinctive name in order to mark the distinction. Note, further, that there is evidently a difference between acting *in consequence* of ignorance and acting *in* ignorance. When a man is drunk or in a passion his actions are not supposed to be the result of ignorance but of one or other of these conditions. But, as he does not realize what he is doing, he is acting *in* ignorance. To be sure every bad man is ignorant of what he ought to do and refrain from doing, and it is just this ignorance that makes people unjust and otherwise wicked. But when we use the word 'involuntary' we do not apply it in a case where the agent does not know what is for his own good. For involuntary acts are not the consequence of ignorance when the ignorance is shown in our choice of ends; what does result from such ignorance is a completely vicious condition. No, what I mean is not general ignorance—which is what gives ground for censure—but particular ignorance, ignorance that is to say of the particular circumstances or the particular persons concerned. In such cases there may be room for pity and pardon, because a man who acts in ignorance of such details is an involuntary agent. It will therefore no doubt be well to define the nature and determine the number of these particular circumstances. They are (1) the agent, (2) the act; (3) that which is the object or within the range of the act. Sometimes we must add (4) the instrument (e.g. a tool), (5) the effect or result (e.g. when a man's life is saved), (6) the manner (e.g. gently or roughly). Now nobody in his right mind could be ignorant of *all* these circumstances. Obviously he cannot be ignorant of (1) the agent—how can he fail to know himself? But a man may fail to know (2) what he is doing, as when people say that a remark 'escaped' them or that they did not know they were betraying secrets. (A good instance is that of Aeschylus' supposed revelation of the Mysteries.) Or like the man who was accused of killing another with a catapult, you might say you only wanted to show him how the thing worked. Then (3) you might mistake, say, your son for an enemy, like Merope in the play, or (4) take a naked spear instead of one with the button on, or a lump of rock in mistake for a pumice stone, or (5) you might be the death of a man with a medicine which you hoped would save his life, or (6) hit your antagonist a blow when you only meant to grip his hand, as in 'open' wrestling. Seeing then that there is the possibility of ignorance in any of these special circumstances, one who has acted in ignorance of any one of them is considered to have acted involuntarily, especially if it was the most important of them that he did not know, which by general agreement are (2) the act and (3) the effect of the act.

An involuntary act being one performed under compulsion or as the result of ignorance, a voluntary act would seem to be one of which the origin or efficient cause lies in the agent, he knowing the particular circumstances in which he is acting. I believe it to be an error to say that acts occasioned by anger or desire are involuntary. For in the first place if we maintain this we shall have to give up the view that any of the lower animals, or even children, are capable of voluntary action. In the second place, when we act from desire or anger are none of our actions voluntary? Or are our fine actions voluntary, our ignoble actions, involuntary? It is an absurd distinction, since the agent is one and the same person. It is surely paradoxical to describe as 'involuntary' acts inspired by sentiments which we quite properly desire to have. There are some things at which we *ought* to feel angry, and others which we *ought* to desire —health, for instance, and the acquisition of knowledge. Thirdly, people assume that what is involuntary must be painful and what falls in with our own wishes must be pleasant. Fourthly, what difference is there in point of voluntariness between wrong actions which are calculated and wrong actions which are done on impulse? Both are to be avoided; and the further reflection suggests itself, that the irrational emotions are no less typically human than our considered judgement. Whence it follows that actions inspired by anger or desire are equally typical of the human being who performs them. Therefore to classify these actions as 'involuntary' is surely a very strange proceeding. . . .

The question is now raised whether it is at all times in our power to be good and to do the right. The answer is yes. And it is also in our power at all times to be vicious.

CHAPTER FIVE

Since then it is the end that is the object of our wishing, and the means to the end that is the object of our deliberating and choosing, the actions which deal with means must be done by choice and must be voluntary. Now when the virtues are exercised it is upon means. So virtue also is attainable by our own exertions. And so is vice. For what it lies in our power to do, it lies in our power not to do; when we can say 'no,' we can say 'yes.' If, then, it is in our power to perform an action when it is right, it will be equally in our power to refrain from performing it when it is wrong; and if it lies with us to refrain from doing a thing when that is right, it will also lie with us to do it when that is wrong. But if it is in our power to do the right or the wrong thing, and equally in our power to refrain from doing so; and if doing right or wrong is, as we saw, the same as being good or bad ourselves, we must conclude that it depends upon ourselves whether we are to be virtuous or vicious. The words

To sin and suffer—that offends us still:
But who is ever blest against his will?

must be regarded as a half-truth. It is true that no one is blest against his will, but untrue that wickedness is involuntary. Otherwise we shall have to deny the truth of what we have just been saying and maintain that a man is not the originator of his own actions, of which he might be described as the begetter. But if he demonstrably is so, and we cannot trace our actions to any other springs than those which are found within ourselves, then actions which have such an origin are themselves within our control and are voluntary. In support of this conclusion it seems possible to call in evidence the practice of both private individuals and of legislators. For they inflict pains and penalties for misbehaviour, except in cases where the offender is not held responsible, because he has acted from ignorance or under duress. On the other hand they bestow honours on those who have done some fine action. Their motive in the first case is to stop evil practices, in the second to encourage the well-doer. Now nobody encourages us to do things which it is not in our power to do and which are not voluntary. It does not help at all to be made to believe that there is no such thing as getting hot, or feeling pain or anger, and so on. We shall feel them all the same. We even find that the circumstance that an offence was committed out of ignorance is made a reason for punishment when the offender is held responsible for his ignorance, as is shown, for instance, by the sentence in a case where the accused had been drunk. It may then be doubled on the ground that the offence originated with the offender, since it was open to him to refrain from getting drunk and his drunkenness was responsible for his not knowing what he was doing when he committed the offence. We punish people, too, for breaking the law through ignorance of some point in it which it was their business to know and which they could have known without much trouble. And punishment follows also when the ignorance is thought to have been due to carelessness, it being held that the guilty party need not have shown this ignorance. He should have noticed what he was doing—it was his duty to notice. You may say that very likely he could not help it, he is just that sort of man. But there is an answer to that. Such people have only themselves to blame for having acquired a character like that by their loose living, just as they have only themselves to blame for being unjust, if they make a practice of unjust behaviour, or intemperate, if they spend their time in drinking or other forms of dissipation. It is their persistent activities in certain directions that make them what they are. This is well illustrated by the behaviour of men who are training for some competition or performance: they devote their whole time to the appropriate exercises. The man, then, must be a perfect fool who is unaware that people's characters take their bias from the steady direction of their activities. If a man, well aware of what he is doing, behaves in such a way that he is bound to become unjust, we can only say that he is voluntarily unjust.

Again, while we cannot fairly argue that when a man behaves unjustly he does not wish to be unjust, or that when he plunges into dissipation he has no wish to be dissipated, it is by no means true that he can stop being unjust or dissolute merely by wishing it. You might as well expect a sick man to get better by wishing it. Yet the illness may be voluntary in the sense that it has been caused by loose living and neglecting the doctor's orders. There was a time when he need not have been ill; but once he let himself go, the opportunity was lost. When once you have thrown a stone, it is gone for good and all. Still it lay with yourself to let it lie instead of picking it up and throwing it; the origin of the act was in you. Similarly it was open to the dishonest and dissolute fellow to avoid becoming such a character; so that his original action was voluntary. But once he is hardened in vice the possibility of reforming disappears. Nor is it only vices of character that are voluntary. It is not rare to find bodily defects which are so too. Doubtless nobody blames a man for being born ugly, but we do blame those who lose their looks from want of exercise and neglect of hygiene. We may have the same feeling when a man's physique is weakened or impaired. Thus blindness is not an object of censure but of compassion when it is the result of a congenital defect or an illness or a blow. But if it is the result of alcoholic poisoning or general debauchery, then no one has any sympathy with the blind man. It comes to this. Physical defects which could have been avoided are blamed, but not those which a man cannot help and for which he is therefore not responsible. But, this granted, we must be held responsible for moral failings which are generally reprobated.

But someone may say, 'We all aim at what appears to us to be good, but over this appearance we have no control. How the end appears is determined by the character of the individual. Now one of two things. Either the individual is in a manner responsible for his moral character or he is not. If he is, he will also be in a manner responsible for the way in which the end—that is the good—appears to him. If he is not, then none of us will be responsible for his own misdeeds. The wrongdoer will be acting wrongly because he is ignorant of the true end and thinks that by such wrongdoing he will attain the highest good. That he should aim at the end in this fashion is not a matter of his own choosing. We must be born with an eye for a moral issue which will enable us to form a correct judgement and choose what is truly good. A man who has this natural gift is one of Nature's favourites, and such an endowment is one of the greatest and noblest in the world. It is something that cannot be acquired or learned; and if a man possess it just as it was when it was bestowed upon him at birth, he will have all the native gifts and graces in their genuine and fullest form.' But if this be a sound argument, how will it be possible to maintain that virtue is more voluntary than vice? To the good and the bad man alike the end presents and establishes itself in the same way, whatever that may be, whether an instinctive process or not; and whatever they do, they do it somehow with reference to the end as they see it. One is driven then to hold one of two positions. Either (a) the view one takes of the end —whatever that view may be—is not imposed on us by Nature but is partly due to oneself. Or (b) the end is given by Nature but virtue is voluntary, because the virtuous man does voluntarily whatever he has left himself to do in order to attain his end. In either case vice will be just as voluntary as virtue. For the free agency of the bad man is just as important for his conduct as the free agency of the good man for his, even if we agree that it does not appear in the bad man's choice of an end. So if we say that the virtues are voluntary, then our vices are voluntary too. The cases are identical. . . .

Our dispositions, however, have a different kind of voluntariness from that of our actions. We are masters of an action of ours from start to finish, and it is present to our minds at every stage, so that we know what we are doing. But with dispositions it is otherwise. Their beginning is something we can control, but as they develop step by step the stages of their development elude our observation—it is like the progress of a disease. They are, however, voluntary in the sense that it was originally in our power to exercise them for good or for evil.

NOTES

1.   There will be an opportunity later of considering what is meant by this formula, in particular what is meant by 'the right principle' and how, in its ethical aspect, it is related to the moral virtues.

2.   If we are to illustrate the material, it must be by concrete images.

SAMUEL   BUTLER

Erewhon*

CURRENT OPINIONS

This is what I gathered. That in that country if a man falls into ill health, or catches any disorder, or fails bodily in any way before he is seventy years old, he is tried before a jury of his countrymen, and if convicted is held up to public scorn and sentenced more or less severely as the case may be. There are subdivisions of illness into crimes and misdemeanours as with offences amongst ourselves—a man being punished very heavily for serious illness, while failure of eyes or hearing in one over sixty-five, who has had good health hitherto, is dealt with by fine only, or imprisonment in default of payment. But if a man forges a cheque, or sets his house on fire, or robs with violence from the person, or does any other such things as are criminal in our own country, he is either taken to a hospital and most carefully tended at the public expense, or if he is in good circumstances, he lets it be known to all his friends that he is suffering from a severe fit of immorality, just as we do when we are ill, and they come and visit him with great solicitude, and inquire with interest how it all came about, what symptoms first showed themselves, and so forth

*From Chapters 10, 12, 18, 19. *Erewhon* was first published in 1872.

—questions which he will answer with perfect unreserve; for bad conduct, though considered no less deplorable than illness with ourselves, and as unquestionably indicating something seriously wrong with the individual who misbehaves, is nevertheless held to be the result of either pre-natal or post-natal misfortune.

The strange part of the story, however, is that though they ascribe moral defects to the effect of misfortune either in character or surroundings, they will not listen to the plea of misfortune in cases that in England meet with sympathy and commiseration only. Ill luck of any kind, or even ill treatment at the hands of others, is con-sidered an offence against society, inasmuch as it makes people uncomfortable to hear of it. Loss of fortune, therefore, or loss of some dear friend on whom another was much de-pendent, is punished hardly less severely than physical delinquency. . . .

MALCONTENTS

I confess that I felt rather unhappy when I got home, and thought more closely over the trial that I had just witnessed. [The trial referred to here is that of a man convicted of consumption. See the quotation of John Hospers' article in this volume, p. 389.] For the time I was carried away by the opinion of those among whom I was. They had no misgivings about what they were doing. There did not seem to be a person in the whole court who had the smallest doubt but that all was exactly as it should be. This universal unsuspect-ing confidence was imparted by sympathy to my-self, in spite of all my training in opinions so widely different. So it is with most of us: that which we observe to be taken as a matter of course by those round us, we take as a matter of course ourselves. And after all, it is our duty to do this, save upon grave occasion.

But when I was alone, and began to think the trial over, it certainly did strike me as betraying a strange and untenable position. Had the judge said that he acknowledged the probable truth, namely, that the prisoner was born of unhealthy parents, or had been starved in infancy, or had met with some accidents which had developed consumption; and had he then gone on to say that though he knew all this, and bitterly regretted that the protection of society obliged him to in-

flict additional pain on one who had suffered so much already, yet that there was no help for it, I could have understood the position, however mistaken I might have thought it. The judge was fully persuaded that the infliction of pain upon the weak and sickly was the only means of pre-venting weakness and sickliness from spreading, and that ten times the suffering now inflicted upon the accused was eventually warded off from others by the present apparent severity. I could therefore perfectly understand his inflicting what-ever pain he might consider necessary in order to prevent so bad an example from spreading fur-ther and lowering the Erewhonian standard; but it seemed almost childish to tell the prisoner that he could have been in good health, if he had been more fortunate in his constitution, and been ex-posed to less hardships when he was a boy.

I write with great diffidence, but it seems to me that there is no unfairness in punishing people for their misfortunes, or rewarding them for their sheer good luck; it is the normal condition of human life that this should be done, and no right-minded person will complain of being subjected to the common treatment. There is no alternative open to us. It is idle to say that men are not responsible for their misfortunes. What is respon-sibility? Surely to be responsible means to be lia-ble to have to give an answer should it be demanded, and all things which live are responsi-ble for their lives and actions should society see fit to question them through the mouth of its authorized agent.

What is the offence of a lamb that we should rear it, and tend it, and lull it into security, for the express purpose of killing it? Its offence is the misfortune of being something which society wants to eat, and which cannot defend itself. This is ample. Who shall limit the right of society except society itself? And what consideration for the individual is tolerable unless society be the gainer thereby? Wherefore should a man be so richly rewarded for having been the son of a mil-lionaire, were it not clearly provable that the common welfare is thus better furthered? We cannot seriously detract from a man's merit in having been the son of a rich father without im-perilling our own tenure of things which we do not wish to jeopardize; if this were otherwise we should not let him keep his money for a single hour; we would have it ourselves at once. For property *is* robbery, but then, we are all robbers or would-be robbers together, and have found it essential to organize our thieving, as we have found it necessary to organize our lust and our revenge. Property, marriage, the law; as the bed to the river, so rule and convention to the instinct; and woe to him who tampers with the banks while the flood is flowing.

But to return. Even in England a man on board a ship with yellow fever is held responsible for his mischance, no matter what his being kept in quarantine may cost him. He may catch the fever and die; we cannot help it; he must take his chance as other people do; but surely it would be desperate unkindness to add contumely to our self-protection, unless, indeed, we believe that contumely is one of our best means of self-protection. Again, take the case of maniacs. We say that they are irresponsible for their actions, but we take good care, or ought to take good care, that they shall answer to us for their insanity, and we imprison them in what we call an asylum (that modern sanctuary!) if we do not like their answers. This is a strange kind of irresponsibility. What we ought to say is that we can afford to be satisfied with a less satisfactory answer from a lunatic than from one who is not mad, because lunacy is less infectious than crime.

We kill a serpent if we go in danger by it, simply for being such and such a serpent in such and such a place; but we never say that the serpent has only itself to blame for not having been a harmless creature. Its crime is that of being a thing which it is: but this is a capital offence, and we are right in killing it out of the way, unless we think it more danger to do so than to let it escape; nevertheless we pity the creature, even though we kill it.

But in the case of him whose trial I have described above, it was impossible that any one in the court should not have known that it was but by an accident of birth and circumstances that he was not himself also in a consumption; and yet none thought that it disgraced them to hear the judge give vent to the most cruel truisms about him. The judge himself was a kind and thoughtful person. He was a man of magnificent and benign presence. He was evidently of an iron constitution, and his face wore an expression of the maturest wisdom and experience; yet for all this, old and learned as he was, he could not see things which one would have thought would have been apparent even to a child. He could not emancipate himself from, nay, it did not even occur to him to feel, the bondage of the ideas in which he had been born and bred.

So was it also with the jury and bystanders; and —most wonderful of all—so was it even with the prisoner. Throughout he seemed fully impressed with the notion that he was being dealt with justly: he saw nothing wanton in his being told by the judge that he was to be punished, not so much as a necessary protection to society (although this was not entirely lost sight of), as because he had not been better born and bred than he was. But this led me to hope that he suffered less than he would have done if he had seen the matter in the same light that I did. And, after all, justice is relative.

I may here mention that only a few years before my arrival in the country, the treatment of all convicted invalids had been much more barbarous than now, for no physical remedy was provided, and prisoners were put to the severest labour in all sorts of weather, so that most of them soon succumbed to the extreme hardships which they suffered; this was supposed to be beneficial in some ways, inasmuch as it put the country to less expense for the maintenance of its criminal class; but the growth of luxury had induced a relaxation of the old severity, and a sensitive age would no longer tolerate what appeared to be an excess of rigour, even towards the most guilty; moreover, it was found that juries were less willing to convict, and justice was often cheated because there was no alternative between virtually condemning a man to death and letting him go free; it was also held that the country paid in recommitals for its over-severity; for those who had been imprisoned even for trifling ailments were often permanently disabled by their imprisonment; and when a man had been once convicted, it was probable that he would seldom afterwards be off the hands of the country.

These evils had long been apparent and recognized; yet people were too indolent, and too indifferent to suffering not their own, to bestir themselves about putting an end to them, until at last a benevolent reformer devoted his whole life to effecting the necessary changes. He divided all illness into three classes—those affecting the head, the trunk, and the lower limbs—and obtained an enactment that all diseases of the head, whether internal or external, should be treated with laudanum, those of the body with castor oil, and those of the lower limbs with an embrocation of strong sulphuric acid and water.

It may be said that the classification was not sufficiently careful, and that the remedies were ill chosen; but it is a hard thing to initiate any reform, and it was necessary to familiarize the public mind with the principle, by inserting the thin end of the wedge first: it is not, therefore, to be wondered at that among so practical a people there should still be some room for improvement. The mass of the nation are well pleased with existing arrangements, and believe that their treatment of criminals leaves little or nothing to be desired; but there is an energetic minority who hold what are considered to be extreme opinions, and who are not at all disposed to rest contented until the principle lately admitted has been carried further.

I was at some pains to discover the opinions of these men, and their reasons for entertaining them. They are held in great odium by the generality of the public, and are considered as subverters of all morality whatever. The malcontents, on the other hand, assert that illness is the inevitable result of certain antecedent causes, which, in the great majority of cases, were beyond the control of the individual, and that therefore a man is only guilty for being in a consumption in the same way as rotten fruit is guilty for having gone rotten. True, the fruit must be thrown on one side as unfit for man's use, and the man in a consumption must be put in prison for the protection of his fellow-citizens; but these radicals would not punish him further than by loss of liberty and a strict surveillance. So long as he was prevented from injuring society, they would allow him to make himself useful by supplying whatever of society's wants he could supply. If he succeeded in thus earning money, they would have him made as comfortable in prison as possible, and would in no way interfere with his liberty more than was necessary to prevent him from escaping, or from becoming more severely indisposed within the prison walls; but they would deduct from his earnings the expenses of his board, lodging, surveillance, and half those of his conviction. If he was too ill to do anything for his support in

prison, they would allow him nothing but bread and water, and very little of that.

They say that society is foolish in refusing to allow itself to be benefited by a man merely because he has done it harm hitherto, and that objection to the labour of the diseased classes is only protection in another form. It is an attempt to raise the natural price of a commodity by saying that such and such persons, who are able and willing to produce it, shall not do so, whereby every one has to pay more for it.

Besides, so long as a man has not been actually killed he is our fellow-creature, though perhaps a very unpleasant one. It is in a great degree the doing of others that he is what he is, or in other words, the society which now condemns him is partly answerable concerning him. They say that there is no fear of any increase of disease under these circumstances; for the loss of liberty, the surveillance, the considerable and compulsory deduction from the prisoner's earnings, the very sparing use of stimulants (of which they would allow but little to any, and none to those who did not earn them), the enforced celibacy, and above all, the loss of reputation among friends, are in their opinion as ample safeguards to society against a general neglect of health as those now resorted to. A man, therefore (so they say), should carry his profession or trade into prison with him if possible; if not, he must earn his living by the nearest thing to it that he can; but if he be a gentleman born and bred to no profession, he must pick oakum, or write art criticisms for a newspaper.

These people say further, that the greater part of the illness which exists in their country is brought about by the insane manner in which it is treated.

They believe that illness is in many cases just as curable as the moral diseases which they see daily cured round them, but that a great reform is impossible till men learn to take a juster view of what physical obliquity proceeds from. Men will hide their illnesses as long as they are scouted on its becoming known that they are ill; it is the scouting, not the physic, which produces the concealment; and if a man felt that the news of his being in ill-health would be received by his neighbours as a deplorable fact, but one as much the result of necessary antecedent causes as though he had broken into a jeweller's shop and stolen a valuable diamond necklace—as a fact which might just as easily have happened to themselves, only that they had the luck to be better born or reared; and if they also felt that they would not be made more uncomfortable in the prison than the protection of society against infection and the proper treatment of their own disease actually demanded, men would give themselves up to the police as readily on perceiving that they had taken smallpox, as they go now to the straightener when they feel that they are on the point of forging a will, or running away with somebody else's wife.

But the main argument on which they rely is that of economy: for they know that they will sooner gain their end by appealing to men's pockets, in which they have generally something of their own, than to their heads, which contain for the most part little but borrowed or stolen property; and also, they believe it to be the readiest test and the one which has most to show for itself. If a course of conduct can be shown to cost a country less, and this by no dishonourable saving and with no indirectly increased expenditure in other ways, they hold that it requires a good deal to upset the arguments in favour of its being adopted, and whether rightly or wrongly I cannot pretend to say, they think that the more medicinal and humane treatment of the diseased of which they are the advocates would in the long run be much cheaper to the country: but I did not gather that these reformers were opposed to meeting some of the more violent forms of illness with the cat-of-nine-tails, or with death; for they saw no effectual way of checking them; they would therefore both flog and hang, but they would do so pitifully.

I have perhaps dwelt too long upon opinions which can have no possible bearing upon our own, but I have not said the tenth part of what these would-be reformers urged upon me. I feel, however, that I have sufficiently trespassed upon the attention of the reader. ...

BIRTH FORMULAE

I heard what follows not from Arowhena, but from Mr. Nosibor and some of the gentlemen who occasionally dined at the house: they told me that the Erwhonians believe in pre-existence; and not only this (of which I will write more fully in the next chapter), but they believe that it is of

their own free act and deed in a previous state that they come to be born into this world at all. They hold that the unborn are perpetually plaguing and tormenting the married of both sexes, fluttering about them incessantly, and giving them no peace either of mind or body until they have consented to take them under their protection. If this were not so (this at least is what they urge), it would be a monstrous freedom for one man to take with another, to say that he should undergo the chances and changes of this mortal life without any option in the matter. No man would have any right to get married at all, inasmuch as he can never tell what frightful misery his doing so may entail forcibly upon a being who cannot be unhappy as long as he does not exist. They feel this so strongly that they are resolved to shift the blame on to other shoulders; and have fashioned a long mythology as to the world in which the unborn people live, and what they do, and arts and machinations to which they have recourse in order to get themselves into our own world. But of this more anon: what I would relate here is their manner of dealing with those who do come.

It is a distinguishing peculiarity of the Erewhonians that when they profess themselves to be quite certain about any matter, and avow it as a base on which they are to build a system of practise, they seldom quite believe in it. If they smell a rat about the precincts of a cherished institution, they will always stop their noses to it *if* they can.

This is what most of them did in this matter of the unborn, for I cannot (and never could) think that they seriously believed in their mythology concerning pre-existence: they did and they did not; they did not know themselves what they believed; all they did know was that it was a disease not to believe as they did. The only thing of which they were quite sure was that it was the pestering of the unborn which caused them to be brought into this world, and that they would not have been here if they would have only let peaceable people alone.

It would be hard to disprove this position, and they might have a good case if they would only leave it as it stands. But this they will not do; they must have assurance doubly sure; they must have the written word of the child itself as soon as it is born, giving the parents indemnity from all responsibility on the score of its birth, and asserting its own pre-existence. They have therefore devised something which they call a birth formula—a document which varies in words according to the caution of parents, but is much the same practically in all cases; for it has been the business of the Erewhonian lawyers during many ages to exercise their skill in perfecting it and providing for every contingency.

These formulae are printed on common paper at a moderate cost for the poor; but the rich have them written on parchment and handsomely bound, so that the getting up of a person's birth formula is a test of his social position. They commence by setting forth, That whereas A. B. was a member of the kingdom of the unborn, where he was well provided for in every way, and had no cause of discontent, etc., etc., he did of his own wanton depravity and restlessness conceive a desire to enter into this present world; that thereon having taken the necessary steps as set forth in laws of the unborn kingdom, he did with malice aforethought set himself to plague and pester two unfortunate people who had never wronged him, and who were quite contented and happy until he conceived this base design against their peace; for which wrong he now humbly entreats their pardon.

He acknowledges that he is responsible for all physical blemishes and deficiencies which may render him answerable to the laws of his country; that his parents have nothing whatever to do with any of these things; and that they have a right to kill him at once if they be so minded, though he entreats them to show their marvellous goodness and clemency by sparing his life. If they will do this, he promises to be their most obedient and abject creature during his earlier years, and indeed all his life, unless they should see fit in their abundant generosity to remit some portion of his service hereafter. And so the formula continues, going sometimes into very minute details, according to the fancies of family lawyers, who will not make it any shorter than they can help.

The deed being thus prepared, on the third or fourth day after the birth of the child, or as they call it, the "final importunity," the friends gather together, and there is a feast held, where they are all very melancholy—as a general rule, I believe, quite truly so—and make presents to the father and mother of the child in order to console them

for the injury which has just been done them by the unborn.

By and by the child himself is brought down by his nurse, and the company begin to rail upon him, upbraiding him for his impertinence, and asking him what amends he proposes to make for the wrong that he has committed, and how he can look for care and nourishment from those who have perhaps already been injured by the unborn on some ten or twelve occasions; for they say of people with large families, that they have suffered terrible injuries from the unborn; till at last, when this has been carried far enough, some one suggests the formula, which is brought out and solemnly read to the child by the family straightener. This gentleman is always invited on these occasions, for the very fact of intrusion into a peaceful family shows a depravity on the part of the child which requires his professional services.

On being teased by the reading and tweaked by the nurse, the child will commonly begin to cry, which is reckoned a good sign, as showing a consciousness of guilt. He is thereon asked, Does he assent to the formula? on which, as he still continues crying and can obviously make no answer, some one of the friends comes forward and undertakes to sign the document on his behalf, feeling sure (so he says) that the child would do it if he only knew how, and that he will release the present signer from his engagement on arriving at maturity. The friend then inscribes the signature of the child at the foot of the parchment, which is held to bind the child as much as though he had signed it himself.

Even this, however, does not fully content them, for they feel a little uneasy until they have got the child's own signature after all. So when he is about fourteen, these good people partly bribe him by promises of greater liberty and good things, and partly intimidate him through their great power of making themselves actively unpleasant to him, so that though there is a show of freedom made, there is really none; they also use the offices of the teachers in the Colleges of Unreason, till at last, in one way or another, they take very good care that he shall sign the paper by which he professes to have been a free agent in coming into the world, and to take all the responsibility of having done so on to his own shoulders. And yet, though this document is ob-

438 RESPONSIBILITY, BLAME, AND PUNISHMENT

viously the most important which any one can sign in his whole life, they will have him do so at an age when neither they nor the law will for many a year allow any one else to bind him to the smallest obligation, no matter how righteously he may owe it, because they hold him too young to know what he is about, and do not consider it fair that he should commit himself to anything that may prejudice him in after years.

I own that all this seemed rather hard, and not a piece with the many admirable institutions existing among them. I once ventured to say a part of what I thought about it to one of the Professors of Unreason. I did it very tenderly, but his justification of the system was quite out of my comprehension. I remember asking him whether he did not think it would do harm to a lad's principles, by weakening his sense of the sanctity of his word and of truth generally, that he should be led into entering upon a solemn declaration as to the truth of things about which all that he can certainly know is that he knows nothing—whether, in fact, the teachers who so led him, or who taught anything as a certainty of which they were themselves uncertain, were not earning their living by impairing the truth-sense of their pupils (a delicate organisation mostly), and by vitiating one of their most sacred instincts.

The Professor, who was a delightful person, seemed greatly surprised at the view which I took, but it had no influence with him whatsoever. No one, he answered, expected that the boy either would or could know all that he said he knew; but the world was full of compromises; and there was hardly any affirmation which would bear being interpreted literally. Human language was too gross a vehicle of thought—thought being incapable of absolute translation. He added, that as there can be no translation from one language into another which shall not scant the meaning somewhat, or enlarge upon it, so there is no language which can render thought without a jarring and a harshness somewhere—and so forth; all of which seemed to come to this in the end, that it was the custom of the country, and that the Erewhonians were a conservative people; that the boy would have to begin compromising sooner or later, and this was part of his education in the art. It was perhaps to be regretted that compromise should be as necessary as it was; still it was necessary, and the sooner the boy got to

understand it the better for himself. But they never tell this to the boy.

From the book of their mythology about the unborn I made the extracts which will form the following chapter.

THE WORLD OF THE UNBORN

... Having waded through many chapters ... I came at last to the unborn themselves, and found that they were held to be souls pure and simple, having no actual bodies, but living in a sort of gaseous yet more or less anthropomorphic existence, like that of a ghost; they have thus neither flesh nor blood nor warmth. Nevertheless they are supposed to have local habitations and cities wherein they dwell, though these are as unsubstantial as their inhabitants; they are even thought to eat and drink some thin ambrosial sustenance, and generally to be capable of doing whatever mankind can do, only after a visionary ghostly fashion as in a dream. On the other hand, as long as they remain where they are they never die—the only form of death in the unborn world being the leaving it for our own. They are believed to be extremely numerous, far more so than mankind. They arrive from unknown planets, full grown, in large batches at a time; but they can only leave the unborn world by taking the steps necessary for their arrival here—which is, in fact, by suicide.

They ought to be an exceedingly happy people, for they have no extremes of good or ill fortune; never marrying, but living in a state much like that fabled by the poets as the primitive condition of mankind. In spite of this, however, they are incessantly complaining; they know that we in this world have bodies, and indeed they know everything else about us, for they move among us whithersoever they will, and can read our thoughts, as well as survey our actions at pleasure. One would think that this should be enough for them; and most of them are indeed alive to the desperate risk which they will run by indulging themselves in that body with "sensible warm motion" which they so much desire; nevertheless, there are some to whom the *ennui* of a disembodied existence is so intolerable that they will venture anything for a change; so they resolve to quit. The conditions which they must accept are so uncertain, that none but the most foolish of the unborn will consent to them; and it is from these, and these only, that our own ranks are recruited.

When they have finally made up their minds to leave, they must go before the magistrate of the nearest town, and sign an affidavit of their desire to quit their then existence. On their having done this, the magistrate reads them the conditions which they must accept, and which are so long that I can only extract some of the principal points, which are mainly the following:

First, they must take a potion which will destroy their memory and sense of identity; they must go into the world helpless, and without a will of their own; they must draw lots for their dispositions before they go, and take them, such as they are, for better or worse—neither are they to be allowed any choice in the matter of the body which they so much desire; they are simply allotted by chance, and without appeal, to two people whom it is their business to find and pester until they adopt them. Who these are to be, whether rich or poor, kind or unkind, healthy or diseased, there is no knowing; they have, in fact, to entrust themselves for many years to the care of those for whose good constitution and good sense they have no sort of guarantee.

It is curious to read the lectures which the wiser heads give to those who are meditating a change. They talk with them as we talk with a spendthrift, and with about as much success.

"To be born," they say, "is a felony—it is a capital crime, for which sentence may be executed at any moment after the commission of the offence. You may perhaps happen to live for some seventy or eighty years, but what is that compared with the eternity you now enjoy? And even though the sentence were commuted, and you were allowed to live on for ever, you would in time become so terribly weary of life that execution would be the greatest mercy to you.

"Consider the infinite risk; to be born of wicked parents and trained in vice! to be born of silly parents, and trained to unrealities! of parents who regard you as a sort of chattel or property, belonging more to them than to yourself! Again, you may draw utterly unsympathetic parents, who will never be able to understand you, and who will do their best to thwart you (as a hen when she has hatched a duckling), and then call you ungrateful because you do not love them; or, again, you may draw parents who look upon you

as a thing to be cowed while it is still young, lest it should give them trouble hereafter by having wishes and feelings of its own.

"In later life, when you have been finally allowed to pass muster as a full member of the world, you will yourself become liable to the pesterings of the unborn—and a very happy life you may be led in consequence! for we solicit so strongly that a few only—nor these the best—can refuse us; and yet not to refuse is much the same as going into partnership with half a dozen different people about whom one can know absolutely nothing beforehand—not even whether one is going into partnership with men or women, nor with how many of either. Delude not yourself with thinking that you will be wiser than your parents. You may be an age in advance of those whom you have pestered, but unless you are one of the great ones you will still be an age behind those who will in their turn pester you.

"Imagine what it must be to have an unborn quartered upon you, who is of an entirely different temperament and disposition to your own; nay, half a dozen such, who will not love you though you have stinted yourself in a thousand ways to provide for their comfort and well-being—who will forget all your self-sacrifice, and of whom you may never be sure that they are not bearing a grudge against you for errors of judgment into which you may have fallen, though you had hoped that such had been long since atoned for. Ingratitude such as this is not uncommon, yet fancy what it must be to bear! It is hard upon the duckling to have been hatched by a hen, but is it not also hard upon the hen to have hatched the duckling?

"Consider it again, we pray you, not for our sake but for your own. Your initial character you must draw by lot; but whatever it is, it can only come to a tolerably successful development after long training; remember that over that training you will have no control. It is possible, and even probable, that whatever you may get in after life which is of real pleasure and service to you, will have to be won in spite of, rather than by the help of, those whom you are now about to pester, and that you will only win your freedom after years of a painful struggle in which it will be hard to say whether you have suffered most injury, or inflicted it.

"Remember also, that if you go into the world you will have free will; that you will be obliged to have it; that there is no escaping it; that you will be fettered to it during your whole life, and must on every occasion do that which on the whole seems best to you at any given time, no matter whether you are right or wrong in choosing it. Your mind will be a balance for considerations, and your action will go with the heavier scale. How it shall fall will depend upon the kind of scales which you may have drawn at birth, the bias which they will have obtained by use, and the weight of the immediate considerations. If the scales were good to start with, and if they have not been outrageously tampered with in childhood, and if the combinations into which you enter are average ones, you may come off well; but there are too many 'ifs' in this, and with the failure of any one of them your misery is assured. Reflect on this, and remember that should the ill come upon you, you will have yourself to thank, for it is your own choice to be born, and there is no compulsion in the matter. . . .

Theories of Punishment

IMMANUEL KANT

The Right of Punishing*

The Right of administering Punishment, is the Right of the Sovereign as the Supreme Power to inflict pain upon a Subject on account of a Crime committed by him. The Head of the State cannot therefore be punished; but his supremacy may be withdrawn from him. Any Transgression of the public law which makes him who commits it incapable of being a Citizen, constitutes a *Crime,* either simply as a private Crime (*crimen*), or also as a *public* Crime (*crimen publicum*). Private crimes are dealt with by a Civil Court; Public Crimes by a Criminal Court.—Embezzlement or peculation of money or goods entrusted in trade, Fraud in purchase or sale, if done before the eyes of the party who suffers, are Private Crimes. On the other hand, Coining false money or forging Bills of Exchange, Theft, Robbery, etc., are Public Crimes, because the Commonwealth, and not merely some particular individual, is endangered thereby. Such Crimes may be divided into those of a *base* character (*indolis abjectae*) and those of a *violent* character (*indolis violentioe*).

Judicial or Juridical Punishment (*poena forensis*) is to be distinguished from Natural Punishment (*poena naturalis*), in which Crime as Vice punishes itself, and does not as such come within the cognizance of the Legislator. Juridical Punishment can never be administered merely as a means for promoting another Good either with regard to the Criminal himself or to Civil Society, but must in all cases be imposed only because the individual on whom it is inflicted *has committed a Crime.* For one man ought never to be dealt with merely as a means subservient to the purpose of another, nor be mixed up with the subjects of Real Right. Against such treatment his Inborn Personality has a Right to protect him, even although he may be condemned to lose his Civil Personality. He must first be found guilty and *punishable,* before there can be any thought of drawing from his Punishment any benefit for

*From Immanuel Kant, *The Philosophy of Law,* trans. W. Hastie (Edinburgh, 1887), pp. 194–201. First published in 1797.

himself or his fellow-citizens. The Penal Law is a Categorical Imperative; and woe to him who creeps through the serpent-windings of Utilitarianism to discover some advantage that may discharge him from the Justice of Punishment, or even from the due measure of it, according to the Pharisaic maxim: 'It is better that *one* man should die than that the whole people should perish.' For if Justice and Righteousness perish, human life would no longer have any value in the world.—What, then, is to be said of such a proposal as to keep a Criminal alive who has been condemned to death, on his being given to understand that if he agreed to certain dangerous experiments being performed upon him, he would be allowed to survive if he came happily through them? It is argued that Physicians might thus obtain new information that would be of value to the Commonweal. But a Court of Justice would repudiate with scorn any proposal of this kind if made to it by the Medical Faculty; for Justice would cease to be Justice, if it were bartered away for any consideration whatever.

But what is the mode and measure of Punishment which Public Justice takes as its Principle and Standard? It is just the Principle of Equality, by which the pointer of the Scale of Justice is made to incline no more to the one side than the other. It may be rendered by saying that the undeserved evil which any one commits on another, is to be regarded as perpetrated on himself. Hence it may be said: 'If you slander another you slander yourself; if you steal from another, you steal from yourself; if you strike another, you strike yourself; if you kill another, you kill yourself.' This is the Right of Retaliation (*jus talionis*); and properly understood, it is the only Principle which in regulating a Public Court, as distinguished from mere private judgment, can definitely assign both the quality and the quantity of a just penalty. All other standards are wavering and uncertain; and on account of other considerations involved in them, they contain no principle comfortable to the sentence of pure and strict Justice. It may appear, however, that difference of social status would not admit the application of the Principle of Retaliation, which is that of 'Like with Like.' But although the application may not in all cases be possible according to the letter, yet as regards the effect it may always be attained in practice, by due regard being given to the disposition and sentiment of the parties in the higher social sphere. Thus a pecuniary penalty on account of a verbal injury, may have no direct proportion to the injustice of slander; for one who is wealthy may be able to indulge himself in this offence for his own gratification. Yet the attack committed on the honour of the party aggrieved may have its equivalent in the pain inflicted upon the pride of the aggressor, especially if he is condemned by the judgment of the Court, not only to retract and apologize, but to submit to some meaner ordeal, as kissing the hand of the injured person. In like manner, if a man of the highest rank has violently assaulted an innocent citizen of the lower orders, he may be condemned not only to apologize but to undergo a solitary and painful imprisonment, whereby, in addition to the discomfort endured, the vanity of the offender would be painfully affected, and the very shame of his position would constitute an adequate Retaliation after the principle of 'Like with Like.' But how then would we render the statement: 'If you *steal* from another, you steal from yourself?' In this way, that whoever steals anything makes the property of all insecure; he therefore robs himself of all security in property, according to the Right of Retaliation. Such a one has nothing, and can acquire nothing, but he has the Will to live; and this is only possible by others supporting him. But as the State should not do this gratuitously, he must for this purpose yield his powers to the state to be used in penal labour; and thus he falls for a time, or it may be for life, into a condition of slavery. —But whoever has committed Murder, must *die*. There is, in this case, no juridical substitute or surrogate, that can be given or taken for the satisfaction of Justice. There is no *Likeness* or proportion between Life, however painful, and Death; and therefore there is no Equality between the crime of Murder and the retaliation of it but what is judicially accomplished by the execution of the Criminal. His death, however, must be kept free from all maltreatment that would make the humanity suffering in his Person loathsome or abominable. Even if a Civil Society resolved to dissolve itself with the consent of all its members —as might be supposed in the case of a People inhabiting an island resolving to separate and scatter themselves throughout the whole world— the last Murderer lying in the prison ought to be executed before the resolution was carried out.

This ought to be done in order that every one may realize the desert of his deeds, and that blood-guiltiness may not remain upon the people; for otherwise they might all be regarded as participators in the murder as a public violation of Justice.

The Equalization of Punishment with Crime, is therefore only possible by the cognition of the Judge extending even to the penalty of Death, according to the Right of Retaliation. This is manifest from the fact that it is only thus that a Sentence can be pronounced over all criminals proportionate to their internal *wickedness;* as may be seen by considering the case when the punishment of Death has to be inflicted, not on account of a murder, but on account of a political crime that can only be punished capitally. A hypothetical case, founded on history, will illustrate this. In the last Scottish Rebellion there were various participators in it—such as Balmerino and others—who believed that in taking part in the Rebellion they were only discharging their duty to the House of Stuart; but there were also others who were animated only by private motives and interests. Now, suppose that the Judgment of this Supreme Court regarding them had been this: that every one should have liberty to choose between the punishment of Death or Penal Servitude for life. In view of such an alternative, I say that the Man of Honour would choose Death, and the Knave would choose servitude. This would be the effect of their human nature as it is; for the honourable man values his Honour more highly than even Life itself, whereas a Knave regards a Life, although covered with shame, as better in his eyes than not to be. The former is, without gainsaying, less guilty than the other; and they can only be proportionately punished by death being inflicted equally upon them both; yet to the one it is a mild punishment when his nobler temperament is taken into account, whereas it is a hard punishment to the other in view of his baser temperament. But, on the other hand, were they all equally condemned to Penal Servitude for life, the honourable man would be too severely punished, while the other, on account of his baseness of nature, would be too mildly punished. In the judgment to be pronounced over a number of criminals united in such a conspiracy, the best Equalizer of Punishment and Crime in the form of public Justice is Death. And besides all this, it has never been

heard of, that a Criminal condemned to death on account of a murder has complained that the Sentence inflicted on him more than was right and just; and any one would treat him with scorn if he expressed himself to this effect against it. Otherwise it would be necessary to admit that although wrong and injustice are not done to the Criminal by the Law, yet the Legislative Power is not entitled to administer this mode of Punishment; and if it did so, it would be in contradiction with itself.

However many they may be who have committed a murder, or have even commanded it, or acted as art and part in it, they ought all to suffer death; for so Justice wills it, in accordance with the Idea of the juridical Power as founded on the universal Laws of Reason. But the number of the Accomplices (*correi*) in such a deed might happen to be so great that the State, in resolving to be without such criminals, would be in danger of soon also being deprived of subjects. But it will not thus dissolve itself, neither must it return to the much worse condition of Nature, in which there would be no external Justice. Nor, above all, should it deaden the sensibilities of the People by the spectacle of Justice being exhibited in the mere carnage of a slaughtering bench. In such circumstances the Sovereign must always be allowed to have it in his power to take the part of the Judge upon himself as a case of Necessity,— and to deliver a Judgment which, instead of the penalty of death, shall assign some other punishment to the Criminals, and thereby preserve a multitude of the People. The penalty of Deportation is relevant in this connection. Such a form of Judgment cannot be carried out according to a public law, but only by an authoritative act of the royal Prerogative, and it may only be applied as an act of grace in individual cases.

Against these doctrines, the Marquis Beccaria has given forth a different view. Moved by the compassionate sentimentality of a humane feeling, he has asserted that all Capital Punishment is wrong in itself and unjust. He has put forward this view on the ground that the penalty of death could not be contained in the original Civil Contract; for, in that case, every one of the People would have had to consent to lose his life if he murdered any of his fellow-citizens. But, it is argued, such a consent is impossible, because no one can thus dispose of his own life.—All this is mere sophistry and perversion of Right. No one undergoes Punishment because he has willed to be punished, but because he has willed *a punishable Action;* for it is in fact no Punishment when any one experiences what he wills, and it is impossible for any one to *will* to be punished. To say, 'I *will* to be punished, if I murder any one,' can mean nothing more than 'I submit myself along with all the other citizens to the Laws'; and if there are any Criminals among the People, these Laws will include Penal Laws. The individual who, as a Co-legislator, enacts *Penal Law,* cannot possibly be the same Person who, as a Subject, is punished according to the Law; for, *qua* Criminal, he cannot possibly be regarded as having a voice in the Legislation, the Legislator being rationally viewed as just and holy. If any one, then, enact a Penal Law against himself as a Criminal, it must be the pure juridically lawgiving (Reason) (*homo noumenon*), which subjects him as capable of crime, and consequently as another person (*homo phenomenon*), along with all the others in the Civil Union, to this Penal Law. In other words, it is not the People taken distributively, but the Tribunal of public Justice, as distinct from the Criminal, that prescribes Capital Punishment; and it is not to be viewed as if the Social Contract contained the Promise of all the individuals to allow themselves to be punished, thus disposing of themselves and their lives. For if the Right to punish must be grounded upon a promise of the wrongdoer, whereby he is to be regarded as being willing to be punished, it ought also to be left to him to find himself deserving to the Punishment; and the Criminal would thus be his own Judge. The chief error (π $\omega\tau o$ ν $\psi\epsilon\hat{\upsilon}\delta os$) of this sophistry consists in regarding the judgment of the Criminal himself, necessarily determined by his Reason, that he is under obligation to undergo the loss of his life, as a judgment that must be grounded on a resolution of his *Will* to take it away himself; and thus the execution of the Right in question is represented as united in one and the same person with the adjudication of the right.

F Y O D O R   D O S T O E V S K Y

Prison Life in Siberia*

That same evening, before the closing of the barracks, when it was already dark, I walked to the side of the palisade. A heavy feeling of sadness weighed upon my soul. During all the time that I passed in the convict prison I never felt myself so miserable as on that evening, though the first day is always the hardest, whether at hard labour or in the prison. One thought in particular had left me no respite since my deportation—a question insoluble then and insoluble now. I reflected on the inequality of the punishments inflicted for the same crimes. Often, indeed, one crime cannot be compared even approximately to another. Two murderers kill a man under circumstances which in each case are minutely examined and weighed. They each receive the same punishment; and yet by what an abyss are their two actions separated! One has committed a murder for a trifle—for an onion. He has killed on the high-road a peasant who was passing, and found on him an onion, and nothing else.

"Well, I was sent to hard labour for a peasant who had nothing but an onion!"

"Fool that you are! an onion is worth a kopeck. If you had killed a hundred peasants you would have had a hundred kopecks, or one rouble." The above is a prison joke.

*From Fyodor Dostoevsky, *The House of the Dead,* trans. H. Sutherland Edwards (London: J. M. Dent; New York: E. P. Dutton, Everyman's Library, 1912), pp. 57–60. Used by permission of E. P. Dutton & Co., Inc.

Another criminal has killed a debauchee who was oppressing or dishonouring his wife, his sister, or his daughter.

A third, a vagabond, half dead with hunger, pursued by a whole band of police, was defending his liberty, his life. He is to be regarded as on an equality with the brigand who assassinates children for his amusement, for the pleasure of feeling their warm blood flow over his hands, of seeing them shudder in a last bird-like palpitation beneath the knife which tears their flesh!

They will all alike be sent to hard labour; though the sentence will perhaps not be for the same number of years. But the variations in the punishment are not very numerous, whereas different kinds of crimes may be reckoned by thousands. As many characters, so many crimes.

Let us admit that it is impossible to get rid of this first inequality in punishment, that the problem is insoluble, and that in connection with personal matters it is the squaring of the circle. Let all that be admitted; but even if this inequality cannot be avoided, there is another thing to be thought of—the consequences of the punishment. Here is a man who is wasting away like a candle; there is another one, on the contrary, who had no idea before going into exile that there could be such a gay, such an idle life, where he would find a circle of such agreeable friends. Individuals of this latter class are to be found in the convict prison.

Now take a man of heart, of cultivated mind, and of delicate conscience. What he feels kills him more certainly than the material punishment. The judgment which he himself pronounces on his crime is more pitiless than that of the most severe tribunal, the most Draconian law. He lives by the side of another convict, who has not once reflected on the murder he is expiating, during the whole time of his sojourn in the convict prison. He, perhaps, even considers himself innocent. Are there not, also, poor devils who commit crimes in order to be sent to hard labour, and thus to escape the liberty which is much more painful than confinement? A man's life is miserable, he has never, perhaps, been able to satisfy his hunger. He worked to death in order to enrich his master. In the convict prison his work will be less severe, less crushing. He will eat as much as he wants, better than he could ever have hoped to eat, had he remained free. On holidays he will have meat, and fine people will give him alms, and his evening's work will bring him in some money. And the society one meets with in the convict prison, is that to be counted for nothing? The convicts are clever, wide-awake people, who are up to everything. The new arrival can scarcely conceal the admiration he feels for his companions in labour. He has seen nothing like it before, and he will consider himself in the best company possible.

Is it possible that men so differently situated can feel in an equal degree the punishment inflicted? But why think about questions that are insoluble? The drum beats, let us go back to barracks.

OLIVER WENDELL HOLMES, JR.

The Criminal Law*

... The desire for vengeance imports an opinion that its object is actually and personally to blame. It takes an internal standard, not an objective or external one, and condemns its victims by that. The question is whether such a standard is still accepted either in this primitive form, or in some more refined development, as is commonly supposed, and as seems not impossible, considering the relative slowness with which the criminal law has improved.

It certainly may be argued, with some force, that it has never ceased to be one object of punishment to satisfy the desire for vengeance. The argument will be made plain by considering those instances in which, for one reason or another, compensation for a wrong is out of the question.

Thus an act may be of such a kind as to make indemnity impossible by putting an end to the principal sufferer, as in the case of murder or manslaughter.

Again, these and other crimes, like forgery, although directed against an individual, tend to make others feel unsafe, and this general insecurity does not admit of being paid for.

Again, there are cases where there are no means of enforcing indemnity. In Macaulay's draft of the Indian Penal Code, breaches of contract for the carriage of passengers, were made

criminal. The palanquin-bearers of India were too poor to pay damages, and yet had to be trusted to carry unprotected women and children through wild and desolate tracts, where their desertion would have placed those under their charge in great danger. In all these cases punishment remains as an alternative. A pain can be inflicted upon the wrong-doer, of a sort which does not restore the injured party to his former situation, or to another equally good, but which is inflicted for the very purpose of causing pain. And so far as this punishment takes the place of compensation, whether on account of the death of the person to whom the wrong was done, the indefinite number of persons affected, the impossibility of estimating the worth of the suffering in money, or the poverty of the criminal, it may be said that one of its objects is to gratify the desire for vengeance. The prisoner pays with his body.

The statement may be made stronger still, and it may be said, not only that the law does, but that it ought to, make the gratification of revenge an object. This is the opinion, at any rate, of two authorities so great, and so opposed in other views, as Bishop Butler and Jeremy Bentham.[1] Sir James Stephen says, "The criminal law stands to the passion of revenge in much the same relation as marriage to the sexual appetite."[2]

The first requirement of a sound body of law is, that it should correspond with the actual feeling and demands of the community, whether right or

*From Oliver Wendell Holmes, Jr., *The Common Law* (Boston: Little, Brown, 1881), pp. 40–51.

wrong. If people would gratify the passion of revenge outside of the law, if the law did not help them, the law has no choice but to satisfy the craving itself, and thus avoid the greater evil of private retribution. At the same time, this passion is not one which we encourage, either as private individuals or as law-makers. Moreover, it does not cover the whole ground. There are crimes which do not excite it, and we should naturally expect that the most important purposes of punishment would be coextensive with the whole field of its application. It remains to be discovered whether such a general purpose exists, and if so what it is. Different theories still divide opinion upon the subject.

It has been thought that the purpose of punishment is to reform the criminal; that it is to deter the criminal and others from committing similar crimes; and that it is retribution. Few would now maintain that the first of these purposes was the only one. If it were, every prisoner should be released as soon as it appears clear that he will never repeat his offence, and if he is incurable he should not be punished at all. Of course it would be hard to reconcile the punishment of death with this doctrine.

The main struggle lies between the other two. On the one side is the notion that there is a mystic bond between wrong and punishment; on the other, that the infliction of pain is only a means to an end. Hegel, one of the great expounders of the former view, puts it, in his quasi-mathematical form, that, wrong being the negation of right, punishment is the negation of that negation, or retribution. Thus the punishment must be equal, in the sense of proportionate to the crime, because its only function is to destroy it. Others, without this logical apparatus, are content to rely upon a felt necessity that suffering should follow wrong-doing.

It is objected that the preventive theory is immoral, because it overlooks the ill-desert of wrong-doing, and furnishes no measure of the amount of punishment, except the lawgiver's subjective opinion in regard to the sufficiency of the amount of preventive suffering.[3] In the language of Kant, it treats man as a thing, not as a person; as a means, not as an end in himself. It is said to conflict with the sense of justice, and to violate the fundamental principle of all free communities, that the members of such communities have equal rights to life, liberty, and personal security.[4]

In spite of all this, probably most English-speaking lawyers would accept the preventive theory without hesitation. As to the violation of equal rights which is charged, it may be replied that the dogma of equality makes an equation between individuals only, not between an individual and the community. No society has ever admitted that it could not sacrifice individual welfare to its own existence. If conscripts are necessary for its army, it seizes them, and marches them, with bayonets in their rear, to death. It runs highways and railroads through old family places in spite of the owner's protest, paying in this instance the market value, to be sure, because no civilized government sacrifices the citizen more than it can help, but still sacrificing his will and his welfare to that of the rest.[5]

If it were necessary to trench further upon the field of morals, it might be suggested that the dogma of equality applied even to individuals only within the limits of ordinary dealings in the common run of affairs. You cannot argue with your neighbor, except on the admission for the moment that he is as wise as you, although you may by no means believe it. In the same way, you cannot deal with him, where both are free to choose, except on the footing of equal treatment, and the same rules for both. The ever-growing value set upon peace and the social relations tends to give the law of social being the appearance of the law of all being. But it seems to me clear that the *ultima ratio*, not only *regum*, but of private persons, is force, and that at the bottom of all private relations, however tempered by sympathy and all the social feelings, is a justifiable self-preference. If a man is on a plank in the deep sea which will only float one, and a stranger lays hold of it, he will thrust him off if he can. When the state finds itself in a similar position, it does the same thing.

The considerations which answer the argument of equal rights also answer the objections to treating a man as a thing, and the like. If a man lives in society, he is liable to find himself so treated. The degree of civilization which a people has reached, no doubt, is marked by their anxiety to do as they would be done by. It may be the destiny of man that the social instincts shall grow to control his actions absolutely, even in anti-social situations. But they have not yet done so, and as the rules of law are or should be based upon a morality which is generally accepted, no rule founded on a theory of absolute unselfishness can be laid down without a breach between law and working beliefs.

If it be true, as I shall presently try to show, that the general principles of criminal and civil liability are the same, it will follow from that alone that theory and fact agree in frequently punishing those who have been guilty of no moral wrong, and who could not be condemned by any standard that did not avowedly disregard the personal peculiarities of the individuals concerned. If punishment stood on the moral grounds which are proposed for it, the first thing to be considered would be those limitations in the capacity for choosing rightly which arise from abnormal instincts, want of education, lack of intelligence, and all the other defects which are most marked in the criminal classes. I do not say that they should not be, or at least I do not need to for my argument. I do not say that the criminal law does more good than harm. I only say that it is not enacted or administered on that theory.

There remains to be mentioned the affirmative argument in favor of the theory of retribution, to the effect that the fitness of punishment following wrong-doing is axiomatic, and is instinctively recognized by unperverted minds. I think that it will be seen, on self-inspection, that this feeling of fitness is absolute and unconditional only in the case of our neighbors. It does not seem to me that any one who has satisfied himself that an act of his was wrong, and that he will never do it again, would feel the least need or propriety, as between himself and an earthly punishing power alone, of his being made to suffer for what he had done, although, when third persons were introduced, he might, as a philosopher, admit the necessity of hurting him to frighten others. But when our neighbors do wrong, we sometimes feel the fitness of making them smart for it, whether they have repented or not. The feeling of fitness seems to me to be only vengeance in disguise, and I have already admitted that vengeance was an element, though not the chief element, of punishment.

But, again, the supposed intuition of fitness does not seem to me to be coextensive with the thing to be accounted for. The lesser punishments are just as fit for the lesser crimes as the greater for the greater. The demand that crime should be followed by its punishment should therefore be equal and absolute in both. Again, a *malum prohibitum* is just as much a crime as a *malum in se.* If there is any general ground for punishment, it must apply to one case as much as to the other. But it will hardly be said that, if the wrong in the case just supposed consisted of a breach of the revenue laws, and the government had been indemnified for the loss, we should feel any internal necessity that a man who had thoroughly repented of his wrong should be punished for it, except on the ground that his act was known to others. If it was known, the law would have to verify its threats in order that others might believe and tremble. But if the fact was a secret between the sovereign and the subject, the sovereign, if wholly free from passion, would undoubtedly see that punishment in such a case was wholly without justification.

On the other hand, there can be no case in which the law-maker makes certain conduct criminal without his thereby showing a wish and purpose to prevent that conduct. Prevention would accordingly seem to be the chief and only universal purpose of punishment. The law threatens certain pains if you do certain things, intending thereby to give you a new motive for not doing them. If you persist in doing them, it has to inflict the pains in order that its threats may continue to be believed.

If this is a true account of the law as it stands, the law does undoubtedly treat the individual as a means to an end, and uses him as a tool to increase the general welfare at his own expense. It has been suggested above, that this course is perfectly proper; but even if it is wrong, our criminal law follows it, and the theory of our criminal law must be shaped accordingly.

Further evidence that our law exceeds the limits of retribution, and subordinates consideration of the individual to that of the public well-being, will be found in some doctrines which cannot be satisfactorily explained on any other ground.

The first of these is, that even the deliberate taking of life will not be punished when it is the only way of saving one's own. This principle is not so clearly established as that next to be mentioned; but it has the support of very great authority.[6] If that is the law, it must go on one of two grounds, either that self-preference is proper in the case supposed, or that, even if it is improper, the law cannot prevent it by punishment, because a threat of death at some future time can never be a sufficiently powerful motive to make a man choose death now in order to avoid the threat. If the former ground is adopted, it admits that a single person may sacrifice another to himself, and *a fortiori* that a people may. If the latter view is taken, by abandoning punishment when it can no longer be expected to prevent an act, the law abandons the retributive and adopts the preventive theory.

The next doctrine leads to still clearer conclusions. Ignorance of the law is no excuse for breaking it. This substantive principle is sometimes put in the form of a rule of evidence, that every one is presumed to know the law. It has accordingly been defended by Austin and others, on the ground of difficulty of proof. If justice requires the fact to be ascertained, the difficulty of doing so is no ground for refusing to try. But every one must feel that ignorance of the law could never be proved by sight and hearing in every case. Furthermore, now that parties can testify, it may be doubted whether a man's knowledge of the law is any harder to investigate than many questions which are gone into. The difficulty, such as it is, would be met by throwing the burden of proving ignorance on the lawbreakers.

The principle cannot be explained by saying that we are not only commanded to abstain from certain acts, but also to find out that we are commanded. For if there were such a second command, it is very clear that the guilt of failing to obey it would bear no proportion to that of disobeying the principal command if known, yet the failure to know would receive the same punishment as the failure to obey the principal law.

The true explanation of the rule is the same as that which accounts for the law's indifference to a man's particular temperament, faculties, and so forth. Public policy sacrifices the individual to the general good. It is desirable that the burden of all should be equal, but it is still more desirable to put an end to robbery and murder. It is no doubt true that there are many cases in which the criminal could not have known that he was breaking the law, but to admit the excuse at all would be to encourage ignorance where the lawmaker has determined to make men know and obey, and justice to the individual is rightly outweighed by the larger interests on the other side of the scales.

If the foregoing arguments are sound, it is already manifest that liability to punishment cannot be finally and absolutely determined by considering the actual personal unworthiness of the criminal alone. That consideration will govern only so far as the public welfare permits or demands. And if we take into account the general result which the criminal law is intended to bring about, we shall see that the actual state of mind accompanying a criminal act plays a different part from what is commonly supposed.

For the most part, the purpose of the criminal law is only to induce external conformity to rule. All law is directed to conditions of things manifest to the senses. And whether it brings those conditions to pass immediately by the use of force, as when it protects a house from a mob by soldiers, or appropriates private property to public use, or hangs a man in pursuance of a judicial sentence, or whether it brings them about mediately through men's fears, its object is equally an external result. In directing itself against robbery or murder, for instance, its purpose is to put a stop to the actual physical taking and keeping of other men's goods, or the actual poisoning, shooting, stabbing, and otherwise putting to death of other men. If those things are not done, the law forbidding them is equally satisfied, whatever the motive.

Considering this purely external purpose of the law together with the fact that it is ready to sacrifice the individual so far as necessary in order to accomplish that purpose, we can see more readily than before that the actual degree of personal guilt involved in any particular transgression cannot be the only element, if it is an element at all, in the liability incurred. So far from its being true, as is often assumed, that the condition of a man's heart or conscience ought to be more considered in determining criminal than civil liability, it might almost be said that it is the very opposite of truth. For civil liability, in its immediate working, is simply a redistribution of an existing loss between two individuals; and it will be argued in the next Lecture that sound policy lets losses lie where they fall, except where a special reason can be shown for interference. The most frequent of such reasons is, that the party who is charged has been to blame.

It is not intended to deny that criminal liability, as well as civil, is founded on blameworthiness. Such a denial would shock the moral sense of any civilized community; or, to put it another way, a law which punished conduct which would not be blameworthy in the average member of the community would be too severe for that community to bear. It is only intended to point out that, when we are dealing with that part of the law which aims more directly than any other at establishing standards of conduct, we should expect there more than elsewhere to find that the tests of liability are external, and independent of the degree of evil in the particular person's motives or intentions. The conclusion follows directly from the nature of the standards to which conformity is required. These are not only external, as was shown above, but they are of general application. They do not merely require that every man should get as near as he can to the best conduct possible for him. They require him at his own peril to come up to a certain height. They take no account of incapacities, unless the weakness is so marked as to fall into well-known exceptions, such as infancy or madness. They assume that every man is as able as every other to behave as they command. If they fall on any one class harder than on another, it is on the weakest. For it is precisely to those who are most likely to err by temperament, ignorance, or folly, that the threats of the law are the most dangerous.

The reconciliation of the doctrine that liability is founded on blameworthiness with the existence of liability where the party is not to blame, will be worked out more fully in the next Lecture. It is found in the conception of the average man, the man of ordinary intelligence and reasonable prudence. Liability is said to arise out of such conduct as would be blameworthy in him. But he is an ideal being, represented by the jury when they are appealed to, and his conduct is an external or objective standard when applied to any given individual. That individual may be morally without stain, because he has less than ordinary intelligence or prudence. But he is required to have those qualities at his peril. If he has them, he will not, as a general rule, incur liability without blameworthiness. . . .

NOTES

1. Butler, *Sermons,* VIII. Bentham, *Theory of Legislation* (Principles of Penal Code, Part 2, ch. 16), Hildreth's tr., p. 309.

2. *General View of the Criminal Law of England,* p. 99.

3. Wharton, *Crim. Law* (8th ed.) § 8, n. 1.

4. *Ibid.,* § 7.

5. Even the law recognizes that his is a sacrifice. *Commonwealth* v. *Sawin,* 2 Pick. (Mass.) 547, 549.

6. Cf. 1 East, P. C. 294; *United States* v. *Holmes,* 1 Wall, Jr. 1; 1 Bishop, *Crim. Law,* §§ 347–349, 845 (6th ed.); 4 Bl. Comm. 31.

J. D. MABBOTT

Punishment*

I propose in this paper to defend a retributive theory of punishment and to reject absolutely all utilitarian considerations from its justification. I feel sure that this enterprise must arouse deep suspicion and hostility both among philosophers (who must have felt that the retributive view is the only moral theory except perhaps psychological hedonism which has been definitely destroyed by criticism) and among practical men (who have welcomed its steady decline in our penal practice).

The question I am asking is this. Under what circumstances is the punishment of some particular person justified and why? The theories of reform and deterrence which are usually considered to be the only alternatives to retribution involve well-known difficulties. These are considered fully and fairly in Dr. Ewing's book *The Morality of Punishment,* and I need not spend long over them. The central difficulty is that both would on occasion justify the punishment of an innocent man, the deterrent theory if he were believed to have been guilty by those likely to commit the crime in future, and the reformatory theory if he were a bad man though not a criminal. To this may be added the point against the deterrent theory that it is the threat of punishment and not punishment itself which deters, and that when deterrence seems to depend on actual punishment, to implement the threat, it

really depends on publication and may be achieved if men believe that punishment has occurred even if in fact it has not. As Bentham saw, for a Utilitarian apparent justice is everything, real justice is irrelevant.

Dr. Ewing and other moralists would be inclined to compromise with retribution in the face of the above difficulties. They would admit that one fact and one fact only can justify the punishment of this man, and that is a *past* fact, that he has committed a crime. To this extent reform and deterrence theories, which look only to the consequences, are wrong. But they would add that retribution can determine only *that* a man should be punished. It cannot determine how or how much, and here reform and deterrence may come in. Even Bradley, the fiercest retributionist of modern times, says "Having once the right to punish we may modify the punishment according to the useful and the pleasant, but these are external to the matter; they cannot give us a right to punish and nothing can do that but criminal desert." Dr. Ewing would maintain that the whole estimate of the amount and nature of a punishment may be effected by considerations of reform and deterrence. It seems to me that this is a surrender which the upholders of retribution dare not make. As I said above, it is publicity and not punishment which deters, and the publicity though often spoken of as "part of a man's punishment" is no more part of it than his arrest or his detention prior to trial, though both these may be also unpleasant and bring him into disre-

*J. D. Mabbott, "Punishment," *Mind,* XLVIII (1939), 152–167. Reprinted by permission of the author and the editor of *Mind.*

pute. A judge sentences a man to three years' imprisonment, not to three years *plus* three columns in the press. Similarly with reform. The visit of the prison chaplain is not part of a man's punishment nor is the visit of Miss Fields or Mickey Mouse.

The truth is that while punishing a man and punishing him justly, it is possible to deter others, and also to attempt to reform him, and if these additional goods are achieved the total state of affairs is better than it would be with the just punishment alone. But reform and deterrence are not modifications of the punishment, still less reasons for it. A parallel may be found in the case of tact and truth. If you have to tell a friend an unpleasant truth you may do all you can to put him at his ease and spare his feelings as much as possible, while still making sure that he understands your meaning. In such a case no one would say that your offer of a cigarette beforehand or your apology afterwards are modifications of the truth still less reasons for telling it. You do not tell the truth in order to spare his feelings, but having to tell the truth you also spare his feelings. So Bradley was right when he said that reform and deterrence were "external to the matter," but therefore wrong when he said that they may "modify the punishment." Reporters are admitted to our trials so that punishments may become public and help to deter others. But the punishment would be no less just were reporters excluded and deterrence not achieved. Prison authorities may make it possible that a convict may become physically or morally better. They cannot ensure either result; and the punishment would still be just if the criminal took no advantage of their arrangements and their efforts failed. Some moralists see this and exclude these "extra" arrangements for deterrence and reform. They say that it must be the punishment *itself* which reforms and deters. But it is just my point that the punishment *itself* seldom reforms the criminal and never deters others. It is only "extra" arrangements which have any chance of achieving either result. As this is the central point of my paper, at the cost of laboured repetition I would ask the upholders of reform and deterrence two questions. Suppose it could be shown that a particular criminal had not been improved by a punishment and also that no other would-be criminal had been deterred by it, would that prove that the

punishment was unjust? Suppose it were discovered that a particular criminal had lived a much better life after his release and that many would-be criminals believing him to have been guilty were influenced by his fate, but yet that the "criminal" was punished for something he had never done, would these excellent results prove the punishment just?

It will be observed that I have throughout treated punishment as a purely legal matter. A "criminal" means a man who has broken a law, not a bad man; an "innocent" man is a man who has not broken the law in connection with which he is being punished, though he may be a bad man and have broken other laws. Here I dissent from most upholders of the retributive theory— from Hegel, from Bradley, and from Dr. Ross. They maintain that the essential connection is one between punishment and moral or social wrong-doing.

My fundamental difficulty with their theory is the question of *status.* It takes two to make a punishment, and for a moral or social wrong I can find no punisher. We may be tempted to say when we hear of some brutal action "that ought to be punished"; but I cannot see how there can be duties which are nobody's duties. If I see a man ill-treating a horse in a country where cruelty to animals is not a legal offence, and I say to him "I shall now punish you," he will reply, rightly, "What has it to do with you? Who made you a judge and ruler over me?" I may have a duty to try to stop him and one way of stopping him may be to hit him, but another way may be to buy the horse. Neither the blow nor the price is a punishment. For a moral offence, God alone has the *status* necessary to punish the offender; and the theologians are becoming more and more doubtful whether even God has a duty to punish wrong-doing.

Dr. Ross would hold that not all wrong-doing is punishable, but only invasion of the rights of others; and in such a case it might be thought that the injured party had a right to punish. His right, however, is rather a right to preparation, and should not be confused with punishment proper.

This connection, on which I insist, between punishment and crime, not between punishment and moral or social wrong, alone accounts for some of our beliefs about punishment, and also meets many objections to the retributive theory as stated in its ordinary form. The first point on which it helps us is with regard to retrospective legislation. Our objection to this practice is unaccountable on reform and deterrence theories. For a man who commits a wrong before the date on which a law against it is passed, is as much in need of reform as a man who commits it afterwards; nor is deterrence likely to suffer because of additional punishments for the same offence. But the orthodox retributive theory is equally at a loss here, for if punishment is given for moral wrongdoing or for invasion of the rights of others, that immorality of invasion existed as certainly before the passing of the law as after it.

My theory also explains, where it seems to me all others do not, the case of punishment imposed by an authority who believes the law in question is a bad law. I was myself for some time disciplinary officer of a college whose rules included a rule compelling attendance at chapel. Many of those who broke this rule broke it on principle. I punished them. I certainly did not want to reform them; I respected their characters and their views. I certainly did not want to drive others into chapel through fear of penalties. Nor did I think there had been a wrong done which merited retribution. I wished I could have believed that I would have done the same thing myself. My position was clear. They had broken a rule; they knew it and I knew it. Nothing more was necessary to make punishment proper.

I know that the usual answer to this is that the judge enforces a bad law because otherwise law in general would suffer and good laws would be broken. The effect of punishing good men for breaking bad laws is that fewer bad men break good laws.

[*Excursus on Indirect Utilitarianism.* The above argument is a particular instance of a general utilitarian solution of all similar problems. When I am in funds and consider whether I should pay my debts or give the same amount to charity, I must choose the former because repayment not only benefits my creditor (for the benefit to him might be less than the good done through charity) but also upholds the general credit system. I tell the truth when a lie might do more good to the parties directly concerned, because I thus increase general trust and confidence. I keep a promise when it might do more immediate good to break it, because indirectly I bring it about that

promises will be more readily made in future and this will outweigh the immediate loss involved. Dr. Ross has pointed out that the effect on the credit system of my refusal to pay a debt is greatly exaggerated. But I have a more serious objection of principle. It is that in all these cases the indirect effects do not result from my wrong action —my lie or defalcation or bad faith—but from the publication of these actions. If in any instance the breaking of the rule were to remain unknown then I could consider only the direct or immediate consequences. Thus in my "compulsory chapel" case I could have considered which of my culprits were law-abiding men generally and unlikely to break any other college rule. Then I could have sent for each of these separately and said "I shall let you off if you will tell no one I have done so." By these means the general keeping of rules would not have suffered. Would this course have been correct? It must be remembered that the proceedings need not deceive everybody. So long as they deceive would-be law-breakers the good is achieved.

As this point is of crucial importance and as it has an interest beyond the immediate issue, and gives a clue to what I regard as the true general nature of law and punishment, I may be excused for expanding and illustrating it by an example or two from other fields. Dr. Ross says that two men dying on a desert island would have duties to keep promises to each other even though their breaking them would not affect the future general confidence in promises at all. Here is certainly the same point. But as I find that desert-island morality always rouses suspicion among ordinary men I should like to quote two instances from my own experience which also illustrate the problem.

(i) A man alone with his father at his death promises him a private and quiet funeral. He finds later that both directly and indirectly the keeping of this promise will cause pain and misunderstanding. He can see no particular positive good that the quiet funeral will achieve. No one yet knows that he has made the promise nor need anyone ever know. Should he therefore act as though it had never been made?

(ii) A college has a fund given to it for the encouragement of a subject which is now expiring. Other expanding subjects are in great need of endowment. Should the authorities divert the money? Those who oppose the diversion have previously stood on the past, the promise. But one day one of them discovers the "real reason" for this slavery to a dead donor. He says "We must consider not only the value of this money for these purposes, since on all direct consequences it should be diverted at once. We must remember the effect of this diversion on the general system of benefactions. We know that benefactors like to endow special objects, and this act of ours would discourage such benefactors in future and leave learning worse off." Here again is the indirect utilitarian reason for choosing the alternative which direct utilitarianism would reject. But the immediate answer to this from the most ingenious member of the opposition was crushing and final. He said, "Divert the money but keep it dark." This is obviously correct. It is not the act of diversion which would diminish the stream of benefactions but the news of it reaching the ears of benefactors. Provided that no possible benefactor got to hear of it no indirect loss would result. But the justification of our action would depend entirely on the success of the measures for "keeping it dark." I remember how I felt and how others felt that whatever answer was right this result was certainly wrong. But it follows that indirect utilitarianism is wrong in all such cases. For its argument can always be met by "Keep it dark."]

The view, then, that a judge upholds a bad law in order that law in general should not suffer is indefensible. He upholds it simply because he has no right to dispense from punishment.

The connection of punishment with law-breaking and not with wrong-doing also escapes moral objections to the retributive theory as held by Kant and Hegel or by Bradley and Ross. It is asked how we can measure moral wrong or balance it with pain, and how pain can wipe out moral wrong. Retributivists have been pushed into holding that pain *ipso facto* represses the worse self and frees the better, when this is contrary to the vast majority of observed cases. But if punishment is not intended to measure or balance or negate moral wrong then all this is beside the mark. There is the further difficulty of reconciling punishment with repentance and with forgiveness. Repentance is the reaction morally appropriate to moral wrong and punishment added to remorse is an unnecessary evil. But if punishment is associated with law-breaking and not with the moral evil the punisher is not entitled to consider whether the criminal is penitent any more than he may consider whether the law is good. So, too, with forgiveness. Forgiveness is not appropriate to law-breaking. (It is noteworthy that when, in divorce cases, the law has to recognize forgiveness it calls it "condonation," which is symptomatic of the difference of attitude.) Nor is forgiveness appropriate to moral evil. It is appropriate to personal injury. No one has any right to forgive me except the person I have injured. No judge or jury can do so. But the person I have injured has no right to punish me. Therefore there is no clash between punishment and forgiveness since these two duties do not fall on the same person nor in connection with the same characteristic of my act. (It is the weakness of vendetta that it tends to confuse this clear line, though even there it is only by personifying the family that the injured party and the avenger are identified. Similarly we must guard against the plausible fallacy of personifying society and regarding the criminal as "injuring society," for then once more the old dilemma about forgiveness would be insoluble.) A clergyman friend of mine catching a burglar red-handed was puzzled about his duty. In the end he ensured the man's punishment by information and evidence, and at the same time showed his own forgiveness by visiting the man in prison and employing him when he came out. I believe any "good Christian" would accept this as representing his duty. But obviously if the punishment is thought of as imposed *by* the victim or *for* the injury or immorality then the contradiction with forgiveness is hopeless.

So far as the question of the actual punishment of any individual is concerned this paper could stop here. No punishment is morally retributive or reformative or deterrent. Any criminal punished for any one of these reasons is certainly unjustly punished. The only justification for punishing any man is that he has broken a law.

In a book which has already left its mark on prison administration I have found a criminal himself confirming these views. *Walls Have Mouths,* by W. F. R. Macartney, is prefaced, and provided with appendices to each chapter, by Compton Mackenzie. It is interesting to notice how the novelist maintains that the proper object of penal servitude should be reformation,[1] whereas the prisoner himself accepts the view I have set out above. Macartney says "To punish a man is to treat him as an equal. To be punished *for an offence against rules* is a sane man's right."[2] It is striking also that he never uses "injustice" to describe the brutality or provocation which he experienced. He makes it clear that there were only two types of prisoner who were *unjustly* imprisoned, those who were insane and not responsible for the acts for which they were punished[3] and those who were innocent and had broken no law.[4] It is irrelevant, as he rightly observes, that some of these innocent men were, like Steinie Morrison, dangerous and violent characters, who on utilitarian grounds might well have been restrained. That made their punishment no whit less unjust.[5] To these general types may be added two specific instances of injustice. First, the sentences on the Dartmoor mutineers. "The Penal Servitude Act ... lays down specific punishments for mutiny and incitement to mutiny, which include flogging. ... Yet on the occasion of the only big mutiny in an English prison, men are not dealt with by the Act specially passed to meet mutiny in prison, but are taken out of gaol and tried under an Act expressly passed to curb and curtail the Chartists—a revolutionary movement."[6] Here again the injustice does not lie in the actual effect the sentences are likely to have on the prisoners (though Macartney has some searching suggestions about that also) but in condemning men for breaking a law they did not break and not for breaking the law they did break. The second specific instance is that of Coulton, who served his twenty years and then was brought back to prison to do another eight years and to die. This is due to the "unjust order that no lifer shall be released unless he has either relations or a job to whom he can go: and it is actually suggested that this is really for the lifer's own good. Just fancy, you admit that the man in doing years upon years in prison had expiated his crime: but, instead of releasing him, you keep him a further time—perhaps another three years—because you say he has nowhere to go. Better a ditch and hedge than prison! True, there are abnormal cases who want to stay in prison, but Lawrence wanted to be a private soldier, and men go into monasteries. Because occasionally a man wants to stay in prison, must every lifer who has lost his family during his sentence (I was doing

only ten years and I lost all my family) be kept indefinitely in gaol after he has paid his debt?"[7] Why is it unjust? Because he has paid his debt. When that is over it is for the man himself to decide what is for his own good. Once again the reform and utilitarian arguments are summarily swept aside. Injustice lies not in bad treatment or treatment which is not in the man's own interest, but in restriction which, according to the law, he has not merited.

It is true that Macartney writes, in one place, a paragraph of general reflection on punishment in which he confuses, as does Compton Mackenzie, retribution with revenge and in which he seems to hold that the retributive theory has some peculiar connection with private property. "Indeed it is difficult to see how, in society as it is to-day constituted, a humane prison system could function. All property is sacred, although the proceeds of property may well be reprehensible, therefore any offence against property is sacrilege and must be punished. Till a system eventuates which is based not on exploitation of man by man and class by class, prisons must be dreadful places, but at least there might be an effort to ameliorate the more savage side of the retaliation, and this could be done very easily."[8] The alternative system of which no doubt he is thinking is the Russian system described in his quotations from *A Physician's Tour in Soviet Russia,* by Sir James Purves-Stewart, the system of "correctional colonies" providing curative "treatment" for the different types of criminal.[9] There are two confusions here, to one of which we shall return later. First, Macartney confuses the retributive system with the punishment of one particular type of crime, offences against property, when he must have known that the majority of offenders against property do not find themselves in Dartmoor or even in Wandsworth. After all his own offence was not one against property—it was traffic with a foreign Power—and it was one for which in the classless society of Russia the punishment is death. It is surely clear that a retributive system may be adopted for any class of crime. Secondly, Macartney confuses injustice within a penal system with the wrongfulness of a penal system. When he pleads for "humane prisons" as if the essence of the prison should be humanity, or when Compton Mackenzie says the object of penal servitude should be reform, both of them are giving up punishment altogether, not altering it. A Russian "correctional colony," if its real object is curative treatment, is no more a "prison" than is an isolation hospital or a lunatic asylum. To this distinction between abolishing injustice in punishment and abolishing punishment altogether we must now turn.

It will be objected that my original question "Why ought X to be punished?" is an illegitimate isolation of the issue. I have treated the whole set of circumstances as determined. X is a citizen of a state. About his citizenship, whether willing or unwilling, I have asked no questions. About the government, whether it is good or bad, I do not enquire. X has broken a law. Concerning the law, whether it is well-devised or not, I have not asked. Yet all these questions are surely relevant before it can be decided whether a particular punishment is just. It is the essence of my position that none of these questions is relevant. Punishment is a corollary of law-breaking by a member of the society whose law is broken. This is a static and an abstract view but I see no escape from it. Considerations of utility come in on two quite different issues. Should there be laws, and what laws should there be? As a legislator I may ask what general types of action would benefit the community, and, among these, which can be "standardized" without loss, or should be standardized to achieve their full value. This, however, is not the primary question since particular laws may be altered or repealed. The choice which is the essential *prius* of punishment is the choice that there should be laws. The choice is not Hobson's. Other methods may be considered. A government might attempt to standardize certain modes of action by means of advice. It might proclaim its view and say "Citizens are requested" to follow this or that procedure. Or again it might decide to deal with each case as it arose in the manner most effective for the common welfare. Anarchists have wavered between these two alternatives and a third—that of doing nothing to enforce a standard of behaviour but merely giving arbitrational decisions between conflicting parties, decisions binding only by consent.

I think it can be seen without detailed examination of particular laws that the method of law-making has its own advantages. Its orders are explicit and general. It makes behaviour reliable and predictable. Its threat of punishment may be so effective as to make punishment unnecessary. It promises to the good citizen a certain security in his life. When I have talked to business men about some inequity in the law of liability they have usually said "Better a bad law than no law, for then we know where we are."

Someone may say I am drawing an impossible line. I deny that punishment is utilitarian; yet now I say that punishment is a corollary of law and we decide whether to have laws and which laws to have on utilitarian grounds. And surely it is only this corollary which distinguishes law from good advice or exhortation. This is a misunderstanding. Punishment is a corollary not of law but of law-breaking. Legislators do not choose to punish. They hope no punishment will be needed. Their laws would succeed even if no punishment occurred. The criminal makes the essential choice: he "brings it on himself." Other men obey the law because they see its order is reasonable, because of inertia, because of fear. In this whole area, and it may be the major part of the state, law achieves its ends without punishment. Clearly, then, punishment is not a corollary of law.

We may return for a moment to the question of amount and nature of punishment. It may be thought that this also is automatic. The law will include its own penalties and the judge will have no option. This, however, is again an initial choice of principle. If the laws do include their own penalties then the judge has no option. But the legislature might adopt a system which left complete or partial freedom to the judge, as we do except in the case of murder. Once again, what are the merits (regardless of particular laws, still more of particular cases) of fixed penalties and variable penalties? At first sight it would seem that all the advantages are with the variable penalties; for men who have broken the same law differ widely in degree of wickedness and responsibility. When, however, we remember that punishment is not an attempt to balance moral guilt this advantage is diminished. But there are still degrees of responsibility; I do not mean degrees of freedom of will but, for instance, degrees of complicity in a crime. The danger of allowing complete freedom to the judicature in fixing penalties is not merely that it lays too heavy a tax on human nature but that it would lead to the judge expressing in his penalty the degree of his own moral aversion to the crime. Or he might tend on deterrent grounds to punish more heavily a crime which was spreading and for which temptation and opportunity were frequent. Or again on deterrent grounds he might "make examples" by punishing ten times as heavily those criminals who are detected in cases in which nine out of ten evade detection. Yet we should revolt from all such punishments if they involved punishing theft more heavily than blackmail or negligence more heavily than premeditated assault. The death penalty for sheep-stealing might have been defended on such deterrent grounds. But we should dislike equating sheep-stealing with murder. Fixed penalties enable us to draw these distinctions between crimes. It is not that we can say how much imprisonment is right for a sheep-stealer. But we can grade crimes in a rough scale and penalties in a rough scale, and keep our heaviest penalties for what are socially the most serious wrongs regardless of whether these penalties will reform the criminal or whether they are exactly what deterrence would require. The compromise of laying down maximum penalties and allowing judges freedom below these limits allows for the arguments on both sides.

To return to the main issue, the position I am defending is that it is essential to a legal system that the infliction of a particular punishment should *not* be determined by the good *that particular punishment* will do either to the criminal or to "society." In exactly the same way it is essential to a credit system that the repayment of a particular debt should not be determined by the good that particular payment will do. One may consider the merits of a legal system or of a credit system, but the acceptance of either involves the surrender of utilitarian considerations in particular cases as they arise. This is in effect admitted by Ewing in one place where he says "It is the penal system as a whole which deters and not the punishment of any individual offender."[10]

To show that the choice between a legal system and its alternatives is one we do and must make, I may quote an early work of Lenin in which he was defending the Marxist tenet that the state is bound to "wither away" with the establishment of a classless society. He considers the possible objection that some wrongs by man against man are not economic and therefore that the abolition of classes would not *ipso facto* eliminate crime.

But he sticks to the thesis that these surviving crimes should not be dealt with by law and judicature. "We are not Utopians and do not in the least deny the possibility and inevitability of excesses by *individual persons,* and equally the need to suppress such excesses. But for this no special machine, no special instrument of repression is needed. This will be done by the armed nation itself as simply and as readily as any crowd of civilized people even in modern society parts a pair of combatants or does not allow a woman to be outraged."[11] This alternative to law and punishment has obvious demerits. Any injury not committed in the presence of the crowd, any wrong which required skill to detect or pertinacity to bring home would go untouched. The lynching mob, which is Lenin's instrument of justice, is liable to error and easily deflected from its purpose or driven to extremes. It must be a mob, for there is to be no "machine." I do not say that no alternative machine to ours could be devised but it does seem certain that the absence of all "machines" would be intolerable. An alternative machine might be based on the view that "society" is responsible for all criminality, and this curative and protective system developed. This is the system of Butler's "Erewhon" and something like it seems to be growing up in Russia except for cases of "sedition."

We choose, then, or we acquiesce in and adopt the choice of others of, a legal system as one of our instruments for the establishment of the conditions of a good life. This choice is logically prior to and independent of the actual punishment of any particular persons or the passing of any particular laws. The legislators choose particular laws within the framework of this predetermined system. Once again a small society may illustrate the reality of these choices and the distinction between them. A Headmaster launching a new school must explicitly make both decisions. First, shall we have any rules at all? Second, what rules shall we have? The first decision is a genuine one and one of great importance. Would it not be better to have an "honour" system, by which public opinion in each house or form dealt with any offence? (This is the Lenin method.) Or would complete freedom be better? Or should he issue appeals and advice? Or should he personally deal with each malefactor individually, as the case arises, in the way most likely to improve his conduct? I can well imagine an idealistic Headmaster attempting to run a school with one of these methods or with a combination of several of them and therefore without punishment. I can even imagine that with a small school of, say, twenty pupils all open to direct personal psychological pressure from authority and from each other, these methods involving no "rules" would work. The pupils would of course grow up without two very useful habits, the habit of having some regular habits and the habit of obeying rules. But I suspect that most Headmasters, especially those of large schools, would either decide at once, or quickly be driven, to realize that some rules were necessary. This decision would be "utilitarian" in the sense that it would be determined by consideration of consequences. The question "what rules?" would then arise and again the issue is utilitarian. What action must be regularized for the school to work efficiently? The hours of arrival and departure, for instance, in a day school. But the one choice which is now no longer open to the Headmaster is whether he shall punish those who break the rules. For if he were to try to avoid this he would in fact simply be returning to the discarded method of appeals and good advice. Yet the Headmaster does not decide to punish. The pupils make the decision there. He decides actually to have rules and to threaten, but only hypothetically, to punish. The one essential condition which makes actual punishment just is a condition he *cannot* fulfil—namely that a rule should be broken.

I shall add a final word of consolation to the practical reformer. Nothing that I have said is meant to counter any movement for "penal reform" but only to insist that none of these reforms have anything to do with punishment. The only type of reformer who can claim to be reforming the system of punishment is a follower of Lenin or of Samuel Butler who is genuinely attacking the *system* and who believes there should be no laws and no punishments. But our great British reformers have been concerned not with punishment but with its accessories. When a man is sentenced to imprisonment he is not sentenced also to partial starvation, to physical brutality, to pneumonia from damp cells and so on. And any movement which makes his food sufficient to sustain health, which counters the permanent tendency to brutality on the part of his warders, which gives him a dry or even a light and well-aired cell, is pure gain and does not touch the theory of punishment. Reformatory influences and prisoners' aid arrangements are also entirely unaffected by what I have said. I believe myself that it would be best if all such arrangements were made optional for the prisoner, so as to leave him in these cases a freedom of choice which would make it clear that they are not part of his punishment. If it is said that every such reform lessens a man's punishment, I think that is simply muddled thinking which, if it were clear, would be mere brutality. For instance, a prisoners' aid society is said to lighten his punishment, because otherwise he would suffer not merely imprisonment but also unemployment on release. But he was sentenced to imprisonment, not imprisonment *plus* unemployment. If I promise to help a friend and through special circumstances I find that keeping my promise will involve upsetting my day's work, I do not say that I really promised to help him and to ruin my day's work. And if another friend carries on my work for me I do not regard him as carrying out part of my promise, nor as stopping me from carrying it out myself. He merely removes an indirect and regrettable consequence of my keeping my promise. So with punishment. The Prisoners' Aid Society does not alter a man's punishment nor diminish it, but merely removes an indirect and regrettable consequence of it. And anyone who thinks that a criminal cannot make this distinction and will regard all the inconvenience to him that comes to him as punishment, need only talk to a prisoner or two to find out how sharply they resent these wanton additions to a punishment which by itself they will accept as just. Macartney's chapter on "Food" in the book quoted above is a good illustration of this point, as are also his comments on Clayton's administration. "To keep a man in prison for many years at considerable expense and then to free him charged to the eyes with uncontrollable venom and hatred generated by the treatment he has received in gaol, does not appear to be sensible." Clayton "endeavoured to send a man out of prison in a reasonable state of mind. 'Well, I've done my time. They were not too bad to me. Prison is prison and not a bed of roses. Still they didn't rub it in. ...' "[12] This "reasonable state of mind" is one in which a prisoner on release feels he has been punished but not *additionally* insulted or ill-treated. I feel convinced that penal reformers would meet with even more support if they were clear that they were *not* attempting to alter the system of punishment but to give its victims "fair play." We have no more right to starve a convict than to starve an animal. We have no more right to keep a convict in a Dartmoor cell "down which the water trickles night and day"[13] than we have to keep a child in such a place. If our reformers really want to alter the system of punishment, let them come out clearly with their alternative and preach, for instance, that no human being is responsible for any wrong-doing, that all the blame is on society, that curative or protective measures should be adopted, forcibly if necessary, as they are with infection or insanity. Short of this let them admit that the essence of prison is deprivation of liberty for the breaking of law, and that deprivation of food or of health or of books is unjust. And if our sentimentalists cry "coddling of prisoners," let us ask them also to come out clearly into the open and incorporate whatever starvation and disease and brutality they think necessary *into the sentences they propose.*[14] If it is said that some prisoners will prefer such reformed prisons, with adequate food and aired cells, to the outer world, we may retort that their numbers are probably not greater than those of the masochists who like to be flogged. Yet we do not hear the same "coddling" critics suggest abolition of the lash on the grounds that some criminals may like it. Even if the abolition from our prisons of all maltreatment other than that imposed by law results in a few down-and-outs breaking a window (as O. Henry's hero did) to get a night's lodging, the country will lose less than she does by her present method of sending out her discharged convicts "charged with venom and

hatred" because of the additional and uncovenanted "rubbing it in" which they have received.

I hope I have established both the theoretical importance and the practical value of distinguishing between penal reform as we know and approve it—that reform which alters the accompaniments of punishment without touching its essence—and those attacks on punishment itself which are made not only by reformers who regard criminals as irresponsible and in need of treatment, but also by every judge who announces that he is punishing a man to deter others or to protect society, and by every juryman who is moved to his decision by the moral baseness of the accused rather than by his legal guilt.

NOTES

1. p. 97.

2. p. 165. My italics.

3. pp. 165–166.

4. p. 298.

5. p. 301.

6. p. 255.

7. p. 400.

8. pp. 166, 167.

9. p. 229.

10. A. C. Ewing, *The Morality of Punishment* (London: Routledge and Kegan Paul, Ltd., 1929), p. 66.

11. *The State and Revolution* (Eng. trans.), p. 93. Original italics.

12. p. 152.

13. *Op. cit.,* p. 258.

14. "One of the minor curiosities of jail life was that they quickly provided you with a hundred worries which left you no time or energy for worrying about your sentence, long or short. . . . Rather as if you were thrown into a fire with spikes in it, and the spikes hurt you so badly that you forget about the fire. But then your punishment would *be* the spikes not the fire. Why did they pretend it was only the fire, when they knew very well about the spikes?" (From *Lifer* by Jim Phelan, p. 40.)

JOHN RAWLS

Punishment*

In this paper I want to show the importance of the distinction between justifying a practice[1] and justifying a particular action falling under it, and I want to explain the logical basis of this distinction and how it is possible to miss its significance. While the distinction has frequently been made,[2] and is now becoming commonplace, there remains the task of explaining the tendency either to overlook it altogether, or to fail to appreciate its importance.

To show the importance of the distinction I am going to defend utilitarianism against those objections which have traditionally been made against it in connection with punishment and the obligation to keep promises. I hope to show that if one uses the distinction in question then one can state utilitarianism in a way which makes it a much better explication of our considered moral judgments than these traditional objections would seem to admit.[3] Thus the importance of the distinction is shown by the way it strengthens the utilitarian view regardless of whether that view is completely defensible or not. . . .

The subject of punishment, in the sense of attaching legal penalties to the violation of legal rules, has always been a troubling moral question.[4] The trouble about it has not been that people disagree as to whether or not punishment is justifiable. Most people have held that, freed from certain abuses, it is an acceptable institution.

Only a few have rejected punishment entirely, which is rather surprising when one considers all that can be said against it. The difficulty is with the justification of punishment: various arguments for it have been given by moral philosophers, but so far none of them has won any sort of general acceptance; no justification is without those who detest it. I hope to show that the use of the aforementioned distinction enables one to state the utilitarian view in a way which allows for the sound points of its critics.

For our purposes we may say that there are two justifications of punishment. What we may call the retributive view is that punishment is justified on the grounds that wrongdoing merits punishment. It is morally fitting that a person who does wrong should suffer in proportion to his wrongdoing. That a criminal should be punished follows from his guilt, and the severity of the appropriate punishment depends on the depravity of his act. The state of affairs where a wrongdoer suffers punishment is morally better than the state of affairs where he does not; and it is better irrespective of any of the consequences of punishing him.

What we may call the utilitarian view holds that on the principle that bygones are bygones and that only future consequences are material to present decisions, punishment is justifiable only by reference to the probable consequences of maintaining it as one of the devices of the social order. Wrongs committed in the past are, as such, not relevant considerations for deciding what to

*From John Rawls, "Two Concepts of Rules," Part I, *Philosophical Review,* LXIV (1955), 3–13. Reprinted by permission of the author and the *Philosophical Review.*

do. If punishment can be shown to promote effectively the interest of society it is justifiable, otherwise it is not.

I have stated these two competing views very roughly to make one feel the conflict between them: one feels the force of *both* arguments and one wonders how they can be reconciled. From my introductory remarks it is obvious that the resolution which I am going to propose is that in this case one must distinguish between justifying a practice as a system of rules to be applied and enforced, and justifying a particular action which falls under these rules; utilitarian arguments are appropriate with regard to questions about practices, while retributive arguments fit the application of particular rules to particular cases.

We might try to get clear about this distinction by imagining how a father might answer the question of his son. Suppose the son asks, "Why was *J* put in jail yesterday?" The father answers, "Because he robbed the bank at *B*. He was duly tried and found guilty. That's why he was put in jail yesterday." But suppose the son had asked a different question, namely, "Why do people put other people in jail?" Then the father might answer, "To protect good people from bad people" or "To stop people from doing things that would make it uneasy for all of us; for otherwise we wouldn't be able to go to bed at night and sleep in peace." There are two very different questions here. One question emphasizes the proper name: it asks why *J* was punished rather than someone else, or it asks what he was punished for. The other question asks why we have the institution of punishment; why do people punish one another rather than, say, always forgiving one another?

Thus the father says in effect that a particular man is punished, rather than some other man, because he is guilty, and he is guilty because he broke the law (past tense). In his case the law looks back, the judge looks back, the jury looks back, and a penalty is visited upon him for something he did. That a man is to be punished, and what his punishment is to be, is settled by its being shown that he broke the law and that the law assigns that penalty for the violation of it.

On the other hand we have the institution of punishment itself, and recommend and accept various changes in it, because it is thought by the (ideal) legislator and by those to whom the law applies that, as a part of a system of law impartially applied from case to case arising under it, it will have the consequence, in the long run, of furthering the interests of society.

One can say, then, that the judge and the legislator stand in different positions and look in different directions: one to the past, the other to the future. The justification of what the judge does, *qua* judge, sounds like the retributive view; the justification of what the (ideal) legislator does, *qua* legislator, sounds like the utilitarian view. Thus both views have a point (this is as it should be since intelligent and sensitive persons have been on both sides of the argument); and one's initial confusion disappears once one sees that these views apply to persons holding different offices with different duties; and situated differently with respect to the system of rules that make up the criminal law.[5]

One might say, however, that the utilitarian view is more fundamental since it applies to a more fundamental office, for the judge carries out the legislator's will so far as he can determine it. Once the legislator decides to have laws and to assign penalties for their violation (as things are there must be both the law and the penalty) an institution is set up which involves a retributive conception of particular cases. It is part of the concept of the criminal law as a system of rules that the application and enforcement of these rules in particular cases should be justifiable by arguments of a retributive character. The decision whether or not to use law rather than some other mechanism of social control, and the decision as to what laws to have and what penalties to assign, may be settled by utilitarian arguments; but if one decides to have laws then one has decided on something whose working in particular cases is retributive in form.[6]

The answer, then, to the confusion engendered by the two views of punishment is quite simple: one distinguishes two offices, that of the judge and that of the legislator, and one distinguishes their different stations with respect to the system of rules which make up the law; and then one notes that the different sorts of considerations which would usually be offered as reasons for what is done under the cover of these offices can be paired off with the competing justifications of punishment. One reconciles the two views by the time-honored device of making them apply to different situations.

But can it really be this simple? Well, this answer allows for the apparent intent of each side. Does a person who advocates the retributive view necessarily advocate, as an *institution,* legal machinery whose essential purpose is to set up and preserve a correspondence between moral turpitude and suffering? Surely not.[7] What retributionists have rightly insisted upon is that no man can be punished unless he is guilty, that is, unless he has broken the law. Their fundamental criticism of the utilitarian account is that, as they interpret it, it sanctions an innocent person's being punished (if one may call it that) for the benefit of society.

On the other hand, utilitarians agree that punishment is to be inflicted only for the violation of law. They regard this much as understood from the concept of punishment itself.[5] The point of the utilitarian account concerns the institution as a system of rules: utilitarianism seeks to limit its use by declaring it justifiable only if it can be shown to foster effectively the good of society. Historically it is a protest against the indiscriminate and ineffective use of the criminal law.[9] It seeks to dissuade us from assigning to penal institutions the improper, if not sacreligious, task of matching suffering with moral turpitude. Like others, utilitarians want penal institutions designed so that, as far as humanly possible, only those who break the law run afoul of it. They hold that no official should have discretionary power to inflict penalties whenever he thinks it for the benefit of society; for on utilitarian grounds an institution granting such power could not be justified.[10]

The suggested way of reconciling the retributive and the utilitarian justifications of punishment seems to account for what both sides have wanted to say. There are, however, two further questions which arise, and I shall devote the remainder of this section to them.

First, will not a difference of opinion as to the proper criterion of just law make the proposed reconciliation unacceptable to retributionists? Will they not question whether, if the utilitarian principle is used as the criterion, it follows that those who have broken the law are guilty in a way which satisfies their demand that those punished deserve to be punished? To answer this difficulty, suppose that the rules of the criminal law are justified on utilitarian grounds (it is only for laws that meet his criterion that the utilitarian can be held responsible). Then it follows that the actions which the criminal law specifies as offenses are such that, if they were tolerated, terror and alarm would spread in society. Consequently, retributionists can only deny that those who are punished deserve to be punished if they deny that such actions are wrong. This they will not want to do.

The second question is whether utilitarianism doesn't justify too much. One pictures it as an engine of justification which, if consistently adopted, could be used to justify cruel and arbitrary institutions. Retributionists may be supposed to concede that utilitarians *intend* to reform the law and to make it more humane; that utilitarians do not *wish* to justify any such thing as punishment of the innocent; and that utilitarians may appeal to the fact that punishment presupposes guilt in the sense that by punishment one understands an institution attaching penalties to the infraction of legal rules, and therefore that it is logically absurd to suppose that utilitarians in justifying *punishment* might also have justified punishment (if we may call it that) of the innocent. The real question, however, is whether the utilitarian, in justifying punishment, hasn't used arguments which commit him to accepting the infliction of suffering on innocent persons if it is for the good of society (whether or not one calls this punishment). More generally, isn't the utilitarian committed in principle to accepting many practices which he, as a morally sensitive person, wouldn't want to accept? Retributionists are inclined to hold that there is no way to stop the utilitarian principle from justifying too much except by adding to it a principle which distributes certain rights to individuals. Then the amended criterion is not the greatest benefit of society *simpliciter,* but the greatest benefit of society subject to the constraint that no one's rights may be violated. Now while I think that the classical utilitarians proposed a criterion of this more complicated sort, I do not want to argue that point here.[11] What I want to show is that there is *another* way of preventing the utilitarian principle from justifying too much, or at least of making it much less likely to do so: namely, by stating utilitarianism in a way which accounts for the distinction between the justification of an institution and the justification of a particular action falling under it.

I begin by defining the institution of punishment as follows: a person is said to suffer punishment whenever he is legally deprived of some of the normal rights of a citizen on the ground that he has violated a rule of law, the violation having been established by trial according to the due process of law, provided that the deprivation is carried out by the recognized legal authorities of the state, that the rule of law clearly specifies both the offense and the attached penalty, that the courts construe statutes strictly, and that the statute was on the books prior to the time of the offense.[12] This definition specifies what I shall understand by punishment. The question is whether utilitarian arguments may be found to justify institutions widely different from this and such as one would find cruel and arbitrary.

This question is best answered, I think, by taking up a particular accusation. Consider the following from Carritt:

... the utilitarian must hold that we are justified in inflicting pain always and only to prevent worse pain or bring about greater happiness. This, then, is all we need to consider in so-called punishment, which must be purely preventive. But if some kind of very cruel crime becomes common, and none of the criminals can be caught, it might be highly expedient, as an example, to hang an innocent man, if a charge against him could be so framed that he were universally thought guilty; indeed this would only fail to be an ideal instance of utilitarian 'punishment' because the victim himself would not have been so likely as a real felon to commit such a crime in the future; in all other respects it would be perfectly deterrent and therefore felicific.[13]

Carritt is trying to show that there are occasions when a utilitarian argument would justify taking an action which would be generally condemned; and thus that utilitarianism justifies too much. But the failure of Carritt's argument lies in the fact that he makes no distinction between the justification of the general system of rules which constitutes penal institutions and the justification of particular applications of these rules to particular cases by the various official whose job it is to administer them. This becomes perfectly clear when one asks who the "we" are of whom Carritt speaks. Who is this who has a sort of absolute authority on particular occasions to decide that an innocent man shall be "punished" if everyone can be convinced that he is guilty? Is this person the legislator, or the judge, or the body of private citizens, or what? It is utterly crucial to know who is to decide such matters, and by what authority, for all of this must be written into the rules of the institution. Until one knows these things one doesn't know what the institution is whose justification is being challenged; and as the utilitarian principle applies to the institution one doesn't know whether it is justifiable on utilitarian grounds or not.

Once this is understood it is clear what the countermove to Carritt's argument is. One must describe more carefully what the *institution* is which his example suggests, and then ask oneself whether or not it is likely that having this institution would be for the benefit of society in the long run. One must not content oneself with the vague thought that, when it's a question of *this* case, it would be a good thing if *somebody* did something even if an innocent person were to suffer.

Try to imagine, then, an institution (which we may call "telishment") which is such that the officials set up by it have authority to arrange a trial for the condemnation of an innocent man whenever they are of the opinion that doing so would be in the best interests of society. The discretion of officials is limited, however, by the rule that they may not condemn an innocent man to undergo such an ordeal unless there is, at the time, a wave of offenses similar to that with which they charge him and telish him for. We may imagine that the officials having the discretionary authority are the judges of the higher courts in consultation with the chief of police, the minister of justice, and a committee of the legislature.

Once one realizes that one is involved in setting up an *institution,* one sees that the hazards are very great. For example, what check is there on the officials? How is one to tell whether or not their actions are authorized? How is one to limit the risks involved in allowing such systematic deception? How is one to avoid giving anything short of complete discretion to the authorities to telish anyone they like? In addition to these considerations, it is obvious that people will come to have a very different attitude towards their penal system when telishment is adjoined to it. They will be uncertain as to whether a convicted man has been punished or telished. They will wonder whether or not they should feel sorry for him. They will wonder whether the same fate won't at any time fall on them. If one pictures how such an institution would actually work, and the enormous risks involved in it, it seems clear that it would serve no useful purpose. A utilitarian justification for this institution is most unlikely.

It happens in general that as one drops off the defining features of punishment one ends up with an institution whose utilitarian justification is highly doubtful. One reason for this is that punishment works like a kind of price system: by altering the prices one has to pay for the performance of actions it supplies a motive for avoiding some actions and doing others. The defining features are essential if punishment is to work in this way; so that an institution which lacks these features, e.g., an institution which is set up to "punish" the innocent, is likely to have about as much point as a price system (if one may call it that) where the prices of things change at random from day to day and one learns the price of something after one has agreed to buy it.[14]

If one is careful to apply the utilitarian principle to the institution which is to authorize particular actions, then there is *less* danger of its justifying too much. Carritt's example gains plausibility by its indefiniteness and by its concentration on the particular case. His argument will only hold if it can be shown that there are utilitarian arguments which justify an institution whose publicly ascertainable offices and powers are such as to permit officials to exercise that kind of discretion in particular cases. But the requirement of having to build the arbitrary features of the particular decision into the institutional practice makes the justification much less likely to go through.

NOTES

1. I use the word "practice" throughout as a sort of technical term meaning any form of activity specified by a system of rules which defines offices, roles, moves, penalties, defenses, and so on, and which gives the activity its structure. As examples one may think of games and rituals, trials and parliaments.

2. The distinction is central to Hume's discussion of justice in *A Treatise of Human Nature*, bk. III, pt. II, esp. secs. 2–4. It is clearly stated by John Austin in the second lecture of *Lectures on Jurisprudence* (4th ed.; London, 1873), I, 116ff. (1st ed., 1832). Also it may be argued that J. S. Mill took it for granted in *Utilitarianism;* on this point cf. J. O. Urmson, "The Interpretation of the Moral Philosophy of J. S. Mill,"

Philosophical Quarterly, vol. III (1953). In addition to the arguments given by Urmson there are several clear statements of the distinction in *A System of Logic* (8th ed.; London, 1872), bk. VI, ch. xii pars. 2, 3, 7. The distinction is fundamental to J. D. Mabbott's important paper, "Punishment," *Mind,* n.s., vol. XLVIII (April, 1939). More recently the distinction has been stated with particular emphasis by S. E. Toulmin in *The Place of Reason in Ethics* (Cambridge, 1950), see esp. ch. xi, where it plays a major part in his account of moral reasoning. Toulmin doesn't explain the basis of the distinction, nor how one might overlook its importance, as I try to in this paper, and in my review of his book (*Philosophical Review,* vol. LX [October, 1951]), as some of my criticisms show, I failed to understand the force of it. See also H. D. Aiken, "The Levels of Moral Discourse," *Ethics,* vol. LXII (1952), A. M. Quinton, "Punishment," *Analysis,* vol. XIV (June, 1954), and P. H. Nowell-Smith, *Ethics* (London, 1954), pp. 236–239, 271–273.

3. On the concept of explication see the author's paper, *Philosophical Review,* vol. LX (April, 1951).

4. While this paper was being revised, Quinton's appeared; footnote 2 supra. There are several respects in which my remarks are similar to his. Yet as I consider some further questions and rely on somewhat different arguments, I have retained the discussion of punishment and promises together as two test cases for utilitarianism.

5. Note the fact that different sorts of arguments are suited to different offices. One way of taking the differences between ethical theories is to regard them as accounts of the reasons expected in different offices.

6. In this connection see Mabbott, *op cit.,* pp. 163–164.

7. On this point see Sir David Ross, *The Right and the Good* (Oxford, 1930), pp. 57–60.

8. See Hobbes's definition of punishment in *Leviathan,* ch. xxviii; and Bentham's definition in *The Principle of Morals and Legislation,* ch. xii, par. 36, ch. xv, par. 28, and in *The Rationale of Punishment,* (London, 1830), bk. I, ch. i. They could agree with Bradley that: "Punishment is punishment only when it is deserved. We pay the penalty, because we owe it, and for no other reason; and if punishment is inflicted for any other reason whatever than because it is merited by wrong, it is a gross immorality, a crying injustice, an abominable crime, and not what it pretends to be." *Ethical Studies* (2nd ed.; Oxford, 1927), pp. 26–27. Certainly by definition it isn't what it pretends to be. The innocent can only be punished by mistake; deliberate "punishment" of the innocent necessarily involves fraud.

9. Cf. Leon Radzinowicz, *A History of English Criminal Law: The Movement for Reform 1750–1833* (London, 1948), esp. ch. xi on Bentham.

10. Bentham discusses how corresponding to a punitory provision of a criminal law there is another provision which stands to it as an antagonist and which needs a name as much as the punitory. He calls it, as one might expect, the *anaetiosostic,* and of it he says: "The punishment of guilt is the object of the former one: the preservation of innocence that of the latter." In the same connection he asserts that it is never thought fit to give the judge the option of deciding whether a thief (that is, a person whom he believes to be a thief, for the judge's belief is what the question must always turn upon) should hang or not, and so the law writes the provision: "The judge shall not cause a thief to be hanged unless he have been duly convicted and sentenced in course of law" (*The Limits of Jurisprudence Defined,* ed. C. W. Everett [New York, 1945], pp. 238–239).

11. By the classical utilitarians I understand Hobbes, Hume, Bentham, J. S. Mill, and Sidgwick.

12. All these features of punishment are mentioned by Hobbes; cf. *Leviathan,* ch. xxviii.

13. *Ethical and Political Thinking* (Oxford, 1947), p. 65.

14. The analogy with the price system suggests an answer to the question how utilitarian considerations insure that punishment is proportional to the offense. It is interesting to note that Sir David Ross, after making the distinction between justifying a penal law and justifying a particular application of it, and after stating that utilitarian considerations have a large place in determining the former, still holds back from accepting the utilitarian justification of punishment on the grounds that justice requires that punishment be proportional to the offense, and that utilitarianism is unable to account for this. Cf. *The Right and the Good,* pp. 61–62. I do not claim that utilitarianism can account for this requirement as Sir David might wish, but it happens, nevertheless, that if utilitarian considerations are followed penalties will be proportional to offenses in this sense: the order of offenses according to seriousness can be paired off with the order of penalties according to severity. Also the absolute level of penalties will be as low as possible. This follows from the assumption that people are rational (i.e., that they are able to take into account the "prices" the state puts on actions), the utilitarian rule that a penal system should provide a motive for preferring the less serious offense, and the principle that punishment as such is an evil. All this was carefully worked out by Bentham in *The Principles of Morals and Legislation,* chs. xiii–xv.

Determinism and Theories of Blame

E L I Z A B E T H   L.   B E A R D S L E Y

Determinism and Moral Perspectives*

Can determinists find a satisfactory rationale for moral praise and blame? On this question, determinists themselves have long been divided. Although the affirmative answer has enjoyed the status of a majority opinion, the negative answer has at times found very effective support. The force of the negative answer emerges clearly in certain recent writings, in which writers sympathetic to determinism vigorously defend the thesis that determinism removes from the concepts of moral praiseworthiness and blameworthiness all legitimate application whatsoever.[1]

The negative answer to the question posed here is unsatisfactory, I think; but in some ways it is preferable to the affirmative answer as the latter is usually given and supported. In this paper, I shall argue that judgments of moral praise and blame; affirmative as well as negative, can be made within the framework of determinism, provided that we accept a more complex account of these judgments and their foundations than is ordinarily supplied or assumed. I shall maintain that judgments concerning the presence or absence of moral praiseworthiness and blameworthiness are made from several different standpoints, which I shall call "moral perspectives." My primary purpose is to show how an understanding of these perspectives and their relations can contribute substantially toward relieving the tension widely felt (even by some who are reluctant to admit it) to exist between determinism and certain of our basic ethical concepts.

The terms "praise" and "blame" will be used here with the meaning of "moral praise" and "moral blame." Praise and blame will be treated as correlative concepts such that, for everything that is said about one, a corresponding statement about the other could be made, though it will usually be unnecessary to make it. The term "affirmative judgment of praise" will be used to

*Elizabeth L. Beardsley, "Determinism and Moral Perspectives," *Philosophy and Phenomenological Research,* XXI (1960), 1–20. Reprinted with permission of the author and the editor of *Philosophy* and *Phenomenological Research.*

refer to any explicit attribution of praiseworthiness to a person. A "negative judgment of praise" is an explicit denial that a person is praiseworthy. The general term "judgment of praise" will refer indifferently to either an affirmative or a negative judgment of praise, and similarly for "judgment of blame." Judgments of praise and blame will be treated here as assertions which are true or false, and not as acts which may be useful or useless to perform.

DETERMINIST VIEWS OF PRAISE AND BLAME

Before discussing judgments of praise and blame, it will be helpful to consider briefly certain moral judgments of a different kind. The standpoint from which we affirm or deny that acts are objectively right or wrong I shall call the "perspective of objective rightness or wrongness." A judgment of objective rightness or wrongness is a judgment made about an act, not an agent; and it does not carry with it any implication about the praiseworthiness or blameworthiness of an agent. Statements like "Smith's act was objectively right, but he deserves no praise for it" not only are self-consistent, but are often true; objectively right acts can be committed inadvertently, or from reprehensible motives.

The judgment that an act is objectively right furnishes insufficient evidence for a judgment that its agent is praiseworthy, because certain key facts concerning the causal antecedents of the right act remain to be supplied. The objective rightness or wrongness of an act does not depend in any way on its causal antecedents, but on other considerations, such as its consequences (for teleologists), or its harmony with the will of God, moral rules, or the like (for formalists). It is therefore appropriate to call this perspective a "noncausal" one, for it takes no account of whether an act had causal antecedents of one kind rather than another, or indeed had completely determining causal antecedents at all.

Most philosophers, I think, would agree that the use of the moral perspective of objective rightness or wrongness presents no particular problem for the determinist. It is true that certain libertarians have apparently seen something profoundly incongruous in the application of any normative predicates at all to the constituent parts of a determined universe; but this line of thought has persuaded so few that it may be disregarded.

Much less harmony prevails among philosophers who have reflected on the relation between determinism and the concepts of moral praise and blame. Litertarians, of course, maintain that because the truth of determinism would invalidate affirmative judgments of praise and blame, determinism is false, and criteria for praiseworthiness and blameworthiness must include the requirement that an agent should have performed his act "freely." Though determinists are united in rejecting the conclusion of the libertarian argument as false, they differ sharply concerning the acceptability of the conditional premise.

Among leading determinists who believe that valid affirmative judgments of praise and blame can be made, a fairly clear account of the criteria for praiseworthiness and blameworthiness seems to have emerged. I shall call those who subscribe to this account "Group I determinists." Details of the account vary, but a substantial area of agreement remains. It is commonly held that if an agent has acted wrongly, without external constraint ("voluntarily"), without ignorance of relevant facts, and from a motive or because of a trait that is undesirable, then, and only then, the agent deserves blame for his act.[2] Similar conditions are held to govern praiseworthiness.[3]

Group I determinists deny that there is anything here to conflict with the truth of determinism. They point out that those who make judgments of praise and blame must indeed attend to several key factors among the causal conditions that produced the acts whose agents are judged. But any *other* causal conditions that may have been present, and, in particular, antecedents of antecedents, are to be completely disregarded. Moral praisers and blamers, on this view, are simply not concerned with the nature, or even the existence, of such additional factors. Determinism is thus fully compatible with attributions of praiseworthiness and blameworthiness.[4]

To determinists of a second group—"Group II determinists"—this account seems seriously oversimplified.[5] They contend that the same reasoning which leads us to withhold praise and blame from agents whose acts were committed involuntarily will, when combined with the thesis of determinism, lead on inexorably to the conclusion that no one ever deserves praise or blame for anything. They are haunted by the knowledge that many of the causal antecedents of acts have not been investigated by those who mete out praise and blame on the grounds specified above; and most particularly they are haunted by the knowledge that not all of the causal antecedents of voluntary acts are voluntary acts. Thus they come to believe that no distinction between "voluntary" and "involuntary" acts that a determinist can consistently make can sustain the moral weight that it must bear if we are to judge men praiseworthy or blameworthy. How, they ask, could we ever be justified in blaming or praising someone for a voluntary act and not an involuntary one, when we know full well that even the voluntary act can be traced back to causes—environmental or hereditary—belonging to a world the agent never made?

I believe that there are elements of truth in each of these brands of determinism, and I shall try to show that this is the case.

THE PERSPECTIVE OF MORAL WORTH

Surely there is no doubt that the conditions for praiseworthiness and blameworthiness set forth in the Group I determinists' account do in fact constitute one important and familiar standard according to which we make judgments of praise and blame. It is highly convenient to introduce a special term for the characteristic of moral value that may be said to belong to an agent who has performed an act that meets the conditions specified. I shall say that an agent has "positive moral worth" if and only if he has acted rightly, voluntarily, with knowledge of relevant facts, and from a desire that is good in its situation.[6] The term "moral worth" will be used to refer to either positive or negative moral worth indifferently, and the standard by which agents are judged to have moral worth (positive or negative) will be called the "standard of moral worth." Elsewhere[7] I have discussed certain features of the concept of moral worth in some detail, and have indicated how conditions for the presence of degrees of moral worth may be set up.

A "judgment of moral worth," which may be affirmative or negative, is a judgment in which moral worth is asserted to be present or absent. We must of course distinguish between a negative judgment of positive moral worth ("Agent A is not morally worthy for act A") and an affirmative judgment of negative moral worth ("Agent Y is morally unworthy for his act B").

I shall call the standpoint from which we make judgments of moral worth the "perspective of moral worth." This is plainly not a wholly non-causal perspective, as is the perspective of objective rightness or wrongness. Because *some* (a strictly limited set) of the circumstances causally relevant to the performance of an act are taken into account when the moral worth of its agent is being judged, this perspective may accurately be called a "causally limited" perspective. The factors taken into account in making judgments from this moral perspective will be termed the "worth-determining" factors.

Group II determinists are likely to feel that the introduction of the term "moral worth" is unobjectionable, and perhaps even useful, provided that judgments of moral worth are not held to imply judgments of praise or blame. Thinkers of this group may be disposed to admit that human beings do indeed have a strong psychological tendency to experience positive feelings when confronted by the gestalt agent-performing-act-under-conditions-for-positive-moral-worth, and to experience negative feelings when confronted by the corresponding negative gestalt. They may contend that, since these feelings cannot be rationally justified, human beings had better try to eliminate them from their psyches as soon as possible. The fact that there is no reason to believe that this has ever been accomplished is not likely to daunt them. In any case, the important point, for the Group II determinist, is that we should avoid the confusion of believing that persons who happen to form part of the pleasant or unpleasant gestalts just mentioned deserve praise or blame for what they do. Because the crucial distinction between voluntary and involuntary acts is bound to collapse in the end, no one ever deserves praise or blame. Perhaps judgments or praise and blame *are* made from the perspective of moral worth, but they *should* not be.[8]

To this Group I determinist will reply that, since the conditions for "moral worth" were originally taken directly from an analysis of conditions for praiseworthiness and blameworthiness, it is highly arbitrary, to say the very least, to attempt to purge judgments of moral worth of all association with judgments of praise and blame. Moreover, he will continue, the assertion that human beings have "feelings" which are merely "positive" or "negative," when they encounter persons exhibiting positive or negative moral worth, is decidedly misleading. The "feelings" referred to consists of definite reactions of a specific sort, to which are added, for most moral judges, quite explicit reflective convictions. Human beings feel—and reserve—a very special kind of approval and disapproval for those members of their species who perform acts that have certain salient features. Furthermore, the majority of those who have reflected on the matter seem to have been convinced that approval and disapproval of this special kind are reactions to which the persons in question have a morally justified claim. It is this claim which is put forth in affirmative judgments of praise and blame. In view of these considerations, a heavy burden of proof rests on the Group II determinist, who proposes to eliminate from moral discourse all affirmative judgments of praise and blame. This burden, the Group I determinist charges, has not been effectively sustained.

The Group I determinist will go on to admit readily that, among those features which an act must have if its agent is to merit praise or blame, the requirement that it be voluntary is indeed crucial. But, he will say, to establish voluntariness we need examine only certain of the immediate causal ancestors of an act.[9] Considerations about more remote causal forebears are as irrelevant here as information about a man's grandparents would be if proffered in reply to a query about his parents. Therefore it is the case, not only that we *do* make judgments of praise and blame from the perspective of moral worth, but that this procedure is entirely legitimate, and is not threatened by determinism. Thus, concludes the Group I determinist, the problem of praise and blame has been solved.

The Group I determinist may seem, on the face of it, to have had the better of the argument in the exchange just described. He is right, I think, in maintaining that judgments of praise and blame, affirmative as well as negative, have an extremely strong claim to be retained in moral discourse. He is right, also, in insisting that the distinction between voluntary and involuntary acts which is needed for affirmative judgments of praise and blame can be made by determinists. Finally, he is right in holding that what has been called here the "standard of moral worth" is the standard on which many affirmative and negative judgments of praise and blame are based.

Where the Group I determinist is wrong is in his tacit assumption that *all* judgments of moral praise and blame are made from the perspective of moral worth, and that when a man has been judged praiseworthy or blameworthy from his perspective there is nothing more to say about his moral claim to be praised or blamed for the act under consideration. The truth, as I shall go on to try to show, is much less simple than this. There is indeed a network of causes stretching out in all directions, far beyond the worth-determining factors on which the Group I determinists so resolutely fix their minds. Moreover, these other causal factors are by no means without moral significance. We cannot hope to set up a genuinely effective defense against the Group II determinist's harsh view of what that significance is, unless some other way of doing justice to these additional causal factors can be found.

THE PERSPECTIVE OF MORAL CREDIT

I want now to examine a second moral perspective from which we appraise agents. It is necessary to explain the operation of this perspective somewhat more fully than was the case for moral worth, because it has received little attention from ethical theorists.

When we examine our affirmative and negative judgments of praise and blame, we find that many are made by the standard of moral worth; but we also find, I think, that many are not. A second standard of appraisal often comes into operation after a judgment based on moral worth has been made, when we go on to ask further questions about the individual situation of an agent who has performed an act for which he is judged morally worthy or unworthy. Here individual circumstances which facilitated or hampered the performance of the act are taken into account. What we do, that is, is to investigate factors which made the performance of a certain act by a certain agent particularly "easy" or "difficult" for *him*. On the basis of this information, a further judgment of praise or blame is made.

How do we ascertain that the performance of act A by agent X was "easy" or "difficult"? Not by endeavoring to estimate the intensity of his subjective feelings of effort. What is needed here is an objective correlate;[10] and this, I think, is provided by the concept of circumstances *favorable* or *unfavorable* to the performance of a certain act, i.e., circumstances in whose presence the performance of such an act is either more or less likely to occur than it is in their absence. Given that an act is one for which its agent has positive or negative moral worth, a judgment is made to the effect that the balance of known circumstances causally relevant to the performance of that act was favorable or unfavorable. We try to decide, that is, whether, in view of all the things we know about him, it was antecedently probable that a certain act should have been performed by its agent. If an agent has performed an act for which he has positive moral worth, and if it was antecedently improbable that he should have performed this act, then he is praiseworthy by our new standard as well as by the standard of moral worth. We say that such an act was performed "in spite of obstacles" or "against odds." Similar remarks, of course, could be made regarding blameworthiness as judged by this new standard; and it is convenient at times, though somewhat unidiomatic, to speak of an act for which an agent is morally unworthy and which was antecedently improbable as having also been performed "against odds."

To those who deny that the performance against odds of an act for which the agent is morally worthy or unworthy earns for that agent special praise or blame the only answer can be an invitation to look again, more closely, at the moral appraisals we all make. Evidence confirming the view defended here can be found on all sides. For example, it was maintained not long ago by Auxiliary Bishop Joseph M. Marling of the Roman Catholic Church that the presence of severe neurosis in certain Catholic saints could be admitted, since it not only did not detract from their saintliness, but actually contributed to it, in that a neurosis constitutes a serious obstacle to the achievement of spiritual perfection.[11]

There are strong reasons, I think, for maintaining that the criteria for moral appraisals now being examined constitute a standard separate and distinct from the standard of moral worth.

The alternative "single-standard" view (the belief that both sets of criteria can be combined into one complex standard) appears to be widely, though casually, held; but I think it is mistaken. My reasons for this conclusion have been given elsewhere.[12]

By our second standard, then, an agent X is praiseworthy for his act A to some degree if and only if: (1) X has positive moral worth to some degree for A, and (2) X's situation at the time of performing A included among the known circumstances a preponderance or balance of circumstances (other than the amount of "effort" put forth by the agent) which are reasonably judged to be unfavorable to the performance of the act. Similar conditions govern the presence of blameworthiness as judged by this second standard. Agents who perform acts under the conditions for praiseworthiness just specified will be said to have "positive moral credit" for their acts. Like moral worth, moral credit may be present in either a positive or a negative form. A "judgment of moral credit" is an assertion or denial that an agent possesses positive or negative moral credit.[13]

The moral perspective from which judgments of moral credit are made may be called the "perspective of moral credit," and judgments of praise and blame based on the moral credits standard may also be said to be made from this perspective. In order to judge from the perspective of moral credit, we investigate the causal antecedents of an act more extensively than is done for judgments made from the perspective of moral worth. Any instance of any kind of factor which can reasonably be judged to be an unfavorable or favorable circumstance for a given kind of act is potentially a "credit-determining" factor for any agent performing an act of that kind, even though in common practice, to be sure, not all potential credit-determining factors are investigated before judgments are made. The perspective of moral credit, accordingly, may be called a "causally extended" perspective, as compared with our causally limited perspective of moral worth, and our noncausal perspective of objective rightness or wrongness.

Judgments made from the perspective of moral credit supplement judgments made from the perspective of moral worth. They do not supplant them, any more than judgments about the objective rightness or wrongness of acts are supplanted by judgments about the moral worth of their agents. The latter are self-contained judgments, perfectly satisfactory and significant in their own right. Nevertheless, the perspective of moral credit does set limits to the perspective of moral worth, in that it is important for those who make judgments by the moral worth standard to remember that such judgments do not give us the whole moral truth about an agent. Even when we do not actually go on to ascertain the moral credit-rating of an agent to whom we ascribe positive or negative moral worth, we must bear in mind that further questions along such lines *could* be asked. Judgments of praise and blame made from the perspective of moral worth will be made less dogmatically, with less show of finality, by those who understand that there is another moral perspective from which an individual can be judged. But those who make judgments from the perspective of moral credit must not forget the importance of the perspective of moral worth. Judges who constantly focus their attention on the "ease" or "difficulty" with which something was accomplished need to be reminded at times, to look at the quality of the moral accomplishment itself. Neither of these two moral perspectives can be said to be superior to the other.

It seems clear that the use of the perspective of moral credit is fully compatible with determinism.[14] And the identification of this new standpoint of moral appraisal as a separate moral perspective lends needed strength to the philosophical position of determinism, principally by revealing it to be less dogmatic and impersonal than it is often taken to be. In a more detailed treatment of these matters, the advantages to determinism of recognizing judgments of praise and blame based on moral credit could be explained more fully.

In the end, however, the convinced Group II determinist will always reply that the effort to set up a perspective of moral credit cannot salvage judgments of praise and blame. He will maintain that judgments of praise and blame based on moral credit are ultimately no more compatible with determinism than are judgments of praise and blame based on moral worth.[15] As before, he may look tolerantly, or even benevolently, on the procedure of setting up a "perspective of moral credit," just so long as judgments of praise and blame are kept out of the picture. Again his reaction springs from his awareness of additional causal factors, this time of causal factors lying behind those taken into account from the perspective of moral credit. The Group II determinists will say that, although those who make judgments based on moral credit may make extensive inquiries into the factors causally relevant to human acts, sooner or later, because of the limits of time or energy or human knowledge, they must bring their investigations to a close. And when they do, they will not have told the whole causal story; and the part that will remain untold will invalidate judgments of praise and blame made from this moral perspective.

I believe that this charge can be answered, but I want to show first how it might be supported. Let us consider a comparison between two individuals, Jones and Smith. Jones has performed an act having a high degree of positive moral worth in spite of very unfavorable circumstances, whereas Smith, confronted by essentially the same kind of circumstances and placed in a very similar situation, has performed an act having a much lower degree of positive moral worth. It is clear that Jones possesses a higher degree of positive moral credit for his act than does Smith for his,[16] since the circumstances and situation constitute greater obstacles for Jones' act than for Smith's.

Now, no matter how strong our psychological tendency to feel a greater admiration for the achievement of Jones, such an attitude, the Group II determinist would claim, is not justifiable. For moral credit is ascribed on the basis of finding that a preponderance of the *known* circumstances in an agent's situation was unfavorable to the performance of a given act. Judgments of moral credit deal with acts whose performance was improbable; nevertheless, they deal with acts that *were* performed, events that *happened.* If determinism is true, these happenings were caused. Therefore for each act for which an agent possesses moral credit there must exist also a cluster of one or more unknown circumstances causally relevant to the performance of the act, and a preponderance of *there* circumstances must have been favorable, rather than unfavorable. It is all very well, then, to judge that Jones performed under great odds an act for which he is morally worthy; but such a judgment is superficial and unstable. For, if determinism is true, these vaunted "odds" disappear upon examination; and Jones is seen to have done only what the causal factors in his situation, unknown as well as known, brought forth. So did Smith, and so do we all. How then can praise and blame by the standard of moral credit be justified?

It is evident that this reasoning is too cogent to be set aside. At the close of the preceding section, it was asserted that the causal factors not dealt with in judgments of moral worth were nevertheless morally significant, and would have to be taken care of in some other way. Many of these "left-over" causal factors have now been shown to provide a basis for judgments of praise and blame made from a second moral perspective, the perspective of moral credit. But the Group II determinist now reminds us that behind even the credit-determining factors lie still others, and that these too have a moral significance that cannot be lightly dismissed. His interpretation of the moral significance of this most distant range of causal factors is, as we have seen, simply that they invalidate all affirmative judgments of praise and blame. In the remainder of this paper, I shall try to show that another interpretation is possible, and that it is to be preferred.

THE PERSPECTIVE OF ULTIMATE MORAL EQUALITY

In the course of our discussion, we have now sorted out three groups of factors causally relevant to human behavior: worth-determining factors, credit-determining factors, and what may be called "ultimate" causal factors, which are simply those factors that are left out of account when we make judgments based on moral worth and moral credit. If determinism is true, we may be said to know, for any given act, *that* there are ultimate causal factors. But we do not know *what* they are: if we did know they would take their place among the potential credit-determining factors for the act in question. It is strange that this shadowy group of unknown circumstances should be morally so significant; but I think that there is no doubt that their moral significance is real.

When we are mindful of the existence of the ultimate causal factors, we look at human beings and their acts in a special way. This was brought out by the example of Jones and Smith. When we look at persons in this special way, they are seen to be equals, as far as their claims to moral praise and blame are concerned, or, rather, they are seen to have passed beyond any point at which discriminations of praiseworthiness or blameworthiness are applicable. Seen in this way, all men are members of a moral or spiritual democracy. This is a realm lying behind our distinctions of moral worth and moral credit, a realm in which each is simply the person he is. When we take into account the full range of factors causally relevant to human acts, we must regard human beings as a flock without goats and without sheep.

I propose to say that this special way of looking at persons, in the light of the existence of ultimate causal factors for their behavior, constitutes another moral perspective. This I shall call the "perspective of ultimate moral equality." From this perspective we look at persons and their acts in the widest possible causal contexts, contexts without limits of any kind. Therefore we may call this a "causally unlimited" perspective. As a moral perspective it is, of course, strikingly different in some respects from the others that we have examined. Judgments made from the perspective of moral worth and the perspective of moral credit are judgments of discrimination. This is obvious in the case of comparative judgments, but it is also true of noncomparative ones. Our interest in knowing that X possesses positive moral worth for his honest act, and Y negative moral credit for his cowardly one, stems in large part from the fact that there are honest acts whose agents do not possess positive moral worth, and cowardly acts whose agents earn no negative moral credit. Judgments of praise and blame based on moral worth and moral credit are answers to questions which can in principle be answered either affirmatively or negatively.

This is not true of judgments made from the perspective of ultimate moral equality. Here all are on the same moral footing: none has any ultimate claim to praise or blame, and the judgments made from this perspective are all negative. No matter what acts a person has performed, all that we can say of him from this final moral perspective is that he deserves no praise for what he has done, or that he deserves no blame.

The statement "X is not ultimately praiseworthy for A" is a negative judgment of praise made from the perspective of ultimate moral equality, whereas "Y is not ultimately blame-worthy for B" is a negative judgment of blame made from the same perspective. Judgments of praise and blame made from this perspective will here be limited in scope to persons whose acts have earned for them moral worth or moral credit. That is to say, the statement "X is not ultimately praiseworthy for A" will be permissible if and only if A is an act for which X possesses either positive moral worth or positive moral credit. And the truth-condition for this statement can be stated very briefly: the statement is true if and only if A has ultimate causes. Similarly, "Y is not ultimately blameworthy for B" is permissible if and only if B is an act for which Y possesses negative moral worth or negative moral credit, and true if and only if BN has ultimate causes.

But, if determinism is true, we know of any event that it has ultimate causes, and we know this without any specific investigation. The behavior of all men is causally determined, and the nature of what we have called the "ultimate" causes is equally unknown in each case. This eradication of all distinctions in the causal status of acts erases all distinctions in the moral status of their agents. Therefore in one way it can never be news that Brown does not ultimately deserve praise for his kind deed, or that Robinson does not ultimately deserve blame for his unkind one.

In another way, however, these assertions *are* news, and important news. The fact that Brown and Robinson are ultimately moral equals is a vital part of the whole moral truth about them. Compare the situation for a factual account.[17] In factual descriptions of human beings we are interested in the qualities in which they differ, to be sure; but we are also interested in the qualities in which they are alike. For some purposes, and in some contexts, the similarities may be legitimately disregarded; but this does not mean that they can always be left out of account. Sometimes they are more significant than the differences, and they are never more significant than they become when we are in danger of assuming that the differences tell the whole factual story. So it is with moral appraisals of human beings. For the whole moral story, judgments of praise and blame based on moral worth and moral credit need to be supplemented by judgments made from the perspective of ultimate moral equality.

Because this is true, we are justified in regarding the perspective of ultimate moral equality as a genuinely "moral" perspective, even though it eradicates moral discriminations. The knowledge that when persons are viewed in relation to the ultimate causal factors of their behavior moral discriminations no longer apply to them is a piece of moral knowledge, at least in being knowledge about moral matters. It is curious that as we go from a causally limited perspective to a causally extended one we increase our power to make moral discriminations, whereas when we come to a causally unlimited perspective these moral discriminations stop altogether. But the knowledge that this is so is moral knowledge, and it has important bearings on the rest of our moral knowledge.

The relation that holds between the perspective of ultimate moral equality and the other moral perspectives from which judgments of praise and blame are made is analogous in certain ways to the relation between the perspective of moral credit and that of moral worth. Judgments based on moral credit, as we have seen, set limits to judgments based on moral worth. Similarly, the knowledge that human beings can be viewed from a perspective which will show them to be morally equal will remind those who make judgments based on moral worth and moral credit that these judgments of moral inequality do not tell the whole story about the individuals being judged. This knowledge, in turn, will affect the attitudes of those who have it: they will regard themselves and each other with more tolerance than before. Feelings of admiration, contempt, guilt, and pride, will all be experienced more moderately by those who know that no man is ever the *first* cause of evil or good deeds, or *finally* responsible for winning or losing when confronted by moral odds. But this is not to say that such feelings will not be experienced at all, or that they should not be.

For the perspective of ultimate moral equality cannot give us the whole truth about the praise-worthiness and blameworthiness of human beings either. The fact that X has negative moral worth for his act, or that Y has positive moral credit for his, is not cancelled by saying that X does not ultimately deserve blame, or that Y does not ultimately deserve praise. We value in a special way those whose acts meet the standards of moral worth and moral credit, and this is something that we cannot change. As Spinoza saw, it is true—even in a determined universe—that "we desire to form for ourselves an idea of man upon which we may look as a model of human nature."[18] The idea of a man who performs a right act voluntarily, knowingly, and from a good desire, and the idea of a man who, when confronted by odds, can still do these things—these *are* the models we have formed. Conformity to these patterns is what we regard as worthy of praise, and deviation from them in certain ways is what we regard as worthy of blame. We cannot feel about persons who thus conform or deviate as we do about animals or inanimate objects which measure up or fail to measure up to certain other standards. All this being so, judgments of praise and blame based on moral worth and moral credit are not only legitimate but vitally necessary parts of moral discourse. They are answers to questions that we cannot help asking.

The full moral truth about a man and his act, then, might run as follows: that he deserves a low degree of praise for it by the standard of moral worth, a high degree of praise for it by the standard of moral credit, and ultimately no praise for it when he is judged from the perspective of ultimate moral equality. There is no reason why the three statements cannot be true simultaneously. Also, these perspectives seem to be genuinely coordinate, and complementary: we need them all. And, if we distinguish between moral perspectives, we shall be able to avoid the doubling of metaphysical perspectives which Kant found necessary in order to reconcile causality and morality. It is easier to regard a man as blameworthy from one point of view but not from another than to say that his act is both caused and uncaused.

The acquiring of moral wisdom, at least as far as moral appraisals are concerned, does not consist only in learning how to make sound judgments from each moral perspective. It consists also in learning under what circumstances each of the moral perspectives should be used—a large and fundamental problem that cannot be dealt with here.[19] Here let us note only that most of the questions about the praiseworthiness and blameworthiness of human beings that are actually asked are questions to which the appropriate answer is a judgment based on moral worth or one based on moral credit. Writers on ethics[20] have

pointed out that we feel something peculiarly objectionable in an attempt by a wrongdoer to exculpate himself on the ground that all his acts were caused and therefore he deserves no blame. Here an inquiry into his blameworthiness is launched from one moral perspective and a reply is made from another. But moral perspectives, however coordinate, are certainly not interchangeable. Questions about praiseworthiness or blameworthiness should be answered from the perspective from which they are asked, whenever it is possible to tell what this is. Sometimes it will be appropriate, and even very desirable, to add to this answer a judgment made from another moral perspective; but often it will not be. Particular caution must be exercised in advancing judgments made from the perspective of ultimate moral equality. These are illuminating, and even inspiring, when made in the right context, and by those who know how to make accurate discriminations by the standards of moral worth and moral credit. Otherwise they are apt to seem shallow, and somehow sentimental, or cheap.[21]

SOME OBJECTIONS AND REPLIES

The account which has been given of the perspective of ultimate moral equality and its relation to our other perspectives of praise and blame seems likely to arouse objections from all sides. Three of these appear to me to be particularly striking, and in this concluding section I shall try to reply briefly to each one in turn.

(1) The first objection that I shall consider is one that will be raised by Group II determinists. Some of what has been said in the preceding will presumably be acceptable to members of this group; but they will want to know how it can be maintained that the perspective of ultimate moral equality is merely *one* of several perspectives from which agents are appraised. It is rather *the* moral perspective, which, because of its special nature, invalidates all others. It is superior to the others because it is broader in its scope. This is the only perspective that is causally unlimited, the only one from which we view acts in the context of *all* their causes, unknown as well as known. And since we are seeing more broadly, it follows that we are seeing more accurately.

The answer here must be that it is not clear that this does follow. Do we see "better" from a height that takes in a large part of the surrounding territory? The only reply can be "Yes and no." Details which were not seen from a height spring back into view when we climb back down and look at objects in the context of a smaller part of their surroundings; and things which looked alike from above manifest striking differences when seen from a position farther down. In this case, one standpoint does not reveal the "real nature" of the objects better than another one does.

But we must not be lured into pressing our optical metaphor of "perspectives" too far. In any case, the Group II determinist may wish to support his basic contention—that the perspective of ultimate moral equality has a privileged status—in another way. He may claim that it will be impossible, psychologically, for those who have viewed persons from the perspective of ultimate moral equality to go on making the same old judgments of praise and blame from other perspectives. How, he will ask, can we throw ourselves into the task of sorting the worthy from the unworthy, the creditable from the discreditable, when we know that from another standpoint these distinctions will disappear altogether? Will not the view from every perspective but that of ultimate moral equality take on the aspect of something unreal, a mirage without power to deceive for more than a moment?

Part of the answer here is that we cannot, indeed, make moral discriminations in exactly the "same old" way, and that we cannot "throw ourselves" into the sorting and grading processes with quite the zeal of those who have never seen human beings as ultimate moral equals. The difference, however, will be in the quality and intensity of the emotions accompanying judgments of praise and blame based on moral worth and moral credit. The judgments themselves will go on being made; human acts will go on being looked at in causal contexts of varying scope. Our models of human nature, in short, will go on being used. To see whether it is psychologically possible to return from the perspective of ultimate moral perspectives, no determinist needs to look farther than his own experience. It is in truth not possible to do anything else.

(2) A second objection is likely to be raised by certain libertarians. It is the charge that our so-called "perspective of ultimate moral equality" is ignoble and degrading. Such a perspective, it will

be said, affords a particularly deplorable example of the levelling tendency which seeks to destroy standards of merit in all areas. Plato's charge against political democracy—that it makes equals of unequals—applies a thousandfold to the "moral democracy" that is claimed to be visible from this distorting perspective. The moral world is hierarchical to the core; to remove the sheep and the goats from the moral landscape is to destroy it. So runs this second charge.

The answer to it divides into two parts. The first point to be made is that moral discriminations have not been permanently eradicated. Viewed from the other moral perspectives (which, as we have seen, are not eliminated by the perspectives of ultimate moral equality), the moral landscape swims back into our ken with sheep and goats intact. Moreover, it is sometimes more appropriate to look at the moral world in this way.

But some will feel that this part of the answer is not enough: that it is wrong *ever* to see all persons as moral equals. Now even though one may be deeply convinced that the perspective of ultimate moral equality, far from being ignoble, is—when appropriately used—exalted and inspiring, it is not altogether easy to know how to argue for this conviction. One may point to the increase in compassion, tolerance, equanimity, that come to those who know how to look at themselves and each other on occasion from the perspective of ultimate moral equality. But it may conceivably be said in reply that these are regarded as benefits only by persons who are antecedently convinced that determinism is, as a matter of fact, true. This reply is not without force. That portion of Spinoza's defense of determinism which shows "what service to our own lives a knowledge of this doctrine is" has not lost its power to move determinists; but what power do his words have over others? If all our acts go back to ultimate causes, then we should indeed look at all human beings with compassion and tolerance; but what if they do not? Libertarians may contend that compassion and tolerance are not spiritual goods if these attitudes are directed toward humans who, because they have misused their freedom, simply do not deserve to be pitied or tolerated. And equanimity in the face of moral iniquity is nothing but extreme moral callousness, particularly unforgivable, it will be said, when the wrongdoer is oneself.

It may prove impossible to disabuse some extreme libertarians of their conviction that human beings should never be regarded as being all morally equal. But it is hard to believe that most people, whatever their metaphysical beliefs, will not find something to which they can respond positively in the attitudes engendered by the perspective of ultimate moral equality. The making of all our judgments of praise and blame with less finality, less assurance that they represent the whole truth, must seem to many an end to be welcomed.[22] Religious teachings which have kept before our eyes the view from something like the perspective of ultimate moral equality ("There but for the grace of God go I") have performed a great service for our moral outlook.[23]

(3) Finally, I want to take note of the contention—in which those of all metaphysical persuasions will doubtless heartily concur—that this account of praise and blame is simply too complicated to be acceptable. How could the average unspeculative mortal ever find his way among such a bewildering variety of moral perspectives? How could he ever make a judgment of praise or blame?

In reply to these questions, two points must be made. First, a single moral judgment arrived at from a single moral perspective is not necessarily made more complicated by the present account than by other accounts.[24] But, secondly, it must be admitted that difficulties do arise when a moral judge is asked to remember that other moral perspectives exist and set limits to the one that he is using at any given time, and when he is asked, as he sometimes must be, to decide on the moral perspective that should be used in a particular situation. We have seen that moral wisdom, on the present view, consists not merely in the ability to make correct moral appraisals from a single perspective, but also in the ability to correlate the perspectives, and, on occasion, to choose among them.

It may well be that few attain this kind of wisdom, yet it is by no means clear that it cannot be attained by unspeculative persons. Perhaps such persons can and do make concrete judgments of moral praise and blame in a balanced and large-minded way, keeping the various relevant considerations in due proportion, and governing their own attitudes accordingly, despite a lack of any grasp of a theoretical basis for what they are doing. But, if it should turn out that we cannot really evade the conclusion that the present account makes moral wisdom harder for an unspeculative person to attain, this conclusion would not necessarily vitiate the account. Why should it not be the case that moral wisdom demands considerable resources of intellect as well as of character?

In this paper, I have been arguing that the question with which we began, "Can determinists find a rationale for moral praise and blame?", can be answered affirmatively. I have tried to show, however, that the unrecognized assumption behind the typical and influential affirmative answers that have been given—the assumption that judgments of praise and blame are made from a single moral perspective—is mistaken. I have maintained that those determinists who give a negative answer to our original question have caught sight of some important truths that the others have missed. In the end, however, with their attempts to set up the perspective of ultimate moral equality as the sole valid perspective for judgments of praise and blame, they have fallen into the same fundamental error as the others. One group eternally confronts the other with the question "How can you deny that human beings can be said to be praiseworthy and blameworthy, in view of the fact that they commit acts that are right or wrong, and at the same time done voluntarily, knowingly, and from good or bad desires?" To which the second group incessantly hurls back a question of its own: "How can you assert that human beings can be said to be praiseworthy or blameworthy, in view of the fact that their acts, like all other events, are wholly subject to causal laws, and must be traced back, in the end, to factors wholly beyond the agents' control?" The account given here, which may be called the "theory of multiple moral perspectives," is designed to help put an end to this durable impasse. I have tried to show that the first group is speaking from the perspective of moral worth, while the second replies from the perspective of ultimate moral equality. Both perspectives are valid; but each perspective is incomplete.

Three moral perspectives are necessary, I have contended, if we are to tell the whole about the praiseworthiness and blameworthiness of human beings. One of these, the perspective of ultimate moral equality, takes form as a consequence of assuming determinism to be true; but its adoption is not without moral and spiritual benefits. The other perspectives can be exhibited in an examination of judgments of praise and blame conducted quite independently of any determinist assumptions; and we can then see that determinism is—at the very least—fully compatible with the use of these moral perspectives. It seems to me that considerable work remains to be done in clarifying and refining these concepts and principles, and in exploring their implications in many directions but if the claims nade here are in essentials justified, it follows that determinists need not feel that old familiar uneasiness when confronted by the concepts of moral praise and blame. On the contrary, it may be that we stand here on solid ground.

NOTES

1. See Paul Edwards, "Hard and Soft Determinism," and John Hospers, "What Means This Freedom?" Both in Sidney Hook, *Determinism and Freedom* (New York University Press, 1958); also W. I. Matson, "On the Irrelevance of Free-will to Moral Responsibility," *Mind*, Vol. LXV (1956), pp. 489–497. Although these writers frame their argument more explicitly in terms of the concept of moral responsibility than in terms of moral praiseworthiness and blameworthiness, the application to the latter concepts is clear. Matson's chief thesis, that libertarianism can validate the concept of moral responsibility no more successfully than determinism can, will not be dealt with in the present paper; the part of his article which bears most directly on what I shall have to say is found in sections 2 and 3.

2. I have found the presentation of this general position by P. H. Nowell-Smith in *Ethics* (London, 1954), particularly helpful here.

3. Note that the terms "blameworthy" and "praiseworthy" have not been defined here and that no definitions of these terms will be offered in this paper.

4. Many would argue, of course, that determinism is much more than merely "compatible" with these judgments, since we cannot speak of an agent's act as "his" act or as arising "from" a motive or trait, unless determinism is assumed to be true. This argument will be deliberately set aside here.

5. My distinction between "Group I" and "Group II" determinism is plainly very similar to Edwards' distinction between "soft" and "hard" determinism. See Edwards, *op. cit.*, and also Edwards and Pap, *A Modern Introduction to Philosophy* (Free Press, 1957), p. 380.

6. I prefer to formulate this last condition in terms of a "desire" rather than of a "trait," because we sometimes make judgments of this kind without having sufficient evidence to ascertain the presence of a trait; but this point is not of central importance here.

7. Moral Worth and Moral Credit," *The Philosophical Review*, Vol. LXVI (1957), pp. 304–328. In the present treatment I have left the term "moral worth" undefined, and I have also introduced it here to refer to an attribute of agents who are praiseworthy or blameworthy *for* acts rather than to refer to an attribute of acts themselves.

8. It is convenient to speak of the point at issue between the Group I and Group II determinists as concerned primarily with the validity of *affirmative* judgments of praise and blame; and I occasionally do this. But it should be understood that the Group II determinist in fact equally denies the validity of any *negative* judgment of praise (or blame) which is made with the assumption that the class of persons who deserve praise (or blame) is not vacuous.

9. If it should be said that so-called "voluntary" acts are not *really* voluntary after all, the Group I determinist would reply in the fashion of Flew, in the latter's discussion of the expression "acting freely." See A. Flew, "Divine Omnipotence and Human Freedom," in Flew and MacIntyre, *New Essays in Philosophical Theology* (Macmillan, 1955), pp. 149–151.

10. There will not, however, be an exact correlation between felt intensity of effort and the criterion proposed.

11. See *Time*, Vol. LXVIII (August 27, 1956), for an account of an address by Auxiliary Bishop Joseph M. Marling of Kansas City, Mo., to the Guild of Catholic Psychiatrists.

12. E. L. Beardsley, *op. cit.*, especially pp. 309–315.

13. See *ibid.* for a detailed discussion of the concept of moral credit and its relation to moral worth. Here I leave "moral credit" undefined, and use it to refer to an attribute of agents rather than of acts.

14. It may be said, I think correctly, that the account of moral credit given here actually presupposes a determinist position, since reliable causal generalizations about human behavior underlie the estimates of probability on which judgments of moral credit, in large part, depend.

15. I disregard here the fact that the Group II determinist would also say that the perspective of moral credit inherits what he takes to be the deficiencies of the perspective of moral worth, since judgments of moral worth are presupposed by judgments of moral credit.

16. On degrees of praiseworthiness by the standard of moral credit, see E. L. Beardsley, *op. cit.*, p. 319.

17. By this manner of speaking I do not mean to rule out the possibility that a naturalistic account of the meaning of basic ethical terms can be given.

18. B. Spinoza, *Ethics* (Oxford Press, 4th ed., 1930), p. 179.

19. One important question to consider in this connection is whether it is ever justifiable to employ the perspective of ultimate moral equality when thinking of one's own future acts and their moral status. Some reflections which bear on this question (though they are not expressed in the language of the present paper) are offered by H. Fingarette in his interesting article "Psychoanalytic Perspectives on Moral Guilt and Responsibility: a Re-Evaluation," *Philosophy and Phenomenological Research*, Vol. XVI (1955–1956), pp. 18–29.

20. See, for example, Nowell-Smith, *op. cit.*, pp. 297–300.

21. Judgments made from the perspective of ultimate moral equality are most effective when directed to individuals whose moral credit has been ascertained, as well as their moral worth. If we go directly from the perspective of moral worth to the perspective of ultimate moral equality without

passing through the perspective of moral credit, it appears that something important has been left out.

22. This end is particularly desirable for those more sweeping judgments in which persons are praised or blamed, not for specified acts, but for their whole characters. Space limitations have precluded the consideration of such judgments here; but their treatment forms an important part of a more detailed examination of moral perspectives.

23. Note that, even though the grace of God may be regarded as being "freely" given, in so far as it is held to constitute a causal determinant of human action, it is treated as essentially similar to what have here been called "ultimate causes." Of considerable interest for further study would be a comparision of the perspective of ultimate moral equality—here described in purely naturalistic terms—with such religious concepts as "equality in the sight of God."

24. Indeed, the distinction between moral worth and moral credit makes it possible to give a simpler account of the judgments made by each standard than the account which proponents of the single standard view would have to give if their position were adequately worked out.

PART 6 SELF-LOVE AND

Suppose you find a wallet containing $5,000 in cash. Surely the morally right thing to do (at least according to the prevailing moral code) would be to return it to its owner. But would this truly be the most reasonable course of action? Think of what you have to gain: an expression of gratitude, some small satisfaction at having done your duty (mixed with nagging doubts that you are a fool), and *maybe* a small reward. Now compare these benefits with what you have to lose—namely, the $5,000 itself. It would seem that the losses involved in doing your "duty" (if that's what it is) far outweigh the gains. (Perhaps the example might be still more convincing if the money belonged not to a private person but to a great corporation or the federal government.) Looking at the matter in this way, wouldn't you be a fool to return the money? Isn't it *unreasonable,* indeed profoundly contrary to reason, voluntarily to choose a loss in preference to a gain for oneself? And yet this is what morality seems continually to require of us: that we put the interests of other people ahead of our own. How, then, can it be reasonable to be moral?

One line of reply to this challenge immediately suggests itself. Not to return the property of others is tantamount to stealing it. If other people ever were to find out that you are, in effect, a thief, their opinion of you would drop drastically, and your reputation might never fully recover. Moreover, if the authorities were to make this discovery about you, the consequences might be still worse. Even if no one ever found you out, you would have to live in continued anxiety and fear; and even if you got over that, you might become just a bit bolder in the face of subsequent temptations, until your very success finally would betray you, and you would be found out. The idea that it ever can *pay* to do what is morally wrong, in short, is always a miscalculation.

Glaucon and Adeimantus, two characters in Plato's *Republic,* are not satisfied with this kind of answer. That there are advantages in having the reputation of being moral and upright (or "just" as they would put it) is perfectly evident; what they wish to learn from Socrates is whether there are corresponding advantages in really being, as opposed to merely seeming, morally upright. If it is reasonable to be honest only *because*

THE CLAIMS OF MORALITY

dishonesty doesn't pay, then, it would seem, it is reasonable to be honest only *when* dishonesty doesn't pay; and the ideally wise man would be he who is able to have the "best of both worlds," by seeming, but not really being, moral. Socrates' answer to the challenge of Glaucon and Adeimantus is developed in considerable detail in *The Republic,* and is too long to be included here. It is given an accurate summary, however, in the first selection from the historian W. E. H. Lecky (1838–1903), though without its elaborate supporting argument.

Plato's *Republic* is typical of much of the classical literature of moral philosophy in that it consists largely of arguments designed to show that there is a necessary and invariant connection between duty and self-interest. Many of the greatest moralists have found unthinkable the notion that a man ever truly profits in the long run from being immoral. Whatever else morality may be, these writers argue, it must be something reasonable. And surely, they go on, it cannot be reasonable for a man deliberately to act contrary to his own interest. Hence, it follows that the dictates of morality (assumed to be reasonable) never require sacrifice of self-interest, appearances to the contrary. Many of the great systems of moral theory, then, are designed to account for this conclusion. The first brief selection from Lecky classifies the ways this task was done in the moral systems of antiquity.

The Oxford moralist H. A. Prichard (1871–1947), in the selection included here, argues that this traditional philosophical undertaking is misguided and unnecessary. There can be only one theoretical motive, he believes, for insisting, in the teeth of common sense, that morality always pays; and that is the conviction, which he thinks Socrates shares with the Sophists, that a desire for one's own happiness or well-being is ultimately the only human motive. If no normal person can be moved to do anything except by an appeal to his own good, then men can be induced to act morally only by being persuaded that it is not contrary to their true interests to do so, that their interests and the claims of morality necessarily coincide. Prichard (whose views, incidentally, fall neatly under Lecky's fourth heading) rejects this theory of human motivation and is able therefore to hold that it is both possible and reasonable for a person to do the right thing, even on those occasions when he has nothing to gain—or even a great deal to lose—by doing so.

The theory that human beings are so constituted by nature that they are incapable of desiring or pursuing anything but their own well-being as an end in itself is called *psychological egoism.* Genuinely disinterested acts of benevolence, on this view, do not exist, although persons sometimes appear to be acting unselfishly when they take the interests of other people to be means to the promotion of their own good. This theory of motivation should be distinguished from the doctrine called *ethical egoism,* which, as its name indicates, is not a theory about how men in fact act but rather a moral doctrine stating how they ought to act. According to this doctrine, one ought to pursue one's own well-being, and only one's own well-being, as an end in itself. One might expect that any *psychological* egoist, insofar as he bothered with ethics at all, would be an *ethical* egoist; for if there is only one thing that we *can* pursue, there cannot be some other thing that we *ought* to pursue. Most psychological egoists, however, have sought some way to reconcile necessarily selfish motivation with the unselfish and even self-sacrificing conduct required by morality. The second brief selection from W. E. H. Lecky summarizes such attempts at reconciliation, made in the heyday of psychological egoism by such distinguished writers as Thomas Hobbes (1588–1679), François de La Rochefoucauld (1613–1680), and Claude Adrien Helvetius (1715–1771).

The essay by the editor on psychological egoism is probably the only article in the book that was not written for publication. It was distributed to students for classroom use only at Brown University, Princeton University, and U.C.L.A. during the period 1958–1966. It contains very elementary distinctions and standard arguments reorganized and put into elementary terms. It might very well be used, because of its pedagogical intent, as the student's introduction to this section, or even perhaps to the whole volume. Many or most students seemed, after much resistance, to be persuaded by its arguments; but some of the best students (especially those who were psychology majors) remained unconvinced to the end. Many of those students would have been pleased by the article by Michael Slote, of Columbia University. Slote maintains that even if all the a priori arguments for psychological egoism are fallacious, there may yet be empirical evidence for egoism derived from psychological learning theory.

Just how much weight should a person's own interests have in determining what he *ought* to do in situations where the interests of others are bound to be affected by his action? This question can be interpreted in such a way that asks us *not* to weigh the rational claims of morality against those of self-interest, but rather to decide just how much of our self-interest is represented by, or included in, the claims of morality. This section concludes with four articles by serious philosophers, none of them *immoralists,* who differ among themselves over what degree of self-sacrifice, if any, and what degree of self-promotion, if any, a rational morality requires.

The theory that morality requires us to look after our own interest exclusively (or primarily) and respect the interests of others not at all (or only secondarily) can be called *ethical egoism;* but we must be very careful in our definitions, since a large number of possible "egoistic" theories do not *exactly* fit this definition. Perhaps the least misleading thing to say is that a moral theory is egoistic *to the extent that* it emphasizes the propriety of pursuing one's own interest. This would allow differences in degree of egoism between theories. Similarly, the theory that morality requires us totally to forget our own interests and selflessly devote ourselves to the interests of others can be called *ethical altruism;* and a particular moral theory is altruistic *to the extent that* it emphasizes the propriety of self-abnegation and devotion to others.

The ethical theory of Jeremy Bentham (1748–1833), usually called *utilitarianism* but sometimes denominated *universalistic hedonism,* is no more altruistic than egoistic. In deciding (better *calculating*) what one ought to do, Bentham tells the reader, "everybody is to count as one and nobody as more than one." That is to say, I should consider the alternative actions open to me and their likely consequences for the interests of all those who will be directly affected by them, including of course *my own.* Then, insofar as my act will promote the happiness of the people (including *me*) it affects, just so far does it tend to be the right act for me to perform; and insofar as it promotes unhappiness (including *my* unhappiness), it tends to be wrong. Ideally, I ought to tally up the scores of the alternative acts open to me, counting my own interests as no more and no less important than anyone else's, and select that act which causes the greatest net balance of pleasure over pain all around.

Utilitarianism thus rules out partiality for self, or for family, or social class, or country, and requires us to consider every human being whose happiness can be affected by our conduct to be exactly on a par. It thus has a certain initial attractiveness; but it is not without its difficulties. Should I really give all my savings to relieve the hunger of distant peoples instead of using them to send my children to college, provided only that I thereby do more good "all around"? Do not—*ought* not—my children have a greater claim on me than does any distant stranger? And don't I owe more to those persons to whom I stand in special relations—creditors, those to whom I have made promises, neighbors, friends, teammates—than to individuals who stand in no special relation to me? And what relation can be more intimate and "special" than one's relation to oneself?

J. O. Urmson, of Oxford, would apply the test of social utility, in some cases, not to individual acts but to rules, practices, and alternative systems of morality. A system of morality, after all, is a kind of human artifact, rational only insofar as it serves to promote human welfare. If our moral rules require too much of us in the way of saintliness, heroism, and self-sacrifice, they will produce no more useful results than our human nature is prepared to yield; moreover, they will bring the "moral law" itself into disrepute, and produce widespread morbid guilt and suffering. Psychological egoists have argued in the past that human nature is such that no one is capable of deliberately and voluntarily sacrificing himself or devoting himself selflessly to a social cause. Sometimes they have gone on to infer from this that no reasonable moral rule, therefore, can *require* the heroism that no one is capable of achieving. Urmson, on the contrary, holds that saintliness and heroism are possible, although, he concedes, they are so difficult that perhaps not many people have it in them to measure up to such lofty standards. For this and other reasons, a rational utilitarian moral system will recognize (as traditional Christianity does) a distinction between basic rules imposing duties and obligations, and ideals of perfection that guide aspiration but are not morally mandatory.

An ethical egoist would reject Urmson's compromise. Not only is it false, according to ethical egoism, that we *must* sacrifice our interests for the sake of others (that is, that self-sacrifice is *required* of us), it is even false that we *ought* to make such sacrifices (that is, that self-sacrifice is even an *ideal of perfection*). Some egoists[1] would concede

---

[1]See, for example, Ayn Rand, "The Ethics of Emergencies," in *The Virtue of Selfishness* (New York: Signet Books, 1961).

the reasonableness of a person's assuming a great risk, or paying a great price, in order (say) to save the life of a *loved one,* but would argue that insofar as the loss of the loved one would make the person's own life miserable, the act in question clearly would *not* be self-sacrificing. These egoists, however, would still maintain that it would be unreasonable for a person to make any sacrifice at all for the sake of a complete stranger. The main point of this softened kind of ethical egoism is not to deny the reasonableness of loving and benevolent acts, but rather to give "love" and "benevolence" themselves an egoistic psychological analysis. (The editor argues in his essay "Psychological Egoism" that such analyses are generally flawed.)

Brian Medlin, of the University of Queensland, Australia, attacks extreme ethical egoism. It is doubtful, however, that the egoism he purports to refute conclusively (that "everyone should look after his own interests regardless of the interests of others") is exactly the same as the "softened egoism" discussed in the preceding paragraph. The importance of precise definition, at this point, should be manifest to the student. Labels *can* cause more confusion than understanding. It would be misleading, for example, to characterize the view of W. D. Falk, of the University of North Carolina, as "ethical egoism" of any kind; yet his eloquent essay argues that purely self-regarding directives must be included in the list of valid precepts by which the man of moral wisdom leads his life.

Why Be Moral?

PLATO

The Immoralists' Challenge*

With these words I was thinking that I had made an end of the discussion; but the end, in truth, proved to be only a beginning. For Glaucon, who is always the most pugnacious of men, was dissatisfied at Thrasymachus' retirement; he wanted to have the battle out. So he said to me: Socrates, do you wish really to persuade us, or only to seem to have persuaded us, that to be just is always better than to be unjust?

I should wish really to persuade you, I replied, if I could.

Then you certainly have not succeeded. Let me ask you now:—How would you arrange goods— are there not some which we welcome for their own sakes, and independently of their consequences, as, for example, harmless pleasures and enjoyments, which delight us at the time, although nothing follows from them?

I agree in thinking that there is such a class, I replied.

Is there not also a second class of goods, such as knowledge, sight, health, which are desirable not only in themselves, but also for their results?

Certainly, I said.

And would you not recognize a third class, such as gymnastic, and the care of the sick, and the physician's art; also the various ways of money-making—these do us good but we regard them as disagreeable; and no one would choose them for their own sakes, but only for the sake of some reward or result which flows from them?

There is, I said, this third class also. But why do you ask?

Because I want to know in which of the three classes you would place justice?

In the highest class, I replied,—among those goods which he who would be happy desires both for their own sake and for the sake of their results.

Then the many are of another mind; they think that justice is to be reckoned in the troublesome class, among goods which are to be pursued for the sake of rewards and of reputation, but in themselves are disagreeable and rather to be avoided.

I know, I said, that this is their manner of thinking, and that this was the thesis which Thrasymachus was maintaining just now, when he censured justice and praised injustice. But I am too stupid to be convinced by him.

I wish, he said, that you would hear me as well as him, and then I shall see whether you and I agree. For Thrasymachus seems to me, like a snake, to have been charmed by your voice sooner than he ought to have been; but to my mind the nature of justice and injustice have not yet been made clear. Setting aside their rewards and results, I want to know what they are in themselves, and how they inwardly work in the soul. If you please, then, I will revive the argument of Thrasymachus. And first I will speak of

*From Plato, *The Republic*, ii. 357A–367E, trans. B. Jowett.

the nature and origin of justice according to the common view of them. Secondly, I will show that all men who practice justice do so against their will, of necessity, but not as a good. And thirdly, I will argue that there is reason in this view, for the life of the unjust is after all better far than the life of the just—if what they say is true, Socrates, since I myself am not of their opinion. But still I acknowledge that I am perplexed when I hear the voices of Thrasymachus and myriads of others dinning in my ears; and, on the other hand, I have never yet heard the superiority of justice to injustice maintained by any one in a satisfactory way. I want to hear justice praised in respect of itself; then I shall be satisfied, and you are the person from whom I think that I am most likely to hear this; and therefore I will praise the unjust life to the utmost of my power, and my manner of speaking will indicate the manner in which I desire to hear you too praising justice and censuring injustice. Will you say whether you approve of my proposal?

Indeed I do; nor can I imagine any theme about which a man of sense would oftener wish to converse.

I am delighted, he replied, to hear you say so, and shall begin by speaking, as I proposed, of the nature and origin of justice.

They say that to do injustice is, by nature, good; to suffer injustice, evil; but that the evil is greater than the good. And so when men have both done and suffered injustice and have had experience of both, not being able to avoid the one and obtain the other, they think that they had better agree among themselves to have neither; hence there arise laws and mutual covenants; and that which is ordained by law is termed by them lawful and just. This they affirm to be the origin and nature of justice;—it is a mean or compromise, between the best of all, which is to do injustice and not be punished, and the worst of all, which is to suffer injustice without the power of retaliation; and justice, being at a middle point between the two, is tolerated not as a good, but as the lesser evil, and honoured by reason of the inability of men to do injustice. For no man who is worthy to be called a man would ever submit to such an agreement if he were able to resist; he would be mad if he did. Such is the received account, Socrates, of the nature and origin of justice.

Now that those who practice justice do so involuntarily and because they have not the power to be unjust will best appear if we imagine something of this kind: having given both to the just and the unjust power to do what they will, let us watch and see whither desire will lead them; then we shall discover in the very act the just and unjust man to be proceeding along the same road, following their interest, which all natures deem to be their good, and are only diverted into the path of justice by the force of law. The liberty which we are supposing may be most completely given to them in the form of such a power as is said to have been possessed by Gyges the ancestor of Croesus the Lydian. According to the tradition, Gyges was a shepherd in the service of the king of Lydia; there was a great storm, and an earthquake made an opening in the earth at the place where he was feeding his flock. Amazed at the sight, he descended into the opening, where, among other marvels, he beheld a hollow brazen horse, having doors, at which he stooping and looking in saw a dead body of stature, as appeared to him, more than human, and having nothing on but a gold ring; this he took from the finger of the dead and reascended. Now the shepherds met together, according to custom, that they might send their monthly report about the flocks to the king; into their assembly he came having the ring on his finger, and as he was sitting among them he chanced to turn the collet of the ring inside his hand, when instantly he became invisible to the rest of the company and they began to speak of him as if he were no longer present. He was astonished at this, and again touching the ring he turned the collet outwards and reappeared; he made several trials of the ring, and always with the same result—when he turned the collet inwards he became invisible, when outwards he reappeared. Whereupon he contrived to be chosen one of the messengers who were sent to the court; where as soon as he arrived he seduced the queen, and with her help conspired against the king and slew him, and took the kingdom. Suppose now that there were two such magic rings, and the just put on one of them and the unjust the other; no man can be imagined to be of such an iron nature that he would stand fast in justice. No man would keep his hands off what was not his own when he could safely take what he liked out of the market, or go into houses and lie with any one at his pleasure, or kill or release from prison whom he would, and in all respects be like a God among men. Then the actions of the just would be as the actions of the unjust; they would both come at last to the same point. And this we may truly affirm to be a great proof that a man is just, not willingly or because he thinks that justice is any good to him individually, but of necessity, for wherever any one thinks that he can safely be unjust, there he is unjust. For all men believe in their hearts that injustice is far more profitable to the individual than justice, and he who argues as I have been supposing, will say that they are right. If you could imagine any one obtaining this power of becoming invisible, and never doing any wrong or touching what was another's, he would be thought by the lookers-on to be a most wretched idiot, although they would praise him to one another's faces, and keep up appearances with one another from a fear that they too might suffer injustice. Enough of this.

Now, if we are to form a real judgment of the life of the just and unjust, we must isolate them; there is no other way; and how is the isolation to be effected? I answer: Let the unjust man be entirely unjust, and the just man entirely just; nothing is to be taken away from either of them, and both are to be perfectly furnished for the work of their respective lives. First, let the unjust be like other distinguished masters of craft; like the skillful pilot or physician, who knows intuitively his own powers and keeps within their limits, and who, if he fails at any point, is able to recover himself. So let the unjust make his unjust attempts in the right way, and lie hidden if he means to be great in his injustice (he who is found out is nobody): for the highest reach of injustice is: to be deemed just when you are not. Therefore I say that in the perfectly unjust man we must assume the most perfect injustice; there is to be no deduction, but we must allow him, while doing the most unjust acts, to have acquired the greatest reputation for justice. If he have taken a false step he must be able to recover himself; he must be one who can speak with effect, if any of his deeds come to light, and who can force his way where force is required by his courage and strength, and command of money and friends. And at his side let us place the just man in his nobleness and simplicity, wishing, as Aeschylus says, to be and not to seem good. There must be

no seeming, for if he seem to be just he will be honoured and rewarded, and then we shall not know whether he is just for the sake of justice or for the sake of honours and rewards; therefore, let him be clothed in justice only, and have no other covering; and he must be imagined in a state of life the opposite of the former. Let him be the best of men, and let him be thought the worst; then he will have been put to the proof; and we shall see whether he will be affected by the fear of infamy and its consequences. And let him continue thus to the hour of death; being just and seeming to be unjust. When both have reached the uttermost extreme, the one of justice and the other of injustice, let judgment be given which of them is the happier of the two.

Heavens! my dear Glaucon, I said, how energetically you polish them up for the decision, first one and then the other, as if they were two statues.

I do my best, he said. And now that we know what they are like there is no difficulty in tracing out the sort of life which awaits either of them. This I will proceed to describe; but as you may think the description a little too coarse, I ask you to suppose, Socrates, that the words which follow are not mine.—Let me put them into the mouths of the eulogists of injustice: They will tell you that the just man who is thought unjust will be scourged, racked, bound—will have his eyes burnt out; and, at last, after suffering every kind of evil, he will be impaled: Then he will understand that he ought to seem only, and not to be, just; the words of Aeschylus may be more truly spoken of the unjust than of the just. For the unjust is pursuing a reality; he does not live with a view to appearances—he wants to be really unjust and not to seem only:—

His mind has a soil deep and fertile,
Out of which spring his prudent counsels.[1]

In the first place, he is thought just, and therefore bears rule in the city; he can marry whom he will, and give in marriage to whom he will; also he can trade and deal where he likes, and always to his own advantage, because he has no misgivings about injustice; and at every contest, whether in public or private, he gets the better of his antagonists, and gains at their expense, and is rich, and out of his gains he can benefit his friends, and harm his enemies; moreover, he can offer sacrifices, and dedicate gifts to the gods abundantly and magnificently, and can honour the gods or any man whom he wants to honour in a far better style than the just, and therefore he is likely to be dearer than they are to the gods. And thus, Socrates, gods and men are said to unite in making the life of the unjust better than the life of the just.

I was going to say something in answer to Glaucon, when Adeimantus, his brother, interposed: Socrates, he said, you do not suppose that there is nothing more to be urged?

Why, what else is there? I answered.

The strongest point of all has not been even mentioned, he replied.

Well, then, according to the proverb, 'Let brother help brother'—if he fails in any part do you assist him; although I must confess that Glaucon has already said quite enough to lay me in the dust, and take from me the power of helping justice.

Nonsense, he replied. But let me add something more: There is another side to Glaucon's argument about the praise and censure of justice and injustice, which is equally required in order to bring out what I believe to be his meaning. Parents and tutors are always telling their sons and their wards that they are to be just; but why? not for the sake of justice, but for the sake of character and reputation; in the hope of obtaining for him who is reputed just some of those offices, marriages, and the like which Glaucon has enumerated among the advantages accruing to the unjust from the reputation of justice. More, however, is made of appearances by this class of persons than by the others; for they throw in the good opinion of the gods, and will tell you of a shower of benefits which the heavens, as they say, rain upon the pious; and this accords with the testimony of the noble Hesiod and Homer, the first of whom says, that the gods make the oaks of the just—

To bear acorns at their summit, and bees in the middle;
And the sheep are bowed down with the weight of their
    fleeces.[2]

and many other blessings of a like kind are provided for them. And Homer has a very similar strain; for he speaks of one whose fame is—

As the fame of some blameless king who, like a god,
Maintains justice; to whom the black earth brings forth
Wheat and barley, whose trees are bowed with fruit,
And his sheep never fail to bear, and the sea gives him
    fish.[3]

Still grander are the gifts of heaven which Musaeus and his son[4] vouchsafe to the just; they take them down into the world below, where they have the saints lying on couches at a feast, everlastingly drunk, crowned with garlands; their idea seems to be that an immortality of drunkenness is the highest meed of virtue. Some extend their rewards yet further; the posterity, as they say, of the faithful and just shall survive to the third and fourth generation. This is the style in which they praise justice. But about the wicked there is another strain; they bury them in a slough in Hades, and make them carry water in a sieve; also while they are yet living they bring them to infamy, and inflict upon them the punishments which Glaucon described as the portion of the just who are reputed to be unjust; nothing else does their invention supply. Such is their manner of praising the one and censuring the other.

Once more, Socrates, I will ask you to consider another way of speaking about justice and injustice, which is not confined to the poets, but is found in prose writers. The universal voice of mankind is always declaring that justice and virtue are honourable, but grievous and toilsome; and that the pleasures of vice and injustice are easy of attainment, and are only censured by law and opinion. They say also that honesty is for the most part less profitable than dishonesty; and they are quite ready to call wicked men happy, and to honour them both in public and private when they are rich or in any other way influential, while they despise and overlook those who may be weak and poor, even though acknowledging them to be better than the others. But most extraordinary of all is their mode of speaking about virtue and the gods: they say that the gods apportion calamity and misery to many good men, and good and happiness to the wicked. And mendicant prophets go to rich men's doors and persuade them that they have a power committed to them by the gods of making an atonement for a man's own or his ancestor's sins by sacrifices or charms, with rejoicings and feasts; and they promise to harm an enemy, whether just or unjust, at a small cost; with magic arts and incantations binding heaven, as they say, to execute their will. And the poets are the authorities to whom they appeal, now smoothing the path of vice with words of Hesiod:—

Vice may be had in abundance without trouble; the way is smooth and her dwelling-place is near. But before virtue the gods have set toil,[5]

and a tedious and uphill road: then citing Homer as a witness that the gods may be influenced by men; for he also says:—

The gods, too, may be turned from their purpose; and men pray to them and avert their wrath by sacrifices and soothing entreaties, and by libations and the odour of fat, when they have sinned and transgressed.[6]

And they produce a host of books written by Musaeus and Orpheus, who were children of the Moon and the Muses—that is what they say—according to which they perform their ritual, and persuade not only individuals, but whole cities, that expiations and atonements for sin may be made by sacrifices and amusements which fill a vacant hour, and are equally at the service of the living and the dead; the latter sort they call mysteries, and they redeem us from the pains of hell, but if we neglect them no one knows what awaits us.

He proceeded: And now when the young hear all this said about virtue and vice, and the way in which gods and men regard them, how are their minds likely to be affected, my dear Socrates,—those of them, I mean, who are quickwitted, and, like bees on the wing, light on every flower, and from all that they hear are prone to draw conclusions as to what manner of persons they should be and in what way they should walk if they would make the best of life? Probably the youth will say to himself in the words of Pindar—

Can I by justice or by crooked ways of deceit ascend a loftier tower which may be a fortress to me all my days?

For what men say is that, if I am really just and am not also thought just, profit there is none, but the pain and loss on the other hand are unmistakable. But if, though unjust, I acquire the reputation of justice, a heavenly life is promised to me. Since then, as philosophers prove, appearance tyrannizes over truth and is lord of happiness, to appearance I must devote myself. I will describe around me a picture and shadow of virtue to be the vestibule and exterior of my house; behind I will trail the subtle and crafty fox, as Archilochus, greatest of sages, recommends. But I hear some one exclaiming that the concealment of wickedness is often difficult; to which I answer, Nothing great is easy. Nevertheless, the argument indicates this, if we would be happy, to be the path along which we should proceed. With a view to concealment we will establish secret brotherhoods and political clubs. And there are professors of rhetoric who teach the art of persuading courts and assemblies; and so, partly by persuasion and partly by force, I shall make unlawful gains and not be punished. Still I hear a voice saying that the gods cannot be deceived, neither can they be compelled. But what if there are no gods? or, suppose them to have no care of human things—why in either case should we mind about concealment? And even if there are gods, and they do care about us, yet we know of them only from tradition and the genealogies of the poets; and these are the very persons who say that they may be influenced and turned by 'sacrifices and soothing entreaties and by offerings.' Let us be consistent then, and believe both or neither. If the poets speak truly, why then we had better be unjust, and offer of the fruits of injustice; for if we are just, although we may escape the vengeance of heaven, we shall lose the gains of injustice; but, if we are unjust, we shall keep the gains, and by our sinning and praying, and praying and sinning, the gods will be propitiated, and we shall not be punished. 'But there is a world below in which either we or our posterity will suffer for our unjust deeds.' Yes, my friend, will be the reflection, but there are mysteries and atoning deities, and these have great power. That is what mighty cities declare; and the children of the gods, who were their poets and prophets, bear a like testimony.

On what principle, then, shall we any longer choose justice rather than the worst injustice? when, if we only unite the latter with a deceitful regard to appearances, we shall fare to our mind both with gods and men, in life and after death, as the most numerous and the highest authorities tell us. Knowing all this, Socrates, how can a man who has any superiority of mind or person or rank or wealth, be willing to honour justice; or indeed to refrain from laughing when he hears justice praised? And even if there should be some one who is able to disprove the truth of my words, and who is satisfied that justice is best, still he is not angry with the unjust, but is very ready to forgive them, because he also knows that men are not just of their own free will; unless, peradventure, there be some one whom the divinity within him may have inspired with a hatred of injustice, or who has attained knowledge of the truth—but no other man. He only blames injustice who, owing to cowardice or age or some weakness, has not the power of being unjust. And this is proved by the fact that when he obtains the power, he immediately becomes unjust as far as he can be.

The cause of all this, Socrates, was indicated by us at the beginning of the argument, when my brother and I told you how astonished we were to find that of all the professing panegyrists of justice—beginning with the ancient heroes of whom any memorial has been preserved to us, and ending with the men of our own time—no one has ever blamed injustice or praised justice except with a view to the glories, honours, and benefits which flow from them. No one has ever adequately described either in verse or prose the true essential nature of either of them abiding in the soul, and invisible to any human or divine eye; or shown that of all the things of a man's soul which he has within him, justice is the greatest good, and injustice the greatest evil. Had this been the universal strain, had you sought to persuade us of this from our youth upwards, we should not have been on the watch to keep one another from doing wrong, but every one would have been his own watchman, because afraid, if he did wrong, of harbouring in himself the greatest of evils. I dare say that Thrasymachus and others would seriously hold the language which I have been merely repeating, and words even stronger than these about justice and injustice, grossly, as I conceive, perverting their true nature. But I speak in this vehement manner, as I must frankly confess to you, because I want to hear from you the opposite side; and I would ask you to show not only the superiority which justice has over injustice, but what effect they have on the possessor of them which makes the one to be a good and the other an evil to him. And please, as Glaucon requested of you, to exclude reputations; for unless you take away from each of them his true reputation and add on the false, we shall say that you do not praise justice, but the appearance of it; we shall think that you are only exhorting us to keep injustice dark, and that you really agree with Thrasymachus in thinking that justice is another's good and the interest of the stronger, and that injustice is a man's own profit and interest, though injurious to the weaker. Now as you have admitted that justice is one of that highest class of goods which are desired indeed for their results, but in a far greater degree for their own sakes—like sight or hearing or knowledge or health, or any other real and natural and not merely conventional good—I would ask you in your praise of justice to regard one point only: I mean the essential good and evil which justice and injustice work in the possessors of them. Let others praise justice and censure injustice, magnifying the rewards and honours of the one and abusing the other; that is a manner of arguing which, coming from them, I am ready to tolerate, but from you who have spent your whole life in the consideration of this question, unless I hear the contrary from your own lips, I expect something better. And therefore, I say, not only prove to us that justice is better than injustice, but show what they either of them do to the possessor of them, which makes the one to be a good and the other an evil, whether seen or unseen by gods and men.

NOTES

1. *Seven against Thebes,* 574.
2. Hesiod, *Works and Days,* 230.
3. Homer, *Od.* xix. 109.
4. Eumolpus.
5. Hesiod, *Works and Days,* 287.
6. Homer, *Iliad,* ix. 493.

W. E. H. L E C K Y

Ancient Views on the Relation between Duty and Self-Interest*

The reader will probably have gathered from the last chapter that there are four distinct motives which moral teachers may propose for the purpose of leading men to virtue. They may argue that the disposition of events is such that prosperity will attend a virtuous life, and adversity a vicious one—a proposition they may prove by pointing to the normal course of affairs, and by asserting the existence of a special Providence in behalf of the good in the present world, and of rewards and punishments in the future. As far as these latter arguments are concerned, the efficacy of such teaching rests upon the firmness with which certain theological tenets are held, while the force of the first considerations will depend upon the degree and manner in which society is organised, for there are undoubtedly some conditions of society in which a perfectly upright life has not even a general tendency to prosperity. The peculiar circumstances of dispositions of individuals will also influence largely the way in which they receive such teaching, and, as Cicero observed, 'what one utility has created, another will often destroy.'

They may argue, again, that vice is to the mind what disease is to the body, and that a state of virtue is in consequence a state of health. Just as

bodily health is desired for its own sake, as being the absence of a painful, or at least displeasing state, so a well-ordered and virtuous mind may be valued for its own sake, and independently of all the external good to which it may lead, as being a condition of happiness; and a mind distracted by passion and vice may be avoided, not so much because it is an obstacle in the pursuit of prosperity, as because it is in itself essentially painful and disturbing. This conception of virtue and vice as states of health or sickness, the one being in itself a good and the other in itself an evil, was a fundamental proposition in the ethics of Plato.[1] It was admitted, but only to a subsidiary place, by the Stoics, and has passed more or less into all the succeeding systems. It is especially favourable to large and elevating conceptions of self-culture, for it leads men to dwell much less upon isolated acts of virtue or vice than upon the habitual condition of mind from which they spring.

It is possible, in the third place, to argue in favour of virtue by offering as a motive that sense of pleasure which follows the deliberate performance of a virtuous act. This emotion is a distinct and isolated gratification following a distinct action, and may therefore be easily separated from that habitual placidity of temper which results from the extinction of vicious and perturbing impulses. It is this theory which is implied in the common exhortations to enjoy 'the luxury of do-

*W. E. H. Lecky *History of European Morals from Augustus to Charlemagne* (New York: George Braziller, 1955), Vol. I, pp. 178–181. First published in 1869.

ing good,' and though especially strong in acts of benevolence, in which case sympathy with the happiness created intensifies the feeling, this pleasure attends every kind of virtue.

These three motives of action have all this common characteristic, that they point as their ultimate end to the happiness of the agent. The first seeks that happiness in external circumstances; the second and third in psychological conditions. There is, however, a fourth kind of motive which may be urged, and which is the peculiar characteristic of the intuitive school of moralists and the stumbling-block of its opponents. It is asserted that we are so constituted that the notion of duty furnishes in itself a natural motive of action of the highest order, wholly distinct from all the refinements and modifications of self-interest. The coactive force of this motive is altogether independent of surrounding circumstances, and of all forms of belief. It is equally true for the man who believes and for the man who rejects the Christian faith, for the believer in a future world and for the believer in the mortality of the soul. It is not a question of happiness or unhappiness, of reward or punishment, but of a generically different nature. Men feel that a certain course of life is the natural end of their being, and they feel bound, even at the expense of happiness, to pursue it. They feel that certain acts are essentially good and noble, and others essentially base and vile, and this perception leads them to pursue the one and to avoid the other, irrespective of all considerations of enjoyment.

NOTES

1. Mr. Grote gives the following very clear summary of Plato's ethical theory, which he believes to be original:— 'Justice is in the mind a condition analogous to good health and strength in the body. Injustice is a condition analogous to sickness, corruption, impotence in the body. . . . To possess a healthy body is desirable for its consequences as a means towards other constituents of happiness, but it is still more desirable in itself as an essential element of happiness *per se*, i.e., the negation of sickness, which would of itself make us miserable. . . . In like manner, the just mind blesses the possessor twice: first and chiefly by bringing to him happiness in itself; next, also, as it leads to ulterior happy results. The unjust mind is a curse to its possessor in itself and apart from results, though it also leads to ulterior results which render it still more a curse to him.'—Grote's *Plato*, vol. iii p. 131. According to Plutarch, Aristo of Chio defined virtue as 'the health of the soul.' *(De Virtute Morali.)*

H. A. PRICHARD

Duty and Interest*

In seeking a subject for an inaugural lecture, I have tried to find one which, without raising too technical issues, is near enough to every one to be of general interest and yet would be considered by philosophers still sufficiently controversial to deserve consideration. This subject I hope I have found in the relation between duty and interest. The topic is, of course, well worn. Nevertheless anyone who considers it closely will find that it has not the simple and straightforward character which at first sight it appears to possess.

A general but not very critical familiarity with the literature of moral philosophy might well lead to the remark that much of it is occupied with attempts either to prove that there is a necessary connexion between duty and interest or in certain cases even to exhibit the connexion as something self-evident. And the remark, even if not strictly accurate, plainly has some truth in it. It might be said in support that Plato's treatment of justice in the *Republic* is obviously such an attempt, and that even Aristotle in the *Ethics* tries to do the same thing, disguised and weak though his attempt may be . . .

*H. A. Prichard, *Duty and Interest* (Oxford: Clarendon Press, 1928), pp. 4–21, 24–25. Reprinted by permission of The Clarendon Press, Oxford. Prichard's more developed views on this and related subjects can be found in his *Moral Obligation, Essays and Lectures* (Oxford: Clarendon Press, 1949), especially in the title essay, written in 1937.

When we read the attempts referred to we naturally cannot help in a way wishing them to succeed; and we might express our wish in the form that we should all like to be able to believe that honesty is the best policy. At the same time we also cannot help feeling that somehow they are out of place, so that the real question is not so much whether they are successful, but whether they ought ever to have been made. And my object is to try to justify our feeling of dissatisfaction by considering what these attempts really amount to, and more especially what they amount to in view of the ideas which have prompted them. . . .

One preliminary remark is necessary. It must not be assumed that what are thus grouped together as attempts either to prove or to exhibit the self-evidence of a connexion between duty and interest are properly described by this phrase, or even that they are all attempts to do one and the same thing. And in particular I shall try to show that the attempts so described really consist of endeavours, based on mutually inconsistent presuppositions, to do one or another of three different things.

On a casual acquaintance with the *Republic,* we should probably say without hesitation that, apart from its general metaphysics, what it is concerned with is justice and injustice, and that, with regard to justice and injustice, its main argument is an elaborate attempt, continued to the end of the book, to show in detail that if we look below the surface and consider what just actions really consist in and also the nature of the soul, and, to a minor degree, the nature of the world in which we have to act, it will become obvious, in spite of appearance to the contrary, that it is by acting justly that we shall really gain or become happy.

Further, if we were to ask ourselves, 'What are Plato's words for right and wrong?'—and plainly the question is fair—we should have in the end to give as the true answer what at first would strike us as a paradox. We should have to allow that Plato's words for right and wrong are not to be found in such words as χρή ['one must'] or δεῖ ['one ought'] and their contraries, as in χρή δίκα ιον εἶναι ['one ought to be just'] or ὄντινα τρό πον χρή ζῆν, ['in whatever manner one ought to live'], where the subject is implied by the context to be τὸν μέλλοντα μακάριον ἔσεσθαι ['he who would be happy or blessed'] but in δίκαιον

['just'] and ἄδικον ['unjust'] themselves. When he says of some action that it is δίκαιον, that is his way of saying that it is right, or a duty, or an act which we are morally bound to do. When he says that it is ἄδικον, that is his way of saying that it is wrong. And in the sense in which we use the terms 'justice' and 'injustice', it is less accurate to describe what Plato is discussing as justice and injustice than as right and wrong. Our previous statement, therefore, might be put in the form that Plato is mainly occupied in the *Republic* with attempting to show it is by doing our duty, or what we are morally bound to do, that we shall become happy.

This is the account of his object which we are more particularly inclined to give if we chiefly have in mind what Socrates in the fourth Book is made to offer as the solution of the main problem. But this solution is preceded by an elaborate statement of the problem itself, put into the mouth of Glaucon and Adeimantus; and if we consider this statement closely, we find ourselves forced to make a substantial revision of this account of Plato's object. Glaucon and Adeimantus make it quite clear that whatever it is that they are asking Socrates to show about what they refer to as justice, their object in doing so is to obtain a refutation of what may be called the Sophistic theory of morality. Consequently, if we judge by what Glaucon and Adeimantus say, whatever Plato is trying to prove must be something which Plato would consider as affording a refutation of the Sophistic theory. But what is this theory as represented by Plato? It almost goes without saying that in the first instance men's attitude towards matters of right and wrong is an unquestioning one. However they have come to do so, and in particular whether their doing so is due to teaching or not, they think, and think without having any doubt, that certain actions are right and that certain others are wrong. No doubt in special cases, they may be doubtful; but, as regards some actions, they have no doubt at all, though to say this is not the same as to say that they are certain. But there comes a time when men are stirred out of this unquestioning frame of mind; and in particular the Sophists, as Plato represents them, were thus stirred by the reflection that the actions which men in ordinary life thought right, such as paying a debt, helping a friend, obeying the government, however they differed in other respects, at least agreed in bringing directly a definite loss to the agent. This reflection led them to wonder whether men were right in thinking these actions duties, i.e. whether they thought so truly. Then, having failed to find indirect advantages of these actions which would more than compensate for the direct loss, i.e. such advantages as are found in what we call prudent actions, they drew the conclusion that these actions cannot really be duties at all, and that therefore what may roughly be described as the moral convictions which they and others held in ordinary life were one gigantic mistake or illusion. Finally, they clinched this conclusion by offering something which they represented as an account of the origin of justice, but which is really an account of how they and others came to make the mistake of thinking these actions just, i.e. right.

This is the theory which on Plato's own showing he wants to refute. It is a theory about certain actions, and, on his own showing, what he has to maintain is the opposite theory about these same actions. But how, if our language is to be accurate, should these actions be referred to? Should they be referred to as *just,* i.e. right, actions, or should they be referred to as those actions which in ordinary life we *think* just, i.e. right? The difference, though at first it may seem unimportant, is really vital. In the unquestioning attitude of ordinary life we must either be *knowing* that certain actions are right or not knowing that they are right, but doing something else for which '*thinking* them right' is perhaps the least unsatisfactory phrase. There is no possibility of what might be suggested as a third alternative, viz. that our activity is one of thinking, which in instances where we are thinking truly is also one of knowing. For, as Plato realized, to think truly is not to know, and to discover that in some particular case we were thinking truly is not to discover that in doing so we were knowing. Moreover, when we are what is described as reflecting on the activity involved in our unquestioning attitude of mind, we are inevitably thinking of it as having a certain definite character, and, in so thinking of it, we must inevitably be implying either that the activity is one of knowing or that it is not. For we must think of this attitude either as one of thinking, or as one of knowing, and if we think of it as one of thinking, we imply that it is not one of knowing,

and *vice versa.* In fact, however we think of the activity, we are committed one way or the other. Now the Sophists clearly implied that this unquestioning attitude is one of thinking and not one of knowing; for it would not have been sense to maintain that those actions which in ordinary life we know to be right are really not right. Their theory, then, must be expressed by saying that those actions which in ordinary life we think, and so do not know, to be right are not really right. Consequently Plato also, since he regards this as the theory to be refuted, is implying that in ordinary life we think, and do not know, that certain actions are right, and that, to this extent, he agrees with the Sophists. And for this reason, if we are to state accurately the problem which he is setting himself, we must represent it as referring not to *just* actions but to those actions which he and others in ordinary life *think* just.

It is clear then that when Plato states through the medium of Glaucon and Adeimantus the problem which he has to solve, he is guilty of an inaccuracy, which, though it may easily escape notice, is important. For Glaucon and Adeimantus persistently refer to the actions of which they ask Socrates to reconsider the profitableness as just and unjust actions, whereas they should have referred to them as the actions which men in ordinary life think just and unjust.

I shall now take it as established that when we judge from Plato's own statement of his problem, worked out as it is by reference to the Sophists, we have to allow that he is presupposing that ordinarily we do not know but think that certain actions are right and that he is thinking of his task as that of having to vindicate the truth of these thoughts against the Sophists' objection. And this is what must be really meant when it is said that Plato's object is to vindicate *morality* against the Sophistic view of it, for here 'morality' can only be a loose phrase for our ordinary moral thoughts or convictions.

Glaucon and Adeimantus, however, do not simply ask Socrates to refute the Sophistic view; they ask him to do so in a particular way, which they imply to be the only way possible, viz. by showing that if we go deeper than the Sophists and consider not merely the gains and losses really due to the reputation for doing what men think just and unjust, but also those which these actions directly bring to the man's own soul, it will become obvious that it is by doing what we think just that we shall really gain. And so far as the rest of the *Republic* is an attempt to satisfy this request, this must be what it is an attempt to show.

Now on a first reading of the *Republic,* it is not likely to strike us that there is anything peculiar or unnatural about this part of the request. Just because Plato takes for granted that this is the only way to refute the Sophists, we are apt in reading him to do the same, especially as our attention is likely to be fully taken up by the effort to follow Plato's thought. But if we can manage to consider Plato's endeavour to refute the Sophists with detachment, what strikes us most is not his dissent from their view concerning the comparative profitableness of the actions which men think just and unjust—great, of course, as his dissent is—but the identity of principle underlying the position of both. The Sophists in reaching their conclusion were presupposing that for an action to be really just, it must be advantageous; for it was solely on this ground that they concluded that what we ordinarily think just is not really just. And what in the end most strikes us is that at no stage in the *Republic* does Plato take the line, or even suggest as a possibility, that the very presupposition of the Sophists' arguments is false, and that therefore the question whether some action which men think just will be profitable to the agent has really nothing to do with the question whether it is right, so that Thrasymachus may enlarge as much as he pleases on the losses incurred by doing the actions we think just without getting any nearer to showing that it is a mere mistake to think them just. Plato, on the contrary, instead of urging that the Sophistic contention that men lose by doing what they think just is simply irrelevant to the question whether these actions are just, throughout treats this contention with the utmost seriousness; and he implies that unless the Sophists can be met on their own ground by being shown that, in spite of appearances to the contrary, these actions will really be for the good of the agent, their conclusion that men's moral convictions are mere conventions must be allowed to stand. He therefore, equally with the Sophists, is implying that it is impossible for any action to be really just, i.e. a duty, unless it is for the advantage of the agent.

This presupposition, however, as soon as we consider it, strikes us as a paradox. For though we may find ourselves quite unable to state what it is that does render an action a duty, we ordinarily think that, whatever it is, it is not conduciveness to our advantage; and we also think that though an action which is a duty may be advantageous it need not be so. And while we may not be surprised to find the presupposition in the Sophists, whose moral convictions are represented as at least shallow, we are surprised to find it in Plato, whose moral earnestness is that of a prophet. At first, no doubt, we may try to mitigate our surprise by emphasizing the superior character of the advantages which Plato had in mind. But to do this does not really help. For after all, whatever be meant by the 'superiority' of the advantages of which Plato was thinking, it is simply as advantages that Plato uses them to show that the actions from which they follow are right.

Yet the presupposition cannot simply be dismissed as obviously untrue. For one thing, any view of Plato's is entitled to respect. For another, there appear to be moments in which we find the presupposition in ourselves. There appear to be moments in which, feeling acutely the weight of our responsibilities, we say to ourselves, 'Why *should* I do all these actions, since after all it is others and not I who will gain by doing them?'.

Moreover, there at least seems to be the same presupposition in the mind of those preachers whose method of exhortation consists in appeal to rewards. When, for instance, they commend a certain mode of life on the ground that it will bring about a peace of mind which the pursuit of worldly things cannot yield, they appear to be giving a resulting gain as the reason why we ought to do certain actions, and therefore to be implying that in general it is advantageousness to ourselves which renders an action one which we are bound to do. In fact the only difference between the view of such preachers and that of the Sophists seems to be that the former, in view of their theological beliefs, think that the various actions which we think right will have certain specific rewards the existence of which the Sophists would deny. And the identity of principle underlying their view becomes obvious if the preacher goes on to maintain, as some have done, that if he were to cease to believe in heaven, he would cease to believe in right and wrong. Again, among philosophers, Plato is far from being alone in presupposing that an action, to be right, must be for the good or advantage of the agent. To go no further afield than a commentator on Plato, we may cite Cook Wilson, whose claim to respect no one in Oxford will deny, and who was, to my mind, one of the acutest of thinkers. In lecturing on the *Republic* he used to insist that when men begin to reflect on morality they not only demand, but also have the right to demand, that any action which is right must justify its claim to be right by being shown to be for their own good; and he used to maintain that Plato took the right and only way of justifying our moral convictions, by showing that the actions which we think right are for the good of the society of which we are members, and that at the same time the good of that society *is* our good, as becomes obvious when the nature of our good is properly understood.

Moreover Plato, if he has been rightly interpreted, does not stand alone among the historical philosophers in presupposing the existence of a necessary connexion between duty and interest. At least Butler, whose thoughtfulness is incontestable, is with him. In fact in this matter he seems at first sight only distinguished from Plato by going further. In a well-known passage in the eleventh *Sermon,* after stating that religion always addresses itself to self-love when reason presides in a man, he says: 'Let it be allowed, though virtue or moral rectitude does indeed consist in affection to and pursuit of what is right and good, as such; yet that when we sit down in a cool hour, we can neither justify to ourselves this or any other pursuit, till we are convinced that it will be for our happiness, or at least not contrary to it.'

Here, if we take the phrase 'justify an action to ourselves' in its natural sense of come to know that we ought to do the action by apprehending a reason why we ought to do it, we seem to have to allow that Butler is maintaining that in the last resort there is one, and only one, reason why we ought to do anything whatever, viz. the conduciveness of the action to our happiness or advantage. And if this is right, Butler is not simply presupposing but definitely asserting a necessary connexion between duty and interest, and going

further than Plato by maintaining that it is actually conduciveness to the agent's interest which renders an action right.

Nevertheless, when we seriously face the view that unless an action be advantageous, it cannot really be a duty, we are forced both to abandon it and also to allow that even if it were true, it would not enable us to vindicate the truth of our ordinary moral convictions.

It is easy to see that if we persist in maintaining that an action, to be right, must be advantageous, we cannot stop short of maintaining that it is precisely advantageousness and nothing else which renders an action right. It is impossible to rest in the intermediate position that, though it is something other than advantageousness which renders an action right, nevertheless an action cannot really be right unless it be advantageous. For if it be held that an action is rendered a duty by the possession of some other characteristic, then the only chance of showing that a right action must necessarily be advantageous must consist either in showing that actions having this other characteristic must necessarily be advantageous or in showing that the very fact that we are bound to do some action, irrespectively of what renders us bound to do it, necessitates that we shall gain by doing it. But the former alternative is not possible. But 'an action' in this context must be meant an activity by which a man brings certain things about. And if the characteristic of an action which renders it right does not consist in its bringing about an advantage to the agent, which we may symbolize by 'an X', it must consist in bringing about something of a different kind, which we may symbolize by 'a Y', say, for the sake of argument, an advantage to a friend, or an improvement in someone's character. There can, however, be no means of showing that when we bring about something of one kind, e.g. a Y, we must necessarily bring about something of a different kind, e.g. an X. The nature of an action as being the bringing about a Y cannot require, i.e. necessitate, it to be also the bringing about an X, i.e. to have an X as its consequence; and whether bringing about a Y in any particular case will bring about an X will depend not only on the nature of the act as being the bringing about a Y, but also on the nature of the agent and of the special circumstances in which the act is done. It may be objected that we could avoid the necessity of having to admit this on one condition, viz. that we knew the existence of a Divine Being who would intervene, where necessary, with rewards. But this knowledge would give the required conclusion only on one condition, viz. that this knowledge was really the knowledge that the fact of being bound to do some action itself necessitated the existence of such a Being as a consequence. For if it were the knowledge of the existence of such a Being based on other grounds, it would not enable us to know that the very fact that some action was the bringing about a *Y itself* necessitated that it would also be the bringing about an *X,* i.e. some advantage to the agent. No doubt if we could successfully maintain not only that an action's being the bringing about a *Y* necessitated its being a duty, but also that an action's being a duty necessitated its being rewarded. But to maintain this is really to fall back on the second alternative; and this alternative will, on consideration, turn out no more tenable than the first. It cannot successfully be maintained that the very fact that some action is a duty necessitates, not that the agent will *deserve* to gain—a conclusion which it is of course easy to draw, but that he *will* gain, unless it can be shown that this very fact necessitates, as a consequence, the existence of a being who will, if necessary, reward it. And this obviously cannot be done. . . .

We are therefore forced to allow that in order to maintain that for an action to be right, it must be advantageous, we have to maintain that advantageousness is what renders an action right. But this is obviously something which no one is going to maintain, if he considers it seriously. For he will be involved in maintaining not only that it is a duty to do whatever is for our advantage, but that this is our only duty. And the fatal objection to maintaining this is simply that no one actually thinks it.

Moreover, as it is easy to see, if we were to maintain this, our doing so, so far from helping us, would render it impossible for us, to vindicate the truth of our ordinary moral convictions. For wherever in ordinary life we think of some particular action as a duty, we are not simply thinking of it as right, but also thinking of its rightness as constituted by the possession of some definite characteristic other than that of being advantageous to the agent. For we think of the action as a particular action *of a certain kind,* the nature of which is indicated by general words contained in the phrase by which we refer to the action, e.g. '*fulfilling the promise* which we made to *X* yesterday', or '*looking after* our *parents'.* And we do not think of the action as right *blindly,* i.e. irrespectively of the special character which we think the act to possess; rather we think of it as being right in virtue of possessing a particular characteristic of the kind indicated by the phrase by which we refer to it. Thus in thinking of our keeping our promise to *X* as a duty, we are thinking of the action as rendered a duty by its being the keeping of our promise. This is obvious because we should never, for instance, think of using as an illustration of an action which we think right, telling *X* what we think of him, or meeting him in London, even though we thought that if we thought of these actions in certain other aspects we should think them right. Consequently if we were to maintain that conduciveness to the agent's advantage is what renders an action right, we should have to allow that any of our ordinary moral convictions, so far from being capable of vindication, is simply a mistake, as being really the conviction that some particular action is rendered a duty by its possession of some characteristic which is not that of being advantageous.

The general moral is obvious. Certain arguments, which would ordinarily be referred to as arguments designed to prove that doing what is right will be for the good of the agent, turn out to be attempts to prove that the actions which in ordinary life we think right will be for the good of the agent. There is really no need to consider in detail whether these arguments are successful; for even if they are successful, they will do nothing to prove what they are intended to prove, viz. that the moral convictions of our ordinary life are true. Further the attempts arise simply out of a presupposition which on reflection anyone is bound to abandon, viz. that conduciveness to personal advantage is what renders an action a duty. What Plato should have said to the Sophists is: 'You may be right in maintaining that in our ordinary unquestioning frame of mind we do not know, but only think, that certain actions are right. These thoughts or convictions may or may not be true. But they cannot be false for the reason which you give. You do nothing whatever to show that they are false by urging that the actions in question are disadvantageous; and I should do nothing to show that they are true, if I were to show that these actions are after all advantageous. Your real mistake lies in presupposing throughout that advantageousness is what renders an action a duty. If you will only reflect you will abandon his presupposition altogether, and then you yourself will withdraw your arguments.'

I next propose to contend that there is also to be found . . . in Plato . . ., besides this attempt to show that actions which we *think* right will be for our good, another attempt which [he does not distinguish] from it and which *is* accurately described as an attempt to prove that *right* actions will be for our good. I also propose to ask what is the idea which led them to make the attempt, and to consider whether it is tenable.

When Plato raises the question 'What is justice?' he does not mean by the question 'What do we *mean* by the terms 'justice' and 'just', or, in our language, 'duty' and 'right'?', as we might ask 'What do we *mean* by the term 'optimism', or again, by the phrase 'living thing'?'. And as a matter of fact if he had meant this, he would have been raising what was only verbally, and not really, a question at all, in that any attempt to ask it would have implied that the answer was already known and that therefore there was nothing to ask. He means 'What is the characteristic the possession of which by an action necessitates that the action is just, i.e. an act which it is our duty, or which we ought, to do?' In short he means 'What renders a just or right action, just or right?'

Now this question really means 'What is the characteristic common to particular just acts which renders them just?' And for anyone even to *ask* this question is to imply that he already *knows* what particular actions are just. For even to *ask* 'What is the character common to certain things?' is to imply that we already *know* what things are of which we are wanting to find the common character. Equally, of course, any attempt to *answer* the question has the same implication. For such an attempt can only consist in considering the particular actions which we know to be just and attempting to discover what is the characteristic common to them all, the vague apprehension of which has led us to apprehend them to be just. Plato therefore, both in representing Socrates as raising with his hearers the ques-

tion 'What is justice?' and also in representing them all as attempting to answer it, is implying, whether he is aware that he is doing so or not, that they will know what particular acts are, and what particular acts are not, just. If on the contrary what he had presupposed was that the members of the dialogue think, instead of knowing, that certain actions are just, his question— whether he had expressed it thus or not—would really have been, not 'What is justice?', but 'What do we *think* that justice is?'; or, more clearly, not 'What renders an act just?' but 'What do we think renders an act just?'. But in that case an answer, whatever its character, would have thrown no light on the question 'What is justice?'; and apart from this, he is plainly not asking 'What do we *think* that justice is?'.

As has been pointed out, however, the view which Plato attributes to the Sophists presupposes that ordinary mankind, which of course includes the members of the dialogue, only thinks and does not know that certain actions are just. Therefore, when Plato introduces this view as requiring refutation and, in doing so, represents the members of the dialogue as not questioning the presupposition, he ought in consistency to have made someone point out that in view of the acceptance of this presupposition Socrates' original question 'What is justice?' required to be amended to the question 'What do we think that justice is?'. But Plato does not do so. In the present context the significant fact is that even after he has introduced the view of the Sophists he still represents the question to be answered as being 'What is justice?', and therefore still implies that the members of the dialogue know what is just in particular. Even in making Glaucon and Adeimantus ask Socrates to refute the Sophists, what he, inconsistently, makes them ask Socrates to exhibit the nature of is not the acts which men think just but just acts. And when Plato in the fourth book goes on to give Socrates' answer, which, of course, is intended to express the truth, he in the same way represents Socrates as offering, and the others as accepting, an account of the nature of *just* acts, viz. that they consist in conferring those benefits on society which a man's nature renders him best suited to confer, and then makes Socrates argue in detail that it is *just* action which will be profitable. In doing so he is of course implying, inconsistently with the implication of his treatment of the Sophists' view, that the members of the dialogue, and therefore also mankind in ordinary life, *know* what is just in particular. For in the end the statement 'Justice is conferring certain benefits on society' can only mean that conferring these benefits is the characteristic the vague apprehension of which in certain actions leads us to know or apprehend them to be just; and the acceptance of this statement by the members of the dialogue must be understood as expressing their recognition that this characteristic is the common character of the particular acts which they already know to be just.

It therefore must be allowed that, although to do so is inconsistent with his view of the way in which the Sophistic theory has to be refuted, Plato is in the fourth book (and of course the same admission must be made about the eighth and ninth) endeavouring to prove that *just,* i.e. *right,* action, will be for the good or advantage of the agent.

Given that this is what Plato wants to prove in the fourth book, the general nature of what he conceives to be the proof is obvious. His idea is that if we start with the knowledge of what right actions consist in, viz., to put it shortly, serving the state, and then consider what the effects of these and other actions will be by taking into account not only the circumstances in which we are placed, but also the various desires of the human soul and the varying amounts of satisfaction to which the realization of these objects will give rise, it will be obvious that it is by doing what is right that, at any rate in the long run, we shall become happy.

Now a particular proof of this kind, such as Plato's naturally provokes two comments. The first is that there is no need to consider its success in detail, since we know on general grounds that it must fail. For it can only be shown that actions characterized by being the bringing about things of one kind, in this case benefits to society, will always have as their consequence things of another kind, in this case elements of happiness in the agent, provided that we can prove, as Plato makes no attempt to do, the existence of a Being who will intervene to introduce suitable rewards where they are needed. The second is that though the establishment of this conclusion, whether with or without the help of theological arguments, would be of the greatest benefit to us, since

we should all be better off if we knew it to be true, yet it differs from the establishment of the corresponding conclusion against the Sophists in that it would throw no light whatever on the question 'What is our duty in detail, and why?'. And this second comment naturally raises the question which seems to be the important one to ask in this connexion, viz. '*Why* did Plato think it important to prove that right action would benefit the agent?'.

The explanation obviously cannot be simply, or even mainly, that the combination in Plato of a desire to do what is right and of a desire to become happy led him to try to satisfy himself that by doing what is right he would be, so to say, having it both ways. The main explanation must lie in a quite different direction. There is no escaping the conclusion that when Plato sets himself to consider not what *should,* but what *actually does* as a matter of fact, lead a man to act, when he is acting deliberately, and not merely in consequence of an impulse, he answers 'The desire for some good to himself and that only'. In other words we have to allow that according to Plato, a man pursues whatever he pursues simply as a good to himself, i.e. really as something which will give him satisfaction, or, as perhaps we ought to say, as an element in what will render him happy. In the *Republic* this view comes to light in the sixth book. He there speaks of τὸ ἀγαθόν as that which every soul pursues and for the sake of which it does all it does, divining that it is something but being perplexed and unable to grasp adequately what it is; and he goes on to say of things that are good (τὰ ἀγαθά) that while many are ready to do and to obtain and to be what only *seems* just, even if it is not, no one is content with obtaining what *seems* good, but endeavours to obtain what is *really* good. It might be objected that these statements do not bear out the view which is attributed to Plato, since Plato certainly did not mean by an ἀγαθόν, a source of satisfaction or happiness to oneself. But to this the answer is that wherever Plato uses the term ἀγαθά (goods) elsewhere in the *Republic* and in other dialogues, such as the *Philebus,* the context always shows that he means by a good a good to oneself, and, this being so, he must really be meaning by an ἀγαθόν, a source of satisfaction, or perhaps, more generally, a source of happiness. The view, however, emerges most clearly in the

Gorgias, where Plato, in order to show that rhetoricians and tyrants do not do what they really wish to do, maintains that in all actions alike, and even when we kill a man or despoil him of his goods we do what we do because we think it will be better for us to do so.

Now if we grant, as we must, that Plato thought this, we can find in the admission a natural explanation of Plato's desire to prove that just action will be advantageous. For plainly he passionately wanted men to do what is right, and if he thought that it was only desire of some good. to themselves which moved them in all deliberate action, it would be natural, and indeed necessary, for him to think that if men are to be induced to do what is just, the only way to induce them is to convince them that thereby they will gain or become better off.

I propose now to take it as established (1) that ... Plato ... [is] really endeavouring to prove that right actions, in the strict sense of 'right actions', will be for the agent's advantage; (2) that [his] reason for doing so lies in the conviction that even where we know some action to be right, we shall not do it unless we think that it will be for our advantage; and (3) that behind this conviction lies the conviction of which it is really a corollary, viz. the conviction that desire for some good to oneself is the only motive of deliberate action.

But are these convictions true? For if it can be shown that they are not, then at least Plato's ... reason for trying to prove the advantageousness of right action will have disappeared.

The conviction that even where we know some action to be right, we shall not do it unless we think we shall be the better off for doing it, of course, strikes us as a paradox. At first no doubt we are apt to mis-state the paradox. We are apt to say that the conviction, implying as it does that we only act out of self-interest, really implies that it is impossible for us to do anything which we ought to do at all, since if we did some action out of self-interest we could not have done anything which was a duty. But to say this is to make the mistake of thinking that the motive with which we do an action can possibly have something to do with its rightness or wrongness. To be morally bound is to be morally bound to *do* something, i.e. to bring something about; and even if it be only from the lowest of motives that we have brought about something which we ought to have brought about, we have still done something which we ought to have done. The fact that I have given A credit in order to spite his rival B, or again, in order to secure future favours from A, has, as we see when we reflect, no bearing whatever on the question whether I ought to have given A credit. The real paradox inherent in the conviction lies in its implication that there is no such thing as moral goodness. If I gave A credit solely to obtain future favours, and even if I gave him credit either thinking or knowing that I ought to do so, but in no way directly or indirectly influenced by my either so thinking or knowing, then even though it has to be allowed that I did something which I was morally bound to do, it has to be admitted that there was no moral goodness whatever about my action. And the conviction in question is really what is ordinarily called the doctrine that morality needs a sanction, i.e. really the doctrine that to stimulate a man into doing some action, it is not merely insufficient but even useless to convince him that he is morally bound to do it, and that, instead, we have to appeal to his desire to become better off.

W. E. H. L E C K Y

The Psychological Egoists*

According to these writers we are governed exclusively by our own interest.[1] Pleasure, they assure us, is the only good,[2] and moral good and moral evil mean nothing more than our voluntary conformity to a law that will bring it to us.[3] To love good simply as good, is impossible.[4] When we speak of the goodness of God, we mean only His goodness to us.[5] Reverence is nothing more than our conviction, that one who has power to do us both good and harm, will only do us good.[6] The pleasures of piety arise from the belief that we are about to receive pleasure, and the pains of piety from the belief that we are about to suffer pain from the Deity.[7] Our very affections, according to some of these writers, are all forms of self-love. Thus charity springs partly from our desire to obtain the esteem of others, partly from the expectation that the favours we have bestowed will be reciprocated, and partly, too, from the gratification of the sense of power, by the proof that we can satisfy not only our own desires but also the desires of others.[8] Pity is an emotion arising from a vivid realisation of sorrow that may befall ourselves, suggested by the sight of the sorrows of others. We pity especially those who have not deserved calamity, because we consider ourselves to belong to that category; and the spectacle of suffering against which no forethought could provide, reminds us most forcibly of what

may happen to ourselves.[9] Friendship is the sense of the need of the person befriended.[10]

From such a conception of human nature it is easy to divine what system of morals must flow. No character, feeling, or action is naturally better than others, and as long as men are in a savage condition, morality has no existence. Fortunately, however, we are all dependent for many of our pleasures upon others. Co-operation and organisation are essential to our happiness, and these are impossible without some restraint being placed upon our appetites. Laws are enacted to secure this restraint, and being sustained by rewards and punishments, they make it the interest of the individual to regard that of the community.
. . .

NOTES

1. 'I conceive that when a man deliberates whether he shall do a thing or not do it, he does nothing else but consider whether it be better for himself to do it or not to do it.'—Hobbes, *On Liberty and Necessity.* 'Good and evil are names that signify our appetites and aversions.'—Ibid. *Leviathan,* part i, ch. xvi. 'Obligation is the necessity of doing or omitting any action in order to be happy.'—Gay's dissertation prefixed to King's *Origin of Evil,* p. 36. 'The only reason or motive by which individuals can possibly be induced to the practice of virtue, must be the feeling immediate or the prospect of future private happiness.'—Brown, *On the Characteristics,* p. 159. 'En tout temps, en tout lieu, tant en matière de morale qu'en matière d'esprit, c'est l'intérêt personnel qui dicte le jugement des particuliers, et l'intérêt général qui dicte celui des nations. ... Tout homme ne prend dans ses jugements conseil que de son intérêt.'—['In all times, at all places, as much in moral as in spiritual matters, it is personal interest that dictates judgments of individuals, and the general interest that of nations ... Each man is guided in the judgments only by his own interest.']—Helvétius, *De l'Esprit,* discours ii. 'Nature has

*From W. E. H. Lecky, *History of European Morals from Augustus to Charlemagne* (New York: George Braziller, 1955), Vol. I, pp. 7–11.

placed mankind under the governance of two sovereign masters, pain and pleasure. It is for them alone to point out what
we ought to do, as well as well as to determine what we shall
do. . . . The principle of utility recognises this subjection, and
assumes it for the foundation of that system, the object of
which is to rear the fabric of felicity by the hands of reason
and of law. Systems which attempt to question it, deal in
sounds instead of sense, in caprice instead of reason, in darkness instead of light.'—Bentham's *Principles of Morals and
Legislation,* ch. i. 'By the principle of utility is meant that
principle which approves or disapproves of every action whatsoever, according to the tendency which it appears to have to
augment or diminish the happiness of the party whose interest
is in question.—Ibid. 'Je regarde l'amour éclairé de nous-
mêmes comme le principe de tout sacrifice moral.'—['I look
upon enlightened self-interest as the fundamental principle of
all moral sacrifice.']—D'Alembert quoted by D. Stewart, *Active and Moral Powers,* vol. i. p. 220.

2. 'Pleasure is in itself a good; nay, even setting aside
immunity from pain, the only good; pain is in itself an evil,
and, indeed, without exception, the only evil, or else the words
good and evil have no meaning.'—Bentham's *Principles of
Morals and Legislation,* ch. x.

3. 'Good and evil are nothing but pleasure and pain, or
that which occasions or procures pleasure or pain to us. Moral
good and evil then is only the conformity or disagreement of
our voluntary actions to some law whereby good or evil is
drawn on us by the will and power of the law maker, which
good and evil, pleasure or pain, attending our observance or
breach of the law by the decree of the law maker, is that we
call reward or punishment.'—Locke's *Essay,* book ii. ch.
xxviii. 'Take away pleasures and pains, not only happiness,
but justice, and duty, and obligation, and virtue, all of which
have been so elaborately held up to view as independent of
them, are so many empty sounds.'—Bentham's *Springs of
Action,* ch. i. § 15.

4. 'Il lui est aussi impossible d'aimer le bien pour le bien,
que d'aimer le mal pour le mal.'—['It is just as impossible for
him to love good for its own sake as it is to love evil for its
own sake.']—Helvétius *De l'Esprit,* disc. ii ch. v.

5. 'Even the goodness which we apprehend in God Almighty, is his goodness to us.'—Hobbes *On Human Nature,*
ch. vii. § 3. So Waterland, 'To love God is in effect the same
thing as to love happiness, eternal happiness; and the love of
happiness is still the love of ourselves.'—*Third Sermon on
Self-love.*

6. 'Reverence is the conception we have concerning another, that he hath the power to do unto us both good and
hurt, but not the will to do us hurt.'—Hobbes, *On Human
Nature,* ch. viii. § 7.

7. 'The pleasures of piety are the pleasures that accompany the belief of a man's being in the acquisition, or in
possession of the goodwill or favour of the Supreme Being;
and as a fruit of it, of his being in the way of enjoying pleasures
to be received by God's special appointment either in this life
or in a life to come.'—Bentham's *Principles of Morals and
Legislation,* ch. v. 'The pains of piety are the pains that accompany the belief of a man's being obnoxious to the displeasure of the Supreme Being, and in consequence to certain pains
to be inflicted by His especial appointment, either in this life

or in a life to come. These may be also called the pains of
religion.'—Ibid.

8. 'There can be no greater argument to a man of his own
power, than to find himself able not only to accomplish his
own desires, but also to assist other men in theirs; and this is
that conception wherein consisteth charity.'—Hobbes, *On
Hum. Nat.* ch. ix. § 17. 'No man giveth but with intention of
good to himself, because gift is voluntary; and of all voluntary
acts, the object to every man is his own good.'—Hobbes'
Leviathan, part i. ch. xv. 'Dream not that men will move their
little finger to serve you, unless their advantage in so doing be
obvious to them. Men never did so, and never will while
human nature is made of its present materials.'—Bentham's
Deontology, vol. ii. p. 133.

9. 'Pity is imagination or fiction of future calamity to
ourselves, proceeding from the sense of another man's
calamity. But when it lighteth on such as we think have not
deserved the same, the compassion is greater, because there
then appeareth more probability that the same may happen
to us; for the evil that happeneth to an innocent man may
happen to every man.'—Hobbes, *On Hum. Nat.* ch. ix. § 10.
'La pitié est souvent un sentiment de nos propres maux dans
les maux d'autrui. C'est une habile prévoyance des malheurs
où nous pouvons tomber. Nous donnons des secours aux
autres pour les engager à nous en donner en de semblables
occasions, et ces services que nous leur rendons sont, à propre-
ment parler des biens que nous nous faisons à nous-mêmes par
avance.'—['Pity is often a perception of our own troubles in
the troubles of others. It is an astute prescience of the misfortunes into which we might fall. We help others in order to
commit them to helping us under similar circumstances; and
these services we render them are, properly speaking, services
we render to ourselves in advance.']—La Rochefoucauld,
Maximes, 264. Butler has remarked that if Hobbes' account
were true, the most fearful would be the most compassionate
nature; but this is perhaps not quite just, for Hobbes' notion
of pity implies the union of two not absolutely identical,
though nearly allied, influences, timidity and imagination.
The theory of Adam Smith, though closely connected with,
differs totally in consequences from that of Hobbes on this
point. He says, 'When I condole with you for the loss of your
son, in order to enter into your grief, I do not consider what
I, a person of such a character and profession, should suffer
if I had a son, and if that son should die—I consider what I
should suffer if I was really you. I not only change circumstances with you, but I change persons and characters. My
grief, therefore, is entirely upon your account. . . . A man may
sympathise with a woman in child-bed, though it is impossible
he should conceive himself suffering her pains in his own
proper person and character.'—*Moral Sentiments,* part vii.
ch. i. § 3.

10.   Ce que les hommes ont nommé amitié n'est qu' une
société, qu'un ménagement réciproque d'intérêts et qu'un
échange de bons offices. Ce n'est enfin qu'un commerce où
l'amour-propre se propose toujours quelque chose à gagner.'
—['What men have called "friendship" is but an "association", a reciprocal management of interests, an exchange of
good offices. It is finally, nothing but a form of commerce
where self-interest always expects to gain'].—La Rochefoucauld, *Max.* 83. See this idea developed at large in Helvétius.

JOEL FEINBERG

Psychological Egoism*

A. THE THEORY

1. "Psychological egoism" is the name given to a theory widely held by ordinary men, and at one time almost universally accepted by political economists, philosophers, and psychologists, according to which all human actions when properly understood can be seen to be motivated by selfish desires. More precisely, psychological egoism is the doctrine that the only thing anyone is capable of desiring or pursuing ultimately (as an end in itself) is his *own* self-interest. No psychological egoist denies that men sometimes do desire things other than their own welfare—the happiness of other people, for example; but all psychological egoists insist that men are capable of desiring the happiness of others only when they take it to be a *means* to their own happiness. In short, purely altruistic and benevolent actions and desires do not exist; but people sometimes appear to be acting unselfishly and disinterestedly when they take the interests of others to be means to the promotion of their own self-interest.

2. This theory is called *psychological* egoism to indicate that it is not a theory about what *ought* to be the case, but rather about what, as a matter of fact, *is* the case. That is, the theory claims to be a description of psychological facts, not a prescription of ethical ideals. It asserts, however, not merely that all men do as a contingent matter of fact "put their own interests first," but also that they are capable of nothing else, human nature being what it is. Universal selfishness is not just an accident or a coincidence on this view; rather, it is an unavoidable consequence of psychological laws.

The theory is to be distinguished from another doctrine, so-called "ethical egoism," according to which all men *ought* to pursue their own well-being. This doctrine, being a prescription of what *ought* to be the case, makes no claim to be a psychological theory of human motives; hence the word "ethical" appears in its name to distinguish it from *psychological* egoism.

3. There are a number of types of motives and desires which might reasonably be called "egoistic" or "selfish," and corresponding to each of them is a possible version of psychological egoism. Perhaps the most common version of the theory is that apparently held by Jeremy Bentham.[1] According to this version, all persons have only one ultimate motive in all their voluntary behavior and that motive is a selfish one; more specifically, it is one particular kind of selfish motive—namely, a desire for one's own *pleasure.* According to this version of the theory, "the only kind of ultimate desire is the desire to get or to prolong pleasant experiences, and to avoid or to cut short unpleasant experiences for oneself."[2] This form of psychological egoism is often given the cumbersome name—*psychological egoistic hedonism.*

*From materials composed for philosophy students at Brown University, 1958. Not previously published.

B. PRIMA FACIE REASONS IN SUPPORT OF THE THEORY

4. Psychological egoism has seemed plausible to many people for a variety of reasons, of which the following are typical:

a. "Every action of mine is prompted by motives or desires or impulses which are *my* motives and not somebody else's. This fact might be expressed by saying that whenever I act I am always pursuing my own ends or trying to satisfy my own desires. And from this we might pass on to—'I am always pursuing something for myself or seeking my own satisfaction.' Here is what seems like a proper description of a man acting selfishly, and if the description applies to all actions of all men, then it follows that all men in all their actions are selfish."[3]

b. It is a truism that when a person gets what he wants he characteristically feels pleasure. This has suggested to many people that what we really want in every case is our own pleasure, and that we pursue other things only as a means.

c. *Self-Deception.* Often we deceive ourselves into thinking that we desire something fine or noble when what we really want is to be thought well of by others or to be able to congratulate ourselves, or to be able to enjoy the pleasures of a good conscience. It is a well-known fact that people tend to conceal their true motives from themselves by camouflaging them with words like "virtue," "duty," etc. Since we are so often misled concerning both our own real motives and the real motives of others, is it not reasonable to suspect that we might *always* be deceived when we think motives disinterested and altruistic? Indeed, it is a simple matter to explain away all allegedly unselfish motives: "Once the conviction that selfishness is universal finds root in a person's mind, it is very likely to burgeon out in a thousand corroborating generalizations. It will be discovered that a friendly smile is really only an attempt to win an approving nod from a more or less gullible recording angel; that a charitable deed is, for its performer, only an opportunity to congratulate himself on the good fortune or the cleverness that enables him to be charitable; that a public benefaction is just plain good business advertising. It will emerge that gods are worshipped only because they indulge men's selfish fears, or tastes, or hopes; that the 'golden rule' is no more than an eminently sound success formula; that social and political codes are created and subscribed to only because they serve to restrain other men's egoism as much as one's own, morality being only a special sort of 'racket' or intrigue using weapons of persuasion in place of bombs and machine guns. Under this interpretation of human nature, the categories of commercialism replace those of disinterested service and the spirit of the horse trader broods over the face of the earth."[4]

d. *Moral Education.* Morality, good manners, decency, and other virtues must be teachable. Psychological egoists often notice that moral education and the inculcation of manners usually utilize what Bentham calls the "sanctions of pleasure and pain."[5] Children are made to acquire the civilizing virtues only by the method of enticing rewards and painful punishments. Much the same is true of the history of the race. People in general have been inclined to behave well only when it is made plain to them that there is "something in it for them." Is it not then highly probable that just such a mechanism of human motivation as Bentham describes must be presupposed by our methods of moral education?

C. CRITIQUE OF PSYCHOLOGICAL EGOISM: CONFUSIONS IN THE ARGUMENTS

5. *Non-Empirical Character of the Arguments.* If the arguments of the psychological egoist consisted for the most part of carefully acquired empirical evidence (well-documented reports of controlled experiments, surveys, interviews, laboratory data, and so on), then the critical philosopher would have no business carping at them. After all, since psychological egoism purports to be a scientific theory of human motives, it is the concern of the experimental psychologist, not the philosopher, to accept or reject it. But as a matter of fact, empirical evidence of the required sort is seldom presented in support of psychological egoism. Psychologists, on the whole, shy away from generalizations about human motives which are so sweeping and so vaguely formulated that they are virtually incapable of scientific testing. It is usually the "armchair scientist" who holds the theory of universal selfishness, and his usual arguments are either based simply on his "impressions" or else are largely of a non-empirical sort. The latter are often shot full of a very subtle kind of logical confusion, and this makes their criti-

cism a matter of special interest to the analytic philosopher.

6. The psychological egoist's first argument (4a, above) is a good example of logical confusion. It begins with a truism—namely, that all of my motives and desires are *my* motives and desires and not someone else's. (Who would deny this?) But from this simple tautology nothing whatever concerning the nature of my motives or the objective of my desires can possibly follow. The fallacy of this argument consists in its violation of the general logical rule that analytic statements (tautologies) cannot entail synthetic (factual) ones.[6] That every voluntary act is prompted by the agent's own motives is a tautology; hence, it cannot be equivalent to "A person is always seeking something for himself" or "All of a person's motives are selfish," which are synthetic. What the egoist must prove is not merely:

(i) Every voluntary action is prompted by a motive of the agent's own.

but rather:

(ii) Every voluntary action is prompted by a motive of a quite particular kind, viz. a selfish one.

Statement (i) is obviously true, but it cannot all by itself give any logical support to statement (ii).

The source of the confusion in this argument is readily apparent. It is not the genesis of an action or the *origin* or its motives which makes it a "selfish" one, but rather the "purpose" of the act or the *objective* of its motives; *not where the motive comes from* (in voluntary actions it always comes from the agent) but *what it aims at* determines whether or not it is selfish. There is surely a valid distinction between *voluntary* behavior, in which the agent's action is motivated by purposes of his own, and *selfish* behavior in which the agent's motives are of one exclusive sort. The egoist's argument assimilates all voluntary action into the class of selfish action, by requiring, in effect, that an unselfish action be one which is not really motivated at all. In the words of Lucius Garvin, "to say that an act proceeds from our own ... desire is only to say that the act is our own. To demand that we should act on motives that are not our own is to ask us to make ourselves living contradictions in terms."[7]

7. But if argument 4a fails to prove its point, argument 4b does no better. From the fact that all our successful actions (those in which we get what we were after) are accompanied or followed by pleasure it does not follow, as the egoist claims, that the *objective* of every action is to get pleasure for oneself. To begin with, the premise of the argument is not, strictly speaking, even true. Fulfillment of desire (simply getting what one was after) is no guarantee of satisfaction (pleasant feelings of gratification in the mind of the agent). Sometimes when we get what we want we *also* get, as a kind of extra dividend, a warm, glowing feeling of contentment; but often, far too often, we get no dividend at all, or, even worse, the bitter taste of ashes. Indeed, it has been said that the characteristic psychological problem of our time is the *dissatisfaction* that attends the fulfillment of our very most powerful desires.

Even if we grant, however, for the sake of argument, that getting what one wants *usually* yields satisfaction, the egoist's conclusion does not follow. We can concede that we normally get pleasure (in the sense of satisfaction) when our desires are satisfied, *no matter what our desires are for;* but it does not follow from this roughly accurate generalization that the only thing we ever desire is our own satisfaction. Pleasure may well be the usual accompaniment of all actions in which the agent gets what he wants; but to infer from this that what the agent always wants is his own pleasure is like arguing, in William James's example,[8] that because an ocean liner constantly consumes coal on its trans-Atlantic passage that therefore the *purpose* of its voyage is to consume coal. The immediate inference from even constant accompaniment to purpose (or motive) is always a *non sequitur.*

Perhaps there is a sense of "satisfaction" (desire fulfillment) such that it is certainly and universally true that we get satisfaction whenever we get what we want. But satisfaction in this sense is simply the "coming into existence of that which is desired." Hence, to say that desire fulfillment always yields "satisfaction" in this sense is to say no more than that we always get what we want when we get what we want, which is to utter a tautology like "a rose is a rose." It can no more entail a synthetic truth in psychology (like the egoistic thesis) than "a rose is a rose" can entail significant information in botany.

8. *Disinterested Benevolence.* The fallacy in argument 4b then consists, as Garvin puts it, "in the supposition that the apparently unselfish desire to benefit others is transformed into a selfish one by the fact that we derive pleasure from carrying it out."[9] Not only is this argument fallacious; it also provides us with a suggestion of a counter-argument to show that its conclusion (psychological egoistic hedonism) is false. Not only is the presence of pleasure (satisfaction) as a by-product of an action no proof that the action was selfish; in some special cases it provides rather conclusive proof that the action was *unselfish.* For in those special cases the fact that we get pleasure from a particular action *presupposes that we desired something else*—something other than our own pleasure—as an end in itself and not merely as a means to our own pleasant state of mind.

This way of turning the egoistic hedonist's argument back on him can be illustrated by taking a typical egoist argument, one attributed (perhaps apocryphally) to Abraham Lincoln, and then examining it closely:

Mr. Lincoln once remarked to a fellow-passenger on an old-time mud-coach that all men were prompted by selfishness in doing good. His fellow-passenger was antagonizing this position when they were passing over a corduroy bridge that spanned a slough. As they crossed this bridge they espied an old razor-backed sow on the bank making a terrible noise because her pigs had got into the slough and were in danger of drowning. As the old coach began to climb the hill, Mr. Lincoln called out, "Driver, can't you stop just a moment?" Then Mr. Lincoln jumped out, ran back and lifted the little pigs out of the mud and water and placed them on the bank. When he returned, his companion remarked: "Now Abe, where does selfishness come in on this little episode?" "Why, bless your soul Ed, that was the very essence of selfishness. I should have had no peace of mind all day had I gone on and left that suffering old sow worrying over those pigs. I did it to get peace of mind, don't you see?"[10]

If Lincoln had cared not a whit for the welfare of the little pigs and their "suffering" mother, but only for his own "peace of mind," it would be difficult to explain how he could have derived pleasure from helping them. The very fact that he did feel satisfaction as a result of helping the pigs presupposes that he had a preexisting desire for something other than his own happiness. Then when *that* desire was satisfied, Lincoln of course derived pleasure. The *object* of Lincoln's desire was not pleasure; rather pleasure was the *consequence* of his preexisting desire for something else. If Lincoln had been wholly indifferent to the plight of the little pigs as he claimed, how could be possibly have derived any pleasure from helping them? He could not have achieved peace of mind from rescuing the pigs, had he not a prior concern—on which his peace of mind depended—for the welfare of the pigs for its own sake.

In general, the psychological hedonist analyzes apparent benevolence into a desire for "benevolent pleasure." No doubt the benevolent man does get pleasure from his benevolence, but in most cases, this is only because he has previously desired the good of some person, or animal, or mankind at large. Where there is no such desire, benevolent conduct is not generally found to give pleasure to the agent.

9. *Malevolence.* Difficult cases for the psychological egoist include not only instances of disinterested benevolence, but also cases of "disinterested malevolence." Indeed, malice and hatred are generally no more "selfish" than benevolence. Both are motives likely to cause an agent to sacrifice his own interests—in the case of benevolence, in order to help someone else, in the case of malevolence in order to harm someone else. The selfish man is concerned ultimately only with his own pleasure, happiness, or power; the benevolent man is often equally concerned with the happiness of others; to the malevolent man, the *injury* of another is often an end in itself—an end to be pursued sometimes with no thought for his own interests. There is reason to think that men have as often sacrificed themselves to injure or kill others as to help or to save others, and with as much "heroism" in the one case as in the other. The unselfish nature of malevolence was first noticed by the Anglican Bishop and moral philosopher Joseph Butler (1692–1752), who regretted that men are no more selfish than they are.[11]

10. *Lack of Evidence for Universal Self-Deception.* The more cynical sort of psychological egoist who is impressed by the widespread phenomenon of self-deception (see 4c above) cannot be so quickly disposed of, for he has committed no *logical* mistakes. We can only argue that the acknowledged frequency of self-deception is insuffi-

cient evidence for his universal generalization. His argument is not fallacious, but inconclusive.

No one but the agent himself can ever be certain what conscious motives really prompted his action, and where motives are disreputable, even the agent may not admit to himself the true nature of his desires. Thus, for every apparent case of altruistic behavior, the psychological egoist can argue, with some plausibility, that the true motivation *might* be selfish, appearance to the contrary. Philanthropic acts are really motivated by the desire to receive gratitude; acts of self-sacrifice, when truly understood, are seen to be motivated by the desire to feel self-esteem; and so on. We must concede to the egoist that all apparent altruism might be deceptive in this way; but such a sweeping generalization requires considerable empirical evidence, and such evidence is not presently available.

11. *The "Paradox of Hedonism" and Its Consequences for Education.* The psychological egoistic Hedonist (e.g., Jeremy Bentham) has the simplest possible theory of human motivation. According to this variety of egoistic theory, all human motives without exception can be reduced to one—namely, the desire for one's own pleasure. But this theory, despite its attractive simplicity, or perhaps because of it, involves one immediately in a paradox. Astute observers of human affairs from the time of the ancient Greeks have often noticed that pleasure, happiness, and satisfaction are states of mind which stand in a very peculiar relation to desire. An exclusive desire for happiness is the surest way to prevent happiness from coming into being. Happiness has a way of "sneaking up" on persons when they are preoccupied with other things; but when persons deliberately and single-mindedly set off in pursuit of happiness, it vanishes utterly from sight and cannot be captured. This is the famous "paradox of hedonism": the single-minded pursuit of happiness is necessarily self-defeating, for *the way to get happiness is to forget it;* then perhaps it will come to you. If you aim exclusively at pleasure itself, with no concern for the things that bring pleasure, then pleasure will never come. To derive satisfaction, one must ordinarily first desire something other than satisfaction, and then find the means to get what one desires.

To feel the full force of the paradox of hedonism the reader should conduct an experiment in his imagination. Imagine a person (let's call him "Jones") who is, first of all, devoid of intellectual curiosity. He has no desire to acquire any kind of knowledge for its own sake, and thus is utterly indifferent to questions of science, mathematics, and philosophy. Imagine further that the beauties of nature leaves Jones cold: he is unimpressed by the autumn foliage, the snow-capped mountains, and the rolling oceans. Long walks in the country on spring mornings and skiing forages in the winter are to him equally a bore. Moreover, let us suppose that Jones can find no appeal in art. Novels are dull, poetry a pain, paintings nonsense and music just noise. Suppose further that Jones has neither the participant's nor the spectator's passion for baseball, football, tennis, or any other sport. Swimming to him is a cruel aquatic form of calisthenics, the sun only a cause of sunburn. Dancing is coeducational idiocy, conversation a waste of time, the other sex an unappealing mystery. Politics is a fraud, religion mere superstition; and the misery of millions of underprivileged human beings is nothing to be concerned with or excited about. Suppose finally that Jones has no talent for any kind of handicraft, industry, or commerce, and that he does not regret that fact.

What then is Jones interested in? He must desire something. To be sure, he does. Jones has an overwhelming passion for, a complete preoccupation with, his own happiness. The one exclusive desire of his life is *to be happy*. It takes little imagination at this point to see that Jones's one desire is bound to be frustrated. People who—like Jones—most hotly pursue their own happiness are the least likely to find it. Happy people are those who successfully pursue such things as aesthetic or religious experience, self-expression, service to others, victory in competitions, knowledge, power, and so on. If none of these things in themselves and for their own sakes mean anything to a person, if they are valued at all then only as a means to one's own pleasant states of mind—then that pleasure can never come. The way to achieve happiness is to pursue something else.

Almost all people at one time or another in their lives feel pleasure. Some people (though perhaps not many) really do live lives which are on the whole happy. But if pleasure and happiness presuppose desires for something other than pleasure and happiness, then the existence of pleasure and happiness in the experience of some people proves that those people have strong desires for something other than their own happiness— egoistic hedonism to the contrary.

The implications of the "paradox of hedonism" for educational theory should be obvious. The parents least likely to raise a happy child are those who, even with the best intentions, train their child to seek happiness directly. How often have we heard parents say:

I don't care if my child does not become an intellectual, or a football star, or a great artist. I just want him to be a plain average sort of person. Happiness does not require great ambitions and great frustrations; it's not worth it to suffer and become neurotic for the sake of science, art, or do-goodism. I just want my child to be happy.

This can be a dangerous mistake, for it is the child (and the adult for that matter) without "outer-directed" interests who is the most likely to be unhappy. The pure egoist would be the most wretched of persons.

The educator might well beware of "life adjustment" as the conscious goal of the educational process for similar reasons. "Life adjustment" can be achieved only as a by-product of other pursuits. A whole curriculum of "life adjustment courses" unsupplemented by couses designed to incite an interest in things other than life adjustment would be tragically self-defeating.

As for moral education, it is probably true that punishment and reward are indispensable means of inculcation. But if the child comes to believe that the *sole* reasons for being moral are that he will escape the pain of punishment thereby and/ or that he will gain the pleasure of a good reputation, then what is to prevent him from doing the immoral thing whenever he is sure that he will not be found out? While punishment and reward then are important tools for the moral educator, they obviously have their limitations. Beware of the man who does the moral thing only out of fear of pain or love of pleasure. He is not likely to be wholly trustworthy. Moral education is truly successful when it produces persons who are willing to do the right thing *simply because it is right,* and not merely because it is popular or safe.

12. *Pleasure as Sensation.* One final argument against psychological hedonism should suffice to put that form of the egoistic psychology to rest once and for all. The egoistic hedonist claims that all desires can be reduced to the single desire for one's own *pleasure.* Now the word "pleasure" is ambiguous. On the one hand, it can stand for a certain indefinable, but very familiar and specific kind of sensation, or more accurately, a property of sensations; and it is generally, if not exclusively, associated with the senses. For example, certain taste sensations such as sweetness, thermal sensations of the sort derived from a hot bath or the feel of the August sun while one lies on a sandy beach, erotic sensations, olfactory sensations (say) of the fragrance of flowers or perfume, and tactual and kinesthetic sensations from a good massage, are all pleasant in this sense. Let us call this sense of "pleasure," which is the converse of "physical pain," pleasure$_1$.

On the other hand, the word "pleasure" is often used simply as a synonym for "satisfaction" (in the sense of gratification, not mere desire fulfillment.) In this sense, the existence of pleasure presupposes the prior existence of desire. Knowledge, religious experience, aesthetic expression, and other so-called "spiritual activities" often give pleasure in this sense. In fact, as we have seen, we tend to get pleasure in this sense whenever we get what we desire, no matter what we desire. The masochist even derives pleasure (in the sense of "satisfaction") from his own physically painful sensations. Let us call the sense of "pleasure" which means "satisfaction"—pleasure$_2$.

Now we can evaluate the psychological hedonist's claim that the sole human motive is a desire for one's own pleasure, bearing in mind (as he often does not) the ambiguity of the word "pleasure." First, let us take the hedonist to be saying that it is the desire for pleasure$_1$ (pleasant sensation) which is the sole ultimate desire of all people and the sole desire capable of providing a motive for action. Now I have little doubt that all (or most) people desire their own pleasure, *sometimes.* But even this familiar kind of desire occurs, I think, rather rarely. When I am very hungry, I often desire to eat, or, more specifically, to eat this piece of steak and these potatoes. Much less often do I desire to eat certain morsels simply for the sake of the pleasant gustatory sensations they might cause. I have, on the other hand, been motivated in the latter way when I have gone to especially exotic (and expensive) French or Chinese restaurants; but normally, pleasant gastronomic sensations are simply a happy consequence or by-product of my eating, not the antecedently desired objective of my eating. There are, of course, others who take gustatory sensations far more seriously: the *gourmet* who eats only to savor the textures and flavors of fine foods, and the wine fancier who "collects" the exquisitely subtle and very pleasant tastes of rare old wines. Such men are truly absorbed in their taste sensations when they eat and drink, and there may even be some (rich) persons whose desire for such sensations is the sole motive for eating and drinking. It should take little argument, however, to convince the reader that such persons are extremely rare.

Similarly, I usually derive pleasure from taking a hot bath, and on occasion (though not very often) I even decide to bathe simply for the sake of such sensations. Even if this is equally true of everyone, however, it hardly provides grounds for inferring that *no one ever* bathes from *any* other motive. It should be empirically obvious that we sometimes bathe simply in order to get clean, or to please others, or simply from habit.

The view then that we are never after anything in our actions but our own pleasure—that all men are complete "gourmets" of one sort or another—is not only morally cynical; it is also contrary to common sense and everyday experience. In fact, the view that pleasant sensations play such an enormous role in human affairs is so patently false, on the available evidence, that we must conclude that the psychological hedonist has the other sense of "pleasure"—satisfaction—in mind when he states his thesis. If, on the other hand, he really does try to reduce the apparent multitude of human motives to the one desire for pleasant sensations, then the abundance of historical counter-examples justifies our rejection out of hand of his thesis. It surely seems incredible that the Christian martyrs were ardently pursuing their own pleasure when they marched off to face the lions, or that what the Russian soldiers at Stalingrad "really" wanted when they doused themselves with gasoline, ignited themselves, and then threw the flaming torches of their own bodies on German tanks, was simply the experience of pleasant physical sensations.

13. *Pleasure as Satisfaction.* Let us consider now the other interpretation of the hedonist's thesis, that according to which it is one's own plea-

sure₂ (satisfaction) and not merely pleasure₁ (pleasant sensation) which is the sole ultimate objective of all voluntary behavior. In one respect, the "satisfaction thesis" is even less plausible than the "physical sensation thesis"; for the latter at least is a genuine empirical hypothesis, testable in experience, though contrary to the facts which experience discloses. The former, however, is so confused that it cannot even be completely stated without paradox. It is, so to speak, defeated in its own formulation. Any attempted explication of the theory that all men at all times desire only their own satisfaction leads to an *infinite regress* in the following way:

> "All men desire only satisfaction."
> "Satisfaction of what?"
> "Satisfaction of their desires."
> "Their desires for what?"
> "Their desires for satisfaction."
> "Satisfaction of what?"
> "Their desires."
> "For what?"
> "For satisfaction"—etc., *ad infinitum.*

In short, psychological hedonism interpreted in this way attributes to all people as their sole motive a wholly vacuous and infinitely self-defeating desire. The source of this absurdity is in the notion that satisfaction can, so to speak, feed on itself, and perform the miracle of perpetual self-regeneration in the absence of desires for anything other than itself.

To summarize the argument of sections 11 and 12: The word "pleasure" is ambiguous. Pleasure₁ means a certain indefinable characteristic of physical sensation. Pleasure₂ refers to the feeling of satisfaction that often comes when one gets what one desires whatever be the nature of that which one desires. Now, if the hedonist means pleasure₁ when he says that one's own pleasure is the ultimate objective of all of one's behavior, then his view is not supported by the facts. On the other hand, if he means pleasure₂, then his theory cannot even be clearly formulated, since it leads to the following infinite regress: "I desire only satisfaction of my desire for satisfaction of my desire for satisfaction ... etc., *ad infinitum.*" I conclude then that psychological hedonism (the most common form of psychological egoism), however interpreted, is untenable.

D. CRITIQUE OF PSYCHOLOGICAL EGOISM: UNCLEAR LOGICAL STATUS OF THE THEORY

14. There remain, however, other possible forms of the egoistic psychology. The egoist might admit that not all human motives can be reduced to the one ultimate desire for one's own pleasure, or happiness, and yet still maintain that our ultimate motives, whether they be desire for happiness (J. S. Mill), self-fulfillment (Aristotle), power (Hobbes) or whatever, are always *self-regarding* motives. He might still maintain that, given our common human nature, wholly disinterested action impelled by exclusively other-regarding motives is psychologically impossible, and that therefore there is a profoundly important sense in which it is true that, whether they be hedonists or not, *all men are selfish*.

Now it seems to me that this highly paradoxical claim cannot be finally evaluated until it is properly understood, and that it cannot be properly understood until one knows what the psychological egoist is willing to accept as evidence either for or against it. In short, there are two things that must be decided: (a) whether the theory is true or false and (b) whether its truth or falsity (its truth value) depends entirely on the *meanings* of the words in which it is expressed or whether it is made true or false by certain *facts,* in this case the facts of psychology.

15. *Analytic Statements.* Statements whose truth is determined solely by the meanings of the words in which they are expressed, and thus can be held immune from empirical evidence, are often called analytic statements or tautologies. The following are examples of tautologies:

(1) All spinsters are unmarried.
(2) All effects have causes.
(3) Either Providence is the capital of Rhode Island or it is not.

The truth of (1) is derived solely from the meaning of the word "spinster," which is defined (in part) as "unmarried woman." To find out whether (1) is true or false we need not conduct interviews, compile statistics. or perform experiments. All empirical evidence is superfluous and irrelevant; for if we know the meanings of "spinster" and "unmarried," then we know not only

that (1) is true, but that is is *necessarily* true—i.e., that it cannot possibly be false, that no future experiences or observations could possibly upset it, that to deny it would be to assert a logical contradiction. But notice that what a tautology gains in certainty ("necessary truth") it loses in descriptive content. Statement (1) imparts no information whatever about any matter of fact; it simply records our determination to use certain words in a certain way. As we say, "It is true by definition."

Similarly, (2) is (necessarily) true solely in virtue of the meanings of the words "cause" and "effect" and thus requires no further observations to confirm it. And of course, no possible observations could falsify it, since it asserts no matter of fact. And finally, statement (3) is (necessarily) true solely in virtue of the meaning of the English expression "either . . . or". Such terms as "either . . . or," "If . . . then," "and," and "not" are called by logicians "logical constants." The *definitions* of logical constants are made explicit in the so-called "laws of thought"—the law of contradiction, the law of the excluded middle, and the law of identity. These "laws" are not laws in the same sense as are (say) the laws of physics. Rather, they are merely consequences of the *definitions* of logical constants, and as such, though they are necessarily true, they impart no information about the world. "Either Providence is the capital of Rhode Island or it is not" tells us nothing about geography; and "Either it is now raining or else it is not" tells us nothing about the weather. You don't have to look at a map or look out the window to know that they are true. Rather, they are known to be true *a priori* (independently of experience); and, like all (or many)[12] *a priori* statements, they are *vacuous,* i.e., devoid of informative content.

The denial of an analytic statement is called a contradiction. The following are typical examples of contradictions: "Some spinsters are married," "Some causes have no effects," "Providence both is and is not the capital of Rhode Island." As in the case of tautologies, the truth value of contradictions (their falsehood) is logically necessary, not contingent on any facts of experience, and uninformative. Their falsity is derived from the meanings (definitions) of the words in which they are expressed.

16. *Synthetic Statements.* On the other hand, statements whose truth or falsity is derived not from the meanings of words but rather from the facts of experience (observations) are called *synthetic.*[13] Prior to experience, there can be no good reason to think either that they are true or that they are false. That is to say, their truth value is *contingent;* and they can be confirmed or disconfirmed only by *empirical* evidence,[14] i.e., controlled observations of the world. Unlike analytic statements, they do impart information about matters of fact. Obviously, "It is raining in Newport now," if true, is more informative than "Either it is raining in Newport now or it is not," even though the former *could* be false, while the latter is necessarily true. I take the following to be examples of synthetic (contingent) statements:

(1')   All spinsters are frustrated.
(2')   All events have causes.
(3')   Providence is the capital of Rhode Island.
(3")   Newport is the capital of Rhode Island.

Statement (3') is true; (3") is false; and (1') is a matter for a psychologist (not for a philosopher) to decide; and the psychologist himself can only decide *empirically.* i.e., by making many observations. The status of (2') is very difficult and its truth value is a matter of great controversy. That is because its truth or falsity depends on *all* the facts ("all events"); and, needless to say, not all of the evidence is in.

17. *Empirical Hypotheses.* Perhaps the most interesting subclass of synthetic statements are those generalizations of experience of the sort characteristically made by scientists; e.g., "All released objects heavier than air fall," "All swans are white," "All men have Oedipus complexes." I shall call such statements "empirical hypotheses" to indicate that their function is to sum up past experience and enable us successfully to predict or anticipate future experience.[15] They are never logically certain, since it is always at least conceivable that future experience will disconfirm them. For example, zoologists once believed that all swans are white, until black swans were discovered in Australia. The most important characteristic of empirical hypotheses for our present purposes is their relation to evidence. A person can be said to understand an empirical hypothesis only if he knows how to recognize evidence against it. *If a person asserts or believes a general statement in such a way that he cannot conceive of any possible experience which he would count as evidence against it, then he cannot be said to be asserting or believing an empirical hypothesis.* We can refer to this important characteristic of empirical hypotheses as *falsifiability in principle.*

Some statements only appear to be empirical hypotheses but are in fact disguised tautologies reflecting the speaker's determination to use words in certain (often eccentric) ways. For example, a zoologist might refuse to allow the existence of "Australian swans" to count as evidence against the generalization that all swans are white, on the grounds that the black Australian swans are not "really" swans at all. This would indicate that he is holding *whiteness* to be part of the definition of "swan," and that therefore, the statement "All swans are white" is, for him, "true by definition"—and thus just as immune from counterevidence as the statement "All spinsters are unmarried." Similarly, most of us would refuse to allow any possible experience to count as evidence against "2 + 2 = 4" or "Either unicorns exist or they do not," indicating that the propositions of arithmetic and logic are not empirical hypotheses.

18. *Ordinary Language and Equivocation.* Philosophers, even more than ordinary men, are prone to make startling and paradoxical claims that take the form of universal generalizations and hence resemble empirical hypotheses. For example, "All things are mental (there are no physical objects)," "All things are good (there is no evil)," "All voluntary behavior is selfish," etc. Let us confine our attention for the moment to the latter which is a rough statement of psychological egoism. At first sight, the statement "All voluntary behavior is selfish" seems obviously false. One might reply to the psychological egoist in some such manner as this:

I *know* some behavior, at least, is unselfish, because I saw my Aunt Emma yesterday give her last cent to a beggar. Now she will have to go a whole week with nothing to eat. Surely, *that* was not selfish of her.

Nevertheless, the psychological egoist is likely not to be convinced, and insist that, in this case, if we knew enough about Aunt Emma, we would learn that her primary motive in helping the beggar was to promote her own happiness or assuage her own conscience, or increase her own self-esteem, etc. We might then present the egoist with even more difficult cases for his theory—saints, martyrs, military heroes, patriots, and others who have sacrificed themselves for a cause. If the psychological egoist nevertheless refuses to accept any of these as examples of unselfish behavior, then we have a right to be puzzled about what he is saying. Until we know what he would count as *unselfish* behavior, we can't very well know what he means when he says that all voluntary behavior is *selfish.* And at this point we may suspect that he is holding his theory in a "privileged position"—that of immunity to evidence, that he would allow no *conceivable* behavior to count as evidence against it. What he says then, if true, must be true in virtue of the way he defines —or redefines—the word "selfish." And in that case, it cannot be an empirical hypothesis.

If what the psychological egoist says is "true by redefinition," then I can "agree" with him and say "It is true that in *your* sense of the word 'selfish' my Aunt Emma's behavior was selfish; but in the ordinary sense of 'selfish,' which implies blameworthiness, she surely was not selfish." There is no point of course in arguing about a mere word. The important thing is not what particular words a man uses, but rather whether what he wishes to say in those words is true. Departures from ordinary language can often be justified by their utility for certain purposes; but they are dangerous when they invite equivocation. The psychological egoist may be saying something which is true when he says that Emma is selfish in *his* sense, but if he doesn't realize that his sense of "selfish" differs from the ordinary one, he may be tempted to infer that Emma is selfish in the ordinary sense which implies blameworthiness; and this of course would be unfair and illegitimate. It is indeed an extraordinary extension of the meaning of the word "self-indulgent" (as G. C. Chesterton remarks somewhere) which allows a philosopher to say that a man is self-indulgent when he wants to be burned at the stake.

19. *The Fallacy of the Suppressed Correlative.* Certain words in the English language operate in pairs—e.g., "selfish-unselfish," "good-bad," "large-small," "mental-physical." To assert that a thing has one of the above characteristics is to *contrast* it with the opposite in the pair. To know the meaning of one term in the pair, we must know the meaning of the correlative term with which it is contrasted. If we could not conceive of what it would be like for a thing to be bad, for example, then we could not possibly understand what is being said of a thing when it is called "good." Similarly, unless we had a notion of what it would be like for an action to be *unselfish,* we could hardly understand the sentence "So-and-so acted selfishly"; for we would have nothing to contrast "selfishly" with. The so-called "fallacy of the suppressed correlative"[16] is committed by a person who consciously or unconsciously redefines one of the terms in a contrasting pair in such a way that its new meaning incorporates the sense of its correlative.

Webster's Collegiate Dictionary defines "selfish" (in part) as "regarding one's own comfort, advantage, etc. in disregard of, or at the expense of that of others." In this ordinary and proper sense of "selfish," Aunt Emma's action in giving her last cent to the beggar certainly was *not* selfish. Emma *disregarded* her *own* comfort (it is not "comfortable" to go a week without eating) and advantage (there is no "advantage" in malnutrition) *for the sake of* (not "at the expense of") another. Similarly, the martyr marching off to the stake is foregoing (not indulging) his "comfort" and indeed his very life for the sake of (not at the expense of) a cause. If Emma and the martyr then are "selfish," they must be so in a strange new sense of the word.

A careful examination of the egoist's arguments (see especially 4b above) reveals what new sense he gives to the word "selfish." He redefines the word so that it means (roughly) "motivated," or perhaps "intentional." "After all," says the egoist, "Aunt Emma had some *purpose* in giving the beggar all her money, and this purpose (desire, intention, motive, aim) was *her* purpose and no one else's. She was out to further some aim of her own, wasn't she? Therefore, she was pursuing her own ends (acting from her own motives); she was after something *for herself* in so acting, and that's what I mean by calling her action selfish. Moreover, all intentional action—action done 'on purpose,' deliberately from the agent's own motives—is selfish in the same sense." We can see now, from this reply, that since the egoist apparently means by "selfish" simply "motivated," when he says that all motivated action is selfish *he is not asserting a synthetic empirical hypothesis about human motives; rather, his statement is a tautology roughly equivalent to "all motivated actions are motivated."* And if that is the case, then what he says is true enough; but, like all tautologies, it is empty, uninteresting, and trivial.

Moreover, in redefining "selfish" in this way, the psychological egoist has committed the fallacy of the suppressed correlative. For what can we now contrast "selfish voluntary action" with? Not only are there no *actual* cases of unselfish voluntary actions on the new definition; there are not even any *theoretically possible* or *conceivable* cases of unselfish voluntary actions. And if we cannot even conceive of what an unselfish voluntary action would be like, how can we give any sense to the expression "selfish voluntary action"? The egoist, so to speak, has so blown up the sense of "selfish" that, like inflated currency, it will no longer buy anything.

20. *Psychological Egoism as a Linguistic Proposal.* There is still one way out for the egoist. He might admit that his theory is not really a psychological hypothesis about human nature designed to account for the facts and enable us to predict or anticipate future events. He may even willingly concede that his theory is really a disguised redefinition of a word. Still, he might argue, he has made no claim to be giving an accurate description of actual linguistic usage. Rather, he is making a proposal to *revise* our usage in the interest of economy and convenience, just as the biologists once proposed that we change the ordinary meaning of "insect" in such a way that spiders are no longer called insects, and the ordinary meaning of "fish" so that whales and seals are no longer called fish.

What are we to say to this suggestion? First of all, stipulative definitions (proposals to revise usage) are never true or false. They are simply useful or not useful. Would it be useful to redefine "selfish" in the way the egoist recommends? It is difficult to see what would be gained thereby. The egoist has noticed some respects in which actions normally called "selfish" and actions normally called "unselfish" are alike, namely they are both motivated and they both can give satisfaction—either in prospect or in retrospect—to the agent. Because of these likenesses, the egoist feels justi-

fied in attaching the label "selfish" to *all* actions. Thus one word—"selfish"—must for him do the work of two words ("selfish" and "unselfish" in their old meanings); and, as a result, a very real distinction, that between actions for the sake of others and actions at the expense of others, can no longer be expressed in the language. Because the egoist has noticed some respects in which two types of actions are alike, he wishes to make it impossible to describe the respects in which they differ. It is difficult to see any utility in this state of affairs.

But suppose we adopt the egoist's "proposal" nevertheless. Now we would have to say that all actions are selfish; but, in addition, we would want to say that there are two different kinds of selfish actions, those which regard the interests of others and those which disregard the interests of others, and, furthermore, that only the latter are blameworthy. After a time our ear would adjust to the new uses of the word "selfish," and we would find nothing at all strange in such statements as "Some selfish actions are morally praiseworthy." After a while, we might even invent two new words, perhaps "selfitic" and "unselfitic," to distinguish the two important classes of "selfish" actions. Then we would be right back where we started, with new linguistic tools ("selfish" for "motivated," "selfitic" for "selfish," and "unselfitic" for "unselfish") to do the same old necessary jobs. That is, until some new egoistic philosopher arose to announce with an air of discovery that "All selfish behavior is really selfitic—there are no truly unselfitic selfish actions." Then, God help us!

NOTES

1. See his *Introduction to the Principles of Morals and Legislation* (1789), Chap. I, first paragraph: "Nature has placed mankind under the governance of two sovereign masters, *pain* and *pleasure.* It is for them alone to point out what we ought to do, as well as to determine what we shall do. . . . They govern us in all we do, in all we say, in all we think: every effort we can make to throw off our subjection will serve but to demonstrate and confirm it."

2. C. D. Broad, *Ethics and the History of Philosophy* (New York: The Humanities Press, 1952), Essay 10—"Egoism as a Theory of Human Motives," p. 218. This essay is highly recommended.

3. Austin Duncan-Jones, *Butler's Moral Philosophy* (London: Penguin Books, 1952), p. 96. Duncan-Jones goes on to reject this argument. See p. 512 f.

4. Lucius Garvin, *A Modern Introduction to Ethics* (Boston: Houghton Mifflin, 1953), p. 37. Quoted here by permission of the author and publisher.

5. *Op. cit.,* Chap. III.

6. See Part D, 15 and 16, below.

7. *Op. cit.,* p. 39.

8. *The Principles of Psychology,* (New York: Henry Holt, 1890), Vol. II, p. 558.

9. *Op. cit.,* p. 39.

10. Quoted from the *Springfield* (Illinois) *Monitor,* by F. C. Sharp in his *Ethics* (New York: Appleton-Century, 1928), p. 75.

11. See his *Fifteen Sermons on Human Nature Preached at the Rolls Chapel* (1726), especially the first and eleventh.

12. Whether or not there are some *a priori* statements that are not merely analytic, and hence *not* vacuous, is still a highly controversial question among philosophers.

13. Some philosophers (those called "rationalists") believe that there are some synthetic statements whose truth can be known *a priori* (see footnote 12). If they are right, then the statement above is not entirely accurate.

14. Again, subject to the qualification in footnotes 12 and 13.

15. The three examples given above all have the generic character there indicated, but they also differ from one another in various other ways, some of which are quite important. For our present purposes however, we can ignore the ways in which they differ from one another and concentrate on their common character as generalizations of experience ("inductive generalizations"). As such they are sharply contrasted with such a generalization as "All puppies are young dogs," which is analytic.

16. The phrase was coined by J. Lowenberg. See his article "What is Empirical?" in the *Journal of Philosophy,* May 1940.

M I C H A E L   A.   S L O T E

An Empirical Basis for Psychological Egoism*

It is commonly believed in the philosophical world today that the age-old problem of psychological egoism is merely a pseudo-problem and that this is true just because the a priori philosophical arguments that have traditionally been given in favor of egoism depend in the main upon confusions about the logic of our ordinary language. It has been claimed, for example, that the well-known argument that we act selfishly even when we want to help others because in such cases we are still attempting to *satisfy our own desire* to help others, is fallaciously generated by misunderstandings of the proper use of terms like 'want', 'satisfy', and 'desire'.[1]

In *Butler's Moral Philosophy,* Austin Duncan-Jones, expressing Butler's view, and, it seems from the context, his own as well, states that if there is something wrong with all the a priori philosophical arguments that have traditionally

been given in favor of egoism (which he has earlier identified with the doctrine that all human acts are selfish),[2] then there is little else to recommend the theory, since "the appearance of things, undistorted by theory," is that men sometimes do act unselfishly, disinterestedly. Only one who already believed in the validity of the philosophical arguments for egoism would have any reason to interpret the facts of human behavior in a way compatible with the doctrine of egoism.[3] Thus Duncan-Jones seems clearly to be ruling out the possibility that the (empirical) facts as they stand could, with any semblance of objectivity, be used to support egoism. And many other contemporary philosophers would, I think, tend to agree with him.

In the present paper I wish to argue that psychological egoism may well have a basis in the empirical facts of human psychology. Certain contemporary learning theorists, e.g., Hull and Skinner, have put forward behavioristic theories of the origin and functioning of human motives which posit a certain number of basically "selfish," unlearned primary drives or motives

*Michael A. Slote, "An Empirical Basis for Psychological Egoism," *Journal of Philosophy,* Vol. 61, No. 18 (October 1, 1964), 530–537. This slightly revised version reprinted by permission of the author and the editors of the *Journal of Philosophy.*

(like hunger, thirst, sleep, elimination, and sex), explain all other, higher-order, drives or motives as derived genetically from the primary ones via certain "laws of reinforcement," and, further, deny the "functional autonomy" of those higher-order drives or motives.[4] Now it is a hotly debated .issue in contemporary learning theory whether any theory such as we have described briefly above could adequately explain adult human behavior. I shall, however, argue only that a theory of the above kind may well be true, and that from such a theory, fortified only by one additional psychological premise, the truth of egoism (non-altruism) logically follows. I hope to show, thereby, that the question of psychological egoism is still an open empirical issue, however fallacious be the *philosophical* arguments for it.

But what is "functional autonomy," and how does the lack of it help to show our actions to be selfish? According to behavioristic learning psychologists a higher-order (acquired) motive is functionally autonomous when it becomes causally independent of primary motives (especially of those motives association with which enabled it to be acquired in the first place) in such a way that one will indefinitely keep acting from that motive, even if rewards for those other, primary, motives are no longer in general associated with such action.[5] We have reason to believe that a given higher-order drive or motive is *not* functionally autonomous, i.e., is functionally dependent, if when we cut off all reinforcement of it by primary rewards (rewards of primary drives) and there are, in addition, both a sufficient number of "extinction trials" (occurrences of acts done from that higher-order motive which are not associated even indirectly, i.e., through other higher-order motives, with primary rewards) and a complete absence, during those extinction trials, of primary rewards for any similar higher-order motives (to eliminate the possibility of generalization of primary rewards from motives other than that being extinguished), the higher-order drive or motive actually does extinguish; i.e., the person whose higher-order motive is being extinguished eventually, even if perhaps only very gradually, ceases to act from that higher-order motive.

It is necessary for a motive *derived genetically* from "selfish" (or at least not *unselfish*) primary drives also to be *functionally dependent* upon

them if we are to be able to say that acts performed from that motive are never unselfish. For the fact that in the past we performed such acts only because they led to the satisfaction of some other non-unselfish motive or motives, i.e., because they were reinforced by primary-drive rewards, does not show that such acts performed *now* are not unselfish. To argue thus would be indeed to commit a "genetic fallacy." An act must *presently* be causally connected in the appropriate way with drives that are not unselfish in order to be considered selfish. Now those who deny functional autonomy are saying in effect that whenever, e.g., one acts benevolently (i.e., from what the psychologist would call the higher-order motive of benevolence), one is performing that act, or, at least, in general performing acts of that kind, only because such benevolent action is in general still associated with and reinforced by the satisfaction of such non-unselfish primary drives as hunger and thirst, whether those drives be the same as or different from the primary drives from which the motive of benevolence actually originated.

I do not, however, wish to maintain that the hypothesis of functional dependence (together with its learning-theoretical underpinnings) entails egoism all by itself. The hypothesis does, indeed, entail that we continue to act "benevolently" or "self-sacrificingly" only because such action on our part is in general reinforced by the rewarding of selfish primary drives. But is it not possible that the primary rewards received, in general, when one acts benevolently or self-sacrificingly are not so great as those relinquished in the doing of such acts? It might, in other words, be the case that a poverty-stricken mother who sacrificed some of her own food so that her child might eat better acted in this way only because she was, in general, receiving (however indirectly) some primary-drive satisfactions for her sacrifices. And yet we would still call her actions unselfish if we thought that the rewards she was sacrificing (reduction of her hunger) were greater than those she was getting in return; for is not the habit of giving more than one asks in return an exemplary case of unselfishness?

I should like now to show that a certain empirical hypothesis that entails the hypothesis of functional dependence also entails the thesis of psychological egoism and rules out the possibility of a case like the above, even if the hypothesis of functional dependence alone does not.[6]

Let us imagine that we have a method for determining empirically which primary rewards a person prefers to which others. We set up various situations where the man has to choose between primary rewards, situations involving no moral factors and no interests of other people, and determine the man's preferences. A learning theorist might claim that it is true as a matter of empirical fact that whenever a man systematically (i.e., as a general rule) continues to sacrifice primary reward x to other people, he does so only because he usually obtains thereby some primary reward y *and* because y ranks higher than x among the person's real preferences, such rank being best determined in situations where no considerations of other people's interests and thus of sacrifice to other people's interests are involved.[7] And the above empirical claim, which involves, but is not exhausted by, the claim that functional dependence exists, entails, I think, the thesis of psychological egoism. For if our conscious acts of benevolence and sympathy and sacrifice, etc., are continuing to be performed by us only because we do not, in performing those acts, in general give away *less* in the way of primary-drive satisfactions than we actually get in return, the inevitable conclusion is that all our acts are fundamentally (or ultimately or "really") motivated by our "selfish" primary drives. If this were the case, then, indeed, none of our actions would ever "really" or fundamentally or ultimately be unselfish. The above-described case of the mother who gives away more in the way of primary-drive satisfaction than she gets for herself in return would just never come up. Psychological egoism would be true.

We have thus shown that egoism (in our sense) would be true if certain psychological hypotheses turned out to be true and that the question of the truth of psychological egoism is an empirical question. But that is not to say that contemporary psychology has been able to prove the truth of these hypotheses or that psychologists are even all agreed that, with the further advancement of psychology as a science, these hypotheses will as a matter of fact be verified. There are many psychologists who think, for example, that some higher-order drives *do* become functionally autonomous. Gordon Allport, for instance, has

brought to light a good deal of psychological evidence in favor of this contention.[8] Furthermore, the hypothesis of functional dependence is very difficult to establish experimentally, for reasons well known to psychologists. In the words of Neal Miller, "a strong learned drive may seem unaffected for many [extinction] trials and still eventually extinguish. When generalization, higher-order reinforcement, and shifts from one reinforcing agent to another are added to this possibility, it can be seen how difficult it is in complex human situations to determine whether a habit [drive] actually is functionally autonomous."[9] In other words, even if there is no functional autonomy, there are many ways in which a functionally dependent drive might *appear* to be autonomous, because of distorting psychological factors that can never with absolute certainty be ruled out in the context of human motivation. However, the question whether some drive is autonomous is still empirical in principle, however difficult it may be in practice, given the current rudimentary state of the science of psychology, to determine whether that drive would extinguish if its association with primary reinforcements were entirely severed.

Consider also the hypothesis that entails both functional dependence egoism, the hypothesis, namely, that even if people sometimes do sacrifice and continue to sacrifice a certain kind of primary reward, they do so only because they in general get some greater primary reward in return. This hypothesis, I think, might also turn out to be empirically false. It might turn out, for example, that, although people never made sacrifices unless they got something in return, they sometimes sacrificed some primary reward x for some other primary reward y even though y ranked lower on their preference scorecard as determined in morally neutral circumstances. In such a case there are two things we can say. We might well say that the scorecard as determined in morally neutral circumstances does not tell us a man's real preferences, for if he prefers x to y in neutral circumstances, but prefers y to x when certain other people's interests are involved, who can say what his real preference is? We might, on the other hand, want to say that what a man prefers in morally neutral circumstances really does tell us fairly accurately what he *really* prefers, so that if his preferences differ where moral considerations are involved, we have a right to say that the man has, in the interests of morality, gone against his own preferences and made an unselfish sacrifice. Whether we should want to say the first or the second of these things would depend a great deal, I think, on a number of other scientifically relevant factors. Anyone who would *in principle* refuse to say the second kind of thing would in effect be considering it to be tautologously true that men do not persist in acting against their own self-interest; that is, he would be making the thesis of egoism into a mere tautology, which, I prefer to think, it is not. It seems that there very well could be circumstances in which it would from a scientific point of view be advisable to say that a man had acted against his own real preferences, had persistently sacrificed a greater for a smaller primary reward out of a sense of duty or a feeling of benevolence. Such circumstances might exist, for example, if we had a detailed knowledge of brain physiology which showed that the brain contained a "preference" center and a "morality" center and that the morality center affected our actions not by directly influencing the preference center, but, rather, by acting as an inhibitor or as a modifer on certain motor impulses sent out by the preference center. Such a physiological theory would make it eminently plausible, I think, to believe that what we did in moral contexts might consistently go against our real preferences. In terms of such a theory, then, it might be possible empirically to refute the hypothesis that we never consistently or systematically sacrifice the greater for the smaller primary reward. Thus it would seem that both "parts" of that psychological theory which, I have claimed, entails psychological egoism, are open to empirical refutation, as well as confirmation.[10]

The psychological theory I have been describing should not be confused with a certain theory of human behavior and motivation put forward in recent years by the psychologist A. H. Maslow, a theory which, I believe, does *not* entail psychological egoism. According to Maslow people will not act from such higher motives as benevolence and love unless certain lower needs like hunger, safety, and elimination have already to some degree been satisfied. But once physiological and other lower needs are satisfied to a reasonable

degree, needs to be benevolent, creative, loving, self-sacrificial, and the like will spring up of their own accord. And one will continue to act benevolently, creatively, etc., just as long as one's lower needs remain satisfied, even if none of one's benevolent or creative activities is actually reinforced by the satisfaction of lower needs (primary drives).[11]

Clearly this theory differs substantially from the one I have been describing. For it does *not* assert that we will persist in acting benevolently, etc., only if and because such acts are in general associated with the satisfaction of selfish primary drives. It says merely that we require a certain amount of primary-drive contentment if we are to become people who constantly act benevolently *whether we are rewarded for doing so or not*. According to Maslow, a man often will habitually act from benevolence even though there is "nothing in it for him." It is clear, then, that his theory does *not* exclude the possibility of unselfish human action. The theory *we* have been discussing, on the other hand, does exclude that possibility, just because it implies that we persist in performing some kind of action only because there is in general something in it for us.

It would seem, then, that, as psychology stands today, there is at least some reason to think that the psychological theory we have been discussing may be true. Consequently, the truth of psychological egoism is still an open empirical question. Duncan-Jones and others are mistaken in their belief that, now that the a priori arguments for egoism seem to have been shown to be fallacious, no further case can possibly be made in its favor. Perhaps the only reason philosophers are thus mistaken is their ignorance of contemporary learning theory, its issues, and its results.[12] It is interesting to note, furthermore, that it is impossible to object to an empirical argument for egoism, the way one so often objects to a priori arguments for egoism, by saying that such arguments end up depriving 'selfish' of the logical possibility of a contrast, thus rendering the word meaningless. For egoism will be false if either part of the psychological theory we have been discussing is false. Thus, in making the truth of egoism depend on the truth of an empirically falsifiable (contingent) psychological theory, I am leaving open at the very least the *logical* possibility that egoism is false, that some acts are unselfish.

I might add, finally, that the explanation I have attempted to give of the possibility of arguing on an empirical basis for egoism may help us to understand why so many people, especially beginning students of philosophy, are so dissatisfied by attempts to discredit egoism by showing the invalidity of the traditional philosophical arguments that have been put forward to prove it, and why the doctrine of egoism keeps cropping up, however many be the philosophical voices that seek to silence it. I am willing to conjecture that egoism will not lie dead, because people in some way see that there may be more in favor of egoism than *a priori arguments.* It is my very tentative suggestion that the reason for this may be that even those with little or no training in psychology believe, however inarticulately, that something like the psychological theory we have been discussing in this paper may well be true, believe that men who act consistently in a benevolent manner, for example, are acting benevolently only because their selfish desires and/or interests are usually satisfied by their doing so.

NOTES

1. See P. H. Nowell-Smith's *Ethics* (New York: Philosophical Library, 1957), ch. 10, *passim.*

2. It has been suggested to me by P. R. Foot that only those of one's acts which are somehow related to the wants or interests of others can correctly be called either selfish or unselfish. If this be so, then Duncan-Jones' definition of egoism will make that doctrine trivially false, just because there are some human actions that are neither selfish nor unselfish. In order to avoid such an eventuality, *I* shall mean by *egoism* the slightly different thesis (perhaps more accurately, but clumsily, designated *non-altruism*) that no human act is ever *unselfish.*

3. See p. 109 of *Butler's Moral Philosophy.*

4. It will not, I think, be necessary for my purposes to be truer to ordinary language or more precise with the concepts of drive and motive than are the learning theorists themselves. Thus, e.g., I shall be using 'drive' and 'motive' interchangeably in this paper.

5. I have given a very brief account of the notions of primary and higher-order drives or motives; but it should be sufficient for the purposes of this paper. A more complete account of these and of the other psychological notions I make use of can be found in practically any textbook of experimental psychology.

6. I am again indebted to Mrs. Foot for the insight that the hypothesis of functional dependence does not itself, alone, entail that no act is unselfish. In addition, I am indebted to discussion with Prof. R. P. Wolff for some of the points I shall be making hereafter.

7. Of course, there are some primary rewards, like sexual gratification, that are very hard to measure in isolation from all moral considerations.

8. See his *Personality: A Psychological Interpretation.*

9. "Learnable Drives and Rewards," In S. S. Stevens, ed., *Handbook of Experimental Psychology,* p. 469.
See also D. C. McClelland, "Functional Autonomy of Motives as an Extinction Phenomenon," *Psychological Review,* 49 (1942): 272–283.

10. There is indeed still another way we have not yet mentioned in which this psychological theory might empirically be refuted, namely, if some theory (like Hume's) which made benevolence or other unselfish motives into basic human instincts (primary drives) turned out to be correct.

11. See Maslow's *Motivation and Personality,* ch. 5, *passim.*

12. I do not, however, wish to suggest that *psychologists* have been totally unaware of the philosophical consequences of their own theories. See, for example, Allport, *op. cit.,* p. 206.

JEREMY BENTHAM

The Principle of Utility and Its Sanctions*

CHAPTER I. THE PRINCIPLE OF UTILITY

I. Nature has placed mankind under the governance of two sovereign masters, *pain* and *pleasure*. It is for them alone to point out what we ought to do, as well as to determine what we shall do. On the one hand the standard of right and wrong, on the other the chain of causes and effects, are fastened to their throne. They govern us in all we do, in all we say, in all we think: every effort we can make to throw off our subjection, will serve but to demonstrate and confirm it. In words a man may pretend to abjure their empire: but in reality he will remain subject to it all the while. The *principle of utility* recognises this subjection, and assumes it for the foundation of that system, the object of which is to rear the fabric of felicity by the hands of reason and of law. Systems which attempt to question it, deal in sounds instead of sense, in caprice instead of reason, in darkness instead of light.

But enough of metaphor and declamation: it is not by such means that moral science is to be improved.

II. The principle of utility is the foundation of the present work: it will be proper therefore at the outset to give an explicit and determinate account of what is meant by it. By the principle of utility is meant that principle which approves or disapproves of every action whatsoever, according to

the tendency which it appears to have to augment or diminish the happiness of the party whose interest is in question: or, what is the same thing in other words, to promote or to oppose that happiness. I say of every action whatsoever; and therefore not only of every action of a private individual, but of every measure of government.

III. By utility is meant that property in any object, whereby it tends to produce benefit, advantage, pleasure, good, or happiness, (all this in the present case comes to the same thing) or (what comes again to the same thing) to prevent the happening of mischief, pain, evil, or unhappiness to the party whose interest is considered: if that party be the community in general, then the happiness of the community: if a particular individual, then the happiness of that individual.

IV. The interest of the community is one of the most general expressions that can occur in the phraseology of morals: no wonder that the meaning of it is often lost. When it has a meaning, it is this. The community is a fictitious *body,* composed of the individual persons who are considered as constituting as it were its *members.* The interest of the community then is, what?—the sum of the interests of the several members who compose it.

V. It is in vain to talk of the interest of the community, without understanding what is the interest of the individual. A thing is said to promote the interest, or to be for the interest, of an individual, when it tends to add to the sum total

*From *An Introduction to The Principles of Morals and Legislation,* chapters 1–4. First published in 1789.

of his pleasures: or, what comes to the same thing, to diminish the sum total of his pains.

VI. An action then may be said to be conformable to the principle of utility, or, for shortness sake, to utility (meaning with respect to the community at large) when the tendency it has to augment the happiness of the community is greater than any it has to diminish it.

VII. A measure of government (which is but a particular kind of action, performed by a particular person or persons) may be said to be conformable to or dictated by the principle of utility, when in like manner the tendency which it has to augment the happiness of the community is greater than any which it has to diminish it.

VIII. When an action, or in particular a measure of government, is supposed by a man to be conformable to the principle of utility, it may be convenient, for the purposes of discourse, to imagine a kind of law or dictate, called a law or dictate of utility: and to speak of the action in question as being conformable to such law or dictate.

IX. A man may be said to be a Partisan of the principle of utility, when the approbation or disapprobation he annexes to any action, or to any measure, is determined by and proportioned to the tendency which he conceives it to have to augment or to diminish the happiness of the community: or in other words, to its conformity or unconformity to the laws or dictates of utility.

X. Of an action that is conformable to the principle of utility one may always say either that it is one that ought to be done, or at least that it is not one that ought not to be done. One may say also, that it is right it should be done; at least that it is not wrong it should be done: that it is a right action; at least that it is not a wrong action. When thus interpreted, the words *ought,* and *right* and *wrong,* and others of that stamp, have a meaning: when otherwise, they have none.

XI. Has the rectitude of this principle been ever formally contested? It should seem that it had, by those who have not known what they have been meaning. Is it susceptible of any direct proof? It should seem not: for that which is used to prove every thing else, cannot itself be proved: a chain of proofs must have their commencement somewhere. To give such proof is as impossible as it is needless.

XII. Not that there is or ever has been that human creature breathing, however stupid or perverse, who has not on many, perhaps on most occasions of his life, deferred to it. By the natural constitution of the human frame, on most occasions of their lives men in general embrace this principle, without thinking of it: if not for the ordering of their own actions, yet for the trying of their own actions, as well as of those of other men. There have been, at the same time, not many, perhaps, even of the most intelligent, who have been disposed to embrace it purely and without reserve. There are even few who have not taken some occasion or other to quarrel with it, either on account of their not understanding always how to apply it, or on account of some prejudice or other which they were afraid to examine into, or could not bear to part with. For such is the stuff that man is made of: in principle and in practice, in a right track and in a wrong one, the rarest of all human qualities is consistency.

XIII. When a man attempts to combat the principle of utility, it is with reasons drawn, without his being aware of it, from that very principle itself.[1] His arguments, if they prove anything, prove not that the principle is *wrong,* but that, according to the applications he supposes to be made of it, it is *misapplied.* Is it possible for a man to move the earth? Yes; but he must first find out another earth to stand upon.

XIV. To disprove the propriety of it by arguments is impossible; but, from the causes that have been mentioned, or from some confused or partial view of it, a man may happen to be disposed not to relish it. Where this is the case, if he thinks the settling of his opinions on such a subject worth the trouble, let him take the following steps, and at length, perhaps, he may come to reconcile himself to it.

1. Let him settle with himself, whether he would wish to discard this principle altogether; if so, let him consider what it is that all his reasonings (in matters of politics especially) can amount to?

2. If he would, let him settle with himself, whether he would judge and act without any principle, or whether there is any other he would judge and act by?

3. If there be, let him examine and satisfy himself whether the principle he thinks he has found

is really any separate intelligible principle; or whether it be not a mere principle in words, a kind of phrase, which at bottom expresses neither more nor less than the mere averment of his own unfounded sentiments; that is, what in another person he might be apt to call caprice?

4. If he is inclined to think that his own approbation or disapprobation, annexed to the idea of an act, without any regard to its consequences, is a sufficient foundation for him to judge and act upon, let him ask himself whether his sentiment is to be a standard of right and wrong, with respect to every other man, or whether every man's sentiment has the same privilege of being a standard to itself?

5. In the first case, let him ask himself whether his principle is not despotical, and hostile to all the rest of human race?

6. In the second case, whether it is not anarchical, and whether at this rate there are not as many different standards of right and wrong as there are men? and whether even to the same man, the same thing, which is right to-day, may not (without the least change in its nature) be wrong to-morrow? and whether the same thing is not right and wrong in the same place at the same time? and in either case, whether all argument is not at an end? and whether, when two men have said, 'I like this,' and 'I don't like it,' they can (upon such a principle) have any thing more to say?

7. If he should have said to himself, No: for that the sentiment which he proposes as a standard must be grounded on reflection, let him say on what particulars the reflection is to turn? if on particulars having relation to the utility of the act, then let him say whether this is not deserting his own principle, and borrowing assistance from that very one in opposition to which he sets it up: or if not on those particulars, on what other particulars?

8. If he should be for compounding the matter, and adopting his own principle in part, and the principle of utility in part, let him say how far he will adopt it?

9. When he has settled with himself where he will stop, then let him ask himself how he justifies to himself the adopting it so far? and why he will not adopt it any farther?

10. Admitting any other principle than the principle of utility to be a right principle, a principle that it is right for a man to pursue; admitting (what is not true) that the word *right* can have a meaning without reference to utility, let him say whether there is any such thing as a *motive* that a man can have to pursue the dictates of it: if there is, let him say what that motive is, and how it is to be distinguished from those which enforce the dictates of utility: if not, then lastly let him say what it is this other principle can be good for?

CHAPTER II. OF PRINCIPLES ADVERSE TO THAT OF UTILITY

I. If the principle of utility be a right principle to be governed by, and that in all cases, it follows from what has been just observed, that whatever principle differs from it in any case must necessarily be a wrong one. To prove any other principle, therefore, to be a wrong one, there needs no more than just to show it to be what it is, a principle of which the dictates are in some point or other different from those of the principle of utility: to state it is to confute it.

II. A principle may be different from that of utility in two ways: 1. By being constantly opposed to it: this is the case with a principle which may be termed the principle of *asceticism*. [2] 2. By being sometimes opposed to it, and sometimes not, as it may happen: this is the case with another, which may be termed the principle of *sympathy* and *antipathy*.

III. By the principle of asceticism I mean that principle, which, like the principle of utility, approves or disapproves of any action, according to the tendency which it appears to have to augment or diminish the happiness of the party whose interest is in question; but in an inverse manner: approving of actions in as far as they tend to diminish his happiness: disapproving of them in as far as they tend to augment it.

IV. It is evident that any one who reprobates any the least particle of pleasure, as such, from whatever source derived, is *pro tanto* a partisan of the principle of asceticism. It is only upon that principle, and not from the principle of utility, that the most abominable pleasure which the vilest of malefactors ever reaped from his crime would be to be reprobated, if it stood alone. The case is, that it never does stand alone; but is necessarily followed by such a quantity of pain (or, what comes to the same thing, such a chance for a certain quantity of pain) that the pleasure in comparison of it, is as nothing: and this is the true and sole, but perfectly sufficient, reason for making it a ground for punishment.

V. There are two classes of men of very different complexions, by whom the principle of asceticism appears to have been embraced; the one a set of moralists, the other a set of religionists. Different accordingly have been the motives which appear to have recommended it to the notice of these different parties. Hope, that is the prospect of pleasure, seems to have animated the former: hope, the ailment of philosophic pride: the hope of honour and reputation at the hands of men. Fear, that is the prospect of pain, the latter: fear, the offspring of superstitious fancy: the fear of future punishment at the hands of a splenetic and revengeful Deity. I say in this case fear: for of the invisible future, fear is more powerful than hope. These circumstances characterize the two different parties among the partisans of the principle of asceticism; the parties and their motives different, the principle the same.

VI. The religious party, however, appear to have carried it farther than the philosophical: they have acted more consistently and less wisely. The philosophical party have scarcely gone farther than to reprobate pleasure: the religious party have frequently gone so far as to make it a matter of merit and of duty to court pain. The philosophical party have hardly gone farther than the making pain a matter of indifference. It is no evil, they have said: they have not said, it is a good. They have not so much as reprobated all pleasure in the lump. They have discarded only what they have called the gross; that is, such as are organical, or of which the origin is easily traced up to such as are organical: they have even cherished and magnified the refined. Yet this, however, not under the name of pleasure: to cleanse itself from the sordes of its impure original, it was necessary it should change its name: the honourable, the glorious, the reputable, the becoming, the *honestum,* the *decorum,* it was to be called: in short, any thing but pleasure.

VII. From these two sources have flowed the doctrines from which the sentiments of the bulk of mankind have all along received a tincture of this principle; some from the philosophical, some from the religious, some from both. Men of education more frequently from the philosophical, as more suited to the elevation of their sentiments: the vulgar more frequently from the superstitious, as more suited to the narrowness of their intellect, undilated by knowledge: and to the abjectness of their condition, continually open to the attacks of fear. The tinctures, however, derived from the two sources, would naturally intermingle, insomuch that a man would not always know by which of them he was most influenced: and they would often serve to corroborate and enliven one another. It was this conformity that made a kind of alliance between parties of a complexion otherwise so dissimilar: and disposed them to unite upon various occasions against the common enemy, the partisan of the principle of utility, whom they joined in branding with the odious name of Epicurean.

VIII. The principle of asceticism, however, with whatever warmth it may have been embraced by its partisans as a rule of private conduct, seems not to have been carried to any considerable length, when applied to the business of government. In a few instances it has been carried a little way by the philosophical party: witness the Spartan regimen. Though then, perhaps, it may be considered as having been a measure of security: and an application, though a precipitate and perverse application, of the principle of utility. Scarcely in any instances, to any considerable length, by the religious: for the various monastic orders, and the societies of the Quakers, Dumplers, Moravians, and other religionists, have been free societies, whose regimen no man has been astricted to without the intervention of his own consent. Whatever merit a man may have thought there would be in making himself miserable, no such notion seems ever to have occurred to any of them, that it may be a merit, much less a duty, to make others miserable: although it should seem, that if a certain quantity of misery were a thing so desirable, it would not matter much whether it were brought by each man upon himself, or by one man upon another. It is true, that from the same source from whence, among the religionists, the attachment to the principle of asceticism took its rise, flowed other doctrines and practices, from which misery in abundance was produced in one man by the instrumentality of another: witness the holy wars, and the persecutions for religion. But the passion for producing misery in these cases proceeded upon some special ground: the exercise of it was confined to persons of particular descriptions: they were tormented, not as men, but as heretics and infidels. To have inflicted the same miseries on their fellow-believers and fellow-sectaries, would have been as blameable in the eyes even of these religionists, as in those of a partisan of the principle of utility. For a man to give himself a certain number of stripes was indeed meritorious: but to give the same number of stripes to another man, not consenting, would have been a sin. We read of saints, who for the good of their souls, and the mortification of their bodies, have voluntarily yielded themselves a prey to vermin: but though many persons of this class have wielded the reins of empire, we read of none who have set themselves to work, and made laws on purpose, with a view of stocking the body politic with the breed of highwaymen, housebreakers, or incendiaries. If at any time they have suffered the nation to be preyed upon by swarms of idle pensioners, or useless placemen, it has rather been from negligence and imbecility, than from any settled plan for oppressing and plundering of the people. If at any time they have sapped the sources of national wealth, by cramping commerce, and driving the inhabitants into emigration, it has been with other views, and in pursuit of other ends. If they have declaimed against the pursuit of pleasure, and the use of wealth, they have commonly stopped at declamation: they have not, like Lycurgus, made express ordinances for the purpose of banishing the precious metals. If they have established idleness by a law, it has been not because idleness, the mother of vice and misery, is itself a virtue, but because idleness (say they) is the road to holiness. If under the notion of fasting, they have joined in the plan of confining their subjects to a diet, thought by some to be of the most nourishing and prolific nature, it has been not for the sake of making them tributaries to the nations by whom that diet was to be supplied, but for the sake of manifesting their own power, and exercising the obedience of the people. If they have established, or suffered to be established, punishments for the breach of celibacy, they have done no more than comply with the petitions of those deluded rigorists, who, dupes to the ambitious and deep-laid policy of their rulers, first laid themselves under that idle obligation by a vow.

IX. The principle of asceticism seems originally to have been the reverie of certain hasty speculators, who having perceived, or fancied, that certain pleasures, when reaped in certain circumstances, have, at the long run, been attended with pains more than equivalent to them, took occasion to quarrel with every thing that offered itself under the name of pleasure. Having then got thus far, and having forgot the point which they set out from, they pushed on, and went so much further as to think it meritorious to fall in love with pain. Even this, we see, is at bottom but the principle of utility misapplied.

X. The principle of utility is capable of being consistently pursued; and it is but tautology to say, that the more consistently it is pursued, the better it must ever be for humankind. The principle of asceticism never was, nor ever can be, consistently pursued by any living creature. Let but one tenth part of the inhabitants of this earth pursue it consistently, and in a day's time they will have turned it into a hell.

XI. Among principles adverse to that of utility, that which at this day seems to have most influence in matters of government, is what may be called the principle of sympathy and antipathy. By the principle of sympathy and antipathy, I mean that principle which approves or disapproves of certain actions, not on account of their tending to augment the happiness, nor yet on account of their tending to diminish the happiness of the party whose interest is in question, but merely because a man finds himself disposed to approve or disapprove of them: holding up that approbation or disapprobation as a sufficient reason for itself, and disclaiming the necessity of looking out for any extrinsic ground. Thus far in the general department of morals: and in the particular department of politics, measuring out the quantum (as well as determining the ground) of punishment, by the degree of the disapprobation.

XII. It is manifest, that this is rather a principle in name than in reality: it is not a positive principle of itself, so much as a term employed to signify the negation of all principle. What one expects to find in a principle is something that points out some external consideration, as a means of warranting and guiding the internal sentiments of approbation and disapprobation: this expectation is but ill fulfilled by a proposition, which does neither more nor less than hold up each of those sentiments as a ground and standard for itself.

XIII. In looking over the catalogue of human actions (says a partisan of this principle) in order to determine which of them are to be marked with the seal of disapprobation, you need but to take counsel of your own feelings: whatever you find in yourself a propensity to condemn, is wrong for that very reason. For the same reason it is also meet for punishment: in what proportion it is adverse to utility, or whether it be adverse to utility at all, is a matter that makes no difference. In that same *proportion* also is it meet for punishment: if you hate much, punish much: if you hate little, punish little: punish as you hate. If you hate not at all, punish not at all: the fine feelings of the soul are not to be overborne and tyrannized by the harsh and rugged dictates of political utility.

XIV. The various systems that have been formed concerning the standard of right and wrong, may all be reduced to the principle of sympathy and antipathy. One account may serve for all of them. They consist all of them in so many contrivances for avoiding the obligation of appealing to any external standard, and for prevailing upon the reader to accept of the author's sentiment or opinion as a reason for itself. The phrases [are] different, but the principle the same.[3]

XV. It is manifest, that the dictates of this principle will frequently coincide with those of utility, though perhaps without intending any such thing. Probably more frequently than not: and hence it is that the business of penal justice is carried on upon that tolerable sort of footing upon which we see it carried on in common at this day. For what more natural or more general ground of hatred to a practice can there be, than the mischievousness of such practice? What all men are exposed to suffer by, all men will be disposed to hate. It is far yet, however, from being a constant ground: for when a man suffers, it is not always that he knows what it is he suffers by. A man may suffer grievously, for instance, by a new tax, without being able to trace up the cause of his sufferings to the injustice of some neighbour, who has eluded the payment of an old one.

XVI. The principle of sympathy and antipathy is most apt to err on the side of severity. It is for applying punishment in many cases which deserve none: in many cases which deserve some, it is for applying more than they deserve. There is no incident imaginable, be it ever so trivial, and so remote from mischief, from which this principle may not extract a ground of punishment. Any difference in taste: any difference in opinion: upon one subject as well as upon another. No disagreement so trifling which perseverance and altercation will not render serious. Each becomes in the other's eyes an enemy, and, if laws permit, a criminal. This is one of the circumstances by which the human race is distinguished (not much indeed to its advantage) from the brute creation.

XVII. It is not, however, by any means unexampled for this principle to err on the side of lenity. A near and perceptible mischief moves antipathy. A remote and imperceptible mischief, though not less real, has no effect. Instances in proof of this will occur in numbers in the course of the work. It would be breaking in upon the order of it to give them here.

XVIII. It may be wondered, perhaps, that in all this while no mention has been made of the *theological* principle; meaning that principle which professes to recur for the standard of right and wrong to the will of God. But the case is, this is not in fact a distinct principle. It is never any thing more or less than one or other of the three before-mentioned principles presenting itself under another shape. The *will* of God here meant cannot be his revealed will, as contained in the sacred writings: for that is a system which nobody ever thinks of recurring to at this time of day, for the details of political administration: and even before it can be applied to the details of private conduct, it is universally allowed, by the most eminent divines of all persuasions, to stand in need of pretty ample interpretations; else to what use are the works of those divines? And for the guidance of these interpretations, it is also allowed, that some other standard must be assumed. The will then which is meant on this occasion, is that which may be called the *presumptive* will: that is to say, that which is presumed to be his will on account of the conformity of its dictates to those of some other principle. What then may be this other principle? It must be one or other of the three mentioned above: for there cannot, as we have seen, be any more. It is plain, therefore, that, setting revelation out of the question, no light can ever be thrown upon the standard of right and wrong, by any thing that can be said upon the question, what is God's will. We may be perfectly sure, indeed, that whatever is right is conformable to the will of God: but so far is that from answering the purpose of showing us what is right, that it is necessary to know first whether a thing is right, in order to know from thence whether it be comformable to the will of God.[4]

XIX. There are two things which are very apt to be confounded, but which it imports us carefully to distinguish:—the motive or cause, which, by operating on the mind of an individual, is productive of any act: and the ground or reason which warrants a legislator, or other by-stander, in regarding that act with an eye of approbation. When the act happens, in the particular instance in question, to be productive of effects which we approve of, much more if we happen to observe that the same motive may frequently be productive, in other instances, of the like effects, we are apt to transfer our approbation to the motive itself, and to assume, as the just ground for the approbation we bestow on the act, the circumstance of its originating from that motive. It is in this way that the sentiment of antipathy has often been considered as a just ground of action. Antipathy, for instance, in such or such a case, is the cause of an action which is attended with good effects: but this does not make it a right ground of action in that case, any more than in any other. Still farther. Not only the effects are good, but the agent sees beforehand that they will be so. This may make the action indeed a perfectly right action: but it does not make antipathy a right ground of action. For the same sentiment of antipathy, if implicitly deferred to, may be, and very frequently is, productive of the very worst effects. Antipathy, therefore, can never be a right ground of action. No more, therefore, can resentment, which, as will be seen more particularly hereafter, is but a modification of antipathy. The only right ground of action, that can possibly subsist, is, after all, the consideration of utility, which, if it is a right principle of action, and of approbation, in any one case, is so in every other. Other principles in abundance, that is, other motives, may be the reasons why such and such an act *has* been done: that is, the reasons or causes of its being done: but it is this alone that can be the reason why it might or ought to have been done. Antipathy or resentment requires always to be regulated, to prevent its doing mischief: to be regulated by what? Always by the principle of utility. The principle of utility neither requires nor admits of any other regulator than itself.

CHAPTER III. OF THE FOUR SANCTIONS OR SOURCES OF PAIN AND PLEASURE

I. It has been shown that the happiness of the individuals, of whom a community is composed, that is their pleasures and their security, is the end and the sole end which the legislator ought to have in view: the sole standard, in conformity to which each individual ought, as far as depends upon the legislator, to be *made* to fashion his behaviour. But whether it be this or any thing else that is to be *done,* there is nothing by which a man can ultimately be *made* to do it, but either pain or pleasure. Having taken a general view of these two grand objects (*viz.* pleasure, and what comes to the same thing, immunity from pain) in the character of *final* causes; it will be necessary to take a view of pleasure and pain itself, in the character of *efficient* causes or means.

II. There are four distinguishable sources from which pleasure and pain are in use to flow: considered separately, they may be termed the *physical,* the *political,* the *moral,* and the *religious:* and inasmuch as the pleasures and pains belonging to each of them are capable of giving a binding force to any law or rule of conduct, they may all of them be termed *sanctions.*[5]

III. If it be in the present life, and from the ordinary course of nature, not purposely modified by the interposition of the will of any human being, nor by any extraordinary interposition of any superior invisible being, that the pleasure or the pain takes place or is expected, it may be said to issue from or to belong to the *physical sanction.*

IV. If at the hands of a *particular* person or set of persons in the community, who under names correspondent to that of *judge,* are chosen for the particular purpose of dispensing it, according to the will of the sovereign or supreme ruling power in the state, it may be said to issue from the *political sanction.*

V. If at the hands of such *chance* persons in the community, as the party in question may happen in the course of his life to have concerns with, according to each man's spontaneous disposition, and not according to any settled or concerted rule, it may be said to issue from the *moral* or *popular sanction.*

VI. If from the immediate hand of a superior invisible being, either in the present life, or in a future, it may be said to issue from the *religious* sanction.

VII. Pleasures or pains which may be expected to issue from the *physical, political,* or *moral* sanctions, must all of them be expected to be experienced, if ever, in the *present* life: those which may be expected to issue from the *religious* sanction, may be expected to be experienced either in the *present* life or in a *future.*

VIII. Those which can be experienced in the present life, can of course be no others than such as human nature in the course of the present life is susceptible of: and from each of these sources may flow all the pleasures or pains of which, in the course of the present life, human nature is susceptible. With regard to these then (with which alone we have in this place any concern) those of them which belong to any one of those sanctions, differ not ultimately in kind from those which belong to any one of the other three: the only difference there is among them lies in the circumstances that accompany their production. A suffering which befalls a man in the natural and spontaneous course of things, shall be styled, for instance, a *calamity;* in which case, if it be supposed to befall him through any imprudence of his, it may be styled a punishment issuing from the physical sanction. Now this same suffering, if inflicted by the law, will be what is commonly called a *punishment;* if incurred for want of any friendly assistance, which the misconduct, or supposed misconduct, of the sufferer has occasioned to be withholden, a punishment issuing from the *moral* sanction; if through the immediate interposition of a particular providence, a punishment issuing from the religious sanction.

IX. A man's goods, or his person, are consumed by fire. If this happened to him by what is called an accident, it was a calamity: if by reason of his own imprudence (for instance, from his neglecting to put his candle out) it may be styled a punishment of the physical sanction: if it happened to him by the sentence of the political magistrate, a punishment belonging to the political sanction; that is, what is commonly called a punishment: if for want of any assistance which his *neighbour* withheld from him out of some dislike to his *moral* character, a punishment of the *moral* sanction: if by an immediate act of *God's* displeasure, manifested on account of some *sin* committed by him, or through any distraction of mind, occasioned by the dread of such displeasure, a punishment of the *religious* sanction.

X. As to such of the pleasures and pains belonging to the religious sanction, as regard a future life, of what kind these may be we cannot know. These lie not open to our observation. During the present life they are matters only of expectation: and, whether that expectation be derived from natural or revealed religion, the particular kind of pleasure or pain, if it be different from all those which lie open to our observation, is what we can have no idea of. The best ideas we can obtain of such pains and pleasures are altogether unliquidated in point of quality. In what other respects our ideas of them *may* be liquidated will be considered in another place.

XI. Of these four sanctions the physical is altogether, we may observe, the ground-work of the political and the moral: so is it also of the religious, in as far as the latter bears relation to the present life. It is included in each of those other three. This may operate in any case, (that is, any of the pains or pleasures belonging to it may operate) independently of *them:* none of *them* can operate but by means of this. In a word, the powers of nature may operate of themselves; but neither the magistrate, nor men at large, *can* operate, nor is God in the case in question *supposed* to operate, but through the powers of nature.

XII. For these four objects, which in their nature have so much in common, it seemed of use to find a common name. It seemed of use, in the first place, for the convenience of giving a name to certain pleasures and pains, for which a name equally characteristic could hardly otherwise have been found: in the second place, for the sake of holding up the efficacy of certain moral forces, the influence of which is apt not to be sufficiently attended to. Does the political sanction exert an influence over the conduct of mankind? The moral, the religious sanctions do so too. In every inch of his career are the operations of the political magistrate liable to be aided or impeded by these two foreign powers: who, one or other of them, or both, are sure to be either his rivals or his allies. Does it happen to him to leave them out in his calculations? He will be sure almost to find himself mistaken in the result. Of all this we shall find abundant proofs in the sequel of this work. It behoves him, therefore, to have them continually before his eyes; and that under such a name as exhibits the relation they bear to his own purposes and designs.

CHAPTER IV. VALUE OF A LOT OF PLEASURE OR PAIN, HOW TO BE MEASURED

I. Pleasures then, and the avoidance of pains, are the *ends* which the legislator has in view: it behoves him therefore to understand their *value*. Pleasures and pains are the *instruments* he has to work with: it behoves him therefore to understand their force, which is again, in other words, their value.

II. To a person considered *by himself*, the value of a pleasure or pain considered *by itself*, will be greater or less, according to the four following circumstances:[6]

1. Its *intensity*.
2. Its *duration*.
3. Its *certainty* or *uncertainty*.
4. Its *propinquity* or *remoteness*.

III. These are the circumstances which are to be considered in estimating a pleasure or a pain considered each of them by itself. But when the value of any pleasure or pain is considered for the purpose of estimating the tendency of any *act* by which it is produced, there are two other circumstances to be taken into the account; these are,

5. Its *fecundity,* or the chance it has of being followed by sensations of the *same* kind: that is, pleasures, if it be a pleasure: pains if it be a pain.

6. Its *purity,* or the chance it has of *not* being followed by sensations of the *opposite* kind: that is, pains, if it be a pleasure: pleasures, if it be a pain.

These two last, however, are in strictness scarcely to be deemed properties of the pleasure or the pain itself; they are not, therefore, in strictness to be taken into the account of the value of that pleasure or that pain. They are in strictness to be deemed properties only of the act, or other event, by which such pleasure or pain has been produced; and accordingly are only to be taken into the account of the tendency of such act or such event.

IV. To a *number* of persons, with reference to each of whom the value of a pleasure or a pain is considered, it will be greater or less, according to seven circumstances: to wit, the six preceding ones; *viz.*

1. Its *intensity*.
2. Its *duration*.
3. Its *certainty* or *uncertainty*.
4. Its *propinquity* or *remoteness*.
5. Its *fecundity*.
6. Its *purity*.

And one other; to wit:

7. Its *extent;* that is, the number of persons to whom it *extends;* or (in other words) who are affected by it.

V. To take an exact account then of the general tendency of any act, by which the interests of a community are affected, proceed as follows. Begin with any one person of those whose interests seem most immediately to be affected by it: and take an account,

1. Of the value of each distinguishable *pleasure* which appears to be produced by it in the *first* instance.

2. Of the value of each *pain* which appears to be produced by it in the *first* instance.

3. Of the value of each pleasure which appears to be produced by it *after* the first. This constitutes the *fecundity* of the first *pleasure* and the *impurity* of the first *pain*.

4. Of the value of each *pain* which appears to be produced by it after the first. This constitutes the *fecundity* of the first *pain,* and the *impurity* of the first pleasure.

5. Sum up all the values of all the *pleasures* on the one side, and those of all the pains on the other. The balance, if it be on the side of pleasure, will give the *good* tendency of the act upon the whole, with respect to the interests of that *individual* person; if on the side of pain, the *bad* tendency of it upon the whole.

6. Take an account of the *number* of persons whose interests appear to be concerned; and repeat the above process with respect to each. *Sum up* the numbers expressive of the degrees of *good* tendency, which the act has, with respect to each individual, in regard to whom the tendency of it is *good* upon the whole: do this again with respect

to each individual, in regard to whom the tendency of it is *good* upon the whole: do this again with respect to each individual, in regard to whom the tendency of it is *bad* upon the whole. Take the *balance;* which, if on the side of *pleasure,* will give the general *good tendency* of the act, with respect to the total number or community of individuals concerned; if on the side of pain, the general *evil tendency,* with respect to the same community.

VI. It is not to be expected that this process should be strictly pursued previously to every moral judgment, or to every legislative or judicial operation. It may, however, be always kept in view: and as near as the process actually pursued on these occasions approaches to it, so near will such process approach to the character of an exact one.

VII. The same process is alike applicable to pleasure and pain, in whatever shape they appear: and by whatever denomination they are distinguished: to pleasure, whether it be called *good* (which is properly the cause or instrument of pleasure) or *profit* (which is distant pleasure, or the cause or instrument of distant pleasure), or *convenience,* or *advantage, benefit, emolument, happiness,* and so forth: to pain, whether it be called *evil,* (which corresponds to *good*) or *mischief,* or *inconvenience,* or *disadvantage,* or *loss,* or *unhappiness,* and so forth.

VIII. Nor is this a novel and unwarranted, any more than it is a useless theory. In all this there is nothing but what the practice of mankind, wheresoever they have a clear view of their own interest, is perfectly conformable to. An article of property, an estate in land, for instance, is valuable, on what account? On account of the pleasures of all kinds which it enables a man to produce, and what comes to the same thing the pains of all kinds which it enables him to avert. But the value of such an article of property is universally understood to rise or fall according to the length or shortness of the time which a man has in it: the certainty or uncertainty of its coming into possession; and the nearness or remoteness of the time at which, if at all, it is to come into possession. As to the *intensity* of the pleasures which a man may derive from it, this is never thought of, because it depends upon the use which each particular person may come to make of it; which cannot be estimated till the particular

pleasures he may come to derive from it, or the particular pains he may come to exclude by means of it, are brought to view. For the same reason, neither does he think of the *fecundity* or *purity* of those pleasures. ...

NOTES

1. 'The principle of utility, (I have heard it said) is a dangerous principle: it is dangerous on certain occasions to consult it.' This is as much as to say, what? that it is not consonant to utility, to consult utility: in short, that it is *not* consulting it, to consult it.

2. Ascetic is a term that has been sometimes applied to Monks. It comes from a Greek, word which signifies *exercise.* The practices by which Monks sought to distinguish themselves from other men were called their Exercises. These exercises consisted in so many contrivances they had for tormenting themselves. By this they thought to ingratiate themselves with the Deity. For the Deity, said they, is a Being of infinite benevolence: now a Being of the most ordinary benevolence is pleased to see others make themselves as happy as they can: therefore to make ourselves as unhappy as we can is the way to please the Deity. If anybody asked them, what motive they could find for doing all this? Oh! said they, you are not to imagine that we are punishing ourselves for nothing: we know very well what we are about. You are to know, that for every grain of pain it costs us now, we are to have a hundred grains of pleasure by and by. The case is, that God loves to see us torment ourselves at present: indeed he has as good as told us so. But this is done only to try us, in order just to see how we should behave: which it is plain he could not know, without making the experiment. Now then, from the satisfaction it gives him to see us make ourselves as unhappy as we can make ourselves in this present life, we have a sure proof of the satisfaction it will give him to see us as happy as he can make us in a life to come.

3. It is curious enough to observe the variety of inventions men have hit upon, and the variety of phrases they have brought forward, in order to conceal from the world, and, if possible, from themselves, this very general and therefore very pardonable self-sufficiency.

A. One man says, he has a thing made on purpose to tell him what is right and what is wrong; and that it is called a *moral sense:* and then he goes to work at his ease, and says, such a thing is right, and such a thing is wrong—why? 'because my moral sense tells me it is.'

B. Another man comes and alters the phrase: leaving out *moral,* and putting in *common,* in the room of it. He then tells you, that his common sense teaches him what is right and wrong, as surely as the other's moral sense did: meaning by common sense, a sense of some kind or other, which, he says, is possessed by all mankind: the sense of those, whose sense is not the same as the author's, being struck out of the account as not worth taking. This contrivance does better than the other; for a moral sense, being a new thing, a man may feel about him a good while without being able to find it out: but common sense is as old as the creation; and there is no man but would be ashamed to be thought not to have as much of it as his neighbours. It has another great advantage: by appearing to share power, it lessens envy. ...

C. Another man comes, and says, that as to a moral sense indeed, he cannot find that he has any such thing: that however he has an *understanding,* which will do quite as well. This understanding, he says, is the standard of right and wrong: it tells him so and so. All good and wise men understand as he does: if other men's understandings differ in any point from his, so much the worse for them: it is a sure sign they are either defective or corrupt.

D. Another man says, that there is an eternal and immutable Rule of Right: that rule of right dictates so and so: and then he begins giving you his sentiments upon any thing that comes uppermost: and these sentiments (you are to take for granted) are so many branches of the eternal rule of right.

E. Another man, or perhaps the same man (it's no matter) says, that there are certain practices conformable, and others repugnant, to the Fitness of Things; and then he tells you, at his leisure, what practices are conformable and what repugnant: just as he happens to like a practice or dislike it.

F. A great multitude of people are continually talking of the Law of Nature; and then they go on giving you their sentiments about what is right and what is wrong: and these sentiments, you are to understand, are so many chapters and sections of the Law of Nature.

G. Instead of the phrase, Law of Nature, you have sometimes, Law of Reason, Right Reason, Natural Justice, Natural Equity, Good Order. Any of them will do equally well. This latter is most used in politics. The three last are much more tolerable than the others, because they do not very explicitly claim to be any thing more than phrases: they insist but feebly upon the being looked upon as so many positive standards of themselves, and seem content to be taken, upon occasion, for phrases expressive of the conformity of the thing in question to the proper standard, whatever that may be. On most occasions, however, it will be better to say *utility: utility* is clearer, as referring more explicitly to pain and pleasure.

H. We have one philosopher, who says, there is no harm in any thing in the world but in telling a lie: and that if, for example, you were to murder your own father, this would only be a particular way of saying, he was not your father. Of course, when this philosopher sees any thing that he does not like, he says, it is a particular way of telling a lie. It is saying, that the act ought to be done, or may be done, when, *in truth,* it ought not to be done.

I. The fairest and openest of them all is that sort of man who speaks out, and says, I am of the number of the Elect: now God himself takes care to inform the Elect what is right: and that with so good effect, and let them strive ever so, they cannot help not only knowing it but practising it. If therefore a man wants to know what is right and what is wrong, he has nothing to do but to come to me.

It is upon the principle of antipathy that such and such acts are often reprobated on the score of their being *unnatural:* the practice of exposing children, established among the Greeks and Romans, was an unnatural practice. Unnatural, when it means any thing, means unfrequent: and there it means something; although nothing to the present purpose. But here it means no such thing: for the frequency of such acts is perhaps the great complaint. It therefore means nothing; nothing, I mean, which there is in the act itself. All it can serve to express is, the disposition of the person who is talking of it: the disposition he is in to be angry at the thoughts of it: Does it merit his anger? Very likely it may: but whether it does or no is a question, which, to be answered rightly, can only be answered upon the principle of utility.

Unnatural, is as good a word as moral sense, or common sense; and would be as good a foundation for a system. Such an act is unnatural; that is, repugnant to nature: for I do not like to practise it: and, consequently, do not practise it. It is therefore repugnant to what ought to be the nature of every body else.

The mischief common to all these ways of thinking and arguing (which, in truth, as we have seen, are but one and the same method, couched in different forms of words) is their serving as a cloke, and pretence, and aliment, to despotism: if not a despotism in practice, a despotism however in disposition: which is but too apt, when pretence and power offer, to show itself in practice. The consequence is, that with intentions very commonly of the purest kind, a man becomes a torment either to himself or his fellow-creatures. If he be of the melancholy cast, he sits in silent grief, bewailing their blindness and depravity: if of the irascible, he declaims with fury and virulence against all who differ from him; blowing up the coals of fanaticism, and branding with the charge of corruption and insincerity, every man who does not think, or profess to think, as he does.

If such a man happens to possess the advantages of style, his book may do a considerable deal of mischief before the nothingness of it is understood.

These principles, if such they can be called, it is more frequent to see applied to morals than to politics: but their influence extends itself to both. In politics, as well as morals, a man will be at least equally glad of a pretence for deciding any question in the manner that best pleases him, without the trouble of inquiry. If a man is an infallible judge of what is right and wrong in the actions of private individuals, why not in the measures to be observed by public men in the direction of those actions? Accordingly (not to mention other chimeras) I have more than once known the pretended law of nature set up in legislative debates, in opposition to arguments derived from the principle of utility. . . .

4. The principle of theology refers every thing to God's pleasure. But what is God's pleasure? God does not, he confessedly does not now, either speak or write to us. How then are we to know what is his pleasure? By observing what is our own pleasure, and pronouncing it to be his. Accordingly, what is called the pleasure of God, is and must necessarily be (revelation apart) neither more nor less than the good pleasure of the person, whoever he be, who is pronouncing what he believes, or pretends, to be God's pleasure. How know you it to be God's pleasure that such or such an act should be abstained from? Whence come you even to suppose as much? 'Because the engaging in it would, I imagine, be prejudicial upon the whole to the happiness of mankind'; says the partisan of the principle of utility: 'Because the commission of it is attended with a gross and sensual, or at least with a trifling and transient satisfaction;' says the partisan of the principle of asceticism: 'Because I detest the thoughts of it; and I cannot, neither ought I to be called upon to tell why;' says he who proceeds upon the principle of antipathy. In the words of one or other of these must that person necessarily answer (revelation apart) who professes to take for his standard the will of God.

5. Sanctio, in Latin, was used to signify the *act of binding,* and, by a common grammatical transition, *any thing which serves to bind a man:* to wit, to the observance of such or such a mode of conduct. According to a Latin grammarian, the import of the word is derived by rather a far-fetched process (such as those commonly are, and in a great measure indeed must be, by which intellectual ideas are derived from sensible ones) from the word *sanguis,* blood: because, among the Romans, with a view to inculcate into the people a persuasion that such or such a mode of conduct would be rendered obligatory upon a man by the force of what I call the religious sanction (that is, that he would be made to suffer by the extraordinary interposition of some superior being, if he failed to observe the mode of conduct in question) certain ceremonies were contrived by the priests: in the course of which ceremonies the blood of victims was made use of.

A Sanction then is a source of obligatory powers or *motives:*

and *pleasures;* which, according as they are
such or such modes of conduct, operate, and
only things which can operate, as *motives.*

6.   These circumstances have since been denominated *elements* or *dimensions* of *value* in a pleasure or a pain.

Not long after the publication of the first edition, the following memoriter verses were framed, in the view of lodging more effectually, in the memory, these points, on which the

whole fabric of morals and legislation may be seen to rest.
Intense, long, certain, speedy, fruitful, pure—

Such marks in *pleasures* and in *pains* endure.
Such pleasures seek if *private* be thy end:
If it be *public,* wide let them *extend.*
Such *pains* avoid, whichever be thy view:
If pains *must* come, let them *extend* to few.

J. O. U R M S O N

Saints and Heroes*

Moral philosophers tend to discriminate, explicitly or implicitly, three types of action from the point of view of moral worth. First, they recognize actions that are a duty, or obligatory, or that we ought to perform, treating these terms as approximately synonymous; second, they recognize actions that are right in so far as they are permissible from a moral standpoint and not ruled out by moral considerations, but that are not morally required of us, like the lead of this or that card at bridge; third, they recognize actions that are wrong, that we ought not to do. Some moral philosophers, indeed, could hardly discriminate even these three types of action consistently with the rest of their philosophy. Moore, for example, could hardly recognize a class of morally indifferent actions, permissible but not enjoined, since it is to be presumed that good or ill of some sort will result from the most trivial of our actions. But most moral philosophers recognize these three types of action and attempt to provide a moral theory that will make intelligible such a threefold classification.

To my mind this threefold classification, or any classification that is merely a variation on or elab-

oration of it, is totally inadequate to the facts of morality; any moral theory that leaves room only for such a classification will in consequence also be inadequate. My main task in this paper will be to show the inadequacy of such a classification by drawing attention to two of the types of action that most conspicuously lie outside such a classification; I shall go on to hazard some views on what sort of theory will most easily cope with the facts to which I draw attention, but the facts are here the primary interest.

We sometimes call a person a saint, or an action saintly, using the word "saintly" in a purely moral sense with no religious implications; also we sometimes call a person a hero or an action heroic. It is too clear to need argument that the words "saint" and "hero" are at least normally used in such a way as to be favorably evaluative; it would be impossible to claim that this evaluation is always moral, for clearly we sometimes call a person a saint when evaluating him religiously rather than morally and may call a person the hero of a game or athletic contest in which no moral qualities were displayed, but I shall take it that no formal argument is necessary to show that at least sometimes we use both words for moral evaluation.

If "hero" and "saint" can be words of moral evaluation, we may proceed to the attempt to

*J. O. Urmson, "Saints and Heroes," in *Essays in Moral Philosophy,* ed. A. I. Melden (Seattle: University of Washington Press, 1958), pp. 198–216. Reprinted by permission of the author and the publisher.

make explicit the criteria that we implicitly employ for their use in moral contexts. It appears that we so use them in more than one type of situation, and that there is a close parallel between the ways in which the two terms "hero" and "saint" are used; we shall here notice three types of situation in which they are used which seem to be sufficiently different to merit distinction. As the first two types of situation to be noticed are ones that can be readily subsumed under the threefold classification mentioned above, it will be sufficient here to note them and pass on to the third type of situation, which, since it cannot be subsumed under that classification, is for the purposes of this paper the most interesting.

A person may be called a saint (1) if he does his duty regularly in contexts in which inclination, desire, or self-interest would lead most people not to do it, and does so as a result of exercising abnormal self-control; parallel to this a person may be called a hero (1) if he does his duty in contexts in which terror, fear, or a drive to self-preservation would lead most men not to do it, and does so by exercising abnormal self-control. Similarly for actions: an action may be called saintly (1) if it is a case of duty done by virtue of self-control in a context in which most men would be led astray by inclination or self-interest, and an action may be called heroic (1) if it is a case of duty done by virtue of self-control in a context in which most men would be led astray by fear or a drive for self-preservation. The only difference between the saintly and the heroic in this sort of situation is that the one involves resistance to desire and self-interest; the other, resistance to fear and self-preservation. This is quite a clear difference, though there may be marginal cases, or cases in which motives were mixed, in which it would be equally appropriate to call an action indifferently saintly or heroic. It is easy to give examples of both the heroic and the saintly as distinguished above: the unmarried daughter does the saintly deed of staying at home to tend her ailing and widowed father; the terrified doctor heroically stays by his patients in a plague-ridden city.

A person may be called a saint (2) if he does his duty in contexts in which inclination or self-interest would lead most men not to do it, not, as in the previous paragraph, by abnormal self-control, but without effort; parallel to this a person may be called a hero (2) if he does his duty in contexts in which fear would lead most men not to do it, and does so without effort. The corresponding accounts of a saintly (2) or heroic (2) action can easily be derived. Here we have the conspicuously virtuous deed, in the Aristotelian sense, as opposed to the conspicuously self-controlled, encratic deed of the previous paragraph. People thus purged of temptation or disciplined against fear may be rare, but Aristotle thought there could be such; there is a tendency today to think of such people as merely lucky or unimaginative, but Aristotle thought more highly of them than of people who need to exercise self-control.

It is clear that, in the two types of situation so far considered, we are dealing with actions that fall under the concept of duty. Roughly, we are calling a person saintly or heroic because he does his duty in such difficult contexts that most men would fail in them. Since for the purposes of this paper I am merely conceding that we do use the term "saintly" and "heroic" in these ways, it is unnecessary here to spend time arguing that we do so use them or in illustrating such uses. So used, the threefold classification of actions whose adequacy I wish to deny can clearly embrace them. I shall therefore pass immediately to a third use of the terms "heroic" and "saintly," which I am not merely willing to concede but obliged to establish.

I contend, then, that we may also call a person a saint (3) if he does actions that are far beyond the limits of his duty, whether by control of contrary inclination and interest or without effort; parallel to this we may call a person a hero (3) if he does actions that are far beyond the bounds of his duty, whether by control of natural fear or without effort. Such actions are saintly (3) or heroic (3). Here, as it seems to me, we have the hero or saint, heroic or saintly deed, par excellence; until now we have been considering but minor saints and heroes. We have considered the, certainly, heroic action of the doctor who does his duty by sticking to his patients in a plague-stricken city; we have now to consider the case of the doctor who, no differently situated from countless other doctors in other places, volunteers to join the depleted medical forces in that city. Previously we were considering the soldier who heroically does his duty in the face of such dangers as would cause most to shirk—the sort of man who is rightly awarded the Military Medal in the British Army; we have now to consider the case of the soldier who does more than his superior officers would ever ask him to do—the man to whom, often posthumously, the Victoria Cross is awarded. Similarly, we have to turn from saintly self-discipline in the way of duty to the dedicated, self-effacing life in the service of others which is not even contemplated by the majority of upright, kind, and honest men, let alone expected of them.

Let us be clear that we are not now considering cases of natural affection, such as the sacrifice made by a mother for her child; such cases may be said with some justice not to fall under the concept of morality but to be admirable in some different way. Such cases as are here under consideration may be taken to be as little bound up with such emotions as affection as any moral action may be. We may consider an example of what is meant by "heroism" (3) in more detail to bring this out.

We may imagine a squad of soldiers to be practicing the throwing of live hand grenades; a grenade slips from the hand of one of them and rolls on the ground near the squad; one of them sacrifices his life by throwing himself on the grenade and protecting his comrades with his own body. It is quite unreasonable to suppose that such a man must be impelled by the sort of emotion that he might be impelled by if his best friend were in the squad; he might only just have joined the squad; it is clearly an action having moral status. But if the soldier had not thrown himself on the grenade would he have failed in his duty? Though clearly he is superior in some way to his comrades, can we possibly say that they failed in their duty by not trying to be the one who sacrificed himself? If he had not done so, could anyone have said to him, "You ought to have thrown yourself on that grenade"? Could a superior have decently ordered him to do it? The answer to all these questions is plainly negative. We clearly have here a case of a moral action, a heroic action, which cannot be subsumed under the classification whose inadequacy we are exposing.

But someone may not be happy with this conclusion, and for more respectable reasons than a desire to save the traditional doctrine. He may

reason as follows: in so far as the soldier had time to feel or think at all, he presumably felt that he ought to do that deed; he considered it the proper thing to do; he, if no one else, might have reproached himself for failing to do his duty if he had shirked the deed. So, it may be argued, if an act presents itself to us in the way this act may be supposed to have presented itself to this soldier, then it is our duty to do it; we have no option. This objection to my thesis clearly has some substance, but it involves a misconception of what is at issue. I have no desire to present the act of heroism as one that is naturally regarded as optional by the hero, as something he might or might not do; I concede that he might regard himself as being obliged to act as he does. But if he were to survive the action only a modesty so excessive as to appear false could make him say, "I only did my duty," for we know, and he knows, that he has done more than duty requires. Further, though he might say to himself that so to act was a duty, he could not say so even beforehand to anyone else, and no one else could ever say it. Subjectively, we may say, at the time of action, the deed presented itself as a duty, but it was not a duty.

Another illustration, this time of saintliness, may help. It is recorded by Bonaventura that after Francis of Assisi had finished preaching to the birds on a celebrated occasion his companions gathered around him to praise and admire. But Francis himself was not a bit pleased; he was full of self-reproach that he had hitherto failed in what he now considered to be his duty to preach to the feathered world. There is indeed no degree of saintliness that a suitable person may not come to consider it to be his duty to achieve. Yet there is a world of difference between this failure to have preached hitherto to the birds and a case of straightforward breach of duty, however venial. First, Francis could without absurdity reproach himself for his failure to do his duty, but it would be quite ridiculous for anyone else to do so, as one could have done if he had failed to keep his vows, for example. Second, it is not recorded that Francis ever reproached anyone else for failure to preach to the birds as a breach of duty. He could claim this action for himself as a duty and could perhaps have exhorted others to preach to the birds; but there could be no question of reproaches for not so acting.

To sum up on this point, then, it seems clear that there is no action, however quixotic, heroic, or saintly, which the agent may not regard himself as obliged to perform, as much as he may feel himself obliged to tell the truth and to keep his promises. Such actions do not present themselves as optional to the agent when he is deliberating; but, since he alone can call such an action of his a duty, and then only from the deliberative viewpoint, only for himself and not for others, and not even for himself as a piece of objective reporting, and since nobody else can call on him to perform such an act as they can call on him to tell the truth and to keep his promises, there is here a most important difference from the rock-bottom duties which are duties for all and from every point of view, and to which anyone may draw attention. Thus we need not deny the points made by our imaginary objector in order to substantiate the point that some acts of heroism and saintliness cannot be adequately subsumed under the concept of duty.

Let us then take it as established that we have to deal in ethics not with a simple trichotomy of duties, permissible actions, and wrong actions, or any substantially similar conceptual scheme, but with something more complicated. We have to add at least the complication of actions that are certainly of moral worth but that fall outside the notion of a duty and seem to go beyond it, actions worthy of being called heroic or saintly. It should indeed be noted that heroic or saintly actions are not the sole, but merely conspicuous, cases of actions that exceed the basic demands of duty; there can be cases of disinterested kindness and generosity, for example, that are clearly more than basic duty requires and yet hardly ask for the high titles, "saintly" and "heroic." Indeed, every case of "going the second mile" is a case in point, for it cannot be one's duty to go the second mile in the same basic sense as it is to go the first —otherwise it could be argued first that it is one's duty to go two miles and therefore that the spirit of the rule of the second mile requires that one go altogether four miles, and by repetition one could establish the need to go every time on an infinite journey. It is possible to go just beyond one's duty by being a little more generous, forbearing, helpful, or forgiving than fair dealing demands, or to go a very long way beyond the basic code of duties with the saint or the hero. When I here

draw attention to the heroic and sain[...] do so merely in order to have conspicuous ca[...] of a whole realm of actions that lie outside the trichotomy I have criticized and therefore, as I believe, outside the purview of most ethical theories.

Before considering the implications for ethics of the facts we have up to now been concerned to note, it might be of value to draw attention to a less exalted parallel to these facts. If we belong to a club there will be rules of the club, written or unwritten, calling upon us to fulfill certain basic requirements that are a condition of membership, and that may be said to be the duties of membership. It may perhaps be such a basic requirement that we pay a subscription. It will probably be indifferent whether we pay this subscription by check or in cash—both procedures will be "right"—and almost certainly it will be quite indifferent what sort of hat we wear at the meetings. Here, then, we have conformity to rule which is the analogue of doing one's duty, breach of rule which is the analogue of wrongdoing, and a host of indifferent actions, in accordance with the traditional trichotomy. But among the rule-abiding members of such a club what differences there can be! It is very likely that there will be one, or perhaps two or three, to whose devotion and loyal service the success of the club is due far more than to the activities of all the other members together; these are the saints and the heroes of the clubs, who do more for them by far than any member could possibly be asked to do, whose many services could not possibly be demanded in the rules. Behind them come a motley selection, varying from the keen to the lukewarm, whose contributions vary in value and descend sometimes to almost nothing beyond what the rules demand. The moral contribution of people to society can vary in value in the same way.

So much, then, for the simple facts to which I have wished to draw attention. They are simple facts and, unless I have misrepresented them, they are facts of which we are all, in a way, perfectly well aware. It would be absurd to suggest that moral philosophers have hitherto been unaware of the existence of saints and heroes and have never even alluded to them in their works. But it does seem that these facts have been neglected in their general, systematic accounts of morality. It is indeed easy to see that on some of the best-known theories there is no room for such facts. If for Moore, and for most utilitarians, any action is a duty that will produce the greatest possible good in the circumstances, for them the most heroic self-sacrifice or saintly self-forgetfulness will be duties on all fours with truth-telling and promise-keeping. For Kant, beyond the counsels of prudence and the rules of skill, there is only the categorical imperative of duty, and every duty is equally and utterly binding on all men; it is true that he recognizes the limiting case of the holy will, but the holy will is not a will that goes beyond duty but a will that is beyond morality through being incapable of acting except in accordance with the imperative. The nearest to an equivalent to a holy will in the cases we have been noting is the saintly will in the second sense we distinguished—the will that effortlessly does its duty when most would fail—but this is not a true parallel and in any case does not fall within the class of moral actions that go beyond duty to which our attention is primarily given. It is also true that Kant recognized virtues and talents as having conditional value, but not moral value, whereas the acts of heroism and saintliness we have considered have full moral worth, and their value is as unconditional as anyone could wish. Without committing ourselves to a scholarly examination of Kant's ethical works, it is surely evident that Kant could not consistently do justice to the facts before us. Intuitionism seems to me so obscurantist that I should not wish to prophesy what an intuitionist might feel himself entitled to say; but those intuitionists with whose works I am acquainted found their theories on an intuition of the fitting, the prima facie duty or the claim; the act that has this character to the highest degree at any time is a duty. While they recognize greater and lesser, stronger and weaker, claims, this is only in order to be able to deal with the problem of the conflict of duties; they assign no place to the act that, while not a duty, is of high moral importance.

Simple utilitarianism, Kantianism, and intuitionism, then, have no obvious theoretical niche for the saint and the hero. It is possible, no doubt, to revise these theories to accommodate the facts, but until so modified successfully they must surely be treated as unacceptable, and the modifications required might well detract from their plausibility. The intuitionists, for example, might lay claim to the intuition of a nonnatural characteristic of saintliness, of heroism, of decency, of sportingness, and so on, but this would give to their theory still more the appearance of utilizing the advantages of theft over honest toil.

Thus as moral theorists we need to discover some theory that will allow for both absolute duties, which, in Mill's phrase, can be exacted from a man like a debt, to omit which is to do wrong and to deserve censure, and which may be embodied in formal rules or principles, and also for a range of actions which are of moral value and which an agent may feel called upon to perform, but which cannot be demanded and whose omission cannot be called wrongdoing. Traditional moral theories, I have suggested, fail to do this. It would be well beyond the scope of this paper, and probably beyond my capacity, to produce here and now a full moral theory designed to accommodate all these facts, including the facts of saintliness and heroism. But I do think that of all traditional theories utilitarianism can be most easily modified to accommodate the facts, and would like before ending this paper to bring forward some considerations tending to support this point of view.

Moore went to great pains to determine exactly the nature of the intrinsically good, and Mill to discover the *summum bonum*, Moore's aim being to explain thereby directly the rightness and wrongness of particular actions and Mill's to justify a set of moral principles in the light of which the rightness or wrongness of particular actions can be decided. But, though there can be very tricky problems of duty, they do not naturally present themselves as problems whose solution depends upon an exact determination of an ultimate end; while the moral principles that come most readily to mind— truth-telling; promise-keeping; abstinence from murder, theft, and violence; and the like—make a nice discrimination of the supreme good seem irrelevant. We do not need to debate whether it is Moore's string of intrinsic goods or Mill's happiness that is achieved by conformity to such principles; it is enough to see that without them social life would be impossible and any life would indeed be solitary, poor, nasty, brutish, and short. Even self-interest (which some have seen as the sole foundation of morality) is sufficient ground to render it wise to preach, if not to practice, such principles. Such considerations as these, which are not novel, have led some utilitarians to treat avoidance of the *summum malum* rather than the achievement of the *summum bonum* as the foundation of morality. Yet to others this has seemed, with some justification, to assign to morality too ignoble a place.

But the facts we have been considering earlier in this paper are surely relevant at this point. It is absurd to ask just what ideal is being served by abstinence from murder; but on the other hand nobody could see in acts of heroism such as we have been considering a mere avoidance of anti-social behavior. Here we have something more gracious, actions that need to be inspired by a positive ideal. If duty can, as Mill said, be exacted from persons as a debt, it is because duty is a minimum requirement for living together; the positive contribution of actions that go beyond duty could not be so exacted.

It may, however, be objected that this is a glorification of the higher flights of morality at the expense of duty, toward which an unduly cynical attitude is being taken. In so far as the suggestion is that we are forgetting how hard the way of duty may be and that doing one's duty can at times deserve to be called heroic and saintly, the answer is that we have mentioned this and acknowledge it; it is not forgotten but irrelevant to the point at issue, which is the place of duty in a moral classification of actions, not the problem of the worth of moral agents. But I may be taken to be acquiescing in a low and circumscribed view of duty which I may be advised to enlarge. We should, it may be said, hitch our wagons to the stars and not be content to say: you must do this and that as duties, and it would be very nice if you were to do these other things but we do not expect them of you. Is it perhaps only an imperfect conception of duty which finds it not to comprise the whole of morality? I want to examine this difficulty quite frankly, and to explain why I think that we properly recognize morality that goes beyond duty; for it seems to me incontestable that properly or improperly we do so.

No intelligent person will claim infallibility for his moral views. But allowing for this one must claim that one's moral code is ideal so far as one can see; for to say, "I recognize moral code A but see clearly that moral code B is superior to it," is but a way of saying that one recognizes moral code B but is only prepared to live up to moral code A. In some sense, then, everybody must be prepared to justify his moral code as ideal; but some philosophers have misunderstood this sense. Many philosophers have thought it necessary, if they were to defend their moral code as ideal, to try to show that it had a superhuman, a priori validity. Kant, for example, tried to show that the moral principles he accepted were such as any rational being, whether man or angel, must inevitably accept; the reputedly empiricist Locke thought that it must be possible to work out a deductive justification of moral laws. In making such claims such philosophers have unintentionally done morality a disservice; for their failure to show that the moral code was ideal in the sense of being a rationally justifiable system independent of time, place, circumstance, and human nature has led many to conclude that there can be no justification of a moral code, that moral codes are a matter of taste or convention.

But morality, I take it, is something that should serve human needs, not something that incidentally sweeps man up with itself, and to show that a morality was ideal would be to show that it best served man—man as he is and as he can be expected to become, not man as he would be if he were perfectly rational or an incorporeal angel. Just as it would be fatuous to build our machines so that they would give the best results according to an abstract conception of mechanical principles, and is much more desirable to design them to withstand to some extent our ham-fistedness, ignorance, and carelessness, so our morality must be one that will work. In the only sense of "ideal" that is of importance in action, it is part of the ideal that a moral code should actually help to contribute to human well-being, and a moral code that would work only for angels (for whom it would in any case be unnecessary) would be a far from ideal moral code for human beings. There is, indeed, a place for ideals that are practically unworkable in human affairs, as there is a place for the blueprint of a machine that will never go into production; but it is not the place of such ideals to serve as a basic code of duties.

If, then, we are aiming at a moral code that will best serve human needs, a code that is ideal in the sense that a world in which such a code is acknowledged will be a better place than a world in which some other sort of moral code is acknowledged, it seems that there are ample grounds why our code should distinguish between basic rules, summarily set forth in simple rules and binding on all, and the higher flights of morality of which saintliness and heroism are outstanding examples. These grounds I shall enumerate at once.

1. It is important to give a special status of urgency, and to exert exceptional pressure, in those matters in which compliance with the demands of morality by all is indispensable. An army without men of heroic valor would be impoverished, but without general attention to the duties laid down in military law it would become a mere rabble. Similarly, while life in a world without its saints and heroes would be impoverished, it would only be poor and not necessarily brutish or short as when basic duties are neglected.

2. If we are to exact basic duties like debts, and censure failure, such duties must be, in ordinary circumstances, within the capacity of the ordinary man. It would be silly for us to say to ourselves, our children, and our fellow men, "This and that you and everyone else must do," if the acts in question are such that manifestly but few could bring themselves to do them, though we may ourselves resolve to try to be of that few. To take a parallel from positive law, the prohibition laws asked too much of the American people and were consequently broken systematically; and as people got used to breaking the law a general lowering of respect for the law naturally followed; it no longer seemed that a law was something that everybody could be expected to obey. Similarly in Britain the gambling laws, some of which are utterly unpractical, have fallen into contempt as a body. So, if we were to represent the heroic act of sacrificing one's life for one's comrades as a basic duty, the effect would be to lower the degree of urgency and stringency that the notion of duty does in fact possess. The basic moral code must not be in part too far beyond the capacity of the ordinary men on ordinary occasions, or a general breakdown of compliance with the moral code would be an inevitable consequence; duty would seem to be something high and unattainable, and not for "the likes of us." Admirers of the Sermon on the Mount do not in

practice, and could not, treat failure to turn the other cheek and to give one's cloak also as being on all fours with breaches of the Ten Commandments, however earnestly they themselves try to live a Christian life.

3. A moral code, if it is to be a code, must be formulable, and if it is to be a code to be observed it must be formulable in rules of manageable complexity. The ordinary man has to apply and interpret this code without recourse to a Supreme Court or House of Lords. But one can have such rules only in cases in which a type of action that is reasonably easy to recognize is almost invariably desirable or undesirable, as killing is almost invariably undesirable and promise-keeping almost invariably desirable. Where no definite rule of manageable complexity can be justified, we cannot work on that moral plane on which types of action can be enjoined or condemned as duty or crime. It has no doubt often been the case that a person who has gone off to distant parts to nurse lepers has thereby done a deed of great moral worth. But such an action is not merely too far beyond average human capacity to be regarded as a duty, as was insisted in (2) above; it would be quite ridiculous for everyone, however circumstanced, to be expected to go off and nurse lepers. But it would be absurd to try to formulate complicated rules to determine in just what circumstances such an action is a duty. This same point can readily be applied to such less spectacular matters as excusing legitimate debts or nursing sick neighbors.

4. It is part of the notion of a duty that we have a right to demand compliance from others even when we are interested parties. I may demand that you keep your promises to me, tell me the truth, and do me no violence, and I may reproach you if you transgress. But however admirable the tending of strangers in sickness may be it is not a basic duty, and we are not entitled to reproach those to whom we are strangers if they do not tend us in sickness; nor can I tell you, if you fail to give me a cigarette when I have run out, that you have failed in your duty to me, however much you may subsequently reproach yourself for your meanness if you do so fail. A line must be drawn between what we can expect and demand from others and what we can merely hope for and receive with gratitude when we get it;

duty falls on one side of this line, and other acts with moral value on the other, and rightly so.

5. In the case of basic moral duties we act to some extent under constraint. We have no choice but to apply pressure on each other to conform in these fundamental matters; here moral principles are like public laws rather than like private ideas. But free choice of the better course of action is always preferable to action under pressure, even when the pressure is but moral. When possible, therefore, it is better that pressure should not be applied and that there should be encouragement and commendation for performance rather than outright demands and censure in the event of nonperformance. There are no doubt degrees in this matter. Some pressure may reasonably be brought to persuade a person to go some way beyond basic duty in the direction of kindliness and forbearance, to be not merely a just man but also not too hard a man. But, while there is nothing whatever objectionable in the idea of someone's being pressed to carry out such a basic duty as promise-keeping, there is something horrifying in the thought of pressure being brought on him to perform an act of heroism. Though the man might feel himself morally called upon to do the deed, it would be a moral outrage to apply pressure on him to do such a deed as sacrificing his life for others.

These five points make it clear why I do not think that the distinction of basic duty from other acts of moral worth, which I claim to detect in ordinary moral thought, is a sign of the inferiority of our everyday moral thinking to that of the general run of moral theorists. It in no way involves anyone in acquiescing in a second best. No doubt from the agent's point of view it is imperative that he should endeavor to live up to the highest ideals of behavior that he can think of, and if an action falls within the ideal it is for him irrelevant whether or not it is a duty or some more supererogatory act. But it simply does not follow that the distinction is in every way unimportant, for it is important that we should not demand ideal conduct from others in the way in which we must demand basic morality from them, or blame them equally for failures in all fields. It is not cynicism to make the minimum positive demands upon one's fellow men; but to characterize an act as a duty is so to demand it.

Thus we may regard the imperatives of duty as prohibiting behavior that is intolerable if men are to live together in society and demanding the minimum of cooperation toward the same end; that is why we have to treat compliance as compulsory and dereliction as liable to public censure. We do not need to ask with Bentham whether pushpin is as good as poetry, with Mill whether it is better to be Socrates dissatisfied or a fool satisfied, or with Moore whether a beautiful world with no one to see it would have intrinsic worth; what is and what is not tolerable in society depends on no such nice discrimination. Utilitarians, when attempting to justify the main rules of duty in terms of a *summum bonum,* have surely invoked many different types of utilitarian justification, ranging from the avoidance of the intolerable to the fulfillment of the last detail of a most rarefied ideal.

Thus I wish to suggest that utilitarianism can best accommodate the facts to which I have drawn attention; but I have not wished to support any particular view about the supreme good or the importance of pleasure. By utilitarianism I mean only a theory that moral justification of actions must be in terms of results. We can be content to say that duty is mainly concerned with the avoidance of intolerable results, while other forms of moral behavior have more positive aims.

To summarize, I have suggested that the trichotomy of duties, indifferent actions, and wrongdoing is inadequate. There are many kinds of action that involve going beyond duty proper, saintly and heroic actions being conspicuous examples of such kinds of action. It has been my main concern to note this point and to ask moral philosophers to theorize in a way that does not tacitly deny it, as most traditional theories have. But I have also been so rash as to suggest that we may look upon our duties as basic requirements to be universally demanded as providing the only tolerable basis of social life. The higher flights of morality can then be regarded as more positive contributions that go beyond what is universally to be exacted; but while not exacted publicly they are clearly equally pressing *in foro interno* on those who are not content merely to avoid the intolerable. Whether this should be called a version of utilitarianism, as I suggest, is a matter of small moment.

BRIAN MEDLIN

Ultimate Principles and Ethical Egoism*

I believe that it is now pretty generally accepted by professional philosophers that ultimate ethical principles must be arbitrary. One cannot derive conclusions about what should be merely from accounts of what is the case; one cannot decide how people ought to behave merely from one's knowledge of how they do behave. To arrive at a conclusion in ethics one must have at least one ethical premiss. This premiss, if it be in turn a conclusion, must be the conclusion of an argument containing at least one ethical premiss. And so we can go back, indefinitely but not for ever. Sooner or later, we must come to at least one ethical premiss which is not deduced but baldly asserted. Here we must be a-rational; neither rational nor irrational, for here there is no room for reason even to go wrong.

But the triumph of Hume in ethics has been a limited one. What appears quite natural to a handful of specialists appears quite monstrous to the majority of decent intelligent men. At any rate, it has been my experience that people who are normally rational resist the above account of the logic of moral language, not by argument—for that can't be done—but by tooth and nail. And they resist from the best motives. They see the philosopher wantonly unravelling the whole fabric of morality. If our ultimate principles are arbitrary, they say, if those principles came out of

thin air, then anyone can hold any principle he pleases. Unless moral assertions are statements of fact about the world and either true or false, we can't claim that any man is wrong, whatever his principles may be, whatever his behaviour. We have to surrender the luxury of calling one another scoundrels. That this anxiety flourishes because its roots are in confusion is evident when we consider that we don't call people scoundrels, anyhow, for being mistaken about their facts. Fools, perhaps, but that's another matter. Nevertheless, it doesn't become us to be high-up. The layman's uneasiness, however irrational it may be, is very natural and he must be reassured.

People cling to objectivist theories of morality from oral motives. It's a very queer thing that by doing so they often thwart their own purposes. There are evil opinions abroad, as anyone who walks abroad knows. The one we meet with most often, whether in pub or parlour, is the doctrine that everyone should look after himself. However refreshing he may find it after the high-minded pomposities of this morning's editorial, the good fellow knows this doctrine is wrong and he wants to knock it down. But while he believes that moral language is used to make statements either true or false, the best he can do is to claim that what the egoist says is false. Unfortunately, the egoist can claim that it's true. And since the supposed fact in question between them is not a publicly ascertainable one, their disagreement can never be resolved. And it is here that even good

*Brian Medlin, "Ultimate Principles and Ethical Egoism," *Australasian Journal of Philosophy*, 35 (1957), 111–118. Reprinted by permission of the author and the editor of the *Australasian Journal of Philosophy*.

fellows waver, when they find they have no refutation available. The egoist's word seems as reliable as their own. Some begin half to believe that perhaps it is possible to supply an egoistic basis for conventional morality, some that it may be impossible to supply any other basis. I'm not going to try to prop up our conventional morality, which I fear to be a task beyond my strength, but in what follows I do want to refute the doctrine of ethical egoism. I want to resolve this disagreement by showing that what the egoist says is inconsistent. It is true that there are moral disagreements which can never be resolved, but this isn't one of them. The proper objection to the man who says 'Everyone should look after his own interests regardless of the interests of others' is not that he isn't speaking the truth, but simply that he isn't speaking.

We should first make two distinctions. This done, ethical egoism will lose much of its plausibility.

UNIVERSAL AND INDIVIDUAL EGOISM

Universal egoism maintains that everyone (including the speaker) ought to look after his own interests and to disregard those of other people except in so far as their interests contribute towards his own.

Individual egoism is the attitude that the egoist is going to look after himself and no one else. The egoist cannot promulgate that he is going to look after himself. He can't even preach that he *should* look after himself and preach this alone. When he tries to convince me that he should look after himself, he is attempting so to dispose me that I shall approve when he drinks my beer and steals Tom's wife. I cannot approve of his looking after himself and himself alone without so far approving of his achieving his happiness, regardless of the happiness of myself and others. So that when he sets out to persuade me that he should look after himself regardless of others, he must also set out to persuade me that I should look after him regardless of myself and others. Very small chance he has! And if the individual egoist cannot promulgate his doctrine without enlarging it, what he has is no doctrine at all.

A person enjoying such an attitude may believe that other people are fools not to look after themselves. Yet he himself would be a fool to tell them

so. If he did tell them, though, he wouldn't consider that he was giving them *moral* advice. Persuasion to the effect that one should ignore the claims of morality because morality doesn't pay, to the effect that one has insufficient selfish motive and, therefore, insufficient motive for moral behaviour is not moral persuasion. For this reason I doubt that we should call the individual egoist's attitude an ethical one. And I don't doubt this in the way someone may doubt whether to call the ethical standards of Satan "ethical" standards. A malign morality is none the less a morality for being malign. But the attitude we're considering is one of mere contempt for all moral considerations whatsoever. An indifference to morals may be wicked, but it is not a perverse morality. So far as I am aware, most egoists imagine that they are putting forward a doctrine in ethics, though there may be a few who are prepared to proclaim themselves individual egoists. If the good fellow wants to know how he should justify conventional morality to an individual egoist, the answer is that he shouldn't and can't. Buy your car elsewhere, blackguard him whenever you meet, and let it go at that.

CATEGORICAL AND HYPOTHETICAL EGOISM

Categorical egoism is the doctrine that we all ought to observe our own interests, *because that is what we ought to do.* For the categorical egoist the egoistic dogma is the ultimate principle in ethics.

The hypothetical egoist, on the other hand, maintains that we all ought to observe our own interests, because . . . if we want such and such an end, we must do so and so (look after ourselves). The hypothetical egoist is not a real egoist at all. He is very likely an unwitting utilitarian who believes mistakenly that the general happiness will be increased if each man looks wisely to his own. Of course, a man may believe that egoism is enjoined on us by God and he may therefore promulgate the doctrine and observe it in his conduct, not in the hope of achieving thereby a remote end, but simply in order to obey God. But neither is *he* a real egoist. He believes, ultimately, that we should obey God, even should God command us to altruism.

An ethical egoist will have to maintain the doctrine in both its universal and categorical forms.

Should he retreat to hypothetical egoism he is no longer an egoist. Should he retreat to individual egoism his doctrine, while logically impregnable, is no longer ethical, no longer even a doctrine. He may wish to quarrel with this and if so, I submit peacefully. Let him call himself what he will, it makes no difference. I'm a philosopher, not a ratcatcher, and I don't see it as my job to dig vermin out of such burrows as individual egoism.

Obviously something strange goes on as soon as the ethical egoist tries to promulgate his doctrine. What is he doing when he urges upon his audience that they should each observe his own interests and those interests alone? Is he not acting contrary to the egoistic principle? It cannot be to his advantage to convince them, for seizing always their own advantage they will impair his. Surely if he does believe what he says, he should try to persuade them otherwise. Not perhaps that they should devote themselves to his interests, for they'd hardly swallow that; but that everyone should devote himself to the service of others. But is not to believe that someone should act in a certain way to try to persuade him to do so? Of course, we don't always try to persuade people to act as we think they should act. We may be lazy, for instance. But in so far as we believe that Tom should do so and so, we have a tendency to induce him to do so and so. Does it make sense to say: "Of course you should do this, but for goodness' sake don't"? Only where we mean: "You should do this for certain reasons, but here are even more persuasive reasons for not doing it." If the egoist believes ultimately that others should mind themselves alone, then, he must persuade them accordingly. If he doesn't persuade them, he is no universal egoist. It certainly makes sense to say: "I know very well that Tom should act in such and such a way. But I know also that it's not to my advantage that he should so act. So I'd better dissuade him from it." And this is just what the egoist must say, if he is to consider his own advantage and disregard everyone else's. That is, he must behave as an individual egoist, if he is to be an egoist at all.

He may want to make two kinds of objection here:

1. That it will not be to his disadvantage to promulgate the doctrine, provided that his audience fully understand what is to their ultimate advantage. This objection can be developed in a number of ways, but I think that it will always be possible to push the egoist into either individual or hypothetical egoism.

2. That it is to the egoist's advantage to preach the doctrine if the pleasure he gets out of doing this more than pays for the injuries he must endure at the hands of his converts. It is hard to believe that many people would be satisfied with a doctrine which they could only consistently promulgate in very special circumstances. Besides, this looks suspiciously like individual egoism in disguise.

I shall say no more on these two points because I want to advance a further criticism which seems to me at once fatal and irrefutable.

Now it is time to show the anxious layman that we have means of dealing with ethical egoism which are denied him; and denied him by just that objectivism which he thinks essential to morality. For the very fact that our ultimate principles must be arbitrary means they can't be anything we please. Just because they come out of thin air they can't come out of hot air. Because these principles are not propositions about matters of fact and cannot be deduced from propositions about matters of fact, they must be the fruit of our own attitudes. We assert them largely to modify the attitudes of our fellows but by asserting them we express our own desires and purposes. This means that we cannot use moral language cavalierly. Evidently, we cannot say something like 'All human desires and purposes are bad.' This would be to express our own desires and purposes, thereby committing a kind of absurdity. Nor, I shall argue, can we say 'Everyone should observe his own interests regardless of the interests of others.'

Remembering that the principle is meant to be both universal and categorical, let us ask what kind of attitude the egoist is expressing. Wouldn't that attitude be equally well expressed by the conjunction of an infinite number of avowals thus?—

I want myself to come out on top and	&	I don't care about Tom, Dick, Harry . . . and
I want Tom to come out on top and	&	I don't care about myself, Dick, Harry . . . and
I want Dick to come out on top	&	I don't care about myself, Tom, Harry . . .

I want Harry to come out on top etc.	&	I don't care about myself, Dick, Tom ... etc.

From this analysis it is obvious that the principle expressing such an attitude must be inconsistent.

But now the egoist may claim that he hasn't been properly understood. When he says 'Everyone should look after himself and himself alone,' he means 'Let each man do what he wants regardless of what anyone else wants.' The egoist may claim that what he values is merely that he and Tom and Dick and Harry should each do what he wants and not care about what anyone else may want and that this doesn't involve his principle in any inconsistency. Nor need it. But even if it doesn't, he's no better off. Just what does he value? Is it the well-being of himself, Tom, Dick and Harry or merely their going on in a certain way regardless of whether or not this is going to promote their well-being? When he urges Tom, say, to do what he wants, is he appealing to Tom's self-interest? If so, his attitude can be expressed thus:

I want myself to be happy and I want Tom to be happy	&	I want myself not to care about Tom, Dick, Harry ...

We need go no further to see that the principle expressing such an attitude must be inconsistent. I have made this kind of move already. What concerns me now is the alternative position the egoist must take up to be safe from it. If the egoist values merely that people should go on in a certain way, regardless of whether or not this is going to promote their well-being, then he is not appealing to the self-interest of his audience when he urges them to regard their own interests. If Tom has any regard for himself at all, the egoist's blandishments will leave him cold. Further, the egoist doesn't even have his own interest in mind when he says that, like everyone else, he should look after himself. A funny kind of egoism this turns out to be.

Perhaps now, claiming that he is indeed appealing to the self-interest of his audience, the egoist may attempt to counter the objection of the previous paragraph. He may move into 'Let each man do what he wants and let each man disregard what others want when their desires clash with his own.' Now his attitude may be expressed thus:

I want everyone to be happy	&	I want everyone to disregard the happiness of others when their happiness clashes with his own.

The egoist may claim justly that a man can have such an attitude and also that in a certain kind of world such a man could get what he wanted. Our objection to the egoist has been that his desires are incompatible. And this is still so. If he and Tom and Dick and Harry did go on as he recommends by saying 'Let each man disregard the happiness of others, when their happiness conflicts with his own,' then assuredly they'd all be completely miserable. Yet he wants them to be happy. He is attempting to counter this by saying that it is merely a fact about the world that they'd make one another miserable by going on as he recommends. The world could conceivably have been different. For this reason, he says, this principle is not inconsistent. This argument may not seem very compelling, but I advance it on the egoist's behalf because I'm interested in the reply to it. For now we don't even need to tell him that the world isn't in fact like that. (What it's like makes no difference.) Now we can point out to him that he is arguing not as an egoist but as a utilitarian. He has slipped into hypothetical egoism to save his principle from inconsistency. If the world were such that we always made ourselves and others happy by doing one another down, then we could find good utilitarian reasons for urging that we should do one another down.

If, then, he is to save his principle, the egoist must do one of two things. He must give up the claim that he is appealing to the self-interest of his audience, that he has even his own interest in mind. Or he must admit that, in the conjunction [above], although 'I want everyone to be happy' refers to ends, nevertheless 'I want everyone to disregard the happiness of others when their happiness conflicts with his own' can refer only to means. That is, his so-called ultimate principle is really compounded of a principle and a moral rule subordinate to that principle. That is, he is really a utilitarian who is urging everyone to go on in a certain way so that everyone may be happy. A utilitarian, what's more, who is ludicrously mistaken about the nature of the world. Things being as they are, his moral rule is a very bad one. Things being as they are, it can only be deduced from his principle by means of an empirical premiss which is manifestly false. Good fellows don't need to fear him. They may rest easy that the world is and must be on their side and the best thing they can do is to be good.

It may be worth pointing out that objections similar to those I have brought against the egoist can be made to the altruist. The man who holds that the principle 'Let everyone observe the interests of others' is both universal and categorical can be compelled to choose between two alternatives, equally repugnant. He must give up the claim that he is concerned for the well-being of himself and others. Or he must admit that, though 'I want everyone to be happy' refers to ends, nevertheless 'I want everyone to disregard his own happiness when it conflicts with the happiness of others' can refer only to means.

I have said from time to time that the egoistic principle is inconsistent. I have not said it is contradictory. This for the reason that we can, without contradiction, express inconsistent desires and purposes. To do so is not to say anything like 'Goliath was ten feet tall and not ten feet tall.' Don't we all want to eat our cake and have it too? And when we say we do we aren't asserting a contradiction. We are not asserting a contradiction whether we be making an avowal of our attitudes or stating a fact about them. We all have conflicting motives. As a utilitarian exuding benevolence I want the man who mows my landlord's grass to be happy, but as a slug-a-bed I should like to see him scourged. None of this, however, can do the egoist any good. For we assert our ultimate principles not only to express our own attitudes but also to induce similar attitudes in others, to dispose them to conduct themselves as we wish. In so far as their desires conflict, people don't know what to do. And, therefore, no expression of incompatible desires can ever serve for an ultimate principle of human conduct.

W.   D.   F A L K

Morality, Self, and Others*

1

In: And how can you say that I never had a moral education? As a child, I was taught that one ought not to maltreat other children, ought to share one's sweets with them, ought to keep tidy and clean; as an adolescent, that one ought to keep one's word, to work, to save, to leave off drink, not to waste the best of years of one's life, to let reason govern one's emotions and actions. Nor did I simply learn that one is *called upon* to

act in these ways by paternal authority and social custom on pain of censure. I learned to appreciate that one *ought* to do these things *on their merits,* and that what one ought to do on its merits does not depend on the request or enjoinders of anyone. The facts in the case themselves make one liable, as a reflective person, to act in these ways of one's own accord: they provide one with choice-supporting reasons sufficient to determine one if one knows them and takes diligent account of them.

Out: I know you were taught all this. But why did your teacher say that you ought to act in these ways?

*Reprinted from *Morality and the Language of Conduct,* ed. Hector-Neri Castañeda and George Nakhnikian, pp. 25–47, by permission of The Wayne State University Press. Copyright © 1963, The Wayne State University Press. Parts 4, 5, and 6 are here omitted.

In: Why? For very cogent reasons. My tutor was a student of the Ancients. The moral man, "the man of practical wisdom," he kept quoting Aristotle, "is the man who knows how to deliberate well about what is good and useful for himself." And surely, he would say, you can see for yourself: if you don't act sociably, who will act sociably towards you? Uncleanliness breeds disease. Without work, how are you to live? Without savings, what about your future? Drink leaves one a wreck. Indulging one's sorrows makes them worse. The wasted years, one day you will regret them when it is too late. People who cannot govern themselves are helpless before fortune, without the aid and comfort of inner strength.

Out: And so you think that you had a moral education? Let me tell you, you never even made a start. For what were you taught? That there are things that you ought to do or to avoid on your own account. But one does not learn about morality that way. What one *morally* ought to do is what one ought to do on account of others, or for the sake of some good state of things in general. Now had you been taught to appreciate that you ought to keep clean so as to be pleasing to others, and that you ought to do what moral custom requires for the sake of the general good, then, and then only, would you have learned the rudiments of moral duty.

In: Very well, my upbringing was too narrow. One would hardly be a human being if the good of others, or of society at large, could not weigh with one as a cogent reason for doing what will promote it. So one has not fully learned about living like a rational and moral being unless one has learned to appreciate that one ought to do things out of regard for others, and not only out of regard for oneself.

Out: No, you have still not got my point. I am saying that only insofar as you ought to do things —no matter whether for yourself or for others— for the sake of others, is the reason a moral reason and the ought a moral ought. Reasons of self-regard are not moral reasons at all, and you can forget about them in the reckoning of your *moral* obligations.

In: But this seems artificial. A moral education surely should teach one all about the principles of orderly living and the reasons which tell in their favor. And if there are also perfectly good personal reasons which tell in their favor, why suppress them? To be sure, in talking to people in ordinary life, we do no such thing. If they say "Why ought I to act sociably?" we say "For the general good as well as your own." If they say "Why ought I to be provident?" we say "For your own good as well as that of others." In short, we offer mixed reasons, and none of these reasons can be spared. One ought not to lie because this is a good social rule, and equally because the habit of evasiveness is destructive of oneself as a person. And one ought not to take a drink or indulge one's sorrows, or waste the best years of one's life primarily out of proper regard for oneself, much as there may be other-regarding reasons as well. If morality were all social service, and one had no moral responsibilities towards oneself or towards others, the moral inconveniences of life would be far less than they are. So I don't see the point of saying "But one has no *moral* commitment to do anything except insofar as one ought to do it on account of others." To say this seems like encouraging people not to bother about doing things insofar as they ought to do them only for personal reasons, as after all this is not a moral ought.

Out: But one does not speak of a moral duty to do things for one's own sake. If one ought to save in order to provide for one's own future, one regards this as a precept not of morals but of prudence. It would be different if one ought to save in order to provide for one's dependents. Moral commitments are those which one has as a moral being, and what makes one a moral being is that one has commitments towards others and does not evade them.

In: Not everyone will agree that as a moral being one has only commitments towards others or that only such commitments are properly "moral." The Greeks, for example, took a wider view. For Plato the equivalent of a moral being was the just or right-living person, and of a moral commitment the right and just course—the one which the right-living person would be led to take. And this right-living person was one who would keep himself in good shape as a sane and self-possessed being, and who would do whatever good and sufficient reasons directed him to do. This is why for Plato and the Greeks temperance and prudence were no less among the just man's commitments than paying his debts and not willfully harming others, and why the one was not treated any less as a moral commitment than the other. The Greeks placed the essence of man as a moral being in his capacity to direct himself on rational grounds; and his commitments as a moral being were therefore all those which he seriously incurred as a properly self-directing being.

Out: Citing the Greeks only shows how distant their concept of morality is from ours. We will not call every rational commitment "moral" or equate the moral with the rational man.

In: This is broadly so, although not entirely. Our concept of morality vacillates between the Greek and the Christian tradition. We associate "moral" with "social" commitment, and the "morally good man" with the "selfless man." But we also speak of man as a "moral agent," of his "moral freedom" and "moral powers"; and here we refer to his whole capacity of self-direction by good and sufficient reasons. One may speak without strain of a personal and social ethic, and refer to the negligent disregard of oneself as a vice, and a sign of moral defect. We call the improvident man "morally weak," and we call the man who can resist drink in company on account of his health or who sticks to his vocation in adversity a man of "moral strength and character." There is certainly little difference in the qualities needed to live up to a social or a personal ought. It takes self-denial to provide for one's future, moral courage to stick to one's vocation. One may show one's mettle as a moral agent here no less than in selfless care for others. There are contemporary moralists who call "moral" any "authentic" commitment of a self-governing person, whether its grounds are social or personal. What justifies them is the broader use of the term which is also part of our language and tradition.

Out: And how eccentric this use is. Our very concept of a moral being is inseparable from the notion of submission of self to a good other than one's own. It is not conceivable that a man should have moral duties on a desert island, devoid of man or beast. Would one say that he still had a moral duty to do what was good for him? You may as well go on and say that if a shipwrecked fellow arrived to share his vegetables, it might be his moral duty to let him starve rather than starve himself.

In: The good of others need not always have the overriding claim on one, if this is what you mean. One could say to a good-hearted and weak-willed person, "For your own sake, you ought to stop neglecting your future, even if this hurts others." This would not be a typically "moral" ought, but one may be giving sound moral advice.

Out: And so, if beneficence had the better of this person, you should call him morally irresponsible and blameworthy. On your showing, he has evaded a moral commitment, and for such evasions one is held morally responsible and liable to censure. But surely, even if I granted your case, one would not call him blameworthy and a morally bad man; as indeed in any case where a person fails to do what his own good requires we do not call him morally bad, but only imprudent, unwise, rash. It is quite a different offense to be slack about brushing one's teeth, than to be negligent about providing dentures for others. And this is so precisely because the second is a moral offense and the first is not and because one is blameworthy for the one and not for the other.

In: I agree that there is a difference. One is only called morally bad and is held answerable to *others* for neglecting what one ought to do out of regard for them. And this is understandable enough. After all, insofar as one fails to do only what one's own good requires, the failing is no one's concern but one's own. But then I should not say that such self-neglect was in no sense morally irresponsible and blameworthy. If it does not call for blame by others, it still calls for self-reproach. A rational person is responsible to himself for not being evasive about anything that he is convinced that he really ought to do. And the lack of moral strength and courage in personal matters, although commonly viewed as an amicable vice, is an amicable vice only in the estimation of others since it is not directly a threat to them.

However, we are not making headway. You find it repugnant to call a commitment "moral" unless its grounds are social and unless its non-observance makes one liable not only to social censure but also to self-reproach; and so be it. Perhaps our disagreement is only verbal, and despite some misgivings, I am ready to settle for your usage. Let us only speak of a moral ought where one ought to do things on account of others. But let us not be misled. For it still does not follow that if one ought to do things on one's own account, this ought may not still be otherwise functioning *like* a moral ought.

Out: How could it be like a moral ought if it is not a moral ought?

In: Because when one thinks of a moral ought, one thinks not only that its grounds are social but also that it has a special force and cogency. A moral ought commits one in all seriousness and in every way, without leaving any reasonable option to act otherwise. Your view comes to saying that if an ought is to be moral it must satisfy two conditions: it must seriously bind one in every way, and it must do so for other-regarding reasons. On your showing, a personal ought cannot be moral, as it cannot satisfy one of these conditions simply by having personal grounds. But it may still satisfy the other condition, and be as cogently binding and action-guiding in its force and function as a moral ought. This is why I can only accept your usage with one proviso: that one may also say that there are other than strictly moral commitments which a right-living person may have to reckon with no less than his strictly moral ones.

Out: Surely you don't expect me to fall for this. When I say "Don't count the purely personal ought as moral" I am not saying "Count it as well, but call it by another name." My point is precisely that it does not function like a moral ought at all. Personal reasons do not commit one to do anything with the same cogency as social reasons. In fact, in calling them reasons of prudence or expediency, we deprecate them. We regard them as inferior, and often disreputable, guides to action. So I won't let you reduce my position to triviality. That only the social commitments are essentially moral must be taken as implying that only they have the characteristic moral force.

In: I thought that this was at the back of our discussion all along. It usually is so with people who are so insistent on your usage, although part of the trouble is that one can never be sure. First one is told that a moral ought is one that commits one on other-regarding grounds and that a personal ought is not a moral ought *for this reason.* But then comes the further suggestion that it is not only different from a moral ought in this way, but is also otherwise inferior. It gives directives, but directives of a somehow shady kind. One way or other, the idea is that a commitment that has personal grounds is either not properly a commitment at all, or, if one in any way, then one that

belongs in some limbo of disrepute. But your argument so far has done nothing to prove this point. From your language rule, it only follows that the personal ought must be unlike a moral ought in one essential respect, but not, except by way of confusion, that it must be therefore also unlike a moral ought in other respects too. You might as well say "Surely a lay-analyst is not a doctor," as one is not a doctor without a medical degree, and take this to be proof that a lay-analyst cannot otherwise cure like a doctor either. "No lay-analyst is a doctor" is strictly and trivially true in one way, and may be misleading and tendentiously false in another. And the same with "No personal ought is a *moral* ought." Your language rule makes this strictly and trivially true; but it does not go to show that a personal ought cannot otherwise be *like* a moral ought by being seriously committing or by taking precedence in a conscientious calculus of action-guiding considerations. My point is that, even if this were so, your appeal to usage cannot settle this matter. Logical grammar can decree that only social reasons are properly called "moral." But it cannot decide what reasons can, or cannot, be seriously committing for human beings.

Out: But what I am saying seems substantially true. What one ought to do on account of others is the prototype of the categorically binding ought. Personal reasons have not got the binding cogency of other-regarding reasons, and one deprecates them as inferior and disreputable.

In: And there is some truth in this. Personal and social reasons are not on the same footing in the economy of action-guiding considerations. Personal reasons are very commonly less thoroughly committing, they are often inferior reasons, and not rarely discreditable. But why this is so is a different matter and has not yet been touched on in any way. What is more, personal reasons need not always be in this inferior position. They are often not intrinsically discreditable, and become inferior guides to action only where there are other reasons in the case deserving of prior considerations. Take someone concerned for his health, or future, or self-respect. Surely these are respectable aspirations and there may be things which he ought to do on account of them without violating other claims. His health requires that he be temperate, his self-respect that he live without evasion. Would it not then be positively remiss of him not to act in these ways? If he did not, one would say that he had failed to do what a man in his position really ought to have done, and precisely for the reason which he had. And, if one can say this, what remains of the blemish?

This is why it remains perplexing to me why commitments on personal grounds should be excluded from the orbit of moral teaching, and why modern moralists, unlike the Ancients, should disdain to mention them as an integral part of the moral life. For they may also be cogent and sometimes overridingly cogent commitments to action. And if they are not the whole of morals, why not count them as part of them? For it also seems natural to say that to teach someone all about morality is to teach him about all the valid directives for action; about all those things which he might not otherwise do readily but which, for good and compelling reasons in the nature in the case, he ought to do and would have to break himself into doing whether for the sake of others or his own.

There is, I agree, one tendency to say that the moral man acts in accordance with precepts of selflessness. But there is also another tendency to say that he is the man to organize his life in accordance with all valid precepts. Our disagreement has exhibited the kind of shuttle-service between rival considerations better known as the dialectic of a problem. It may be that this shuttle-service is maintained by a cleft in the very concept of morality. This concept may have grown from conflicting or only partially overlapping observations, which are not fully reconciled in ordinary thinking.

Out: If this is so, I would have to be shown, for common sense still seems to me right in its disparagement of personal reasons.

In: Very well, then we shall have to consider why personal reasons should function as a less cogent guide to action than social ones. I shall admit that in more ways than one the personal ought presents a special case, but not that it presents a case for disparagement except in special contexts. After this, the question of whether the personal ought is properly called moral or not will appear less important, partly because it will have become plainer why there is a question. Nor shall I try to offer a ruling on this point. With a background of discourse as intricate and full of

nuance as in this case, discretion is the better part of valor, and clarification is a safer bet than decision.

2

Whenever one remarks that clearly there are things which one ought to avoid or do if only for one's own sake, someone is sure to say, "No doubt; but any such ought is only a precept of prudence or expediency." It is a textbook cliché against Hobbes that his account of morality comes to just this. And this is said as if it were an obvious truth and enough to discredit all such precepts in one go. This assumes a great deal and settles nothing.

What it assumes is this: that everything that one ever does for one's own sake, one does as a matter of prudence *or* expediency; that there is no difference between these two; that morality always differs from prudence as a scent differs from a bad smell; and that everyone knows how so and why.

None of this will do.

In the first place, not everything done for oneself is done for reasons of prudence. That one ought to insure one's house, save for one's old age, not put all one's money into one venture, are precepts of prudence. But it is not a precept of prudence, though it may be a good precept, that someone ought to undergo a dangerous operation as a long shot to restoring his health rather than linger under a disability forever after.

The point is that prudence is only one way of looking after oneself. To act prudently is to play safe, for near-certain gains at small risks. But some good things one cannot get in this way. To get them at all one has to gamble, taking the risk of not getting them even so, or of coming to harm in the process. If one values them enough, one will do better by oneself to throw prudence to the winds, to play for high stakes, knowing full well the risk and the price of failure. Explorers, artists, scientists, mountaineers are types who may serve themselves better by this course. So will most people at some juncture. Thus, if someone values security, then that he ought to save in order to be secure is a precept of prudence. But that someone ought to stick to his vocation when his heart is in it enough to make it worth risking security or health or life itself is not a precept of *prudence*, but of *courage*.

One says sometimes, "I ought to save, as I *want* to be prudent," but sometimes "as I *ought* to be prudent." One may also decide that in one's own best interests one ought to be prudent rather than daring, or daring rather than prudent, as the case may be. Now, that one ought to do something as it would be prudent is a dictate of prudence. But that one really ought to be prudent, in one's own best interests, would not be a dictate of prudence again. One then ought to play safe in order to serve oneself *best* and not in order to serve oneself *safely.*

A dictate of prudence where one wants to be prudent but ought to be courageous in one's own best interests is a dictate of timidity. A dictate of courage, where one feels reckless but ought to be prudent, is a dictate of foolhardiness. Both will then plainly be morally imperfect precepts. But there is nothing obviously imperfect about a dictate of prudence where one ought to be prudent, or a dictate of courage where one ought to be daring. Such precepts seem near-moral enough to allow one to call the habit of acting on them a virtue. The Ancients considered both prudence and courage as moral virtues. Oddly enough, in our time, one is more ready to view courage on one's own behalf as a moral virtue than prudence. It needs the reminder that precepts of self-protection may be precepts of courage as well as of prudence for one to see that any precept of self-protection may have a moral flavor. I think that the dim view which we take of prudence corresponds to a belief that to be daring is harder than to be level-headed, a belief most likely justified within our own insurance-minded culture. But such belief would have seemed strange to Bishop Butler and the fashionable eighteenth-century gentlemen to whom he addressed himself. Prudence in Butler's time, as throughout the ancient world, was not yet the cheap commodity which it is with us; and the price of virtue varies with the market.

There are other precepts of self-protection which are not "just a matter of prudence" either. That one ought not to take to drugs or drink, indulge oneself in one's sorrows, waste one's talents, commit suicide just in the despair of the moment, are precepts made of sterner stuff. One wants to say, "Surely, it is more than just a matter of prudence that one ought to avoid these things." And rightly so. The effect on oneself of taking to drugs or drink, or of any of the others, is not conjectural, but quite certain. To avoid them is therefore more than a matter of *taking no risks.* Sometimes, when one looks down a precipice, one feels drawn to jump. If one refrains, it will hardly be said of one, "How prudent he is, he takes no chances." The avoidance of excesses of all kinds in one's own best interests is in this class. The habit of avoiding them the Greeks called temperance, a virtue distinct from prudence.

Another error is to equate the prudent with the expedient, and, again, the expedient with everything that is for one's own good. To save may be prudent; but whether it is expedient or convenient to start now is another matter. With a lot of money to spare at the moment it will be expedient; otherwise it will not. But it may be prudent all the same. Again, one marries in the hope of finding happiness; but marriage in this hope is not a marriage of convenience. The point is that reasons of expediency are reasons of a special sort: reasons for doing something on the ground that it is incidentally at hand to serve one's purpose, or because it serves a purpose quite incidental to the purpose for which one would normally be doing this thing. One marries for reasons of expediency when one marries for money, but not when in hope of finding happiness. Hobbes said that "men never act except with a view to some good to themselves." This would be quite different from saying that "they never act except with a view to what is expedient."

There is also this difference between the prudent and the expedient: one can speak of "rules of prudence," but less well of "rules of expediency." The expedient is what happens to serve. It is not therefore easily bottled in rules.

The word "prudence" is used too freely in still one more context. When one wishes to justify the social virtues to people, a traditional and inviting move is to refer them, among other things at least, to their own good. "You ought to hold the peace, be honest, share with others." "Why?" "Because an order in which such practices were universal is of vital concern to you; and your one hope of helping to make such an order is in doing your share." The classical formulation of this standard move is Hooker's, quoted with approval by Locke: "If I cannot but wish to receive good ... how should I look to have any part of my desire herein satisfied, unless I myself be careful to satisfy the like desire: my desire therefore to be loved of my equals in nature, as much as possible may be, imposes upon me a *natural duty* of bearing to themward fully the like affection."

Now, it is said again, "So defended, the social duties come to no more than precepts of prudence"; and this goes with the veiled suggestion that it is morally improper to use this defense. But, even if so defended, the social duties are not necessarily reduced purely to precepts of prudence. For they may be recommended in this way either as mere *rules* or as *principles* of self-protection; and as principles they would be misdescribed as mere precepts of prudence. The distinction is this: When one says, "People ought to practice the social virtues, if only for their own benefit," one may be saying, "They ought to practice them for this reason as a *rule,* i.e., normally, as much as each time this is likely to be for their own good." Or one may be saying, "They ought to practice them for this reason not merely as a rule but as a *matter of principle,* i.e., every time, whether at that time this is likely to be for their good or not." And one might defend the adoption of this principle by saying, "Because your best, even if slim, hope of contributing to a society fit for you to live in lies in adding to the number of principled people who will do their share each time, without special regard for their good at that time."

Now this seems to me a precept of courage rather than one of prudence. The game of attempting by one's actions to make society a place fit for one to live in is a gamble worth the risk only because of the known price of not attempting it. This gamble is a root condition of social living. One is sure to give hostages to fortune, but again, what other hope has one got? Hence, if a man practiced the social virtues, thinking that he ought to as a matter of principle, and on these grounds, one will praise him for his *wisdom,* his firm grasp of vital issues, his steadfastness, his courage. But one will not necessarily congratulate him on his prudence. For many times the prudent course might have been otherwise. It may be wise to persist in being honest with cheats, or forbearing with the aggressive, or helpful to those slow to require helpfulness; but it might have been more prudent to persist for no longer than there was requital, or not even to start before requital was assured.

Now would it be a moral precept or not that, if only out of proper care for oneself, one ought to act on principles of wisdom and courage? That one ought to risk life in order to gain it? And, assuming a society of men acting fixedly on these principles but no others, would it or would it not contain men of moral virtue? One might as well ask, "Is a ski an article of footwear?" There is no more of a straight answer here than there. One may say, "Not quite"; and the point of saying this needs going into. But it would be more misleading to say, "Not at all." For it is part of the meaning of "moral precept" that it prescribes what a man would do in his wisdom—if he were to consider things widely, looking past the immediate concerns of self and giving essentials due weight before incidentals. As it is also part of what is meant by one's moral capacities that one can live by such considerations, it becomes fruitless after a time to press the point whether such precepts are properly called moral.

There are then varieties of the personal ought, differing in the considerations on which they are based and the qualities needed to follow them; and they all seem at least akin to a "moral" ought in their action-guiding force and function. But I grant that one does not want to speak of more than a kinship, and the point of this needs considering. One's hesitancy derives from various sources which have to be traced one by one.

Some of the hesitancy comes from contexts where one can say disparagingly, "He did this *only* for reasons of prudence, *only* for reasons of expediency, *only* for himself." This plainly applies sometimes, but it does not apply always. One would hardly say of someone without dependents, "He thought that he ought to save, but *only* for reasons of prudence"; or of someone, "He thought that he ought to have the carpenter in along with the plumber, but *only* for reasons of expediency or convenience"; or "He thought that he ought to become a doctor, but *only* because the career would suit him." "Only" has no point here. Why else should a man without dependents save, except to be prudent? Why else should anyone have the carpenter in along with the plumber, except for convenience? What better reason is there normally for choosing a career than that it will suit one? On the other hand, there is point in saying, "He held the peace only because it was prudent," "He saved only because it was convenient," "He practices the social virtues only for self-protection." It is plain why "only" applies here and is disparaging. One says "only" because something is done for the wrong or for not quite the right reason—done for *one* reason where there is *another* and nearer reason for doing it anyway. Personal reasons are often in this position, and then they are disparaged as inferior. One saves "only" because it is expedient, if one ought to have saved anyway for reasons of prudence. One holds the peace "only" because it was prudent when one ought to have done so anyway as a matter of principle and even if it had not been prudent. And one practices the social virtues "only" for self-protection when one does not *also* practice them for the general good.

The last case is different from the others. Plainly, one ought to practice the social virtues as principles of general good. But on none but perhaps pure Christian principles would it hold, or necessarily hold, that one ought to practice them on this ground unconditionally, however great the provocation to oneself. The case for the social virtues is weakened when the social environment becomes hostile and intractable by peaceable means; it is correspondingly strengthened where they can also be justified as wise principles of self-protection. That someone practices forbearance "only" as a wise principle of self-protection is not therefore to say that he practices it for a reason which is neither here nor there; but rather for a reason which falls short of all the reason there is. This was, in effect, the view of the Old Natural Law moralists—Hooker, Grotius, Puffendorf: the social virtues derive joint support from our natural concern for our own good and for that of society. Hobbes streamlined this account by denying the second, which provoked subsequent moralists to deny the first. Both Hobbes's sophistical toughness and the well-bred innocence of the academic moralists since are distorted visions which are less convincing than the unsqueamish common sense of the philosophers and divines of earlier times.

3

So far we have met no reason for deprecating every personal ought. Men often have cause to be temperate, courageous, wise for their own good. This is often the only, or the nearest, reason why they should. It is then pointless to go on complaining, " But they still only act so for their own sakes." "Only" is a dangerous word.

Even so one feels that somehow a commitment that has only personal grounds is morally inferior. "One ought to risk one's life in order to gain it" seems near-moral enough. But compare it with "One ought to risk one's life in order to save others." This still seems different. And this is so not only because the one has a personal reason and the other has not, but also because where the reason is social rather than personal, the ought itself feels different—more binding, more relentless, and more properly called "moral" for this reason. The real inferiority of the personal ought seems here to lie in a lack of formal stringency.

There are such differences of stringency between "I ought to save, as I *want* to provide for my future" and "I ought to save, as I *ought* to provide for my children." The first prescribes saving as a means to an end which one *is* seeking; the second as a means to an end which in turn one *ought* to seek. The first therefore commits one formally less than the second. It leaves one at liberty to escape the commitment by renouncing the ultimate end, which the second does not. One may, as Kant did, call the first ought hypothetical and non-moral, and the second categorical and moral on account of this difference. The distinction is made to rest on a formal difference of the binding force and not at all on any material difference in the justifying grounds. The formally "moral" commitment is to an ultimate end or rule of life and to what one ought to do on account of it in any particular case.

Now the personal ought comes more typically as non-moral and the social ought as moral in form. One says, "You don't *want* to make your misery worse, so you ought not to dwell on it"; "You *want* to secure your future, so you ought to be prudent and save." One might also say "You *want* to provide for your children, so you ought to save"; and then formally this too would be a non-moral ought although its grounds are other-regarding. But this is the less typical case. One is often more grudging about the needs of others than one's own. So there is here less occasion for saying, "You ought to do this on account of an end which you *are* seeking"; and more for saying, "You ought to do it on account of an end which in turn you *ought* to seek."

This typical difference between the personal and the social ought raises two questions: one, whether it is an inherent feature of the personal ought to be never more than non-moral in form; the other, whether, even if this were so, it would be any the worse as a possibly serious commitment. Both of these positions have been taken. One's own good one always seeks. It is not therefore among the ends which one ever ought to seek in the absence of a sufficient inclination. But with the good of others, or the avoidance of harm to them, it is different. Here are ends which one does not always seek, but ought to seek all the same: ends which one may still have reason for seeking on their own account; which one would be led to seek on a diligently comprehending and imaginative review of them (of what doing good, or harm, inherently amount to). Only the social ought, therefore, may bind one to the choice of the final end as well as of the means, while the personal ought binds one only to the means on account of an end which one wants already. The personal ought is therefore only non-moral in form, and "only" once again signifies a defect. But all this is misleading. One does not always seek one's own good as much as one has reasonable ground for seeking it, and about this I shall say more later. But even supposing that one did, then all precepts of self-regard would prescribe what one ought to do consistently with an already desired end. But they would not therefore be negligible or improper all the time.

It is true that what one ought to do consistently with a desired end need not be what one really ought to do at all. The end, or the means towards it, may prove undesirable on further scrutiny either by reason of what it is in itself or of the special circumstances of the case. I ought to save as I wish for security, and there is nothing inherently wrong with the end or the means, and so far so good. But I also ought to support my mother, and I cannot do both. Then maybe I ought not to do *all told* what otherwise I ought to have done. But in this case, the precept of prudence would have been less than "only" non-moral. It would have been invalid all told, and counter-moral altogether. But surely not every case is like this.

For often there is nothing wrong with the things which one cares for on one's own behalf, and one really does care for them. Even if one had the abstract option to give them up, one has no serious wish to do so. One often does care for one's life or health or career or the regard of others and one often *may* without violating other claims. And one always *may* care, if one does, for one's peace of mind or self-respect. And so what one ought to do as far as these ends go one really ought to do. As one wants to live, one really ought to look after one's health. As one wants to be liked by others, one really ought to keep a civil tongue. As one wants to live after one's own fashion, one really ought to stick to one's vocation in ‸adversity. As one wants to be able to respect oneself or, in Hume's phrase, "bear one's own survey," one really ought to conduct oneself as one thinks that one has good reasons for doing. All these precepts tell one what one ought to do consistently with a personal end which one actually has at heart; and where they hold after scrutiny, they hold no less validly and conclusively than any fully "moral" precept. The conscientious man would have to take notice of them no less than of the others. They deserve to be called "semi-moral" at least.

I keep allowing that a distinction remains. "I ought to work hard, as I *want* to succeed" is still a different kind of commitment from "I ought to work hard as I *ought* to provide for others." The difference is partly in the end, personal in the one case, impersonal in the other. But this quite apart, there is another reason for the difference. The second ought has a quality of sternness which is lacking from the first, and which is a product of its *form,* not of its *content.* For the second is an ought twice over. It says that one ought to take steps for an end which one ought to pursue ultimately. The first is an ought only once; it says that one ought to take steps for an end with regard to which one is at liberty as far as it goes. So the second ought subjects one to a regimen which is complete. It commits one *through and through,* whereas the semi-moral ought does not. And this through-and-throughness gives to the moral ought its notorious stern flavor. It makes it more imposing and often more onerous. One is having one's socks pulled up all over. And additional qualities are required of one for appreciating it and acting on it: not only forethought and consistency, but also the ability to appreciate an end as committing by reason of its own nature, which, among other things, requires sympathetic understanding and imagination. No wonder that a moral ought inspires those confronted with it with awe. The semi-moral ought cannot compete with this, though when it comes to the precepts of wisdom and courage on one's own behalf they come near enough.

However, having given the formally moral ought its due, I want to add that respect for it should be no reason for slighting the other. For in the first place, and as a reassurance to those who regard lack of onerousness as a defect, though the semi-moral ought is not so bad, it may be bad enough. How hard it is to pull up one's socks does not necessarily depend on their number; two commodious socks may respond more readily than one shrunken one. One semi-moral and one moral case may serve as examples. If one really *wants* to do a thing and do it well, one ought to take trouble. And if one really *ought* to do good to the sick, one ought to telephone and inquire how they are getting on. The first requires a lot: putting oneself into harness, forgoing all sorts of things which one would rather do, particularly at that moment, coping with aches and pains and anxieties, playing the endless game of snakes and ladders with achievement, and yet going on, nursing one's purpose. The second, though in form a commitment through and through, requires nothing but getting up and dialing a number. It may need a great deal not to put things off, not to dwell on one's miseries, not to spend improvidently, all simply because one really ought not to in one's own best interest. The ought that lays down the law on these things may be little imposing in form. But such is the bulk of the stuff which compounds the "moral" inconveniences of ordinary life. And one also measures oneself and others by the show that is made on this front.

But then it is not the lack of onerousness as much as that of formal stringency that is felt to discredit the semi-moral ought. It still is not binding like the moral ought, simply as it is not committing through and through. Moreover, its very subservience to an end which is only desired seems something amiss, as if a man should rather act always for the sake of ends which he ultimately ought to seek, and not just of ends which he happens to be seeking even if nothing is wrong with them.

This sense of guilt about the non-obligatory rests partly on excessive zeal for original sin. What the natural man in one desires never can be quite as it should. It is always "Tell me what you want to do, and I shall tell you what you ought to do instead." But there is also a failure to see that not every semi-moral commitment is renounceable at will. Not every situation need confront one with a commitment through and through, and it is improper to demand that it should or to deplore that it does not.

When one ought to do a thing on account of some desired end, then one need not always be at liberty to escape the commitment by renouncing the end. It depends on whether one is free to give up the end itself, and this is not always so. One says of some ends, "If you want to seek it you may, and if you don't want to you need not." There is here no reason against seeking the end, nor reason enough to tell one to seek it in the absence of a desire for it. And one is free to escape a commitment on account of such an end simply by giving up the end. But in the case of other ends one will say, "If you want to seek it you may, but if you do not want to you still ought to all the same." Again there is no reason against seeking the end if one wants to, but here there would be still reason for seeking it even if one did not want to. A commitment on account of such an end one may not escape at will as one is not here free to give up the end. It is arguable whether commitments on personal grounds are not often in this position. One ought to be temperate as one wants to preserve one's health. And although this is a semi-moral ought as far as it goes, one need not be free to get out of it at will. For even if one ceased to care about the end, one might still here have reasonable ground for caring, and ought to care all the same.

An ought of this kind commits one on account of an end which one seeks as well as ought to seek. And this makes it like an ought through and through, but still not quite. There can be ends which one seeks and ought to seek. But insofar as one *is* seeking such an end, it is strained to say that one also *ought* to seek it at the same time. One would rather say that if one were not seeking it already, then one ought to be seeking it all the same. This is why, if someone is perfectly willing about an end, a commitment on account of this end would still not for him have the form of a commitment through and through; and this although it is potentially such a commitment and would turn into one as soon as he ceased to be readily inclined towards the end.

The point is that ought applies only where there is a case for pulling one's socks up. The same action may be viewed in otherwise the same circumstances either as one which one ought to do, or as one which one wants to and may do, according to the psychological starting point. One normally wants to have one's breakfast, and one would find it improper to have it put before one with the remark, "You ought to eat this morning." "Why ought I? Don't I eat every morning anyway?" But if one were convalescent, the remark would be in place. Nor would one say to a notoriously indulgent parent, "You ought not to be harsh with your children" (though one might wonder whether he *may* be so indulgent). The remark applies to a parent bad at controlling his temper. If I resolved to become an early riser and succeeded, I might report in retrospect, "For the first month it was a duty, but afterwards it ceased to be a duty and became a habit, if not a pleasure."

None of this should be surprising. Ought is an action-guiding concept. It expresses the notion that one is liable to direction by reasons in the case which would motivate one if one gave them due consideration. And one cannot be *liable* to direction by reasons except in a matter of doing what one is not fully motivated to do already. This is why it cannot be an obligation for one to do what one wants to do anyway, much as it might become an obligation for one to do it if one ceased to want to. This is also why, when one really wants to do something, the natural question to ask is not, "And *ought* I to do this thing?" but rather, "And *may* I do it?" or "Would there be anything wrong with it?" or "Ought I perhaps *not* to do it?" One looks for possible reasons against, not for possible reasons for. And what point would there be in doing anything more? When one really wants to do something, one already has, *for* doing it, all the reason one needs. And this is also why one only says "You ought to" to others when one only says "You ought to" to others when one takes it that there is a case for changing their present frame of mind. But to wonder whether one ought to (as distinct from wondering whether one may, or perhaps ought not to) where one already wants to would be like wondering whether to sit down when seated; and

to say "You ought to" to someone quite ready to, would be like advising a sitting man to take a seat.

There is no ought for those blessed with wants which are not wrong.

One may object: "But surely one can say that everyone ought to do good, and if there were benevolent people this would not make this false." And this is correct, but no refutation. What raises a problem are general statements like "People ought to do good," "One ought to be tolerant." But one may make a general statement without having to specify all the conditions when it shall or shall not hold. One says in general, "Butter will melt in the sun"; and if someone interjected, "But *not* when one has just melted it on the kitchen stove," this would be no rebuttal. "*This* butter will melt in the sun," when I am bringing it dripping from the kitchen, would be different. This particular butter is not *liable* to melt, even though it remains true that butter is. The same with "People ought to do good." This is a general statement, and one need not state the obvious: that it will not apply to someone whose heart needs no melting as it is soft already. Nor does one use "one ought to" directively to people, except for general purposes of propaganda. "I ought to" and "you ought to" are in a logically different class.

One makes general ought-statements about standard ends and practices towards which people commonly have no sufficient inclination. These ought-statements apply particularly to doing things for others, and less so to doing things for oneself. And this alone could explain why one normally does not say that people ought to care for their own good. For the question of whether they *ought* to does not here normally arise. They can be trusted with a modicum of well adjustment towards this end—they seek it, and, within limits, they may seek it. Hence, what one ought to do on account of one's own good is commonly a commitment on account of a desired end, much as it might also turn into a commitment through and through with a loss of immediate interest in the end. Nor could one reasonably hope that such commitments were more imposing in form than they are. On the contrary, one may say that the less imposing the ought, the better designed for living the man.

Suggestions for Further Reading

PART 1. REASON AND RELIGIOUS BELIEF

Virtually all the important writings on the ontological argument from St. Anselm to the present have recently been brought together in one volume, *The Ontological Argument*, edited by Alvin Plantinga, with an introduction by Richard Taylor (New York: Doubleday Anchor Books, 1965). The leading contemporary proponent of the argument is Charles Hartshorne. See his *Man's Vision of God* (New York: Harper & Row, 1941), and *The Logic of Perfection* (La Salle, Ill.: The Open Court Publishing Co., 1963).

For recent versions and defenses of the arguments of St. Thomas Aquinas, see G. H. Joyce, *The Principles of Natural Theology* (New York: Longmans, Green, 1951) and D. J. B. Hawkins, *The Essentials of Theism* (New York: Sheed and Ward, 1949). Anthony Kenny's *Five Ways: St. Thomas Aquinas's Proofs of God's Existence* (London: Routledge & Kegan Paul, 1969) is an excellent and thorough commentary by a skilled English analytic philosopher. A very useful collection of critical essays on the first cause argument and other arguments similar in form to it can be found in *The Cosmological Arguments*, edited by Donald Burrill (New York: Doubleday Anchor Books, 1967).

A classic statement and defense of the argument from design is found in William Paley's *Evidences of the Existence and Attributes of the Deity* (1802). See also the discussion in John Stuart Mill's "Theism" in his *Three Essays on Religion* (1875). David Hume's writings on religion have been gathered together in a useful volume with an excellent introductory essay by Richard Wollheim, *David Hume on Religion* (Meridian Books, 1964). The definitive edition and commentary on Hume's *Dialogues* is that of Nelson Pike (Indianapolis: Bobbs-Merrill, 1971).

For the problem of evil see *God and Evil,* edited by Nelson Pike (Englewood Cliffs, N.J.: Prentice-Hall, 1964) and the helpful bibliography contained therein.

For contemporary discussions of the meaning of religious statements, verification, falsifiability, and related problems, see the following excellent collections: *New Essays in Philosophical Theology,* edited by Antony Flew and Alasdair MacIntyre (New York: Macmillan, 1955); *Faith and Logic,* edited by Basil Mitchell (London: Allen and Unwin, 1957); *Faith and the Philosophers,* edited by John Hick (New York: St. Martin's Press, 1964); and *New Essays on Religious Language,* edited by Dallas M. High (New York: Oxford University Press, 1969). See also Alasdair MacIntyre's "The Logical Status of Religious Belief" in *Metaphysical Beliefs* (London: S. C. M. Press, 1957) and Frederick Ferré's *Language, Logic, and God* (London: Eyre & Spottiswoode, 1962). John Wisdom's "Gods" in *Philosophy and Psychoanalysis* (Oxford: Blackwell, 1957) is a very important article.

For sympathetic discussions of religious mysticism, see W. R. Inge, *Mysticism in Religion* (Chicago: University of Chicago Press, 1948) and W. T. Stace, *Mysticism and Philosophy* (Philadelphia: Lippincott, 1960). For an unsympathetic discussion based on psychological analysis, see J. H. Leuba, *The Psychology of Religious Mysticism* (New York: Harcourt, Brace & World, 1925). For discussions of the religious significance of drugs, consult the footnote references in Huston Smith's article above. An important recent book on this subject is R. C. Zaehner's *Zen, Drugs, and Mysticism* (New York: Pantheon Books, 1972).

For views opposed to William James's on the reasonableness of beliefs based on no adequate evidence, see W. K. Clifford's "The Ethics of Belief" in his *Lectures and Essays,* Vol. II (London: Macmillan, 1879). The classic statement of "agnosticism" (that in the absence of evidence belief should be suspended) is T. H. Huxley's in his *Essays Upon Controversial Questions* (1889).

There is an important fideist tradition in modern Protestant theology which is often called "Christian Existentialism." Its clearest statements can be found in Soren Kierkegaard's *Concluding Unscientific Postscript,* as selected by E.

L. Miller in his valuable collection, *Philosophical and Religious Issues* (Belmont, Calif.: Dickenson Publishing Co., 1972), and in *Dynamics of Faith* by Paul Tillich (New York: Harper & Row, 1957).

Many of the topics in Part I are discussed in the following recent important books: John Hick, *Faith and Knowledge* (Ithaca, N.Y.: Cornell University Press, 1957); Alvin Plantinga, *God and Other Minds* (Ithaca, N.Y.: Cornell University Press, 1968); James F. Ross, *Philosophical Theology* (Indianapolis, Bobbs-Merrill, 1969); Wallace I. Matson, *The Existence of God* (Ithaca, N. Y.: Cornell University Press, 1965); and Antony Flew, *God and Philosophy* (London: Hutchinson and Co., 1966). The books by Hick, Plantinga, and Ross are sympathetic to religious belief; those by Matson and Flew are written from nontheistic points of view. Two good elementary texts are: John Hick, *Philosophy of Religion* (Englewood Cliffs, N.J.: Prentice-Hall, 1963) and John King-Farlow, *Reason and Religion* (London: Darton, Longman & Todd, 1969). Terence Penelhum's *Religion and Rationality* (New York: Random House 1971) is an important contribution to its subject, and readily accessible to the beginner.

PART 2. HUMAN KNOWLEDGE: ITS GROUNDS AND LIMITS

For general introductions to the problems of epistemology (the theory of knowledge) the following books are recommended: A. J. Ayer, *The Problem of Knowledge* (Baltimore: Penguin Books, 1956); R. M. Chisholm, *Theory of Knowledge* (Englewood Cliffs, N.J.: Prentice-Hall, 1966); John Hospers, *Introduction to Philosophical Analysis* (Englewood Cliffs, N.J.: Prentice-Hall, 1953), Chaps. 2, 3, 6; Bertrand Russell, *The Problems of Philosophy* (London: Oxford University Press, 1912); C. H. Whiteley, *An Introduction to Metaphysics* (London: Methuen, 1949); A. D. Woozley, *Theory of Knowledge* (London: Hutchinson's University Library, 1949). *Meaning and Knowledge,* edited by Ernest Nagel and Richard B. Brandt (New York: Harcourt, Brace & World, 1965) is an excellent collection of primary materials from classical and contemporary sources divided by problems.

For general accounts of the period from Descartes through Mill in histories of philosophy, see

Frederick Copleston, S. J., *A History of Philosophy* (Westminster, Md.: Westminster Press, 1960), Vols. IV, V, VI; Frank Thilly and Ledger Wood, *A History of Philosophy,* 3rd ed. (New York: Holt, 1957); and W. Windelband, *A History of Philosophy* (New York: Macmillan, 1893), Part V.

Norman Kemp Smith has written valuable commentaries on Descartes and Hume: *Studies in the Cartesian Philosophy* (London, 1902); *New Studies in the Philosophy of Descartes* (London, 1953); and *The Philosophy of David Hume* (London, 1941). The following are also valuable studies of individual philosophers: D. J. O'Connor, *John Locke* (Baltimore: Penguin Books, 1955); G. J. Warnock, *Berkeley* (Baltimore: Penguin Books, 1953); A. H. Basson, *David Hume* (Baltimore: Penguin Books, 1958); and D. F. Pears, ed., *David Hume, A Symposium* (London: Macmillan, 1963). Keith Lehrer's "Scottish Influences on Contemporary American Philosophy," in *The Philosophical Journal,* Vol. 5 (1968) contains, among other things, a very clear account of Reid's critique of Hume's theory of perception.

John Locke's theory of perception is found in *An Essay Concerning Human Understanding,* especially Book II, Chaps. 8, 9, and Book IV, Chap. 11. For an illuminating discussion of the kind of argument used in Berkeley's first dialogue, see A. J. Ayer, *The Foundations of Empirical Knowledge,* Chap. 1. Ayer is criticized in turn by J. L. Austin in *Sense and Sensibilia* (New York: Oxford University Press, 1964). A classic exposition of phenomenalism is Karl Pearson's *The Grammar of Science* (London, 1892). See also: A. J. Ayer, *Philosophical Essays* (London: Macmillan, 1954), Chaps. 4–6; C. D. Broad, "Phenomenalism," *Proceedings of the Aristotelian Society,* Vol. 15 (1914–15); C. I. Lewis, *An Analysis of Knowledge and Valuation* (La Salle, Ill.: Open Court, 1946), chaps. 7–9; Paul Marhenke, "Phenomenalism," in Max Black (ed.), *Philosophical Analysis* (Ithaca, N.Y.: Cornell University Press, 1950); and C. H. Whiteley, "Physical Objects," *Philosophy,* Vol. 34 (1959). Important recent books on perceptual knowledge include: D. M. Armstrong, *Perception and the Physical World* (London: Routledge and Kegan Paul, 1961); Roderick M. Chisholm, *Perceiving* (Ithaca, N.Y.: Cornell University Press, 1957); R. J. Hirst, *The Problems of Perception* (London: Allen & Unwin,

1959); H. H. Price, *Perception* (London: Methuen, 1933); and Wilfrid Sellars, *Science, Perception, and Reality* (London: Routledge and Kegan Paul, 1963), Chap. 3. A very clear and thorough treatment of the philosophy of perception for beginners can be found in James Cornman and Keith Lehrer, *Philosophical Problems and Arguments: An Introduction* (New York: Macmillan, 1968).

Recent efforts to deal with Hume's skeptical doubts about induction include: Max Black, "The Justification of Induction" in *Language and Philosophy* (Ithaca, N.Y.: Cornell University Press, 1949); Arthur W. Burks, "On the Presuppositions of Induction," *Review of Metaphysics,* Vol. 8 (1955); Hans Reichenbach, *Experience and Prediction* (Chicago: University of Chicago Press, 1938); Bertrand Russell, *Human Knowledge* (New York: Simon & Schuster, 1948), Part 5; and Wesley C. Salmon, *The Foundations of Scientific Inference* (Pittsburgh: University of Pittsburgh Press, 1967).

The grounds for the belief in other minds are discussed in the following articles and books: Bruce Aune, "On Thought and Feeling," *Philosophical Quarterly,* Vol. 13 (1963); Stuart Hampshire, "The Analogy of Feeling," *Mind,* Vol. 61 (1952); Norman Malcolm, "Knowledge of Other Minds," in *Knowledge and Certainty* (Englewood Cliffs, N.J.: Prentice-Hall, 1963); Bertrand Russell, *Human Knowledge* (New York: Simon & Schuster, 1948), Part 6, Chap. 8; P. F. Strawson, *Individuals* (London: Methuen, 1959), Chap. 3; and James Thomson, "The Argument from Analogy and Our Knowledge of Other Minds," *Mind,* Vol. 60 (1951). An astute comparison of proposed justifications for our belief in other minds and the belief in God is found in Alvin Plantinga's *God and Other Minds: A Study of the Rational Justification of Belief in God* (Ithaca, N.Y.: Cornell University Press, 1968). See also the more complete bibliography of works on this subject at the conclusion of Sydney Shoemaker's article in this volume.

An excellent connection of important articles on the a priori is a recent volume edited by L. W. Sumner and John Woods, *Necessary Truth* (New York: Random House, 1969).

Additional statements of pragmatism are found in William James, *Pragmatism* (New York: Longmans, Green, 1907), and John Dewey, *Reconstruction in Philosophy* (New York: Henry Holt, 1920). W. B. Gallie's *Peirce and Pragmatism* is a helpful commentary. A. J. Ayer's *The Origins of Pragmatism* (London: Macmillan, 1968) is a thorough critical exposition of the philosophies of Peirce and James by an important British philosopher who is renowned for the clarity and precision of his style. A definitive collection of the leading statements and criticisms of pragmatism from the time of Peirce to the present in an inexpensive paperback edition is Amelie Rorty's *Pragmatic Philosophy* (Garden City, N.Y.: Doubleday, 1966).

PART 3. MIND AND ITS PLACE IN NATURE

The philosophy of mind has been greatly enriched in the last few decades largely because of the stimulation of Ludwig Wittgenstein. The beginning student will experience difficulties with Wittgenstein's *Philosophical Investigations* (Oxford: Basil Blackwell, 1958) but he will find useful guides in George Pitcher's *The Philosophy of Wittgenstein* (Englewood Cliffs, N.J.: Prentice-Hall, 1964) and *The Private-Language Problem* by John Turk Saunders and Donald F. Henze (New York: Random House; 1967). Another great influence on recent work is Gilbert Ryle's *The Concept of Mind* (New York: Barnes & Noble, 1949). Important articles on the mind-body problem and related topics have been widely anthologized. See, for example, the following paperback collections: V. C. Chappell, (ed.), *The Philosophy of Mind* (Englewood Cliffs, N.J.: Prentice-Hall, 1962); Donald Gustafson (ed.), *Essays in Philosophical Psychology* (Garden City, N.Y.: Doubleday Anchor, 1964); Stuart Hampshire (ed.), *Philosophy of Mind* (New York: Harper & Row, 1966); Sidney Hood (ed.), *Dimensions of Mind* (New York: New York University Press, 1960); and Anthony Flew (ed.), *Body, Mind, and Death* (New York: Macmillan, 1964). A very large and useful collection of articles on the mind-body problem from Descartes to an article written in 1961 is G. N. A. Vesey's *Body and Mind* (London: George Allen & Unwin, 1964). Clear and helpful elementary books on the subject are Jerome Shaffer's *Philosophy of Mind* (Englewood Cliffs, N.J.: Prentice-Hall, 1967) and Alan R. White's *The Philosophy of Mind* (New York: Random House, 1967).

Descartes's views on the relation between mind and body are also found in *On the Passions of the Soul* (1630). For an account of Gassendi's own positive views see *The Philosophy of Gassendi* by G. S. Brett (New York, 1908).

Among twentieth-century works defending interactionism are John Laird's *Our Minds and Their Bodies* (London: Oxford University Press, 1925) and J. B. Pratt's *Matter and Spirit* (New York: Macmillan, 1926). Important and subtle recent books emphasizing the unity of mind and body are P. F. Strawson, *Individuals* (London: Methuen, 1959), Part I, and G. N. A. Vesey, *The Embodied Mind* (London: George Allen & Unwin, 1965).

A fuller statement of J. J. C. Smart's theory of brain-mind identity is found in his book *Philosophy and Scientific Realism* (London: Routledge & Kegan Paul; New York: Humanities Press, 1963). An important early statement of the theory which influenced Smart is: U. T. Place, "Is Consciousness a Brain Process?," *British Journal of Psychology*, XLVII (February, 1956). A classic source for the theory is Herbert Feigl's "The 'Mental' and the 'Physical' " in H. Feigl, M. Scriven, and G. Maxwell (eds.), *Minnesota Studies in the Philosophy of Science*, Vol. 2 (Minneapolis: University of Minnesota Press, 1958). Critical discussions of the identity theory are found in the various anthologies mentioned above. Others worthy of note include: Jaegwon Kim, "On the Psycho-Physical Identity Theory," *American Philosophical Quarterly*, Vol. 3 (1966); Norman Malcolm, "Scientific Materialism and the Identity Theory," *Dialogue*, Vol. 3 (1964); J. A. Shaffer, "Mental Events and the Brain," *Journal of Philosophy*, Vol. 60 (1963); and J. T. Stevenson, "Sensations and Brain Processes: A Reply to J. J. C. Smart," *Philosophical Review*, Vol. 69 (1960). A recent defense and elaboration of the theory is found in D. M. Armstrong, *A Materialist Theory of the Mind* (London: Routledge & Kegan Paul; New York: Humanities Press, 1968). For a very useful paperback collection of articles devoted exclusively to the identity theory, some friendly and some antagonistic, see: John O'Connor (ed.), *Modern Materialism: Readings on Mind-Body Identity* (New York: Harcourt, Brace & World, 1969).

Classic statements of the other form of materialism (epiphenomenalism) are found in T. H. Huxley's "On the Hypothesis That Animals Are Automata and Its History" in *Methods and Results* (London and New York: Appleton, 1874), and in Shadworth Hodgson, *The Metaphysics of Experience* (London: Longmans, Green, 1898), Vol. II. Epiphenomenalism finds expression in the form of a beautiful parable in George Santayana's "Normal Madness," in *Dialogues in Limbo* (New York: Scribners, 1926). The latest important work to suggest a theory like epiphenomenalism is Keith Campbell's *Body and Mind* (New York: Doubleday Anchor Books, 1971).

C. J. Ducasse's conceptions of mind and the prospects of its survival of the death of the body are spelled out in more detail in his book, *A Critical Examination of the Belief in a Life After Death* (Springfield, Ill.: Charles C. Thomas, 1961). See also his *Nature, Mind, and Death* (La Salle, Ill.: Open Court, 1951), Chaps. 20 and 21 and H. H. Price, "Personal Identity and Survival" (London: Society for Psychical Research, 1958). For the case against survival, see Corliss Lamont, *The Illusion of Immortality* (New York: G. P. Putnam's, 1935) and C. Cohen, *The Other Side of Death* (London: The Pioneer Press, 1922). *Man's Concern With Death* containing original articles by Arnold Toynbee, A. K. Mant, Ninian Smart, John Hinton, Simon Yudkin, Eric Rhode, Rosalind Heywood, and H. H. Price (London: Hodder & Stoughton, 1968) is an excellent collection. Terence Penelhum's *Survival and Disembodied Existence* (New York: Humanities Press, 1970) is a very clear discussion of the conceptual problems raised by the doctrine of survival.

For classical theories of personal identity opposed in various ways to that of John Locke, see: David Hume, *A Treatise of Human Nature* (Oxford, 1888), Book I, Part IV, Section VI; and Thomas Reid, *Essays on the Intellectual Powers of Man*, edited by A. D. Woozley (London, 1941). A recent argument for a position like Butler's is Bernard Williams's "The Self and the Future," *Philosophical Review* (1970). Leading modern theories are found in William James's *The Principles of Psychology* (New York: Henry Holt, 1890), Vol. I, Chap. X and Sydney Shoemaker, *Self-Knowledge and Self-Identity* (Ithaca, N.Y.: Cornell University Press, 1963). The view in Shoemaker's important book has some affinities with that of Locke, as do "Personal Identity" by

H. P. Grice, *Mind* (1941) and "The Soul" by Anthony Quinton, *Journal of Philosophy* (1962). See also Derek Parfit's ingenious "Personal Identity," *Philosophical Review* (1971) and John Perry's "Can the Self Divide?," *Journal of Philosophy* (1972).

Many of the most important recent articles on mentality and machines are found in two excellent paperback anthologies: *Minds and Machines,* edited by Alan Ross Anderson (Englewood Cliffs, N.J.: Prentice-Hall, 1964) and *Dimensions of Mind,* edited by Sidney Hook. The Anderson volume also contains a very helpful bibliography. Three important new books on the subject are Keith Gunderson's *Mentality and Machines* (New York: Doubleday, 1971), Kenneth M. Sayre, *Consciousness, A Philosophical Study of Minds and Machines* (New York: Random House, 1969), and Hubert L. Dreyfus, *What Computers Can't Do: A Critique of Artificial Reason* (New York: Harper & Row, 1973). Other articles of interest include: Keith Gunderson, "Interview With a Robot," *Analysis* (1964); D. M. MacKay, "The Epistemological Problem for Automata," *Automata Studies* (Princeton, N.J.: Princeton University Press, 1956); R. Puccetti, "On Thinking Machines and Feeling Machines," *British Journal for the Philosophy of Science,* Vol. 18 (1967); and Denis Thompson, "Can A Machine Be Conscious?," *British Journal for the Philosophy of Science,* Vol. 16 (1965).

PART 4. DETERMINISM, FREEDOM, AND RESPONSIBILITY

Hospers' account of explanation is of the sort that finds its classic statement in "Studies in the Logic of Explanation," by Carl G. Hempel and Paul Oppenheim, *Philosophy of Science,* Vol. 15 (1948). Also see Hempel's elementary text, *The Philosophy of Natural Science* (Englewood Cliffs, N.J.: Prentice-Hall, 1966) and Ernest Nagel's *The Structure of Science* (New York: Harcourt, Brace, & World, 1961), Chaps. 2, 3. For critical discussions of the Hempel-Oppenheim theory, especially as it applies to historical explanation, see *Philosophy and History,* edited by Sidney Hook (New York: New York University Press, 1963), especially Part III. Other useful articles are: "Why Questions," by Sylvain Bromberger in *Mind and Cosmos,* edited by R. Colodny (Pitts-

burgh, 1965), and "Explanation in Everyday Life, in Science, and in History," by John Passmore, *History and Theory,* Vol. II (1962).

Almost all the important recent work on the explanation of human actions is contained in one or the other of two remarkably thorough recent anthologies: *Readings in the Theory of Action,* edited by Norman S. Care and Charles Landesman (Bloomington, Ind.: Indiana University Press, 1968), and *The Nature of Human Action,* edited by Myles Brand (Glenview, Ill.: Scott, Foresman and Co., 1970). The leading presentation, perhaps, of the position opposed to that of the R. S. Peters selection in the text is included in both these volumes. It is Donald Davidson's "Actions, Reasons, and Causes."

At least five very valuable symposia on the problem of determinism and free will have appeared in recent years: *Free Will and Determinism,* edited by Bernard Berofsky (New York: Harper & Row, 1966); *Determinism and Freedom in the Age of Modern Science,* edited by Sidney Hook (New York: New York University Press, 1958); *Freedom and Determinism,* edited by Keith Lehrer (New York: Random House, 1966); *Free Will,* edited by Sidney Morgenbesser and James Walsh (Englewood Cliffs, N.J., Prentice-Hall, 1962), all of which are inexpensive paperbacks; and *Freedom and the Will,* edited by D. F. Pears (London: Macmillan; New York: St. Martin's Press, 1963). Most of the essays in the Pears volume originated as talks in the Third Programme of the British Broadcasting Corporation.

The reconciling determinist position is defended in Thomas Hobbes's *Leviathan* (1651), Chap. 21; in David Hume's *Treatise of Human Nature,* Book II, Part III; and in John Stuart Mill's *System of Logic* (1843), Book VI, Chap. 2. Recent influential arguments for the theory are found in Chapter 7 of Moritz Schlick's *Problems of Ethics* (Englewood Cliffs, N.J.: Prentice-Hall, 1939); in Chapter 14 of Charles L. Stevenson's *Ethics and Language* (New Haven, Conn.: Yale University Press, 1944); in R. B. Hobart's "Free-Will as Involving Determinism and Inconceivable without It," *Mind,* 1934; and in Frederick Vivian, *Human Freedom and Responsibility* (London: Chatto & Windus, 1964).

Deterministic theories of a relatively nonreconciling kind are found in Baruch Spinoza's *Ethics,*

Part III; in *System of Nature* by Baron D'Holbach (1770); and in essays by Paul Edwards and John Hospers in the Sidney Hook anthology mentioned above. See also the speeches of the great criminal lawyer Clarence Darrow, in *Attorney for the Damned,* edited by Arthur Weinberg (New York: Simon & Schuster, 1957), especially Part One.

A good collection of materials in and about existentialism is *Existential Philosophy,* edited by James A. Gould and Willis H. Truitt (Belmont, Calif.: Dickenson Publishing Co., 1973). Perhaps the best treatment in English of the existentialist theory of freedom and choice is Frederick A. Olafson, *Principles and Persons: An Ethical Interpretation of Existentialism* (Baltimore: Johns Hopkins University Press, 1967) Chap. 7.

For the debate over deliberation and foreknowledge see the books and articles cited in the footnotes of Goldman's article, especially the works by Cranston, Canfield, Cox, and R. Taylor. See also Michael Scriven's "An Essential Unpredictability in Human Behavior," in *Scientific Psychology: Principles and Approaches,* edited by B. B. Wolman and E. Nagel (New York, 1965) and "Scriven on Human Unpredictability," by David K. Lewis and Jane Shelby Richardson in *Philosophical Studies,* Vol. 17 (1966). A kind of precursor of the Ginet article is "Decision, Intention, and Certainty," by H. L. A. Hart and Stuart Hampshire, *Mind,* Vol. 67 (1958).

Indeterminist theories are defended in Henri Bergson, *Time and Free Will* (New York: Macmillan, 1921); Isaiah Berlin, *Historical Inevitability* (London: Oxford University Press, 1954); C. A. Campbell, *Skepticism and Construction* (London: Allen & Unwin, 1931) and *On Selfhood and Godhood* (London: Allen & Unwin; New York: Macmillan, 1957), Lecture IX; Stuart Hampshire, *Freedom of the Individual* (New York: Harper & Row, 1965); William James, "The Dilemma of Determinism," first published in 1884 and now widely anthologized; Charles S. Peirce, "The Doctrine of Necessity Examined," reprinted in *The Philosophy of Peirce,* edited by J. Buchler (New York: Harcourt, Brace, 1950); Thomas Reid, *Essays on the Powers of the Human Mind* (1812), Vol. III; and Jean-Paul Sartre, *Being and Nothingness* (New York: Philosophical Library, 1956).

PART 5. RESPONSIBILITY, BLAME, AND PUNISHMENT

For a large and unusually complete collection of readings on criminal punishment and other problems concerning responsibility in law and morals, see Herbert Morris (ed.), *Freedom and Responsibility* (Stanford, Calif.: Stanford University Press, 1961). Excellent general discussions of the topics of this and the preceding section are also found in Richard B. Brandt, *Ethical Theory* (Englewood Cliffs, N.J.: Prentice-Hall, 1959), Chap. 18–20 and in John Hospers, *Human Conduct* (Harcourt, Brace & World, 1961), Chap. 9 and 10.

For a general account of Aristotle's ethics, see W. D. Ross, *Aristotle* (New York: Meridian Books, 1959), Chap. 7 and W. F. R. Hardie, *Aristotle's Ethical Theory* (Oxford: Clarendon Press, 1968). An excellent analysis of Aristotle's theory of personal responsibility against the background of centuries of Greek thought on the subject is found in Arthur W. H. Adkins, *Merit and Responsibility* (Oxford: Clarendon Press, 1960), Chap. 15.

Classical sources of the utilitarian theory of punishment are: Jeremy Bentham, *An Introduction to the Principles of Morals and Legislation* (Oxford: Basil Blackwell, 1948) and *The Rationale of Punishment* (1830). An excellent little commentary is David Lyons's *Jeremy Bentham* (London: Macmillan, 1972). See also the Marquis de Beccaria, *An Essay on Crimes and Punishments* (Indianapolis: Bobbs-Merrill, 1963), first published in 1764; Hastings Rashdall, *Theory of Good and Evil* (Oxford: Clarendon Press, 1924), Vol. I, Chap. 9; and H. Wechsler and J. Michael, "A Rationale of the Law of Homicide," *Columbia Law Review,* 1937.

Views similar to those of Butler's Erewhonian "malcontents" are expressed in Plato's *Protagoras* (324–325), *Gorgias* (479–480 and 525–526), and *Republic* (380); in Robert Owen, *Letters to the Human Race* (London, 1850) and in Leo Tolstoy, *What I Believe* (Oxford Centenary Edition, 1933), Vol. II. See also Tolstoy's novel *Resurrection.* For recent versions of the view that all crime is sickness, see Benjamin Karpman, "Criminality, Insanity, and the Law," *Journal of Criminal Law and Criminology* (1939), and *The Criminal Mind,* by Philip Q. Roche, M.D. (New York:

Grove Press, 1958). For the contrary view, that only some criminals are mentally ill, see Paul Schilder, *Psychoanalysis, Man, and Society* (New York: Norton, 1951). For analyses of the concepts of mental health and illness, see Joseph Margolis, *Psychotherapy and Morality* (New York: Random House, 1966), Chaps. 1–3, Georg von Wright, *The Varieties of Goodness* (London: Routledge & Kegan Paul, 1963), Chap. III, and Jonathan Glover, *Responsibility* (New York: Humanities Press, 1970).

For the moralistic (Kantian) version of the retributive theory, see Josef Kohler, *Philosophy of Law* (Boston: Boston Book Co., 1914), and Rudolf Stammler, *The Theory of Justice* (New York: Macmillan, 1925). The leading American Kantian was Francis Wharton. See his *A Treatise On Criminal Law,* 8th ed. (Philadelphia, 1880).

The main source of Hegel's theory of punishment is *Hegel's Philosophy of Right,* translated by T. M. Knox (Oxford, 1953), especially sections 90–104. An excellent critique of retributivism is found in Chapter I of A. C. Ewing's *The Morality of Punishment* (London: Kegan Paul, 1929). Refined versions of retributivism are expressed in "The Retributivist Hits Back," by K. G. Armstrong, *Mind,* Vol. 70 (1961); H. J. McCloskey, "A Non-Utilitarian Approach to Punishment," *Inquiry* (1965); and Herbert Morris, "Persons and Punishment," *The Monist* (October, 1968).

For discussions sympathetic to the view that vengeance is a legitimate function of criminal punishment, see James Fitzjames Stephen, *History of the Criminal Law* (1883), Vol. I, p. 478 and Vol. II, pp. 81–82 *et passim* and G. de Tarde, *Penal Philosophy* (Boston: Little, Brown, 1912).

A developed theory of the sort suggested by the Mabbott and Rawls selections is to be found in S. I. Benn and R. S. Peters, *Social Principles and the Democratic State* (London: Allen & Unwin, 1959), Chap. 8.

For discussions of blame and blameworthiness, consult the footnote references in Elizabeth Beardsley's article included here. See also Chap. 18 of Richard Brandt's *Ethical Theory* (Englewood Cliffs, N.J.: Prentice-Hall, 1958), and the following articles: R. B. Brandt, "Blameworthiness and Obligation," in A. I. Melden (ed.) *Essays in Moral Philosophy* (Seattle: University of Washington Press, 1958); E. L. Beardsley, "A Plea for

Deserts," *American Philosophical Quarterly,* Vol. 6 (1969), and "Moral Disapproval and Moral Indignation," *Philosophy and Phenomenological Research,* Vol. 31 (1970); L. Kenner, "On Blaming," *Mind,* Vol. 76 (1967); and J. E. R. Squires, "Blame," *The Philosophical Quarterly,* Vol. 18, (1968).

The following are new books on the philosophy of punishment and the criminal law: H. B. Acton (ed.), *The Philosophy of Punishment* (Blackwell's, 1969); Gertrude Ezorsky, editor, *Philosophical Perspectives on Punishment* (Albany, N.Y.: State of New York University Press, 1972); Joel Feinberg, *Doing and Deserving,* (Princeton, N.J.: Princeton University Press, 1970); H. L. A. Hart, *Punishment and Responsibility* (New York and Oxford: Oxford University Press, 1968); Ted Honderich, *Punishment, The Supposed Justifications* (London: Hutchinson, 1969); John Kleinig, *Punishment and Desert* (The Hague: Martinus Nijhoff, 1973); Karl Menninger, *The Crime of Punishment* (New York: Viking Press, 1966); Sir Walter Moberly, *The Ethics of Punishment* (London: Faber & Faber, 1968); Herbert L. Packer, *The Limits of the Criminal Sanction* (Stanford, Calif.: Stanford University Press, 1968); and Edmund L. Pincoffs, *The Rationale of Legal Punishment* (New York: Humanities Press, 1966).

PART 6. SELF-LOVE AND THE CLAIMS OF MORALITY

For commentaries on Plato's *Republic,* see A. E. Taylor, *Plato, the Man and His Work* (New York: Humanities Press, 1927), Chap. XI; and R. C. Cross and A. D. Woozley, *Plato's Republic, A Philosophical Commentary* (London: Macmillan, 1964).

For various answers to, and discussions of, the question "Why Should I Be Moral?" see the following: Kurt Baier, *The Moral Point of View* (Ithaca, N.Y.: Cornell University Press, 1958), Chap. 11, 12; F. H. Bradley, *Ethical Studies* (Oxford, 1876), Essay II; John Hospers, *Human Conduct* (New York: Harcourt, Brace & World, 1961), Chap. 4; Frank C. Sharp, *Ethics* (New York: Appleton-Century, 1928), Chap. 22, 23.

Other discussions of ethical egoism are contained in Richard C. Brandt, *Ethical Theory,* Chap. 14; G. E. Moore, *Principia Ethica*

(Cambridge: Cambridge University Press, 1903), Chap. III C; James B. Pratt, *Reason in the Art of Living* (New York: Macmillan, 1949), Chap. 10; Moritz Schlick, *Problems of Ethics* (Englewood Cliffs, N.J.: Prentice-Hall, 1939), Chap. 3; and Henry Sidgwick, *The Methods of Ethics,* 7th ed. (New York and London: Macmillan, 1907), Book II.

For classical statements of psychological egoism, consult the authors quoted in the footnotes of the second selection from Lecky. See also Bernard De Mandeville's *The Fable of the Bees, or Private Vices, Public Benefits* (London, 1723). Mandeville believed that human beings are incorrigibly greedy, conceited, and vainglorious; yet these very vices, he argued, can be motives for the noblest conduct. "The moral virtues," he concluded, "are the political offspring which flattery begot on pride."

Philosophical works arguing against psychological egoism are legion. Among the best of them are: C. D. Broad, "Egoism as a Theory of Human Motives," in *Ethics and the History of Philosophy* (New York: Humanities Press, 1952); Joseph Butler, *Fifteen Sermons Upon Human Nature* (London, 1729), especially Sermon Eleven—"Upon the Love of Our Neighbor"; Austin Duncan-Jones, *Butler's Moral Philosophy* (Harmondsworth: Penguin Books, 1952), Chap. 4; Lucius Garvin, *A Modern Introduction to Ethics* (Boston: Houghton Mifflin, 1953), Chap. 2; William James, *The Principles of Psychology* (New York: Henry Holt, 1890; Vol. II, Chap. XXVI; Hastings Rashdall, *The Theory of Good and Evil* (London: Oxford University Press, 1924), Vol. I, Chap. 2; Frank C. Sharp, *Ethics* (New York: Appleton-Century, 1928), Book III; and Henry Sidgwick, *Methods of Ethics,* Book I, Chap. 4.

More thorough discussions of the logic behind some of the arguments in the final part of Feinberg's "Psychological Egoism" can be found in Norman Malcolm's "Moore and Ordinary Language" in *The Philosophy of G. E. Moore,* edited by P. A. Schilpp (Evanston, Ill.: Northwestern University Press, 1942), and in John Wisdom's "Philosophical Perplexity" in *Philosophy and Psychoanalysis* (Oxford: Basil Blackwell, 1957).

The classic sources of utilitarian moral philosophy after Bentham include John Stuart Mill's *Utilitarianism,* first published in 1861, now available in several paperback editions; Henry Sidgwick, *Methods of Ethics* (London: Macmillan Papermac, 1963), first published in 1874; and G. E. Moore, *Ethics* (London: Oxford University Press, 1912). An excellent paperback collection of important recent papers on utilitarianism is Michael D. Bayles (ed.), *Contemporary Utilitarianism* (Garden City, N.Y.: Doubleday Anchor, 1968). A bibliography of articles on duty and supererogation, including some articles criticizing Urmson's "Saints and Heroes" can be found in Joel Feinberg (ed.), *Moral Concepts* (Oxford: Oxford University Press, 1969).

Two excellent recent books on the problems of Part 6 are Thomas Nagel, *The Possibility of Altruism* (Oxford: Clarendon Press, 1970) and Robert G. Olson, *The Morality of Self-Interest* (New York: Harcourt, Brace & World, 1965). The Nagel book is of the first importance but it will be difficult for the beginner. *Morality and Rational Self-Interest,* edited by D. P. Gautier (Englewood Cliffs, N.J.: Prentice-Hall, 1970), and *Egoism and Altruism,* edited by Ronald D. Milo (Belmont, Calif.: Wadsworth, 1973) are useful anthologies.